NOVEL & SHORT
WRITER'S MARKET
2019

Includes a one-year online subscription to **Novel & Short Story Writer's Market** on

WritersMarket.com

Where & How to Sell What You Write

THE ULTIMATE MARKET RESEARCH TOOL FOR WRITERS

To register your *Novel & Short Story Writer's Market 2019* and **start your one-year online subscription**, scratch off the block below to reveal your activation code*, then go to WritersMarket.com. Find the box that says "Purchased a Deluxe Edition?" then click on "Activate Your Account" and enter the activation code. It's that easy!

WITHDRAWN

UPDATED MARKET LISTINGS

EASY-TO-USE, SEARCHABLE DATABASE • RECORD-KEEPING TOOLS

PROFESSIONAL TIPS & ADVICE • INDUSTRY NEWS

Your purchase of *Novel & Short Story Writer's Market* gives you access to updated listings related to literary agents (valid through 12/31/19). For just $9.99, you can upgrade your subscription and get access to listings from all of our best-selling Market Books. Visit **WritersMarket.com** for more information.

WritersMarket.com

Where & How to Sell What You Write

Activate your WritersMarket.com subscription to get instant access to:

- **UPDATED LISTINGS IN YOUR WRITING GENRE:** Find additional listings that didn't make it into the book, updated contact information, and more. WritersMarket.com provides the most comprehensive database of verified markets available anywhere.

- **EASY-TO-USE, SEARCHABLE DATABASE:** Looking for a specific magazine or book publisher? Just type in its name. Or widen your prospects with the Advanced Search. You can also search for listings that have been recently updated!

- **PERSONALIZED TOOLS:** Store your best-bet markets, and use our popular recording-keeping tools to track your submissions. Plus, get new and updated market listings, query reminders, and more every time you log in!

- **PROFESSIONAL TIPS & ADVICE:** From pay-rate charts to sample query letters, how-to articles to Q&As with literary agents, we have all the resources writers need.

YOU'LL GET ALL OF THIS WITH THE INCLUDED SUBSCRIPTION TO

WritersMarket.com

Where & How to Sell What You Write

OCT 0 1 2018

‹ 38ᵀᴴ ANNUAL EDITION ›

NOVEL & SHORT STORY WRITER'S MARKET

Robert Lee Brewer, Editor

WRITER'S DIGEST
BOOKS
WritersDigest.com
Cincinnati, Ohio

NOVEL & SHORT STORY WRITER'S MARKET 2019. Copyright © 2018 F+W Media, Inc. Published by Writer's Digest Books, an imprint of F+W Media, Inc., 10151 Carver Road, Suite 300, Blue Ash, Ohio 45242. Printed and bound in the United States of America.

Writer's Market website: www.writersmarket.com
Writer's Digest website: www.writersdigest.com

Distributed in the U.K. and Europe by F&W Media International
Pynes Hill Court, Pynes Hill, Rydon Lane
Exeter, EX2 5AZ, United Kingdom
Tel: (+44) 1392-797680, Fax: (+44) 1626-323319
E-mail: postmaster@davidandcharles.co.uk

ISSN: 0897-9812
ISBN-13: 978-1-4403-5437-3
ISBN-10: 1-4403-5437-5

Attention Booksellers: This is an annual directory of F+W Media, Inc. Return deadline for this edition is December 31, 2019.

Edited by: Robert Lee Brewer
Designed by: Alexis Estoye and Katelyn Summers
Production coordinated by: Debbie Thomas

CONTENTS

FROM
THE EDITOR

//

In this edition of *Novel & Short Story Writer's Market*, I had two goals: Squeeze in as many fiction market listings as possible and include some great articles on the craft and business of writing fiction.

For the craft, there are articles on mastering the art of complexity, incorporating conflict in fiction, and creating antagonistic settings. Plus, Jack Smith shares the anatomy of successful short stories. On the business side, we take a look at using Patreon, choosing an attorney, and getting an agent. There are also insightful interviews with the likes of George Saunders, Kristin Hannah, Leigh Bardugo, and Roxane Gay.

Of course, the fiction listings are still "where it's at" with *Novel & Short Story Writer's Market*, and I tried to pack as many into this year's book as possible. You'll find fiction listings for book publishers, literary agents, magazines, contests, and more.

Also, be sure to take advantage of the webinar for *Novel & Short Story Writer's Market* readers. Learn more at www.writersmarket.com/2019-nsswm-webinar.

Until next we meet, keep writing and marketing what you write.

Robert Lee Brewer
Senior Content Editor
Novel & Short Story Writer's Market
http://writersdigest.com/editor-blogs/poetic-asides
http://blog.writersmarket.com
http://twitter.com/robertleebrewer

HOW TO USE
NSSWM

//

To make the most of *Novel & Short Story Writer's Market*, you need to know how to use it. And with more than five hundred pages of fiction publishing markets and resources, a writer could easily get lost amid the information. This quick-start guide will help you navigate through the pages of *Novel & Short Story Writer's Market*—as well as the fiction-publishing process—and accomplish your dream of seeing your work in print.

1. READ, READ, READ. Read numerous magazines, fiction collections, and novels to determine if your fiction compares favorably with work currently being published. If your fiction is at least the same caliber as what you're reading, then move on to step two. If not, postpone submitting your work and spend your time polishing your fiction. Reading the work of others is one of the best ways to improve your craft.

You'll find advice and inspiration from best-selling authors and seasoned writers in the articles found in the first few sections of this book (**Craft & Technique**, **Interviews**, and **The Business of Fiction Writing**). *Novel & Short Story Writer's Market* also includes listings for **Literary Agents** who accept fiction submissions, **Book Publishers** and **Magazines** that publish fiction in a variety of genres, **Contests & Awards** to enter, and **Conferences & Workshops** where you can meet fellow writers and attend instructive sessions to hone your skills.

2. ANALYZE YOUR FICTION. Determine the type of fiction you write to target markets most suitable for your work. Do you write literary, genre, mainstream, or one of many other categories of fiction? For definitions and explanations of genres and subgenres, check out the **Glossary** and the **Genre Glossary** in the **Resources** section of the book. Many magazines and presses are currently seeking specialized work in each of these areas as well as numerous others.

For editors and publishers with specialized interests, see the **Category Index** in the back of the book.

3. LEARN ABOUT THE MARKET. Read *Writer's Digest* magazine; *Publishers Weekly*, the trade magazine of the publishing industry; and *Independent Publisher*, which contains information about small- to medium-size independent presses. And don't forget the Internet. The number of sites for writers seems to grow daily, and among them you'll find www.writersmarket.com and www.writersdigest.com.

4. FIND MARKETS FOR YOUR WORK. There are a variety of ways to locate markets for fiction. The periodical section in bookstores and libraries is a great place to discover new journals and magazines that might be open to your type of short stories. Read writing-related magazines and newsletters for information about new markets and publications seeking fiction submissions. Also, frequently browse bookstore shelves to see what novels and short story collections are being published and by whom. Check acknowledgment pages for names of editors and agents, too. Online journals often have links to the websites of other journals that may publish fiction. And last, but certainly not least, read the listings found here in *Novel & Short Story Writer's Market*.

5. SEND FOR GUIDELINES. In the listings in this book, we try to include as much submission information as we can get from editors and publishers. Over the course of the year, however, editors' expectations and needs may change. Therefore, it is best to obtain a copy of the submission guidelines. You can check each magazine's and press's website—they usually contain a page with guideline information. Or you can do it the old-fashioned way and send a self-addressed, stamped envelope (SASE) with a request for them.

6. BEGIN YOUR PUBLISHING EFFORTS WITH JOURNALS AND CONTESTS OPEN TO BEGINNERS. If this is your first attempt at publishing your work, your best bet is to begin with local publications or those you

KEY TO ICONS & ABBREVIATIONS

- Ⓐ market accepts agented submissions only
- ⊘ market does not accept unsolicited submissions
- award-winning market
- Canadian market
- market located outside of the U.S. and Canada
- Ⓢ market pays (in magazine sections)
- comment from the editor of *Novel & Short Story Writer's Market*
- ◯ actively seeking new writers
- ◑ seeks both new and established writers
- prefers working with established writers, mostly referrals
- ◉ market has a specialized focus
- imprint, subsidiary, or division of larger book publishing house (in book publishers section)
- publisher of graphic novels or comics

know are open to beginning writers. After you have built a publication history, you can try submitting to the more prestigious and nationally distributed magazines. For markets most open to beginners, look for the ◯ symbol preceding listing titles. Also look for the ◑ symbol, which identifies markets open to exceptional work from beginners as well as work from experienced, previously published writers.

7. SUBMIT YOUR FICTION IN A PROFESSIONAL MANNER. Take the time to show editors that you care about your work and are serious about publishing. By following a publication's or book publisher's submission guidelines and practicing standard submission etiquette, you can increase your chances that an editor will want to take the time to read your work and consider it for publication. Remember: First impressions matter. A carelessly assembled submission packet can jeopardize your chances before your story or novel manuscript has had a chance to speak for itself.

8. KEEP TRACK OF YOUR SUBMISSIONS. Know when and where you have sent fiction and how long you need to wait before expecting a reply. If an editor does not respond in the time indicated in his or her market listing or guidelines, wait a few more weeks before following up with an e-mail or letter (with SASE) asking when the editor anticipates making a decision. If you do not receive a reply from the editor within a month or two, send a letter withdrawing your work from consideration and move on to the next market on your list.

9. LEARN FROM REJECTION. Rejection is the hardest part of the publication process. Unfortunately rejection happens to every writer, and every writer needs to learn to deal with the negativity involved. Believe it or not, rejection can be valuable when used as a teaching tool rather than a reason to doubt yourself and your work. If an editor offers suggestions with his or her rejection slip, take those comments into consideration. You don't have to agree with an editor's opinion of your work. It may be that the editor has a different perspective on the piece than you do. Or you may find that the editor's suggestions give you new insight into your work and help you improve your craft.

10. DON'T GIVE UP. The best advice we can offer you as you try to get published is to be persistent and to always believe in yourself and your work. By continually reading other writers' work, constantly working on the craft of fiction writing, and relentlessly submitting your work, you will eventually find that magazine or book publisher that's the perfect match for your fiction. *Novel & Short Story Writer's Market* will be here to help you every step of the way.

GUIDE TO LISTING FEATURES

Below is an example of the market listings contained in *Novel & Short Story Writer's Market,* with callouts identifying the various format features of the listings. (For an explanation of the icons used, see the sidebar on page 3.)

---

❶❷❸ THE SOUTHERN REVIEW

Old President's House, Louisiana State University, Baton Rouge, LA 70803-5001. (225)578-5108. Fax: (225)578-5098. E-mail: southernreview@lsu.edu. **Website:** www.lsu.edu/thesouthern review.

Contact Cara Blue Adams, editor. Magazine: 6¼ × 10; 240 pages; 50 lb. Glatfelter paper; 65 lb. #1 grade cover stock. Quarterly. Circ. 3,000.

• Several stories published in *The Southern Review* were Pushcart Prize selections.

NEEDS Literary. "We select fiction that conveys a unique and compelling voice and vision." Receives approximately 300 unsolicited mss/month. Accepts 4-6 mss/issue. Reading period: September-June. Publishes ms 6 months after acceptance. Agented fiction 1%. Publishes 10-12 new writers/year. Recently published work by Jack Driscoll, Don Lee, Peter Levine, and Debbie Urbanski. Also publishes literary essays, literary criticism, poetry, and book reviews.

HOW TO CONTACT Mail hard copy of ms with cover letter and SASE. No queries. ("Prefer brief letters giving author's professional information, including recent or notable publications. Biographical info not necessary." Responds in 10 weeks to mss. Sample copy for $8. Writer's guidelines online. Reviews fiction, poetry.

PAYMENT/TERMS Pays $30/page. Pays on publication for first North American serial rights. Sends page proof to author via e-mail. Sponsors awards/contests.

TIPS "Careful attention to craftsmanship and technique combined with a developed sense of the creation of story will always make us pay attention."

Callouts:

- AT-A-GLANCE REFERENCE ICONS
- E-MAIL AND WEBSITE INFORMATION
- SPECIFIC CONTACT NAMES
- DETAILED SUBMISSION GUIDELINES
- TIPS FOR SUBMISSION

MASTERING THE ART OF COMPLEXITY

by Fred D. White

//

Fiction illuminates the complexity of human nature by plunging the reader into the minds and hearts of the characters and showing, with a degree of clarity and perceptiveness often lacking in everyday life, how they interact among themselves, grapple with their inner demons, and overcome enormous obstacles. Situations overly complicated or incoherent in real life become understandable as well as engrossing through the lens of fiction—not by simplifying human nature but by capturing something of its subtlety and inner turmoil—that is to say, its complexity.

I use the word lens to call attention to the ability of a well-made story to focus sharply on the particulars of the moment, the outer behavior and emotional turbulence of the characters. Orchestrating these variables skillfully creates verisimilitude—the magic of entering the story's world and becoming a part of it.

DEFINING COMPLEXITY

According to the *American Heritage Dictionary*, something complex is "composed of interconnected or interwoven parts." Applied to human behavior, complexity encompasses habits of mind, impulses, repressed desires, logical thinking colliding with irrational longings—and most importantly, the manner in which those facets of behavior interconnect. In fiction, complexity encompasses not only the turbulent actions and impulses of the characters, but the many layered consequences of interacting with others in a particular social milieu.

WHY COMPLEXITY IS IMPORTANT

Whether you're writing a fast-paced crime story, a psychological portrait of an artist, or a multi-generational saga, complexity is elemental. Of course, there are degrees of complexity. You may not be able to give your characters the depth and intrigue of Dostoevsky's egotistical (and murderous) protagonist Raskolnikov in *Crime and Punishment* if you are working on a crime short story, but you still have plenty of room to imbue your protagonist with enough complexity—a past mistake that threatens to undermine her credibility, for example—to enable readers to identify with and care about her. Lacking complexity, characters will seem more like stereotypes, cardboard props, than authentic persons.

THE ELEMENTS OF COMPLEXITY IN FICTION

I identify three major kinds of complexity: emotional, narrative/descriptive, and situational. Let's consider each kind in turn:

Emotional complexity. Human behavior is never what it seems; but a good story places it under intense scrutiny. Novice writers tend to gloss over delineating emotional experience, assuming that merely telling readers about what he or she is feeling will suffice. For example, to indicate a young man's growing infatuation for a young lady, a novice might write, "Day after day, I could not stop thinking about her, or imagining how I'd one day express my feelings to her." And that would be that. But now look at how James Joyce handles such an emotional moment in "Araby," one of his *Dubliners* stories:

> Her name sprang to my lips . . . in strange prayers and praises which I myself did not understand. My eyes were often full of tears . . . , and at times a flood from my heart seemed to pour itself out into my bosom. I thought little of the future. I did not know whether I would ever speak to her or not, or, if I spoke to her, how I could tell her of my confused adoration. But my body was like a harp and her words and gestures were like fingers running upon the wires.

Joyce delves deeper into the emotional complexity of his young narrator, a complexity that, by the way, resonates with the other elements of the story, such as the social milieu and the narrator's situation.

Narrative and descriptive complexity: I place these two elements together because they almost always intertwine. To put it another way, the narrative progression of events include descriptions of what is unfolding. In his 1997 bestselling novel, *Memoirs of a Geisha*, Arthur Golden not only lets you see in vivid detail the transformation of a woman into a geisha as she applies her special makeup, but simultaneously conveys a great deal of information about Geisha culture:

> Hatsumomo [the narrator's cruel rival] . . . sang quietly to herself as she opened a jar of pale yellow cream. You may not believe me when I tell you that this cream was made from nightingale droppings, but it's true. Many geisha used it as a face cream in those days, because it was believed to be very good for the skin; but it was so ex-

> pensive that Hatsumomo put only a few dots around her eyes and mouth. Then she
> tore a small piece of wax from one of the bars and, after softening it in her fingertips,
> rubbed it into the skin of her face, neck and chest. She took some time to wipe her
> hands clean on a rag, and then moistened one of her flat makeup brushes in a dish
> of water and rubbed it in the makeup until she had a chalky white paste. She used it
> to paint her face and neck, but left her eyes bare, as well as the area around her lips
> and nose. . . .After this she looked as if she'd fallen face first into a bin of rice flour, for
> her whole face was ghastly white. She looked like the demon she was, but even so, I
> was sick with jealousy and shame. Because I knew that in an hour or so, men would
> be gazing with astonishment at that face; and I would still be there in the okiya [a
> boarding house for geishas], looking sweaty and plain.

The power of this passage lies in the artful description of Hatsumomo's makeup and how
she applies it, intertwined with the narrator's complex emotional response to it.

Situational complexity. Just as human behavior is never what it seems to be on the
surface, the situations that comprise a memorable short story or novel often are richer in
consequence than meets the eye. If Captain Yossarian, in Joseph Heller's *Catch-22* (1961),
were to claim insanity to avoid having to go on a bombing mission, why, then his insanity
would make him ideal for the mission! Heller's pitting the struggle for sanity amid the insanity of warfare is what makes this novel so memorable. In Jerzy Kosinski's *Being There*
(1971), a satiric parable of a mentally deficient gardener's rise from homelessness to political stardom through a series of chance encounters and by mimicking words and manner-
isms from TV (which he watches habitually), the tale, so simple on its surface, is complex
in situational irony. When Chance, recuperating from an accident in the Washington,
DC home of a financier, meets with the President, the latter asks him, "What do you think
about the bad season on [Wall] Street?"

> Chance stared at the carpet. Finally, he spoke: 'In a garden . . . growth has its season.
> There are spring and summer, but there are also fall and winter. And then spring and
> summer again. As long as the roots are not severed, all is well and all will be well.'
> He raised is eyes. Rand [the financier] was looking at him, nodding. The President
> seemed quite pleased.
>
> 'I must admit . . .' the President said, "that what you've just said is one of the most
> refreshing and optimistic statements I've heard in a very, very long time. Many of us
> forget that nature and society are one!'

Chance, of course, has no capacity for understanding or appreciating metaphor; ironically, the President understands metaphor to a fault, and goes on to use Chance's garden
metaphors (in an address to the nation) in hopes that such figurative language would con-

vince the nation that the economy is healthy when it isn't. Irony, then, is a powerful tool for injecting complexity into a story.

HOW TO USE COMPLEXITY TO DEVELOP A STORY

Now you're probably wondering what steps you can take to imbue your characters and plots with the complexity needed to make them realistic and engaging. Here's what I suggest:

1. *To create emotional complexity*, prepare in-depth psychological and behavioral profiles of your protagonist and antagonist. Go into as much detail as possible; include old and recent traumatic experiences, frustrations, grudges, sorrows, obsessions; temperament; successes and failures; bad and good habits. Behavior is destiny; people's actions largely determine their lot in life.
2. *To create narrative/descriptive complexity*, write a one- or two-page descriptions of key scenes in which a character is engaged in an activity that reveals some aspect of his or her personality. For example, imagine that your protagonist is a sculptor who exploits his wife's beauty for his own selfish advances while ignoring her needs and ambitions. What goes through his mind as he shapes and reshapes the clay? What goes through her mind as she poses for him?
3. *To create situational complexity*, write a one- or two-page dramatic incident that captures something about the clash between protagonist and antagonist. Keep in mind that people often possess ulterior, undisclosed motives or hidden agendas that belie what they say or do overtly. To continue with the example of the self-centered sculptor and his unhappy wife, dramatize a moment when she can no longer endure his insensitivity, and asks him point blank if he really loves her or is just using her.

CONCLUDING REFLECTIONS

A good story captivates because it enables readers to become part of an imagined world that illuminates facets of the real world that nonfiction, with its emphasis on outward events, cannot penetrate. Historians can give us vivid accounts of Civil War battles, but they cannot put us into the mind of a solider caught in the terrifying moments of combat, as Stephen Crane has done with his protagonist in *The Red Badge of Courage* (1895):

> He fought an intense battle with his body. His dulled senses wished him to swoon and he opposed them stubbornly, his mind portraying unknown dangers and mutilations if he should fall. . . . Around him he could hear the grumble of jolted cannon as the scurrying horses were lashed toward the front. Once, a young officer on a besplashed charger nearly ran him down.

Stephen Crane was born six years after the Civil War ended; he had never experienced combat firsthand. And yet he possessed the fiction writer's ability to probe deeply enough into human nature to sense what it must be like to partake in the trauma of combat. More than that, he possessed the ironist's ability to capture the stark contrast between the desolate human situation and nature's indifference to it:

> As he gazed around him the youth felt a flash of astonishment at the blue, pure sky and the sun-gleamings on the trees and fields. It was surprising that Nature had gone tranquilly on with her golden process in the midst of such much devilment.

By becoming adept at the art of complexity—the art of capturing the vicissitudes of characters, story progression and conflict—you will be well on your way to becoming a masterful writer of fiction.

Fred D. White is a professor of English, emeritus, at Santa Clara University. He has published numerous short works of fiction and humor, most recently in *Every Day Fiction*, *Praxis*, *Aphelion*, *Brilliant Flash Fiction*, and *Clockwise Cat*. He is the author of several books on writing, including *The Daily Writer*, *The Writer's Idea Thesaurus*, and *Writing Flash*.

HOW TO INCORPORATE CONFLICT INTO YOUR FICTION

....

by Janice Hussein

With characterization, conflict runs hand-in-hand as one of the key ingredients of writing fiction, yet many writers, especially new writers, aren't clear about this crucial link between the two and how it functions to create stories that editors and readers will love. Writers shouldn't just think, I'm going to take this kind of (just) place-holding main character and I want this cool list of things to happen in the book, without reference to the character and their back story/background, not having the one work off the other.

This article will first cover briefly how conflict functions and then explain how the link between it and characters works, what is needed to make it work, and offer illustrations taken from one book and its characters, and transpose them into another book/story to show how this is the case—how using just any character, placed within any story, doesn't work.

The purpose of conflict is to provide an opportunity for growth and change for one of the main characters over the course of the novel. The protagonist(s) must have a goal to achieve and a wound to resolve. The playing field for that conflict in a novel requires at least a three-act structure, with a minimum of 3 major reversals.

Certain elements are needed in a novel to make the conflict/character link work. First, the protagonist's desire or goal must be the antagonist's desire as well. The antagonist may be a specific person or may be a set way of thinking—a worldview that is triggered by and due to an event or events that have happened to the protagonist in the past.

There must be a match, a conflict lock—such that both protagonist and antagonist are working to get the same goal, yet only one can succeed. Each works against the other. The antagonist, along with fate, places obstacles, setbacks, and reversals in the path of the protagonists during their quest to achieve what they desire. In the process, at least one of the protagonists works through an internal problem or wound, a problem that requires fairly specific obstacles and setbacks for it to be resolved. For example, in a romance, it can be any number of things—the heroine was jilted at the altar and thus humiliated; the heroine went through an abusive marriage and thus doesn't want to get involved again; or the heroine (and/or hero) came from a broken home and doesn't want to relive that experience.

The key element of this link is incorporating all three types of conflict into your fiction. Those three types of conflict are external, internal, and in-between conflict, with subplot conflict using these same types but on a smaller scale. The story opens with the character having external conflict that isn't resolved until the end. The external plot forces the protagonists into situations that illuminate the internal conflict and focuses them to deal specifically with that internal conflict. Thus the internal conflict is what drives the external conflict, because the external conflict must be designed to help resolve that specific internal conflict. Internal conflict should correspond in some way to the external conflict. In-between conflict, unlike internal conflict, is conflict that occurs because of other differences between the characters—such as societal, socio-economic, cultural, or professional (law officer vs. criminal)—that determine how they approach life, and how they would approach a problem. The subplot conflict should resonate with the main conflict, showing different facets of the theme.

External conflict has 4 main types: 1) Relational; 2) Social; 3) Situational; and, 4) Cosmic that can be used in a novel. Relational is between family and friends; social is group; situational is the problem in your immediate area—neighborhood/town; and cosmic is like a hurricane or other natural disaster.

In a romance novel, the author must develop conflict for both hero and heroine. If hero and heroine have separate external conflicts, they must be related. In a long book, both hero and heroine will have internal conflict.

Another element is the ongoing interdependent interaction between conflict and character, as reflected within action, dialogue, and narrative, and serves to deepen the conflict and up the stakes—both the emotional and the external or plot stakes—while also necessarily revealing character. We are our choices, and our choices and our subsequent actions and reactions, especially in situations of importance to us, reveal who we really are. The conflict via this interaction can introduce the relationships between characters, the characters themselves, and why readers should like the protagonists, pull for them, and dislike the antagonist(s). Conflict helps to flesh out the characters so that they are more complex. And each character that is introduced can serve to also widen and deepen the conflict, to up the stakes—moving generally from least impactful to most impactful.

With each introduction of character and conflict, readers can be introduced to different facets of why we should hate the villains, from the different perspectives of several characters, and this make the main conflict more complex, giving valid believable reasons for why the different characters are invested in taking on the villains. This increases readers' emotional investment in both the novel and the characters, and serves to up the stakes.

The movie *Silverado* illustrates this interdependent interaction between conflict and character in the scenes where the five heroes take on retrieving the money stake of the homesteaders who came to the territory to put up fences and to farm the land. This action brings them into direct conflict with the area's cattlemen who are, in this case, the villains, and creates another facet of conflict for the main heroes—it ups the stakes, and intensifies the conflict.

....

Another different character, with a similar or different internal conflict or wound, placed in similar circumstances, might decide to take vastly different steps to resolve or avoid the conflict, and thus, the novel about their journey would be different.

....

This interaction must be developed over the course of the novel, via the conflict, so that at the climax of the book, the character(s) must acknowledge the wound or flaw and deal with it. The steps that a character chooses to take to avoid or resolve the conflict depends on their personality, their background and experiences, and subsequently on the results of each of those decisions—further setbacks, obstacles, and reversals and the reactions from other characters or the antagonists to what happens after each of those steps. Another different character, with a similar or different internal conflict or wound, placed in similar circumstances, might decide to take vastly different steps to resolve or avoid the conflict, and thus, the novel about their journey would be different.

How the conflict/conflict link works can be illustrated when an element of the link—either conflict or character—is taken from one book and its characters, and transposed into another book/story, and serves to show how using just any character, placed within any story, doesn't work. To provide an example of this link, below are two books, their summaries, and then what happens when their elements are transposed.

In Linda Howard's novel *Up, Close, and Dangerous*, the character Bailey Wingate—smart, sophisticated, and cautious—avoids getting close to anyone. Though not a professional investor, she manages a private trust fund for her step-children. From her background of observing her parents marry so many times, with the resulting half-siblings and step-siblings, she believes love and sexual attraction cause stupidity. And in any possible relationship, she chooses to always cautious and smart, and to be the one who would reject first before anyone can reject her. She has a problem with trust and believes love doesn't last. She would distance herself, both physically and emotionally, from anyone who might approach her in an even vaguely romantic way. She's never been in love. But her avoidant approach to relationships is challenged when she finds herself in a bid for survival after a private plane crash leaves her stranded with pilot Cam Justice in the snowy ice-cold Idaho mountains. This results in a romantic entanglement from which she can't just physically remove herself.

In Julie James' novel *It Happened One Wedding*, the character Sydney Sinclair, a director of a private equity fund, is searching for that special someone, applying the same instincts and tactics she used in her job, testing each potential date against a 20-item checklist—the key to her approach to solving her dating problem—which suitors must pass, and which she put together after she was jilted at the altar by her fiancé Brodie. When her sister Isabel and the hero's brother Simon decide to get married, with Sydney as the maid of honor and hero FBI agent Vaughn Roberts as the best man, they are constantly thrown together. Despite the checklist, Sydney is sufficiently attracted to Vaughn—who couldn't imagine settling down to one woman and abandoning the fun of serial relationships—to become at least sexually involved with him, a Mr. Wrong—the casual no-strings-attached fling perfectly fine with Vaughn—while she dates potential Mr. Rights.

To illustrate how transposing the characters wouldn't work: If Bailey were the protagonist in the book *It Happened One Wedding*, it would be a different novel or not a novel at all—Bailey wouldn't be dating, she wouldn't have a 20-item checklist, and while she would be polite to the hero, she would have avoided FBI agent Vaughn Roberts, whatever the circumstances. She definitely wouldn't have had a fling with him. Only if Bailey were forced into a situation—such as being stranded in the wilderness with the hero—where she could not avoid close proximity to the hero, would she get emotionally involved. And if Bailey ever decided to date, her strategy for dating would likely not include a 20-item checklist—one that private equity fund director Sydney developed to hedge her dating risks. Though if Bailey were to date, she would definitely weigh her risks, but in a different way. To resolve Bailey's internal conflict, it would take a different set of conflicts and a different hero than those in the novel *It Happened One Wedding*.

Further, the heroes in the books are looking for different things. For example, hero Cam Justice, in *Up, Close, and Dangerous*, discovers that behind heroine Bailey's emotional walls and the rather cool polite front she displays, she is strong-minded and resourceful even in extreme circumstances, full of ingenious yet practical ideas, and totally giving of herself—a marshmallow who is altruistic. That is the kind of heroine you want in a survival situation and the kind that a strong, commanding hero like Cam Justice would fall for—he wants a woman with whom he doesn't have "to hold himself back to keep from… overwhelming her."

The character/conflict link requires a unique pairing of character and conflict—external, internal, and in-between. The above example illustrates how using just any character, placed within any story, doesn't work. The three types of conflict work hand-in-glove with particular character(s) to build a unique story, through the ongoing interdependent interaction between conflict and character, the interaction deepening the conflict and upping the stakes, in order to resolve the particular internal conflict through the gauntlet of external conflict.

....

Janice Hussein is a freelance writer and editor, with more than a decade of freelance experience, and a Master's degree in Writing and publishing. She edits and copyedits short stories and novels, and offers classes and workshops, at conferences and elsewhere, to writers at all levels. She is a member of NW Independent Editors Guild, the National Writers Union, EFA, RWA, and she networks on Twitter, Facebook, LinkedIn, and Google+. Several of her articles have been previously published in the *Writer's Market*, and the *Novel & Short Story Writer's Market*.

....

CREATING AN ANTAGONISTIC SETTING

....

by DiAnn Mills

//

An antagonistic setting is as much a gift to the reader as an unpredictable plot. The explosion of an unforeseen or modified environment forces the protagonist to dig deep for ways to survive. When setting becomes a predator, a character's true inner landscape is revealed, one he cannot deny.

I welcome the task of increasing the stakes to provide an obscure setting. The work is worth every drop of perspiration—and your readers will love you for the professional touch.

Writers search for ways to raise the stakes for the protagonist. We mine weaknesses to make him squirm and pressure him to grow into a true hero—or heroine. Sometimes he fails and sometimes he succeeds. In each instance, the protagonist is caught off guard, and every breath is met with potential disaster.

We writers often turn to obvious means of adding stress, tension, and conflict through characterization, dialogue, plot twists, symbolism, and emotive conflict. These are powerful tools, and our stories must contain stellar treatment of each literary technique to ensure our protagonists are continuously challenged.

Why not add more to defy the protagonist's resolve?

Establishing an antagonistic setting as an additional means of growth and change requires skill. But once mastered, the method offers a new dimension to the story by creating additional stumbling points that add barriers to the character's goal.

Making life easy doesn't keep the reader engaged. I prefer keeping my readers up all night trying to figure out what will happen next.

An antagonistic setting means shaky ground for the protagonist. The problem creeps up to catch the character unaware, stalking him with devious tactics. Survival extends beyond defeating a villain, either mental, physical, or spiritual.

Mental Antagonistic Setting:

- A dream world
- An unconscious state
- A hallucination
- Altered thinking as in mental illness or depression
- A phobia

Phobias provide an ideal backdrop for a hostile setting. The person suffering from one of these fears can experience physical symptoms that can be life-threatening. Dizziness, dread, nausea, chest pains, panic attacks, and a host of other reactions can stop the character and debilitate him from moving forward.

Take a look at a few of these phobias as a possible way to heighten a weakness associated with setting:

- Acrophobia - fear of heights
- Astraphobia - fear of storms
- Claustrophobia - fear of being stuck in a small space
- Ophidiophobia - fear of snakes
- Pteromerhanophobia: fear of flying
- Social Phobia - fear of interacting with people

To ensure a tight, high-stakes scene, use inner and outer fears against him. This intimidates the character to not only struggle but also face an inner and outer antagonist: fear and setting. Watch plot twists emerge that will add levels to the story line. Seek ways to ensure the he faces one difficult situation after another with paralyzing fright.

Physical Antagonistic Setting:

- An unexpected storm
- A rough and foreign terrain
- A natural disaster
- An explosive work or home life
- An otherwise harmonious situation that turns hostile
- A limitation of mobility

Spiritual Antagonistic Setting:

- A belief system that supports superiority of a single race, creed, or culture
- A religious conviction that practices persecution of others

- An ideology presented in childhood has the potential to instill prejudice and strong biases that can be difficult to overcome. An aversion to others who embrace other forms of faith.

An unanticipated change in an environment reveals the true inner self by displaying strengths or weaknesses. Does he run or stand and fight? Sometimes fleeing is a form of courage. The adversity can be obvious or hidden but include the deception in ways that compel him to make tough decisions and then accept responsibility for the consequences.

A wise writer shows enough setting for the reader to envision the story world—and no more. Information overload cheats the reader of vicariously living the adventure of the character and closes the door on imagination. Readers today crave a story of adventure, growth, and unforeseen events.

How does a writer accomplish an antagonistic setting? View the location's description as though it were a characterization sketch. Concentrate on an antagonist's personality traits and use them to disguise what looks like an enticing environment:

- Determination
- Power
- Beauty
- Charm
- Manipulation
- Deception

Setting is vital and full of spirit. Let the character's surroundings whisper, "Be careful for what is ahead." Associate the location with sensory perception, for in the depths of the five senses lie emotions and memories that have the ability to paralyze.

Sight - What does he perceive around him that can alter reality?

A man dreamed of one day living in the mountains. He spent his entire savings building a cabin. During a wildfire, he was forced to evacuate and couldn't find his dog. How does this memory affect his choices today: where will he live or will he ever own another dog?

Smell - What smells trigger pleasant or unpleasant memories? If the smell is unfamiliar, how does the character react?

A twelve-year-old girl was sent to her grandparents' farm at the beginning of summer. She loved helping her grandmother pick strawberries and make preserves. She learned the reason for the visit was so her parents could work out details of a divorce. To this day, the smell of strawberries makes her ill.

Taste - What tastes draw the character to the past? Can a unique taste shake his conscious or unconscious reaction to what is going on around him?

Consider a man who was celebrating his birthday at a restaurant. The meal was served, a steak cooked to perfection, and he received a call that his mother had died. How would he view his birthday, the restaurant, or steak in the future?

Hear - What sounds soothe or disturb the character? Where did the sounds originate to pinpoint the reaction?

A woman's father worked as a professional organist. He played in churches, theaters, and private events, entertaining and inspiring everyone he met. The woman is involved in a high-stress law firm, and the only way she can relax is by listening to organ music.

Feel - How was the character touched in the past that evokes positive or negative memories?

A man was never touched as a child. He was born premature, abandoned in the hospital, and later placed in a foster care home where he didn't receive affection. As he grew, he sought inappropriate means for attention. Now he's considering a serious crime.

When plotting with setting in mind, a writer chooses at least one of the following scenarios to create a story with visceral impact:

- Man vs. man
- Man vs. animal
- Man vs. nature
- Man vs. society
- Man vs. survival
- Man vs. technology
- Man vs. God

Every situation above requires a distinct setting in which the writer can harvest the gems of antagonism. The opposition is often more than one scenario. Write the scene in the point of view of the character who has the most to lose, using staggering conflict. Use dialogue that anchors voice and responses.

A character who is familiar with a particular setting will not make the same observations or mistakes as a novice.

- A veteran police officer understands the demands and evolving nature of his job better than a rookie, who can be either nervous, apprehensive, or overconfident.
- A seasoned teacher welcomes the new school year with experience and wisdom. A new teacher is fearful about her first teaching position. Is she too strong a disciplinarian? Are her students learning? Is she offering them exciting teaching venues?

The following are instances of an antagonistic setting in a few popular genres.

Contemporary: A beautiful afternoon in a park for a family reunion is interrupted when a young girl brings her fiancé, a man who is of a different race and culture. Her father is enraged, and a fight breaks out among family members. The young girl is killed when she attempts to stop the conflict.

Fantasy: In a land faraway, a kindly king is replaced by a tyrant who levies heavy taxes upon his subjects. One man chooses to free the people of the greedy king, but he must find a way to enter the heavily guarded castle.

Historical: A wagon train pulls into a peaceful valley where the weary travelers can rest before heading across a vast prairie. A pack of hungry wolves attack the horses and livestock stopping the travelers from continuing their journey.

Romance: A couple honeymoons on an exotic, deserted island. The white sandy beaches and the call of seagulls appear to be a paradise. An unexpected storm rises, bringing high winds and twenty-foot waves. The couple is trapped with no means of contacting help.

Sci-Fi: An isolated, peaceful planet is invaded by highly intelligent aliens who require the inhabitant's water supply for their own survival. Who can help the weaker people overcome insurmountable odds?

Suspense: A heroine refers to her backyard as a haven. A tall, stone wall frames nature's display of green and flowering plants. But when a killer chases her inside the garden, she is trapped by what she thought was her respite. Can anyone help her?

Thriller: An aid to a popular politician is invited to an isolated mountain retreat center with other staff members. The aid discovers the politician plans to unleash a virus on American citizens that will kill many innocent people. The politician confiscates all devices leaving the aid helpless to tell the world of the devastation to come.

Whatever the setting, the writer strives to keep characters—and the plot—moving in unpredictable directions.

Why place your hero or heroine in an idyllic environment that makes solving the goal easy and pain free? Why not muddy the waters and create an antagonistic setting that keeps readers on the edge of their seats?

DiAnn Mills is a bestselling author who believes her readers should expect an adventure. She combines unforgettable characters with unpredictable plots to create action-packed, suspense-filled novels. Her titles have appeared on the CBA and ECPA bestseller lists; won two Christy Awards; and been finalists for the RITA, Daphne Du Maurier, Inspirational Readers' Choice, and Carol award contests. Firewall, the first book in her Houston: FBI series, was listed by Library Journal as one of the best Christian Fiction books of 2014. DiAnn is a founding board member of the American Christian Fiction Writers, a member of Advanced Writers and Speakers Association, Sisters in Crime, and International Thriller Writers. She is co-director of The Blue Ridge Mountain Christian Writers Conference and The Mountainside Marketing Conference with social media specialist Edie Melson where she continues her passion of helping other writers be successful. Learn more at www.diannmills.com.

ANATOMY OF A GREAT SHORT STORY

by Jack Smith

Many writers, at least literary fiction writers, begin their writing career with the short story, sending off work to magazines and journals, trying to get published. The competition, they discover, is "maddening," to borrow from Willy Loman's comment about the business world in *Death of a Salesman*. This is the first thing a writer discovers when s/he submits stories. Magazines often taken no more than two percent of what they receive—and they receive a lot, as market blurbs reveal.

How do you compete in that world?

If you submit and submit and submit, you will eventually—if you get the craft down. Ask published writers—it's the way it is.

But outside of the matter of publication—which can become a goal in itself, robbing a writer of the joy of writing—what about the story itself? Let's start there. What makes a good short story? What makes a great one? If you're a writer, you need to put that first. As they say, the rest will follow.

What is a short story, exactly? Short stories run different lengths, some short, some long, some bordering on the novella. James Joyce's "The Dead" has been called both short story and novella. The same for William Faulkner's "The Bear."

The short story is all about compression. It's got to be a whole story, not half-baked. It's got to round things out, have a plot, have a character arc. But it affords a small space in which to pull all this off, and that's what makes it so tough—to make a work that has fullness but sparseness too.

But let's begin with the process, not the product.

THE PROCESS

Experientially, what is the act of composition like? How is it different from writing a longer work, or is it?

Peter Selgin, author of *Drowning Lessons*, winner of the Flannery O'Connor Award for Fiction, illuminates the essential nature of the short story by contrasting it with the novel. "I've heard the difference described as that between a sprint and a marathon, or a one-night-stand versus a marriage (though I prefer to think of a story not as a one-night-stand, but as something more romantic, a brief affair)." But if we move beyond the most obvious difference—time span—what else separates these two? Perhaps a difference in intensity? No, says Selgin: "Surely a novel can be just as intense, just as urgent, though obviously the urgency has to be spread over more pages, and—usually—a wider scope of time." For him, one radical difference between the two forms is the drafting process for each, and this is a matter of intensity: "I think a big part of the difference comes down to how stories are actually written, not to the intensity of subject matter, character motivation, or plot, but the intensity brought to the composition process itself, the swift concentrated attack as opposed to a process of slow deliberation." Second, the time frame it takes to complete the work also makes the process for these two quite different: "With a novel, you may hack away at the thing for months and even years," says Selgin, "whereas a story is more like a karate chop: swift and ruthless, with the effort all concentrated into what Poe called the story's 'singular effect.'" Third, the mental activity that goes into creating a novel is much different from that of a short story: "Where writing a novel might involve as much rumination as composition, with a story it's probably better to not ruminate at all, to grab hold of the thing—that initial impulse or idea or whatever—and run it down, chase it into its lair." Or, shifting metaphors, Selgin states, "You hold your nose, take the plunge. Fitzgerald said, 'All good writing is swimming underwater and holding your breath.' His words apply especially to the short story, I think."

HALLMARKS OF THE GREAT STORY

In terms of artistic method, then, the short story may require an activity all its own. But what about its properties? What makes the successful short story? And how about the great one? Are there any reliable standards you can go by? Any criteria you can follow?

According to Robert Garner McBrearty, winner of the Sherwood Anderson Foundation Fiction Award and author of three story collections, it would be reductive to try to set forth criteria for such a complex work as the short story. "Because short stories come in so many different types, from flash fictions to longer, fully-developed stories, from the realistic to the surreal, there really isn't a one-size-fits-all description of a successful short story." Viewing flash fiction as a subgenre, he states, "For instance, the expectations about character development would be different in a flash fiction than they would be in a long story. In general, though, one would expect to find certain elements in most successful short stories." Bottom line? It comes down to the craft, says McBrearty, including "vivid characters and setting, lively dialogue, a strong writing style, the sense of something important at stake, and an interesting conflict building to a climax and resolution, even if there is not full resolution of the conflict." Still, you can have all the right stuff, you can handle the fictional elements masterfully, and yet the story can "still come off flat," says McBrearty. It seems a "great mystery," but he believes it has to do with three aspects that separate the successful story from the really great one: tone, voice, and vision. The great story, McBrearty believes, is not only superb in craft but equally strong in its overall vision: representing "the unique way the writer looks at the world."

Like McBrearty, other short story writers tend to judge a story's quality on a basis that includes but also exceeds technical performance. Donna Baier Stein, author of *Sympathetic People*, prefers stories that "reveal the complexities of our inner worlds, that show us how multi-faceted our minds and hearts really are." Besides a skill with language and a way of pulling one into the world of the story, for her the great short story writer "has psychological insight, a keenly observant eye." She finds these qualities in two of her favorite short story writers, Flannery O'Connor and Richard Bausch.

For Kerry Neville, author of two collections of short stories, a story's greatness depends on its memorability, which has much to do with the nature of the language. The great story, she says, "approaches the lyrical compression of poetry: it is vigilant in terms of the cadences of sentences, the collisions of words pressed against each other." With this in mind, she values James Joyce's "The Dead." She especially loves the closing line for its fine lyricism: "'His soul swooned slowly as he heard the snow falling faintly through the universe and faintly falling, like the descent of their last end, upon all the living and the dead.'" The stories that stay with Neville are the ones that raise her consciousness much like a lyric poem does: "a quick, intense illumination of an overlooked or forgotten spot of time in the world that might, in fact, change the way I understand myself in the world or the world's presence inside myself."

Melissa Pritchard is the Flannery O'Connor, O. Henry and Pushcart Prize winning author of four story collections and five novels. One seldom writes the enduring short story, she states. Though she's read a lot of "marvelous" stories, she's encountered only a few that are "deeply memorable, worth returning to, sharing and teaching." Even among favorite writers, says Pritchard, we find certain stories we admire far more than others. She found this to be true of William Trevor's short fiction. "Once, after I had made my way, reverently, through one of his volumes of collected stories, I discovered that though every one of his seventy stories was beautifully polished and brilliantly written, only a handful were what I considered masterpieces, enduring works of art." This discovery surprised her, but at the same time she found it "oddly comforting." It gave her insight into her own work: "What it said was that one must write prolifically, knowing not every story will be perfect, but that perhaps after the seventh or eighth or ninth story, the tenth might turn out to be the one with lasting magic."

But what does "lasting magic" look like? For Pritchard, "There is something rare and haunting about a masterful story. I believe it comes from the writer succeeding at what I call 'lofting' the story out of its immediate setting and dilemma of character or characters into a larger ethical question about human experience—a question that 'floats' above the story, ultimately unanswerable, but emotionally recognized by readers."

So, again, the really great story, the kind anthologized as "literature," is about more than craft. The craft must be there, of course, and much of what makes it great is attributable to its expert handling of craft. But the great short story has an even larger reach than that. Because of its distinctive vision and flash of insight, it has a staying power that haunts us long after we've finished reading it.

ACHIEVING COMPRESSION

As a literary form, the short story is known for its compression. It can usually be read in one sitting. In terms of space, it's confined, not expanded; it's a small world, not a vast, global one. And yet, restrained as it is, the short story, paradoxically, has enormous potential to achieve both depth and range. But how do you manage to pack so much into such a small space?

For McBrearty, there are many different ways of writing stories, but he usually tries to get the characters and the action moving quickly, and to watch out for bloated backstory: "Where we start the story is particularly important. Early drafts tend to contain too much background. Ask yourself: where does the story really start? Where does it start getting interesting? Start the story there! Or just before." Second, he says, watch out for excessive description. "A whole lot of physical details about a character may not be needed. There may be one or two striking details that will be more vivid if we leave out some of the other details." With setting, McBrearty's description tends to be spare and impressionistic. "I just want to give a sense, but a strong sense, of the environment where the story is taking place." He achieves further economy by bringing in setting details as characters engage in action instead of creating setting and then placing them in it. "Compressing the story," he says, "doesn't mean making it tight and restricted, but making it even livelier as we highlight the essential elements."

If you're a short story writer, says Baier Stein, you have to make every word count. This means being "very careful in what you choose to include." For this reason, she advises her creative writing students to limit their story to one protagonist and one point of view. You must find further ways to focus, she says: "Don't try to cover one character's entire life. Focus on a few hours, a day, a week." Time-frame wise, she recommends starting a story "close to its ending." There are, of course, exceptions, as she notes. For example, Alice Munro: "She may start a story with a scene that happens completely separate from the main plot's timeframe." There's much to learn from great writers, but Baier Stein does recommend that at least "in the early stories you write, you keep the parameters simple with a limited time frame."

Neville offers us an intriguing analogy: "A short story is like an arrow shot straight through the heart: direct and intentional. So, every sentence must serve this intent. No extraneous matter. Character details should not only allow us to 'see' a character in the moment, but to feel the weight of time that has come before and will come after for the character." Short stories tend to focus on the ordinary events of life, not the big ones, she says. Great short stories deal with the "ordinary moments made extraordinary through a writer's intentional caretaking."

"I think a short story must not take on too much in the way of plot,' says Selgin, "that ideally as little as possible should happen." For him, the old adage "less is more" is true. "John Gardner called it the 'rule of elegance and efficiency.'" Keeping this in mind, Selgin offers this advice: "If you can tell a story with two characters, don't have three; if you can tell it in one scene, don't write two scenes, and so on." An excellent story to read for compression, he believes, is John Cheever's "The Swimmer." "When Cheever sends Ned Merrill off on his symbolic journey across a river of swimming pools, he does so not across a distance of months, years, or decades, but on one summer day that, by a twist of suburban magical realism, turns into a lifetime." This isn't a prescription for all stories, though, because "other stories demand greater complexity," states Selgin. Still, in general, he says, "Do with as little complexity as possible. Trust simplicity."

According to Pritchard, compression is about tension and pressure. In a traditional story, she says, "you will be putting your main character under so much pressure, internally and externally, that she is forced to act, choose, to think and risk in radical ways." This applies to both the internal sphere, the character's mind, and the external, the world the character enters into, and such pressure leads to suspense, which is a must, Pritchard states, regardless of the kind of fiction you're writing. "Suspense is not confined to genre fiction—it is imperative in literary fiction as well. What is she going to do, what will she choose or refuse, how will she be transformed or changed by the wringing-out process you, the author, the creator of this story, have designed for her?"

If a short story is all about compression, there is no single way to achieve this—and certainly no single way to create the great story, the memorable one, the one with that lasting magic. For Selgin, "Every truly distinguished short story is a laboratory experiment, an engineered mutation that invents its own rules, that finds its own form."

WRAPPING UP

Every story you write can't be a great one. Even the greats may write only a half dozen or dozen really great ones in their life. But writing the truly great one can be your goal. Meanwhile, learn the craft. Learn how to handle the very demanding compression of the short story form. Read a lot of short stories, and find out what is good, and what is truly great. Which stories do you remember the most? Which ones linger on, stay with you, hold you fast? Study those. What is it about them? Where's the magic?

Jack Smith has published four novels: *Miss Manners for War Criminals*, *Being*, *Icon*, and *Hog to Hog*. Besides his writing, Smith was fiction editor of *The Green Hills Literary Lantern*, published by Truman State University, for 25 years.

GEORGE SAUNDERS

The Big Short

....

by Tyler Moss

//

Superlatives.

George Saunders is used to those.

A 2013 profile in *The New York Times Magazine* called him "the writer of our time." The late David Foster Wallace once dubbed him "the most exciting writer in America," and Saunders' fellow novelist and teaching peer Mary Karr named him "the best short story writer in English—not 'one of,' not 'arguably,' but the Best." Zadie Smith deemed his latest work "a masterpiece," and he's been hailed as the heir to Pynchon and Vonnegut.

A former MacArthur Genius Fellow, Saunders has written nearly two dozen pieces—both fiction and nonfiction—for *The New Yorker*, demonstrating his talent across category. His 2013 *New York Times* bestselling short story collection, "Tenth of December," was a National Book Award Finalist and was named one of the best books of the year by such venues as NPR, *Entertainment Weekly* and *New York* magazine.

Unwilling to be defined by his concision alone, Saunders' first foray into full-length fiction—2017's Man Booker Prize–winning *Lincoln in the Bardo*—is an existential exercise in human suffering, sentimentality and historical re-examination, with a dash of his trademark humor. The novel follows young Willie Lincoln who, after perishing from typhoid at age 11, awakens in the "bardo" (a liminal state after death pulled from Buddhist tradition), bringing readers along as he meets other ghosts still struggling to sort out their previous life's baggage. Honest Abe himself makes an appearance, grief and guilt drawing him to his son's crypt. Defying the conventions of genre and format, the book is simply the latest trophy in Saunders' crowded case.

Yet despite all the accolades, the 59-year-old is remarkably humble. It's a modesty hewn from early years of struggle in developing his own voice, with his acclaimed first collection, 1996's "CivilWarLand in Bad Decline," written in his off-hours while he worked full time as a technical writer in Rochester, N.Y. That humility translates into an abundant generosity of spirit. Saunders teaches at Syracuse University's Master of Fine Arts program—the same program through which the distinguished writers Tobias Wolff and Douglas Unger mentored him in the late 1980s.

His sense of altruism—an openness to share from his well of wisdom—manifests itself in a craft-based conversation with WD that runs nearly 10,000 words. Read an excerpt of that interview over the following pages—which covers the inventive structure of *Lincoln in the Bardo* (now available in paperback), Saunders' formula for conflict and his aversion to outlines—and find the extended version online at writersdigest.com/aug-18.

Lincoln in the Bardo has such an innovative structure: excerpts from history books, sections that read like a stage play, character monologues that are self-contained vignettes. How did you land on that format?

This book took me, in total, about 20-something years to write. During the first 16 of that, I was mostly just thinking about it and a little terrified of it, and also trying to avoid it. I would think, *I'll do that Lincoln book*, then I'd think, *I don't know how to start*. I guess the short answer to your question is: Structure is a way that allows you to do the things you're good at, and avoid the things you're not so good at. In this case, I was really afraid that the Lincoln subject would necessitate or cause the book to be a little stiff and 19th century. For example, I thought of writing it in Lincoln's voice, [but] that seemed really boring. I couldn't think of any way to make that enjoyable.

I thought about telling it in a distant third-person, [but] that didn't excite me at all. I stalled out for many years because I couldn't think of any structure that would let me have fun, basically. I had tried to write a book in this theatrical format before and had put it aside, but when I crossed that idea with the Lincoln idea, I got excited all of the sudden.

The one piece of advice I would give: If it's not exciting to you, it probably won't work out. In this case, it was just waiting for a structure that would get me excited.

I just read a great quote by Grace Paley, who said something like: It's not that you should write what you know, you should write what you don't know about what you know. I trust a lot in that feeling of an intrigued confusion.

What was your process like piecing it all together?

As I remember it, I started with the ghosts talking back and forth theatrically. There were two doubts I had about that: One was that I knew the reason I was excited about this book had a lot to do with the moment in history when the whole thing happened, this event where Lincoln went into his son's crypt. It happened in the middle of the Civil War. The circumstances around his son's death were very tragic and sad and specific. I knew I had to get the history in. Then, at the same time, after some number of weeks of writing the ghosts, I started to get that drifty feeling like, *Well, since they're ghosts, you can do anything.*

That's actually the enemy of good writing, I think. Good writing thrives on some kind of constraint. When you're saying, "OK, they're ghosts from any historical period and they can do any physical thing," that's really hard. Also, I felt as if my imagined or projected reader would be getting a little impatient with the absence of constraint. If anything goes, nothing happens, basically. Those two ideas arrived at the same time, and I thought, *I've got to put some history in there, just for grounding. Just so the ghosts will suddenly actually seem more believable.* If you have a ghost and a fact, the ghost seems more factual somehow.

One day I had one of these neurotic conversations with myself, which is like me talking back and forth to me. I said, "OK, do you think this history stuff has to go in there?"

"I do."

"OK. How do you think it can go in there?"

"I don't know, I tried everything I can do."

"OK, how do you know that history?"

"Well, I read it in all those history books."

"Well, why not just put it in there verbatim?"

Then there was an awkward silence and I'm like, "Can I do that?" And the other me said, "Well, it's your stupid book, you can do whatever you like."

That was another moment of excitement and a little bit of transgression—to say a part of my "writing" process was going to be typing up other people's words, editing them, rearranging them and injecting them into my book. Again, something about the almost suspect nature of that got me excited. The idea of using other sources suddenly seemed like sampling in music, or something like that. I've learned to trust that feeling. If I'm being a little dangerous or a little naughty or a little transgressive, and not just for the sake of it, then I know to go in that direction.

How much of a story's arc do you know before you begin?

My normal idea on stories is to try to know as little as possible at every step, because then you're open to the actual energy that's coming off the page. If you want the story to go left, but it really wants to go right, you'd better let it go right. If I don't have a whole lot of preconceptions about it, it's easier for me to make that swerve. Having said that, it always varies. Some stories, like one called "The End of Firpo in the World," I knew the whole arc, just in an instant. This Lincoln book … here's what my outline was: On one level, Lincoln comes into the crypt, holds the body and eventually leaves the graveyard. That would either happen in one night, or three times in three successive nights. The second arc was: Willie dies, is for some reason stuck in this bardo zone, and either is liberated from it in a positive way—or isn't. That was my whole outline. It was like a vague hallway I could walk down and try to find the particulars.

My sense of most younger writers that I meet is they put too much stock in knowing the whole thing before they start, which takes a lot of different forms. Sometimes it's outlines, sometimes it's a lot of discursive thought about thematics: *My book is going to be about this, and it's going to show this.* Speaking anecdotally, in most cases, that's too much. It actually is an elaborate ruse by the subconscious to keep you from finding the thing you should write about. It's almost like somebody walking through Paris with a map right in front of their face. They're concentrating on the map, but they're not really seeing the actual Paris.

You've called prose, when done right, "empathy training wheels." What are those "right" elements that need to be in place for the story to truly elicit empathy?

One of the symptoms of good writing—and also one of the causes of good writing—is that it takes the reader and the writer and puts them on the same footing. For example, a bad story is usually one where the writer is talking down to the reader. Leading him around by the nose, manipulating. The reader feels that, and just like if you were in a relationship with somebody who was constantly talking down to you, you would resist. It really is just the old-fashioned stuff of being clear, residing in your text long enough to know if you're defying logic in some way or if you're finding the optimal path through the material.

One of the symptoms of good writing—and also one of the causes of good writing—is that it takes the reader and the writer and puts them on the same footing.

Sometimes there's a tendency to overdo this idea of empathy, as if you have to make every story a demonstration of selfless compassion or something. But I think the empathy, so called, is mostly in your relation to the reader. You're trying to imagine that person as being every bit as smart and worldly and talented and curious as you are. If you do that, the level of your discourse will come up, and that person will feel honored by your attention.

When I read Dickens, I feel him as an empathetic writer. I just feel that he thinks well of me. He thinks that I'm as smart as he is, so he's telling the story very honestly and very frankly. Dickens resided long enough in that story to really find out why Scrooge was so stingy, then to supply exactly the right medicine in the form of those three ghosts to bring Scrooge up. He was loving Scrooge all along, even when Scrooge was a stinker. Dickens had that beautiful attitude of saying, "I know there's more to you than that, Ebenezer. Let me just keep looking at you."

You've said that you like to "take a human situation and make it come to a boil." How do you go about planting the seeds for conflict?

The truth is, it has to do with line-to-line revision. It has to do with … it's hard for me to explain this, but it's basically revising enough that the situation you're describing seems to you 100 percent real. You know how sometimes when you're in an early draft, it feels like typing—it doesn't become a human event yet? I feel like my job is to revise it until it feels like something that really happened. That has to do sometimes with the way the prose sounds, that compulsion we talked about earlier. If you power through a section of prose and have no doubts, then it seems like it happened.

Within that, there's another thing, which has to do with what I would call "narrative logic." It's like, OK, if you're reading a story of mine, you're doing that complicated work of projecting yourself into my main character. In other words, you're becoming my main character, and so am I. We're walking along together with this, and then in person, and we're both being that person. I have a little more control than you, so I say, "Jim came to the mud puddle," and you say, "OK, we're standing in front of a mud puddle." And then I say, "He took off all his clothes and rolled around in the mud on his way to work."

Now, part of your mind is going, "No, he didn't." The reason you're saying that is because you wouldn't do that. We can tolerate some of that [separation], and that's how we make a character distinct from ourselves—but I think if there are hundreds of moments like that in a story where I'm looking at you and saying, "Would you accept that the character would do Action A?" If you say yes, then we're still right next to each other and we're experiencing the story together. If you say, "I don't know," we've separated a bit. Some of that separation is necessary, because our characters aren't identical to us, but in a badly told story, the writer is asking the reader to accept things that a human being wouldn't do. That affects the reader's belief in the story, so that when you get to the climatic moment, the reader isn't fully invested because the writer has given her so many off-ramps.

In other words, when you read a description of a mental state in a story, and the reader goes, "Yeah, I've had that feeling," that's a good bonding agent. When you describe a physical sensation or item really well, the reader goes, "Oh yeah, I know that." Every time you can do that, you pull the reader in a little closer to you. I think the idea is to get to the very end of the story and have the reader still standing foot-to-foot with you. You haven't given her any reasons to disavow the truth of the story. That's what we talk about when we say climactic moments. The climactic moments feel powerful as long as we're still standing close together. In fact, even a fairly small climax can feel huge if the reader and writer are close.

I take a lot of consolation in that. If a story isn't working, we sometimes think we have to make it bigger, make a bigger escalation—an explosion, an alien invasion.

Often, that impulse just means that we sense that we've lost the reader early. It's almost like if you had a really terrible date with somebody and it wasn't going well, so you thought, "OK, I'll rent a string quartet at the very end."

You've said you're at a point now that when you don't have any story ideas, you find joy in that moment, instead of considering it a crisis. The possibility of running out of ideas terrifies most writers. Where does that optimism come from?

It's a mistake to think that a story is a result of ideas. I don't think I've ever written a good story that came out of an idea, really. Or if I start it that way, I abandon it quickly. A story is actually a system of meaning that creates meaning by reacting to itself. In other words, you don't actually need an external idea to write a story, you need an inciting something or other. For me, that can be a phrase or a vague idea of a theme park, or whatever. Sometimes it's just a diction that I want to use; I just want to talk in a certain voice.

This notion that we have to have an idea is deadly. It always has been for me. I think if you do have an idea for a story, your wish should be that the story would burn that idea away and three weeks in, you go, "What a facile idea that was. That wasn't enough." As a starting point it was great, but I think the idea is always that the story would overflow its banks in some way and become about something that you didn't even know it was going be about. Actually, it's probably too harsh to say you start a story with no ideas. You start [with] a nice idea, almost like when you say, "Let's take a trip to California." That's an idea—an idea that will get you started in the right direction, but hopefully you're going to have some complicated fun along the way, and you won't just get in a car and drive right to California. There will be some adventure [en route].

What I'm saying is, I find it really helpful to my process to say, "You don't have to have any ideas. You don't have to have any themes. You don't have to have any notions of where a story's going. You need one little chunk of text that's interesting to you, then you're going to go in there and start goofing with it and trying to make it sound better, and the story will reveal itself in that way."

I'm working on a story now—I have no idea what it's about. I don't know where it's going. There's some good lines in it, and I have confidence that if I just get in there and sit down and start working on it, it'll show me the path. It's almost like if you were going to dinner with a really good friend. I don't think you would feel inclined to sketch out your conversational plans. You would just trust that there's enough energy there that you're going to find out what the conversation is, and you're good enough on your feet that you can move with it and the result of that conversation when you both bring your sincere interest to the table and let it rip, that's going to be much more joyful and full of life than if you had talking points.

What's the most important bit of wisdom writers can take away from this interview?

We look for writing advice because it's such an uncom-fortable, frightening profession—so subjective and so iffy. The [sought after] writing advice will be somewhat helpful, encouraging us to go ahead and try something, but the real truth is the only writing advice that actually matters is the stuff that you discover 12 years into your journey, which strangely is almost impossible to talk about.

The real experience of writing a book or a story, if you think of it, is made up of thousands of tiny intuitive leaps. That moment when an image pops into your head and converts into language. You adjust that and boom, you typed it, and it's good or it's bad. That's an almost indescribable thing.

Tyler Moss is the editor-in-chief of *Writer's Digest,* in which this interview originally appeared.

KRISTIN HANNAH

New Territory

....

by Jessica Strawser

For a great many years before she was a household name, Kristin Hannah's fiction-writing career was an enviable kind of steady. In search of a more family-friendly pursuit than her law practice, as a young mother she made her first sale (1991's *A Handful of Heaven*, now out of print) and kept on selling—roughly a book a year, give or take a few, becoming a staple on the women's fiction shelves and, eventually, on the bestseller lists.

It was a slow, modest burn, the kind of "breakout" success that is built over time and fed with ever-better writing, increasingly complex stories, and an eye for both the intimate and the universal. Her 2008 release, *Firefly Lane*, the story of a tight but tested friendship spanning three decades, sold more than 1.2 million copies—catching by surprise only those who hadn't been paying attention. Within a few years, she became one of the first authors to have two novels appear on five *New York Times* bestseller lists simultaneously, with 2011's *Night Road* (the heartbreaking story of one bad decision's consequences, and the capacity to forgive) and 2012's *Home Front* (illuminating the toll of modern-day war on a military family).

And then, more than 20 novels in, Hannah blew her deadline.

She was writing something different, something more research-intensive, more sweeping and more in-depth than anything she'd written before—a World War II–era tale of two French sisters with very different approaches to living under Nazi occupation. But halfway through the manuscript, it became clear her usual timeline wasn't going to cut it.

"I called my editor and told her that I thought I had a potentially special book, but that there was no way I could write it in the amount of time I had on my deadline," Hannah says. "I asked her to roll the dice with me and give me another year to see if I couldn't make this book as special as I felt it could be." The editor—Jennifer Enderlin at

St. Martin's Press—said yes.

It was a good call.

Leaping into the No. 1 spot on bestsellers lists across the board and making itself at home there, 2015's *The Nightingale* moved readers worldwide. It was named a Best Book of the Year by *The Wall Street Journal*, Amazon, Goodreads, *Library Journal*, *BuzzFeed* and *The Week*, snagging the People's Choice Award and Audiobook of the Year Award on the way. As of this writing, the novel has more than 35,000 customer reviews on Amazon with a full 5-star average, and a Hollywood adaptation is in development with TriStar Pictures.

Now comes the long-awaited follow-up. Hannah's February release, *The Great Alone*, takes readers into the remote backcountry of Alaska in the wake of the Vietnam War, when a former prisoner of war takes his wife and daughter, young protagonist Leni, to restart their lives on the homestead of a fallen comrade. Hannah spoke with WD's editor-at-large, fellow novelist Jessica Strawser, about the evolution of her process, waiting for the right story, and much more.

After a smash hit like The Nightingale, I would imagine there's a lot of pressure surrounding what you're going to write next. How did you land on this story, and were there others you considered in the meantime?

You know, that is an interesting thing, how you follow up a success like *The Nightingale*. The one thing I can say is, I feel so incredibly grateful that it happened two decades into my career—but even so, even with the fact that I had written a lot of books before and, you know, sort of learned how to handle the writing business—it still was difficult. And I did put a lot of pressure on myself.

My original thought was that I wanted to write something that couldn't be compared to *The Nightingale*. Something completely different, its own kind of book. That took me down a rabbit hole, and I ended up having to throw a book away after almost two years of working on it. Because not only did it not live up to *The Nightingale*, it just didn't feel like it ever coalesced into a book that I believed in 110 percent.

You never know if a book is going to succeed or fail, so what matters ultimately is how you feel about it, and whether you, the author, are willing to bet the farm on this novel. And I just never quite was with that one.

So after I threw the first one away, I calmed down a bit and decided that what I needed to do was what I always do, which is simply take what I had learned from writing *The Nightingale*, and take what I felt were better skills and understanding of my strengths for writing powerful female characters, and let that be my guide.

I decided I wanted to sort of come home to America and write about something I knew pretty intimately. That led me to this novel set in the 1970s in Alaska, which is a time and place that I know very well and is, in its way, as much a secret world or an unusual world as anything I've ever done before.

Was that a difficult conversation with your publisher when you threw that first book away? Did you have to call them up and say, "That's not happening?"

Yeah [laughs], that's really what it comes down to. I've been lucky in my partnership with St. Martin's. … I said, "Nobody wants me to publish this book. We don't want this to be the next Kristin Hannah book because it's just not good enough. And I don't think working another year will make it good enough." So I was really lucky that they trusted me and said, "OK, take the time that you need." It helped, of course, that The Nightingale hadn't even rolled over into paperback yet. [But] the whole team there, I just think they really care about their books from the top of the list to the bottom. As a writer, you can't ask for much more than that.

You said that you knew the topic pretty well, but even so, The Great Alone reflects so much meticulous detail about the time period, the homesteading life, Alaska's seasons, the wildlife—how did you approach the research element of this project from the beginning?

Well, it was a lot of research. My family owns a sport fishing lodge up there, so we've been going to Alaska as a family since the early '80s. My dad's partner is a homesteading family. I know the geography, I know the people, I grew up and came of age at the same time that [Leni] did, and that helped a great deal.

But even though I had grown up during [the '70s], because I was young and my parents kind of sheltered me, I didn't really realize until I did the research what a turbulent time it was with the hijackings, and the kidnappings, and the bombings, and all of this. The more research I did about the '70s, the more it felt relevant to today—like the world was as unsettled then as it sometimes feels now. That's when I knew that I had a book—a fascinating look into a world that we haven't read about a lot.

How long did it take you to write, once you hit on the new idea?

Well, the good news was the book that I threw away was set in modern-day Alaska, so a lot of that original research was able to be repurposed. But it took probably 18 months to write this second version. And I'm a very fast writer.

That does seem fast—it's a large book!

I know. I ran out of words very quickly. I tend to throw literally hundreds of pages away.

What is your process for what gets left on the cutting room floor? With a story that spans so many years, I would assume it's a challenge to decide what to keep in and what to leave out.

I have an eye that is drawn to the intimate. I'm interested in day-to-day happenings in my characters, and I tend to think that every moment in their lives is important. So in the first draft, I write a lot of scenes that are mostly me discovering who the character is, and what this world looks like on a very intimate level.

Then, once I've found the characters and found the story, the arc, then the job is to amp everything up, so that the conflict becomes hopefully almost unbearable, and then to cut away everything that isn't absolutely necessary. That's how I tend to find the pacing that I like, combined with the depth of characterization that I'm looking for. That's the balance.

Your website says you typically do 10 drafts—is that still true?
Probably well more than that.

And I know you write longhand. At what point does a computer come into play? Are you revising in longhand too?
What happens is I write longhand on my yellow legal pad, and then that gets entered into the computer. Then I get a printout, and generally for the first five to seven drafts, the changes are so extensive that I'm still using the yellow pad. I'll get to the end of a paragraph and say, "insert here," and rewrite the book on the yellow legal pad, inserting the manuscript as it goes. When I'm getting closer to the end, it's light enough that it can all be done on the printed pages from the computer.

Is that how you've always worked?
In early days when my books were simpler and more straightforward, and I was just trying to learn the craft of writing, no—I would not have been able to do it this way, and I didn't do it this way. In those days, I spent a lot of time doing outlines and character biographies, and escalations-of-scene kind of research, and then I sat down and wrote the book that I intended to write. As the books have gotten bigger and more complex, they just require a messier process, I guess.

I have to say, I don't find that comforting …
[Laughs.] Neither do I! I'm always saying to people, if anyone has a new process, I am definitely looking for it.

Right! The way I work is such a mess, too—what we all want to hear is that you can figure it out more easily with experience.
You know what? A lot of it does get easier. The problem is that while you become more adept at knowing what's going to work in the beginning, and more adept at a sentence-by-sentence kind of thing and creating characters quickly, I think that as a writer, you also grow. As you grow, you ask more and more of yourself. And so you end up writing novels that you never imagined you'd be capable of writing in the be-

ginning. It's just sort of a one-foot-in-front-of-the-other kind of process, where you never stop asking yourself to do more or be more.

Aside from the stories themselves being more ambitious, are there other things you can qualify where you feel your craft has improved or changed?

You know, I think that the single most important thing [has been] aging, and motherhood, and going through life and understanding what it is I have to say. When I started writing, I was young—my first book was published when I was 29, I think—so the biggest thing is knowing more about the world and being more confident, more fervent in my own opinions. I think that's the biggest thing.

They talk about the evolution of voice as if it's about sentences, and certainly it is—I believe that I'm a significantly better writer now than I was when I started. But I think it's more about what I have to say now.

Everyone talks about The Nightingale being on a whole different level, but looking back at your career up to this point, what are the moments that stand out most to you?

Well, there's nothing that really ever eclipses that first sale, that first year where you get the call. First you get an agent and then someone buys it and a year later you see it on the shelves and you realize that it's possible: This job, this career, this passion can all come true. So, that still remains probably the biggest moment.

Then: I wrote *Firefly Lane* about 10 years ago, and that was probably the most personal of all of my novels. That changed the course of my career; that's when I began to truly find my voice and what it was I had to say.

With *The Nightingale*, to see what the novel has meant to people—especially people who have lived through this or have family members who have lived through it and have told me what the novel means to them—that's been a pretty special experience.

And it's really still going on.

It is, yes. I guess next would be the movie—[which] is in production, so that'll be a pretty amazing moment.

I saw an interview where you noted that a lot of times people don't take newer writers seriously because they assume you're going to give up—and that the important thing is just to stay with it. Perseverance is advice that you often hear for newer writers, but it seems like it's good advice for any stage in a writing career.

You know, that's what it's all about. You have to believe in this career, you have to believe in yourself, and you have to move with great determination forward, because it doesn't matter whether you're trying to sell your first book or your 50th book, or you're trying to redefine your career, or you're trying to reinvent what it is you do, it's always going to be difficult. There are always going to be naysayers, and it's always going to be easier to either give up or follow the path of least resistance or write what appears to be the easy answer for success at that moment.

Those skills that you develop as an unpublished writer—your discipline, your dedication—I think all of that holds you in really good stead as you continue forward and transition from a beginning writer to a working writer to a career novelist.

Jessica Strawser (jessicastrawser.com) is editor-at-large for WD and the author of the novels *Almost Missed You* and *Not That I Could Tell*, both from St. Martin's Press. This interview originally appeared in *Writer's Digest*.

LEIGH BARDUGO

Unstoppable

....

by Baihley Gentry

Leigh Bardugo has always written the stories she wanted to write.

When querying her debut, *Shadow and Bone*—in which she introduced readers to a Czarist Russia-inspired world where individuals called Grisha have the mystical ability to manipulate matter—Bardugo was faced with a publishing-industry reality. Although young adult novels were popular at the time, and her premise was unique and compelling, no literary agents seemed interested in epic or high fantasy books for young readers.

She forged ahead anyway.

"I knew very little about the market. I learned that many [agents] would not even entertain the idea of that kind of book," she says. "It's wise to know what's out there, [but don't] let that hinder you. If you have an idea, pursue it. [Think] about things that make your story a story that only you could tell—those are the things that will stand out."

The strength of that story did eventually resonate with a rep, and the series was sold in a three-book deal in 2010. Within a week of its release in 2012, *Shadow and Bone* skyrocketed to the top of *The New York Times* bestseller list—as did her six books after that: 2013's *Siege and Storm* and 2014's *Ruin and Rising*, which rounded out the Grisha trilogy; 2015's *Six of Crows* and 2016's *Crooked Kingdom*, a "heist-con" duology Bardugo likens to "*Ocean's 11* meets *Game of Thrones*"; and her two latest stand-alones in 2017: *The Language of Thorns*, her first short story collection, and *Wonder Woman: Warbringer*, about the superhero's teen years.

In sum, her books have sold more than 1 million copies combined internationally, and have earned such accolades as RT Reviewers Choice Awards in 2012 and 2015, and multiple starred reviews from *Publishers Weekly*, *Kirkus Reviews* and *School Library Journal*. Bardugo regularly writes short stories for Tor.com, and she has appeared in various anthologies, including *Last Night a Superhero Saved My Life* with notable names like Jodi

Picoult and Neil Gaiman, and *Slasher Girls & Monster Boys* alongside Jonathan Maberry and Kendare Blake.

Despite the impressive trajectory of her career, the path from aspiring author to bestseller was a circuitous one.

Born in Jerusalem and raised in Southern California, Bardugo's lifelong aspiration to be a writer led her to earn a degree in journalism from Yale. While struggling for years to finish a first draft of a novel ("I didn't know yet that I was an outliner, and how badly I needed structure in order to work"), she took jobs in copywriting, advertising and as a Hollywood makeup and special effects artist.

It wasn't until she brushed off "some pretty wonky ideas" espoused by media, TV and film about what it meant to produce creative work that Bardugo was able to embrace a "terrible, messy, ugly first draft." That experience taught her something valuable: "Let go of the idea that somehow you can outsmart a first draft," she says. "Because I have never met anybody who can."

The YA fantasy maestro took a break from promoting *The Language of Thorns* and *Wonder Woman: Warbringer* to talk world-building, personal perseverance and more.

The runaway success of a debut can put a lot of pressure on subsequent follow-ups. How did you manage to cope with that so gracefully?

When a book lists, there's the illusion of runaway success. My [first book] listed, but it's not as if you hit *The New York Times* bestseller list and all of a sudden they give you the keys to a magical clubhouse and you've suddenly arrived. That's one book, and a book does not make a career. Certainly, I had a wonderful push from my publisher and got very lucky. I'm very aware of what it means to have a publisher back you. But your job as a writer, no matter what else is happening, is to continue to produce work—whether you're succeeding or failing. [You have to put] aside ideas about sales or success or ambition, and just work.

You know, I think I have a journey that looks smooth from the outside. And I'm always a little hesitant to talk about it because I don't want people to get a false impression about what it takes to get published. But [up until the point of publishing *Shadow and Bone*], I did face plenty of rejection, and even after I signed with [my agent], every single one of those rejections stung. Because the marvel of the information age is that you're still getting email rejections months and months after you sent them. [Laughs]. And so, until *Shadow and Bone* came out, I would read those rejections—because, of course, I had to read every single one of them—and I would think, *Well, maybe they're right and everybody else is wrong.* Part of the journey is that horrific balance of, you know, delusions of grandeur and abject humility that I think writers walk the line of all the time.

You've talked about losing faith in your ability to become a professional writer. What would you tell others who are struggling with that same feeling?

I want to be really clear about something: I think we kind of fetishize the creative life. We have the vision of what it means to be an author, where you sit in your garret or looking out at your view and you give everything to your art and you commit fully to it. But the reality is that most of us have bills to pay. We have loans to pay off. We have educations to pay for. Some of us have children to take care of or other relatives or dependents or responsibilities.

And the idea that somehow you're not a real writer if you are pursuing taking care of yourself and your life, as you pursue your art, is an incredibly damaging one. Very few people have the wherewithal or the safety net to be able to pursue writing full time from moment one. And I want people to understand that you can absolutely work a job, sometimes two jobs, and have those responsibilities—and still write. I didn't fail to become a writer, and therefore had to take a job. I had to take a job to keep a roof over my head because I had student loans to pay off. And that's the way it works.

For writers trying to balance life and art, how would you encourage them to stay motivated in pursuing their passion?

Set realistic goals. Sometimes that means doing something like NaNoWriMo, or it means saying, "I'm just going to write 500 words a day, but I'm going to write 500 words a day." Or "I'm going to do writing sprints for 30 minutes before work." Or in the 45 minutes when my kid is napping, or whatever it is. Carve out a time, find a process that works for you and don't compare yourself to anybody else.

[And] get offline. Stop reading about what other authors are doing. Stop reading reviews. Let yourself be immersed in the story that you're writing.

Remember: There is no expiration date on your talent. I did not publish my first book until I was 35 years old. If you have a story to tell, it doesn't matter when you tell it. Just get it onto the page and let go of any of the ideas that somehow it's less worthwhile because it took you a little longer to get there than it took others.

Man, you're inspiring me!

[Laughs.] Oh, good. Do it. Do it.

You've said before that there is no right way to write a book. You've been publishing at least one book per year since 2012, which is an impressive output. Describe your process.

I'm an outliner. I write through a three-act structure. I build all of my books in pretty much the exact same way: I have the idea, I write it out onto a single page so that I essentially have a book that is one-page long, and then I begin to fill in all of the things that I know. I build this kind of ramshackle zero-draft, that operates as an extended outline, and that is what becomes the musculature of the book. Now, when I get into the work of actually writing the scenes and revising the book into something that it can be, that process changes a little depending on the project.

....

A big part of writing is the discomfort of the work not being what you want it to be and the feelings of doubt or failure that come with not being able to make the idea instantly into what you want it to be.

....

Everybody processes differently, but [the exact method] is something you can keep coming back to when you feel psychologically embattled. A big part of writing is the discomfort of the work not being what you want it to be and the feelings of doubt or failure that come with not being able to make the idea instantly into what you want it to be.

Your books have very elaborate, well-rounded worlds. I haven't read a book in a long time where I felt so there. When world-building, where do you typically begin?

I start with my characters and with the story, the plot. When a reader enters the first chapter of your book, they're trying to get their bearings. It's our job as authors to give them the signals they need in order to be able to navigate that world. The great challenge of world-building is not building the world. You could build a world with maps and languages and all these things [and still be missing something]. It's releasing that information to the reader. The world-building that really falls into place first is what I always describe as the sense of power—helping readers understand how power flows in the book. That could mean governmental power, personal power, magical power, whatever. But [determining how power flows] is going to determine how your characters behave on the page, and what they're able or not able to do.

You had help creating the Grisha Trilogy's Ravkan language from David Peterson, who assisted with developing the Dothraki language in HBO's Game of Thrones. What was that like?

David and I met at Worldcon several years ago. I went to a presentation of his on Dothraki. He has been kind enough to be a resource for me as we've worked through the

[Grisha] books, although we do occasionally butt heads because he wants me to be much more ambitious in my language in the book, and he's very probably right.

You write a lot of diverse characters without falling victim to stereotypes. Do you think attitudes about diversity in publishing have shifted, or does the industry still have a ways to go?

I think both of those things are true. I think that there's a new dedication to making sure that not only is representation better, but that marginalized authors and voices that maybe didn't have voices before are increasingly given platforms in publishing. And that is not only as writers, but as editors and in everything from publicity to sales. That said, I don't think there's any question that there's a long way to go because that is a long process and because until the fundamental power structures change, until the gatekeepers are different, I don't think we're going to see the kind of change that we really need to see—in the way not only that stories are told, but in the way they reach readers.

I'm sure many authors ask you what's trending in YA. What do you think is the ideal balance of writing what you're passionate about and understanding what's drawing readers in the industry?

You have to know the market. So you have to know what's selling, what isn't selling anymore, what people are fatigued by. But that doesn't mean you can say, "Oh, well, I [can't write that ever]." There was a period of time where people would say, "Oh, no more vampire books," or "no more dystopians," or no more this or that. But that is really false because what that actually meant was no more of that particular kind of story. We need a different take on vampires or we need to see a dystopian that is simply described as science fiction. YA shifts and moves faster than most other categories because so much work is being generated and consumed so quickly. And to be frank, I think if I brought *Shadow and Bone* out now, it would not have the same reception it had in 2012. Be aware of the market, but really, being aware of the market is just one part of being a storyteller and thinking about craft.

What's next for you?

Well, *King of Scars* is the first book in my upcoming duology that continues the story of the Grishaverse, and will pick up the story of Nikolai Lantsov, the young king of Ravka. And I'm [also working on] *Ninth House,* my first novel for adults. It is the start of a series set at Yale, a dark fantasy that focuses on the secret societies among East Coast elites. I've got a couple of other things cooking, but nothing I can discuss just yet.

I heard you have a band, which is probably the coolest side hustle ever. What type of music do you play?

Our lead guitarist would probably punch me for this, but I've always described it as "geek rock." It's sort of like if you put the Pixies and the New Pornographers and a little bit of They Might Be Giants in a blender. I mostly sing. Unfortunately, all of our lives got taken over by adulthood: Our guitarist had a baby. Our bassist had a baby. Our drummer bought a house. I landed my dream job. But we do occasionally meet up for band brunch and one of these days we'll have a reunion show.

I think that when you're writing, being creative in other ways is really useful and therapeutic. And whether that's creating visual art or making music—or hell, even baking—as long as you're doing something that's keeping you engaged and keeping you from chewing over reviews on Goodreads, I think you're better off.

....

Baihley Gentry is the associate editor of *Writer's Digest*, in which this interview originally appeared.

....

ROXANE GAY

Something to Say

....

by Sharon Short

//

No matter what kind of reading you're drawn to—long-form journalism, short stories, novels, cultural criticism, personal reflection, even comic books—you've probably come across some beautifully woven words by the prolific and wide-ranging Roxane Gay. She has published hundreds of pieces in top venues, from women's magazines (*Elle, Glamour, xoJane*) to literary journals (including *Tin House, McSweeney's* and her own co-founded *PANK*) to popular online hubs (among them *Salon, Buzzfeed* and, most famously, *The Rumpus*, where she served as the original essays editor) to long-standing newspapers (*The Guardian, The Wall Street Journal* and *The New York Times*, where she is now a contributing opinion writer entrusted with book reviews for such talked-about titles as Jodi Picoult's *Small Great Things*).

Whether on social media or instructing young writers as an associate professor of creative writing at Purdue University, she is skilled at engaging an audience no matter the venue, with more than 200,000 followers on Twitter alone.

She was a darling of literary journals when her first collection of short fiction, *Ayiti,* was released in 2011. By the publication of her next books in 2014—her critically acclaimed debut novel, *An Untamed State*, and runaway hit essay collection, *Bad Feminist*—Gay had distinguished herself as a literary star and astute cultural observer who pulls no punches in sharing her point of view.

This year brings another pair of new titles from Gay: the fiction collection *Difficult Women* and her much-awaited memoir, *Hunger*, published in June. *Hunger* is perhaps her most personal book yet, exploring with candor Gay's experiences with weight, self-image and an act of violence in her youth that shaped her worldview.

In my role as executive director of the Antioch Writers' Workshop at the University of Dayton, I've met Gay three times. The first was shortly after *Ayiti* was published, when she served on a panel of editors at one of our events. A few years later, she led an afternoon session on fiction writing for our weeklong summer workshop. By 2016, when she was our keynote speaker, Gay's fame and respect in the literary world had skyrocketed. Yet in terms of how she interacts with budding writers—witty, gracious and kind, yet instructive, without sugarcoating any of the challenges of either the craft or the business of creative writing—she hasn't changed a bit.

Congratulations on Difficult Women and Hunger. How did these projects come to fruition?

Difficult Women is actually the first book I ever tried to sell—the book I got my first agent with. I wrote most of the stories while in graduate school, writing fiction as way of creating something different [while] I got my degree in an unrelated field.

Editors said that they really enjoyed *Difficult Women* but that the relentless darkness made them feel hopeless and want to die. And I thought, That's exactly what I'm going for! So, I wasn't willing to compromise. After *An Untamed State*, my fiction publisher made an offer on *Difficult Women* and the book came into the world.

Hunger is a memoir of my body. It's a book that looks at trauma, and obesity as a response to trauma. I decided to write it because whenever women write about weight it is always at the end of a weight-loss journey. We never really seem to see narratives from the middle of the weight-loss journey, where you want to lose weight, have lost weight, and are working on it but still have a long way to go.

You seem at home in so many genres and forms. Is it easy to switch from one to another? Do you know which form is right for an idea, or do you experiment first?

It's relatively easy in that storytelling is storytelling. Crafting a narrative is oftentimes the same whether it's fiction or nonfiction. In terms of determining which genre, I know up front. It's not like I think, *I want to write about food, which way do I go?* I just know.

....

With fiction, I get to make everything up.

....

I'm relatively new to writing nonfiction, so I do find writing that to be more challenging. Right or wrong, I feel like there is more at stake. With fiction, I get to make everything up. You can certainly make mistakes, but in fiction, you're dealing with truths. In nonfiction, you're dealing with the truth. And truth matters, especially in this day and age. So I'm always thinking about maintaining the integrity of what I'm saying, reporting my arguments in ethical ways, making sure I'm offering nuance, and hopefully at my best respecting other points of view while making it clear I disagree with them.

You recently wrote for the World of Wakanda Marvel Comics series. What do you think other writers can learn from comic books and graphic novels?

I read Archie Comics religiously as a kid. I'm new to reading adult comics—and [am] enjoying them very much.

World of Wakanda was an unexpected opportunity. I was a writer on a five-issue arc about Ayo and Aneka, members of Dora Milaje, an all-female fighting guard for Black Panther, the king of Wakanda. What I liked about the experience was exploring a new way of telling a story. It forced me to think in terms of scene and about how to get my characters from one moment to the next because you can't take that for granted in a comic form.

Writers can learn a lot from reading comic books and graphic novels, such as about brevity. Of course, comics do have the benefit of imagery. That said, the importance of scene can't be understated. I'm always telling my students: Show us moments instead of wildly narrating an entire story and describing what's happening. Try to find ways to immerse the reader.

You're known as a cultural critic, clear-voiced in your views on women's issues, LGBTQ issues, politics and so forth. How does that impact your writing?

My views are a natural part of my writing. I am who I am. That shapes how I see the world and how I narrate it. I don't know that there's any separating one's views from one's writing. Journalists often talk about impartiality and treat it as a holy grail—but I don't know that anyone is impartial. We've all been enculturated in very specific ways and I think that always informs what we do, think and say. I don't know that it's useful to try to get away from that.

In your essays and certainly in Hunger, you share your experiences with raw, relatable honesty. What's your approach to giving personal writing a universal feel?

I'm always thinking about looking both inward and outward and making sure it's not just about me wrestling with my demons and working toward catharsis. That's something you do in therapy. So, in general you want to think about, *What is the necessity of this personal detail? How does it illuminate something that is bigger than myself—some sort of question that people other than myself might be grappling with?* That's always where I start.

[For example], when I write about trauma I think about silence and the ways in which people across the gender spectrum are oftentimes very silent when it comes to the ways in which we've suffered—there's a lot of shame around it. It's hard to know how to begin a conversation about something that is so painful and personal. That inspires me to say, *OK, I'll go first. I'll offer up my story so that people might feel more comfortable in sharing theirs.*

Do you ever feel nervous about sharing so much in print?

Absolutely. The only way I really have the courage or stupidity to share my writing is by believing that no one is going to read it. I have to tell myself that because I'm actually very shy and private in real life. It's hard to share such personal stories. But here I am!

It's difficult at this point to maintain the delusion. It was much easier when I was publishing in small literary magazines and nobody knew who I was.

How do you set boundaries for your privacy?

I'm clear with myself on what I will and won't share. I also think very carefully about how I write about the people in my life, because it's one thing for me to make this choice to write about myself, but it's another thing to involve my loved ones—they didn't ask for this. I am not going to compromise those relationships.

You also review books and movies. Does that help with your own craft? Is it something you'd recommend other writers do?

When I'm writing critiques of other creative work, I make a mental list of things I should be aware of and that I should be thinking more carefully about in my own creative work. Writing the critiques makes me a sharper thinker.

Often, writers are told they have to write reviews. You don't. I think writers should write exactly what they want to write, and nothing more, nothing less. So I always encourage writers not to feel pressure to write criticism. Only write criticism if you feel called to it. But, I think it's a great idea to write criticism of a book or television show or movie in a journal, because that's just for you, and you can learn from it.

Do you ever find it awkward to be in the position of unfavorably reviewing another writer's book, when you might cross paths with that author in certain circles on the same side of the table?

Yes. But it goes both ways. It's awkward if I've encountered someone who has written a negative review of my work. But that's fine. When we put our work into the world, criticism is part of the bargain. We don't write into a vacuum.

....

When we put our work into the world, criticism is part of the bargain. We don't write into a vacuum.

....

In my critiques, I focus on the work, and make sure I'm not personal. I feel like I've been fair. I don't feel I've ever slandered anyone. I tried to find the good. I've had conversations with people I've critiqued. After I wrote a review of her book *Lean In*, Sheryl Sandberg and I had a really great conversation about my critique, and what she agreed and disagreed with. It was very genial—wonderful, actually—and one of best conversations I've ever had.

You have an impressive if not formidable list of bylines. Did you accumulate those as a conscious strategy in building a platform for a book?

Not at all. I've always loved writing and so I just wrote and would submit to magazines. Ignorance is bliss—I remember the first magazine I submitted to was *The Paris Review*. I was just a kid and I really thought it was an option! I didn't even know about the magazine's reputation. I just had a copy of *Writer's Market*, and I loved the idea of Paris even though I'd never been. I even wrote that I speak French in the cover letter.

Eventually, I started publishing in online magazines such as *Word Riot* and *Monkeybicycle*. Shorter pieces can be great stepping stones. Without those early publications, I would be nothing today. Online magazines don't get enough respect. Frankly, that is where your work is going to be read. There's no limit to how many people might read your work in an online magazine if your work gets traction.

Shorter pieces also give you experience, build credits and build stronger work.

My ambition, though, was always to write a novel or short story collection. I really wanted to have a book in the world. But I didn't know how to articulate a dream beyond that, even when An Untamed State was published. Now I have more of a plan. And to this day I'd love to be published in *The Paris Review*!

As a teacher of creative writing, what advice do you most enjoy giving students about pursuing a life with writing as its heart and soul?

A writing life can look a lot of different ways. Don't listen to the naysayers who say it's not possible. I think it's incredibly hypocritical that people who have achieved success as a writer love to tell young writers, "You won't be able to do it today. The markets have changed and the world has changed." You can still make a life as a writer.

That said, I think it's important to have a day job. I still have a day job. Financial security and being able to pay my bills makes it easier for me to create. But I was always a writer when I was working an office job or any number of the other jobs I've held. That doesn't take away from your writing. I think more writers need to hear that.

Do you view social media as an important part of outreach to readers?

It's optional. Writers should only engage in social media if they want to. If you don't want to or if you're doing it halfheartedly, it shows. I think it's important for writers to not think in terms of platform. It's not healthy. I only think about it now because I recognize that with [so many] Twitter followers, yes I have a platform, and it would be disingenuous to deny that. But in terms of getting to that place, I was just myself. I talked about other writers more than myself, because I read a lot and love to talk about what I'm reading.

I think it is useful for writers to connect to other writers and other readers. But some writers build a platform just by having their work out in the world, and that's OK, too.

Given your prolific work and teaching/speaking schedule, what are your tips for time management?

I can give tips on many things, but not productivity and time management. One thing I do is make time. Everyone loves talking about how busy they are. But there are 24 hours in a day. Make a half-hour or hour in a day, or an hour in a week, for writing. Just make sure you have at least one designated time—however long it is, given your constraints—to focus on writing.

I treat my writing like a job, and I don't mean that in a bad way. I mean I give it the respect of a professional endeavor, not a hobby. Even when it was a hobby, I treated it like a job. It is important to do that because craft takes time and demands respect.

. . . .

Sharon Short is the executive editor of the Antioch Writers' Workshop at the University of Dayton and the author of the novel *My One Square Inch of Alaska*. This interview originally appeared in *Writer's Digest*.

. . . .

BUSINESS BASICS

Successfully Submit Your Novels & Short Stories

It's true there are no substitutes for talent and hard work. A writer's first concern must always be attention to craft. No matter how well presented, a poorly written story or novel has little chance of being published. On the other hand, a well-written piece may be equally hard to sell in today's competitive publishing market. Talent alone is just not enough.

To be successful, writers need to study the field and pay careful attention to finding the right market. While the hours spent perfecting your writing are usually hours spent alone, you're not alone when it comes to developing your marketing plan. *Novel & Short Story Writer's Market* provides you with detailed listings containing the essential information you'll need to locate and contact the markets most suitable for your work.

Once you've determined where to send your work, you must turn your attention to presentation. We can help here, too. We've included the basics of manuscript preparation, along with information on submission procedures and how to approach markets. We also include tips on promoting your work. No matter where you're from or what level of experience you have, you'll find useful information here on everything from presentation to mailing to selling rights to promoting your work—the "business" of fiction.

APPROACHING MAGAZINE MARKETS

A query letter by itself is usually not required by most magazine fiction editors. If you are approaching a magazine to find out if fiction is accepted, a query is fine, but editors looking for short fiction want to see the actual piece. A cover letter can be useful as a letter of introduction, but the key here is brevity. A successful cover letter is no more than one page (20-lb. bond paper). It should be single-spaced with a double space between paragraphs, proofread carefully, and neatly typed in a standard typeface (not script or italic). The writer's name, address, phone number, and e-mail address must appear at the top, and the letter should be addressed, ideally, to a specific editor. (If the editor's name is unavailable, use "Fiction Editor.")

The body of a successful cover letter contains the name and word count of the story, a brief list of previous publications, if you have any, and the reason you are submitting to this particular publication. Mention that you have enclosed a self-addressed, stamped envelope for reply. Also, let the editor know if you are sending a disposable manuscript (not to be returned; more and more editors prefer disposable manuscripts that save them time and save you postage). Finally, don't forget to thank the editor for considering your story.

Note that more and more publications prefer to receive electronic submissions, both as e-mail attachments and through online submission forms. See individual listings for specific information on electronic submission requirements, and always visit magazines' websites for up-to-date guidelines.

APPROACHING BOOK PUBLISHERS

Some book publishers ask for queries first, but most want a query plus sample chapters or an outline or, occasionally, the complete manuscript. Again, make your letter brief. Include the essentials about yourself: name, address, phone number, e-mail address, and publishing experience. Include a three- or four-sentence "pitch" and only the personal information related to your story. Show that you have researched the market with a few sentences about why you chose this publisher.

BOOK PROPOSALS

A book proposal is a package sent to a publisher that includes a cover letter and one or more of the following: sample chapters, outline, synopsis, author bio, publications list. When asked to send sample chapters, send up to three consecutive chapters. An outline covers the highlights of your book chapter by chapter. Be sure to include details on main characters, the plot, and subplots. Outlines can run up to thirty pages, depending on the length of your novel. The object is to tell what happens in a concise but clear manner. A synopsis is a shorter summary of your novel, written in a way that expresses the emotion of the story in addition to just explaining the essential points. Evan Marshall, literary agent and author of *The Marshall Plan for Getting Your Novel Published* (Writer's Digest Books), suggests you aim for a page of synopsis for every twenty-five pages of manuscript. Marshall also advises you write the synopsis as one unified narrative, without section heads, subheads, or chapters to break up the text. The terms *synopsis* and *outline* are sometimes used interchangeably, so be sure to find out exactly what each publisher wants.

ABOUT OUR POLICIES

We occasionally receive letters asking why a certain magazine, publisher, or contest is not in the book. Sometimes when we contact listings, the editors do not want to be listed because they:

- do not use very much fiction.
- are overwhelmed with submissions.
- are having financial difficulty or have been recently sold.
- use only solicited material.
- accept work from a select group of writers only.
- do not have the staff or time for the many unsolicited submissions a listing may bring.

Some of the listings do not appear because we have chosen not to list them. We investigate complaints of unprofessional conduct in editors' dealings with writers and misrepresentation of information provided to us by editors and publishers. If we find these reports to be true after a thorough investigation, we will delete the listing from future editions.

There is no charge to the companies that list in this book. Listings appearing in *Novel & Short Story Writer's Market* are compiled from detailed questionnaires, phone interviews, and information provided by editors, publishers, and directors of awards and conferences. The publishing industry is volatile, and changes of address, editor, policies, and needs happen frequently. To keep up with the changes between editions of the book, we suggest you check the market information on the Writer's Market website at www.writersmarket.com. Many magazine and book publishers offer updated information for writers on their websites. Check individual listings for those website addresses.

Organization newsletters and small magazines devoted to helping writers also list market information. Several offer online bulletin boards, message centers, and chat lines with up-to-the-minute changes and happenings in the writing community.

We rely on our readers, as well, for new markets and information about market conditions. E-mail us if you have any new information or if you have suggestions on how to improve our listings to better suit your writing needs.

A FEW WORDS ABOUT AGENTS

Agents are not usually needed for short fiction and most do not handle it unless they already have a working relationship with you. For novels, you may want to consider working with an agent, especially if you intend to market your book to publishers who do not look at unsolicited submissions. For more on approaching agents and to read listings of agents willing to work with beginning and established writers, see our **Literary Agents** section. You can also refer to this year's edition of *Guide to Literary Agents*, edited by Robert Lee Brewer.

MANUSCRIPT MECHANICS

A professionally presented manuscript will not guarantee publication. But a sloppy, hard-to-read manuscript will not be read—publishers simply do not have the time. Here's a list of suggested submission techniques for polished manuscript presentation:

- For a short story manuscript, your first page should include your name, address, phone number, and e-mail address (single spaced) in the upper left corner. In the upper right, indicate an approximate word count. Center the name of your story about one-third of the way down the page, skip a line, and center your byline (the byline is optional). Skip four lines and begin your story. On subsequent pages, put your last name and page number in the upper right corner.
- For book manuscripts, use a separate title page. Put your name, address, phone number, and e-mail address in the lower right corner and word count in the upper right. If you have representation, list your agent's name and address in the lower right. (This bumps your name and contact information to the upper left corner.) Center your title and byline about halfway down the page. Start your first chapter on the next page. Center the chapter number and title (if there is one) one-third of the way down the page. Include your last name and the novel's title in all caps in the upper left header, and put the page number in the upper right header of this page and each page to follow. Start each chapter with a new page.
- Proofread carefully. Keep a dictionary, thesaurus, and stylebook handy and use the spell-check function on your computer.
- Include a word count. Your word processing program can likely give you a word count.
- Suggest art where applicable. Most publishers do not expect you to provide artwork and some insist on selecting their own illustrators, but if you have suggestions, let them know. Magazine publishers work in a very visual field and are usually open to ideas.
- Keep accurate records. This can be done in a number of ways, but be sure to keep track of where your stories are and when you sent them out. Write down submission dates. If you do not hear about your submission for a long time—about one to two months longer than the reporting time stated in the listing—you may want to contact the publisher. When you do, you will need an accurate record for reference.

Electronic Submissions

- If sending electronic submissions via e-mail or online submission form, check the publisher's website first for specific information and follow the directions carefully.

Hard-Copy Submissions

- Many publications no longer accept hard-copy submissions. Make sure to read the submission guidelines carefully.
- Use white 8½" × 11" bond paper, preferably 16- or 20-lb. weight. The paper must be heavy enough not to show pages underneath and strong enough to take handling by several people.
- Type your manuscript on a computer and print it out using a laser or ink-jet printer (or, if you must, use a typewriter with a new ribbon).
- An occasional spot of white-out is okay, but don't send a marked-up manuscript with many typos.
- Always double-space and leave a 1" margin on all sides of the page.
- Don't forget word count. If you are using a typewriter, there are several ways to count the number of words in your piece. One way is to count the words in five lines and divide that number by five to find an average. Then count the number of lines and multiply to find the total words. For long pieces, you may want to count the words in the first three pages, divide by three, and multiply by the number of pages you have.
- Always keep a copy. Manuscripts do get lost. To avoid expensive mailing costs, send only what is required. If you are including artwork or photos but you are not positive they will be used, send photocopies. Artwork is hard to replace.
- Enclose a self-addressed, stamped envelope (SASE) if you want a reply or if you want your manuscript returned. For most letters, a business-size (#10) envelope will do. Avoid using any envelope too small for an 8½" × 11" sheet of paper. For manuscripts, be sure to include enough postage and an envelope large enough to contain it. If you are requesting a sample copy of a magazine or a book publisher's catalog, send an appropriately sized envelope.
- Consider sending a disposable manuscript that saves editors time (this will also save you money).

RIGHTS

The Copyright Law states that writers are selling one-time rights (in almost all cases) unless they and the publisher have agreed otherwise. A list of various rights follows. Be sure you know exactly what rights you are selling before you agree to the sale.

Copyright is the legal right to exclusive publication, sale, or distribution of a literary work. As the writer or creator of a written work, you need simply to include your name and the date on your piece in order to copyright it. Be aware, however, that most editors today consider placing the copyright symbol on your work the sign of an amateur and many are even offended by it.

To get specific answers to questions about copyright (but not legal advice), you can call the Copyright Public Information Office at (202)707-3000 weekdays between 8:30 A.M. and 5 P.M. EST. Publications listed in *Novel & Short Story Writer's Market* are copyrighted unless otherwise stated. In the case of magazines that are not copyrighted, be sure to keep a copy of your manuscript with your notice printed on it. For more information on copyrighting your work, see *The Copyright Handbook: What Every Writer Needs to Know, 11th edition*, by Stephen Fishman (Nolo Press, 2011).

Some people are under the mistaken impression that copyright is something they have to send away for and that their writing is not properly protected until they have "received" their copyright from the government. The fact is, you don't have to register your work with the Copyright Office in order for your work to be copyrighted; all writing is copyrighted the moment it is put to paper.

Although it is generally unnecessary, registration is a matter of filling out an application form (for writers, that's Form TX). The Copyright Office now recommends filing an online claim at www.copyright.gov/forms. The online service carries a basic claim fee of $35. If you opt for snail mail, send the completed form, a nonreturnable copy of the work in question, and a check for $65 to the Library of Congress, Copyright Office-TX, 101 Independence Ave. SE, Washington, DC 20559-6000. If the thought of paying $35 each to register every piece you write does not appeal to you, you can cut costs by registering a group of your works with one form, under one title, for one $65 fee.

Most magazines are registered with the Copyright Office as single collective entities themselves; that is, the individual works that make up the magazine are not copyrighted individually in the names of the authors. You'll need to register your article yourself if you wish to have the additional protection of copyright registration.

For more information, visit the U.S. Copyright Office online at www.copyright.gov.

First Serial Rights

This means the writer offers a newspaper or magazine the right to publish the article, story, or poem for the first time in a particular periodical. All other rights to the material remain with the writer. The qualifier "North American" is often added to this phrase to specify a geographical limit to the license.

When material is excerpted from a book scheduled to be published and it appears in a magazine or newspaper prior to book publication, this is also called first serial rights.

One-Time Rights

A periodical that licenses one-time rights to a work (also known as simultaneous rights) buys the nonexclusive right to publish the work once. That is, there is nothing to stop the author from selling the work to other publications at the same time. Simultaneous sales would typically be to periodicals with different audiences.

Second Serial (Reprint) Rights

This gives a newspaper or magazine the opportunity to print an article, poem, or story after it has already appeared in another newspaper or magazine. Second serial rights are nonexclusive; that is, they can be licensed to more than one market.

All Rights

This is just what it sounds like. All rights means a publisher may use the manuscript anywhere and in any form, including movie and book club sales, without further payment to the writer (although such a transfer, or assignment, of rights will terminate after thirty-five years). If you think you'll want to use the material more than once, you must avoid submitting to such markets or refuse payment and withdraw your material. Ask the editor whether he is willing to buy first rights instead of all rights before you agree to an assignment or sale. Some editors will reassign rights to a writer after a given period, such as one year. It's worth an inquiry in writing.

Subsidiary Rights

These are the rights, other than book publication rights, that should be covered in a book contract. These may include various serial rights; movie, television, audiotape, and other electronic rights; translation rights, etc. The book contract should specify who controls these rights (author or publisher) and what percentage of sales from the licensing of these subrights goes to the author.

Dramatic, Television, and Motion Picture Rights

This means the writer is selling his material for use on the stage, in television, or in the movies. Often a one-year option to buy such rights is offered (generally for 10 percent of the total price). The interested party then tries to sell the idea to actors, directors, studios, or television networks. Some properties are optioned over and over again, but most fail to become dramatic productions. In such cases, the writer can sell his rights again and again—as long as there is interest in the material.

Electronic Rights

These rights cover usage in a broad range of electronic media, from online magazines and databases to interactive games. The editor should state in writing the specific electronic rights he is requesting. The presumption is that the writer keeps unspecified rights.

Compensation for electronic rights is a major source of conflict between writers and publishers, as many book publishers seek control of them and many magazines routinely include electronic rights in the purchase of print rights, often with no additional payment. Writers can suggest an alternative way of handling this issue by asking for an additional

15 percent to purchase first rights and a royalty system based on the number of times an article is accessed from an electronic database.

MARKETING AND PROMOTION

Everyone agrees writing is hard work whether you are published or not. Yet once you achieve publication, the work changes. Now not only do you continue writing and revising your next project, you must also concern yourself with getting your book into the hands of readers. It's time to switch hats from artist to salesperson.

While even best-selling authors whose publishers have committed big bucks to marketing are asked to help promote their books, new authors may have to take it upon themselves to plan and initiate some of their own promotion, usually dipping into their own pockets. While this does not mean that every author is expected to go on tour, sometimes at their own expense, it does mean authors should be prepared to offer suggestions for promoting their books.

Depending on the time, money, and personal preferences of the author and publisher, a promotional campaign could mean anything from mailing out press releases to setting up book signings to hitting the talk-show circuit. Most writers can contribute to their own promotion by providing contact names—reviewers, hometown newspapers, civic groups, organizations—that might have a special interest in the book or the writer.

Above all, when it comes to promotion, be creative. What is your book about? Try to capitalize on it. Focus on your potential audiences and how you can help them connect with your book.

IMPORTANT LISTING INFORMATION

- Listings are not advertisements. Although the information here is as accurate as possible, the listings are not endorsed or guaranteed by the editors of *Novel & Short Story Writer's Market*.
- *Novel & Short Story Writer's Market* reserves the right to exclude any listing that does not meet its requirements.

HOW TO USE PATREON TO ENGAGE FANS

by Rekaya Gibson

Patreon is a web-based, membership platform for artists and creators to run a subscription content service. Fans become paying members, or 'patrons', of creators in one of 15 categories, including writing, podcasting, and video & film. Co-founded in 2013 by musician Jack Conte of the band Pomplamoose, more than 50,000 creators use this service each year and over 1 million monthly patrons support the creative efforts.

Having a Patreon page is a great way for you to identify loyal fans. It allows you to create an exclusive community for them where they have direct access to you – the artist and creator – establishing two-way communication on an ongoing basis. Knowing you have patrons can boost productivity and keep you and other artists and creators motivated. It's definitely something worthwhile to explore further.

Writers can setup their free Patreon pages, so fans can pay them monthly or every time they release something new, like a novel or short story. For example, if contributors pay a dollar per chapter and the writer releases four chapters in December, then each of the patrons will pay four-dollars that month. Patreon takes a small processing fee, and then creators have access to the funds after they cash out. Funds are sent to their designated PayPal account. Fans become what many would call patrons of the arts. It's in the creator's best interest to keep these supporters engaged.

BUILD AND USE A PATREON PAGE

By touching on the main components of building and using a Patreon page, creators should gain insight and examples to help them get started. A Patreon page should be fun and easy to navigate. Most importantly, it should be appealing and convincing, so that fans return often to interact with their favorite creator. When going through the Patreon setup process, creators will be prompted to create a URL. Make it memorable by using your name, if available. That way, people can find you easily.

Develop a Project Description

Prepare a brief description for the About section. Introduce yourself and let people know what you are writing about. Tell them why you are using Patreon and explain the challenges you face with limited resources. List what their funds will support. Summarize the benefits in becoming a patron. This can include the rewards each creator sets at different monetary levels and the types of content the creator will release. Both are explained in the reward section. According to Patreon's website, creators should avoid using 'support' or 'help', so that they don't sound needy. Instead, it recommends 'get access' or 'join my exclusive community'. Lastly, limit the use of hyperlinks to keep people from leaving your page. Make sure to update the description so that it appears active.

'Welcome' Video Message

Next, create a brief Welcome video message. People like to put a face to the name/project, and some prefer to watch a video when they visit your page. This video is similar to the About section, so include some of the same information. Here is where you can also explain how Patreon works. Breakdown what you will be using the funding for and mention some of the rewards. Encourage visitors to browse the page. Remember to keep the video short; a minute or less is a good rule of thumb.

Select Rewards

Rewards act as incentives to persuade fans into becoming patrons. The creator can set the number of rewards and the pledge amounts. Some people start with three levels and select one, three, and five dollars; while others, choose five levels at five, ten, twenty-five, fifty and one-hundred dollars. Each reward level has a description. As writers, rewards might include items such as an alternative ending to a current novel, swag bag of book/author items, or a book cover first look. If patrons pay per-creation, offer a short story every set amount of days. If the patron pledges two dollars per short story and the creator releases three per month, that's six dollars. Select rewards that you can provide with little to no cost or offer something that you do on a regular basis. For example, at the one-dollar level, the patron gets a thank-you email, at the three-dollar level, the person gets the dollar reward plus a shout out on social media; and at the five-dollar level, the patron gets everything already mentioned, plus an advanced e-copy of the writer's book.

Keep in mind, creators can limit the quantity of reward levels. Perhaps, offer only two rewards at the twenty-five dollars per month level. Also, creators can denote if a shipping address is required in order to send goodies, such as cover art, books, and t-shirts to the patron. Furthermore, creators can always ask fans what rewards they would like to see. If they are reasonable, add them to the appropriate level or levels. That's a great way to keep fans signed up as regular patrons.

Create Banner Images and Thumbnails

Give your page some visual appeal. Creators can do so by adding a page banner and reward-tier images. Author Keith Kareem Williams used a vibrant red banner that includes a picture of himself surrounded by his books. He placed a quote on it that details what he writes. It's the first thing fans see when they visit his Patreon page. This makes fans want to scroll down to see the rest. Creators can also add a square thumb-size image to each reward tier. Use something relatable to that tier to draw attention. Williams placed the reward amounts and circular medal levels as his images: bronze, silver, gold, platinum, and diamond. It gives the page a cohesive look and fans start thinking right away about which reward levels to consider.

Set Goals

In this case, goals are not time sensitive. They are used as milestones. Start by setting a monetary goal. It should be practical and meet the challenges that the creator is facing. Then, add a goal description. Summarize it using one to three sentences. For example, if the creator's goal is to raise $600 per month, then the goal's description might read, "When I reach this goal, I will be able to hire a professional editor." If creators do not reach their goals, whatever they have raised is still theirs to keep. They can maintain the account as long they like. If they reach their goals, they can set up another one. Goals can be edited or deleted at any time. Reaching your goals may take time. Continue to produce content and keep fans engaged. Over time, monthly contributions add up, and then you will be able to hire that editor. Stay encouraged!

Write a 'Thank You' Message

After a fan has become a patron, take time to send them a 'Thank you' message. Complete Patreon's customizable page with a few words or create and add a video. Whatever you decide, make it a point to complete this task. Every patron deserves a thank you, and it shows appreciation. Recently, a friend became a patron of four projects; she has yet to receive such a note. Here are five tips for writing the 'Thank you' message:

1. Don't forget to say, "Thank you."
2. Let fans know what their patronage means to you and/your project.
3. Welcome them to the community.
4. In the closing statement, invite them to return to the page for their exclusive content or rewards.
5. Sign off with an appropriate salutation, such as "Kind regards" or "Sincerely", and then your name. Remember, the goal is to keep fans engaged. Gratitude shows patrons that you care and you're nice. Who doesn't want to support nice people?

WAYS TO REACH AND MAINTAIN PATRONS

While building your Patreon page, you should be spreading the word about it. Explain to people how it works and what to expect. You can do this by using a newsletter, social media, a blog post, YouTube video, and/or podcast. Then, when you launch, it won't be foreign to them. Once the page is up and running, ask family and friends individually to become patrons. It adds a personal touch and they might feel honored to help out versus just seeing a post about it on social media. Share the big news with your email newsletter subscribers and include a call to action. For example, ask for feedback on your page, invite them to check out the rewards you're offering, or offer a chance to get an excerpt of your latest work on the Patreon page. Promote your page on all your social media channels. Get creative and use memes, images, or videos. Some platforms use hashtags to attract new audiences. Search for popular ones that are appropriate for your content and experiment with them. Some believe engagement decreases on Twitter the more hashtags you use, so stick around two or three. Use up to 30 hashtags to attract attention on Instagram.

Once the page is up and running, ask family and friends individually to become patrons. It adds a personal touch and they might feel honored to help out versus just seeing a post about it on social media.

Once fans have signed up to become patrons, how do you keep them engaged? It's very important to deliver exclusive content or rewards as promised. Use the post feature found on the dashboard to keep patrons informed about your work. There are several post types, including text, images, videos, live streams, audio, and a poll feature. On a regular basis, share news and/or progress reports about your current project(s) using any one of these methods. Continue to offer access to content that fans cannot find anywhere else, like voting on characters' names or cool sticker printouts. This unique content makes your community exclusive. Think of it as investing in patrons who invest in you. If you only have ten patrons, show them the love and respect, just as if you had 100,000.

How writers set up their page will determine the number of patron engagements that will occur. Fans look for rewards that fill a void they can't fulfill anywhere else. If writers are mindful of the way they utilize Patreon, they too can reap the monthly benefits that thousands already enjoy.

Rekaya Gibson has penned three articles for Writer's Digest Books, two of which featured other authors. She's also contributed content for Amtrak, *Cuisine Noir* Magazine, and various lifestyle magazines. In addition, she's penned and published six books of her own. When Gibson is not writing, she's hosting a sports podcast and maintaining a Patreon page.

GETTING AN AGENT 101

by Jennifer D. Foster

///

Considered the "gatekeepers" to (large) publishing houses, literary agents are often your best bet to getting your foot in the door and making a name for yourself in the book (and even the motion picture, but that's another story!) world. But do you really need an agent? And exactly how do you find one? What are the tell-tale signs of a reputable (and not-so-reputable) literary agent? And how do you make the author-agent relationship work? Key insights, helpful tips and sound advice from authors, editors, publishing consultants, editorial directors, literary agents, writing instructors and heads of professional writing organizations give you the inside track.

WHAT LITERARY AGENTS DO

While the Writers' Union of Canada website states that "about 70 per cent of the books published in Canada do not have an agent-assisted contract," it's a radically different story in the United States. In her book *Publishing 101: A First-Time Author's Guide to Getting Published, Marketing and Promoting Your Book, and Building a Successful Career* (Jane Friedman, 2015), Jane Friedman reveals that "in today's market, probably about 80 per cent of books that the New York publishers acquire are sold to them by agents." But before taking the often-challenging plunge of getting a literary agent, do your homework to determine it you actually need one to get your manuscript published. And in order to figure that out, it's necessary to understand what, exactly, literary agents are and what they do. Jennifer Croll, editorial director of Greystone Books in Vancouver, explains it this way: "Agents act as both scouts and filters—they sort through what's out there and actively search to find the authors and proposals that are most likely to be published." Linden MacIntyre, award-winning journalist, internationally bestselling and Scotiabank Giller

Prize–winning author and former host of the fifth estate, concurs. "Agents know the world of publishing, who matters, and established agents are known and recognized by editors and publishers. A recommendation from a credible agent will usually assure that someone of influence in publishing will read the manuscript."

Trevor Cole, Toronto, Ontario–based, award-winning author of *The Whisky King*, *Hope Makes Love* and *Practical Jean*, further clarifies. An agent is beneficial "if you are committed to producing well-crafted book-length prose on a consistent professional basis." And, he says, "if the agent is part of a large house, they will have international contacts and sub-agents who can give your book its best chance at international distribution." Quite simply, "if an agent loves a book you've written, they will go to bat for it hard," he says, adding, "and once an editor agrees to buy the book, the agent's job is to get the best possible financial deal for you." Geoffrey Taylor, director of the International Festival of Authors in Toronto, Ontario, says that "an agent is the conduit for an author's work. This could mean anything from national to world rights. It could include all print forms, electronic and video/film platforms." He says that agents have a lot of "experience with contracts and can usually negotiate better terms and a higher cash advance against future sales." Terence Green explains further. "A book contract can easily be twenty pages or more. An agent familiar with the publishing business understands which clauses are negotiable, and to what degree, and can customize the boilerplate contracts often tendered as a matter of rote to ones that are more palatable and fair-minded to all parties." Martha Kanya-Forstner, editor-in-chief of Doubleday Canada, and McClelland & Stewart, and vice-president of Penguin Random House Canada, reveals that "it is exceptionally difficult for authors to negotiate the value of their own work, [and it is] much better to have an agent secure the best deal possible and ensure that all terms of that deal are then met."

Martha Webb, proprietor and literary agent with CookeMcDermid in Toronto, Ontario, sees the agent's role as that of career guide and activist. "We are an author's advocate throughout the life of their work, and the liaison between the author and publisher. Our goal is to find the best possible publishing arrangements for the author's work… to support and advocate for their interests throughout the process and to advise them throughout their writing career." Carolyn Forde, literary agent and international rights director for Westwood Creative Artists in Toronto, Ontario, sums up the advocate role this way: "The agent supports and advises their clients. We do many, many contracts a year, and most authors won't do more than one a year (and even that would be considered a lot), so we do know what's industry standard, what's author friendly and what isn't."

In an online interview with Authornomics, agent Katherine Sands, with the Sarah Jane Freymann Literary Agency in New York, takes it even further, explaining that "literary agent now means content manager…the work is hands-on with a role in developing and marketing an author's name and material for print, digital and other media—not just centered around a book deal." She believes "the digital age is revolutionizing every-thing and reinvented agents are now far more involved in creating opportunities for writ-ing clients' content in emerging markets: for books, to be used online, with partners, in podcasts, in products, and in digital media to accrue sales. The new agent focus is on how writers can market and maximize their works across a wide slate." Lori Hahnel, Calgary-based author of *After You've Gone*, *Love Minus Zero* and *Nothing Sacred* and creative writ-ing teacher at Mount Royal University and the Alexandra Writers' Centre Society, notes another role of the agent—that of editor. "Today more than ever, agents are taking on an editorial role. As publishers employ fewer and fewer editors, they need the manuscripts they get from agents to be in nearly publishable form when they're submitted."

Agents also handle other types of administrative and editorial-type tasks, such as checking royalty statements and hunting down overdue royalty checks; submitting books to reviewers and literary contests; and submitting future manuscripts to editors/publish-ers.

DETERMINING NEED

"Academic writing, and those working in less commercially successful genres likely don't need an agent," says Webb. Friedman, in her blog post "How to Find a Literary Agent for Your Book," adds that "if you're writing for a niche market (e.g., vintage automobiles) or wrote an academic or literary work, then you might not need an agent." Why? "Agents are motivated to take on clients based on the size of the advance they think they can get. If your project doesn't command a decent advance, then you may not be worth an agent's time, and you'll have to sell the project on your own." Kelsey Attard, managing editor of Freehand Books in Calgary, Alberta, says that "it depends on your goals…and also it depends on your genre. There are virtually no agents who represent poets, for example." Anita Purcell, executive director of the Canadian Authors Association, expounds further. "If you write poetry, short stories, or novellas, agents are not likely to take you on, and you have a better chance pitching directly to smaller presses that specialize in your particu-lar genre." And, she adds, "authors who have been offered a contract with a publisher may want to get an agent to represent their interests before actually signing the contract. It is far easier to land an agent when you've got a firm offer from a publisher in hand."

Croll notes that those who want to work with an independent (indie) publisher can most likely get by without an agent. But, literary representation is essential for any writer wanting to make money by accessing most major publishing houses and editors, especial-ly since the merging of many publishing companies has resulted in huge conglomerates with multiple imprints. "Editors often review agented submission first—and give them more consideration—because those submissions have already gone through a sort of vet-ting process," says Croll. And, shares Attard, "those biggest publishers typically don't accept unsolicited submissions from unagented authors." In the same online interview with Authornomics, Sands paints this picture: "Try this test at home: call a leading publisher tomorrow and try to get anyone to discuss your work. An agent has the greenlight to do this, but a civilian is unlikely to penetrate the publisher's robotic turnaround, shielding editors from unrepresented writers." And, she poses, "betcha you can't find out which newly-hired editor would really love your literotic chiller about a sexy ichthyologist who must solve eco-system crime in Namibia."

Dawn Green, British Columbia–based author of *In the Swish* and *How Samantha Became a Revolutionary*, has this perspective. "I think any author who wants to just be an author, just be writing novels full time, requires an agent who will allow them time to focus on their craft." Stephanie Sinclair, senior literary agent with Transatlantic Agency in Toronto, Ontario, shares Dawn Green's sentiment: "The contracts are often very tricky, and without an agent, the process can end up taking up so much time, the author has no time/energy left to write! My job is to help my authors, so they can just focus on the writing." Like Sands, Dawn Green also holds that "an agent needs to help a writer market and brand themselves. It's that classic difference between art and business." And, she adds, "today, it seems that more time needs to be put into the social media and networking side of things, and that is not easy for most introverted writers to do."

Taylor Brown, Wilmington, North Carolina–based bestselling author of the novels *Fallen Land, The River of Kings* and *Gods of Howl Mountain*, views the author-agent relationship from this lens. "Once your work has been published in book form, your agent's help only becomes that much more important. I think of an agent as a 'corner man' or woman of sorts." As well, he says, "they can do everything from giving feedback on manuscripts to helping interpret communications from your publisher to acting as a sounding board for important career changes. I could hardly imagine this career without an agent."

BEFORE THE QUERY

Most (good) literary agents receive hundreds of submissions a week from prospective clients, so time is precious, and second chances are rare. Part of doing your homework in finding an agent, before even entering the literary agent querying process, is ensuring your manuscript is the absolute best it can be. You want to be ready to hit "Send" as soon as an agent requests pages. In a guest blog post about finding a literary agent for The Writers' Workshop, novelist Harry Bingham says that means having a rock-solid product. "Write a good book. A stunning one. A dazzling one. One that echoes in the consciousness. One that makes a professional reader (i.e. agent/editor) sit up late with tears in their eyes." Sands agrees. In her book *Making the Perfect Pitch: How to Catch a Literary Agent's*

Eye (The Writer Books, 2004), she says, "Literary agents must be enchanted, seduced, and won over to take you on as a client."

But how do you ensure this? Have your manuscript professionally evaluated; give it to trusted beta readers for invaluable constructive feedback. "They will find idiosyncrasies in your manuscript that will surprise you and also offer suggestions. Then after you make the edits, send the manuscript to a copy editor. Agents can spot professionalism a mile away," says Lynne Wiese Sneyd, owner of LWS Literary Services in Tucson, Arizona, and literary consultant for the Tucson Festival of Books. Hiring a professional editor will ensure the manuscript is error-free and at-the-ready for agent consideration. Brown shares Wiese Sneyd's philosophy. "A professional editor who has a record of helping shepherd books to publication is simply invaluable. You cannot depend on the agent seeing the potential in your work. They are not looking for potential. They are looking for a book they can sell right now."

THE QUERY: SOME DOS AND DON'TS

Also, make sure your pitch to an agent is bang-on in every aspect. If you can't write an enticing query letter, you may not convince a literary agent that you can write a compelling book. Jan Kardys, a literary agent at Black Hawk Literary Agency LLC in Redding, Connecticut, and chairman of the Unicorn Writers' Conference, offers these tips for honing your query and book summary: "It is helpful for writers to study book publishers' websites and study catalogue copy. Once you study author's bio(s) and read the descriptions of their books, you get great ideas." Sinclair explains the pitch process this way: "Know who you are submitting to. When people send letters referencing some of my other clients and my taste, I know they have done their homework, which makes me immediately pay close attention." According to Sands, "it's the pitch and nothing but the pitch that gets a writer selected from the leaning tower of queries in a literary agent's office… The writing you do about your writing is as important as the writing itself." It is "part 'hello,' part cover letter, part interview for the coveted job of book author," she says. Agents, she stresses, "are looking first for a reason to keep reading, then for a reason to represent you…you want your pitch to give crystal clear answers—fast."

Some of those answers, says Croll, include being able to clearly describe the market for your book—who is going to buy it. "Selling your manuscript to a publisher is how an agent makes a living—that is their source of income. They are motivated to take on authors who will create work they can actually sell." And remember that your query letter is a form of communication, "so try to come across as a real person and not a pitching robot following a formula," advises Webb. Purcell couldn't agree more. "Always personalize your letter: make sure you use the agent's name and spell it correctly. If possible, find something you share in common, whether it's having the same birthplace, a mutual love of horror, or having met at a writers' conference." Like Webb, Purcell says "the query letter should not read like a form letter that is sent to every agent and publisher."

Hahnel, like Wiese Sneyd, suggests soliciting feedback from respected beta readers. The input will help "polish your query and your sample chapters until they shine." Purcell suggests taking it a step further. Writers "should ask experienced authors to review their query letter before submitting it." Why go to all this effort? "The bar is very, very high now, and so anything you can do to put your best foot forward is in your best interest," stresses Forde.

Hahnel also recommends having "a synopsis ready. Not all agents ask for them, but some will." As for a query letter, she says "don't clutter it with unnecessary information, such as courses you've taken or retreats you've gone on." Be polite and professional, says Hahnel, and ensure a confident and positive tone. "Don't say negative things like, 'I'm not sure if you'll like this.' or 'You probably won't want to read all of this.'" Attard recommends this: "Be brief, engaging, and also (at least for literary writing) let your manuscript be the star." Forde offers similar sound advice for a query. "Keep it short and concise—tell me about the book and about you. Don't try to be cute or memorable. Don't compare your book to the best book in the genre. If you say it's the next Harry Potter, what I hear is that you have unrealistic expectations." Purcell has this sage query-writing advice. "Agents often say that what catches their interest most is when writers manage to avoid some of the pitfalls of new writers, such as telling the agent that they're good writers (show, don't tell), or that all their family and friends loved the manuscript (of course they did, they love you), or that they've been wanting to be published authors since they were six years old (few writers haven't)." She says what also catches agents' interest is "when writers seem to have a strong understanding of their genre, as well as the distinction between commercial, upmarket, and literary writing."

A FEW WISE WORDS ON PLATFORM

Purcell says that it's all about branding right now "And writers should look at their social media platforms and their website, if they have one, with a critical eye that asks: 'What is my current brand and how appealing is that brand to a potential agent or publisher? Are there any posts or images that might turn an agent or publisher off?' And, she adds, "if they're unpublished, writers need to think about what makes them stand out as good candidates for representation by the agent. Have they won any writing competitions? Are they authorities on the subject matter?"

WHERE TO FIND AGENTS

Once your manuscript is ultra-polished and ready for publication, and you've decided to take the leap and find an agent, one way is to conduct online research. "I think a writer should be a good sleuth," says Dawn Green. "And most agents/agencies are clear on their websites about what they are looking for." She also suggests researching to see if agents have given (online) interviews and made additional comments about what they're looking for in a manuscript.

Publishers Marketplace is a helpful online research tool. For a $25 monthly membership, writers/authors can get snapshots of top literary agencies, seeing which books agents have sold and editors' buying patterns. A membership also offers industry news updates and deal reports. The "Dealmaker" lists a contact database and a rights and proposals board posting—all helpful for determining which agent to pitch and also for knowing how to entice each one. "It's one of the most extensive databases of agents," says Wiese Sneyd. "It's an amazing resource."

Word of mouth is also helpful. Ask authors (especially in your genre) you know and trust, and whose work you respect who their agent is and request a candid assessment of their professional and personal style. "Referrals from existing clients are also an excellent way to get an agent's attention, so if you are able to ask an established writer, do so," recommends Forde. With Brown, he's the one making the connection for the writer. "In several cases, I have come across an unrepresented writer whose work I admire and recommended them to my agent."

Another method is to read the acknowledgment section of books with a similar audience or vibe to yours, as well as those of your favorite authors, who often list their agent with a huge "thank you." In a *Forbes'* blog post by contributor Nick Morgan, he succinctly explains the process: "Find books that are similar to what you hope yours will be, and that you like, and read the acknowledgements. Every writer thanks her agent fulsomely in the acknowledgements, or she'll never publish again."

Writers' conferences are also another viable route to find agents who are actively seeking new titles/authors. These agents are often speakers/panelists there, offering writers the chance to meet with them one-on-one to pitch their manuscript. "Face-to-face meetings with agents can help you get a foot in the door—as long as you keep it professional and respectful," notes Purcell. Hahnel knows "two people who were able to sign with agents at 'speed-dating' sessions at conferences," but, she stresses, "I understand it's not a super-common occurrence." Taylor says to attend myriad industry events, including in-store appearances, book launches and festivals. "Talk to people. Often those in attendance are part of the book industry. Always tell people you are an author. You never know who you may be talking to."

QueryTracker.net has helped more than 2,400 authors find a literary agent. Among its many online freebies are a detailed database of more than 1,500 agent profiles, including author comments from their experience with said agent; an agent query-tracking feature; and data that lists agent reply rates, typical response times, etc. Writersdigest.com also offers a handy online feature called "New Agency Alerts" that profiles "new literary agents actively seeking writers, books, and queries now. These agents are building their client lists." Agentquery.com, which says it's "the internet's largest free database of literary agents," lets you search for agents (around one thousand of them) by category, offers an online social networking community (great for the query process) and provides agent and agency updates. Attard maintains that authors and writers should check out the deal listings on *Publishers Weekly*, and *Quill & Quire*, investigating the agents listed in those deal announcements. And annual print directories, such as the *Literary Market Place: The Directory of the American Book Publishing Industry* (which offers listings to "reach the people who publish, package, review, represent, edit, translate, typeset, illustrate, design, print, bind, promote, publicize, ship, and distribute"), are often available in your local library's reference section, says Purcell.

Brown suggests submitting to literary magazines and contests. "These publications still attract the attention of agents," he assures. He also recommends using social media. Brown "drew the attention of a couple of agents after becoming active on Twitter." Why? "I believe some of the younger literary agents monitor social media for young writers who are making waves with their essays or stories." Attard is in agreement. "Some agents are active on social media, so follow a few and get a sense of what they like and don't like, and what you should avoid doing! It can be really valuable to get a sense of how they work."

And while a seasoned, big-name agent may be able to get you an impressive advance on your book and secure an ironclad contract, don't be afraid to go with a newer literary agent, someone who's "hungry" and will most likely have more time and offer a high level of personal attention to champion not only your book, but also your literary career. Attard suggests that "if an agent is new without many prior sales, consider their history in the industry. Do they have the connections necessary to be successful?" And, cautions Webb, "a junior agent—and everyone needs to start somewhere—should be a junior agent within a reputable agency, who has the support of more senior agents behind her." In the same vein is the size of the literary agency. "This doesn't necessarily correlate with the quality of the agent or the size of the deal you can expect," verifies Friedman in her blog post "How to Find a Literary Agent for Your Book."

THE "GOOD" AGENT

What are the signs of a good literary agent? According to the website of the Canadian Authors Association, "reputable agents will be up to date on current publishing trends… and serve as experts in market sales, so they will help ensure your book gets a good cover design, and more attention from the publisher's publicity department." Purcell affirms that agents "represent you [the author], not the publisher, and will negotiate for more money, subsidiary rights, and protection clauses. Good agents are also in it for the long haul: they are as interested in building the author's career as they are in selling the first book."

MacIntyre shares the same mindset. He says that many writers aren't interested in the "bureaucracy and the fine points of the book business," so a good agent, "in addition to possessing literary instincts and professional connections, has a mercenary skill set. An agent should be a partner and a friend, but strong enough to speak truth to vanity. An agent will offer an essential service but is not a servant." He also says good agents attend myriad international book fairs; have strong professional relationships with influential editors; "play bad-cop where money matters matter; play mom/dad when the creative muse becomes petulant and sulky; pick up the tab (now and then); offer tactful commentary and advice (but not instruction) on creative issues; and know the difference between momentary insecurity and reality-based despair." MacIntyre also believes good agents have "the sensibilities and judgment of an editor; the skills of an accountant; the temerity of a union boss; a sense of humour, irony; good taste in food, drink and literature; and patience."

Kanya-Forstner stresses that "the best agents search widely and actively for new, diverse and challenging voices; for writers who bring something essential to the conversations in which they participate." She says that "the best agents are the most discerning, taking on only those clients whose work they know they can champion with the utmost integrity and confidence. The work they then submit comes with the weight of their endorsement and credibility." To Kanya-Forstner, "the best agents make it their business to be familiar with the sensibilities and interests of individual editors and with the publishing identity and strengths of individual imprints. The best agents pride themselves on being successful matchmakers."

Kardys says a "talented agent" will suggest to a writer several tactics, such as building a platform before the book deal—social media, contact lists, and doing events or writing articles/stories; provide ideas on how to market the book; and edit the writer's book summary." For her, "ideally, the best literary agents have a background as a former book editor, subsidiary rights experience at a book publisher, or the agent has started their publishing career by working for another literary agency before leaving to start their own agency."

Cole sees a good agent as "someone who seems to 'get' your work, who understands what you're writing now, and what you want to write in the future." And, adds Kanya-Forstner, since "publishing is a constantly changing business, the best agents stay on top of market trends, shifts in buying habits and retail practices." Terence Green describes the good agent in these terms: "A good agent knows editors and what they are looking for. They can provide shortcuts to editors. Many editors won't even look at unsolicited manuscripts, trusting the judgment of respected agents." So, the good agent, he says, is "in essence, the editor's first reader, winnowing the field appropriately for the editor." Friedman believes a good agent is not only an author's business manager, but also an author's "mentor and cheerleader." She shares these wise sentiments in her blog post: Literary agents are "also there to hold your hand when things go wrong with the editor or publisher. They prop you up when you're down, they celebrate your successes publicly, they look for opportunities you might not see, and they attend to your financial best interests as well as your big-picture career growth." Purcell stresses that "because the bulk of their work involves sales and negotiation, [editors] should be confident and assertive in their dealings, but always professional and respectful in their treatment of people, including you." She also believes agents should be "strategic thinkers" with strong social media skills. And "being well-organized is also a useful quality in a literary agent, since they need to juggle a variety of authors, editors and projects."

THE "BAD" AGENT

While the list of qualities and skills of a good agent is long, the list for a "bad" one is comparable. Since there is no worldwide professional organization responsible for vetting agents and maintaining agent standards, virtually anyone can hang out their "Agent" shingle. Beware of sweet-talking scammers, secretive behavior, those who don't treat you as a business partner, those who don't communicate respectfully and clearly, and those who don't reply in a timely manner. They aren't legit agents. Never, ever give a literary agent money upfront—not as a retainer, not for administrative expenses and not for a reading fee/feedback. An agent only gets paid—somewhere between 10 and 15 percent of an author's earnings—when an author gets paid and the publisher's advance is received. And 20 to 25 percent is standard for foreign sales (when translation rights are licensed to foreign book publishers), since the commission is often split between foreign and domestic agents. Cole says that "if you send a manuscript to an agent and she doesn't respond after a few months, that's an agent I wouldn't bother approaching further." And, he stresses, "if you're working with an agent, and she can't give you a list of the publishers she's sent your manuscript to, that's an agent who probably isn't working hard for you." Similarly, Taylor says that "if your agent is not directing you towards a deal, perhaps it is not the best fit."

Kardys feels the following are red flags: "A writer should not work with an agent who has no experience in the book field or hasn't offered suggested changes in the manuscript." However, she says, "if the book requires major work, an agent shouldn't sign up a writer as a client." And "if the agent doesn't know the basic points of a contract, the payment structures for an advance and the latest changes in the book marketplace, you should be cautious," she warns. Friedman, in her blog post, stresses that "if an agent passes you a publisher's boilerplate contact to sign with no changes, you may be in big trouble." Hahnel says to avoid agents with "non-existent client lists or sales history." And, she alerts, "beware of agents who only work with a few publishers."

According to a Science Fiction & Fantasy Writers of America blog post by A.C. Crispin, "real agents don't advertise. They don't have to. If you see an agency name in a sponsored Google ad or in the back of a writer's magazine, odds are they're a scam." And, says Crispin in that same post, "any agent that claims their client list is 'confidential' should be regarded with wariness, and their credentials should be investigated with extra care." Also, avoid agents who don't help with improving your query and/or proposal package. In her blog post, Friedman says only a few authors can put together a "crackerjack proposal." She stresses that "an agent should be ensuring the pitch or proposal is primed for success, and this almost always requires at least one round of feedback and revision."

Membership in the newly founded Professional Association of Canadian Literary Agents (PACLA), which only permits established literary agents to join and has a strict Code of Practice, or in the Association of Authors' Representatives, Inc. (AAR), for which its some 400 member must meet the highest standards and subscribe to its bylaws and Canon of Ethics, is a positive sign, but not necessarily a guarantee. Friedman states that "people in the industry should recognize the name of your agent." She also warns that if no online mention or reference to your agent can be found and if the agent isn't a member of the AAR, "that's a red flag. Check his track record carefully. See who he's sold to and how recently." And, forewarns Purcell, "generally speaking, if an agent is pursuing you rather than the other way around, think twice—most agents already have a stable of promising authors and rarely need to be the wooer." These are all reasons why, says, Terence Green, "one must do one's 'due diligence' in the matter, just as one would before venturing into any business investment."

HOW TO KEEP THE GOOD ONES

If you do secure a literary agent, be mindful that, like in any good relationship, the author-agent "marriage" can only thrive on mutual trust and respect, shared enthusiasm and open communication. Says Purcell: "I think it's important to have a connection with your literary agent. If there isn't a genuine and mutual feeling of respect and liking for one another, the relationship may sour over time." Sinclair thinks "it's important that you can enjoy a meal together. It's an intimate relationship in a way, so you want to be sure you like each other!" Cole advises to "be reliable, meet your deadlines and appreciate [your agent's] hard work." And Webb says to "be open to feedback and trust that your agent wants to make a success of your book and your career." But, don't' expect to sit back and let your agent do all of the legwork. "Be proactive about your career, boosting your platform whenever you can, and be someone who editors want to work with," she advises. Wiese Sneyd concurs. "Learn the business ahead of time. Respect an agent's time. Avoid excessive emails. Don't expect an agent to teach you the ins and outs of publishing. You'll have questions, of course, but enter the relationship as a savvy author."

Kardys advises to "always put in writing the obligations and duties of the writer and the agent" and to "encourage open communication and timelines." She also stresses to "listen carefully when your agent tells you to build your social media platform and make a list of email contacts, as later you will not have time to do this intense work when your book is published." Brown's suggestions are also a list of dos. Only a small percentage of writers get to have an agent represent their work, he says, and "there will be ups and downs and stressors of all kinds." But, he notes, "it's important to keep in mind that many writers only dream of having such problems! So try to enjoy the whole experience, even the worries and frustrations. They are all part of the story."

MAKING THE FINAL DECISION

Kanya-Forstner advises that "agents are only as good as the authors they represent, or for new agents, as good as the writers whose work they champion on social platforms and in public discourse about books." Refer to an agent's client list, which rights they've sold, when and in which countries, view their photograph, their (literary) likes and dislikes (Goodreads is a good resource to check), their Twitter feed, their website or their company's website, and weigh it all with any kind of gut feeling you may have to help you make your final choice. It all boils down to feelings and sensibilities—a kind of personal chemistry. MacIntyre concurs: "Basically, it will come down to a gut-level response, based on impressions and the compatibility of personalities." Author Chuck Sambuchino takes a similar stance. In his online WritersDigest.com article entitled "11 Steps to Finding the Agent Who'll Love your Book," he says that, after making your list of agents to contact, "rank agents in the likelihood of a love match."

THE SUBMISSION PROCESS IN A NUTSHELL

After doing your research into finding suitable agents, it's absolutely essential to find out what each agent wants in a submission. "Be professional, read about the formatting details the agency wants and let your story do the selling," says Dawn Green. Purcell shares in her tips, adding, "it's important to find out what their preferences are and to follow their guidelines faithfully. If they want the manuscript double-spaced in the courier font with one-inch margins, that's what you should give them. You're sending them a message if you don't." Sambuchino concurs in his online piece. "Getting through the front door is often about playing by the rules. Don't send anything less—or more—than each agent has asked for." If the agent specifies that they don't want attachments, "that means they want the query letter and up to ten pages of the manuscript imbedded in the body of the email, even if that looks ugly," says Purcell. Also, says Sambuchino, be sure you're submitting to four to eight agents only at a time, giving each agent their own separate email or mailed package. "Keep things professional. No gimmicks." And don't argue if/when you get a "no thank you" reply. "An agent is not attacking you. They know the business, they know what sells, and they are honestly trying to help your words get noticed," says Dawn Green, adding not to take agent criticism personally. Taylor suggests that if you receive a "no," be sure to "follow up with a thank you and ask if they might suggest who might be interested. Sometimes advice comes your way, or even your work gets a second look. Often publishing is luck and timing."

BEYOND THE QUERY

Be sure to keep track of your submissions and their results. Sambuchino says that "if you aren't getting any page requests, your query needs work. If you're getting partial requests but then nothing, your first draft pages aren't snagging the reader. If you're getting full requests but no nibbles, it's time to take a look at the full manuscript again." Use each rejection and any feedback you may get from an agent to fine-tune your next set of submissions. "This is not an easy business, and rejection is the norm, not the exception. I like to think of rejections as marks of honor," says Brown. "It's not how many times you get knocked down; it's how many times you get back up. Each rejection is one step closer to publication. Keep the faith. Keep going. It's worth it." And be prepared to wait for as long as it takes to find your perfect match. "My experience," clarifies Terence Green, "has always been that this is not a business for the impatient."

Perhaps the best advice to keep in mind during this journey comes from Cole: "Too many beginning writers with a half-finished manuscript think the first thing they need to do is get an agent, as if that will solve everything and ensure a flourishing writing career. It doesn't work that way," he warns. "The first thing you need to do is master your craft and produce a damn good book. An agent can't make you a good writer. An agent can't make you a success. That's up to you."

....

Jennifer D. Foster is a Toronto-based freelance writer, editor, and content strategist. Find her online at lifeonplanetword.wordpress.com.

....

WHAT TO LOOK FOR WHEN CHOOSING AN ATTORNEY

by Francine A. Gargano, Esq.

Some people go through life never having to acquire the legal services of an attorney. Unfortunately, for those who do find it necessary, it is often because of an unhappy or emergent situation. In those cases people often rush to hire someone without giving it much thought.

For our purposes, let's assume that you will want an attorney that will be available to help you with either your writing career or your personal affairs that are affected by your career. This article will assist you in choosing the attorney that is right for you and your particular situation.

IS THE ATTORNEY QUALIFIED TO HANDLE YOUR SITUATION?

In order to decide if an attorney is qualified to handle your particular situation you need to know what you want the attorney to do for you. Writers will need an attorney for positive things like setting up their business structure (yes, writing is a business and should be established as such). You may also need an attorney to help you protect your work product through copyrighting. Attorneys are necessary for reviewing and negotiating contracts on those big book deals. Unfortunately, an attorney may also have to be retained to sue to collect on those contracts where you have not been compensated as promised, to renegotiate the terms of a contract or to sue someone who is infringing on your copyrighted material.

In your personal life you will we need an attorney to prepare your Estate Plan to protect all of your works and royalties so that your family can benefit after you have departed this earth. In the case of a divorce, writers need an attorney who can protect their work from their spouses. As you can see, writers will definitely have occasion to use an attorney in their lifetime.

Given the different circumstances that may bring you to an attorney, it is important to understand exactly what you need them to do. Once you understand what it is you need, you can begin to look for the properly qualified attorney.

Not all attorneys are created equal. An attorney can be a great divorce attorney but not understand the nuances of the writing business enough to argue for the protection of your works. A good divorce attorney may know nothing about copyrights and therefore should not be the person you choose. A good contract attorney may still not know enough about the writing business to properly negotiate that big deal. On the other hand, the contract may be simple enough for any contract attorney to handle.

For the above reasons, the first thing to look for when choosing an attorney is to find out if they are qualified to deal with your legal issue - as it applies to your writing business. The person does not have to be an "expert" in a field to necessarily help you. There are good general attorneys who may know enough about the industry to help you on more than one issue. A good general attorney should be able to help you set up your business, review simple contracts, and write your estate plan to protect your writings and royalties.

There are several ways to find out about an attorney's qualifications. You can ask the attorney directly if he or she has dealt with an issue likes yours. You can check with local, county, state or federal bar associations. Most can easily be found online.

Another source of good information is Martindale-Hubbell which can be found at www.martindale.com or in your local library. It is rich with information about attorneys. Some libraries also carry the Lawyer's Diary and Manuel (which is available for New Jersey, New York, Florida, Massachusetts and New Hampshire) which has information regarding attorneys and their expertise.

You should also consider consulting your writers' organizations and materials which may carry information regarding attorneys who work with writers. Of course, word-of-mouth through friends and family members can be an important resource as well.

DO YOU WANT TO WORK WITH A LAW FIRM OR A SOLO PRACTITIONER?

Your next decision is whether or not you want to go with a law firm or a solo practitioner. That decision is entirely up to you but what you should know is the difference between them and the pros and cons of both. Law firms generally tend to charge higher fees, bill in larger minimum increments and are more aggressive with their billing. Also, with law firms you often will interview with a partner who you think will be your attorney but you will very rarely ever see them again. You will be passed off to associates and parale-gals and may end up with multiple people making it confusing and costly. The benefit of a law firm is that there are more people so if your attorney cannot attend a court hearing for some reason there is another person who can take over. It can also be beneficial for ex-tremely large cases that may require a lot of expenditures because you have the money of the firm behind you.

With solo practitioners you get one attorney that is handling your case. You may also have paralegals to deal with there as well but you will have more communication and more of a relationship with the actual attorney. You usually have more access to the attor-ney as well.

Solo practitioners tend to have lower fees and are more likely to work with you on payment plans and in finding ways to minimize your costs.

WHAT WILL YOU HAVE TO PAY IN LEGAL FEES?

Legal fees are not free unless you do not earn much money and only for very specific types of matters. Contingent fees (where you only pay your attorney when they win a case) is rare and again, for specific types of cases. For our purposes it is safe to assume you will have to pay your attorney and you will need to know how much that will be.

Most attorneys require a retainer which is a lump sum amount of money that is paid BEFORE any work is started. You can however occasionally find an attorney who will let you pay in installments. It is wise to start putting money aside now for future legal fees so you are not caught without the funds you need to get proper legal services.

The attorney should provide you with a retainer agreement which will set forth whether you are being charged a flat fee (which is a set amount of money for the matter) or an hourly fee (which is where you are billed in increments of an hour and pay for each thing the attorney does). It should list the hourly fee for the partner, associates, paralegals, and secretaries.

The retainer should let you know what expenses, if any, you have to pay. Typically you will pay for all outside third parties, i.e. court costs, deposition costs and expert fees. You may also be charged for copies, faxes, emails, texts and travel costs. Make sure you un-derstand what you will be billed so that you can decide if this is an attorney you want to hire. It will also help you to figure out how you can minimize your costs while maximiz-ing your service.

The fees you will be billed by an attorney is important but should not be your decid-ing factor. I see more people give up a trusted and loyal attorney for what they think will be lower fees only to be disappointed by the results. Understand that attorney fees are based upon the number of years an attorney is in practice, whether they are with a firm or a solo practitioner and if the subject matter is a specialty.

The longer an attorney is in practice the higher the hourly fee will be. You are paying for the experience and knowledge of the attorney. If you have an attorney you know and trust, that is worth more than the money you think you will save.

Going to an attorney who charges less money, does not always save you money. I know a person who gave up their family attorney because they said they were too expensive. They went to a law firm believing they would save money because the work would be done by a paralegal. This is like saying I am giving up one doctor so I can be treated by the receptionist at a different doctor's office instead.

In the end, the people involved in this transition found that the work done by the firm was not right and the people ended up spending way more money than they had figured. Make sure you balance out fees with quality of service and familiarity with the attorney.

ARE YOU AND THE ATTORNEY COMPATIBLE?

In my opinion the most important thing to look for in an attorney is compatibility. This may sound strange but think about it. You and your attorney have to work hand-in-hand in order to be successful in your endeavors together. You may spend many hours with them in close quarters preparing a case.

Like a good friend or a lover, you need to be able to feel comfortable confiding in your attorney. We all have secrets and sometimes they need to be exposed to the attorney. If you do not feel comfortable with the attorney, you will be reluctant to fully discuss certain issues.

One thing you will want to consider is if they work the same hours as you? For me, I have clients who are on the West Coast so they need me to be available in what is the evening for me on the East Coast. Some clients need evening and weekend hours. If you do you need to know if your attorney can accommodate that.

Compatibility these days also involves electronics and the digital world. However, not everyone is comfortable with it. If you need an attorney who will see you physically in the office, talk to you on the phone and send you paperwork in the mail, you need to make sure the one you hire can do this. There are attorneys right now who are completely paperless so they will not be able to accommodate some of your needs. This also means they will not hold original documents for you like wills or divorce decrees.

On the other hand if you like being able to speak in "k", "LOL" and "ttyl" via text, make sure you have an attorney who can accommodate that. In my case most of my clients want to see me as little as possible and want me as electronically savvy as they are. I still have, however, older clients who are completely the opposite and I have to make sure I can accommodate both types of clients.

You also need to be on the same page as your attorney. If you do not like to fight and are willing to give in, make sure you have an attorney who can work with that. If you are aggressive and want to go for that proverbial "jugular", you do not want a weak person working for you. Remember, you may want an attorney who is aggressive in the court-room but that does not mean you want them to necessarily be that way with you. I once saw an attorney throw his briefcase down and start screaming at his client in the court-house. Unless you want someone who will treat you like that, find an attorney who will save the hostility for your adversaries.

I personally made the mistake once of hiring an attorney with whom I had nothing in common. I chose him because I thought he had the expertise I needed. I can tell you it was not a successful match and it cost my dearly. Do not make the same mistake that I did.

If you follow my advice you will have a greater chance at success with your legal en-deavors. Happy Lawyer Hunting!

Francine Gargano is an attorney who has a general practice in Somerville, NJ. Ms. Gargano is a member of the NJ State Bar Association, former Trustee of the Somerset County Bar Associa-tion, the Past Chair of the Somerset County Bar Foundation and President of the Vicinage XIII Women's Bar Association. Ms. Gargano is an activist who has in the past received a Congres-sional Volunteer Award ran a legal clinic, worked with numerous organizations and received an American Bar Association Commendation. She has testified in hearings, taught paralegal stud-ies and has written numerous articles on the law.

LITERARY AGENTS

///

Many publishers are willing to look at unsolicited submissions, but most feel having an agent is in the writer's best interest. In this section we include agents who specialize in or represent fiction.

The commercial fiction field is intensely competitive. Many publishers have small staffs and little time. For that reason, many book publishers rely on agents for new talent. Some publishers even rely on agents as "first readers" who must wade through the deluge of submissions from writers to find the very best. For writers a good agent can be a foot in the door—someone willing to do the necessary work to put your manuscript in the right editor's hands.

It would seem today that finding a good agent is as hard as finding a good publisher. Yet writers who have agents say they are invaluable. Not only can an agent help you make your work more marketable, an agent also acts as your business manager and adviser, protecting your interests during and after contract negotiations.

Still, finding an agent can be very difficult for a new writer. If you are already published in magazines, you have a better chance than someone with no publishing credits. (Some agents read periodicals searching for new writers.) Although many agents do read queries and manuscripts from unpublished authors without introduction, referrals from their writer clients can be a big help. If you don't know any published authors with agents, attending a conference is a good way to meet agents. Some agents even set aside time at conferences to meet new writers.

Almost all the agents listed here have said they are open to working with new, previously unpublished writers as well as published writers. They do not charge a fee to cover the time and effort involved in reviewing a manuscript or a synopsis and chapters, but their time is still extremely valuable. Send an agent your work only when you feel it is as complete and polished as possible.

⊘ DOMINICK ABEL LITERARY AGENCY, INC.

146 W. 82nd St., #1A, New York NY 10024. (212)877-0710. **Fax:** (212)595-3133. **E-mail:** agency@dalainc.com. **Website:** dalainc.com. **Contact:** Dominick Abel. Estab. 1975. Member of AAR. Represents 50 clients.

REPRESENTS Fiction, novels. **Considers these fiction areas:** action, adventure, crime, detective, mystery, police.

HOW TO CONTACT Query via e-mail. No attachments. "If you wish to submit fiction, describe what you have written and what market you are targeting (you may find it useful to compare your work to that of an established author). Include a synopsis of the novel and the first two or three chapters. If you wish to submit nonfiction, you should, in addition, detail your qualifications for writing this particular book. Identify the audience for your book and explain how your book will be different from and better than already published works aimed at the same market." Accepts simultaneous submissions. Responds in 2-3 weeks.

ADAMS LITERARY

7845 Colony Rd., C4 #215, Charlotte NC 28226. (704)542-1440. **Fax:** (704)542-1450. **E-mail:** info@adamsliterary.com. **Website:** www.adamsliterary.com. **Contact:** Tracey Adams, Josh Adams. Estab. 2004. Member of AAR. Other memberships include SCBWI and WNBA.

MEMBER AGENTS Tracey Adams, Josh Adams, Lorin Oberweger.

REPRESENTS **Considers these fiction areas:** middle grade, picture books, young adult.

HOW TO CONTACT **Submit through online form on website only.** Send e-mail if that is not operating correctly. All submissions and queries should first be made through the online form on website. Will not review—and will promptly recycle—any unsolicited submissions or queries received by mail. Before submitting work for consideration, review complete guidelines online, as the agency sometimes shuts off to new submissions. Accepts simultaneous submissions. Responds in 6 weeks if interested. "While we have an established client list, we do seek new talent—and we accept submissions from both published and aspiring authors and artists."

TERMS Agent receives 15% commission on domestic sales; 20% on foreign sales. Offers written contract.

RECENT SALES *The Cruelty*, by Scott Bergstrom (Feiwel & Friends); *The Little Fire Truck*, by Margery Cuyler (Christy Ottaviano); *Unearthed*, by Amie Kaufman and Meagan Spooner (Disney-Hyperion); *A Handful of Stars*, by Cynthia Lord (Scholastic); *Under Their Skin*, by Margaret Peterson Haddix (Simon & Schuster); *The Secret Horses of Briar Hill*, by Megan Shepherd (Delacorte); *The Secret Subway*, by Shana Corey (Schwartz & Wade); *Impyrium*, by Henry Neff (HarperCollins).

TIPS "Guidelines are posted (and frequently updated) on our website."

THE AHEARN AGENCY, INC.

2021 Pine St., New Orleans LA 70118. (504)861-8395. **Fax:** (504)866-6434. **E-mail:** pahearn@aol.com. **Website:** www.ahearnagency.com. **Contact:** Pamela G. Ahearn. Estab. 1992. Other memberships include MWA, RWA, ITW. Represents 30 clients.

REPRESENTS Novels. **Considers these fiction areas:** crime, detective, romance, suspense, thriller.

HOW TO CONTACT Query with SASE or via e-mail. Please send a one-page query letter stating the type of book you're writing, word length, where you feel your book fits into the current market, and any writing credentials you may possess. Please do not send ms pages or synopses if they haven't been previously requested. If you're querying via e-mail, send no attachments unless requested. Accepts simultaneous submissions. Responds in 2 months on submissions, 4 months on queries. Obtains most new clients through recommendations from others, solicitations, conferences.

TERMS Agent receives 15% commission on domestic sales; 20% commission on foreign sales. Offers written contract, binding for 1 year; renewable by mutual consent.

RECENT SALES *Paper Ghosts*, by Julia Heaberlin; *The Secret of Flirting*, by Sabrina Jeffries; *Mister Tender's Girl*, by Carter Wilson; *Married at Midnight*, by Gerri Russell; *The Ripper's Shadow*, by Laura Joh Rowland; *The Husband Hunter's Guide to London*, by Kate Moore; *Just a Breath Away*, by Carlene Thompson.

WRITERS CONFERENCES Romance Writers of America, Thrillerfest, Bouchercon.

TIPS "Be professional! Always send in exactly what an agent/editor asks for—no more, no less. Keep query letters brief and to the point, giving your writing credentials and a very brief summary of your book. If 1 agent rejects you, keep trying—there are a lot of us out there!"

❺ AITKEN ALEXANDER ASSOCIATES

291 Gray's Inn Rd., Kings Cross, London WC1X 8QJ United Kingdom. (020)7373-8672. **Fax:** (020)7373-6002. **E-mail:** reception@aitkenalexander.co.uk. **E-mail:** submissions@aitkenalexander.co.uk. **Website:** www.aitkenalexander.co.uk. Estab. 1976.

MEMBER AGENTS Gillon Aitken; Clare Alexander (literary, commercial, memoir, narrative nonfiction, history); Matthew Hamilton (literary fiction, suspense, music, politics, and sports); Gillie Russell (middle grade, young adult); Mary Pachnos; Anthony Sheil; Lucy Luck (quality fiction and nonfiction); Lesley Thorne; Matias Lopez Portillo; Shruti Debi; Leah Middleton.

REPRESENTS Nonfiction, novels. **Considers these fiction areas:** commercial, literary, mainstream, middle grade, suspense, thriller, young adult.

HOW TO CONTACT "If you would like to submit your work to us, please e-mail your covering letter with a short synopsis and the first 30 pages (as a Word document) to submissions@aitkenalexander.co.uk indicating if there is a specific agent who you would like to consider your work. Although every effort is made to respond to submissions, if we have not responded within three months please assume that your work is not right for the agency's list. Please note that the Indian Office does not accept unsolicited submissions." Accepts simultaneous submissions. Obtains most new clients through recommendations from others, solicitations.

RECENT SALES *A Country Row, A Tree*, by Jo Baker (Knopf); *Noonday*, by Pat Barker (Doubleday); *Beatlebone*, by Kevin Barry (Doubleday); *Spill Simmer Falter Wither*, by Sara Baume (Houghton Mifflin).

⊘ ALIVE LITERARY AGENCY

7680 Goddard St., Suite 200, Colorado Springs CO 80920. (719)260-7080. **Fax:** (719)260-8223. **E-mail:** info@aliveliterary.com. **E-mail:** submissions@aliveliterary.com. **Website:** www.aliveliterary.com. **Contact:** Rick Christian. Estab. 1989. Member of AAR. Other memberships include Authors Guild.

MEMBER AGENTS Rick Christian president (blockbusters, bestsellers); Andrea Heinecke (thoughtful/inspirational nonfiction, women's fiction/nonfiction, popular/commercial nonfiction & fiction); Bryan Norman (popular nonfiction, biography/memoir/autobiography, spiritual growth, inspirational, literary); Lisa Jackson (popular nonfiction, biography/memoir/autobiography, spiritual growth, inspirational, literary, women's nonfiction).

REPRESENTS Nonfiction, fiction, novels, short story collections, novellas. **Considers these fiction areas:** adventure, contemporary issues, family saga, historical, humor, inspirational, literary, mainstream, mystery, religious, romance, satire, sports, suspense, thriller, young adult.

HOW TO CONTACT "Because all our agents have full client loads, they are only considering queries from authors referred by clients and close contacts. Please refer to our guidelines at http://aliveliterary.com/submissions. Authors referred by an Alive client or close contact are invited to send proposals to submissions@aliveliterary.com." Your submission should include a referral (name of referring Alive client or close contact in the e-mail subject line. In the e-mail, please describe your personal or professional connection to the referring individual), a brief author biography (including recent speaking engagements, media appearances, social media platform statistics, and sales histories of your books), a synopsis of the work for which you are seeking agency representation (including the target audience, sales and marketing hooks, and comparable titles on the market), and the first 3 chapters of your manuscript. Alive will respond to queries meeting the above guidelines within 8-10 weeks.

TERMS Agent receives 15% commission on domestic sales. Offers written contract; two-month notice must be given to terminate contract.

TIPS Rewrite and polish until the words on the page shine. Endorsements, a solid platform, and great connections may help, provided you can write with power and passion. Hone your craft by networking with publishing professionals, joining critique groups, and attending writers' conferences.

AMBASSADOR LITERARY AGENCY

P.O. Box 50358, Nashville TN 37205. (615)370-4700. **E-mail:** info@ambassadoragency.com. **Website:** www.ambassadorspeakers.com/acp/index.aspx. **Contact:** Wes Yoder. Represents 25-30 clients.

REPRESENTS Nonfiction, novels. **Considers these fiction areas:** contemporary issues, religious.

HOW TO CONTACT Authors should e-mail a short description of their ms with a request to submit their work for review. Official submission guidelines will be sent if we agree to review a ms. Direct all inquiries and submissions to info@ambassadoragency.com. Accepts simultaneous submissions.

BETSY AMSTER LITERARY ENTERPRISES

607 Foothill Blvd. #1061, La Canada Flintridge CA 91012. **E-mail:** b.amster.assistant@gmail.com (for adult titles); b.amster.kidsbooks@gmail.com (for children's and young adult). **Website:** www.amsterlit.com; www.cummingskidlit.com. **Contact:** Betsy Amster (adult); Mary Cummings (children's and young adult). Estab. 1992. Member of AAR. Represents more than 75 clients.

REPRESENTS Nonfiction, novels, juvenile books. **Considers these fiction areas:** crime, detective, family saga, juvenile, literary, middle grade, multicultural, mystery, picture books, police, suspense, thriller, women's, young adult.

HOW TO CONTACT "For adult fiction or memoirs, please embed the first 3 pages in the body of your e-mail. For nonfiction, please embed the overview of your proposal. For children's picture books, please embed the entire text in the body of your e-mail. For longer middle-grade and YA fiction and nonfiction, please embed the first 3 pages." Accepts simultaneous submissions. Responds in 1 month to queries; 2 months to mss. Obtains most new clients through recommendations from others, solicitations, and conferences.

TERMS Agent receives 15% commission on domestic sales; 20% commission on foreign sales. Offers written contract, binding for 1 year; three-month notice must be given to terminate contract. Charges for photocopying, postage, messengers, galleys/books used in submissions to foreign and film agents and to magazines for first serial rights. (Please note that it is rare to incur much in the way of expenses now that most submissions are made by e-mail.)

RECENT SALES Betsy Amster: *Kachka: A Return to Russian Cooking*, by Bonnie Frumkin Morales with Deena Prichep (Flatiron); *It Takes One to Tango*, by Winifred Reilly (Touchstone); *Good Trouble*, by Christopher Noxon (Abrams); *The Lost Gutenberg*, by Margaret Leslie Davis (Avery). **Mary Cummings**: *Where is My Balloon?*, by Ariel Bernstein (Paula Wiseman Books/Simon & Schuster); *When Numbers Met*

Letters, by Lois Barr (Holiday House); *Do Not Go in There!*, by Ariel Horn (Macmillan/Imprint); *Bike and Trike*, by Elizabeth Verdick (Paula Wiseman Books/Simon & Schuster).

APONTE LITERARY AGENCY

E-mail: agents@aponteliterary.com. **Website:** aponteliterary.com. **Contact:** Natalia Aponte. Member of AAR. Signatory of WGA.

MEMBER AGENTS Natalia Aponte (any genre of mainstream fiction and nonfiction, but she is especially seeking women's novels, historical novels, supernatural and paranormal fiction, fantasy novels, political and science thrillers); Victoria Lea (any category, especially interested in women's fiction, science fiction and speculative fiction).

REPRESENTS Novels. **Considers these fiction areas:** fantasy, historical, paranormal, science fiction, supernatural, thriller, women's.

HOW TO CONTACT E-query. Accepts simultaneous submissions. Responds in 6 weeks if interested.

RECENT SALES *The Nightingale Bones*, by Ariel Swan; *An Irish Doctor in Peace and At War*, by Patrick Taylor; *Siren's Treasure*, by Debbie Herbert.

⊘ THE AUGUST AGENCY, LLC

Website: www.augustagency.com. **Contact:** Cricket Freemain, Jeffery McGraw. Estab. 2004. Represents 25-40 clients.

MEMBER AGENTS Jeffery McGraw, Cricket Freeman.

REPRESENTS Novels. **Considers these fiction areas:** crime, mainstream.

HOW TO CONTACT Currently closed to submissions.

THE AXELROD AGENCY

55 Main St., P.O. Box 357, Chatham NY 12037. (518)392-2100. **E-mail:** steve@axelrodagency.com. **Website:** www.axelrodagency.com. **Contact:** Steven Axelrod. Member of AAR. Represents 15-20 clients.

MEMBER AGENTS Steven Axelrod, representation; Lori Antonson, subsidiary rights.

REPRESENTS Novels. **Considers these fiction areas:** crime, mystery, new adult, romance, women's.

HOW TO CONTACT Query via e-mail. Accepts simultaneous submissions. Obtains most new clients through recommendations from others.

TERMS Agent receives 15% commission on domestic sales; 20% commission on foreign sales. No written contract.

WRITERS CONFERENCES RWA National Conference.

AZANTIAN LITERARY AGENCY

E-mail: queries@azantianlitagency.com. **Website:** www.azantianlitagency.com. **Contact:** Jennifer Azantian. Estab. 2014.

REPRESENTS Novels. **Considers these fiction areas:** fantasy, horror, middle grade, science fiction, urban fantasy, young adult.

HOW TO CONTACT During open submission windows only: send your query letter, 1-2 page synopsis, and first 10-15 pages all pasted in an e-mail (no attachments). Please note in the e-mail subject line if your work was requested at a conference, is an exclusive submission, or was referred by a current client. Accepts simultaneous submissions. Responds within 6 weeks. Please check the submissions page of the agency website before submitting to make sure Ms. Azantian is currently open to queries.

BARONE LITERARY AGENCY

385 North St., Batavia OH 45103. (513)732-6740. **Fax:** (513)297-7208. **E-mail:** baroneliteraryagency@roadrunner.com. **Website:** www.baroneliteraryagency.com. **Contact:** Denise Barone. Estab. 2010. Member of AAR. Signatory of WGA. Member of RWA. Represents 11 clients.

REPRESENTS Nonfiction, fiction, novels. **Considers these fiction areas:** action, adventure, cartoon, comic books, commercial, confession, contemporary issues, crime, detective, erotica, ethnic, experimental, family saga, fantasy, feminist, frontier, gay, glitz, hi-lo, historical, horror, humor, inspirational, juvenile, lesbian, literary, mainstream, metaphysical, military, multicultural, multimedia, mystery, new adult, New Age, occult, paranormal, plays, police, psychic, regional, religious, romance, satire, science fiction, spiritual, sports, supernatural, suspense, thriller, translation, urban fantasy, war, westerns, women's, young adult.

HOW TO CONTACT "Please send a query letter via e-mail. If I like your query letter, I will ask for the first 3 chapters and a synopsis as attachments." Accepts simultaneous submissions. "I make every effort to respond within 4 months." Obtains new clients by queries/submissions via e-mail only.

TERMS Agency receives 15% commission on domestic sales; 20% on foreign sales. Offers written contract.

RECENT SALES *The Beekeeper*, by Robert E. Hoxie (Six Gun Pictures); *All The Glittering Bones*, by Anna Snow (Entangled Publishing); *Devon's Choice*, by Cathy Bennett (Clean Reads); *Molly's Folly*, by Denise Gwen (Clean Reads); *In Deep*, by Laurie Albano (Solstice Publishing).

WRITERS CONFERENCES Annual Conference of Romance Writers of America, Orlando, Florida, 2017; Lori Foster's Readers and Authors' Get-Together, West Chester, Ohio; A Weekend with the Authors, Nashville, Tennessee; Willamette Writers' Conference, Portland, Oregon.

TIPS "The best writing advice I ever got came from a fellow writer, who wrote, 'Learn how to edit yourself,' when signing her book to me."

BAROR INTERNATIONAL, INC.

P.O. Box 868, Armonk NY 10504. **E-mail:** heather@barorint.com. **Website:** www.barorint.com. **Contact:** Danny Baror; Heather Baror-Shapiro. Represents 300 clients.

MEMBER AGENTS Danny Baror; Heather Baror-Shapiro.

REPRESENTS Fiction. **Considers these fiction areas:** fantasy, literary, science fiction, young adult, adult fiction, commerical.

HOW TO CONTACT Submit by e-mail or mail (with SASE); include a cover letter and a few sample chapters Accepts simultaneous submissions.

⚫ LORELLA BELLI LITERARY AGENCY (LBLA)

54 Hartford House, 35 Tavistock Crescent, Notting Hill, London England W11 1AY United Kingdom. (44)(207)727-8547. **Fax:** (44)(870)787-4194. **E-mail:** info@lorellabelliagency.com. **Website:** www.lorellabelliagency.com. **Contact:** Lorella Belli. Estab. 2002. Membership includes AAA (this is the British Association of Authors Agents), Crime Writers' Association, Romantic Novelists Association, The Book Society, Women in Publishing.

REPRESENTS Nonfiction, fiction, novels, juvenile books. **Considers these fiction areas:** action, adventure, commercial, contemporary issues, crime, detective, family saga, feminist, historical, inspirational, literary, mainstream, multicultural, mystery, new adult, police, romance, suspense, thriller, women's, young adult.

HOW TO CONTACT E-query. Do not send a proposal or ms before it's requested. Please send an initial brief query via e-mail. Accepts simultaneous submissions.

TERMS Agent receives 15% commission on domestic sales; 20% commission on foreign sales.

RECENT SALES Follow us on Twitter and Facebook to see all sales.

THE BENT AGENCY

19 W. 21st St., #201, New York NY 10010. **E-mail:** info@thebentagency.com. **E-mail:** Please see website. **Website:** www.thebentagency.com. **Contact:** Jenny Bent. Estab. 2009. Member of AAR.

MEMBER AGENTS Jenny Bent (adult fiction, including women's fiction, romance, and crime/suspense; she particularly likes novels with magical or fantasy elements that fall outside of genre fiction; young adult and middle-grade fiction; memoir; humor); Nicola Barr (literary and commercial fiction for adults and children, and nonfiction in the areas of sports, popular science, popular culture, and social and cultural history); Molly Ker Hawn (young adult and middle-grade books, including contemporary, historical, fantasy, science fiction, thrillers, and mystery); Gemma Cooper (all ages of children's and young adult books, including picture books; likes historical, contemporary, thrillers, mystery, humor, and science fiction); Louise Fury (children's fiction: picture books, literary middle-grade, and all young adult; adult fiction: speculative fiction, suspense/thriller, commercial fiction, and all subgenres of romance including erotic; nonfiction: cookbooks and pop culture); Sarah Manning (commercial and accessible literary adult fiction and nonfiction in the area of memoir, lifestyle, and narrative nonfiction); Beth Phelan (young adult, thrillers, suspense and mystery, romance and women's fiction, literary and general fiction, cookbooks, lifestyle, and pets/animals); Victoria Cappello (commercial and literary adult fiction as well as narrative nonfiction); Heather Flaherty (young adult and middle-grade fiction: all genres; select adult fiction: upmarket fiction, women's fiction, and female-centric thrillers; select nonfiction: pop culture, humorous, and social media–based projects, as well as teen memoir).

REPRESENTS Nonfiction, novels, short story collections, juvenile books. **Considers these fiction areas:** adventure, commercial, crime, erotica, fantasy, feminist, historical, horror, humor, juvenile, literary, mainstream, middle grade, multicultural, mystery, new adult, picture books, romance, short story collections, suspense, thriller, women's, young adult.

HOW TO CONTACT "Tell us briefly who you are, what your book is, and why you're the one to write it. Then include the first 10 pages of your material in the body of your e-mail. We respond to all queries; please resend your query if you haven't had a response within 4 weeks." Accepts simultaneous submissions.

RECENT SALES *Caraval*, by Stephanie Garber (Flatiron); *Rebel of the Sands*, by Alwyn Hamilton (Viking Children's/Penguin BFYR); *The Square Root of Summer*, by Harriet Reuter Hapgood (Roaring Brook/Macmillan); *Dirty Money*, by Lisa Renee Jones (Simon & Schuster); *True North*, by Liora Blake (Pocket Star).

VICKY BIJUR LITERARY AGENCY

27 W. 20th St., Suite 1003, New York NY 10011. **E-mail:** queries@vickybijuragency.com. **Website:** www.vickybijuragency.com. Estab. 1988. Member of AAR.

MEMBER AGENTS Vicky Bijur; Alexandra Franklin.

REPRESENTS Nonfiction, novels. **Considers these fiction areas:** commercial, literary, mystery, new adult, thriller, women's, young adult, Campus novels, coming-of-age.

HOW TO CONTACT "Please send a query letter of no more than 3 paragraphs on what makes your book special and unique, a very brief synopsis, its length and genre, and your biographical information, along with the first 10 pages of your manuscript. Please let us know in your query letter if it is a multiple submission, and kindly keep us informed of other agents' interest and offers of representation. If sending electronically, paste the pages in an e-mail as we don't open attachments from unfamiliar senders. If sending by hard copy, please include an SASE for our response. If you want your material returned, include an SASE large enough to contain pages and enough postage to send back to you." Accepts simultaneous submissions. "We generally respond to all queries within 8 weeks of receipt."

RECENT SALES *That Darkness*, by Lisa Black; *Long Upon the Land*, by Margaret Maron; *Daughter of Ashes*, by Marcia Talley.

DAVID BLACK LITERARY AGENCY

335 Adams St., Suite 2707, Brooklyn NY 11201. (718)-852-5500. **Fax:** (718)852-5539. **Website:** www.davidblackagency.com. **Contact:** David Black, owner. Estab. 1989. Member of AAR. Represents 150 clients.

MEMBER AGENTS David Black; Jenny Herrera; Gary Morris; Joy E. Tutela (narrative nonfiction, memoir, history, politics, self-help, investment, business, science, women's issues, GLBT issues, parenting, health and fitness, humor, craft, cooking and wine, lifestyle and entertainment, commercial fiction, literary fiction, MG, YA); Susan Raihofer (commercial fiction and nonfiction, memoir, pop culture, music, inspirational, thrillers, literary fiction); Sarah Smith (memoir, biography, food, music, narrative history, social studies, literary fiction).

REPRESENTS Nonfiction, novels. **Considers these fiction areas:** commercial, literary, middle grade, thriller, young adult.

HOW TO CONTACT "To query an individual agent, please follow the specific query guidelines outlined in the agent's profile on our website. Not all agents are currently accepting unsolicited queries. To query the agency, please send a 1-2 page query letter describing your book, and include information about any previously published works, your audience, and your platform." Do not e-mail your query unless an agent specifically asks for an e-mail. Accepts simultaneous submissions. Responds in 2 months to queries.

RECENT SALES Some of the agency's best-selling authors include: Erik Larson, Stuart Scott, Jeff Hobbs, Mitch Albom, Gregg Olsen, Jim Abbott, and John Bacon.

BOND LITERARY AGENCY

4340 E. Kentucky Ave., Suite 471, Denver CO 80246. (303)781-9305. **E-mail:** queries@bondliteraryagency.com. **Website:** www.bondliteraryagency.com. **Contact:** Sandra Bond.

MEMBER AGENTS Sandra Bond, agent (fiction: adult commercial and literary, mystery/thriller/suspense, women's, historical, young adult; nonfiction: narrative, history, science, business); Becky LeJeune, associate agent (fiction: horror, mystery/thriller/suspense, science fiction/fantasy, historical, general fiction, young adult).

REPRESENTS Nonfiction, fiction, novels, juvenile books. **Considers these fiction areas:** commercial, crime, detective, family saga, fantasy, historical, hor-

ror, juvenile, literary, mainstream, middle grade, multicultural, mystery, police, science fiction, suspense, thriller, urban fantasy, women's, young adult.

HOW TO CONTACT Please submit query by e-mail (absolutely no attachments unless requested). No unsolicited mss. "They will let you know if they are interested in seeing more material. No phone calls, please." Accepts simultaneous submissions.

RECENT SALES *The Past is Never*, by Tiffany Quay Tyson; *Cold Case: Billy the Kid*, by W.C. Jameson; *Women in Film: The Truth and the Timeline*, by Jill S. Tietjen and Barbara Bridges; Books 7 & 8 in the Hiro Hattori Mystery Series, by Susan Spann.

BOOK CENTS LITERARY AGENCY, LLC

121 Black Rock Turnpike, Suite #499, Redding Ridge CT 06876. **E-mail:** cw@bookcentsliteraryagency.com. **Website:** www.bookcentsliteraryagency.com. **Contact:** Christine Witthohn. Estab. 2005. Member of AAR. RWA, MWA, SinC, KOD.

REPRESENTS Novels. **Considers these fiction areas:** commercial, mainstream, multicultural, mystery, paranormal, romance, suspense, thriller, urban fantasy, women's, young adult.

HOW TO CONTACT Submit via form on website. Does not accept mail or e-mail submissions.

TIPS Sponsors the International Women's Fiction Festival in Matera, Italy. See www.womensfictionfestival.com for more information. Ms. Witthohn is also the U.S. rights and licensing agent for leading French publisher Bragelonne, German publisher Egmont, and Spanish publisher Edebe.

BOOKENDS LITERARY AGENCY

Website: www.bookendsliterary.com. **Contact:** Jessica Faust, Kim Lionetti, Jessica Alvarez, Moe Ferrara, Tracy Marchini, Rachel Brooks, Natascha Morris, Beth Campbell, James McGowan. Estab. 1999. Member of AAR. RWA, MWA, SCBWI, SFWA. Represents 50+ clients.

MEMBER AGENTS Jessica Faust (women's fiction, mysteries, thrillers, suspense); Kim Lionetti (romance, women's fiction, young adult); Jessica Alvarez (romance, women's fiction, mystery, suspense, thrillers, and nonfiction); Beth Campbell (fantasy, science fiction, young adult, suspense, romantic suspense, and mystery); Moe Ferrara (middle-grade, young adult, and adult: romance, science fiction, fantasy, horror); Tracy Marchini (picture book, middle-grade, and young adult: fiction and nonfiction); Rachel Brooks (young adult, romance, women's fiction, cozy mysteries); Natascha Morris (young adult, middle grade, picture book).

REPRESENTS Nonfiction, novels, juvenile books. **Considers these fiction areas:** adventure, comic books, crime, detective, erotica, fantasy, gay, historical, horror, juvenile, lesbian, mainstream, middle grade, multicultural, mystery, paranormal, picture books, police, romance, science fiction, supernatural, suspense, thriller, urban fantasy, women's, young adult.

HOW TO CONTACT Visit website for the most up-to-date guidelines and current preferences. BookEnds agents accept all submissions through their personal Query Manager forms. These forms are accessible on the agency website under Submissions. Accepts simultaneous submissions. "Our response time goals are 6 weeks for queries and 12 weeks on requested partials and fulls."

THE BOOK GROUP

20 W. 20th St., Suite 601, New York NY 10011. (212)803-3360. **E-mail:** submissions@thebookgroup. com. **Website:** www.thebookgroup.com. Estab. 2015. Member of AAR. Signatory of WGA.

MEMBER AGENTS Julie Barer; Faye Bender; Brettne Bloom (fiction: literary and commercial fiction, select young adult; nonfiction, including cookbooks, lifestyle, investigative journalism, history, biography, memoir, and psychology); Elisabeth Weed (upmarket fiction, especially plot-driven novels with a sense of place); Rebecca Stead (innovative forms, diverse voices, and open-hearted fiction for children, young adults, and adults); Dana Murphy (story-driven fiction with a strong sense of place, narrative nonfiction/essays with a pop-culture lean, and YA with an honest voice).

REPRESENTS Considers these fiction areas: commercial, literary, mainstream, women's, young adult.

HOW TO CONTACT Send a query letter and 10 sample pages to submissions@thebookgroup.com, with the first and last name of the agent you are querying in the subject line. All material must be in the body of the e-mail, as the agents do not open attachments. "If we are interested in reading more, we will get in touch with you as soon as possible." Accepts simultaneous submissions.

RECENT SALES *This Is Not Over*, by Holly Brown; *Perfect Little World*, by Kevin Wilson; *City of Saints*

& Thieves, by Natalie C. Anderson; *The Runaway Midwife*, by Patricia Harman; *Always*, by Sarah Jio; *The Young Widower's Handbook*, by Tom McAllister.

BOOKS & SUCH LITERARY MANAGEMENT

52 Mission Circle, Suite 122, PMB 170, Santa Rosa CA 95409. **E-mail:** representation@booksandsuch.com. **Website:** www.booksandsuch.com. **Contact:** Janet Kobobel Grant, Wendy Lawton, Rachel Kent, Rachelle Gardner, Cynthia Ruchti. Estab. 1996. CBA, American Christian Fiction Writers Represents 250 clients.

REPRESENTS Nonfiction, fiction, novels, juvenile books. **Considers these fiction areas:** adventure, commercial, crime, family saga, frontier, historical, inspirational, juvenile, literary, mainstream, middle grade, mystery, religious, romance, spiritual, suspense, women's, young adult.

HOW TO CONTACT Query via e-mail only; no attachments. Accepts simultaneous submissions. Responds in 1 month to queries. "If you don't hear from us asking to see more of your writing within 30 days after you have sent your e-mail, please know that we have read and considered your submission but determined that it would not be a good fit for us." Obtains most new clients through recommendations from others, conferences.

TERMS Agent receives 15% commission on domestic sales; 20% commission on foreign sales. Offers written contract; two-month notice must be given to terminate contract. No additional charges.

RECENT SALES A full list of this agency's clients (and the awards they have won) is on the agency website.

WRITERS CONFERENCES Mount Hermon Christian Writers Conference, American Christian Fiction Writers Conference, San Francisco Writers Conference.

TIPS "Our agency highlights personal attention to individual clients that includes coaching on how to thrive in a rapidly changing publishing climate, grow a career, and get the best publishing offers possible."

Ø GEORGES BORCHARDT, INC.

136 E. 57th St., New York NY 10022. (212)753-5785. **Website:** www.gbagency.com. Estab. 1967. Member of AAR. Represents 200+ clients.

MEMBER AGENTS Anne Borchardt, Georges Borchardt, Valerie Borchardt, Samantha Shea.

REPRESENTS Nonfiction, fiction, novels, short story collections, novellas.

HOW TO CONTACT No unsolicited submissions. Obtains most new clients through recommendations from others.

TERMS Agent receives 15% commission on domestic sales; 20% commission on foreign sales. Offers written contract.

RECENT SALES *The Relive Box and Other Stories*, by T.C. Boyle; *Nutshell*, by Ian McEwan; *What It Means When a Man Falls From the Sky*, by Lesley Nneka Arimah.

BRADFORD LITERARY AGENCY

5694 Mission Center Rd., #347, San Diego CA 92108. (619)521-1201. **E-mail:** queries@bradfordlit.com. **Website:** www.bradfordlit.com. **Contact:** Laura Bradford, Natalie Lakosil, Sarah LaPolla, Monica Odom. Estab. 2001. Member of AAR. RWA, SCBWI, ALA Represents 130 clients.

MEMBER AGENTS Laura Bradford (romance [historical, romantic suspense, paranormal, category, contemporary, erotic], mystery, women's fiction, thrillers/suspense, middle grade & YA); Natalie Lakosil (children's literature [from picture book through teen and New Adult], romance [contemporary and historical], cozy mystery/crime, upmarket women's/general fiction and select children's nonfiction); Sarah LaPolla (YA, middle grade, literary fiction, science fiction, magical realism, dark/psychological mystery, literary horror, and upmarket contemporary fiction); Monica Odom (nonfiction by authors with demonstrable platforms in the areas of: pop culture, illustrated/graphic design, food and cooking, humor, history and social issues; narrative nonfiction, memoir, literary fiction, upmarket commercial fiction, compelling speculative fiction and magic realism, historical fiction, alternative histories, dark and edgy fiction, literary psychological thrillers, and illustrated/picture books).

REPRESENTS Nonfiction, fiction, novels, juvenile books. **Considers these fiction areas:** commercial, crime, ethnic, gay, historical, juvenile, lesbian, literary, mainstream, middle grade, multicultural, mystery, new adult, paranormal, picture books, romance, science fiction, thriller, women's, young adult.

HOW TO CONTACT Accepts e-mail queries only; For submissions to Laura Bradford or Natalie Lakosil, send to queries@bradfordlit.com. For submissions to

Sarah LaPolla, send to sarah@bradfordlit.com. For submissions to Monica Odom, send to Monica@bradfordlit.com. The entire submission must appear in the body of the e-mail and not as an attachment. The subject line should begin as follows: "QUERY: (the title of the ms or any short message that is important should follow)." For fiction: e-mail a query letter along with the first chapter of ms and a synopsis. Include the genre and word count in your query letter. Nonfiction: e-mail full nonfiction proposal including a query letter and a sample chapter. Accepts simultaneous submissions. Responds in 4 weeks to queries; 10 weeks to mss. Obtains most new clients through queries.

TERMS Agent receives 15% commission on domestic sales; 25% commission on foreign sales. Offers written contract. Charges for extra copies of books for foreign submissions.

RECENT SALES Sold 115 titles in the last year, including *Snowed In With Murder*, by Auralee Wallace (St. Martin's); *All the Secrets We Keep*, by Megan Hart (Montlake); *The Notorious Bargain*, by Joanna Shupe (Avon); *Allegedly*, by Tiffany Jackson (Katherine Tegen Books); *Wives of War*, by Soraya Lane (Amazon); *The Silver Gate*, by Kristin Bailey (Katherine Tegen Books); *Witchtown*, by Cory Putman Oakes (Houghton Mifflin Harcourt); *Under Her Skin*, by Adriana Anders (Sourcebooks); *The Fixer*, by HelenKay Dimon (Avon); *Too Hard To Forget*, by Tessa Bailey (Grand Central); *In A Daze Work*, by Siobhan Gallagher (Ten Speed); *Piper Morgan Makes A Splash*, by Stephanie Faris (Aladdin); *The Star Thief*, by Lindsey Becker (Little, Brown); *Vanguard*, by Ann Aguirre (Feiwel & Friends); *Gray Wolf Island*, by Tracey Neithercott (Knopf); *Single Malt*, by Layla Reyne (Carina Press); *Whiskey Sharp: Unraveled*, by Lauren Dane (HQN).

WRITERS CONFERENCES RWA National Conference, Romantic Times Booklovers Convention.

BRANDT & HOCHMAN LITERARY AGENTS, INC.

1501 Broadway, Suite 2310, New York NY 10036. (212)840-5760. **Fax:** (212)840-5776. **Website:** brandthochman.com. **Contact:** Gail Hochman. Member of AAR. Represents 200 clients.

MEMBER AGENTS Gail Hochman (works of literary fiction, idea-driven nonfiction, literary memoir and children's books); Marianne Merola (fiction, nonfiction and children's books with strong and unique narrative voices); Bill Contardi (voice-driven young adult and middle grade fiction, commercial thrillers, psychological suspense, quirky mysteries, high fantasy, commercial fiction and memoir); Emily Forland (voice-driven literary fiction and nonfiction, memoir, narrative nonfiction, history, biography, food writing, cultural criticism, graphic novels, and young adult fiction); Emma Patterson (fiction from dark, literary novels to upmarket women's and historical fiction; narrative nonfiction that includes memoir, investigative journalism, and popular history; young adult fiction); Jody Kahn (literary and upmarket fiction; narrative nonfiction, particularly books related to sports, food, history, science and pop culture—including cookbooks, and literary memoir and journalism); Henry Thayer (nonfiction on a wide variety of subjects and fiction that inclines toward the literary). The e-mail addresses and specific likes of each of these agents is listed on the agency website.

REPRESENTS Nonfiction, novels. **Considers these fiction areas:** fantasy, historical, literary, middle grade, mystery, suspense, thriller, women's, young adult.

HOW TO CONTACT "We accept queries by e-mail and regular mail; however, we cannot guarantee a response to e-mailed queries. For queries via regular mail, be sure to include a SASE for our reply. Query letters should be no more than 2 pages and should include a convincing overview of the book project and information about the author and his or her writing credits. Address queries to the specific Brandt & Hochman agent whom you would like to consider your work. Agent e-mail addresses and query preferences may be found at the end of each agent profile on the 'Agents' page of our website." Accepts simultaneous submissions. Obtains most new clients through recommendations from others.

TERMS Agent receives 15% commission on domestic sales; 20% commission on foreign sales.

RECENT SALES This agency sells 40-60 new titles each year. A full list of their hundreds of clients is on the agency website.

TIPS "Write a letter which will give the agent a sense of you as a professional writer—your long-term interests as well as a short description of the work at hand."

THE BRATTLE AGENCY

P.O. Box 380537, Cambridge MA 02238. (617)721-5375. **E-mail:** christopher.vyce@thebrattleagency.com. **E-mail:** submissions@thebrattleagency.com.

Website: thebrattleagency.com. **Contact:** Christopher Vyce. Member of AAR. Signatory of WGA.

REPRESENTS Nonfiction, fiction. **Considers these fiction areas:** literary, graphic novels.

HOW TO CONTACT Query by e-mail. Include cover letter, brief synopsis, brief CV. Accepts simultaneous submissions. Responds to queries in 72 hours. Responds to approved submissions in 6-8 weeks.

BARBARA BRAUN ASSOCIATES, INC.

7 E. 14th St., #19F, New York NY 10003. **Fax:** (212)604-9023. **E-mail:** bbasubmissions@gmail.com. **Website:** www.barbarabraunagency.com. **Contact:** Barbara Braun. Member of AAR. Authors Guild, PEN Center USA

REPRESENTS Nonfiction, novels. **Considers these fiction areas:** commercial, historical, literary, multicultural, mystery, thriller, women's, young adult, Art-related fiction.

HOW TO CONTACT "We no longer accept submissions by regular mail. Please send all queries via e-mail, marked 'Query' in the subject line. Your query should include: a brief summary of your book, word count, genre, any relevant publishing experience, and the first 5 pages of your manuscript pasted into the body of the e-mail. (No attachments—we will not open these.)" Accepts simultaneous submissions.

TERMS Agent receives 15% commission on domestic sales; 20% commission on foreign sales. No reading fees.

TIPS "Our clients' books are represented throughout Europe, Asia, and Latin America by various subagents. We are also active in selling motion picture rights to the books we represent, and work with various Hollywood agencies."

BRESNICK WEIL LITERARY AGENCY

115 W. 29th St., Third Floor, New York NY 10001. (212)239-3166. **Fax:** (212)239-3165. **E-mail:** query@bresnickagency.com. **Website:** bresnickagency.com. **Contact:** Paul Bresnick.

MEMBER AGENTS Paul Bresnick; Susan Duff (women's health, food and wine, fitness, humor, memoir); Lisa Kopel (narrative nonfiction, memoir, pop culture, and both commercial and literary fiction); Matthew MiGangi (music, American history, sports, politics, weird science, pop/alternative culture, video games, and fiction).

REPRESENTS Nonfiction, novels. **Considers these fiction areas:** commercial, literary.

HOW TO CONTACT Electronic submissions only. For fiction, submit query and 2 chapters. For nonfiction, submit query with proposal. Accepts simultaneous submissions.

CURTIS BROWN, LTD.

10 Astor Place, New York NY 10003. (212)473-5400. **Fax:** (212)598-0917. **Website:** www.curtisbrown.com. Member of AAR. Signatory of WGA.

MEMBER AGENTS Noah Ballard (literary debuts, upmarket thrillers, narrative nonfiction, always looking for honest and provocative new writers); Tess Callero (young adult, upmarket commercial women's fiction, mysteries/ thrillers, romance, nonfiction: pop culture, business, cookbooks, humor, biography, self-help, and food narrative projects); Ginger Clark (science fiction, fantasy, paranormal romance, literary horror, and young adult and middle grade fiction); Kerry D'Agostino (literary and commercial fiction, as well as narrative nonfiction and memoir); Katherine Fausset (literary fiction, upmarket commercial fiction, journalism, memoir, popular science, and narrative nonfiction); Holly Frederick; Peter Ginsberg, president; Elizabeth Harding, vice president (represents authors and illustrators of juvenile, middle-grade and young adult fiction); Ginger Knowlton, executive vice president (authors and illustrators of children's books in all genres—picture book, middle grade, young adult fiction and nonfiction); Timothy Knowlton, CEO; Jonathan Lyons (biographies, history, science, pop culture, sports, general narrative nonfiction, mysteries, thrillers, science fiction and fantasy, and young adult fiction); Sarah Perillo (middle grade fiction and commercial fiction for adults, nonfiction:history, politics, science, pop culture, and humor, and is especially fond of anything involving animals or food); Laura Blake Peterson, vice president (memoir and biography, natural history, literary fiction, mystery, suspense, women's fiction, health and fitness, children's and young adult, faith issues and popular culture); Steven Salpeter (literary fiction, fantasy, graphic novels, historical fiction, mysteries, thrillers, young adult, narrative nonfiction, gift books, history, humor, and popular science); Maureen Walters, senior vice president (working primarily in women's fiction and nonfiction projects on subjects as eclectic as parenting & child care, popular psychology, inspirational/motivational volumes as well as a few medical/nutritional books); Mitchell Waters (literary and commercial fiction and nonfiction, including mystery, history, biography, memoir, young adult, cookbooks, self-help and popular culture); Monika Woods (plot-driven literary novels, non-fiction that is creatively critical, unique perspectives, a great cookbook, and above all, original prose).

REPRESENTS Nonfiction, fiction, novels, short story collections, juvenile books. **Considers these fiction areas:** fantasy, horror, humor, juvenile, literary, mainstream, middle grade, mystery, paranormal, picture books, religious, romance, spiritual, sports, suspense, thriller, women's, young adult.

HOW TO CONTACT Please refer to the "Agents" page on the website for each agent's submission guidelines. Accepts simultaneous submissions. Responds in 3 weeks to queries; 5 weeks to mss. Obtains most new clients through recommendations from others, solicitations, conferences.

TERMS Agent receives 15% commission on domestic sales; 20% on foreign sales. Offers written contract. 75-day notice must be given to terminate contract. Charges for some postage (overseas, etc.).

RECENT SALES This agency prefers not to share information on specific sales.

BROWNE & MILLER LITERARY ASSOCIATES

52 Village Place, Hinsdale IL 60521. (312) 922-3063. **E-mail:** mail@browneandmiller.com. **Website:** www.browneandmiller.com. **Contact:** Danielle Egan-Miller, president. Estab. 1971. Member of AAR. RWA, MWA, Authors Guild.

REPRESENTS Nonfiction, fiction, novels. **Considers these fiction areas:** commercial, crime, detective, erotica, family saga, historical, inspirational, literary, mainstream, mystery, police, religious, romance, suspense, thriller, women's, Christian/inspirational fiction.

HOW TO CONTACT Query via e-mail only; no attachments. Do not send unsolicited mss. Accepts simultaneous submissions.

ANDREA BROWN LITERARY AGENCY, INC.

E-mail: andrea@andreabrownlit.com; caryn@andreabrownlit.com; lauraqueries@gmail.com; jennifer@andreabrownlit.com; kelly@andreabrownlit.com; jennL@andreabrownlit.com; jamie@andreabrownlit.com; jmatt@andreabrownlit.com; kathleen@andreabrownlit.com; lara@andreabrownlit.com; soloway@

andreabrownlit.com. **Website:** www.andreabrownlit. com. Member of AAR.

MEMBER AGENTS Andrea Brown (president); Laura Rennert (executive agent); Caryn Wiseman (senior agent); Jennifer Laughran (senior agent); Jennifer Rofé (senior agent); Kelly Sonnack (senior agent); Jamie Weiss Chilton (senior agent); Jennifer Mattson (agent); Kathleen Rushall (agent); Lara Perkins (associate agent, digital manager); Jennifer March Soloway (associate agent).

REPRESENTS Juvenile books. **Considers these fiction areas:** juvenile, middle grade, picture books, young adult, middle-grade, all juvenile genres.

HOW TO CONTACT For picture books, submit a query letter and complete ms in the body of the e-mail. For fiction, submit a query letter and the first 10 pages in the body of the e-mail. For nonfiction, submit proposal, first 10 pages in the body of the e-mail. Illustrators: submit a query letter and 2-3 illustration samples (in jpeg format), link to online portfolio, and text of picture book, if applicable. "We only accept queries via e-mail. No attachments, with the exception of jpeg illustrations from illustrators." Visit the agents' bios on our website and choose only one agent to whom you will submit your e-query. Send a short e-mail query letter to that agent with "QUERY" in the subject field. Accepts simultaneous submissions. "If we are interested in your work, we will certainly follow up by e-mail or by phone. However, if you haven't heard from us within 6 to 8 weeks, please assume that we are passing on your project." Obtains most new clients through referrals from editors, clients and agents. Check website for guidelines and information.

TERMS Agent receives 15% commission on domestic sales; 25% commission on foreign sales. Offers written contract.

RECENT SALES *The Scorpio Races*, by Maggie Stiefvater (Scholastic); *The Future of Us*, by Jay Asher; *Triangles*, by Ellen Hopkins (Atria); *Crank*, by Ellen Hopkins (McElderry/S&S); *Burned*, by Ellen Hopkins (McElderry/S&S); *Impulse*, by Ellen Hopkins (McElderry/S&S); *Glass*, by Ellen Hopkins (McElderry/S&S); *Tricks*, by Ellen Hopkins (McElderry/S&S); *Fallout*, by Ellen Hopkins (McElderry/S&S); *Perfect*, by Ellen Hopkins (McElderry/S&S); *The Strange Case of Origami Yoda*, by Tom Angleberger (Amulet/Abrams); *Darth Paper Strikes Back*, by Tom Angleberger (Amulet/Abrams);

Becoming Chloe, by Catherine Ryan Hyde (Knopf); Sasha Cohen autobiography (HarperCollins); *The Five Ancestors*, by Jeff Stone (Random House); *Thirteen Reasons Why*, by Jay Asher (Penguin); *Identical*, by Ellen Hopkins (S&S).

WRITERS CONFERENCES SCBWI, Asilomar; Maui Writers' Conference, Southwest Writers' Conference, San Diego State University Writers' Conference, Big Sur Children's Writing Workshop, William Saroyan Writers' Conference, Columbus Writers' Conference, Willamette Writers' Conference, La Jolla Writers' Conference, San Francisco Writers' Conference, Hilton Head Writers' Conference, Pacific Northwest Conference, Pikes Peak Conference.

TRACY BROWN LITERARY AGENCY

P.O. Box 772, Nyack NY 10960. **Fax:** (914)931-1746. **E-mail:** tracy@brownlit.com. **Contact:** Tracy Brown. Estab. 2003. Represents 35 clients.

REPRESENTS Nonfiction.

HOW TO CONTACT Submit outline/proposal, synopsis, and author bio. Accepts simultaneous submissions. Responds in 2 weeks to queries. Obtains most new clients through referrals.

TERMS Agent receives 15% commission on domestic sales. Agent receives 20% commission on foreign sales. Offers written contract.

SHEREE BYKOFSKY ASSOCIATES, INC.

P.O. Box 706, Brigantine NJ 08203. **E-mail:** shereebee@aol.com. **Website:** www.shereebee.com. **Contact:** Sheree Bykofsky. Estab. 1991. Member of AAR. Author's Guild, Atlantic City Chamber of Commerce, PRC Council Represents 1,000+ clients.

MEMBER AGENTS Sheree Bykofsky, Janet Rosen.

REPRESENTS Nonfiction, novels, scholarly books. **Considers these fiction areas:** commercial, contemporary issues, crime, detective, literary, mainstream, mystery, women's.

HOW TO CONTACT Query via e-mail to submitbee@aol.com. "We only accept e-queries. We respond only to those queries in which we are interested. No attachments, snail mail, or phone calls, please. We do not open attachments." Fiction: one-page query, one-page synopsis, and first three pages of ms in body of the e-mail. Nonfiction: one-page query in the body of the e-mail. Currently we are focusing much more on our nonfiction portfolio. Accepts simultaneous submissions. Responds in 1 month to requested mss.

Obtains most new clients through referrals but still reads all submissions closely.

TERMS Agent receives 15% commission on domestic sales. Agent receives 15% commission on foreign sales, plus international co-agent receives another 10%. Offers written contract, binding for 1 year. Charges for international postage.

RECENT SALES *Virtual Billions: The Genius, the Drug Lord, and the Ivy League Twins Behind the Rise of Bitcoin* by Eric Geissinger (Prometheus Books), *Thank You, Teacher: Grateful Students Tell the Stories of the Teachers Who Changed Their Lives* by Holly and Bruce Holbert (New World Library), *The Type B Manager: Leading Successfully in a Type A World* by Victor Lipman (Prentice Hall), *Let the Story Do the Work: The Art of Storytelling for Business Success* by Esther Choy (Amacom), *Convicting Avery: The Bizarre Laws and Broken System Behind "Making a Murderer"* by Michael D. Cicchini (Prometheus Books), *The Curious Case of Kiryas Joel: The Rise of a Village Theocracy and the Battle to Defend the Separation of Church and State* by Louis Grumet with John Caher (Chicago Review Press), *Cells are the New Cure* by Robin L. Smith, M.D. and Max Gomez, Ph.D.; dozens of international sales

WRITERS CONFERENCES Truckee Meadow Community College Keynote, ASJA Writers Conference, Asilomar, Florida Suncoast Writers' Conference, Whidbey Island Writers' Conference, Florida First Coast Writers' Festival, Agents and Editors Conference, Columbus Writers' Conference, Southwest Writers' Conference, Willamette Writers' Conference, Dorothy Canfield Fisher Conference, Maui Writers' Conference, Pacific Northwest Writers' Conference, IWWG.

KIMBERLEY CAMERON & ASSOCIATES

1550 Tiburon Blvd., #704, Tiburon CA 94920. (415)789-9191. **Website:** www.kimberleycameron. com. **Contact:** Kimberley Cameron. Member of AAR. Signatory of WGA.

MEMBER AGENTS Kimberley Cameron; Elizabeth Kracht (temporarily closed to submissions); Amy Cloughley (literary and upmarket fiction, women's, historical, narrative nonfiction, travel or adventure memoir); Mary C. Moore (fantasy, science fiction, upmarket "book club," genre romance, thrillers with female protagonists, and stories from marginalized voices); Lisa Abellera (currently closed to unsolicited submissions); Douglas Lee, douglas@kimberlycam-

eron.com (only accepting submissions via conference and in-person meetings in the Bay Area); Dorian Maffei (only open to submissions requested through Twitter pitch parties, conferences, or #MSWL).

REPRESENTS Considers these fiction areas: commercial, fantasy, historical, literary, mystery, romance, science fiction, thriller, women's, young adult, LGBTQ.

HOW TO CONTACT Prefers queries via site. Only query one agent at a time. For fiction, fill out the correct submissions form for the individual agent and attach the first 50 pages and a synopsis (if requested) as a Word doc or PDF. For nonfiction, fill out the correct submission form of the individual agent and attach a full book proposal and sample chapters (includes the first chapter and no more than 50 pages) as a Word doc or PDF. Accepts simultaneous submissions. Obtains new clients through recommendations from others, solicitations.

CYNTHIA CANNELL LITERARY AGENCY

54 W. 40th St., New York NY 10018. (212)396-9595. **Website:** www.cannellagency.com. **Contact:** Cynthia Cannell. Estab. 1997. Member of AAR. Women's Media Group and the Authors Guild

REPRESENTS Nonfiction, fiction.

HOW TO CONTACT "Please query us with an e-mail or letter. If querying by e-mail, send a brief description of your project with relevant biographical information including publishing credits (if any) to info@cannellagency.com. Do not send attachments. If querying by conventional mail, enclose an SASE." Responds if interested. Accepts simultaneous submissions.

RECENT SALES Check the website for an updated list of authors and sales.

CAPITAL TALENT AGENCY

1330 Connecticut Ave. NW, Suite 271, Washington DC 20036. (202)429-4785. **Fax:** (202)429-4786. **E-mail:** literary.submissions@capitaltalentagency.com. **Website:** capitaltalentagency.com/html/literary.shtml. **Contact:** Cynthia Kane. Estab. 2014. Member of AAR. Signatory of WGA.

MEMBER AGENTS Cynthia Kane; Roger Yoerges; Michelle Muntifering; J. Fred Shiffman.

REPRESENTS Nonfiction, fiction, movie scripts, stage plays.

HOW TO CONTACT "We accept submissions only by e-mail. We do not accept queries via postal mail or fax. For fiction and nonfiction submissions, send a query letter in the body of your e-mail. Please note that while we consider each query seriously, we are unable to respond to all of them. We endeavor to respond within 6 weeks to projects that interest us." Accepts simultaneous submissions. 6 weeks

MARIA CARVAINIS AGENCY, INC.

Rockefeller Center, 1270 Avenue of the Americas, Suite 2915, New York NY 10020. (212)245-6365. **Fax:** (212)245-7196. **E-mail:** mca@mariacarvainisagency.com. **E-mail:** mca@mariacarvainisagency.com. **Website:** www.mariacarvainisagency.com. Estab. 1977. Member of AAR. Authors Guild, Women's Media Group, ABA, MWA, RWA Represents 75 clients.

MEMBER AGENTS Maria Carvainis, president/literary agent; Elizabeth Copps, associate agent.

REPRESENTS Nonfiction, novels. **Considers these fiction areas:** action, adventure, commercial, contemporary issues, crime, family saga, historical, horror, humor, juvenile, literary, mainstream, middle grade, multicultural, mystery, romance, suspense, thriller, women's, young adult.

HOW TO CONTACT If you would like to query the agency, please send a query letter, a synopsis of the work, first 5-10 pages, and note of any writing credentials. Please e-mail queries to mca@mariacarvainisagency.com. All attachments must be either Word documents or PDF files. The agency also accepts queries by mail to Maria Carvainis Agency, Inc., Attention: Query Department. If you want the materials returned to you, please enclose a SASE. Otherwise, please be sure to include your e-mail address. There is no reading fee. Accepts simultaneous submissions. Responds to queries within 1 month. Obtains most new clients through recommendations from others, conferences, query letters.

TERMS Agent receives 15% commission on domestic sales. Agent receives 20% commission on foreign sales. Offers written contract. Charges clients for foreign postage.

RECENT SALES *Someone To Love* by Mary Balogh (Signet), *Sting* by Sandra Brown (Grand Central), *Enraptured* by Candace Camp (Pocket Books), *If You Only Knew* by Kristan Higgins (HQN Books), *Palindrome* by E.Z. Rinsky (Witness Impulse), *Almost*

Paradise by Corabel Shofner (Farrar Straus & Giroux Books for Young Readers).

CHALBERG & SUSSMAN

115 W. 29th St., Third Floor, New York NY 10001. (917)261-7550. **Website:** www.chalbergsussman.com. Member of AAR. Signatory of WGA.

MEMBER AGENTS Terra Chalberg; Rachel Sussman (narrative journalism, memoir, psychology, history, humor, pop culture, literary fiction); Nicole James (plot-driven fiction, psychological suspense, uplifting female-driven memoir, upmarket self-help, and lifestyle books); Lana Popovic (young adult, middle grade, contemporary realism, speculative fiction, fantasy, horror, sophisticated erotica, romance, select nonfiction, international stories).

REPRESENTS Nonfiction, fiction, novels. **Considers these fiction areas:** erotica, fantasy, horror, literary, middle grade, romance, science fiction, suspense, young adult, contemporary realism, speculative fiction.

HOW TO CONTACT To query by e-mail, please contact one of the following: terra@chalbergsussman.com, rachel@chalbergsussman.com, nicole@chalbergsussman.com, lana@chalbergsussman.com. To query by regular mail, please address your letter to one agent and include SASE. Accepts simultaneous submissions.

RECENT SALES The agents' sales and clients are listed on their website.

CHASE LITERARY AGENCY

11 Broadway, Suite 1010, New York NY 10004. (212)477-5100. **E-mail:** farley@chaseliterary.com. **Website:** www.chaseliterary.com. **Contact:** Farley Chase.

MEMBER AGENTS Farley Chase.

REPRESENTS Nonfiction, fiction, novels. **Considers these fiction areas:** commercial, historical, literary, mystery.

HOW TO CONTACT E-query farley@chaseliterary.com. If submitting fiction, please include the first few pages of the ms with the query. "I do not response to queries not addressed to me by name. I'm keenly interested in both fiction and nonfiction. In fiction, I'm looking for both literary or commercial projects in either contemporary or historical settings. I'm open to anything with a strong sense of place, voice, and, especially plot. I don't handle science fiction, romance, supernatural or young adult. In nonfiction, I'm especially interested in narratives in history, memoir, journalism, natural science, military history, sports, pop culture, and humor. Whether by first-time writers or long time journalists, I'm excited by original ideas, strong points of view, detailed research, and access to subjects which give readers fresh perspectives on things they think they know. I'm also interested in visually-driven and illustrated books. Whether they involve photography, comics, illustrations, or art I'm taken by creative storytelling with visual elements, four color or black and white." Accepts simultaneous submissions.

RECENT SALES *Devil in the Grove: Thurgood Marshall, the Groveland Boys, and the Dawn of a New America* , by Gilbert King (Harper); *Heads in Beds: A Reckless Memoir of Hotels, Hustles, and So-Called Hospitality*, by Jacob Tomsky (Doubleday); *And Every Day Was Overcast*, by Paul Kwiatowski (Black Balloon); *The Badlands Saloon*, by Jonathan Twingley (Scribner).

CHENEY ASSOCIATES, LLC

78 Fifth Ave., 3rd Floor, New York NY 10011. (212)277-8007. **Fax:** (212)614-0728. **E-mail:** submissions@cheneyliterary.com. **Website:** www.cheneyliterary.com. **Contact:** Elyse Cheney; Adam Eaglin; Alex Jacobs; Alice Whitwham.

MEMBER AGENTS Elyse Cheney; Adam Eaglin (literary fiction and nonfiction, including history, politics, current events, narrative reportage, biography, memoir, and popular science); Alexander Jacobs (narrative nonfiction [particularly in the areas of history, science, politics, and culture], literary fiction, crime, and memoir); Alice Whitwham (literary and commercial fiction, as well as voice-driven narrative nonfiction, cultural criticism, and journalism).

REPRESENTS Nonfiction, novels. **Considers these fiction areas:** commercial, crime, family saga, historical, literary, short story collections, suspense, women's.

HOW TO CONTACT Query by e-mail or snail mail. For a snail mail responses, include a SASE. Include up to 3 chapters of sample material. Do not query more than one agent. Accepts simultaneous submissions.

RECENT SALES *The Love Affairs of Nathaniel P.*, by Adelle Waldman (Henry Holt & Co.); *This Town*, by Mark Leibovich (Blue Rider Press); *Thunder & Lightning*, by Lauren Redniss (Random House).

THE CHUDNEY AGENCY

72 N. State Rd., Suite 501, Briarcliff Manor NY 10510. (914)465-5560. **E-mail:** steven@thechudneyagency.com. **Website:** www.thechudneyagency.com. **Contact:** Steven Chudney. Estab. 2001. SCBWI

REPRESENTS Novels, juvenile books. **Considers these fiction areas:** commercial, family saga, gay, historical, juvenile, lesbian, literary, middle grade, picture books, regional, suspense, thriller, young adult.

HOW TO CONTACT No snail mail submissions. Queries only. Submission package info to follow should we be interested. For children's picture books, we only want author/illustrator projects. Submit a pdf with full text and at least 5-7 full-color illustrations. Accepts simultaneous submissions. Responds if interested in 2-3 weeks to queries.

CK WEBBER ASSOCIATES

E-mail: carlie@ckwebber.com. **Website:** ckwebber.com. **Contact:** Carlisle Webber. Member of AAR. Signatory of WGA.

REPRESENTS Novels, juvenile books. **Considers these fiction areas:** action, adventure, commercial, contemporary issues, crime, detective, family saga, fantasy, feminist, horror, literary, mainstream, middle grade, mystery, new adult, romance, science fiction, suspense, thriller, westerns, women's, young adult.

HOW TO CONTACT Accepts queries via e-mail only. To submit your work for consideration, please send a query letter, synopsis, and the first 30 pages or 3 chapters of your work, whichever is more, to carlie@ckwebber.com and put the word "query" in the subject line of your e-mail. Please include your materials in the body of your e-mail. Blank emails that include an attachment will be deleted unread. Accepts simultaneous submissions.

WM CLARK ASSOCIATES

54 W. 21st St., Suite 809, New York NY 10010. (212)675-2784. **E-mail:** general@wmclark.com. **Website:** www.wmclark.com. **Contact:** William Clark. Estab. 1997. Member of AAR.

REPRESENTS Nonfiction, novels. **Considers these fiction areas:** historical, literary.

HOW TO CONTACT Accepts queries via online query form only. "We will endeavor to respond as soon as possible as to whether or not we'd like to see a proposal or sample chapters from your manuscript." Responds in 1-2 months to queries.

TERMS Agent receives 15% commission on domestic sales; 20% commission on foreign sales. Offers written contract.

WRITERS CONFERENCES London Book Fair, Frankfurt Book Fair.

TIPS "Translation rights are sold directly in the German, Italian, Spanish, Portuguese, Latin American, French, Dutch, and Scandinavian territories; and through corresponding agents in China, Bulgaria, Czech Republic, Latvia, Poland, Hungary, Russia, Japan, Greece, Israel, Turkey, Korea, Taiwan, Vietnam, and Thailand."

FRANCES COLLIN, LITERARY AGENT

P.O. Box 33, Wayne PA 19087-0033. **E-mail:** queries@ francescollin.com. **Website:** www.francescollin.com. Estab. 1948. Member of AAR. Represents 50 clients.

MEMBER AGENTS Frances Collin; Sarah Yake.

REPRESENTS Nonfiction, fiction, novels. **Considers these fiction areas:** adventure, commercial, experimental, feminist, historical, juvenile, literary, middle grade, multicultural, science fiction, women's, young adult.

HOW TO CONTACT "We ask that writers send a traditional query e-mail describing the project and copy and paste the first 5 pages of the manuscript into the body of the e-mail. We look forward to hearing from you at queries@francescollin.com. Please send queries to that e-mail address. Any queries sent to another e-mail address within the agency will be deleted unread." Accepts simultaneous submissions. Responds in 1-4 weeks for initial queries, longer for full mss.

⊘ COMPASS TALENT

(646)376-7747. **Website:** www.compasstalent.com. **Contact:** Heather Schroder. Member of AAR. Signatory of WGA.

REPRESENTS **Considers these fiction areas:** commercial, literary, mainstream.

HOW TO CONTACT This agency is currently closed to unsolicited submissions. Accepts simultaneous submissions.

RECENT SALES A full list of agency clients is available on the website.

DON CONGDON ASSOCIATES INC.

110 William St., Suite 2202, New York NY 10038. (212)645-1229. **Fax:** (212)727-2688. **E-mail:** dca@ doncongdon.com. **Website:** doncongdon.com. Estab. 1983. Member of AAR.

MEMBER AGENTS Cristina Concepcion (crime fiction, narrative nonfiction, political science, journalism, history, books on cities, classical music, biography, science for a popular audience, philosophy, food and wine, iconoclastic books on health and human relationships, essays, and arts criticism); Michael Congdon (commercial and literary fiction, suspense, mystery, thriller, history, military history, biography, memoir, current affairs, and narrative nonfiction [adventure, medicine, science, and nature]); Katie Grimm (literary fiction, historical, women's fiction, short story collections, graphic novels, mysteries, young adult, middle-grade, memoir, science, academic); Katie Kotchman (business [all areas], narrative nonfiction [particularly popular science and social/cultural issues], self-help, success, motivation, psychology, pop culture, women's fiction, realistic young adult, literary fiction, and psychological thrillers); Maura Kye-Casella (narrative nonfiction, cookbooks, women's fiction, young adult, self-help, and parenting); Susan Ramer (literary fiction, upmarket commercial fiction [contemporary and historical], narrative nonfiction, social history, cultural history, smart pop culture [music, film, food, art], women's issues, psychology and mental health, and memoir).

REPRESENTS Nonfiction, novels, short story collections. **Considers these fiction areas:** crime, hi-lo, historical, literary, middle grade, mystery, short story collections, suspense, thriller, women's, young adult.

HOW TO CONTACT "For queries via e-mail, you must include the word 'query' and the agent's full name in your subject heading. Please also include your query and sample chapter in the body of the e-mail, as we do not open attachments for security reasons. Please query only one agent within the agency at a time. If you are sending your query via regular mail, please enclose a SASE for our reply. If you would like us to return your materials, please make sure your postage will cover their return." Accepts simultaneous submissions.

RECENT SALES This agency represents many bestselling clients such as David Sedaris and Kathryn Stockett.

JILL CORCORAN LITERARY AGENCY

2150 Park Place, Suite 100, El Segundo CA 90245. **Website:** jillcorcoranliteraryagency.com. **Contact:** Jill Corcoran. Estab. 2013.

MEMBER AGENTS Jill Corcoran, Adah Nuchi, Silvia Arienti, Eve Porinchak.

REPRESENTS Nonfiction, novels, juvenile books. **Considers these fiction areas:** commercial, crime, juvenile, middle grade, picture books, romance, young adult.

HOW TO CONTACT Please go online to the agency submissions page and submit to the agent you feel would best represent your work. Accepts simultaneous submissions.

CORVISIERO LITERARY AGENCY

275 Madison Ave., at 40th, 14th Floor, New York NY 10016. (646)856-4032. **Fax:** (646)217-3758. **E-mail:** consult@corvisieroagency.com. **Website:** www.corvisieroagency.com. **Contact:** Marisa A. Corvisiero, Founder, Senior Agent, Attorney. Estab. 2012.

MEMBER AGENTS Marisa A. Corvisiero, senior agent and literary attorney (contemporary romance, thrillers, adventure, paranormal, urban fantasy, science fiction, MG, YA, picture books, Christmas themes, time travel, space science fiction, nonfiction, self-help, science, business); Saritza Hernandez, senior agent (all kinds of romance, GLBT, YA, erotica); Doreen Thistle (do not query); Cate Hart (YA, fantasy, magical realism, MG, mystery, fantasy, adventure, historical romance, LGBTQ, erotic, history, biography); Veronica Park (dark or edgy YA/NA, Commercial adult, adult romance and romantic suspense, and funny and/or current/controversial nonfiction); Kelly Peterson (MG, fantasy, paranormal, sci-fi, YA, steampunk, historical, dystopian, sword and sorcery, romance, historical romance, adult, fantasy, romance); Justin Wells; Kaitlyn Johnson (upper MG, YA, NA, and Adult; fantasy, urban fantasy, romance, historical fiction, contemporary, LGBTQ); Kortney Price (MG, YA, and Adult; fantasy, steampunk, science fiction, mystery, thriller, contemporary); Jennifer Haskin (Fiction only, YA, NA, fantasy, sci-fi, dystopian, steampunk, thriller, LGBTQ, romance, dark).

REPRESENTS Nonfiction, fiction, novels, juvenile books. **Considers these fiction areas:** action, adventure, erotica, family saga, fantasy, feminist, gay, historical, humor, juvenile, lesbian, metaphysical, middle grade, multicultural, mystery, new adult, New Age, occult, paranormal, picture books, psychic, religious, romance, science fiction, spiritual, suspense, thriller, urban fantasy, women's, young adult, magical realism, steampunk, dystopian, sword and sorcery.

HOW TO CONTACT Accepts submissions via QueryManager. Include query letter, 5 pages of complete and polished ms, and a 1-2 page synopsis. For nonfiction, include a proposal instead of the synopsis. Each agent profile on website has a button for direct submissions. Accepts simultaneous submissions.

WRITERS CONFERENCES SCWC (San Diego); AuthorPreneur Workshop Charlotte; NJ Fiction Writers; Muse and the Marketplace; RT Convention; LI Romance Writers; BEA; DFW Fort Worth; Thrillerfest NYC; RWA; Writers Digest NYC; AuthorPreneur Workshop Red Bank; SCWC (Los Angeles); NJ Romance Writers.

CREATIVE BOOK SERVICES

111 W. 19th St., Sixth Floor, New York NY 10011. (212)226-1936. **E-mail:** bob.mecoy@gmail.com. **Contact:** Bob Mecoy, owner. Estab. 2001.

REPRESENTS Nonfiction, novels. **Considers these fiction areas:** action, adventure, cartoon, comic books, crime, detective, fantasy, literary, mainstream, mystery, new adult, romance, science fiction, sports, urban fantasy, war.

HOW TO CONTACT Query with sample chapters and synopsis. Accepts simultaneous submissions.

CREATIVE MEDIA AGENCY, INC.

(212)812-1494. **E-mail:** paige@cmalit.com. **Website:** www.cmalit.com. **Contact:** Paige Wheeler. Estab. 1997. Member of AAR. WMG, RWA, MWA, Authors Guild. Represents about 30 clients.

REPRESENTS Nonfiction, fiction, novels. **Considers these fiction areas:** commercial, crime, detective, historical, inspirational, mainstream, middle grade, mystery, new adult, romance, suspense, thriller, women's, young adult, general fiction.

HOW TO CONTACT E-query. Write "query" in your e-mail subject line. For fiction, paste in the first 5 pages of the ms after the query. For nonfiction, paste in an extended author bio as well as the marketing section of your book proposal after the query. Accepts simultaneous submissions. Responds in 4-6 weeks.

⊘ CREATIVE TRUST, INC.

210 Jamestown Park Dr., Suite 200, Brentwood TN 37027. (615)297-5010. **Fax:** (615)297-5020. **E-mail:**

info@creativetrust.com. **Website:** www.creative-trust.com.

REPRESENTS Nonfiction, novels, movie scripts, multimedia, other.

HOW TO CONTACT "Creative Trust Literary Group does not accept unsolicited manuscripts or book proposals from unpublished authors. We do accept unsolicited inquiries from previously published authors under the following requisites; email inquiries only, which must not be accompanied by attachments of any kind, to info@creativetrust.com. Please indicate 'Literary Submission' in your subject line. Due to the volume of queries we receive, we are not able to respond except to request additional materials." Accepts simultaneous submissions.

⊘ 🖐 RICHARD CURTIS ASSOCIATES, INC.

200 E. 72nd St., Suite 28J, New York NY 10021. (212)772-7363. **Fax:** (212)772-7393. **Website:** www.curtisagency.com. Member of AAR. RWA, MWA, ITW, SFWA. Represents 100 clients.

REPRESENTS Nonfiction, fiction, novels, juvenile books. **Considers these fiction areas:** commercial, fantasy, romance, science fiction, thriller, young adult.

HOW TO CONTACT Use submission procedure on website. "We also read one-page query letters accompanied by SASE." Accepts simultaneous submissions.

TERMS Agent receives 15% commission on domestic sales; 25% commission on foreign sales. Offers written contract. Charges for photocopying, express mail, international freight, book orders.

RECENT SALES Sold 100 titles in the last year, including *The Library*, by D.J. MacHale; *Tylers of Texas*, by Janet Dailey; and *Death of an Heir*, by Philip Jett.

D4EO LITERARY AGENCY

7 Indian Valley Rd., Weston CT 06883. (203)544-7180. **Fax:** (203)544-7160. **Website:** www.d4eoliteraryagency.com. **Contact:** Bob Diforio. Estab. 1990.

MEMBER AGENTS Bob Diforio; Joyce Holland; Pam Howell; Quressa Robinson; Kelly Van Sant.

REPRESENTS Nonfiction, novels. **Considers these fiction areas:** adventure, detective, erotica, juvenile, literary, mainstream, middle grade, mystery, new adult, romance, sports, thriller, young adult.

HOW TO CONTACT Each of these agents has a different submission e-mail and different tastes regarding how they review material. See all on their individual agent pages on the agency website. Responds in 1 week to queries if interested. Obtains most new clients through recommendations from others.

TERMS Offers written contract, binding for 2 years; automatic renewal unless 60 days notice given prior to renewal date. Charges for photocopying and submission postage.

LAURA DAIL LITERARY AGENCY, INC.

121 W. 27th St., Suite 1201, New York NY 10001. (212)239-7477. **E-mail:** literary@ldlainc.com. **E-mail:** queries@ldlainc.com. **Website:** www.ldlainc.com. Member of AAR.

MEMBER AGENTS Laura Dail; Tamar Rydzinski; Elana Roth Parker.

REPRESENTS Nonfiction, fiction, novels, juvenile books. **Considers these fiction areas:** commercial, contemporary issues, crime, detective, ethnic, fantasy, feminist, gay, historical, juvenile, lesbian, mainstream, middle grade, multicultural, mystery, picture books, thriller, women's, young adult.

HOW TO CONTACT "If you would like, you may include a synopsis and no more than 10 pages. If you are mailing your query, please be sure to include a self-addressed, stamped envelope; without it, you may not hear back from us. To save money, time and trees, we prefer queries by e-mail to queries@ldlainc.com. We get a lot of spam and are wary of computer viruses, so please use the word 'Query' in the subject line and include your detailed materials in the body of your message, not as an attachment." Accepts simultaneous submissions. Responds in 2-4 weeks.

DARHANSOFF & VERRILL LITERARY AGENTS

133 W. 72nd St., Room 304, New York NY 10023. (917)305-1300. **E-mail:** submissions@dvagency.com. **Website:** www.dvagency.com. Member of AAR.

MEMBER AGENTS Liz Darhansoff; Chuck Verrill; Michele Mortimer; Eric Amling.

REPRESENTS Nonfiction, novels. **Considers these fiction areas:** literary, middle grade, suspense, young adult.

HOW TO CONTACT Send queries via e-mail. Accepts simultaneous submissions.

RECENT SALES A full list of clients is available on their website.

🌀 CAROLINE DAVIDSON LITERARY

AGENCY

5 Queen Anne's Gardens, London W4 1TU United Kingdom. (44)(0)(20)8995-5768. **Fax:** (44)(0)(20)8994-2770. **E-mail:** enquiries@cdla.co.uk. **Website:** www.cdla.co.uk. **Contact:** Ms. Caroline Davidson. AAA

REPRESENTS Nonfiction, fiction.

HOW TO CONTACT Send preliminary letter with CV and detailed well thought-out book proposal/synopsis and/or first 50 pages and last 10 pages of novel in hard copy only. No e-mail submissions will be accepted or replied to. No reply without large SASE with correct return postage. No reading fee. Please refer to website for further information. CDLA does not acknowledge or reply to e-mail inquiries. No telephone inquiries.

LIZA DAWSON ASSOCIATES

121 W. 27th St., Suite 1201, New York NY 10001. (212)465-9071. **Website:** www.lizadawsonassociates.com. **Contact:** Caitie Flum. Member of AAR. MWA, Women's Media Group. Represents 50+ clients.

MEMBER AGENTS Liza Dawson, queryliza@lizadawsonassociates.com (plot-driven literary and popular fiction, historical, thrillers, suspense, history, psychology [both popular and clinical], politics, narrative nonfiction, and memoirs); Caitlin Blasdell, querycaitlin@lizadawsonassociates.com (science fiction, fantasy [both adult and young adult], parenting, business, thrillers, and women's fiction); Hannah Bowman, queryhannah@lizadawsonassociates.com (commercial fiction [especially science fiction and fantasy, young adult] and nonfiction in the areas of mathematics, science, and spirituality); Monica Odom, querymonica@lizadawsonassociates.com (nonfiction in the areas of Social Studies, including topics of: identity, race, gender, sexual orientation, socioeconomics, civil rights and social justice, advice/relationships, self-help/self-reflection, how-to, crafting/creativity, food and cooking, humor, pop culture, lifestyle, fashion & beauty, biography, memoir, narrative, business, politics and current affairs, history, science and literary fiction and upmarket fiction, Illustrators with demonstrable platforms, preferably author/illustrators, working on nonfiction, graphic memoirs or graphic novels); Caitie Flum, querycaitie@lizadawsonassociates.com (commercial fiction, especially historical, women's fiction, mysteries, crossover fantasy, young adult, and middle-grade; nonfiction in the areas of theater, current affairs, and pop culture).

REPRESENTS Nonfiction, novels. **Considers these fiction areas:** action, adventure, commercial, contemporary issues, crime, detective, ethnic, family saga, fantasy, feminist, gay, historical, horror, humor, juvenile, lesbian, mainstream, middle grade, multicultural, mystery, new adult, police, romance, science fiction, supernatural, suspense, thriller, urban fantasy, women's, young adult.

HOW TO CONTACT Query by e-mail only. No phone calls. Each of these agents has their own specific submission requirements, which you can find online at the agency's website. Obtains most new clients through recommendations from others, conferences, and queries.

TERMS Agent receives 15% commission on domestic sales; 20% commission on foreign sales. Offers written contract.

THE JENNIFER DE CHIARA LITERARY AGENCY

299 Park Ave., 6th Floor, New York NY 10171. (212)739-0803. **E-mail:** jenndec@aol.com. **Website:** www.jdlit.com. **Contact:** Jennifer De Chiara. Estab. 2001.

MEMBER AGENTS Jennifer De Chiara, jenndec@aol.com (fiction interests include literary, commercial, women's fiction [no bodice-rippers, please], chick-lit, mystery, suspense, thrillers, funny/quirky picture books, middle-grade, and young adult; nonfiction interests include celebrity memoirs and biographies, LGBT, memoirs, books about the arts and performing arts, behind-the-scenes-type books, and books about popular culture); Stephen Fraser, fraserstephena@gmail.com (one-of-a-kind picture books; strong chapter book series; whimsical, dramatic, or humorous middle-grade; dramatic or high-concept young adult; powerful and unusual nonfiction on a broad range of topics; Marie Lamba, marie.jdlit@gmail.com (young adult and middle-grade fiction, along with general and women's fiction and some memoir; interested in established illustrators and picture book authors); Roseanne Wells, queryroseanne@gmail.com (picture book, middle grade, young adult, select literary fiction, narrative nonfiction, select memoir, science (popular or trade, not academic), history, religion (not inspirational or Christian market), travel, humor, food/cooking, and similar subjects); Victoria Selvaggio, vickiaselvaggio@gmail.com (board books, picture books, chapter books, middle-grade, young adult, new adult, and adult; interested in nonfiction and fiction in all genres); Damian McNicholl, damianmcnichollvarney@gmail.com (accessible literary fiction, memoir, narrative nonfiction [especially biography, investigative journalism, cultural, legal, and LGBT]); Alexandra Weiss, alexweiss.jdlit@gmail.com (voice-driven young adult in all genres, silly and smart middle-grade fiction, chapter books, fiction and nonfiction picture books, especially science-based stories, select literary fiction); Cari Lamba, cari.jdlit.@gmail.com (middle-grade fiction, especially contemporary and quirky, fiction and nonfiction picture books, commercial fiction, mysteries, cozies, and foodie novels); David Laurell, dclaurell@gmail.com (celebrity memoir, pop culture, television, broadcasting, all genres of entertainment and sports, inspirational, collecting and strong character-driven fiction).

REPRESENTS Nonfiction, fiction, novels, juvenile books. **Considers these fiction areas:** commercial, contemporary issues, crime, ethnic, family saga, fantasy, feminist, gay, historical, horror, humor, inspirational, juvenile, lesbian, literary, mainstream, middle grade, multicultural, mystery, new adult, New Age, paranormal, picture books, science fiction, suspense, thriller, urban fantasy, women's, young adult.

HOW TO CONTACT Each agent has their own e-mail submission address and submission instructions; check the website for the current updates, as policies do change. Accepts simultaneous submissions. Obtains most new clients through recommendations from others, conferences, query letters.

TERMS Agent receives 15% commission on domestic sales. Offers written contract.

DEFIORE & COMPANY

47 E. 19th St., 3rd Floor, New York NY 10003. (212)925-7744. **Fax:** (212)925-9803. **E-mail:** info@defliterary.com, submissions@defliterary.com. **Website:** www.defliterary.com. Member of AAR. Signatory of WGA.

MEMBER AGENTS Brian DeFiore (popular nonfiction, business, pop culture, parenting, commercial fiction); **Laurie Abkemeier** (memoir, parenting, business, how-to/self-help, popular science); **Matthew Elblonk** (young adult, popular culture, narrative nonfiction); **Caryn Karmatz-Rudy** (popular fiction, self-help, narrative nonfiction); **Adam Schear** (commercial fiction, humor, young adult, smart thrillers, historical fiction, quirky debut literary novels, popu-

lar science, politics, popular culture, current events); **Meredith Kaffel Simonoff** (smart upmarket women's fiction, literary fiction [especially debut], literary thrillers, narrative nonfiction, nonfiction about science and tech, sophisticated pop culture/humor books); **Rebecca Strauss** (literary and commercial fiction, women's fiction, urban fantasy, romance, mystery, young adult, memoir, pop culture, select nonfiction); **Lisa Gallagher** (fiction and nonfiction); **Nicole Tourtelot** (narrative and prescriptive nonfiction, food, lifestyle, wellness, pop culture, history, humor, memoir, select young adult and adult fiction); **Ashely Collom** (women's fiction, children's and young adult, psychological thrillers, memoir, politics, photography, cooking, narrative nonfiction, LGBT issues, feminism, occult); **Miriam Altshuler** (adult literary and commercial fiction, narrative nonfiction, middle-grade, young adult, memoir, narrative nonfiction, self-help, family sagas, historical novels); **Reiko Davis** (adult literary and upmarket fiction, narrative nonfiction, young adult, middle-grade, memoir).

REPRESENTS Nonfiction, novels, short story collections, juvenile books, poetry books. **Considers these fiction areas:** comic books, commercial, ethnic, feminist, gay, lesbian, literary, mainstream, middle grade, mystery, paranormal, picture books, poetry, romance, short story collections, suspense, thriller, urban fantasy, women's, young adult.

HOW TO CONTACT Query with SASE or e-mail to submissions@defliterary.com. "Please include the word 'query' in the subject line. All attachments will be deleted; please insert all text in the body of the e-mail. For more information about our agents, their individual interests, and their query guidelines, please visit our 'About Us' page on our website." Accepts simultaneous submissions. Obtains most new clients through recommendations from others.

TERMS Agent receives 15% commission on domestic sales. Agent receives 20% commission on foreign sales. Offers written contract; 10-day notice must be given to terminate contract. Charges clients for photocopying and overnight delivery (deducted only after a sale is made).

JOELLE DELBOURGO ASSOCIATES, INC.

101 Park St., Montclair NJ 07042. (973)773-0836. **E-mail:** joelle@delbourgo.com. **E-mail:** submissions@delbourgo.com. **Website:** www.delbourgo.com. **Con-**

tact: Joelle Delbourgo. Estab. 1999. Member of AAR. Represents more than 500 clients.

MEMBER AGENTS Joelle Delbourgo; Jacqueline Flynn.

REPRESENTS Nonfiction, fiction, novels. **Considers these fiction areas:** adventure, commercial, contemporary issues, crime, detective, fantasy, feminist, juvenile, literary, mainstream, middle grade, military, mystery, new adult, New Age, romance, science fiction, thriller, urban fantasy, women's, young adult.

HOW TO CONTACT It's preferable if you submit via e-mail to a specific agent. Query 1 agent only. No attachments. Put the word "Query" in the subject line. "While we do our best to respond to each query, if you have not received a response in 60 days you may consider that a pass. Please do not send us copies of self-published books unless requested. Let us know if you are sending your query to us exclusively or if this is a multiple submission. For nonfiction, let us know if a proposal and sample chapters are available; if not, you should probably wait to send your query when you have a completed proposal. For fiction and memoir, embed the *first* 10 pages of manuscript into the e-mail after your query letter. Please no attachments. If we like your first pages, we may ask to see your synopsis and more manuscript. Please do not cold call us or make a follow-up call unless we call you." Accepts simultaneous submissions.

TERMS Agent receives 15% commission on domestic sales and 20% commission on foreign sales as well as television/film adaptation when a co-agent is involved. Offers written contract. Charges clients for postage and photocopying.

RECENT SALES *Prison 865: The Search for Hitler's Death Camp Guards in America*, by Debbie Cenziper (Hachette Books); *Hushed in Death*, by Stephen P. Kelly (Pegasus); *Hypersext: Keeping Our Children Safe in a Sexualized World*, by Jillian P. Roberts PhD with Sara Au (Quarto); *The Griffins of Castle Cary*, by Heather Shumaker (Simon & Schuster Children's); *Biscuit: 50 California-Style Recipes*, by Michael Volpatt (Running Press); *Husbands and Other Sharp Objects*, by Marilyn Simon Rothstein (Lake Union).

WRITERS CONFERENCES Unicorn Conference.

TIPS "Do your homework. Do not cold call. Read and follow submission guidelines before contacting us. Do not call to find out if we received your material. No e-mail queries. Treat agents with respect, as you would

any other professional, such as a doctor, lawyer or financial advisor."

SANDRA DIJKSTRA LITERARY AGENCY
1155 Camino del Mar, PMB 515, Del Mar CA 92014. **E-mail:** queries@dijkstraagency.com. **Website:** www.dijkstraagency.com. Member of AAR. Authors Guild, Organization of American Historians, RWA. Represents 200+ clients.

MEMBER AGENTS President: Sandra Dijkstra (adult only). Acquiring Associate agents: Elise Capron (adult only); Jill Marr (adult only); Thao Le (adult and YA); Roz Foster (adult and YA); Jessica Watterson (subgenres of adult romance, and women's fiction); Suzy Evans (adult and YA); Jennifer Kim (adult and YA).

REPRESENTS Nonfiction, fiction, novels, short story collections, juvenile books, scholarly books. **Considers these fiction areas:** commercial, contemporary issues, detective, family saga, fantasy, feminist, historical, horror, juvenile, literary, mainstream, middle grade, multicultural, mystery, new adult, romance, science fiction, short story collections, sports, suspense, thriller, urban fantasy, women's, young adult.

HOW TO CONTACT "Please see guidelines on our website, www.dijkstraagency.com. Please note that we only accept e-mail submissions. Due to the large number of unsolicited submissions we receive, we are only able to respond those submissions in which we are interested." Accepts simultaneous submissions. Responds to queries of interest within 6 weeks.

TERMS Works in conjunction with foreign and film agents. Agent receives 15% commission on domestic sales and 20% commission on foreign sales. Offers written contract. No reading fee.

TIPS "Remember that publishing is a business. Do your research and present your project in as professional a way as possible. Only submit your work when you are confident that it is polished and ready for prime-time. Make yourself a part of the active writing community by getting stories and articles published, networking with other writers, and getting a good sense of where your work fits in the market."

DONAGHY LITERARY GROUP
(647)527-4353. **E-mail:** stacey@donaghyliterary.com. **Website:** www.donaghyliterary.com. **Contact:** Stacey Donaghy. RWA, PACLA.

MEMBER AGENTS Stacey Donaghy (women's fiction, romantic suspense, LGBTQ, Diverse and #Own-voice, thriller, mystery, contemporary romance, and YA); Valerie Noble (historical, science fiction and fantasy [think Kristin Cashore and Suzanne Collins] for young adults and adults); Sue Miller (YA, urban fantasy, contemporary romance); Amanda Ayers Barnett (mystery/thrillers and middle-grade, young adult, new adult and women's fiction).

REPRESENTS Fiction, novels, juvenile books. **Considers these fiction areas:** commercial, contemporary issues, crime, detective, ethnic, family saga, fantasy, feminist, gay, historical, horror, juvenile, lesbian, literary, mainstream, middle grade, multicultural, mystery, new adult, paranormal, police, psychic, romance, science fiction, sports, supernatural, suspense, thriller, urban fantasy, women's, young adult.

HOW TO CONTACT Visit agency website for "new submission guidelines" Do not e-mail agents directly. This agency only accepts submissions through the QueryManager database system. Accepts simultaneous submissions. Time may vary depending on the volume of submissions.

TERMS Agent receives 15% commission on domestic sales; 20% commission on foreign sales. Offers written contract, 30-day notice must be given to terminate contract.

WRITERS CONFERENCES Romantic Times Booklovers Convention, Windsor International Writers Conference, OWC Ontario Writers Conference, SoCal Writers Conference, WD Toronto Writer's Workshop.

TIPS "Only submit to one DLG agent at a time, we work collaboratively and often share projects that may be better suited to another agent at the agency."

JIM DONOVAN LITERARY

5635 SMU Blvd., Suite 201, Dallas TX 75206. **E-mail:** jdliterary@sbcglobal.net. **Contact:** Melissa Shultz, agent. Estab. 1993. Represents 34 clients.

MEMBER AGENTS Jim Donovan (history—particularly American, military and Western; biography; sports; popular reference; popular culture; fiction—literary, thrillers and mystery); Melissa Shultz (all subjects listed above [like Jim], along with parenting and women's issues).

REPRESENTS Nonfiction, fiction, novels. **Considers these fiction areas:** action, adventure, commercial, crime, detective, frontier, historical, mainstream, multicultural, mystery, police, suspense, thriller, war, westerns.

HOW TO CONTACT "For nonfiction, I need a well-thought-out query letter telling me about the book: What it does, how it does it, why it's needed now, why it's better or different than what's out there on the subject, and why the author is the perfect writer for it. For fiction, the novel has to be finished, of course; a short (2- to 5-page) synopsis—not a teaser, but a summary of all the action, from first page to last—and the first 30-50 pages is enough. This material should be polished to as close to perfection as possible." Accepts simultaneous submissions. Responds in 2 weeks to queries; 1 month to mss. Obtains most new clients through recommendations from others.

TERMS Agent receives 15% commission on domestic sales. Agent receives 20% commission on foreign sales. Offers written contract, binding for 1 year; 30-day notice must be given to terminate contract. This agency charges for things such as overnight delivery and manuscript copying. Charges are discussed beforehand.

RECENT SALES *The Road to Jonestown*, by Jeff Guinn (S&S); *The Earth Is All That Lasts*, by Mark Gardner (HarperCollins); *As Good as Dead*, by Stephen Moore (NAL); *James Monroe*, by Tim McGrath (NAL); *The Greatest Fury*, by William C. Davis (NAL); *The Hamilton Affair*, by Elizabeth Cobbs (Arcade); *Resurrection Pass*, by Kurt Anderson (Kensington).

TIPS "Get published in short form—magazine reviews, journals, etc.—first. This will increase your credibility considerably, and make it much easier to sell a full-length book."

DUNHAM LITERARY, INC.

110 William St., Suite 2202, New York NY 10038. (212)929-0994. **E-mail:** query@dunhamlit.com. **Website:** www.dunhamlit.com. **Contact:** Jennie Dunham. Estab. 2000. Member of AAR. SCBWI Represents 50 clients.

MEMBER AGENTS Jennie Dunham, Bridget Smith, Leslie Zampetti.

REPRESENTS Nonfiction, fiction, novels, short story collections, juvenile books. **Considers these fiction areas:** family saga, fantasy, feminist, gay, historical, humor, juvenile, lesbian, literary, mainstream, middle grade, multicultural, mystery, picture books, science fiction, short story collections, sports, urban fantasy, women's, young adult.

HOW TO CONTACT E-mail queries preferred, with all materials pasted in the body of the e-mail. Attachments will not be opened. Paper queries are also accepted. Please include a SASE for response and return of materials. Please include the first 5 pages with the query. Accepts simultaneous submissions. Responds in 4 weeks to queries; 2 months to mss. Obtains most new clients through recommendations from others, solicitations.

TERMS Agent receives 15% commission on domestic sales; 20% commission on foreign sales.

RECENT SALES *The Bad Kitty Series*, by Nick Bruel (Macmillan); *The Christmas Story*, by Robert Sabuda (Candlewick); *The Gollywhopper Games* and Sequels, by Jody Feldman (HarperCollins); *Foolish Hearts*, by Emma Mills (Macmillan); *Learning Not To Drown*, by Anna Shinoda (Simon & Schuster); *Gangster Nation*, by Tod Goldberg (Counterpoint); *A Shadow All of Light*, by Fred Chappell (Tor).

DUNOW, CARLSON, & LERNER AGENCY

27 W. 20th St., Suite 1107, New York NY 10011. (212)645-7606. **E-mail:** mail@dclagency.com. **Website:** www.dclagency.com. Member of AAR.

MEMBER AGENTS Jennifer Carlson (narrative nonfiction writers and journalists covering current events and ideas and cultural history, as well as literary and upmarket commercial novelists); Henry Dunow (quality fiction–literary, historical, strongly written commercial–and with voice-driven nonfiction across a range of areas–narrative history, biography, memoir, current affairs, cultural trends and criticism, science, sports); Erin Hosier (nonfiction: popular culture, music, sociology and memoir); Betsy Lerner (nonfiction writers in the areas of psychology, history, cultural studies, biography, current events, business; fiction: literary, dark, funny, voice driven); Yishai Seidman (broad range of fiction: literary, postmodern, and thrillers; nonfiction: sports, music, and pop culture); Amy Hughes (nonfiction in the areas of history, cultural studies, memoir, current events, wellness, health, food, pop culture, and biography; also literary fiction); Eleanor Jackson (literary, commercial, memoir, art, food, science and history); Julia Kenny (fiction—adult, middle grade and YA—and is especially interested in dark, literary thrillers and suspense); Edward Necarsulmer IV (strong new voices in teen & middle grade as well as picture books); Stacia Decker; Arielle Datz (fiction—adult, YA, or middle-grade—literary and commercial, nonfiction—essays, unconventional memoir, pop culture, and sociology).

REPRESENTS Nonfiction, fiction, novels, short story collections. **Considers these fiction areas:** commercial, literary, mainstream, middle grade, mystery, picture books, thriller, young adult.

HOW TO CONTACT Query via snail mail with SASE, or by e-mail. E-mail preferred, paste 10 sample pages below query letter. No attachments. Will respond only if interested. Accepts simultaneous submissions. Responds in 4-6 weeks if interested.

RECENT SALES A full list of agency clients is on the website.

DYSTEL, GODERICH & BOURRET LLC

1 Union Square W., Suite 904, New York NY 10003. (212)627-9100. **Fax:** (212)627-9313. **Website:** www.dystel.com. Estab. 1994. Member of AAR. Other membership includes SCBWI. Represents 600+ clients.

MEMBER AGENTS Jane Dystel; Miriam Goderich, miriam@dystel.com (literary and commercial fiction as well as some genre fiction, narrative nonfiction, pop culture, psychology, history, science, art, business books, and biography/memoir); Stacey Glick, sglick@dystel.com (adult narrative nonfiction including memoir, parenting, cooking and food, psychology, science, health and wellness, lifestyle, current events, pop culture, YA, middle grade, children's nonfiction, and select adult contemporary fiction); Michael Bourret, mbourret@dystel.com (middle grade and young adult fiction, commercial adult fiction, and all sorts of nonfiction, from practical to narrative; he's especially interested in food and cocktail related books, memoir, popular history, politics, religion (though not spirituality), popular science, and current events); Jim McCarthy, jmccarthy@dystel.com (literary women's fiction, underrepresented voices, mysteries, romance, paranormal fiction, narrative nonfiction, memoir, and paranormal nonfiction); Jessica Papin, jpapin@dystel.com (plot-driven literary and smart commercial fiction, and narrative non-fiction across a range of subjects, including history, medicine, science, economics and women's issues); Lauren Abramo, labramo@dystel.com (humorous middle grade and contemporary YA on the children's side, and upmarket commercial fiction and well-paced literary fiction on the adult side; adult narrative nonfiction, especially pop culture, psychology, pop science, reportage, media, and contemporary culture; in nonfiction, has a strong preference for interdisciplinary approaches, and in all categories she's especially interested in underrepresented voices); John Rudolph, jrudolph@dystel.com (picture book author/illustrators, middle grade, YA, select commercial fiction, and narrative nonfiction—especially in music, sports, history, popular science, "big think", performing arts, health, business, memoir, military history, and humor); Sharon Pelletier, spelletier@dystel.com (smart commercial fiction, from upmarket women's fiction to domestic suspense to literary thrillers, and strong contemporary romance novels; compelling nonfiction projects, especially feminism and religion); Michael Hoogland, mhoogland@dystel.com (thriller, SFF, YA, upmarket women's fiction, and narrative nonfiction); Erin Young, eyoung@dystel.com (YA/MG, literary and intellectual commercial thrillers, memoirs, biographies, sport and science narratives); Amy Bishop, abishop@dystel.com (commercial and literary women's fiction, fiction from diverse authors, historical fiction, YA, personal narratives, and biographies); Kemi Faderin, kfaderin@dystel.com (smart, plot-driven YA, historical fiction/non-fiction, contemporary women's fiction, and literary fiction).

REPRESENTS Considers these fiction areas: commercial, ethnic, gay, lesbian, literary, mainstream, middle grade, mystery, paranormal, romance, suspense, thriller, women's, young adult.

HOW TO CONTACT Query via e-mail and put "Query" in the subject line. "Synopses, outlines or sample chapters (say, one chapter or the first 25 pages of your manuscript) should either be included below the cover letter or attached as a separate document. We won't open attachments if they come with a blank e-mail." Accepts simultaneous submissions. Responds in 6 to 8 weeks to queries; within 8 weeks to mss. Obtains most new clients through recommendations from others, solicitations, conferences.

TERMS Agent receives 15% commission on domestic sales; 19% commission on foreign sales. Offers written contract.

WRITERS CONFERENCES Backspace Writers' Conference, Pacific Northwest Writers' Association, Pike's Peak Writers' Conference, Writers League of Texas, Love Is Murder, Surrey International Writers Conference, Society of Children's Book Writers and Illustrators, International Thriller Writers, Willamette Writers Conference, The South Carolina Writers Workshop Conference, Las Vegas Writers Conference, Writer's Digest, Seton Hill Popular Fiction, Romance Writers of America, Geneva Writers Conference.

TIPS "DGLM prides itself on being a full-service agency. We're involved in every stage of the publishing process, from offering substantial editing on mss and proposals, to coming up with book ideas for authors looking for their next project, negotiating contracts and collecting monies for our clients. We follow a book from its inception through its sale to a publisher, its publication, and beyond. Our commitment to our writers does not, by any means, end when we have collected our commission. This is one of the many things that makes us unique in a very competitive business."

EDEN STREET LITERARY
P.O. Box 30, Billings NY 12510. **E-mail:** info@edenstreetlit.com. **E-mail:** submissions@edenstreetlit.com. **Website:** www.edenstreetlit.com. **Contact:** Liza Voges. Member of AAR. Signatory of WGA. Represents over 40 clients.

REPRESENTS Nonfiction, fiction, novels, juvenile books. **Considers these fiction areas:** juvenile, middle grade, picture books, young adult.

HOW TO CONTACT E-mail a picture book ms or dummy; a synopsis and 3 chapters of a MG or YA novel; a proposal and 3 sample chapters for nonfiction. Accepts simultaneous submissions. Responds only to submissions of interest.

RECENT SALES *Dream Dog*, by Lou Berger; *Biscuit Loves the Library*, by Alyssa Capucilli; *The Scraps Book*, by Lois Ehlert; *Two Bunny Buddies*, by Kathryn O. Galbraith; *Between Two Worlds*, by Katherine Kirkpatrick.

JUDITH EHRLICH LITERARY MANAGEMENT, LLC
146 Central Park W., 20E, New York NY 10023. (646)505-1570. **Fax:** (646)505-1570. **E-mail:** jehrlich@judithehrlichliterary.com. **Website:** www.judithehrlichliterary.com. Estab. 2002. Member of the Author's Guild and the American Society of Journalists and Authors.

MEMBER AGENTS Judith Ehrlich, jehrlich@judithehrlichliterary.com (upmarket, literary and quality commercial fiction, nonfiction: narrative, women's, business, prescriptive, medical and health-related topics, history, and current events).

REPRESENTS Nonfiction, fiction, novels, short story collections, juvenile books. **Considers these fiction areas:** adventure, commercial, contemporary issues, crime, detective, family saga, historical, humor, juvenile, literary, middle grade, mystery, picture books, short story collections, suspense, thriller, women's, young adult.

HOW TO CONTACT E-query, with a synopsis and some sample pages. The agency will respond only if interested. Accepts simultaneous submissions.

RECENT SALES Fiction: *The Bicycle Spy*, by Yona Zeldis McDonough (Scholastic); *The House on Primrose Pond*, by Yona McDonough (NAL/Penguin); *You Were Meant for Me*, by Yona McDonough (NAL/Penguin); *Echoes of Us: The Hybrid Chronicles*, Book 3 by Kat Zhang (HarperCollins); *Once We Were: The Hybrid Chronicles* Book 2, by Kat Zhang (HarperCollins). Nonfiction: *Listen to the Echoes: The Ray Bradbury Interviews (Deluxe Edition)*, by Sam Weller (Hat & Beard Press); *What are The Ten Commandments?*, by Yona McDonough (Grosset & Dunlap); *Little Author in the Big Woods: A Biography of Laura Ingalls Wilder*, by Yona McDonough (Christy Ottaviano Books/Henry Holt); *Ray Bradbury: The Last Interview: And Other Conversations*, by Sam Weller (Melville House); *Who Was Sojourner Truth?*, by Yona McDonough (Grosset & Dunlap); *Power Branding: Leveraging the Success of the World's Best Brands*, by Steve McKee (Palgrave Macmillan); *Confessions of a Sociopath: A Life Spent Hiding in Plain Sight*, by M.E. Thomas (Crown); *Luck and Circumstance: A Coming of Age in New York* and *Hollywood* and *Points Beyond*, by Michael Lindsay-Hogg (Knopf).

EINSTEIN LITERARY MANAGEMENT

27 W. 20th St., No. 1003, New York NY 10011. (212)221-8797. **E-mail:** info@einsteinliterary.com. **E-mail:** submissions@einsteinliterary.com. **Website:** http://einsteinliterary.com. **Contact:** Susanna Einstein. Estab. 2015. Member of AAR. Signatory of WGA.

MEMBER AGENTS Susanna Einstein, Susan Graham, Shana Kelly.

REPRESENTS Nonfiction, fiction, novels, short story collections, juvenile books. **Considers these fiction areas:** comic books, commercial, crime, fantasy, historical, juvenile, literary, middle grade, mystery, picture books, romance, science fiction, suspense, thriller, women's, young adult.

HOW TO CONTACT Please submit a query letter and the first 10 double-spaced pages of your manuscript in the body of the e-mail (no attachments). Does not respond to mail queries or telephone queries or queries that are not specifically addressed to this agency. Accepts simultaneous submissions. Responds in 6 weeks if interested.

EMPIRE LITERARY

115 W. 29th St., 3rd Floor, New York NY 10001. (917)213-7082. **E-mail:** abarzvi@empireliterary.com. **E-mail:** queries@empireliterary.com. **Website:** www.empireliterary.com. Estab. 2013. Member of AAR. Signatory of WGA.

MEMBER AGENTS Andrea Barzvi; Carrie Howland; Kathleen Schmidt; Penny Moore.

REPRESENTS Nonfiction, novels. **Considers these fiction areas:** literary, middle grade, women's, young adult.

HOW TO CONTACT Please only query one agent at a time. "If we are interested in reading more we will get in touch with you as soon as possible." Accepts simultaneous submissions.

FELICIA ETH LITERARY REPRESENTATION

555 Bryant St., Suite 350, Palo Alto CA 94301-1700. **E-mail:** feliciaeth.literary@gmail.com. **Website:** eth-literary.com. **Contact:** Felicia Eth. Member of AAR.

REPRESENTS Nonfiction, fiction, novels. **Considers these fiction areas:** contemporary issues, historical, literary, mainstream, suspense.

HOW TO CONTACT For fiction: Please write a query letter introducing yourself, your book, your writing background. Don't forget to include degrees you may have, publishing credits, awards and endorsements. Please wait for a response before including sample pages. "We only consider material where the manuscript for which you are querying is complete, unless you have previously published." For nonfiction: A query letter is best, introducing idea and what you have written already (proposal, manuscript?). "For writerly nonficiton (narratives, bio, memoir) please let us know if you have a finished manuscript. Also it's important you include information about yourself, your background and expertise, your platform and notoriety, if any. We do not ask for exclusivity in most instances but do ask that you inform us if other agents are considering the same material." Accepts simultaneous submissions. Responds in ideally 2 weeks for query, a month if more.

TERMS Agent receives 15% commission on domestic sales; 20% commission on foreign and film sales. Charges clients for photocopying and express mail service

RECENT SALES *Bumper Sticker Philosophy*, by Jack Bowen (Random House); *Boys Adrift*, by Leonard Sax (Basic Books); *The Memory Thief*, by Emily Colin (Ballantine Books); *The World is a Carpet*, by Anna Badkhen (Riverhead).

WRITERS CONFERENCES "Wide array—from Squaw Valley to Mills College."

MARY EVANS INC.

242 E. Fifth St., New York NY 10003. (212)979-0880. **Fax:** (212)979-5344. **E-mail:** info@maryevansinc.com. **Website:** maryevansinc.com. Member of AAR.

MEMBER AGENTS Mary Evans (progressive politics, alternative medicine, science and technology, social commentary, American history and culture); Julia Kardon (literary and upmarket fiction, narrative nonfiction, journalism, and history); Tom Mackay (nonfiction that uses sport as a platform to explore other issues and playful literary fiction).

REPRESENTS Nonfiction, novels. **Considers these fiction areas:** literary, upmarket.

HOW TO CONTACT Query by mail or e-mail. If querying by mail, include a SASE. If querying by e-mail, put "Query" in the subject line. For fiction: Include the first few pages, or opening chapter of your novel as a single Word attachment. For nonfiction: Include your book proposal as a single Word attachment. Accepts simultaneous submissions. Responds within 4-8 weeks.

EVATOPIA, INC.

8447 Wilshire Blvd., Suite 401, Beverly Hills CA 90211. **E-mail:** submissions@evatopia.com. **Website:** www.evatopia.com. **Contact:** Margery Walshaw. Estab. 2004. BAFTA, IBPA, NetGalley Represents 15 clients.

MEMBER AGENTS Mary Kay (story development); Jamie Davis (story editor); Jill Jones (story editor).

REPRESENTS Nonfiction, fiction, novels, juvenile books, movie scripts, feature film, TV movie of the week. **Considers these fiction areas:** crime, detective, fantasy, juvenile, new adult, paranormal, romance, supernatural, thriller, women's, young adult, Projects aimed at women, teens and children. REPRESENTS Screenplays and novels; provides self-publishing support to novelists.

HOW TO CONTACT Submit via online submission form at www.evatopiaentertainment.com. Accepts simultaneous submissions. Obtains most new clients through recommendations.

TERMS Agent receives 15% commission on domestic sales. Agent receives 15% commission on foreign sales. Offers written contract; 30-day notice must be given to terminate contract.

TIPS "Remember that you only have 1 chance to make that important first impression. Make your loglines original and your synopses concise. The secret to a screenwriter's success is creating an original story and telling it in a manner that we haven't heard before."

FAIRBANK LITERARY REPRESENTATION

P.O. Box Six, Hudson NY 12534-0006. (617)576-0030. **E-mail:** queries@fairbankliterary.com. **Website:** www.fairbankliterary.com and www.publishersmarketplace.com/members/SorcheFairbank/. **Contact:** Sorche Elizabeth Fairbank. Estab. 2002. Member of AAR. Author's Guild, the Agents Round Table, and Grub Street's Literary Advisory Council.

MEMBER AGENTS Sorche Fairbank (narrative nonfiction, commercial and literary fiction, memoir, food and wine); Matthew Frederick, matt@fairbankliterary.com (scout for sports nonfiction, architecture, design).

REPRESENTS Nonfiction, novels, short story collections. **Considers these fiction areas:** commercial, feminist, literary, mainstream, mystery, picture books, short story collections, sports, suspense, thriller, women's, International voices. Southern voices.

HOW TO CONTACT Query by e-mail queries@fairbankliterary.com or by mail with SASE. Accepts simultaneous submissions. Obtains most new clients through recommendations from others, solicitations, conferences, ideas generated in-house.

TERMS Agent receives 15% commission on domestic sales; 20% commission on foreign sales. Offers written contract, binding for 12 months; 45-day notice must be given to terminate contract.

RECENT SALES 3-book deal for Terry Border for picture books to Philomel; 2-book deal for Lisa Currie, *Surprise Yourself* and a 2nd book scheduled for 2019 to Marian Lizzi at Tarcher Perigee; scratch & sniff spinoff and an early reader adaptation of Terry Border's best-selling *Peanut Butter & Cupcake* to Grosset and Dunlap/Penguin; 4-book deal for Matthew Frederick for his best-selling *101 Things I Learned Series* moving to Crown.

TIPS "Be professional from the very first contact. There shouldn't be a single typo or grammatical flub in your query. Show me that you know your audience—and your competition. Have the writing and/or proposal at the very, very best it can be before starting the querying process. Don't assume that if someone likes it enough they'll 'fix' it. The biggest mistake new writers make is starting the querying process before they—and the work—are ready. Take your time and do it right."

LEIGH FELDMAN LITERARY

E-mail: assistant@lfliterary.com. **E-mail:** query@lfliterary.com. **Website:** http://lfliterary.com. **Contact:** Leigh Feldman. Estab. 2014. Member of AAR. Signatory of WGA.

REPRESENTS Nonfiction, fiction, novels, short story collections. **Considers these fiction areas:** contemporary issues, family saga, feminist, gay, historical, lesbian, literary, multicultural, short story collections, women's, young adult.

HOW TO CONTACT E-query. "Please include 'query' in the subject line. Due to large volume of submissions, we regret that we can not respond to all queries individually. Please include the first chapter or the first 10 pages of your manuscript (or proposal) pasted after your query letter. I'd love to know what led you to query me in particular, and please let me know if you are querying other agents as well." Accepts simultaneous submissions.

RECENT SALES List of recent sales and best known sales are available on the agency website.

THE FIELDING AGENCY, LLC

1550G Tiburon Blvd., #528, Tiburon CA 94920. **E-mail:** wlee@fieldingagency.com. **Website:** www.fieldingagency.com. **Contact:** Whitney Lee.

REPRESENTS Nonfiction, fiction, juvenile books.

HOW TO CONTACT Accepts simultaneous submissions.

DIANA FINCH LITERARY AGENCY

116 W. 23rd St., Suite 500, New York NY 10011. (917)544-4470. **E-mail:** diana.finch@verizon.net. **Website:** dianafinchliteraryagency.blogspot.com. **Contact:** Diana Finch. Estab. 2003. Member of AAR. Represents approximately 40 active clients clients.

REPRESENTS Nonfiction, fiction, novels, scholarly books. **Considers these fiction areas:** action, adventure, contemporary issues, crime, detective, ethnic, fantasy, historical, literary, mainstream, middle grade, multicultural, new adult, police, science fiction, sports, thriller, urban fantasy, young adult.

HOW TO CONTACT This agency prefers submissions via its online form. Accepts simultaneous submissions. Obtains most new clients through recommendations from others.

TERMS Agent receives 15% commission on domestic sales; 20% commission on foreign sales. Offers written contract. "I charge for overseas postage, galleys, and books purchased, and try to recoup these costs from earnings received for a client, rather than charging outright."

RECENT SALES *The Journeys of the Trees*, by Zach St George (W. W. Norton); *Owls of the Eastern Ice*, by Jonathan SIaght (FSG/Scientific American); *Uncolor: on toxins in personal products*, by Ronnie Citron-Fink (Island Press); *Cutting School*, by Professor Noliwe Rooks (The New Press); *Merchants of Men*, by Loretta Napoleoni (Seven Stories Press); *Beyond $15*, by Jonathan Rosenblum (Beacon Press); *The Age of Inequality*, by the Editors of In These Times (Verso Books); *Seeds of Resistance*, by Mark Schapiro (Hot Books/Skyhorse).

WRITERS CONFERENCES Washington Writers Conference; Writers Digest NYC Conference; CLMP/New School conference, and others on an individual basis.

TIPS "Do as much research as you can on agents before you query. Have someone critique your query letter before you send it. It should be only 1 page and describe your book clearly—and why you are writing it—but also demonstrate creativity and a sense of your writing style."

FINEPRINT LITERARY MANAGEMENT

207 W. 106th St., Suite 1D, New York NY 10025. (212)279-1282. **Website:** www.fineprintlit.com. Estab. 2007. Member of AAR.

MEMBER AGENTS Peter Rubie, CEO, peter@fineprintlit.com (nonfiction interests include narrative nonfiction, popular science, spirituality, history, biography, pop culture, business, technology, parenting, health, self help, music, and food; fiction interests include literate thrillers, crime fiction, science fiction and fantasy, military fiction and literary fiction, middle grade and boy-oriented YA fiction); Stephany Evans, stephany@fineprintlit.com (nonfiction: health and wellness, spirituality, lifestyle, food and drink, sustainability, running and fitness, memoir, and narrative nonfiction; fiction interests include mystery/crime, women's fiction, from literary to commercial to romance); Laura Wood, laura@fineprintlit.com (serious nonfiction, especially in the areas of science and nature, along with substantial titles in business, history, religion, and other areas by academics, experienced professionals, and journalists; select genre fiction only (no poetry, literary fiction or memoir) in the categories of science fiction & fantasy and mystery); June Clark, june@fineprintlit.com (nonfiction projects in the areas of entertainment, self-help, parenting, reference/how-to books, food and wine, style/beauty, and prescriptive business titles); Jacqueline Murphy, jacqueline@fineprintlit.com.

REPRESENTS Nonfiction, fiction, novels, short story collections. **Considers these fiction areas:** commercial, crime, fantasy, historical, literary, mainstream, middle grade, mystery, romance, science fiction, suspense, thriller, women's, young adult.

HOW TO CONTACT E-query. For fiction, send a query, synopsis, bio, and 30 pages pasted into the e-mail. No attachments. For nonfiction, send a query only; proposal requested later if the agent is interested. Accepts simultaneous submissions. Obtains most new clients through recommendations from others, solicitations.

TERMS Agent receives 15% commission on domestic sales; 20% commission on foreign sales.

JAMES FITZGERALD AGENCY

118 Waverly Place, #1B, New York NY 10011. **E-mail:** submissions@jfitzagency.com. **Website:** www.jfitzagency.com. **Contact:** James Fitzgerald.

MEMBER AGENTS James Fitzgerald; Dylan Lowy.

REPRESENTS Nonfiction, fiction, novels, juvenile books, scholarly books, graphic novles, packaged books. **Considers these fiction areas:** action, adventure, cartoon, comic books, crime, detective, fantasy, frontier, historical, humor, juvenile, literary, mainstream, middle grade, mystery, picture books, science fiction, sports, supernatural, suspense, thriller, translation, war, westerns, young adult.

HOW TO CONTACT Query via e-mail or snail mail. This agency's online submission guidelines page explains all the elements they want to see when you submit a nonfiction book proposal. Accepts simultaneous submissions.

RECENT SALES A full and diverse list of titles are on this agency's website.

FLANNERY LITERARY

1140 Wickfield Ct., Naperville IL 60563. **E-mail:** jennifer@flanneryliterary.com. **Website:** flanneryliterary.com. **Contact:** Jennifer Flannery. Estab. 1992. Represents 40 clients.

REPRESENTS Nonfiction, fiction, novels, juvenile books. **Considers these fiction areas:** juvenile, middle grade, new adult, picture books, young adult.

HOW TO CONTACT Query by e-mail only. "Multiple queries are fine, but please inform us. Please no attachments. If you're sending a query about a novel, please embed in the e-mail the first 5-10 pages; if it's a picture book, please embed the entire text in the e-mail. We do not open attachments unless they have been requested." Accepts simultaneous submissions. Responds in 2-4 weeks to queries; 1 month to mss. Obtains new clients through referrals and queries.

TERMS Agent receives 15% commission on domestic sales; 20% commission on foreign sales. Offers written contract, binding for life of book in print.

TIPS "Write an engrossing, succinct query describing your work. We are always looking for a fresh new voice."

FLETCHER & COMPANY

78 Fifth Ave., 3rd Floor, New York NY 10011. **E-mail:** info@fletcherandco.com. **Website:** www.fletcherandco.com. **Contact:** Christy Fletcher. Estab. 2003. Member of AAR.

MEMBER AGENTS Christy Fletcher (referrals only); Melissa Chinchillo (select list of her own authors); Rebecca Gradinger (literary fiction, up-market commercial fiction, narrative nonfiction, self-help, memoir, Women's studies, humor, and pop culture); Gráinne Fox (literary fiction and quality commercial authors, award-winning journalists and food writers, American voices, international, literary crime, upmarket fiction, narrative nonfiction); Lisa Grubka (fiction—literary, upmarket women's, and young adult; and nonfiction — narrative, food, science, and more); Sylvie Greenberg (literary fiction, business, sports, science, memoir and history); Donald Lamm (history, biography, investigative journalism, politics, current affairs, and business); Todd Sattersten (business books); Eric Lupfer; Sarah Fuentes; Veronica Goldstein; Mink Choi; Erin McFadden.

REPRESENTS Nonfiction, novels. **Considers these fiction areas:** commercial, crime, literary, women's, young adult.

HOW TO CONTACT Send queries to info@fletcherandco.com. Please do not include e-mail attachments with your initial query, as they will be deleted. Address your query to a specific agent. No snail mail queries. Accepts simultaneous submissions.

RECENT SALES *The Profiteers*, by Sally Denton; *The Longest Night*, by Andrea Williams; *Disrupted: My Misadventure in the Start-Up Bubble*, by Dan Lyons; *Free Re-Fills: A Doctor Confronts His Addiction*, by Peter Grinspoon, M.D.; *Black Man in a White Coat: A Doctor's Reflections on Race and Medicine*, by Damon Tweedy, M.D.

FOLIO LITERARY MANAGEMENT, LLC

The Film Center Building, 630 Ninth Ave., Suite 1101, New York NY 10036. (212)400-1494. **Fax:** (212)967-0977. **Website:** www.foliolit.com. Member of AAR. Represents 100+ clients.

MEMBER AGENTS Claudia Cross (romance novels, commercial women's fiction, cooking and food writing, serious nonfiction on religious and spiritual topics); Scott Hoffman (literary and commercial fiction, journalistic or academic nonfiction, narrative nonfiction, pop culture books, business, history, politics, spiritual or religious-themed fiction and nonfiction, sci-fi/fantasy literary fiction, heartbreaking memoirs, humorous nonfiction); Jeff Kleinman (book-club fiction (not genre commercial, like mysteries or romances), literary fiction, thrillers and suspense novels, narrative nonfiction, memoir); Dado Derviskadic (nonfiction: cultural history, biography, memoir, pop science, motivational self-help, health/nutrition, pop culture, cookbooks; fiction that's gritty, introspective, or serious); Frank Weimann (biography, business/investing/finance, history, religious, mind/body/spirit, health, lifestyle, cookbooks, sports, African-American, science, memoir, special forces/CIA/FBI/mafia, military, prescriptive nonfiction, humor, celebrity; adult and children's fiction); Michael Harriot (commercial non-fiction (both narrative and prescriptive) and fantasy/science fiction); Erin Harris (book club, historical fiction, literary, narrative nonfiction, psychological suspense, young adult); Katherine Latshaw (blogs-to-books, food/cooking, middle grade, narra-

tive and prescriptive nonfiction); Annie Hwang (literary and upmarket fiction with commercial appeal; select nonfiction: popular science, diet/health/fitness, lifestyle, narrative nonfiction, pop culture, and humor); Erin Niumata (fiction: commercial women's fiction, romance, historical fiction, mysteries, psychological thrillers, suspense, humor; nonfiction: self-help, women's issues, pop culture and humor, pet care/pets, memoirs, and anything blogger); Ruth Pomerance (narrative nonfiction and commercial fiction); Marcy Posner (adult: commercial women's fiction, historical fiction, mystery, biography, history, health, and lifestyle, commercial novels, thrillers, narrative nonfiction; children's: contemporary YA and MG, mystery series for boys, select historical fiction and fantasy); Jeff Silberman (narrative nonfiction, biography, history, politics, current affairs, health, lifestyle, humor, food/cookbook, memoir, pop culture, sports, science, technology; commercial, literary, and book club fiction); Steve Troha; Emily van Beek (YA, MG, picture books), Melissa White (general nonfiction, literary and commercial fiction, MG, YA); John Cusick (middle grade, picture books, YA); Jamie Chambliss.

REPRESENTS Nonfiction, novels. **Considers these fiction areas:** commercial, fantasy, horror, literary, middle grade, mystery, picture books, religious, romance, thriller, women's, young adult.

HOW TO CONTACT Query via e-mail only (no attachments). Read agent bios online for specific submission guidelines and e-mail addresses, and to check if someone is closed to queries. "All agents respond to queries as soon as possible, whether interested or not. If you haven't heard back from the individual agent within the time period that they specify on their bio page, it's possible that something has gone wrong, and your query has been lost–in that case, please e-mail a follow-up."

TIPS "Please do not submit simultaneously to more than one agent at Folio. If you're not sure which of us is exactly right for your book, don't worry. We work closely as a team, and if one of our agents gets a query that might be more appropriate for someone else, we'll always pass it along. It's important that you check each agent's bio page for clear directions as to how to submit, as well as when to expect feedback."

FOUNDRY LITERARY + MEDIA

33 W. 17th St., PH, New York NY 10011. (212)929-5064. **Fax:** (212)929-5471. **Website:** www.foundry-media.com.

MEMBER AGENTS Peter McGuigan, pmsubmissions@foundrymedia.com (smart, offbeat voices in all genres of fiction and nonfiction); Yfat Reiss Gendell, yrgsubmissions@foundrymedia.com (practical nonfiction: health and wellness, diet, lifestyle, how-to, and parenting; range of narrative nonfiction that includes humor, memoir, history, science, pop culture, psychology, and adventure/travel stories; unique commercial fiction, including young adult fiction, that touch on her nonfiction interests, including speculative fiction, thrillers, and historical fiction); Chris Park, cpsubmissions@foundrymedia.com (memoirs, narrative nonfiction, sports books, Christian nonfiction and character-driven fiction); Hannah Brown Gordon, hbgsubmissions@foundrymedia.com (stories and narratives that blend genres, including thriller, suspense, historical, literary, speculative, memoir, pop-science, psychology, humor, and pop culture); Brandi Bowles, bbsubmissions@foundrymedia.com (nonfiction list ranges from cookbooks to prescriptive books, science, pop culture, and real-life inspirational stories; high-concept novels that feature strong female bonds and psychological or scientific themes); Kirsten Neuhaus, knsubmissions@foundrymedia.com (platform-driven narrative nonfiction, in the areas of memoir, business, lifestyle (beauty/fashion/relationships), current events, history and stories with strong female voices, as well as smart fiction that appeals to a wide market); Jessica Regel, jrsubmissions@foundrymedia.com (young adult and middle grade books, as well as a select list of adult general fiction, women's fiction, and adult nonfiction); Anthony Mattero, amsubmissions@foundrymedia.com (smart, platform-driven nonfiction particularly in the genres of pop culture, humor, music, sports, and pop-business); Peter Steinberg, pssubmissions@foundrymedia.com (narrative nonfiction, commercial and literary fiction, memoir, health, history, lifestyle, humor, sports, and young adult); Roger Freet, rfsubmissions@foundrymedia.com (narrative and idea-driven nonfiction clients in the areas of religion, spirituality, memoir, and cultural issues by leading scholars, pastors, historians, activists and musicians); Adriann Ranta, arsubmissions@foundrymedia.com (accepts all genres and age groups; loves gritty, realistic, true-to-life narratives; women's fiction and nonfiction; accessible, pop nonfiction in science, history, and craft; and smart, fresh, genre-bending works for children).

REPRESENTS Considers these fiction areas: commercial, historical, humor, literary, middle grade, suspense, thriller, women's, young adult.

HOW TO CONTACT Target one agent only. Send queries to the specific submission e-mail of the agent. For fiction: send query, synopsis, author bio, first 3 chapters—all pasted in the e-mail. For nonfiction, send query, sample chapters, TOC, author bio (all pasted). "We regret that we cannot guarantee a response to every submission we receive. If you do not receive a response within 8 weeks, your submission is not right for our lists at this time." Accepts simultaneous submissions.

FOX LITERARY

110 W. 40th St., Suite 2305, New York NY 10018. **E-mail:** submissions@foxliterary.com. **Website:** foxliterary.com.

MEMBER AGENTS Diana Fox.

REPRESENTS Nonfiction, fiction, novels, short story collections, juvenile books, scholarly books, graphic novels. **Considers these fiction areas:** action, adventure, comic books, commercial, confession, contemporary issues, crime, detective, erotica, fantasy, feminist, gay, historical, juvenile, lesbian, literary, mainstream, middle grade, multicultural, mystery, new adult, paranormal, romance, science fiction, short story collections, spiritual, suspense, thriller, urban fantasy, women's, young adult, general.

HOW TO CONTACT E-mail query and first 5 pages in body of e-mail. E-mail queries preferred. For snail mail queries, must include an e-mail address for response and no response means no. Do not send SASE. No e-mail attachments. Accepts simultaneous submissions.

SARAH JANE FREYMANN LITERARY AGENCY

(212)362-9277. **E-mail:** sarah@sarahjanefreymann.com. **E-mail:** submissions@sarahjanefreymann.com. **Website:** www.sarahjanefreymann.com. **Contact:** Sarah Jane Freymann, Steve Schwartz.

MEMBER AGENTS Sarah Jane Freymann (nonfiction: spiritual, psychology, self-help, women/men's issues, books by health experts [conventional and alternative], cookbooks, narrative non-fiction, natural science, nature, memoirs, cutting-edge journalism, travel, multicultural issues, parenting, lifestyle, fiction: literary, mainstream YA); Jessica Sinsheimer, jessica@sarahjanefreymann.com; Steven Schwartz, steve@sarahjanefreymann.com (popular fiction [crime, thrillers, and historical novels], world and national affairs, business books, self-help, psychology, humor, sports and travel).

REPRESENTS Nonfiction, fiction, novels. **Considers these fiction areas:** crime, historical, literary, mainstream, thriller, young adult, Popular fiction.

HOW TO CONTACT Query via e-mail. No attachments. Below the query, please paste the first 10 pages of your work. Accepts simultaneous submissions.

TERMS Charges clients for long distance, overseas postage, photocopying. 100% of business is derived from commissions on ms sales.

FREDRICA S. FRIEDMAN AND CO., INC.

857 Fifth Ave., New York NY 10065. (212)639-9455. **E-mail:** info@fredricafriedman.com. **E-mail:** submissions@fredricafriedman.com. **Website:** www.fredricafriedman.com. **Contact:** Ms. Chandler Smith.

REPRESENTS Nonfiction, fiction.

HOW TO CONTACT Submit e-query, synopsis; be concise, and include any pertinent author information, including relevant writing history. If you are a fiction writer, submit the first 10 pages of your manuscript. Keep all material in the body of the e-mail. Accepts simultaneous submissions. Responds in 6 weeks.

REBECCA FRIEDMAN LITERARY AGENCY

E-mail: brandie@rfliterary.com. **Website:** www.rfliterary.com. Estab. 2013. Member of AAR. Signatory of WGA.

MEMBER AGENTS Rebecca Friedman (commercial and literary fiction with a focus on literary novels of suspense, women's fiction, contemporary romance, and young adult, as well as journalistic nonfiction and memoir); Susan Finesman, susan@rfliterary.com (fiction, cookbooks, and lifestyle); Abby Schulman, abby@rfliterary.com (YA and nonfiction related to health, wellness, and personal development); Brandie Coonis, brandie@rfliterary.com (MG, YA, SFF, and writers that defy genre).

REPRESENTS Nonfiction, fiction, novels. **Considers these fiction areas:** commercial, family saga, fantasy, feminist, frontier, gay, historical, horror, literary, middle grade, mystery, new adult, romance, science fiction, suspense, thriller, women's, young adult.

HOW TO CONTACT Please submit your brief query letter and first chapter (no more than 15 pages, double-spaced). No attachments. Accepts simultaneous submissions. Tries to respond in 6-8 weeks.

RECENT SALES A complete list of agency authors is available online.

THE FRIEDRICH AGENCY

19 W. 21st St., Suite 201, New York NY 10010. (212)317-8810. **E-mail:** mfriedrich@friedrichagency.com; lcarson@friedrichagency.com; kwolf@friedrichagency.com. **Website:** www.friedrichagency.com. **Contact:** Molly Friedrich; Lucy Carson; Kent D. Wolf. Estab. 2006. Member of AAR. Signatory of WGA. Represents 50+ clients.

MEMBER AGENTS Molly Friedrich, founder and agent (open to queries); Lucy Carson, TV/film rights director and agent (open to queries); Kent D. Wolf, foreign rights director and agent (open to queries).

REPRESENTS Nonfiction, fiction, novels, short story collections. **Considers these fiction areas:** commercial, detective, family saga, feminist, literary, multicultural, short story collections, suspense, women's, young adult.

HOW TO CONTACT Query by e-mail only. Please query only 1 agent at this agency. Accepts simultaneous submissions. Responds in 2-4 weeks.

RECENT SALES *W is For Wasted*, by Sue Grafton; *Olive Kitteridge*, by Elizabeth Strout. Other clients include Frank McCourt, Jane Smiley, Esmeralda Santiago, Terry McMillan, Cathy Schine, Ruth Ozeki, Karen Joy Fowler, and more.

FULL CIRCLE LITERARY, LLC

San Diego CA **Website:** www.fullcircleliterary.com. **Contact:** Stefanie Von Borstel. Estab. 2005. Member of AAR. Society of Children's Books Writers & Illustrators, Authors Guild. Represents 100+ clients.

MEMBER AGENTS Stefanie Sanchez Von Borstel; Adriana Dominguez; Taylor Martindale Kean; Lilly Ghahremani.

REPRESENTS **Considers these fiction areas:** literary, middle grade, multicultural, young adult.

HOW TO CONTACT Online submissions only via submissions form online. Please complete the form and submit cover letter, author information and sample writing. For sample writing: fiction please include the first 10 ms pages. For nonfiction, include a proposal with 1 sample chapter. Accepts simultaneous submissions. "Due to the high volume of submissions, please keep in mind we are no longer able to personally respond to every submission. However, we read every submission with care and often share for a second read within the office. If we are interested, we will contact you by email to request additional materials (such as a complete manuscript or additional manuscripts). Please keep us updated if there is a change in the status of your project, such as an offer of representation or book contract." If you have not heard from us in 6-8 weeks, your project is not right for our agency at the current time and we wish you all the best with your writing. Thank you for considering Full Circle Literary, we look forward to reading! Obtains most new clients through recommendations from others and conferences.

TERMS Agent receives 15% commission on domestic sales; 25% commission on foreign sales. Offers written contract which outlines responsibilities of the author and the agent.

FUSE LITERARY

Foreword Literary, Inc. dba FUSE LITERARY, P.O. Box 258, La Honda CA 94020. **E-mail:** info@fuseliterary.com. **E-mail:** query[firstnameofagent]@fuseliterary.com. **Website:** www.fuseliterary.com. **Contact:** Contact each agent directly via e-mail. Estab. 2013. RWA, SCBWI. Represents 100+ clients.

MEMBER AGENTS Laurie McLean (only accepting referral inquiries and submissions requested at conferences or online events); Gordon Warnock, querygordon@fuseliterary.com (fiction: high-concept commercial fiction, literary fiction (adults through YA), graphic novels (adults through MG); nonfiction: memoir (adult, YA, NA, graphic), cookbooks/food narrative/food studies, illustrated/art/photography (especially graphic nonfiction), political and current events, pop science, pop culture (especially punk culture and geek culture), self-help, how-to, humor, pets, business and career); Connor Goldsmith, queryconnor@fuseliterary.com (fiction: sci-fi/fantasy/horror, thrillers, and upmarket commercial fiction with a unique and memorable hook; books by and about people from marginalized perspectives, such as LGBT people and/or racial minorities; nonfiction (from recognized experts with established platforms): history (particularly of the ancient world), theater, cinema, music, television, mass media, popular culture, feminism and gender studies, LGBT issues, race relations, and the sex industry); Michelle Richter, querymichelle@fuseliterary.com (primarily seeking fiction, specifically book club reads, literary fiction, and mystery/suspense/thrillers; for nonfiction, seeking fashion, pop culture, science/medicine, sociology/social trends, and economics); Emily S. Keyes, queryemily@fuseliterary.com (picture books, middle grade and young adult children's books, plus select commercial fiction, including fantasy & science fiction, women's fiction, new adult fiction, pop culture and humor); Tricia Skinner, querytricia@fuseliterary.com (Romance: science fiction, futuristic, fantasy, military/special ops, medieval historical; brand new relationships; diversity); Margaret Bail, querymargaret@fuseliterary.com (adult fiction in the genres of romance [no Christian or inspirational, please], science fiction [soft sci-fi rather than hard], mystery, thrillers, action adventure, historical fiction [not a fan of WWII era], and fantasy. In nonfiction, memoirs with a unique hook, and cookbooks with a strong platform); Carlisle Webber, querycarlisle@fuseliterary.com (high-concept commercial fiction in middle grade, young adult, and adult; dark thrillers, mystery, horror, dark women's fiction, dark pop/mainstream fiction; especially interested in diverse authors and their stories).

REPRESENTS Nonfiction, fiction, novels, juvenile books, scholarly books, poetry books. **Considers these fiction areas:** action, adventure, cartoon, comic books, commercial, confession, contemporary issues, crime, detective, erotica, ethnic, experimental, family saga, fantasy, feminist, frontier, gay, glitz, hi-lo, historical, horror, humor, inspirational, juvenile, lesbian, literary, mainstream, metaphysical, middle grade, multicultural, multimedia, mystery, new adult, New Age, occult, paranormal, picture books, plays, poetry, poetry in translation, police, psychic, regional, romance, satire, science fiction, spiritual, sports, supernatural, suspense, thriller, urban fantasy, westerns, women's, young adult. "We are committed to expanding storytelling into a wide variety of formats other than books, including video games, movies, television shows, streaming videos, enhanced ebooks, VR, etc."

HOW TO CONTACT E-query an individual agent. Check the website to see if any individual agent has closed themselves to submissions, as well as for a description of each agent's individual submission preferences. (You can find these details by clicking on each agent's photo.) Usually responds in 4-6 weeks, but sometimes more if an agent is exceptionally busy. Check each agent's bio/submissions page on the website. Only accepts e-mailed queries that follow our online guidelines.

TERMS "We earn 15% on negotiated deals for books and with our co-agents earn between 20-30% on foreign translation deals depending on the territory; 20% on TV/Movies/Plays; other multimedia deals are so new there is no established commission rate. The author has the last say, approving or not approving all deals." After the initial 90-day period, there is a 30-day termination of the agency agreement clause. No fees.

RECENT SALES Seven-figure and six figure deals for NYT bestseller Julie Kagawa (YA); six-figure deal for debut Melissa D. Savage (MG); six-figure deal for Kerry Lonsdale (suspense).

WRITERS CONFERENCES Agents from this agency attend many conferences. A full list of their appearances is available on the agency website.

GALLT AND ZACKER LITERARY AGENCY

273 Charlton Ave., South Orange NJ 07079. (973)761-6358. **Website:** www.galltzacker.com. **Contact:** Nancy Gallt, Marietta Zacker. Estab. 2000. Represents 80 clients.

MEMBER AGENTS Nancy Gallt; Marietta Zacker; Linda Camacho; Beth Phelan.

REPRESENTS Nonfiction, fiction, novels, juvenile books, scholarly books, poetry books. **Considers these fiction areas:** juvenile, middle grade, picture books, young adult.

HOW TO CONTACT Submit through online submission form on agency website. No e-mail queries, please. Accepts simultaneous submissions. Obtains new clients through submissions, conferences and recommendations from others.

TERMS Agent receives 15% commission on domestic sales; 20% commission on foreign sales. Offers written contract; 30-day notice must be given to terminate contract.

RECENT SALES Rick Riordan's Books (Hyperion); *Trace*, by Pat Cummings (Harper); *What Gloria Heard*, illustrated by Daria Peoples (Bloomsbury); *Gondra's Treasure*, illustrated by Jennifer Black Reinhardt (Clarion/HMH); *Caterpillar Summer*, by Gillian McDunn (Bloomsbury); *It Wasn't Me*, by Dana Alison Levy (Delacorte/Random House); *Namesake*, by Paige Britt (Scholastic); *The Turning*, by Emily Whit-

man (Harper); *Rot*, by Ben Clanton (Simon & Schuster). *The Year They Fell*, by David Kreizman (Imprint/Macmillan); *Manhattan Maps*, by Jennifer Thermes (Abrams); *The Moon Within*, by Aida Salazar (Scholastic); *Artist in Space*, by Dean Robbins (Scholastic); *Lucy McGee*, by Mary Amato (Holiday House); *Where Are You From?*, by Yamile Saied Méndez (Harper); *The Artist*, by Selina Alko (Scholastic).

TIPS "Writing and illustrations stand on their own, so submissions should tell the most compelling stories possible—whether visually, in narrative, or both."

MAX GARTENBERG LITERARY AGENCY

912 N. Pennsylvania Ave., Yardley PA 19067. (215)295-9230. **Website:** www.maxgartenberg.com. **Contact:** Anne Devlin (nonfiction). Estab. 1954. Represents 100 clients.

MEMBER AGENTS Anne G. Devlin (current events, education, politics, true crime, women's issues, sports, parenting, biography, environment, narrative nonfiction, health, lifestyle, and celebrity).

REPRESENTS Nonfiction, juvenile books, scholarly books, textbooks.

HOW TO CONTACT Writers desirous of having their work handled by this agency may query by e-mail to agdevlin@aol.com. Accepts simultaneous submissions. Responds in 2 weeks to queries; 6 weeks to mss.

TERMS Agent receives 15% commission on sales.

RECENT SALES *The Enlightened College Applicant*, by Andrew Belasco (Rowman and Littlefield); *Beethoven for Kids: His Life and Music*, by Helen Bauer (Chicago Review Press); *Portrait of a Past Life Skeptic*, by Robert L. Snow (Llewellyn Books); *Beyond Your Baby's Checkup*, by Luke Voytas, MD (Sasquatch Books); *Unorthodox Warfare: The Chinese Experience*, by Ralph D. Sawyer (Westview Press); *Encyclopedia of Earthquakes and Volcanoes*, by Alexander E. Gates (Facts on File); *Pandas!: Step Into Reading*, by David Salomon (Random House Children's Bookss).

TIPS "We have recently expanded to allow more access for new writers."

GELFMAN SCHNEIDER / ICM PARTNERS

850 7th Ave., Suite 903, New York NY 10019. **E-mail:** mail@gelfmanschneider.com. **Website:** www.gelfmanschneider.com. **Contact:** Jane Gelfman, Deborah Schneider. Member of AAR. Represents 300+ clients.

MEMBER AGENTS Deborah Schneider (all categories of literary and commercial fiction and nonfiction); Jane Gelfman; Heather Mitchell (particularly interested in narrative nonfiction, historical fiction and young debut authors with strong voices); Penelope Burns, penelope.gsliterary@gmail.com (literary and commercial fiction and nonfiction, as well as a variety of young adult and middle grade).

REPRESENTS Nonfiction, fiction, juvenile books. **Considers these fiction areas:** commercial, fantasy, historical, literary, mainstream, middle grade, mystery, science fiction, suspense, women's, young adult.

HOW TO CONTACT Query. Check Submissions page of website to see which agents are open to queries and further instructions. Accepts simultaneous submissions.

TERMS Agent receives 15% commission on domestic sales; 20% commission on foreign sales; 15% commission on film sales. Offers written contract. Charges clients for photocopying and messengers/couriers.

THE GERNERT COMPANY

136 E. 57th St., New York NY 10022. (212)838-7777. **E-mail:** info@thegernertco.com. **Website:** www.thegernertco.com. Estab. 1996.

MEMBER AGENTS Sarah Burnes (literary fiction and nonfiction; children's fiction); Stephanie Cabot (represents a variety of genres, including crime/thrillers, commercial and literary fiction, latte lit, and nonfiction); Chris Parris-Lamb (nonfiction, literary fiction); Seth Fishman (looking for the new voice, the original idea, the entirely breathtaking creative angle in both fiction and nonfiction); Alia Hanna Habib (narrative nonfiction, literary fiction, and culinary titles); Will Roberts (smart, original thrillers with distinctive voices, compelling backgrounds, and fast-paced narratives); Erika Storella (nonfiction projects that make an argument, narrate a history, and/or provide a new perspective); Sarah Bolling (literary fiction, smart genre fiction —particularly sci-fi— memoir, pop culture, and style); Julia Eagleton (literary fiction and nonfiction: science, politics, nature, and memoir); Anna Worrall (smart women's literary and commercial fiction, psychological thrillers, and narrative nonfiction); Ellen Coughtrey (women's literary and commercial fiction, historical fiction, narrative nonfiction and smart, original thrillers, plus. well-written Southern Gothic anything); Jack Gernert (stories about heroes—both real and imagined); Libby McGuire (distinctive storytelling in both fiction and nonfiction, across a wide range of genres). At this time, Courtney Gatewood and Rebecca Gardner are closed to queries. See the website to find out the tastes of each agent.

REPRESENTS Nonfiction, novels. **Considers these fiction areas:** commercial, crime, fantasy, historical, literary, middle grade, science fiction, thriller, women's, young adult.

HOW TO CONTACT Please send us a query letter by e-mail to info@thegernertco.com describing the work you'd like to submit, along with some information about yourself and a sample chapter if appropriate. Please indicate in your letter which agent you are querying. Please do not send e-mails directly to individual agents. It's our policy to respond to your query only if we are interested in seeing more material, usually within 4-6 weeks. See company website for more instructions. Accepts simultaneous submissions. Obtains most new clients through recommendations from others, solicitations.

RECENT SALES *Partners*, by John Grisham; *The River Why*, by David James Duncan; *The Thin Green Line*, by Paul Sullivan; *A Fireproof Home for the Bride*, by Amy Scheibe; *The Only Girl in School*, by Natalie Standiford.

GHOSH LITERARY

E-mail: submissions@ghoshliterary.com. **Website:** www.ghoshliterary.com. **Contact:** Anna Ghosh. Member of AAR. Signatory of WGA.

REPRESENTS Nonfiction, fiction.

HOW TO CONTACT E-query. Please send an e-mail briefly introducing yourself and your work. Although no specific format is required, it is helpful to know the following: your qualifications for writing your book, including any publications and recognition for your work; who you expect to buy and read your book; similar books and authors. Accepts simultaneous submissions.

GLASS LITERARY MANAGEMENT

138 W. 25th St., 10th Floor, New York NY 10001. (646)237-4881. **E-mail:** alex@glassliterary.com; rick@glassliterary.com. **Website:** www.glassliterary.com. **Contact:** Alex Glass or Rick Pascocello. Estab. 2014. Member of AAR. Signatory of WGA.

MEMBER AGENTS Alex Glass; Rick Pascocello.

REPRESENTS Nonfiction, novels.

HOW TO CONTACT "Please send your query letter in the body of an e-mail and if we are interested, we will respond and ask for the complete manuscript or proposal. No attachments." Accepts simultaneous submissions.

RECENT SALES *100 Days of Cake*, by Shari Goldhagen; *The Red Car*, by Marcy Dermansky; *The Overnight Solution*, by Dr. Michael Breus; *So That Happened: A Memoir*, by Jon Cryer; *Bad Kid*, by David Crabb; *Finding Mr. Brightside*, by Jay Clark; *Strange Animals*, by Chad Kultgen.

GLOBAL LION INTELLECTUAL PROPERTY MANAGEMENT

P.O. Box 669238, Pompano Beach FL 33066. **E-mail:** queriesgloballionmgt@gmail.com. **Website:** www.globallionmanagement.com. **Contact:** Peter Miller. Estab. 2013. Member of AAR. Signatory of WGA.

HOW TO CONTACT E-query. Global Lion Intellectual Property Management. Inc. accepts exclusive submissions only. "If your work is under consideration by another agency, please do not submit it to us." Below the query, paste a one page synopsis, a sample of your book (20 pages is fine), a short author bio, and any impressive social media links.

BARRY GOLDBLATT LITERARY LLC

320 7th Ave. #266, Brooklyn NY 11215. **E-mail:** query@bgliterary.com. **Website:** www.bgliterary.com. **Contact:** Barry Goldblatt; Jennifer Udden. Estab. 2000. Member of AAR. Signatory of WGA.

MEMBER AGENTS Barry Goldblatt; Jennifer Udden, query.judden@gmail.com (speculative fiction of all stripes, especially innovative science fiction or fantasy; contemporary/erotic/LGBT/paranormal/historical romance; contemporary or speculative YA; select mysteries, thrillers, and urban fantasies).

REPRESENTS Fiction. **Considers these fiction areas:** fantasy, middle grade, mystery, romance, science fiction, thriller, young adult.

HOW TO CONTACT "E-mail queries can be sent to query@bgliterary.com and should include the word 'query' in the subject line. To query Jen Udden specifically, e-mail queries can be sent to query.judden@gmail.com. Please know that we will read and respond to every e-query that we receive, provided it is properly addressed and follows the submission guidelines below. We will not respond to e-queries that are addressed to no one, or to multiple recipients. Your e-mail query should include the following within the body of the e-mail: your query letter, a synopsis of the book, and the first 5 pages of your manuscript. We will not open or respond to any e-mails that have attachments. If we like the sound of your work, we will request more from you. Our response time is 4 weeks on queries, 6-8 weeks on full manuscripts. If you haven't heard from us within that time, feel free to check in via e-mail." Accepts simultaneous submissions. Obtains clients through referrals, queries, and conferences.

TERMS Agent receives 15% commission on domestic sales; 20% on foreign and dramatic sales. Offers written contract. 60 days notice must be given to terminate contract.

TIPS "We're a hands-on agency, focused on building an author's career, not just making an initial sale. We don't care about trends or what's hot; we just want to sign great writers."

FRANCES GOLDIN LITERARY AGENCY, INC.

214 W. 29th St., Suite 410, New York NY 10001. (212)777-0047. **Fax:** (212)228-1660. **Website:** www.goldinlit.com. Estab. 1977. Member of AAR.

MEMBER AGENTS Frances Goldin, founder/president; Ellen Geiger, vice president/principal (nonfiction: history, biography, progressive politics, photography, science and medicine, women, religion and serious investigative journalism; fiction: literary thriller, and novels in general that provoke and challenge the status quo, as well as historical and multicultural works. Please no New Age, romance, how-to or right-wing politics); Matt McGowan, agent/rights director, mm@goldinlit.com, (literary fiction, essays, history, memoir, journalism, biography, music, popular culture & science, sports [particularly soccer], narrative nonfiction, cultural studies, as well as literary travel, crime, food, suspense and sci-fi); Sam Stoloff, vice president/principal, (literary fiction, memoir, history, accessible sociology and philosophy, cultural studies, serious journalism, narrative and topical nonfiction with a progressive orientation); Ria Julien, agent/counsel; Nina Cochran, literary assistant.

REPRESENTS Nonfiction, novels. **Considers these fiction areas:** historical, literary, mainstream, multicultural, suspense, thriller.

HOW TO CONTACT There is an online submission process you can find online. Responds in 4-6 weeks to queries.

IRENE GOODMAN LITERARY AGENCY

27 W. 24th St., Suite 700B, New York NY 10010. **E-mail:** miriam.queries@irenegoodman.com, barbara.queries@irenegoodman.com, rachel.queries@irenegoodman.com, kim.queries@irenegoodman.com, victoria.queries@irenegoodman.com, irene.queries@irenegoodman.com, brita.queries@irenegoodman.com. **E-mail:** submissions@irenegoodman.com. **Website:** www.irenegoodman.com. **Contact:** Brita Lundberg. Estab. 1978. Member of AAR. Represents 150 clients.

MEMBER AGENTS Irene Goodman, Miriam Kriss, Barbara Poelle, Rachel Ekstrom, Kim Perel, Brita Lundberg, Victoria Marini.

REPRESENTS Nonfiction, fiction, novels, juvenile books. **Considers these fiction areas:** action, crime, detective, family saga, historical, horror, middle grade, mystery, romance, science fiction, suspense, thriller, urban fantasy, women's, young adult.

HOW TO CONTACT Query. Submit synopsis, first 10 pages pasted into the body of the email. E-mail queries only! See the website submission page. No e-mail attachments. Query 1 agent only. Accepts simultaneous submissions. Responds in 2 months to queries. Consult website for each agent's submission guidelines.

TERMS 15% commission.

TIPS "We are receiving an unprecedented amount of e-mail queries. If you find that the mailbox is full, please try again in two weeks. E-mail queries to our personal addresses will not be answered. E-mails to our personal inboxes will be deleted."

DOUG GRAD LITERARY AGENCY, INC.

156 Prospect Park West, #3L, Brooklyn NY 11215. (718)788-6067. **E-mail:** query@dgliterary.com. **Website:** www.dgliterary.com. **Contact:** Doug Grad. Estab. 2008. Member of AAR. Signatory of WGA. Represents 50+ clients.

MEMBER AGENTS Doug Grad (narrative nonfiction, military, sports, celebrity memoir, thrillers, mysteries, cozies, historical fiction, music, style, business, home improvement, cookbooks, science and theater).

REPRESENTS Nonfiction, fiction, novels. **Considers these fiction areas:** action, adventure, commercial, crime, detective, historical, horror, literary, mainstream, military, mystery, police, romance, science fiction, suspense, thriller, war, young adult.

HOW TO CONTACT Query by e-mail first. No sample material unless requested; no printed submissions by mail. Accepts simultaneous submissions. Due to the volume of queries, it's impossible to give a response time.

RECENT SALES *The Next Greatest Generation*, by Joseph L. Galloway and Marvin J. Wolf (Thomas Nelson); *Game Face: A Lifetime of Hard-Learned Lessons On and Off the Basketball Court*, by Bernard King with Jerome Preisler (Da Capo); Dan Morgan thriller series, by Leo Maloney (Kensington); Cajun Country cozy mystery series, by Ellen Byron (Crooked Lane); *Please Don't Feed the Mayor* and *Alaskan Catch*, by Sue Pethick (Kensington).

SANFORD J. GREENBURGER ASSOCIATES, INC.

55 Fifth Ave., New York NY 10003. (212)206-5600. **Fax:** (212)463-8718. **Website:** www.greenburger.com. Member of AAR. Represents 500 clients.

MEMBER AGENTS Matt Bialer, querymb@sjga.com (fantasy, science fiction, thrillers, and mysteries as well as a select group of literary writers, and also loves smart narrative nonfiction including books about current events, popular culture, biography, history, music, race, and sports); Brenda Bowen, querybb@sjga.com (literary fiction, writers and illustrators of picture books, chapter books, and middle-grade and teen fiction); Faith Hamlin, fhamlin@sjga.com (receives submissions by referral); Heide Lange, queryhl@sjga.com (receives submissions by referral); Daniel Mandel, querydm@sjga.com (literary and commercial fiction, as well as memoirs and nonfiction about business, art, history, politics, sports, and popular culture); Rachael Dillon Fried, rfried@sjga.com (both fiction and nonfiction authors, with a keen interest in unique literary voices, women's fiction, narrative nonfiction, memoir, and comedy); Stephanie Delman, sdelman@sjga.com (literary/upmarket contemporary fiction, psychological thrillers/suspense, and atmospheric, near-historical fiction); Ed Maxwell, emaxwell@sjga.com (expert and narrative nonfiction authors, novelists and graphic novelists, as well as children's book authors and illustrators).

REPRESENTS Nonfiction, fiction, novels, juvenile books. **Considers these fiction areas:** commercial, crime, family saga, fantasy, feminist, historical, literary, middle grade, multicultural, mystery, picture books, romance, science fiction, thriller, women's, young adult.

HOW TO CONTACT E-query. "Please look at each agent's profile page for current information about what each agent is looking for and for the correct email address to use for queries to that agent. Please be sure to use the correct query e-mail address for each agent." Agents may not respond to all queries; will respond within 6-8 weeks if interested. Obtains most new clients through recommendations from others.

TERMS Agent receives 15% commission on domestic sales; 20% commission on foreign sales. Charges for photocopying and books for foreign and subsidiary rights submissions.

THE GREENHOUSE LITERARY AGENCY

E-mail: submissions@greenhouseliterary.com. **Website:** www.greenhouseliterary.com. **Contact:** Sarah Davies. Estab. 2008. Member of AAR. Other memberships include SCBWI. Represents 50 clients.

MEMBER AGENTS Sarah Davies, vice president (fiction and nonfiction by North American authors, chapter books through to middle grade and young adult); Polly Nolan, agent (fiction by UK, Irish, Commonwealth–including Australia, NZ and India–authors, plus European authors writing in English, author/illustrators (texts under 1,000 words) to young fiction series, through middle grade and young adult).

REPRESENTS Juvenile books. **Considers these fiction areas:** juvenile, young adult.

HOW TO CONTACT Query 1 agent only. Put the target agent's name in the subject line. Paste the first 5 pages of your story after the query. Accepts simultaneous submissions.

TERMS Agent receives 15% commission on domestic sales; 25% commission on foreign sales. Offers written contract. This agency occasionally charges for submission copies to film agents or foreign publishers.

RECENT SALES *The Preacher Woods*, by Ashley Elston (Disney-Hyperion); *The Science of Breakable Things*, by Tae Keller (Random House); *We Speak in Storms*, by Natalie Lund (Philomel); *When We Wake*, by Elle Cosimano; *Secrets of Topsea* , by Kir Fox & M. Shelley Coats; *The Bigfoot Files*, by Lindsay Eagar (Candlewick); *Wanted: Women Mathematicians*, by Tami Lewis Brown & Debbie Loren Dunn (Disney-Hyperion); *Fake*, by Donna Cooner (Scholastic).

WRITERS CONFERENCES Bologna Children's Book Fair, ALA and SCBWI conferences, BookExpo America.

TIPS "Before submitting material, authors should visit the Greenhouse Literary Agency website and carefully read all submission guidelines."

KATHRYN GREEN LITERARY AGENCY, LLC

157 Columbus Ave., Suite 510, New York NY 10023. (212)245-4225. **E-mail:** query@kgreenagency.com. **Website:** www.kathryngreenliteraryagency.com. **Contact:** Kathy Green. Estab. 2004. Other memberships include Women's Media Group.

REPRESENTS Nonfiction, fiction, novels, short story collections, juvenile books. **Considers these fiction areas:** commercial, crime, detective, family saga, historical, humor, juvenile, literary, mainstream, middle grade, multicultural, mystery, police, romance, satire, suspense, thriller, women's, young adult.

HOW TO CONTACT Query by e-mail. Send no attachments unless requested. Do not send queries via regular mail. Responds in 4 weeks. "Queries do not have to be exclusive; however if further material is requested, please be in touch before accepting other representation." Accepts simultaneous submissions. Obtains most new clients through recommendations from others, solicitations, conferences.

TERMS Agent receives 15% commission on domestic sales; 20% commission on foreign sales.

RECENT SALES *Jigsaw Jungle*, by Kristin Levine; *Jane, Anonymous*, by Laurie Faria, Stolarz; *To Woo a Wicked Widow*, by Jenna Jaxon.

GREGORY & COMPANY AUTHORS' AGENTS

David Higham Associates, Waverley House, 7–12 Noel St., London W1F 8GQ England. 020 7434 5900. **E-mail:** laura@gregoryandcompany.co.uk; sara@gregoryandcompany.co.uk; info@gregoryandcompany.co.uk. **E-mail:** maryjones@gregoryandcompany.co.uk. **Website:** www.gregoryandcompany.co.uk. **Contact:** Laura Darpetti. Estab. 1987. Other memberships include AAA. Represents 60 clients.

MEMBER AGENTS Jane Gregory (English language and Film and TV sales); Claire Morris (Translation rights sales); Stephanie Glencross and Mary Jones (Editorial); Sara Langham (Editorial Assistant); Laura Darpetti (Rights Assistant).

REPRESENTS Fiction, novels. **Considers these fiction areas:** commercial, crime, detective, historical, literary, mystery, police, suspense, thriller, women's.

HOW TO CONTACT Submit outline of the complete plot, the first three chapters or up to 50 pages by e-mail or by post together with publishing history, and a brief author biography. Send submissions to Mary Jones, submissions editor: maryjones@gregoryandcompany.co.uk. If by post, include a SASE. Accepts simultaneous submissions. Allow 3 or 4 weeks for a response. Returns materials only with SASE. Obtains most new clients through recommendations from others.

TERMS Agent receives 15% commission on domestic sales and 20% commission on foreign sales. Offers written contract; 1-month notice must be given to terminate contract. Charges clients for photocopying of whole typescripts and copies of book for submissions.

GREYHAUS LITERARY

3021 20th St., Pl. SW, Puyallup WA 98373. **E-mail:** scott@greyhausagency.com. **E-mail:** submissions@greyhausagency.com. **Website:** www.greyhausagency.com. **Contact:** Scott Eagan, member RWA. Estab. 2003. Member of AAR. Signatory of WGA.

REPRESENTS Novels. **Considers these fiction areas:** new adult, romance, women's.

HOW TO CONTACT Submissions to Greyhaus can be done in one of three ways: 1) A standard query letter via email. If using this method, do not attach documents or send anything else other than a query letter. 2) Use the Submission Form found on the website on the Contact page. Or 3) send a query, the first 3 pages and a synopsis of no more than 3-5 pages (and a SASE), using a snail mail submission. Accepts simultaneous submissions. Responds in up to 3 months.

JILL GRINBERG LITERARY MANAGEMENT

392 Vanderbilt Ave., Brooklyn NY 11238. (212)620-5883. **E-mail:** info@jillgrinbergliterary.com. **Website:** www.jillgrinbergliterary.com. Estab. 1999. Member of AAR.

MEMBER AGENTS Jill Grinberg; Cheryl Pientka; Katelyn Detweiler; Sophia Seidner.

REPRESENTS Nonfiction, fiction, novels. **Considers these fiction areas:** fantasy, historical, juvenile, literary, mainstream, middle grade, multicultural, picture books, romance, science fiction, women's, young adult.

HOW TO CONTACT "Please send queries via e-mail to info@jillgrinbergliterary.com–include your query letter, addressed to the agent of your choice, along with the first 50 pages of your ms pasted into the body of the e-mail or attached as a doc. or docx. file. We also accept queries via mail, though e-mail is preferred. Please send your query letter and the first 50 pages of your ms by mail, along with a SASE, to the attention of your agent of choice. Please note that unless a SASE with sufficient postage is provided, your materials will not be returned. As submissions are shared within the office, please only query one agent with your project." Accepts simultaneous submissions.

TIPS "We prefer submissions by electronic mail."

JILL GROSJEAN LITERARY AGENCY

1390 Millstone Rd., Sag Harbor NY 11963. (631)725-7419. **E-mail:** jilllit310@aol.com. **Contact:** Jill Grosjean. Estab. 1999.

REPRESENTS Novels. **Considers these fiction areas:** historical, literary, mainstream, mystery, women's.

HOW TO CONTACT E-mail queries preferred, no attachments. No cold calls, please. Accepts simultaneous submissions, though when manuscript requested, requires exclusive reading time. Accepts simultaneous submissions. Responds in 1 week to queries; month to mss. Obtains most new clients through recommendations and through recommendations and solicitations.

TERMS Agent receives 15% commission on domestic sales; 20% commission on foreign and film sales.

RECENT SALES *The Gold Pawn*, by L.A. Chandlar (Kensington Books); *Caught in Time*, by Julie McEwain (Pegasus Books); *A Murder in Time*, by Julie McEwain (Pegasus Books); *A Twist in Time*, by Julie McEwain (Pegasus Books); *The Silver Gun*, by LA Chandlar (Kensington Books); *The Edison Effect*, by Bernadette Pajer (Poison Pen Press); *Threading the Needle*, by Marie Bostwick (Kensington Publishing); *Tim Cratchit's Christmas Carol: A Novel of Scrooge's Legacy*, by Jim Piecuch (Simon & Schuster); *The Lighterman's Curse*, by Loretta Marion (Crooked Lane Books).

WRITERS CONFERENCES Thrillerfest, Texas Writer's League, Book Passage Mystery's Writer's Conference, Writer's Market Conference.

LAURA GROSS LITERARY AGENCY

E-mail: assistant@lg-la.com. **Website:** www.lg-la.com. Estab. 1988. Represents 30 clients.

REPRESENTS Nonfiction, novels.

HOW TO CONTACT Queries accepted online via online form on LGLA Submittable site. No e-mail queries. "On the submission form, please include a concise but substantive cover letter. You may include the first 6,000 words of your manuscript in the form as well. We will request further sample chapters from you at a later date, if we think your work suits our list." There may be a delay of several weeks in responding to your query. Accepts simultaneous submissions.

TERMS Agent receives 15% commission on domestic sales; 20% commission on foreign sales. Offers written contract.

HARTLINE LITERARY AGENCY

123 Queenston Dr., Pittsburgh PA 15235-5429. (412)829-2483. **E-mail:** jim@hartlineliterary.com. **Website:** www.hartlineliterary.com. **Contact:** James D. Hart. Estab. 1992. ACFW Represents 400 clients.

MEMBER AGENTS Jim Hart, principal agent (jim@hartlineliterary.com); Joyce Hart, founder (joyce@hartlineliterary.com); Diana Flegal (diana@hartlineliterary.com); Linda Glaz (linda@hartlineliterary.com); Cyle Young (cyle@hartlineliterary.com).

REPRESENTS Nonfiction, fiction, novels, novellas, juvenile books, scholarly books. **Considers these fiction areas:** action, adventure, commercial, contemporary issues, crime, detective, family saga, fantasy, frontier, historical, humor, inspirational, literary, mystery, new adult, religious, romance, science fiction, suspense, thriller, urban fantasy, westerns, women's, young adult.

HOW TO CONTACT E-query preferred, USPS to the Pittsburgh office. Target one agent only. "All e-mail submissions sent to Hartline Agents should be sent as a MS Word doc attached to an e-mail with 'submission: title, authors name and word count' in the subject line. A proposal is a single document, not a collection of files. Place the query letter in the email itself. Do not send the entire proposal in the body of the e-mail or send PDF files." Further guidelines online. Accepts simultaneous submissions. Responds in 2 months to queries; 3 months to mss. Obtains most new clients through recommendations from others, and at conferences.

TERMS Agent receives 15% commission on domestic sales. Offers written contract.

WRITERS CONFERENCES ACFW; Oregon Christian Writers; Realm Makers; Blue Ridge Mountain Christian Writers; Florida Christian Writers; Write to Publish; Mount Hermon Conference; Taylor's Professional Writing Conference; Maranatha Christian Writers Conference; Write His Answer Christian Conferences.

TIPS Please follow the guidelines on our web site www.hartlineliterary for the fastest response to your proposal. E-mail proposals only.

ANTONY HARWOOD LIMITED

103 Walton St., Oxford OX2 6EB United Kingdom. (44)(018)6555-9615. **E-mail:** mail@antonyharwood.com. **Website:** www.antonyharwood.com. **Contact:** Antony Harwood; James Macdonald Lockhart; Jo Williamson. Estab. 2000. Represents 52 clients.

MEMBER AGENTS Antony Harwood, James Macdonald Lockhart, Jo Williamson (children's).

REPRESENTS Nonfiction, novels. **Considers these fiction areas:** action, adventure, cartoon, comic books, confession, crime, detective, erotica, ethnic, experimental, family saga, fantasy, feminist, frontier, gay, hi-lo, historical, horror, humor, lesbian, literary, mainstream, military, multicultural, multimedia, mystery, occult, picture books, plays, police, regional, religious, romance, satire, science fiction, spiritual, sports, suspense, thriller, translation, war, westerns, young adult, gothic.

HOW TO CONTACT "We are happy to consider submissions of fiction and nonfiction in every genre and category except for screenwriting and poetry. If you wish to submit your work to us for consideration, please send a covering letter, brief outline and the opening 50 pages by e-mail. If you want to post your material to us, please be sure to enclose an SAE or the cost of return postage." Replies if interested. Accepts simultaneous submissions. Responds in 2 months to queries.

TERMS Agent receives 15% commission on domestic sales; 20% commission on foreign sales.

JOHN HAWKINS & ASSOCIATES, INC.

80 Maiden Ln., Suite 1503, New York NY 10038. (212)807-7040. **E-mail:** jha@jhalit.com. **Website:** www.jhalit.com. **Contact:** Moses Cardona (rights and translations); Annie Kronenberg (permissions);

Warren Frazier, literary agent; Anne Hawkins, literary agent; William Reiss, literary agent. Estab. 1893. Member of AAR. The Author Guild Represents 100+ clients.

MEMBER AGENTS Moses Cardona, moses@jhalit.com (commercial fiction, suspense, business, science, and multicultural fiction); Warren Frazier, frazier@jhalit.com (fiction; nonfiction, specifically technology, history, world affairs and foreign policy); Anne Hawkins, ahawkins@jhalit.com (thrillers to literary fiction to serious nonfiction; interested in science, history, public policy, medicine and women's issues).

REPRESENTS Nonfiction, fiction, novels, short story collections, novellas, juvenile books. **Considers these fiction areas:** commercial, historical, literary, multicultural, suspense, thriller.

HOW TO CONTACT Query. Include the word "Query" in the subject line. For fiction, include 1-3 chapters of your book as a single Word attachment. For nonfiction, include your proposal as a single attachment. E-mail a particular agent directly if you are targeting one. Accepts simultaneous submissions. Responds in 1 month to queries. Obtains most new clients through recommendations from others.

TERMS Agent receives 15% commission on domestic sales; 20% commission on foreign sales. Charges clients for photocopying.

RECENT SALES *Forty Rooms*, by Olga Grushin; *A Book of American Martyrs*, by Joyce Carol Oates; *City on Edge*, by Stefanie Pintoff; *Cold Earth*, by Ann Cleeves; *The Good Lieutenant*, by Whitney Terrell; *Grief Cottage*, by Gail Godwin.

☺ HELEN HELLER AGENCY INC.

4-216 Heath St. W., Toronto ON M5P 1N7 Canada. (416)489-0396. **E-mail:** info@helenhelleragency.com. **Website:** www.helenhelleragency.com. **Contact:** Helen Heller. Represents 30+ clients.

MEMBER AGENTS Helen Heller, helen@helenhelleragency.com (thrillers and front-list general fiction); Sarah Heller, sarah@helenhelleragency.com (front list commercial YA and adult fiction, with a particular interest in high concept historical fiction); Barbara Berson, barbara@helenhelleragency.com (literary fiction, nonfiction, and YA).

REPRESENTS Nonfiction, novels. **Considers these fiction areas:** commercial, crime, historical, literary, mainstream, thriller, young adult.

HOW TO CONTACT E-mail info@helenhelleragency.com. Submit a brief synopsis, publishing history, author bio, and writing sample, pasted in the body of the e-mail. No attachments with e-queries. Accepts simultaneous submissions. Responds within 3 months if interested. Accepts simultaneous submissions. Obtains most new clients through recommendations from others, solicitations.

TIPS "Whether you are an author searching for an agent, or whether an agent has approached you, it is in your best interest to first find out who the agent represents, what publishing houses has that agent sold to recently and what foreign sales have been made. You should be able to go to the bookstore, or search online and find the books the agent refers to. Many authors acknowledge their agents in the front or back or their books."

RICHARD HENSHAW GROUP

145 W. 28th St., 12th Floor, New York NY 10001. (212)414-1172. **E-mail:** submissions@henshaw.com. **Website:** www.richardhenshawgroup.com. **Contact:** Rich Henshaw. Member of AAR.

REPRESENTS Novels. **Considers these fiction areas:** fantasy, historical, horror, literary, mainstream, mystery, police, romance, science fiction, thriller, young adult.

HOW TO CONTACT "Please feel free to submit a query letter in the form of an e-mail of fewer than 250 words to submissions@henshaw.com address." No snail mail queries. Accepts simultaneous submissions. Obtains most new clients through recommendations from others, solicitations, conferences.

TERMS Agent receives 15% commission on domestic sales; 20% commission on foreign sales. No written contract. Charges clients for photocopying and book orders.

TIPS "While we do not have any reason to believe that our submission guidelines will change in the near future, writers can find up-to-date submission policy information on our website. Always include a SASE with correct return postage."

HILL NADELL LITERARY AGENCY

6442 Santa Monica Blvd., Suite 201, Los Angeles CA 90038. (310)860-9605. **E-mail:** queries@hillnadell.com. **Website:** www.hillnadell.com. Represents 100 clients.

MEMBER AGENTS Bonnie Nadell (nonfiction books include works on current affairs and food as well as memoirs and other narrative nonfiction; in fiction, she represents thrillers along with upmarket women's and literary fiction); Dara Hyde (literary and genre fiction, narrative nonfiction, graphic novels, memoir and the occasional young adult novel).

REPRESENTS Nonfiction, novels. **Considers these fiction areas:** literary, mainstream, thriller, women's, young adult.

HOW TO CONTACT Send a query and SASE. If you would like your materials returned, please include adequate postage. To submit electronically: Send your query letter and the first 5-10 pages to queries@hillnadell.com. No attachments. Due to the high volume of submissions the agency receives, it cannot guarantee a response to all e-mailed queries. Accepts simultaneous submissions.

TERMS Agent receives 15% commission on domestic and film sales; 20% commission on foreign sales. Charges clients for photocopying and foreign mailings.

HOLLOWAY LITERARY

P.O. Box 771, Cary NC 27512. **E-mail:** submissions@hollowayliteraryagency.com. **Website:** hollowayliteraryagency.com. **Contact:** Nikki Terpilowski. Estab. 2011. Member of AAR. Signatory of WGA. International Thriller Writers and Romance Writers of America Represents 26 clients.

MEMBER AGENTS Nikki Terpilowski (romance, women's fiction, Southern fiction, historical fiction, cozy mysteries, lifestyle no-fiction (minimalism, homesteading, southern, etc.) commercial, upmarket/book club fiction, African-American fiction of all types, literary); Rachel Burkot (young adult contemporary, women's fiction, upmarket/book club fiction, contemporary romance, Southern fiction, nonfiction).

REPRESENTS Nonfiction, fiction, movie scripts, feature film. **Considers these fiction areas:** action, adventure, commercial, contemporary issues, crime, detective, ethnic, family saga, fantasy, glitz, historical, inspirational, literary, mainstream, metaphysical, middle grade, military, multicultural, mystery, new adult, New Age, regional, romance, short story collections, spiritual, suspense, thriller, urban fantasy, war, women's, young adult.

HOW TO CONTACT Send query and first 15 pages of ms pasted into the body of e-mail to submissions@hollowayliteraryagency.com. In the subject header write: (Insert Agent's Name)/Title/Genre. Holloway Literary does accept submissions via mail (query letter and first 50 pages). Expect a response time of at least 3 months. Include e-mail address, phone number, social media accounts, and mailing address on your query letter. Accepts simultaneous submissions. Responds in 6-8 weeks. If the agent is interested, he/she'll respond with a request for more material.

HSG AGENCY

37 W. 28th St., 8th Floor, New York NY 10001. **E-mail:** channigan@hsgagency.com; jsalky@hsgagency.com; jgetzler@hsgagency.com; sroberts@hsgagency.com; leigh@hsgagency.com. **Website:** hsgagency.com. **Contact:** Carrie Hannigan; Jesseca Salky; Josh Getzler; Soumeya Roberts; Leigh Eisenman. Estab. 2011. Member of AAR. Signatory of WGA.

MEMBER AGENTS Carrie Hannigan (children's books, illustrators, YA and MG); Jesseca Salky (literary and mainstream fiction); Josh Getzler (foreign and historical fiction; both women's fiction, straightahead historical fiction, and thrillers and mysteries); Soumeya Roberts (literary fiction and narrative nonfiction); Leigh Eisenman (literary and upmarket fiction, foodie/cookbooks, health and fitness, lifestyle, and select narrative nonfiction).

REPRESENTS Nonfiction, fiction, novels, short story collections, juvenile books. **Considers these fiction areas:** adventure, commercial, contemporary issues, crime, detective, ethnic, experimental, family saga, fantasy, feminist, historical, humor, juvenile, literary, mainstream, middle grade, multicultural, mystery, picture books, science fiction, suspense, thriller, translation, women's, young adult.

HOW TO CONTACT Please send a query letter and the first 5 pages of your ms (within the e-mail–no attachments please) to the appropriate agent for your book. If it is a picture book, please include the entire ms. If you were referred to us, please mention it in the first line of your query. Please note that we do not represent screenplays, romance fiction, or religious fiction. If Carrie and Jesseca have not responded to your query within 10 weeks of submission, please consider this a pass. Due to the volume of queries Leigh receives, she will only respond to those in which she's interested.Soumeya will not be accepting new unsolicited queries until May 1, 2018. All queries received during that time will be deleted. All agents are open to new clients.

⃠ ICM PARTNERS

65 E. 55th St., New York NY 10022. (212)556-5600. **Website:** www.icmtalent.com. **Contact:** Literary Department. Member of AAR. Signatory of WGA.

REPRESENTS Nonfiction, fiction, novels.

HOW TO CONTACT Accepts simultaneous submissions.

INKLINGS LITERARY AGENCY

3419 Virginia Beach Blvd. #183, Virginia Beach VA 23452. **E-mail:** michelle@inklingsliterary.com. **E-mail:** query@inklingsliterary.com. **Website:** www. inklingsliterary.com. Estab. 2013. RWA, SinC, HRW.

MEMBER AGENTS Michelle Johnson, michelle@inklingsliterary.com (in adult and YA fiction, contemporary, suspense, thriller, mystery, horror, fantasy — including paranormal and supernatural elements within those genres), romance of every level, nonfiction in the areas of memoir and true crime); Dr. Jamie Bodnar Drowley, jamie@inklingsliterary.com (new adult fiction in the areas of romance [all subgenres], fantasy [urban fantasy, light sci-fi, steampunk], mystery and thrillers—as well as young adult [all subgenres] and middle grade stories); Naomi Davis, naomi@inklingsliterary.com (romance of any variety—including paranormal, fresh urban fantasy, general fantasy, new adult and light sci-fi; young adult in any of those same genres; memoirs about living with disabilities, facing criticism, and mental illness); Whitley Abell, whitley@inklingsliterary.com (young adult, middle grade, and select upmarket women's fiction); Alex Barba, alex@inklingsliterary.com (YA fiction).

REPRESENTS Nonfiction, fiction, novels, juvenile books. **Considers these fiction areas:** action, adventure, commercial, contemporary issues, crime, detective, erotica, ethnic, fantasy, feminist, gay, historical, horror, juvenile, lesbian, mainstream, metaphysical, middle grade, military, multicultural, multimedia, mystery, new adult, New Age, occult, paranormal, police, psychic, regional, romance, science fiction, spiritual, sports, supernatural, suspense, thriller, urban fantasy, war, women's, young adult.

HOW TO CONTACT E-queries only. To query, type "Query (Agent Name)" plus the title of your novel in the subject line, then please send your query letter, short synopsis, and first 10 pages pasted into the body

of the e-mail to query@inklingsliterary.com. Check the agency website to make sure that your targeted agent is currently open to submissions. Accepts simultaneous submissions. For queries, no response in 3 months is considered a rejection.

TERMS Agent takes 15% domestic, 20% subsidiary commission. Charges no fees.

INKWELL MANAGEMENT, LLC

521 Fifth Ave., Suite 2600, New York NY 10175. (212)922-3500. **Fax:** (212)922-0535. **E-mail:** info@inkwellmanagement.com. **E-mail:** submissions@inkwellmanagement.com. **Website:** www.inkwellmanagement.com. Represents 500 clients.

MEMBER AGENTS Stephen Barbara (select adult fiction and nonfiction); William Callahan (nonfiction of all stripes, especially American history and memoir, pop culture and illustrated books, as well as voice-driven fiction that stands out from the crowd); Michael V. Carlisle; Catherine Drayton (bestselling authors of books for children, young adults and women readers); David Forrer (literary, commercial, historical and crime fiction to suspense/thriller, humorous nonfiction and popular history); Alexis Hurley (literary and commercial fiction, memoir, narrative nonfiction and more); Nathaniel Jacks (memoir, narrative nonfiction, social sciences, health, current affairs, business, religion, and popular history, as well as fiction—literary and commercial, women's, young adult, historical, short story, among others); Jacqueline Murphy; (fiction, children's books, graphic novels and illustrated works, and compelling narrative nonfiction); Richard Pine; Eliza Rothstein (literary and commercial fiction, narrative nonfiction, memoir, popular science, and food writing); David Hale Smith; Kimberly Witherspoon; Jenny Witherell; Charlie Olson; Liz Parker (commercial and upmarket women's fiction and narrative, practical, and platform-driven nonfiction); George Lucas; Lyndsey Blessing; Claire Draper; Kate Falkoff; Claire Friedman; Michael Mungiello; Jessica Mileo; Corinne Sullivan; Maria Whelan.

REPRESENTS Novels. **Considers these fiction areas:** commercial, crime, historical, literary, middle grade, picture books, romance, short story collections, suspense, thriller, women's, young adult.

HOW TO CONTACT "In the body of your e-mail, please include a query letter and a short writing sample (1-2 chapters). We currently accept submissions in all genres except screenplays. Due to the volume of queries we receive, our response time may take up to 2 months. Feel free to put 'Query for [Agent Name]: [Your Book Title]' in the e-mail subject line." Accepts simultaneous submissions. Obtains most new clients through recommendations from others.

TERMS Agent receives 15% commission on domestic sales; 20% commission on foreign sales. Offers written contract.

TIPS "We will not read mss before receiving a letter of inquiry."

INTERNATIONAL TRANSACTIONS, INC.

P.O. Box 97, Gila NM 88038-0097. (845)373-9696. **E-mail:** Info@internationaltransactions.us. **Website:** www.intltrans.com. **Contact:** Peter Riva. Estab. 1975.

MEMBER AGENTS Peter Riva with Sandra Riva (part-time); JoAnn Collins (women's fiction, medical fiction).

REPRESENTS Nonfiction, fiction, novels, short story collections, juvenile books, scholarly books, illustrated books, anthologies. **Considers these fiction areas:** action, adventure, commercial, crime, detective, erotica, experimental, family saga, feminist, gay, historical, humor, inspirational, lesbian, literary, mainstream, middle grade, military, multicultural, mystery, new adult, picture books, police, satire, science fiction, spiritual, sports, suspense, thriller, translation, war, westerns, women's, young adult, chick lit.

HOW TO CONTACT In 2018, we will be extremely selective of new projects. First, e-query with an outline or synopsis. E-queries only. Put "Query: [Title]" in the e-mail subject line. Submissions or emails received without these conditions met are automatically discarded. Responds in 3 weeks to queries if interested; 5 weeks to ms after follow-up request. Obtains most new clients through recommendations from others.

TERMS Agent receives 15% (25%+ on illustrated books) commission on domestic sales; 20% commission on foreign sales and media rights. Offers written contract; 100-day notice must be given to terminate contract. No additional fees, ever.

JABBERWOCKY LITERARY AGENCY

49 W. 45th St., 12th Floor, New York NY 10036. **Website:** www.awfulagent.com. **Contact:** Joshua Bilmes. Estab. 1990. Other memberships include SFWA. Represents 80 clients.

MEMBER AGENTS Joshua Bilmes; Eddie Schneider; Lisa Rodgers.

REPRESENTS Nonfiction, fiction, novels, novellas, juvenile books. **Considers these fiction areas:** action, adventure, contemporary issues, crime, detective, ethnic, family saga, fantasy, feminist, gay, glitz, historical, horror, humor, juvenile, lesbian, literary, mainstream, middle grade, mystery, new adult, paranormal, police, psychic, regional, romance, satire, science fiction, sports, supernatural, thriller, women's, young adult.

HOW TO CONTACT "We are currently open to unsolicited queries. No e-mail, phone, or fax queries, please. Query with SASE. Please check our website, as there may be times during the year when we are not accepting queries. Query letter only; no manuscript material unless requested." Accepts simultaneous submissions. Responds in 3-6 weeks to queries. Obtains most new clients through solicitations, recommendation by current clients.

TERMS Agent receives 15% commission on domestic sales; 20% commission on foreign sales. Offers written contract, binding for 1 year. Charges clients for book purchases, photocopying, international book/ms mailing.

TIPS "In approaching with a query, the most important things to us are your credits and your biographical background to the extent it's relevant to your work. I (and most agents) will ignore the adjectives you may choose to describe your own work."

JANKLOW & NESBIT ASSOCIATES

285 Madison Ave., 21st Floor, New York NY 10017. (212)421-1700. **Fax:** (212)355-1403. **E-mail:** info@janklow.com. **E-mail:** submissions@janklow.com. **Website:** www.janklowandnesbit.com. Estab. 1989.

MEMBER AGENTS Morton L. Janklow; Anne Sibbald; Lynn Nesbit; Luke Janklow; PJ Mark (interests are eclectic, including short stories and literary novels. His nonfiction interests include journalism, popular culture, memoir/narrative, essays and cultural criticism); Paul Lucas (literary and commercial fiction, focusing on literary thrillers, science fiction and fantasy; also seeks narrative histories of ideas and objects, as well as biographies and popular science); Emma Parry (nonfiction by experts, but will consider outstanding literary fiction and upmarket commercial fiction); Kirby Kim (formerly of WME); Marya Spence; Allison Hunter; Melissa Flashman; Stefanie Lieberman.

REPRESENTS Nonfiction, fiction.

HOW TO CONTACT Be sure to address your submission to a particular agent. For fiction submissions, send an informative cover letter, a brief synopsis and the first 10 pages. "If you are sending an e-mail submission, please include the sample pages in the body of the e-mail below your query. For nonfiction submissions, send an informative cover letter, a full outline, and the first 10 pages of the ms. If you are sending an e-mail submission, please include the sample pages in the body of the e-mail below your query. For picture book submissions, send an informative cover letter, full outline, and include a picture book dummy and at least one full-color sample. If you are sending an e-mail submission, please attach a picture book dummy as a PDF and the full-color samples as JPEGs or PDFs." Accepts simultaneous submissions. Due to the volume of submissions received, please note that we cannot respond to every query. We shall contact you if we wish to pursue your submission. Obtains most new clients through recommendations from others.

TIPS "Please send a short query with first 10 pages or artwork."

J DE S ASSOCIATES, INC.

9 Shagbark Rd., Norwalk CT 06854. (203)838-7571. **E-mail:** jdespoel@aol.com. **Website:** www.jdesassociates.com. **Contact:** Jacques de Spoelberch. Estab. 1975.

REPRESENTS Novels. **Considers these fiction areas:** crime, detective, frontier, historical, juvenile, literary, mainstream, mystery, New Age, police, suspense, westerns, young adult.

HOW TO CONTACT "Brief queries by regular mail and e-mail are welcomed for fiction and nonfiction, but kindly do not include sample proposals or other material unless specifically requested to do so." Accepts simultaneous submissions. Responds in 2 months to queries. Obtains most new clients through recommendations from authors and other clients.

TERMS Agent receives 15% commission on domestic sales; 20% commission on foreign sales. Charges clients for foreign postage and photocopying.

RECENT SALES Joshilyn Jackson's new novel *A Grown-Up Kind of Pretty* (Grand Central); Margaret George's final Tudor historical *Elizabeth I* (Penguin); the fifth in Leighton Gage's series of Brazilian thrillers *A Vine in the Blood* (Soho); Genevieve Graham's romance *Under the Same Sky* (Berkley Sensation); Hil-

ary Holladay's biography of the early Beat Herbert Huncke, *American Hipster* (Magnus); Ron Rozelle's *My Boys and Girls Are In There: The 1937 New London School Explosion* (Texas A&M); the concluding novel in Dom Testa's YA science fiction series, *The Galahad Legacy* (Tor); and Bruce Coston's new collection of animal stories *The Gift of Pets* (St. Martin's Press).

THE CAROLYN JENKS AGENCY

30 Cambridge Park Dr. Unit 3140, Cambridge MA 02140. (617)233-9130. **E-mail:** carolynjenks@comcast.net. **Website:** www.carolynjenksagency.com. **Contact:** Carolyn Jenks. Estab. 1987. Signatory of WGA. Represents 48 clients.

REPRESENTS Nonfiction, fiction, novels, short story collections, novellas, feature film, episodic drama, documentary, miniseries, theatrical stage play. **Considers these fiction areas:** contemporary issues, crime, detective, ethnic, family saga, fantasy, feminist, gay, historical, lesbian, literary, mainstream, mystery, short story collections, thriller, women's.

HOW TO CONTACT Please submit a one page query including a brief bio via the form on the agency website. Queries are reviewed on a rolling basis, and we will follow up directly with the author if there is interest. No cold calls.

TERMS Offers written contract, 1-3 years depending on the project. Standard agency commissions. No fees.

RECENT SALES *Snafu*, by Miryam Sivan, Cuidano Press; *The Land of Forgotten Girls*, by Erin Kelly, Harper Collins; *The Christos Mosaic*, by Vincent Czyz, Blank Slate Press; *A Tale of Two Maidens*, by Anne Echols, Bagwyn Books; *Esther*, by Rebecca Kanner, Simon and Schuster; *Magnolia City*, by Duncan Alderson, Kensington Books.

TIPS E-mail contact only. Do not query for more than one property at a time. Response within two weeks unless otherwise notified.

JERNIGAN LITERARY AGENCY

P.O. Box 741624, Dallas TX 75374. (972)722-4838. **E-mail:** jerniganliterary@gmail.com. **Contact:** Barry Jernigan. Estab. 2010. Represents 45 clients.

MEMBER AGENTS Barry Jernigan (eclectic tastes in nonfiction and fiction; nonfiction interests include women's issues, gay/lesbian, ethnic/cultural, memoirs, true crime; fiction interests include mystery, suspense and thriller).

REPRESENTS Nonfiction, fiction, novels, movie scripts, feature film. **Considers these fiction areas:** historical, mainstream, mystery, romance, thriller.

HOW TO CONTACT E-mail your query with a synopsis, brief bio and the first few pages embedded (no attachments). "We do not accept unsolicited manuscripts. We accept submissions via e-mail only. No snail mail accepted." Accepts simultaneous submissions. Responds in 2 weeks to queries; 6 weeks to mss. Obtains new clients through conferences and word of mouth.

TERMS Agent receives 15% commission.

JET LITERARY ASSOCIATES

941 Calle Mejia, #507, Santa Fe NM 87501. (505)780-0721. **E-mail:** etp@jetliterary.com. **Website:** www.jetliterary.wordpress.com. **Contact:** Liz Trupin-Pulli. Estab. 1975.

MEMBER AGENTS Liz Trupin-Pulli (adult fiction/nonfiction; romance, mysteries, parenting); Jim Trupin (adult fiction/nonfiction, military history, pop culture).

REPRESENTS Nonfiction, fiction, novels, short story collections.

HOW TO CONTACT Only an e-query should be sent at first. Accepts simultaneous submissions. Responds in 1 week to queries; 8-12 weeks to mss. Obtains most new clients through recommendations from others, solicitations, conferences.

TERMS Agent receives 15% commission on domestic sales; 10% commission on foreign sales, while foreign agent receives 10%. Offers written agency contract, binding for 3 years. This agency charges for reimbursement of mailing and any photocopying.

TIPS "Do not write cute queries; stick to a straightforward message that includes the title and what your book is about, why you are suited to write this particular book, and what you have written in the past (if anything), along with a bit of a bio."

LAWRENCE JORDAN LITERARY AGENCY

231 Lenox Ave., Suite One, New York NY 10027. (212)662-7871. **Fax:** (212)865-7171. **E-mail:** ljlagency@aol.com. **Contact:** Lawrence Jordan, president.

REPRESENTS Novels.

HOW TO CONTACT Online submissions only. Please note that the agency takes on only a few new clients each year. Accepts simultaneous submissions.

TERMS Agent receives 15% commission on domestic sales; 20% commission on foreign and film sales. Charges for long-distance calls, photocopying, foreign submission costs, postage, cables, messengers.

⊘ NATASHA KERN LITERARY AGENCY

White Salmon WA 98672. **E-mail:** via website. **Website:** www.natashakern.com. **Contact:** Natasha Kern. Estab. 1986. Other memberships include RWA, MWA, SinC, The Authors Guild, and American Society of Journalists and Authors. Represents 40 clients.

REPRESENTS Fiction, novels. **Considers these fiction areas:** commercial, historical, inspirational, mainstream, multicultural, mystery, romance, suspense, women's, Only Inspirational fiction in these genres.

HOW TO CONTACT This agency is currently closed to unsolicited fiction and nonfiction submissions. Submissions only via referral. Obtains new clients by referral only.

TERMS Agent receives 15% commission on domestic sales; 20% commission on foreign sales; 15% commission on film sales.

WRITERS CONFERENCES RWA National Conference; ACFW Conference.

TIPS "Your chances of being accepted for representation will be greatly enhanced by going to our website first. Our idea of a dream client is someone who participates in a mutually respectful business relationship, is clear about needs and goals, and communicates about career planning. If we know what you need and want, we can help you achieve it. A dream client has a storytelling gift, a commitment to a writing career, a desire to learn and grow, and a passion for excellence. We want clients who are expressing their own unique voice and truly have something of their own to communicate. This client understands that many people have to work together for a book to succeed and that everything in publishing takes far longer than one imagines. Trust and communication are truly essential."

HARVEY KLINGER, INC.

300 W. 55th St., Suite 11V, New York NY 10019. (212)581-7068. **E-mail:** queries@harveyklinger.com. **Website:** www.harveyklinger.com. **Contact:** Harvey Klinger. Estab. 1977. Member of AAR. PEN Represents 100 clients.

MEMBER AGENTS Harvey Klinger, harvey@harveyklinger.com; David Dunton, david@harveyklinger.com (popular culture, music-related books, literary fiction, young adult, fiction, and memoirs); Andrea Somberg, andrea@harveyklinger.com (literary fiction, commercial fiction, romance, sci-fi/fantasy, mysteries/thrillers, young adult, middle grade, quality narrative nonfiction, popular culture, how-to, self-help, humor, interior design, cookbooks, health/fitness); Wendy Silbert Levinson, wendy@harveyklinger.com (literary and commercial fiction, occasional children's YA or MG, wide variety of nonfiction); Rachel Ridout, rachel@harveyklinger.com (children's MG and YA).

REPRESENTS Nonfiction, fiction, novels, juvenile books. **Considers these fiction areas:** action, adventure, commercial, contemporary issues, crime, detective, erotica, family saga, fantasy, gay, glitz, historical, horror, juvenile, lesbian, literary, mainstream, middle grade, mystery, new adult, police, romance, suspense, thriller, women's, young adult.

HOW TO CONTACT Use online e-mail submission form on the website, or query with SASE via snail mail. No phone or fax queries. Don't send unsolicited mss or e-mail attachments. Make submission letter to the point and as brief as possible. Accepts simultaneous submissions. Responds in 2-4 weeks to queries, if interested. Obtains most new clients through recommendations from others.

TERMS Agent receives 15% commission on domestic sales; 25% commission on foreign sales. Offers written contract. Charges for photocopying mss and overseas postage for mss.

RECENT SALES *Land of the Afternoon Sun*, by Barbara Wood; *I Am Not a Serial Killer*, by Dan Wells; *Me, Myself and Us*, by Brian Little; *The Secret of Magic*, by Deborah Johnson; *Children of the Mist*, by Paula Quinn. Other clients include George Taber, Terry Kay, Scott Mebus, Jacqueline Kolosov, Jonathan Maberry, Tara Altebrando, Alex McAuley, Eva Nagorski, Greg Kot, Justine Musk, Michael Northrup, Nina LaCour, Ashley Kahn, Barbara De Angelis, Robert Patton, Augusta Trobaugh, Deborah Blum, Jonathan Skariton.

KNEERIM & WILLIAMS

90 Canal St., Boston MA 02114. **Website:** www.kwlit.com. Also located in Santa Fe, NM, with affiliated office in NYC. Estab. 1990.

MEMBER AGENTS Katherine Flynn, kflynn@kwlit.com (history, biography, politics, current affairs, adventure, nature, pop culture, science, and psychology for nonfiction and particularly loves exciting narrative nonfiction; literary and commercial fiction with urban or foreign locales, crime novels, insight into women's lives, biting wit, and historical settings); Jill Kneerim, jill@kwlit.com (narrative history; big ideas; sociology; psychology and anthropology; biography; women's issues; and good writing); John Taylor ("Ike") Williams, jtwilliams@kwblit.com (biography, history, politics, natural science, and anthropology); Carol Franco, carolfranco@comcast.net (business; nonfiction; distinguished self-help/how-to); Lucy Cleland, lucy@kwlit.com (literary/commercial fiction, Y/A novels, history, narrative); Carolyn Savarese, carolyn@kwlit.com (riveting narratives in science, technology and medicine; unknown history; big think subjects; memoir; lifestyle and design, literary fiction and short stories); Hope Denekamp (agency manager); Emma Hamilton (literary fiction).

HOW TO CONTACT E-query an individual agent. Send no attachments. Put "Query" in the subject line. Accepts simultaneous submissions. Obtains most new clients through recommendations from others.

THE KNIGHT AGENCY

232 W. Washington St., Madison GA 30650. **E-mail:** deidre.knight@knightagency.net. **E-mail:** submissions@knightagency.net. **Website:** http://knightagency.net/. **Contact:** Deidre Knight. Estab. 1996. Member of AAR. SCWBI, WFA, SFWA, RWA Represents 200+ clients.

MEMBER AGENTS Deidre Knight (romance, women's fiction, erotica, commercial fiction, inspirational, m/m fiction, memoir and nonfiction narrative, personal finance, true crime, business, popular culture, self-help, religion, and health); Pamela Harty (romance, women's fiction, young adult, business, motivational, diet and health, memoir, parenting, pop culture, and true crime); Elaine Spencer (romance (single title and category), women's fiction, commercial "book-club" fiction, cozy mysteries, young adult and middle grade material); Lucienne Diver (fantasy, science fiction, romance, suspense and young adult); Nephele Tempest (literary/commercial fiction, women's fiction, fantasy, science fiction, romantic suspense, paranormal romance, contemporary romance, historical fiction, young adult and middle grade fiction); Melissa Jeglinski (romance [contemporary, category, historical, inspirational], young adult, middle grade, women's fiction and mystery); Kristy Hunter (romance, women's fiction, commercial fiction, young adult and middle grade material), Travis Pennington (young adult, middle grade, mysteries, thrillers, commercial fiction, and romance [nothing paranormal/fantasy in any genre for now]).

REPRESENTS Nonfiction, fiction, novels. **Considers these fiction areas:** commercial, crime, erotica, fantasy, gay, historical, juvenile, lesbian, literary, mainstream, middle grade, multicultural, mystery, new adult, paranormal, psychic, romance, science fiction, thriller, urban fantasy, women's, young adult.

HOW TO CONTACT E-queries only. "Your submission should include a one page query letter and the first five pages of your manuscript. All text must be contained in the body of your e-mail. Attachments will not be opened nor included in the consideration of your work. Queries must be addressed to a specific agent. Please do not query multiple agents." Accepts simultaneous submissions. Responds in 1-2 weeks on queries, 6-8 weeks on submissions.

TERMS 15% Simple agency agreement with open-ended commitment. 15% commission on all domestic sales, 20% on foreign and film.

STUART KRICHEVSKY LITERARY AGENCY, INC.

6 E. 39th St., Suite 500, New York NY 10016. (212)725-5288. **Fax:** (212)725-5275. **Website:** www.skagency.com. Member of AAR.

MEMBER AGENTS Stuart Krichevsky, query@skagency.com (emphasis on narrative nonfiction, literary journalism and literary and commercial fiction); Ross Harris, rhquery@skagency.com (voice-driven humor and memoir, books on popular culture and our society, narrative nonfiction and literary fiction); David Patterson, dpquery@skagency.com (writers of upmarket narrative nonfiction and literary fiction, historians, journalists and thought leaders); Mackenzie Brady Watson, mbwquery@skagency.com (narrative nonfiction, science, history, sociology, investigative journalism, food, business, memoir, and select upmarket and literary YA fiction); Hannah Schwartz, hsquery@skagency; Laura Usselman, luquery@skagency.com.

REPRESENTS Nonfiction, novels. **Considers these fiction areas:** commercial, contemporary issues, literary, young adult.

HOW TO CONTACT Please send a query letter and the first few (up to 10) pages of your ms or proposal in the body of an e-mail (not an attachment) to one of the e-mail addresses. No attachments. Responds if interested. Accepts simultaneous submissions. Obtains most new clients through recommendations from others, solicitations.

KT LITERARY, LLC

9249 S. Broadway, #200-543, Highlands Ranch CO 80129. **E-mail:** contact@ktliterary.com. **E-mail:** katequery@ktliterary.com, saraquery@ktliterary.com, reneequery@ktliterary.com, hannahquery@ktliterary.com, hilaryquery@ktliterary.com. **Website:** www.ktliterary.com. **Contact:** Kate Schafer Testerman, Sara Megibow, Renee Nyen, Hannah Fergesen, Hilary Harwell. Estab. 2008. Member of AAR. Other agency memberships include SCBWI, YALSA, ALA, SFWA and RWA. Represents 75 clients.

MEMBER AGENTS Kate Testerman (middle grade and young adult); Renee Nyen (middle grade and young adult); Sara Megibow (middle grade, young adult, romance, science fiction and fantasy); Hannah Fergesen (middle grade, young adult and speculative fiction); and Hilary Harwell (middle grade and young adult). Always LGBTQ and diversity friendly!.

REPRESENTS Fiction. **Considers these fiction areas:** fantasy, middle grade, romance, science fiction, young adult.

HOW TO CONTACT "To query us, please select one of the agents at kt literary at a time. If we pass, you can feel free to submit to another. Please e-mail your query letter and the first 3 pages of your manuscript in the body of the e-mail to either Kate at katequery@ktliterary.com, Sara at saraquery@ktliterary.com, Renee at reneequery@ktliterary.com, Hannah at hannahquery@ktliterary.com, or Hilary at hilaryquery@ktliterary.com. The subject line of your e-mail should include the word 'Query' along with the title of your manuscript. Queries should not contain attachments. Attachments will not be read, and queries containing attachments will be deleted unread. We aim to reply to all queries within 4 weeks of receipt. For examples of query letters, please feel free to browse the About My Query archives on the KT Literary website. In addition, if you're an author who is sending a new query, but who previously submitted a novel to us for which we requested chapters but ultimately declined, please do say so in your query letter. If we like your query, we'll ask for the first 5 chapters and a complete synopsis. For our purposes, the synopsis should include the full plot of the book including the conclusion. Don't tease us. Thanks! We are not accepting snail mail queries or queries by phone at this time. We also do not accept pitches on social media." Accepts simultaneous submissions. Responds in 2-4 weeks to queries; 2 months to mss. Obtains most new clients through query slush pile.

TERMS Agent receives 15% commission on domestic sales; 20% commission on foreign sales. Offers written contract; 30-day notice must be given to terminate contract.

THE LA LITERARY AGENCY

1264 North Hayworth Ave., Suite 10, Los Angeles CA 90046. (323)654-5288. **E-mail:** maureen@laliteraryagency.com. **E-mail:** ann@laliteraryagency.com. **Website:** www.laliteraryagency.com; www.labookeditor.com. **Contact:** Ann Cashman.

MEMBER AGENTS Ann Cashman, Eric Lasher, Maureen Lasher.

REPRESENTS Nonfiction, fiction, novels. **Considers these fiction areas:** action, adventure, commercial, confession, contemporary issues, crime, detective, family saga, feminist, historical, literary, mainstream, mystery, sports, suspense, thriller, war, westerns, women's.

HOW TO CONTACT Nonfiction: query letter and book proposal. Fiction: query letter and full ms as an attachment. Accepts simultaneous submissions.

PETER LAMPACK AGENCY, INC.

The Empire State Building, 350 Fifth Ave., Suite 5300, New York NY 10118. (212)687-9106. **Fax:** (212)687-9109. **E-mail:** andrew@peterlampackagency.com. **Website:** www.peterlampackagency.com. **Contact:** Andrew Lampack.

REPRESENTS Nonfiction, fiction, novels. **Considers these fiction areas:** action, adventure, commercial, crime, detective, literary, mainstream, mystery, police, suspense, thriller.

HOW TO CONTACT The Peter Lampack Agency no longer accepts material through conventional mail. E-queries only. When submitting, you should include a cover letter, author biography and a 1 or 2 page synopsis. Please do not send more than 1 sample chapter of your ms at a time. "Due to the extremely high volume of submissions, we ask that you allow 4-6 weeks for a response." Accepts simultaneous submissions.

Obtains most new clients through referrals made by clients.

TERMS Agent receives 15% commission on domestic sales. Agent receives 20% commission on foreign sales.

THE STEVE LAUBE AGENCY

24 W. Camelback Rd., A-635, Phoenix AZ 85013. (602)336-8910. **E-mail:** krichards@stevelaube.com. **Website:** www.stevelaube.com. Estab. 2004. Represents 250+ clients.

MEMBER AGENTS Steve Laube (president), Tamela Hancock Murray, Dan Balow, Bob Hostetler.

REPRESENTS Nonfiction, fiction, novels. **Considers these fiction areas:** fantasy, inspirational, religious, science fiction, Christian.

HOW TO CONTACT Consult website for guidelines, because queries are sent to assistants, and the assistants' e-mail addresses may change. Submit proposal package, outline, 3 sample chapters, SASE. For e-mail submissions, attach as Word doc or PDF. Accepts simultaneous submissions. Responds in 6-8 weeks to queries. Obtains most new clients through recommendations from others, solicitations, conferences.

TERMS Agent receives 15% commission on domestic sales; 20% commission on foreign sales. Offers written contract; 30-day notice must be given to terminate contract.

LAUNCHBOOKS LITERARY AGENCY

E-mail: david@launchbooks.com. **Website:** www.launchbooks.com. **Contact:** David Fugate. Represents 45 clients.

REPRESENTS Nonfiction, fiction, novels. **Considers these fiction areas:** action, adventure, commercial, crime, fantasy, horror, humor, mainstream, military, paranormal, satire, science fiction, sports, suspense, thriller, urban fantasy, war, westerns, young adult.

HOW TO CONTACT Query via e-mail. Accepts simultaneous submissions. Responds in 1 week to queries; 4 weeks to mss. Obtains most new clients through recommendations from others, solicitations.

TERMS Agent receives 15% commission on domestic sales; 25% commission on foreign sales. Offers written contract; 30-day notice to terminate contract. Charges occur very seldom. This agency's agreement limits any charges to $50 unless the author gives a written consent.

SUSANNA LEA ASSOCIATES

28, rue Bonaparte, 75006 Paris France. **E-mail:** inquiries@susannalea.com. **E-mail:** ny@susannalea.com; london@susannalea.com; paris@susannalea.com. **Website:** www.susannalea.com. **Contact:** Submissions Department. 331 W. 20th St., New York NY 10011.

REPRESENTS Novels.

HOW TO CONTACT To submit your work, please send the following by e-mail: a concise query letter, including your e-mail address, telephone number, any relevant information about yourself (previous publications, etc.), a brief synopsis, and the first 3 chapters and/or proposal. Accepts simultaneous submissions.

THE NED LEAVITT AGENCY

70 Wooster St., Suite 4F, New York NY 10012. (212)334-0999. **Website:** www.nedleavittagency.com. **Contact:** Ned Leavitt; Jillian Sweeney. Member of AAR. Represents 40+ clients.

MEMBER AGENTS Ned Leavitt, founder and agent; Britta Alexander, agent; Jillian Sweeney, agent.

REPRESENTS Novels.

HOW TO CONTACT This agency now only takes queries/submissions through referred clients. Do not cold query. Accepts simultaneous submissions.

ROBERT LECKER AGENCY

4055 Melrose Ave., Montreal QC H4A 2S5 Canada. **E-mail:** robert.lecker@gmail.com. **Website:** www.leckeragency.com. **Contact:** Robert Lecker. Estab. 2013. PACLA Represents 50 clients.

MEMBER AGENTS Robert Lecker (popular culture, music); Mary Williams (travel, food, popular science).

REPRESENTS Nonfiction, novels, syndicated material. **Considers these fiction areas:** action, adventure, crime, detective, erotica, literary, mainstream, mystery, police, suspense, thriller.

HOW TO CONTACT E-query. In the subject line, write: "New Submission QUERY." Accepts simultaneous submissions. Responds in 2 weeks to queries; 1 month to mss. Obtains most new clients through recommendations from others, conferences, interest in website.

TERMS Agent receives 15% commission on domestic sales; 15-20% commission on foreign sales. Offers written contract, binding for 1 year; 6-month notice must be given to terminate contract.

THE LESHNE AGENCY

New York NY **E-mail:** info@leshneagency.com. **E-mail:** submissions@leshneagency.com. **Website:** www.leshneagency.com. **Contact:** Lisa Leshne, agent and owner. Estab. 2011. Member of AAR. Women's Media Group

MEMBER AGENTS Lisa Leshne, agent and owner; Sandy Hodgman, director of foreign rights.

REPRESENTS Nonfiction, fiction, novels. **Considers these fiction areas:** commercial, middle grade, young adult.

HOW TO CONTACT The Leshne Agency is seeking new and existing authors across all genres. "We are especially interested in narrative; memoir; prescriptive nonfiction, with a particular interest in sports, health, wellness, business, political and parenting topics; and truly terrific commercial fiction, young adult and middle-grade books. We are not interested in screenplays; scripts; poetry; and picture books. If your submission is in a genre not specifically listed here, we are still open to considering it, but if your submission is for a genre we've mentioned as not being interested in, please don't bother sending it to us. All submissions should be made through the Authors.me portal by clicking on this link: https://app.authors.me/#submit/the-leshne-agency." Accepts simultaneous submissions.

LEVINE GREENBERG ROSTAN LITERARY AGENCY, INC.

307 Seventh Ave., Suite 2407, New York NY 10001. (212)337-0934. **Fax:** (212)337-0948. **E-mail:** submit@lgrliterary.com. **Website:** www.lgrliterary.com. Member of AAR. Represents 250 clients.

MEMBER AGENTS Jim Levine (nonfiction, including business, science, narrative nonfiction, social and political issues, psychology, health, spirituality, parenting); Stephanie Rostan (adult and YA fiction; nonfiction, including parenting, health & wellness, sports, memoir); Melissa Rowland; Daniel Greenberg (nonfiction: popular culture, narrative nonfiction, memoir, and humor; literary fiction); Victoria Skurnick; Danielle Svetcov (nonfiction); Lindsay Edgecombe (narrative nonfiction, memoir, lifestyle and health, illustrated books, as well as literary fiction); Monika Verma (nonfiction: humor, pop culture, memoir, narrative nonfiction and style and fashion titles; some young adult fiction (paranormal, historical, contemporary)); Kerry Sparks (young adult and middle grade; select adult fiction and occasional nonfiction); Tim Wojcik (nonfiction, including food narratives, humor, pop culture, popular history and science; literary fiction); Arielle Eckstut (no queries); Sarah Bedingfield (literary and upmarket commercial fiction, Epic family dramas, literary novels with notes of magical realism, darkly gothic stories, psychological suspense).

REPRESENTS Nonfiction, novels. **Considers these fiction areas:** commercial, literary, mainstream, middle grade, suspense, young adult.

HOW TO CONTACT E-query to submit@lgrliterary.com, or online submission form. "If you would like to direct your query to one of our agents specifically, please feel free to name them in the online form or in the email you send." Cannot respond to submissions by mail. Do not attach more than 50 pages. "Due to the volume of submissions we receive, we are unable to respond to each individually. If we would like more information about your project, we'll contact you within 3 weeks (though we do get backed up on occasion!)." Accepts simultaneous submissions. Obtains most new clients through recommendations from others.

TERMS Agent receives 15% commission on domestic sales; 20% commission on foreign sales. Offers written contract. Charges clients for out-of-pocket expenses—telephone, fax, postage, photocopying—directly connected to the project.

RECENT SALES *Notorious RBG*, by Irin Carmon and Shana Knizhnik; *Pogue's Basics: Life*, by David Pogue; *Invisible City*, by Julia Dahl; *Gumption*, by Nick Offerman; *All the Bright Places*, by Jennifer Niven.

WRITERS CONFERENCES ASJA Writers' Conference.

TIPS "We focus on editorial development, business representation, and publicity and marketing strategy."

PAUL S. LEVINE LITERARY AGENCY

1054 Superba Ave., Venice CA 90291. (310)450-6711. **Fax:** (310)450-0181. **E-mail:** paul@paulslevinelit.com. **Website:** www.paulslevinelit.com. **Contact:** Paul S. Levine. Estab. 1992. Other memberships include the State Bar of California. Represents over 100 clients.

MEMBER AGENTS Paul S. Levine (children's and young adult fiction and nonfiction, adult fiction and nonfiction except sci-fi, fantasy, and horror); Loren R. Grossman (archeology, art/photography, architecture, child guidance/parenting, coffee table books, gardening, education/academics, health/medicine/science/technology, law, religion, memoirs, sociology).

REPRESENTS Nonfiction, fiction, novels, TV movie of the week, episodic drama, sitcom, animation, documentary, miniseries, syndicated material, variety show, comic books; graphic novels. **Considers these fiction areas:** adventure, ethnic, mainstream, mystery, romance, thriller, young adult.

HOW TO CONTACT E-mail preferred; "snail mail" with SASE is also acceptable. Send a 1-page, single-spaced query letter. In your query letter, note your target market, with a summary of specifics on how your work differs from other authors' previously published work. Accepts simultaneous submissions. Responds in 1 day to queries; 6-8 weeks to mss. Obtains most new clients through conferences, referrals, giving classes and seminars, and listings on various websites and in directories.

TERMS Agent receives 15% commission on domestic sales. Offers written contract. Charges for postage and actual, out-of-pocket costs only.

● LIMELIGHT CELEBRITY MANAGEMENT LTD.

10 Filmer Mews, 75 Filmer Rd., London SW6 7JF United Kingdom. (44)(0)207-384-9950. **E-mail:** mail@limelightmanagement.com. **Website:** www.limelightmanagement.com. **Contact:** Fiona Lindsay. Estab. 1991. Other memberships include AAA.

MEMBER AGENTS Fiona Lindsay.

REPRESENTS Selected fiction. **Considers these fiction areas:** crime, historical, literary, mystery, suspense, thriller, women's.

HOW TO CONTACT All work should be typed with double spacing. Ensure that the word "Submission" is clearly marked in the subject line and that any attachments include the title of your work. E-mail a brief synopsis and the first 3 chapters only as a Word or Open Document attachment. Only handles film and TV scripts for existing clients. Accepts simultaneous submissions. Obtains most new clients through recommendations from others.

TERMS Agent receives 15% commission on domestic sales; 25% commission on foreign sales; 10-20% commission on TV and radio deals.

LITERARY SERVICES, INC.

P.O. Box 888, Barnegat NJ 08005. **E-mail:** jwlitagent@msn.com. **E-mail:** john@literaryservicesinc.com. **Website:** www.literaryservicesinc.com. **Contact:** John Willig. Estab. 1991. Other memberships include Author's Guild. Represents 90 clients.

MEMBER AGENTS John Willig (business, personal growth, history, health and lifestyle, science and technology, politics, psychology, current events, food and travel, reference and gift books, true crime, humor, historical fiction).

REPRESENTS Considers these fiction areas: historical, literary, mystery, translation.

HOW TO CONTACT Query with SASE. For starters, a one-page outline sent via e-mail is acceptable. See our website and our Submissions section to learn more about our questions. Do not send a ms unless requested. Accepts simultaneous submissions. Thankfully, obtains most new clients through recommendations from others, solicitations, writer's conferences.

TERMS Agent receives 15% commission on domestic sales; 15% commission on foreign sales. Offers written contract. This agency charges an administrative fee for copying, postage, etc.

LKG AGENCY

60 Riverside Blvd., #1101, New York NY 10069. **E-mail:** query@lkgagency.com. **E-mail:** mgya@lkgagency.com (MG/YA); nonfiction@lkgagency.com (nonfiction). **Website:** lkgagency.com. **Contact:** Lauren Galit; Caitlen Rubino-Bradway. Estab. 2005.

MEMBER AGENTS Lauren Galit (nonfiction, middle grade, young adult); Caitlen Rubino-Bradway (middle grade and young adult, some nonfiction).

REPRESENTS Nonfiction, juvenile books. **Considers these fiction areas:** middle grade, young adult.

HOW TO CONTACT For nonfiction submissions, please send a query letter to nonfiction@lkgagency.com, along with a TOC and 2 sample chapters. The TOC should be fairly detailed, with a paragraph or 2 overview of the content of each chapter. Please also make sure to mention any publicity you have at your disposal. For middle grade and young adult submissions, please send a query, synopsis, and the three (3) chapters, and address all submissions to mgya@lkgagency.com. On a side note, while both Lauren and Caitlen consider young adult and middle grade, Lauren tends to look more for middle grade, while Caitlen deals more with young adult fiction. Please note: due

to the high volume of submissions, we are unable to reply to every one. If you do not receive a reply, please consider that a rejection. Accepts simultaneous submissions.

STERLING LORD LITERISTIC, INC.

115 Broadway, New York NY 10006. (212)780-6050. **Fax:** (212)780-6095. **E-mail:** info@sll.com. **Website:** www.sll.com. Estab. 1987. Member of AAR. Signatory of WGA.

MEMBER AGENTS Philippa Brophy (represents journalists, nonfiction writers and novelists, and is most interested in current events, memoir, science, politics, biography, and women's issues); Laurie Liss (represents authors of commercial and literary fiction and nonfiction whose perspectives are well developed and unique); Sterling Lord; Peter Matson (abiding interest in storytelling, whether in the service of history, fiction, the sciences); Douglas Stewart (primarily fiction for all ages, from the innovatively literary to the unabashedly commercial); Neeti Madan (memoir, journalism, popular culture, lifestyle, women's issues, multicultural books and virtually any intelligent writing on intriguing topics); Robert Guinsler (literary and commercial fiction (including YA), journalism, narrative nonfiction with an emphasis on pop culture, science and current events, memoirs and biographies); Jim Rutman; Celeste Fine (expert, celebrity, and corporate clients with strong national and international platforms, particularly in the health, science, self-help, food, business, and lifestyle fields); Martha Millard (fiction and nonfiction, including well-written science fiction and young adult); Mary Krienke (literary fiction, memoir, and narrative nonfiction, including psychology, popular science, and cultural commentary); Jenny Stephens (nonfiction: cookbooks, practical lifestyle projects, transportive travel and nature writing, and creative nonfiction; fiction: contemporary literary narratives strongly rooted in place); Alison MacKeen (idea-driven research books: social scientific, scientific, historical, relationships/parenting, learning and education, sexuality, technology, the life-cycle, health, the environment, politics, economics, psychology, geography, and culture; literary fiction, literary nonfiction, memoirs, essays, and travel writing); John Maas (serious nonfiction, specifically business, personal development, science, self-help, health, fitness, and lifestyle); Sarah Passick (commercial nonfiction in the celebrity, food, blogger, lifestyle, health, diet, fitness and fashion categories).

REPRESENTS Nonfiction, fiction. **Considers these fiction areas:** commercial, juvenile, literary, middle grade, picture books, science fiction, young adult.

HOW TO CONTACT Query via snail mail. "Please submit a query letter, a synopsis of the work, a brief proposal or the first 3 chapters of the manuscript, a brief bio or resume, and SASE for reply. Original artwork is not accepted. Enclose sufficient postage if you wish to have your materials returned to you. We do not respond to unsolicited e-mail inquiries." Accepts simultaneous submissions.

TERMS Agent receives 15% commission on domestic sales; 20% commission on foreign sales. Offers written contract.

LOWENSTEIN ASSOCIATES INC.

115 E. 23rd St., Floor 4, New York NY 10010. (212)206-1630. **E-mail:** assistant@bookhaven.com. **Website:** www.lowensteinassociates.com. **Contact:** Barbara Lowenstein. Member of AAR.

MEMBER AGENTS Barbara Lowenstein, president (nonfiction interests include narrative nonfiction, health, money, finance, travel, multicultural, popular culture, and memoir; fiction interests include literary fiction and women's fiction); Mary South (literary fiction and nonfiction on subjects such as neuroscience, bioengineering, women's rights, design, and digital humanities, as well as investigative journalism, essays, and memoir).

REPRESENTS Nonfiction, fiction, novels, short story collections. **Considers these fiction areas:** commercial, literary, middle grade, science fiction, women's, young adult.

HOW TO CONTACT "For fiction, please send us a 1-page query letter, along with the first 10 pages pasted in the body of the message by e-mail to assistant@bookhaven.com. If nonfiction, please send a 1-page query letter, a table of contents, and, if available, a proposal pasted into the body of the e-mail. Please put the word 'QUERY' and the title of your project in the subject field of your e-mail and address it to the agent of your choice. Please do not send an attachment as the message will be deleted without being read and no reply will be sent." Accepts simultaneous submissions. Will respond if interested. Obtains most new clients through recommendations from others, solicitations, conferences.

TERMS Agent receives 15% commission on domestic sales; 20% commission on foreign sales. Offers written contract. Charges for large photocopy batches, messenger service, international postage.

TIPS "Know the genre you are working in and read!"

ANDREW LOWNIE LITERARY AGENCY, LTD.

36 Great Smith St., London SW1P 3BU England. (44)(207)222-7574. **Fax:** (44)(207)222-7576. **E-mail:** lownie@globalnet.co.uk; david.haviland@andrewlownie.co.uk. **Website:** www.andrewlownie.co.uk. **Contact:** Andrew Lownie (nonfiction); David Haviland (fiction). Estab. 1988. Society of Authors Represents 200 clients.

REPRESENTS Nonfiction, fiction, novels. **Considers these fiction areas:** action, adventure, commercial, contemporary issues, crime, detective, ethnic, experimental, family saga, feminist, frontier, gay, glitz, hi-lo, historical, horror, humor, inspirational, juvenile, lesbian, literary, mainstream, metaphysical, middle grade, military, multicultural, mystery, new adult, paranormal, police, romance, satire, science fiction, sports, supernatural, suspense, thriller, translation, war, westerns, women's, young adult.

HOW TO CONTACT Query by e-mail only. For nonfiction, submit outline and one sample chapter. For fiction, a synopsis and the first 3 chapters. Accepts simultaneous submissions. Responds in 1 week to queries; 1 month to mss. Obtains most new clients through recommendations from others and unsolicited through website.

TERMS Agent receives 15% commission on domestic sales; 20% commission on foreign sales. Offers written contract; 30-day notice must be given to terminate contract.

DONALD MAASS LITERARY AGENCY

1000 Dean St., Suite 252, Brooklyn NY 11238. (212)727-8383. **E-mail:** query.dmaass@maassagency.com. **Website:** www.maassagency.com. Estab. 1980. Member of AAR. Other memberships include SFWA, MWA, RWA. Represents more than 200 clients.

MEMBER AGENTS Donald Maass (mainstream, literary, mystery/suspense, science fiction, romance, women's fiction); Jennifer Jackson (science fiction and fantasy for both adult and YA markets, thrillers that mine popular and controversial issues, YA that challenges traditional thinking); Cameron McClure (literary, mystery/suspense, urban, fantasy, narrative nonfiction and projects with multicultural, international, and environmental themes, gay/lesbian); Katie Shea Boutillier (women's fiction/book club, edgy/dark, realistic/contemporary YA, commercial-scale literary fiction, and celebrity memoir); Paul Stevens (science fiction, fantasy, horror, mystery, suspense, and humorous fiction, LBGT a plus); Jennie Goloboy (fun, innovative, diverse, and progressive science fiction and fantasy for adults); Caitlin McDonald (SF/F - YA/MG/Adult, genre-bending/cross-genre fiction, diversity); Michael Curry (science fiction and fantasy, near future thrillers).

REPRESENTS Nonfiction, fiction, novels, juvenile books. **Considers these fiction areas:** commercial, contemporary issues, crime, detective, ethnic, fantasy, feminist, gay, historical, horror, juvenile, lesbian, literary, mainstream, middle grade, military, multicultural, mystery, paranormal, police, regional, romance, science fiction, supernatural, suspense, thriller, urban fantasy, westerns, women's, young adult.

HOW TO CONTACT Query via e-mail only. All the agents have different submission addresses and instructions. See the website and each agent's online profile for exact submission instructions. Accepts simultaneous submissions.

TERMS Agency receives 15% commission on domestic sales; 20% commission on foreign sales.

GINA MACCOBY LITERARY AGENCY

P.O. Box 60, Chappaqua NY 10514. (914)238-5630. **E-mail:** query@maccobylit.com. **Website:** www.publishersmarketplace.com/members/ginamaccoby/. **Contact:** Gina Maccoby. Estab. 1986. Member of AAR. AAR Board of Directors; Royalties and Ethics and Contracts subcommittees; Authors Guild, SCBWI.

REPRESENTS Nonfiction, fiction, novels, juvenile books. **Considers these fiction areas:** crime, detective, family saga, historical, juvenile, literary, mainstream, middle grade, multicultural, mystery, new adult, thriller, women's, young adult.

HOW TO CONTACT Query by e-mail only. Accepts simultaneous submissions. Owing to volume of submissions, may not respond to queries unless interested. Obtains most new clients through recommendations.

TERMS Agent receives 15% commission on domestic sales; 20-25% commission on foreign sales, which includes subagents commissions. May recover certain costs, such as purchasing books, shipping books overseas by airmail, legal fees for vetting motion picture contracts, bank fees for electronic funds transfers, overnight delivery services.

CAROL MANN AGENCY

55 Fifth Ave., 18th Floor, New York NY 10003. (212)206-5635. **Fax:** (212)675-4809. **E-mail:** submissions@carolmannagency.com. **Website:** www.carolmannagency.com. **Contact:** Agnes Carlowicz. Member of AAR. Represents Roughly 200 clients.

MEMBER AGENTS Carol Mann (health/medical, religion, spirituality, self-help, parenting, narrative nonfiction, current affairs); Laura Yorke; Gareth Esersky; Myrsini Stephanides (nonfiction areas of interest: pop culture and music, humor, narrative nonfiction and memoir, cookbooks; fiction areas of interest: offbeat literary fiction, graphic works, and edgy YA fiction); Joanne Wyckoff (nonfiction areas of interest: memoir, narrative nonfiction,personal narrative, psychology, women's issues, education, health and wellness, parenting, serious self-help, natural history; also accepts fiction); Lydia Shamah (edgy, modern fiction and timely nonfiction in the areas of business, self-improvement, relationship and gift books, particularly interested in female voices and experiences); Tom Miller (narrative nonfiction, self-help/psychology, popular culture, body-mind-spirit, wellness, business, and literary fiction).

REPRESENTS Nonfiction, fiction, novels. **Considers these fiction areas:** commercial, literary, young adult, graphic works.

HOW TO CONTACT Please see website for submission guidelines. Accepts simultaneous submissions. Responds in 4 weeks to queries.

TERMS Agent receives 15% commission on domestic sales; 20% commission on foreign sales. Offers written contract.

MANUS & ASSOCIATES LITERARY AGENCY, INC.

425 Sherman Ave., Suite 200, Palo Alto CA 94306. (650)470-5151. **Fax:** (650)470-5159. **E-mail:** manuslit@manuslit.com. **Website:** www.manuslit.com. **Contact:** Jillian Manus, Jandy Nelson, Penny Nelson. NYC address: 444 Madison Ave., 39th Floor, New York NY 10022. Member of AAR.

MEMBER AGENTS Jandy Nelson (currently not taking on new clients); Jillian Manus, jillian@manuslit.com (political, memoirs, self-help, history, sports, women's issues, thrillers); Penny Nelson, penny@manuslit.com (memoirs, self-help, sports, nonfiction).

REPRESENTS Nonfiction, novels. **Considers these fiction areas:** thriller.

HOW TO CONTACT Snail mail submissions welcome. E-queries also accepted. For nonfiction, send a full proposal via snail mail. For fiction, send a query letter and 30 pages (unbound) if submitting via snail mail. Send only an e-query if submitting fiction via e-mail. If querying by e-mail, submit directly to one of the agents. Accepts simultaneous submissions. Responds in 3 months. Obtains most new clients through recommendations from others, solicitations, conferences.

TERMS Agent receives 15% commission on domestic sales; 20-25% commission on foreign sales. Offers written contract, binding for 2 years; 60-day notice must be given to terminate contract. Charges for photocopying and postage/UPS.

⚫ MARJACQ SCRIPTS LTD

Box 412, 19/12 Crawford St., London W1H 1PJ United Kingdom. (44)(207)935-9499. **Fax:** (44)(207)935-9115. **E-mail:** enquiries@marjacq.com. **E-mail:** subs@marjacq.com or (preferably) individual agent as shown on website. **Website:** www.marjacq.com. **Contact:** Submissions: individual agent. Business matters: Guy Herbert. Estab. 1974. AAA Represents 120 clients.

MEMBER AGENTS Philip Patterson (thrillers, commercial fiction and nonfiction); Sandra Sawicka (commercial, genre, speculative and upmarket fiction); Diana Beaumont (commercial and accessible literary fiction and nonfiction); Imogen Pelham (literary fiction and nonfiction); Catherine Pellegrino (children's, middle grade and young adult).

REPRESENTS Nonfiction, fiction, novels, short story collections, novellas, juvenile books, scholarly books.

HOW TO CONTACT Submit outline, synopsis, 3 sample chapters, bio, covering letter, SASE. "Do not bother with fancy bindings and folders. Keep synopses, bio, and covering letter short." Accepts simultaneous submissions. Responds in 4-6 weeks to mss. Don't send queries without sample. Obtains most new clients through recommendations from others, solicitations, conferences.

TERMS Agent receives 15% commission on direct book sales; 20% on foreign rights, film etc Offers writ-

ten contract. Services include in-house business affairs consultant. No service fees other than commission. Recharges bank fees for money transfers.

MARSAL LYON LITERARY AGENCY, LLC

PMB 121, 665 San Rodolfo Dr. 124, Solana Beach CA 92075. **E-mail:** jill@marsallyonliteraryagency.com, kevan@marsallyonliteraryagency.com, patricia@marsallyonliteraryagency.com, Deborah@marsallyonliteraryagency.com; shannon@marsallyonliteraryagency.com. **Website:** www.marsallyonliteraryagency.com. Estab. 2009. Represents See agency website for a client listing clients.

MEMBER AGENTS Kevan Lyon (women's fiction, with an emphasis on commercial women's fiction, young adult fiction and all genres of romance); Jill Marsal (all types of women's fiction, book club fiction, stories of family, friendships, relationships, secrets, and stories with strong emotion; mystery, cozy, suspense, psychological suspense, thriller; romance-contemporary, romantic suspense, historical, and category; nonfiction in the areas of current events, business, health, self-help, relationships, psychology, parenting, history, science, and narrative non-fiction); Patricia Nelson (literary fiction and commercial fiction, all types of women's fiction, contemporary and historical romance, young adult and middle grade fiction, LGBTQ fiction for both YA and adult); Deborah Ritchken (lifestyle books, specifically in the areas of food, design and entertaining; pop culture; women's issues; biography; and current events; her niche interest is projects about France, including fiction); Shannon Hassan (literary and commercial fiction, young adult and middle grade fiction, and select nonfiction).

REPRESENTS Nonfiction, fiction, novels, juvenile books. **Considers these fiction areas:** commercial, juvenile, literary, mainstream, middle grade, multicultural, mystery, paranormal, romance, suspense, thriller, women's, young adult.

HOW TO CONTACT Query by e-mail. Query only one agent at this agency at a time. "Please visit our website to determine who is best suited for your work. Write 'query' in the subject line of your e-mail. Please allow up to several weeks to hear back on your query." Accepts simultaneous submissions. Query response time is generally up to 2 weeks and submission time varies by agent.

THE EVAN MARSHALL AGENCY

1 Pacio Ct., Roseland NJ 07068-1121. (973)287-6216. **E-mail:** evan@evanmarshallagency.com. **Website:** www.evanmarshallagency.com, www.themarshall-plan.net. **Contact:** Evan Marshall. Estab. 1987. Member of AAR. Novelists, Inc. Represents 50+ clients.

REPRESENTS Fiction, novels. **Considers these fiction areas:** action, adventure, crime, detective, erotica, ethnic, family saga, fantasy, feminist, frontier, gay, glitz, historical, horror, humor, inspirational, lesbian, literary, mainstream, military, multicultural, multimedia, mystery, new adult, New Age, occult, paranormal, police, psychic, regional, religious, romance, satire, science fiction, spiritual, sports, supernatural, suspense, thriller, translation, urban fantasy, war, westerns, women's, young adult, romance (contemporary, gothic, historical, regency).

HOW TO CONTACT E-mail query letter, synopsis and first 3 chapters of novel within body of e-mail. Will request full manuscript if interested. Accepts simultaneous submissions. Responds in 1 week to queries if interested. Responds in 2 months to mss. Obtains new clients through queries and through recommendations from editors and current clients.

TERMS Agent receives 15% commission on domestic sales; 20% commission on foreign and film/TV sales. Offers written contract.

THE MARTELL AGENCY

1350 Avenue of the Americas, Suite 1205, New York NY 10019. **Fax:** (212)317-2676. **E-mail:** submissions@themartellagency.com. **Website:** www.themartellagency.com. **Contact:** Alice Martell.

REPRESENTS Nonfiction, fiction, novels.

HOW TO CONTACT E-query Alice Martell. This should include a summary of the project and a short biography and any information, if appropriate, as to why you are qualified to write on the subject of your book, including any publishing credits. Accepts simultaneous submissions.

MARTIN LITERARY AND MEDIA MANAGEMENT

914 164th St. SE, Suite B12, #307, Mill Creek WA 98012. **E-mail:** sharlene@martinlit.com. **Website:** www.martinlit.com. **Contact:** Sharlene Martin. Estab. 2002.

MEMBER AGENTS Sharlene Martin (nonfiction); Clelia Gore (children's, middle grade, young adult);

Adria Goetz (Christian books, lifestyle books, children and YA); Natalie Grazian (adult fiction).

REPRESENTS Nonfiction. **Considers these fiction areas:** adventure, contemporary issues, fantasy, feminist, historical, humor, literary, middle grade, science fiction, supernatural, suspense, urban fantasy, women's, young adult.

HOW TO CONTACT Query via e-mail with MS Word only. No attachments on queries; place letter in body of e-mail. Accepts simultaneous submissions. Responds in 2 weeks to queries; 3-4 weeks to mss. Obtains most new clients through recommendations from others.

TERMS Agent receives 15% commission on domestic sales. We are exclusive for foreign sales to Taryn Fagerness Agency. Offers written contract, binding for 1 year; 1-month notice must be given to terminate contract. 99% of materials are sent electronically to minimize charges to author for postage and copying.

MASSIE & MCQUILKIN

27 W. 20th St., Suite 305, New York NY 10011. **E-mail:** info@lmqlit.com. **Website:** www.lmqlit.com.

MEMBER AGENTS Laney Katz Becker, laney@lmqlit.com (book club fiction, upmarket women's fiction, suspense, thrillers and memoir); Ethan Bassoff, ethan@lmqlit.com (literary fiction, crime fiction, and narrative nonfiction in the areas of history, sports writing, journalism, science writing, pop culture, humor, and food writing); Jason Anthony, jason@lmqlit.com (commercial fiction of all types, including young adult, and nonfiction in the areas of memoir, pop culture, true crime, and general psychology and sociology); Will Lippincott, will@lmqlit.com (narrative nonfiction and nonfiction in the areas of politics, history, biography, foreign affairs, and health); Rob McQuilkin, rob@lmqlit.com (literary fiction; narrative nonfiction and nonfiction in the areas of memoir, history, biography, art history, cultural criticism, and popular sociology and psychology; Rayhane Sanders, rayhane@lmqlit.com (literary fiction, historical fiction, upmarket commercial fiction [including select YA], narrative nonfiction [including essays], and select memoir); Stephanie Abou (literary and upmarket commercial fiction (including select young adult and middle grade), crime fiction, memoir, and narrative nonfiction); Julie Stevenson (literary and upmarket fiction, narrative nonfiction, YA and children's books).

REPRESENTS Nonfiction, fiction, novels. **Considers these fiction areas:** commercial, contemporary issues, crime, literary, mainstream, middle grade, suspense, thriller, women's, young adult.

HOW TO CONTACT E-query preferred. Include the word "Query" in the subject line of your e-mail. Review the agency's online page of agent bios (lmqlit.com/contact.html), as some agents want sample pages with their submissions and some do not. If you have not heard back from the agency in 4 weeks, assume they are not interested in seeing more. Accepts simultaneous submissions. Obtains most new clients through recommendations from others, solicitations, conferences.

TERMS Agent receives 15% commission on domestic sales; 20% commission on foreign sales. Offers written contract; 30-day notice must be given to terminate contract. Only charges for reasonable business expenses upon successful sale.

MARGRET MCBRIDE LITERARY AGENCY

P.O. Box 9128, La Jolla CA 92038. (858)454-1550. **E-mail:** staff@mcbridelit.com. **Website:** www.mcbridel-iterary.com. Estab. 1981. Member of AAR. Other memberships include Authors Guild.

MEMBER AGENTS Margret McBride; Faye Atchison.

REPRESENTS Nonfiction, fiction, novels. **Considers these fiction areas:** action, adventure, comic books, commercial, confession, contemporary issues, crime, detective, family saga, feminist, historical, horror, juvenile, mainstream, multicultural, multimedia, mystery, new adult, paranormal, police, psychic, regional, supernatural, suspense, thriller, young adult.

HOW TO CONTACT Please check our website, as instructions are subject to change. Only e-mail queries are accepted: staff@mcbridelit.com. In your query letter, provide a brief synopsis of your work, as well as any pertinent information about yourself. We recommend that authors look at book jacket copy of professionally published books to get an idea of the style and content that should be included in a query letter. Essentially, you are marketing yourself and your work to us, so that we can determine whether we feel we can market you and your work to publishers. There are detailed nonfiction proposal guidelines on our website, but we recommend author's get a copy of How to Write a Book Proposal by Michael Larsen for further instruction. **Please note: The McBride Agency**

will not respond to queries sent by mail, and will not be responsible for the return of any material submitted by mail. Accepts simultaneous submissions. Responds within 8 weeks to queries; 6-8 weeks to requested mss. "You are welcome to follow up by phone or e-mail after 6 weeks if you have not yet received a response."

TERMS Agent receives 15% commission on domestic sales; 25% commission on translation rights sales (15% to agency, 10% to sub-agent). Charges for overnight delivery and photocopying.

SEAN MCCARTHY LITERARY AGENCY

E-mail: submissions@mccarthylit.com. **Website:** www.mccarthylit.com. **Contact:** Sean McCarthy. Estab. 2013.

REPRESENTS Considers these fiction areas: juvenile, middle grade, picture books, young adult.

HOW TO CONTACT E-query. "Please include a brief description of your book, your biography, and any literary or relevant professional credits in your query letter. If you are a novelist: Please submit the first 3 chapters of your manuscript (or roughly 25 pages) and a 1-page synopsis in the body of the e-mail or as a Word or PDF attachment. If you are a picture book author: Please submit the complete text of your manuscript. We are not currently accepting picture book manuscripts over 1,000 words. If you are an illustrator: Please attach up to 3 JPEGs or PDFs of your work, along with a link to your website." Accepts simultaneous submissions.

MCCORMICK LITERARY

37 W. 20th St., New York NY 10011. (212)691-9726. **E-mail:** queries@mccormicklit.com. **Website:** mccormicklit.com. Member of AAR. Signatory of WGA.

MEMBER AGENTS David McCormick; Pilar Queen (narrative nonfiction, practical nonfiction, and commercial women's fiction); Bridget McCarthy (literary and commercial fiction, narrative nonfiction, memoir, and cookbooks); Alia Hanna Habib (literary fiction, narrative nonfiction, memoir and cookbooks); Edward Orloff (literary fiction and narrative nonfiction, especially cultural history, politics, biography, and the arts); Daniel Menaker; Leslie Falk; Emma Borges-Scott.

REPRESENTS Nonfiction, novels. **Considers these fiction areas:** literary, women's.

HOW TO CONTACT Snail mail queries only. Send an SASE. Accepts simultaneous submissions.

⚙⊘ ANNE MCDERMID & ASSOCIATES, LTD

320 Front St. W., Suite 1105, Toronto ON M5V 3B6 Canada. (647)788-4016. **Fax:** (416)324-8870. **E-mail:** admin@mcdermidagency.com. **E-mail:** info@mc-dermidagency.com. **Website:** www.mcdermidagency. com. **Contact:** Anne McDermid. Estab. 1996.

MEMBER AGENTS Anne McDermid, Martha Webb, Monica Pacheco, Chris Bucci.

REPRESENTS Novels.

HOW TO CONTACT Query via e-mail or mail with a brief bio, description, and first 5 pages of project only. Accepts simultaneous submissions. *No unsolicited manuscripts.* Obtains most new clients through recommendations from others.

MCINTOSH & OTIS, INC.

353 Lexington Ave., New York NY 10016. (212)687-7400. **Fax:** (212)687-6894. **E-mail:** info@mcintoshandotis.com. **Website:** www.mcintoshandotis.com. **Contact:** Elizabeth Winick Rubinstein. Estab. 1928. Member of AAR. Signatory of WGA. SCBWI

MEMBER AGENTS Elizabeth Winick Rubinstein, ewrquery@mcintoshandotis.com (literary fiction, women's fiction, historical fiction, and mystery/suspense, along with narrative nonfiction, spiritual/self-help, history and current affairs); Christa Heschke, CHquery@mcintoshandotis.com (picture books, middle grade, young adult and new adult projects); Adam Muhlig, AMquery@mcintoshandotis.com (music–from jazz to classical to punk–popular culture, natural history, travel and adventure, and sports).

REPRESENTS Considers these fiction areas: fantasy, historical, horror, literary, middle grade, mystery, new adult, paranormal, picture books, romance, science fiction, suspense, urban fantasy, women's, young adult.

HOW TO CONTACT E-mail submissions only. Each agent has their own e-mail address for subs. For fiction: Please send a query letter, synopsis, author bio, and the first 3 consecutive chapters (no more than 30 pages) of your novel. For nonfiction: Please send a query letter, proposal, outline, author bio, and 3 sample chapters (no more than 30 pages) of the ms. For children's & young adult: Please send a query letter, synopsis and the first 3 consecutive chapters (not to exceed 25 pages) of the ms. Accepts simultaneous submissions. Obtains clients through recommendations from others, editors, conferences and queries.

TERMS Agent receives 15% commission on domestic sales; 20% on foreign sales.

MENDEL MEDIA GROUP, LLC

115 W. 30th St., Suite 209, New York NY 10001. (646)239-9896. **E-mail:** query@mendelmedia.com. **Website:** www.mendelmedia.com. Estab. 2002. Member of AAR. Represents 60-90 clients.

REPRESENTS Nonfiction, fiction, novels. **Considers these fiction areas:** action, adventure, contemporary issues, crime, detective, erotica, ethnic, feminist, gay, glitz, historical, humor, inspirational, juvenile, lesbian, literary, mainstream, mystery, picture books, police, religious, romance, satire, sports, thriller, young adult, commercial and literary fiction.

HOW TO CONTACT You should e-mail your work to query@mendelmedia.com. We no longer accept or read submissions sent by mail, so please do not send inquiries by any other method. If we want to read more or discuss your work, we will respond to you by e-mail or phone. Fiction queries: If you have a novel you would like to submit, please paste a synopsis and the first twenty pages into the body of your email, below a detailed letter about your publication history and the history of the project, if it has been submitted previously to publishers or other agents. Please do not use attachments, as we will not open them. Nonfiction queries: If you have a completed nonfiction book proposal and sample chapters, you should paste those into the body of an e-mail, below a detailed letter about your publication history and the history of the project, if it has been submitted previously to any publishers or other agents. Please do not use attachments, as we will not open them. If we want to read more or discuss your work, we will call or e-mail you directly. If you do not receive a personal response within a few weeks, we are not going to offer representation. In any case, however, please do not call or email to inquire about your query. Accepts simultaneous submissions. Responds within a few weeks, if interested. Obtains most new clients through referrals.

TERMS Agent receives 15% commission on domestic sales; 20% commission on foreign sales.

WRITERS CONFERENCES BookExpo America; Frankfurt Book Fair; London Book Fair; RWA National Conference; Modern Language Association Convention; Jerusalem Book Fair.

TIPS "While I am not interested in being flattered by a prospective client, it does matter to me that she knows why she is writing to me in the first place. Is one of my clients a colleague of hers? Has she read a book by one of my clients that led her to believe I might be interested in her work? Authors of descriptive nonfiction should have real credentials and expertise in their subject areas, either as academics, journalists, or policy experts, and authors of prescriptive nonfiction should have legitimate expertise and considerable experience communicating their ideas in seminars and workshops, in a successful business, through the media, etc."

THE STUART M. MILLER CO.

11684 Ventura Blvd., #225, Studio City CA 91604. (818)506-6067. **E-mail:** smmco@aol.com. **Contact:** Stuart Miller. Memberships include Signatory of WGA, DGA, Association of Talent Agents (ATA).

REPRESENTS Nonfiction, fiction, novels, scholarly books, movie scripts, feature film, TV scripts, TV movie of the week, animation, miniseries. **Considers these fiction areas:** adventure, detective, historical, literary, mainstream, military, mystery, police, satire, short story collections, sports, suspense, thriller, war.

HOW TO CONTACT For screenplays, query via e-mail, narrative outline (2-3 pages). For books, e-mail narrative outline (5-10 pages). Accepts simultaneous submissions. "If requests full screenplay or mss, requires reasonable exclusivity period." Responds in 5 days to queries; 2-3 weeks to screenplays and 4-6 weeks to mss.

TERMS Screenplays, teleplays—10%, All books and other underlying rights—15% Written contract, binding for 2 years for WGA, DGA members, 3 years for non-guild & authors.

RECENT SALES This agency prefers not to share information on specific sales.

TIPS "Always include an e-mail address with query letters. Agents are incredibly busy; make it easy to respond."

HOWARD MORHAIM LITERARY AGENCY

30 Pierrepont St., Brooklyn NY 11201. (718)222-8400. **Fax:** (718)222-5056. **E-mail:** info@morhaimliterary.com. **Website:** www.morhaimliterary.com. Member of AAR.

MEMBER AGENTS Howard Morhaim, howard@morhaimliterary.com; Kate McKean, kmckean@morhaimliterary.com; DongWon Song, dongwon@morhaimliterary.com; Kim-Mei Kirtland, kimmei@morhaimliterary.com.

REPRESENTS Considers these fiction areas: fantasy, historical, literary, middle grade, new adult, romance, science fiction, women's, young adult, LGBTQ young adult, magical realism, fantasy should be high fantasy, historical fiction should be no earlier than the 20th century.

HOW TO CONTACT Query via e-mail with cover letter and 3 sample chapters. See each agent's listing for specifics. Accepts simultaneous submissions.

MOVEABLE TYPE MANAGEMENT

244 Madison Ave., Suite 334, New York NY 10016. **E-mail:** achromy@movabletm.com. **Website:** www.movabletm.com. **Contact:** Adam Chromy. Estab. 2002.

REPRESENTS Nonfiction, fiction, novels. **Considers these fiction areas:** action, commercial, crime, detective, erotica, hi-lo, historical, literary, mainstream, mystery, romance, satire, science fiction, sports, suspense, thriller, women's.

HOW TO CONTACT E-queries only. Responds if interested. For nonfiction: Send a query letter in the body of an e-mail that precisely introduces your topic and approach, and includes a descriptive bio. For journalists and academics, please also feel free to include a CV. Fiction: Send your query letter and the first 10 pages of your novel in the body of an e-mail. Your subject line needs to contain the word "Query" or your message will not reach the agency. No attachments and no snail mail. Accepts simultaneous submissions.

RECENT SALES *The Wedding Sisters*, by Jamie Brenner (St. Martin's Press); *Rage*, by (AmazonCrossing); *Sons Of Zeus*, by Noble Smith (Thomas Dunne Books); *World Made By Hand And Too Much Magic*, by James Howard Kunstler (Grove/Atlantic Press); *Dirty Rocker Boys*, by Bobbie Brown (Gallery/S&S).

JEAN V. NAGGAR LITERARY AGENCY, INC.

JVNLA, Inc., 216 E. 75th St., Suite 1E, New York NY 10021. (212)794-1082. **Website:** www.jvnla.com. **Contact:** Jennifer Weltz. Estab. 1978. Member of AAR. Other memberships include Women's Media Group, SCBWI, Pace University's Masters in Publishing Board Member. Represents 450 clients.

MEMBER AGENTS Jennifer Weltz (well-researched and original historicals, thrillers with a unique voice, wry dark humor, and magical realism; enthralling narrative nonfiction; voice driven young adult, middle grade); Alice Tasman (literary, commercial, YA, middle grade, and nonfiction in the categories of narrative, biography, music or pop culture); Ariana Philips (nonfiction both prescriptive and narrative).

REPRESENTS Nonfiction, fiction, novels, short story collections, novellas, juvenile books, scholarly books, poetry books.

HOW TO CONTACT "Visit our website to send submissions and see what our individual agents are looking for. No snail mail submissions please!" Accepts simultaneous submissions. Depends on the agent. No responses for queries unless the agent is interested.

TERMS Agent receives 15% commission on domestic sales; 20% commission on foreign sales. Offers written contract. Charges for overseas mailing, messenger services, book purchases, photocopying—all deductible from royalties received.

RECENT SALES *Mort(e)*, by Robert Repino; *The Paying Guests*, by Sarah Waters; *The Third Victim*, by Phillip Margolin; *Every Kind of Wanting*, by Gina Frangello; *The Lies They Tell*, by Gillian French; *Dietland*, by Sarai Walker; *Mr. Rochester*, by Sarah Shoemaker; *Not If I See You First*, by Eric Lindstrom.

TIPS "We recommend courage, fortitude, and patience: the courage to be true to your own vision, the fortitude to finish a novel and polish it again and again before sending it out, and the patience to accept rejection gracefully and wait for the stars to align themselves appropriately for success."

NELSON LITERARY AGENCY

1732 Wazee St., Suite 207, Denver CO 80202. (303)292-2805. **E-mail:** query@nelsonagency.com. **E-mail:** querykristin@nelsonagency.com; querydanielle@nelsonagency.com; queryjoanna@nelsonagency.com; queryquressa@nelsonagency.com. **Website:** www.nelsonagency.com. **Contact:** Kristin Nelson, President. Estab. 2002. Member of AAR. RWA, SCBWI, SFWA. Represents 79 clients.

MEMBER AGENTS Danielle Burby; Joanna MacKenzie; Quressa Robinson.

REPRESENTS Fiction, novels, young adult, middle grade, literary commercial, upmarket women's fiction, single-title romance, science fiction, fantasy. **Considers these fiction areas:** commercial, fantasy, historical, horror, literary, mainstream, middle grade, romance, science fiction, suspense, thriller, urban fantasy, women's, young adult.

HOW TO CONTACT "Please visit our website and carefully read our submission guidelines. We do not accept any queries on Facebook or Twitter. Query by e-mail only. Write the word 'Query' in the e-mail subject line along with the title of your novel. Send no attachments, but please paste the first 10 pages of your novel in the body of the e-mail beneath your query letter." Accepts simultaneous submissions. Makes best efforts to respond to all queries within 3 weeks. Response to full mss requested can take up to 3 months.

TERMS Agent charges industry standard commission.

TIPS "If you would like to learn how to write an awesome pitch paragraph for your query letter or would like any info on how publishing contracts work, please visit Kristin's popular industry blog Pub Rants: http://nelsonagency.com/pub-rants/."

NEW LEAF LITERARY & MEDIA, INC.

110 W. 40th St., Suite 2201, New York NY 10018. (646)248-7989. **Fax:** (646)861-4654. **E-mail:** query@newleafliterary.com. **Website:** www.newleafliterary.com. Estab. 2012. Member of AAR.

MEMBER AGENTS Joanna Volpe (women's fiction, thriller, horror, speculative fiction, literary fiction and historical fiction, young adult, middle grade, art-focused picture books); Kathleen Ortiz, Director of Subsidiary Rights and literary agent (new voices in YA and animator/illustrator talent); Suzie Townsend (new adult, young adult, middle grade, romance [all subgenres], fantasy [urban fantasy, science fiction, steampunk, epic fantasy] and crime fiction [mysteries, thrillers]); Pouya Shahbazian, Director of Film and Television (no unsolicited queries); Janet Reid, janet@newleafliterary.com; Jaida Temperly (all fiction: magical realism, historical fiction; literary fiction; stories that are quirky and fantastical; nonfiction: niche, offbeat, a bit strange; middle grade; JL Stermer (nonfiction, smart pop culture, comedy/satire, fashion, health & wellness, self-help, and memoir).

REPRESENTS Nonfiction, fiction, novels, novellas, juvenile books, poetry books. **Considers these fiction areas:** crime, fantasy, historical, horror, literary, mainstream, middle grade, mystery, new adult, paranormal, picture books, romance, thriller, women's, young adult.

HOW TO CONTACT Send query via e-mail. Please do not query via phone. The word "Query" must be in the subject line, plus the agent's name, i.e.–Subject: Query, Suzie Townsend. You may include up to 5 double-spaced sample pages within the body of the e-mail. No attachments, unless specifically requested.

Include all necessary contact information. You will receive an auto-response confirming receipt of your query. "We only respond if we are interested in seeing your work." Responds only if interested. All queries read within 1 month.

RECENT SALES *Carve the Mark*, by Veronica Roth (HarperCollins); *Red Queen*, by Victoria Aveyard (HarperCollins); *Lobster is the Best Medicine*, by Liz Climo (Running Press); *Ninth House*, by Leigh Bardugo (Henry Holt); *A Snicker of Magic*, by Natalie Lloyd (Scholastic).

DANA NEWMAN LITERARY

1800 Avenue of the Stars, 12th Floor, Los Angeles CA 90067. **E-mail:** dananewmanliterary@gmail.com. **Website:** dananewman.com. **Contact:** Dana Newman. Estab. 2009. Member of AAR. California State Bar. Represents 29 clients.

MEMBER AGENTS Dana Newman (narrative nonfiction, business, lifestyle, current affairs, parenting, memoir, pop culture, sports, health, literary, and upmarket fiction).

REPRESENTS Nonfiction, novels, short story collections. **Considers these fiction areas:** commercial, contemporary issues, family saga, feminist, historical, literary, multicultural, sports, women's.

HOW TO CONTACT E-mail queries only. For both nonfiction and fiction, please submit a query letter including a description of your project and a brief biography. "If we are interested in your project, we will contact you and request a full book proposal (nonfiction) or a synopsis and the first 25 pages (fiction)." Accepts simultaneous submissions. "If we have requested your materials after receiving your query, we usually respond within 4 weeks." Obtains new clients through recommendations from others, queries, and submissions.

TERMS Obtains 15% commission on domestic sales; 20% on foreign sales. Offers 1 year written contract. Notice must be given 1 month prior to terminate a contract.

HAROLD OBER ASSOCIATES

425 Madison Ave., New York NY 10017. (212)759-8600. **Fax:** (212)759-9428. **Website:** www.haroldober.com. **Contact:** Appropriate agent. Member of AAR. Represents 250 clients.

MEMBER AGENTS Phyllis Westberg; Craig Tenney (few new clients, mostly Ober backlist and foreign rights).

HOW TO CONTACT Submit concise query letter addressed to a specific agent with the first 5 pages of the ms or proposal and SASE. No fax or e-mail. Does not handle filmscripts or plays. Responds as promptly as possible. Obtains most new clients through recommendations from others.

TERMS Agent receives 15% commission on domestic sales; 20% commission on foreign sales. Charges clients for express mail/package services.

PARK LITERARY GROUP, LLC

270 Lafayette St., Suite 1504, New York NY 10012. (212)691-3500. **Fax:** (212)691-3540. **E-mail:** info@parkliterary.com. **E-mail:** queries@parkliterary.com. **Website:** www.parkliterary.com. Estab. 2005.

MEMBER AGENTS Theresa Park (plot-driven fiction and serious nonfiction); Abigail Koons (popular science, history, politics, current affairs and art, and women's fiction); Peter Knapp (children's and YA).

REPRESENTS Nonfiction, novels. **Considers these fiction areas:** juvenile, middle grade, suspense, thriller, women's, young adult.

HOW TO CONTACT Please specify the first and last name of the agent to whom you are submitting in the subject line of the e-mail. All materials must be in the body of the e-mail. Responds if interested. For fiction submissions, please include a query letter with short synopsis and the first 3 chapters of your work. Accepts simultaneous submissions.

RECENT SALES This agency's client list is on their website. It includes bestsellers Nicholas Sparks, Soman Chainani, Emily Giffin, and Debbie Macomber.

⊘ PAVILION LITERARY MANAGEMENT

660 Massachusetts Ave., Suite 4, Boston MA 02118. (617)792-5218. **E-mail:** jeff@pavilionliterary.com. **Website:** www.pavilionliterary.com. **Contact:** Jeff Kellogg.

REPRESENTS Nonfiction, novels. **Considers these fiction areas:** adventure, fantasy, juvenile, mystery, thriller.

HOW TO CONTACT No unsolicited submissions. If the agency has requested your submission: Query first by e-mail (no attachments). The subject line should specify fiction or nonfiction and include the title of the work. If submitting nonfiction, include a book proposal (no longer than 75 pages), with sample chapters. Accepts simultaneous submissions.

L. PERKINS AGENCY

5800 Arlington Ave., Riverdale NY 10471. (718)543-5344. **E-mail:** submissions@lperkinsagency.com. **Website:** lperkinsagency.com. Estab. 1987. Member of AAR. Represents 150 clients.

MEMBER AGENTS Tish Beaty, ePub agent (erotic romance–including paranormal, historical, gay/lesbian/bisexual, and light-BDSM fiction; also, she seeks new adult and YA); Sandy Lu, sandy@lperkinsagency.com (fiction: she is looking for dark literary and commercial fiction, mystery, thriller, psychological horror, paranormal/urban fantasy, historical fiction, YA, historical thrillers or mysteries set in Victorian times; nonfiction: narrative nonfiction, history, biography, pop science, pop psychology, pop culture [music/theatre/film], humor, and food writing); Lori Perkins (not currently taking new clients); Leon Husock (science fiction & fantasy, as well as young adult and middle-grade); Rachel Brooks (picture books, all genres of young adult and new adult fiction, as well as adult romance—especially romantic suspense [NOTE: Rachel is currently closed to unsolicited submissions]); Maximilian Ximinez (fiction: science fiction, fantasy, horror, thrillers; nonfiction: popular science, true crime, arts and trends in developing fields and cultures).

REPRESENTS Nonfiction, fiction, novels, short story collections. **Considers these fiction areas:** commercial, crime, detective, erotica, fantasy, feminist, gay, historical, horror, lesbian, literary, middle grade, mystery, new adult, paranormal, picture books, romance, science fiction, short story collections, supernatural, thriller, urban fantasy, women's, young adult.

HOW TO CONTACT E-queries only. Include your query, a 1-page synopsis, and the first 5 pages from your novel pasted into the e-mail, or your proposal. No attachments. Submit to only 1 agent at the agency. No snail mail queries. "If you are submitting to one of our agents, please be sure to check the submission status of the agent by visiting their social media accounts listed [on the agency website]." Accepts simultaneous submissions. Obtains most new clients through recommendations from others, solicitations, conferences.

TERMS Agent receives 15% commission on domestic sales; 20% commission on foreign sales. No written contract. Charges clients for photocopying.

RUBIN PFEFFER CONTENT

648 Hammond St., Chestnut Hill MA 02467. **E-mail:** info@rpcontent.com. **Website:** www.rpcontent.com.

Contact: Rubin Pfeffer. Estab. 2014. Member of AAR. Signatory of WGA.

MEMBER AGENTS Melissa Nasson is an associate agent at Rubin Pfeffer Content and an attorney. She previously interned at Zachary Shuster Harmsworth, Perseus Books Group, and East-West Literary Agency before joining Rubin Pfeffer Content. Melissa also works as contracts director at Beacon Press.

REPRESENTS Considers these fiction areas: juvenile, middle grade, picture books, young adult.

HOW TO CONTACT Note: Rubin Pfeffer accepts submissions by referral only. Melissa Nasson is open to queries for picture books, middle-grade, and young adult fiction and nonfiction. To query Melissa, email her at melissa@rpcontent.com, include the query letter in the body of the email, and attach the first 50 pages as a Word doc or PDF. If you wish to query Rubin Pfeffer by referral only, specify the contact information of your reference when submitting. Authors/illustrators should send a query and a 1-3 chapter ms via e-mail (no postal submissions). The query, placed in the body of the e-mail, should include a synopsis of the piece, as well as any relevant information regarding previous publications, referrals, websites, and biographies. The ms may be attached as a .doc or a .pdf file. Specifically for illustrators, attach a PDF of the dummy or artwork to the e-mail. Accepts simultaneous submissions. Strives to respond within 6-8 weeks.

🌑 PONTAS LITERARY & FILM AGENCY

Sèneca, 31, principal 08006, Barcelona Spain. (34)(93)218-2212. **E-mail:** submissions@pontas-agency.com. **Website:** www.pontas-agency.com. Estab. 1992. Represents 70 clients.

REPRESENTS Fiction, novels. **Considers these fiction areas:** action, adventure, commercial, confession, contemporary issues, crime, detective, ethnic, experimental, family saga, feminist, frontier, gay, historical, horror, inspirational, lesbian, literary, mainstream, multicultural, mystery, regional, satire, thriller, translation, women's, young adult.

HOW TO CONTACT When submitting work, include a brief cover letter with your name and title of your mss in the e-mail subject, a detailed synopsis of your plot, your biography, and the full work in PDF or Word format. Accepts simultaneous submissions. "Due to the enormous and increasing volume of submissions that we receive, we cannot guarantee a reply. If you do not receive a response 6 weeks from the date of your submission, you can assume we're not interested. It's also important to note that we don't provide specific reasons nor editorial feedback on the submissions received."

PRENTIS LITERARY

PMB 496 6830 NE Bothell Way, Kenmore WA 98028. **Website:** prentisliterary.com. **Contact:** Autumn Frisse, acquisitions; Terry Johnson, business manager. Represents 12-15 clients.

REPRESENTS Nonfiction, fiction, novels. **Considers these fiction areas:** adventure, ethnic, fantasy, gay, historical, horror, humor, lesbian, literary, mainstream, middle grade, mystery, paranormal, romance, science fiction, supernatural, thriller, urban fantasy, young adult.

HOW TO CONTACT No phone or fax queries. No surface mail. For submission use our submission form posted on our submission page or e-mail acquisitions afrisse@prentisliterary.com. For other business business questions e-mail: tjohnson@prentisliterary.com. Accepts simultaneous submissions. Obtains most new clients through recommendations from others, solicitations.

TERMS Agent receives 15% commission on domestic sales; 20% commission on foreign sales. Offers written contract; 60-day notice must be given to terminate contract.

AARON M. PRIEST LITERARY AGENCY

200 W. 41st St., 21st Floor, New York NY 10036. (212)818-0344. **Fax:** (212)573-9417. **E-mail:** info@aaronpriest.com. **Website:** www.aaronpriest.com. Estab. 1974. Member of AAR.

MEMBER AGENTS Aaron Priest, querypriest@aaronpriest.com (thrillers, commercial fiction, biographies); Lisa Erbach Vance, queryvance@aaronpriest.com (contemporary fiction, thrillers/suspense, international fiction, narrative nonfiction); Lucy Childs, querychilds@aaronpriest.com (literary and commercial fiction, memoir, edgy women's fiction); Mitch Hoffman, queryhoffman@aaronpriest.com (thrillers, suspense, crime fiction, and literary fiction, as well as narrative nonfiction, politics, popular science, history, memoir, current events, and pop culture).

REPRESENTS **Considers these fiction areas:** commercial, contemporary issues, crime, literary, middle grade, suspense, thriller, women's, young adult.

HOW TO CONTACT Query one of the agents using the appropriate e-mail listed on the website. "Please

do not submit to more than 1 agent at this agency. We urge you to check our website and consider each agent's emphasis before submitting. Your query letter should be about one page long and describe your work as well as your background. You may also paste the first chapter of your work in the body of the e-mail. Do not send attachments." Accepts simultaneous submissions. Responds in 4 weeks, only if interested.

TERMS Agent receives 15% commission on domestic sales.

PROSPECT AGENCY

551 Valley Rd., PMB 377, Upper Montclair NJ 07043. (718)788-3217. **Fax:** (718)360-9582. **Website:** www.prospectagency.com. Estab. 2005. Member of AAR. Signatory of WGA. Represents 130+ clients.

MEMBER AGENTS Emily Sylvan Kim, esk@prospectagency.com (romance, women's, commercial, young adult, new adult); Rachel Orr, rko@prospectagency.com (picture books, illustrators, middle grade, young adult); Becca Stumpf, becca@prospectagency.com (young adult and middle grade [all genres, including fantasy/SciFi, literary, mystery, contemporary, historical, horror/suspense], especially MG and YA novels featuring diverse protagonists and life circumstances. Adult SciFi and Fantasy novels with broad appeal, upmarket women's fiction, smart, spicy romance novels); Carrie Pestritto, carrie@prospectagency.com (narrative nonfiction, general nonfiction, biography, and memoir; commercial fiction with a literary twist, women's fiction, romance, upmarket, historical fiction, high-concept YA and upper MG); Kirsten Carleton, kcarleton@prospectagency.com (upmarket speculative, thriller, and literary fiction for adult and YA).

REPRESENTS Nonfiction, fiction, novels, novellas, juvenile books, scholarly books, textbooks. **Considers these fiction areas:** commercial, contemporary issues, crime, ethnic, family saga, fantasy, feminist, gay, historical, horror, humor, juvenile, lesbian, literary, mainstream, middle grade, multicultural, mystery, new adult, picture books, romance, science fiction, suspense, thriller, urban fantasy, women's, young adult.

HOW TO CONTACT All submissions are electronic and must be submitted through the portal at prospectagency.com/submissions. We do not accept any submissions through snail mail. Accepts simultaneous submissions. Obtains new clients through conferences, recommendations, queries, and some scouting.

TERMS Agent receives 15% on domestic sales, 20% on foreign sales sold directly and 25% on sales using a subagent. Offers written contract.

�« » P.S. LITERARY AGENCY

2010 Winston Park Dr., 2nd Floor, Oakville ON L6H 5R7 Canada. **E-mail:** info@psliterary.com. **E-mail:** query@psliterary.com. **Website:** www.psliterary.com. **Contact:** Curtis Russell, principal agent; Carly Watters, senior agent; Maria Vicente, literary agent; Eric Smith; literary agent; Kurestin Armada, associate agent. Estab. 2005.

MEMBER AGENTS Curtis Russell (literary/commercial fiction, mystery, thriller, suspense, romance, young adult, middle grade, picture books, business, history, politics, current affairs, memoirs, health/wellness, sports, humor, pop culture, pop science, pop psychology); Carly Watters (upmarket/commercial fiction, women's fiction, book club fiction, literary thrillers, cookbooks, health/wellness, memoirs, humor, pop science, pop psychology); Maria Vicente (young adult, middle grade, illustrated picture books, graphic novels, pop culture, science, lifestyle, design); Kurestin Armada (magic realism, science fiction, fantasy, illustrated picture books, middle grade, young adult, graphic novels, romance, design, cookbooks, pop psychology, photography, nature, science); Eric Smith (young adult, new adult, literary/commercial fiction, cookbooks, pop culture, humor, essay collections).

REPRESENTS Nonfiction, fiction, novels, juvenile books. **Considers these fiction areas:** action, adventure, comic books, commercial, crime, detective, erotica, ethnic, experimental, family saga, fantasy, feminist, gay, historical, horror, humor, inspirational, juvenile, lesbian, literary, mainstream, middle grade, multicultural, mystery, new adult, New Age, paranormal, picture books, police, romance, satire, science fiction, sports, supernatural, suspense, thriller, urban fantasy, women's, young adult.

HOW TO CONTACT Query letters should be directed to query@psliterary.com. PSLA does not accept or respond to phone, paper, or social media queries. Responds in 4-6 weeks to queries/proposals. Obtains most new clients through solicitations.

TERMS Agent receives 15% commission on domestic sales; 25% commission on foreign sales. "We offer a written contract, with 30-days notice to terminate."

TIPS "Please review our website for the most up-to-date submission guidelines. We do not charge reading fees. We do not offer a critique service."

⊘ PUBLICATION RIOT GROUP

E-mail: submissions@priotgroup.com. **Website:** www.priotgroup.com. **Contact:** Donna Bagdasarian. Member of AAR. Signatory of WGA.

REPRESENTS Nonfiction, novels. **Considers these fiction areas:** ethnic, historical, literary, mainstream, thriller, women's.

HOW TO CONTACT Currently closed to all submissions. Accepts simultaneous submissions.

THE PURCELL AGENCY

E-mail: tpaqueries@gmail.com. **Website:** www.the-purcellagency.com. **Contact:** Tina P. Schwartz. Estab. 2012. SCBWI Represents 42 clients.

MEMBER AGENTS Tina P. Schwartz, Kim Blair McCollum, Catherine Hedrick.

REPRESENTS Nonfiction, fiction, novels, juvenile books. **Considers these fiction areas:** juvenile, middle grade, women's, young adult.

HOW TO CONTACT Check the website to see if agency is open to submissions and for submission guidelines. Accepts simultaneous submissions.

RECENT SALES *Seven Suspects*, by Renee James; *A Kind of Justice*, by Renee James; *Adventures at Hound Hotel*, by Shelley Swanson Sateren; *Adventures at Tabby Towers*, by Shelley Swanson Sateren; *Keys to Freedom*, by Karen Meade.

QUEEN LITERARY AGENCY

30 E. 60th St., Suite 1004, New York NY 10022. (212)974-8333. **Fax:** (212)974-8347. **E-mail:** submissions@queenliterary.com. **Website:** www.queenliterary.com. **Contact:** Lisa Queen.

REPRESENTS Novels. **Considers these fiction areas:** commercial, historical, literary, mystery, thriller.

HOW TO CONTACT E-query. Accepts simultaneous submissions.

RECENT SALES A full list of this agency's clients and sales is available on their website.

RED SOFA LITERARY

P.O. Box 40482, St. Paul MN 55104. (651)224-6670. **E-mail:** dawn@redsofaliterary.com laura@redsofaliterary.com; amanda@redsofaliterary.com; stacey@ redsofaliterary.com; erik@redsofaliterary.com; liz@ redsofaliterary.com. **Website:** www.redsofaliterary. com. **Contact:** Dawn Frederick, owner/literary agent; Laura Zats, literary agent; Amanda Rutter, associate literary agent; Stacey Graham, associate literary agent; Erik Hane, associate literary agent; Liz Rahn, subrights agent. Estab. 2008. Authors Guild and the MN Publishers Round Table Represents 125 clients.

MEMBER AGENTS Laura Zats; Amanda Rutter; Stacey Graham; Erik Hane; Liz Rahn.

REPRESENTS Nonfiction, fiction, novels, juvenile books. **Considers these fiction areas:** action, adventure, commercial, contemporary issues, detective, erotica, ethnic, fantasy, feminist, gay, humor, juvenile, lesbian, literary, mainstream, middle grade, multicultural, mystery, picture books, romance, science fiction, suspense, thriller, urban fantasy, young adult.

HOW TO CONTACT Query by e-mail or mail with SASE. No attachments, please. Submit full proposal (for nonfiction especially, for fiction it would be nice) plus 3 sample chapters (or first 50 pages) and any other pertinent writing samples upon request by the specific agent. Do not sent within or attached to the query letter. Pdf/doc/docx is preferred, no rtf documents please. Accepts simultaneous submissions. Obtains new clients through queries, also through recommendations from others, solicitations.

TERMS Agent receives 15% commission on domestic sales; 20% commission on foreign sales. Offers written contract.

REES LITERARY AGENCY

14 Beacon St., Suite 710, Boston MA 02108. (617)227-9014. **E-mail:** lorin@reesagency.com. **Website:** reesagency.com. Estab. 1983. Member of AAR. Represents more than 100 clients.

MEMBER AGENTS Ann Collette, agent10702@aol. com (fiction: literary, upscale commercial women's, crime [including mystery, thriller and psychological suspense], upscale western, historical, military and war, and horror; nonfiction: narrative, military and war, books on race and class, works set in Southeast Asia, biography, pop culture, books on film and opera, humor, and memoir); Lorin Rees, lorin@reesagency.com (literary fiction, memoirs, business books, self-help, science, history, psychology, and narrative nonfiction); Rebecca Podos, rebecca@reesagency.com (young adult and middle grade fiction, particularly

books about complex female relationships, beautifully written contemporary, genre novels with a strong focus on character, romance with more at stake than "will they/won't they," and LGBTQ books across all genres).

REPRESENTS Novels. **Considers these fiction areas:** commercial, crime, historical, horror, literary, middle grade, mystery, suspense, thriller, westerns, women's, young adult.

HOW TO CONTACT Consult website for each agent's submission guidelines and e-mail addresses, as they differ. Accepts simultaneous submissions. Obtains most new clients through recommendations from others, conferences, submissions.

TERMS Agent receives 15% commission on domestic sales; 20% commission on foreign sales.

REGAL HOFFMANN & ASSOCIATES LLC

242 W. 38th St., Floor 2, New York NY 10018. (212)684-7900. **Fax:** (212)684-7906. **E-mail:** submissions@rhaliterary.com. **Website:** www.rhaliterary.com. Estab. 2002. Member of AAR. Represents 70 clients.

MEMBER AGENTS Claire Anderson-Wheeler (nonfiction: memoirs and biographies, narrative histories, popular science, popular psychology; adult fiction: primarily character-driven literary fiction, but open to genre fiction, high-concept fiction; all genres of young adult / middle grade fiction); Markus Hoffmann (international and literary fiction, crime, [pop] cultural studies, current affairs, economics, history, music, popular science, and travel literature); Joseph Regal (literary fiction, international thrillers, history, science, photography, music, culture, and whimsy); Stephanie Steiker (serious and narrative nonfiction, literary fiction, graphic novels, history, philosophy, current affairs, cultural studies, biography, music, international writing); Grace Ross (literary fiction, historical fiction, international narratives, narrative nonfiction, popular science, biography, cultural theory, memoir).

REPRESENTS Nonfiction, fiction, novels, short story collections, juvenile books, scholarly books. **Considers these fiction areas:** literary, mainstream, middle grade, short story collections, thriller, women's, young adult.

HOW TO CONTACT Query with SASE or via e-mail to submissions@rhaliterary.com. No phone calls. Submissions should consist of a 1-page query letter detailing the book in question, as well as the qualifications of the author. For fiction, submissions may also include the first 10 pages of the novel or one short story from a collection. Responds if interested. Accepts simultaneous submissions. Responds in 4-8 weeks.

TERMS Agent receives 15% commission on domestic sales; 20% commission on foreign sales. We charge no reading fees.

⊘ THE AMY RENNERT AGENCY

1550 Tiburon Blvd., #302, Tiburon CA 94920. **E-mail:** queries@amyrennert.com. **Website:** www.publishersmarketplace.com/members/amyrennert/. **Contact:** Amy Rennert.

REPRESENTS Nonfiction, novels. **Considers these fiction areas:** literary, mainstream, mystery.

HOW TO CONTACT Amy Rennert is not currently accepting unsolicited submissions. Accepts simultaneous submissions.

TIPS "Due to the high volume of submissions, it is not possible to respond to each and every one. Please understand that we are only able to respond to queries that we feel may be a good fit with our agency."

◑ THE LISA RICHARDS AGENCY

108 Upper Leeson St., Dublin 4 Ireland. (03)(531)637-5000. **Fax:** (03)(531)667-1256. **E-mail:** info@lisarichards.ie. **Website:** www.lisarichards.ie. Estab. 1989.

MEMBER AGENTS Faith O'Grady (literary).

REPRESENTS Nonfiction, fiction, juvenile books. **Considers these fiction areas:** commercial, literary, middle grade, young adult.

HOW TO CONTACT Contact If sending fiction, please limit your submission to the first three or four chapters, and include a covering letter and an SASE if required. If sending nonfiction, please send a detailed proposal about your book, a sample chapter and a cover letter. Every effort will be made to respond to submissions within 3 months of receipt. Accepts simultaneous submissions.

RECENT SALES Clients include Arlene Hunt, Roisin Ingle, Declan Lynch, Kevin Rafter.

◔ THE RIGHTS FACTORY

P.O. Box 499, Station C, Toronto ON M6J 3P6 Canada. (416)966-5367. **Website:** www.therightsfactory.com. Estab. 2004. Represents ~150 clients.

MEMBER AGENTS Sam Hiyate (President: fiction, nonfiction and graphic novel); Ali McDonald (Kidlit Agent: YA and children's literature of all kinds); Olga Filina (Associate Agent: commercial and historical fiction; great genre fiction in the area of romance and mystery; nonfiction in the field of business, wellness, lifestyle and memoir; and young adult and middle grade novels with memorable characters); Cassandra Rogers (Associate Agent: adult literary and commercial women's fiction; historical fiction; nonfiction on politics, history, science, and finance; humorous, heartbreaking and inspiring memoir); Lydia Moed (Associate Agent: science fiction and fantasy, historical fiction, diverse voices; narrative nonfiction on a wide variety of topics, including history, popular science, biography and travel); Natalie Kimber (Associate Agent: literary and commercial fiction and creative nonfiction in categories such as memoir, cooking, pop-culture, spirituality, and sustainability); Harry Endrulat (Associate Agent: children's literature, especially author/illustrators and Canadian voices); Haskell Nussbaum (Associate Agent: literature of all kinds); Anna Trader (Associate Agent: literary, general and women's fiction; nonfiction in self-help and memoir).

REPRESENTS Nonfiction, fiction, novels, short story collections, novellas, juvenile books. **Considers these fiction areas:** commercial, crime, family saga, fantasy, gay, hi-lo, historical, horror, juvenile, lesbian, literary, mainstream, middle grade, multicultural, mystery, new adult, paranormal, picture books, romance, science fiction, short story collections, suspense, thriller, urban fantasy, women's, young adult.

HOW TO CONTACT There is a submission form on this agency's website. Accepts simultaneous submissions. Responds in 3-6 weeks.

ANGELA RINALDI LITERARY AGENCY

P.O. Box 7875, Beverly Hills CA 90212-7875. (310)842-7665. **Fax:** (310)837-8143. **E-mail:** info@rinaldiliterary.com. **Website:** www.rinaldiliterary.com. **Contact:** Angela Rinaldi. Member of AAR.

REPRESENTS Nonfiction, novels, TV and motion picture rights (for clients only). **Considers these fiction areas:** commercial, historical, literary, mainstream, mystery, suspense, thriller, women's, contemporary, gothic, women's book club fiction.

HOW TO CONTACT E-queries only. Include the word "Query" in the subject line. For fiction, please send a brief synopsis and paste the first 10 pages into an e-mail. Nonfiction queries should include a detailed cover letter, your credentials and platform information as well as any publishing history. Tell us if you have a completed proposal. Accepts simultaneous submissions. Responds in 2-4 weeks.

TERMS Agent receives 15% commission on domestic sales; 25% commission on foreign sales. Offers written contract.

ANN RITTENBERG LITERARY AGENCY, INC.

15 Maiden Lane, Suite 206, New York NY 10038. (212)684-6936. **E-mail:** info@rittlit.com. **Website:** www.rittlit.com. **Contact:** Ann Rittenberg, president. Estab. 1992. Member of AAR. Represents 30 clients.

MEMBER AGENTS Ann Rittenberg, Rosie Jonker.

REPRESENTS Nonfiction, fiction, novels, juvenile books. **Considers these fiction areas:** crime, detective, family saga, literary, mainstream, mystery, suspense, thriller, women's.

HOW TO CONTACT Query via e-mail or postal mail (with SASE). Submit query letter with 3 sample chapters pasted into the body of the e-mail. If you query by e-mail, we will only respond if interested. If you are making a simultaneous submission, you must tell us in your query. Accepts simultaneous submissions. Responds in 6-8 weeks. However, as noted above, if you don't receive a response to an emailed query, that means it was a pass. Obtains most new clients through referrals from established writers and editors.

TERMS Agent receives 15% commission on domestic sales, and 20% commission on foreign and film deals. This 20% is shared with co-agents. Offers written contract. No charges except for PDFs or finished books for foreign and film submissions.

RECENT SALES *Since We Fell*, by Dennis Lehane; *Your First Novel - Revised and Expanded Edition*, by Ann Rittenberg and Laura Whitcomb with Camille Goldin; *Paradise Valley*, by C.J. Box; *The Field Guide to Dumb Birds of North America*, by Matt Kracht; *Stay Hidden*, by Paul Doiron.

TIPS "Refrain from sending enormous bouquets of red roses. Elegant bouquets of peonies, tulips, ranunculus, calla lily, and white roses are acceptable."

RIVERSIDE LITERARY AGENCY

41 Simon Keets Rd., Leyden MA 01337. (413)772-0067. **Fax:** (413)772-0969. **E-mail:** rivlit@sover.net. **Website:** www.riversideliteraryagency.com. **Contact:** Susan Lee Cohen. Estab. 1990.

REPRESENTS Nonfiction, fiction.

HOW TO CONTACT E-query. Accepts simultaneous submissions. Obtains most new clients through referrals.

TERMS Agent receives 15% commission on domestic sales. Offers written contract. Charges clients for foreign postage, photocopying large mss, express mail deliveries, etc.

RLR ASSOCIATES, LTD.

420 Lexington Ave., Suite 2532, New York NY 10170. (212)541-8641. **E-mail:** website.info@rlrassociates. net. **Website:** www.rlrassociates.net. **Contact:** Scott Gould. Member of AAR. Represents 50 clients.

REPRESENTS Nonfiction, novels. **Considers these fiction areas:** commercial, literary, mainstream, middle grade, picture books, romance, women's, young adult, genre.

HOW TO CONTACT Query by snail mail. For fiction, send a query and 1-3 chapters (pasted). For nonfiction, send query or proposal. Accepts simultaneous submissions. "If you do not hear from us within 3 months, please assume that your work is out of active consideration." Obtains most new clients through recommendations from others.

TERMS Agent receives 15% commission on domestic sales; 20% commission on foreign sales. Offers written contract.

RECENT SALES Clients include Shelby Foote, The Grief Recovery Institute, Don Wade, David Plowden, Nina Planck, Karyn Bosnak, Gerald Carbone, Jason Lethcoe, Andy Crouch.

TIPS "Please check out our website for more details on our agency."

BJ ROBBINS LITERARY AGENCY

5130 Bellaire Ave., North Hollywood CA 91607-2908. **E-mail:** robbinsliterary@gmail.com. **Website:** www. bjrobbinsliterary.com. **Contact:** (Ms.) BJ Robbins. Estab. 1992. Member of AAR.

REPRESENTS Nonfiction, fiction. **Considers these fiction areas:** contemporary issues, crime, detective, ethnic, historical, literary, mainstream, multicultural, mystery, sports, suspense, thriller, women's.

HOW TO CONTACT E-query with no attachments. For fiction, okay to include first 10 pages in body of e-mail. Accepts simultaneous submissions. Only responds to projects if interested. Obtains most new clients through conferences, referrals.

TERMS Agent receives 15% commission on domestic sales; 20% commission on foreign sales. Offers written contract. No fees.

⊘ THE ROBBINS OFFICE, INC.

405 Park Ave., 9th Floor, New York NY 10022. (212)223-0720. **Fax:** (212)223-2535. **Website:** www.robbinsoffice.com. **Contact:** Kathy P. Robbins, owner.
MEMBER AGENTS Kathy P. Robbins; David Halpern.

REPRESENTS Novels.

HOW TO CONTACT Accepts submissions by referral only. Do not cold query this market. Accepts simultaneous submissions.

TERMS Agent receives 15% commission on domestic, foreign, and film sales. Bills back specific expenses incurred in doing business for a client.

RODEEN LITERARY MANAGEMENT

3501 N. Southport #497, Chicago IL 60657. **E-mail:** info@rodeenliterary.com. **E-mail:** submissions@rodeenliterary.com. **Website:** www.rodeenliterary.com. **Contact:** Paul Rodeen. Estab. 2009. Member of AAR. Signatory of WGA.

REPRESENTS Nonfiction, novels, juvenile books, illustrations, graphic novels. **Considers these fiction areas:** juvenile, middle grade, picture books, young adult, graphic novels, comics.

HOW TO CONTACT Unsolicited submissions are accepted by e-mail only. Cover letters with synopsis and contact information should be included in the body of your e-mail. An initial submission of 50 pages from a novel or a longer work of nonfiction will suffice and should be pasted into the body of your e-mail. Accepts simultaneous submissions.

THE ROSENBERG GROUP

23 Lincoln Ave., Marblehead MA 01945. (781)990-1341. **Fax:** (781)990-1344. **Website:** www.rosenberggroup.com. **Contact:** Barbara Collins Rosenberg. Estab. 1998. Member of AAR. Recognized agent of the RWA. Represents 25 clients.

REPRESENTS Nonfiction, novels, textbooks, college textbooks only. **Considers these fiction areas:** romance, women's, chick lit.

HOW TO CONTACT Query via snail mail. Your query letter should not exceed one page in length. It should include the title of your work, the genre and/or sub-genre; the manuscript's word count; and a brief description of the work. If you are writing category romance, please be certain to let her know the line for which your work is intended. Accepts simultaneous submissions. Obtains most new clients through recommendations from others, solicitations, conferences.

TERMS Agent receives 15% commission on domestic and foreign sales. Offers written contract; 1-month notice must be given to terminate contract. Charges maximum of $350/year for postage and photocopying.

ANDY ROSS LITERARY AGENCY

767 Santa Ray Ave., Oakland CA 94610. (510)238-8965. **E-mail:** andyrossagency@hotmail.com. **Website:** www.andyrossagency.com. **Contact:** Andy Ross. Estab. 2008. Member of AAR. Represents See website for client list. clients.

REPRESENTS Nonfiction, fiction, novels, juvenile books, scholarly books. **Considers these fiction areas:** commercial, contemporary issues, historical, juvenile, literary, middle grade, picture books, young adult.

HOW TO CONTACT Queries should be less than half page. Please put the word "query" in the title header of the e-mail. In the first sentence, state the category of the project. Give a short description of the book and your qualifications for writing. Accepts simultaneous submissions. Responds in 1 week to queries.

TERMS Agent receives 15% commission on domestic sales; 20% commission on foreign sales or other deals made through a sub-agent. Offers written contract.

RECENT SALES See my website.

JANE ROTROSEN AGENCY LLC

85 Broad St., 28th Floor, New York NY 10004. (212)593-4330. **Fax:** (212)935-6985. **Website:** www.janerotrosen.com. Estab. 1974. Member of AAR. Other memberships include Authors Guild. Represents more than 100 clients.

MEMBER AGENTS Jane Rotrosen Berkey (not taking on clients); Andrea Cirillo, acirillo@janerotrosen.com (general fiction, suspense, and women's fiction); Annelise Robey, arobey@janerotrosen.com (women's fiction, suspense, mystery, literary fiction, and select nonfiction); Meg Ruley, mruley@janerotrosen.com (commercial fiction, including suspense, mysteries, romance, and general fiction); Christina Hogrebe, chogrebe@janerotrosen.com (young adult, new adult, book club fiction, romantic comedies, mystery, and suspense); Amy Tannenbaum, atannenbaum@janerotrosen.com (contemporary romance, psychological suspense, thrillers, and new adult, as well as women's fiction that falls into that sweet spot between literary and commercial, memoir, narrative and prescriptive non-fiction in the areas of health, business, pop culture, humor, and popular psychology); Rebecca Scherer rscherer@janerotrosen.com (women's fiction, mystery, suspense, thriller, romance, upmarket/literary-leaning fiction); Jessica Errera (assistant to Christina and Rebecca).

REPRESENTS Nonfiction, novels. **Considers these fiction areas:** commercial, literary, mainstream, mystery, new adult, romance, suspense, thriller, women's, young adult.

HOW TO CONTACT Check website for guidelines. Accepts simultaneous submissions. Obtains most new clients through recommendations from others.

TERMS Agent receives 15% commission on domestic sales; 20% commission on foreign sales. Offers written contract, binding for 3 years; 2-month notice must be given to terminate contract. Charges clients for photocopying, express mail, overseas postage, book purchase.

THE RUDY AGENCY

825 Wildlife Ln., Estes Park CO 80517. (970)577-8500. **E-mail:** mak@rudyagency.com; claggett@rudyagency.com. **Website:** www.rudyagency.com. **Contact:** Maryann Karinch. Estab. 2004. Adheres to AAR canon of ethics. Represents 24 clients.

MEMBER AGENTS Maryann Karinch and Hilary Claggett (selected nonfiction).

REPRESENTS Nonfiction, fiction, novels, scholarly books. **Considers these fiction areas:** action, adventure, commercial, contemporary issues, crime, erotica, feminist, gay, historical, inspirational, lesbian, literary, military, multicultural, sports, thriller, women's.

HOW TO CONTACT "Query us. If we like the query, we will invite a complete proposal (or complete ms if writing fiction). No phone queries, please. We won't hang up on you, but it makes it easier if you send us a note first." Accepts simultaneous submissions. Responds in under 3 weeks to non-fiction proposals and 8 weeks to invited manuscripts. Obtains most new clients through recommendations from others, solicitations.

TERMS Agent receives 15% commission on domestic sales. Offers written contract, binding for 1 year.

RECENT SALES *Isadora Duncan's Neck*, by Tim Rayborn (Skyhorse); *Control the Conversation*, by

James O. Pyle (Red Wheel/Weiser); *Unavailable Men*, by Marni Feuerman (New World Library).

TIPS "Present yourself professionally. Know what we need to see in a query and what a proposal for a work of non-fiction must contain before you contact us."

VICTORIA SANDERS & ASSOCIATES

440 Buck Rd., Stone Ridge NY 12484. (212)633-8811. **E-mail:** queriesvsa@gmail.com. **Website:** www.victoriasanders.com. **Contact:** Victoria Sanders. Estab. 1992. Member of AAR. Signatory of WGA. Represents 135 clients.

MEMBER AGENTS Victoria Sanders; Bernadette Baker-Baughman; Jessica Spivey.

REPRESENTS Nonfiction, fiction, novels, short story collections, juvenile books. **Considers these fiction areas:** action, adventure, cartoon, comic books, contemporary issues, crime, detective, ethnic, family saga, feminist, gay, historical, humor, inspirational, juvenile, lesbian, literary, mainstream, middle grade, multicultural, multimedia, mystery, new adult, picture books, suspense, thriller, women's, young adult.

HOW TO CONTACT Authors who wish to contact us regarding potential representation should send a query letter with the first 3 chapters (or about 25 pages) pasted into the body of the message to queriesvsa@gmail.com. We will only accept queries via e-mail. Query letters should describe the project and the author in the body of a single, 1-page e-mail that does not contain any attached files. Important note: Please paste the first 3 chapters of your manuscript (or about 25 pages, and feel free to round up to a chapter break) into the body of your e-mail." Accepts simultaneous submissions. Responds in 1-4 weeks, although occasionally it will take longer. "We will not respond to e-mails with attachments or attached files."

TERMS Agent receives 15% commission on domestic sales; 20% commission on foreign/film sales. Offers written contract.

TIPS "Limit query to letter (no calls) and give it your best shot. A good query is going to get a good response."

SCHIAVONE LITERARY AGENCY, INC.

236 Trails End, West Palm Beach FL 33413-2135. (561)966-9294. **Fax:** (561)966-9294. **E-mail:** profschia@aol.com. **Website:** www.publishersmarketplace.com/members/profschia; www.schiavoneliteraryagencyinc.blogspot.com. **Contact:** Dr. James Schiavone, CEO, corporate offices in Florida; Jennifer

DuVall, president, New York office. Estab. 1996. Other memberships include National Education Association. Represents 40+ clients.

MEMBER AGENTS James Schiavone, profschia@aol.com; Jennifer DuVall, jendu77@aol.com.

REPRESENTS Nonfiction, fiction, novels, scholarly books, We specialize in Celebrity memoirs. **Considers these fiction areas:** literary, mainstream, mystery, romance, suspense, thriller, young adult.

HOW TO CONTACT "One-page e-mail queries only. Absolutely no attachments. Postal queries are not accepted. No phone calls. We do not consider poetry, short stories, anthologies or children's books. Celebrity memoirs only. No scripts or screen plays. We handle dramatic, film and TV rights, options, and screen plays for books we have agented. We are not interested in work previously published in any format (e.g., self-published; online; e-books; Print On Demand). E-mail queries may be addressed to any of the agency's agents." Accepts simultaneous submissions. Responds in 2 weeks to queries; 6 weeks to mss. Obtains most new clients through referrals.

TERMS Agent receives 15% commission on domestic sales; 20% commission on foreign sales. Offers written contract. No fees.

WENDY SCHMALZ AGENCY

402 Union St., #831, Hudson NY 12534. (518)672-7697. **E-mail:** wendy@schmalzagency.com. **Website:** www.schmalzagency.com. **Contact:** Wendy Schmalz. Estab. 2002. Member of AAR.

REPRESENTS Juvenile books. **Considers these fiction areas:** middle grade, young adult.

HOW TO CONTACT Accepts only e-mail queries. Paste synopsis into the e-mail. Do not attach the ms or sample chapters or synopsis. Replies to queries only if they want to read the ms. If you do not hear from this agency within 2 weeks, consider that a no. Accepts simultaneous submissions. Obtains clients through recommendations from others.

TERMS Agent receives 15% commission on domestic sales; 20% on foreign sales; 25% for Asia.

SUSAN SCHULMAN LITERARY AGENCY LLC

454 W. 44th St., New York NY 10036. (212)713-1633. **E-mail:** susan@schulmanagency.com. **E-mail:** queries@schulmanagency.com. **Website:** www.publishersmarketplace.com/members/schulman/. **Contact:** Susan Schulman. Estab. 1980. Member of AAR. Sig-

natory of WGA. Other memberships include Dramatists Guild, Writers Guild of America, East, New York Women in Film, Women's Media Group, Agents' Roundtable, League of New York Theater Women.

REPRESENTS Nonfiction, fiction, novels, juvenile books, feature film, TV scripts, theatrical stage play. **Considers these fiction areas:** commercial, contemporary issues, juvenile, literary, mainstream, new adult, religious, women's, young adult.

HOW TO CONTACT "For fiction: query letter with outline and three sample chapters, resume and SASE. For nonfiction: query letter with complete description of subject, at least one chapter, resume and SASE. Queries may be sent via regular mail or e-mail. Please do not submit queries via UPS or Federal Express. Please do not send attachments with e-mail queries Please incorporate the chapters into the body of the e-mail." Accepts simultaneous submissions. Responds in less than 1 week generally to a full query and 6 weeks to a full ms. Obtains most new clients through recommendations from others, solicitations, conferences.

TERMS Agent receives 15% commission on domestic sales; 20% commission on foreign sales. Offers written contract; 30-day notice must be given to terminate contract.

SCOVIL GALEN GHOSH LITERARY AGENCY, INC.

276 Fifth Ave., Suite 708, New York NY 10001. (212)679-8686. **Fax:** (212)679-6710. **E-mail:** info@sgglit.com. **Website:** www.sgglit.com. **Contact:** Russell Galen. Estab. 1992. Member of AAR. Represents 300 clients.

MEMBER AGENTS Russell Galen, russellgalen@sgglit.com (novels that stretch the bounds of reality; strong, serious nonfiction books on almost any subject that teach something new; no books that are merely entertaining, such as diet or pop psych books; serious interests include science, history, journalism, biography, business, memoir, nature, politics, sports, contemporary culture, literary nonfiction, etc.); Jack Scovil, jackscovil@sgglit.com; Anna Ghosh, annaghosh@sgglit.com (nonfiction proposals on all subjects, including literary nonfiction, history, science, social and cultural issues, memoir, food, art, adventure, and travel; adult commercial and literary fiction); Ann Behar, annbehar@sgglit.com (juvenile books for all ages).

HOW TO CONTACT E-mail queries only. Note how each agent at this agency has their own submission e-mail. Accepts simultaneous submissions.

SECRET AGENT MAN

P.O. Box 1078, Lake Forest CA 92609-1078. (949)354-8411. **E-mail:** scott@secretagentman.net. **Website:** www.secretagentman.net. **Contact:** Scott Mortenson. Estab. 1999.

REPRESENTS Nonfiction, fiction, novels. **Considers these fiction areas:** action, crime, detective, horror, literary, mainstream, mystery, paranormal, psychic, religious, science fiction, spiritual, supernatural, suspense, thriller, westerns.

HOW TO CONTACT Query via e-mail only; include sample chapters, synopsis and/or outline. Prefers to read the real thing rather than a description, but a synopsis helps with getting an overall feel of the MS. Accepts simultaneous submissions. Responds in 2-6 weeks. Obtains most new clients through recommendations from others.

⊘ SELECTIC ARTISTS

9 Union Square, #123, Southbury CT 06488. **E-mail:** christopher@selectricartists.com. **E-mail:** query@selectricartists.com. **Website:** www.selectricartists.com. **Contact:** Christopher Schelling. Estab. 2011.

REPRESENTS Nonfiction, fiction, novels, short story collections, juvenile books. **Considers these fiction areas:** commercial, fantasy, feminist, gay, historical, horror, humor, juvenile, lesbian, literary, mainstream, science fiction, short story collections, suspense, thriller, young adult.

HOW TO CONTACT E-mail only. Consult agency website for status on open submissions. Accepts simultaneous submissions.

LYNN SELIGMAN, LITERARY AGENT

400 Highland Ave., Upper Montclair NJ 07043. (973)783-3631. **E-mail:** seliglit@aol.com. **Contact:** Lynn Seligman. Estab. 1986. Women's Media Group Represents 35 clients.

REPRESENTS Nonfiction, fiction, novels. **Considers these fiction areas:** commercial, ethnic, fantasy, feminist, historical, horror, humor, literary, mainstream, mystery, new adult, romance, science fiction, women's, young adult.

HOW TO CONTACT Query with SASE or via e-mail with no attachments. Prefers to read materials exclusively but if not, please inform. Answers written

queries, but does not respond to e-mail queries if not appropriate for the agency. Accepts simultaneous submissions. Responds in 2 weeks to queries; 2 months to mss. Obtains new clients through referrals from other writers and editors as well as unsolicited queries.

TERMS Agent receives 15% commission on domestic sales; 25% commission on foreign sales. Charges clients for photocopying, unusual postage, express mail, telephone expenses (checks with author first).

RECENT SALES Sold 12 titles in 2017 including novels by Dee Ernst, Alexandra Hawkins, and Terra Little.

SERENDIPITY LITERARY AGENCY, LLC

305 Gates Ave., Brooklyn NY 11216. **E-mail:** rbrooks@serendipitylit.com; info@serendipitylit.com. **Website:** www.serendipitylit.com; facebook.com/serendipitylit. **Contact:** Regina Brooks. Estab. 2000. Member of AAR. Signatory of WGA. Represents 150 clients.

MEMBER AGENTS Regina Brooks; Dawn Michelle Hardy (nonfiction, including sports, pop culture, blog and trend, music, lifestyle and social science); Folade Bell (literary and commercial women's fiction, YA, literary mysteries & thrillers, historical fiction, African-American issues, gay/lesbian, Christian fiction, humor and books that deeply explore other cultures; nonfiction that reads like fiction, including blog-to-book or pop culture); Nadeen Gayle (romance, memoir, pop culture, inspirational/ religious, women's fiction, parenting, young adult, mystery and political thrillers, and all forms of nonfiction); Rebecca Bugger (narrative nonfiction, investigative journalism, memoir, inspirational self-help, religion/spirituality, international, popular culture, and current affairs; literary and commercial fiction); Christina Morgan (literary fiction, crime fiction, and narrative nonfiction in the categories of pop culture, sports, current events and memoir); Jocquelle Caiby (literary fiction, horror, middle grade fiction, and children's books by authors who have been published in the adult market, athletes, actors, journalists, politicians, and musicians).

REPRESENTS Nonfiction, fiction, novels. **Considers these fiction areas:** commercial, gay, historical, lesbian, literary, middle grade, mystery, romance, thriller, women's, young adult, Christian.

HOW TO CONTACT Check the website, as there are online submission forms for fiction, nonfiction and juvenile. Website will also state if we're temporarily closed to submissions to any areas. Accepts simultaneous submissions. Obtains most new clients through conferences, referrals.

TERMS Agent receives 15% commission on domestic sales; 20% commission on foreign sales. Offers written contract; 2-month notice must be given to terminate contract. Charges clients for office fees, which are taken from any advance.

THE SEYMOUR AGENCY

475 Miner St., Canton NY 13617. (239) 398-8209. **E-mail:** nicole@theseymouragency.com; julie@theseymouragency.com. **Website:** www.theseymouragency.com. Member of AAR. Signatory of WGA. Other memberships include RWA, Authors Guild, RWA, ACFW, HWA, MWA, SCBWI.

MEMBER AGENTS Nicole Rescinti, nicole@theseymouragency.com; Julie Gwinn, julie@theseymouragency.com; Tina Wainscott, tina@theseymouragency.com; Jennifer Wills, jennifer@theseymouragency.com; Lesley Sabga, lesley@theseymourageency.com.

REPRESENTS Nonfiction, fiction, novels, juvenile books. **Considers these fiction areas:** action, adventure, commercial, contemporary issues, erotica, ethnic, experimental, family saga, fantasy, feminist, frontier, gay, horror, humor, inspirational, lesbian, literary, mainstream, metaphysical, middle grade, military, multicultural, multimedia, mystery, new adult, New Age, occult, paranormal, picture books, police, religious, romance, science fiction, spiritual, sports, supernatural, suspense, thriller, translation, urban fantasy, war, westerns, women's, young adult.

HOW TO CONTACT Accepts e-mail queries. Check online for guidelines. Accepts simultaneous submissions. Responds in 1 month to queries; 3 months to mss.

TERMS Agent receives 12-15% commission on domestic sales.

DENISE SHANNON LITERARY AGENCY, INC.

20 W. 22nd St., Suite 1603, New York NY 10010. **E-mail:** info@deniseshannonagency.com. **E-mail:** submissions@deniseshannonagency.com. **Website:** www.deniseshannonagency.com. **Contact:** Denise Shannon. Estab. 2002. Member of AAR.

REPRESENTS Nonfiction, novels. **Considers these fiction areas:** literary.

HOW TO CONTACT "Queries may be submitted by post, accompanied by a SASE, or by e-mail to submissions@deniseshannonagency.com. Please include a description of the available book project and a brief bio including details of any prior publications. We will reply and request more material if we are interested. We request that you inform us if you are submitting material simultaneously to other agencies." Accepts simultaneous submissions.

⊘ KEN SHERMAN & ASSOCIATES

1275 N. Hayworth Ave., Suite 103, Los Angeles CA 90046. (310)273-8840. **E-mail:** kenshermanassociates@gmail.com. **E-mail:** ksasubmissions@gmail.com. **Website:** www.kenshermanassociates.com. **Contact:** Ken Sherman. Estab. 1989. BAFTA (British Academy of Film and Television Arts). Represents 35 clients.

REPRESENTS Nonfiction, fiction, novels, movie scripts, feature film, TV scripts, TV movie of the week, miniseries, teleplays, life rights, film/TV rights to books and life rights. **Considers these fiction areas:** action, adventure, commercial, crime, detective, family saga, gay, literary, mainstream, middle grade, mystery, police, romance, satire, science fiction, suspense, thriller, women's, young adult.

HOW TO CONTACT Contact by referral only, please. Reports in approximately 1 month. Accepts simultaneous submissions. Obtains most new clients through recommendations from others.

TERMS Agent receives 15% commission on domestic and foreign sales; 10-15% commission on film sales. Offers written contract. Charges clients for reasonable office expenses (postage, photocopying, etc.).

WRITERS CONFERENCES Maui Writers' Conference; Squaw Valley Writers' Workshop; Santa Barbara Writers' Conference; Screenwriting Conference in Santa Fe; Aspen Summer Words Literary Festival including The Aspen Institute, the San Francisco Writer's Conference, Eugene International Film Festival, The Chautauqua Institute - Writer's Conference, La Jolla Writer's Conference, Central Coast Writer's Conference (California), etc.

WENDY SHERMAN ASSOCIATES, INC.

138 W. 25th St., Suite 1018, New York NY 10001. (212)279-9027. **E-mail:** submissions@wsherman.com. **Website:** www.wsherman.com. **Contact:** Wendy Sherman. Estab. 1999. Member of AAR.

MEMBER AGENTS Wendy Sherman (women's fiction that hits that sweet spot between literary and mainstream, Southern voices, suspense with a well-developed protagonist, anything related to food, dogs, mothers and daughters).

REPRESENTS Nonfiction, fiction, novels, juvenile books. **Considers these fiction areas:** mainstream, Mainstream fiction that hits the sweet spot between literary and commercial.

HOW TO CONTACT Query via e-mail only. "We ask that you include your last name, title, and the name of the agent you are submitting to in the subject line. For fiction, please include a query letter and your first 10 pages copied and pasted in the body of the e-mail. We will not open attachments unless they have been requested. For nonfiction, please include your query letter and author bio. Due to the large number of e-mail submissions that we receive, we only reply to e-mail queries in the affirmative. We respectfully ask that you do not send queries to our individual e-mail addresses." Accepts simultaneous submissions. Obtains most new clients through recommendations from other writers.

TERMS Agent receives standard 15% commission. Offers written contract.

BEVERLEY SLOPEN LITERARY AGENCY

131 Bloor St. W., Suite 711, Toronto ON M5S 1S3 Canada. (416)964-9598. **E-mail:** beverly@slopenagency.ca. **Website:** www.slopenagency.com. **Contact:** Beverley Slopen. Represents 70 clients.

REPRESENTS Nonfiction, novels. **Considers these fiction areas:** commercial, literary, mystery, suspense.

HOW TO CONTACT Query by e-mail. Returns materials only with SASE (Canadian postage only). To submit a work for consideration, e-mail a short query letter and a few sample pages. Submit only one work at a time. "If we want to see more, we will contact the writer by phone or e-mail." Accepts simultaneous submissions. Responds in 1 month to queries only if interested.

TERMS Agent receives 15% commission on domestic sales; 10% commission on foreign sales. Offers written contract, binding for 2 years; 3-month notice must be given to terminate contract.

TIPS "Please, no unsolicited manuscripts."

SPECTRUM LITERARY AGENCY

320 Central Park W., Suite 1-D, New York NY 10025. (212)362-4323. **Fax:** (212)362-4562. **Website:** www.spectrumliteraryagency.com. **Contact:** Eleanor

Wood, president. Estab. 1976. SFWA Represents 90 clients.

MEMBER AGENTS Eleanor Wood (referrals only; commercial fiction: science fiction, fantasy, suspense, as well as select nonfiction); Justin Bell (science fiction, mysteries, and select nonfiction).

REPRESENTS Novels. **Considers these fiction areas:** commercial, fantasy, mystery, science fiction, suspense.

HOW TO CONTACT Unsolicited mss are not accepted. Send snail mail query with SASE. "The letter should describe your book briefly and include publishing credits and background information or qualifications relating to your work, and the first 10 pages of your work. Our response time is generally 2-3 months." Responds in 1-3 months to queries. Obtains most new clients through recommendations from authors.

TERMS Agent receives 15% commission on domestic sales. Deducts for photocopying and book orders.

TIPS "Spectrum's policy is to read only book-length manuscripts that we have specifically asked to see. Unsolicited manuscripts are not accepted. The letter should describe your book briefly and include publishing credits and background information or qualifications relating to your work, if any."

SPEILBURG LITERARY AGENCY

E-mail: speilburgliterary@gmail.com. **Website:** speilburgliterary.com. **Contact:** Alice Speilburg. Estab. 2012. SCBWI; MWA; RWA.

MEMBER AGENTS Alice Speilburg worked for John Wiley & Sons and Howard Morhaim Literary Agency, before launching Speilburg Literary. She is a member of Romance Writers of America, Mystery Writers of America, and Society of Children's Book Writers and Illustrators, and she is a board member of Louisville Literary Arts. She represents novels and narrative nonfiction. Eva Scalzo has a B.A. in the Humanities from the University of Puerto Rico and a M.A. in Publishing and Writing from Emerson College. She has spent her career in scholarly publishing, working for Houghton Mifflin, Blackwell Publishing, John Wiley & Sons, and Cornell University in a variety of roles. Eva is looking to represent all subgenres of Romance, with the exclusion of inspirational romance, as well as Young Adult fiction.

REPRESENTS Nonfiction, fiction, novels. **Considers these fiction areas:** adventure, commercial, detective, fantasy, feminist, historical, horror, mainstream, mystery, police, romance, science fiction, suspense, urban fantasy, westerns, women's, young adult.

HOW TO CONTACT In the subject line of your query e-mail, please include "Query [AGENT'S FIRST NAME]" followed by the title of your project. For fiction, please send the query letter and the first three chapters. For nonfiction, please send the query letter and a proposal, which should include a detailed TOC and a sample chapter. Accepts simultaneous submissions.

SPENCERHILL ASSOCIATES

8131 Lakewood Main St., Building M, Suite 205, Lakewood Ranch FL 34202. (941)907-3700. **E-mail:** submission@spencerhillassociates.com. **Website:** www. spencerhillassociates.com. **Contact:** Karen Solem, Nalini Akolekar, Amanda Leuck, Sandy Harding, and Ali Herring. Member of AAR.

MEMBER AGENTS Karen Solem; Nalini Akolekar; Amanda Leuck; Sandy Harding; Ali Herring.

REPRESENTS Fiction, novels, juvenile books. **Considers these fiction areas:** commercial, contemporary issues, crime, detective, erotica, family saga, feminist, gay, historical, inspirational, lesbian, literary, mainstream, middle grade, multicultural, mystery, new adult, paranormal, police, religious, romance, suspense, thriller, women's, young adult.

HOW TO CONTACT "We accept electronic submissions only. Please send us a query letter in the body of an e-mail, pitch us your project and tell us about yourself: Do you have prior publishing credits? Attach the first three chapters and synopsis preferably in .doc, rtf or txt format to your email. Send all queries to submission@spencerhillassociates.com. Or submit through the QueryManager link on our website. We do not have a preference for exclusive submissions, but do appreciate knowing if the submission is simultaneous. We receive thousands of submissions a year and each query receives our attention. Unfortunately, we are unable to respond to each query individually. If we are interested in your work, we will contact you within 12 weeks." Accepts simultaneous submissions. Responds in approximately 12 weeks.

TERMS Agent receives 15% commission on domestic sales; 20% commission on foreign sales. Offers written contract; 3-month notice must be given to terminate contract.

RECENT SALES A full list of sales and clients is available on the agency website.

THE SPIELER AGENCY

27 W. 20 St., Suite 302, New York NY 10011. (212)757-4439, ext. 1. **Fax:** (212)333-2019. **Website:** thespieleragency.com. **Contact:** Joe Spieler. Represents 160 clients.

MEMBER AGENTS Victoria Shoemaker, victoria@thespieleragency.com (environment and natural history, popular culture, memoir, photography and film, literary fiction and poetry, and books on food and cooking); John Thornton, john@thespieleragency.com (nonfiction); Joe Spieler, joe@thespieleragency.com (nonfiction and fiction and books for children and young adults); Helen Sweetland, helen@thespieleragency.com (children's from board books through young adult fiction; adult general-interest nonfiction, including nature, green living, gardening, architecture, interior design, health, and popular science).

REPRESENTS Nonfiction, novels, juvenile books. **Considers these fiction areas:** literary, middle grade, New Age, picture books, thriller, young adult.

HOW TO CONTACT "Before submitting projects to the Spieler Agency, check the listings of our individual agents and see if any particular agent shows a general interest in your subject (e.g. history, memoir, YA, etc.). Please send all queries either by e-mail or regular mail. If you query us by regular mail, we can only reply to you if you include a SASE." Accepts simultaneous submissions. Cannot guarantee a personal response to all queries. Obtains most new clients through recommendations, listing in *Guide to Literary Agents*.

TERMS Agent receives 15% commission on domestic sales. Charges clients for messenger bills, photocopying, postage.

WRITERS CONFERENCES London Book Fair.

PHILIP G. SPITZER LITERARY AGENCY, INC

50 Talmage Farm Ln., East Hampton NY 11937. (631)329-3650. **Fax:** (631)329-3651. **E-mail:** lukas. ortiz@spitzeragency.com; annelise.spitzer@spitzeragency.com. **E-mail:** kim.lombardini@spitzeragency. com. **Website:** www.spitzeragency.com. **Contact:** Lukas Ortiz. Estab. 1969. Member of AAR.

MEMBER AGENTS Philip G. Spitzer; Anne-Lise Spitzer; Lukas Ortiz.

REPRESENTS Novels. **Considers these fiction areas:** literary, mainstream, suspense, thriller.

HOW TO CONTACT E-mail query containing synopsis of work, brief biography, and a sample chapter (pasted into the e-mail). Be aware that this agency openly says their client list is quite full. Obtains most new clients through recommendations from others.

TERMS Agent receives 15% commission on domestic sales; 20% commission on foreign sales.

RECENT SALES *The Jealous Kind*, by James Lee Burke (Simon & Schuster); *The Ex*, by Alafair Burke (HarperCollins); *Townie*, by Andre Dubus III (Norton); *The Wrong Side of Goodbye*, by Michael Connelly (Little, Brown & Co); *The Emerald Lie*, Ken Bruen (Mysterious Press/Grove-Atlantic); *Terror in the City of Champions*, by Tom Stanton (Lyons Press); *The Brain Defense*, by Kevin Davis (Penguin Press); *The Silent Girls*, by Eric Rickstad (HarperCollins); *Assume Nothing*, Gar Anthony Haywood (Severn House); *The Hanged Man*, by Gary Inbinder (Norton); *Cold Black Earth*, by Sam Reaves (Thomas & Mercer); *Mexico*, by Josh Barkan (Hogarth).

WRITERS CONFERENCES London Bookfair, Frankfurt, BookExpo America, Bouchercon.

NANCY STAUFFER ASSOCIATES

P.O. Box 1203, Darien CT 06820. (203)202-2500. **E-mail:** nancy@staufferliterary.com. **Website:** www.publishersmarketplace.com/members/nstauffer. **Contact:** Nancy Stauffer Cahoon. Other memberships include Authors Guild.

REPRESENTS **Considers these fiction areas:** literary.

HOW TO CONTACT Accepts simultaneous submissions. Obtains most new clients through referrals from existing clients.

TERMS Agent receives 15% commission on domestic sales.

STONESONG

270 W. 39th St. #201, New York NY 10018. (212)929-4600. **E-mail:** editors@stonesong.com. **E-mail:** submissions@stonesong.com. **Website:** stonesong.com. Member of AAR. Signatory of WGA.

MEMBER AGENTS Alison Fargis; Ellen Scordato; Judy Linden; Emmanuelle Morgen; Leila Campoli (business, science, technology, and self improvement); Maria Ribas (cookbooks, self-help, health, diet, home, parenting, and humor, all from authors with demonstrable platforms; she's also interested in narrative nonfiction and select memoir); Melissa Edwards (children's fiction and adult commercial fiction, as well as select pop-culture nonfiction); Alyssa Jennette (children's and adult fiction and picture books, and has dabbled in humor and pop culture nonfiction); Madelyn Burt (adult and children's fiction, as well as select historical nonfiction).

REPRESENTS Nonfiction, fiction, novels, juvenile books. **Considers these fiction areas:** action, adventure, commercial, confession, contemporary issues, ethnic, experimental, family saga, fantasy, feminist, gay, historical, horror, humor, juvenile, lesbian, literary, mainstream, middle grade, military, multicultural, mystery, new adult, New Age, occult, paranormal, regional, romance, satire, science fiction, supernatural, suspense, thriller, urban fantasy, women's, young adult.

HOW TO CONTACT Accepts electronic queries for fiction and nonfiction. Submit query addressed to a specific agent. Include first chapter or first 10 pages of ms. Accepts simultaneous submissions.

RECENT SALES *Sweet Laurel*, by Laurel Gallucci and Claire Thomas; *Terrain: A Seasonal Guide to Nature at Home*, by Terrain; *The Prince's Bane*, by Alexandra Christo; *Deep Listening*, by Jillian Pransky; *Change Resilience*, by Lior Arussy; *A Thousand Words*, by Brigit Young.

⊘ STRACHAN LITERARY AGENCY

P.O. Box 2091, Annapolis MD 21404. **E-mail:** query@strachanlit.com. **Website:** www.strachanlit.com. **Contact:** Laura Strachan. Estab. 1998.

REPRESENTS Nonfiction, fiction, novels, short story collections, juvenile books. **Considers these fiction areas:** feminist, literary, multicultural, short story collections, translation, young adult.

HOW TO CONTACT Please query with description of project and short biographical statement. Do not paste or attach sample pages. Accepts simultaneous submissions.

ROBIN STRAUS AGENCY, INC.

The Wallace Literary Agency, 229 E. 79th St., Suite 5A, New York NY 10075. (212)472-3282. **Fax:** (212)472-3833. **E-mail:** info@robinstrausagency.com. **Website:** www.robinstrausagency.com. **Contact:** Ms. Robin Straus. Estab. 1983. Member of AAR.

REPRESENTS Considers these fiction areas: commercial, contemporary issues, fantasy, feminist, literary, mainstream, science fiction, translation, women's.

HOW TO CONTACT E-query only. No physical mail accepted. See our website for full submission instructions. Email us a query letter with contact information, an autobiographical summary, a brief synopsis or description of your book project, submission history, and information on competition. If you wish, you may also include the opening chapter of your manuscript (pasted). While we do our best to reply to all queries, you can assume that if you haven't heard from us after six weeks, we are not interested. Accepts simultaneous submissions.

TERMS Agent receives 15% commission on domestic sales; 20% commission on foreign sales. Offers written contract.

THE STRINGER LITERARY AGENCY LLC

P.O. Box 111255, Naples FL 34108. **E-mail:** mstringer@stringerlit.com. **Website:** www.stringerlit.com. **Contact:** Marlene Stringer. Estab. 2008. Member of AAR. Signatory of WGA. RWA, MWA, ITW, SBCWI Represents 50 clients.

REPRESENTS Fiction, novels. **Considers these fiction areas:** commercial, crime, detective, fantasy, historical, horror, mainstream, multicultural, mystery, new adult, paranormal, police, romance, science fiction, suspense, thriller, urban fantasy, women's, young adult, No space opera SF.

HOW TO CONTACT Electronic submissions through website submission form only. Please make sure your ms is as good as it can be before you submit. Agents are not first readers. For specific information on what we like to see in query letters, refer to the information at www.stringerlit.com under the heading "Learn." Accepts simultaneous submissions. "We strive to respond quickly, but current clients' work always comes first." Obtains new clients through referrals, submissions, conferences.

TERMS Standard commission. "We do not charge fees."

THE STROTHMAN AGENCY, LLC

63 E. 9th St., 10X, New York NY 10003. **E-mail:** info@strothmanagency.com. **E-mail:** strothmanagency@gmail.com. **Website:** www.strothmanagency.com. **Contact:** Wendy Strothman, Lauren MacLeod. Estab. 2003. Member of AAR. Represents 100+ clients.

MEMBER AGENTS Wendy Strothman (history, narrative nonfiction, narrative journalism, science and nature, and current affairs); Lauren MacLeod (young adult fiction and nonfiction, middle grade novels, as well as adult narrative nonfiction, particularly food writing, science, pop culture and history).

REPRESENTS Nonfiction, juvenile books. **Considers these fiction areas:** middle grade, young adult.

HOW TO CONTACT Accepts queries only via e-mail. See submission guidelines online. Accepts simultaneous submissions. "All e-mails received will be responded to with an auto-reply. If we have not replied to your query within 6 weeks, we do not feel that it is right for us." Accepts simultaneous submissions. Obtains most new clients through recommendations from others.

TERMS Agent receives 15% commission on domestic sales; 20% commission on foreign sales. Offers written contract; 30-day notice must be given to terminate contract.

THE STUART AGENCY

260 W. 52 St., #25C, New York NY 10019. (212)586-2711. **E-mail:** andrew@stuartagency.com. **Website:** stuartagency.com. **Contact:** Andrew Stuart. Estab. 2002.

MEMBER AGENTS Andrew Stuart (history, science, narrative nonfiction, business, current events, memoir, psychology, sports, literary fiction); Christopher Rhodes, christopher@stuartagency.com (literary and upmarket fiction [including thriller and horror]; connected stories/essays [humorous and serious]; memoir; creative/narrative nonfiction; history; religion; pop culture; and art & design); Rob Kirkpatrick, rob@stuartagency.com (memoir, biography, sports, music, pop culture, current events, history, and pop science).

REPRESENTS Nonfiction, novels. **Considers these fiction areas:** horror, literary, thriller.

HOW TO CONTACT Query via online submission form on the agency website. Accepts simultaneous submissions.

EMMA SWEENEY AGENCY, LLC

245 E 80th St., Suite 7E, New York NY 10075. **E-mail:** info@emmasweeneyagency.com. **E-mail:** queries@emmasweeneyagency.com. **Website:** www.emmasweeneyagency.com. Estab. 2006. Member of AAR.

Other memberships include Women's Media Group. Represents 80 clients.

MEMBER AGENTS Emma Sweeney, president; Margaret Sutherland Brown (commercial and literary fiction, mysteries and thrillers, narrative nonfiction, lifestyle, and cookbook); Kira Watson (children's literature).

REPRESENTS Nonfiction, fiction, novels, juvenile books. **Considers these fiction areas:** commercial, contemporary issues, crime, historical, horror, juvenile, literary, mainstream, middle grade, mystery, new adult, suspense, thriller, women's, young adult.

HOW TO CONTACT "We accept only electronic queries, and ask that all queries be sent to queries@ emmasweeneyagency.com rather than to any agent directly. Please begin your query with a succinct (and hopefully catchy) description of your plot or proposal. Always include a brief cover letter telling us how you heard about ESA, your previous writing credits, and a few lines about yourself. We cannot open any attachments unless specifically requested, and ask that you paste the first 10 pages of your proposal or novel into the text of your e-mail." Accepts simultaneous submissions.

STEPHANIE TADE LITERARY AGENCY

P.O. Box 235, Durham PA 18039. (610)346-8667. **E-mail:** submissions@stephanietadeagency.com. **Website:** stephanietadeagency.com. **Contact:** Stephanie Tade.

MEMBER AGENTS Stephanie Tade, president and principal agent; Colleen Martell, editorial director and associate agent (cmartell@stadeagency.com).

REPRESENTS Nonfiction, fiction.

HOW TO CONTACT Query by e-mail or mail with SASE. "When you write to the agency, please include information about your proposed book, your publishing history and any media or online platform you have developed." Accepts simultaneous submissions.

TALCOTT NOTCH LITERARY

31 Cherry St., Suite 100, Milford CT 06460. (203)876-4959. **Fax:** (203)876-9517. **E-mail:** editorial@talcottnotch.net. **Website:** www.talcottnotch.net. **Contact:** Gina Panettieri, President. Represents 150 clients.

MEMBER AGENTS Gina Panettieri, gpanettieri@ talcottnotch.net (history, business, self-help, science, gardening, cookbooks, crafts, parenting, memoir, true crime and travel, YA, MG and women's fiction, paranormal, urban fantasy, horror, science fiction, historical, mystery, thrillers and suspense); Paula Munier, pmunier@talcottnotch.net (mystery/thriller, SF/fantasy, romance, YA, memoir, humor, pop culture, health & wellness, cooking, self-help, pop psych, New Age, inspirational, technology, science, and writing); Saba Sulaiman, ssulaiman@talcottnotch.net (upmarket literary and commercial fiction, romance [all subgenres except paranormal], character-driven psychological thrillers, cozy mysteries, memoir, young adult [except paranormal and sci-fi], middle grade, and nonfiction humor).

REPRESENTS Nonfiction, fiction, novels, short story collections, novellas, juvenile books. **Considers these fiction areas:** action, adventure, commercial, contemporary issues, crime, ethnic, fantasy, feminist, gay, hi-lo, historical, horror, juvenile, lesbian, literary, mainstream, middle grade, multicultural, multimedia, mystery, new adult, New Age, paranormal, police, romance, science fiction, short story collections, suspense, thriller, urban fantasy, women's, young adult.

HOW TO CONTACT Query via e-mail (preferred) with first 10 pages of the ms pasted within the body of the e-mail, not as an attachment. Accepts simultaneous submissions. Responds in 2 weeks to queries; 6-10 weeks to mss.

TERMS Agent receives 15% commission on domestic sales; 20% commission on foreign sales. Offers written contract, binding for 1 year.

TESSLER LITERARY AGENCY, LLC

27 W. 20th St., Suite 1003, New York NY 10011. (212)242-0466. **Website:** www.tessleragency.com. **Contact:** Michelle Tessler. Estab. 2004. Member of AAR. Women's Media Group.

REPRESENTS Nonfiction, fiction, novels. **Considers these fiction areas:** commercial, ethnic, family saga, historical, literary, multicultural, women's.

HOW TO CONTACT Submit query through online query form only. Accepts simultaneous submissions. New clients by queries/submissions through the website and recommendations from others.

TERMS Receives 15% commission on domestic sales; 20% on foreign sales. Offers written contract.

THOMPSON LITERARY AGENCY

115 W. 29th St., Third Floor, New York NY 10001. (347)281-7685. **E-mail:** submissions@thompsonliterary.com. **Website:** thompsonliterary.com. **Con-**

tact: Meg Thompson, founder. Estab. 2014. Member of AAR. Signatory of WGA.

MEMBER AGENTS Cindy Uh, senior agent; Kiele Raymond, senior agent; John Thorn, affiliate agent; Sandy Hodgman, director of foreign rights.

REPRESENTS Nonfiction, fiction, novels, juvenile books. **Considers these fiction areas:** commercial, contemporary issues, experimental, fantasy, feminist, historical, juvenile, literary, middle grade, multicultural, picture books, women's, young adult.

HOW TO CONTACT "For fiction: Please send a query letter, including any salient biographical information or previous publications, and attach the first 25 pages of your manuscript. For nonfiction: Please send a query letter and a full proposal, including biographical information, previous publications, credentials that qualify you to write your book, marketing information, and sample material. You should address your query to whichever agent you think is best suited for your project." Accepts simultaneous submissions. Responds in 6 weeks if interested.

THREE SEAS LITERARY AGENCY

P.O. Box 444, Sun Prairie WI 53590. (608)834-9317. **E-mail:** queries@threeseaslit.com. **Website:** threeseasagency.com. **Contact:** Michelle Grajkowski, Cori Deyoe. Estab. 2000. Member of AAR. Other memberships include RWA (Romance Writers of America), SCBWI Represents 55 clients.

MEMBER AGENTS Michelle Grajkowski (romance, women's fiction, young adult and middle grade fiction, select nonfiction projects); Cori Deyoe (all sub-genres of romance, women's fiction, young adult, middle grade, picture books, thrillers, mysteries and select nonfiction); Linda Scalissi (women's fiction, thrillers, young adult, mysteries and romance).

REPRESENTS Nonfiction, novels. **Considers these fiction areas:** middle grade, mystery, picture books, romance, thriller, women's, young adult.

HOW TO CONTACT E-mail queries only; no attachments, unless requested by agents. For fiction, please e-mail the first chapter and synopsis along with a cover letter. Also, be sure to include the genre and the number of words in your manuscript, as well as pertinent writing experience in your query letter. For nonfiction, e-mail a complete proposal, including a query letter and your first chapter. For picture books, query with complete text. Accepts simultaneous submissions. Obtains most new clients through recommendations from others, conferences.

TERMS Agent receives 15% commission on domestic sales; 20% commission on foreign sales. Offers written contract.

RECENT SALES REPRESENTS Bestselling authors, including Jennifer Brown, Katie MacAlister, Kerrelyn Sparks, and C.L. Wilson.

☉ TRANSATLANTIC LITERARY AGENCY

2 Bloor St. E., Suite 3500, Toronto ON M4W 1A8 Canada. (416)488-9214. **E-mail:** info@transatlanticagency.com. **Website:** transatlanticagency.com.

MEMBER AGENTS Trena White (upmarket, accessible non-fiction: current affairs, business, culture, politics, technology, and the environment); Amy Tompkins (adult: literary fiction, historical fiction, women's fiction including smart romance, narrative non-fiction, and quirky or original how-to books; children's: early readers, middle grade, young adult, and new adult); Stephanie Sinclair (literary fiction, upmarket women's and commercial fiction, literary thriller and suspense, YA crossover; narrative non-fiction, memoir, investigative journalism and true crime); Samantha Haywood (literary fiction and upmarket commercial fiction, specifically literary thrillers and upmarket mystery, historical fiction, smart contemporary fiction, upmarket women's fiction and cross-over novels; narrative nonfiction, including investigative journalism, politics, women's issues, memoirs, environmental issues, historical narratives, sexuality, true crime; graphic novels (fiction/nonfiction): preferably full length graphic novels, story collections considered, memoirs, biographies, travel narratives); Jesse Finkelstein (nonfiction: current affairs, business, culture, politics, technology, religion, and the environment); Marie Campbell (middle grade fiction); Shaun Bradley (referrals only; adult literary fiction and narrative nonfiction, primarily science and investigative journalism); Sandra Bishop (fiction; nonfiction: biography, memoir, and positive or humorous how-to books on advice/relationships, mind/body/spirit, religion, healthy living, finances, life-hacks, traveling, living a better life); Fiona Kenshole (children's and young adult; only accepting submissions from referrals or conferences she attends as faculty); Lynn Bennett (not accepting submissions or new clients); David Bennett (children's, young adult, adult).

REPRESENTS Nonfiction, novels, juvenile books.

HOW TO CONTACT Always refer to the website, as guidelines will change, and only various agents are open to new clients at any given time. Obtains most new clients through recommendations from others.

TERMS Agent receives 15% commission on domestic sales; 20% commission on foreign sales. Offers written contract; 45-day notice must be given to terminate contract. This agency charges for photocopying and postage when it exceeds $100.

RECENT SALES Sold 250 titles in the last year.

TRIADA US

P.O. Box 561, Sewickley PA 15143. (412)401-3376. **E-mail:** uwe@triadaus.com; brent@triadaus.com; laura@triadaus.com; lauren@triadaus.com; amelia@triadaus.com. **Website:** www.triadaus.com. **Contact:** Dr. Uwe Stender, President. Estab. 2004. Member of AAR.

MEMBER AGENTS Uwe Stender; Brent Taylor; Laura Crockett; Lauren Spieller; Amelia Appel.

REPRESENTS Nonfiction, fiction, novels, juvenile books. **Considers these fiction areas:** action, adventure, comic books, commercial, contemporary issues, crime, detective, ethnic, family saga, fantasy, gay, historical, horror, juvenile, lesbian, literary, mainstream, middle grade, multicultural, mystery, new adult, occult, picture books, police, suspense, thriller, urban fantasy, women's, young adult.

HOW TO CONTACT E-mail queries preferred. Please paste your query letter and the first 10 pages of your ms into the body of a message e-mailed to the agent of your choice. Please note: a rejection from 1 Triada US agent is a rejection from all. Triada US agents personally respond to all queries and requested material and pride themselves on having some of the fastest response times in the industry. Obtains most new clients through submission inbox (query letters and requested mss), client referrals, and conferences.

TERMS Triada US retains 15% commission on domestic sales and 20% commission on foreign and translation sales. Offers written contract; 30-day notice must be given prior to termination.

RECENT SALES *The Hemingway Thief*, by Shaun Harris (Seventh Street); *Finder's Fee*, by Summer Heacock (Mira); *Not Perfect*, by Elizabeth LaBan (Lake Union); *Sometime After Midnight*, by L. Philips (Viking); *The Diminished*, by Kaitlyn Sage Patterson (Harlequin Teen); *A Short History of the Girl Next Door*, by Jared Reck (Knopf); *Chaotic Good*, by Whitney Gardner (Knopf); *Project Pandora*, by Aden Polydoros (Entangled Teen); *Skulls!*, by Blair Thornburgh (Atheneum).

TRIDENT MEDIA GROUP

41 Madison Ave., 36th Floor, New York NY 10010. (212)333-1511. **Website:** www.tridentmediagroup.com. **Contact:** Ellen Levine. Member of AAR.

MEMBER AGENTS Kimberly Whalen, ws.assistant@tridentmediagroup (commercial fiction and nonfiction, including women's fiction, romance, suspense, paranormal, and pop culture); Alyssa Eisner Henkin (picture books through young adult fiction, including mysteries, period pieces, contemporary school-settings, issues of social justice, family sagas, eerie magical realism, and retellings of classics; children's/YA nonfiction: history, STEM/STEAM themes, memoir) Scott Miller, smiller@tridentmediagroup.com (commercial fiction, including thrillers, crime fiction, women's, book club fiction, middle grade, young adult; nonfiction, including military, celebrity and pop culture, narrative, sports, prescriptive, and current events); Melissa Flashman, mflashman@tridentmediagroup.com (nonfiction: pop culture, memoir, wellness, popular science, business and economics, technology; fiction: adult and YA, literary and commercial); Don Fehr, dfehr@tridentmediagroup.com (literary and commercial fiction, young adult fiction, narrative nonfiction, memoirs, travel, science, and health); John Silbersack, silbersack.assistant@tridentmediagroup.com (fiction: literary fiction, crime fiction, science fiction and fantasy, children's, thrillers/suspense; nonfiction: narrative nonfiction, science, history, biography, current events, memoirs, finance, pop culture); Erica Spellman-Silverman; Ellen Levine, levine.assistant@tridentmediagroup.com (popular commercial fiction and compelling nonfiction, including memoir, popular culture, narrative nonfiction, history, politics, biography, science, and the odd quirky book); Mark Gottlieb (fiction: science fiction, fantasy, young adult, graphic novels, historical, middle grade, mystery, romance, suspense, thrillers; nonfiction: business, finance, history, religious, health, cookbooks, sports, African-American, biography, memoir, travel, mind/body/spirit, narrative nonfiction, science, technology); Alexander Slater, aslater@tridentmdiagroup.com (children's, middle grade, and young adult fiction); Amanda O'Connor, aoconnor@tridentmediagroup.com; Tara Carberry, tcarberry@tridentmediagroup.com (women's commercial fiction, romance, new adult, young adult, and select nonfiction); Alexa Stark, astark@tridentmedia-group.com (literary fiction, upmarket commercial fiction, young adult, memoir, narrative nonfiction, popular science, cultural criticism and women's issues).

REPRESENTS Considers these fiction areas: commercial, crime, fantasy, historical, juvenile, literary, middle grade, mystery, new adult, paranormal, picture books, romance, science fiction, suspense, thriller, women's, young adult.

HOW TO CONTACT Submit through the agency's online submission form on the agency website. Query only one agent at a time. If you e-query, include no attachments. Accepts simultaneous submissions.

TIPS "If you have any questions, please check FAQ page before e-mailing us."

THE UNTER AGENCY

23 W. 73rd St., Suite 100, New York NY 10023. (212)401-4068. **E-mail:** jennifer@theunteragency. com. **Website:** www.theunteragency.com. **Contact:** Jennifer Unter. Estab. 2008. Member of AAR. Women Media Group

REPRESENTS Nonfiction, fiction, novels, short story collections, juvenile books. **Considers these fiction areas:** action, adventure, cartoon, commercial, family saga, inspirational, juvenile, mainstream, middle grade, mystery, paranormal, picture books, thriller, women's, young adult.

HOW TO CONTACT Send an e-query. There is also an online submission form. If you do not hear back from this agency within 3 months, consider that a no. Accepts simultaneous submissions. Responds in 3 months.

RECENT SALES A full list of recent sales/titles is available on the agency website.

UPSTART CROW LITERARY

244 Fifth Avenue, 11th Floor, New York NY 10001. **E-mail:** danielle.submission@gmail.com. **Website:** www.upstartcrowliterary.com. **Contact:** Danielle Chiotti, Alexandra Penfold. Estab. 2009. Member of AAR. Signatory of WGA.

MEMBER AGENTS Michael Stearns (not accepting submissions); Danielle Chiotti (all genres of young adult and middle grade fiction; adult upmarket commercial fiction [not considering romance, mystery/suspense/thriller, science fiction, horror, or erotica]; nonfiction in the areas of narrative/memoir, lifestyle,

relationships, humor, current events, food, wine, and cooking); Ted Malawer (not accepting submissions); Alexandra Penfold (not accepting submissions); Susan Hawk (books for children and teens only).

REPRESENTS Considers these fiction areas: commercial, mainstream, middle grade, picture books, young adult.

HOW TO CONTACT Submit a query and 20 pages pasted into an e-mail. Accepts simultaneous submissions.

VERITAS LITERARY AGENCY

601 Van Ness Ave., Opera Plaza, Suite E, San Francisco CA 94102. (415)647-6964. **Fax:** (415)647-6965. **E-mail:** submissions@veritasliterary.com. **Website:** www.veritasliterary.com. **Contact:** Katherine Boyle. Member of AAR. Other memberships include Author's Guild and SCBWI.

MEMBER AGENTS Katherine Boyle, kboyle@veritasliterary.com (literary fiction, middle grade, young adult, narrative nonfiction/memoir, historical fiction, crime/suspense, history, pop culture, popular science, business/career); Michael Carr, michael@veritasliterary.com (historical fiction, women's fiction, science fiction and fantasy, nonfiction).

REPRESENTS Nonfiction, novels. **Considers these fiction areas:** commercial, crime, fantasy, historical, literary, middle grade, new adult, science fiction, suspense, women's, young adult.

HOW TO CONTACT This agency accepts short queries or proposals via e-mail only. "Fiction: Please include a cover letter listing previously published work, a one-page summary and the first 5 pages in the body of the e-mail (not as an attachment). Nonfiction: If you are sending a proposal, please include an author biography, an overview, a chapter-by-chapter summary, and an analysis of competitive titles. We do our best to review all queries within 4-6 weeks; however, if you have not heard from us in 12 weeks, consider that a no." Accepts simultaneous submissions. If you have not heard from this agency in 12 weeks, consider that a no.

WADE & CO. LITERARY AGENCY, LTD

33 Cormorant Lodge, Thomas More St., London E1W 1AU United Kingdom. (44)(207)488-4171. **Fax:** (44) (207)488-4172. **E-mail:** rw@rwla.com. **Website:** www. rwla.com. **Contact:** Robin Wade. Estab. 2001.

MEMBER AGENTS Robin Wade.

HOW TO CONTACT New proposals for full length adult and young adult books (excluding children's books or poetry) are always welcome. We much prefer to receive queries and submissions by e-mail, although we do, of course, accept proposals by post. There is no need to telephone in advance. Please provide a few details about yourself, a synopsis (i.e. a clear narrative summary of the complete story, of between say 1 and 6 pages in length) and the first 10,000 words or so (ideally as word.doc or PDF attachments) over e-mail. Accepts simultaneous submissions. Responds in 1 week to queries; 1 month to mss.

TERMS Agent receives 15% commission on domestic sales; 20% commission on foreign sales. Offers written contract; 1-month notice must be given to terminate contract.

TIPS "We seek manuscripts that are well written, with strong characters and an original narrative voice. Our absolute priority is giving the best possible service to the authors we choose to represent, as well as maintaining routine friendly contact with them as we help develop their careers."

WALES LITERARY AGENCY, INC.

1508 10th Ave. E. #401, Seattle WA 98102. (206)284-7114. **E-mail:** waleslit@waleslit.com. **Website:** www.waleslit.com. **Contact:** Elizabeth Wales; Neal Swain. Estab. 1990. Member of AAR. Other memberships include Authors Guild.

MEMBER AGENTS Elizabeth Wales; Neal Swain.

REPRESENTS Nonfiction, fiction, novels.

HOW TO CONTACT E-query with no attachments. Submission guidelines can be found at the agency website along with a list of current clients and titles. Accepts simultaneous submissions. Responds in 2 weeks to queries, 2 months to mss.

TERMS Agent receives 15% commission on domestic sales; 20% commission on foreign sales.

WATERSIDE PRODUCTIONS, INC.

2055 Oxford Ave., Cardiff CA 92007. (760)632-9190. **Fax:** (760)632-9295. **E-mail:** admin@waterside.com. **Website:** www.waterside.com. Estab. 1982.

MEMBER AGENTS Bill Gladstone (big nonfiction books); Margot Maley Hutchinson (computer, health, psychology, parenting, fitness, pop culture, and business); Carole Jelen, carole@jelenpub.com (innovation and thought leaders especially in business, technology, lifestyle and self-help); David Nelson; Jill Kramer, watersideagentjk@aol.com (quality fiction with empowering themes for adults and YA (including crossovers); nonfiction, including mind-body-spirit, self-help, celebrity memoirs, relationships, sociology, finance, psychology, health and fitness, diet/nutrition, inspiration, business, family/parenting issues); Brad Schepp (e-commerce, social media and social commerce, careers, entrepreneurship, general business, health and fitness); Natasha Gladstone, (picture books, books with film tie-ins, books with established animated characters, and educational titles); Johanna Maaghul, johanna@waterside.com (nonfiction and select fiction); Kimberly Brabec, rights@waterside.com (Director of International Rights).

REPRESENTS Considers these fiction areas: mainstream, picture books, young adult.

HOW TO CONTACT "Please read each agent bio [on the website] to determine who you think would best represent your genre of work. When you have chosen your agent, please write his or her name in the subject line of your e-mail and send it to admin@waterside.com with your query letter in the body of the e-mail, and your proposal or sample material as an attached word document." Nonfiction submission guidelines are available on the website. Accepts simultaneous submissions. Obtains most new clients through referrals from established client and publisher list.

TIPS "For new writers, a quality proposal and a strong knowledge of the market you're writing for goes a long way toward helping us turn you into a published author. We like to see a strong author platform."

⊘ WATKINS LOOMIS AGENCY, INC.

P.O. Box 20925, New York NY 10025. (212)532-0080. **Fax:** (646)383-2449. **E-mail:** assistant@watkinsloomis.com. **Website:** www.watkinsloomis.com. Estab. 1980. Represents 50+ clients.

MEMBER AGENTS Gloria Loomis, president; Julia Masnik, junior agent.

REPRESENTS Nonfiction, novels.

HOW TO CONTACT *No unsolicited mss.* This agency does not guarantee a response to queries.

TERMS Agent receives 15% commission on domestic sales; 20% commission on foreign sales.

WAXMAN LEAVELL LITERARY AGENCY,

INC.

443 Park Ave. S, Suite 1004, New York NY 10016. (212)675-5556. **Fax:** (212)675-1381. **Website:** www.waxmanleavell.com.

MEMBER AGENTS Scott Waxman (nonfiction: history, biography, health and science, adventure, business, inspirational sports); Byrd Leavell (narrative nonfiction, sports, humor, and select commercial fiction); Holly Root (middle grade, young adult, women's fiction (commercial and upmarket), urban fantasy, romance, select nonfiction); Larry Kirschbaum (fiction and nonfiction; select self-published breakout books); Rachel Vogel (nonfiction: subject-driven narratives, memoirs and biography, journalism, popular culture and the occasional humor and gift book; selective fiction); Taylor Haggerty (young adult, historical, contemporary and historical romance, middle grade, women's, new adult); Cassie Hanjian (new adult novels, plot-driven commercial and upmarket women's fiction, historical fiction, psychological suspense, cozy mysteries and contemporary romance; for nonfiction, mind/body/spirit, self-help, health and wellness, inspirational memoir, food/wine (narrative and prescriptive), and a limited number of accessible cookbooks); Fleetwood Robbins (fantasy and speculative fiction—all subgenres); Molly O'Neill (middle grade and YA fiction and picture book author/illustrators, and—more selectively—narrative nonfiction [including children's/YA/MG, pop science/pop culture, and lifestyle/food/travel/cookbook projects by authors with well-established platforms]).

REPRESENTS Nonfiction, novels. **Considers these fiction areas:** fantasy, historical, literary, mainstream, middle grade, mystery, paranormal, romance, science fiction, suspense, thriller, urban fantasy, women's, young adult.

HOW TO CONTACT To submit a project, please send a query letter only via e-mail to one of the addresses included on the website. Do not send attachments, though for fiction you may include 5-10 pages of your manuscript in the body of your e-mail. "Due to the high volume of submissions, agents will reach out to you directly if interested. The typical time range for consideration is 6-8 weeks." "Please do not query more than 1 agent at our agency simultaneously." (To see the types of projects each agent is looking for, refer to the Agent Biographies page on website.) Use these e-mails: scottsubmit@waxmanleavell.com; byrdsub-

mit@waxmanleavell.com; hollysubmit@waxmanleavell.com; rachelsubmit@waxmanleavell.com; and larrysubmit@waxmanleavell.com; taylorsubmit@waxmanleavell.com; cassiesubmit@waxmanleavell.com; mollysubmit@waxmanleavell.com. Accepts simultaneous submissions.

TERMS Agent receives 15% commission on domestic sales; 10% commission on foreign sales. Offers written contract; 2-month notice must be given to terminate contract.

⊘ CHERRY WEINER LITERARY AGENCY

925 Oak Bluff Ct., Dacula GA 30019-6660. (732)446-2096. **Fax:** (732)792-0506. **E-mail:** cherry8486@aol.com. **Contact:** Cherry Weiner. Estab. 1977. Represents 40 clients.

REPRESENTS Fiction, novels. **Considers these fiction areas:** action, adventure, commercial, contemporary issues, crime, detective, family saga, fantasy, frontier, gay, historical, horror, literary, mainstream, military, mystery, paranormal, police, psychic, romance, science fiction, supernatural, suspense, thriller, urban fantasy, westerns, women's.

HOW TO CONTACT Only wishes to receive submissions from referrals and from writers she has met at conferences/events. Responds in 1 week to queries; 2 months to requested mss.

TERMS Agent receives 15% commission on domestic sales; 15% commission on foreign sales. Offers written contract. Charges clients for extra copies of mss, first-class postage for author's copies Mailing of books first class, express mail for important documents/mss.

RECENT SALES This agency prefers not to share information on specific sales.

WRITERS CONFERENCES Western Writers of America; BoucherCon; World Science Fiction Writers Conference; World Fantasy Conference; and many writer group workshops.

TIPS "Meet agents and publishers at conferences. Establish a relationship, then get in touch with them and remind them of the meeting and conference."

THE WEINGEL-FIDEL AGENCY

310 E. 46th St., 21E, New York NY 10017. (212)599-2959. **Contact:** Loretta Weingel-Fidel.

REPRESENTS Novels. **Considers these fiction areas:** literary, mainstream.

HOW TO CONTACT Accepts writers by referral only. *No unsolicited mss.* Accepts simultaneous submissions.

TERMS Agent receives 15% commission on domestic sales; 20% commission on foreign sales. Offers written contract, binding for 1 year with automatic renewal.

TIPS "A very small, selective list enables me to work very closely with my clients to develop and nurture talent. I only take on projects and writers about which I am extremely enthusiastic."

WELLS ARMS LITERARY

New York NY **E-mail:** info@wellsarms.com. **Website:** www.wellsarms.com. Estab. 2013. Member of AAR. SCBWI, Society of Illustrators. Represents 25 clients.

REPRESENTS Nonfiction, fiction, novels, juvenile books, children's book illustrators. **Considers these fiction areas:** juvenile, middle grade, new adult, picture books, young adult.

HOW TO CONTACT E-query. Put "query" and your title in your e-mail subject line addressed to info@wellsarms.com. Accepts simultaneous submissions. We try to respond in a month's time. If no response, assume it's a no.

☮ WESTWOOD CREATIVE ARTISTS, LTD.

386 Huron St., Toronto ON M5S 2G6 Canada. (416)964-3302. **E-mail:** wca_office@wcaltd.com. **Website:** www.wcaltd.com. Represents 350+ clients.

MEMBER AGENTS Carolyn Ford (literary fiction, commercial, women's/literary crossover, thrillers, serious narrative nonfiction, pop culture); Jackie Kaiser (President and COO); Michael A. Levine (Chairman); Hilary McMahon (Executive Vice President, fiction, nonfiction, children's); John Pearce (fiction and nonfiction); Bruce Westwood (Founder, Managing Director and CEO).

REPRESENTS Nonfiction, fiction, novels. **Considers these fiction areas:** commercial, juvenile, literary, thriller, women's, young adult.

HOW TO CONTACT E-query only. Include credentials, synopsis, and no more than 10 pages. No attachments. Accepts simultaneous submissions.

TIPS "We will reject outright complete, unsolicited manuscripts, or projects that are presented poorly in the query letter. We prefer to receive exclusive submissions and request that you do not query more than one agent at the agency simultaneously. It's often best if you approach WCA after you have accumulated some publishing credits."

WHIMSY LITERARY AGENCY, LLC

49 N. 8th St., 6G, Brooklyn NY 11249. (212)674-7162. **E-mail:** whimsynyc@aol.com. **Contact:** Jackie Meyer. Represents 30 clients.

MEMBER AGENTS Jackie Meyer.

REPRESENTS Nonfiction. **Considers these fiction areas:** commercial, inspirational, New Age, paranormal, picture books, psychic.

HOW TO CONTACT Send your proposal via e-mail to whimsynyc@aol.com (include your media platform, table of contents with full description of each chapter). First-time authors: "We appreciate proposals that are professional and complete. Please consult the many fine books available on writing book proposals. We are not considering poetry, or screenplays. Please Note: Due to the volume of queries and submissions, we are unable to respond unless they are of interest to us." Accepts simultaneous submissions. Responds "quickly, but only if interested" to queries. *Does not accept unsolicited mss.* Obtains most new clients through recommendations from others, solicitations.

TERMS Agent receives 15% commission on domestic sales; 20% commission on foreign sales. Offers written contract.

WOLF LITERARY SERVICES, LLC

E-mail: queries@wolflit.com. **Website:** wolflit.com. Estab. 2008. Member of AAR. Signatory of WGA.

MEMBER AGENTS Kirsten Wolf (no queries); Kate Johnson (literary and upmarket fiction, memoir, cultural history, pop science, narrative nonfiction); Allison Devereux (literary and upmarket fiction, narrative nonfiction, cultural history and criticism, memoir, and biography); Rachel Crawford (literary fiction; high concept YA; and narrative nonfiction, particularly environmental and science journalism, ecological memoir, and queer and feminist pop culture).

REPRESENTS Nonfiction, fiction, novels. **Considers these fiction areas:** commercial, contemporary issues, family saga, fantasy, feminist, gay, historical, horror, lesbian, literary, science fiction, suspense, thriller, young adult, LGBTI+.

HOW TO CONTACT To submit a project, please send a query letter along with a 50-page writing sample (for fiction) or a detailed proposal (for nonfiction) to queries@wolflit.com. Samples may be submitted as an attachment or embedded in the body of the e-mail. Accepts simultaneous submissions.

WOLFSON LITERARY AGENCY

P.O. Box 266, New York NY 10276. **E-mail:** query@wolfsonliterary.com. **Website:** www.wolfsonliterary.com. **Contact:** Michelle Wolfson. Estab. 2007. Adheres to AAR canon of ethics.

REPRESENTS Nonfiction, fiction. **Considers these fiction areas:** commercial, mainstream, new adult, romance, thriller, women's, young adult.

HOW TO CONTACT E-queries only. Accepts simultaneous submissions. Responds only if interested. Positive response is generally given within 2-4 weeks. Responds in 3 months to mss. Obtains most new clients through queries or recommendations from others.

TERMS Agent receives 15% commission on domestic sales; 25% commission on foreign sales. Offers written contract; 30-day notice must be given to terminate contract.

TIPS "Be persistent."

WORDSERVE LITERARY GROUP

7061 S. University Blvd., Suite 307, Centennial CO 80122. **E-mail:** admin@wordserveliterary.com. **Website:** www.wordserveliterary.com. **Contact:** Greg Johnson. Represents 100 clients.

MEMBER AGENTS Greg Johnson, Nick Harrison, Sarah Freese.

REPRESENTS Nonfiction, fiction, novels. **Considers these fiction areas:** historical, inspirational, literary, mainstream, religious, spiritual, suspense, thriller, women's, young adult.

HOW TO CONTACT E-query admin@wordserveliterary.com. In the subject line, include the word "query." All queries should include the following three elements: a pitch for the book, information about you and your platform (for nonfiction) or writing background (for fiction), and the first 5 (or so) pages of the manuscript pasted into the e-mail. Please view our website for full guidelines: http://www.wordserveliterary.com/submission-guidlines/. Accepts simultaneous submissions. Response within 60 days. Obtains most new clients through recommendations from others.

TERMS Agent receives 15% commission on domestic sales; 10-15% commission on foreign sales. Offers

written contract; up to 60-day notice must be given to terminate contract.

TIPS "We are looking for good proposals, great writing and authors willing to market their books. We specialize in projects with a faith element bent. See the website before submitting."

WRITERS HOUSE

21 W. 26th St., New York NY 10010. (212)685-2400. **Fax:** (212)685-1781. **Website:** www.writershouse.com. Estab. 1973. Member of AAR.

MEMBER AGENTS Amy Berkower; Stephen Barr; Susan Cohen; Dan Conaway; Lisa DiMona; Susan Ginsburg; Susan Golomb; Merrilee Heifetz; Brianne Johnson; Daniel Lazar; Simon Lipskar; Steven Malk; Jodi Reamer, Esq.; Robin Rue; Rebecca Sherman; Geri Thoma; Albert Zuckerman; Alec Shane; Stacy Testa; Victoria Doherty-Munro; Beth Miller; Andrea Morrison; Soumeya Roberts.

REPRESENTS Nonfiction, novels. **Considers these fiction areas:** commercial, fantasy, juvenile, literary, mainstream, middle grade, picture books, science fiction, women's, young adult.

HOW TO CONTACT Individual agent email addresses are available on the website. "Please e-mail us a query letter, which includes your credentials, an explanation of what makes your book unique and special, and a synopsis. Some agents within our agency have different requirements. Please consult their individual Publisher's Marketplace (PM) profile for details. We respond to all queries, generally within six to eight weeks." If you prefer to submit my mail, address it to an individual agent, and please include SASE for our reply. (If submitting to Steven Malk: Writers House, 7660 Fay Ave., #338H, La Jolla, CA 92037.) Accepts simultaneous submissions. "We respond to all queries, generally within 6-8 weeks." Obtains most new clients through recommendations from authors and editors.

TERMS Agent receives 15% commission on domestic sales. Agent receives 20% commission on foreign sales. Offers written contract, binding for 1 year. Agency charges fees for copying mss/proposals and overseas airmail of books.

JASON YARN LITERARY AGENCY

3544 Broadway, No. 68, New York NY 10031. **E-mail:** jason@jasonyarnliteraryagency.com. **Website:** www.jasonyarnliteraryagency.com. Member of AAR. Signatory of WGA.

REPRESENTS Nonfiction, fiction. **Considers these fiction areas:** commercial, fantasy, literary, middle grade, science fiction, suspense, thriller, young adult, graphic novels, comics.

HOW TO CONTACT Please e-mail your query to jason@jasonyarnliteraryagency.com with the word "Query" in the subject line, and please paste the first 10 pages of your manuscript or proposal into the text of your e-mail. Do not send any attachments. "Visit the About page for information on what we are interested in, and please note that JYLA does not accept queries for film, TV, or stage scripts." Accepts simultaneous submissions.

⊘ ZACHARY SHUSTER HARMSWORTH

19 W. 21st St., Suite 501, New York NY 10010. (212)765-6900. **Website:** www.zshliterary.com. Alternate address: 545 Boylston St., 11th Floor, Boston MA 02116. (617)262-2400. Fax: (617)262-2468.

MEMBER AGENTS Lane Zachary (memoir, current events, history, biography and psychology); Todd Shuster (nonfiction: current affairs, biography, true-crime, popular science, adventure, politics and civil rights, history, memoir, business, health, parenting, and psychology; fiction: literary and "crossover" commercial novels, including mysteries and thrillers); Esmond Harmsworth (fiction: literary fiction mystery, crime, mainstream fiction, young adult, middle grade; nonfiction, including business, politics, psychology, culture, society, science); Jennifer Gates (nonfiction, including literary and inspirational memoir, narrative nonfiction, current affairs, history, pop culture, business, science, and psychology; literary and commercial fiction and children's); Janet Silver (literary fiction and narrative nonfiction, including memoir, biography, history, and cultural studies); Bridget Wagner Matzie (nonfiction and commercial fiction); Jane Von Mehren (nonfiction: business, cooking, health, history, memoir, parenting, psychology, and science; fiction: YA and Middle Grade literature, thrillers, and women's, book club, and historical fiction); Elias Altman (narrative nonfiction, memoirs, history, literary fiction, cultural criticism); Lori Galvin (cookbooks, narratives about food and drink (memoir or cultural commentary), lifestyle, self-help); Albert Lee (narrative journalism, current affairs, pop culture, music, business and technology, titles with strong book-to-film/TV potential); Michelle Brower (literary fiction, thrillers and literary mysteries, smart women's fiction, "book club" fiction, paranormal/fantasy, selective YA; nonfiction: subject-driven narratives, memoirs, and journalism); Sarah Levitt (nonfiction: biography, cultural history, memoir, science, "ideas" books, reportage, narrative; literary fiction); Jen Marshall; David Granger.

REPRESENTS Novels.

HOW TO CONTACT "We regret that we cannot accept unsolicited submissions under any circumstances except for short queries sent by e-mail." Use the online agency submission form to send e-mail to anyone on our staff. Accepts simultaneous submissions. Obtains most new clients through recommendations from others.

TERMS Agent receives 15% commission on domestic sales; 20% commission on foreign sales. Offers written contract, binding for 1 work only; 30-day notice must be given to terminate contract.

HELEN ZIMMERMANN LITERARY AGENCY

E-mail: submit@zimmagency.com. **Website:** www.zimmermannliterary.com. **Contact:** Helen Zimmermann. Estab. 2003.

REPRESENTS Nonfiction, fiction. **Considers these fiction areas:** family saga, literary, mainstream.

HOW TO CONTACT Accepts e-mail queries only. "For nonfiction queries, initial contact should just be a pitch letter. For fiction queries, I prefer a summary, your bio, and the first chapter as text in the email (not as an attachment). If I express interest I will need to see a full proposal for nonfiction and the remainder of the manuscript for fiction." Accepts simultaneous submissions. Responds in 2 weeks to queries, only if interested. Obtains most new clients through recommendations from others, solicitations.

TERMS Agent receives 15% commission on domestic sales. Offers written contract; 30-day notice must be given to terminate contract.

MAGAZINES

This section contains magazine listings that fall into one of several categories: literary, consumer, small circulation, and online. Our decision to combine magazines under one section was twofold: All of these magazines represent markets specifically for short fiction, and many magazines now publish both print and online versions, making them more difficult to subcategorize.

Selecting the Right Magazine

Once you have browsed through this section and have a list of journals you might like to submit to, read those listings again carefully. Remember, this is information editors provide to help you submit work that fits their needs. Note that you will find some magazines that do not read submissions all year long. Whether limited reading periods are tied to a university schedule or meant to accommodate the capabilities of a very small staff, those periods are noted within listings (when the editors notify us). The staffs of university journals are usually made up of student editors and a managing editor who is also a faculty member. These staffs often change every year. Whenever possible, we indicate this in listings and give the name of the current editor and the length of that editor's term. Also be aware that the schedule of a university journal usually coincides with that university's academic year, meaning that the editors of most university publications are difficult or impossible to reach during the summer.

FURTHERING YOUR SEARCH

Most of the magazines listed here are published in the U.S. You will also find some English-speaking markets from around the world. These foreign publications are denoted with a ◐ symbol at the beginning of listings. To make it easier to find Canadian markets, we include a ◌ symbol at the start of those listings.

5_TROPE

Website: www.5trope.com. **Contact:** Doren Robbins, editor. Estab. 1999. "Our intention is to seek out guest editors who will solicit excellent experimental work from their colleagues, which we will then publish. In this way each issue will become the fruit of a single editor's labour and guidance, a thematically united work of Internet art in its own right. Let us call this *5_trope*'s overarching experiment: to discover what happens when editorship and authorship collide. We welcome applications for guest editorship, but please be aware that applications will not be considered from novice writers and that we may not be able to respond to every person we do not select. Applications may be sent to: editor.5trope@gmail.com. Give us your best pitch."

30 N

North Central College, Naperville IL 60540. **E-mail:** 30north@noctrl.edu. **Website:** 30northblog.wordpress.com. **Contact:** Katie Draves, Crystal Ice. *30 N*, published semiannually, considers work in all literary genres, including occasional interviews, from undergraduate writers globally. The journal's goal is for college-level, emerging creative writers to share their work publicly and create a conversation with each other.

○ Contributors must be currently enrolled as undergraduates at a two- or four-year institution at the time of submission. Reads submissions September-March, with deadlines in February and October.

NEEDS Length: up to 5,000 words.

HOW TO CONTACT Submit complete ms via online submissions manager. "You must be a currently enrolled undergraduate at a two- or four-year institution at the time of submission. Please submit using your .edu e-mail address, your institution, and your year." Include brief bio written in third person.

PAYMENT/TERMS Pays 2 contributor's copies.

TIPS "Don't send anything you just finished moments ago—rethink, revise, and polish. Avoid sentimentality and abstraction. That said, *30 N* publishes beginners, so don't hesitate to submit and, if rejected, submit again."

● 34THPARALLEL MAGAZINE

Reality & Fiction, Paris , France. **E-mail:** 34thparallel@gmail.com. **Website:** www.34thparallel.net. **Contact:** Martin Chipperfield. Estab. 2007. *34thParallel Magazine*, monthly in digital and print editions, publishes new and emerging writers.

NEEDS Submit via online submissions manager (Submittable).

TIPS "It's all about getting your story out there looking good: your reality (creative nonfiction), fiction, journalism, essays, screenplays, poetry (writing that isn't prose), hip-hop, art, photography, photo stories or essays, graphic stories, comics, or cartoons."

580 SPLIT

A Journal of Arts and Letters, Mills College, Graduate English Department, 5000 MacArthur Blvd., Oakland CA 94613-0982. **E-mail:** five80split@gmail.com. **Website:** www.580split.org. Estab. 1998. "*580 Split* is an online literary journal published by graduate students of the English Department at Mills College. This national literary journal includes innovative and risk-taking fiction, creative nonfiction, poetry, and art.

NEEDS Length: up to 5,000 words.

HOW TO CONTACT Submit complete ms via online submissions manager. No e-mailed or mailed submissions are accepted. Please submit .doc or .docx files.

PAYMENT/TERMS Annual prose contest pays a cash prize.

TIPS "Get a hold of a past issue, read through it, find out what we are about. Check the website for most recent information."

A&U

Art & Understanding, Inc., 25 Monroe St., Suite 205, Albany NY 12210-2729. (518)426-9010. **Fax:** (518)436-5354. **E-mail:** chaelneedle@mac.com. **Website:** www.aumag.org. **Contact:** Chael Needle, managing editor. Estab. 1991. Each summer, *A&U* publishes a summer reading issue. Writers are encouraged to submit work to the Christopher Hewitt Literary Award contest, held annually. Submissions for the contest open in the spring.

NEEDS Literary electronic submissions, as Word attachments, may be mailed to Brent Calderwood, literary editor, at aumaglit@gmail.com. Pay rate schedule available upon request. Length: up to 1,500 words.

HOW TO CONTACT Send complete ms.

PAYMENT/TERMS Pays $50.

TIPS "We're looking for more articles on youth and HIV/AIDS; more international coverage; celebrity interviews; more coverage of how the pandemic is affecting historically underrepresented communities. We are also looking for literary submissions that address the past and present AIDS epidemic in fresh ways. Each year, we sponsor the Christopher Hewitt Award, given to the best poem, short story, creative nonfiction piece, and drama submitted."

ABLE MUSE

Able Muse Press, 467 Saratoga Ave., #602, San Jose CA 95129-1326. **E-mail:** submission@ablemuse.com. **Website:** www.ablemuse.com. **Contact:** Alex Pepple, editor. Estab. 1999. *Able Muse: A Review of Poetry, Prose & Art*, published twice/year, predominantly publishes metrical poetry complemented by art and photography, fiction, and nonfiction, including essays, book reviews, and interviews with a focus on metrical and formal poetry.

○ Sponsors 2 annual contests: The Able Muse Write Prize for Poetry & Fiction and The Able Muse Book Award for Poetry (in collaboration with Able Muse Press at www.ablemusepress. com). See website for details.

NEEDS "Our emphasis is on literary fiction; *Able Muse* is not a venue for fantasy, romance, horror, action-adventure, gratuitous violence, or inspirational/sentimental genres." Length: up to 4,000 words/ms.

HOW TO CONTACT Send up to 2 ms via online submission form or e-mail. "We will consider longer pieces of exceptional merit."

THE ADIRONDACK REVIEW

Stanhope St., Brooklyn NY 11237, United States. **E-mail:** editors@theadirondackreview.com. **Website:** www.theadirondackreview.com; www.theadirondackreview.submittable.com. **Contact:** Angela Leroux-Lindsey, editor in chief; Nicholas Samaras, poetry editor; Giovanni Appruzzese, translations editor; Sarah Escue, associate editor. Estab. 2000. *The Adirondack Review* is an online quarterly literary magazine featuring poetry, fiction, art, photography, and translations.

NEEDS Length: up to 6,000 words.

HOW TO CONTACT Submit via online submissions manager.

TIPS "*The Adirondack Review* accepts submissions all year long, so send us your poetry, fiction, nonfiction, translation, reviews, interviews, and art and photography."

AFRICAN VOICES

African Voices Communications, Inc., 270 W. 96th St., New York NY 10025. (212)865-2982. **E-mail:** africanvoicesart@gmail.com. **Website:** www.africanvoices. com. **Contact:** Angela Kinemore, poetry editor. Estab. 1992. *African Voices*, published quarterly, is an "art and literary magazine that highlights the work of people of color. We publish literature and poetry on any subject. We also consider all themes and styles: avant-garde, free verse, haiku, light verse, and traditional. We do not wish to limit the reader or author." *African Voices* is about 48 pages, magazine-sized, professionally printed, saddle-stapled, with paper cover. Receives about 150 submissions/year, accepts about 30%.

NEEDS Length: 500-2,500 words.

HOW TO CONTACT Send complete ms. Include short bio. Accepts submissions by postal mail. Send SASE for return of ms.

PAYMENT/TERMS Pays contributor's copies.

TIPS "A manuscript stands out if it is neatly typed with a well-written and interesting storyline or plot. Originality is encouraged. We are interested in more horror, erotic, and drama pieces. *AV* wants to highlight the diversity in our culture. Stories must touch the humanity in us all. We strongly encourage new writers/poets to send in their work. Accepted contributors are encouraged to subscribe."

AFTER HAPPY HOUR REVIEW

150 Hallock St., Floor 1, Pittsburgh PA 15211. **E-mail:** hourafterhappyhour@gmail.com. **Website:** afterhappyhourreview.com. **Contact:** Mike Good. Estab. 2014. The *After Happy Hour Review* is an independent, online literary journal that publishes poetry, fiction, creative nonfiction, and visual art. Our headquarters are based in Pittsburgh, and we have published writers from around the United States alongside international writers. Curated by the Hour After Happy Hour Writing Workshop, our editors come from varying backgrounds with their own inclinations, tastes, and preferences. Take your time, read an issue, and send us your best work. We aim to respond as quickly as possible to all submissions and nominate work for all major awards, including the Pushcart Prize and Best of Net."

NEEDS "*AHHR* sets the limit at 6,000, but excessive length is the top reason why we tend to reject short fiction pieces. Oftentimes we run into stories that start strong, but simply go on for too many pages to maintain their effectiveness. Make sure your piece has no fat to cut and send it in. Give us original ideas and uncompromising language. Make an impact and make it early." Length: 6,000 words max.

PAYMENT/TERMS No payment.

AFTER THE PAUSE

Indianapolis Indiana **E-mail:** afterthepause@gmail. com. **Website:** afterthepause.com. **Contact:** Michael Prihoda, founding editor. Estab. 2014. "We are open to reading or viewing anything. Give us the wildest pieces of your imagination! Literary ephemera of all kinds welcome. We feature experimental poetry, flash fiction, visual poetry, and visual art from new, emerging, and veteran writers."

NEEDS Send up to 3 flash fiction pieces of no more than 1,000 words each in an attached Word document or in the body of an e-mail. Anything over 1,000 words will not be considered. Length: up to 1,000 words.

TIPS "If we receive something too close to publication of an issue, it is automatically considered for the following issue."

AGNI

Boston University, 236 Bay State Rd., Boston MA 02215. **E-mail:** agni@bu.edu. **Website:** www.agnimagazine.org. **Contact:** Sven Birkerts, editor. Estab. 1972. Eclectic literary magazine publishing first-rate poems, essays, translations, and stories.

Reading period is September 1-May 31 only. Online magazine carries original content not found in print edition. All submissions are considered for both. Founding editor Askold Melnyczuk won the PEN/Nora Magid Lifetime Achievement Award for Magazine Editing. Work from *AGNI* has been included and cited regularly in the *Pushcart Prize*, *O. Henry*, and *Best American* anthologies.

NEEDS No genre scifi, horror, mystery, or romance.

HOW TO CONTACT Submit online or by regular mail, no more than 1 story at a time. E-mailed submissions will not be considered. Include a SASE or your e-mail address if sending by mail.

PAYMENT/TERMS Pays $20/page up to $300, plus a one-year subscription, and, for print publication, 2 contributor's copies and 4 gift copies.

TIPS "We're also looking for extraordinary translations from little-translated languages. It is important

to read work published in *AGNI* before submitting, to see if your own might be compatible."

ALASKA QUARTERLY REVIEW

University of Alaska Anchorage, 3211 Providence Dr., Anchorage AK 99508. **E-mail:** uaa_aqr@uaa.alaska. edu. **Website:** www.uaa.alaska.edu/aqr. **Contact:** Ronald Spatz, editor in chief. Estab. 1982. "*Alaska Quarterly Review* is a literary journal devoted to contemporary literary art, publishing fiction, short plays, poetry, photo essays, and literary nonfiction in traditional and experimental styles. The editors encourage new and emerging writers, while continuing to publish award-winning and established writers."

Magazine: 6x9; 232-300 pages; 60 lb. Glatfelter paper; 12 pt. C15 black ink or 4-color; varnish cover stock; photos on cover and photo essays. Reads mss August 15-May 15.

NEEDS "Works in *AQR* have certain characteristics: freshness, honesty, and a compelling subject. The voice of the piece must be strong—idiosyncratic enough to create a unique persona. We look for craft, putting it in a form where it becomes emotionally and intellectually complex. Many pieces in *AQR* concern everyday life. We're not asking our writers to go outside themselves and their experiences to the absolute exotic to catch our interest. We look for the experiential and revelatory qualities of the work. We will champion a piece that may be less polished or stylistically sophisticated if it engages me, surprises me, and resonates for me. The joy in reading such a work is in discovering something true. Moreover, in keeping with our mission to publish new writers, we are looking for voices our readers do not know, voices that may not always be reflected in the dominant culture and that, in all instances, have something important to convey." No romance, children's, or inspirational/religious. Length: up to 50 pages.

HOW TO CONTACT Submit complete ms by mail. Include cover letter with contact information and SASE for return of ms.

PAYMENT/TERMS Pays contributor's copies and honoraria when funding is available.

TIPS "Although we respond to e-mail queries, we cannot review electronic submissions."

ALBEDO ONE

8 Bachelor's Walk, Dublin 1 , Ireland. **E-mail:** bobn@ yellowbrickroad.ie. **Website:** www.albedo1.com. **Contact:** Bob Nielson. Estab. 1993. "We are always

looking for thoughtful, well-written fiction. Our definition of what constitutes science fiction, horror, and fantasy is extremely broad, and we love to see material which pushes at the boundaries or crosses between genres."

NEEDS Length: 2,000-8,000 words.

HOW TO CONTACT Submit complete ms by mail or e-mail.

PAYMENT/TERMS Pays €6/1,000 words, to a maximum of 8,000 words, and 1 contributor's copy.

TIPS "We look for good writing, good plot, good characters. Read the magazine, and don't give up."

✪ ALBERTA VIEWS

Alberta Views, Ltd., Suite 208, 320 23rd Ave. SW, Calgary AB T2S 0J2, Canada. (403)243-5334; (877)212-5334. **Fax:** (403)243-8599. **E-mail:** queries@albertaviews.ab.ca. **Website:** www.albertaviews.ab.ca. **Contact:** Evan Osenton, editor. Estab. 1997. "We are a regional magazine providing thoughtful commentary and background information on issues of concern to Albertans. Most of our writers are Albertans."

○   No phone queries.

NEEDS Only fiction by Alberta writers via the annual *Alberta Views* fiction contest. Length: 2,500-4,000 words.

HOW TO CONTACT Send complete ms.

PAYMENT/TERMS Pays up to $1,000.

THE ALEMBIC

Providence College, English Department, ATTN: The Alembic Editors, 1 Cunningham Square, Providence RI 02918-0001. **Website:** www.providence.edu/english/pages/alembic.aspx. **Contact:** Magazine has revolving editor. Editorial term: 1 year. Estab. 1940. "*The Alembic* is an international literary journal featuring the work of both established and student writers and photographers. It is published each April by Providence College in Providence, Rhode Island."

○   Magazine: 6x9, 80 pages. Contains illustrations, photographs.

NEEDS "We are open to all styles of fiction." Does not read December 1-July 31. Published Bruce Smith, Robin Behn, Rane Arroyo, Sharon Dolin, Jeff Friedman, and Khalid Mattawa. Length: up to 6,000 words.

HOW TO CONTACT Send complete ms with cover letter. Include brief bio. Send SASE (or IRC) for return of ms. Does not accept online submissions.

PAYMENT/TERMS Pays 2 contributor's copies.

TIPS "We're looking for stories that are wise, memorable, grammatical, economical, poetic in the right places, and end strongly. Take Heraclitus' claim that 'character is fate' to heart and study the strategies, styles, and craft of such masters as Anton Chekov, J. Cheever, Flannery O'Connor, John Updike, Rick Bass, Phillip Roth, Joyce Carol Oates, William Treavor, Lorrie Moore, and Ethan Canin."

ALIMENTUM

The Literature of Food, P.O. Box 210028, Nashville TN 37221. **E-mail:** editor@alimentumjournal.com. **Website:** www.alimentumjournal.com. **Contact:** Peter Selgin, fiction and nonfiction editor; Esther Cohen, poetry editor. Estab. 2005. "*Alimentum* celebrates the literature and art of food. We welcome work from like-minded writers, musicians, and artists."

○   Essays appearing in *Alimentum* have appeared in *Best American Essays* and *Best Food Writing*.

NEEDS Has published Mark Kurlansky, Oliver Sacks, Dick Allen, Ann Hood, and Carly Sachs. Publishes short shorts. Also publishes literary essays, poetry, spot illustrations. Rarely comments on/critiques rejected mss. Length: up to 2,000 words.

HOW TO CONTACT Send complete ms by mail. Please include SASE.

PAYMENT/TERMS Pays 1 contributor's copy.

TIPS "No e-mail submissions, only snail mail. Mark outside envelope to the attention of Poetry, Fiction, or Nonfiction Editor."

ALITERATE

Genre, Ltd., P.O. Box 380020, Cambridge MA 02238. **E-mail:** editor@aliterate.org. **E-mail:** submissions@aliterate.org. **Website:** www.aliterate.org. Estab. 2016. *Aliterate* is a production of Genre, Ltd., a small nonprofit publisher based in Cambridge, Massachusetts. "Much has been said about the gulf between literary and genre literature. *Aliterate* seeks to publish works that span this divide, blending tight prose with the fantastical. *Aliterate* reads during March and April."

NEEDS *Aliterate* is a publisher of literary genre fiction and publishes only science fiction, fantasy, Westerns, pulps, thrillers, horror, romance, etc. "We consider 'comedy' to be a fairly large genre; if you submit a comedy, please ensure it is also falls within another genre." Submissions should be of a 'literary' character, with an emphasis on character and language over clever plotting. Does not want poetry, inspirational, erotica, gore, polemics, fan fiction, or young adult. Length: 3,000-12,000 words.

HOW TO CONTACT Review is conducted by blind jury. Remove all identifying information from your submission. No need to include a cover letter; we'll solicit biographic information on acceptance. The subject line of your e-mail will be used to track your story in our review system. Submit only 1 ms in each reading period. Submission is open to all writers, apart from residents of Crimea, Cuba, Iran, North Korea, Sudan, and Syria.

PAYMENT/TERMS Pays 6¢/word.

TIPS "We've been asked for examples of authors who would fit the tone of *Aliterate*; they include Samuel Delany, Margaret Atwood, and Walter J. Miller Jr. While we love writers like Asimov, *Aliterate* doesn't aim to be a venue primarily for hard science fiction."

ALIVE NOW

1908 Grand Ave., P.O. Box 340004, Nashville TN 37203. (615)340-7254. **E-mail:** alivenow@upperroom.org. **Website:** www.alivenow.org; alivenow.upperroom.org. **Contact:** Beth A. Richardson, editor. Estab. 1971. *Alive Now*, published bimonthly, is a devotional magazine that invites readers to enter an ever-deepening relationship with God. "*Alive Now* seeks to nourish people who are hungry for a sacred way of living. Submissions should invite readers to see God in the midst of daily life by exploring how contemporary issues impact their faith lives. Each word must be vivid and dynamic and contribute to the whole. We make selections based on a list of upcoming themes. Mss which do not fit a theme will be returned."

NEEDS Length: 400-500 words.

HOW TO CONTACT Prefers electronic submissions attached as Word document. Postal submissions should include SASE. Include name, address, theme on each sheet.

PAYMENT/TERMS Pays $35 minimum.

THE ALLEGHENY REVIEW

Allegheny College Box 32, 520 N. Main St., Meadville PA 16335. **E-mail:** review@allegheny.edu. **Website:** alleghenyreview.wordpress.com. **Contact:** Senior editor. Estab. 1983. "*The Allegheny Review* is one of America's only nationwide literary magazines exclusively for undergraduate works of poetry, fiction, and nonfiction. Our intended audience is persons interested in quality literature."

Annual. Magazine: 6x9; 100 pages; illustrations; photos. Has published work by Dianne Page, Monica Stahl, and DJ Kinney.

NEEDS Receives 50 unsolicited mss/month. Accepts 3 mss/issue. Publishes ms 2 months after deadline. Publishes roughly 90% new writers/year. Also publishes short shorts (up to 20 pages), nonfiction, and poetry. Does not want "fiction not written by undergraduates—we accept nothing but fiction by currently enrolled undergraduate students. We consider anything catering to an intellectual audience." Length: up to 20 pages, double-spaced.

HOW TO CONTACT Submit complete ms via online submissions manager.

PAYMENT/TERMS Pays 1 contributor's copy; additional copies $3. Sponsors awards/contests; reading fee $5.

TIPS "We look for quality work that has been thoroughly revised. Unique voice, interesting topic, and playfulness with the English language. Revise, revise, revise! And be careful how you send it—the cover letter says a lot. We definitely look for diversity in the pieces we publish."

ALLEGORY

P.O. Box 2714, Cherry Hill NJ 08034. **E-mail:** submissions@allegoryezine.com. **Website:** www.allegoryezine.com. **Contact:** Ty Drago, publisher and managing editor. Estab. 1998. "We are an e-zine by writers for writers. Our articles focus on the art, craft, and business of writing. Our links and editorial policy all focus on the needs of fiction authors." *Allegory* (as Peridot Books) won the Page One Award for Literary Contribution.

NEEDS Receives 150 unsolicited mss/month. Accepts 12 mss/issue; 24 mss/year. Agented fiction 5%. Publishes 10 new writers/year. Also publishes literary essays, literary criticism. Often comments on rejected mss. "No media tie-ins (*Star Trek*, *Star Wars*, etc., or space opera, vampires)." Length: 1,500-7,500 words; average length: 2,500 words.

HOW TO CONTACT "All submissions should be sent by e-mail (no letters or telephone calls) in either text or RTF format. Please place 'Submission [Title]-[first and last name]' in the subject line. Include the following in both the body of the e-mail and the attachment: your name, name to use on the story (byline) if different, your preferred e-mail address, your mailing address, the story's title, and the story's word count."

PAYMENT/TERMS Pays $15/story.

TIPS "Give us something original, preferably with a twist. Avoid gratuitous sex or violence. Funny always scores points. Be clever and imaginative, but be able to tell a story with proper mood and characterization. Put your name and e-mail address in the body of the story. Read the site and get a feel for it before submitting."

ALLIGATOR JUNIPER

Prescott College, 220 Grove Ave., Prescott AZ 86301. (928)350-2012. **Website:** alligatorjuniper.org. "*Alligator Juniper* features contemporary poetry, fiction, creative nonfiction, and b&w photography. We encourage submissions from writers and photographers at all levels: emerging, early career, and established." Annual magazine comprised of the winners and finalists of national contests. "All entrants pay an $18 submission fee and receive a complementary copy of that year's issue in the spring. First-place winning writers in each genre receive a $1,000 prize. The first-place winner in photography receives a $500 award. Finalists in writing and images are published and paid in contributor copies. There is currently no avenue for submissions other than the annual contest."

NEEDS "No children's literature or genre work." Length: up to 30 pages, double-spaced.

HOW TO CONTACT Accepts submissions only through annual contest. Submit via online submission form or regular mail. If submitting by regular mail, include $18 entry fee payable to *Alligator Juniper* for each story. Include cover letter with name, address, phone number, and e-mail. Mss should be typed with numbered pages, double-spaced, 12-point font, and 1" margins. Include author's name on first page. "Double-sided submissions are encouraged." No e-mail submissions.

AMBIT MAGAZINE

Staithe House, Main Rd., Brancaster Staithe, Norfolk PE31 8PB, United Kingdom. **E-mail:** contact@ambitmagazine.co.uk. **Website:** www.ambitmagazine.co.uk. **Contact:** Briony Bax, editor; Ralf Webb, poetry editor; Kate Pemberton, fiction editor; Olivia Bax and Jean Philippe Dordolo, art editors. Estab. 1959. *Ambit Magazine* is a literary and artwork quarterly published in the UK and read internationally. *Ambit* is put together entirely from unsolicited, previously unpublished poetry and short fiction submissions. "Please read the guidelines on our website carefully concerning submission windows and policies."

NEEDS Length: up to 5,000 words. "We're very enthusiastic about flash and very short fiction, which is under 1,000 words. Stories should not be published elsewhere, including blogs and online."

HOW TO CONTACT Submit complete ms via Submittable. No e-mail submissions.

PAYMENT/TERMS Payment details on website.

TIPS "Read a copy of the magazine before submitting!"

AMERICAN LITERARY REVIEW

University of North Texas, 1155 Union Circle #311307, Denton TX 76203. **E-mail:** americanliteraryreview@gmail.com. **Website:** www.americanliteraryreview.com. **Contact:** Bonnie Friedman, editor in chief. Estab. 1990. "*The American Literary Review* publishes "excellent poetry, fiction, and nonfiction by writers at all stages of their careers." Beginning in fall 2013, *ALR* became an online publication."

Reading period is from October 1-May 1.

NEEDS "We would like to see more short shorts and stylistically innovative and risk-taking fiction. We like to see stories that illuminate the various layers of characters and their situations with great artistry. Give us distinctive character-driven stories that explore the complexities of human existence." Looks for "the small moments that contain more than at first possible, that surprise us with more truth than we thought we had a right to expect." Has published work by Marylee MacDonald, Michael Isaac Shokrian, Arthur Brown, Roy Bentley, Julie Marie Wade, and Karin Forfota Poklen. No genre works. Length: up to 8,000 words.

HOW TO CONTACT Submit 1 complete ms through online submissions manager for a fee of $3. Does not accept submissions via e-mail or mail.

TIPS "We encourage writers and artists to examine our journal."

THE AMERICAN READER

E-mail: fiction@theamericanreader.com; poetry@theamericanreader.com; criticism@theamericanreader.com. **Website:** theamericanreader.com. **Contact:** Uzoamaka Maduka, editor in chief. *The American Reader* is a bimonthly print literary journal. The magazine is committed to inspiring literary and critical conversation among a new generation of readers, and restoring literature to its proper place in American cultural discourse.

NEEDS Does not accept unsolicited novel excerpts.

HOW TO CONTACT Submit by e-mail: fiction@ theamericanreader.com.

ⓢ AMERICAN SHORT FICTION

Badgerdog Literary Publishing, P.O. Box 301209, Austin TX 78703. **E-mail:** editors@americanshortfiction. org. **Website:** www.americanshortfiction.org. **Contact:** Rebecca Markovits and Adeena Reitberger, editors. Estab. 1991. "Issued triannually, *American Short Fiction* publishes work by emerging and established voices: stories that dive into the wreck, that stretch the reader between recognition and surprise, that conjure a particular world with delicate expertise—stories that take a different way home."

🗨 Stories published by *American Short Fiction* are anthologized in *Best American Short Stories*, *Best American Non-Required Reading*, *The O. Henry Prize Stories*, *The Pushcart Prize: Best of the Small Presses*, and elsewhere.

NEEDS "Open to publishing mystery or speculative fiction if we feel it has literary value." Does not want young adult or genre fiction. Length: open.

HOW TO CONTACT *American Short Fiction* seeks "short fiction by some of the finest writers working in contemporary literature, whether they are established, new, or lesser-known authors." Also publishes stories under 2,000 words online. Submit 1 story at a time via online submissions manager ($3 fee). No paper submissions.

PAYMENT/TERMS Writers receive $250-500, 2 contributor's copies, free subscription to the magazine. Additional copies $5.

TIPS "We publish fiction that speaks to us emotionally, uses evocative and precise language, and takes risks in subject matter and/or form. Try to read a few issues of *American Short Fiction* to get a sense of what we like. Also, to be concise is a great virtue."

ⓢ ANALOG SCIENCE FICTION & FACT

Dell Magazines, 44 Wall St., Suite 904, New York NY 10005-2401. **E-mail:** analogsf@dellmagazines.com. **Website:** www.analogsf.com. **Contact:** Trevor Quachri, editor. Estab. 1930. *Analog* seeks "solidly entertaining stories exploring solidly thought-out speculative ideas. But the ideas, and consequently the stories, are always new. Real science and technology have always been important in *ASF,* not only as the foundation of its fiction but as the subject of articles about real research with big implications for the future."

🗨 Fiction published in *Analog* has won numerous Nebula and Hugo Awards.

NEEDS "Basically, we publish science fiction stories. That is, stories in which some aspect of future science or technology is so integral to the plot that, if that aspect were removed, the story would collapse. The science can be physical, sociological, psychological. The technology can be anything from electronic engineering to biogenetic engineering. But the stories must be strong and realistic, with believable people (who needn't be human) doing believable things—no matter how fantastic the background might be." No fantasy or stories in which the scientific background is implausible or plays no essential role. Length: 2,000-7,000 words for short stories, 10,000-20,000 words for novelettes and novellas, and 40,000-80,000 for serials.

HOW TO CONTACT Send complete ms via online submissions manager (preferred) or postal mail. Does not accept e-mail submissions.

PAYMENT/TERMS Analog pays 8-10¢/word for short stories up to 7,500 words, 8-8.5¢ for longer material, 6¢/word for serials.

TIPS "I'm looking for irresistibly entertaining stories that make me think about things in ways I've never done before. Read several issues to get a broad feel for our tastes, but don't try to imitate what you read."

ⓢ ANCIENT PATHS

E-mail: skylarburris@yahoo.com. **Website:** www.editorskylar.com/magazine/table.html. **Contact:** Skylar H. Burris, editor. Estab. 1998. *Ancient Paths* provides "a forum for quality spiritual poetry and short fiction. We consider works from writers of all religions, but poets and authors should be comfortable appearing in a predominantly Christian publication. Works published in *Ancient Paths* explore themes such as redemption, sin, forgiveness, doubt, faith, gratitude for the ordinary blessings of life, spiritual struggle, and spiritual growth. Please, no overly didactic works. Subtlety is preferred." Please send seasonally themed works for Lent and Advent at least 1 month prior to the start of each season. Works on other themes may be sent at any time.

NEEDS E-mail submissions only. Paste short fiction directly in the e-mail message. Use the subject heading "AP Online Submission (title of your work)." Include name and e-mail address at top of e-mail. Previously published works accepted, provided they are not currently available online. Please indicate if your work has been published elsewhere. Length: under 800 words preferred; up to 2,000 words.

PAYMENT/TERMS Pays $1.25/work published. Published authors also receive discount code for $3 off 2 printed back issues.

TIPS "Read the great religious poets: John Donne, George Herbert, T.S. Eliot, Lord Tennyson. Remember not to preach. This is a literary magazine, not a pulpit. This does not mean you do not communicate morals or celebrate God. It means you are not overbearing or simplistic when you do so."

◐❺ THE ANNALS OF SAINT ANNE DE BEAUPRE

9795 St. Anne Blvd., St. Anne de Beaupre QC G0A 3C0, Canada. (418)827-4538. **Fax:** (418)827-4530. **E-mail:** mag@revuesainteanne.ca. **Website:** www.annalsofsaintanne.ca. Estab. 1885. "The purpose of The Annals of Saint Anne is to effectively communicate the word of God in the Catholic Tradition by growing and expanding our outreach to Catholics of all ages through print and electronic media. Since the very first publication of The Annals of Saint Anne, our aim was to lead Catholic families toward a deeper union with God through prayer, communion with one another, and a joyful practice of their faith."

HOW TO CONTACT "Be sure to include your complete name, address, phone and/or fax number, and e-mail address. The editing committee will acknowledge your proposal as soon as possible. Please do not send additional material unless it is requested. In the event your manuscript is not accepted, if you want us to return it you, include SASE."

ANOTHER CHICAGO MAGAZINE

P.O. Box 408439, Chicago IL 60640. **E-mail:** editors@anotherchicagomagazine.net. **Website:** www.anotherchicagomagazine.net. **Contact:** Caroline Eick Kasner, managing editor; Matt Rowan, fiction editor; David Welch, poetry editor; Colleen O'Connor, nonfiction editor. Estab. 1977. "*Another Chicago Magazine* is a biannual literary magazine that publishes work by both new and established writers. We look for work that goes beyond the artistic and academic to include and address the larger world. The editors read submissions in fiction, poetry, and creative nonfiction year round. The best way to know what we publish is to read what we publish. If you haven't read *ACM* before, order a sample copy to know if your work is appropriate." Sends prepublication galleys.

◒ Work published in *ACM* has been included frequently in *The Best American Poetry* and *The Pushcart Prize* anthologies. **Charges $3 submissions fee.**

NEEDS Length: up to 7,500 words.

HOW TO CONTACT Submit complete ms via online submissions manager.

TIPS "Support literary publishing by subscribing to at least 1 literary journal—if not ours, another. Get used to rejection slips, and don't get discouraged. Keep introductory letters short. Make sure ms has name and address on every page, and that it is clean, neat, and proofread. We are looking for stories with freshness and originality in subject angle and style, and work that encounters the world."

◐❺ THE ANTIGONISH REVIEW

St. Francis Xavier University, P.O. Box 5000, Immaculata Hall, Room 413, Antigonish NS B2G 2W5, Canada. (902)867-3962. **Fax:** (902)867-5563. **E-mail:** tar@stfx.ca. **Website:** www.antigonishreview.com. **Contact:** Gerald Trites, editor. Estab. 1970. *The Antigonish Review*, published quarterly, features the writing of new and emerging writers as well as the ideas of established and innovative thinkers through poetry, stories, essays, book reviews and interviews."

NEEDS Send complete ms only through Submittable on our website. No erotica. Length: 500-5,000 words.

HOW TO CONTACT Send complete ms.

PAYMENT/TERMS Pays $50, 1 print edition and 1 digital edition for stories.

TIPS Contact by e-mail (tar@stfx.ca) and submit through the website using Submittable. There is a submission fee.

❺ ANTIOCH REVIEW

P.O. Box 148, Yellow Springs OH 45387-0148. (937)769-1365. **E-mail:** review@antiochcollege.edu. **Website:** www.antiochreview.org. **Contact:** Robert S. Fogarty, editor; Judith Hall, poetry editor. Estab. 1941. Literary and cultural review of contemporary issues and literature for general readership. *The Antioch Review* "is an independent quarterly of critical and creative thought. For well over 75 years, prominent and promising authors, poets, and thinkers have found a friendly reception—regardless of formal reputation.

The Antioch Review, founded in 1941, is one of the oldest, continuously publishing literary magazines in America. We publish fiction, essays, and poetry from both emerging as well as established authors. Authors published in our pages are consistently included in Best American anthologies and Pushcart prizes. We continue to serve our readers and our authors and to encourage others to publish the "best words in the best order." We receive thousands of submissions each year from established and emerging authors. The competition is keen. Form and content are so inseparable and reaction is so personal, it is difficult to state requirements or limitations. Studying issues of *The Antioch Review* and reviewing our "Writer's Guidelines should be helpful."

NEEDS Quality fiction only, distinctive in style with fresh insights into the human condition. No science fiction, fantasy, or confessions.

HOW TO CONTACT Send complete ms with SASE, preferably mailed flat. Fiction submissions are not accepted between June 1-August 31.

PAYMENT/TERMS Pays $20/printed page, plus 2 contributor's copies.

APALACHEE REVIEW

Apalachee Press, P.O. Box 10469, Tallahassee FL 32302. (850) 644-9114. **E-mail:** mtrammell@fsu.edu. **E-mail:** arsubmissions@gmail.com (for queries outside the U.S.). **Website:** apalacheereview.org. **Contact:** Michael Trammell, Alicia Casey, and Jenn Bronson, chief editors; Kathleen Laufenberg, nonfiction editor; Mary Jane Ryals, fiction editor; Chris Hayes, poetry editor. Estab. 1976. "At *Apalachee Review*, we are interested in outstanding literary fiction, but we especially like poetry, fiction, and nonfiction that address intercultural issues in a domestic or international setting or context."

○ *Apalachee Review*, published annually, is 90 pages, digest-sized, professionally printed, perfect-bound, with card cover. Press run is 300-400. Includes photographs. Member CLMP.

NEEDS Receives 60-100 mss/month. Accepts 5-10 mss/issue. Agented fiction: 0.5%. Publishes 1-2 new writers/year. "We prefer fiction that is no longer than 15 pages in length." Has published Michael Martone, Lu Vickers, Joe Clark, Joe Taylor, Jane Arrowsmith Edwards, Vivian Lawry, Linda Frysh, Charles Harper Webb, Reno Raymond Gwaltney. Also publishes short

shorts. Does not want cliché-filled, genre-oriented fiction. Length: 600-3,300 words; average length: 2,200 words. Average length of short shorts: 250 words.

HOW TO CONTACT Send complete ms with cover letter. Include brief bio, list of publications. Send either SASE (international authors should see website for "international" guidelines: no IRCs, please) for return of ms, or disposable copy of ms and #10 SASE for reply only.

PAYMENT/TERMS Pays 2 contributor's copies.

⑤ APEX MAGAZINE

Apex Publications, LLC, P.O. Box 24323, Lexington KY 40524. **E-mail:** lesley@apex-magazine.com. **Website:** www.apex-magazine.com. **Contact:** Lesley Conner, managing editor. Estab. 2004. "An elite repository for new and seasoned authors with an other-worldly interest in the unquestioned and slightly bizarre parts of the universe. We want science fiction, fantasy, horror, and mash-ups of all three of the dark, weird stuff down at the bottom of your little literary heart."

NEEDS Length: 100-7,500 words.

HOW TO CONTACT Send complete ms.

PAYMENT/TERMS Pays 6¢/word.

APPALACHIAN HERITAGE

CPO 2166, Berea KY 40404. **E-mail:** appalachianheritage@berea.edu. **Website:** appalachianheritage.net. **Contact:** Jason Howard, editor. Estab. 1973. "We are seeking poetry, short fiction, literary criticism and biography, book reviews, and creative nonfiction, including memoirs, opinion pieces, and historical sketches. Unless you request not to be considered, all poems, stories, and articles published in *Appalachian Heritage* are eligible for our annual Plattner Award. All honorees are rewarded with a sliding bookrack with an attached commemorative plaque from Berea College Crafts, and first-place winners receive an additional stipend of $200."

○ Submission period: August 15-December 15.

NEEDS "We do not want to see fiction that has no ties to Southern Appalachia." No genre fiction. Length: up to 7,500 words.

HOW TO CONTACT Submit through online submissions manager only.

PAYMENT/TERMS Pays 3 contributor's copies.

TIPS "Sure, we are *Appalachian Heritage* and we do appreciate the past, but we are a forward-looking contemporary literary quarterly, and, frankly, we receive too many nostalgic submissions. Please spare us the 'Papaw Was Perfect' poetry and the 'Mamaw Moved Mountains' manuscripts and give us some hard-hitting prose, some innovative poetry, some inventive photography, and some original art. Help us be the ground-breaking, stimulating kind of quarterly we aspire to be."

⟳ APPLE VALLEY REVIEW

A Journal of Contemporary Literature, 88 South Third St., Suite 336, San Jose CA 95113. **E-mail:** editor@leah-browning.net. **Website:** www.applevalleyreview.com. **Contact:** Leah Browning, editor. Estab. 2005. *Apple Valley Review: A Journal of Contemporary Literature*, published semiannually online, features "beautifully crafted poetry, short fiction, and essays."

NEEDS Receives 100+ mss/month. Accepts 1-4 mss/issue; 2-8 mss/year. Published Siamak Vossoughi, Arndt Britschgi, Robert Radin, Sue Hyon Bae, Jessica Rafalko, Thomas Andrew Green, and Inderjeet Mani. Also publishes short shorts/flash. Does not want strict genre fiction, erotica, work containing explicit language, or anything "particularly violent or disturbing." Length: 100-4,000 words. Average length: 2,000 words. Average length of short shorts: 800 words.

HOW TO CONTACT Send complete ms with cover letter.

ARKANSAS REVIEW

A Journal of Delta Studies, Department of English and Philosophy, P.O. Box 1890, Office: Humanities and Social Sciences, State University AR 72467-1890. (870)972-3043; (870)972-2210. **Fax:** (870)972-3045. **E-mail:** mtribbet@astate.edu. **E-mail:** jcollins@astate.edu; arkansasreview@astate.edu. **Website:** arkreview.org. **Contact:** Dr. Marcus Tribbett, general editor. Estab. 1998. "All material, creative and scholarly, published in the *Arkansas Review* must evoke or respond to the natural and/or cultural experience of the Mississippi River Delta region." *Arkansas Review* is 92 pages, magazine-sized, photo offset-printed, saddle-stapled, with 4-color cover. Press run is 500; 50 distributed free to contributors.

NEEDS Receives 30-50 unsolicited mss/month. Accepts 2-3 mss/issue; 5-7 mss/year. Agented fiction 1%. Publishes 3-4 new writers/year. Has published work by Susan Henderson, George Singleton, Scott Ely, and Pia Erhart. "No genre fiction. Must have a Delta focus." Length: up to 10,000 words.

HOW TO CONTACT Send complete ms.

PAYMENT/TERMS Pays 3 contributor's copies.

TIPS "Immerse yourself in the literature of the Delta, but provide us with a fresh and original take on its land, its people, its culture. Surprise us. Amuse us. Recognize what makes this region particular as well as universal, and take risks. Help us shape a new Delta literature."

⑤ ARTS & LETTERS JOURNAL OF CONTEMPORARY CULTURE

Georgia College & State University, Milledgeville GA 31061. (478)445-1289. **Website:** al.gcsu.edu. **Contact:** Laura Newbern, editor; Faith Thompson, managing editor. Estab. 1999. *Arts & Letters Journal of Contemporary Culture*, published semiannually, is devoted to publishing contemporary work from established and emerging writers. Our editors seek work that doesn't try too hard to grab our attention, but rather guides it toward the human voice and its perpetual struggle into language. We're open to both formal and experimental fiction, nonfiction, and poetry; we're also open to work that defies classification. Above all, we look for work in which we can feel writers surprising themselves. Work published in *Arts & Letters Journal* has received the Pushcart Prize.

NEEDS No genre fiction. Length: up to 25 pages typed and double-spaced.

HOW TO CONTACT Submit complete ms via online submissions manager.

PAYMENT/TERMS Pays $10/printed page (minimum payment: $50) and 1 contributor's copy.

⑤ ART TIMES

arttimesjournal, P.O. Box 730, Mount Marion NY 12456. (845)246-6944. **Fax:** (845)246-6944. **E-mail:** info@arttimesjournal.com. **Website:** www.arttimesjournal.com. **Contact:** Raymond J. Steiner, editor. Estab. 1984. "*Art Times*, now an online-only publication, covers the arts fields with essays about music, dance, theater, film, and art, and includes short fiction and poetry as well as editorials. Our readers are creatives looking for resources and people who appreciate good writing."

NEEDS Looking for quality short fiction that aspires to be literary. Publishes up to 4 stories a month. Nothing violent, sexist, erotic, juvenile, racist, romantic, political, off-beat, or related to sports or juvenile fiction. Length: up to 1,000 words.

HOW TO CONTACT Send complete ms.

PAYMENT/TERMS Pays $25.

ASCENT ASPIRATIONS

Friday's Poems, 1560 Arbutus Dr., Nanoose Bay BC C9P 9C8, Canada. **E-mail:** ascentaspirations@shaw. ca. **Website:** www.davidpfraser.ca. **Contact:** David Fraser, editor. Estab. 1997. *"Ascent Aspirations* magazine publishes weekly online and in print annually. The print issues are operated as contests or as anthologies of a year's accepted submissions. Please refer to current guidelines before submitting. *Ascent Aspirations* is a quality electronic publication dedicated to the promotion and encouragement of aspiring writers of poetry. For Friday's Poems we accept submissions all the time, publish 3 poems per week, and archive then after that week is over. Magazine: 3 electronic pages; photos. Receives 100-200 unsolicited mss/month. Accepts 3 mss/issue; 156 mss/year. Publishes 10-50 new writers/year. Has published work by Taylor Graham, Janet Buck, Jim Manton, Steve Cartwright, Don Stockard, Penn Kemp, Sam Vargo, Vernon Waring, Margaret Karmazin, Bill Hughes, and spoken-word artists Sheri-D Wilson, Missy Peters, Ian Ferrier, Cathy Petch, and Bob Holdman.

TIPS "Poetry should use language lyrically and effectively, be experimental in either form or content, and take the reader into realms where they can analyze and think about the human condition. Write with passion for your material, be concise and economical, and let the reader work to unravel your story. In terms of editing, always proofread to the point where what you submit is the best it possibly can be. Never be discouraged if your work is not accepted; it may just not be the right fit for a current publication."

ASIMOV'S SCIENCE FICTION

Dell Magazines, 44 Wall St., Suite 904, New York NY 10005. **E-mail:** asimovs@dellmagazines.com. **Website:** www.asimovs.com. **Contact:** Sheila Williams, editor; Victoria Green, senior art director. Estab. 1977. "Magazine consists of science fiction and fantasy stories for adults and young adults. Publishes the best short science fiction available."

NEEDS Wants "science fiction primarily. Some fantasy and humor. It is best to read a great deal of material in the genre to avoid the use of some very old ideas." Submit ms via online submissions manager or postal mail; no e-mail submissions. No horror or psychic/supernatural, sword and sorcery, explicit sex or violence that isn't integral to the story. Would like to see more hard science fiction. Length: 750-15,000 words.

PAYMENT/TERMS Pays 8-10¢/word for short stories up to 7,500 words; 8-8.5¢/word for longer material. Works between 7,500-10,000 words by authors who make more than 8¢/word for short stories will receive a flat rate that will be no less than the payment would be for a shorter story.

TIPS "In general, we're looking for 'character-oriented' stories, those in which the characters, rather than the science, provide the main focus for the reader's interest. Serious, thoughtful, yet accessible fiction will constitute the majority of our purchases, but there's always room for the humorous as well."

ASSIGNMENT

The Literary Magazine of Southern New Hampshire University, 2500 N. River Rd., Manchester NH 03106. **E-mail:** assignmentlitmag@gmail.com. **Website:** www.assignmentmag.com. **Contact:** Benjamin Nugent, editor. Estab. 2015. *"Assignment* is a literary magazine published annually by Southern New Hampshire University. It's so named because, in addition to short stories and essays by established and up-and-coming authors, and interviews, it will include creative writing assignments (i.e., exercises) generated by the contributors. Said assignments might be as conventional as 'Write a story entirely in dialogue,' or as unconventional as 'Walk across Europe.' Each issue will also feature the winner of the annual contest for students of SNHU's Master in Fine Arts program."

Assignment is not accepting unsolicited submissions at this time.

THE ATA MAGAZINE

11010 142nd St. NW, Edmonton Alberta T5N 2R1, Canada. (780)447-9400. **Fax:** (780)455-6481. **E-mail:** government@teachers.ab.ca. **Website:** www.teachers. ab.ca. Estab. 1920.

THE ATLANTIC MONTHLY

The Watergate, 600 New Hampshire Ave., NW, Washington DC 20037. (202)266-6000. **Fax:** (202)266-6001. **E-mail:** submissions@theatlantic.com; pitches@theatlantic.com. **Website:** www.theatlantic.com. **Contact:** Scott Stossel, magazine editor; Ann Hulbert, literary editor. Estab. 1857. General magazine for an educated readership with broad cultural and public-affairs interests. *"The Atlantic* considers unsolicited mss, either fiction or nonfiction. A general familiarity with what we have published in the past is the best guide to our needs and preferences."

NEEDS "Seeks fiction that is clear, tightly written with strong sense of 'story' and well-defined characters." No longer publishes fiction in the regular magazine. Instead, it will appear in a special newsstand-only fiction issue. Receives 1,000 unsolicited mss/month. Accepts 7-8 mss/year. **Publishes 3-4 new writers/year.** Preferred length: 2,000-6,000 words.

HOW TO CONTACT Submit via e-mail with Word document attachment to submissions@theatlantic.com. Mss submitted via postal mail must be typewritten and double-spaced.

PAYMENT/TERMS Payment varies.

TIPS "Writers should be aware that this is not a market for beginner's work (nonfiction and fiction), nor is it truly for intermediate work. Study this magazine before sending only your best, most professional work. When making first contact, cover letters are sometimes helpful, particularly if they cite prior publications or involvement in writing programs. Common mistakes: melodrama, inconclusiveness, lack of development, unpersuasive characters and/or dialogue."

AUTHORSHIP

National Writers Association, 10940 S. Parker Rd., #508, Parker CO 80134. **E-mail:** natlwritersassn@hotmail.com. **Website:** www.nationalwriters.com. Estab. 1950s. "Association magazine targeted to beginning and professional writers. Covers how-to, humor, marketing issues. Disk and e-mail submissions preferred."

TIPS "Members of National Writers Association are given preference."

THE AVALON LITERARY REVIEW

CCI Publishing, P.O. Box 780696, Orlando FL 32878. (407)574-7355. **E-mail:** submissions@avalonliteraryreview.com. **Website:** www.avalonliteraryreview.com. **Contact:** Valerie Rubino, managing editor. Estab. 2011. "*The Avalon Literary Review* welcomes work from both published and unpublished writers and poets. We accept submissions of poetry, short fiction, and personal essays. While we appreciate the genres of fantasy, historical romance, science fiction, and horror, our magazine is not the forum for such work." Quarterly magazine.

NEEDS No erotica, science fiction, or horror. Length: 250-2,500 words.

HOW TO CONTACT Submit complete ms. Only accepts electronic submissions.

PAYMENT/TERMS Pays 5 contributor's copies.

TIPS "The author's voice and point of view should be unique and clear. We seek pieces that spring from the author's life and experiences. Fiction submissions that explore both the sweet and bitter of life with a touch of humor, and poetry with vivid imagery, are a good fit for our review."

THE AWAKENINGS REVIEW

Awakenings Project, The, P.O. Box 177, Wheaton IL 60187. (630)606-8732. **E-mail:** ar@awakeningsproject.org. **Website:** www.awakeningsproject.org. **Contact:** Robert Lundin, editor. Estab. 1999. *The Awakenings Review* is published by the Awakenings Project. Begun in cooperation with the University of Chicago Center for Psychiatric Rehabilitation in 2000, *The Awakenings Review* has been acclaimed internationally and draws writers from all over the United States and from several other countries including Israel, South Africa, Australia, Finland, Switzerland, the United Kingdom, and Canada.

NEEDS Length: 5,000 words max.

HOW TO CONTACT No e-mail submissions. Cover letter is preferred. Include SASE and short bio.

PAYMENT/TERMS Pays 1 contributor's copy, plus discount on additional copies.

🜲 BABYBUG

Cricket Media, Inc., 7926 Jones Branch Dr., Suite 870, McLean VA 22102. (703)885-3400. **Website:** www.cricketmedia.com. Estab. 1994. "*Babybug*, a look-and-listen magazine, presents simple poems, stories, nonfiction, and activities that reflect the natural playfulness and curiosity of babies and toddlers."

NEEDS Wants very short, clear fiction. Length: up to 6 sentences.

HOW TO CONTACT Submit complete ms via online submissions manager.

PAYMENT/TERMS Pays up to 25¢/word.

TIPS "We are particularly interested in mss that explore simple concepts, encourage very young children's imaginative play, and provide opportunities for adult readers and babies to interact. We welcome work that reflects diverse family cultures and traditions."

🜲 THE BALTIMORE REVIEW

6514 Maplewood Rd., Baltimore MD 21212. **E-mail:** editor@baltimorereview.org. **Website:** www.baltimorereview.org. **Contact:** Barbara Westwood Diehl, senior editor. Estab. 1996. *The Baltimore Review* publishes poetry, fiction, and creative nonfiction from Baltimore and beyond. Submission periods are August 1-November 30 and February 1-May 31.

NEEDS Length: 100-5,000 words.

HOW TO CONTACT Send complete ms using online submission form. Publishes 16-20 mss (combination of poetry, fiction, and creative nonfiction) per online issue. Work published online is also published in annual anthology.

PAYMENT/TERMS Pays $40.

TIPS "See editor preferences on staff page of website."

● THE BANGALORE REVIEW

Spanning Minds, No. 149, 2nd Floor, 4th Cross, Kasturi Nagar, Bangalore Karnataka , India. **E-mail:** info@bangalorereview.com. **E-mail:** submissions@bangalorereview.com. **Website:** www.bangalorereview.com. **Contact:** Suhail Rasheed, managing editor; Maitreyee Choudhury and Fehmida Zakeer, co-editors; Mithun Jayaram, arts editor. Estab. 2013. *The Bangalore Review* is a monthly online magazine aimed at promoting literature, arts, culture, criticism, and philosophy at a deeper level.

NEEDS Does not want erotica. Length: 250-5,000.

HOW TO CONTACT Query with complete ms.

PAYMENT/TERMS Does not offer payment.

BARBARIC YAWP

BoneWorld Publishing, 3700 County Rt. 24, Russell NY 13684. **Website:** www.boneworldpublishing.com. Estab. 1997. "We publish what we like. Fiction should include some bounce and surprise. Our publication is intended for the intelligent, open-minded reader."

● *Barbaric Yawp*, published quarterly, is digest-sized; 44 pages; matte cover stock.

NEEDS "We don't want any pornography, gratuitous violence, or whining."

HOW TO CONTACT Submit complete ms by mail. Send SASE for reply and return of ms, or send a disposable copy of ms. Accepts simultaneous, multiple submissions, and reprints.

PAYMENT/TERMS Pays 1 contributor's copy; additional copies $3.

TIPS "Don't give up. Read much, write much, submit much. Observe closely the world around you. Don't borrow ideas from TV or films. Revision is often necessary—grit your teeth and do it. Never fear rejection."

● THE BARCELONA REVIEW

Correu Vell 12-2, Barcelona 08002, Spain. (00 34) 93 319 15 96. **E-mail:** editor@barcelonareview.com. **Website:** www.barcelonareview.com. **Contact:** Jill Adams, editor. Estab. 1997. *The Barcelona Review* is "the Web's first multilingual review of international, contemporary, cutting-edge fiction. *TBR* is actually 3 separate reviews—English, Spanish, and Catalan—with occasional translations from 1 language to another. Original texts of other languages are presented along with English and Spanish translations as available."

● "We cannot offer money to contributors, but in lieu of pay we can sometimes offer an excellent Spanish translation (worth quite a bit of money in itself). Work is showcased along with 2 or more known authors in a high-quality literary review with an international readership."

NEEDS Length: up to 4,500 words.

HOW TO CONTACT Submit 1 story at a time. To submit via e-mail, send an attached document. Do not send in the body of an e-mail. Include "Submission/Author Name" in the subject box. Accepts hard copies, but they will not be returned. Double-space ms.

TIPS "Send top-drawer material that has been drafted 2, 3, 4 times—whatever it takes. Then sit on it for a while and look at it afresh. Keep the text tight. Grab the reader in the first paragraph and don't let go. Keep in mind that a perfectly crafted story that lacks a punch of some sort won't cut it. Make it new, make it different. Surprise the reader in some way. Read the best of the short fiction available in your area of writing to see how yours measures up. Don't send anything off until you feel it's ready, and then familiarize yourself with the content of the review/magazine to which you are submitting."

BARKING SYCAMORES

Autonomous Press, 3488 Gateway Lakes Dr., Grove City OH 43123. **E-mail:** barkingsycamores@gmail.com. **Website:** barkingsycamores.wordpress.com. **Contact:** N.I. Nicholson and V. E. Maday, editors. Estab. 2014. *Barking Sycamores* is a literary journal whose mission is to publish poetry, short fiction (1,000 words or less), creative nonfiction, hybrid genre, and artwork by neurodivergent contributors. "We also seek to add positively to the public discussion about neurodivergence as a whole in the form of essays on literature and the interrelationship between it and the creative process. Additionally, we also publish book reviews (1,000 words or less) of titles either written by or focused on neurodivergent individuals. We pay contributors once their work is included in the yearly print anthology. Payment comes from the Autonomous Press anthology fund."

PAYMENT/TERMS We pay contributors once their work is included in the yearly print anthology. Payment comes from the Autonomous Press anthology fund.

BARRELHOUSE

E-mail: yobarrelhouse@gmail.com. **Website:** www.barrelhousemag.com. **Contact:** Dave Housley, Joe Killiany, and Matt Perez, fiction editors; Tom McAllister, nonfiction editor; Dan Brady, poetry editor. Estab. 2004. *Barrelhouse* is a biannual print journal featuring fiction, poetry, interviews, and essays about music, art, and the detritus of popular culture.

○ Stories originally published in *Barrelhouse* have been featured in *The Best American Nonrequired Reading*, *The Best American Science Fiction and Fantasy*, and the Million Writer's Award.

NEEDS Length: open, but prefers pieces under 8,000.

HOW TO CONTACT Submit complete ms via online submissions manager. DOC or RTF files only.

PAYMENT/TERMS Pays $50 and 2 contributor copies.

BATEAU

105 Eden St., Bar Harbor ME 04609. **E-mail:** dan@bateaupress.org. **Website:** bateaupress.org. **Contact:** Daniel Mahoney, editor in chief. Estab. 2007. "*Bateau*, published annually, subscribes to no trend but serves to represent as wide a cross-section of contemporary writing as possible. For this reason, readers will most likely love and hate at least something in each issue. We consider this a good thing. To us, it means *Bateau* is eclectic, open-ended, and not mired in a particular strain."

○ *Bateau* is around 80 pages, digest-sized, offset print, perfect-bound, with a 100% recycled letterpress cover. Press run is 250.

HOW TO CONTACT Submit via online submissions manager. Brief bio is encouraged but not required.

PAYMENT/TERMS Pays contributor's copies.

TIPS "Send us your best work. Send us funny work, quirky work, outstanding work, work that is well punctuated or lacks punctuation. Fearless work. Work that wants to crash on our sofa."

BAYOU

Department of English, University of New Orleans, 2000 Lakeshore Dr., New Orleans LA 70148. **E-mail:** bayou@uno.edu. **Website:** bayoumagazine.org. **Contact:** Joanna Leake, editor in chief. Estab. 2002. "A nonprofit journal for the arts, each issue of *Bayou* contains beautiful fiction, nonfiction, and poetry. From quirky shorts to more traditional stories, we are committed to publishing solid work, regardless of style. At *Bayou* we are always interested first in a well-told tale. Our poetry and prose are filled with memorable characters observing their world, acknowledging both the mundane and the sublime, often at once and always with an eye toward beauty. *Bayou* is packed with a range of material from established, award-winning authors as well as new voices on the rise. Recent contributors include Eric Trethewey, Virgil Suarez, Marilyn Hacker, Sean Beaudoin, Tom Whalen, Mark Doty, Philip Cioffari, Lyn Lifshin, Timothy Liu, and Gaylord Brewer. In 1 issue every year, *Bayou* features the winner of the annual Tennessee Williams/New Orleans Literary Festival One-Act Play Competition."

○ Accepts submissions on Submittable and by mail. Reads submissions September 1-May 1.

NEEDS "Flash fiction and short shorts are welcome. No novel excerpts, please, unless they can stand alone as short stories." No horror, gothic, or juvenile fiction. Length: up to 7,500 words.

HOW TO CONTACT Send complete ms via online submission system or postal mail.

PAYMENT/TERMS Pays 2 contributor's copies.

TIPS "Do not submit in more than 1 genre at a time. Don't send a second submission until you receive a response to the first."

THE BEAR DELUXE MAGAZINE

Orlo, 240 N. Broadway, #112, Portland OR 97227. **E-mail:** beardeluxe@orlo.org. **Website:** www.orlo.org. **Contact:** Tom Webb, editor-in-chief; Kristin Rogers Brown, art director. Estab. 1993. "*The Bear Deluxe Magazine* is a national independent environmental arts magazine publishing significant works of reporting, creative nonfiction, literature, visual art, and design. Based in the Pacific Northwest, it reaches across cultural and political divides to engage readers on vital issues effecting the environment. Published twice per year, *The Bear Deluxe* includes a wider array and a higher percentage of visual artwork and design than many other publications. Artwork is included both as editorial support and as standalone or independent art. It has included nationally recognized artists as well as emerging artists. As with any publication, artists are encouraged to review a sample copy for a clearer understanding of the magazine's approach. Unsolicited submissions and samples are accepted and encouraged."

NEEDS "We are most excited by high-quality writing that furthers the magazine's goal of engaging new and divergent readers. We appreciate strong aspects of storytelling and are open to new formats, though we wouldn't call ourselves publishers of 'experimental fiction.'" No traditional sci-fi, horror, romance, or crime/action. Length: up to 4,000 words.

HOW TO CONTACT Query or send complete ms. Prefers postal mail submissions.

PAYMENT/TERMS Pays free subscription to the magazine, contributor's copies, and $25-400, depending on piece; additional copies for postage.

TIPS "Offer to be a stringer for future ideas. Get a copy of the magazine and guidelines, and query us with specific nonfiction ideas and clips. We're looking for original, magazine-style stories, not fluff or PR. Fiction, essay, and poetry writers should know we have an open and blind review policy and they should keep sending their best work even if rejected once. Be as specific as possible in queries."

BEATDOM

Beatdom Books, 426 Blowrie St., Dundee Scotland DD3 1AH, United Kingdom. **E-mail:** editor@beatdom.com. **Website:** www.beatdom.com. **Contact:** David Wills, editor. Estab. 2007. Beatdom is a Beat Generation-themed literary journal that publishes essays, short stories, and poems related to the Beats. "We publish studies of Beat texts, figures, and legends; we look at writers and movements related to the Beats; we support writers of the present who take their influence from the Beats."

NEEDS Length: up to 5,000 words.

HOW TO CONTACT Submit complete ms via e-mail.

PAYMENT/TERMS Pays $50.

BELLEVUE LITERARY REVIEW

NYU Langone Medical Center, Department of Medicine, 550 First Ave., OBV-A612, New York NY 10016. (212)263-3973. **E-mail:** info@blreview.org. **Website:** www.blreview.org. **Contact:** Stacy Bodziak, managing editor. Estab. 2001. *Bellevue Literary Review*, published semiannually, prints "works of fiction, nonfiction, and poetry that touch upon relationships to the human body, illness, health, and healing."

Work published in *Bellevue Literary Review* has appeared in *The Pushcart Prize* and *Best American Short Stories*. Recently published work by Francine Prose, Molly Peacock, and Chard deNiord. Closed to submissions in July and August.

NEEDS *BLR* "seeks character-driven fiction with original voices and strong settings. While we are always interested in creative explorations in style, we do lean toward classic short stories." No genre fiction. Length: up to 5,000 words. Average length: 2,500 words.

HOW TO CONTACT Submit via online submissions manager.

PAYMENT/TERMS Pays 2 contributor's copies, one-year subscription, and one-year gift subscription.

BELLINGHAM REVIEW

Mail Stop 9053, Western Washington University, Bellingham WA 98225. (360)650-4863. **E-mail:** bellingham.review@wwu.edu. **Website:** www.bhreview.org. **Contact:** Susanne Paola Antonetta, editor-in-chief; Mike Oliphant, managing editor. Estab. 1977. Nonprofit magazine published once/year in the spring. Seeks "literature of palpable quality: poems, stories, and essays so beguiling they invite us to touch their essence. *Bellingham Review* hungers for a kind of writing that nudges the limits of form or executes traditional forms exquisitely." The editors are actively seeking submissions of creative nonfiction, as well as stories that push the boundaries of the form. Open submission period is from September 15-December 1.

NEEDS Length: up to 6,000 words. For prose that is 1,500 words or fewer, submit up to three in one entry. Does not want anything nonliterary. Length: up to 6,000 words.

HOW TO CONTACT Submit complete ms via online submissions manager.

PAYMENT/TERMS Pays as funds allow, plus contributor's copies.

TIPS "The *Bellingham Review* holds 3 annual contests: the 49th Parallel Award for poetry, the Annie Dillard Award for Nonfiction, and the Tobias Wolff Award for Fiction. See the individual listings for these contests under Contests & Awards for full details."

BELOIT FICTION JOURNAL

Box 11, Beloit College, 700 College St., Beloit WI 53511. (608)363-2079. **E-mail:** bfj@beloit.edu. **Website:** www.beloit.edu/bfj. **Contact:** Chris Fink, editor-in-chief. Estab. 1985. "*The Beloit Fiction Journal* publishes the best in contemporary short fiction. Traditional and experimental narratives find a home in our pages. We publish new writers alongside established writers. Our fiction-only format allows us to consider very long as well as very short stories. We occasionally publish excerpts."

○ Reading period: August 1-December 1. Work first appearing in *Beloit Fiction Journal* has been reprinted in award-winning collections, including the Flannery O'Connor and the Milkweed Fiction Prize collections, and has won the Iowa Short Fiction award. Has published work by Dennis Lehane, Silas House, and David Harris Ebenbach.

NEEDS Receives 200 unsolicited mss/month. Accepts 14 mss/year. Publishes ms 9 months after acceptance. **Publishes new writers every year.** Sometimes comments on rejected mss. Wants more experimental and short shorts. Would like to see more "stories with a focus on both language and plot, unusual metaphors and vivid characters." No pornography, religious dogma, science fiction, horror, political propaganda, or genre fiction. Length: 1-60 pages.

HOW TO CONTACT Submit complete ms via online submissions manager ($3 fee) or postal mail.

PAYMENT/TERMS Pays contributor copies.

TIPS "Many of our contributors are writers whose work we had previously rejected. Don't let 1 rejection slip turn you away from our—or any—magazine."

BERKELEY FICTION REVIEW

Berkeley Fiction Review, c/o ASUC Student Union FMO, 432 Eshleman, MC 4500, University of California, Berkeley, Berkeley CA 94720, United States. **E-mail:** berkeleyfictionreview@gmail.com. **Website:** berkeleyfictionreview.com. Estab. 1981. "The *Berkeley Fiction Review* is a UC Berkeley undergraduate, student-run publication. We look for innovative short fiction that plays with form and content, as well as tra-

ditionally constructed stories with fresh voices and original ideas."

○ *BFR* nominates to O.Henry, *Best American Short Stories* and *Pushcart* prizes. Sponsored by the ASUC.

NEEDS Length: no more than 25 pages.

HOW TO CONTACT Submit via e-mail with "Submission: Name, Title" in subject line. Include cover letter in body of e-mail, with story as an attachment.

PAYMENT/TERMS Pays 1 contributor's copy.

TIPS "Our criteria is fiction that resonates. Voices that are strong and move a reader. Clear, powerful prose (either voice or rendering of subject) with a point. Unique ways of telling stories—these capture the editors. Work hard, don't give up. Ask an honest person to point out your writing weaknesses, and then work on them. We look forward to reading fresh new voices."

BEST NEW WRITING

Hopewell Publications, LLC, P.O. Box 11, Titusville NJ 08560-0011. **E-mail:** info@bestnewwriting.com. **Website:** www.bestnewwriting.com. **Contact:** Brittany Fonte, managing editor. Estab. 2006. "*Best New Writing* is an annual anthology of fiction and creative nonfiction, including the winner of the Gover Story Prize for fiction and creative nonfiction of less than 10,000 words. Edited by award-winning authors, editors, and masters of the writing craft, *Best New Writing* showcases new works of outstanding literary value that are found outside of the commercial publishing establishment. Entries are previously unpublished (or published with a circulation of less than 500) and nominated by the writing community and the public at large. To submit books or prose or to view previous winners, please visit Best New Writing site (www.bestnewwriting.com). Send mss electronically."

NEEDS Length: up to 10,000 words.

HOW TO CONTACT Send complete ms.

TIPS "Read the guidelines. Read any issue of *Best New Writing*."

⑤ BEYOND CENTAURI

White Cat Publications, LLC, 33080 Industrial Rd., Suite 101, Livonia MI 48150. (734)237-8522. **Fax:** (313)557-5162. **E-mail:** beyondcentauri@whitecatpublications.com. **Website:** www.whitecatpublications.com/guidelines/beyond-centauri. Estab. 2003. *Beyond Centauri*, published quarterly, contains fantasy, science fiction, sword and sorcery, very mild horror short stories, poetry, and illustrations for readers ages 10 and up.

○ *Beyond Centauri* is 44 pages, magazine-sized, offset printed, perfect-bound, with paper cover for color art, includes ads. Press run is 100; 5 distributed free to reviewers.

NEEDS Looks for themes of science fiction or fantasy. "Science fiction and especially stories that take place in outer space will find great favor with us." Length: up to 2,500 words.

HOW TO CONTACT Submit in the body of an e-mail, or as an RTF attachment.

PAYMENT/TERMS Pays $6/story, $3/reprints, and $2/flash fiction (under 1,000 words), plus 1 contributor's copy.

BIG BRIDGE

Big Bridge Press, P.O. 2724, Tallahassee FL 32304. **E-mail:** walterblue@bigbridge.org. **Website:** www.bigbridge.org. **Contact:** Michael Rothenberg and Terri Carrion, editors. "*Big Bridge* is one of the oldest and most respected online literary arts magazines. For over 20 years, Big Bridge has published the best in poetry, fiction, nonfiction essays, journalism, and art (photos, line drawings, performance, installations, site-works, comics, graphics)."

HOW TO CONTACT Only accepts electronic submissions. Submit via e-mail.

TIPS "Big Bridge publishes one very big issue each year. Each issue features an online chapbook. We are interested in anthology concepts and thematic installations as well as individual submissions. Send query to propose installations and anthology ideas for consideration. All individual submissions should include a bio and bio photo."

BIG MUDDY

A Journal of the Mississippi River Valley, Southeast Missouri State University Press, One University Plaza, MS 2650, Cape Girardeau MO 63701. (573)651-2044. **E-mail:** upress@semo.edu. **Website:** www.semopress.com/bigmuddy/. Estab. 2000. "*Big Muddy* explores multidisciplinary, multicultural issues, people, and events mainly concerning, but not limited to, the 10-state area that borders the Mississippi River. We publish fiction, poetry, historical essays, creative nonfiction, environmental essays, biography, regional events, photography, art, etc."

NEEDS No romance, fantasy, or children's.

PAYMENT/TERMS Pays 2 contributor's copies; additional copies $5. Annual short story ($1,000) and flash fiction ($500) contests.

TIPS "We look for clear language, avoidance of clichés, a fresh vision of the theme or issue. Find some excellent and honest readers to comment on your work-in-progress and final draft. Consider their viewpoints carefully. Revise if needed."

BIG PULP

Exter Press, P.O. Box 92, Cumberland MD 21501. **E-mail:** editors@bigpulp.com. **Website:** www.bigpulp.com. **Contact:** Bill Olver, editor. Estab. 2008. *Big Pulp* defines "pulp fiction" very broadly: It's lively, challenging, thought provoking, thrilling, and fun, regardless of how many or how few genre elements are packed in. It doesn't subscribe to the theory that genre fiction is disposable; a great deal of literary fiction could easily fall under one of their general categories. Places a higher value on character and story than genre elements.

○ "Submissions are only accepted during certain reading periods. Our website is updated to reflect when we are and are not reading, and what we are looking for."

NEEDS Does not want generic slice-of-life, memoirs, inspirational, political, pastoral odes. Length: up to 2,500 words.

HOW TO CONTACT Submit complete ms.

PAYMENT/TERMS Pays $5-25.

TIPS "We like to be surprised, and we have few boundaries. Fantasy writers may focus on the mundane aspects of a fantastical creature's life or the magic that can happen in everyday life. Romances do not have to be requited or have happy endings, and the object of one's obsession may not be a person. Mysteries need not focus on 'whodunit?' We're always interested in science or speculative fiction focusing on societal issues, but writers should avoid being partisan or shrill. We also like fiction that crosses genre; for example, a science fiction romance or a fantasy crime story. We have an online archive for fiction and poetry and encourage writers to check it out. That said, *Big Pulp* has a strong editorial bias in favor of stories with monkeys. Especially talking monkeys."

BILINGUAL REVIEW

Arizona State University, Hispanic Research Center, P.O. Box 875303, Tempe AZ 85287-5303. (480)965-

3867. **Fax:** (480)965-0315. **E-mail:** brp@asu.edu. **Website:** www.asu.edu/brp/submit. **Contact:** Gary Francisco Keller, publisher. Estab. 1974. *Bilingual Review* is "committed to publishing high-quality writing by both established and emerging writers."

○ Magazine: 7x10; 96 pages; 55 lb. acid-free paper; coated cover stock.

NEEDS Receives 50 unsolicited mss/month. Accepts 3 mss/issue; 9 mss/year. "We do not publish literature about tourists in Latin America and their perceptions of the 'native culture.' We do not publish fiction about Latin America unless there is a clear tie to the U.S."

HOW TO CONTACT Submit via mail. Send 2 copies of complete ms with SAE and loose stamps. Does not usually accept e-mail submissions except through special circumstance/prior arrangement.

PAYMENT/TERMS Pays 2 contributor's copies; 30% discount for additional copies.

THE BITTER OLEANDER

4983 Tall Oaks Dr., Fayetteville NY 13066. **E-mail:** info@bitteroleander.com. **Website:** www.bitteroleander.com. **Contact:** Paul B. Roth, editor and publisher. "We're reading to find a language uncommitted to the commonplace and more integrated with the natural world. A language that helps define the same particulars in nature that exist in us and have not been socialized out of us." Biannual magazine covering poetry and short fiction and translations of contemporary poetry and short fiction.

NEEDS Wants short, imaginative fiction of no more than 2,500 words Does not want family or college stories with moralistic plots or fantasy that involve hyper-reality of any sort. Length: up to 2,500 words.

HOW TO CONTACT Submit through online Submittable portal.

PAYMENT/TERMS Pays 1 contributor's copy.

TIPS "If you are writing poems or short fiction in the tradition of 98% of all journals publishing in this country, then your work will usually not fit for us. If within the first 400 words my mind drifts, the rest rarely makes it. Be yourself, and listen to no one but yourself."

BLACKBIRD

Virginia Commonwealth University Department of English, P.O. Box 843082, Richmond VA 23284. (804)827-4729. **E-mail:** blackbird@vcu.edu. **Website:** www.blackbird.vcu.edu. Estab. 2001. *Blackbird* is published twice a year. Reading period: November 15-April 15.

NEEDS "We primarily look for short stories, but novel excerpts are acceptable if self-contained."

HOW TO CONTACT Submit using online submissions manager or by mail. Online submission is preferred.

TIPS "We like a story that invites us into its world, that engages our senses, soul, and mind. We are able to publish long works in all genres, but query *Blackbird* before you send a prose piece over 8,000 words or a poem exceeding 10 pages."

⑤ BLACK WARRIOR REVIEW

P.O. Box 862936, Tuscaloosa AL 35486. (205)348-4518. **E-mail:** interns.bwr@gmail.com. **Website:** www.bwr.ua.edu. **Contact:** Cat Ingrid Leeches, editor. Estab. 1974. "We publish contemporary fiction, poetry, reviews, essays, and art for a literary audience. We publish the freshest work we can find." Work that appeared in the *Black Warrior Review* has been included in the *Pushcart Prize* anthology, *Harper's Magazine*, *Best American Short Stories*, *Best American Poetry*, and *New Stories from the South*.

NEEDS "We are open to good experimental writing and short-short fiction. No genre fiction please." Publishes novel excerpts if under contract to be published. Length: up to 7,000 words.

HOW TO CONTACT One story/chapter per envelope. Wants work that is conscious of form and well-crafted.

PAYMENT/TERMS Pays one-year subscription and nominal lump-sum fee.

TIPS "We look for attention to language, freshness, honesty, a convincing and sharp voice. Send us a clean, well-printed, proofread ms. Become familiar with the magazine prior to submission."

BLUE COLLAR REVIEW

Partisan Press, P.O. Box 11417, Norfolk VA 23517. **E-mail:** red-ink@earthlink.net. **Website:** www.partisanpress.org. **Contact:** A. Markowitz, editor; Mary Franke, co-editor. Estab. 1997. *Blue Collar Review (Journal of Progressive Working Class Literature)*, published quarterly, contains poetry, short stories, and illustrations "reflecting the working-class experience—a broad range from the personal to the societal. Our purpose is to promote and expand working-class literature and an awareness of the connections between workers of all occupations and the social context in which we live. Also to inspire the creativity and latent talent in 'common' working people."

NEEDS Submit ms via mail. Name and address should appear on every page. Cover letter is helpful but not required. Size 10 SASE is required for response. Length: up to 1,000 words.

PAYMENT/TERMS Pays contributor's copies.

BLUELINE

120 Morey Hall, SUNY Potsdam, Postdam NY 13676. **E-mail:** blueline@potsdam.edu. **Website:** bluelinemagadk.com. **Contact:** Donald J. McNutt, editor and nonfiction editor; Caroline Downing, art editor; Stephanie Coyne-DeGhett, fiction editor; Rebecca Lehmann, poetry editor. Estab. 1979. "*Blueline* seeks poems, stories, and essays relating to the Adirondacks and regions similar in geography and spirit, or focusing on the shaping influence of nature. Submission period is July-November. *Blueline* welcomes electronic submissions as Word document (DOC or DOCX) attachments. Please identify genre in subject line. Please avoid using compression software." Annual literary magazine publishing fiction, poetry, personal essays, book reviews, and quality visual art for those interested in the Adirondacks or well-crafted nature writing in general.

- "Proofread all submissions. It is difficult for our editors to get excited about work containing typographical and syntactic errors."

NEEDS Receives 8-10 unsolicited mss/month. Accepts 2-3 mss/issue. Does not read January-June. Publishes 2 new writers/year. Recently published work by Jim Meirose, Amber Timmerman, Gail Gilliland, Matthew J. Spireng, Roger Sheffer, and Mason Smith. No urban stories or erotica. Length: 500-3,000 words. Average length: 2,500 words.

PAYMENT/TERMS Pays 1 contributor's copy; charges $9 each for 3 or more copies.

TIPS "We look for concise, clear, concrete prose that tells a story and touches upon a universal theme or situation. We prefer realism to romanticism but will consider nostalgia if well done. Pay attention to grammar and syntax. Avoid murky language, sentimentality, cuteness, or folksiness. We would like to see more good, creative nonfiction centered on the literature and/or culture of the Adirondacks, Northern New York, New England, or Eastern Canada. If ms has potential, we work with author to improve and reconsider for publication. Our readers prefer fiction to poetry (in general) or reviews. Write from your own experience, be specific and factual (within the bounds of your story), and if you write about universal features such as love, death, change, etc., write about them in a fresh way. You'll catch our attention if your writing is interesting, vigorous, and polished."

BLUE MESA REVIEW

Department of Language and Literature, Humanities Building, Second Floor, MSC03 2170, 1 University of New Mexico, Albuquerque NM 87131. **Website:** bluemesareview.org. **Contact:** Has rotating editorial board; see website for current masthead. Estab. 1989. "Originally founded by Rudolfo Anaya, Gene Frumkin, David Johnson, Patricia Clark Smith, and Lee Bartlette in 1989, the *Blue Mesa Review* emerged as a source of innovative writing produced in the Southwest. Over the years the magazine's nuance has changed, sometimes shifting towards more craft-oriented work, other times realigning with its original roots."

- Open for submissions from September 30-March 31. Contest: June 1-August 31. Only accepts submissions through online submissions manager.

NEEDS Length: up to 6,000 words.

HOW TO CONTACT Submit via online submissions manager.

TIPS "In general, we are seeking strong voices and lively, compelling narrative with a fine eye for craft. We look forward to reading your best work!"

BLUESTEM

English Deptartment, Eastern Illinois University, **Website:** www.bluestemmagazine.com. **Contact:** Olga Abella, editor. Estab. 1966. *Bluestem*, formerly known as *Karamu*, produces a quarterly online issue (December, March, June, September) and an annual spring print issue.

- Only accepts submissions through online submissions manager.

NEEDS Length: up to 5,000 words.

HOW TO CONTACT Submit only 1 short story at a time. Include bio (less than 100 words) with submission. Query if longer than 5,000 words.

PAYMENT/TERMS Pays 1 contributor's copy and discount for additional copies.

BODY LITERATURE

Website: bodyliterature.com. Estab. 2012. *BODY* is an international online literary journal. "We publish the highest-quality poetry and prose from emerging and established writers.

NEEDS Length: up to 10 pages typed and double-spaced.

HOW TO CONTACT Submit through online submissions manager. Include short cover letter and short third-person bio.

BOMBAY GIN

Naropa University, Creative Writing and Poetics Department, 2130 Arapahoe Ave., Boulder CO 80302. **E-mail:** bgin@naropa.edu. **Website:** www.bombayginjournal.com. **Contact:** Jade Lascelles, editor in chief. Estab. 1974. *Bombay Gin*, published annually, is the literary journal of the Jack Kerouac School of Disembodied Poetics at Naropa University. Produced and edited by MFA students, *Bombay Gin* publishes established writers alongside unpublished and emerging writers. We have a special interest in works that push conventional literary boundaries. Submissions of poetry, prose, visual art, translation, and works involving hybrid forms and cross-genre exploration are encouraged. Translations are also considered. Guidelines are the same as for original work. Translators are responsible for obtaining any necessary permissions."

　　Bombay Gin is 150-200 pages, digest-sized, professionally printed, perfect-bound, with color card cover. Has published work by Amiri Baraka, Lisa Robertson, CA Conrad, Sapphire, Fred Moten, Anne Waldman, Diane di Prima and bell hooks, among others.

NEEDS Length: up to 15 pages.

HOW TO CONTACT Submit through online submissions manager. Include 100-word bio, e-mail, and mailing address.

BOMB MAGAZINE

80 Hanson Place, Ste. 703, Brooklyn NY 11217. (718)636-9100. **Fax:** (718)636-9200. **E-mail:** saul@bombsite.com. **Website:** www.bombmagazine.com. **Contact:** Saul Anton, senior editor. Estab. 1981. "Written, edited, and produced by industry professionals and funded by those interested in the arts, *BOMB Magazine* publishes work which is unconventional and contains an edge, whether it be in style or subject matter."

NEEDS No genre fiction: romance, science fiction, horror, western. Length: up to 25 pages.

HOW TO CONTACT *BOMB Magazine* accepts unsolicited poetry and prose submissions for our literary supplement *First Proof* by online submission manager in January and August. Submissions sent outside these months will not be read. Submit complete ms via online submission manager. E-mailed submissions will not be considered.

PAYMENT/TERMS Pays $100 and contributor's copies.

TIPS "Mss should be typed, double-spaced, and proofread, and should be final drafts. Purchase a sample issue before submitting work."

✪ BOSTON REVIEW

P.O. Box 425786, Cambridge MA 02142. (617)324-1360. **E-mail:** review@bostonreview.net. **Website:** www.bostonreview.net. **Contact:** Deborah Chasman and Joshua Cohen, editors. Estab. 1975. The editors are committed to a society that fosters human diversity and a democracy in which we seek common grounds of principle amidst our many differences. In the hope of advancing these ideals, *Boston Review* acts as a forum that seeks to enrich the language of public debate.

　　Boston Review is a recipient of the Pushcart Prize in Poetry.

NEEDS Currently closed to general fiction submissions but assembling a special issue of fiction on global dystopias, edited by Junot Díaz. See submission page for details. Length: up to 5,000 words, but can be much shorter.

HOW TO CONTACT Send complete ms.

PAYMENT/TERMS Pays $100-300 and contributor's copies.

TIPS "The best way to get a sense of the kind of material *Boston Review* is looking for is to read the magazine. It is all available online for free."

✪ BOULEVARD

Opojaz, Inc., 6614 Clayton Rd., Box 325, Richmond Heights MO 63117. **E-mail:** editors@boulevardmagazine.org. **Website:** www.boulevardmagazine.org; boulevard.submittable.com/submit. **Contact:** Jessica Rogen, editor. Estab. 1985. Hosts the Short Fiction Contest for Emerging Writers. **Prize:** $1,500 and publication in *Boulevard*. **Postmarked deadline:** December 31. **Entry fee:** $15 for each individual story, with no limit per author. Entry fee includes a one-year subscription to *Boulevard* (1 per author). Make check payable to *Boulevard*. For contests, make check payable to *Boulevard* or submit online at boulevard.submittable.com/submit. "*Boulevard* is a diverse literary magazine presenting original creative work by well-known authors as well as by writers of exciting promise." Triannual magazine featuring fiction, poetry, and essays. Sometimes comments on rejected mss. *Boulevard* has been called "one of the half-dozen best literary journals" by Poet Laureate Daniel Hoffman in *The Philadelphia Inquirer*. "We strive to publish the finest in poetry, fiction, and nonfiction. We frequently publish writers with previous credits, and we are very interested in publishing less experienced or unpublished writers with exceptional promise. We've published everything from John Ashbery to Donald Hall to a wide variety of styles from new or lesser known poets. We're eclectic. We are interested in original, moving poetry written from the head as well as the heart. It can be about any topic." *Boulevard* is 175-250 pages, digest-sized, flat-spined, with glossy card cover. Receives over 600 unsolicited mss/month. Accepts about 10 mss/issue. Publishes 10 new writers/year. Recently published work by Joyce Carol Oates, Floyd Skloot, John Barth, Stephen Dixon, David Guterson, Albert Goldbarth, Molly Peacock, Bob Hicok, Alice Friman, Dick Allen, and Tom Disch.

NEEDS Submit by mail or Submittable. Accepts multiple submissions. Does not accept mss May 1-October 1. SASE for reply. "We do not want erotica, science fiction, romance, western, horror, or children's stories." Length: up to 8,000 words.

PAYMENT/TERMS Pays $50-500 (sometimes higher) for accepted work.

TIPS "Read the magazine first. The work *Boulevard* publishes is generally recognized as among the finest in the country. We continue to seek more good literary or cultural essays. Send only your best work."

BRAIN, CHILD

Erielle Media, LLC, 341 Newtown Turnpike, Wilton CT 06897. **E-mail:** editorial@brainchildmag.com. **Website:** www.brainchildmag.com. **Contact:** Marcelle Soviero, editor in chief. Estab. 2000. "*Brain, Child: The Magazine for Thinking Mothers*, reflects modern motherhood—the way it really is. It is the largest print literary magazine devoted to motherhood. *Brain, Child* is a community for and by mothers who like to think about what raising kids does for (and to) the mind and soul. *Brain, Child* isn't your typical parenting magazine. We couldn't cupcake-decorate our way out of a paper bag. We are more 'literary' than 'how-to,' more *New Yorker* than *Parents*. We shy away from expert advice on childrearing in favor of first-hand reflections by great writers (Jane Smiley, Barbara Ehrenreich, Anne Tyler) on life as a mother. Each quarterly issue is full of essays, features, humor, reviews, fiction, art, cartoons, and our readers' own stories. Our philosophy is pretty simple: Motherhood is worthy of literature. And there are a lot of ways to mother, all of them interesting. We're proud to be publishing articles and essays that are smart, down to earth, sometimes funny, and sometimes poignant."

NEEDS "We publish fiction that has a strong motherhood theme." No genre fiction. Length: 800-4,000 words.

HOW TO CONTACT Send complete ms.

PAYMENT/TERMS Payment varies.

TIPS "We are excited by great writing. It makes our day when we hear from an established writer or publish an author for the first time."

THE BRIAR CLIFF REVIEW

3303 Rebecca St., Sioux City IA 51104. (712)279-1651. **E-mail:** tricia.currans-sheehan@briarcliff.edu. **Website:** bcreview.org. **Contact:** Tricia Currans-Sheehan, editor; Jeanne Emmons, poetry editor; Phil Hey, fiction editor; Paul Weber, Siouxland and nonfiction editor. Estab. 1989. *The Briar Cliff Review*, published annually in April, is "an attractive, eclectic literary/art magazine." It focuses on, but is not limited to, "Siouxland writers and subjects. We are happy to proclaim ourselves a regional publication. It doesn't diminish us; it enhances us."

🖸 Member: CLMP, Humanities International Complete.

NEEDS Accepts 5 mss/year. **Publishes 10-14 new writers/year.** Publishes ms 3-4 months after acceptance. Recently published work by Leslie Barnard, Daryl Murphy, Patrick Hicks, Siobhan Fallon, Shelley Scaletta, Jenna Blum, Brian Bedard, Rebecca Tuch, Scott H. Andrews, and Josip Novakovich. "No romance, horror, or alien stories." Length: up to 5,000 words.

HOW TO CONTACT Submit by (send SASE for return of ms) or online submissions manager. Does not accept e-mail submissions (unless from overseas). Seldom comments on rejected mss.

PAYMENT/TERMS Pays 2 contributor's copies; additional copies available for $12.

TIPS "So many stories are just telling. We want some action. It has to move. We prefer stories in which there is no gimmick, no mechanical turn of events, no moral except the one we would draw privately."

BRILLIANT CORNERS: A JOURNAL OF JAZZ & LITERATURE

Lycoming College, 700 College Place, Williamsport PA 17701. **Website:** www.lycoming.edu/brilliantcorners. **Contact:** Sascha Feinstein, editor. Estab. 1996. "We publish jazz-related literature—fiction, poetry, and nonfiction. We are open as to length and form." Semiannual.

○ Reading period: September 1-May 15.

NEEDS Receives 10-15 unsolicited mss/month. Accepts 1-2 mss/issue; 2-3 mss/year.

HOW TO CONTACT Submit with SASE for return of ms, or send disposable copy of ms. Accepts unpublished work only. No e-mail or fax submissions. Cover letter is preferred.

TIPS "We look for clear, moving prose that demostrates a love of both writing and jazz. We primarily publish established writers, but we read all submissions carefully and welcome work by outstanding young writers."

THE BROADKILL REVIEW

c/o John Milton & Company, 104 Federal St., Milton DE 19968. **E-mail:** broadkillreview@gmail.com. **Website:** broadkillreview.com, www.thebroadkillreview.blogspot.com; sites.google.com/site/thebroadkillreview. **Contact:** James C.L. Brown, founding editor; Stephen Scott Whitaker, managing editor; Linda Blaskey, poetry and interview editor, HA Maxson, fiction editor. Estab. 2005.

○ "*The Broadkill Review* accepts the best fiction, poetry, and nonfiction by new and established writers. We have published Pushcart-nominated fiction and poetry." *TBR* publishes many writers from the Mid-Atlantic region, but does not limit itself to work from this region, as they are an internationally read publication that publishes a wide variety of work from around the globe, including Canada, U.S., Western and Eastern Europe, China, Vietnam, Australia, and Pakistan.

NEEDS No erotica, fantasy, science fiction "unless these serve some functional literary purpose; most do not." Length: up to 6,000 words.

HOW TO CONTACT Send complete ms with cover letter through online submissions manager. Include estimated word count, brief bio, list of publications.

PAYMENT/TERMS Pays contributor's copy.

TIPS "Query the editor first. Visit our website to familiarize yourself with the type of material we publish. Request and read a copy of the magazine first!"

○ BROKEN PENCIL

P.O. Box 203, Station P, Toronto ON M5S 2S7, Canada. **E-mail:** editor@brokenpencil.com. **Website:** www.brokenpencil.com. **Contact:** Alison Lang, editor. Estab. 1995. "*Broken Pencil* is one of the few magazines in the world devoted exclusively to underground culture and the independent arts. We are a great resource and a lively read! *Broken Pencil* reviews the best zines, books, websites, videos, and artworks from the underground and reprints the best articles from the alternative press. From the hilarious to the perverse, *Broken Pencil* challenges conformity and demands attention."

○ "Please read our magazine (you can order a free trial issue at brokenpencil.com/freeissue) or browse our content at brokenpencil.com before submitting any fiction, nonfiction, or story ideas!"

NEEDS "We're particularly interested in work from emerging writers." Reads fiction submissions February 1-September 15. Length: 50-3,000 words.

HOW TO CONTACT Submit via online submissions manager.

PAYMENT/TERMS Pays $30-300.

TIPS "Remember, we are a guide to alternative and independent culture. We don't want your thoughts on Hollywood movies or your touching tale about coming of age on the prairies! Make sure you have some sense of the kind of work we use before getting in touch. Never send us something if you haven't at least read *Broken Pencil*. Always include your address, phone number, and e-mail, so we know where to find you, and a little something about yourself, so we know who you are."

BUENOS AIRES REVIEW

E-mail: editors@buenosairesreview.org. **Website:** buenosairesreview.org. *The Buenos Aires Review* presents the best and latest work by emerging and established writers from the Americas, in both Spanish and English. "We value translation and conversation. We're bilingual. And we're passionate about the art and craft that allows us to be, so we provide a dedicated space for translators to discuss their recent projects."

⊛ BUGLE

Rocky Mountain Elk Foundation, 5705 Grant Creek, Missoula MT 59808. (406)523-4500. **Fax:** (800)225-5355. **E-mail:** bugle@rmef.org. **E-mail:** conservationeditor@rmef.org; huntingeditor@rmef.org; assistanteditor@rmef.org; photos@rmef.org. **Website:** www.rmef.org. Estab. 1984. *Bugle* is the membership publication of the Rocky Mountain Elk Foundation, a nonprofit wildlife conservation group. "Our readers are predominantly hunters, many of them conservationists who care deeply about protecting wildlife habitat." Bimonthly. Magazine: 114-212 pages; 55 lb. Escanaba paper; 80 lb. Sterling cover, b&w, 4-color illustrations; photos.

NEEDS "We accept fiction and nonfiction stories pertaining in some way to elk, other wildlife, hunting, habitat conservation, and related issues. We would like to see more humor." Length: 1,500-5,000 words; average length: 2,500 words.

HOW TO CONTACT Query or submit complete ms to appropriate e-mail address; see website for guidelines.

PAYMENT/TERMS Pays 30¢/word and 3 contributor's copies.

TIPS "Hunting stories and essays should celebrate the hunting experience, demonstrating respect for wildlife, the land, and the hunt. Articles on elk behavior or elk habitat should include personal observations and should entertain as well as educate. No freelance product reviews or formulaic how-to articles accepted. Straight action-adventure hunting stories are in short supply, as are 'Situation Ethics' mss."

⊛ BURNSIDE REVIEW

P.O. Box 1782, Portland OR 97207. **Website:** www.burnsidereview.org. **Contact:** Sid Miller, founder and editor; Dan Kaplan, managing editor. Estab. 2004. *Burnside Review*, published every 9 months, prints "the best poetry and short fiction we can get our hands on. We tend to publish writing that finds beauty in truly unexpected places; that combines urban and natural imagery; that breaks the heart."

Burnside Review is 80 pages, 6x6, professionally printed, perfect-bound. Charges a $3 submission fee to cover printing costs.

NEEDS "We like bright, engaging fiction that works to surprise and captivate us." Length: up to 5,000 words.

HOW TO CONTACT Submit complete ms via online submissions manager.

PAYMENT/TERMS Pays $25 and 1 contributor's copy.

BUST MAGAZINE

Bust, Inc., 253 36th St., Suite C307, Brooklyn NY 11232. **E-mail:** debbie@bust.com. **E-mail:** submissions@bust.com. **Website:** www.bust.com. **Contact:** Debbie Stoller, editor in chief/publisher. Estab. 1993. "*Bust* is the groundbreaking, original women's lifestyle magazine and website that is unique in its ability to connect with bright, cutting-edge, influential young women."

"Please include your full name, e-mail address, mailing address, and day and night phone number in your submission. If you're e-mailing your submission, please send it as an attachment. If you're mailing your submission and want us to return it to you, please include a SASE. If we're interested in running your piece, we'll get back to you about it. If we aren't, we will try to let you know, but it may take a very long time and we can't promise you that we'll be able to. *Bust* does not accept poetry. If you are submitting a story idea rather than a story, please also send us clips of your previous writing."

NEEDS "We only publish erotic fiction. All other content is nonfiction." Length: 1,000-1,500 words.

HOW TO CONTACT Query with published clips.

PAYMENT/TERMS Pays up to $50

TIPS "We are always looking for stories that are surprising, and that 'bust' stereotypes about women."

⊛ THE CAFE IRREAL

E-mail: editors@cafeirreal.com. **Website:** www.cafeirreal.com. **Contact:** G.S. Evans and Alice Whittenburg, co-editors. Estab. 1998. "Our audience is composed of people who read or write literary fiction with fantastic themes, similar to the work of Franz Kafka, Kobo Abe, or Ana María Shua. This is a type of fiction (irreal) that has difficulty finding its way into print in the English-speaking world and defies many of the conventions of American literature especially. As a result, ours is a fairly specialized literary publication, and we would strongly recommend that prospective writers look at our current issue and guidelines carefully." Recently published work by Jiří Kratochvil, Vanessa Gebbie, Paul Blaney, Venita Blackburn, Ian Seed, BE Turner, Hernán Ortiz.

NEEDS Accepts submissions by e-mail. No attachments; include submission in body of e-mail. Include estimated word count. Accepts 6-8 mss/issue; 24-32 mss/year. No horror or "slice-of-life" stories; no genre or mainstream science fiction or fantasy. Length: up to 2,000 words.

PAYMENT/TERMS Pays 1¢/word, $2 minimum.

TIPS "Forget formulas. Write about what you don't know, take me places I couldn't possibly go, don't try to make me care about the characters. Read short fiction by writers such as Franz Kafka, Jorge Luis Borges, Donald Barthelme, Leonora Carrington, Magnus Mills, and Stanislaw Lem. Also read our website and guidelines."

CALLALOO

A Journal of African Diaspora Arts & Letters, Texas A&M University, 249 Blocker Hall, College Station TX 77843-4212, United States. (979)458-3108. **Fax:** (979)458-3275. **E-mail:** callaloo@tamu.edu. **Website:** callaloo.tamu.edu. Estab. 1976. *Callaloo: A Journal of African Diaspora Arts & Letters*, published quarterly, is devoted to poetry dealing with the African Diaspora, including North America, Europe, Africa, Latin and Central America, South America, and the Caribbean. Features about 15-20 poems (all forms and styles) in each issue along with short fiction, interviews, literary criticism, and concise critical book reviews.

NEEDS Would like to see more experimental fiction, science fiction, and well-crafted literary fiction particularly dealing with the black middle class, immigrant communities, and/or the black South. Accepts 3-5 mss/issue; 10-20 mss/year. **Publishes 5-10 new writers/year.** Recently published work by Charles Johnson, Edwidge Danticat, Thomas Glave, Nallo Hopkinson, John Edgar Wideman, Jamaica Kincaid, Percival Everett, and Patricia Powell. Also publishes poetry. Length: up to 10,000 words excluding title page, abstract, bio, and references.

HOW TO CONTACT Submit ms via online submissions manager: callaloo.expressacademic.org/login.php. All fiction submissions are now limited to 1 manuscript per submission with a maximum of 3 submissions by a single author per calendar year.

TIPS "We look for freshness of both writing and plot, strength of characterization, plausibility of plot. Read what's being written and published, especially in journals such as *Callaloo*."

CALYX

P.O. Box B, Corvallis OR 97339. (541)753-9384. **E-mail:** info@calyxpress.org; editor@calyxpress.org. **Website:** www.calyxpress.org. **Contact:** Brenna Crotty, senior editor. Estab. 1976. *"CALYX exists to publish fine literature and art by women and is dedicated to publishing the work of all women, including women of color, older women, working-class women and other voices that need to be heard. We are committed to discovering and nurturing developing writers."*

○ Annual open submission (poetry and prose) period is October 1 - December 31. Lois Cranston Memorial Poetry Prize ($300 cash prize) is open March 1 - June 30. Margarita Donnelly Prize for Prose Writing ($500 cash prize) is open July 1 - September 30.

NEEDS Length: no more than 5,000 words.

HOW TO CONTACT All submissions should include author's name on each page and be accompanied by a brief (50-word or less) biographical statement, phone number, and e-mail address. Submit using online submissions manager.

PAYMENT/TERMS Pays in contributor's copies and one-volume subscription.

TIPS "A forum for women's creative work—including work by women of color, lesbian and queer women, young women, old women—*CALYX* breaks new ground. Each issue is packed with new poetry, short stories, full-color artwork, photography, essays, and reviews."

○○ THE CAPILANO REVIEW

102-281 Industrial Ave., Vancouver BC V6A 2P2, Canada. **E-mail:** contact@thecapilanoreview.ca. **E-mail:** online through submittable. **Website:** www.thecapilanoreview.com. **Contact:** Matea Kulic, managing editor. Estab. 1972. Triannual visual and literary arts magazine that "publishes only what the editors consider to be the very best fiction, poetry, drama, or visual art being produced. *TCR* editors are interested in fresh, original work that stimulates and challenges readers. Over the years, the magazine has developed a reputation for pushing beyond the boundaries of traditional art and writing. We are interested in work that is new in concept and in execution. We no longer accept submissions by mail. Please review our submission guidelines on our website and submit online through submittable."

NEEDS No traditional, conventional fiction. Wants to see more innovative, genre-blurring work. Length: up to 5,000 words.

PAYMENT/TERMS Pays $50-150.

⑤ ORSON SCOTT CARD'S INTERGALACTIC MEDICINE SHOW

Hatrack River Publications, P.O. Box 18184, Greensboro NC 27419. **Website:** intergalacticmedicineshow.com; oscigms.com. **Contact:** Edmund R. Schubert, editor. Estab. 2005. "*Orson Scott Card's InterGalactic Medicine Show* is an online fantasy and science fiction magazine. We are a bimonthly publication featuring content from both established and talented new authors. In addition to our bimonthly issues, we offer weekly columns and reviews on books, movies, video games, and writing advice."

NEEDS "We like to see well-developed milieus and believable, engaging characters. We also look for clear, unaffected writing." Length: up to 17,000 words.

HOW TO CONTACT Submit via online submission form. Submit only 1 story at a time. Include estimated word count, e-mail address.

PAYMENT/TERMS Pays 6¢/word.

TIPS "Please note: *IGMS* is a PG-13 magazine and website. That means that while stories can deal with intense and adult themes, we will not accept stories with explicit or detailed sex of the sort that would earn a movie rating more restrictive than PG-13; nor will there be language of the sort that earns an R rating."

THE CARIBBEAN WRITER

University of the Virgin Islands, RR 1, P.O. Box 10,000, Kingshill, St. Croix USVI 00850. (340)692-4152. **E-mail:** info@thecaribbeanwriter.org. **Website:** www.thecaribbeanwriter.org. **Contact:** Alscess Lewis-Brown, editor in chief. Estab. 1986. *The Caribbean Writer* features new and exciting voices from the region and beyond that explore the diverse and multi-ethnic culture in poetry, short fiction, personal essays, creative nonfiction, and plays. Social, cultural, economic, and sometimes controversial issues are also explored, employing a wide array of literary devices.

☯ Poetry published in *The Caribbean Writer* has appeared in *The Pushcart Prize*. *The Caribbean Writer* is 300+ pages, digest-sized, handsomely printed on heavy stock, perfect-bound, with glossy card cover. Press run is 1,200.

NEEDS Submit complete ms through online submissions manager. Name, address, phone number, e-mail address, and title of ms should appear in cover letter along with brief bio. Title only on ms. All submissions are eligible for the Virgin Islands Daily News Prize ($500) for a fiction or nonfiction essay to an author residing in the U.S. or British Virgin Islands, the David Hough Literary Prize to a Caribbean author ($500), the Canute A. Brodhurst Prize for Fiction ($400), the Cecile Dejongh Literary Prize to an author whose work best expresses the spirit of the Caribbean ($500), and the Marvin Williams Literary Prize for first-time publication in the Caribbean ($500). Length: up to 3,500 words or 10 pages.

PAYMENT/TERMS Pays 1 contributor's copy.

THE CAROLINA QUARTERLY

CB #3520 Greenlaw Hall, University of North Carolina, Chapel Hill NC 27599-3520. (919)408-7786. **E-mail:** carolina.quarterly@gmail.com. **Website:** www.thecarolinaquarterly.com; thecarolinaquarterly.submittable.com/submit. **Contact:** Sarah George-Waterfield, editor-in-chief; Travis Alexander, nonfiction editor; Laura Broom, fiction editor; Calvin Olsen, poetry editor. Estab. 1948. *The Carolina Quarterly*, published 2 times/year, prints fiction, poetry, reviews, nonfiction, and visual art. No specifications regarding form, length, subject matter, or style. Considers translations of work originally written in languages other than English. *The Carolina Quarterly* is about 100 pages, digest-sized, professionally printed, perfect-bound, with glossy cover; includes ads. Press run is 1,000. Accepts submissions September through May.

NEEDS Length: up to 7,500 words.

HOW TO CONTACT Submit 1 complete ms via online submissions manager or postal mail (address submissions to Fiction Editor).

CAVEAT LECTOR

400 Hyde St., #606, San Francisco CA 94109. **E-mail:** caveatlectormagazine@gmail.com. **Website:** www.caveat-lector.org. **Contact:** Christopher Bernard, co-

editor. Estab. 1989. *Caveat Lector*, published 2 times/year, is devoted to the arts and cultural and philosophical commentary. As well as literary work, it publish art, photography, music, streaming audio of selected literary pieces, and short films. Poetry, fiction, artwork, music, and short films are posted on the website. "Don't let those examples limit your submissions. Send what you feel is your strongest work, in any style and on any subject." All submissions should be sent with a brief bio and SASE, or submitted electronically at caveatlectormagazine@gmail.com. (Poetry submissions are only accepted through postal mail.) Reads poetry submissions February 1-June 30; reads all other submissions year round.

NEEDS Accepts prose submissions (short stories, excerpts from longer works) throughout the year. Submit complete ms, preferably by e-mail. Interested in authors who have a distinct, engaging voice, regardless of subject or genre.

PAYMENT/TERMS Pays contributor's copies.

CC&D: CHILDREN, CHURCHES & DADDIES

The Unreligious, Non-Family-Oriented Literary and Art Magazine, Scars Publications and Design, 1316 Porterfield Dr., Austin TX 78753. **E-mail:** ccandd96@scars.tv. **Website:** scars.tv/ccd. **Contact:** Janet Kuypers. Estab. 1993. "Our biases are works that relate to issues such as politics, sexism, society, and the like, but are definitely not limited to such. We publish good work that makes you think, that makes you feel like you've lived through a scene instead of merely reading it. If it relates to how the world fits into a person's life (political story, a day in the life, coping with issues people face), it will probably win us over faster. We have received comments from readers and other editors saying that they thought some of our stories really happened. They didn't, but it was nice to know they were so concrete, so believable that people thought they were nonfiction. Do that to our readers." Publishes every other month online and in print; issues sold via Amazon.com throughout the U.S., U.K., and continental Europe. Publishes short shorts, essays, and stories. Also publishes poetry. Always comments on/critiques rejected mss if asked. Has published Patrick Fealey, Linda M. Crate, Kenneth DiMaggio, Linda Webb Aceto, Brian Looney, Joseph Hart, Fritz Hamilton, G.A. Scheinoha, and Ken Dean.

NEEDS Does not want religious, rhyming, or family-oriented material. Average length: 1,000 words.

"Contact us if you are interested in submitting very long stories or parts of a novel. (If you are accepted, it would appear in parts in multiple issues.)"

HOW TO CONTACT Send complete ms with cover letter, or query with clips of published work. Prefers submissions by e-mail. "If you have e-mail and send us a snail-mail submission, we will accept writing only if you e-mail it to us. 99.5% of all submissions are via e-mail only, so if you do not have electronic access, there is a strong chance you will not be considered. We recommend you e-mail submissions to us, either as an attachment (TXT, RTF, DOC, or DOCX, but not PDF) or by placing it directly in the e-mail letter). Send either SASE (or IRC) for return of ms or disposable copy of ms and #10 SASE for reply only." Reviews fiction, essays, journals, editorials, short fiction.

CEMETERY MOON

Fortress Publishing, Inc., 3704 Hartzdale Dr., Camp Hill PA 17011. **E-mail:** cemeterymoon@yahoo.com. **Website:** www.fortresspublishinginc.com. *Cemetery Moon* is a magazine filled with short stories and poetry devoted to horror, suspense, and Gothic. This magazine brings to light what lurks in the darkness.

NEEDS Length: up to 5,000 words.

HOW TO CONTACT Send complete ms with cover letter by e-mail only.

TIPS "We want compelling stories—if we stop reading your story, so will the reader. We don't care about trick or twist endings; we're more concerned about how you take us there. Don't try to reinvent the wheel. Listen to advice with an open mind. Read your story, reread it, then read it again before you send it anywhere."

CHA

Hong Kong **E-mail:** editors@asiancha.com; j@asiancha.com; submissions@asiancha.com. **Website:** www.asiancha.com. **Contact:** Tammy Ho Lai-Ming, founding co-editor; Jeff Zroback, founding co-editor; Eddie Tay, reviews editor. Estab. 2007. *Cha* is the first Hong Kong-based English online literary journal; it is dedicated to publishing quality poetry, fiction, creative non-fiction, reviews, photography & art. *Cha* has a strong focus on Asian-themed creative work and work done by Asian writers and artists. It also publishes established and emerging writers/artists from around the world. *Cha* is an affiliated organisation of the Asia-Pacific Writing Partnership and it is catalogued in the School of Oriental and African Studies (SOAS)

Library, among other universities. *Cha* was named Best New Online Magazine of 2008. "At this time, we can only accept work in English or translated into English. If you want to review a book for *Cha*, please also write for further information."

NEEDS Length: 100-5,000 words.

HOW TO CONTACT Submit via e-mail.

TIPS "Please read the guidelines on our website carefully before you submit work to us. Do not send attachments in your e-mail. Include all writing in the body of e-mail. Include a brief biography (100 words)."

THE CHAFFIN JOURNAL

E-mail: nancy.jensen@eku.edu. **Website:** www.english.eku.edu/chaffin_journal. **Contact:** Nancy Jensen, editor. Estab. 1998; revised and re-established in 2017. *The Chaffin Journal* is a print journal for literary fiction, poetry, and creative nonfiction, published annually through the English Department at Eastern Kentucky University. "We seek diverse and original poetry, fiction, and creative nonfiction rooted in literary tradition. We value strong voices, freshness of vision, precision in language, and a sense of urgency in the literary fiction, poetry, and creative nonfiction we publish." Online submission period: April 1-July 15. Use the Submittable link on website. No postal mail or e-mailed submissions will be considered.

NEEDS Wants literary fiction, primarily short stories. Novel excerpts that can stand alone may be considered. No children's fiction, young adult fiction, formula fiction, fanfiction, or erotica. Length: up to 6,000 words

HOW TO CONTACT Submit 1 work of fiction up to 6,000 words per reading period.

PAYMENT/TERMS Pays 1 contributor's copy.

THE CHARITON REVIEW

Truman State University Press, 100 E. Normal Ave., Kirksville MO 63501. (660)785-7336. **Fax:** (660)785-4480. **E-mail:** chariton@truman.edu. **Website:** tsup.truman.edu/product/chariton-review/. Estab. 1975. *The Chariton Review* is an international literary journal publishing the best in short fiction, essays, poetry, and translations in 2 issues each year.

NEEDS No flash fiction. Length: up to 7,000 words.

HOW TO CONTACT Submit 1 complete ms through online submissions manager. English only.

CHAUTAUQUA

Chautauqua Institution and University of North Carolina at Wilmington, Department of Creative Writing, 601 S. College Rd., Wilmington NC 28403. **E-mail:** chautauquajournal@gmail.com. **Website:** ciweb.org. **Contact:** Jill Gerard and Philip Gerard, editors. Estab. 2003. *Chautauqua*, published annually in June, prints poetry, short fiction, and creative nonfiction. The editors actively solicit writing that expresses the values of Chautauqua Institution broadly construed: a sense of inquiry into questions of personal, social, political, spiritual, and aesthetic importance, regardless of genre. Considers the work of any writer, whether or not affiliated with Chautauqua Institution. Looking for a mastery of craft, attention to vivid and accurate language, a true lyric "ear," an original and compelling vision, and strong narrative instinct. Above all, it values work that is intensely personal, yet somehow implicitly comments on larger public concerns, like work that answers every reader's most urgent question: Why are you telling me this? Reads submissions February 15-April 15 and August 15-November 15. Work published in *Chautauqua* has been included in *The Pushcart Prize* anthology; notable work in Best American Series; notable issues Best American Series.

NEEDS "*Chautauqua* short stories, self-contained novel excerpts, or flash fiction demonstrate a sound storytelling instinct, using suspense in the best sense, creating a compulsion in the reader to continue reading. Wants to engage readers' deep interest in the characters and their actions, unsettled issues of action or theme, or in some cases simple delight at the language itself. A superior story will exhibit the writer's attention to language—both in style and content—and should reveal a masterful control of diction and syntax." Length: up to 25 double-spaced pages or 7,000 words.

HOW TO CONTACT Submit through online submissions manager.

PAYMENT/TERMS Pays 2 contributor's copies.

TIPS "*Chautauqua* has added a new section, which celebrates young writers, ages 12-18. Work should be submitted by a teacher, mentor, or parent. Please confirm on the entry that the piece can be classified as a Young Voices entry. We ask that young writers consider the theme. Essays and stories should remain under 1,500 words. For poetry, please submit no more than 3 poems and/or no more than 6 pages."

CHICAGO QUARTERLY REVIEW

517 Sherman Ave., Evanston IL 60202. **E-mail:** cqr@ icogitate.com. **Website:** www.chicagoquarterlyreview. com. **Contact:** S. Afzal Haider and Elizabeth McKenzie, senior editors. Estab. 1994. "The *Chicago Quarterly Review* is a nonprofit, independent literary journal publishing the finest short stories, poems, translations, and essays by both emerging and established writers. We hope to stimulate, entertain, and inspire."

The *Chicago Quarterly Review* is 6x9; 225 pages; illustrations; photos. Receives 250 unsolicited mss/month. Accepts 10-15 mss/issue; 20-30 mss/year. Agented fiction 5%. **Publishes 8-10 new writers/year.**

NEEDS Length: up to 5,000 words; average length: 2,500 words.

HOW TO CONTACT Submit through online submissions manager only.

PAYMENT/TERMS Pays 2 contributor's copies.

TIPS "The writer's voice ought to be clear and unique and should explain something of what it means to be human. We want well-written stories that reflect an appreciation for the rhythm and music of language, work that shows passion and commitment to the art of writing."

CHICAGO REVIEW

Taft House, 935 E. 60th St., Chicago IL 60637. **E-mail:** editors@chicagoreview.org. **Website:** chicagoreview. org. **Contact:** Gerónimo Sarmiento Cruz, managing editor. Estab. 1946. "Since 1946, *Chicago Review* has published a range of contemporary poetry, fiction, and criticism. Each year typically includes two single issues and a double issue with a special feature section."

NEEDS "We will consider work in any literary style but are typically less interested in traditional narrative approaches." Length: up to 5,000 words.

HOW TO CONTACT Submit 1 short story or up to 5 short short stories submitted in 1 file. Submit via online submissions manager. Prefers electronic submissions.

PAYMENT/TERMS Pays contributor's copies.

TIPS "We strongly recommend that authors familiarize themselves with recent issues of *Chicago Review* before submitting. Submissions that demonstrate familiarity with the journal tend to receive more attention than those that appear to be part of a carpet-bombing campaign."

CHIRON REVIEW

Chiron, Inc., 522 E. South Ave., St. John KS 67576-2212. **E-mail:** editor@chironreview.com. **Website:** www.chironreview.com. **Contact:** Michael Hathaway, publisher. Estab. 1982 as *The Kindred Spirit. Chiron Review*, published quarterly, presents the widest possible range of contemporary creative writing—fiction and nonfiction, traditional and off-beat—in an attractive, perfect-bound digest, including artwork and photographs. No taboos.

NEEDS Submit complete ms by mail with SASE, or by e-mail as DOC attachment. Length: up to 2,500 words.

PAYMENT/TERMS Pays 1 contributor's copy.

TIPS "Please check our website to see if we are open to submissions. When you do send submissions, please have mercy on the editors and follow the guidelines noted here and on our website."

CIMARRON REVIEW

205 Morrill Hall, English Department, Oklahoma State University, Stillwater OK 74078. **E-mail:** cimarronreview@okstate.edu. **Website:** cimarronreview.okstate.edu. **Contact:** Toni Graham, editor and fiction editor; Lisa Lewis, poetry editor; Sarah Beth Childers, nonfiction editor. Estab. 1967. "One of the oldest quarterlies in the nation, *Cimarron Review* publishes work by writers at all stages of their careers, including Pulitzer Prize winners, writers appearing in the Best American Series and the Pushcart anthologies, and winners of national book contests. Since 1967, *Cimarron* has showcased poetry, fiction, and nonfiction with a wide-ranging aesthetic. Our editors seek the bold and the ruminative, the sensitive and the shocking, but above all they seek imagination and truth-telling, the finest stories, poems, and essays from working writers across the country and around the world."

Cimarron Review is 6.5x8.5; 110 pages. Accepts 3-5 mss/issue; 12-15 mss/year. Publishes 2-4 new writers/year. Eager to receive mss from both established and less experienced writers "who intrigue us with their unusual perspective, language, imagery, and character." Has published work by Molly Giles, Gary Fincke, David Galef, Nona Caspers, Robin Beeman, Edward J. Delaney, William Stafford, John Ashbery, Grace Schulman, Barbara Hamby,

Patricia Fargnoli, Phillip Dacey, Holly Prado, and Kim Addonizio.

NEEDS "We are interested in any strong writing of a literary variety but are especially partial to fiction in the modern realist tradition and poetry that engages the reader through a distinctive voice—be it lyric, narrative, etc. When submitting fiction, please do not include a summary of your story in the cover letter. Allow the work to stand on its own." No juvenile or genre fiction. "We have no set page lengths for any genre, but we seldom publish short shorts or pieces longer than 25 pages. There are, however, exceptions to every rule. Our guiding aesthetic is the quality of the work itself."

HOW TO CONTACT Send complete ms with SASE, or submit online through submission manager; include cover letter.

PAYMENT/TERMS Pays 2 contributor's copies.

TIPS "All electronic and postal submissions should include a cover letter. Postal submissions must include a SASE. We do not accept submissions by e-mail. Please follow our guidelines as they appear on our website. In order to get a feel for the kind of work we publish, please read several issues before submitting."

⊛ THE CINCINNATI REVIEW

P.O. Box 210069, Cincinnati OH 45221-0069. (513)556-3954. **Fax:** (513)556-3959. **E-mail:** editors@cincinnatireview.com. **Website:** www.cincinnatireview.com. **Contact:** Michael Griffith, fiction editor; Don Bogen, poetry editor; Kristen Iversen, nonfiction editor. Estab. 2003. A journal devoted to publishing the best new literary fiction, creative nonfiction, and poetry, as well as book reviews, essays, and interviews.

◯ *The Cincinnati Review* is 180-200 pages, digest-sized, perfect-bound, with matte paperback cover with full-color art. Press run is 1,000. Reads submissions August 15-March 15.

NEEDS Does not want genre fiction. Length: up to 40 double-spaced pages.

HOW TO CONTACT Submit complete ms via online submissions manager only.

PAYMENT/TERMS Pays $25/page.

TIPS "Each issue includes a translation feature. For more information on translations, please see our website."

◑ THE CLAREMONT REVIEW

1581-H Hillside Ave., Suite 101, Victoria BC V8T 2C1, Canada. **E-mail:** claremontreview@gmail.com. **Website:** www.theclaremontreview.ca. **Contact:** Ali Blythe, Editor-in-chief. Estab. 1992. The editors of *The Claremont Review* publish the best poetry, short stories, visual art and photography by youth ages 13-19, from anywhere in the English-speaking world. "We publish work in many styles that range from traditional to modern. We prefer edgy pieces that take chances, show your commitment to craft, explore real characters, and reveal authentic emotion. Read the samples in our resources or in past issues for a clearer understanding of what we accept. We strongly encourage readers to subscribe to our magazine, to read, connect with and support youth writing from all over the world."

NEEDS Only accepts submissions from writers ages 13-19. Length: up to 2,000 words.

PAYMENT/TERMS Pays $10.

TIPS "We love: Wild minds like yours.don't be afraid to try something new with form or thinking. Images, metaphor, leaps, research, specificity, images, sensory details, images. Writing that reveals YOUR artistic spirit.are you formal? Tricky? Elusive? Allusive? Quiet? Bold? Clean writing: read your piece word by word, then line by line, and fix spelling or grammatical errors. Entries that meet all our guidelines, read them."

CLOUD RODEO

E-mail: jakesyersak@gmail.com. **E-mail:** submit@cloudrodeo.org. **Website:** cloudrodeo.org. **Contact:** Jake Syersak, editor. "*Cloud Rodeo* is an irregularly published journal of the irregular. So let's get weird."

HOW TO CONTACT Submit 1 prose piece via e-mail as a DOC or PDF attachment.

COAL CITY REVIEW

Coal City Press, English Department, University of Kansas, Lawrence KS 66045. **Website:** coalcitypress.wordpress.com. **Contact:** Brian Daldorph, editor. *Coal City Review*, published annually, usually late in the year, publishes poetry, short stories, reviews: "the best material I can find."

NEEDS Accepts mainly mainstream fiction: "Please don't send 'experimental' work our way." Length: up to 4,000 words.

PAYMENT/TERMS Pays contributor's copies.

COLD MOUNTAIN REVIEW

Department of English, Appalachian State University, ASU Box 32052, Boone NC 28608. **E-mail:** coldmountain@appstate.edu. **Website:** www.coldmountainreview.org. **Contact:** Kathryn Kirkpatrick, editor; Katherine Abrams, managing editor; Samantha Hunter, assistant editor. *Cold Mountain Review*, published twice/year (in spring and fall), features fiction, nonfiction, poetry, and b&w art. "Themed fall issues rotate with general spring issues, but all work is considered beneath our broad ecological–ecojustice umbrella." *Cold Mountain Review* is about 130 pages, digest-sized, perfect-bound, with light cardstock cover. Reading period is August-May.

NEEDS Considers novel excerpts if the submissions is "an exemplary stand-alone piece." Length: up to 6,000 words.

HOW TO CONTACT Submit 1 piece at a time through online submissions manager or by mail.

PAYMENT/TERMS Pays contributor's copies.

THE COLLAGIST

Dzanc Books, **E-mail:** editor@thecollagist.com; poetry@thecollagist.com; bookreviews@thecollagist.com. **Website:** thecollagist.com. **Contact:** Gabriel Blackwell, editor in chief; Marielle Prince, poetry editor; Michael Jauchen, book review editor. Estab. 2009. *The Collagist* is a monthly journal published on the 15th of each month, containing short fiction, poetry, essays, book reviews, and one of more excerpts from novels forthcoming from (mostly) independent presses.

HOW TO CONTACT Submit short stories through online submissions manager.

🟢 COLORADO REVIEW

Center for Literary Publishing, Colorado State University, 9105 Campus Delivery, Fort Collins CO 80523. (970)491-5449. **E-mail:** creview@colostate.edu. **Website:** coloradoreview.colostate.edu. **Contact:** Stephanie G'Schwind, editor-in-chief and nonfiction editor; Steven Schwartz, fiction editor; Don Revell, Sasha Steensen, and Matthew Cooperman, poetry editors; Harrison Candelaria Fletcher, nonfiction editor; Dan Beachy-Quick, poetry book review editor; Jennifer Wisner Kelly, fiction and nonfiction book review editor. Estab. 1956. Literary magazine published 3 times/year. Work published in *Colorado Review* has been included in *Best American Essays, Best American Short Stories, Best American Poetry, Best New American*

Voices, Best Travel Writing, Best Food Writing, and the *Pushcart Prize Anthology*.

NEEDS No genre fiction. Length: up to 10,000 words.

HOW TO CONTACT Send complete ms. Fiction mss are read August 1-April 30. Mss received May 1-July 31 will be returned unread. Send no more than 1 story at a time.

PAYMENT/TERMS Pays $200.

COLUMBIA

A Journal of Literature and Art, Columbia University, New York NY 10027. **E-mail:** info@columbiajournal.org. **Website:** columbiajournal.org. **Contact:** Staff rotates each year. Estab. 1977. "*Columbia: A Journal of Literature and Art* is an annual publication that features the very best in poetry, fiction, nonfiction, and art. We were founded in 1977 and continue to be one of the few national literary journals entirely edited, designed, and produced by students. You'll find that our minds are open, our interests diverse. We solicit mss from writers we love and select the most exciting finds from our virtual submission box. Above all, our commitment is to our readers—to producing a collection that informs, surprises, challenges, and inspires."

🔵 Reads submissions March 1-September 15.

NEEDS Accepts all forms of short fiction: short stories, flash fiction, prose poetry. Length: up to 5,000 words.

HOW TO CONTACT Submit complete ms via online submissions manager. Include short bio.

COMMON GROUND REVIEW

Western New England University, H-5132, Western New England University, 1215 Wilbraham Rd., Springfield MA 01119. **E-mail:** editors@cgreview.org. **Website:** cgreview.org. **Contact:** Janet Bowdan, editor. Estab. 1999. *Common Ground Review*, published twice yearly (Spring/Summer, Fall/Winter), prints poetry and 1 short nonfiction piece in the Fall issue and 1 short fiction piece in the Spring issue. Holds annual poetry contest.

NEEDS Length: up to 12 pages double-spaced.

HOW TO CONTACT Submit via online submissions manager or mail.

PAYMENT/TERMS Pays 1 contributor's copy.

TIPS "For poems, use a few good images to ground and convey ideas; take ideas further than the initial thought. Poems should be condensed and concise, free from words that do not contribute. The subject matter should be worthy of the reader's time and should appeal to a wide range of readers. Form should be an extension of content. Sometimes the editors may suggest possible revisions."

🟢 CONCEIT MAGAZINE

Perry Terrell Publishing, P.O. Box 884223, San Francisco CA 94188-4223. **E-mail:** conceitmagazine2007@yahoo.com. **Website:** https://sites.google.com/site/conceitmagazine/ and http://conceitmagazine.weebly.com. **Contact:** Perry Terrell, editor. Estab. 2006. We are a literary sharing organization. Magazine publishes poetry, short stories, articles, cartoons and essays. Very few guidelines—let me see your creative work. We will decide after reading.

NEEDS List of upcoming themes available for SASE and on website. Receives 60-70 mss/month. Accepts 20-30 mss/issue; up to 640+ mss/year. Ms published 3-10 months after acceptance. Publishes 250 new writers/year. Published D. Neil Simmers, Tamara Fey Turner, Eve J. Blohm, Barbara Hantman, David Body, Milton Kerr, Marlon Jackson, Michael Shane Love and Juanita Torrence-Thompson. Does not want profanity, porn, gruesomeness. Length: 100-4,000 words. Average length: 1,500-2,000 words. Publishes short shorts. Average length of short shorts: 50-500 words.

HOW TO CONTACT Will read and review your books. "Send review copies to Perry Terrell." Query first or send complete ms with cover letter. Accepts submissions by e-mail and snail mail. Include estimated word count, brief bio, list of publications.

PAYMENT/TERMS Pays 1 contributor's copy. Additional copies $4.50. Pay via PayPal to conceitmagazine@yahoo.com. Pays writers through contests. Monthly contests in 2018. Send SASE or check blog on websites for details."

TIPS "We are a 'literary sharing' organization. Uniqueness and creativity make a ms stand out. Be brave and confident. Let me see what you created. Also, patience is ultimately required."

CONCHO RIVER REVIEW

Angelo State University, ASU Station #10894, San Angelo TX 76909. **E-mail:** ageyer@usca.edu; haleya@acu.edu; jerry.bradley@lamar.edu; roger.jackson@angelo.edu. **Website:** conchoriverreview.org. **Contact:** R. Mark Jackson, general editor and book review editor; Andrew Geyer, fiction editor; Albert Haley, nonfiction editor; Jerry Bradley, poetry editor. Estab. 1987.

"*CRR* aims to provide its readers with escape, insight, laughter, and inspiration for many years to come. We urge authors to submit to the journal and readers to subscribe to our publication."

NEEDS "Editors tend to publish traditional stories with a strong sense of conflict, finely drawn characters, and crisp dialogue." Length: 1,500-5,000 words.

HOW TO CONTACT Submit only 1 ms at a time. Electronic submissions preferred. See website for appropriate section editor.

PAYMENT/TERMS Pays 1 contributor's copy.

🟢 CONFRONTATION

English Department, LIU Post, Brookville NY 11548. **E-mail:** confrontationmag@gmail.com. **Website:** www.confrontationmagazine.org. **Contact:** Jonna G. Semeiks, editor in chief; Belinda Kremer, poetry editor; Terry Kattleman, publicity director/production editor. Estab. 1968. "*Confrontation* has been in continuous publication since 1968. Our taste and our magazine is eclectic, but we always look for excellence in style, an important theme, a memorable voice. We enjoy discovering and fostering new talent. Each issue contains work by both well-established and new writers. We read August 16-April 15. Do not send mss or e-mail submissions between April 16 and August 15."

Confrontation has garnered a long list of awards and honors, including the Editor's Award for Distinguished Achievement from CLMP (given to Martin Tucker, the founding editor of the magazine) and NEA grants. Work from the magazine has appeared in numerous anthologies, including the *Pushcart Prize*, *Best Short Stories*, and *The O. Henry Prize Stories*. "We also publish the work of 1 visual artist per issue, selected by the editors."

NEEDS "We judge on quality of writing and thought or imagination, so we will accept genre fiction. However, it must have literary merit or must transcend or challenge genre." No "proselytizing" literature or conventional genre fiction. Length: up to 7,200 words.

HOW TO CONTACT Send complete ms.

PAYMENT/TERMS Pays $175-250; more for commissioned work.

TIPS "We look for literary merit. Keep honing your skills, and keep trying."

CONJUNCTIONS

Bard College, 21 E. 10th St., #3E, New York NY 10003. **E-mail:** conjunctions@bard.edu. **Website:** www.conjunctions.com. Estab. 1981. "We provide a forum for writers & artists whose work challenges acccepted forms and modes of expression, experiments with language and thought, and is fully realized art." Unsolicited mss cannot be returned unless accompanied by SASE. Electronic and simultaneous submissions will not be considered.

TIPS "Final selection of the material is made based on the literary excellence, originality, and vision of the writing. We have maintained a consistently high editorial and production quality with the intention of attracting a large and varied audience."

CONNOTATION PRESS

Website: www.connotationpress.com. **Contact:** Ken Robidoux, publisher. *Connotation Press* accepts submissions in poetry, fiction, creative nonfiction, playwriting, screenplay, interview, book review, music review, etc. "Basically, we're looking at virtually every genre or crossover genre you can create."

NEEDS Submit 1 story of any length, a chapter or excerpt from a novel, or 1-5 flash fiction pieces through online submission manager. Include headshot and short bio.

⑤ CONTRARY

The Journal of Unpopular Discontent, Chicago IL **E-mail:** chicago@contrarymagazine.com. **Website:** www.contrarymagazine.com. **Contact:** Jeff McMahon, editor; Frances Badgett, fiction editor; Shaindel Beers, poetry editor. Estab. 2003. *Contrary* publishes fiction, poetry, and literary commentary, and prefers work that combines the virtues of all those categories. Founded at the University of Chicago, it now operates independently and not-for-profit on the South Side of Chicago. Quarterly. Member CLMP. "We like work that is not only contrary in content but contrary in its evasion of the expectations established by its genre. Our fiction defies traditional story form. For example, a story may bring us to closure without ever delivering an ending. We don't insist on the ending, but we do insist on the closure. And we value fiction as poetic as any poem."

NEEDS Receives 650 mss/month. Accepts 6 mss/issue; 24 mss/year. Publishes 14 new writers/year. Has published Sherman Alexie, Andrew Coburn, Amy Reed, Clare Kirwan, Stephanie Johnson, Laurence

Davies, and Edward McWhinney. Length: up to 2,000 words. Average length: 750 words. Publishes short shorts. Average length of short shorts: 750 words.

HOW TO CONTACT Accepts submissions through website only. Include estimated word count, brief bio, list of publications.

PAYMENT/TERMS Pays $20-60.

TIPS "Beautiful writing catches our eye first. If we realize we're in the presence of unanticipated meaning, that's what clinches the deal. Also, we're not fond of expository fiction. We prefer to be seduced by beauty, profundity, and mystery than to be presented with the obvious. We look for fiction that entrances, that stays the reader's finger above the mouse button. That is, in part, why we favor microfiction, flash fiction, and short shorts. Also, we hope writers will remember that most editors are looking for very particular species of work. We try to describe our particular species in our mission statement and our submission guidelines, but those descriptions don't always convey nuance. That's why many editors urge writers to read the publication itself, in the hope that they will intuit an understanding of its particularities. If you happen to write that particular species of work we favor, your submission may find a happy home with us. If you don't, it does not necessarily reflect on your quality or your ability. It usually just means that your work has a happier home somewhere else."

CONVERGENCE

An Online Journal of Poetry and Art, **E-mail:** clinville@csus.edu. **Website:** www.convergence-journal.com. **Contact:** Cynthia Linville, managing editor/designer. Estab. 2003. "We look for well-crafted work with fresh images and a strong voice. Work from a series or with a common theme has a greater chance of being accepted. Seasonally themed work is appreciated (spring and summer for the January deadline, fall and winter for the June deadline). Please include a 75-word bio with your work (bios may be edited for length and clarity). A cover letter is not needed. Absolutely no simultaneous or previously published submissions."

◓ Deadlines are January 5 and June 5.

HOW TO CONTACT Submit up to 5 fiction pieces, no longer than 1,000 words each. Accepts e-mail submissions only; put "Convergence" in subject line.

PAYMENT/TERMS Acquires first rights.

THE COPPERFIELD REVIEW

A Journal for Readers and Writers of Historical Fiction, **E-mail:** copperreview@aol.com. **E-mail:** copperreview@aol.com. **Website:** www.copperfieldreview.com. **Contact:** Meredith Allard, executive editor. Estab. 2000. "We are a quarterly online literary journal that publishes historical fiction, reviews, and interviews related to historical fiction. We believe that by understanding the lessons of the past through historical fiction, we can gain better insight into the nature of our society today, as well as a better understanding of ourselves."

○ "Remember that we are a journal for readers and writers of historical fiction. We only consider submissions that are historical in nature."

NEEDS "We will consider submissions in most fiction categories, but the setting must be historical in nature. We don't want to see anything not related to historical fiction." Receives 40 unsolicited mss/month. Publishes 30-40% new writers/year. Publishes short shorts. Length: 500-3,000 words.

HOW TO CONTACT Send complete ms. Name and e-mail address should appear on the first page of the submission. Accepts submissions pasted into an e-mail only. "Do not query first. Send the complete ms according to our guidelines."

TIPS "We wish to showcase the very best in historical fiction. Stories that use historical periods to illuminate universal truths will immediately stand out. We are thrilled to receive thoughtful work that is polished, poised, and written from the heart. Be professional, and only submit your very best work. Be certain to adhere to a publication's submission guidelines, and always treat your e-mail submissions with the same care you would use with a traditional publisher."

COPPER NICKEL

English Department, Campus Box 175, CU Denver, P.O. Box 173364, Denver CO 80217. **E-mail:** wayne.miller@ucdenver.edu. **Website:** copper-nickel.org. **Contact:** Wayne Miller, editor/managing editor; Brian Barker and Nicky Beer, poetry editors; Joanna Luloff, fiction and nonfiction editor; Teague Bohlen, fiction editor. Estab. 2002. *Copper Nickel*—the national literary journal housed at the University of Colorado Denver—was founded by poet Jake Adam York in 2002. Work published in *Copper Nickel* has appeared in *Best American Poetry*, *Best American Short Stories*, and *Pushcart Prize* anthologies. Contributors to *Copper Nickel* have received numerous honors for their work, including the National Book Critics Circle Award; the Kingsley Tufts Poetry Award; the American, California, Colorado, Minnesota, and Washington State Book Awards; the Georg Büchner Prize; the T.S. Eliot and Forward Poetry Prizes; the Anisfield-Wolf Book Award; the Whiting Writers Award; the Alice Fay Di Castagnola Award; the Lambda Literary Award; and fellowships from the National Endowment for the Arts; the Guggenheim, Ingram Merrill, Witter Bynner, Soros, Rona Jaffe, Bush, and Jerome Foundations; the Bunting Institute; Cave Canem; and the American Academy in Rome. Submission period: August 15-April 15.

HOW TO CONTACT Submit 1 story or 3 pieces of flash fiction at a time through online submissions manager.

PAYMENT/TERMS Pays $30/printed page, 2 contributor's copies, and a one-year subscription.

CRAB CREEK REVIEW

7315 34th Ave. NW, Seattle WA 98117. **E-mail:** crabcreekreview@gmail.com. **Website:** www.crabcreekreview.org. **Contact:** Jenifer Lawrence, editor-in-chief; Laura Read, poetry editor. Estab. 1983. *Crab Creek Review* is a 100-page, perfect-bound paperback. "We are a literary journal based in the Pacific Northwest that is looking for poems, stories, and essays that pay attention to craft. We appreciate risk-taking, wild originality, and consummate craftsmanship. We publish established and emerging writers." Nominates for the Pushcart Prize. Annual *Crab Creek Review* poetry prize: $500.

NEEDS Accepts only the strongest fiction. 2,500 word maximum; prefers shorter work and flash fiction (750 word max). Has published fiction by Shann Ray, Sharma Shields, Daniel Homan, Leyna Krow. Length: 2,500 words.

HOW TO CONTACT Send complete ms.

PAYMENT/TERMS Pays 1 contributor's copy.

⑤ CRAB ORCHARD REVIEW

Southern Illinois University Carbondale, Department of English, Faner Hall 2380, Mail Code 4503, 1000 Faner Dr., Carbondale IL 62901. (618)453-6833. **Fax:** (618)453-8224. **E-mail:** jtribble@siu.edu. **Website:** www.craborchardreview.siu.edu. **Contact:** Allison Joseph, editor in chief and poetry editor; Carolyn Alessio, prose editor; Jon Tribble, managing editor. Estab. 1995. "We are a general-interest literary journal published twice/year. We strive to be a journal that writers admire and readers enjoy. We publish fiction, poetry, creative nonfiction, fiction translations, interviews, and reviews."

NEEDS No science fiction, romance, western, horror, gothic, or children's. Wants more novel excerpts that also stand alone. Length: up to 25 pages double-spaced.

HOW TO CONTACT Submit through online submissions manager.

PAYMENT/TERMS Pays $25/published magazine page ($100 minimum), 2 contributor's copies, and one-year subscription.

CRAZYHORSE

College of Charleston, Department of English, 66 George St., Charleston SC 29424. (843)953-4470. **E-mail:** crazyhorse@cofc.edu. **Website:** crazyhorse. cofc.edu. **Contact:** Jonathan Bohr Heinen, managing editor; Emily Rosko, poetry editor; Anthony Varallo, fiction editor; Bret Lott, nonfiction editor. Estab. 1960. "We like to print a mix of writing regardless of its form, genre, school, or politics. We're especially on the lookout for original writing that doesn't fit the categories and that engages in the work of honest communication."

○ Reads submissions September 1-May 31.

NEEDS "We are open to all narrative styles and forms, and are always on the lookout for something we haven't seen before. Send a story we won't be able to forget." Submit 1 story through online submissions manager. Length: 2,500-8,500 words.

PAYMENT/TERMS Pays $20/page ($200 maximum) and 2 contributor's copies.

TIPS "Write to explore subjects you care about. The subject should be one in which something is at stake. Before sending, ask, 'What's reckoned with that's important for other people to read?'"

CREAM CITY REVIEW

University of Wisconsin-Milwaukee, Department of English, P.O. Box 413, Milwaukee WI 53201. **E-mail:** info@creamcityreview.org. **Website:** uwm. edu/creamcityreview. **Contact:** Loretta McCormick, editor in chief; Mollie Boutell, managing editor. Estab. 1975. *Cream City Review* publishes "memorable and energetic fiction, poetry, and creative nonfiction. Features reviews of contemporary literature and criticism as well as author interviews and artwork. We are

interested in camera-ready art depicting themes appropriate to each issue."

○ Reading periods: August 1-November 1 for fall/ winter issue; January 1-April 1 for spring/summer issue.

NEEDS "We would like to see more quality fiction. No horror, formulaic, racist, sexist, pornographic, homophobic, science fiction, romance." Length: up to 20 pages.

HOW TO CONTACT Submit ms via online submissions manager.

PAYMENT/TERMS Pays one-year subscription beginning with the issue in which the author's work appears.

CREATIVE WITH WORDS PUBLICATIONS

P.O. Box 223226, Carmel CA 93922. **E-mail:** geltrich@ mbay.net. **Website:** creativewithwords.tripod.com. **Contact:** Brigitta Gisella Geltrich-Ludgate, publisher and editor. Estab. 1975. *Creative with Words* publishes "poetry, prose, illustrations, photos by all ages."

NEEDS No violence or erotica, overly religious fiction, or sensationalism. Length: up to 800 words.

HOW TO CONTACT Submit complete ms by mail or e-mail. Always include SASE and legitimate address with postal submissions. Cover letter preferred.

TIPS "We offer a great variety of themes. We look for clean family-type fiction and poetry. Also, we ask the writer to look at the world from a different perspective, research the topic thoroughly, be creative, apply brevity, tell the story from a character's viewpoint, tighten dialogue, be less descriptive, proofread before submitting, and be patient. We will not publish every ms we receive. It has to be in standard English, well written, and proofread. We do not appreciate receiving mss where we have to do the proofreading and correct the grammar."

CRUCIBLE

Barton College, P.O. Box 5000, Wilson NC 27893. **E-mail:** crucible@barton.edu. **Website:** www.barton. edu/crucible. Estab. 1964. *Crucible*, published annually in the fall, publishes poetry and fiction as part of its Poetry and Fiction Contest run each year. Deadline for submissions is May 1.

○ *Crucible* is under 100 pages, digest-sized, professionally printed on high-quality paper, with matte card cover. Press run is 500.

NEEDS Length: up to 8,000 words.

HOW TO CONTACT Submit ms by e-mail. Do not include name on ms. Include separate bio.

PAYMENT/TERMS Pays $150 for first prize, $100 for second prize, contributor's copies.

CUMBERLAND RIVER REVIEW

Trevecca Nazarene University, Department of English, 333 Murfreesboro Rd., Nashville TN 37210. **E-mail:** crr@trevecca.edu. **Website:** crr.trevecca.edu. **Contact:** Graham Hillard, editor; Amanda Johnson, managing editor. *The Cumberland River Review* is a quarterly online publication of new poetry, fiction, essays, and art. The journal is produced by the department of English at Trevecca Nazarene University and welcomes submissions from both national and international writers and artists. Reading period: September through April.

NEEDS Length: up to 5,000 words.

HOW TO CONTACT Submit 1 story through online submissions manager or mail (include SASE).

CURA

A Literary Magazine of Art and Action, 441 E. Fordham Rd., English Department, Dealy 541W, Bronx NY 10548. **E-mail:** curamag@fordham.edu. **Website:** www.curamag.com. **Contact:** Sarah Gambito, editor. Estab. 2011. *CURA: A Literary Magazine of Art and Action* is a multimedia initiative based at Fordham University committed to integrating the arts and social justice. Featuring creative writing, visual art, new media, and video in response to current news, we seek to enable an artistic process that is rigorously engaged with the world at the present moment. *CURA* is taken from the Ignatian educational principle of "cura personalis," care for the whole person. On its own, the word *cura* is defined as guardianship, solicitude, and significantly, written work.

Reading period: October 15-March 15.

NEEDS Length: up to 6,000 words.

HOW TO CONTACT Submit complete ms through online submissions manager.

PAYMENT/TERMS Pays 1 contributor's copy.

CURRENT ACCOUNTS

Current Accounts, Apt. 2D, Bradshaw Hall, Hardcastle Gardens, Bolton BL2 4NZ, UK. **E-mail:** fjameshartnell@aol.com. **Website:** www.bankstreetwriters.uk. **Contact:** James Hartnell, editor. Estab. 1994. *Current Accounts*, an online publication, prints poetry, drama, fiction, and nonfiction by members of Bank Street Writers, and other contributors. E-mail submissions please. Receives about 200 poems and stories/plays per year; accepts about 5%.

NEEDS Length: up to 1,500 words, and preferably under 1,000 words for short stories. Plays should be 1 act and no longer than 4 minutes read aloud.

HOW TO CONTACT E-mail submissions only. "Stories need to be well-constructed with good believable characters, an awareness of 'show, don't tell' dialogue that is real, a plot that moves along, and an ending that is neither obvious nor ridiculously far-fetched. Too many stories are overwritten and leave nothing unexplained for the reader to work out and enjoy. All genres (within the word length) are acceptable. We don't get enough plays."

PAYMENT/TERMS Pays 1 contributor's copy.

TIPS Bank Street Writers meets once/month and offers workshops, guest speakers, and other activities. E-mail for details. "We like originality of ideas, images, and use of language. No inspirational or religious verse unless it's also good in poetic terms."

CUTTHROAT

A Journal of the Arts, P.O. Box 2414, Durango CO 81302. (970)903-7914. **E-mail:** cutthroatmag@gmail.com. **Website:** www.cutthroatmag.com. **Contact:** Pamela Uschuk, editor in chief; Beth Alvarado, fiction editor; William Luvaas, online fiction editor; William Pitt Root, poetry editor. Estab. 2005. Sponsors the Rick DeMarinis Short Fiction Prize ($1,250 first prize). See separate listing and website for more information. "We publish only high-quality fiction, creative nonfiction, and poetry. We are looking for the cutting edge, the endangered word, fiction with wit, heart, soul, and meaning." *CUTTHROAT* is a literary magazine/journal and "one separate online edition of poetry, translations, short fiction, essays, and book reviews yearly." Member CLMP.

NEEDS Send review copies to Pamela Uschuk. List of upcoming themes available on website. Receives 100+ mss/month. Accepts 6 mss/issue; 10-12 mss/year. Does not read October 1-March 1 and June 1-July 15. **Publishes 5-8 new writers/year.** Published Michael Schiavone, Rusty Harris, Timothy Rien, Summer Wood, Peter Christopher, Jamey Genna, Doug Frelke, Sally Bellerose, and Marc Levy. Publishes short shorts and book reviews. Does not want romance, horror, historical, fantasy, religious, teen, or juvenile. Length: 500-5,000 words.

HOW TO CONTACT Submit complete ms through online submissions manager (preferred) or mail (include SASE).

PAYMENT/TERMS Pays contributor copies. Additional copies: $10.

TIPS "Read our magazine, and see what types of work we've published. The piece must have heart and soul, excellence in craft. "

☼ THE DALHOUSIE REVIEW

Dalhousie University, Halifax NS B3H 4R2, Canada. **E-mail:** dalhousie.review@dal.ca. **Website:** dalhousiereview.dal.ca. **Contact:** Lynne Evans, production manager. Estab. 1921. *Dalhousie Review*, published 3 times/year, is a journal of criticism publishing poetry and fiction. Considers works from both new and established writers.

☼   *Dalhousie Review* is 144 pages, digest-sized. Press run is 500.

NEEDS Length: up to 8,000 words.

HOW TO CONTACT Submit by e-mail. Writers are encouraged "to follow whatever canons of usage might govern the particular work in question and to be inventive with language, ideas, and form."

PAYMENT/TERMS Pays 2 contributor's copies.

DARGONZINE

E-mail: dargon@dargonzine.org. **Website:** dargonzine.org. **Contact:** Jon Evans, editor. "*DargonZine* is an e-zine that prints original fantasy fiction by aspiring fantasy writers. The Dargon Project is a shared world anthology whose goal is to provide a way for aspiring fantasy writers to meet and improve their writing skills through mutual contact and collaboration as well as through contact with a live readership via the Internet. Our goal is to write fantasy fiction that is mature, emotionally compelling, and professional. Membership in the Dargon Project is a requirement for publication."

☼   Publishes 1-3 new writers/year.

NEEDS Must be a member of the Dargon Project to submit fiction for publication. See website for details and guidelines.

PAYMENT/TERMS "As a strictly noncommercial magazine, our writers' only compensation is their growth and membership in a lively writing community."

TIPS "The Readers and Writers FAQs on our website provide much more detailed information about our mission, writing philosophy, and the value of writing for *DargonZine*."

☉ THE DARK

Prime Books, P.O. Box 1152, Germantown MD 20875. **E-mail:** thedarkmagazine@gmail.com. **Website:** www.thedarkmagazine.com. **Contact:** Silvia Moreno-Garcia and Sean Wallace, editors. Estab. 2013. Stories featured in *The Dark* have appeared in *The Best Horror of the Year*, *The Year's Best Dark Fantasy & Horror: 2016*, and *The Year's Best Weird Fiction*.

NEEDS "Don't be afraid to experiment or to deviate from the ordinary; be different—try us with fiction that may fall out of 'regular' categories. However, it is also important to understand that despite the name, *The Dark* is not a market for graphic, violent horror." Length: 2,000-6,000 words.

HOW TO CONTACT Send complete ms by e-mail attached in Microsoft Word DOC only. No multiple submissions.

PAYMENT/TERMS Pays 3¢/word.

TIPS "All fiction must have a dark, surreal, fantastical bend to it. It should be out of the ordinary and/or experimental. Can also be contemporary."

THE DEAD MULE SCHOOL OF SOUTHERN LITERATURE

The Dead Mule Literary Journal, NC 27889. **E-mail:** deadmule@gmail.com. **Website:** www.deadmule.com. **Contact:** Valerie MacEwan, publisher and editor. Estab. 1996. The *Mule* sponsors flash fiction contests with no entry fees. See the site for specifics. Chapbooks published by invitation, also short fiction compilations. "No good southern fiction is complete without a dead mule." *The Dead Mule* is one of the oldest, if not *the* oldest, continuously published online literary journals alive today. Publisher and editor Valerie MacEwan welcomes submissions. *The Dead Mule School of Southern Literature* wants flash fiction, visual poetry, essays, and creative nonfiction. Twenty-one Years Online, 1996-2017. Celebrate With a Dead Mule. 2017 means 21 years online—that's a century in cyber-time. "*The Dead Mule School of Southern Literature* Institutional Alumni Association recruits year round. We love reading what you wrote."

NEEDS "We welcome the ingenue and the established writer. It's mostly about you entertaining us and capturing our interest. Everyone is South of Somewhere; go ahead, check us out." No soft porn, no erotica, no ethnic slurs and all that the term implies. The Dead Mule is read in high schools, writers are encouraged to consider the audience when they submit. 2,500 word limit, but we're flexible. We love short fiction, 750 words or less.

HOW TO CONTACT All submissions must be accompanied by a "southern legitimacy statement," details of which can be seen within each page on *The Dead Mule* and within the submishmash entrypage.

PAYMENT/TERMS Pays sporadically "whenever CafePress/*Dead Mule* sales reach an agreeable amount."

TIPS "Read the site to get a feel for what we're looking to publish. Read the guidelines. We look forward to hearing from you. We are nothing if not for our writers. *The Dead Mule* strives to deliver quality writing in every issue. It is in this way that we pay tribute to our authors. Send us something original."

⑤ DECEMBER

A Literary Legacy Since 1958, December Publishing, P.O. Box 16130, St. Louis MO 63105-0830. (314)301-9980. **E-mail:** editor@decembermag.org. **Website:** decembermag.org. **Contact:** Gianna Jacobson, editor; Jennifer Goldring, managing editor. Estab. 1958. Committed to distributing the work of emerging writers and artists, and celebrating more seasoned voices through a semiannual nonprofit literary magazine featuring fiction, poetry, creative nonfiction, and visual art.

NEEDS Does not want genre fiction. Length: up to 10,000 words.

HOW TO CONTACT Send complete ms.

PAYMENT/TERMS Pays $10/page (minimum $40; maximum $200).

⑤ DELAWARE BEACH LIFE

Endeavours LLC, P.O. Box 417, Rehoboth Beach DE 19971. (302)227-9499. **E-mail:** info@delaware-beachlife.com. **Website:** www.delawarebeachlife.com. **Contact:** Terry Plowman, publisher/editor. Estab. 2002. "*Delaware Beach Life* focuses on coastal Delaware: Fenwick to Lewes. You can go slightly inland as long as there's water and a natural connection to the coast, e.g., Angola or Long Neck."

○ "*Delaware Beach Life* is the only full-color glossy magazine focused on coastal Delaware's culture and lifestyle. Created by a team of the best freelance writers, the magazine takes a deeper look at the wealth of topics that inter-

est coastal residents. *Delaware Beach Life* features such top-notch writing and photography that it inspires 95% of its readers to save it as a 'coffee-table' magazine."

NEEDS Does not want anything not coastal. Length: 1,000-2,000 words.

HOW TO CONTACT Query with published clips.

DENVER QUARTERLY

University of Denver, 2000 E. Asbury, Denver CO 80208. (303) 871-2892. **E-mail:** denverquarterly@gmail.com. **Website:** www.du.edu/denverquarterly. **Contact:** Laird Hunt, editor. Estab. 1965. Publishes fiction, articles, and poetry for a generally well-educated audience primarily interested in literature and the literary experience. Audience reads *DQ* to find something a little different from a strictly academic quarterly or a creative writing outlet.

○ *Denver Quarterly* received an Honorable Mention for Content from the American Literary Magazine Awards, and selections have been anthologized in the *Pushcart Prize* anthologies. Reads September 15-May 15. Mss submitted between May 15 and September 15 will regretfully be returned unread.

NEEDS "We are interested in experimental fiction (minimalism, magic realism, etc.) as well as realistic fiction and writing about fiction. No sentimental, science fiction, romance, or spy thrillers." Length: up to 15 pages.

HOW TO CONTACT Submit by mail or online submissions manager.

PAYMENT/TERMS Pays 2 contributor's copies.

DESCANT

Fort Worth's Journal of Poetry and Fiction, TCU Department of English, Box 297270, Ft. Worth TX 76129. **E-mail:** descant@tcu.edu. **Website:** www.descant.tcu.edu. **Contact:** Matthew Pitt, editor in chief and fiction editor; Alex Lemon, poetry editor. Estab. 1956. "*descant* seeks high-quality poems and stories in both traditional and innovative form."

○ Member CLMP. Magazine: 6x9; 120-150 pages; acid-free paper; paper cover. Reading period: September 1-April 1. Offers 4 annual cash awards for work already accepted for publication in the journal: The $500 Frank O'Connor Award for the best story in an issue, the $250 Gary Wilson Award for an outstanding story in an issue, the $500 Betsy Colquitt Award for the best poem in an issue, and the $250 Basker-ville Publishers Award for outstanding poem in an issue. Several stories first published by *descant* have appeared in *Best American Short Stories.*

NEEDS Receives 20-30 unsolicited mss/month. Accepts 3-5 mss/year. Publishes ms 1 year after acceptance. Publishes 50% new writers/year. Recently published work by William Harrison, Annette Sanford, Miller Williams, Patricia Chao, Vonesca Stroud, and Walt McDonald. No horror, romance, fantasy, erotica. Length: up to 5,000 words.

HOW TO CONTACT Send complete ms through online submissions manager or mail.

PAYMENT/TERMS Pays 2 contributor's copies; additional copies $6.

TIPS "We look for character and quality of prose. Send your best short work."

DEVIL'S LAKE

600 N. Park St., Suite 6195, Madison WI 53706. **E-mail:** devilslake.editor@gmail.com. **Website:** english. wisc.edu/devilslake.

NEEDS Length: up to 4,500 words.

HOW TO CONTACT Submit complete ms through online submissions manager.

DIAGRAM

Department of English, University of Arizona, P.O. Box 210067, Tucson AZ 85721-0067. **E-mail:** editor@ thediagram.com. **Website:** www.thediagram.com. **Contact:** Ander Monson, editor; T. Fleischmann and Nicole Walker, nonfiction editors; Sarah Blackman and Thomas Mira y Lopez, fiction editors; Heidi Gotz, Rafael Gonzalez, and Katie Jean Shinkle, poetry editors. Estab. 2000. "*DIAGRAM* is an electronic journal of text and art, found and created. We're interested in representations, naming, indicating, schematics, labeling and taxonomy of things; in poems that masquerade as stories; in stories that disguise themselves as indices or obituaries. We specialize in work that pushes the boundaries of traditional genre or work that is in some way schematic. We do publish traditional fiction and poetry, too, but hybrid forms (short stories, prose poems, indexes, tables of contents, etc.) are particularly welcome! We also publish diagrams and schematics (original and found)." Publishes 6 new writers/year. Bimonthly. Member CLMP. "We cosponsor a yearly chapbook contest for prose, po-etry, or hybrid work with New Michigan Press with a Spring deadline. Guidelines on website."

NEEDS Receives 200 unsolicited mss/month. Accepts 3-4 mss/issue; 20 mss/year. "We don't publish genre fiction unless it's exceptional and transcends the genre boundaries." Length: open.

HOW TO CONTACT Send complete ms. Accepts submissions by online submissions manager; no e-mail. If sending by snail mail, send SASE for return of the ms or send disposable copy of the ms and #10 SASE for reply only.

TIPS "Submit interesting text, images, sound, and new media. We value the insides of things, vivisec-tion, urgency, risk, elegance, flamboyance, work that moves us, language that does something new, or does something old—well. We like iteration and reitera-tion. Ruins and ghosts. Mechanical, moving parts, balloons, and frenzy. We want art and writing that demonstrates interaction; the processes of things; how functions are accomplished; how things become or expire, move or stand. We'll consider anything."

THE DOS PASSOS REVIEW

Briery Creek Press, Longwood University, Depart-ment of English and Modern Languages, 201 High St., Farmville VA 23909. **E-mail:** brierycreek@gmail. com. **E-mail:** dospassosreview@gmail.com. **Website:** brierycreekpress.wordpress.com/the-dos-passos-re-view. **Contact:** Managing Editor. "We are looking for writing that demonstrates characteristics found in the work of John Dos Passos, such as an intense and original exploration of specifically American themes, an innovative quality, and a range of literary forms, especially in the genres of fiction and creative nonfic-tion. We are not interested in genre fiction or prose that is experiment for the sake of experiment. We are also not interested in nonfiction that is scholarly or critical in nature. Send us your best unpublished lit-erary prose or poetry."

○ Reading periods: April 1-July 31 for Fall issue; February 1-May 31 for Spring issue.

NEEDS No genre fiction. Length: up to 3,000 words for short stories; up to 1,000 for flash fiction.

HOW TO CONTACT Submit 1 short story or 3 flash fiction pieces by e-mail as attachment. Include cover letter and brief bio.

PAYMENT/TERMS Pays 2 contributor's copies.

DOWN IN THE DIRT

E-mail: dirt@scars.tv. **Website:** www.scars.tv/dirt. **Contact:** Janet Kuypers, editor. Estab. 2000. *Down in the Dirt*, published every other month online and in print issues sold via Amazon.com throughout the U.S., U.K., and continental Europe, prints "good work that makes you think, that makes you feel like you've lived through a scene instead of merely read it." Also considers poems. *Down in the Dirt* is published "electronically as well as in print, either as printed magazines sold through our printer over the Internet, on the Web, or sold through our printer. And for prose, because we get so much of it, all we can suggest is, the shorter the better." Has published work by Mel Waldman, Ken Dean, Jon Brunette, John Ragusa, and Liam Spencer.

NEEDS No religious, rhyming, or family-oriented material. Average length: 1,000 words. "Contact us if you are interested in submitting very long stories or parts of a novel (if accepted, it would appear in parts in multiple issues)."

HOW TO CONTACT Query editor with e-mail submission. "99.5% of all submissions are via e-mail only, so if you do not have electronic access, there is a strong chance you will not be considered. We recommend you e-mail submissions to us, either as an attachment (TXT, RTF, DOC, or DOCX files, but not PDF) or by placing it directly in the e-mail letter. For samples of what we've printed in the past, visit our website."

DOWNSTATE STORY

1825 Maple Ridge, Peoria IL 61614. (309)688-1409. E-mail: ehopkins7@prodigy.net. **Website:** www.downstatestory.com; www.wiu.edu/users/mfgeh/dss. Estab. 1992.

NEEDS Does not want porn. Length: 300-2,000 words.

HOW TO CONTACT Submit complete ms with cover letter and SASE via postal mail.

TIPS "We want more political fiction. We also publish short shorts and literary essays."

DRAMATICS MAGAZINE

Educational Theatre Association, 2343 Auburn Ave., Cincinnati OH 45219. (513)421-3900. **E-mail:** gbossler@schooltheatre.org. **Website:** schooltheatre.org. **Contact:** Gregory Bossler, editor-in-chief. Estab. 1929. *Dramatics* is for students (mainly high school age) and teachers of theater. The magazine wants student readers to grow as theater artists and become a more discerning and appreciative audience. Material is directed to both theater students and their teachers, with strong student slant. Tries to portray the theater community in all its diversity.

NEEDS Young adults: drama (one-act and full-length plays). "We prefer unpublished scripts that have been produced at least once." Does not want to see plays that show no understanding of the conventions of the theater. No plays for children, no Christmas or didactic "message" plays. Length: 10 minutes to full length.

HOW TO CONTACT Submit complete ms. Buys 5-9 plays/year. Emerging playwrights have better chances with résumé of credits.

PAYMENT/TERMS Pays $100-500 for plays.

TIPS "Obtain our writer's guidelines and look at recent back issues. The best way to break in is to know our audience—drama students, teachers, and others interested in theater—and write for them. Writers who have some practical experience in theater, especially in technical areas, have an advantage, but we'll work with anybody who has a good idea. Some freelancers have become regular contributors."

DUCTS

P.O. Box 3203, Grand Central Station, New York NY 10163. **E-mail:** vents@ducts.org. **Website:** www.ducts.org. **Contact:** Mary Cool, editor in chief; Tim Tomlinson, fiction editor; Lisa Kirchner, memoir editor; Amy Lemmon, poetry editor; Jacqueline Bishop, art editor. Estab. 1999. *Ducts* is a semiannual webzine of personal stories, fiction, essays, memoirs, poetry, humor, profiles, reviews, and art. "*Ducts* was founded in 1999 with the intent of giving emerging writers a venue to regularly publish their compelling, personal stories. The site has been expanded to include art and creative works of all genres. We believe that these genres must and do overlap. *Ducts* publishes the best, most compelling stories, and we hope to attract readers who are drawn to work that rises above."

NEEDS No novel excerpts.

HOW TO CONTACT Submit by e-mail to julie@ducts.org.

PAYMENT/TERMS Pays $20.

TIPS "We prefer writing that tells a compelling story with a strong narrative drive."

ECLECTICA MAGAZINE

E-mail: editors@eclectica.org. **Website:** www.eclectica.org. **Contact:** Tom Dooley, managing editor. Estab. 1996. "*Eclectica* is a sterling-quality quarterly electronic literary magazine on the World Wide Web, not bound by formula or genre, harnessing technology to further the reading experience without distracting from its dynamic, global content. Founded in 1996, *Eclectica* has been devoted to showcasing the best writing on the Web regardless of genre for over two decades, and it remains one of a handful of still active publications from the earliest days of the Internet. 'Literary' and 'genre' work appear side-by-side in each issue, along with pieces blurring the distinctions between such categories. Pushcart Prize, National Poetry Series, and Pulitzer Prize winners, as well as Nebula Award nominees, have shared issues with previously unpublished authors. On the fiction front, *Eclectica* has been recognized for more Million Writers Award notable and top ten stories than any other site." Submission deadlines: December 1 for January/February issue, March 1 for April/May issue, June 1 for July/August issue, September 1 for October/November issue.

NEEDS Needs "high-quality work in any genre." Accepts short stories and novellas. Length: up to 20,000 words for short fiction; longer novella-length pieces accepted.

HOW TO CONTACT Submit via online submissions manager.

TIPS "We pride ourselves on giving everyone (high schoolers, convicts, movie executives, etc.) an equal shot at publication, based solely on the quality of their work. Because we like eclecticism, we tend to favor the varied perspectives that often characterize the work of international authors, people of color, women, alternative lifestylists—but others who don't fit into these categories often surprise us."

ECOTONE, REIMAGINING PLACE

University of North Carolina Wilmington, Department of Creative Writing, 601 S. College Rd., Wilmington NC 28403. **E-mail:** info@ecotonejournal.com. **Website:** www.ecotonemagazine.org. **Contact:** David Gessner, editor in chief. Estab. 2005. "*Ecotone, Reimagining Place* is a literary journal of place seeking to publish creative work that illuminates the edges between science and literature, the urban and rural, and the personal and biological." Semiannual.

Literary magazine/journal: 6x9. Reading period: August 15-October 1, December 15-February 1. "*Ecotone* charges a small fee for electronic submissions. If you are unable to pay this fee, please submit by postal mail."

NEEDS Has published Kevin Brockmeier, Michael Branch, Brock Clarke, Daniel Orozco, Steve Almond, and Pattiann Rogers. Does not want genre (fantasy, horror, science fiction, etc.) or young adult fiction. Length: up to 30 pages. "We are now considering shorter prose works (under 2,500 words) as well."

HOW TO CONTACT Submit via online submissions manager or postal mail with SASE. Include brief cover letter, listing both the title of the piece and the word count. Do not include identifying information on or within the ms itself. Also publishes literary essays, poetry.

ELLIPSIS

Westminster College, 1840 S. 1300 E., Salt Lake City UT 84105. (801)832-2321. **E-mail:** ellipsis@westminstercollege.edu. **Website:** ellipsis.westminstercollege.edu. Estab. 1965. *Ellipsis*, published annually in April, needs good literary poetry, fiction, essays, plays, and visual art.

Reads submissions August 1-November 1. Staff changes each year; check website for an updated list of editors. *Ellipsis* is 120 pages, digest-sized, perfect-bound, with color cover. Accepts about 5% of submissions received. Press run is 2,000; most distributed free through college.

NEEDS Length: up to 6,000 words.

HOW TO CONTACT Submit complete ms via online submissions manager. Include cover letter.

PAYMENT/TERMS Pays $50 and 2 contributor's copies.

EPOCH

251 Goldwin Smith Hall, Cornell University, Ithaca NY 14853-3201. (607)255-3385. **Website:** www.epoch.cornell.edu. **Contact:** Michael Koch, editor; Heidi E. Marschner, managing editor. Estab. 1947. Looking for well-written literary fiction, poetry, personal essays. Newcomers welcome. Open to mainstream and avant-garde writing.

Magazine: 6×9; 128 pages; good quality paper; good cover stock. Receives 500 unsolicited mss/month. Accepts 15-20 mss/issue. Reads unsolicited submissions September 15-April

15. Publishes 3-4 new writers/year. Has published work by Antonya Nelson, Doris Betts, Heidi Jon Schmidt.

NEEDS No genre fiction. Would like to see more Southern fiction (Southern U.S.).

HOW TO CONTACT Send complete ms. Considers fiction in all forms, short short to novella length.

PAYMENT/TERMS Pay varies; pays up to $150/unsolicited piece.

TIPS "Tell your story, speak your poem, straight from the heart. We are attracted to language and to good writing, but we are most interested in what the good writing leads us to, or where."

EVANSVILLE REVIEW

University of Evansville Creative Writing Department, 1800 Lincoln Ave., Evansville IN 47722. (812)488-1042. **E-mail:** evansvillereview@evansville.edu. **Website:** https://theevansvillereview.submittable.com/submit. **Contact:** Amanda Alexander, editor in chief; Sari Baum, editor in chief; Brittney Kaleri, nonfiction editor; William Capella, fiction editor; Beth Brunmeier, poetry editor. Estab. 1990. "*The Evansville Review* is an annual literary journal published at the University of Evansville. Our award-winning journal includes poetry, fiction, nonfiction, plays, and interviews by a wide range of authors, from emerging writers to Nobel Prize recipients. Past issues have included work by Joyce Carol Oates, Arthur Miller, John Updike, Joseph Brodsky, Elia Kazan, Edward Albee, Willis Barnstone, Shirley Ann Grau, and X.J. Kennedy."

◯ Reading period: September 1-October 31.

NEEDS "We are open to a wide range of styles, though our aim is always the highest literary quality. Hit us with your best language, your most compelling characters. Make us remember your story." Does not want erotica, fantasy, experimental, or children's fiction. Submit up to 3 pieces of flash fiction (1,000 words each) or 1 story (up to 9,000 words).

HOW TO CONTACT Submit online at theevansvillereview.submittable.com/submit.

PAYMENT/TERMS Pays contributor's copies.

EVENING STREET REVIEW

Evening Street Press, Inc., 2701 Corabel Ln., #27, Sacramento CA 95821. (614)937-2124. **E-mail:** editor@eveningstreetpress.com. **Website:** www.eveningstreetpress.com. **Contact:** Barbara Bergmann, managing editor. Estab. 2007. "Intended for a general audience, *Evening Street Press* is centered on Elizabeth Cady Stanton's 1848 revision of the Declaration of Independence: 'that all men and women are created equal,' with equal rights to 'life, liberty, and the pursuit of happiness.' It focuses on the realities of experience, personal and historical, from the most gritty to the most dreamlike, including awareness of the personal and social forces that block or develop the possibilities of this new culture."

HOW TO CONTACT Send complete ms. E-mail submissions preferred.

PAYMENT/TERMS Pays 1 contributor's copy.

TIPS "Does not want to see male chauvinism. Mss are read year round. See website for chapbook and book competitions."

EXOTIC MAGAZINE

XMAG, LLC, 818 SW Third Ave., Suite 1324, Portland OR 97204. (503)241-4317. **Fax:** (503)914-0439. **E-mail:** editorial@xmag.com; info@xmag.com. **Website:** www.xmag.com. **Contact:** John R. Voge, editor. Estab. 1993. "*Exotic* is pro-sex, informative, amusing, mature, and intelligent. Our readers rent and/or buy adult videos, visit strip clubs, and are interested in topics related to the adult entertainment industry and sexuality/culture. Don't talk down to them or fire too far over their heads. Many readers are computer literate and well-traveled. We're also interested in insightful fetish material. We are not a 'hard core' publication."

NEEDS "We are currently overwhelmed with fiction submissions. Please only send fiction if it's really amazing." Length: 1,000-1,800 words.

HOW TO CONTACT Send complete ms.

PAYMENT/TERMS Pays 10¢/word, up to $150.

TIPS "Read adult publications, spend time in the clubs doing more than just tipping and drinking. Look for new insights in adult topics. For the industry to continue to improve, those who cover it must also be educated consumers and affiliates. Please type, spell-check, and be realistic about how much time the editor can take 'fixing' your ms."

FAILBETTER.COM

2022 Grove Ave., Richmond VA 23221. **E-mail:** submissions@failbetter.com. **Website:** www.failbetter.com. **Contact:** Thom Didato, editor. Estab. 2000. "We are a quarterly online magazine published in the spirit of a traditional literary journal—dedicated to publishing quality fiction, poetry, and artwork. While the Web plays host to hundreds, if not thousands, of genre-related sites (many of which have merit), we are not one of them."

NEEDS "If you're sending a short story or novel excerpt, send only 1 at a time. Wait to hear from us before sending another."

HOW TO CONTACT Submit work by pasting it into the body of an e-mail. Must put "Submission" in e-mail's subject line. Do not send attachments. Also accepts postal mail submissions.

TIPS "Read an issue. Read our guidelines! We place a high degree of importance on originality, believing that even in this age of trends it is still possible. We are not looking for what is current or momentary. We are not concerned with length: One good sentence may find a home here, as the bulk of mediocrity will not. Most importantly, know that what you are saying could only come from you. When you are sure of this, please feel free to submit."

FAULTLINE

University of California at Irvine, Department of English, 435 Humanities Instructional Building, Irvine CA 92697. (949)824-1573. **E-mail:** faultline@uci.edu. **Website:** faultline.sites.uci.edu. **Contact:** Stefan Karlsson, poetry editor; Kathleen Mackay, fiction editor. Estab. 1992.

○ Reading period is October 15-February 15. Submissions sent at any other time will not be read. Editors change in September of each year.

NEEDS Length: up to 20 pages.

HOW TO CONTACT Submit complete ms via online submissions manager or mail. "While simultaneous submissions are accepted, multiple submissions are not accepted. Please restrict your submissions to 1 story at a time, regardless of length."

PAYMENT/TERMS Pays contributor copies.

TIPS "Our commitment is to publish the best work possible from well-known and emerging authors with vivid and varied voices."

FEMINIST STUDIES

4137 Susquehanna Hall, University of Maryland, College Park MD 20742. (301)405-7415. **Fax:** (301)405-8395. **E-mail:** info@feministstudies.org; brittany@feministstudies.org. **E-mail:** kmantilla@feministstudies.org. **Website:** www.feministstudies.org. **Con**tact: Ashwini Tambe, editorial director; Karla Mantilla, managing editor. Estab. 1974. Over the years, *Feminist Studies* has been a reliable source of significant writings on issues that are important to all classes and races of women. Those familiar with the literature on women's studies are well aware of the importance and vitality of the journal and the frequency with which articles first published in *Feminist Studies* are cited and/or reprinted elsewhere. Indeed, no less than 4 anthologies have been created from articles originally published in *Feminist Studies*: *Clio's Consciousness Raised: New Perspectives on the History of Women*; *Sex and Class in Women's History*; *U.S. Women in Struggle: A Feminist Studies Anthology*; and *Lesbian Subjects: A Feminist Studies Reader. Feminist Studies* is committed to publishing an interdisciplinary body of feminist knowledge that sees intersections of gender with racial identity, sexual orientation, economic means, geographical location, and physical ability as the touchstone for our politics and our intellectual analysis. Whether work is drawn from the complex past or the shifting present, the articles and essays that appear in *Feminist Studies* address social and political issues that intimately and significantly affect women and men in the United States and around the world."

NEEDS "We are interested in work that addresses questions of interest to the Feminist Studies audience, particularly work that pushes past the boundaries of what has been done before." Length: up to 15 pages or 5,500 words.

HOW TO CONTACT Submit complete ms by mail and e-mail (creative@feministstudies.org). FS has published Meena Alexander, Nicole Brossard, Jayne Cortez, Toi Derricotte, Diane Glancy, Marilyn Hacker, Lyn Hejinian, June Jordan, Audre Lorde, Cherrie Moraga, Sharon Olds, Grace Paley, Ruth Stone, and Mitsuye Yamada, among others.

FICTION

Department of English, City College of New York, Convent Ave. & 138th St., New York NY 10031. **E-mail:** fictionmageditors@gmail.com. **Website:** www.fictioninc.com. **Contact:** Mark J. Mirsky, editor. Estab. 1972. "As the name implies, we publish only fiction; we are looking for the best new writing available, leaning toward the unconventional. *Fiction* has traditionally attempted to make accessible the inaccessible, to bring the experimental to a broader audience." Reading period for unsolicited mss is September 15-June 15.

◐ Stories first published in *Fiction* have been selected for the *Pushcart Prize: Best of the Small Presses*, *O. Henry Prize Stories*, and *Best American Short Stories*.

NEEDS No romance, science fiction, etc. Length: reads any length, but encourages lengths under 5,000 words.

HOW TO CONTACT Submit complete ms via mail or online submissions manager.

TIPS "The guiding principle of *Fiction* has always been to go to terra incognita in the writing of the imagination and to ask that modern fiction set itself serious questions, if often in absurd and comedic voices, interrogating the nature of the real and the fantastic. It represents no particular school of fiction, except the innovative. Its pages have often been a harbor for writers at odds with each other. As a result of its willingness to publish the difficult, experimental, and unusual, while not excluding the well known, *Fiction* has a unique reputation in the U.S. and abroad as a journal of future directions."

FICTION INTERNATIONAL

San Diego State University, San Diego State University, Department of English and Comp. Lit, 5500 Campanile Dr., San Diego CA 92182-6020. **E-mail:** fictioninternational@gmail.com. **E-mail:** https://fictioninternational.submittable.com/submit. **Website:** fictioninternational.sdsu.edu. **Contact:** Harold Jaffe, editor. Estab. 1973. "*Fiction International* is the only literary journal in the United States emphasizing formal innovation and social activism. Each issue revolves around a theme and features a wide variety of fiction, nonfiction, indeterminate prose, and visuals by leading writers and artists from around the world." Has published works by William Burroughs, Clarice Lispector (Brazil), Robert Coover, Edmund White, Joyce Carol Oates, Walter Abish, and Kathy Acker.

NEEDS Each issue is themed; see website for details. No genre fiction. Length: up to 5,500 words.

HOW TO CONTACT Submit complete ms via online submissions manager.

FICTION TERRIFICA

7956 Cross Creek Dr., Glen Burnie MD 21061. (443)875-4524. **E-mail:** dschaff@fictionterrifica.com. **E-mail:** subs@fictionterrifica.com. **Website:** www.fictionterrifica.com. **Contact:** Dana Schaff, managing editor. Estab. 2014. "*Fiction Terrifica* is a website/bimonthly e-zine dedicated to helping small press writers and previously unpublished writers publish their mss. We are a royalty-based publishing site. We promote writers on Facebook and Twitter, along with any works they may have currently for sale. Our only requirement for acceptance is that the work be horror, dark fiction, science fiction, or fantasy related. We host links to our authors works available at other sites. We also offer Kindle publishing on a royalty basis."

NEEDS Length: 1,500-15,000 words.

HOW TO CONTACT Query before submitting.

TIPS "The best advice I can give is to write a good story, article, or personal experience publishing piece and submit it. We are always looking to promote new and upcoming writers. Have your piece polished and ready for publication."

◐$ THE FIDDLEHEAD

Campus House, 11 Garland Crt, PO Box 4400, University of New Brunswick, Fredericton NB E3B 5A3, Canada. **E-mail:** fiddlehd@unb.ca. **Website:** www.thefiddlehead.ca. **Contact:** Kathryn Taglia, managing editor; Ian LeTourneau, secretary/graphic designer. Estab. 1945. *The Fiddlehead* is open to good writing in English or translations into English from all over the world and in a variety of styles, including experimental genres. Our editors are always happy to see new unsolicited works in fiction (including novel excerpts), creative nonfiction, and poetry. We also publish reviews, and occasionally other selected creative work such as excerpts from plays. Work is read on an ongoing basis; the acceptance rate is around 1-2% (we are, however, famous for our rejection notes!). We particularly welcome submissions from Indigenous writers, writers of colour, writers with disabilities, LGBTQQIA+ writers, and writers from other intersectional and under-represented communities. If you are comfortable identifying yourself as one or more of the above, please feel free to mention this in your cover letter. *The Fiddlehead*'s mandate is to publish accomplished poetry, short fiction, and Canadian literature reviews; to discover and promote new writing talent; to represent the Atlantic Canada's lively cultural and literary diversity; and to place the best of new and established Canadian writing in an international context. *The Fiddlehead* has published works from a long list of Canadian authors including Margaret Atwood, George Elliott Clarke, Kayla Czaga, Eden Robinson,

Gregory Scofield, and Clea Young alongside international authors such as Jorie Graham, Jaki McCarrick, Thylias Moss, Les Murray, and Daniel Woodrell. *The Fiddlehead* also sponsors an annual writing contest in poetry and short fiction.

NEEDS A short fiction submission should be one story, double spaced. Unless a story is very, very short (under 1,000 words), please send only one story per submission. Please specify at the top of the first page the number of words in the story submitted. No fiction aimed at children. Length: up to 6,000 words. Rarely publishes flash fiction.

HOW TO CONTACT Send SASE with **Canadian** postage for response or self-addressed envelope with cheque/money to cover postage (US or CA dollars). May request email response if you do not want ms. returned. No e-mail or faxed submissions. Simultaneous submissions only if stated on cover letter; must contact immediately if accepted elsewhere. *The Fiddlehead* is phasing in a move to an online submission system in 2018, please check website for details.

PAYMENT/TERMS Pays up to $60 (Canadian)/published page and 2 contributor's copies.

TIPS "If you are serious about submitting to *The Fiddlehead*, you should subscribe or read several issues to get a sense of the journal. Contact us if you would like to order sample back issues."

⑤ THE FIFTH DI...

P.O. Box 782, Cedar Rapids IO 52406-0782. **E-mail:** thefifthdi@yahoo.com. **Website:** www.nomadicdeliriumpress.com/fifth.htm. Estab. 1994. *The Fifth Di.*, published quarterly online, features fiction from the science fiction and fantasy genres.

NEEDS Open to most forms, but all submissions must be science fiction or fantasy. Does not want horror, or anything that is not science fiction or fantasy. Length: up to 7,500 words.

HOW TO CONTACT Submit by e-mail with .RTF attachment only; no .DOC or .DOCX submissions. Include the word "Submission" in subject line.

PAYMENT/TERMS Pays $10 per story.

⑤ THE FIRST LINE

Blue Cubicle Press, LLC, P.O. Box 250382, Plano TX 75025. (214)455-4324. **E-mail:** info@thefirstline.com. **E-mail:** submission@thefirstline.com. **Website:** www.thefirstline.com. **Contact:** Robin LaBounty, manuscript coordinator. Estab. 1999. "*The First Line* is an exercise in creativity for writers and a chance for readers to see how many different directions we can take when we start from the same place. The purpose of *The First Line* is to jump start the imagination—to help writers break through the block that is the blank page. Each issue contains short stories that stem from a common first line; it also provides a forum for discussing favorite first lines in literature."

NEEDS "We only publish stories that start with the first line provided. We are a collection of tales—of different directions writers can take when they start from the same place." "Stories that do not start with our first line." Length: 300-5,000 words.

HOW TO CONTACT Submit complete ms.

PAYMENT/TERMS Pays $25-50.

TIPS "Don't just write the first story that comes to mind after you read the sentence. If it is obvious, chances are other people are writing about the same thing. Don't try so hard. Be willing to accept criticism."

FIVE CHAPTERS

Five Chapters, Wales. **Website:** www.fivechapters.com. FiveChapters.com is the home of the most exciting original fiction on the web. A 5-part story will be published every week, serial-style, beginning on Monday and with a new installment every weekday.

HOW TO CONTACT Send complete ms.

FIVE POINTS

Georgia State University, P.O. Box 3999, Atlanta GA 30302-3999. **Website:** www.fivepoints.gsu.edu. **Contact:** David Bottoms, co-editor. Estab. 1996. *Five Points*, published 3 times/year, is committed to publishing work that compels the imagination through the use of fresh and convincing language.

○ Magazine: 6x9; 200 pages; cotton paper; glossy cover; photos. Has published Alice Hoffman, Natasha Tretheway, Pamela Painter, Billy Collins, Philip Levine, George Singleton, Hugh Sheehy, and others. All submissions received outside of our reading periods are returned unread.

NEEDS Receives 250 unsolicited mss/month. Accepts 4 mss/issue; 15-20 mss/year. Reads fiction August 15-December 1 and January 3-March 31. Publishes 1 new writer/year. Sometimes comments on rejected mss. Sponsors awards/contests. Length: up to 7,500 words.

HOW TO CONTACT Submit through online sub-missions manager. Include cover letter.

PAYMENT/TERMS Pays $15/page ($250 maximum), plus free subscription to magazine and 2 contributor's copies; additional copies $4.

TIPS "We place no limitations on style or content. Our only criteria is excellence. If your writing has an original voice, substance, and significance, send it to us. We will publish distinctive, intelligent writing that has something to say and says it in a way that captures and maintains our attention."

FLINT HILLS REVIEW

Department of English, Modern Languages, and Journalist, Emporia State University, 1 Kellogg Circle, Emporia KS 66801. **E-mail:** awebb@emporia.edu. **E-mail:** bluestem@emporia.edu. **Website:** www.emporia.edu/fhr. **Contact:** Amy Sage Webb and Kevin Rabas, editors. Estab. 1996. *Flint Hills Review*, published annually, is "a regionally focused journal presenting writers of national distinction alongside new authors. *FHR* seeks work informed by a strong sense of place or region, especially Kansas and the Great Plains region. We seek to provide a publishing venue for writers of the Great Plains and Kansas while also publishing authors whose work evidences a strong sense of place, writing of literary quality, and accomplished use of language and depth of character development." Magazine: 6x9; 75-200 pages; perfect-bound; 60 lb. paper; glossy cover; illustrations; photos. Has published work by Julene Bair, Elizabeth Dodd, Dennis Etzel Jr., Patricia Lawson, and Amanda Frost. Reads mss November to mid-March.

NEEDS Wants writing of literary quality with a strong sense of place. Publishes short stories and flash fiction. Include short bio (150 words or less). No religious, inspirational, children's. Length: 1-3 pages for short shorts; 7-25 pages for short stories.

HOW TO CONTACT Submit complete ms by mail or as e-mail attachment.

PAYMENT/TERMS Pays 1 contributor's copy; additional copies at discounted price.

TIPS "Submit writing that has strong imagery and voice, writing that is informed by place or region, writing of literary quality with depth of character development. Hone the language to the most literary depiction possible in the shortest space that still provides depth of development without excess length."

THE FLORIDA REVIEW

Department of English, University of Central Florida, P.O. Box 161346, Orlando FL 32816-1346. **E-mail:** fl-review@ucf.edu. **Website:** floridareview.cah.ucf.edu. **Contact:** Lisa Roney, editor. Estab. 1972. "*The Florida Review* publishes exciting new work from around the world from writers both emerging and well known. We are not Florida-exclusive, though we acknowledge having a jungle mentality and a preference for grit, and we have provided and continue to offer a home for many Florida writers."

○ Has published work by Gerald Vizenor, Billy Collins, Sherwin Bitsui, Kelly Clancy, Denise Duhamel, Tony Hoagland, Baron Wormser, Marcia Aldrich, and Patricia Foster. Accepts mailed submissions only if author does not have regular access to the Internet.

NEEDS No genre fiction. Length: 3-25 pages.

HOW TO CONTACT Submit complete ms via on-line submissions manager.

TIPS "We're looking for writers with fresh voices and original stories. We like risk."

FLORIDA SPORTSMAN

Wickstrom Communications, Intermedia Outdoors, 2700 S. Kanner Hwy., Stuart FL 34994. (772)219-7400. **Fax:** (772)219-6900. **E-mail:** editor@floridasportsman.com. **Website:** www.floridasportsman.com. **Contact:** Jeff Weakley, executive editor. Edited for the boat owner and offshore, coastal, and fresh water fisherman. It provides a how, when, and where approach in its articles, which also includes occasional camping, diving, and hunting stories—plus ecology (in-depth articles and editorials attempting to protect Florida's wilderness, wetlands, and natural beauty).

TIPS "Feature articles are sometimes open to free-lancers; however there is little chance of acceptance unless contributor is an accomplished and avid out-doorsman *and* a competent writer-photographer with considerable experience in Florida."

FLOYD COUNTY MOONSHINE

720 Christiansburg Pike, Floyd VA 24091. (540)745-5150. **E-mail:** floydshine@gmail.com. **Website:** www.floydcountymoonshine.com. **Contact:** Aaron Lee Moore, editor-in-chief. Estab. 2008. *Floyd County Moonshine*, published biannually, is a "literary and arts magazine in Floyd, Virginia, and the New River Valley. We accept poetry, short stories, and essays addressing all manner of themes; however, preference is

given to those works of a rural or Appalachian nature. *Floyd County Moonshine* publishes a variety of home-grown Appalachian writers in addition to writers from across the country. The mission of *Floyd County Moonshine* is to publish thought-provoking, well-crafted, free-thinking, uncensored prose and poetry. Our literature explores the dark and Gothic as well as the bright and pleasant in order to give an honest portrayal of the human condition. We aspire to publish quality literature in the local color genre, specifically writing that relates to Floyd, Virginia, and the New River Valley. Floyd and local Appalachian authors are given priority consideration; however, to stay versatile we also aspire to publish some writers from all around the country in every issue. We publish both well-established and beginning writers." Wants literature addressing rural or Appalachian themes. Has published poetry by Steve Kistulentz, Louis Gallo, Ernie Wormwood, R.T. Smith, Chelsea Adams, and Justin Askins.

NEEDS "Any and all subject matter is welcome, although we gravitate toward Local Color (especially stories set in Floyd, the New River Valley, or a specific rural setting) and the Southern Gothic." Length: up to 8,000 words.

HOW TO CONTACT Accepts e-mail (preferred). Submit a Word document as attachment. Accepts previously published works and simultaneous submissions on occasion. Cover letter is unnecessary. Include brief bio. Reads submissions year round.

PAYMENT/TERMS Pays 1 contributor's copy.

TIPS "If we favor your work, it may appear in several issues, so prior contributors are also encouraged to re-submit. Every year we choose at least 1 featured author for an issue. We also nominate for Pushcart prizes, and we will do book reviews if you mail us the book."

FLYLEAF

Flyleaf, LLC, 6627 Old Oaks Blvd., Pearland TX 77584. **E-mail:** info@flyleafjournal.com. **E-mail:** submissions@flyleafjournal.com. **Website:** www.flyleaf.journal.com. **Contact:** Matthew Jankiewicz, editor; Parker Stockman, managing editor. Estab. 2014. *Flyleaf Journal* is a literary periodical that publishes one short story every month. Each story is produced as a two-sided, four-panel gatefold that opens up to reveal a literary and graphic landscape. Each story is integrated with the photographs and illustrations of a graphic collaborator, designed exclusively for that story.

NEEDS Length: 500-2,000 words.

HOW TO CONTACT Send complete ms.

PAYMENT/TERMS Pays $50 per story.

TIPS "We love to read unique and memorable voices in fiction. We want to receive stories written out of love, passion, or anger. If it doesn't move the writer, we will most likely not be moved as well. Our fiction celebrates the short memories in life that make the biggest impact on us."

FLYWAY

Journal of Writing and Environment, Department of English, 206 Ross Hall, Iowa State University, Ames IA 50011-1201. (515)294-8273. **Fax:** (515)294-6814. **E-mail:** flywayjournal@gmail.com. **Website:** www.flywayjournal.org. **Contact:** Zachary Lisabeth, managing editor. Estab. 1995. Based out of Iowa State University, *Flyway: Journal of Writing and Environment* publishes poetry, fiction, nonfiction, and visual art exploring the many complicated facets of the word environment—at once rural, urban, and suburban—and its social and political implications. Also open to all different interpretations of environment.Reading period is August 15-May 15. Has published work by Rick Bass, Jacob M. Appel, Madison Smartt Bell, Jane Smiley. Also sponsors the annual fall Notes from the Field contest in creative nonfiction, the spring Sweet Corn Prize in Fiction and Poetry contest and a themed winter contest. Details on website. "We look for stories that bring in environment as a character or central element. Does this mean we only take stories about ecology/nature/treehuggers? Nope. We want stories that wouldn't be remarkable or couldn't happen in another place than where they happen. We want writing that shows tension between character and surroundings, that shows how changes in living space affect actions and interactions in that living space. This environment could be an abandoned school, a strip mall comic bookstore, a thinning forest or a hiking trail—if it shapes the characters, affects events, and if it's of interest to us. We are open to work of all genres and subjects if it fits our aesthetic, and we are always happy to be surprised."

NEEDS Length: up to 5,000 words. Average length: 3,000 words. Also publishes short shorts of up to 1,000 words. Average length: 500 words.

HOW TO CONTACT Submit mss only via online submission manager. Receives 50-100 mss monthly. Accepts 3-5 stories per issue; up to 10 per year. Also reviews novels and short-story collections. Submit 1 short story or up to 3 short shorts.

PAYMENT/TERMS Pays one-year subscription to *Flyway*.

TIPS "For *Flyway*, there should be tension between the environment or setting of the story and the characters in it. A well-known place should appear new, even alien and strange through the eyes and actions of the characters. We want to see an active environment, too—a setting that influences actions, triggers its own events."

🚫 FOGGED CLARITY

Fogged Clarity and Nicotine Heart Press, P.O. Box 1016, Muskegon MI 49443-1016. (231)670-7033. **E-mail:** editor@foggedclarity.com; submissions@foggedclarity.com. **Website:** www.foggedclarity.com. **Contact:** Editors. Estab. 2008. "*Fogged Clarity* is an arts review that accepts submissions of poetry, fiction, nonfiction, music, visual art, and reviews of work in all mediums. We seek art that is stabbingly eloquent. Our print edition is released once every year, while new issues of our online journal come out at the beginning of every month. Artists maintain the copyrights to their work until they are monetarily compensated for said work. If your work is selected for our print edition and you consent to its publication, you will be compensated."

○ "By incorporating music and the visual arts and releasing a new issue monthly, *Fogged Clarity* aims to transcend the conventions of a typical literary journal. Our network is extensive, and our scope is as broad as thought itself; we are, you are, unconstrained. With that spirit in mind, *Fogged Clarity* examines the work of authors, artists, scholars, and musicians, providing a home for exceptional art and thought that warrants exposure."

NEEDS Length: up to 8,000 words.

HOW TO CONTACT Submit 1-2 complete ms by e-mail (submissions@foggedclarity.com) as attached .DOC or .DOCX file. Subject line should be formatted as: "Last Name: Medium of Submission." For example, "Evans: Fiction." Include brief cover letter, complete contact information, and a third-person bio.

TIPS "The editors appreciate artists communicating the intention of their submitted work and the influences behind it in a brief cover letter. Any artists with proposals for features or special projects should feel free to contact Ben Evans directly at editor@foggedclarity.com."

FOLIATE OAK LITERARY MAGAZINE

University of Arkansas-Monticello, Arts & Humanities, 562 University Dr., Monticello AR 71656. (870)460-1247. **E-mail:** foliateoak@gmail.com. **Website:** www.foliateoak.com. **Contact:** Diane Payne, faculty advisor. Estab. 1973. The *Foliate Oak Literary Magazine* is an online student-run magazine accepting hybrid prose, poetry, fiction, flash, creative nonfiction, and artwork. "After you receive a rejection/acceptance notice, please wait 1 month before submitting new work. **Submission Period: August 1-April 24**. We do not read submissions during summer break. If you need to contact us for anything other than submitting your work, please write to foliateoak@gmail.com." No e-mail submissions.

NEEDS Does not want pornographic, racist, or homophobic content. We avoid genre fiction. Length: 200-2,500 words.

HOW TO CONTACT Send complete ms through online submission manager. "Remember to include your brief third-person bio."

TIPS "Please submit all material via our online submission manager. Read our guidelines before submitting. We are eager to include multimedia submissions of videos, music, and collages. Submit your best work."

FOLIO

A Literary Journal at American University, Department of Literature, American University, Washington DC 20016. (202)885-2971. **Fax:** (202)885-2938. **E-mail:** folio.editors@gmail.com. **Website:** www.american.edu/cas/literature/folio. **Contact:** Editor in chief. Estab. 1984. "*Folio* is a nationally recognized literary journal sponsored by the College of Arts and Sciences at American University in Washington, DC. Since 1984, we have published original creative work by both new and established authors. Past issues have included work by Michael Reid Busk, Billy Collins, William Stafford, and Bruce Weigl, and interviews with Michael Cunningham, Charles Baxter, Amy Bloom, Ann Beattie, and Walter Kirn. We look for well-crafted poetry and prose that is bold and memorable."

○ Poems and prose are reviewed by editorial staff and senior editors. Reads submissions in the fall of each year. To submit, please visit: https://foliolitjournal.submittable.com/submit.

NEEDS Length: up to 5,000 words.

HOW TO CONTACT Submit via online submission form at foliolitjournal.submittable.com/submit. Cover letters must contain all of the following: brief bio, e-mail address, snail mail address, phone number, and title(s) of work enclosed.

FORWARD IN CHRIST

WELS Communication Services, 2929 N. Mayfair Rd., Milwaukee WI 53222. (414)256-3210. **Fax:** (414)256-3899. **E-mail:** fic@wels.net. **Website:** www.wels.net. **Contact:** Julie K. Wietzke, managing editor; John A. Braun, executive editor. Estab. 1913.

TIPS "Topics should be of interest to the majority of the members of the synod—the people in the pews. Articles should have a Christian viewpoint, but we don't want sermons. We suggest you carefully read at least 5 or 6 issues with close attention to the length, content, and style of the features."

FOURTEEN HILLS

Department of Creative Writing, San Francisco State University, 1600 Holloway Ave., San Francisco CA 94137. **E-mail:** hills@sfsu.edu. **Website:** www.14hills. net. Estab. 1994. "*Fourteen Hills* publishes the highest-quality innovative fiction and poetry for a literary audience."

○ Semiannual magazine: 6x9; 200 pages; 60 lb. paper; 10-point C15 cover. Reading periods: September 1-December 1 for summer issue; March 1-June 1 for winter issue.

NEEDS Has published work by Susan Straight, Yiyun Li, Alice LaPlante, Terese Svoboda, Peter Rock, Stephen Dixon, and Adam Johnson. Length: up to 6,000 words or 20 pages for short stories; up to 1,000 words or 10 pages each for flash fiction.

HOW TO CONTACT Submit 1 short story or 3 flash fiction pieces via online submissions manager.

PAYMENT/TERMS Pays 2 contributor's copies and offers discount on additional copies.

TIPS "Please read an issue of *Fourteen Hills* before submitting."

THE FOURTH RIVER

Chatham University, Woodland Rd., Pittsburgh PA 15232. **E-mail:** 4thriver@gmail.com. **Website:** thefourthriver.com. Estab. 2005. *The Fourth River*, an annual publication of Chatham University's MFA in Creative Writing Programs, features literature that engages and explores the relationship between humans and their environments. Wants writings that

are richly situated at the confluence of place, space, and identity, or that reflect upon or make use of landscape and place in new ways.

○ *The Fourth River* is digest-sized, perfect-bound, with full-color cover by various artists. Reading periods: November 1-January 1 (fall online issue) and July 1-September 1 (spring print issue).

NEEDS Length: up to 7,000 words.

HOW TO CONTACT Submit complete ms via online submissions manager.

○$ FREEFALL MAGAZINE

FreeFall Literary Society of Calgary, 460, 1720 29th Ave. SW, Calgary AB T2T 6T7, Canada. **E-mail:** editors@freefallmagazine.ca. **Website:** www.freefallmagazine.ca. **Contact:** Ryan Stromquist, managing editor. Estab. 1990. Magazine published triannually containing fiction, poetry, creative nonfiction, essays on writing, interviews, and reviews. "We are looking for exquisite writing with a strong narrative."

NEEDS Length: up to 4,000 words.

HOW TO CONTACT Submit via online submissions manager.

PAYMENT/TERMS Pays $10/printed page in the magazine ($100 maximum) and 1 contributor's copy.

TIPS "Our mission is to encourage the voices of new, emerging, and experienced Canadian writers and provide a platform for their quality work."

○ FREEXPRESSION

Peter F Pike T/As FreeXpresSion, P.O. Box 4, West Hoxton NSW 2171, Australia. 0425-273-703. **E-mail:** editor@freexpression.com.au. **Website:** www.freexpression.com.au. **Contact:** Peter F. Pike, managing editor. Estab. 1993. *FreeXpresSion*, published monthly, contains creative writing, how-to articles, short stories, and poetry, including cinquain, haiku, etc., and bush verse. Open to all forms. "Christian themes OK. Humorous material welcome. No gratuitous sex; bad language OK. We don't want to see anything degrading." *FreeXpresSion* also publishes books up to 200 pages **through subsidy arrangements with authors**. Some poems published throughout the year are used in *Yearbooks* (annual anthologies). *FreeXpresSion* is 32 pages, magazine-sized, offset-printed, saddle-stapled, full color. Receives about 3,500 poems/year, accepts about 30%.

HOW TO CONTACT Submit prose via e-mail.

THE FRIEND MAGAZINE

The Church of Jesus Christ of Latter-day Saints, 50 E. North Temple St., Salt Lake City UT 84150. (801)240-2210. **Fax:** (801)240-2270. **E-mail:** friend@ldschurch. org. **Website:** www.lds.org/friend. **Contact:** Paul B. Pieper, editor; Mark W. Robison, art director. Estab. 1971. "The *Friend* is published by The Church of Jesus Christ of Latter-day Saints for boys and girls up to 3-12 years of age."

NEEDS Wants illustrated stories and "For Little Friends" stories. See guidelines online.

THE FROGMORE PAPERS

The Frogmore Press, 21 Mildmay Rd., Lewes, East Sussex BN7 1PJ, England. **E-mail:** frogmorepress@gmail. com (accepted from outside UK only). **Website:** www. frogmorepress.co.uk. **Contact:** Jeremy Page, editor. Estab. 1983. *The Frogmore Papers*, published semiannually, is a literary magazine with emphasis on new poetry, short stories and flash fiction. *The Frogmore Papers* is 42 pages, photocopied in photo-reduced typescript, saddle-stapled, with matte card cover. Accepts 2% of poetry received. Press run is 500. Reading periods: October 1-31 for March issue and April 1-30 for September issue.

NEEDS Length: up to 2,000 words.

HOW TO CONTACT Submit by e-mail or mail (email submissions only accepted from outside the UK).

PAYMENT/TERMS Pays 1 contributor's copy.

FUGUE LITERARY JOURNAL

200 Brink Hall, University of Idaho, P.O. Box 44110, Moscow ID 83844. **E-mail:** fugue@uidaho.edu. **Website:** www.fuguejournal.com. **Contact:** Alexandra Teague, faculty advisor. Estab. 1990. "Begun in 1990 by the faculty in the Department of English at University of Idaho, *Fugue* has continuously published poetry, plays, fiction, essays, and interviews from established and emerging writers biannually. We take pride in the work we print, the writers we publish, and the presentation of each and every issue. Working in collaboration with local and national artists, our covers display some of the finest art from photography and digital art to ink drawings and oil paintings. We believe that each issue is a print and digital artifact of the deepest engagement with our culture, and we make it our personal goal that the writing we select and presentation of each issue reflect the reverence we have for art and letters." Work published in *Fugue*

has won the Pushcart Prize and has been cited in *Best American Essays*. Submissions are accepted online only. Poetry, fiction, and nonfiction submissions are accepted September 1-May 1. All material received outside of this period will not be read. $3 submission fee per entry. See website for submission instructions.

HOW TO CONTACT Submit complete ms via online submissions manager. "Please send no more than 2 short shorts or 1 story at a time. Submissions in more than 1 genre should be submitted separately. All multiple submissions will be returned unread. Once you have submitted a piece to us, wait for a response on this piece before submitting again."

PAYMENT/TERMS Pays 1 contributor's copy and $15 per published piece.

TIPS "The best way, of course, to determine what we're looking for is to read the journal. As the name *Fugue* indicates, our goal is to present a wide range of literary perspectives. We like stories that satisfy us both intellectually and emotionally, with fresh language and characters so captivating that they stick with us and invite a second reading. We are also seeking creative literary criticism which illuminates a piece of literature or a specific writer by examining that writer's personal experience."

FUNNY TIMES

Funny Times, Inc., P.O. Box 18530, Cleveland Heights OH 44118. (216)371-8600. **E-mail:** info@funnytimes. com. **Website:** www.funnytimes.com. **Contact:** Ray Lesser and Susan Wolpert, publishers. Estab. 1985. "*Funny Times* is a monthly review of America's funniest cartoonists and writers. We are a unique voice in modern American humor with a progressive/peace-oriented/environmental/politically activist slant."

NEEDS Wants anything funny. Length: 600-800 words.

HOW TO CONTACT Query with published clips.

PAYMENT/TERMS Pays $50-150.

TIPS "Send us a small packet (1-3 items) of only your very funniest stuff. If this makes us laugh, we'll be glad to ask for more. We particularly welcome previously published material that has been well received elsewhere."

GARBLED TRANSMISSIONS MAGAZINE

5813 NW 20th St., Margate FL 33063. **E-mail:** jamesrobertpayne@yahoo.com. **E-mail:** editor@garbledtransmission.com. **Website:** www.garbledtransmission.com. **Contact:** James Payne, editor in chief. Estab. 2011. Daily online literary magazine featuring fiction and book, movie, and comic book reviews.

○ "Stories should have a dark/strange/twisted slant to them and should be original ideas, or have such a twist to them that they redefine the genre. We like authors with an original voice. That being said, we like Stephen King, Richard Matheson, Neil Gaiman, A. Lee Martinez, Chuck Palahniuk, and Clive Barker. Movies and TV shows that inspire us include "Lost," *The Matrix*, *Fight Club*, *3:10 to Yuma*, *Dark City*, *The Sixth Sense*, "X-Files," and *Super 8*."

NEEDS "No romance or corny sci-fi or fantasy. Nothing contrived or a blatant rip-off." Length: 500-15,000 words.

HOW TO CONTACT Send complete ms by e-mail with subject line "Garbled Transmissions Submission."

TIPS "The best way to see what we like is to visit our website and read some of the stories we've published to get a taste of what style we seek."

GARGOYLE

Paycock Press, 3819 13th St. N, Arlington VA 22201. (703) 380-4893. **E-mail:** rchrdpeabody9@gmail.com. **Website:** www.gargoylemagazine.com. **Contact:** Richard Peabody, editor/publisher. Estab. 1976. "*Gargoyle* has always been a scallywag magazine, a maverick magazine, a bit too academic for the underground and way too underground for the academics. We are a writer's magazine in that we are read by other writers and have never worried about reaching the masses." Annual. The submission window opens each year in August and remains open until full. Recently published works by: Jill Adams, Roberta Allen, Cathy Alter, Jacob Appel, Donna Baier Stein, Stacy Barton, C.L. Bledsoe, Caroline Bock, Jamie Brown, Grace Cavalieri, Laura Cesarco Eglin, Patrick Chapman, Juliet Cook, Rachel Dacus, Michael Dailey, Kristina Marie Darling, William Virgil Davis, Glenn Deutsch, Andrew Gifford, Sid Gold, Suzanne Feldman, Heather Fowler, Susan Gubernat, Myronn Hardy, Abhay K. George Kalamaras, Jesse Lee Kercheval, Leonard Kress, W. F. Lantry, Lyn Lifshin, Susan Neville, Kevin O'Cuinn, Donaji Olmedo, Frances Park, Pedro Ponce, Glen Pouricau, Melissa Reddish, Aria Riding, Bruce Sager, John Saul, Marija Stajic, Liza Nash Taylor, Susan Tepper, Sally Toner, Gretchen A. Van Lente, Idea

Vilarino, Jesse Waters, Kathleen Wheaton, Andrea Wyatt, Katherine E. Young, and Bonnie ZoBell.

NEEDS Wants "edgy realism or experimental works. We run both." Wants to see more Canadian, British, Australian, and Third World fiction. Receives 300 unsolicited mss/week during submission period. Accepts 20-50 mss/issue. Agented fiction 5%. **Publishes 2-3 new writers/year.** Publishes 1-2 titles/year. Format: trade paperback originals. No romance, horror, science fiction. Length: up to 5,000 words. "We have run 2 novellas in the past 40 years."

PAYMENT/TERMS Pays 1 contributor's copy and offers 50% discount on additional copies.

TIPS "We have to fall in love with a particular fiction."

A GATHERING OF THE TRIBES

P.O. Box 20693, Tompkins Square Station, New York NY 10009. (212)777-2038. **E-mail:** gatheringofthetribes@gmail.com. **E-mail:** tribes.editor@gmail.com. **Website:** www.tribes.org. **Contact:** Steve Cannon. Estab. 1992. *A Gathering of the Tribes* is a multicultural and multigenerational publication featuring poetry, fiction, interviews, essays, visual art, and musical scores. The audience is anyone interested in the arts from a diverse perspective."

○ Magazine: 8.5x10; 130 pages; glossy paper and cover; illustrations; photos. Receives 20 unsolicited mss/month. Publishes 40% new writers/year. Has published work by Carl Watson, Ishle Park, Wang Pang, and Hanif Kureishi. Sponsors awards/contests.

NEEDS "Would like to see more satire/humor. We are open to all work; just no poor writing/grammar/syntax." Length: 2,500-5,000 words.

HOW TO CONTACT Send complete ms by postal mail or e-mail.

PAYMENT/TERMS Pays 1 contributor's copy.

TIPS "Make sure your work has substance."

THE GEORGIA REVIEW

The University of Georgia, Main Library, Room 706A, 320 S. Jackson St., Athens GA 30602. (706)542-3481. **Fax:** (706)542-0047. **E-mail:** garev@uga.edu. **Website:** thegeorgiareview.com. **Contact:** Stephen Corey, editor. Estab. 1947. "*The Georgia Review* is a literary quarterly committed to the art of editorial practice. We collaborate equally with established and emerging authors of essays, stories, poems, and reviews in the pursuit of extraordinary works that engage with the evolving concerns and interests of intellectually curious readers from around the world. Our aim in curating content is not only to elevate literature, publishing, and the arts, but also to help facilitate socially conscious partnerships in our surrounding communities." $3 online submission fee waived for subscribers. No fees for manuscripts submitted by post. Reading period: August 15-May 15.

NEEDS "We seek original, excellent short fiction not bound by type. Ordinarily we do not publish novel excerpts or works translated into English, and we discourage authors from submitting these."

HOW TO CONTACT Send complete ms via online submissions manager or postal mail.

PAYMENT/TERMS Pays $50/published page.

GERTRUDE

Queer Literary Journal and Book Club, 4857 NE 13th Ave., Portland OR 97211. **E-mail:** editorgertrudepress@gmail.com. **Website:** www.gertrudepress.org. **Contact:** Tammy Lynne Stoner. Estab. 1999. *Gertrude* is a "literary journal featuring the voices and visions of LGBTQA writers and artists" whose editors also make selections from the best of new and notable queer, literary novels for GERTIE - their 'quarterly, queer book club.'"

NEEDS Had published over 300 writers from 10 countries, launching many careers. romance. christian. erotica. abuse stories. Length: up to 3,000 words.

HOW TO CONTACT Submit 1-2 pieces via online submissions manager, double-spaced. Include word count for each piece in cover letter.

TIPS "We look for strong characterization and imagery, and new, unique ways of writing about universal experiences. Or anything bizarre."

THE GETTYSBURG REVIEW

Gettysburg College, Gettysburg College, 300 N. Washington St., Gettysburg PA 17325. (717)337-6770. **E-mail:** mdrew@gettysburg.edu. **Website:** www.gettysburgreview.com. **Contact:** Mark Drew, editor; Jess L. Bryant, managing editor. Estab. 1988. Published quarterly, *The Gettysburg Review* considers unsolicited submissions of poetry, fiction, and essays. "Our concern is quality. Mss submitted here should be extremely well written." Reading period September 1-May 31.

NEEDS Wants high-quality literary fiction. "We require that fiction be intelligent and aesthetically written." No genre fiction. Length: 2,000-7,000 words.

HOW TO CONTACT Send complete ms with SASE.

PAYMENT/TERMS Pays $25/printed page, a one-year subscription, and 1 contributor's copy.

GINOSKO LITERARY JOURNAL

Ginosko, P.O. Box 246, Fairfax CA 94978. (415)785-3160. **E-mail:** editorginosko@aol.com. **Website:** www.ginoskoliteraryjournal.com. **Contact:** Robert Paul Cesaretti, editor. Estab. 2002. *Ginosko* Flash Fiction Contest: Deadline is March 1; $5 entry fee; $250 prize. "*Ginosko* (ghin-océ-koe): To perceive, understand, realize, come to know; knowledge that has an inception, a progress, an attainment. The recognition of truth by experience." Accepting short fiction and poetry, creative nonfiction, interviews, social justice concerns, and literary insights for www.ginoskoliteraryjournal.com. Reads year round. Length of articles flexible; accepts excerpts. Publishing as semiannual e-zine. Print anthology every 2 years. Check downloadable issues on website for tone and style. Downloads free; accepts donations. Member CLMP.

NEEDS Download issue for tone and style. Length: 25-5,000 words.

HOW TO CONTACT Submit via postal mail, e-mail (prefers attachments: WPS, DOC, or RTF), or online submissions manager Submittable (ginosko.submittable.com/submit).

PAYMENT/TERMS No payment.

TIPS "Read several issues for tone and style."

GIRLS' LIFE

3 S. Frederick St., Suite 806, Baltimore MD 21202. (410)426-9600. **Fax:** (866)793-1531. **E-mail:** writeforgl@girlslife.com. **Website:** www.girlslife.com. **Contact:** Karen Bokram, founding editor and publisher; Kelsey Haywood, senior editor; Chun Kim, art director. Estab. 1994.

NEEDS "We accept short fiction. They should be stand-alone stories and are generally 2,500-3,500 words."

TIPS "Send thought-out queries with published writing samples and detailed résumé. Have fresh ideas and a voice that speaks to our audience—not down to them. And check out a copy of the magazine or visit girlslife.com before submitting."

❸ GLIMMER TRAIN STORIES

Glimmer Train Press, Inc., P.O. Box 80430, Portland OR 97280. **Fax:** (503)221-0837. **E-mail:** eds@glimmertrain.org. **Website:** www.glimmertrain.org. **Contact:** Susan Burmeister-Brown. Estab. 1991. "We are interested in literary short stories, particularly by new and emerging writers."

○ Recently published work by Benjamin Percy, Laura van den Berg, Manuel Muñoz, Claire Vaye Watkins, Abby Geni, Peter Ho Davies, William Trevor, Thisbe Nissen, and Yiyun Li.

NEEDS Length: 500-20,000 words.

HOW TO CONTACT Submit via the website at www.glimmertrain.org. In a pinch, send a hard copy and include SASE for response. Receives 36,000 unsolicited mss/year. Accepts 15 mss/issue; 45 mss/year. Agented fiction 1%. Publishes 20 new writers/year.

PAYMENT/TERMS Pays $700 for standard submissions, up to $3,000 for contest-winning stories.

TIPS "In the last 2 years, over half of the first-place stories have been their authors' very first publications. See our contest listings in Contests & Awards section."

❸ GRASSLIMB

P.O. Box 420816, San Diego CA 92142. **E-mail:** editor@grasslimb.com. **Website:** www.grasslimb.com. **Contact:** Valerie Polichar, editor. Estab. 2002. *Grasslimb* publishes literary prose, poetry, and art. Fiction is best when it is short and avant-garde or otherwise experimental.

NEEDS "Fiction in an experimental, avant-garde, or surreal mode is often more interesting to us than a traditional story." "Although general topics are welcome, we're less likely to select work regarding romance, sex, aging, and children." Length: up to 2,500 words; average length: 1,500 words.

HOW TO CONTACT Send complete ms via e-mail or postal mail with SASE.

PAYMENT/TERMS Pays $10-70 and 2 contributor's copies.

TIPS "We publish brief fiction work that can be read in a single sitting over a cup of coffee. Work is generally 'literary' in nature rather than mainstream. Experimental work welcome. Remember to have your work proofread and to send short work. We cannot read over 3,000 words and prefer under 2,000 words. Include word count."

GREEN HILLS LITERARY LANTERN

Truman State University, Department of English, Truman State University, Kirksville MO 63501. **E-mail:** adavis@truman.edu. **Website:** ghll.truman.edu. **Contact:** Adam Brooke Davis, prose editor/managing editor; Joe Benevento, poetry editor. Estab. 1990. *Green Hills Literary Lantern* is published annually, in June, by Truman State University. Historically, the print publication ran between 200-300 pages, consisting of poetry, fiction, reviews, and interviews. The digital magazine is of similar proportions and artistic standards. Open to the work of new writers, as well as more established writers.

NEEDS "We are interested in stories that demonstrate a strong working knowledge of the craft. Not especially interested in genre fiction, inspirational, or religious fiction—but if you've got something in those categories that goes beyond the conventions in interesting ways, send it. Otherwise, we are open to short stories of various settings, character conflict, and styles, including experimental." No word limit.

HOW TO CONTACT Submit complete ms.

GREEN MOUNTAINS REVIEW

Johnson State College, 337 College Hill, Johnson VT 05656. (802)635-1350. **E-mail:** gmr@jsc.edu. **Website:** greenmountainsreview.com. **Contact:** Elizabeth Powell, editor; Jessica Hendry Nelson, nonfiction editor; Jacob White, fiction editor; Ben Aleshire, assistant poetry editor. Semiannual magazine covering poems, stories, and creative nonfiction by both well-known authors and promising newcomers.

○ The editors are open to a wide range of styles and subject matter. Open reading period: September 1-March 1.

NEEDS Recently published work by Tracy Daugherty, Terese Svoboda, Walter Wetherell, T.M. McNally, J. Robert Lennon, Louis B. Jones, and Tom Whalen. Publishes short shorts. Also publishes literary criticism, poetry. Sometimes comments on rejected mss. Length: up to 25 pages, double-spaced.

HOW TO CONTACT Submit ms via online submissions manager.

PAYMENT/TERMS Pays contributor's copies, one-year subscription, and small honorarium, depending on grants.

TIPS "We encourage you to order some of our back issues to acquaint yourself with what has been accepted in the past."

GREENPRINTS

P.O. Box 1355, Fairview NC 28730. (828)628-1902. **E-mail:** pat@greenprints.com. **Website:** www.green-prints.com. **Contact:** Pat Stone, managing editor. Estab. 1990. "*GreenPrints* is the 'Weeder's Digest.' We share the human—*not* how-to—side of gardening. We publish true personal gardening stories and essays: humorous, heartfelt, insightful, inspiring. We love good, true, well-told personal *stories*—all must be about gardening!"

NEEDS "We run very little fiction."

HOW TO CONTACT Submit complete ms.

PAYMENT/TERMS Pays $75-200.

TIPS Wants "a great, true, *unique* personal *story* with dialogue, a narrative, and something special that happens to make it truly stand out."

THE GREENSBORO REVIEW

MFA Writing Program, 3302 MHRA Building, UNC-Greensboro, Greensboro NC 27402. **E-mail:** jlclark@uncg.edu. **Website:** tgronline.net. **Contact:** Jim Clark, editor. Estab. 1965. "A local lit mag with an international reputation. We've been 'old school' since 1965."

○ Stories for *The Greensboro Review* have been included in *Best American Short Stories, The O. Henry Awards Prize Stories, New Stories from the South* and *Pushcart Prize*. Does not accept e-mail submissions.

NEEDS Length: up to 7,500 words.

HOW TO CONTACT Submit complete ms via online submission form or postal mail. Include cover letter and estimated word count.

PAYMENT/TERMS Pays contributor's copies.

TIPS "We want to see the best being written regardless of theme, subject, or style."

THE GRIFFIN

Gwynedd Mercy University, 1325 Sumneytown Pike, P.O. Box 901, Gwynedd Valley PA 19437-0901. **E-mail:** garber.r@gmercyu.edu. **Website:** www.gmer-cyu.edu/about-gwynedd-mercy/publications/griffin. **Contact:** Dr. Donna M. Allego, editor. Estab. 1999. Published by Gwynedd Mercy University, *The Griffin* is a literary journal for the creative writer—subscribing to the belief that improving the human condition requires dedication to and respect for the individual and the community. Seeks works which explore universal qualities—truth, justice, integrity, compassion, mercy. Publishes poetry, short stories, short plays, and reflections.

NEEDS All genres considered. No slashers, graphic violence, or sex, however. Length: up to 2,500 words.

HOW TO CONTACT Submit complete ms via e-mail or on disk with a hard copy. Include short author bio.

TIPS "Pay attention to the word length requirements, the mission of the magazine, and how to submit ms as set forth. These constitute the writer's guidelines listed online."

GRIST

English Dept., 301 McClung Tower, Univ. of Tennessee, Knoxville TN 37996-0430. **E-mail:** gristeditors@gmail.com. **Website:** www.gristjournal.com. Estab. 2007. *Grist* is a nationally distributed journal of fiction, nonfiction, poetry, interviews, and craft essays. We seek work of high literary quality from both emerging and established writers, and we welcome all styles and aesthetic approaches. Each issue is accompanied by Grist Online, which features some of the best work we receive during our reading period. In addition to general submissions, *Grist* holds the Pro-Forma Contest every spring, recognizing unpublished creative work that explores the relationship between content and form, whether in fiction, nonfiction, poetry, or a hybrid genre. Throughout the year, we publish interviews, craft essays, and reviews on our blog, The Writing Life.

NEEDS Length: 7,000 words.

HOW TO CONTACT Send complete ms.

PAYMENT/TERMS 1 cent per word up to $50.

TIPS "*Grist* seeks work from both emerging and established writers, whose work is of high literary quality."

GUD MAGAZINE

Greatest Uncommon Denominator Publishing, P.O. Box 1537, Laconia NH 03247. **E-mail:** spiderbait1@gudmagazine.com. **Website:** www.gudmagazine.com. Estab. 2006. L "*GUD Magazine* transcends and encompasses the audiences of both genre and literary fiction by featuring fiction, art, poetry, essays and reports, comics, and short drama."

NEEDS Length: up to 15,000 words.

HOW TO CONTACT Submit via online submissions manager.

PAYMENT/TERMS Pays a minimum of $5/piece, or 3¢/word for longer pieces.

TIPS "We publish work in any genre, plus artwork, factual articles, and interviews. We'll publish something as short as 20 words or as long as 15,000, as long as it grabs us. Be warned: We read a lot. We've seen it all before. We are not easy to impress. Is your work original? Does it have something to say? Read it again. If you genuinely believe it to be so, send it. We do accept simultaneous submissions, as well as multiple submissions, but read the guidelines first."

GUERNICA MAGAZINE

112 W. 27th St., Suite 600, New York NY 10001. **E-mail:** editors@guernicamag.com; publisher@guernicamag.com. **Website:** www.guernicamag.com. **Contact:** see masthead online for specific editors. Estab. 2004. *Guernica* is called a 'great online literary magazine' by *Esquire*. *Guernica* contributors come from dozens of countries and write in nearly as many languages.

Received Caine Prize for African Writing, Best of the Net.

NEEDS *Guernica* strongly prefers fiction with a diverse international outlook—or if American, from an underrepresented or alternative perspective. (No stories about American tourists in other countries, please.) Has published Jesse Ball, Elizabeth Crane, Josh Weil, Justo Arroyo, Sergio Ramírez Mercado, Matthew Derby, E.C. Osondu (Winner of the 2009 Caine Prize for African Writing). No genre fiction or satire. Length: 1,200-4,500 words.

HOW TO CONTACT Submit complete ms via online submissions manager.

TIPS "Please read the magazine first before submitting. Most stories that are rejected simply do not fit our approach. Submission guidelines available online."

GULF COAST

A Journal of Literature and Fine Arts, 4800 Calhoun Rd., Houston TX 77204-3013. (713)743-3223. **E-mail:** editors@gulfcoastmag.org. **Website:** www.gulfcoastmag.org. **Contact:** Luisa Muradyan Tannahill, editor; Michele Nereim, managing editor; Georgia Pearle, digital editor; Henk Rossouw, Dan Chu, and Erika Jo Brown, poetry editors; Alex McElroy, Charlotte Wyatt, and Corey Campbell, fiction editors; Alex Naumann and Nathan Stabenfeldt, nonfiction editors; Jonathan Meyer, online fiction editor; Carolann

Madden, online poetry editor; Melanie Brkich, online nonfiction editor. Estab. 1986.

Magazine: 7x9; approximately 300 pages; stock paper, gloss cover; illustrations; photos.

NEEDS "Please do not send multiple submissions; we will read only 1 submission per author at a given time, except in the case of our annual contests." No children's, genre, religious/inspirational.

HOW TO CONTACT *Gulf Coast* reads general submissions, submitted by post or through the online submissions manager, September 1-March 1. Submissions e-mailed directly to the editors or postmarked March 1-September 1 will not be read or responded to. "Please visit our contest page for contest submission guidelines." Receives 500 unsolicited mss/month. Accepts 6-8 mss/issue; 12-16 mss/year. Agented fiction: 5%. Publishes 2-8 new writers/year. Recently published work by Alan Heathcock, Anne Carson, Bret Anthony Johnston, John D'Agata, Lucie Brock-Broido, Clancy Martin, Steve Almond, Sam Lipsyte, Carl Phillips, Dean Young, and Eula Biss. Publishes short shorts.

PAYMENT/TERMS Pays $50/page.

TIPS "Submit only previously unpublished works. Include a cover letter. Online submissions are strongly preferred. Stories or essays should be typed, double-spaced, and paginated with your name, address, and phone number on the first page and the title on subsequent pages. Poems should have your name, address, and phone number on the first page of each." The Annual Gulf Coast Prizes award publication and $1,500 each in poetry, fiction, and nonfiction; opens in December of each year. Honorable mentions in each category will receive a $250 second prize. Postmark/online entry deadline: March 22 of each year. Winners and honorable mentions will be announced in May. **Entry fee:** $23 (includes one-year subscription). Make checks payable to *Gulf Coast*. Guidelines available on website.

GULF STREAM MAGAZINE

English Department, FIU, Biscayne Bay Campus, 3000 NE 151 St., AC1-335, North Miami FL 33181. **E-mail:** gulfstreamlitmag@gmail.com. **Website:** www.gulfstreamlitmag.com. **Contact:** T.C. Jones, editor in chief. Estab. 1989. "*Gulf Stream Magazine* has been publishing emerging and established writers of exceptional fiction, nonfiction, and poetry since 1989. We also publish interviews and book reviews. Past contributors include Sherman Alexie, Steve Almond, Jan Beatty, Lee Martin, Robert Wrigley, Dennis Lehane, Liz Robbins, Stuart Dybek, David Kirby, Ann Hood, Ha Jin, B.H. Fairchild, Naomi Shihab Nye, F. Daniel Rzicznek, and Connie May Fowler. *Gulf Stream Magazine* is supported by the Creative Writing Program at Florida International University in Miami, Florida."

NEEDS Does not want romance, historical, juvenile, or religious work.

HOW TO CONTACT "Submit online only. Please read guidelines on website in full. Submissions that do not conform to our guidelines will be discarded. We do not accept e-mailed or mailed submissions. We read from September 1-November 1 and January 1-March 1."

PAYMENT/TERMS Pays contributor's copies.

TIPS "We look for fresh, original writing: well-plotted stories with unforgettable characters, fresh poetry, and experimental writing."

HADASSAH MAGAZINE

Hadassah, WZOA, 40 Wall St., Eighth Floor, New York NY 10005. **Fax:** (212)451-6257. **E-mail:** magazine@hadassah.org. **Website:** www.hadassahmagazine.org. **Contact:** Elizabeth Barnea. Bimonthly publication of the Hadassah Women's Zionist Organization of America. Emphasizes Jewish life, Israel. Readers are 85% females who travel and are interested in Jewish affairs, average age 59.

NEEDS Wants short stories with strong plots and positive Jewish values. Receives 20-25 unsolicited mss/month. Publishes some new writers/year. No personal memoirs, "schmaltzy" or shelter magazine fiction. Length: 1,500-2,000 words.

PAYMENT/TERMS Pays $500 minimum.

TIPS "Stories on a Jewish theme should be neither self-hating nor schmaltzy."

HAIGHT ASHBURY LITERARY JOURNAL

558 Joost Ave., San Francisco CA 94127. (415)584-8264. **E-mail:** haljeditor@gmail.com. **Website:** haightashburyliteraryjournal.wordpress.com. **Contact:** Alice Rogoff and Cesar Love, editors. Estab. 1979. *Haight Ashbury Literary Journal*, publishes well-written poetry and fiction. *HALJ*'s voices are often of people who have been marginalized, oppressed, or abused. *HALJ* strives to bring literary arts to the general public, to the San Francisco community of writers, to the Haight Ashbury neighborhood, and to peo-ple of varying ages, genders, ethnic groups, and sexual preferences. The Journal is produced as a tabloid to maintain an accessible price for low-income people.

NEEDS Submit 1-3 short stories or 1 long story. Submit only once every 6 months. No e-mail submissions (unless overseas); postal submissions only. "Put name and address on first page, and include SASE. No bio." Sometimes publishes theme issues (each issue changes its theme and emphasis).

HOW TO CONTACT Submit under 20 pages.

HANGING LOOSE

Hanging Loose Press, 231 Wyckoff St., Brooklyn NY 11217. (347)529-4738. **Fax:** (347)227-8215. **E-mail:** print225@aol.com. **Website:** www.hangingloosepress.com. **Contact:** Robert Hershon and Mark Pawlak, editors. Estab. 1966. *Hanging Loose*, published in April and October, concentrates on the work of new writers. Wants excellent, energetic poems and short stories.

Hanging Loose is 120 pages, offset-printed on heavy stock, flat-spined, with 4-color glossy card cover.

HOW TO CONTACT Submit 1 complete ms by postal mail with SASE.

PAYMENT/TERMS Pays small fee and 2 contributor's copies.

HARPER'S MAGAZINE

666 Broadway, 11th Floor, New York NY 10012. (212)420-5720. **E-mail:** readings@harpers.org; scg@harpers.org. **Website:** www.harpers.org. **Contact:** Ellen Rosenbush, editor. Estab. 1850. *Harper's Magazine* encourages national discussion on current and significant issues in a format that offers arresting facts and intelligent opinions. By means of its several shorter journalistic forms—Harper's Index, Readings, Forum, and Annotation—as well as with its acclaimed essays, fiction, and reporting, *Harper's* continues the tradition begun with its first issue in 1850: to inform readers across the whole spectrum of political, literary, cultural, and scientific affairs.

Harper's Magazine will neither consider nor return unsolicited nonfiction mss that have not been preceded by a written query. *Harper's* will consider unsolicited fiction. Unsolicited poetry will not be considered or returned. No queries or mss will be considered unless they are accompanied by a SASE. All submissions and written queries (with the exception of Readings submissions) must be sent by mail to above address.

NEEDS Will consider unsolicited fiction. Has published work by Rebecca Curtis, George Saunders, Haruki Murakami, Margaret Atwood, Allan Gurganus, Evan Connell, and Dave Bezmosgis. Length: 3,000-5,000 words.

HOW TO CONTACT Submit complete ms by postal mail.

PAYMENT/TERMS Generally pays 50¢-$1/word.

TIPS "Some readers expect their magazines to clothe them with opinions in the way that Bloomingdale's dresses them for the opera. The readers of *Harper's Magazine* belong to a different crowd. They strike me as the kind of people who would rather think in their own voices and come to their own conclusions."

HARPUR PALATE

English Department, Binghamton University, P.O. Box 6000, Binghamton NY 13902-6000. **E-mail:** harpur.palate@gmail.com. **Website:** harpurpalate.com. **Contact:** Heather Humphrey, editor in chief; Bernadette Roe, nonfiction editor; Brian Kelly, poetry editor; Amanda Biltucci, poetry edito. Estab. 2000. *Harpur Palate*, published biannually, is "dedicated to publishing the best poetry and prose, regardless of style, form, or genre. We have no restrictions on subject matter or form. Quite simply, send us your highest-quality fiction and poetry."

Submission periods are September 1-November 15 for the Winter issue and February 1-April 15 for the Summer issue.

NEEDS Receives 400 unsolicited mss/month. Accepts 5-10 mss/issue; 12-20 mss/year. Publishes 5 new writers/year. Has published work by Darryl Crawford and Tim Hedges, Jesse Goolsby, Ivan Faute, and Keith Meatto. Does not accept novel excerpts. Length: up to 6,000 words.

HOW TO CONTACT Prefers submissions through online submissions manager, or send complete ms by postal mail with SASE. No more than 1 submission per envelope.

PAYMENT/TERMS Pays 2 contributor copies.

TIPS "We are interested in high-quality writing of all genres but especially literary poetry and fiction. We also sponsor a fiction contest for the Summer issue and a poetry and nonfiction contest for the Winter issue with $500 prizes."

HARVARD REVIEW

Harvard University, Lamont Library, Harvard University, Cambridge MA 02138. (617)495-9775. **E-mail:** info@harvardreview.org. **Website:** harvardreview.fas.harvard.edu. **Contact:** Christina Thompson, editor; Suzanne Berne, fiction editor; Major Jackson, poetry editor; Chloe Garcia Roberts, managing editor. Estab. 1992. Semiannual magazine covering poetry, fiction, essays, drama, graphics, and reviews in the spring and fall by an eclectic range of international writers. "Previous contributors include John Updike, Alice Hoffman, Joyce Carol Oates, Miranda July, and Jim Crace. We also publish the work of emerging and previously unpublished writers." Does not accept e-mail submissions. Reading period: November 1-May 31.

NEEDS No genre fiction (romance, horror, detective, etc.). Length: up to 7,000 words.

HOW TO CONTACT Submit by online submissions manager or mail (with SASE).

TIPS "Writers at all stages of their careers are invited to apply; however, we can only publish a very small fraction of the material we receive. We recommend that you familiarize yourself with *Harvard Review* before you submit your work."

HAWAI'I PACIFIC REVIEW

1060 Bishop St., Honolulu HI 96813. **Website:** hawaiipacificreview.org. **Contact:** Tyler McMahon, editor; Christa Cushon, managing editor. Estab. 1987. "*Hawai'i Pacific Review* is the online literary magazine of Hawai'i Pacific University. It features poetry and prose by authors from Hawai'i, the mainland, and around the world. *HPR* was started as a print annual in 1987. In 2013, it began to publish exclusively online. *HPR* publishes work on a rolling basis. Poems, stories, and essays are posted 1 piece at a time, several times a month. All contents are archived on the site."

NEEDS Prefers literary work to genre work. Length: up to 4,000 words.

HOW TO CONTACT Submit 1 ms via online submissions manager.

TIPS "We look for the unusual or original plot, and prose with the texture and nuance of poetry. Character development or portrayal must be unusual/original; humanity shown in an original, insightful way (or characters); sense of humor where applicable. Be sure it's a draft that has gone through substantial changes, with supervision from a more experienced writer, if you're a beginner. Write about intense emotion and feeling, not just about someone's divorce or shaky relationship. No soap-opera-like fiction."

HAWAI'I REVIEW

University of Hawaii Board of Publications, 2445 Campus Rd., Hemenway Hall 107, Honolulu HI 96822. (808)956-3030. **Fax:** (808)956-3083. **E-mail:** hawaiireview@gmail.com. **Website:** http://hawaiireview.org/. Estab. 1973. *Hawai'i Review* is a student-run biannual literary and visual arts print journal featuring national and international writing and visual art, as well as regional literature and visual art of Hawai'i and the Pacific.

○ Accepts submissions online through Submittable only. Offers yearly award with $500 prizes in poetry and fiction.

NEEDS Length: up to 7,000 words for short stories, up to 2,500 words for flash fiction.

HOW TO CONTACT Send 1 short story or 2 pieces of flash fiction via online submission manager.

TIPS "Make it new."

HAYDEN'S FERRY REVIEW

Arizona State University, c/o Dept. of English,, Arizona State University, P.O. Box 870302, Tempe AZ 85287. **E-mail:** hfr@asu.edu. **Website:** haydensferryreview.com. **Contact:** Editorial staff changes every year; see website for current masthead. Estab. 1986. "*Hayden's Ferry Review* publishes the best-quality fiction, poetry, and creative nonfiction from new, emerging, and established writers." Work from *Hayden's Ferry Review* has been selected for inclusion in *Pushcart Prize* anthologies and *Best Creative Nonfiction*. No longer accepts postal mail or e-mail submissions (except in the case of the incarcerated and the visually impaired).

NEEDS Does not want genre fiction. Word length open, but typically does not accept submissions over 25 pages.

HOW TO CONTACT Send complete ms via online submissions manager.

PAYMENT/TERMS Pays 1 contributor's copy.

HEARING HEALTH

Hearing Health Foundation, 363 Seventh Ave., 10th Floor, New York NY 10001. (866)454-3924. **E-mail:** info@hhf.org. **E-mail:** info@hearinghealthfoundation.org. **Website:** www.hearinghealthfoundation.org. **Contact:** Yishane Lee, editor. Magazine covering issues and concerns pertaining to hearing health and hearing loss.

NEEDS All submissions should reflect the publication's mission: to raise awareness of real-world applications of hearing-related research, technology, and trends and to educate people about the effects of hearing loss on health and quality of life.

HOW TO CONTACT Send complete ms by e-mail (preferred), mail electronic files on a disk or CD, or fax ms.

PAYMENT/TERMS Pays contributor's copies.

HELIOTROPE

E-mail: heliotropeditor@gmail.com. **Website:** www.heliotropemag.com. Estab. 2006. *Heliotrope* is a quarterly e-zine that publishes fiction, articles, and poetry.

NEEDS "If your story is something we can't label, we're interested in that, too." Length: up to 5,000 words.

HOW TO CONTACT Submit complete ms via e-mail.

PAYMENT/TERMS Pays 10¢/word.

THE HELIX

Central Connecticut State University, 1615 Stanley St., New Britain CT 06053. **E-mail:** helixmagazine@gmail.com. **Website:** helixmagazine.org. **Contact:** See website for current editorial staff. "The *Helix* is a Central Connecticut State University undergraduate publication that puts out an issue every semester. The magazine features writing from CCSU students, writing from the Hartford County community, and an array of submissions from all over the world. The magazine publishes multiple genres of literature and art, including poetry, fiction, drama, nonfiction, paintings, photography, watercolor, collage, stencil, and computer-generated artwork. It is a student-run publication and is funded by the university."

NEEDS Length: up to 3,000 words.

HOW TO CONTACT Submit by online submissions manager.

TIPS "Please see our website for specific deadlines, as it changes every semester based on a variety of factors, but we typically leave the submission manager open sometime starting in the summer to around the end of October for the Fall issue, and during the winter to late February or mid-March for the Spring issue. Contributions are invited from all members of the campus community, as well as the literary community at large."

HELLOHORROR

Houston TX (512)537-0504. **E-mail:** info@hello-horror.com. **E-mail:** submissions@hellohorror.com. **Website:** www.hellohorror.com. **Contact:** Brent Armour, editor-in-chief. Estab. 2012. "*HelloHorror* is an online literary magazine. We are currently in search of literary pieces, photography, and visual art, including film from writers and artists that have a special knack for inducing goose bumps and raised hairs. This genre has become, especially in film, noticeably saturated in gore and high shock-value aspects as a crutch to avoid the true challenge of bringing about real psychological fear to an audience that's persistently more and more numb to its tactics. While we are not opposed to the extreme, blood and guts need bones and cartilage. Otherwise it's just a sloppy mess. Specifically, we are looking for pieces grounded in psychological fear induced by surreal situations unusual to horror rather than gore. We will not automatically pass on a gore-drenched story, but it needs to have its foundations in psychological horror."

NEEDS "We don't want fiction that can in no way be classified as horror. Some types of dark science fiction are acceptable, depending on the story." Length: 6-20 pages for short stories; up to 1,000 words for flash fiction.

HOW TO CONTACT Submit complete ms via e-mail.

TIPS "We like authors that show consideration for their readers. A great horror story leaves an impression on the reader long after it is finished. Consider your reader and consider yourself. What really scares you as opposed to what's stereotypically supposed to scare you? Bring us and our readers into that place of fear with you."

HIGHLIGHTS FOR CHILDREN

803 Church St., Honesdale PA 18431. (570)253-1080. **Fax:** (570)251-7847. **E-mail:** eds@highlights.com (Do not send submissions to this address.). **E-mail:** Highlights.submittable.com. **Website:** www.highlights.com. **Contact:** Christine French Cully, Editor in Chief. Estab. 1946. "This book of wholesome fun is dedicated to helping children grow in basic skills and knowledge, in creativeness, in ability to think and reason, in sensitivity to others, in high ideals, and worthy ways of living—for children are the world's most important people. We publish stories and articles for beginning and advanced readers. Up to 400 words for beginning readers, up to 750 words for advanced readers."

NEEDS Stories appealing to girls and boys ages 6-12. Vivid, full of action. Engaging plot, strong characterization, lively language. Prefers stories in which a child protagonist solves a dilemma through his or her own resources. No stories glorifying war, crime or violence. Up to 475 words for beginning readers. Up to 750 words for advanced readers.

HOW TO CONTACT See Highlights.submittable.com.

PAYMENT/TERMS Pays $175 and up.

TIPS "We update our guidelines and current needs regularly at Highlights.submittable.com. Read several recent issues of the magazine before submitting. In addition to fiction, nonfiction, and poetry, we purchase crafts, puzzles, and activities that will stimulate children mentally and creatively. We judge each submission on its own merits. Expert reviews and complete bibliography are required for nonfiction. Include special qualifications, if any, of author. Speak to today's kids. Avoid didactic, overt messages. Even though our general principles haven't changed over the years, we are contemporary in our approach to issues."

ALFRED HITCHCOCK'S MYSTERY MAGAZINE

Dell Magazines, 44 Wall St., Suite 904, New York NY 10005. **E-mail:** alfredhitchcockmm@dellmagazines.com. **Website:** www.themysteryplace.com/ahmm. Estab. 1956.

NEEDS Wants "original and well-written mystery and crime fiction. Because this is a mystery magazine, the stories we buy must fall into that genre in some sense or another. We are interested in nearly every kind of mystery: stories of detection of the classic kind, police procedurals, private eye tales, suspense, courtroom dramas, stories of espionage, and so on. We ask only that the story be about crime (or the threat or fear of one). We sometimes accept ghost stories or supernatural tales, but those also should involve a crime." No sensationalism. Length: up to 12,000 words.

HOW TO CONTACT Send complete ms.

PAYMENT/TERMS Payment varies.

TIPS "No simultaneous submissions, please. Submissions sent to *Alfred Hitchcock's Mystery Magazine* are not considered for or read by *Ellery Queen's Mystery Magazine*, and vice versa."

HOBART

P.O. Box 1658, Ann Arbor MI 48103. **E-mail:** aaron@hobartpulp.com. **Website:** www.hobartpulp.com. **Contact:** Aaron Burch, editor. Also accepts comics submissions; see online examples. "We tend to like quirky stories like truck driving, mathematics, and vagabonding. We like stories with humor (humorous but engaging, literary but not stuffy). We want to get excited about your story and hope you'll send your best work."

○ All submissions must go through online submissions manager. Only accepting submissions for online journal.

NEEDS "We publish nonstuffy, unpretentious, high-quality fiction that never takes itself too serious and always entertains." Length: up to 2,000 words; prefers submissions of about 1,000 words.

HOW TO CONTACT Submit complete ms via online submissions manager.

TIPS "We'd love to receive fewer run-of-the-mill relationship stories and more stories concerning truck drivers, lumberjacks, carnival workers, and gunslingers. In other words, surprise us. Show us a side of life rarely depicted in literary fiction."

HOME PLANET NEWS ONLINE

E-mail: homeplanetnewsol@gmail.com. **Website:** homeplanetnews.org/AOnLine.html. **Contact:** Frank Murphy, chief editor. Estab. 1979. *Home Planet News* publishes mainly poetry along with some fiction, as well as reviews (books, theater, and art) and articles of literary interest. Home Planet News Online was created when the print edition could no longer be published. Donald Lev ask Frank Murphy (who had been doing an online version of some of the magazine) to continue the magazine online. We have just finished our 5th Issue.

NEEDS Length: 500-2,500 words; average length: 2,000 words.

TIPS "Read an Issue before sending in to us. It will give you an idea of what we are looking for."

⑨ HOOT

A Postcard Review of (Mini) Poetry and Prose, 4234 Chestnut St., Apt. 1 R, Philadelphia PA 19104. **E-mail:** info@hootreview.com. **Website:** www.hootreview.com. **Contact:** Jane-Rebecca Cannarella, editor in chief; Amanda Vacharat and Dorian Geisler, editors/co-founders. Estab. 2011. *HOOT* publishes 1 piece of writing, designed with original art and/or photographs, on the front of a postcard every month, as well as 2-3 pieces online. The postcards are intended for sharing, to be hung on the wall, etc. Therefore, *HOOT* looks for very brief, surprising-yet-gimmick-free writing that can stand on its own, that also follows "The Refrigerator Rule"—something that you would hang on your refrigerator and would want to read and look at for a whole month. This rule applies to online content as well.

○ Costs $2 to submit up to 2 pieces of work. Submit through online submissions manager or postal mail.

NEEDS Length: up to 150 words.

HOW TO CONTACT Submit complete ms.

PAYMENT/TERMS Pays $10-100 for print publication.

TIPS "We look for writing with audacity and zest from authors who are not afraid to take risks. We appreciate work that is able to go beyond mere description in its 150 words. We offer free online workshops every other Wednesday for authors who would like feedback on their work from the *HOOT* editors. We also often give feedback with our rejections. We publish roughly 6-10 new writers each year."

HORIZONS MAGAZINE

Presbyterian Women in the PC(USA), Inc., 100 Witherspoon St., Louisville KY 40202. (844)797-2872. **E-mail:** yvonne.hileman@pcusa.org. **Website:** www.presbyterianwomen.org. **Contact:** Yvonne Hileman, assistant editor. Estab. 1988. *Horizons* magazine provides information, inspiration, and education from the perspectives of women who are committed to Christ, the church, and faithful discipleship. *Horizons* brings current issues dealing with family life, the mission of the church, and the challenges of culture and society to its readers. Interviews, feature articles, Bible study resources, and departments offer help and insight for up-to-date, day-to-day concerns of the church and individual Christians.

TIPS See www.presbyterianwomen.org/horizons for writer guidelines and themes. The magazine has a Reformed theological perspective.

HOTEL AMERIKA

Columbia College Chicago, The Department of Creative Writing, 600 S. Michigan Ave., Chicago IL 60605.

(312)369-8175. **Website:** www.hotelamerika.net. **Contact:** David Lazar, editor; Jenn Tatum, managing editor. Estab. 2002. *Hotel Amerika* is a venue for both well-known and emerging writers. Publishes exceptional writing in all forms. Strives to house the most unique and provocative poetry, fiction, and nonfiction available.

Mss will be considered between September 1 and May 1. Materials received after May 1 and before September 1 will be returned unread. Work published in *Hotel Amerika* has been included in *The Pushcart Prize* and *The Best American Poetry*, and featured on *Poetry Daily*.

NEEDS Welcomes submissions in all genres of creative writing, generously defined. Does not publish book reviews as such, although considers review-like essays that transcend the specific objects of consideration.

HOW TO CONTACT Submit complete ms through online submissions manager.

THE HUDSON REVIEW

33 W. 67th St., New York NY 10023. (212)650-0020. **E-mail:** info@hudsonreview.com. **Website:** hudsonreview.com. **Contact:** Paula Deitz, editor. Estab. 1948. Since its beginning, the magazine has dealt with the area where literature bears on the intellectual life of the time and on diverse aspects of American culture. It has no university affiliation and is not committed to any narrow academic aim or to any particular political perspective. The magazine serves as a major forum for the work of new writers and for the exploration of new developments in literature and the arts. It has a distinguished record of publishing little-known or undiscovered writers, many of whom have become major literary figures. Each issue contains a wide range of material including poetry, fiction, essays on literary and cultural topics, book reviews, reports from abroad, and chronicles covering film, theater, dance, music, and art. *The Hudson Review* is distributed in 25 countries. Unsolicited mss are read according to the following schedule: April 1 through June 30 for poetry, September 1 through November 30 for fiction, and January 1 through March 31 for nonfiction.

NEEDS If you go through our archives, most of the short stories fall into the nebulous category of "literary fiction." Many stories have elements of mystery, romance, historical fiction, etc. For novel excerpts, we ask that the work be able to stand on its own. For genre stories, we ask that the work go beyond its genre—a religious story would have to be more than a conversion narrative or cautionary tale; a comic story would ideally have a little pathos; a romance or mystery or sci-fi story would have some ambiguities or aesthetic concerns or experimentation. In general, we want stories that a writer has put a lot of thought into, and that readers will think about long after they've finished. Length: up to 10,000 words.

HOW TO CONTACT Send complete ms by mail or online submissions manager from **September 1 through November 30** only.

TIPS "We do not specialize in publishing any particular 'type' of writing; our sole criterion for accepting unsolicited work is literary quality. The best way for you to get an idea of the range of work we publish is to read a current issue. Unsolicited mss submitted outside of specified reading times will be returned unread. Do not send submissions via e-mail."

⑤ HUNGER MOUNTAIN

Vermont College of Fine Arts, 36 College St., Montpelier VT 05602. (802)828-8517. **E-mail:** hungermtn@vcfa.edu. **Website:** www.hungermtn.org. **Contact:** Cameron Finch, managing editor. Estab. 2002. Accepts high-quality work from unknown, emerging, or successful writers. Publishing fiction, creative nonfiction, poetry, and young adult & children's writing. Four writing contests annually. *Hunger Mountain* is a print and online journal of the arts. The print journal is about 200 pages, 7x9, professionally printed, perfect-bound, with full-bleed color artwork on cover. Press run is 1,000. Over 10,000 visits online monthly. Uses online submissions manager (Submittable). Member: CLMP.

NEEDS "We look for work that is beautifully crafted and tells a good story, with characters that are alive and kicking, storylines that stay with us long after we've finished reading, and sentences that slay us with their precision." No genre fiction, meaning science fiction, fantasy, horror, detective, erotic, etc. Length: up to 10,000 words.

HOW TO CONTACT Submit ms using online submissions manager: https://hungermtn.submittable.com/submit.

PAYMENT/TERMS Pays $50 for general fiction.

TIPS "Mss must be typed, prose double-spaced. Poets submit poems as one document. No multiple genre submissions. Fresh viewpoints and human interest are very important, as is originality and diversity. We are committed to publishing an outstanding journal of the arts. Do not send entire novels, mss, or short story collections. Do not send previously published work."

I-70 REVIEW

Writing from the Middle and Beyond, 913 Joseph Dr., Lawrence KS 66049. **E-mail:** i70review@gmail.com. **Website:** www.fieldinfoserv.com. **Contact:** Gary Lechliter, Maryfrances Wagner, Greg Field, and Gay Dust, editors; Jan Duncan-O'Neal editor emeritus. Estab. 1998. *I-70 Review* is an annual literary magazine. "Our interests lie in writing grounded in fresh language, imagery, and metaphor. We prefer free verse in which the writer pays attention to the sound and rhythm of the language. We appreciate poetry with individual voice and a good lyric or a strong narrative. In fiction, we like short pieces that are surprising and uncommon. We want writing that captures the human spirit with unusual topics or familiar topics with different perspective or approaches. We reject stereotypical and clichéd writing, as well as sentimental work or writing that summarizes and tells instead of shows. We look for writing that pays attention to words, sentences, and style. We publish literary writing. We do not publish anything erotic, religious, or political." Open submission period is July 1-December 31.

NEEDS Rejects anything over 1,500 words, unless solicited. Not interested in anything political, religious, spiritual, didactic, or erotic. Accepts mainly flash fiction and very short literary fiction. Pays in contributor copies. Length: up to 1,500 words.

HOW TO CONTACT Submit complete ms by e-mail.

PAYMENT/TERMS Pays contributor copies.

TIPS "Read a copy of the issue or check our website to see writers we've featured to get a good idea of what we publish."

ICONOCLAST

1675 Amazon Rd., Mohegan Lake NY 10547-1804. **Website:** www.iconoclastliterarymagazine.com. **Contact:** Phil Wagner, editor and publisher. Estab. 1992. *Iconoclast* seeks and chooses the best new writing and poetry available—of all genres and styles and entertainment levels. Its mission is to provide a serious publishing opportunity for unheralded, unknown, but deserving creators, whose work is often overlooked or trampled in the commercial, university, or Internet marketplace.

NEEDS "Subjects and styles are completely open (within the standards of generally accepted taste—though exceptions, as always, can be made for unique and visionary works)." No slice-of-life stories, stories containing alcoholism, incest, and domestic or public violence. Accepts most genres, "with the exception of mysteries."

HOW TO CONTACT Submit by mail; include SASE. Cover letter not necessary.

PAYMENT/TERMS Pays 1¢/word and 2 contributor's copies. Contributors get 40% discount on extra copies.

TIPS "Please don't send preliminary drafts—rewriting is half the job. If you're not sure about the story, don't truly believe in it, or are unenthusiastic about the subject (we will not recycle your term papers or thesis), then don't send it. This is not a lottery (luck has nothing to do with it)."

THE IDAHO REVIEW

Boise State University, 1910 University Dr., Boise ID 83725. **E-mail:** mwieland@boisestate.edu. **Website:** idahoreview.org. **Contact:** Mitch Wieland, editor. Estab. 1998. *The Idaho Review* is the literary journal of Boise State University. Recent stories appearing in *The Idaho Review* have been reprinted in *The Best American Short Stories, The O. Henry Prize Stories, The Pushcart Prize*, and *New Stories from the South*. Recent contributors include Joyce Carol Oates, Rick Moody, Ann Beattie, T.C. Boyle, and Joy Williams. Reading period: September 15-March 15.

NEEDS No genre fiction of any type. Length: up to 25 double-spaced pages.

HOW TO CONTACT Submit through online submissions manager.

PAYMENT/TERMS Pays $300-$500/story and contributor's copies.

TIPS "We look for strongly crafted work that tells a story that needs to be told. We demand vision and intelligence and mystery in the fiction we publish."

IDIOM 23

Central Queensland University, P.O. Box 172, 554-700 Yaamba Rd., Rockhampton QLD 4702, Australia. **E-mail:** idiom@cqu.edu.au; n.anae@cqu.edu.au. **Website:** www.cqu.edu.au/idiom23. **Contact:** Dr. Nicole Anae, editor. Estab. 1988. *Idiom 23*, published annually, is "named for the Tropic of Capricorn and is dedicated to developing the literary arts throughout the Central Queensland region. Submissions of original short stories, poems, articles, and b&w drawings and photographs are welcomed by the editorial collective. *Idiom 23* is not limited to a particular viewpoint but, on the contrary, hopes to encourage and publish a broad spectrum of writing. The collective seeks out creative work from community groups with as varied backgrounds as possible."

NEEDS Length: up to 3,000 words.

HOW TO CONTACT Submit complete ms via online submissions manager.

ILLUMINATIONS

Department of English, College of Charleston, 66 George St., Charleston SC 29424-0001. (843)953-1920. **E-mail:** illuminations@cofc.edu. **Website:** illuminations.cofc.edu. **Contact:** Simon Lewis, editor. Estab. 1982. "Over these many years, *Illuminations* has remained consistently true to its mission statement to publish new writers alongside some of the world's finest, including Nadine Gordimer, James Merrill, Carol Ann Duffy, Dennis Brutus, Allen Tate, interviews with Tim O'Brien, and letters from Flannery O'Connor and Ezra Pound. A number of new poets whose early work appeared in *Illuminations* have gone on to win prizes and accolades, and we at *Illuminations* sincerely value the chance to promote the work of emerging writers."

○ "As a magazine devoted primarily to poetry, we publish only 1-2 pieces of short fiction and/or nonfiction in any given year, and sometimes publish none at all. "

HOW TO CONTACT Submit complete ms by mail, e-mail, or online submissions manager.

PAYMENT/TERMS Pays 2 contributor's copies of current issue and 1 copy of subsequent issue.

⊙ IMAGE

3307 Third Ave. W., Seattle WA 98119. (206)281-2988. **Fax:** (206)281-2979. **E-mail:** image@imagejournal.org. **Website:** www.imagejournal.org. **Contact:** Gregory Wolfe, publisher and editor. Estab. 1989. "*Image* is a unique forum for the best writing and artwork that is informed by—or grapples with—religious faith. We have never been interested in art that merely regurgitates dogma or falls back on easy answers or didacticism. Instead, our focus has been on writing and visual artwork that embody a spiritual struggle, that seek

to strike a balance between tradition and a profound openness to the world. Each issue explores this relationship through outstanding fiction, poetry, painting, sculpture, architecture, film, music, interviews, and dance. *Image* also features 4-color reproductions of visual art." Magazine: 7×10; 136 pages; glossy cover stock; illustrations; photos.

NEEDS No sentimental, preachy, moralistic, obvious stories, or genre stories (unless they manage to transcend their genre). Length: 3,000-6,000 words.

HOW TO CONTACT Send complete ms by postal mail (with SASE for reply or return of ms) or online submissions manager at www.imagejournal.org/journal/submit. Does not accept e-mail submissions.

PAYMENT/TERMS Pays $20/page and 4 contributor's copies.

TIPS "Fiction must grapple with religious faith, though subjects need not be overtly religious."

⊙ INDIANA REVIEW

Ballantine Hall 529, 1020 E. Kirkwood Ave., Indiana University, Bloomington IN 47405. **E-mail:** inreview@indiana.edu. **Website:** indianareview.org. **Contact:** See masthead for current editorial staff. Estab. 1976. "*Indiana Review*, a nonprofit organization run by IU graduate students, is a journal of innovative fiction, nonfiction, and poetry. We're interested in energy, originality, and careful attention to craft. While we publish many well-known authors, we also welcome new and emerging poets and fiction writers." See website for open reading periods.

NEEDS "We look for daring stories which integrate theme, language, character, and form. We like polished writing, humor, and fiction which has consequence beyond the world of its narrator." No genre fiction. Length: up to 8,000 words.

HOW TO CONTACT Submit via online submissions manager.

PAYMENT/TERMS Pays $5/page ($10 minimum), plus 2 contributor's copies.

TIPS "We're always looking for more nonfiction. We enjoy essays that go beyond merely autobiographical revelation and utilize sophisticated organization and slightly radical narrative strategies. We want essays that are both lyrical and analytical, where confession does not mean nostalgia. Read us before you submit. Back issues are available for $10. Our most recent issues have online previews available for free and accessible through the "Shop" page on our website. Often reading is slower in summer and holiday months. Submit work that 'stacks up' with the work we've published."

INTERNATIONAL EXAMINER

409 Maynard Ave. S., #203, Seattle WA 98104. (206)624-3925. **Fax:** (206)624-3046. **E-mail:** editor@ iexaminer.org. **Website:** www.iexaminer.org. **Contact:** Travis Quezon, editor in chief. Estab. 1974. "*International Examiner* is about Asian American issues and things of interest to Asian Americans. We do not want stuff about Asian things (stories on your trip to China, Japanese Tea Ceremony, etc. will be rejected). Yes, we are in English."

NEEDS Asian American authored fiction by or about Asian Americans only.

HOW TO CONTACT Query.

TIPS "Write decent, suitable material on a subject of interest to the Asian American community. All submissions are reviewed; all good ones are contacted. It helps to call and run an idea by the editor before or after sending submissions."

⬤ INTERPRETER'S HOUSE

'Scrimshaw', 63 Strait Path, Gardenstown Aberdeenshire AB45 3ZQ, Scotland. **E-mail:** theinterpretershouse@aol.com. **Website:** www.theinterpretershouse.com. **Contact:** Martin Malone, editor. Estab. 1996. *The Interpreter's House*, published 3 times/year spring, summer, and autumn, prints short stories and poetry. Submission windows: October for the Spring issue, February for the Summer issue, June for the Autumn issue.

NEEDS Length: up to 2,000 words.

HOW TO CONTACT Submit up to 2 short stories by mail (with SASE) or e-mail.

PAYMENT/TERMS Pays contributor's copies.

⬤ THE IOWA REVIEW

308 EPB, The University of Iowa, Iowa City IA 52242. (319)335-0462. **E-mail:** iowa-review@uiowa.edu. **Website:** www.iowareview.org. **Contact:** Harilaos Stecopoulos. Estab. 1970. *The Iowa Review*, published 3 times/year, prints fiction, poetry, essays, reviews, and, occasionally, interviews. Receives about 5,000 submissions/year, accepts up to 100. Press run is 2,900; 1,500 distributed to stores.

◗ This magazine uses the help of colleagues and graduate assistants. Its reading period for unsolicited work is September 1-December 1.

From January through April, the editors read entries to the annual Iowa Review Awards competition. Check the website for further information.

NEEDS "We are open to a range of styles and voices and always hope to be surprised by work we then feel we need." Receives 600 unsolicited mss/month. Accepts 4-6 mss/issue; 12-18 mss/year. Does not read mss January-August. Publishes ms an average of 12-18 months after acceptance. Agented fiction less than 2%. **Publishes some new writers/year.** Recently published work by Johanna Hunting, Bennett Sims, and Pedro Mairal.

HOW TO CONTACT Send complete ms with cover letter. Don't bother with queries. SASE for return of ms. Accepts mss by snail mail (SASE required for response) and online submission form at iowareview. submittable.com/submit; no e-mail submissions.

PAYMENT/TERMS Pays 8¢/word ($100 minimum), plus 2 contributor's copies.

TIPS "We publish essays, reviews, novel excerpts, stories, poems, and photography. We have no set guidelines regarding content but strongly recommend that writers read a sample issue before submitting."

IRIS

E-mail: submissions@creatingiris.org. **E-mail:** editorial@creatingiris.org. **Website:** www.creatingiris. org. Estab. 2014. "*Iris* seeks works of fiction and poetry that speak to LGBT young adults and their allies. We are interested in creative, thoughtful, original work that engages our young readers. We seek writing that challenges them and makes them think. We're looking for stories that capture their imaginations and characters that are relatable. We think there's a need in the young adult literary market for writing that speaks to the everyday experiences of LGBT adolescents: Themes of identity, friendship, coming out, families, etc., are especially welcome. The protagonist need not identify as LGBT, but we do ask that there be some kind of LGBT angle to your story. We welcome all genres of fiction and poetry!"

◗ "Because we publish for a young demographic, work submitted to *Iris* may not include depictions of sex, drug use, and violence. They can certainly be discussed and referenced, but not directly portrayed."

NEEDS Length: up to 3,000 words.

HOW TO CONTACT Submit complete ms via e-mail as attachment. Include cover letter in text of e-mail.

ISLAND

Island Magazine, P.O. Box 4703, Hobart Tasmania 7000, Australia. (+61)(03)6234-1462. **E-mail:** admin@islandmag.com. **Website:** www.islandmag.com. **Contact:** Kate Harrison, general manager. Estab. 1979. *Island* seeks quality fiction, poetry, and essays. It is "one of Australia's leading literary magazines, tracing the contours of our national, and international, culture while still retaining a uniquely Tasmanian perspective." Only publishes the work of subscribers; you can submit if you are not currently a subscriber, but if your piece is chosen, the subscription will be taken from the fee paid for the piece.

NEEDS "Although we are not strict about word limits, we tend not to publish flash fiction or microfiction at time. In terms of upper limits, we are less likely to publish works longer than 5,000 words. This is a general guideline: We do not have a formal cut-off for submissions. However, please be aware that if you submit a work longer than 4,000 words, we may not read beyond this length if we feel certain the work is not suited for publication with us."

HOW TO CONTACT Submit 1 piece via online submissions manager.

PAYMENT/TERMS Pay varies.

JABBERWOCK REVIEW

Department of English, Mississippi State University, Drawer E, Mississippi State MS 39762. **E-mail:** jabberwockreview@english.msstate.edu. **Website:** www.jabberwock.org.msstate.edu. **Contact:** Becky Hagenston, editor. Estab. 1979. *Jabberwock Review* is a literary journal published semi-annually by students and faculty of Mississippi State University. The journal consists of poetry, fiction, and nonfiction from around the world. Funding is provided by the Office of the Provost, the College of Arts & Sciences, the Shackouls Honors College, the Department of English, and subscriptions. Submissions accepted August 15-October 20 and January 15-March 15.

NEEDS Does not publish romance or erotica. There is no word limit, but we rarely publish works of more than 30 pages. The entire journal is about 100 pages.

HOW TO CONTACT Submit no more than 1 story at a time.

PAYMENT/TERMS Pays contributor's copies.

TIPS "It might take a few months to get a response from us, but your work will be read with care. Our editors enjoy reading submissions (really!) and will remember writers who are persistent and committed to getting a story 'right' through revision."

JACK AND JILL

U.S. Kids, P.O. Box 88928, Indianapolis IN 46208. (317)634-1100. **E-mail:** jackandjill@uskidsmags.com. **Website:** www.uskidsmags.com. Estab. 1938. *Jack and Jill* is an award-winning magazine for children ages 6-12. It promotes the healthy educational and creative growth of children through interactive activities and articles. The pages are designed to spark a child's curiosity in a wide range of topics through articles, games, and activities. Inside you will find: current real-world topics in articles in stories; challenging puzzles and games; and interactive entertainment through experimental crafts and recipes. Please do not send artwork. "We prefer to work with professional illustrators of our own choosing. Write entertaining and imaginative stories for kids, not just about them. Writers should understand what is funny to kids, what's important to them, what excites them. Don't write from an adult 'kids are so cute' perspective. We're also looking for health and healthful lifestyle stories and articles, but don't be preachy."

NEEDS Submit complete ms via postal mail; no e-mail submissions. The tone of the stories should be fun and engaging. Stories should hook readers right from the get-go and pull them through the story. Humor is very important! Dialogue should be witty instead of just furthering the plot. The story should convey some kind of positive message. Possible themes could include self-reliance, being kind to others, appreciating other cultures, and so on. There are a million positive messages, so get creative! Kids can see preachy coming from a mile away, though, so please focus on telling a good story over teaching a lesson. The message—if there is one—should come organically from the story and not feel tacked on. Length: 600-800 words.

PAYMENT/TERMS Pays $25 minimum.

TIPS "We are constantly looking for new writers who can tell good stories with interesting slants—stories that are not full of outdated and time-worn expressions. We like to see stories about kids who are smart and capable but not sarcastic or smug. Problem-solving skills, personal responsibility, and integrity are good topics for us. Obtain current issues of the magazine and study them to determine our present needs and editorial style."

JERRY JAZZ MUSICIAN

2207 NE Broadway, Portland OR 97232. **Website:** www.jerryjazzmusician.com. Estab. 1997. *"Jerry Jazz Musician's* mission is to explore the culture of 20th-century America with, as noted jazz critic Nat Hentoff wrote, 'jazz as the centerpiece.' We focus on publishing content geared toward readers with interests in jazz music, its rich history, and the culture it influenced—and was influenced by. We regularly publish original interviews, poetry, literature, and art, and encourage readers to share their own perspectives."

JEWISH CURRENTS

P.O. Box 111, Accord NY 12404. (845)626-2427. **E-mail:** editor@jewishcurrents.org. **Website:** jewishcurrents.org. **Contact:** Lawrence Bush, editor; Jacob Plitman, associate editor. Estab. 1946. *Jewish Currents*, published 4 times/year, is a progressive Jewish quarterly magazine that carries on the insurgent tradition of the Jewish left through independent journalism, political commentary, and a 'countercultural' approach to Jewish arts and literature. Our website is an active magazine in its own right, with new material published daily. *Jewish Currents* is 88 pages, magazine-sized, offset-printed, saddle-stapled with a full-color arts section, "JCultcha & Funny Pages." The Winter issue is a 12-month arts calendar.

HOW TO CONTACT Send complete ms with cover letter. "Writers should include brief biographical information."

PAYMENT/TERMS Pays contributor's copies or small honoraria.

J JOURNAL: NEW WRITING ON JUSTICE

524 W. 59th St., Seventh Floor, New York NY 10019. (212)237-8697. **E-mail:** jjournal@jjay.cuny.edu. **E-mail:** submissionsjjournal@gmail.com. **Website:** www.jjournal.org. **Contact:** Adam Berlin and Jeffrey Heiman, editors. Estab. 2008. *"J Journal* publishes literary fiction, creative nonfiction, and poetry on the justice theme—social, political, criminal, gender, racial, religious, economic. While the justice theme is specific, it need not dominate the work. We're interested in innovative writing that examines justice from all creative perspectives. Tangential connections to justice are often better than direct." Several works

from *J Journal* have been recognized in *Pushcart Prize* anthologies.

NEEDS Receives 100 mss/month. Accepts 5-8 mss/issue; 10-16 mss/year. Length: 750-6,000 words. Average length: 4,000 words.

HOW TO CONTACT Send complete ms with cover letter. Include estimated word count, brief bio, list of publications.

PAYMENT/TERMS Pays 2 contributor's copies. Additional copies $10.

TIPS "We're looking for literary fiction, memoir, personal narrative, or poetry with a connection, direct or tangential, to the theme of justice."

❸ THE JOURNAL

The Ohio State University, 164 Annie and John Glenn Ave., Columbus OH 43210. **E-mail:** managingeditor@thejournalmag.org. **Website:** thejournalmag.org. Estab. 1973. "We are interested in quality fiction, poetry, nonfiction, art, and reviews of new books of poetry, fiction, and nonfiction. We impose no restrictions on category, type, or length of submission for fiction, poetry, and nonfiction. We are happy to consider long stories and self-contained excerpts of novels. Please double-space all prose submissions. Please send 3-5 poems in 1 submission. We only accept online submissions and will not respond to mailed submissions."

◗ "We're open to all forms; we tend to favor work that gives evidence of a mature and sophisticated sense of the language."

NEEDS No romance, science fiction, or religious/devotional. Length: up to 10,000 words.

HOW TO CONTACT Send full ms via online submissions manager. "Mss are rejected because of lack of understanding of the short story form, shallow plots, undeveloped characters. Cure: Read as much well-written fiction as possible. Our readers prefer 'psychological' fiction rather than stories with intricate plots. Take care to present a clean, well-typed submission."

PAYMENT/TERMS Pays 2 contributor's copies and one-year subscription.

KAIMANA

Literary Arts Hawai'i, Hawai'i Literary Arts Council, P.O. Box 11213, Honolulu HI 96828. **E-mail:** reimersa001@hawaii.rr.com. **Website:** www.hawaii.edu/hlac. Estab. 1974. *Kaimana: Literary Arts Hawai'i*, published annually, is the magazine of the Hawai'i Literary Arts Council. Wants submissions with "some

Pacific reference—Asia, Polynesia, Hawai'i—but not exclusively."

○ *Kaimana* is 64-76 pages, 7.5x10, saddle-stapled, with high-quality printing. Press run is 1,000. "Poets published in *Kaimana* have received the Pushcart Prize, the Hawaii Award for Literature, the Stefan Baciu Award, the Cades Award, and the John Unterecker Award."

HOW TO CONTACT Submit ms with SASE. No e-mail submissions. Cover letter is preferred.

PAYMENT/TERMS Pays 2 contributor's copies.

TIPS "Hawai'i gets a lot of 'travelling regionalists,' visiting writers with inevitably superficial observations. We also get superb visiting observers who are careful craftsmen anywhere. *Kaimana* is interested in the latter, to complement our own best Hawai'i writers."

⑤ KALEIDOSCOPE

United Disability Services, 701 S. Main St., Akron OH 44311-1019. (330)762-9755. **Fax:** (330)762-0912. **E-mail:** kaleidoscope@udsakron.org. **Website:** www.kaleidoscopeonline.org. **Contact:** Gail Willmott, editor in chief. Estab. 1979. Kaleidoscope magazine creatively focuses on the experiences of disability through literature and the fine arts. As a pioneering literary resource for the field of disability studies, this award-winning publication expresses the diversity of the disability experience from a variety of perspectives including: individuals, families, friends, caregivers, educators, and healthcare professionals, among others."

○ Kaleidoscope has received awards from the Great Lakes Awards Competition and Ohio Public Images; received the Ohioana Award of Editorial Excellence.

NEEDS Wants short stories with a well-crafted plot and engaging characters. No fiction that is stereotypical, patronizing, sentimental, erotic, or maudlin. No romance, religious or dogmatic fiction; no children's literature. Length: up to 5,000 words.

HOW TO CONTACT Submit complete ms by website or e-mail. Include cover letter.

PAYMENT/TERMS Pays $25.

TIPS "The material chosen for Kaleidoscope challenges and overcomes stereotypical, patronizing, and sentimental attitudes about disability. We accept the work of writers with and without disabilities; however the work of a writer without a disability must focus on some aspect of disability. The criteria for good writing apply: effective technique, thought-provoking subject matter, and, in general, a mature grasp of the art of storytelling. Writers should avoid using offensive language and always put the person before the disability."

KANSAS CITY VOICES

Whispering Prairie Press, P.O. Box 410661, Kansas City MO 64141. **E-mail:** info@wppress.org. **Website:** www.wppress.org. **Contact:** Tom Sullivan, managing editor. Estab. 2003. *Kansas City Voices*, published annually, features an eclectic mix of fiction, poetry, and art. "We seek exceptional written and visual creations from established and emerging voices." Submission period: December 15 through March 15. Note: We will not be publishing KCV in 2018. Our next submission period begins December 15, 2018, for publication in 2019.

NEEDS Length: up to 2,500 words.

HOW TO CONTACT Submit up to 2 complete mss via online submissions manager.

PAYMENT/TERMS Pays small honorarium and 1 contributor's copy.

TIPS "There is no 'type' of work we are looking for, and while we would love for you to read through our previous issues, it is not an indicator of what kind of work we actively seek. Our editors rotate, our tastes evolve, and good work is just *good work*. We want to feel something when we encounter a piece. We want to be excited, surprised, thoughtful, and interested. We want to have a reaction. We want to share the best voices we find. Send us that one."

○ KASMA MAGAZINE

E-mail: editors@kasmamagazine.com. **Website:** www.kasmamagazine.com. **Contact:** Alex Korovessis, editor. Estab. 2009. Online magazine. "We publish the best science fiction from promising new and established writers. Our aim is to provide stories that are well written, original, and thought provoking."

NEEDS No erotica or excessive violence/language. Length: 1,000-5,000 words.

HOW TO CONTACT Submit complete ms via e-mail.

PAYMENT/TERMS Pays $25 CAD.

TIPS "The type of stories I enjoy the most usually come as a surprise: I think I know what is happening, but the underlying reality is revealed to me as I read on. That said, I've accepted many stories that don't fit this model. Sometimes I'm introduced to a new story structure. Sometimes the story I like reminds me of another story, but it introduces a slightly different spin on it. Other times, the story introduces such interesting and original ideas that structure and style don't seem to matter as much."

THE KELSEY REVIEW

Liberal Arts Division, Mercer County Community College, P.O. Box 17202, Trenton NJ 08690. **E-mail:** kelsey.review@mccc.edu. **Website:** www.mccc.edu/community_kelsey-review.shtml; kelseyreview.com. **Contact:** Jacqueline Vogtman, editor. Estab. 1988. *The Kelsey Review*, published annually in print and online formats by Mercer County Community College, serves as an outlet for literary talent of people living and working in the larger Mercer County, New Jersey, area. Submissions are open between January 1-May 1 via our Submittable site.

NEEDS Has no specifications as to form, subject matter, or style. Length: up to 4,000 words.

HOW TO CONTACT Submit via online submissions manager. Submissions are limited to people who live, work, or give literary readings in Mercer County, New Jersey.

TIPS "See *The Kelsey Review* website for current guidelines. Note: We only accept submissions from the Mercer County, New Jersey, area."

⑤ KENTUCKY MONTHLY

Vested Interest Publications, P.O. Box 559, 100 Consumer Lane, Frankfort KY 40602-0559. (502)227-0053; (888)329-0053. **Fax:** (502)227-5009. **E-mail:** kymonthly@kentuckymonthly.com; steve@kentuckymonthly.com. **E-mail:** patty@kentuckymonthly.com. **Website:** www.kentuckymonthly.com. **Contact:** Stephen Vest, editor; Patricia Ranft, associate editor. Estab. 1998. "We publish stories about Kentucky and by Kentuckians, including stories written by those who live elsewhere."

NEEDS We publish stories about Kentucky and by Kentuckians, including stories written by those who live elsewhere." Length: 1,000-5,000 words.

HOW TO CONTACT Query with published clips. Accepts submissions by e-mail.

PAYMENT/TERMS Pays $50-500.

TIPS "Please read the magazine to get the flavor of what we're publishing each month. We accept articles via e-mail. Approximately 70% of articles are assigned."

⑤ THE KENYON REVIEW

Finn House, 102 W. Wiggin, Gambier OH 43022. (740)427-5208. **Fax:** (740)427-5417. **E-mail:** kenyonreview@kenyon.edu. **Website:** www.kenyonreview.org. **Contact:** Alicia Misarti. Estab. 1939. "An international journal of literature, culture, and the arts, dedicated to an inclusive representation of the best in new writing (fiction, poetry, essays, interviews, criticism) from established and emerging writers." *The Kenyon Review* receives about 8,000 submissions/year. Also publishes *KR Online*, a separate and complementary online literary magazine.

NEEDS Receives 800 unsolicited mss/month. Unsolicited mss accepted September 15-November 1 only. Recently published work by Leslie Blanco, Karl Taro Greenfeld, Charles Johnson, Amit Majmudar, Joyce Carol Oates, and Rion Amilcar Scott. Length: 3-15 typeset pages preferred.

HOW TO CONTACT Only accepts mss via online submissions manager; visit website for instructions. Do not submit via e-mail or mail.

PAYMENT/TERMS Pays 8¢/published word of prose (minimum payment $80; maximum payment $450); word count does not include title, notes, or citations.

TIPS "We no longer accept mailed or e-mailed submissions. Work will only be read if it is submitted through our online program on our website. Reading period is September 15 through November 1. We look for strong voice, unusual perspective, and power in the writing."

KEYS FOR KIDS DEVOTIONAL

Keys for Kids Ministries, 2060 43rd St. SE, Grand Rapids MI 49508. **E-mail:** editorial@keysforkids.org. **Website:** www.keysforkids.org. **Contact:** Courtney Lasater, editor. Estab. 1982. Daily devotional featuring stories and Scripture verses for children ages 6-12 that help kids dig into God's Word and apply it to their lives. Please put your name and contact information on the first page of your submission. We strongly prefer receiving submissions via our website. Story length is typically 340-375 words. To see full guidelines or submit a story, please go to www.keysforkids.org/writersguidelines.

NEEDS Need short contemporary stories with spiritual applications for kids. Please suggest a key verse and an appropriate Scripture passage, generally 3-10 verses, to reinforce the theme of your story. Length: Up to 375 words.

PAYMENT/TERMS Pays $30.

⑤ LADY CHURCHILL'S ROSEBUD WRISTLET

Small Beer Press, 150 Pleasant St., #306, Easthampton MA 01027. **E-mail:** info@smallbeerpress.com. **Website:** www.smallbeerpress.com/lcrw. **Contact:** Gavin Grant, editor. Estab. 1996. *Lady Churchill's Rosebud Wristlet* accepts fiction, nonfiction, poetry, and b&w art. "The fiction we publish tends toward, but is not limited to, the speculative. This does not mean only quietly desperate stories. We will consider items that fall out with regular categories. We do not accept multiple submissions." Semiannual.

NEEDS Receives 100 unsolicited mss/month. Accepts 4-6 mss/issue; 8-12 mss/year. Publishes 2-4 new writers/year. Also publishes literary essays, poetry. Has published work by Ted Chiang, Gwenda Bond, Alissa Nutting, and Charlie Anders. "We do not publish gore, sword and sorcery, or pornography. We can discuss these terms if you like. There are places for them all; this is not one of them." Length: 200-7,000 words.

HOW TO CONTACT Send complete ms with a cover letter. Include estimated word count. Send SASE (or IRC) for return of ms, or send a disposable copy of ms and #10 SASE for reply only.

PAYMENT/TERMS Pays $0.03 per word, $25 minimum.

TIPS "We recommend you read *Lady Churchill's Rosebud Wristlet* before submitting. You can pick up a copy from our website or from assorted book shops."

LAKE EFFECT

An International Literary Journal, School of Humanities & Social Sciences, Penn State Erie, The Behrend College, Erie PA 16563-1501. **E-mail:** gol1@psu.edu; alp248@psu.edu. **Website:** psbehrend.psu.edu/school-of-humanities-social-sciences/academic-programs-1/creative-writing/cw-student-organizations/lake-effect. **Contact:** George Looney, editor in chief. Estab. 1978. *Lake Effect* is a publication of the School of Humanities and Social Sciences at Penn State Erie, The Behrend College.

NEEDS "*Lake Effect* is looking for stories that emerge from character and language as much as from plot. *Lake Effect* does not, in general, publish genre fiction, but literary fiction. *Lake Effect* seeks work from both

established and new and emerging writers." Query first for stories longer than 15 pages.

HOW TO CONTACT Submit via online submissions manager.

⑤ LAKE SUPERIOR MAGAZINE

Lake Superior Port Cities, Inc., P.O. Box 16417, Duluth MN 55816-0417. (218)722-5002. **Fax:** (218)722-4096. **E-mail:** edit@lakesuperior.com. **Website:** www.lakesuperior.com. **Contact:** Konnie LeMay, editor. Estab. 1979. We are a family-owned business sustained with book and magazine publications as well as a Lake Superior Collection of retail items.

NEEDS Must be targeted regionally. Wants stories that are Lake Superior related. Rarely uses fiction stories. Length: 300-2,500 words.

HOW TO CONTACT Query with published clips.

PAYMENT/TERMS Pays $50-125.

TIPS "Well-researched queries are attended to. We actively seek queries from writers in Lake Superior communities. We prefer queries. Provide enough information on why the subject is important to the region and our readers, or why and how something is unique. We want details. The writer must have a thorough knowledge of the subject and how it relates to our region. We prefer a fresh, unused approach to the subject that provides the reader with an emotional involvement. Almost all of our articles feature quality photography in color or b&w. It is a prerequisite of all nonfiction. All submissions should include a *short* biography of author/photographer; mug shot sometimes used. Blanket submissions need not apply."

THE LAND

Free Press Co., P.O. Box 3169, Mankato MN 56002-3169. (507)345-4523. **E-mail:** editor@thelandonline.com. **Website:** www.thelandonline.com. Estab. 1976. "Although we're not tightly focused on any one type of farming, our articles must be of interest to farmers. In other words, will your article topic have an impact on people who live and work in rural areas?" Prefers to work with Minnesota or Iowa writers.

TIPS "Be enthused about rural Minnesota and Iowa life and agriculture, and be willing to work with our editors. We try to stress relevance. When sending me a query, convince me the story belongs in a Minnesota farm publication."

☻ LANDFALL: NEW ZEALAND ARTS AND LETTERS

Otago University Press, P.O. Box 56, Dunedin 9054, New Zealand. (64)(3)479-4155. **E-mail:** landfall. press@otago.ac.nz. **Website:** www.otago.ac.nz/press/landfall. **Contact:** Editor. Estab. 1947. *Landfall: New Zealand Arts and Letters* contains literary fiction and essays, poetry, extracts from works-in-progress, commentary on New Zealand arts and culture, work by visual artists including photographers and reviews of local books. (*Landfall* does not accept unsolicited reviews.)

☐ Deadlines for submissions: January 10 for the May issue, July 10 for the November issue. "*Landfall* is open to work by New Zealand and Pacific writers or by writers whose work has a connection to the region in subject matter or location. Work from Australian writers is occasionally included as a special feature."

NEEDS Length: up to 3,000 words.

HOW TO CONTACT Submit up to 3 pieces at a time. Prefers e-mail submissions. Include cover letter with contact info and bio of about 30 words.

THE LAUREL REVIEW

Northwest Missouri State University, Dept. of Language, Literature, and Writing, 800 University Dr., Maryville MO 64468. (660)562-1739. **Website:** laurel-review.org. **Contact:** John Gallaher and Luke Rolfes, editors; Daniel Biegelson and Richard Sonnenmoser, associate editors. Estab. 1960. "We publish poetry and fiction of high quality, from the traditional to the avant-garde. We are eclectic, open, and flexible. Good writing is all we seek."

☐ Biannual magazine: 6x9; 124-128 pages; good-quality paper. Reading period: September 1-May 1.

HOW TO CONTACT Submit complete ms via online submission manager or postal mail.

PAYMENT/TERMS Pays 2 contributor's copies and one-year subscription.

TIPS "Nothing really matters to us except our perception that the story presents something powerfully felt by the writer and communicated intensely to a serious reader. (We believe, incidentally, that comedy is just as serious a matter as tragedy, and we don't mind a bit if something makes us laugh out loud; we get too little that makes us laugh, in fact.) We try to reply promptly, though we don't always manage that.

In short, we want good poems and good stories. We hope to be able to recognize them, and we print what we believe is the best work submitted."

❸ LEADING EDGE MAGAZINE

4087 JKB, Provo UT 84602. **E-mail:** editor@leading-edgemagazine.com; fiction@leadingedgemagazine.com; art@leadingedgemagazine.com; poetry@leadingedgemagazine.com; nonfiction@leadingedgemagazine.com. **Website:** www.leadingedgemagazine.com. **Contact:** Heather White, editor-in-chief. Estab. 1981. "*Leading Edge* is a magazine dedicated to new and upcoming talent in the fields of science fiction and fantasy. We strive to encourage developing and established talent and provide high-quality speculative fiction to our readers." Does not accept mss with sex, excessive violence, or profanity. Accepts unsolicited submissions.

NEEDS Length: up to 15,000 words.

HOW TO CONTACT Send complete ms with cover letter and SASE. Include estimated word count.

PAYMENT/TERMS Pays 1¢/word; $50 maximum.

TIPS "Buy a sample issue to know what is currently selling in our magazine. Also, make sure to follow the writer's guidelines when submitting."

LE FORUM

University of Maine, Franco-American Center, Orono ME 04469-5719. (207)581-3789. **Fax:** (207)581-3791. **E-mail:** lisa_michaud@umit.maine.edu. **Website:** umaine.edu/francoamerican/le-forum. **Contact:** Lisa Desjardins Michaud, editor. Estab. 1972. "We will consider any type of short fiction, poetry, and critical essay having to do with the Franco-American experience. They must be of good quality in French or English. We are also looking for Canadian writers with French-North American experiences."

HOW TO CONTACT Include SASE.

PAYMENT/TERMS Pays 3 contributor's copies.

TIPS "Write honestly. Start with a strongly felt personal Franco-American experience. If you make us feel what you have felt, we will publish it. We stress that this publication deals specifically with the Franco-American experience."

LIGHTHOUSE DIGEST

Lighthouse Digest, P.O. Box 250, East Machias ME 04630. (207)259-2121. **E-mail:** Editor@Lighthouse-Digest.com. **Website:** www.lighthousedigest.com.

Contact: Tim Harrison, editor. Estab. 1989. Full color lighthouse news and history magazine.

NEEDS 2,500 words maximum.

HOW TO CONTACT Send complete ms.

TIPS "Read our publication and visit the website."

✪ LIGUORIAN

One Liguori Dr., Liguori MO 63057. (636)223-1538. **Fax:** (636)223-1595. **E-mail:** liguorianeditor@liguori. org. **Website:** www.liguorian.org. **Contact:** Elizabeth Herzing, managing editor. Estab. 1913. "Our purpose is to lead our readers to a fuller Christian life by helping them better understand the teachings of the gospel and the church and by illustrating how these teachings apply to life and the problems confronting them as members of families, the church, and society."

NEEDS Length: 1,500-2,200 words.

HOW TO CONTACT Send complete ms.

PAYMENT/TERMS Pays 12-15¢/word and 5 contributor's copies.

TIPS "First read several issues containing short stories. We look for originality and creative input in each story we read. Consideration requires the author studies the target market and presents a carefully polished manuscript. We publish 1 fiction story per issue. Compare this with the 25 or more we receive over the transom each month. We believe fiction is a highly effective mode for transmitting the Christian message; however, many fiction pieces are written without a specific goal or thrust—an interesting incident that goes nowhere is not a story."

LILITH MAGAZINE: INDEPENDENT, JEWISH & FRANKLY FEMINIST

119 West 57th St., Suite 1210, New York NY 10019. (212)757-0818. **Fax:** (212)757-5705. **E-mail:** info@lilith.org. **Website:** www.lilith.org. **Contact:** Susan Weidman Schneider, editor in chief; Naomi Danis, managing editor. Estab. 1976. *Lilith Magazine: Independent, Jewish & Frankly Feminist*, published quarterly, welcomes submissions of high-quality, lively writing: reportage, opinion pieces, memoirs, fiction, and poetry on subjects of interest to Jewish women.

○ *Lilith Magazine* is 48 pages, magazine-sized, with glossy color cover. Press run is about 10,000 (about 6,000 subscribers). Subscription: $26/year. For all submissions: Make sure name and contact information appear on each page of mss. Include a short bio (1-2 sentences),

written in third person. Accepts submissions year round.

NEEDS Length: up to 3,000 words.

HOW TO CONTACT Send complete ms via online submissions form or mail.

TIPS "Read a copy of the publication before you submit your work. Please be patient."

THE LISTENING EYE

Kent State University Geauga Campus, 14111 Claridon-Troy Rd., Burton OH 44021. (440)286-3840. **E-mail:** grace_butcher@msn.com. **E-mail:** Only from other countries. **Contact:** Grace Butcher, editor. Estab. 1970. "We look for powerful, unusual imagery, content, and plot in our short stories. In poetry, we look for tight lines that don't sound like prose, unexpected images or juxtapositions, the unusual use of language, noticeable relationships of sounds, a twist in viewpoint, an ordinary idea in extraordinary language, an amazing and complex idea simply stated, play on words and with words, an obvious love of language. Poets need to read the 'Big Three'—Cummings, Thomas, Hopkins—to see the limits to which language can be taken. Then read the 'Big Two'—Dickinson to see how simultaneously tight, terse, and universal a poem can be, and Whitman to see how sprawling, cosmic, and personal. Then read everything you can find that's being published in literary magazines today, and see how your work compares to all of the above."

○ Magazine: 5.5×8.5; 60 pages; photographs. "We publish the occasional very short stories (750 words/3 pages double-spaced) in any subject and any style, but the language must be strong, unusual, free from cliché and vagueness. We are a shoestring operation from a small campus, but we publish high-quality work." Reads submissions January 1-April 15 only.

NEEDS "Pretty much anything will be considered except porn." Recently published work by Simon Perchik, Lyn Lifshin, and John Hart. Publishes short shorts. Also publishes poetry. Sometimes comments on rejected mss.

HOW TO CONTACT Send SASE for return of ms or disposable copy of ms with SASE for reply only.

LITERAL LATTÉ

200 E. 10th St., Ste. 240, New York NY 10003. (212)260-5532. **E-mail:** litlatte@aol.com. **Website:** www.literal-latte.com. **Contact:** Jenine Gordon Bockman and Jeffrey Michael Bockman, editors and pub-

lishers. Estab. 1994. Bimonthly online publication. Print anthologies featuring the best of the website. "We want great writing in all styles and subjects. A feast is made of a variety of flavors."

NEEDS Accepts all styles and genres. Length: up to 10,000 words.

HOW TO CONTACT Submit via online submissions manager or postal mail.

PAYMENT/TERMS Pays anthology copies. Cash prizes for contests.

TIPS "Keeping free thought free and challenging entertainment are not mutually exclusive. Words make a ms stand out, words beautifully woven together in striking and memorable patterns."

LITERARY JUICE

Seattle WA , USA. **E-mail:** info@literaryjuice.com. **Website:** www.literaryjuice.com. **Contact:** Sara Rajan, editor in chief; Andrea O'Connor and Dinesh Rajan, managing editors. Estab. 2011. Bimonthly online literary magazine that publishes original, unpublished works of fiction, poetry, art, and photography. Does not publish works of nonfiction, essays, or interviews.

NEEDS "We do not publish works with intense sexual content." Length: 100-2,000 words.

HOW TO CONTACT Submit complete ms via online submissions manager.

TIPS Looking for works that are not only thought-provoking, but venture into unconventional territory as well. Avoid submitting mainstream stories and poems (stories about zombies or politics fall into this category). Instead, take the reader to a new realm that has yet to be explored.

LITERARY MAMA

E-mail: lminfo@literarymama.com. **E-mail:** Specific to departments; see website. **Website:** www.literary-mama.com. **Contact:** Karna Converse, editor-in-chief. Estab. 2003. Online monthly magazine that features writing about the complexities and many faces of motherhood. Departments include columns, creative nonfiction, fiction, literary reflections, poetry, profiles, and book reviews. "We prefer previously unpublished work and are interested in work that offers a fresh perspective."

○   "*Literary Mama* is not currently a paying market. We are all volunteers here: editors, writers, and editorial assistants. With the publication of each issue, we make a concerted effort to promote the work of our contributors via Facebook, Twitter, and our newsletter."

NEEDS "We love stories with strong narrative structure, great characters, interesting settings, beautiful language, and complicated themes." Length: up to 5,000 words.

THE LITERARY REVIEW

285 Madison Ave., Madison NJ 07940. (973)443-8564. **E-mail:** info@theliteraryreview.org. **Website:** www.theliteraryreview.org. **Contact:** Minna Proctor, editor. Estab. 1957. *The Literary Review* is published by Fairleigh Dickinson University. Work published in *The Literary Review* has been included in *Editor's Choice*, *Best American Short Stories*, and *Pushcart Prize* anthologies. Uses online submissions manager.

NEEDS Wants works of high literary quality only. Does not want to see "overused subject matter or pat resolutions to conflicts." Length: up to 7,000 words.

HOW TO CONTACT Submit electronically only. Does not accept paper submissions.

PAYMENT/TERMS Pays 2 contributor's copies and a one-year subscription.

TIPS "We want original dramatic situations with complex moral and intellectual resonance and vivid prose. We don't want versions of familiar plots and relationships. Too much of what we are seeing today is openly derivative in subject, plot, and prose style. We pride ourselves on spotting new writers with fresh insight and approach."

LITTLE PATUXENT REVIEW

P.O. Box 6084, Columbia MD 21045. **E-mail:** editor@littlepatuxentreview.org. **Website:** www.littlepatuxentreview.org. **Contact:** Steven Leyva, editor. Estab. 2006. "*Little Patuxent Review* (*LPR*) is a community-based, biannual print journal devoted to literature and the arts, primarily in the Mid-Atlantic region. We profile the work of a major poet or fiction writer and a visual artist in each issue. We celebrate the launch of each issue with a series of readings and broadcast highlights on *LPR*'s YouTube channel. All forms and styles considered. Please see our website for the current theme." *LPR* is about 120 pages; digest-sized; 100# finch cover; artwork (varies depending on featured artist). Has published poetry by Lucille Clifton, Martín Espada, Donald Hall, Joy Harjo, Marie Howe, Myra Sklarew, Clarinda Harriss, and Alan King.

NEEDS Length: up to 5,000 words.

HOW TO CONTACT Submit complete ms by online submissions manager; no mail or e-mail submissions. Include word count and 75-word bio.

PAYMENT/TERMS Pays 1 contributor's copy.

TIPS "Please see our website for the current theme. Poetry and prose must exhibit the highest quality to be considered. Please read a sample issue before submitting."

💲 LIVE

Gospel Publishing House, 1445 N. Boonville Ave., Springfield MO 65802-1894. (417)862-1447. **E-mail:** rl-live@gph.org. **Website:** www.gospelpublishing.com. Estab. 1928. "*LIVE* is a take-home paper distributed weekly in young adult and adult Sunday school classes. We seek to encourage Christians in living for God through fiction and true stories which apply Biblical principles to everyday problems."

NEEDS No preachy fiction, fiction about Bible characters, or stories that refer to religious myths (e.g., Santa Claus, Easter Bunny, etc.). No science or Bible fiction. No controversial stories about such subjects as feminism, war, or capital punishment. Length: 800-1,200 words.

HOW TO CONTACT Send complete ms.

PAYMENT/TERMS Pays 7-10¢/word.

TIPS "Don't moralize or be preachy. Provide human interest articles with Biblical life application. Stories should consist of action, not just thought-life, interaction, or insight. Heroes and heroines should rise above failures, take risks for God, prove that scriptural principles meet their needs. Conflict and suspense should increase to a climax! Avoid pious conclusions. Characters should be interesting, believable, and realistic. Avoid stereotypes. Characters should be active, not just pawns to move the plot along. They should confront conflict and change in believable ways. Describe the character's looks and reveal his personality through his actions to such an extent that the reader feels he has met that person. Readers should care about the character enough to finish the story. Feature racial, ethnic, and regional characters in rural and urban settings."

🌐💲 THE LONDON MAGAZINE

11 Queen's Gate, London SW7 5EL, United Kingdom. (44)(0)20 7584 5977. **E-mail:** info@thelondonmagazine.org. **Website:** www.thelondonmagazine.org. **Contact:** Steven O'Brien, editor. Estab. 1732. "The Oldest Literary Magazine, established 1732. We publish literary writing of the highest quality. We look for poetry and short fiction that startles and entertains us. Reviews, essays, memoir pieces, and features should be erudite, lucid, and incisive. We are obviously interested in writing that has a London focus, but not exclusively so, since London is a world city with international concerns."

NEEDS "Short fiction should address mature and sophisticated themes. Moreover, it should have an elegance of style, structure and characterization. We do not normally publish science fiction or fantasy writing, or erotica." Length: up to 4,000 words.

HOW TO CONTACT Send complete ms. Submit via online submissions manager, e-mail (as an attachment), or postal mail (enclose SASE).

TIPS "Please look at *The London Magazine* before you submit work so that you can see the type of material we publish."

LONG LIFE

Longevity through Technology, The Immortalist Society, 24355 Sorrentino Ct., Clinton Township MI 48035. **E-mail:** info@cryonics.org. **Website:** www.cryonics.org/resources/long-life-magazine. Estab. 1968. "*Long Life* magazine is a publication for people who are particularly interested in cryonic suspension: the theory, practice, legal problems, etc. associated with being frozen when you die in the hope of eventual restoration to life and health. Many people who receive the publication have relatives who have undergone cryonic preparation or have made such arrangements for themselves or are seriously considering this option. Readers are also interested in other aspects of life extension such as anti-aging research and food supplements that may slow aging. Articles we publish include speculation on what the future will be like; problems of living in a future world, and science in general, particularly as it may apply to cryonics and life extension."

NEEDS "We occasionally publish short fiction, but cryonics and life extension should be essential to the story. We are not interested in horror, in stories where the future is portrayed as gloom and doom, end-of-the-world stories, or those with an inspirational theme." Length: up to 2,500 words.

PAYMENT/TERMS Pays 1 contributor's copy.

TIPS "We are a small magazine but with a highly intelligent and educated readership which is socially and economically diverse. We currently don't pay for material but are seeking new authors and provide contributors with copies of the magazine with the contributor's published works. Look over a copy of *Long Life*, or talk with the editor to get the tone of the publication. There is an excellent chance that your ms will be accepted if it is well written and 'on theme.' Pictures to accompany the article are always welcome, and we like to publish photos of the authors with their first ms."

LONG STORY SHORT, AN E-ZINE FOR WRITERS

P.O. Box 475, Lewistown MT 59457. **E-mail:** alongstory_short@aol.com. **Website:** www.alongstoryshort. net. **Contact:** Anisa Claire, Kim Bussey, editors. Estab. 2003. *Long Story Short, An E-zine for Writers* publishes "the best fiction and poetry from both emerging and established writers.

☐ Free newsletter with poetry of the month chosen by poetry editor; includes author's bio and web page listed in the e-zine. Offers light critique of submissions upon request and a free writing forum.

NEEDS Accepts all genres of flash fiction or prose. Length: up to 2,000 words.

HOW TO CONTACT Submit by e-mail; no attachments.

PAYMENT/TERMS Pays $10-15 and 1 contributor's copy for short stories 1,000-2,000 words. Pays 1 contributor's copy for flash fiction.

THE LOS ANGELES REVIEW

P.O. Box 2458, Redmond WA 98073. (626)356-4760. **Fax:** (626)356-9974. **E-mail:** lareview.trager.editor@ gmail.com. **Website:** losangelesreview.org. **Contact:** Alisa Trager, managing editor. Estab. 2003.

NEEDS "We're looking for hard-to-put-down shorties under 500 words and lengthier shorts up to 4,000 words—lively, vivid, excellent literary fiction." Does not accept multiple submissions. Does not want pornography. Length: 500-4,000 words.

HOW TO CONTACT "Submishmash, our online submission form, is now our preferred method of submission, though you may still submit through postal mail. Please see our guidelines online."

TIPS "Read a few recent issues to see what we're about. Pay close attention to the submission guidelines. We like cover letters, but please keep them brief."

LOST LAKE FOLK OPERA

Shipwreckt Books Publishing Company, 309 W. Stevens Ave., Rushford MN 55971. **E-mail:** contact@ shipwreckbooks.com. **Website:** www.shipwreckt-books.com. **Contact:** Tom Driscoll, managing editor. Estab. 2013. *Lost Lake Folk Opera* magazine, published twice annually, accepts submissions of critical journalism, short fiction, poetry, B&W photography and graphic art. Seeks high-quality submissions. For journalistic pieces, please query first.

NEEDS Length: 250-5000 words.

HOW TO CONTACT Query with sample.

PAYMENT/TERMS Pays contributor copy.

TIPS "When in doubt, edit and cut. Please remember to read your submission. Don't expect *LLFO* to wash your car and detail it. Send clean copies of your work."

LOUISIANA LITERATURE

SLU Box 10792, Hammond LA 70402. **E-mail:** lalit@ selu.edu. **Website:** www.louisianaliterature.org. **Contact:** Jack B. Bedell, editor. Estab. 1984. "Since 1984, *Louisiana Literature* has featured some of the finest writing published in America. The journal has always striven to spotlight local talent alongside nationally recognized authors. Whether it's work from established writers or from first-time publishers, *Louisiana Literature* is always looking to print the finest poetry and fiction available."

☐ Biannual magazine: 6x9; 150 pages; 70 lb. paper; card cover; illustrations. Receives 100 unsolicited mss/month. May not read mss June-July. Publishes 4 new writers/year. Publishes theme issues. Has published work by Anthony Bukowski, Aaron Gwyn, Robert Phillips, and R.T. Smith. Work first published in *Louisiana Literature* is regularly reprinted in collections and is nominated for prizes from the National Book Awards for both genres and the Pulitzer. Recently, stories by Aaron Gwyn and Robert Olen Butler were selected for inclusion in *New Stories from the South*.

NEEDS Reviews fiction. "No sloppy, ungrammatical mss." Length: 1,000-6,000 words; average length: 3,500 words.

HOW TO CONTACT Submit ms via online submissions manager. Ms should be double-spaced.

PAYMENT/TERMS Pays 2 contributor's copies.

TIPS "Cut out everything that is not a functioning part of the story. Make sure your ms is professionally presented. Use relevant, specific detail in every scene. We love detail, local color, voice, and craft. Any professional ms stands out."

THE LOUISIANA REVIEW

Louisiana State University Eunice, Division of Liberal Arts, P.O. Box 1129, Eunice LA 70535. (337)550-1315. **E-mail:** bfonteno@lsue.edu. **Website:** web.lsue.edu/la-review. **Contact:** Dr. Billy Fontenot, editor and fiction editor; Dr. Jude Meche, poetry editor; Dr. Diane Langlois, art editor. Estab. 1999. *The Louisiana Review*, published annually during the fall or spring semesters, offers "Louisiana poets, writers, and artists a place to showcase their most beautiful pieces. Others may submit Louisiana- or Southern-related poetry, stories, and art. Publishes photographs. Sometimes publishes nonfiction." Wants "strong imagery, metaphor, and evidence of craft."

○ *The Louisiana Review* is 100 pages, digest-sized, professionally printed, perfect-bound. Press run is 300-600.

NEEDS Receives 25 unsolicited mss/month. Accepts 5-7 mss/issue. Reads year round. Has published work by Ronald Frame, Tom Bonner, Laura Cario, and Sheryl St. Germaine. Also publishes short shorts. No length restrictions.

HOW TO CONTACT Send SASE for return of ms. Accepts multiple submissions.

PAYMENT/TERMS Pays 1 contributor's copy.

TIPS "We do like to have fiction play out visually as a film would rather than be static and undramatized. Louisiana or Gulf Coast settings and themes preferred."

LULLWATER REVIEW

Emory University, P.O. Box 122036, Atlanta GA 30322. **E-mail:** emorylullwaterreview@gmail.com. **Website:** emorylullwaterreview.com. **Contact:** Aneyn M. O'Grady, editor in chief. Estab. 1990. "We're a small, student-run literary magazine published out of Emory University in Atlanta, Georgia, with 2 issues yearly—once in the fall and once in the spring. You can find us in the *Index of American Periodical Verse*, the *American Humanities Index* and as a member of the Council of Literary Magazines and Presses. We welcome work that brings a fresh perspective, whether through language or the visual arts."

NEEDS Recently published work by Greg Jenkins, Thomas Juvik, Jimmy Gleacher, Carla Vissers, and Judith Sudnolt. No romance or science fiction, please. Length: up to 5,000 words.

HOW TO CONTACT Send complete ms via e-mail. *Does not accept postal mail submissions.*

PAYMENT/TERMS Pays 3 contributor's copies.

TIPS "We at the *Lullwater Review* look for clear, cogent writing, strong character development, and an engaging approach to the story in our fiction submissions. Stories with particularly strong voices and well-developed central themes are especially encouraged. Be sure that your ms is ready before mailing it to us. Revise, revise, revise! Be original, honest, and, of course, keep trying."

LUMINA JOURNAL

Sarah Lawrence College, 1 Mead Way, Bronxville NY 10708. **E-mail:** lumina@gm.slc.edu. **Website:** lumina-journal.com. **Contact:** Victoria Johnson, editor-in-chief. Estab. 2000. "*LUMINA*'s mission is to provide a journal where emerging and established writers and visual artists come together in exploration of the new and appreciation of the traditional. We want to see sonnets sharing space with experimental prose; we want art that pushes boundaries and bends rules with eloquence."

NEEDS Length: up to 5,000 words.

HOW TO CONTACT Submit via online submissions manager. All submissions are read blind; do not include personal information on submission documents.

LUNGFULL!MAGAZINE

316 23rd St., Brooklyn NY 11215. **E-mail:** customerservice@lungfull.org. **Website:** lungfull.org. **Contact:** Brendan Lorber, editor/publisher. Estab. 1994. "*LUNGFULL!* Magazine World Headquarters in Brooklyn is home to a team of daredevils who make it their job to bring you only the finest in typos, misspellings, and awkward phrases. That's because *LUNGFULL!magazine* is the only literary and art journal in America that prints the rough drafts of people's work so you can see the creative process as it happens."

NEEDS Publishes rough drafts.

HOW TO CONTACT Submit up to 15 pages of prose. Include cover letter.

⑤ LYRICAL PASSION POETRY E-ZINE

Arlington VA **E-mail:** lpezinesubmissions@gmail.com. **Website:** lyricalpassionpoetry.yolasite.com.

Contact: Raquel D. Bailey, founder & editor-in-chief. Estab. 2007. Founded by award-winning poet Raquel D. Bailey, *Lyrical Passion Poetry E-Zine* is an attractive monthly online literary magazine specializing in Japanese short-form poetry. Publishes quality artwork, well-crafted short fiction, and poetry in English by emerging and established writers. Literature of lasting literary value will be considered. Welcomes the traditional to the experimental. Poetry works written in German will be considered if accompanied by translations. Offers annual short fiction and poetry contests.

HOW TO CONTACT Send complete ms, typed in the body of your email or as pdf attachment. Cover letter preferred.

❸ MᴀNOA

A Pacific Journal of International Writing, University of Hawaii at Mānoa, English Department, Honolulu HI 96822. **E-mail:** mjournal-l@lists.hawaii.edu. **Website:** manoajournal.hawaii.edu. **Contact:** Frank Stewart, editor. Estab. 1989. *Mānoa* is seeking high-quality literary fiction, poetry, essays, and translations for an international audience. In general, each issue is devoted to new work from an area of the Asia-Pacific region. Because we feature different places and have guest editors, please contact us to see if your submission is appropriate for what we're working on. *Mānoa* has received numerous awards, and work published in the magazine has been selected for prize anthologies. See website for recently published issues.

NEEDS Query first. No Pacific exotica. Length: 1,000-7,500 words.

HOW TO CONTACT Send complete ms.

PAYMENT/TERMS Pays $100-500 ($25/printed page).

TIPS "Not accepting unsolicited mss at this time because of commitments to special projects. Please query before sending mss as e-mail attachments."

THE MACGUFFIN

Schoolcraft College, 18600 Haggerty Rd., Livonia MI 48152. (734)462-4400, ext. 5327. **E-mail:** macguffin@schoolcraft.edu. **Website:** www.schoolcraft.edu/macguffin. **Contact:** Steven A. Dolgin, editor; Gordon Krupsky, managing editor;. Estab. 1984. "Our purpose is to encourage, support, and enhance the literary arts in the Schoolcraft College community, the region, the state, and the nation. We also sponsor annual literary events and give voice to deserving new writers as well as established writers."

NEEDS Preferences range from flash and experimental to mainstream. Length: up to 5,000 words.

HOW TO CONTACT Submit ms via e-mail or postal mail. Ms should be double-spaced.

PAYMENT/TERMS Pays 2 contributor's copies.

MAD HATTERS' REVIEW

Edgy and Enlightened Art, Literature and Music in the Age of Dementia, **E-mail:** askalice@madhatarts.com; marc@madhatarts.com. **Website:** www.madhattersreview.com. **Contact:** Marc Vincenz, publisher and editor in chief. *Mad Hatters' Review* "seeks to foster the work of writers and poets: explosive, lyrical, passionate, deeply wrought voices and aesthetic experiments that stretch the boundaries of language, narrative, and image, vital and enduring literary voices that sing on the page as well as in the mind. The name of our annual reflects our view of the world as essentially demented and nonsensical, too frequently a nightmare or 'non-dream' that needs to be exposed to the light for what it is, as well as what it is not. We're particularly interested in risky, thematically broad (i.e., saying something about the world and its creatures), psychologically and philosophically sophisticated works. Humor, satire, irony, magical realism, and surrealism are welcome. We look for originality, surprise, intellectual and emotional strength, lyricism, and rhythm. We love writers who stretch their imaginations to the limits and challenge conventional notions of reality and style; we care little for categories. We also adore collaborative ventures, between/among writers, visual artists, and composers."

NEEDS Submissions are open briefly for each issue: check guidelines periodically for dates. **Publishes 1 new writer/year.** Has published Alastair Gray, Kass Fleisher, Vanessa Place, Harold Jaffe, Andrei Codrescu, Sheila Murphy, Simon Perchik, Terese Svoboda, Niels Hav, Martin, Nakell, and Juan Jose Millas (translated from the Spanish). Does not want mainstream prose/story that doesn't exhibit a love of language and a sophisticated mentality. No religious or inspirational writings, confessionals, boys sowing oats, sentimental and coming-of-age stories. Length: up to 3,000 words. Average length: 1,500-2,500 words. Publishes short shorts. Average length of short shorts: 500-800 words.

HOW TO CONTACT Submit via online submissions manager.

TIPS "Imagination, skill with and appreciation of language, inventiveness, rhythm, sense of humor/irony/satire, and compelling style make a manuscript stand out. Read the magazine. Don't necessarily follow the rules you've been taught in the usual MFA program or workshop."

THE MADISON REVIEW

University of Wisconsin, 600 N. Park St., 6193 Helen C. White Hall, Madison WI 53706. **E-mail:** madisonrevw@gmail.com. **Website:** www.english.wisc.edu/madisonreview. **Contact:** Abigail Zemach and John McCracken, fiction editors; Fiona Sands and Kiyoko Reidy, poetry editors. Estab. 1972. *The Madison Review* is a student-run literary magazine that looks to publish the best available fiction and poetry.

    Does not publish unsolicited interviews or genre fiction. Send all submissions through online submissions manager.

NEEDS Wants well-crafted, compelling fiction featuring a wide range of styles and subjects. Does not read May-September. No genre: horror, fantasy, erotica, etc. Length: 500-30,000 words, up to 30 pages.

HOW TO CONTACT Send complete ms.

PAYMENT/TERMS Pays 2 contributor's copies, $5 for additional copies.

TIPS "Our editors have very eclectic tastes, so don't specifically try to cater to us. Above all, we look for original, high-quality work."

💲 THE MAGAZINE OF FANTASY & SCIENCE FICTION

P.O. Box 3447, Hoboken NJ 07030. (201)876-2551. **E-mail:** fandsf@aol.com. **Website:** www.fandsf.com; submissions.ccfinlay.com/fsf. **Contact:** C.C. Finlay, editor. Estab. 1949. *The Magazine of Fantasy & Science Fiction* publishes various types of science fiction and fantasy short stories and novellas, making up about 80% of each issue. The balance of each issue is devoted to articles about science fiction, a science column, book and film reviews, cartoons, and competitions. Bimonthly.

    The Magazine of Fantasy & Science Fiction is one of the oldest and most prestigious magazines in the field, having published Isaac Asimov, Ray Bradbury, Shirley Jackson, Robert Heinlein, Kurt Vonnegut, Joyce Carol Oates, Harlan Ellison, Samuel R. Delany, James Tiptree Jr., Ursula K. Le Guin, Karen Joy Fowler, Ted Chiang, and many others. Many stories published by *F&SF* receive award nominations and are reprinted in Year's Best anthologies. Alaya Dawn Johnson's "A Guide to the Fruits of Hawai'i" won the Nebula Award for Best Novelet in 2015.

NEEDS *F&SF* has no formula for fiction. The speculative element may be slight, but it should be present. We prefer character-oriented stories, whether it's fantasy, science fiction, horror, humor, or another genre. *F&SF* is open to diverse voices and perspectives, and has published writers from all over the world. Length: up to 25,000 words.

HOW TO CONTACT Send complete ms.

PAYMENT/TERMS Pays 7-12¢/word.

TIPS Good storytelling makes a submission stand out. We like to be surprised by stories, either by the character insights, ideas, plots, or prose. Even though we prefer electronic submissions, we need stories in standard mss format (like that described here: www.sfwa.org/writing/vonda/vonda.htm). Read an issue of the magazine before submitting to get a sense of the range of our tastes and interests.

THE MAGNOLIA QUARTERLY

P.O. Box 10294, Gulfport MS 39505. **E-mail:** writerpllevin@gmail.com. **Website:** www.gcwriters.org. **Contact:** Phil Levin, editor. Estab. 1985. *The Magnolia Quarterly* publishes poetry, fiction, nonfiction, and reviews. **For members of GCWA only.**

    The Magnolia Quarterly is 40 pages, pocket-sized, stapled, with glossy cover, includes ads. Editing service offered on all prose.

NEEDS Length: about 700 words.

HOW TO CONTACT E-mail submissions in DOC format as attachments.

PAYMENT/TERMS No payment.

THE MAIN STREET RAG

Douglass-Rausch, Ent. LLC, P.O. Box 690100, Charlotte NC 28227-7001. (704)573-2516. **E-mail:** editor@mainstreetrag.com. **Website:** www.mainstreetrag.com. **Contact:** M. Scott Douglass, publisher/managing editor. Estab. 1996. *The Main Street Rag*, published quarterly, prints "poetry, short fiction, essays, interviews, reviews, photos, and art. We like publishing good material from people who are interested in more than notching another publishing credit, people who support small independent publishers like ourselves." Will consider "almost anything," but prefers "writing with an edge—either gritty or bitingly humorous. Contributors are advised to visit our website prior to submission to confirm current needs." *The Main Street Rag* receives about 5,000 submissions/year; publishes 50+ poems and 3-5 stories per issue, a featured interview, photos, and an occasional nonfiction piece. Press run is about 500 (250 subscribers, 15 libraries).

NEEDS Length: up to 6,000 words.

HOW TO CONTACT No hard copy submissions—all electronic. See website for details.

PAYMENT/TERMS Pays 1 contributor's copy.

◐ ❸ THE MALAHAT REVIEW

The University of Victoria, P.O. Box 1700, STN CSC, Victoria BC V8W 2Y2, Canada. (250)721-8524. **E-mail:** malahat@uvic.ca (for queries only). **Website:** www.malahatreview.ca. **Contact:** John Barton, editor. Estab. 1967. Quarterly magazine covering poetry, fiction, creative nonfiction, and reviews. "We try to achieve a balance of views and styles in each issue. We strive for a mix of the best writing by both established and new writers."

NEEDS Length: up to 8,000 words.

HOW TO CONTACT Submit via online submissions manager.

PAYMENT/TERMS Pays $60/magazine page.

TIPS "Please do not send more than 1 submission at a time: 3-5 poems, 1 piece of creative nonfiction, or 1 short story (do not mix poetry and prose in the same submission). See *The Malahat Review*'s Open Season Awards for poetry and short fiction, creative nonfiction, long poem, and novella contests in the Awards section of our website."

❸ THE MASSACHUSETTS REVIEW

University of Massachusetts, Photo Lab 309, 211 Hicks Way, Amherst MA 01003. (413)545-2689. **E-mail:** massrev@external.umass.edu. **Website:** www.massreview.org. **Contact:** Emily Wojcik, managing editor. Estab. 1959. Seeks a balance between established writers and promising new ones. Interested in material of variety and vitality relevant to the intellectual and aesthetic questions of our time. Aspire to have a broad appeal.

◐   Does not respond to mss without SASE.

NEEDS Wants short stories. Accepts 1 short story per submission. Include name and contact information on the first page. Encourages page numbers. Has

published work by Ahdaf Soueif, Elizabeth Denton, and Nicholas Montemarano. Length: up to 30 pages or 8,000 words.

HOW TO CONTACT Send complete ms.

PAYMENT/TERMS Pays $50 and 2 contributor's copies.

TIPS "No manuscripts are considered May-September. Electronic submission process can be found on website. No fax or e-mail submissions. Shorter rather than longer stories preferred (up to 28-30 pages)." Looks for works that "stop us in our tracks." Manuscripts that stand out use "unexpected language, idiosyncrasy of outlook, and are the opposite of ordinary."

MCCROSKEY MEMORIAL INTERNET PLAYHOUSE

MMIP, 416 101st Ave SE #308, Bellevue WA 98004. (206)417-5965. **E-mail:** administrator@theinternetplayhouse.com. **E-mail:** submissions@theinternetplayhouse.com. **Website:** www.theinternetplayhouse.com. **Contact:** Jim Snowden, artistic director. Quarterly. Circ. 500. Publisher of short story collections, novellas and novels. "We publish two short fiction collections per year, based on a theme posted on our website. We also take novels and novella length fiction. Query first. In addition, short stories selected for the anthology will be assigned to actors in the Seattle area and read for our podcast and in our live performance venue in Seattle." Payment: royalties. See guidelines for specifics. Publication is copyrighted. Acquires first English Anthology Rights (including e-book rights), one time podcast performance rights.

NEEDS erotica, ethnic/multicultural (general), experimental, feminist, gay, historical (general), humor/satire, lesbian, literary, science fiction (other), translations. Does not want religious, romance, or fanfic. For upcoming themes, check the website. Accepts 6 mss/issue; 24 mss/year. Manuscript published 2 months after acceptance. Length: 2,000 words (min)-8,000 words (max). Also publishes poetry. Rarely comments on/critiques rejected manuscripts.

HOW TO CONTACT Please e-mail all submissions. Use .rtf, .doc, or Pages format for all manuscripts. Cover letters aren't required, but are welcome. Include brief bio, list of publications. Responds to mss in 3 months. Considers simultaneous submissions, previously published submissions, multiple submissions. Guidelines available on website. Please email all submissions. Use .rtf, .doc, or Pages format for all manuscripts. Cover letters aren't required, but are welcome.

PAYMENT/TERMS Writers receive 3 contributor's copies in the form of CD. Pays on publication. Acquires electronic rights. Sends galleys to author. Publication is not copyrighted.

TIPS "We're looking for a strong and original voice, a willingness to tackle uncomfortable subject matter, suitability for the all-audio format. Read the guidelines, read your work out loud, read everything you can, and send your best."

MCSWEENEY'S

849 Valencia St., San Francisco CA 94110. **E-mail:** letters@mcsweeneys.net (website submissions). **E-mail:** websubmissions@mcsweeneys.net (humor website); https://mcsweeneysquarterly.submittable.com/submit (print quarterly). **Website:** www.mcsweeneys.net. **Contact:** Christopher Monks, humor website editor; Claire Boyle, print editor. Estab. 1998. Online literary journal. "Timothy McSweeney's *Internet Tendency* is an offshoot of Timothy McSweeney's *Quarterly Concern*, a journal created by nervous people in relative obscurity, and published four times a year."

NEEDS literate humor. Sometimes comments on rejected mss. Sometimes comments on rejected mss. Length: 1,500 words maximum; preference for pieces significantly shorter (700-1,000 words).

HOW TO CONTACT For submissions to the website, paste the entire piece into the body of an e-mail.

TIPS "Please read the writer's guidelines before submitting, and send your submissions to the appropriate address. Do not submit your work to both the print submissions address and the Web submissions address, as seemingly hundreds of writers have been doing lately. If you submit a piece of writing intended for the magazine to the web submissions address, you will confuse us, and if you confuse us, we will accidentally delete your work without reading it."

MENSBOOK JOURNAL

Strategen, P.O. Box 200, West Yarmouth MA 02675. **E-mail:** mensbookfeatures@gmail.com. **Website:** www.mensbook.com. **Contact:** Payson Fitch, editor/publisher. Estab. 2008. Gay-owned and operated company with arms in publishing and advertising.

NEEDS "Our audience comprises bright, inquisitive, discerning gay men looking for a blend of mature and reasoned voices and stories across an array of gay subject matter." Does not want "sexcapades or pointless trash." Length: 750-3,500 words.

HOW TO CONTACT Accepts variable amounts of fiction mss/year. Send complete ms by e-mail.

TIPS "Be a tight writer with a cogent, potent message. Structure your work with well-organized progressive sequencing. Edit everything down before you send it over so we know it is your best work, and we'll work together from there."

MERIDIAN

University of Virginia, P.O. Box 400145, Charlottesville VA 22904-4145. **E-mail:** meridianuva@gmail.com; meridianpoetry@gmail.com; meridianfiction@gmail.com. **Website:** www.readmeridian.org. Estab. 1998. *Meridian* Editors' Prize Contest offers annual $1,000 award. Submit online only; see website for formatting details. **Entry fee:** $8.50, includes one-year electronic subscription to *Meridian* for all U.S. entries or 1 copy of the prize issue for all international entries. **Deadline:** December or January; see website for current deadline. *Meridian*, published semiannually, prints poetry, fiction, nonfiction, interviews, and reviews. "*Meridian* is interested in writing that is vibrant, moving, and alive, and welcomes contributions from a variety of aesthetic approaches. Has published such poets as Alexandra Teague, Gregory Pardlo, Sandra Meek, and Bob Hicok, and such fiction writers as Matt Bell, Kate Milliken, and Ron Carlson. Has recently interviewed C. Michael Curtis, Ann Beatty, and Claire Messud, among other luminaries. Also publishes a recurring feature called 'Lost Classic,' which resurrects previously unpublished work by celebrated writers and which has included illustrations from the mss of Jorge Luis Borges, letters written by Elizabeth Bishop, Stephen Crane's deleted chapter from *The Red Badge of Courage*, and a letter written by Flannery O'Connor about her novel *Wise Blood*."

Meridian is 130 pages, digest-sized, offset-printed, perfect-bound, with color cover. Receives about 2,500 poems/year, accepts about 40 (less than 1%). Press run is 1,000 (750 subscribers, 15 libraries, 200 shelf sales); 150 distributed free to writing programs. Work published in *Meridian* has appeared in *The Best American Poetry* and *The Pushcart Prize Anthology*.

NEEDS Submit complete ms via online submissions manager. Length: up to 6,500 words.

PAYMENT/TERMS Pays 2 contributor's copies (additional copies available at discount).

🟢 MICHIGAN QUARTERLY REVIEW

0576 Rackham Bldg., 915 E. Washington, Ann Arbor MI 48109-1070. (734)764-9265. **E-mail:** mqr@umich. edu. **Website:** www.michiganquarterlyreview.com. **Contact:** Jonathan Freedman, editor; Vicki Lawrence, managing editor. Estab. 1962. *Michigan Quarterly Review* is an eclectic interdisciplinary journal of arts and culture that seeks to combine the best of poetry, fiction, and creative nonfiction with outstanding critical essays on literary, cultural, social, and political matters. The flagship journal of the University of Michigan, *MQR* draws on lively minds here and elsewhere, seeking to present accessible work of all varieties for sophisticated readers from within and without the academy.

○ The Laurence Goldstein Award is a $500 annual award to the best poem published in *MQR* during the previous year. The Lawrence Foundation Award is a $1,000 annual award to the best short story published in *MQR* during the previous year. The Page Davidson Clayton Award for Emerging Poets is a $500 annual award given to the best poet appearing in *MQR* during the previous year who has not yet published a book.

NEEDS "No restrictions on subject matter or language. We are very selective. We like stories that are unusual in tone and structure, and innovative in language. No genre fiction written for a market. Would like to see more fiction about social, political, and cultural matters, not just centered on a love relationship or dysfunctional family." Receives 300 unsolicited mss/month. Accepts 3-4 mss/issue; 12-16 mss/year. Publishes 1-2 new writers/year. Has published work by Rebecca Makkai, Peter Ho Davies, Laura Kasischke, Gerald Shapiro, and Alan Cheuse. Length: 1,500-7,000 words; average length: 5,000 words.

HOW TO CONTACT Send complete ms.

PAYMENT/TERMS Payment varies but is usually in the range of $50-$150.

TIPS "Read the journal and assess the range of contents and the level of writing. We have no guidelines to offer or set expectations; every ms is judged on its unique qualities. On essays, query with a very thorough description of the argument and a copy of the first page. Watch for announcements of special issues, which are usually expanded issues and draw upon a lot of freelance writing. Be aware that this is a university quarterly that publishes a limited amount of fiction and poetry and that it is directed at an educated audience, one that has done a great deal of reading in all types of literature."

MID-AMERICAN REVIEW

Bowling Green State University, Department of English, Bowling Green OH 43403. (419)372-2725. **E-mail:** mar@bgsu.edu. **E-mail:** marsubmissions.bgsu. edu. **Website:** www.bgsu.edu/midamericanreview. **Contact:** Abigail Cloud, editor-in-chief; Bridget Adams, fiction editor. Estab. 1981. "We aim to put the best possible work in front of the biggest possible audience. We publish contemporary fiction, poetry, creative nonfiction, translations, and book reviews." Contests: The Fineline Competition for Prose Poems, Short Shorts, and Everything In Between (June 1 deadline, $10 per 3 pieces, limit 500 words each); The Sherwood Anderson Fiction Award (November 1 deadline, $10 per piece); and the James Wright Poetry Award (November 1 deadline, $10 per 3 pieces).

NEEDS Publishes traditional, character-oriented, literary, experimental, prose poem, and short-short stories. No genre fiction. Length: up to 6,000 words.

HOW TO CONTACT Submit ms by mail with SASE, or through online submission manager. Agented fiction 5%. Recently published work by Mollie Ficek and J. David Stevens.

TIPS "We are seeking translations of contemporary authors from all languages into English; submissions must include the original and proof of permission to translate. We would also like to see more creative nonfiction."

MIDWAY JOURNAL

216 Banks St. #2, Cambridge MA 02138. (763)516-7463. **E-mail:** editors@midwayjournal.com. **Website:** www.midwayjournal.com. **Contact:** Christopher Lowe, nonfiction editor; Ralph Pennel, fiction editor; Paige Riehl, poetry editor. Estab. 2006. "Just off of I-94 and on the border between St. Paul and Minneapolis, the Midway, like any other state fairgrounds, is alive with a mix of energies and people. Its position as mid-way, as a place of boundary crossing, also reflects our vision for this journal. The work here complicates and questions the boundaries of genre, binary, and aesthetic. It offers surprises and ways of re-seeing, re-thinking, and re-feeling: a veritable banquet of lit-

erary fare. Which is why, in each new issue, we are honored to present work by both new and established writers alike." Member CLMP.

NEEDS No length limit.

HOW TO CONTACT Submit 1 piece of fiction or 2 pieces of flash/sudden fiction via online submissions manager.

TIPS "An interesting story with engaging writing, both in terms of style and voice, make a ms stand out. Round characters are a must. Writers who take chances either with content or with form grab an editor's immediate attention. Spend time with the words on the page. Spend time with the language. The language and voice are not vehicles; they, too, are tools."

MINAS TIRITH EVENING-STAR: JOURNAL OF THE AMERICAN TOLKIEN SOCIETY

American Tolkien Society, P.O. Box 97, Highland MI 48357-0097, U.S.A. **E-mail:** editor@americantolkiensociety.org; americantolkiensociety@yahoo.com. **E-mail:** editor@americantolkiensociety.org. **Website:** www.americantolkiensociety.org. **Contact:** Amalie A. Helms, editor. Estab. 1967. *Minas Tirith Evening-Star: Journal of the American Tolkien Society*, published occasionally, publishes poetry, book reviews, essays, and fan fiction. *Minas Tirith Evening-Star* is digest-sized, offset-printed from typescript, with cartoon-like b&w graphics. Press run is 400. Single copy: $3.50; subscription: $12.50. Sample: $3. Make checks payable to American Tolkien Society.

HOW TO CONTACT Submit complete ms by mail or e-mail.

PAYMENT/TERMS Pays 1 contributor's copy.

THE MINNESOTA REVIEW

Virginia Tech, **E-mail:** editors@theminnesotareview.org. **E-mail:** submissions@theminnesotareview.org. **Website:** minnesotareview.wordpress.com. **Contact:** Janell Watson, editor. Estab. 1960. *The Minnesota Review*, published biannually, is a journal featuring creative and critical work from writers on the rise or who are already established. Each issue is about 200 pages, digest-sized, flat-spined, with glossy card cover. Press run is 1,000 (400 subscribers). Also available online. Subscription: $30 for 2 years for individuals, $60/year for institutions. Sample: $15.

◐ Open to submissions August 1-November 1 and January 1-April 1.

NEEDS Length: up to 5,000 words for short stories, up to 1,000 words for short shorts or flash fiction.

HOW TO CONTACT Submit up to 1 short story or 4 short shorts or flash fiction pieces per reading period via online submissions manager.

PAYMENT/TERMS Pays 2 contributor's copies.

❸ THE MISSOURI REVIEW

357 McReynolds Hall, University of Missouri, Columbia MO 65211. (573)882-4474. **E-mail:** question@moreview.com. **Website:** www.missourireview.com. **Contact:** Kate McIntyre. Estab. 1978. The William Peden Prize of $1,000 is awarded annually to the best piece of fiction to have appeared in the previous volume year. The winner is chosen by an outside judge. There is no separate application process. Publishes contemporary fiction, poetry, interviews, personal essays, and special features—such as History as Literature series, Found Text series, and Curio Cabinet art features—for the literary and the general reader interested in a wide range of subjects.

NEEDS Length: No restrictions, but longer mss (9,000-12,000 words) or flash fiction ms (up to 2,000 words) must be truly exceptional to be published.

HOW TO CONTACT Send complete ms.

PAYMENT/TERMS Pays $40/printed page.

TIPS "Send your best work."

MOBIUS

The Journal of Social Change, 149 Talmadge St., Madison WI 53704. **E-mail:** fmschep@charter.net. **E-mail:** fmschep@charter.net (fiction); demiurge@fibitz.com (poetry). **Website:** www.mobiusmagazine.com. **Contact:** Fred Schepartz, publisher and executive editor. Estab. 1989. *Mobius: The Journal of Social Change* is an online-only journal, published quarterly in March, June, September, and December. "At *Mobius* we believe that writing is power and good writing empowers both the reader and the writer. We feel strongly that alternatives are needed to an increasingly corporate literary scene. *Mobius* strives to provide an outlet for writers disenfranchised by a bottom-line marketplace and challenging writing for those who feel that today's literary standards are killing us in a slow, mind-numbing fashion."

NEEDS Wants fiction dealing with themes of social change. "We like social commentary, but mainly we like good writing. No porn or work that is racist, sexist or any other kind of -*ist*. No Christian or spirituality proselytizing fiction." Length: up to 5,000 words.

HOW TO CONTACT Submit up to 1 story at a time via e-mail (preferred) or mail.

TIPS "We like high impact. We like plot- and character-driven stories that function like theater of the mind. We look first and foremost for good writing. Prose must be crisp and polished; the story must pique my interest and make me care due to a certain intellectual, emotional aspect. *Mobius* is about social change. We want stories that make some statement about the society we live in, either on a macro or micro level. Not that your story needs to preach from a soapbox (actually, we prefer that it doesn't), but it needs to have something to say."

THE MOCHILA REVIEW

Missouri Western State University, Department of English & Modern Languages, 4525 Downs Dr., St. Joseph MO 64507. **E-mail:** mochila@missouriwestern. edu. **Website:** www.missouriwestern.edu/orgs/mochila/homepage.htm. **Contact:** Dr. Marianne Kunkel, editor in chief. Estab. 2000. "*The Mochila Review* is an annual international undergraduate journal published with support from the English and Modern Languages department at Missouri Western State University. Our goal is to publish the best short stories, poems, and essays from the next generation of important authors: student writers. Our staff, comprised primarily of undergraduate students, understands the publishing challenges that emerging writers face and is committed to helping talented students gain wider audiences in the pages of *The Mochila Review* and on our website."

NEEDS Length: up to 5,000 words.

HOW TO CONTACT Submit complete ms via online submissions manager.

PAYMENT/TERMS Pays contributor's copies.

TIPS "Mss with fresh language, energy, passion, and intelligence stand out. Study the craft, and be entertaining and engaging."

🌑 MORPHEUS TALES

E-mail: morpheustales@gmail.com. **Website:** morpheustales.wixsite.com/morpheustales. **Contact:** Adam Bradley, publisher. Estab. 2008. "We publish the best in horror, science fiction, and fantasy—both fiction and nonfiction."

NEEDS Length: 800-3,000 words.

HOW TO CONTACT Send complete ms.

🌑💲 MSLEXIA

Mslexia Publications Ltd., P.O. Box 656, Newcastle upon Tyne NE99 1PZ, United Kingdom. (44)(191)204-8860. **E-mail:** submissions@mslexia.co.uk; postbag@mslexia.co.uk; debbie@mslexia.co.uk. **Website:** www.mslexia.co.uk. **Contact:** Debbie Taylor, editorial director. Estab. 1997. "*Mslexia* tells you all you need to know about exploring your creativity and getting into print. No other magazine provides *Mslexia*'s unique mix of advice and inspiration; news, reviews, interviews; competitions, events, grants; all served up with a challenging selection of new poetry and prose. *Mslexia* is read by authors and absolute beginners. A quarterly master class in the business and psychology of writing, it's the essential magazine for women who write. We accept submissions from any woman from any country writing in English. There are 14 ways of submitting to the magazine, for every kind of writing, and we pay for everything we publish. Submissions guidelines are on our website. We also run a series of women's fiction competitions with top cash prizes and career development opportunities for finalists."

NEEDS See guidelines on website. "Submissions not on 1 of our current themes will be returned (if submitted with a SASE) or destroyed." Length: 50-2,200 words.

HOW TO CONTACT Send complete ms.

PAYMENT/TERMS Pays £15 per 1,000 words prose plus contributor's copies.

TIPS "Read the magazine; subscribe if you can afford it. *Mslexia* has a particular style and relationship with its readers which is hard to assess at a quick glance. The majority of our readers live in the UK, so feature pitches should be aware of this. We never commission work without seeing a written sample first. We rarely accept unsolicited manuscripts, but prefer a short letter suggesting a feature, plus a brief bio and writing sample."

💲 MUZZLE BLASTS

P.O. Box 67, Friendship IN 47021. (812)667-5131. **Fax:** (812)667-5136. **E-mail:** llarkin@nmlra.org. **Website:** www.nmlra.org. **Contact:** Lee A. Larkin, editor. Estab. 1939. "Articles must relate to muzzleloading or the muzzleloading era of American history."

NEEDS Must pertain to muzzleloading. Length: 2,500 words.

HOW TO CONTACT Query.

PAYMENT/TERMS Pays $50-300.

N+1

The Editors, 68 Jay St., Suite 405, Brooklyn NY 11201. **E-mail:** editors@nplusonemag.com. **E-mail:** submissions@nplusonemag.com. **Website:** www.nplusonemag.com. **Contact:** Nikil Saval and Dayna Tortorici, editors.

NEEDS Submit queries or finished pieces by e-mail.

TIPS "Most of the slots available for a given issue will have been filled many months before publication. If you would like to brave the odds, the best submission guidelines are those implied by the magazine itself. Read an issue or two through to get a sense of whether your piece might fit into *n+1*."

🚫 NA'AMAT WOMAN

21515 Vanowen Street, Suite 102, Canoga Park CA 91303. (818)431-2200. **E-mail:** naamat@naamat.org; judith@naamat.org. **Website:** www.naamat.org. **Contact:** Judith Sokoloff, editor. Estab. 1926. "Magazine covering a wide variety of subjects of interest to the Jewish community—including political and social issues, arts, profiles; many articles about Israel and women's issues. Fiction must have a Jewish theme. Readers are the American Jewish community." Circ. 15,000. "Magazine covering a wide variety of subjects of interest to the Jewish community— including political and social issues, arts, profiles; many articles about Israel and women's issues. Fiction must have a Jewish theme. Readers are the American Jewish community."

NEEDS Ethnic/multicultural, historical, humor/satire, literary, novel excerpts, women-oriented. Receives 10 unsolicited mss/month. Accepts 1-3 mss/year. "We want serious fiction, with insight, reflection and consciousness." "We do not want fiction that is mostly dialogue. No corny Jewish humor. No Holocaust fiction." Length: 2,000-3,000 words.

HOW TO CONTACT Query with published clips or send complete mss. Responds in 6 months to queries; 6 months to mss. Sample copy for 9×11½ SAE and $2 postage or look online. Sample copy for $2. Writer's guidelines for #10 SASE, or by e-mail. Query with published clips or send complete ms.

PAYMENT/TERMS Pays 10¢/word and 2 contributor's copies. Pays on publication for first North American serial, first, one time, second serial (reprint) rights,

makes work-for-hire assignments. Pays 10-20¢/word for assigned articles and for unsolicited articles.

TIPS "No maudlin nostalgia or romance; no hackneyed Jewish humor."

NARRATIVE MAGAZINE

2443 Fillmore St., #214, San Francisco CA 94115. **E-mail:** contact@narrativemagazine.com. **Website:** www.narrativemagazine.com. **Contact:** Michael Croft, senior editor; Mimi Kusch, managing editor; Michael Wiegers, poetry editor. Estab. 2003. "*Narrative* publishes high-quality contemporary literature in a full range of styles, forms, and lengths. Submit poetry, fiction, and nonfiction, including stories, short shorts, novels, novel excerpts, novellas, personal essays, humor, sketches, memoirs, literary biographies, commentary, reportage, interviews, and short audio recordings of short-short stories and poems. We welcome submissions of previously unpublished mss of all lengths, ranging from short-short stories to complete book-length works for serialization. In addition to submissions for issues of *Narrative* itself, we also encourage submissions for our Story of the Week, Poem of the Week, literary contests, and Readers' Narratives. Please read our Submission Guidelines for all information on mss formatting, word lengths, author payment, and other policies. We accept submissions only through our electronic submission system. We do not accept submissions through postal services or e-mail. You may send us mss for the following submission categories: General Submissions, Narrative Prize, Story of the Week, Poem of the Week, Readers' Narrative, iPoem, iStory, Six-Word Story, or a specific Contest. Your mss must be in one of the following file forms: DOC, RTF, PDF, DOCX, TXT, WPD, ODF, MP3, MP4, MOV, or FLV."

🔵 *Narrative* has received recognitions in *New Stories from the South*, *Best American Mystery Stories*, *O. Henry Prize Stories*, *Best American Short Stories*, *Best American Essays*, and the *Pushcart Prize Collection*. In an article on the business of books, the National Endowment for the Arts featured *Narrative* as the model for the evolution of both print and digital publishing.

NEEDS Has published work by Alice Munro, Tobias Wolff, Marvin Bell, Jane Smiley, Joyce Carol Oates, E.L. Doctorow, and Min Jin Lee. Publishes new and emerging writers.

HOW TO CONTACT Send complete ms.

PAYMENT/TERMS Pays on publication between $150-1,000, $1,000-5,000 for book length, plus annual prizes of more than $28,000.

TIPS "Log on and study our magazine online. Narrative fiction, graphic art, and multimedia are selected, first and foremost, for quality."

THE NASSAU REVIEW

Nassau Community College, Nassau Community College, English Department, 1 Education Dr., Garden City NY 11530. **E-mail:** nassaureview@ncc.edu. **Website:** www.ncc.edu/nassaureview. **Contact:** Christina M. Rau, editor in chief. Estab. 1964. *The Nassau Review* welcomes submissions of many genres, preferring work that is "innovative, captivating, well-crafted, and unique, work that crosses boundaries of genre and tradition. You may be serious. You may be humorous. You may be somewhere in between. We are looking simply for quality. New and seasoned writers are welcome."

○ All open submissions are under consideration for the Writer Awards.

NEEDS Accepts simultaneous submissions: "Please let us know they are simultaneous when you submit them." Does not want "children's literature; cliché, unoriginal work; fan fiction." Length: 100-3,000 words.

HOW TO CONTACT Submit via online submissions manager. Include title, word count, and bio of up to 100 words.

PAYMENT/TERMS Pays 1 contributor's copy.

NATURAL BRIDGE

Department of English, University of Missouri-St. Louis, 1 University Blvd., St. Louis MO 63121. **E-mail:** natural@umsl.edu. **Website:** www.umsl.edu/~natural. Estab. 1999. *Natural Bridge*, published biannually in April and December, invites submissions of poetry, fiction, personal essays, and translations.

○ No longer accepts submissions via e-mail. Accepts submissions through online submission manager and postal mail only.

NEEDS Submit year round; however, "we do not read May 1-August 1." Recently published work by Tayari Jones, Steve Stern, Jamie Wriston Colbert, Lex Williford, and Mark Jay Mirsky. Also publishes literary essays, poetry. Sometimes comments on rejected mss.

HOW TO CONTACT Submit 1 ms through online submissions manager ($3 fee for nonsubscribers) or postal mail (free).

PAYMENT/TERMS Pays 2 contributor's copies and one-year subscription.

NEBO

Arkansas Tech University, Department of English, Russellville AR 72801. **E-mail:** nebo@atu.edu. **E-mail:** nebo@atu.edu. **Website:** www.atu.edu/world-languages/Nebo.php. **Contact:** Editor. Estab. 1983. *Nebo*, published in the spring and fall, publishes fiction, poetry, creative nonfiction, drama, comics, and art from Arkansas Tech students and unpublished writers as well as nationally known writers.

○ Reads submissions August 15-May 1.

NEEDS Accepts all genres. Length: up to 5,000 words.

HOW TO CONTACT Submit complete ms by e-mail or postal mail.

TIPS "Avoid pretentiousness. Write something you genuinely care about. Please edit your work for spelling, grammar, cohesiveness, and overall purpose. Many of the mss we receive should be publishable with a little polishing. Mss should never be submitted handwritten or on 'onion skin' or colored paper."

◐⊘ NEON MAGAZINE

Neon Books, UK. **E-mail:** info@neonmagazine.co.uk. **E-mail:** subs@neonmagazine.co.uk. **Website:** www.neonmagazine.co.uk. **Contact:** Krishan Coupland. Twice-yearly online and print magazine featuring alternative work of any form of poetry and prose, short stories, flash fiction, artwork, and reviews. "*Neon* sits on the edge of horror and science-fiction, but with strong literary leanings. If you have a taste for the magical realist or uncanny, *Neon* is the magazine for you."

NEEDS "No nonsensical prose; we are not appreciative of sentimentality." No word limit.

HOW TO CONTACT Full guidelines online.

PAYMENT/TERMS Pays royalties.

TIPS "Send several poems, 1-2 pieces of prose, or several images via form e-mail. Include the word 'submission' in your subject line. Include a short biographical note (up to 100 words). Read submission guidelines before submitting your work."

THE NEW CRITERION

900 Broadway, Ste. 602, New York NY 10003. **Website:** www.newcriterion.com. **Contact:** Roger Kimball, editor and publisher; David Yezzi, poetry editor. Estab. 1982. "A monthly review of the arts and intellectual life, *The New Criterion* began as an experiment in critical audacity—a publication devoted to engaging, in Matthew Arnold's famous phrase, with 'the best that has been thought and said.' This also meant engaging with those forces dedicated to traducing genuine cultural and intellectual achievement, whether through obfuscation, politicization, or a commitment to nihilistic absurdity. We are proud that *The New Criterion* has been in the forefront both of championing what is best and most humanely vital in our cultural inheritance and in exposing what is mendacious, corrosive, and spurious. Published monthly from September through June, *The New Criterion* brings together a wide range of young and established critics whose common aim is to bring you the most incisive criticism being written today."

- *The New Criterion* is 90 pages, 7x10, flat-spined. Single copy: $12.

NEW DELTA REVIEW

University of Louisiana English Dept., Baton Rouge LA 70803. **Website:** ndrmag.org. Estab. 1984. "We seek vivid and exciting work from new and established writers. We have published fiction from writers such as National Book Award finalist Patricia Smith, Pushcart Prize winner Stacey Richter, and former poet laureate Billy Collins."

- Semiannual. Editors change every year; check website. Online only. *New Delta Review* also sponsors the Matt Clark Prizes for fiction and poetry, the annual Ryan Gibbs Awards for short fiction and photography, and an annual chapbook contest. Work from the magazine has been included in the *Pushcart Prize* anthology.

NEEDS "We publish fiction in wildly different styles and modes. It's easy to say, "Please read our journal to get a sense of our aesthetic," so we will! After you've read, please send us fiction that is emotionally engaging and structurally sound. We also appreciate (carefully considered) risks with language, content, and form. We also have a special interest in flash fiction, and brief series of flash pieces." "No Elvis stories, over-wrought 'Southern' fiction, or cancer stories." Length: up to 3,000 words.

PAYMENT/TERMS Offers no payment, but all published pieces are eligible for yearly editor's prize of $250.

TIPS "Our staff is open-minded and youthful. We base decisions on merit, not reputation. The ms that's most enjoyable to read gets the nod. Be bold, take risks, surprise us."

NEW ENGLAND REVIEW

Middlebury College, Middlebury VT 05753. (802)443-5075. **E-mail:** nereview@middlebury.edu. **Website:** www.nereview.com. **Contact:** Marcia Parlow, managing editor. Estab. 1978. *New England Review* is a prestigious, nationally distributed literary journal. Reads September 1-May 31 (postmarked dates). *New England Review* is 200+ pages, 7x10, printed on heavy stock, flat-spined, with glossy cover with art. Receives 3,000-4,000 poetry submissions/year, accepts about 70-80 poems/year. Receives 550 unsolicited mss/month, accepts 6 mss/issue, 24 fiction mss/year. Does not accept mss June-August, December-January. Agented fiction less than 5%.

NEEDS Send 1 story at a time, unless it is very short. Wants only serious literary fiction and novel excerpts. Publishes approximately 10 new writers/year. Has published work by Steve Almond, Christine Sneed, Roy Kesey, Thomas Gough, Norman Lock, Brock Clarke, Carl Phillips, Lucia Perillo, Linda Gregerson, and Natasha Trethewey. Length: not strict on word count.

HOW TO CONTACT Send complete ms via online submission manager. No e-mail submissions. "Will consider simultaneous submissions, but it must be stated as such and you must notify us immediately if the ms is accepted for publication elsewhere."

PAYMENT/TERMS Pays $20/page ($20 minimum), and 2 contributor's copies.

TIPS "We consider short fiction, including short shorts, novellas, and self-contained extracts from novels in both traditional and experimental forms. In nonfiction, we consider a variety of general and literary but not narrowly scholarly essays; we also publish long and short poems, screenplays, graphics, translations, critical reassessments, statements by artists working in various media, testimonies, and letters from abroad. We are committed to exploration of all forms of contemporary cultural expression in the U.S.

and abroad. With few exceptions, we print only work not published previously elsewhere."

⑤ NEW LETTERS

University of Missouri-Kansas City, 5101 Rockhill Rd., Kansas City MO 64110. (816)235-1168. **Fax:** (816)235-2611. **E-mail:** newletters@umkc.edu. **Website:** www.newletters.org. **Contact:** Robert Stewart, editor-in-chief. Estab. 1934. "*New Letters*, published quarterly, continues to seek the best new writing, whether from established writers or those ready and waiting to be discovered. In addition, it supports those writers, readers, and listeners who want to experience the joy of writing that can both surprise and inspire us all." Submissions are not read May 1 through October 1.

NEEDS No genre fiction. Length: up to 5,000 words.

HOW TO CONTACT Send complete ms.

PAYMENT/TERMS Pays $30-75.

TIPS "We aren't interested in essays that are footnoted or essays usually described as scholarly or critical. Our preference is for creative nonfiction or personal essays. We prefer shorter stories and essays to longer ones (an average length is 3,500-4,000 words). We have no rigid preferences as to subject, style, or genre, although commercial efforts tend to put us off. Even so, our only fixed requirement is good writing."

NEW MADRID

Journal of Contemporary Literature, Murray State University, Department of English and Philosophy, 7C Faculty Hall, Murray KY 42071-3341. (270)809-4730. **E-mail:** msu.newmadrid@murraystate.edu. **Website:** newmadridjournal.org. **Contact:** Ann Neelon, editor; Jacque E. Day, managing editor. "*New Madrid* is the national journal of the low-residency MFA program at Murray State University. It takes its name from the New Madrid seismic zone, which falls within the central Mississippi Valley and extends through western Kentucky."

○   See website for guidelines and upcoming themes. "We have 2 reading periods, August 15-October 15 and January 15-March 15." Also publishes poetry and creative nonfiction. Rarely comments on/critiques rejected mss.

NEEDS Length: up to 20 pages double-spaced.

HOW TO CONTACT Accepts submissions by online submissions manager only. Include brief bio, list of publications. Considers multiple submissions.

PAYMENT/TERMS Pays 2 contributor's copies.

TIPS "Quality is the determining factor for breaking into *New Madrid*. We are looking for well-crafted, compelling writing in a range of genres, forms, and styles."

⑤ NEW OHIO REVIEW

English Department, 79 S. Court St.; Lindley Hall, Ohio University, Athens OH 45701. (740)707-3191. **E-mail:** noreditors@ohio.edu. **Website:** www.ohiou.edu/nor. **Contact:** David Wanczyk, editor. Estab. 2007. *New Ohio Review*, published biannually in spring and fall, publishes fiction, nonfiction, and poetry. Member CLMP. Reading period is September 15-December 15 and January 15-April 15. Annual contests, Jan 15th-Apr 15th ($1,000 prizes).

NEEDS Considers literary short fiction; no novel excerpts.

HOW TO CONTACT Send complete ms.

PAYMENT/TERMS Pays $30 minimum in addition to 2 contributor's copies and one-year subscription.

⑤ NEW ORLEANS REVIEW

Box 195, Loyola University, New Orleans LA 70118. (504)865-2295. **E-mail:** noreview@loyno.edu. **Website:** neworleansreview.org. **Contact:** Heidi Braden, managing editor; Mark Yakich, fiction editor. Estab. 1968. *New Orleans Review* is an annual journal of contemporary literature and culture, publishing new poetry, fiction, nonfiction, art, photography, film, and book reviews.

○   The journal has published an eclectic variety of work by established and emerging writers, including Walker Percy, Pablo Neruda, Ellen Gilchrist, Nelson Algren, Hunter S. Thompson, John Kennedy Toole, Richard Brautigan, Barry Spacks, James Sallis, Jack Gilbert, Paul Hoover, Rodney Jones, Annie Dillard, Everette Maddox, Julio Cortazar, Gordon Lish, Robert Walser, Mark Halliday, Jack Butler, Robert Olen Butler, Michael Harper, Angela Ball, Joyce Carol Oates, Diane Wakoski, Dermot Bolger, Roddy Doyle, William Kotzwinkle, Alain Robbe-Grillet, Arnost Lustig, Raymond Queneau, Yusef Komunyakaa, Michael Martone, Tess Gallagher, Matthea Harvey, D. A. Powell, Rikki Ducornet, and Ed Skoog.

NEEDS Length: up to 6,500 words.

HOW TO CONTACT Submit complete ms using online submissions manager ($3 fee).

PAYMENT/TERMS Pays 2 contributor's copies.

TIPS "We're looking for dynamic writing that demonstrates attention to the language and a sense of the medium, writing that engages, surprises, moves us. We're not looking for genre fiction or academic articles. We subscribe to the belief that in order to truly write well, one must first master the rudiments: grammar and syntax, punctuation, the sentence, the paragraph, the line, the stanza. We receive about 3,000 mss a year and publish about 3% of them. Check out a recent issue, send us your best, proofread your work, be patient, be persistent."

○ ❸ THE NEW QUARTERLY

St. Jerome's University, 290 Westmount Rd. N., Waterloo ON N2L 3G3, Canada. (519)884-8111, ext. 28290. **E-mail:** editor@tnq.ca; info@tnq.ca. **Website:** www.tnq.ca. Estab. 1981. "Emphasis on emerging writers and genres, but we publish more traditional work as well if the language and narrative structure are fresh." Open to Canadian writers only. Reading periods: March 1-August 31; September 1-February 28.

NEEDS *"Canadian work only.* We are not interested in genre fiction. We are looking for innovative, beautifully crafted, deeply felt literary fiction."

HOW TO CONTACT Send complete ms with submission cover sheet and bio. Does not accept submissions by e-mail. Accepts simultaneoues submissions if indicated in cover letter.

PAYMENT/TERMS Pays $250/story.

TIPS "Reading us is the best way to get our measure. We don't have preconceived ideas about what we're looking for other than that it must be Canadian work (Canadian writers, not necessarily Canadian content). We want something that's fresh, something that will repay a second reading, something in which the language soars and the feeling is complexly rendered."

NEW SOUTH

Georgia State University, Campus Box 1894, MSC 8R0322 Unit 8, Atlanta GA 30303-3083. **E-mail:** newsoutheditors@gmail.com. **Website:** www.newsouthjournal.com. Estab. 1980. Semiannual magazine dedicated to finding and publishing the best work from artists around the world. Wants original voices searching to rise above the ordinary. Seeks to publish high-quality work, regardless of genre, form, or regional ties. *New South* is 160+ pages. Press run is 1,500, and free to GSU students. The *New South* An-

nual Writing Contest offers $1,000 for the best poem and $1,000 for the best story or essay; one-year subscription to all who submit. Submissions must be unpublished. Submit up to 3 poems, 1 story, or 1 essay on any subject or in any form. Guidelines available online. Competition receives 300 entries. Past judges include Sharon Olds, Jane Hirschfield, Anthony Hecht, Phillip Levine, Mark Doty, and Jake Adam York. Winners will be published in the Fall issue.

NEEDS Receives 200 unsolicited mss/month. Publishes and welcomes short shorts. Length: up to 9,000 words (short stories); up to 1,000 words (short shorts).

HOW TO CONTACT Submit 1 short story or up to 5 short shorts through Submittable.

PAYMENT/TERMS Pays 2 contributor's copies.

TIPS "We want what's new, what's fresh, and what's different—whether it comes from the Southern United States, the South of India, or the North, East or West of Anywhere."

❸ NEW WELSH REVIEW

P.O. Box 170, Aberystwyth, Ceredigion SY23 1 WZ, United Kingdom. 01970-628410. **E-mail:** editor@newwelshreview.com. **E-mail:** submissions@newwelshreview.com. **Website:** www.newwelshreview.com. **Contact:** Gwen Davies, editor. *"New Welsh Review,* a literary magazine published 3 times/year and ranked in the top 5 British literary magazines, publishes stories, poems, and critical essays. The best of Welsh writing in English, past and present, is celebrated, discussed, and debated. We seek poems, short stories, reviews, special features/articles, and commentary."

HOW TO CONTACT Submit complete ms by e-mail.

PAYMENT/TERMS Pays direct to account or sends check on publication and 1 copy at discounted contributor's rate of £5 inc p&p."

❸ THE NEW YORKER

1 World Trade Center, New York NY 10007. **E-mail:** themail@newyorker.com. **E-mail:** poetry@newyorker.com. **Website:** www.newyorker.com. **Contact:** David Remnick, editor in chief. Estab. 1925. A quality weekly magazine of distinct news stories, articles, essays, and poems for a literate audience.

○ *The New Yorker* receives approximately 4,000 submissions per month.

NEEDS Publishes 1 ms/issue.

HOW TO CONTACT Send complete ms by e-mail (as PDF attachment) or mail (address to Fiction Editor).

PAYMENT/TERMS Payment varies.

TIPS "Be lively, original, not overly literary. Write what you want to write, not what you think the editor would like."

NIMROD

International Journal of Prose and Poetry, University of Tulsa, 800 S. Tucker Dr., Tulsa OK 74104-3189. (918)631-3080. **Fax:** (918)631-3033. **E-mail:** nimrod@utulsa.edu. **Website:** www.utulsa.edu/nimrod. **Contact:** Eilis O'Neal, editor-in-chief; Cassidy McCants, associate editor. Estab. 1956. Since its founding in 1956 at The University of Tulsa, *Nimrod International Journal of Prose and Poetry*'s mission has been the discovery, development, and promotion of new writing. On a national and international scale, *Nimrod* helps new writers find their audiences through publication in our semiannual journal. We offer new and promising work that may be unfamiliar to readers, such as writing from countries not well represented in the American mainstream, writing in translation, and writing from people of under-represented ages, races, and sexual identities. On a personal scale, we continue our longstanding dedication to a full review of every submission to *Nimrod* by at least two readers from our Editorial Board. We also remain committed to responding personally to the hundreds of submissions we receive, often offering direct editorial feedback geared to helping writers expand their craft. *Nimrod* supports and defends the literary tradition of small magazines, spotlighting lesser-known poets and writers and providing foundations for their literary careers. We promote a living literature, believing that it is possible to search for, recognize, and reward contemporary writing of imagination, substance, and skill. Semiannual magazine: 200 pages; perfect-bound; 4-color cover. Receives 300 unsolicited mss/month. **Publishes 50-120 new writers/year.** Reading period: January 1 through November 30. Online submissions accepted at nimrodjournal.submittable.com/submit. Does not accept submissions by -mail unless the writer is living outside the U.S. and cannot submit using the submissions manager.

NEEDS Wants "vigorous writing, characters that are well developed, dialogue that is realistic without being banal." Length: up to 7,500 words.

HOW TO CONTACT Submit complete ms by mail or through the online submissions manager. Include SASE for work submitted by mail.

PAYMENT/TERMS Pays 2 contributor's copies.

🌑 NINTH LETTER

Department of English, University of Illinois, 608 S. Wright St., Urbana IL 61801. **E-mail:** info@ninthletter.com; editor@ninthletter.com; fiction@ninthletter.com; poetry@ninthletter.com; nonfiction@ninthletter.com. **Website:** www.ninthletter.com. **Contact:** Editorial staff rotates; contact genre-specific e-mail address with inquiries. "*Ninth Letter* accepts submissions of fiction, poetry, and essays from September 1-February 28 (postmark dates). *Ninth Letter* is published semiannually at the University of Illinois, Urbana-Champaign. We are interested in prose and poetry that experiment with form, narrative, and nontraditional subject matter, as well as more traditional literary work."

⊙ *Ninth Letter* won Best New Literary Journal 2005 from the Council of Editors of Learned Journals (CELJ) and has had poetry selected for *Best American Poetry*, *The Pushcart Prize*, *Best New Poets*, and *The Year's Best Fantasy and Horror*.

NEEDS Length: up to 8,000 words.

HOW TO CONTACT "Please send only 1 story at a time. All mailed submissions must include an SASE for reply."

PAYMENT/TERMS Pays $25/printed page and 2 contributor's copies.

NITE-WRITER'S INTERNATIONAL LITERARY ARTS JOURNAL

158 Spencer Ave., Suite 100, Pittsburgh PA 15227. **E-mail:** nitewritersliteraryarts@gmail.com. **Website:** sites.google.com/site/nitewriterinternational/home. **Contact:** John Thompson. Estab. 1994. *Nite-Writer's International Literary Arts Journal* is "dedicated to the emotional intellectual with a creative perception of life."

⊙ Journal is open to beginners as well as professionals.

NEEDS Length: up to 1,200 words.

HOW TO CONTACT All literary works should be in DOC format in 12-point font.

TIPS "Read a lot of what you write—study the market. Don't fear rejection, but use it as a learning tool to strengthen your work before resubmitting."

THE NORMAL SCHOOL

The Press at the California State University - Fresno, 5245 North Backer Ave., M/S PB 98, Fresno CA 93740-8001. **E-mail:** editors@thenormalschool.com. **Website:** thenormalschool.com. **Contact:** Sophie Beck, managing editor. Estab. 2008. Semiannual magazine that accepts outstanding work by beginning and established writers.

Mss are read September 1-December 1 and January 15-April 15. Address submissions to the appropriate editor. Charges $3 fee for each online submission, due to operational costs.

NEEDS "We consider literary short fiction with contemporary themes and styles. We tend to prefer character-driven work and pieces that explore marginalized voices." Does not want any genre writing. Length: up to 7,000 words.

HOW TO CONTACT Submit complete ms via online submissions manager.

PAYMENT/TERMS Pays 2 contributor's copies and one-year subscription.

NORTH AMERICAN REVIEW

University of Northern Iowa, 1222 W. 27th St., Cedar Falls IA 50614. (319)273-6455. **E-mail:** nar@uni.edu. **Website:** northamericanreview.org. Estab. 1815. "The *North American Review* is the oldest literary magazine in America and one of the most respected; though we have no prejudices about the subject matter of material sent to us, our first concern is quality."

This is the oldest literary magazine in the country and one of the most prestigious. Also one of the most entertaining—and a tough market for the young writer.

NEEDS Wants to see more "well-crafted literary stories that emphasize family concerns. We'd also like to see more stories engaged with environmental concerns." Reads fiction mss during academic year. **Publishes 2 new writers/year.** Recently published work by Lee Ann Roripaugh, Dick Allen, and Rita Welty Bourke. "No flat narrative stories where the inferiority of the character is the paramount concern." Length: up to 30 pages.

HOW TO CONTACT Submit ms via online submissions manager.

TIPS "We like stories that start quickly and have a strong narrative arc. Poems that are passionate about subject, language, and image are welcome, whether they are traditional or experimental, whether in formal or free verse (closed or open form). Nonfiction should combine art and fact with the finest writing."

NORTH CAROLINA LITERARY REVIEW

East Carolina University, Mailstop 555 English, Greenville NC 27858-4353. (252)328-1537. **Fax:** (252)328-4889. **E-mail:** bauerm@ecu.edu; nclruser@ecu.edu. **E-mail:** nclrsubmissions@ecu.edu. **Website:** www.nclr.ecu.edu. **Contact:** Margaret Bauer. Estab. 1992. "Articles should have a North Carolina slant. Fiction, creative nonfiction, and poetry accepted through yearly contests. First consideration is always for quality of work. Although we treat academic and scholarly subjects, we do not wish to see jargon-laden prose; our readers, we hope, are found as often in bookstores and libraries as in academia. We seek to combine the best elements of a magazine for serious readers with the best of a scholarly journal." Accepts submissions through Submittable.

NEEDS Length: up to 6,000 words.

HOW TO CONTACT Submit fiction for the Doris Betts Fiction Prize competition via Submittable.

PAYMENT/TERMS First-place winners of contests receive a prize of $250. Other writers whose stories are selected for publication receive contributor's copies.

TIPS "By far the easiest way to break in is with special issue sections. We are especially interested in reports on conferences, readings, meetings that involve North Carolina writers, and personal essays or short narratives with a strong sense of place. See back issues for other departments. Interviews are probably the other easiest place to break in; no discussions of poetics/theory, etc., except in reader-friendly (accessible) language. Interviews should be personal, more like conversations, and extensive, exploring connections between a writer's life and his or her work."

NORTH DAKOTA QUARTERLY

University of North Dakota, 276 Centennial Dr. Stop 7209, Merrifield Hall Room 15, Grand Forks ND 58202. (701)777-3322. **E-mail:** ndq@und.edu. **Website:** www.ndquarterly.org. **Contact:** William Caraher, editor; Gilad Elbom, fiction editor; Heidi Czerwiec, poetry editor; Sharon Carson, book reviews editor. Estab. 1911. *North Dakota Quarterly* strives to publish the best fiction, poetry, and essays that in our estimation we can. Our tastes and interests are best reflected in what we have been recently publishing, and we suggest that you look at some current issues for guidance.

○ Work published in *North Dakota Quarterly* was selected for inclusion in *The O. Henry Prize Stories*, *The Pushcart Prize Series*, and *Best American Essays*.

NEEDS Literary preferences are very subjective. There are no fixed, universal, or objective criteria that we use when we read fiction submissions. In recent issues of NDQ we have published stories in which the setting is clearly identified, characters are properly named and introduced, the action progresses on a linear axis, and things, generally speaking, are far from confusing. We're not against that. But we've also published a partially hallucinatory story about an incompetent broomball player, a theologically equivocal story about a Jesuit novice on an Indian reservation, a story from the perspective of a twice-kidnapped boy, a 4,000-word one-sentence story, a story about an imaginary novel, and a story about sheep in Scotland—from the perspective of a sheep. Ultimately, we're looking for multiple perspectives, different voices, and a variety of approaches to fiction. These approaches can revolve around uncertainty, ambiguity, fragmentation, polyphony, contradictory information, structural experimentation, and all the other things that teachers of freshman composition tell us we must eliminate or avoid. In other words, we value the willingness to treat fiction as textual art and take literary risks. Naturally, there is no guarantee that innovation will yield good results. But when it comes to art, it might be better to fail with something original than to play it safe with a predictable formula. No length restrictions.

HOW TO CONTACT Submit completed manuscript via https://ndquarterly.submittable.com/submit/112686/north-dakota-quarterly-fiction-submissions

⑤ NOTRE DAME REVIEW

University of Notre Dame, B009C McKenna Hall, Notre Dame IN 46556. **Website:** ndreview.nd.edu. Estab. 1995. "The *Notre Dame Review* is an independent, noncommercial magazine of contemporary American and international fiction, poetry, criticism, and art. Especially interested in work that takes on big issues by making the invisible seen, that gives voice to the voiceless. In addition to showcasing celebrated authors like Seamus Heaney and Czelaw Milosz, the *Notre Dame Review* introduces readers to authors they may have never encountered before but who are doing innovative and important work. In conjunction with the *Notre Dame Review*, the online companion to the printed magazine, the *nd[re]view*, engages readers as a community centered in literary rather than commercial concerns, a community we reach out to through critique and commentary as well as aesthetic experience."

○ Does not accept e-mail submissions. Only reads hardcopy submissions September through November and January through March.

NEEDS "We're eclectic. Upcoming theme issues planned. List of upcoming themes or editorial calendar available for SASE." No genre fiction. Length: up to 3,000 words.

HOW TO CONTACT Submit complete ms via online submissions manager.

PAYMENT/TERMS Pays $5-25.

TIPS "Excellence is our sole criteria for selection, although we are especially interested in fiction and poetry that take on big issues."

NOW & THEN

The Appalachian Magazine, East Tennessee State University, Box 70556, Johnson City TN 37614-1707. (423)439-5348. **Fax:** (423)439-7074. **E-mail:** nowandthen@etsu.edu; sandersr@etsu.edu. **Website:** www.etsu.edu/cas/cass/nowandthen. **Contact:** Randy Sanders, managing editor. Estab. 1984. *Now & Then* accepts a variety of writing genres: fiction, poetry, nonfiction, essays, interviews, memoirs, and book reviews. All submissions must relate to Appalachia and to the issue's specific theme. Readership is educated and interested in the region.

○ "At this time, the magazine is in the process of transitioning to an online-only publication. Therefore, we are currently not accepting submissions. Follow our progress by visiting the *Now & Then* website at www.etsu.edu/cas/cass/nowandthen."

NTH DEGREE

2770 Buckstone Dr., Powhatan VA 23139. **E-mail:** submissions@nthzine.com. **Website:** www.nthzine.com. **Contact:** Michael D. Pederson. Estab. 2002. Free online fanzine to promote up-and-coming new science fiction and fantasy authors and artists. Also supports the world of fandom and conventions. No longer accepts hard copy submissions.

NEEDS Length: up to 7,500 words.

HOW TO CONTACT Submit complete ms via e-mail.

PAYMENT/TERMS Pays in contributor's copies.

TIPS "Don't submit anything that you may be ashamed of 10 years later."

NUTHOUSE

P.O. Box 119, Ellenton FL 34222. **Website:** www.nuthousemagazine.com. *Nuthouse*, published every 3 months, uses humor of all kinds, including homespun and political.

○ *Nuthouse* is 12 pages, digest-sized, photocopied from desktop-published originals. Receives about 500 poems/year, accepts about 100. Press run is 100. Subscription: $5 for 4 issues.

NEEDS "We publish all genres, from the homespun to the horrific. We don't automatically dismiss crudity or profanity. We're not prudes. Yet we consider such elements cheap and insulting unless essential to the gag. *NuTHOuSe* seeks submissions that are original, tightly written, and laugh-out-loud funny." Length: up to 1,000 words. "The shorter, the better."

HOW TO CONTACT Send complete ms with SASE and cover letter. Include estimated word count, bio (paragraph), and list of publications. No e-mail submissions.

PAYMENT/TERMS Pays 1 contributor's copy.

OBSIDIAN

Brown University, **E-mail:** obsidianatbrown@gmail.com. **Website:** obsidian-magazine.tumblr.com. **Contact:** Staff rotates each year; see website for current masthead. Estab. 1975. *Obsidian* is a "literary and visual space to showcase the creativity and experiences of black people, specifically at Brown University, formed out of the need for a platform made for us, by us." It is "actively intersectional, safe, and open: a space especially for the stories and voices of black women, black queer and trans people, and black people with disabilities."

NEEDS Length: up to 4,000 words.

HOW TO CONTACT Submit by e-mail as attachment. Include brief bio up to 3 sentences long.

TIPS "Following proper format is essential. Your title must be intriguing and text clean. Never give up."

Some of the writers we publish were rejected many times before we published them."

OHIO TEACHERS WRITE

Department of English, University of Dayton, 300 College Park, Dayton OH 45469. (937)229-3463. **E-mail:** pthomas1@udayton.edu. **Website:** octela.org/publications/ohio-teachers-write. **Contact:** Patrick Thomas. Estab. 1995. "*Ohio Teachers Write* is a literary magazine published annually by the Ohio Council of Teachers of English Language Arts. This publication seeks to promote both poetry and prose of Ohio teachers and to provide an engaging collection of writing for our readership of educators and other like-minded adults. Invites electronic submissions from both active and retired Ohio educators for our annual literary print magazine."

NEEDS Submissions are limited to Ohio Educators. Length: up to 1,500 words.

HOW TO CONTACT Submit by e-mail.

PAYMENT/TERMS Pays 2 contributor's copies.

TIPS Check website for yearly theme.

OLD RED KIMONO

Georgia Highlands College, 3175 Cedartown Hwy. SE, Rome GA 30161. **E-mail:** napplega@highlands.edu. **Website:** www.highlands.edu/site/ork. **Contact:** Dr. Nancy Applegate. Estab. 1972. *Old Red Kimono*, published annually, prints original, high-quality poetry and fiction. *Old Red Kimono* is 72 pages, magazine-sized, professionally printed, color cover and 16 color pages. Receives about 250 submissions/year, accepts about 60-70. Sample: $3. Contributors receive two copies.

NEEDS Length: up 1,500 words.

HOW TO CONTACT Submit via mail or e-mail.

PAYMENT/TERMS Pays 2 contributor's copies.

⑤ ONE STORY

232 3rd St., #A108, Brooklyn NY 11215. **Website:** www.one-story.com. **Contact:** Maribeth Batcha, publisher. Estab. 2002. "*One Story* is a literary magazine that contains, simply, 1 story. Approximately every 3-4 weeks, subscribers are sent *One Story* in the mail. *One Story* is artfully designed, lightweight, easy to carry, and ready to entertain on buses, in bed, in subways, in cars, in the park, in the bath, in the waiting rooms of doctor's offices, on the couch, or in line at the supermarket. Subscribers also have access to a website where they can learn more about *One Story* authors

and hear about *One Story* readings and events. There is always time to read *One Story*."

○   Reading period: September 1-May 31.

NEEDS *One Story* only accepts short stories. Do not send excerpts. Do not send more than 1 story at a time. Length: 3,000-8,000 words.

HOW TO CONTACT Send complete ms using online submission form.

PAYMENT/TERMS Pays $500 and 25 contributor's copies.

TIPS "*One Story* is looking for stories that are strong enough to stand alone. Therefore they must be very good. We want the best you can give."

✪ ON SPEC

P.O. Box 4727, Station South, Edmonton AB T6E 5G6, Canada. (780)628-7121. **E-mail:** onspec@onspec.ca. **Website:** www.onspec.ca. Estab. 1989. . "We publish speculative fiction and poetry by new and established writers, with a strong preference for Canadian-authored works."

○   See website guidelines for submission announcements. "Please refer to website for information regarding submissions, as we are not open year round."

NEEDS No media tie-in or shaggy-alien stories. No condensed or excerpted novels, religious/inspirational stories, fairy tales. Length: 1,000-6,000 words.

HOW TO CONTACT Send complete ms. Electronic submissions preferred.

TIPS "We want to see stories with plausible characters, a well-constructed, consistent, and vividly described setting, a strong plot, and believable emotions; characters must show us (not tell us) their emotional responses to each other and to the situation and/or challenge they face. Also: Don't send us stories written for television. We don't like media tie-ins, so don't watch TV for inspiration! Read instead! Strong preference given to submissions by Canadians."

❸ ON THE PREMISES: A GOOD PLACE TO START

On the Premises, LLC, 4323 Gingham Court, Alexandria VA 22310. **E-mail:** questions@onthepremises.com. **Website:** www.onthepremises.com. **Contact:** Tarl Roger Kudrick or Bethany Granger, co-publishers. Estab. 2006. Stories published in *On the Premises* are winning entries in contests that are held every 6 months. Each contest challenges writers to produce a great story based on a broad premise that our editors supply as part of the contest.*On the Premises* aims to promote newer and/or relatively unknown writers who can write what we feel are creative, compelling stories told in effective, uncluttered, and evocative prose. Entrants pay no fees, and winners receive cash prizes in addition to publication. Also holds four "mini-contests" a year in which authors are asked to write extremely short fiction (50 words or so) in accordance with special challenges.

○   Does not read March or September. Receives 50-150 mss/month. Accepts 4-7 mss/issue; 8-14 mss/year. Has published a few well-known authors such as multiple award-winner Ken Liu, as well as dozens of lesser known authors and quite a few first-time fiction sellers. Member Small Press Promotions.

NEEDS Themes are announced the day each contest is launched. List of past and current premises available on website. "All genres considered. All stories must be based on the broad premise supplied as part of the contest. Sample premise, taken from the first issue: 'One or more characters are traveling in a vehicle, and never reach their intended destination. Why not? What happens instead?'" No young adult, children's, or "preachy" fiction. "In general, we don't like stories that were written solely to make a social or political point, especially if the story seems to assume that no intelligent person could possibly disagree with the author. Save the ideology for editorial and opinion pieces, please. But above all, we *never ever* want to see stories that do not use the contest premise! Use the premise, and make it 'clear' and 'obvious' that you are using the premise." Length: 1,000-5,000 words. Average length: 3,500 words.

HOW TO CONTACT Submit stories only via submission form at onthepremises.submittable.com/submit. "We no longer accept e-mailed submissions."

PAYMENT/TERMS Pays $60-220.

TIPS "Make sure you use the premise, not just interpret it. If the premise is 'must contain a real live dog,' then think of a creative, compelling way to use a real dog. Revise your draft, then revise again and again. Remember, we judge stories blindly, so craftmanship and creativity matter, not how well known you are."

✪ OPEN MINDS QUARTERLY

36 Elgin St., 2nd Floor, Sudbury ON P3C 5B4, Canada. (705)222-6472, ext. 303. **E-mail:** openminds@nisa.

on.ca. **Website:** www.openmindsquarterly.com. **Contact:** Sarah Mann, editor. Estab. 1997. *Open Minds Quarterly* provides a venue for individuals who have experienced mental illness to express themselves via poetry, short fiction, essays, first-person accounts of living with mental illness, and book/movie reviews. Wants unique, well-written, provocative work. Does not want overly graphic or sexual violence.

○ *Open Minds Quarterly* is 24 pages, magazine-sized, saddle-stapled, with 100 lb. stock cover with original artwork, includes ads. Press run is 550; 150 distributed free to potential subscribers, published writers, NISA member, advertisers, and conferences and events.

NEEDS Length: 1,000-3,000 words.

HOW TO CONTACT Submit through website. Cover letter is required. Information in cover letter: indicate your lived experience with mental illness. Reads submissions year round.

PAYMENT/TERMS Pays contributor's copies.

⚫ ORBIS

17 Greenhow Ave., West Kirby Wirral CH48 5EL, United Kingdom. **E-mail:** carolebaldock@hotmail.com. **Website:** www.orbisjournal.com. **Contact:** Carole Baldock, editor; Noel Williams, reviews editor. Estab. 1969. "*Orbis* has long been considered one of the top 20 small-press magazines in the U.K. We are interested in social inclusion projects and encouraging access to the arts, young people, under 20s, and 20-somethings. Subjects for discussion: 'day in the life,' technical, topical."

○ Please see guidelines on website before submitting.

NEEDS Submit by postal mail or e-mail (overseas submissions only). Include cover letter. Length: up to 1,000 words.

TIPS "Any publication should be read cover to cover because it's the best way to improve your chances of getting published. Enclose SAE with all correspondence. Overseas: 2 IRCs, 3 if work is to be returned."

OUTER-ART

The University of New Mexico, 705 Gurley Ave., Gallup NM 87301. **Website:** www.gallup.unm.edu/~smarandache/a/outer-art.htm. Estab. 2000. "*Outer-Art* is a movemet set up as a protest against, or to ridicule, the random modern art which states that everything is ... art! It was initiated by Florentin Smarandache in the 1990s, who ironically called

for an upside-down artwork: to do art in a way it is not supposed to be done, i.e. to make art as ugly, as silly, as wrong as possible, and generally as impossible as possible."

💲 OVERTIME

Blue Cubicle Press, LLC, P.O. Box 250382, Plano TX 75025. **E-mail:** overtime@workerswritejournal.com. **Website:** www.workerswritejournal.com/overtime.htm. **Contact:** David LaBounty, editor. Estab. 2006.

NEEDS Length: 5,000-12,000 words.

HOW TO CONTACT Query; send complete ms.

PAYMENT/TERMS Pays $35-50 and one-year print subscription.

OXFORD MAGAZINE

Miami University, Oxford OH 45056. **E-mail:** ox-mag@miamioh.edu. **Website:** www.oxfordmagazine.org. Estab. 1984. *Oxford Magazine*, published annually online in May, is open in terms of form, content, and subject matter. "Since our premiere in 1984, our magazine has received Pushcart Prizes for both fiction and poetry and has published authors such as Charles Baxter, William Stafford, Robert Pinsky, Stephen Dixon, Helena Maria Viramontes, Andre Dubus, and Stuart Dybek."

○ Work published in *Oxford Magazine* has been included in the *Pushcart Prize* anthology. Does not read submissions July through August.

NEEDS Length: up to 3,000 words.

HOW TO CONTACT Submit complete ms via online submissions manager.

OYEZ REVIEW

Roosevelt University, Dept. of Literature & Languages, 430 S. Michigan Ave., Chicago IL 60605. **E-mail:** oyezreview@roosevelt.edu. **Website:** oyezreview.wordpress.com. Estab. 1965. Annual magazine of the Creative Writing Program at Roosevelt University, publishing fiction, creative nonfiction, poetry, and art. There are no restrictions on style, theme, or subject matter.

○ Reading period is August 1-October 1. Each issue has 104 pages: 92 pages of text and an 8-page spread of 1 artist's work (in color or b&w). Work by the issue's featured artist also appears on the front and back cover, totaling 10 pieces. The journal has featured work from such writers as Charles Bukowski, James McManus, Carla Panciera, Michael Onofrey, Tim

Foley, John N. Miller, Gary Fincke, and Barry Silesky, and visual artists Vivian Nunley, C. Taylor, Jennifer Troyer, and Frank Spidale. Accepts queries by e-mail.

NEEDS "We publish short stories and flash fiction on their merit as contemporary literature rather than the category within the genre." Length: up to 5,000 words.

HOW TO CONTACT Send complete ms via online submissions manager or postal mail.

PAYMENT/TERMS Pays 2 contributor's copies.

OYSTER BOY REVIEW

P.O. Box 1483, Pacifica CA 94044. **E-mail:** email@oysterboyreview.com. **Website:** www.oysterboyreview.com. **Contact:** Damon Sauve, editor/publisher. Estab. 1993. Electronic and print magazine. *Oyster Boy Review*, published annually, is interested in "the underrated, the ignored, the misunderstood, and the varietal. We'll make some mistakes."

NEEDS Wants fiction that revolves around characters in conflict with themselves or each other; a plot that has a beginning, a middle, and an end; a narrative with a strong moral center (not necessarily 'moralistic'); a story with a satisfying resolution to the conflict; and an ethereal something that contributes to the mystery of a question but does not necessarily seek or contrive to answer it. Submit complete ms by postal mail or e-mail. No genre fiction.

PAYMENT/TERMS Pays 2 contributor's copies.

TIPS "Keep writing, keep submitting, keep revising."

PACIFICA LITERARY REVIEW

E-mail: pacificalitreview@gmail.com. **Website:** www.pacificareview.com. **Contact:** Matt Muth, editor-in-chief; Sarina Sheth and Paul Vega, managing editors. Estab. 2012. "*Pacifica Literary Review* is a small literary arts magazine based in Seattle. *Pacifica* publishes three web issues annually in September, January, and May, and one print editon. *PLR* is now accepting submissions of poetry, fiction, creative nonfiction, author interviews, and b&w photography. Submission period: year-round."

NEEDS Wants literary fiction and flash fiction. Length: up to 5,000 words for literary fiction; 300-1,000 words for flash fiction.

HOW TO CONTACT Submit complete ms.

PAYMENT/TERMS Pays copy of issue in which author was published and copy of next issue.

PACIFIC REVIEW

SDSU Press, Dept. of English and Comparative Literature, San Diego State University, 5500 Campanile Dr., MC6020, San Diego CA 92182-6020. **E-mail:** pacrevjournal@gmail.com. **E-mail:** info.pacrev@gmail.com. **Website:** pacificreview.sdsu.edu. **Contact:** Hari Alluri, Editor. Estab. 1977. Pacific Review accepts poems, fiction (short stories, flash fiction and excerpts that stand alone), memoir, creative non-fiction, essays, comics, visual art, photography, documented performance and hybrid.

○ Current theme: Errant Mythologies. For details and to submit, please see our Submittable page - https://pacrev.submittable.com/submit. Simultaneous submissions permitted with immediate notification of acceptance elsewhere.

NEEDS Length: up to 5,000 words.

HOW TO CONTACT Submit ms via online submissions manager. Include cover letter with name, postal address, e-mail addresss, phone number, and short bio.

PAYMENT/TERMS Pays 1 contributor's copy.

TIPS "We welcome all submissions as long as they fit the theme and represent work that the author loves and believes we may love."

PACKINGTOWN REVIEW

111 S. Lincoln St., Batavia IL 60510. **E-mail:** packingtownreview@gmail.com. **Website:** www.packingtownreview.com. Estab. 2008. *Packingtown Review* publishes imaginative and critical prose and poetry by emerging and established writers. Welcomes submissions of poetry, scholarly articles, drama, creative nonfiction, fiction, and literary translation, as well as genre-bending pieces.

○ Literary magazine/journal: 8.5 x 11, 250 pages. Press run: 500.

NEEDS Does not want to see uninspired or unrevised work. Wants to avoid fantasy, science fiction, overtly religious, or romantic pieces. Length: up to 4,000 words.

HOW TO CONTACT Send complete ms as attachment. Include cover letter in body of e-mail.

PAYMENT/TERMS Pays 2 contributor's copies.

TIPS "We are looking for well-crafted prose. We are open to most styles and forms. We are also looking for prose that takes risks and does so successfully. We will consider articles about prose."

PAINTED BRIDE QUARTERLY

Drexel University, Department of English and Philosophy, 3141 Chestnut St., Philadelphia PA 19104. **E-mail:** info@pbqmag.org. **Website:** pbqmag.org. **Contact:** Kathleen Volk Miller and Marion Wrenn, editors. Estab. 1973. *Painted Bride Quarterly* seeks literary fiction (experimental and traditional), poetry, and artwork and photographs.

NEEDS Publishes theme-related work; check website. Holds annual fiction contests. Length: up to 5,000 words.

HOW TO CONTACT Send complete ms through online submissions manager.

PAYMENT/TERMS Pays $20.

TIPS "We look for freshness of idea incorporated with high-quality writing. We receive an awful lot of nicely written work with worn-out plots. We want quality in whatever—we hold experimental work to as strict standards as anything else. Many of our readers write fiction; most of them enjoy a good reading. We hope to be an outlet for quality. A good story gives, first, enjoyment to the reader. We've seen a good many of them lately, and we've published the best of them."

PANK

PANK, Department of Humanities, 1400 Townsend Dr., Houghton MI 49931-1200. **Website:** www.pankmagazine.com. Estab. 2006. "*PANK* Magazine fosters access to emerging and experimental poetry and prose, publishing the brightest and most promising writers for the most adventurous readers. To the end of the road, up country, a far shore, the edge of things, to a place of amalgamation and unplumbed depths, where the known is made and unmade, and where unimagined futures are born, a place inhabited by contradictions, a place of quirk and startling anomaly. *PANK*, no soft pink hands allowed."

NEEDS "Bright, new, energetic, passionate writing, writing that pushes our tender little buttons and gets us excited. Push our tender buttons, excite us, and we'll publish you."

HOW TO CONTACT Send complete ms through online submissions manager.

PAYMENT/TERMS Pays $20, a one-year subscription, and a *PANK* t-shirt.

TIPS "To read *PANK* is to know *PANK*. Or, read a lot within the literary magazine and small-press universe—there's plenty to choose from. Unfortunately, we see a lot of submissions from writers who have clearly read neither *PANK* nor much else. Serious writers are serious readers. Read. Seriously."

PAPERPLATES

19 Kenwood Ave., Toronto ON M6C 2R8, Canada. **E-mail:** magazine@paperplates.org. **Website:** www.paperplates.org. **Contact:** Bernard Kelly, publisher. Estab. 1990. *paperplates* is a literary journal published once a year. "We make no distinction between veterans and beginners. Some of our contributors have published several books; some have never before published a single line." No longer accepts IRCs.

NEEDS Length: no more than 7,500 words.

HOW TO CONTACT Submit by mail or e-mail. "Do not send fiction as an e-mail attachment. Copy the first 300 words or so into the body of your message. If you prefer not to send a fragment, you have the option of using surface mail." Include short bio with submission.

THE PARIS REVIEW

544 West 27th St., New York NY 10001. (212)343-1333. **E-mail:** queries@theparisreview.org. **Website:** www.theparisreview.org. **Contact:** Lorin Stein, editor; Robyn Creswell, poetry editor. *The Paris Review* publishes "fiction and poetry of superlative quality, whatever the genre, style, or mode. Our contributors include prominent, as well as less well-known and previously unpublished writers. The Writers at Work interview series includes important contemporary writers discussing their own work and the craft of writing."

Address submissions to proper department. Do not make submissions via e-mail.

NEEDS Study the publication. Annual Plimpton Prize award of $10,000 given to a new voice published in the magazine. Recently published work by Ottessa Moshfegh, John Jeremiah Sullivan, and Lydia Davis. Length: no limit.

HOW TO CONTACT Send complete ms.

PAYMENT/TERMS Pays $1,000-3,000.

PASSAGER

Passager, 1420 N. Charles St., Baltimore MD 21201. **E-mail:** editors@passagerbooks.com. **Website:** www.passagerbooks.com. **Contact:** Kendra Kopelke, Mary Azrael, Christine Drawl. Estab. 1990. "*Passager* has a special focus on older writers. Its mission is to encourage, engage, and strengthen the imagination well into old age and to give mature readers opportunities that are sometimes closed off to them in our youth-oriented culture. We are dedicated to honoring the creativity that takes hold in later years and to making public the talents of those over the age of 50." *Passager* publishes 2 issues/year, an Open issue (fall/winter) and a Poetry Contest issue (spring/summer). Open to writers over 50.

NEEDS Accepts literary fiction submissions from writers over 50. Length: up to 4,000 words.

HOW TO CONTACT Send complete ms with cover letter, or use Submittable. Check website for guidelines. Include estimated word count, brief bio, list of publications. Send either SASE (or IRC) for return of ms, or disposable copy of ms and #10 SASE for reply only.

PAYMENT/TERMS Pays 1 contributor's copy.

TIPS "Stereotyped images of old age will be rejected immediately. Write humorous, tongue-in-cheek essays. Read the publication, or at least visit the website."

PASSAGES NORTH

English Department, Northern Michigan University, 1401 Presque Isle Ave., Marquette MI 49855. (906)227-1203. **E-mail:** passages@nmu.edu. **Website:** www.passagesnorth.com. **Contact:** Jennifer A. Howard, editor-in-chief; Ethan Brightbill & Willow Grosz, managing editors; Matthew Gavin Frank & Rachel May, non-fiction and hybrids editors; Patricia Killelea, poetry editor; Monica McFawn, fiction editor. Estab. 1979. *Passages North*, published annually in spring, prints poetry, short fiction, creative nonfiction, essays, hybrids, and interviews.

  Magazine: 7×10; 200-350 pgs; 60 lb. paper. Publishes work by established and emerging writers.

NEEDS "Don't be afraid to surprise us." Length: up to 7,000 words.

HOW TO CONTACT Send 1 short story or as many as 3 short-short stories (paste them all into 1 document).

TIPS "We look for voice, energetic prose, writers who take risks. We look for an engaging story in which the author evokes an emotional response from the reader through carefully rendered scenes, complex characters, and a smart, narrative design. Revise, revise. Read what we publish."

THE PATERSON LITERARY REVIEW

Passaic County Community College, 1 College Blvd., Paterson NJ 07505. (973)684-6555. **Website:** www.patersonliteraryreview.com. **Contact:** Maria Mazziotti Gillan, editor/executive director. *Paterson Literary Review*, published annually, is produced by the The Poetry Center at Passaic County Community College.

  Work for *PLR* has been included in the *Pushcart Prize* anthology and *Best American Poetry*.

NEEDS "We are interested in quality short stories, with no taboos on subject matter." Receives 60 unsolicited mss/month. Publishes 5% new writers/year. Length: up to 1,500 words.

HOW TO CONTACT Send SASE for reply or return of ms. "Indicate whether you want story returned."

PAYMENT/TERMS Pays contributor's copies.

THE PEDESTAL MAGAZINE

6815 Honors Court, Charlotte NC 28210. **E-mail:** pedmagazine@carolina.rr.com. **Website:** www.thepedestalmagazine.com. **Contact:** John Amen, editor in chief. Estab. 2000. Committed to promoting diversity and celebrating the voice of the individual.

  See website for reading periods for different forms. Member: CLMP.

NEEDS "We are receptive to all sorts of high-quality literary fiction. Genre fiction is encouraged as long as it crosses or comments upon its genre and is both character-driven and psychologically acute. We encourage submissions of short fiction, no more than 3 flash fiction pieces at a time. There is no need to query prior to submitting; please submit via online submissions manager—no e-mail to the editor." Length: up to 4,000 words for short stories; up to 1,000 words for flash fiction.

PAYMENT/TERMS Pays 3¢/word.

TIPS "If you send us your work, please wait for a response to your first submission before you submit again."

PENNINE INK MAGAZINE

1 Neptune St., Burnley BB11 1SF, England. **E-mail:** piwwmag40@gmail.com. **Website:** www.pennine-ink.weebly.com. **Contact:** Alex Marsh, compiling editor. Estab. 1983. *Pennine Ink*, published annually in November, prints poems and short prose pieces. *Pennine Ink* is 48 pages, A5, with b&w illustrated cover. Receives about 400 poems/year, accepts about 40. Press run is 200. "Contributors wishing to purchase

a copy of *Pennine Ink* should go to the Amazon website and search for Pennine Ink. More information on our website."

PAYMENT/TERMS Pays 1 contributor's copy.

PENNSYLVANIA ENGLISH

Indiana University of Pennsylvania, Department of English, Indiana University of Pennsylvania, HSS 506A, 981 Grant St., Indiana PA 15705. **E-mail:** mtwill@iup.edu. **Website:** paenglish.submittable. com/submit. **Contact:** Dr. Michael T. Williamson, editor (mtwill@iup.edu); Dr. Michael Cox, creative prose editor (mwcox@pitt.edu); Tony Vallone, MFA, poetry editor (avallone@psu.edu); Dr. John Marsden (marsden@iup.edu) and Dr. Michael T. Williamson, literary criticism editors. Estab. 1985. *Pennsylvania English*, published annually, is "sponsored by the Pennsylvania College English Association. Our philosophy is quality. We publish literary fiction (and poetry and nonfiction) and essays about literature. Our intended audience includes people who love literature and writing, university professors, college professors, Community College professors, temporary faculty, K-12 teachers, and literate readers from around the world. *Pennsylvania English* is 6x9 up to 175 pages, perfect-bound, full-color cover featuring the artwork of a Pennsylvania artist. Reads mss during the summer. Publishes 4-6 new writers/year. Has published work by Dave Kress, Dan Leone, Paul West, Liz Rosenberg, Walt MacDonald, Amy Pence, Jennifer Richter, and Jeff Schiff.

NEEDS No genre fiction or romance.

HOW TO CONTACT Submit via online submissions manager. "For all submissions, please include a brief bio for the contributors' page. Be sure to include your name, address, phone number, e-mail address, institutional affiliation (if you have one), the title of your short story, and any other relevant information. We will edit if necessary for space."

PAYMENT/TERMS Pays 1 contributor's copy.

TIPS "Quality of the writing is our only measure. We're not impressed by long-winded cover letters detailing awards and publications we've never heard of. Beginners and professionals have the same chance with us. We receive stacks of competently written but boring fiction. For a story to rise from the rejection pile, it takes more than the basic competence."

PENNSYLVANIA LITERARY JOURNAL

Anaphora Literary Press, 1108 W 3rd St., Quanah TX 79252. (470)289-6395. **E-mail:** director@anaphoraliterary.com. **Website:** anaphoraliterary.com. **Contact:** Anna Faktorovich, editor/director. Estab. 2009. *Pennsylvania Literary Journal* is a printed, peer-reviewed journal that publishes critical essays, book reviews, short stories, interviews, photographs, art, and poetry. Published tri-annually, it features special issues on a wide variety of different fields from film studies to literary criticism to interviews with bestsellers. Submissions in all genres from emerging and established writers are warmly welcomed.

NEEDS Detailed, descriptive, and original short stories are preferred. No word limit.

HOW TO CONTACT Send complete ms via e-mail.

PAYMENT/TERMS Does not provide payment.

TIPS "We are just looking for great writing. Send your materials; if they are good and you don't mind working for free, we'll take it."

PENNY DREADFUL

Tales & Poems of Fantastic Terror, P.O. Box 719, Radio City Station, Hell's Kitchen NY 10101-0719. **E-mail:** mmpendragon@aol.com. **Website:** www.mpendragon.com/pennydreadful.html. Estab. 1996. *Penny Dreadful: Tales & Poems of Fanastic Terror*, published irregularly (about once a year), features goth-romantic poetry and prose. Publishes poetry, short stories, essays, letters, listings, reviews, and b&w artwork "which celebrate the darker aspects of Man, the World, and their Creator." Wants "literary horror in the tradition of Poe, M.R. James, Shelley, M.P. Shiel, and LeFanu—dark, disquieting tales and verses designed to challenge the reader's perception of human nature, morality, and man's place within the Darkness. Stories and poems should be set prior to 1910 and/or possess a timeless quality." Does not want "references to 20th- and 21st-century personages/events, graphic sex, strong language, excessive gore and shock elements."

◯   "Works appearing in *Penny Dreadful* have been reprinted in *The Year's Best Fantasy and Horror*." *Penny Dreadful* nominates best tales and poems for Pushcart Prizes. *Penny Dreadful* is over 100 pages, digest-sized, desktop-published, perfect-bound. Press run is 200.

NEEDS Length: up to 5,000 words.

HOW TO CONTACT Submit complete ms by mail or e-mail. "Mss should be submitted in the standard, professional format: typed, double-spaced, name and address on the first page, name and title of work on all subsequent pages, etc. Include SASE for reply. Also include brief cover letter with a brief bio and publication history."

PAYMENT/TERMS Pays 1 contributor's copy.

❸ PENTHOUSE VARIATIONS

FriendFinder Networks, 20 Broad St., 14th Floor, New York NY 10005. **Website:** penthouse.com. Estab. 1978. A digest-sized print and digital magazine publishing erotic short stories; publishes 12 issues/year.

NEEDS Send complete first-person, past-tense ms; no queries. No poetry. No serialized fiction. Length: 3,000-3,500 words.

PAYMENT/TERMS Pays $400.

TIPS "*Variations* publishes first-person, sex-positive narratives in which the author fully describes sex scenes squarely focused within 1 of the magazine's usual categories, in highly explicit erotic detail. To submit material to *Variations* you must be 18 years of age or older."

PEREGRINE

Amherst Writers & Artists Press, P.O. Box 1076, Amherst MA 01004. (413)253-3307. **E-mail:** peregrinejournal@gmail.com. **E-mail:** peregrine@amherstwriters.com. **Website:** amherstwriters.info/peregrine. **Contact:** Kate Eliza Frank, managing editor; Milo Muise, fiction editor, Rachelle Parker, poetry editor. Estab. 1983. *Peregrine*, published annually, features poetry and fiction. "*Peregrine* has provided a forum for national and international writers since 1983 and is committed to finding excellent work by emerging as well as established writers. We welcome work reflecting diversity of voice. We like to be surprised. We look for writing that is honest, unpretentious, and memorable. All decisions are made by the editors."

◯ Reading period: March 15-May 15.

NEEDS Length: up to 750 words.

HOW TO CONTACT Submit via e-mail. Include word count on first page of submissions. "Shorter stories have a better chance."

PAYMENT/TERMS Pays 2 contributor's copies.

TIPS "Check guidelines before submitting your work. Familiarize yourself with *Peregrine*. We look for heart and soul as well as technical expertise. Trust your own voice."

PERMAFROST: A LITERARY JOURNAL

America's Farthest North Literary Magazine, University of Alaska Fairbanks, c/o English Dept., Univ. of Alaska Fairbanks, P.O. Box 755720, Fairbanks AK 99775. **E-mail:** editor@permafrostmag.com. **Website:** permafrostmag.uaf.edu. Estab. 1977. *Permafrost Magazine*, a literary journal, contains poems, short stories, hybrid pieces, creative nonfiction, b&w drawings, photographs, and prints. We print both new and established writers, hoping and expecting to see the best work out there. We have published work by E. Ethelbert Miller, W. Loran Smith, Peter Orlovsky, Jim Wayne Miller, Allen Ginsberg, and Andy Warhol. *Permafrost* is about 200 pages, digest-sized, professionally printed, flat-spined. Also publishes summer online edition.

NEEDS Length: up to 8,000 words.

HOW TO CONTACT Submit complete ms via online submissions manager at permafrostmag.submittable.com; "e-mail submissions will not be read."

PAYMENT/TERMS Pays 1 contributor's copy. Reduced contributor rate of $5 on additional copies.

PERSIMMON TREE: MAGAZINE OF THE ARTS BY WOMEN OVER SIXTY

1534 Campus Dr., Berkeley CA 94708. (510)486-2332. **E-mail:** editor@persimmontree.org. **E-mail:** submissions@persimmontree.org. **Website:** www.persimmontree.org. **Contact:** Sue Leonard, editor. *Persimmon Tree*, an online magazine, is a showcase for the creativity and talent of women over sixty. Too often older women's artistic work is ignored or disregarded, and only those few who are already established receive the attention they deserve. Yet many women are at the height of their creative abilities in their later decades and have a great deal to contribute. *Persimmon Tree* is committed to bringing this wealth of fiction, nonfiction, poetry, and art to a broader audience, for the benefit of all.

NEEDS Length: under 3,500 words.

HOW TO CONTACT Submit complete ms via e-mail. Note: You must be signed onto the e-mail newsletter to be considered for publication.

TIPS "High quality of writing and an interesting or unique point of view make a manuscript stand out. Make it clear that you're familiar with the magazine. Tell us why the piece would work for our audience."

PERSPECTIVES

c/o Jason Lief, Dordt College, 498 4th Ave. NE, Sioux Center IA 51250. **E-mail:** editors@perspectivesjournal.org. **E-mail:** submissions@perspectivesjournal.org. **Website:** perspectivesjournal.org. **Contact:** Jason Lief. "*Perspectives* is a journal of theology in the broad Reformed tradition. We seek to express the Reformed faith theologically; to engage issues that Reformed Christians meet in personal, ecclesiastical, and societal life; and thus to contribute to the mission of the church of Jesus Christ.The editors are interested in submissions that contribute to a contemporary Reformed theological discussion. Our readers tend to be affiliated with the Presbyterian Church (USA), the Reformed Church in America, and the Christian Reformed Church. Some of our subscribers are academics or pastors, but we also gear our articles to thoughtful, literate laypeople who want to engage in Reformed theological reflection on faith and culture."

NEEDS Length: up to 3,000 words.

HOW TO CONTACT Submit complete ms by e-mail.

PHILADELPHIA STORIES

Fiction/Nonfiction/Art/Poetry of the Delaware Valley, 93 Old York Rd., Suite 1/#1-753, Jenkintown PA 19046. **Website:** www.philadelphiastories.org. **Contact:** Christine Weiser, executive director/co-publisher. Estab. 2004. *Philadelphia Stories*, published quarterly, publishes "fiction, poetry, creative nonfiction, and art written by authors living in, or originally from, Pennsylvania, Delaware, or New Jersey. *Philadelphia Stories* also hosts 2 national writing contests: The Marguerite McGlinn Short Story Contest ($2,500 first-place prize; $750 second-place prize; $500 third-place prize) and the Sandy Crimmins National Poetry Contest ($1,000 first-place prize, 3 $100 runner-up prizes). Visit our website for details." Literary magazine/journal: 8.5x11; 32 pages; 70# matte text, all 4-color paper; 70# matte text cover. Contains illustrations, photographs. Subscription: "We offer $20 memberships that include home delivery." Make checks payable to *Philadelphia Stories*. Member: CLMP.

NEEDS Receives 45-80 mss/month. Accepts 3-4 mss/issue for print, additional 1-2 online; 12-16 mss/year for print, 4-8 online. Publishes 50% new writers/year. "We will consider anything that is well written but are most inclined to publish literary or mainstream fiction. We are *not* particularly interested in most genres (science fiction, fantasy, romance, etc.)." Length: up to 5,000 words; 4,000 words average. Also publishes short shorts; average length: 800 words.

PAYMENT/TERMS Pays $25 honorarium from the Conrad Weiser Author Fund and 2 contributor's copies.

TIPS "We look for exceptional, polished prose, a controlled voice, strong characters and place, and interesting subjects. Follow guidelines. We cannot stress this enough. Read every guideline carefully and thoroughly before sending anything out. Send out only polished material. We reject many quality pieces for various reasons; try not to take rejection personally. Just because your piece isn't right for one publication doesn't mean it's bad. Selection is an extremely subjective process."

PHOEBE

A Journal of Literature and Art, MSN 2C5, George Mason University, 400 University Dr., Fairfax VA 22030. **Website:** www.phoebejournal.com. **Contact:** Andrew Cartwright and Ryan McDonald, nonfiction editors; Sarah Bates, fiction editor, and Joseph Kuhn, assistant fiction editor; Doug Luman, poetry editor, and Janice Majewski, assistant. Estab. 1971. Publishes poetry, fiction, nonfiction, and online content. "*Phoebe* prides itself on supporting up-and-coming writers, whose style, form, voice, and subject matter demonstrate a vigorous appeal to the senses, intellect, and emotions of our readers."

NEEDS No romance or erotica. Length: up to 4,000 words.

HOW TO CONTACT Submit 1 fiction submission via online submission manager.

PAYMENT/TERMS Pays 2 contributor's copies and $400 for contest winner.

PILGRIMAGE MAGAZINE

Colorado State University-Pueblo, Dept. of English, 2200 Bonforte Blvd., Pueblo CO 81001. **E-mail:** info@pilgrimagepress.org. **Website:** www.pilgrimagepress.org. **Contact:** Juan Morales, editor. Estab. 1976. Serves an eclectic fellowship of readers, writers, artists, naturalists, contemplatives, activists, seekers, adventurers, and other kindred spirits.

NEEDS Length: up to 6,000 words. "Shorter works are easier to include, due to space constraints."

TIPS "Our interests include wildness in all its forms; inward and outward explorations; home ground, the open road, service, witness, peace, and justice;

symbols, story, and myth in contemporary culture; struggle and resilience; insight and transformation; wisdom wherever it is found; and the great mystery of it all. We like good storytellers and a good sense of humor. No e-mail submissions, please."

THE PINCH

English Department, University of Memphis, Memphis TN 38152. **E-mail:** editor@pinchjournal.com. **Website:** www.pinchjournal.com. Estab. 1980. Semiannual literary magazine. "We publish fiction, creative nonfiction, poetry, and art of literary quality by both established and emerging artists."

○ "The Pinch Literary Awards in Fiction, Poetry, and Nonfiction offer a $1,000 prize and publication. Check our website for details."

NEEDS Wants "character-based" fiction with a "fresh use of language." No genre fiction. Length: up to 5,000 words.

HOW TO CONTACT Submit complete ms (or up to 3 flash fiction pieces) via online submissions manager.

PAYMENT/TERMS Pays 2 contributor's copies. "One work from each genre will be awarded a $200 Featured Writer award, as determined by the editors."

TIPS "We have a new look and a new edge. We're soliciting work from writers with a national or international reputation as well as strong, interesting work from emerging writers."

THE PINK CHAMELEON

The Pink Chameleon On Line, **E-mail:** dpfreda@juno.com. **Website:** www.thepinkchameleon.com. **Contact:** Dorothy Paula Freda, editor/publisher. Estab. 2000. *The Pink Chameleon*, published annually online, contains family-oriented, upbeat poetry, stories, essays, and articles, any genre in good taste that gives hope for the future. Reading period is February 1-March 31 and September 1-October 31.

NEEDS Accepts fiction that follows *The Pink Chameleon* online guidelines. No violence for the sake of violence. No novels or novel excerpts. Length: 500-2,500 words; average length: 2,000 words.

HOW TO CONTACT Send complete ms in the body of the e-mail. No attachments. Accepts reprints as long as author retains rights to reprints. Has published work by Deanne F. Purcell, Martin Green, Albert J. Manachino, James W. Collins, Ron Arnold, Sally Kosmalski, Susan Marie Davniero, and Glenn D. Hayes, among many others.

PAYMENT/TERMS No payment.

TIPS Wants "simple, honest, evocative emotion; upbeat fiction and nonfiction submissions that give hope for the future; well-paced plots; stories, poetry, articles, essays that speak from the heart. Read guidelines carefully. Use a good, but not ostentatious, opening hook. Stories should have a beginning, middle, and end that make the reader feel the story was worth his or her time. This also applies to articles and essays. In the latter 2, wrap your comments and conclusions in a neatly packaged final paragraph. Turnoffs include violence and bad language. Simple, genuine, and sensitive work does not need to shock with vulgarity to be interesting and enjoyable."

PISGAH REVIEW

Division of Humanities, Brevard College, 1 Brevard College Dr., Brevard NC 28712. (828)577-8324. **E-mail:** tinerjj@brevard.edu. **Website:** www.pisgahreview.com. **Contact:** Jubal Tiner, editor. Estab. 2005. *"Pisgah Review* publishes primarily literary short fiction, creative nonfiction, and poetry. Our only criteria is quality of work; we look for the best." Has published Ron Rash, Thomas Rain Crowe, Joan Conner, Gary Fincke, Steve Almond, and Fred Bahnson. Also published Rick Bass Marjorie Hudson, Jane Smiley and others in our Looking Glad Rock Writer's Conference special issues.

NEEDS Receives 85 mss/month. Accepts 6-8 mss/issue; 12-15 mss/year. Publishes 5 new writers/year. Does not want genre fiction or inspirational stories. Length: 2,000-7,500 words. Accepts Flash Fiction as well.

HOW TO CONTACT "Send complete ms to our submission manager on our website."

PAYMENT/TERMS Writers receive 2 contributor's copies. Additional copies $7.

TIPS "We select work of only the highest quality. Grab us from the beginning and follow through. Engage us with your language and characters. A clean ms goes a long way toward acceptance. Stay true to the vision of your work, revise tirelessly, and submit persistently."

●⊖ PLANET: THE WELSH INTERNATIONALIST

Berw Ltd., P.O. Box 44, Aberystwyth Ceredigion SY23 3ZZ, United Kingdom. 01970 622408. **E-mail:** admin@planetmagazine.org.uk. **E-mail:** submissions@planetmagazine.org.uk. **Website:** www.planetmagazine.org.uk. **Contact:** Emily Trahair, editor.

Estab. 1970. A literary/cultural/political journal centered on Welsh affairs but with a strong interest in minority cultures in Europe and elsewhere. *Planet: The Welsh Internationalist*, published quarterly, is a cultural magazine centered on Wales, but with broader interests in arts, sociology, politics, history, and science. *Planet* is 96 pages, A5, professionally printed, perfect-bound, with glossy colour card cover. Receives about 500 submissions/year, accepts about 5%. Press run is 1,000 (800 subscribers, about 10% libraries, 200 shelf sales).

NEEDS Would like to see more inventive, imaginative fiction that pays attention to language and experiments with form. No magical realism, horror, science fiction. Length: 1,500-2,750 words.

HOW TO CONTACT Submit complete ms via mail or e-mail (with attachment). For postal submissions, no submissions returned unless accompanied by an SASE. Writers submitting from abroad should send at least 3 IRCs for return of typescript; 1 IRC for reply only.

PAYMENT/TERMS Pays £50/1,000 words.

TIPS "We do not look for fiction that necessarily has a 'Welsh' connection, which some writers assume from our title. We try to publish a broad range of fiction, and our main criterion is quality. Try to read copies of any magazine you submit to. Don't write out of the blue to a magazine which might be completely inappropriate for your work. Recognize that you are likely to have a high rejection rate, as magazines tend to favor writers from their own countries."

PLEIADES

Literature in Context, University of Central Missouri, Department of English, Martin 336, 415 E. Clark St., Warrensburg MO 64093. (660)543-4268. **E-mail:** clintoncrockettp@gmail.com (nonfiction inquiries); pnguyen@ucmo.edu (fiction inquiries); pleiadespoetryeditor@gmail.com (poetry inquiries). **Website:** www.pleiadesmag.com. **Contact:** Clinton Crockett Peters, nonfiction editor; Phong Nguyen, fiction editor; and Jenny Molberg, poetry editor. Estab. 1991. "We publish contemporary fiction, poetry, interviews, literary essays, special-interest personal essays, and reviews for a general and literary audience from authors from around the world." Reads in the months of July for the summer issue and December for the winter issue.

NEEDS Reads fiction year-round. No science fiction, fantasy, confession, erotica. Length: 2,000-6,000 words.

HOW TO CONTACT Send complete ms via online submission manager.

PAYMENT/TERMS Pays $10 and contributor's copies.

TIPS "Submit only 1 genre at a time to appropriate editors. Show care for your material and your readers—submit quality work in a professional format. Cover art is solicited directly from artists. We accept queries for book reviews."

PLOUGHSHARES

Emerson College, 120 Boylston St., Boston MA 02116. (617)824-3757. **E-mail:** pshares@pshares.org. **Website:** www.pshares.org. **Contact:** Ladette Randolph, editor-in-chief/executive director; Ellen Duffer, managing editor. Estab. 1971. *Ploughshares* publishes issues four times a year. 2 of these issues are guest-edited by different, prominent authors. A third issue, a mix of both prose and poetry, is edited by our staff editors. The fourth issue is a collection of longform work edited by our Editor-in-chief, Ladette Randolph; these stories and essays are first published as e-books known as Ploughshares Solos. Translations are welcome if permission has been granted. We accept electronic submissions—there is a $3 fee per submission, which is waived if you are a subscriber. Ploughshares is 200 pages, digest-sized. Receives about 11,000 poetry, fiction, and essay submissions/year. Reads submissions June 1-January 15 (postmark); hosts the Emerging Writer's Contest, for writers who have yet to publish a book-length work, March 1-May 15; mss submitted at all other times will be returned unread. A competitive and highly prestigious market. Rotating and guest editors make cracking the line-up even tougher, since it's difficult to know what is appropriate to send.

NEEDS Has published work by ZZ Packer, Antonya Nelson, and Stuart Dybek. Length: up to 6,000 words

HOW TO CONTACT Submit via online submissions form or by mail.

PAYMENT/TERMS Pays $45/printed page ($90 minimum, $450 maximum); 2 contributor's copies; and one-year subscription.

PMS

University of Alabama at Birmingham, HB 217, 1530 Third Ave. S., Birmingham AL 35294. (205)934-2641. **Fax:** (205)975-8125. **E-mail:** poemmemoirstory@gmail.com. **Website:** www.uab.edu/cas/englishpublications/pms-poemmemoirstory. **Contact:** Kerry Madden, editor in chief. "*PMS poemmemoirstory* appears once a year. We accept unpublished, original submissions of poetry, memoir, and short fiction during our January 1-March 31 reading period. We accept simultaneous submissions; however, we ask that you please contact us immediately if your piece is published elsewhere so we may free up space for other authors. While *PMS* is a journal of exclusively women's writing, the subject field is wide open."

○ "*PMS* has gone all-digital on Submittable. There is now a $3 fee, which covers costs associated with our online submissions system. Please send all submissions to poemmemoirstory.submittable.com/submit."

NEEDS Length: up to 15 pages or 4,300 words.

HOW TO CONTACT Submit through online submissions manager.

PAYMENT/TERMS Pays 2 contributor's copies.

TIPS "We strongly encourage you to familiarize yourself with *PMS* before submitting. You can find links to some examples of what we publish in the pages of *PMS 8* and *PMS 9*. We look forward to reading your work."

⑤ POCKETS

The Upper Room, P.O. Box 340004, Nashville TN 37203. (615)340-7333. **E-mail:** pockets@upperroom.org. **Website:** pockets.upperroom.org. **Contact:** Lynn W. Gilliam, editor. Estab. 1981. In addition to receiving regular submissions, *Pockets* sponsors a fiction contest each year. Magazine published 11 times/year. "*Pockets* is a Christian devotional magazine for children ages 6-12. All submissions should address the broad theme of the magazine. Each issue is built around a theme with material which can be used by children in a variety of ways. Scripture stories, fiction, poetry, prayers, art, graphics, puzzles and activities are included. Submissions do not need to be overtly religious. They should help children experience a Christian lifestyle that is not always a neatly wrapped moral package but is open to the continuing revelation of God's will. Seasonal material, both secular and liturgical, is desired."

○ Does not accept e-mail or fax submissions.

NEEDS "Stories should contain lots of action, use believable dialogue, be simply written, and be relevant to the problems faced by this age group in everyday life." Length: 600-1,000 words.

HOW TO CONTACT Submit complete ms by mail. No e-mail submissions.

TIPS "Theme stories, role models, and retold scripture stories are most open to freelancers. Poetry is also open. It is very helpful if writers read our writers' guidelines and themes on our website."

POETICA MAGAZINE

Contemporary Jewish Writing, Mizmor L'David Anthology, 5215 Colley Ave. #138, Norfolk VA 23508. (757)617-0821. **E-mail:** poeticapublishing@aol.com. **Website:** www.poeticamagazine.com. **Contact:** Michal Mahgerefteh, publisher. Estab. 2002. *Poetica Magazine, Contemporary Jewish Writing*, is the publisher of the annual Mizmor L'David Anthology, offers "an outlet for the many writers who draw from their Jewish background and experiences to create poetry/prose/short stories, giving both emerging and recognized writers the opportunity to share their work with the larger community." *Poetica* is 80 pages, perfect-bound, full-color cover. Receives about 300 poems/year, accepts about 80%. Press run is 350.

HOW TO CONTACT Submit ms through online submissions manager. Include e-mail, bio, and mailing address.

TIPS "We publish original, unpublished works by Jewish and non-Jewish writers alike. We are interested in works that have the courage to acknowledge, challenge, and celebrate modern Jewish life beyond distinctions of secular and sacred. We like accessible works that find fresh meaning in old traditions that recognize the challenges of our generation. We evaluate works on several levels, including its skillful use of craft, its ability to hold interest, and layers of meaning."

POETS & WRITERS MAGAZINE

90 Broad St., Suite 2100, New York NY 10004. (212)226-3586. **E-mail:** editor@pw.org. **Website:** www.pw.org/magazine. **Contact:** Kevin Larimer, editor. Estab. 1987.

○ No poetry or fiction submissions.

TIPS "We typically assign profiles to coincide with an author's forthcoming book publication. We are not looking for the Get Rich Quick or 10 Easy Steps variety of writing and publishing advice."

POINTED CIRCLE

Portland Community College, Cascade Campus, SC 206, 705 N. Killingsworth St., Portland OR 97217. **Website:** www.pcc.edu/about/literary-magazines/pointed-circle. **Contact:** Wendy Bourgeois, faculty advisor. Estab. 1980. Publishes "anything of interest to educationally/culturally mixed audience. We will read whatever is sent, but we encourage writers to remember we are a quality literary/arts magazine intended to promote the arts in the community. No pornography, nothing trite. Be mindful of deadlines and length limits." Accepts submissions by e-mail, mail; artwork in high-resolution digital form.

○ Reading period: October 1-February 7. Magazine: 80 pages; b&w illustrations; photos.

NEEDS Length: up to 3,000 words.

HOW TO CONTACT Submitted materials will not be returned; include SASE for notification only. Accepts multiple submissions.

PAYMENT/TERMS Pays 2 contributor's copies.

POLYPHONY H.S.

An International Student-Run Literary Magazine for High School Writers and Editors, Polyphony High School, 1514 Elmwood Ave., Suite 2, Evanston IL 60201. (224)307-4623. **E-mail:** info@polyphonyhs.com. **Website:** www.polyphonyhs.com. **Contact:** Billy Lombardo, co-founder and managing editor. Estab. 2005. "Our mission is to create a high-quality literary magazine written, edited, and published by high school students. We believe that when young writers put precise and powerful language to their lives it helps them better understand their value as human beings. We believe the development of that creative voice depends upon close, careful, and compassionate attention. Helping young editors become proficient at providing thoughtful and informed attention to the work of their peers is essential to our mission. We believe this important exchange between young writers and editors provides each with a better understanding of craft, of the writing process, and of the value of putting words to their own lives while preparing them for participation in the broader literary community. We strive to build respectful, mutually beneficial writer-editor relationships that form a community devoted to improving students' literary skills in the areas of poetry, fiction, and creative nonfiction." Does not accept hard-copy entries; submit only through online submissions form.

NEEDS Length: up to 1,500 words.

HOW TO CONTACT Submit complete ms via online submissions form.

PAYMENT/TERMS Pays 1 contributor's copy.

TIPS "We manage the Claudia Ann Seaman Awards for Young Writers; cash awards for the best poem, best story, best essay. See website for details."

PORTLAND MONTHLY

165 State St., Portland ME 04101. (207)775-4339. **E-mail:** staff@portlandmonthly.com. **Website:** www.portlandmagazine.com. **Contact:** Colin Sargent, editor. Estab. 1985. Monthly city lifestyle magazine—fiction, style, business, real estate, controversy, fashion, cuisine, interviews, and art relating to the Maine area.

NEEDS Length: up to 1,000 words.

HOW TO CONTACT Submit via online submission manager.

TIPS "Our target audience is our 100,000 readers, ages 18-90. We write for our readers alone, and while in many cases we're delighted when our interview subjects enjoy our stories once they're in print, we are not writing for them but only for our readers. Interview subjects may not ever read or hear any portion of our stories before the stories are printed, and in the interest of objective distance, interview subjects are never to be promised complimentary copies of the magazine. It is the writer's responsibility to return all materials such as photos or illustrations to the interview subjects providing them."

THE PORTLAND REVIEW

Portland State University, P.O. Box 751, Portland OR 97207. **E-mail:** editor@portlandreview.org. **Website:** portlandreview.org. **Contact:** Alex Dannemiller, eidor-in-chief. Estab. 1956. Portland Review has been publishing exceptional writing and artwork by local and international artists since 1956.

NEEDS Publishes 40 manuscripts per year.

PAYMENT/TERMS Pays contributor's copies.

TIPS "Please visit portlandreview.org for access to our submission manager and for more information."

POST ROAD

P.O. Box 600725, Newtown MA 02460. **Website:** www.postroadmag.com. **Contact:** Chris Boucher, managing editor. *Post Road,* published twice yearly, accepts unsolicited poetry, fiction, nonfiction, short plays and monologues, and visual-art submissions. Reads

March 1-April 30 for the winter issue and July 1-August 31 for the summer issue.

○ Work from *Post Road* has received the following honors: honorable mention in the 2001 O. Henry Prize Issue guest-edited by Michael Chabon, Mary Gordon, and Mona Simpson; the Pushcart Prize; honorable mention in *The Best American Nonfiction* series; and inclusion in the *Best American Short Stories* 2005.

HOW TO CONTACT Submit ms via online submission form.

PAYMENT/TERMS Pays 2 contributor's copies.

TIPS "We are looking for interesting narrative, sharp dialogue, and deft use of imagery and metaphor. Be persistent, and be open to criticism."

POTOMAC REVIEW

A Journal of Arts & Humanities, Montgomery College, 51 Mannakee St., MT/212, Rockville MD 20850. (240)567-4100. **E-mail:** PotomacReviewEditor@montgomerycollege.edu. **E-mail:** potomacreview.submittable.com. **Website:** blogs.montgomerycollege.edu/potomacreview/. **Contact:** Julie Wakeman-Linn, editor-in-chief; Kathleen Smith, poetry editor; John W. Wang, fiction editor. Estab. 1994. *Potomac Review: A Journal of Arts & Humanities*, published semiannually in August and February, welcomes poetry and fiction from across the spectrum, both traditional and nontraditional poetry, free verse and in-form (translations accepted). "We like traditional fiction and experimental or meta fiction and flash fiction. Essays and creative nonfiction are also welcome."

○ Reading period: Year round, although slower in the summer. Has published work by David Wagoner, Ryan Ridge, Sandra Beasley, Marilyn Kallet, Katie Cortese, and Amy Holman.

NEEDS Length: up to 5,000 words.

HOW TO CONTACT Submit electronically through website.

○⑤ THE PRAIRIE JOURNAL

A Magazine of Canadian Literature, P.O. Box 68073, 28 Crowfoot Terrace NW, Calgary AB T3G 3N8, Canada. **E-mail:** editor@prairiejournal.org (queries only); prairiejournal@yahoo.com. **Website:** www.prairiejournal.org. **Contact:** Anne Burke, literary editor. Estab. 1983. "The audience is literary, university, library, scholarly, and creative readers/writers. We welcome newcomers and unsolicited submission of writing and artwork. In addition to the print issues, we publish online long poems, fiction, interviews, drama, and reviews."

NEEDS No genre: romance, horror, western—sagebrush or cowboys—erotic, science fiction, or mystery. Length: 100-3,000 words.

HOW TO CONTACT Send complete ms. No e-mail submissions.

PAYMENT/TERMS Pays $10-75.

TIPS "We publish many, many new writers and are always open to unsolicited submissions because we are 100% freelance. Do not send U.S. stamps; always use IRCs. We have poems, interviews, stories, and reviews online (query first)."

PRAIRIE SCHOONER

University of Nebraska–Lincoln, 123 Andrews Hall, Lincoln NE 68588. (402)472-0911. **Fax:** (402)472-1817. **E-mail:** prairieschooner@unl.edu. **Website:** prairieschooner.unl.edu. **Contact:** Ashley Strosnider, managing editor. Estab. 1926. "We look for the best fiction, poetry, and nonfiction available to publish, and our readers expect to read stories, poems, and essays of extremely high quality. We try to publish a variety of styles, topics, themes, points of view, and writers with a variety of backgrounds in all stages of their careers. We like work that is compelling—intellectually or emotionally—either in form, language, or content."

○ Submissions must be received between September 1 and May 1. Poetry published in *Prairie Schooner* has been selected for inclusion in *The Best American Poetry* and the *Pushcart Prize* anthologies. "All mss published in *Prairie Schooner* will automatically be considered for our annual prizes." These include The Strousse Award for Poetry ($500), the Bernice Slote Prize for Beginning Writers ($500), the Hugh J. Luke Award ($250), the Edward Stanley Award for Poetry ($1,000), the Virginia Faulkner Award for Excellence in Writing ($1,000), the Glenna Luschei Prize for Excellence ($1,500), and the Jane Geske Award ($250). Also, each year 10 Glenna Luschei Awards ($250 each) are given for poetry, fiction, and nonfiction. All contests are open only to those writers whose work was published in the magazine the previous year. Editors serve as judges. Also sponsors The *Prairie Schooner* Book Prize.

NEEDS "We try to remain open to a variety of styles, themes, and subject matter. We look for high-quality writing, 3-D characters, well-wrought plots, setting, etc. We are open to realistic and/or experimental fiction."

HOW TO CONTACT Send complete ms through mail, e-mail, or online submissions manager.

PAYMENT/TERMS Pays 3 copies of the issue in which the writer's work is published.

TIPS "Send us your best, most carefully crafted work, and be persistent. Submit again and again. Constantly work on improving your writing. Read widely in literary fiction, nonfiction, and poetry. Read *Prairie Schooner* to know what we publish."

PREMONITIONS

13 Hazely Combe, Arrenton Isle of Wight PO30 3AJ, United Kingdom. **E-mail:** mail@pigasuspress.co.uk. **Website:** www.pigasuspress.co.uk. **Contact:** Tony Lee, editor. "Science fiction and horror stories, plus genre poetry and fantastic artwork."

NEEDS Wants "original, high-quality SF/fantasy. Horror must have a science fiction element and be psychological or scary, rather than simply gory. Cutting-edge SF and experimental writing styles (cross-genre scenarios, slipstream, etc.) are always welcome." "No supernatural fantasy-horror." Length: 500-6,000 words. Send 1 story at a time.

HOW TO CONTACT Submit via mail and include SAE or IRC if you want material returned. "Use a standard manuscript format: double-spaced text, no right-justify, no staples." Do not send submissions via e-mail, unless by special request from editor. Include personalized cover letter with brief bio and publication credits.

PAYMENT/TERMS Pays minimum $5 or £5 per 1,000 words, plus copy of magazine.

TIPS "Potential contributors are advised to study recent issues of the magazine."

PRISM INTERNATIONAL

Dept. of Creative Writing, Buch E462, 1866 Main Mall, University of British Columbia, Vancouver BC V6T 1Z1, Canada. (604)822-2514. **Fax:** (604)822-3616. **E-mail:** prismcirculation@gmail.com. **Website:** www.prismmagazine.ca. Estab. 1959. A quarterly international journal of contemporary writing—fiction, poetry, drama, creative nonfiction and translation. *PRISM international* is digest-sized, elegantly printed, flat-spined, with original colour artwork on a nylon card cover. Readership: public and university libraries, individual subscriptions, bookstores—a world-wide audience concerned with the contemporary in literature. "We have no thematic or stylistic allegiances: Excellence is our main criterion for acceptance of manuscripts." Receives 1,000 submissions/year, accepts about 80. Circulation is for 1,200 subscribers. Subscription: $35/year for Canadian subscriptions, $40/year for US subscriptions, $45/year for international. Sample: $13.

NEEDS Experimental, traditional. New writing that is contemporary and literary. Short stories and self-contained novel excerpts (up to 25 double-spaced pages). Works of translation are eagerly sought and should be accompanied by a copy of the original. Would like to see more translations. "No gothic, confession, religious, romance, pornography, or sci-fi." Also looking for creative nonfiction that is literary, not journalistic, in scope and tone. Receives over 100 unsolicited mss/month. Accepts 70 mss/year. "PRISM publishes both new and established writers; our contributors have included Franz Kafka, Gabriel Garciía Maárquez, Michael Ondaatje, Margaret Laurence, Mark Anthony Jarman, Gail Anderson-Dargatz and Eden Robinson." Publishes ms 4 months after acceptance. **Publishes 7 new writers/year.** Recently published work by Ibi Kaslik, Melanie Little, Mark Anthony Jarman. Publishes short shorts. Also publishes poetry. For Drama: one-acts/excerpts of no more than 1,500 words preferred. Also interested in seeing dramatic monologues. "New writing that is contemporary and literary. Short stories and self-contained novel excerpts. Works of translation are eagerly sought and should be accompanied by a copy of the original. Would like to see more translations. No gothic, confession, religious, romance, pornography, or science fiction." Length: 25 pages maximum.

HOW TO CONTACT "Keep it simple. U.S. contributors take note: Do not send SASEs with U.S. stamps, they are not valid in Canada. Send International Reply Coupons instead." Responds in 4 months to queries; 3-6 months to mss. Sample copy for $13 or on website. Writer's guidelines online. Send complete ms.

PAYMENT/TERMS Pays $20/printed page of prose, $40/printed page of poetry, and 2 copies of issue. Pays on publication for first North American serial rights. Selected authors are paid an additional $10/page for digital rights. Cover art pays $300 and 2 copies of issue. Sponsors awards/contests, including annual short fiction, poetry, and nonfiction contests. Pays $30/printed page, and 2 copies of issue.

TIPS "We are looking for new and exciting fiction. Excellence is still our No. 1 criterion. As well as poetry, imaginative nonfiction and fiction, we are especially open to translations of all kinds, very short fiction pieces and drama which work well on the page. Translations must come with a copy of the original language work."

ⓢ PSEUDOPOD

Escape Artists, Inc., P.O. Box 965609, Marietta GA 30066. **E-mail:** editor@pseudopod.org. **Website:** pseudopod.org. **Contact:** Shawn M. Garrett and Alex Hofelich, co-editors. Estab. 2006. "*Pseudopod* is the premier horror podcast magazine. Every week we bring you chilling short stories from some of today's best horror authors, in convenient audio format for your computer or MP3 player."

NEEDS Guidelines available at pseudopod.org/guidelines/. Submit via pseudopod.submittable.com/submit. Length: 2,000-6,000 words (short fiction); 500-1,500 words (flash fiction).

PAYMENT/TERMS Pays 6¢/word for original fiction, $100 for short fiction reprints, $20 for flash fiction.

TIPS "Let the writing be guided by a strong sense of who the (hopefully somewhat interesting) protagonist is, even if zero time is spent developing any other characters. Preferably, tell the story using standard past tense, third person, active voice."

A PUBLIC SPACE

323 Dean St., Brooklyn NY 11217. (718)858-8067. **E-mail:** general@apublicspace.org. **Website:** www.apublicspace.org. **Contact:** Brigid Hughes, founding editor; Anne McPeak, managing editor. *A Public Space*, published quarterly, is an independent magazine of literature and culture. "In an era that has relegated literature to the margins, we plan to make fiction and poetry the stars of a new conversation. We believe that stories are how we make sense of our lives and how we learn about other lives. We believe that stories matter."

◌   Accepts unsolicited submissions from September 15-April 15. Submissions accepted through Submittable or by mail (with SASE).

NEEDS No word limit.

HOW TO CONTACT Submit 1 complete ms via online submissions manager.

PUERTO DEL SOL

New Mexico State University, English Dept., P.O. Box 30001, MSC 3E, Las Cruces NM 88003. **E-mail:** puertodelsoljournal@gmail.com. **Website:** www.puertodelsol.org. **Contact:** Richard Greenfield, editor-in-chief; Emily Alex, prose editor; Nate Wilkerson, poetry editor; Brady Richards, managing editor. Estab. 1964. Publishes innovative work from emerging and established writers and artists. Wants poetry, fiction, nonfiction, drama, theory, artwork, interviews, reviews, and interesting combinations thereof. *Puerto del Sol* is 150 pages, digest-sized, professionally printed, flat-spined, with matte card cover with art. Press run is 1,250 (300 subscribers, 25-30 libraries). Reading period for the print issue is June-October 15. General submissions reading period is variable.

NEEDS Accepts 8-12 mss/issue; 16-24 mss/year. Publishes several new writers/year. Has published work by David Trinidad, Molly Gaudry, Ray Gonzalez, Cynthia Cruz, Steve Tomasula, Denise Leto, Rae Bryant, Joshua Cohen, Blake Butler, Trinie Dalton, and Rick Moody.

HOW TO CONTACT Send 1 short story or 2-4 short short stories at a time through online submission manager.

PAYMENT/TERMS Pays 1 contributor copy.

TIPS "We are especially pleased to publish emerging writers who work to push their art form or field of study in new directions."

QUARTER AFTER EIGHT

Ohio University, 342 Lindley Hall, Athens OH 45701. **E-mail:** editor@quarteraftereight.org. **Website:** www.quarteraftereight.org. **Contact:** Derek Robbins, editor; Kristin Distel, assistant editor. "*Quarter After Eight* is an annual literary journal devoted to the exploration of innovative writing. We celebrate work that directly challenges the conventions of language, style, voice, or idea in literary forms. In its aesthetic commitment to diverse forms, *QAE* remains a unique publication among contemporary literary magazines." Reading period: October 15-April 15. Holds annual short prose (any genre) contest with grand prize of $1,008.15. Deadline is November 30.

HOW TO CONTACT Submit through online submissions manager.

TIPS "We look for prose and poetry that is innovative, exploratory, and—most importantly—well written. Please subscribe to our journal and read what is published to get acquainted with the *QAE* aesthetic."

ⓢ QUARTERLY WEST

University of Utah, 255 S. Central Campus Dr., Room 3500, Salt Lake City UT 84112. **E-mail:** quarterlywest@gmail.com. **Website:** www.quarterlywest.com. **Contact:** Sara Eliza Johnson and J.P. Grasser, editors. Estab. 1976. "We publish fiction, poetry, nonfiction, and new media in long and short formats, and will consider experimental as well as traditional works."

○ *Quarterly West* was awarded first place for Editorial Content from the American Literary Magazine Awards. Work published in the magazine has been selected for inclusion in the *Pushcart Prize* anthology, the *Best of the Net* anthology, and *The Best American Short Stories* anthology.

NEEDS No preferred lengths; interested in longer, fuller short stories and short shorts. Accepts 6-10 mss/year. No detective, science fiction, or romance.

HOW TO CONTACT Send complete ms using online submissions manager only.

TIPS "We publish a special section of short shorts every issue, and we also sponsor an annual novella contest. We are open to experimental work—potential contributors should read the magazine! Don't send more than 1 story per submission. Novella competition guidelines available online. We prefer work with interesting language and detail—plot or narrative are less important. We don't do religious work."

ⓢ ELLERY QUEEN'S MYSTERY MAGAZINE

44 Wall St., Suite 904, New York NY 10005-2401. **E-mail:** elleryqueenmm@dellmagazines.com. **Website:** www.themysteryplace.com/eqmm. Estab. 1941. "*Ellery Queen's Mystery Magazine* welcomes submissions from both new and established writers. We publish every kind of mystery short story: the psychological suspense tale, the deductive puzzle, the private eye case—the gamut of crime and detection from the realistic (including the policeman's lot and stories of police procedure) to the more imaginative (including 'locked rooms' and 'impossible crimes'). We look for strong writing, an original and exciting plot, and professional craftsmanship. We encourage writers whose

work meets these general criteria to read an issue of *EQMM* before making a submission."

NEEDS "We always need detective stories. Special consideration given to anything timely and original." Publishes ms 6-12 months after acceptance. Agented fiction 50%. **Publishes 10 new writers/year.** Recently published work by Jeffery Deaver, Joyce Carol Oates, and Margaret Maron. Sometimes comments on rejected mss. No explicit sex or violence, no gore or horror. Seldom publishes parodies or pastiches. "We do not want true detective or crime stories." Length: 2,500-8,000 words, but occasionally accepts longer and shorter submissions—including minute mysteries of 250 words, stories up to 12,000 words, and novellas of up to 20,000 words from established authors.

HOW TO CONTACT "*EQMM* uses an online submission system (eqmm.magazinesubmissions.com) that has been designed to streamline our process and improve communication with authors. We ask that all submissions be made electronically, using this system, rather than on paper. All stories should be in standard ms format and submitted in .DOC format. We cannot accept .DOCX, .RTF, or .TXT files at this time."

PAYMENT/TERMS Pays 5-8¢/word; occasionally higher for established authors.

TIPS "*EQMM*'s range in the mystery genre is extensive: Almost any story that involves crime or the threat of crime comes within our purview. However, like all magazines, *EQMM* has a distinctive tone and style, and you can only get a sense of whether your work will suit us by reading an issue."

⊘ⓢ QUEEN'S QUARTERLY

402D - Douglas Library, 93 University Ave., Queen's University, Kingston ON K7L 5v4, Canada. (613)533-2667. **E-mail:** queens.quarterly@queensu.ca. **Website:** www.queensu.ca/quarterly. **Contact:** Dr. Boris Castel, editor; Joan Harcourt, literary editor. Estab. 1893. *Queen's Quarterly* is "a general-interest intellectual review featuring articles on science, politics, humanities, arts and letters, extensive book reviews, and some poetry and fiction." Has published work by Gail Anderson-Dargatz, Tim Bowling, Emma Donohue, Viktor Carr, Mark Jarman, Rick Bowers, and Dennis Bock.

NEEDS Length: up to 2,500 words.

HOW TO CONTACT Send complete ms with SASE and/or IRC. No reply with insufficient postage. Accepts 2 mss/issue; 8 mss/year. Publishes 5 new writers/year.

PAYMENT/TERMS "Payment to new writers will be determined at time of acceptance."

QUIDDITY INTERNATIONAL LITERARY JOURNAL AND PUBLIC-RADIO PROGRAM

Quiddity, PO Box 1046, Murphysboro IL 62966. **E-mail:** quidditylit@gmail.com. **Website:** www.quidditylit.com. **Contact:** Joanna Beth Tweedy, founding editor; John McCarthy, managing editor. *Quiddity*, published semi-annually, is a print journal and public-radio program featuring poetry, prose, and artwork by new, emerging, and established contributors from around the world. Has published work by J.O.J. Nwachukwu-Agbada, Kevin Stein, Karen An-Hwei Lee, and Haider Al-Kabi. *Quiddity* is 176 pages, 7X9, perfect-bound, with 60 lb. full color cover. Receives about 3,500 poems/year, accepts about 3%. Press run is 1,000. Single copy: $9; subscription: $15/year. Make checks payable to *Quiddity*. Each work selected is considered for public-radio program feature offered by NPR-member station. International submissions are encouraged.

NEEDS Length: 5,000 word-max.

HOW TO CONTACT Send complete ms. Submit online through submissions manager.

THE RAG

P.O. Box 17463, Portland OR 97217. **E-mail:** submissions@raglitmag.com; seth@raglitmag.com. **Website:** raglitmag.com. **Contact:** Seth Porter, managing editor; Dan Reilly, editor. Estab. 2011. *The Rag* focuses on the grittier genres that tend to fall by the wayside at more traditional literary magazines. *The Rag*'s ultimate goal is to put the literary magazine back into the entertainment market while rekindling the social and cultural value short fiction once held in North American literature.

○ Fee to submit online ($3) is waived if you subscribe or purchase a single issue.

NEEDS Accepts all styles and themes. Length: up to 10,000 words.

HOW TO CONTACT Send complete ms.

PAYMENT/TERMS Pays 5¢/word, $250 average/story.

TIPS "We like gritty material: material that is psychologically believable and that has some humor in it, dark or otherwise. We like subtle themes, original characters, and sharp wit."

❸ RAINBOW RUMPUS

P.O. Box 6881, Minneapolis MN 55406. **Website:** www.rainbowrumpus.org. **Contact:** Liane Bonin Starr, editor in chief and fiction editor. Estab. 2005. "*Rainbow Rumpus* is the world's only online literary magazine for children and youth with lesbian, gay, bisexual, and transgender (LGBT) parents. We are creating a new genre of children's and young adult fiction. Please carefully read and observe the guidelines on our website."

NEEDS "Stories should be written from the point of view of children or teens with lesbian, gay, bisexual, or transgender parents or other family members, or who are connected to the LGBT community. Stories featuring families of color, bisexual parents, transgender parents, family members with disabilities, and mixed-race families are particularly welcome." Length: 800-2,500 words for stories for 4- to 12-year-olds; up to 5,000 words for stories for 13- to 18-year-olds.

HOW TO CONTACT Query editor through website's Contact page. Be sure to select the Submissions category.

PAYMENT/TERMS Pays $300/story.

TIPS "Emerging writers encouraged to submit. You do not need to be a member of the LGBT community to participate."

RALEIGH REVIEW LITERARY & ARTS MAGAZINE

Box 6725, Raleigh NC 27628-6725. **E-mail:** info@raleighreview.org. **Website:** www.raleighreview.org. **Contact:** Rob Greene, editor; Landon Houle, fiction editor; Bryce Emley, poetry editor. Estab. 2010. "*Raleigh Review* is a national nonprofit magazine of poetry, short fiction (including flash), and art. We believe that great literature inspires empathy by allowing us to see the world through the eyes of our neighbors, whether across the street or across the globe. Our mission is to foster the creation and availability of accessible yet provocative contemporary literature. We look for work that is emotionally and intellectually complex."

NEEDS "We prefer work that is physically grounded and accessible, though complex and rich in emotional or intellectual power. We delight in stories from unique voices and perspectives. Any fiction that is born from a relatively unknown place grabs our attention. We are not opposed to genre fiction, so long as it has real, human characters and is executed artfully."

Length: 250-7,500 words. "While we accept fiction up to 7,500 words, we are more likely to publish work in the 4,500- to 5,000-word range."

HOW TO CONTACT Submit complete ms.

PAYMENT/TERMS Pays $10 maximum.

TIPS "Please be sure to read the guidelines and look at sample work on our website. Every piece is read for its intrinsic value, so new/emerging voices are often published alongside nationally recognized, award-winning authors."

🅢 RATTAPALLAX

Rattapallax Press, 217 Thompson St., Suite 353, New York NY 10012. **E-mail:** devineni@rattapallax.com. **Website:** www.rattapallax.com. **Contact:** Ram Devineni, founder & president; Flávia Rocha, editor in chief. Estab. 1999. Receives 15 unsolicited mss/month. Accepts 3 mss/issue; 6 mss/year. Agented fiction 15%. Receives about 5,000 poems/year; accepts 2%. Publishes 3 new writers/year. Has published work by Stuart Dybek, Howard Norman, Molly Giles, Rick Moody, Anthony Hecht, Sharon Olds, Lou Reed, Marilyn Hacker, Billy Collins, and Glyn Maxwell. *Rattapallax*, published semiannually, is named for "Wallace Stevens's word for the sound of thunder. The magazine includes a DVD featuring poetry films and audio files. *Rattapallax* is looking for the extraordinary in modern poetry and prose that reflect the diversity of world cultures. Our goals are to create international dialogue using literature and focus on what is relevant to our society."

🅞 *Rattapallax* is 112 pages, magazine-sized, offset-printed, perfect-bound, with 12-pt. CS1 cover; some illustrations; photos. Press run is 2,000 (100 subscribers, 50 libraries, 1,200 shelf sales); 200 distributed free to contributors, reviews, and promos.

NEEDS Length: up to 2,000 words.

HOW TO CONTACT Submit via online submissions manager at rattapallax.submittable.com/submit.

PAYMENT/TERMS Pays 2 contributor's copies.

RATTLING WALL

c/o PEN USA, 269 S. Beverly Dr. #1163, Beverly Hills CA 90212. **E-mail:** therattlingwall@penusa.org. **Website:** therattlingwall.com. **Contact:** Michelle Meyering, editor. Estab. 2010.

🅞 Magazine: 6x9, square bound.

NEEDS Length: up to 15 pages.

HOW TO CONTACT Submit 1 complete story; no excerpts. Submissions should be double-spaced. Include cover letter with contact information, brief bio, writing sample.

PAYMENT/TERMS Pays 2 contributor's copies.

🅢 THE RAVEN CHRONICLES

A Journal of Art, Literature, & the Spoken Word, 15528 12th Ave. NE, Shoreline WA 98155. (206)941-2955. **E-mail:** editors@ravenchronicles.org. **E-mail:** https://ravenchronicles.submittable.com/submit. **Website:** www.ravenchronicles.org. **Contact:** Phoebe Bosché, managing editor; Priscilla Long, nonfiction editor; Kathleen Alcalá, fiction editor; Gary Lilley, poetry editor. Estab. 1991. "*The Raven Chronicles* publishes work which reflects the cultural diversity of the Pacific Northwest, Canada, and other areas of North America. We promote art, literature, and the spoken word for an audience that is hip, literate, funny, informed, and lives in a society that has a multicultural sensibility. We publish fiction, talk art/spoken word, poetry, essays, reflective articles, reviews, interviews, and contemporary art. We look for work that reflects the author's experiences, perceptions, and insights."

NEEDS "Experimental work is always of interest." Length: up to 4,000 words, or 3 flash fiction/lyric prose fiction. "Check with us for maximum length. We sometimes print longer pieces."

HOW TO CONTACT Submit complete ms via online submissions manager.

🅢 THE READER

The Reader Organisation, Calderstones Mansion, Calderstones Park, Liverpool L18 3JB, United Kingdom. **E-mail:** magazine@thereader.org.uk; info@thereader.org.uk. **Website:** www.thereader.org.uk. **Contact:** Grace Frame. Estab. 1997. "*The Reader* is a quarterly literary magazine aimed at the intelligent 'common reader'—from those just beginning to explore serious literary reading to professional teachers, academics, and writers. As well as publishing short fiction and poetry by new writers and established names, the magazine features articles on all aspects of literature, language, and reading; regular features, including a literary quiz and a section on the Reading Revolution, reporting on The Reader Organisation's outreach work; reviews; and readers' recommendations of books that have made a difference to them. *The Reader* is unique among literary magazines in its focus on reading as a creative, important, and pleasurable activity, and in its combination of high-quality material and presentation with a genuine commitment to ordinary but dedicated readers." Also publishes literary essays, literary criticism, poetry.

NEEDS Wants short fiction and (more rarely) novel excerpts. Has published work by Karen King Arbisala, Ray Tallis, Sasha Dugdale, Vicki Seal, David Constantine, Jonathan Meades, and Ramesh Avadhani. Length: 1,000-2,500 words. Average length: 2,300 words. Publishes short shorts. Average length of short shorts: 1,500 words.

HOW TO CONTACT No e-mail submissions. Send complete ms with cover letter. Include estimated word count, brief bio, list of publications.

TIPS "The style or polish of the writing is less important than the deep structure of the story (though, of course, it matters that it's well written). The main persuasive element is whether the story moves us—and that's quite hard to quantify. It's something to do with the force of the idea and the genuine nature of enquiry within the story. When fiction is the writer's natural means of thinking things through, that'll get us. "

REAL

Regarding Arts & Letters, Stephen F. Austin State University, Nacogdoches TX 75962-3007. **Website:** regardingartsandletters.wordpress.com. **Contact:** Mark Sanders, editor. Estab. 1968. "*REAL: Regarding Arts & Letters* was founded in 1968 as an academic journal which occasionally published poetry. Now, it is an international creative magazine dedicated to publishing the best contemporary fiction, poetry, and nonfiction." Features both established and emerging writers. Magazine: semiannual, 120 pages, perfect-bound.

NEEDS "We're not interested in genre fiction—science fiction or romance or the like—unless you're doing some cheeky genre-bending. Otherwise, send us your best literary work." Publishes short shorts. Length: up to 6,000 words.

HOW TO CONTACT Submit via online submissions manager.

PAYMENT/TERMS Pays contributor's copies

TIPS "We are looking for the best work, whether you are established or not."

REDIVIDER

Department of Writing, Literature, and Publishing, Emerson College, 120 Boylston St., Boston MA 02116. **E-mail:** editor@redividerjournal.org. **Website:**

www.redividerjournal.org. Estab. 1986. *Redivider*, a journal of literature and art, is published twice a year by graduate students in the Writing, Literature, and Publishing Department of Emerson College. Prints new art, fiction, nonfiction, and poetry from new, emerging, and established artists and writers. Every spring, *Redivider* hosts the Beacon Street Prize Writing Contest, awarding a cash prize and publication to the winning submission in fiction, poetry, and nonfiction categories. Hosts the Blurred Genre Contest each fall, awarding cash prizes and publication for flash fiction, flash nonfiction, and prose poetry. See website for details.

NEEDS Length: up to 8,000 words.

HOW TO CONTACT Submit via online submissions manager.

PAYMENT/TERMS Pays 2 contributor's copies.

TIPS "To get a sense of what we publish, pick up an issue!"

RED ROCK REVIEW

College of Southern Nevada, CSN Department of English, J2A, 3200 E. Cheyenne Ave., North Las Vegas NV 89030. (702)651-4094. **Fax:** (702)651-4455. **E-mail:** redrockreview@csn.edu. **Website:** sites.csn.edu/english/redrockreview. **Contact:** Todd Moffett, senior editor; Erica Vital-Lazare, associate editor. Estab. 1994. Dedicated to the publication of fine contemporary literature. Accepts fine poetry and short fiction year round.

○ *Red Rock Review* is about 130 pages, magazine-sized, professionally printed, perfect-bound, with 10-pt. CS1 cover.

NEEDS "We're looking for the very best literature. Stories need to be tightly crafted, strong in character development, built around conflict." Length: up to 5,000 words.

HOW TO CONTACT Send ms via e-mail as Word, RTF, or PDF file attachment.

PAYMENT/TERMS Pays 2 contributor's copies.

RED WHEELBARROW

De Anza College, 21250 Stevens Creek Blvd., Cupertino CA 95014. **Website:** www.deanza.edu/redwheelbarrow. Estab. 1976 as *Bottomfish*; 2000 as *Red Wheelbarrow*.

○ "We seek to publish a diverse range of styles and voices from around the country and the world." Publishes a student edition and a national edition.

NEEDS Length: up to 4,000 words.

HOW TO CONTACT Send complete ms by mail (include SASE) or e-mail with brief bio.

TIPS "Write freely, rewrite carefully. Resist clichés and stereotypes. We are not affiliated with Red Wheelbarrow Press or any similarly named publication."

REED MAGAZINE

San Jose State University, Dept. of English, One Washington Square, San Jose CA 95192. **E-mail:** mail@reedmag.org; cathleen.miller@sjsu.edu. **Website:** www.reedmag.org. **Contact:** Cathleen Miller, editor-in-chief. Estab. 1867. *Reed Magazine* is California's oldest literary journal. "We publish works of short fiction, nonfiction, poetry, and art, and offer cash prizes in each category." Accepts electronic submissions only.

NEEDS Does not want children's, young adult, fantasy, or erotica. Length: up to 5,000 words.

HOW TO CONTACT Submit complete ms via online submissions manager.

PAYMENT/TERMS Contest contributors receive 1 free copy; additional copies: $15.

TIPS "Well-writen, original, clean grammatical prose is essential. We are interested in established authors as well as fresh new voices. Keep submitting!"

RHINO

The Poetry Forum, Inc., P.O. Box 591, Evanston IL 60204. **E-mail:** editors@rhinopoetry.org. **Website:** rhinopoetry.org. **Contact:** Ralph Hamilton, editor-in-chief. "This independent, eclectic annual journal of 40 plus years accepts poetry, flash fiction (up to 500 words), and poetry-in-translation that experiments, provokes, compels. Emerging and established poets are showcased." Accepts general submissions April 1-July 31 and Founders' Prize submissions September 1-October 31.

NEEDS Length: up to 500 words.

PAYMENT/TERMS Pays 1 contributor's copy and offers contributor discounts for additional copies.

TIPS "Our diverse group of editors looks for the very best in contemporary writing, and we have created a dynamic process of soliciting and reading new work by local, national, and international writers. We are open to all styles and look for idiosyncratic, rigorous, well-crafted, lively, and passionate work."

RIVER STYX MAGAZINE

Big River Association, 3139A Grand Blvd., Suite 203, St. Louis MO 63118. **E-mail:** bigriver@riverstyx.org. **Website:** www.riverstyx.org. **Contact:** Theresa Brickman, Managing Editor. Estab. 1975. Sponsors an annual Microfiction Contest, judged by the editors. Deadline: December 31. Guidelines available for SASE or on website. "*River Styx* publishes the highest-quality poetry, fiction, interviews, essays, and visual art. We are an internationally distributed multicultural literary magazine."

Work published in *River Styx* has been selected for inclusion in past volumes of *New Stories from the South*, *The Best American Poetry*, *Best New Poets*, *New Poetry from the Midwest*, and *The Pushcart Prize Anthology*.

NEEDS Recently published work by George Singleton, Philip Graham, Katherine Min, Richard Burgin, Nancy Zafris, Jacob Appel, and Eric Shade. Sponsors an annual microfiction contest. No genre fiction, less thinly veiled autobiography. Length: no more than 23-30 manuscript pages.

HOW TO CONTACT Send complete ms with SASE.

PAYMENT/TERMS Pays 2 contributor copies, plus one-year subscription. Cash payment as funds permit.

R.KV.R.Y. QUARTERLY LITERARY JOURNAL

90 Meetings in 90 Days Press, 499 North Canon Dr., Suite 400, Beverly Hills CA 90210. **E-mail:** r.kv.r.y.editor@gmail.com. **Website:** www.rkvry.com. **Contact:** Mary Akers, editor-in-chief. Estab. 2004. "*r.kv.r.y.* publishes 3 short stories of high literary quality every quarter. We publish fiction that varies widely in style. We prefer stories of character development, psychological penetration, and lyricism, without sentimentality or purple prose. We ask that all submissions address issues related to recovery from any type of physical, psychological, or cultural loss, dislocation or oppression. We include but do not limit ourselves to issues of substance abuse. We do not publish the standard 'what it was like, what happened and what it is like now' recovery narrative. Works published by *r.kv.r.y.* embrace almost every area of adult interest related to recovery. Material should be presented in a fashion suited to a quarterly that is neither journalistic nor academic. We welcome academic articles from varying fields. We encourage our academic contributors to free themselves from the constraints imposed by academic journals, letting their knowledge,

wisdom, and experience rock and roll on these pages. Our intended audience is people of discriminating taste, original ideas, heart, and love of narrative and language."

NEEDS Receives 30 stories/month. Accepts 3 stories/issue; 12 stories/year. Agented fiction 10%. Publishes 5-6 new writers/year. Published Anthony Doerr, Margaret Atwood, Dylan Landis, T.J. Forrester, Kim Chinquee, Alicia Gifford, Andrew Tibbets, Jason Schneiderman. Length: 3,000 words (max). Average length: 2,000 words. Average length of short shorts: 1,000 words.

HOW TO CONTACT "Submit complete ms with cover letter through our online submission system."

TIPS "Wants strong focus on character development and lively writing style with strong voice. Read our present and former issues (archived online)."

⑤ ROANOKE REVIEW

221 College Lane, Miller Hall, Salem VA 24153. E-mail: review@roanoke.edu. **Website:** http://roanokereview.org. Estab. 1967. "The *Roanoke Review* is an online literary journal that is dedicated to publishing new and established voices in fiction, nonfiction, and poetry. Humor is encouraged; humility as well." Recent work by Henry Taylor, Adrian Blevins, Lucy Jane Bledsoe, John Sibley Williams, and Karl Harshbarger.

NEEDS Length: 1,000-5,000 words. Average length: 3,000 words.

HOW TO CONTACT Submit via Submittable, e-mail, or send SASE for reply only.

TIPS "Send us something you love."

THE ROCKFORD REVIEW

Rockford Writers' Guild, P.O. Box 858, Rockford IL 61105. **E-mail:** editor@rockfordwritersguild.org. **Website:** www.rockfordwritersguild.org. **Contact:** Connie Kuntz. Estab. 1947. Since 1947, Rockford Writers' Guild has published The Rockford Review twice a year. Anyone may submit to the winter-spring edition of The Rockford Review from July 15-October 15. If published, payment is one contributor copy of journal and $5 per published piece. We also publish a "Members Only" edition in the summer which is open to members of Rockford Writers' Guild. Anyone may be a member of RWG and we have 170 members from the United States, England, Canada, and Mexico. Members are guaranteed publication at least once

a year. Check website for frequent updates at www.rockfordwritersguild.org. Follow us Facebook under Rockford Writers' Guild or Twitter and Instagram @ guildypleasures. Poetry 50 lines or less, prose 1,300 words or less. No racist, supremacist, or sexist content. If published in the winter-spring edition of *The Rockford Review*, payment is one copy of journal and $5 per published piece. Pays on publication. Credit line given. Buys first North American serial rights.

NEEDS Prose should express fresh insights into the human condition. No sexist, pornographic, or supremacist content. Length: no more than 1,300 words.

TIPS "We're wide open to new and established writers alike."

ROMANCE FLASH

Romance Flash, 1112 Dakota Street, Watertown WI 53094. **E-mail:** info@romanceflash.com. **E-mail:** submissions@romanceflash.com. **Website:** www.romanceflash.com. **Contact:** Kat de Falla and Rachel Green, editors. Estab. 2010. Monthly online magazine featuring romantic flash fiction stories of 1,000 words or fewer.

NEEDS No heavy erotica. Length: 1,000 words or less.

PAYMENT/TERMS Pays $3 per story (paid via PayPal only).

◑⑤ ROOM

West Coast Feminist Literary Magazine Society, P.O. Box 46160, Station D, Vancouver BC V6J 5G5, Canada. **E-mail:** contactus@roommagazine.com. **Website:** www.roommagazine.com. Estab. 1975. "*Room* is Canada's oldest feminist literary journal. Published quarterly by a collective based in Vancouver, *Room* showcases fiction, poetry, reviews, artwork, interviews, and profiles by writers and artists who identify as women or genderqueer. Many of our contributors are at the beginning of their writing careers, looking for an opportunity to get published for the first time. Some later go on to great acclaim. *Room* is a space where women can speak, connect, and showcase their creativity. Each quarter we publish original, thought-provoking works that reflect women's strength, sensuality, vulnerability, and wit."

◑ *Room* is digest-sized; contains illustrations, photos. Press run is 1,600 (900 subscribers, 50-100 libraries, 100-350 shelf sales).

NEEDS Accepts literature that illustrates the female experience—short stories, creative nonfiction, poetry—by, for, and about women.

HOW TO CONTACT Submit complete ms via online submissions manager.

PAYMENT/TERMS Pays $50-120 CAD, 2 contributor's copies, and a one-year subscription.

ROSEBUD

N3310 Asje Rd., Cambridge WI 53523. (608)423-9780. **Website:** www.rsbd.net. **Contact:** Rod, managing editor. Estab. 1993. *Rosebud*, published 3 times/year in April, August, and December, has presented many of the most prominent voices in the nation and has been listed as among the very best markets for writers.

⊙ *Rosebud* is elegantly printed with full-color cover. Press run is 10,000.

NEEDS Has published work by Ray Bradbury, X.J. Kennedy, and Nikki Giovanni. Publishes short shorts. Also publishes literary essays. Often comments on rejected mss. "No formula pieces."

HOW TO CONTACT Send up to 3 stories to Roderick Clark by postal mail. Include SASE for return of ms and $1 handling fee.

TIPS "Each issue has 6 or 7 flexible departments (selected from a total of 16 departments that rotate). We are seeking stories; articles; profiles; and poems of love, alienation, travel, humor, nostalgia, and unexpected revelation. Something has to 'happen' in the pieces we choose, but what happens inside characters is much more interesting to us than plot manipulation. We like good storytelling, real emotion, and authentic voice."

THE SAINT ANN'S REVIEW

Saint Ann's School, 129 Pierrepont St., Brooklyn NY 11201. (718)522-1660 ext. 317. **Fax:** (718)522-2599. **E-mail:** sareview@saintannsny.org. **Website:** www.saintannsreview.com. Estab. 2000. "*The Saint Ann's Review* publishes short fiction, poetry, essays, drama, novel excerpts, reviews, translations, interviews, and experimental works."

⊙ We seek honed work that gives the reader a sense of its necessity.

NEEDS Length: up to 6,000 words for short stories; up to 25 pages for excerpts.

HOW TO CONTACT Guidelines available online.

PAYMENT/TERMS Pays 2 contributor's copies.

ST. ANTHONY MESSENGER

Franciscan Media, 28 W. Liberty St., Cincinnati OH 45202-6498. (513)241-5615. **Fax:** (513)241-0399. **E-mail:** magazineeditors@franciscanmedia.org. **Website:** www.stanthonymessenger.org. **Contact:** Pat McCloskey, OFM, Franciscan Editor. Estab. 1893. *St. Anthony Messenger* is a Catholic family magazine which aims to help its readers lead more fully human and Christian lives. "We publish articles that report on a changing church and world, opinion pieces written from the perspective of Christian faith and values, personality profiles, and fiction which entertains and informs. Take our writer's guidelines very seriously. We do!"

NEEDS "We do not want mawkishly sentimental or preachy fiction. Stories are most often rejected for poor plotting and characterization, bad dialogue (listen to how people talk), and inadequate motivation. Many stories say nothing, are 'happenings' rather than stories. No fetal journals, no rewritten Bible stories." Length: 2,000 words maximum.

HOW TO CONTACT Send complete ms.

PAYMENT/TERMS Pays 20¢/word.

TIPS "The freelancer should consider why his or her proposed article would be appropriate for us, rather than for *Redbook* or *Saturday Review*. We treat human problems of all kinds, but from a religious perspective. Articles should reflect Catholic theology, spirituality, and employ a Catholic terminology and vocabulary. We need more articles on prayer, scripture, Catholic worship. Get authoritative information (not merely library research); we want interviews with experts. Write in popular style; use lots of examples, stories, and personal quotes. Word length is an important consideration."

SALMAGUNDI

Skidmore College, 815 N. Broadway, Saratoga Springs NY 12866. **Fax:** (518)580-5188. **E-mail:** salmagun@skidmore.edu. **Website:** https://salmagundi.skidmore.edu. **Contact:** Marc Woodworth, associate editor. Estab. 1965. "*Salmagundi* publishes an eclectic variety of materials, ranging from short-short fiction to novellas from the surreal to the realistic, as well as poems, essays, symposia and interviews. Authors include Allan Gurganus, Phillip Lopate, Lincoln Perry, Max Nelson, David Bromwich, J.M. Coerzee, Russell Banks, Rick Moody, Binnie Kirschenbaum, Akeel Bilgrami, Carolyn Forché, Chase Twichell, Linda Pastan, Debora Greger, William Logan, Bina Gogenini, Thomas Chatterton Williams, Marilynne Robinson, Orlando Patterson, Gordon Lish, Anthony Appiah, Clark Blaise, Henri Cole, Mary Gordon, Frank Bidart, Louise Glück, George Steiner, Robert Pinsky, Joyce Carol Oates, Mary Gaitskill, Amy Hempel, Nadine Gordimer, George Scialabba, Rochelle Gurstein, Catherine Pond, Richard Howard, Jennifer Delton and Cynthia Ozick. Our audience is a generally literate population of people who read for pleasure and enjoy the occasional bracing argument." Magazine: 8x5; illustrations; photos. *Salmagundi* authors are regularly represented in *Pushcart* collections and *Best American Short Story* collections. Reading period: November 1-December 1.

NEEDS Length: up to 12,000 words.

HOW TO CONTACT Submit hard copy only by snail mail with SASE.

PAYMENT/TERMS Pays 6-10 contributor's copies and one-year subscription.

TIPS "I look for excellence and a very unpredictable ability to appeal to the interests and tastes of the editors. Be brave. Don't be discouraged by rejection. Keep stories in circulation. Of course, it goes without saying: Work hard on the writing. Revise tirelessly. Study other magazines as well as this one, and send only to those whose sensibility matches yours."

SALT HILL JOURNAL

Creative Writing Program, Syracuse University, English Deptartment, 401 Hall of Languages, Syracuse University, Syracuse NY 13244. **Website:** salthilljournal.net. **Contact:** Jakob Maier, Jono Naito, editors-in-chief. "*Salt Hill* is published through Syracuse University's Creative Writing MFA program. We strive to publish a mix of the best contemporary and emerging talent in poetry, fiction, and nonfiction. Your work, if accepted, would appear in a long tradition of exceptional contributors, including Steve Almond, Mary Caponegro, Kim Chinquee, Edwidge Danticat, Denise Duhamel, Brian Evenson, B.H. Fairchild, Mary Gaitskill, Terrance Hayes, Bob Hicok, Laura Kasischke, Etgar Keret, Phil Lamarche, Dorianne Laux, Maurice Manning, Karyna McGlynn, Ander Monson, David Ohle, Lucia Perillo, Tomaž Šalamun, Zachary Schomburg, Christine Schutt, David Shields, Charles Simic, Patricia Smith, Dara Wier, and Raúl Zurita, among many others." Only accepts submissions by

online submission form; does not accept unsolicited e-mail submissions.

NEEDS Length: up to 30 pages.

HOW TO CONTACT Submit via online submissions manager; contact fiction editor via e-mail for retractions and queries only.

THE SAME

P.O. Box 494, Mount Union PA 17066. **E-mail:** editors@thesamepress.com. **E-mail:** submissions@thesamepress.com. **Website:** www.thesamepress.com. **Contact:** Nancy Eldredge, managing editor. Estab. 2000. *The Same*, published biannually, prints nonfiction (essays, reviews, literary criticism), poetry, and short fiction.

○   *The Same* is 50-100 pages, desktop-published, perfect-bound.

HOW TO CONTACT Query before submitting.

THE SANDY RIVER REVIEW

University of Maine at Farmington, 114 Prescott St., Farmington ME 04938. **E-mail:** thesandyriverreview@gmail.com. **E-mail:** sandyriversubmissions@gmail.com. **Website:** sandyriverreview.com. **Contact:** Alexandra Dupuis and Elayna Chamberlin, print editors; Richard Southard and Meagan Jones, the River editors. "*The Sandy River Review* seeks prose, poetry, and art submissions once a year for our annual print issue. *The River*, our regularly flowing stream of high-quality digital content, accepts these as well, along with podcasts and music. Deadline for the print issue is in December, while *The River* has rolling submissions. Prose submissions may be either fiction or creative nonfiction and should be a maximum of 3,500 words in length, 12-point, Times New Roman font, and double-spaced. Most of our art is published in b&w and must be submitted as 300-dpi quality, CMYK color mode, and saved as a TIFF file. We publish a wide variety of work from students as well as professional, established writers. Your submission should be polished and imaginative with strongly drawn characters and an interesting, original narrative. The review is the face of the University of Maine at Farmington's venerable BFA Creative Writing program, and we strive for the highest quality prose and poetry standard."

NEEDS Submit via e-mail. "The review is a literary journal—please, no horror, science fiction, romance." Length: up to 3,5000 words.

HOW TO CONTACT Send complete ms.

PAYMENT/TERMS Pays 3 contributor's copies.

TIPS "We recommend that you take time with your piece. As with all submissions to a literary journal, submissions should be fully completed, polished final drafts that require minimal to no revision once accepted. Double-check your prose pieces for basic grammatical errors before submitting."

SANTA MONICA REVIEW

Santa Monica College, 1900 Pico Blvd., Santa Monica CA 90405. **Website:** www.smc.edu/sm_review. **Contact:** Andrew Tonkovich, editor. Estab. 1988. The *Santa Monica Review*, published twice yearly in fall and spring, is a nationally distributed literary arts journal sponsored by Santa Monica College. It currently features fiction and nonfiction.

NEEDS "No crime and detective, mysogyny, footnotes, TV, dog stories. We want more self-conscious, smart, political, humorous, digressive, meta-fiction."

HOW TO CONTACT Submit complete ms with SASE. No e-mail submissions.

PAYMENT/TERMS Pays contributor's copies and subscription.

THE SARANAC REVIEW

Dept. of English, SUNY Plattsburgh, 101 Broad St., Plattsburgh NY 12901. (518)564-2241. **Fax:** (518)564-2140. **E-mail:** saranacreview@plattsburgh.edu. **Website:** www.saranacreview.com. **Contact:** J.L. Torres, executive editor. Estab. 2004. "*The Saranac Review* is committed to dissolving boundaries of all kinds, seeking to publish a diverse array of emerging and established writers from Canada and the U.S. *The Saranac Review* aims to be a textual clearing in which a space is opened for cross-pollination between American and Canadian writers. In this way the magazine reflects the expansive, bright spirit of the etymology of its name, Saranac, meaning 'cluster of stars.' *The Saranac Review* is digest-sized, with color photo or painting on cover. Publishes both digital and print-on-demand versions. Has published Lawrence Raab, Jacob M. Appel, Marilyn Nelson, Tom Wayman, Colette Inez, Louise Warren, Brian Campbell, Gregory Pardlo, Myfanwy Collins, William Giraldi, Xu Xi, Julia Alvarez, and other fine emerging and established writers." Published annually.

NEEDS "We're looking for well-crafted fiction that demonstrates respect for and love of language. Fiction that makes us feel and think, that edifies without being didactic or self-indulgent and ultimately connects us to our sense of humanity." No genre material (fantasy, sci-fi, etc.) or light verse. Length: up to 7,000 words.

HOW TO CONTACT Submit complete ms via online submissions manager (Submittable).

❍❸ THE SAVAGE KICK LITERARY MAGAZINE

Murder Slim Press, 29 Alpha Rd., Gorleston Norfolk NR31 0LQ, United Kingdom. **E-mail:** moonshine@murderslim.com. **Website:** www.murderslim.com. Estab. 2005. "*Savage Kick* primarily deals with viewpoints outside the mainstream: honest emotions told in a raw, simplistic way. It is recommended that you are very familiar with the *SK* style before submitting. Ensure you have a distinctive voice and story to tell."

NEEDS "Real-life stories are preferred, unless the work is distinctively extreme within the crime genre. No poetry of any kind. No mainstream fiction, Oprah-style fiction, Internet/chat language, teen issues, excessive Shakespearean language, surrealism, overworked irony, or genre fiction (horror, fantasy, science fiction, western, erotica, etc.)." Length: up to 8,000 words.

HOW TO CONTACT Send complete ms via postal mail or e-mail.

PAYMENT/TERMS Pays £15 (U.K.) or $25 (international).

SCREAMINMAMAS

Harmoni Productions, LLC, 1911 Cleveland St., Hollywood FL 33020. **E-mail:** screaminmamas@gmail.com. **Website:** www.screaminmamas.com. **Contact:** Darlene Pistocchi, editor; Lena, submissions coordinator. Estab. 2012. "We are the voice of everyday moms. We share their stories, revelations, humorous rants, photos, talent, children, ventures, etc."

NEEDS Does not want vulgar, obscene, derogatory, or negative fiction. Length: 800-1,200 words.

HOW TO CONTACT Send complete ms.

TIPS "Visit our submissions page and themes page on our website."

THE SEATTLE REVIEW

Box 354330, University of Washington, Seattle WA 98195. (206)543-2302. **E-mail:** seattlereview@gmail.com. **Website:** www.seattlereview.org. **Contact:** Andrew Feld, editor in chief. Estab. 1978. *The Seattle Review* includes poetry, fiction, and creative nonfiction.

⊙ *The Seattle Review* will only publish long works. Poetry must be 10 pages or longer, and prose must be 40 pages or longer. *The Seattle Review* is 8x10; 175-250 pages. Receives 200 unsolicited mss/month. Accepts 10-15 mss/issue; 20-30 mss/year. Publishes ms 6 months-1 year after acceptance.

NEEDS Only publishes novellas. "Currently, we do not consider, use, or have a place for genre fiction (sci-fi, detective, etc.) or visual art." Length: at least 40 double-spaced pages.

HOW TO CONTACT Send complete ms. Accepts electronic submissions only.

PAYMENT/TERMS Pays 2 contributor's copies and 1-year subscription.

TIPS "Know what we publish; no genre fiction. Look at our magazine and decide if your work might be appreciated. Beginners do well in our magazine if they send clean, well-written manuscripts. We've published a lot of 'first stories' from all over the country and take pleasure in discovery."

⊛ SEEK

Standard Publishing, 4050 Lee Vance View Dr., Colorado Springs CO 80918. (800)323-7543. **E-mail:** seek@standardpublishing.com. **Website:** www.standard-pub.com. Estab. 1970. "Inspirational stories of faith-in-action for Christian adults; a Sunday School take-home paper." Quarterly.

⊙ Magazine: 5.5×8.5; 8 pages; newsprint paper; art and photo in each issue.

NEEDS List of upcoming themes available online. Accepts 150 mss/year. Send complete ms. Prefers submissions by e-mail. "*SEEK* corresponds to the topics of Standard Publishing's adult curriculum line and is designed to further apply these topics to everyday life." Unsolicited mss must be written to a theme list. Does not want poetry. Length: 850-1,000 words.

HOW TO CONTACT Send complete ms. Prefers submissions by e-mail.

PAYMENT/TERMS Pays 7¢/word.

TIPS "Write a credible story with a Christian slant—no preachments; avoid overworked themes such as joy in suffering, generation gaps, etc. Most mss are rejected by us because of irrelevant topic or message, unrealistic story, or poor character and/or plot development. We use fiction stories that are believable."

SEEMS

Lakeland University, W 3718 South Dr., Plymouth WI 53073-4878. (920)565-1000 or (920)565-3871. **Fax:** (920)565-1206. **E-mail:** seems@lakeland.edu. **Website:** seemsmagazine.wixsite.com/seems. Estab. 1971. *SEEMS*, published irregularly, prints poetry, fiction, and essays. Focuses on work that integrates economy of language, "the musical phrase," forms of resemblance, and the sentient. Will consider unpublished poetry, fiction, and creative nonfiction. See the editor's website at www.karlelder.com. "Links to my work and an interview may provide insight for the potential contributor."

NEEDS Length: up to 5,000 words.

HOW TO CONTACT Submit by mail or e-mail.

PAYMENT/TERMS Pays 1 contributor's copy.

SEQUESTRUM

Sequestrum Publishing, 1023 Garfield Ave., Ames IA 50014. **E-mail:** sequr.info@gmail.com. **Website:** www.sequestrum.org. **Contact:** R.M. Cooper, managing editor. Estab. 2014. All publications are paired with a unique visual component. Regularly holds contests and features well-known authors, as well as promising new and emerging voices.

NEEDS Length: 12,000 words max.

HOW TO CONTACT Submit complete ms via online submissions manager.

PAYMENT/TERMS Pays $10-15/story.

TIPS "Reading a past issue goes a long way; there's little excuse not to. Our entire archive is available online to preview, and subscription rates are variable. Send your best, most interesting work. General submissions are always open, and we regularly hold contests and offer awards which are themed."

THE SEWANEE REVIEW

735 University Ave., Sewanee TN 37383. (931)598-1246. **E-mail:** sewaneereview@sewanee.edu. **Website:** thesewaneereview.com. **Contact:** Adam Ross, editor. Estab. 1892. *The Sewanee Review* is America's oldest continuously published literary quarterly. Publishes original fiction, poetry, essays, and interviews. Does not read mss June 1-July 31.

NEEDS Length: up to 10,000 words.

HOW TO CONTACT Submit complete ms via online submissions manager.

PAYMENT/TERMS Pays $25/page, $300 minimum.

SHENANDOAH

Washington and Lee University, Lexington VA 24450. (540)458-8908. **E-mail:** shenandoah@wlu.edu. **Website:** shenandoahliterary.org. **Contact:** R.T. Smith, editor; William Wright, assistant editor. Estab. 1950. Sponsors the Shenandoah Prize for Fiction, awarded annually to the best story published in a volume year of *Shenandoah*, and the Bevel Summers Prize for the Short Short Story, awarded annually to the best short short story of up to 1,000 words. Prizes for both contests are $1,000. For more than half a century, *Shenandoah* has been publishing splendid poems, stories, essays, and reviews which display passionate understanding, formal accomplishment, and serious mischief.

NEEDS No sloppy, hasty, slight fiction. Length: up to 20 pages.

HOW TO CONTACT Send complete ms via online submissions manager.

PAYMENT/TERMS Pays $25/page ($250 maximum), one-year subscription, and 1 contributor's copy.

SHINE BRIGHTLY

GEMS Girls' Clubs, 1333 Alger St., SE, Grand Rapids MI 49507. (616)241-5616. **Fax:** (616)241-5558. **E-mail:** shinebrightly@gemsgc.org. **Website:** www.gemsgc.org. **Contact:** Kelli Gilmore, managing editor. Estab. 1970. "Our purpose is to lead girls into a living relationship with Jesus Christ and to help them see how God is at work in their lives and the world around them. Puzzles, crafts, stories, and articles for girls ages 9-14."

NEEDS Does not want "unrealistic stories and those with trite, easy endings. We are interested in manuscripts that show how real girls can change the world." Believable only. Nothing too preachy. Length: 700-900 words.

HOW TO CONTACT Submit complete ms in body of e-mail. No attachments.

PAYMENT/TERMS Pays up to $35, plus 2 copies.

TIPS Writers: "Please check our website before submitting. We have a specific style and theme that deals with how girls can impact the world. The stories should be current, deal with pre-adolescent problems and joys, and help girls see God at work in their lives through humor as well as problem-solving." Prefers not to see anything on the adult level, secular material, or violence. Writers frequently oversimplify the articles and often write with a Pollyanna attitude. An author should be able to see his/her writing style as exciting and appealing to girls ages 9-14. The style can be fun, but also teach a truth. Subjects should be current and important to *SHINE brightly* readers. Use our theme update as a guide. We would like to receive material with a multicultural slant."

SHORT STORY AMERICA

Short Story America, LLC, 2121 Boundary St., Suite 204, Beaufort SC 29902. (843)597-3220. **E-mail:** editors@shortstoryamerica.com. **Website:** www.shortstoryamerica.com. **Contact:** Tim Johnston, editor. Estab. 2010. "Our readers are fans of the short story. Our audience simply wants to enjoy reading great stories."

NEEDS No erotica. Length: 500-12,000 words.

HOW TO CONTACT Submit complete ms via online submissions form.

PAYMENT/TERMS Pays $25-50.

TIPS "We want stories readers will remember and want to read again. If your story entertains from the first page forward, and the pacing and conflict engages the reader's interest from plot, character, and thematic standpoints, then please submit your story today! If the reader genuinely wants to know what eventually happens in your story and is still thinking about it 10 minutes after finishing, then your story works."

SHORT STUFF

Bowman Publications, 2001 I St., #5, Fairbury NE 68352. (402)587-5003. **E-mail:** shortstf89@aol.com. Estab. 1989. "We are perhaps an enigma in that we publish only clean stories in any genre. We'll tackle any subject but don't allow obscene language or pornographic description. Our magazine is for grownups, not X-rated 'adult' fare."

NEEDS Receives 500 unsolicited mss/month. Accepts 9-12 mss/issue; 76 mss/year. Has published work by Bill Hallstead, Dede Hammond, and Skye Gibbons. No erotica; nothing morbid or pornographic. Length: 500-1,500 words.

HOW TO CONTACT Send complete ms.

PAYMENT/TERMS Payment varies.

TIPS "We are holiday oriented; mark on outside of envelope if story is for Easter, Mother's Day, etc. We receive 500 mss each month. This is up about 200%. Because of this, I implore writers to send 1 ms at a time. I would not use stories from the same author more than once an issue, and this means I might keep the others too long. Please don't e-mail your stories! If you have an e-mail address, please include that with the cover letter so we can contact you. If no SASE, we destroy the ms."

SIERRA NEVADA REVIEW

999 Tahoe Blvd., Incline Village NV 89451. **E-mail:** sncreview@sierranevada.edu. **Website:** blog.sierranevada.edu/sierranevadareview. Estab. 1990. "*Sierra Nevada Review*, published annually in May, features poetry, short fiction, and literary nonfiction by new and established writers. Wants "writing that leans toward the unconventional, surprising, and risky." Reads submissions September 1-February 15 only.

NEEDS Length: up to 4,000 words.

HOW TO CONTACT Submit ms via online submissions manager.

PAYMENT/TERMS Pays 2 contributor's copies.

SINISTER WISDOM

2333 McIntosh Rd., Dover FL 33527. (813)502-5549. **E-mail:** julie@sinisterwisdom.org. **Website:** www.sinisterwisdom.org. Estab. 1976. *Sinister Wisdom* is a quarterly lesbian-feminist journal providing fiction, poetry, drama, essays, journals, and artwork. Past issues include "Lesbians of Color," "Old Lesbians/Dykes," and "The Lesbian Body." *Sinister Wisdom* is 5.5x8.5; 128-144 pages; 55 lb. stock; 10 pt. C1S cover; with illustrations, photos.

NEEDS List of upcoming themes available on website. Receives 30 unsolicited mss/month. Accepts 6 mss/issue; 24 mss/year. Recently published work by Jacqueline Miranda, Amanda Esteva, and Sharon Bridgforth. No heterosexual or male-oriented fiction; no 1970s Amazon adventures; nothing that stereotypes or degrades women. Length: 500-5,000 words; average length: 2,000 words.

HOW TO CONTACT Send complete ms. Strongly prefers submissions through online submissions manager. Publishes short shorts. Also publishes literary essays, literary criticism, poetry. Sometimes comments on rejected mss. Reviews fiction.

PAYMENT/TERMS Pays 1 contributor's copy and one-year subscription.

TIPS *Sinister Wisdom* is "a multicultural lesbian journal reflecting the art, writing, and politics of our communities."

SKIPPING STONES

A Multicultural Literary Magazine, Skipping Stones. Inc., P.O. Box 3939, Eugene OR 97403-0939. (541)342-4956. **E-mail:** editor@skippingstones.org. **Website:** www.skippingstones.org. **Contact:** Arun Toké, editor. Estab. 1988. "*Skipping Stones* is an award-winning multicultural, nonprofit magazine designed to promote cooperation, creativity and celebration of cultural and ecological richness. We encourage submissions by children of color, minorities and underrepresented populations. We want material meant for children and young adults/teenagers with multicultural or ecological awareness themes. Think, live and write as if you were a child, tween or teen. We want material that gives insight to cultural celebrations, lifestyle, customs and traditions, glimpse of daily life in other countries and cultures. Photos, songs, artwork are most welcome if they illustrate/highlight the points. Translations are invited if your submission is in a language other than English." Themes may include cultural celebrations, living abroad, challenging disability, hospitality customs of various cultures, cross-cultural understanding, African, Asian and Latin American cultures, humor, international understanding, turning points and magical moments in life, caring for the earth, spirituality, and multicultural awareness. *Skipping Stones* is magazine-sized, saddle-stapled, printed on recycled paper. Published quarterly during the school year (4 issues).

NEEDS Middle readers, young adult/teens: contemporary, meaningful, humorous. All levels: folktales, multicultural, nature/environment. Multicultural needs include: bilingual or multilingual pieces; use of words from other languages; settings in other countries, cultures or multi-ethnic communities. No suspense or romance stories. Length: 1,000 words maximum.

HOW TO CONTACT Send complete ms.

PAYMENT/TERMS Pays 6 contributor's copies.

TIPS "Be original and innovative. Use multicultural, nature, or cross-cultural themes. Multilingual submissions are welcome."

SLOW TRAINS LITERARY JOURNAL

P.O. 4741, Denver CO 80155. **E-mail:** editor@slowtrains.com. **Website:** www.slowtrains.com. **Contact:** Susannah Grace Indigo, editor. Estab. 2000. Looking for fiction, essays, and poetry that reflect the spirit of adventure, the exploration of the soul, the energies of imagination, and the experience of Big Fun. Music, travel, sex, humor, love, loss, art, spirituality, childhood/coming of age, baseball, and dreams, but most of all, *Slow Trains* wants to read about the things you are passionate about.

NEEDS Genre writing is not encouraged. No sci-fi, erotica, horror, romance, though elements of those may naturally be included. Length: up to 5,000 words.

HOW TO CONTACT Submit via e-mail only.

SNREVIEW

197 Fairchild Ave., Fairfield CT 06825-4856. **E-mail:** editor@snreview.org. **Website:** www.snreview.org. **Contact:** Joseph Conlin, editor. Estab. 1999. *SNReview* is a quarterly literary e-zine created for writers of non-genre fiction, nonfiction, and poetry. Quarterly.

NEEDS Receives 300 unsolicited mss/month. Accepts 40+ mss/issue; 150 mss/year. Publishes 75 new writers/year. Has published work by Frank X. Walker, Adrian Louis, Barbara Burkhardt, E. Lindsey Balkan, Marie Griffin, and Jonathan Lerner. "No romance, mystery, science fiction, fantasy, or horror genre fiction." Length: up to 7,000 words.

HOW TO CONTACT Submit via e-mail; label the e-mail "SUB: Name of Story." Copy and paste work into the body of the e-mail. Don't send attachments. Include 100-word bio and list of publications.

SONORA REVIEW

University of Arizona, Dept. of English, Tucson AZ 85721. **Website:** sonorareview.com/. Estab. 1980. "We look for the highest-quality poetry, fiction, and nonfiction, with an emphasis on emerging writers. Our magazine has a long-standing tradition of publishing the best new literature and writers. Check out our website for a sample of what we publish and our submission guidelines."

NEEDS Length: up to 4,000 words.

HOW TO CONTACT Send complete ms via online submissions manager.

PAYMENT/TERMS Pays 2 contributor's copies.

SO TO SPEAK

George Mason University, 4400 University Dr., MSN 2C5, Fairfax VA 22030. **E-mail:** sotospeak@sotospeakjournal.org. **Website:** sotospeakjournal.org. **Contact:** Kristen Brida, editor in chief. Estab. 1993. *So to Speak*, published semiannually, prints "high-quality work relating to feminism, including poetry, fiction, nonfiction (including book reviews and in-

terviews), photography, artwork, collaborations, lyrical essays, and other genre-questioning texts." Wants "work that addresses issues of significance to women's lives and movements for women's equality. Especially interested in pieces that explore issues of race, class, and sexuality in relation to gender."

○ *So to Speak* is 100-128 pages, digest-sized, photo-offset-printed, perfect-bound, with glossy cover; includes ads. Press run is 1,000 (75 subscribers, 100 shelf sales); 500 distributed free to students/contributors. Reads submissions September 15-November 15 for spring issue and January 1-April 15 for fall issue.

NEEDS Receives 100 unsolicited mss/month. Accepts 3-5 mss/issue; 6-10 mss/year. **Publishes 7 new writers/year.** Sponsors awards/contests. No science fiction, mystery, genre romance. Length: up to 4,000 words.

HOW TO CONTACT Submit ms via online submissions manager. Include cover letter.

PAYMENT/TERMS Pays 2 contributor's copies.

TIPS "Every writer has something they do exceptionally well; do that and it will shine through in the work. We look for quality prose with a definite appeal to a feminist audience. We are trying to move away from strict genre lines. We want high-quality fiction, nonfiction, poetry, art, innovative and risk-taking work."

SOUL FOUNTAIN

E-mail: soulfountain@antarcticajournal.com. **Website:** www.antarcticajournal.com/soul-fountain/. **Contact:** Tone Bellizzi, editor. Estab. 1997. *Soul Fountain* is produced by The Antarctica Journal, a not-for-profit arts project of the Hope for the Children Foundation, committed to empowering young and emerging artists of all disciplines at all levels to develop and share their talents through performance, collaboration, and networking. Digitally publishes poetry, art, photography, short fiction, and essays on the antarcticajournal.com website. Open to all. Publishes quality submitted work, and specializes in emerging voices. Favors visionary, challenging, and consciousness-expanding material.

HOW TO CONTACT Submit by e-mail only. No cover letters, please.

SOUNDINGS EAST

Salem State University, English Department, MH249, 352 Lafayette St., Salem MA 01970. **E-mail:** soundingseast@salemstate.edu. **Website:** www.salemstate.

edu/soundingseast. Estab. 1973. *Soundings East* is the literary journal of Salem State University, published annually with support from the Center for Creative and Performing Arts.

○ Reading period: September 1-Feburary 15.

NEEDS Length: up to 10,000 words.

HOW TO CONTACT Submit ms via online submissions manager or by postal mail.

THE SOUTH CAROLINA REVIEW

Center for Electronic and Digital Publishing, 801 Strode Tower, Clemson SC 29634-0522. **Fax:** (864)656-1345. **E-mail:** screv@clemson.edu. **Website:** https://www.clemson.edu/centers-institutes/press/journals-annuals/south-carolina-review/. **Contact:** Elizabeth Stansell, managing editor. Estab. 1967. Since 1968, *The South Carolina Review* has published fiction, poetry, interviews, unpublished letters and mss, essays, and reviews from well-known and aspiring scholars and writers. *The South Carolina Review* is 7.5 x 9.25; 150-200 pages. Semiannual. Does not read mss June-August or December.

NEEDS Submit complete ms as PDF or Word file. Cover letter is preferred. Do not submit during June, July, August, or December. Recently published work by Thomas E. Kennedy, Ronald Frame, Dennis Mc-Fadden, Dulane Upshaw Ponder, and Stephen Jones. Rarely comments on rejected mss.

SOUTH DAKOTA REVIEW

The University of South Dakota, Dept. of English, 414 E. Clark St., Vermillion SD 57069. (605)677-5184. **E-mail:** sdreview@usd.edu. **Website:** www.usd.edu/sdreview. **Contact:** Lee Ann Roripaugh, editor-in-chief. Estab. 1963. "*South Dakota Review*, published quarterly, is committed to cultural and aesthetic diversity. First and foremost, we seek to publish exciting and compelling work that reflects the full spectrum of the contemporary literary arts. Since its inception in 1963, *South Dakota Review* has maintained a tradition of supporting work by contemporary writers writing from or about the American West. We hope to retain this unique flavor through particularly welcoming works by American Indian writers, writers addressing the complexities and contradictions of the 'New West,' and writers exploring themes of landscape, place, and/or eco-criticism in surprising and innovative ways. At the same time, we'd like to set these ideas and themes in dialogue with and within the context of larger global literary communities. Single copy:

$12; subscription: $40/year, $65/2 years. Sample: $8. Writing from *South Dakota Review* has appeared in *Pushcart* and *Best American Essays* anthologies. Press run is 500-600 (more than 500 subscribers, many of them libraries).

NEEDS "Our aesthetic is eclectic, but we tend to favor deft use of language in both our poetry and prose selections, nuanced characterization in our fiction, and either elegantly or surprisingly executed formal strategies. As part of our unique flavor, a small handful works in each issue will typically engage with aspects of landscape, ecocritical issues, or place (oftentimes with respect to the American West)." Length: up to 6,000 words.

HOW TO CONTACT Submit via online submissions manager. Include cover letter.

PAYMENT/TERMS Pays 2 contributor's copies.

THE SOUTHEAST REVIEW

Department of English, Florida State University, Tallahassee FL 32306. **E-mail:** southeastreview@gmail.com. **Website:** southeastreview.org. **Contact:** Alex Quinlan, editor in chief. Estab. 1979. "The mission of *The Southeast Review* is to present emerging writers on the same stage as well-established ones. In each semiannual issue, we publish literary fiction, creative nonfiction, poetry, interviews, book reviews, and art. With nearly 60 members on our editorial staff who come from throughout the country and the world, we strive to publish work that is representative of our diverse interests and aesthetics, and we celebrate the eclectic mix this produces. We receive approximately 400 submissions per month, and we accept less than 1-2% of them."

NEEDS Submit Length: up to 7,500 words.

HOW TO CONTACT Submit complete ms through online submissions manager. "All submissions must be typed (prose should be double-spaced) and properly formatted, then uploaded to our online submissions manager as a DOC or RTF file only. Submission manager restricts you from sending us your work more than twice per year. Please wait until you receive a reply regarding a submission before you upload the next." Does not accept e-mail, paper, or previously published submissions.

PAYMENT/TERMS Pays 2 contributor's copies.

TIPS "Avoid trendy experimentation for its own sake (present-tense narration, observation that isn't also revelation). Fresh stories, moving and interesting characters, and a sensitivity to language are still fiction mainstays. We also publish the winner and runners-up of the World's Best Short Story Contest, Poetry Contest, and Creative Nonfiction Contest."

SOUTHERN HUMANITIES REVIEW

Auburn University, 9088 Haley Center, Auburn University AL 36849. (334)844-9088. **Fax:** (334)844-9027. **E-mail:** shr@auburn.edu. **Website:** www.southern-humanitiesreview.com. **Contact:** Aaron Alford, managing editor. Estab. 1967. *Southern Humanities Review* publishes fiction, essays, and poetry.

THE SOUTHERN REVIEW

338 Johnston Hall, Louisiana State University, Baton Rouge LA 70803. (225)578-5104. **Fax:** (225)578-6461. **E-mail:** southernreview@lsu.edu. **Website:** thesouthernreview.org. **Contact:** Jessica Faust, co-editor and poetry editor; Emily Nemens, co-editor and prose editor. Estab. 1935. "*The Southern Review* is one of the nation's premiere literary journals. Hailed by *Time* as 'superior to any other journal in the English language,' we have made literary history since our founding in 1935. We publish a diverse array of fiction, nonfiction, and poetry by the country's—and the world's—most respected contemporary writers." Reading period: September 1 through December 1 (prose); September 1 through February 1 (poetry). All mss submitted during outside the reading period will be recycled.

NEEDS Wants short stories of lasting literary merit, with emphasis on style and technique; novel excerpts. "We emphasize style and substantial content. No mystery, fantasy, or religious mss." Length: up to 8,000 words.

HOW TO CONTACT Submit 1 ms at a time by mail or through online submission form. "We rarely publish work that is longer than 8,000 words. We consider novel excerpts if they stand alone."

PAYMENT/TERMS Pays $25/printed page (max $200), 2 contributor's copies, and 1-year subscription.

TIPS "Careful attention to craftsmanship and technique combined with a developed sense of the creation of story will always make us pay attention."

SOUTHWESTERN AMERICAN LITERATURE

Center for the Study of the Southwest, Texas State University, Brazos Hall, 601 University Dr., San Marcos TX 78666-4616. (512)245-2224. **Fax:** (512)245-7462. **E-mail:** wj13@txstate.edu. **Website:** www.txstate.edu/cssw/publications/sal.html. **Contact:** William Jensen,

editor. Estab. 1971. *Southwestern American Literature* is a biannual scholarly journal that includes literary criticism, fiction, poetry, and book & film reviews concerning the Greater Southwest. "We are interested only in material dealing with the **Southwest**."

NEEDS Fiction must deal with the Southwest. Stories set outside our region will be rejected. We are always looking for stories that examine the relationship between the tradition of Southwestern American literature and the writer's own imagination. We like stories that move beyond stereotype. Length: no more than 6,000 words/25 pages.

HOW TO CONTACT Submit using online submissions manager.

PAYMENT/TERMS Pays 2 contributor's copies.

TIPS "**Fiction and poetry must deal with the greater Southwest.** We look for crisp language, an interesting approach to material. Read widely, write often, revise carefully. We seek stories that, as William Faulkner noted in his Nobel Prize acceptance speech, treat subjects central to good literature—the old verities of the human heart, such as honor and courage and pity and suffering, fear and humor, love and sorrow."

SOU'WESTER

Department of English, Box 1438, Southern Illinois University Edwardsville, Edwardsville IL 62026. **Website:** souwester.org. **Contact:** Joshua Kryah, poetry editor; Valerie Vogrin, prose editor. Estab. 1960. *Sou'wester* appears biannually in spring and fall.

○ *Sou'wester* is professionally printed, flat-spined, with textured matte card cover, press run is 300 for 500 subscribers of which 50 are libraries. Open to submissions in mid-August for fall and spring issues.

HOW TO CONTACT Submit 1 piece of prose at a time. Will consider a suite of 2-3 flash fiction pieces.

PAYMENT/TERMS Pays 2 contributor's copies and a one-year subscription.

⑤ SPACE AND TIME

458 Elizabeth Ave., Somerset NJ 08873. **Website:** www.spaceandtimemagazine.com. **Contact:** Hildy Silverman, publisher. Estab. 1966. *Space and Time* is the longest continually published small-press genre fiction magazine still in print. "We pride ourselves in having published the first stories of some of the great writers in science fiction, fantasy, and horror."

"We love stories that blend elements—horror and science fiction, fantasy with science fiction elements, etc. We challenge writers to try something new and send us their hard to classify works-—what other publications reject because the work doesn't fit in their 'pigeonholes.'"

NEEDS "We are looking for creative blends of science fiction, fantasy, and/or horror." "Do not send children's stories." Length: 1,000-10,000 words. Average length: 6,500 words. Average length of short shorts: 1,000 words.

HOW TO CONTACT Submit electronically as a Word doc or .rtf attachment only during open reading periods. Anything sent outside those period will be rejected out of hand.

PAYMENT/TERMS Pays 1¢/word.

SPITBALL

The Literary Baseball Magazine, 536 Lassing Way, Walton KY 41094. **E-mail:** spitball5@hotmail.com. **Website:** www.spitballmag.com. **Contact:** Mike Shannon, editor-in-chief. Estab. 1981. *Spitball: The Literary Baseball Magazine*, published semiannually, is a unique magazine devoted to poetry, fiction, and book reviews exclusively about baseball. Newcomers are very welcome, but they must know the subject. "Perhaps a good place to start for beginners is one's personal reactions to the game, a game, a player, etc., and take it from there." Writers submitting to *Spitball* for the first time must buy a sample copy (waived for subscribers). "This is a one-time-only fee, which we regret, but economic reality dictates that we insist those who wish to be published in *Spitball* help support it, at least at this minimum level." *Spitball* is 48 pages, digest-sized, computer-typeset, perfect-bound. Receives about 1,000 submissions/year, accepts about 40. Press run is 1,000.

NEEDS Length: 5-15 pages, double-spaced. Short stories longer than 20 pages must be exceptionally good.

HOW TO CONTACT Submit ms with bio and SASE.

PAYMENT/TERMS Pays 2 contributor's copies.

TIPS "Take the subject seriously. We do. In other words, get a clue (if you don't already have one) about the subject and about the poetry that has already been done and published about baseball. Learn from it—think about what you can add to the canon that is original and fresh—and don't assume that just anybody with the feeblest of efforts can write a baseball poem worthy of publication. And most importantly, stick with it. Genius seldom happens on the first try."

SPORTS AFIELD

Field Sports Publishing, P.O. Box 271305, Fort Collins CO 80527. **Website:** www.sportsafield.com. Estab. 1887. "We cater to the upscale hunting market, especially hunters who travel to exotic destinations like Alaska and Africa. We are not a deer hunting magazine, and we do not cover fishing."

SPOTLIGHT ON RECOVERY MAGAZINE

R. Graham Publishing Company, 9602 Glenwood Rd., #140, Brooklyn NY 11236. (347)831-9373. **E-mail:** rgraham_100@msn.com. **Website:** www.spotlightonrecovery.com. **Contact:** Robin Graham, publisher and editor-in-chief. Estab. 2001. "This is the premiere outreach and resource magazine in New York. Its goal is to be the catalyst for which the human spirit could heal. Everybody knows somebody who has mental illness, substance abuse issues, parenting problems, educational issues, or someone who is homeless, unemployed, physically ill, or the victim of a crime. Many people suffer in silence. *Spotlight on Recovery* will provide a voice to those who suffer in silence and begin the dialogue of recovery."

TIPS "Send a query and give a reason why you would choose the subject posted to write about."

STAND MAGAZINE

School of English, University of Leeds, Leeds LS2 9JT, United Kingdom. (44)(113)343-4794. **E-mail:** editors@standmagazine.org. **Website:** www.standmagazine.org. **Contact:** Jon Glover, managing editor. Estab. 1952. *Stand Magazine* is concerned with what happens when cultures and literatures meet, with translation in its many guises, with the mechanics of language, with the processes by which the policy receives or disables its cultural makers. *Stand* promotes debate of issues that are of radical concern to the intellectual community worldwide. U.S. submissions can be made through the Virginia office (see separate listing). Does not accept e-mail submissions except from subscribers.

NEEDS Does not want genre fiction. Length: up to 3,000 words.

HOW TO CONTACT Submit ms by mail. Include SASE if from U.K; email address otherwise

STEPPING STONES MAGAZINE

P.O. Box 902, Norristown PA 19404-0902. **E-mail:** info@ssmalmia.com. **Website:** ssmalmia.com. **Contact:** Trinae Ross, publisher. Estab. 1996. "*Stepping Stones Magazine* is a not-for-profit organization dedicated to presenting awesome writing and art created by people from all lifestyles." Publishes fiction, nonfiction, and poetry."

◔ Has published poetry by Richard Fenwick, Karlanna Lewis, and Stephanie Kaylor. Receives about 600 poems/year, accepts about 10-15%.

NEEDS Fiction should be able to hold the reader's interest in the first paragraph and sustain that interest throughout the rest of the story. Length: up to 4,000 words.

HOW TO CONTACT Send up to 3 mss via postal mail, e-mail (fiction@ssmalmia.com), or online submissions manager. Include brief bio.

STILL CRAZY

(614)746-0859. **E-mail:** editor@crazylitmag.com. **Website:** www.crazylitmag.com. **Contact:** Barbara Kussow, editor. Estab. 2008. *Still Crazy*, published biannually in January and July, features poetry, short stories, and essays written by or about people over age 50. The editor is particularly interested in material that challenges the stereotypes of older people and that portrays older people's inner lives as rich and rewarding. Wants writing by people over age 50 and writing by people of any age if the topic is about people over 50.

◔ Accepts 3-4 short stories per issue; 5-7 essays; 12-14 poems. Reads submissions year round.

NEEDS Publishes short shorts. Ms published 6-12 months after acceptance. Sometimes features a "First Story," a story by an author who has not been published before. Does not want material that is "too sentimental or inspirational, 'Geezer' humor, or anything too grim." Length: up to 3,500 words, but stories fewer than 3,000 words are more likely to be published.

HOW TO CONTACT Upload submissions via submissions manager on website. Include estimated word count, brief bio, age of writer or "Over 50."

PAYMENT/TERMS Pays 1 contributor's copy.

TIPS Looking for interesting characters and interesting situations that might interest readers of all ages. Humor and lightness welcomed.

STIRRING

Sundress Publications, **E-mail:** stirring@sundress-publications.com. **E-mail:** stirring.nonfiction@gmail.com; reviews@sundresspublications.com; stirring.fiction@gmail.com; stirring.poetry@gmail.com; stirring.artphoto@gmail.com. **Website:** www.stirringlit.com. **Contact:** Luci Brown and Andrew Koch, managing editors and poetry editors; Shaun Turner, fiction editor; Donna Vorreyer, reviews editor; Gabe Montesanti, nonfiction editor. Estab. 1999. "*Stirring* is one of the oldest continually published literary journals on the Web. *Stirring* is a monthly literary magazine that publishes poetry, short fiction, creative nonfiction, and photography by established and emerging writers."

NEEDS Length: up to 5,000 words.

HOW TO CONTACT Submit complete ms by e-mail to stirring.fiction@gmail.com

STONE SOUP

The magazine inspiring creative kids around the world, Children's Art Foundation, P.O. Box 83, Santa Cruz CA 95063-0083. **E-mail:** editor@stonesoup.com. **Website:** https://stonesoup.com. **Contact:** Emma Wood, editor. Estab. 1973. *Stone Soup*, a digital magazine with a print annual, is the national magazine of writing and art by kids, founded in 1973. Receives 5,000 poetry submissions/year, accepts about 20. Subscription: $24.99/year (U.S.). "We have a preference for writing and art based on real-life experiences; no formula stories or poems. We only publish writing by children up to (and including) age 13. We do not publish writing by adults." Subscription includes downloadable PDFs of each issue as well as more than 15 years of back issues online.

NEEDS "We do not like assignments or formula stories of any kind." Length: 150-5,000 words.

HOW TO CONTACT We only accept submissions through Submittable.

PAYMENT/TERMS Pays in a contributor copy of the print annual (a collection of the years' issues along with bonus content from the blogs), discounted subscription rates.

TIPS "All writing we publish is by young people ages 13 and under. We do not publish any writing by adults. We can't emphasize enough how important it is to read a couple of issues of the magazine. You can read stories and poems from past issues online. We have a strong preference for writing on subjects that mean a lot to the author. If you feel strongly about something that happened to you or something you observed, use that feeling as the basis for your story or poem. Stories should have good descriptions, realistic dialogue, and a point to make. In a poem, each word must be chosen carefully. Your poem should present a view of your subject, and a way of using words that are special and all your own."

STORIE

Via Suor Celestina Donati 13/E, Rome 00167, Italy. **E-mail:** info@storie.it. **Website:** www.storie.it/english. Estab. 1986. *Storie* is one of Italy's leading cultural and literary magazines. Committed to a truly cross-over vision of writing, the bilingual (Italian/English) review publishes high-quality fiction and poetry, interspersed with the work of alternative wordsmiths such as filmmakers and musicians. Through writings bordering on narratives and interviews with important contemporary writers, it explores the culture and craft of writing.

HOW TO CONTACT "Manuscripts may be submitted directly by regular post without querying first; however, we do not accept unsolicited manuscripts via e-mail. Please query via e-mail first. We only contact writers if their work has been accepted. We also arrange for and oversee a high-quality, professional translation of the piece."

PAYMENT/TERMS Pays $30-600 and 2 contributor's copies.

TIPS "More than erudite references or a virtuoso performance, we're interested in a style merging news writing with literary techniques in the manner of new journalism. *Storie* reserves the right to include a brief review of interesting submissions not selected for publication in a special column of the magazine."

STORY BYTES

E-mail: editor@storybytes.com. **Website:** www.storybytes.com. **Contact:** Mark Stanley Bubein. "A monthly e-zine and weekly electronic mailing list presenting the Internet's (and the world's) shortest stories—fiction ranging from 2 to 2,048 words. Just as eyes, art often provides a window to the soul. *Story Bytes'* very short stories offer a glimpse through this window into brief vignettes of life, often reflecting or revealing those things which make us human."

NEEDS "Story length must fall on a power of 2. That's 2, 4, 8, 16, 32, 64, 128, 256, 512, 1,024, and 2,048 words long. Stories must match one of these lengths exactly."

See website for examples. No sexually explicit material. Length: 2-2,048 words.

HOW TO CONTACT Submit story as plain text via e-mail. "The easiest way to do so is to simply copy it from your word processor and paste it into an e-mail message. Specify the word count below the title."

TIPS "In *Story Bytes* the very short stories themselves range in topic. Many explore a brief event—a vignette of something unusual, unique, and at times even commonplace. Some stories can be bizarre, while others quite lucid. Some are based on actual events, while others are entirely fictional. Try to develop conflict early on (in the first sentence if possible!), and illustrate or resolve this conflict through action rather than description."

STORYSOUTH

3302 MHRA Building, UNCG, Greensboro NC 27412, USA. **E-mail:** terry@storysouth.com; fiction@storysouth.com; poetry@storysouth.com;. **Website:** www.storysouth.com. **Contact:** Terry Kennedy, editor; Cynthia Nearman, creative nonfiction editor; Drew Perry, fiction editor; Luke Johnson, poetry editor. Estab. 2001. "*storySouth* accepts unsolicited submissions of fiction, poetry, and creative nonfiction during 2 submission periods annually: May 15-July 1 and November 15-January 1. Long pieces are encouraged. Please make only 1 submission in a single genre per reading period."

NEEDS No word-count limit.

HOW TO CONTACT Submit 1 story via online submissions manager.

TIPS "What really makes a story stand out is a strong voice and a sense of urgency—a need for the reader to keep reading the story and not put it down until it is finished."

THE STORYTELLER

65 Highway 328 W., Maynard AR 72444. (870)647-2137. **E-mail:** storytelleranthology@gmail.com. **Website:** www.thestorytellermagazine.com. **Contact:** Regina Riney, editor. Estab. 1996. "We are here to help writers however we can and to help start them on their publishing career. Proofread! Make sure you know what we take and what we don't and also make sure you know the word count."

NEEDS Does not want pornography, erotica, horror, graphic language or violence, children's stories, or anything deemed racial or biased toward any religion, race, or moral preference. 3,000

HOW TO CONTACT Send complete ms with cover letter and SASE.

TIPS "*The Storyteller* is one of the best places you will find to submit your work, especially new writers. Our best advice, be professional. You have one chance to make a good impression. Don't blow it by being unprofessional."

THE STRAND MAGAZINE

P.O. Box 1418, Birmingham MI 48012-1418. (800)300-6652. **E-mail:** strandmag@strandmag.com. **Website:** www.strandmag.com. Estab. 1998. "After an absence of nearly half a century, the magazine known to millions for bringing Sir Arthur Conan Doyle's ingenious detective, Sherlock Holmes, to the world has once again appeared on the literary scene. First launched in 1891, *The Strand* included in its pages the works of some of the greatest writers of the 20th century: Agatha Christie, Dorothy Sayers, Margery Allingham, W. Somerset Maugham, Graham Greene, P.G. Wodehouse, H.G. Wells, Aldous Huxley, and many others. In 1950, economic difficulties in England caused a drop in circulation, which forced the magazine to cease publication."

NEEDS "We are interested in mysteries, detective stories, tales of terror and the supernatural as well as short stories. Stories can be set in any time or place, provided they are well written, the plots interesting and well thought." Occasionally accepts short shorts and short novellas. "We are not interested in submissions with any sexual content." Length: 2,000-6,000 words.

HOW TO CONTACT Submit complete ms by postal mail. Include SASE. No e-mail submissions.

PAYMENT/TERMS Pays $25-150.

TIPS "No gratuitous violence, sexual content, or explicit language, please."

⊖ STRANGE HORIZONS

Strange Horizons, Inc., P.O. Box 1693, Dubuque IA 52004-1693. **E-mail:** management@strangehorizons.com; fiction@strangehorizons.com. **Website:** strangehorizons.com. **Contact:** Jane Crowley and Kate Dollarhyde, editors-in-chief. Estab. 2000. **E-mail:** fiction@strangehorizons.com. "*Strange Horizons* is a magazine of and about speculative fiction and related nonfiction. Speculative fiction includes science fiction, fantasy, horror, slipstream, and other flavors of fantastica." Work published in *Strange Horizons* has been shortlisted for or won Hugo, Nebula, Rhysling, Theodore Sturgeon, James Tiptree Jr., and World Fantasy Awards.

NEEDS "We love, or are interested in, fiction from or about diverse perspectives and traditionally under-represented groups, settings, and cultures, written from a nonexoticizing and well-researched position; unusual yet readable styles and inventive structures and narratives; stories that address political issues in complex and nuanced ways, resisting oversimplification; and hypertext fiction." No excessive gore. Length: up to 10,000 words (under 5,000 words preferred).

HOW TO CONTACT Submit via online submissions manager; no e-mail or postal submission accepted.

PAYMENT/TERMS Pays 8¢/word, $50 minimum.

O STRAYLIGHT

UW-Parkside, English Department, University of Wisconsin-Parkside, 900 Wood Rd., Kenosha WI 53141. **E-mail:** submissions@straylightmag.com. **Website:** www.straylightmag.com. Estab. 2005. *Straylight*, published biannually, seeks fiction and poetry of almost any style "as long as it's inventive."

Ⓠ Literary magazine/journal: 6x9, 115 pages, quality paper, uncoated index stock cover. Contains illustrations, photographs.

NEEDS "*Straylight* is interested in publishing high-quality, character-based fiction of any style. We tend not to publish strict genre pieces, though we may query them for future special issues. We do not publish erotica." Publishes short shorts and novellas. Does not read May through August. Agented fiction 10%. Length: 1,000-5,000 words for short stories; under 1,000 words for flash fiction; 17,500-45,000 words for novellas. Average length: 1,500-3,000 words.

HOW TO CONTACT Send complete ms with cover letter. Accepts submissions by online submission manager or mail (send either SASE or IRC for return of ms, or disposable copy of ms and #10 SASE for reply only). Include brief bio, list of publications.

PAYMENT/TERMS Pays 2 contributor's copies.

TIPS "We tend to publish character-based and inventive fiction with cutting-edge prose. We are unimpressed with works based on strict plot twists or novelties. Read a sample copy to get a feel for what we publish."

STRAYLIGHT ONLINE

University of Wisconsin-Parkside, English Department, University of Wisconsin-Parkside, 900 Wood Rd., Box 2000, Kenosha WI 53414-2000. (262) 595-2139. **Fax:** (262) 595-2271. **E-mail:** villa@straylight-mag.com. **Website:** straylightmag.com. **Contact:** appropriate genre editor (revolving editors). Estab. 2008. *Straylight Online* is the web counterpart to *Straylight Literary Arts Journal*. It does not mirror the content of the print edition but is dedicated to exploring narrative of all fashion.

NEEDS "We look for stories with a strong sense of place and moments that are character-centered rather than those that rely on plot turns and literary tricks. We welcome submissions that cross genre boundaries as well as those that explore the way visual art, music, and literature combine to produce new manifestations of story and verse." Length: up to 1,000 words for short stories, 17,500-45,000 words for novellas.

HOW TO CONTACT Submit complete ms via online submissions manager. Include brief bio.

STRUGGLE

A Magazine of Proletarian Revolutionary Literature, P.O. Box 28536, Detroit MI 48228. (313)273-9039. **E-mail:** timhall11@yahoo.com. **Website:** www.strugglemagazine.net. **Contact:** Tim Hall, editor. Estab. 1985. "Irregularly published now after 30 years of existence funded solely by writers and activists, but planning to resume as a twice-yearly magazine featuring African American, Latino, and other writers of color; prisoners; disgruntled workers; activists in the anti-war, anti-racist, and other mass movements; and many writers discontented with the Democrats and with the Republicans, their joint austerity campaign against the workers and the poor, the racist police murders against people of color, the unending destruction of the environment, and their continuing aggressive wars and drone murders abroad. While we urge literature in the direction of revolutionary working-class politics and a vision of socialism as embodying a genuine workers' power, in distinction to the state-capitalist regimes of the former Soviet Union, present-day China, North Korea, Cuba, etc., we accept a broader range of rebellious viewpoints in order to encourage creativity and dialogue."

NEEDS "Readers would like fiction about anti-globalization, the fight against racism, global militarism including the war dangers under Trump, the struggle of immigrants, and the disillusionment with the Democratic and Republican administrations as they reveal their craven service to the rich billionaires. Would also like to see more fiction that depicts life, work, and struggle of the working class of every background, especially young workers in the struggle for a $15/hour wage and unionization in fast food and Walmart; also the struggles of the 1930s and 1960s illustrated and brought to life." No romance, psychic, mystery, western, erotica, or religious. Length: 4,000 words; average length: 1,000-3,000 words.

HOW TO CONTACT Submit ms via e-mail or postal mail.

PAYMENT/TERMS Pays 1 contributor's copy.

STUDIO

A Journal of Christians Writing, 727 Peel St., Albury NSW 2640, Australia. (61)(2)6021-1135. **E-mail:** studio00@bigpond.net.au. **Contact:** Paul Grover, publisher. Estab. 1980. *Studio, A Journal of Christians Writing*, published three times a year, prints poetry and prose of literary merit, offering a venue for previously published, new, and aspiring writers and seeking to create a sense of community among Christians writing. Also publishes occasional articles as well as news and reviews of writing, writers, and events of interest to members. People who send material should be comfortable being published under this banner: *Studio, A Journal of Christians Writing. Studio* is 60-80 pages, digest-sized, professionally printed on high-quality paper, saddle-stapled, with matte card cover. Press run is 300 (all subscriptions).

NEEDS Cover letter is required. Include brief details of previous publishing history, if any. SAE with IRC required. "Submissions must be typed and double-spaced on 1 side of A4 white paper. Name and address must appear on the reverse side of each page submitted."

PAYMENT/TERMS Pays 1 contributor's copy.

SUBTERRAIN

Strong Words for a Polite Nation, P.O. Box 3008, MPO, Vancouver British Columbia V6B 3X5, Canada. (604)876-8710. **Fax:** (604)879-2667. **E-mail:** subter@portal.ca. **Website:** www.subterrain.ca. **Contact:** Brian Kaufman, editor-in-chief; Natasha Sanders-Kay, managing editor. Estab. 1988. "*subTerrain* magazine is published 3 times/year from modest offices just off of Main Street in Vancouver, BC. We strive to produce a stimulating fusion of fiction, poetry, photography, and graphic illustration from uprising Canadian, U.S., and international writers and artists."

○ Magazine: 8.5×11; 80 pages; colour matte stock paper; colour matte cover stock; illustrations; photos. "Strong words for a polite nation."

NEEDS Receives 100 unsolicited mss/month. Accepts 4 mss/issue; 10-15 mss/year. Recently published work by J.O. Bruday, Lisa Pike, and Peter Babiak. Does not want genre fiction or children's fiction. **3,000 words max.**

HOW TO CONTACT Send complete ms. Include disposable copy of the ms and SASE for reply only. Accepts multiple submissions.

PAYMENT/TERMS Pays $50/page for prose.

TIPS "Read the magazine first. Get to know what kind of work we publish."

⑨ SUBTROPICS

University of Florida, P.O. Box 112075, 4008 Turlington Hall, Gainesville FL 32611-2075. **E-mail:** subtropics@english.ufl.edu. **Website:** www.english.ufl.edu/subtropics. **Contact:** David Leavitt, editor. Estab. 2005. *Subtropics* seeks to publish the best literary fiction, essays, and poetry being written today, both by established and emerging authors. Will consider works of fiction of any length, from short shorts to novellas and self-contained novel excerpts. Gives the same latitude to essays. Appreciates work in translation and, from time to time, republishes important and compelling stories, essays, and poems that have lapsed out of print by writers no longer living. Member: CLMP.

○ Literary magazine/journal: 9x6, 160 pages. Includes photographs. Submissions accepted from September 1-April 15.

NEEDS Does not read May 1-August 31. Agented fiction 33%. **Publishes 1-2 new writers/year.** Has published John Barth, Ariel Dorfman, Tony D'Souza, Allan Gurganus, Frances Hwang, Kuzhali Manickavel, Eileen Pollack, Padgett Powell, Nancy Reisman, Jarret Rosenblatt, Joanna Scott, and Olga Slavnikova. No genre fiction. Length: up to 15,000 words. Average length: 5,000 words. Average length of short shorts: 400 words.

HOW TO CONTACT Submit complete ms via online submissions manager.

PAYMENT/TERMS Pays $500 for short shorts; $1,000 for full stories; 2 contributor's copies.

TIPS "We publish longer works of fiction, including novellas and excerpts from forthcoming novels. Each issue includes a short-short story of about 250 words on the back cover. We are also interested in publishing works in translation for the magazine's English-speaking audience."

THE SUMMERSET REVIEW

25 Summerset Dr., Smithtown NY 11787. **E-mail:** editor@summersetreview.org. **Website:** www.summersetreview.org. **Contact:** Joseph Levens, editor. Estab. 2002. "Our goal is simply to publish the highest-quality literary fiction, nonfiction, and poetry intended for a general audience. This is a simple online literary journal of high-quality material, so simple you can call it unique."

○ Magazine: illustrations and photographs. Periodically releases print issues. Quarterly.

NEEDS No sci-fi, horror, or graphic erotica. Length: up to 8,000 words; average length: 3,000 words. Publishes short shorts.

HOW TO CONTACT Send complete ms by e-mail as attachment or by postal mail with SASE.

TIPS "Style counts. We prefer innovative or at least very smooth, convincing voices. Even the dullest premises or the complete lack of conflict make for an interesting story if it is told in the right voice and style. We like to find little, interesting facts and/or connections subtly sprinkled throughout the piece. Harsh language should be used only if/when necessary. If we are choosing between light and dark subjects, the light will usually win."

THE SUN

107 N. Roberson St., Chapel Hill NC 27516. (919)942-5282. **Fax:** (919)932-3101. **Website:** www.thesunmagazine.org. **Contact:** Sy Safransky, editor. Estab. 1974. *The Sun* publishes essays, interviews, fiction, and poetry. "We are open to all kinds of writing, though we favor work of a personal nature."

NEEDS Open to all fiction. Receives 800 unsolicited mss/month. Accepts 20 short stories/year. Recently published work by Sigrid Nunez, Susan Straight, Lydia Peelle, Stephen Elliott, David James Duncan, Linda McCullough Moore, and Brenda Miller. No science fiction, horror, fantasy, or other genre fiction. "Read an issue before submitting." Length: up to 7,000 words.

HOW TO CONTACT Send complete ms. Accepts reprint submissions.

PAYMENT/TERMS Pays $300-1,500 and 1-year subscription.

TIPS "Do not send queries except for interviews. We're open to unusual work. Read the magazine to get a sense of what we're about. Our submission rate is extremely high. Please be patient after sending us your work and include return postage."

SUSPENSE MAGAZINE

Suspense Publishing, 26500 W. Agoura Rd., Suite 102-474, Calabasas CA 91302. **E-mail:** editor@suspensemagazine.com; john@suspensemagazine.com. **E-mail:** stories@suspensemagazine.com. **Website:** www.suspensemagazine.com. **Contact:** John Raab, publisher/CEO/editor-in-chief. Estab. 2007. *Suspense Magazine* was designed to bring fans closer to the authors they love. We cover the entire suspense, thriller, mystery, horror genre not only with our magazine but with Suspense Radio. We have something for everyone that loves to dive into the unknown. We also have a publishing company that has published several bestsellers and won several awards. When you submit either a short story or a manuscript to Suspense Publishing, the one thing the author needs to make sure of? Editing! I can't say this strong enough. Almost 80% of our entries have not been edited and it shows. If you misspell a word in your query letter, we are not to excited to read your manuscript or short story. And most times we never get that far, we just simply reject it. Just write the absolute best book you can. Don't worry about trends in the market, etc. If you write a great book, people will find it. Just be patient.

NEEDS No explicit scenes. Length: 1,500-5,000 words.

HOW TO CONTACT Submit story in body of e-mail. "Attachments will not be opened."

TIPS "Unpublished writers are welcome and encouraged to query. Our emphasis is on horror, suspense, thriller, and mystery."

SYCAMORE REVIEW

Purdue University Department of English, 500 Oval Dr., West Lafayette IN 47907. (765) 494-3783. **Fax:** (765) 494-3780. **E-mail:** sycamore@purdue.edu. **Website:** www.sycamorereview.com. **Contact:** Anthony Sutton, editor in chief; Bess Cooley, managing editor. *Sycamore Review* is Purdue University's internationally acclaimed literary journal, affiliated with Purdue's College of Liberal Arts and the Dept. of English. Strives to publish the best writing by new and estab-

lished writers. Looks for well-crafted and engaging work, works that illuminate our lives in the collective human search for meaning. Would like to publish more work that takes a reflective look at national identity and how we are perceived by the world. Looks for diversity of voice, pluralistic worldviews, and political and social context.

Reading period: September 1-March 31.

NEEDS No genre fiction.

HOW TO CONTACT Submit complete ms via online submissions manager.

PAYMENT/TERMS Pays in contributor's copies and $50/short story.

TIPS "We look for originality, brevity, significance, strong dialogue, and vivid detail. We sponsor the Wabash Prize for Poetry (deadline: December 1) and Fiction (deadline: April 17), $1,000 award for each. All contest submissions will be considered for regular inclusion in the *Sycamore Review*."

TAKAHĒ

P.O. Box 13-335, Christchurch 8141, New Zealand. **E-mail:** admin@takahe.org.nz. **E-mail:** essays@takahe.org.nz; fiction@takahe.org.nz; poetry@takahe.org.nz. **Website:** www.takahe.org.nz. **Contact:** Jane Seaford and Rachel Smith, fiction editors. *Takahē* magazine is a New Zealand-based literary and arts magazine that appears 3 times/year with a mix of print and online issues. It publishes short stories, poetry, and art by established and emerging writers and artists as well as essays, interviews, and book reviews (by invitation) in these related areas. The Takahē Collective Trust is a nonprofit organization that aims to support emerging and published writers, poets, artists, and cultural commentators.

NEEDS "We look for stories that have something special about them: an original idea, a new perspective, an interesting narrative style or use of language, an ability to evoke character and/or atmosphere. Above all, we like some depth, an extra layer of meaning, an insight—something more than just an anecdote or a straightforward narration of events." Length: 1,500-3,000 words, "Stories up to 5,000 words may be considered for publication in the online magazine only."

HOW TO CONTACT E-mail submissions are preferred (fiction@takahe.org.nz). Overseas submissions are only accepted by e-mail.

PAYMENT/TERMS Pays small honorarium.

TIPS "Editorials, book reviews, artwork, and literary commentaries are by invitation only."

TALKING RIVER

Lewis-Clark State College, 500 Eighth Ave., Lewiston ID 83501. (208)792-2716. **E-mail:** talkingriver@lcmail.lcsc.edu. **Website:** www.lcsc.edu/talking-river. **Contact:** Kevin Goodan, editorial advisor. Estab. 1994. "*Talking River*, Lewis-Clark State College's literary journal, seeks examples of literary excellence and originality. Theme may and must be of your choosing. Send us your mss of poetry, fiction, and creative nonfiction. The journal is a national publication, featuring creative work by some of this country's best contemporary writers."

Reads mss August 1-April 1 only.

NEEDS Wants more well-written, character-driven stories that surprise and delight the reader with fresh, arresting yet un-self-conscious language, imagery, metaphor, revelation. Recently published work by Chris Dombrowski, Sherwin Bitsui, and Lia Purpura, Jim Harrison, David James Duncan, Dan Gerber, Alison Hawthorne Deming. No stories that are sexist, racist, homophobic, erotic for shock value; no genre fiction. Length: up to 4,000 words.

HOW TO CONTACT Send complete ms with cover letter by postal mail. Include estimated word count, two-sentence bio, and list of publications. Send SASE for reply and return of ms, or send disposable copy of ms.

PAYMENT/TERMS Pays contributor's copies; additional copies $6.

TIPS "We look for the strong, the unique; we reject clichéd images and predictable climaxes."

TAMPA REVIEW

University of Tampa Press, 401 W. Kennedy Blvd., Tampa FL 33606. (813)253-6266. **Fax:** (813)258-7593. **E-mail:** utpress@ut.edu. **Website:** www.ut.edu/tampareview. **Contact:** Richard Mathews, editor; Daniel Dooghan, nonfiction editor; Shane Hinton and Yuly Restrepo, fiction editors; Geoff Bouvier and Elizabeth Winston, poetry editors. Estab. 1988. An international literary journal publishing art and literature from Florida and Tampa Bay as well as new work and translations from throughout the world. "We no longer accept paper submissions. Please submit all work via the online submission manager. You will find it on our website under the link titled 'How to Submit.'"

NEEDS "We are far more interested in quality than in genre. Nothing sentimental as opposed to genuinely moving, nor self-conscious style at the expense of human truth." Length: up to 5,000 words.

HOW TO CONTACT Send complete ms via online submissions manager. We no longer accept submissions by mail.

PAYMENT/TERMS Pays $10/printed page, 1 contributor's copy, and offers 40% discount on additional copies.

TIPS "Send a clear cover letter stating previous experience or background. Our editorial staff considers submissions between September and December for publication in the following year."

TEARS IN THE FENCE

Portman Lodge, Durweston, Blandford Forum, Dorset DT11 0QA, United Kingdom. **E-mail:** tearsinthefence@gmail.com. **Website:** tearsinthefence.com. Estab. 1984. *Tears in the Fence*, published 3 times/year, is a "small-press magazine of poetry, prose poetry, creative non-fiction, fiction, interviews, essays, and reviews. We are open to a wide variety of poetic styles and work that shows social and poetic awareness whilst prompting close and divergent readings." *Tears in the Fence* is 184 pages, A5, digitally printed on 110-gms. paper, perfect-bound, with matte card cover. Press run is 600.

NEEDS Length: up to 3,000 words.

HOW TO CONTACT Submit complete ms via e-mail as attachment.

PAYMENT/TERMS Pays 1 contributor's copy.

TELLURIDE MAGAZINE

Big Earth Publishing, Inc., P.O. Box 888, Telluride CO 81435. (970)728-4245. **Fax:** (866)936-8406. **E-mail:** deb@telluridemagazine.com. **Website:** www.telluridemagazine.com. **Contact:** Deb Dion Kees, editor in chief. Estab. 1982. "*Telluride Magazine* speaks specifically to Telluride and the surrounding mountain environment. Telluride is a resort town supported by the ski industry in winter, festivals in summer, outdoor recreation year round, and the unique lifestyle all of that affords. As a National Historic Landmark District with a colorful mining history, it weaves a tale that readers seek out. The local/visitor interaction is key to Telluride's success in making profiles an important part of the content. Telluriders are an environmentally minded and progressive bunch who appreciate efforts toward sustainability and protecting the natural landscape and wilderness that are the region's number one draw."

NEEDS "Please contact us; we are very specific about what we will accept." Length: 800-1,200 words.

HOW TO CONTACT Query with published clips.

TERRAIN.ORG: A JOURNAL OF THE BUILT + NATURAL ENVIROMENTS

Terrain.org, P.O. Box 19161, Tucson AZ 85731-9161. **E-mail:** contact2@terrain.org. **Website:** www.terrain. org. **Contact:** Simmons B. Buntin, editor in chief. Receives 25 mss/month. Accepts 12-15 mss/year. Agented fiction 5%. **Publishes 1-3 new writers/year.** Published Al Sim, Jacob MacAurthur Mooney, T.R. Healy, Deborah Fries, Andrew Wingfield, Braden Hepner, Chavawn Kelly, Tamara Kaye Sellman. *Terrain.org* is based on, and thus welcomes quality submissions from, new and experienced authors and artists alike. Our online journal accepts only the finest poetry, essays, fiction, articles, artwork, and other contributions' material that reaches deep into the earth's fiery core, or humanity's incalculable core, and brings forth new insights and wisdom. *Terrain.org* is searching for that interface—the integration among the built and natural environments, that might be called the soul of place. The works contained within *Terrain.org* ultimately examine the physical realm around us and how those environments influence us and each other physically, mentally, emotionally, and spiritually."

○ Beginning March 2014, publication schedule is rolling; we will no longer be issue-based. Sends galleys to author. Publication is copyrighted. Sponsors *Terrain.org* Annual Contest in Poetry, Fiction, and Nonfiction. **Deadline:** August 1. Submit via online submissions manager.

NEEDS Does not want erotica. Length: up to 6,000 words. Average length: 5,000 words. Publishes short shorts. Average length of short shorts: 750 words.

HOW TO CONTACT Accepts submissions online at sub.terrain.org. Include brief bio. Send complete ms with cover letter. Reads September 1-May 30 for regular submissions; contest submissions open year round.

TIPS "We have 3 primary criteria in reviewing fiction: (1) The story is compelling and well crafted. (2) The story provides some element of surprise; whether in content, form, or delivery we are unexpectedly delighted in what we've read. (3) The story meets an upcoming theme, even if only peripherally. Read fic-

tion in the current issue and perhaps some archived work, and if you like what you read—and our overall enviromental slant—then send us your best work. Make sure you follow our submission guidelines (including cover note with bio), and that your mss is as error-free as possible."

TEXAS REVIEW

Texas Review Press, Department of English, Sam Houston State University, Box 2146, Huntsville TX 77341-2146. (936)294-1992. **Fax:** (936)294-3070. **E-mail:** eng_pdr@shsu.edu; cww006@shsu.edu. **Website:** www.shsu.edu/~www_trp. **Contact:** Dr. Paul Ruffin, editor/director; Greg Bottoms, essay editor; Eric Miles Williamson, fiction editor; Nick Lantz, poetry editor. Estab. 1976. "We publish top-quality poetry, fiction, articles, interviews, and reviews for a general audience." Semiannual.

○ Does not read mss May-September. A member of the Texas A&M University Press consortium.

NEEDS "We are eager enough to consider fiction of quality, no matter what its theme or subject matter. No juvenile fiction."

HOW TO CONTACT Send complete ms. No mss accepted via fax. Send disposable copy of ms and #10 SASE for reply only. Accepts multiple submissions.

PAYMENT/TERMS Pays contributor's copies and one-year subscription.

⑤ THEMA

Thema Literary Society, P.O. Box 8747, Metairie LA 70011-8747. **E-mail:** thema@cox.net. **E-mail:** For writers living outside the U.S. **Website:** themaliterarysociety.com. **Contact:** Virginia Howard, editor; Gail Howard, poetry editor. Estab. 1988. *"THEMA* is designed to stimulate creative thinking by challenging writers with unusual 'themes, such as "Is There a Word for That?' and 'The Face in the Photograph.' Appeals to writers, teachers of creative writing, artists, photographers, and general reading audience." *THEMA* is 100 pages, digest-sized professionally printed, with glossy card cover. Receives about 400 poems/year, accepts about 8%. Press run is 400 (230 subscribers, 30 libraries). Subscription: $30 U.S./$40 foreign. Has published poetry by Beverly Boyd, John Grey, James B. Nicola, and Matthew Spireng.

NEEDS All stories must relate to one of *THEMA*'s upcoming themes (**indicate the target theme on submission of manuscript**). See website for themes. No erotica. Length: 300-6,000 words (1-20 double-spaced pages).

HOW TO CONTACT Send complete ms with SASE, cover letter; include "name and address, brief introduction, **specifying the intended target issue for the mss**." SASE. Accepts simultaneous, multiple submissions, and reprints. Does not accept e-mailed submissions except from non-USA addresses.

PAYMENT/TERMS Payment: $10 for under 1,000 words; $25 for stories over 1,000 words, plus one contributor copy.

THIRD COAST

Western Michigan University, English Department, Kalamazoo MI 49008-5331. **E-mail:** editors@thirdcoastmagazine.com. **Website:** www.thirdcoastmagazine.com. **Contact:** S.Marie LaFata-Clay, editor in chief. Estab. 1995. Sponsors an annual fiction contest. First prize: $1,000 and publication. Guidelines available on website. **Entry fee:** $16, which includes one-year subscription to *Third Coast*. "*Third Coast* publishes poetry, fiction (including traditional and experimental fiction, shorts, and novel excerpts, but not genre fiction), creative nonfiction (including reportage, essay, memoir, and fragments), drama, and translations."

○ *Third Coast* is 176 pages, digest-sized, professionally printed, perfect-bound, with 4-color cover with art. Reads mss from September through December of each year.

NEEDS Has published work by Bonnie Jo Campbell, Peter Ho Davies, Robin Romm, Lee Martin, Caitlin Horrocks, and Peter Orner. No genre fiction. Length: up to 7,500 words or 25 pages. Query for longer works.

HOW TO CONTACT Send complete ms via online submissions manager.

PAYMENT/TERMS Pays 2 contributor's copies and one-year subscription.

TIPS "We will consider many different types of fiction and favor those exhibiting a freshness of vision and approach."

⑤ THREE-LOBED BURNING EYE

Portland OR **Website:** www.3lobedmag.com. Estab. 1999. *Three-Lobed Burning Eye* is a speculative fiction magazine published online twice per year (usually spring and fall) and as a print anthology every other year. Each issue features six stories.

NEEDS "We are looking for quality speculative fiction, in the vein of horror and dark fantasy, what you might call magical realism, slipstream, cross genre, or weird fiction. We will consider the occasional science fiction, suspense, or western story, though we prefer that it contain some speculative element. Sword and sorcery, hard SF, space opera, and extreme horror are hard sells. We like voices both literary and pulpy, with unique and flowing but not experimental styles. All labels aside, we want stories that expand genre, that value originality in character, narrative, and plot." Has published work by Gemma Files, DF Lewis, Laird Barron, Brenden Connell, Amy Grech, Neil Ayres, and Tim Waggoner. Does not want fan or franchise tie-in fiction (*Star Trek, Buffy, D&D*, etc.), serial stories, or novel excerpts. No erotica. Length: up to 7,000 for short stories; 500-1,000 words for flash fiction.

HOW TO CONTACT Submit via online submissions manager.

PAYMENT/TERMS Pays 3¢/word, up to $35.

TIPS "Send only your best fiction, distinct and remarkable tales that the reader cannot forget. We encourage diverse authors, characters and points of view, inclusive of all races, cultures, genders, and orientations."

THE THREEPENNY REVIEW

P.O. Box 9131, Berkeley CA 94709. (510)849-4545. **E-mail:** wlesser@threepennyreview.com. **Website:** www.threepennyreview.com. **Contact:** Wendy Lesser, editor. Estab. 1980. "We are a general-interest, national literary magazine with coverage of politics, the visual arts, and the performing arts." Reading period: January 1-June 30.

NEEDS No fragmentary, sentimental fiction. Length: 800-4,000 words.

HOW TO CONTACT Send complete ms.

PAYMENT/TERMS Pays $400.

TIPS "Nonfiction (political articles, memoirs, reviews) is most open to freelancers."

TIMBER JOURNAL

University of Colorado Boulder, **E-mail:** timberjournal@gmail.com. **Website:** www.colorado.edu/timberjournal. **Contact:** Staff changes regularly; see website for current staff members. *Timber* is a literary journal run by students in the MFA program at the University of Colorado Boulder and dedicated to the promotion of innovative literature. Publishes work that explores the boundaries of poetry, fiction, creative nonfiction, and digital literatures. Produces both an online journal that explores the potentials of the digital medium and an annual print anthology.

Reading period: August-March (submit once during this time).

NEEDS Length: up to 4,000 words.

HOW TO CONTACT Submit via online submissions manager. Include 30- to 50-word bio.

PAYMENT/TERMS Pays 1 contributor's copy.

TIPS "We are looking for innovative poetry, fiction, creative nonfiction, and digital lit (screenwriting, digital poetry, multimedia lit, etc.)."

TIN HOUSE

McCormack Communications, P.O. Box 10500, Portland OR 97296. (503)219-0622. **E-mail:** info@tinhouse.com. **Website:** www.tinhouse.com. **Contact:** Cheston Knapp, managing editor; Holly MacArthur, founding editor. Estab. 1999. "We are a general-interest literary quarterly. Our watchword is quality. Our audience includes people interested in literature in all its aspects, from the mundane to the exalted."

Reading period: September 1-May 31.

NEEDS Length up to 10,000 words.

HOW TO CONTACT Submit via online submissions manager or postal mail. Include cover letter with word count.

PAYMENT/TERMS Pays $200-800.

TOASTED CHEESE

E-mail: editors@toasted-cheese.com. **E-mail:** submit@toasted-cheese.com. **Website:** www.toasted-cheese.com. Estab. 2001. *Toasted Cheese* accepts submissions of previously unpublished fiction, flash fiction, creative nonfiction, poetry, and book reviews. See site for book review requirements and guidelines. "Our focus is on quality of work, not quantity. Some issues will therefore contain fewer or more pieces than previous issues. We don't restrict publication based on subject matter. We encourage submissions from innovative writers in all genres and actively seek diverse voices." No simultaneous submissions. Be mindful that final notification of acceptance or rejection may take four months. No chapters or excerpts unless they read as a stand-alone story. No first drafts.

NEEDS Toasted Cheese actively seeks submissions from those with diverse voices. See site for submission guidelines and samples of what Toasted Cheese publishes. No fan fiction. No chapters or excerpts unless they read as a stand-alone story. No first drafts.

HOW TO CONTACT See site for submission guidelines and samples of what Toasted Cheese publishes.

PAYMENT/TERMS Toasted Cheese is a non-paying market.

TIPS "We are looking for clean, professional work from writers and poets of any experience level. Accepted stories and poems will be concise and compelling with a strong voice. We're looking for writers who are serious about the craft: tomorrow's literary stars before they're famous. See site for submission guidelines and samples of what Toasted Cheese publishes."

TORCH JOURNAL

Torch Literary Arts, **E-mail:** torchliteraryarts@gmail.com. **E-mail:** torchliteraryarts@gmail.com. **Website:** www.torchliteraryarts.org. **Contact:** Amanda Johnston, Founder / Editor. Estab. 2006. *TORCH Journal*, published semiannually online, provides "a place to publish contemporary poetry, prose, and short stories by experienced and emerging writers alike. We prefer our contributors to take risks, and offer a diverse body of work that examines and challenges preconceived notions regarding race, ethnicity, gender roles, and identity." Has published poetry by Sharon Bridgforth, Patricia Smith, Crystal Wilkinson, Tayari Jones, and Natasha Trethewey. Reads submissions April 15-August 31 only. Sometimes comments on rejected poems. Always sends prepublication galleys. No payment. "Within *TORCH*, we offer a special section called Flame that features an interview, biography, and work sample by an established writer as well as an introduction to their Spark—an emerging writer who inspires them and adds to the boundless voice of creative writing by Black women." A free online newsletter is available; see website.

TRAIL OF INDISCRETION

Fortress Publishing, Inc., Lemoyne PA 17011. **E-mail:** realm.beyond@yahoo.com. **Website:** www.fortress-publishinginc.com. **Contact:** Brian Koscienski, editor. *Trail of Indiscretion* publishes fantasy, science fiction, and horror short stories.

NEEDS No profanity or graphic scenes. Length: up to 5,000 words.

HOW TO CONTACT E-mail Word document.

PAYMENT/TERMS Pays contributor's copies.

TIPS "If it's a story about a 13-year-old girl named Mary coping with the change to womanhood while poignantly reflecting the recent passing of her favorite aunt Gertrude, we DON'T want it! Now, if Mary is the 13-year-old daughter of a vampire cowboy who stumbles upon a government conspiracy involving aliens and unicorns while investigating, hard-boiled style, the grisly murder of her favorite aunt, Gertrude, then we'll take a look at it."

TRANSITION: AN INTERNATIONAL REVIEW

104 Mount Auburn St., 3R, Cambridge MA 02138. (617)496-2845. **Fax:** (617)496-2877. **E-mail:** transition@fas.harvard.edu. **Website:** http://hutchinscenter.fas.harvard.edu/transition. **Contact:** Sara Bruya, managing editor. Estab. 1961. *Transition Magazine* is a trimestrial international review known for compelling and controversial writing from and about Africa and the Diaspora. This prestigious magazine is edited at the Hutchins Center for African American Research at Harvard University.

HOW TO CONTACT "For all submissions, please include the following information in your e-mail or cover letter and in the top left corner of the first page of all documents: name, address, e-mail address, word count, date of submission. Please also include a title with each work."

PAYMENT/TERMS Pays 1 contributor's copy.

TIPS "We look for a nonwhite, alternative perspective dealing with issues of race, ethnicity, and identity in an unpredictable, provocative way."

TRIQUARTERLY

School of Professional Studies, Northwestern University, 339 E. Chicago Ave., Chicago IL 60611. **E-mail:** triquarterly@northwestern.edu. **Website:** www.triquarterly.org. **Contact:** Carrie Muehle, managing editor. Estab. 1964. "*TriQuarterly*, the literary magazine of Northwestern University, welcomes submissions of fiction, creative nonfiction, poetry, short drama, and hybrid work. We also welcome short-short prose pieces." Reading period: November 15-May 1.

NEEDS Length: up to 5,000 words.

HOW TO CONTACT Submit complete ms via online submissions manager.

PAYMENT/TERMS Pays honoraria.

TIPS "We are especially interested in work that embraces the world and continues, however subtly, the ongoing global conversation about culture and society that *TriQuarterly* pursued from its beginning in 1964."

TRUE CONFESSIONS

105 E. 34th St., Box 141, New York NY 10016. **E-mail:** shazell@truerenditionsllc.com. **E-mail:** trueswriters@yahoo.com. **Website:** www.truerenditionsllc.com. **Contact:** Samantha Hazell, editor. "*True Confessions* is a women's magazine featuring true-to-life stories about working-class women and their families. The stories must be in first-person and generally deal with family problems, relationship issues, romances, single moms, abuse, and any other realistic issue women face in our society. The stories we look for are true or at least believable. We look for stories that evoke some sort of emotion, be it happiness or sadness, but in the end there needs to be some sort of moral or lesson learned."

NEEDS "Stories should be written in first person and past tense. We generally look for more serious stories. The underlying theme is overcoming adversities in life. These are supposed to be 'true' stories—or at least stories that could be true!" Length: 3,000-7,000 words.

HOW TO CONTACT E-mail submissions preferred (trueswriters@yahoo.com). Include contact information and brief synopsis of story. To submit by postal mail, include disk saved in Word, a hard copy, and SASE for return of materials.

PAYMENT/TERMS Pays 3¢/word.

TULANE REVIEW

Tulane University, Suite G08A Lavin-Bernick Center, Tulane University, New Orleans LA 70118. **E-mail:** litsoc@tulane.edu. **Website:** www.tulane.edu/~litsoc/index.html. Estab. 1988. *Tulane Review*, published biannually, is a national literary journal seeking quality submissions of prose, poetry, and art.

NEEDS Length: up to 4,000 words.

HOW TO CONTACT Submit via online submissions manager only. Include a brief biography, an e-mail address, and a return address in cover letter.

PAYMENT/TERMS Pays 2 contributor's copies.

UPSTREET

Ledgetop Publishing, P.O. Box 105, Richmond MA 01254-0105. (413)441-9702. **E-mail:** editor@upstreet-mag.org. **Website:** www.upstreet-mag.org. **Contact:** Vivian Dorsel, Founding Editor/Publisher. Estab. 2005.

NEEDS Does not want run-of-the-mill genre, children's, anything but literary. Length: 5,000 words.

HOW TO CONTACT Send complete ms.

PAYMENT/TERMS Pays $50-250.

TIPS "Get sample copy, submit electronically, and follow guidelines."

💲 U.S. CATHOLIC

Claretian Publications, 205 W. Monroe St., Chicago IL 60606. (312)236-7782. **Fax:** (312)236-8207. **E-mail:** literaryeditor@uscatholic.org. **E-mail:** submissions@claretians.org. **Website:** www.uscatholic.org. Estab. 1935. "*U.S. Catholic* puts faith in the context of everyday life. With a strong focus on social justice, we offer a fresh and balanced take on the issues that matter most in our world, adding a faith perspective to such challenges as poverty, education, family life, the environment, and even pop culture."

🖸 Please include SASE with written ms.

NEEDS Accepts short stories. "Topics vary, but unpublished fiction should be no longer than 1,500 words and should include strong characters and cause readers to stop for a moment and consider their relationships with others, the world, and/or God. Specifically religious themes are not required; subject matter is not restricted. E-mail submissions@uscatholic.org." Length: 700-1,500 words.

HOW TO CONTACT Send complete ms.

PAYMENT/TERMS Pays minimum $200.

VAMPIRES 2 MAGAZINE

Man's Story 2 Publishing Co., 1321 Snapfinger Rd., Decatur GA 30032. **E-mail:** vampires2com2@aol.com. **Website:** www.vampires2.us. **Contact:** Carlos Dunn, founder and editor. Estab. 1999. "Online e-zine that strives to re-create vampire romance in the pulp fiction style of the 1920s through the 1970s with strong emphasis on 3D graphic art." Also features illustrated stories, online magazine, online photo galleries, and more.

🖸 "We publish books, publish online, and operate websites. In 2000 we became one of *Writer's Digest*'s top 100 markets for fiction writers and have since become listed with 20 other outstanding writers organizations."

NEEDS Length: up to 3,500 words or up to 10,000 words (two options offered; see website for details).

HOW TO CONTACT Send complete ms via e-mail as a .doc attachment. Include short summary of story.

TIPS "Your story must come to us edited, error free, and ready to publish. We prefer stories that have a strong romantic angle and a tastefully written lovemaking scene. Your story must have a compelling plot, nonstop action, and a satisfying ending, and you must tell a story well."

🌑 VAN GOGH'S EAR

Best World Poetry & Prose, French Connection Press, 12 Rue Lamartine, Paris 75009, France. (33)(1)4016-1147. **E-mail:** tinafayeayres@gmail.com. **Website:** www.frenchcx.com/press; theoriginalvangoghsear-anthology.com. Estab. 2002. *Van Gogh's Ear*, published annually in April, is an anthology series "devoted to publishing powerful poetry and prose in English and English translations by major voices and innovative new talents from around the globe."

🖸 *Van Gogh's Ear* is 280 pages, digest-sized, offset-printed, perfect-bound, with 4-color matte cover with commissioned artwork. Poetry published in *Van Gogh's Ear* has appeared in *The Best American Poetry*.

NEEDS Length: up to 1,500 words.

HOW TO CONTACT Submit up to 2 prose pieces by e-mail. Cover letter is preferred, along with a brief bio of up to 120 words.

PAYMENT/TERMS Pays 1 contributor's copy.

TIPS "As a 501(c)(3) nonprofit enterprise, *Van Gogh's Ear* needs the support of individual poets, writers, and readers to survive. Any donation, large or small, will help *Van Gogh's Ear* continue to publish the best cross-section of contemporary poetry and prose. Because of being an anglophone publication based in France, *Van Gogh's Ear* is unable to get any grants or funding. Your contribution will be tax-deductible. Make donation checks payable to Committee on Poetry-*VGE*, and mail them (donations **only**) to the Allen Ginsberg Trust, P.O. Box 582, Stuyvesant Station, New York NY 10009."

💲 VANILLEROTICA LITERARY EZINE

Cleveland OH 44102. (216)799-9775. **E-mail:** talentdripseroticpublishing@yahoo.com. **Website:** eroticatalentdrips.wordpress.com. **Contact:** Kimberly Steele, founder. Estab. 2007. *Vanillerotica*, published monthly online, focuses solely on showcasing new erotic fiction.

NEEDS Length: 5,000-10,000 words.

HOW TO CONTACT Submit short stories by e-mail to talentdripseroticpublishing@yahoo.com. Stories should be pasted into body of message. Reads submissions during publication months only.

PAYMENT/TERMS Pays $15 for each accepted short story.

TIPS "Please read our take on the difference between *erotica* and *pornography*; it's on the website. *Vanillerotica* does not accept pornography. And please keep poetry 30 lines or less."

⬤ VERANDAH LITERARY & ART JOURNAL

Faculty of Arts, Deakin University, 221 Burwood Hwy., Burwood, Victoria 3125, Australia. (61)(3)9251-7134. **E-mail:** verandah@deakin.edu.au. **Website:** verandahjournal.wordpress.com/. Estab. 1985. *Verandah*, published annually in August, is a high-quality literary journal edited by professional writing students. It aims to give voice to new and innovative writers and artists.

○ Submission period: February 1 through June 5. Has published work by Christos Tsiolka, Dorothy Porter, Seamus Heaney, Les Murray, Ed Burger, and John Muk Muk Burke. *Verandah* is 120 pages, professionally printed on glossy stock, flat-spined, with full-color glossy card cover.

NEEDS Length: 350-2,500 words.

HOW TO CONTACT Submit by mail or e-mail. However, electronic version of work must be available if accepted by *Verandah*. Do not submit work without the required submission form (available for download on website). Reads submissions by June 5 deadline (postmark).

PAYMENT/TERMS Pays 1 contributor's copy, "with prizes awarded accordingly."

VESTAL REVIEW

P.O. Box 35369, Brighton MA 02135. **E-mail:** submissions@vestalreview.net. **Website:** www.vestalreview.org. **Contact:** Mark Budman, editor. Estab. 2000. Semi-annual print magazine specializing in flash fiction. The oldest magazine of flash fiction. A paying market. Our reading periods are February-May and August-November.

NEEDS Only flash fiction under 500 words. No porn, racial slurs, excessive gore, or obscenity. No children's or preachy stories. Nothing over 500 words. Length: 50-500 words.

HOW TO CONTACT Publishes flash fiction. "We accept submissions only through our submission manager."

PAYMENT/TERMS Pays $25 and 1 contributor's copy.

TIPS "We like literary fiction with a plot that doesn't waste words. Don't send jokes masked as stories."

🌀 THE VIRGINIA QUARTERLY REVIEW

VQR, P.O. Box 400223, Charlottesville VA 22904. **E-mail:** editors@vqronline.org. **Website:** www.vqronline.org. **Contact:** Allison Wright, executive editor. Estab. 1925. "*VQR*'s primary mission has been to sustain and strengthen Jefferson's bulwark, long describing itself as 'A National Journal of Literature and Discussion.' And for good reason. From its inception in prohibition, through depression and war, in prosperity and peace, *The Virginia Quarterly Review* has been a haven—and home—for the best essayists, fiction writers, and poets, seeking contributors from every section of the United States and abroad. It has not limited itself to any special field. No topic has been alien: literary, public affairs, the arts, history, the economy. If it could be approached through essay or discussion, poetry or prose, *VQR* has covered it." Press run is 4,000.

NEEDS "We are generally not interested in genre fiction (such as romance, science fiction, or fantasy)." Length: 2,000-10,000 words.

HOW TO CONTACT Accepts online submissions only at virginiaquarterlyreview.submittable.com/submit.

PAYMENT/TERMS Pays $1,000-2,500 for short stories; $1,000-4,000 for novellas and novel excerpts.

VIRTUE IN THE ARTS

Randy Mate, P.O. Box 11081, Glendale CA 91226. **E-mail:** info@virtueinthearts.com. **Website:** www.virtueinthearts.com. Estab. 2006. Each publication features short stories, articles, poetry and artwork relating to a different virtue each time (such as honesty, compassion, trustworthiness, etc.).

○ "The goal of this publication is to provide an entertaining showcase of diverse writers and artists who promote a new and better civilization through their work. Each issue has works by author Becky Mate along with winners of the New Civilization Theme Contest sponsored by

New Castle Remodeling, Inc. of Los Angeles, California."

NEEDS Fiction shedding a positive light on the current theme (a virtue) in an entertaining way. Length: 300-1,500 words.

HOW TO CONTACT Send complete ms.

PAYMENT/TERMS Pays $7.

TIPS We're looking for material that promotes virtue. If you promote virtue, you get virtue. Find out the current deadline and the current virtue, then send us your submission.

WEB DEL SOL

Wed del Sol Association, 2020 Pennsylvania Ave. NW, Suite 443, Washington D.C. 20006. **E-mail:** editor@ webdelsol.com. **Website:** www.webdelsol.com. **Contact:** Michael Neff, editor in chief. Estab. 1994. Electronic magazine. "The goal of *Web Del Sol* is to use the medium of the Internet to bring the finest in contemporary literary arts to a larger audience. To that end, *WDS* not only web-publishes collections of work by accomplished writers and poets, but hosts over 25 literary arts publications on the WWW such as *Del Sol Review*, *North American Review*, *Global City Review*, *The Literary Review*, and *The Prose Poem*." Estab. 1994.

NEEDS Literary. "*WDS* publishes work considered to be literary in nature, i.e. non-genre fiction. *WDS* also publishes poetry, prose poetry, essays and experimental types of writing." **Publishes 100-200 new writers/ year.**

HOW TO CONTACT "Submissions by e-mail from September through November and from January through March only. Submissions must contain some brief bio, list of prior publications (if any), and a short work or portion of that work, neither to exceed 1,000 words. Editors will contact if the balance of work is required." Sample copy online.

TIPS "*WDS* wants fiction that is absolutely cutting edge, unique and/or at a minimum, accomplished with a crisp style and concerning subjects not usually considered the objects of literary scrutiny. Read works in such publications as *Conjunctions* (www.conjunctions.com) and *North American Review* (webdelsol. com/NorthAmReview/NAR) to get an idea of what we are looking for."

WEBER

The Contemporary West, Weber State University, 1395 Edvalson St., Dept. 1405, Ogden UT 84408-1405.

E-mail: weberjournal@weber.edu. **Website:** www. weber.edu/weberjournal. **Contact:** Kristin Jackson, managing editor. Estab. 1983. *Weber: The Contemporary West*, published 2 times/year, "spotlights personal narrative, commentary, fiction, nonfiction, and poetry that speaks to the environment and culture of the American West and beyond."

Poetry published in *Weber* has appeared in *The Best American Poetry*. *Weber* is 150 pages, off-set-printed on acid-free paper, perfect-bound, with color cover. Receives about 250-300 poems/year, accepts 30-40. Press run is 1,000; 80% libraries.

WEST BRANCH

Stadler Center for Poetry, Bucknell University, Lewisburg PA 17837-2029. (570)577-1853. **Fax:** (570)577-1885. **E-mail:** westbranch@bucknell.edu. **Website:** www.bucknell.edu/westbranch. **Contact:** G.C. Waldrep, editor. *West Branch* publishes poetry, fiction, and nonfiction in both traditional and innovative styles.

Reading period: August 15 through April 1. No more than 3 submissions from a single contributor in a given reading period.

NEEDS No genre fiction. Length: no more than 30 pages.

HOW TO CONTACT Send complete ms.

PAYMENT/TERMS Pays 5¢/word, with a maximum of $100.

TIPS "All submissions must be sent via our online submission manager. Please see website for guidelines. We recommend that you acquaint yourself with the magazine before submitting."

WESTERLY MAGAZINE

University of Western Australia, The Westerly Centre (M202), Crawley WA 6009, Australia. (61)(8)6488-3403. **Fax:** (61)(8)6488-1030. **E-mail:** westerly@uwa. edu.au. **Website:** westerlymag.com.au. **Contact:** Catherine Noske, editor. Estab. 1956. *Westerly*, published in July and November, prints quality short fiction, poetry, literary criticism, socio-historical articles, and book reviews with special attention given to Australia, Asia, and the Indian Ocean region. "We assume a reasonably well-read, intelligent audience. Past issues of *Westerly* provide the best guides. Not consciously an academic magazine."

Westerly is about 200 pages, digest-sized. Online Special Issues complement the print publication. Subscription information available on website. Deadline for July edition: March 31; deadline for November edition: August 31.

NEEDS Length: up to 3,500 words.

HOW TO CONTACT Submit complete ms by mail, e-mail, or online submissions form.

PAYMENT/TERMS Pays $150 and contributor's copies.

WESTERN HUMANITIES REVIEW

University of Utah, 3528 LNCO / English Department, 255 S. Central Campus Dr., Salt Lake City UT 84112-0494. (801)581-6168. **Fax:** (801)585-5167. **E-mail:** managingeditor.whr@gmail.com. **Website:** www.westernhumanitiesreview.com. **Contact:** Michael Mejia, editor; Emily Dyer Barker, managing editor. Estab. 1947. *Western Humanities Review* is a journal of contemporary literature and culture housed in the University of Utah English Department. Publishes poetry, fiction, nonfiction essays, artwork, and work that resists categorization. Reading period: September 1 through April 15. All submissions must be sent through online submissions manager.

NEEDS Does not want genre (romance, science fiction, etc.). Length: 5,000 words.

HOW TO CONTACT Send complete ms.

PAYMENT/TERMS Pays $5/published page (when funds available).

TIPS "Because of changes in our editorial staff, we urge familiarity with recent issues of the magazine. We do not publish writer's guidelines because we think that the magazine itself conveys an accurate picture of our requirements. Please, no e-mail submissions."

WHISKEY ISLAND MAGAZINE

English Dept., Cleveland State University, 2121 Euclid Ave., Cleveland OH 44115. (216)687-3951. **E-mail:** whiskeyisland@csuohio.edu. **Website:** whiskeyislandmagazine.com. **Contact:** Dan Dorman. *Whiskey Island* is a nonprofit literary magazine that has been published in one form or another by students of Cleveland State University for over 30 years.

Reading periods: August 15 through November 15 and January 15 through April 15. Paper and e-mail submissions are not accepted. No multiple submissions.

NEEDS No translations, please. Length: 1,500-8,000 words for short stories; up to 1,500 words for flash fiction.

HOW TO CONTACT Submit via online submissions manager.

PAYMENT/TERMS Pays 2 contributor's copies.

WHITE FUNGUS: AN EXPERIMENTAL ARTS MAGAZINE

Room 5, Floor 9, 420 Nantun Rd., Section 2, Nantun District, Taichung City Taiwan +886 987 208 516. **E-mail:** mail@whitefungus.com. **Website:** www.whitefungus.com. Estab. 2004. "*White Fungus* is an art magazine based in Taichung City, Taiwan. Founded by brothers Ron and Mark Hanson in Wellington in 2004 as a quasi-political manifesto, copies of the first issue were produced on a photocopier, wrapped in Christmas paper, and hurled anonymously through the entrances of businesses throughout the city. Now a magazine featuring interviews, writing on art, new music, history, and politics, *White Fungus* takes a dialogical approach to the work it covers. The name of the publication comes from a can of 'white fungus' the Hansons found in their local supermarket in the industrial zone of Taichung City."

HOW TO CONTACT Query.

WICKED ALICE

Dancing Girl Press & Studio, 410 S. Michigan #921, Chicago IL 60605. **E-mail:** wickedalicepoetry@yahoo.com. **Website:** www.sundresspublications.com/wickedalice. **Contact:** Kristy Bowen, editor. Estab. 2001. "*Wicked Alice* is a women-centered online journal dedicated to publishing quality work by both sexes, depicting and exploring the female experience." Wants "work that has a strong sense of image and music. Work that is interesting and surprising, with innovative, sometimes unusual, use of language. We love humor when done well, strangeness, wackiness. Hybridity, collage, intertexuality."

HOW TO CONTACT Submit complete ms by e-mail.

WILD VIOLET

P.O. Box 39706, Philadelphia PA 19106. **E-mail:** wildvioletmagazine@yahoo.com. **Website:** www.wildviolet.net. **Contact:** Alyce Wilson, editor. Estab. 2001. *Wild Violet*, published monthly online, aims "to make the arts more accessible, to make a place for the arts in modern life, and to serve as a creative forum for writers and artists. Our audience includes English-speaking readers from all over the world who are interested in both 'high art' and pop culture."

NEEDS Receives 30 unsolicited mss/month. Accepts 3-5 mss/issue; 135 mss/year. **Publishes 70 new writers/year.** Recently published work by Aaron Sokoloff, Josh Karaczewski, Jason Howell and Megan Sierra Smith. Also publishes literary essays, literary criticism, poetry. Sometimes comments on rejected mss. "No stories where sexual or violent content is just used to shock the reader. No racist writings." Length: 500-6,000 words; average length: 3,000 words.

HOW TO CONTACT Send complete ms. Accepts submissions by e-mail and postal mail. Include estimated word count and brief bio. Send SASE for return of ms or send a disposable copy of ms and #10 SASE for reply only. Accepts simultaneous, multiple submissions.

PAYMENT/TERMS Writers receive bio and links on contributor's page. Sponsors awards/contests.

TIPS "We look for stories that are well-paced and show character and plot development. Even short shorts should do more than simply paint a picture. Manuscripts stand out when the author's voice is fresh and engaging. Avoid muddying your story with too many characters, and don't attempt to shock the reader with an ending you have not earned. Experiment with styles and structures, but don't resort to experimentation for its own sake."

WILLARD & MAPLE

375 Maple Street, Burlington VT 05401. **E-mail:** willardandmaple@champlain.edu. **Website:** willardandmaple.com. Estab. 1994. *Willard & Maple*, published annually in spring, is a student-run literary magazine from Champlain College's Professional Writing Program that considers short fiction, essays, reviews, fine art, and poetry by adults, children, and teens. Wants creative work of the highest quality.

○ *Willard & Maple* is 200 pages, digest-sized, digitally printed, perfect-bound. Receives about 500 poems/year, accepts about 20%. Press run is 600 (80 subscribers, 4 libraries); 200 are distributed free to the Champlain College writing community.

HOW TO CONTACT Send complete ms via e-mail or postal mail. Send SASE for return of ms or send disposable copy of mss and #10 SASE for reply only.

PAYMENT/TERMS Pays 2 contributor's copies.

TIPS "The power of imagination makes us infinite."

WILLOW REVIEW

College of Lake County Publications, College of Lake County, 19351 W. Washington St., Grayslake IL 60030-1198. (847)543-2956. **E-mail:** com426@clcillinois.edu. **Website:** www.clcillinois.edu/community/willowreview.asp. **Contact:** Michael Latza, editor. Estab. 1969. Prizes totaling $400 are awarded to the best poetry and short fiction/creative nonfiction in each issue. *Willow Review*, published annually, is interested in poetry, creative nonfiction, and fiction of high quality. "We have no preferences as to form, style, or subject, as long as each piece stands on its own as art and communicates ideas." The editors award prizes for best poetry and prose in the issue. Prize awards vary contingent on the current year's budget but normally range from $100-400. There is no reading fee or separate application for these prizes. All accepted mss are eligible."*Willow Review* can be found on EBSCOhost databases, assuring a broader targeted audience for our authors' work. *Willow Review* is a nonprofit journal partially supported by a grant from the Illinois Arts Council (a state agency), College of Lake County Publications, private contributions, and sales."

NEEDS Accepts short fiction. Considers simultaneous submissions "if indicated in the cover letter" and multiple submissions.

HOW TO CONTACT Send complete ms with cover letter. Include estimated word count, brief bio, list of publications. Send either SASE (or IRC) for return of ms or disposable copy of ms and #10 SASE for reply only.

PAYMENT/TERMS Pays 2 contributor's copies.

⑤ WILLOW SPRINGS

668 N. Riverpoint Blvd. #259, Spokane WA 99202. (509)828-1486. **E-mail:** willowspringsewu@gmail.com. **Website:** willowsprings.ewu.edu. **Contact:** Samuel Ligon, editor. Estab. 1977. *Willow Springs* is a semiannual magazine covering poetry, fiction, literary nonfiction and interviews of notable writers. Published twice a year, in spring and fall. Reading period: September 1 through May 31 for fiction and poetry; year-round for nonfiction. Reading fee: $3/submission.

NEEDS "We accept any good piece of literary fiction. Buy a sample copy." Does not want to see genre fiction that does not transcend its subject matter. Length: open for short stories; up to 750 words for short shorts.

HOW TO CONTACT Submit via online submissions manager.

PAYMENT/TERMS Pays $100 and 2 contributor's copies for short stories; $40 and 2 contributor's copies for short shorts.

TIPS "While we have no specific length restrictions, we generally publish fiction and nonfiction no longer than 10,000 words and poetry no longer than 120 lines, though those are not strict rules. *Willow Springs* values poems and essays that transcend the merely autobiographical and fiction that conveys a concern for language as well as story."

THE WINDHOVER

P.O. Box 8008, 900 College St., Belton TX 76513. (254)295-4563. **E-mail:** windhover@umhb.edu. **Website:** undergrad.umhb.edu/english/windhover-journal. **Contact:** Dr. Nathaniel Hansen, editor. Estab. 1997. "*The Windhover* is dedicated to promoting poetry, fiction and creative nonfiction that considers Christian perspectives and engages spiritual themes."

◐ Reading periods are 2/1-4/15 & 8/1-10/15.

NEEDS Length: 500-4,000 words. Average length: 3,000 words.

PAYMENT/TERMS Pays 1 contributor's copy.

TIPS "We are looking for writing that avoids the didactic, the melodramatic, the trite, the obvious. Eschew tricks and gimmicks. We want writing that invites rereading."

WISCONSIN REVIEW

University of Wisconsin Oshkosh, 800 Algoma Blvd., Oshkosh WI 54901. (920)424-2267. **E-mail:** wisconsinreview@uwosh.edu. **Website:** www.uwosh.edu/wisconsinreview. Estab. 1966. *Wisconsin Review*, published biannually, is a "contemporary poetry, prose, and art magazine run by students at the University of Wisconsin Oshkosh."

◐ *Wisconsin Review* is around 100 pages, digest-sized, perfect-bound, with 4-color glossy coverstock. Receives about 400 poetry submissions/year, accepts about 50; Press run is 1,000. Reading period: May through October for Spring issue; November through April for Fall issue.

NEEDS "Standard or experimental styles will be considered, although we look for outstanding characterization and unique themes." Submit via postal mail (include SASE) or online submission manager. There is a $2 reading fee for online submissions. Length: up to 15 pages, double-spaced with 12-point font.

PAYMENT/TERMS Pays 2 contributor's copies.

TIPS "We are open to any poetic form and style, and look for outstanding imagery, new themes, and fresh voices—poetry that induces emotions."

WITCHES AND PAGANS

BBI Media, Inc., P.O. Box 687, Forest Grove OR 97116. (503)430-8817. **E-mail:** editor2@bbimedia.com. **Website:** www.witchesandpagans.com. **Contact:** Anne Newkirk Niven. Estab. 2002. "Devoted exclusively to promoting and covering contemporary Pagan culture, *W&P* features exclusive interviews with the teachers, writers, and activists who create and lead our traditions, visits to the sacred places and people who inspire us, and in-depth discussions of our ever-evolving practices. You'll also find practical daily magic, ideas for solitary ritual and devotion, God/dess-friendly craft-projects, Pagan poetry and short fiction, reviews, and much more in every 88-page issue. *W&P* is available in either traditional paper copy sent by postal mail or as a digital PDF e-zine download that is compatible with most computers and readers."

NEEDS Does not want faction (fictionalized retellings of real events). Avoid gratuitous sex, violence, sentimentality, and pagan moralizing. Don't beat our readers with the Rede or the Threefold Law. Length: 1,000-5,000 words.

HOW TO CONTACT Send complete ms.

TIPS "Read the magazine, do your research, write the piece, send it in. That's really the only way to get started as a writer; everything else is window dressing."

WOMAN'S WORLD

Bauer Publishing, 270 Sylvan Ave., Englewood Cliffs NJ 07632. (201)569-6699. **Fax:** (201)569-3584. **E-mail:** dearww@womansworldmag.com. **E-mail:** wwfeatures@womansworldmag.com; circleofkindness@womansworldmag.com; moneysavingrecipe@womansworldmag.com; angels@womansworldmag.com; happiness@womansworldmag.com; loveandlaughter@womansworldmag.com. **Website:** www.womansworldmag.com. Estab. 1980. Publishes short romances and mini-mysteries for all women, ages 18-68.

◐ *Woman's World* is not looking for freelancers to take assigments generated by the staff, but it will assign stories to writers who have made a successful pitch.

NEEDS Wants romance and mainstream short stories of 800 words and mini-mysteries of 1,000 words. Each of story should have a light romantic theme and can be written from either a masculine or feminine point of view. Women characters may be single, married, or divorced. Plots must be fast moving with vivid dialogue and action. The problems and dilemmas inherent in them should be contemporary and realistic, handled with warmth and feeling. The stories must have a positive resolution. Specify Fiction on envelope. Always enclose SASE. Mini-mysteries may revolve around anything from a theft to murder. Not interested in sordid or grotesque crimes. Emphasis should be on intricacies of plot rather than gratuitous violence. The story must include a resolution that clearly states the villain is getting his or her come-uppance. Submit complete mss. Specify Mini-Mystery on envelope. Not interested in science fiction, fantasy, historical romance, or foreign locales. No explicit sex, graphic language, or steamy settings. Romances: 800 words; mysteries: 1,000 words.

HOW TO CONTACT Send complete ms.

PAYMENT/TERMS Pays $1,000.

TIPS The whole story should be sent when submitting fiction. Stories slanted for a particular holiday should be sent at least 6 months in advance. "Familiarize yourself totally with our format and style. Read at least a year's worth of *Woman's World* fiction. Analyze and dissect it. Regarding romances, scrutinize them not only for content but tone, mood, and sensibility."

WOODS READER

P.O. Box 46, Warren MN 56762. **E-mail:** editor@woodsreader.com. **Website:** www.woodsreader.com. **Contact:** S Sedgwick. Estab. 2017. A quarterly publication for those who love woodland areas: whether a public preserve, forest, tree farm, backyard woodlot or other patch of trees and wildlife. Will only consider articles based on woodlands. "We are looking for positive, whimsical, interesting articles. Our readers like to hear about others' experiences and insights. Please visit submissions page on website. We encourage stories of personal experience. We also buy forest ecology mss of general interest, DIY (photos must accompany), personal essays, book reviews (query first)."

NEEDS Short fiction based on woodland setting. Will buy longer fiction for serialization over four issues. Length: 500-2,000 words.

PAYMENT/TERMS Payment varies.

THE WORCESTER REVIEW

P.O. Box 804, Worcester MA 01613. **E-mail:** editor.worcreview@gmail.com. **Website:** www.theworcesterreview.org. **Contact:** Diane Vanaskie Mulligan, managing editor. Estab. 1972. *The Worcester Review*, published annually by the Worcester County Poetry Association, encourages "critical work with a New England connection; no geographic limitation on poetry and fiction." Wants "work that is crafted, intuitively honest and empathetic. We like high-quality, creative poetry, artwork, and fiction. Critical articles should be connected to New England." *The Worcester Review* is 160 pages, digest-sized, professionally printed in dark type on quality stock, perfect-bound, with matte card cover. Press run is 600.

NEEDS Accepts about 5% unsolicited mss. Length: 1,000-4,000 words. Average length: 2,000 words.

HOW TO CONTACT Send complete ms via online submissions manager. "Send only 1 short story—reading editors do not like to read 2 by the same author at the same time. We will use only 1."

PAYMENT/TERMS Pays 2 contributor's copies and honorarium if possible.

TIPS "We generally look for creative work with a blend of craftsmanship, insight, and empathy. This does not exclude humor. We won't print work that is shoddy in any of these areas."

💲 WORKERS WRITE!

Blue Cubicle Press, LLC, P.O. Box 250382, Plano TX 75025. **E-mail:** info@workerswritejournal.com. **Website:** www.workerswritejournal.com. **Contact:** David LaBounty, managing editor. Estab. 2005. "*Workers Write!* is an annual print journal published by Blue Cubicle Press, an independent publisher dedicated to giving voice to writers trapped in the daily grind. Each issue focuses on a particular workplace; check website for details. Submit your stories via e-mail or send a hard copy."

NEEDS "We need your stories (5,000-12,000 words) about the workplace from our Overtime series. Every 3 months, we'll release a chapbook containing 1-2 related stories that center on work." Length: 500-5,000 words.

HOW TO CONTACT Send complete ms.

PAYMENT/TERMS Payment: $5-50 (depending on length and rights requested).

THE WRITE PLACE AT THE WRITE TIME

E-mail: questions@thewriteplaceatthewritetime.org. **E-mail:** submissions@thewriteplaceatthewritetime.org. **Website:** www.thewriteplaceatthewritetime.org. **Contact:** Nicole M. Bouchard, editor-in-chief. Estab. 2008. Online literary magazine, published 3 times/year. Publishes fiction, personal nonfiction, craft essays by professionals, and poetry that "speaks to the heart and mind. Our writers come from around the world and range from previously unpublished to having written for *The New York Times, Time* magazine, *The New Yorker, The Wall Street Journal, Glimmer Train, Newsweek, Business Week*, Random House, and Simon and Schuster. Interview subjects include *NYT* best-selling authors such as Tracy Chevalier, Dennis Lehane, Mona Simpson, Janet Fitch, Alice Hoffman, Joanne Harris, Arthur Golden, Jodi Picoult, and Frances Mayes."

NEEDS Considers literary and most genre fiction if thought-provoking and emotionally evocative. No erotica, explicit horror/gore/violence, political. Length: up to 3,500 words. Average length of stories: 3,000 words. Average length of short-shorts: 1,000 words. "If we feel the strength of the submission merits added length, we are happy to consider exceptions."

HOW TO CONTACT Send complete ms with cover letter by e-mail—no attachments. Include estimated word count and brief bio. Accepts multiple submissions, up to 3 stories at a time. Accepts simultaneous submissions if indicated; other publications must be notified immediately upon acceptance. "If accepted elsewhere, we must be notified." Accepts 90-100 mss/year; receives 500-700 mss/year.

TIPS "Through our highly personalized approach to content, feedback, and community, we aim to give a very human visage to the publishing process. We wish to speak deeply of the human condition through pieces that validate the entire spectrum of emotions and the real circumstances of life. Every piece has a unique power and presence that stands on its own; we've had writers write about surviving an illness, losing a child, embracing a foreign land, learning of their parent's suicide, discovering love, finding humor in dark hours, and healing from abuse. Our collective voice, from our aesthetic to our artwork to the words, looks at and highlights aspects of life through a storytelling lens that allows for or promotes a universal understanding."

WRITER'S BLOC

MSC 162, Fore Hall Rm. 110, 700 University Blvd., Texas A&M University-Kingsville, Kingsville TX 78363. (361)593-2516. **E-mail:** kfmrj00@tamuk.edu; connie.salgado@tamuk.edu. **E-mail:** WritersBloc-LitMag@hotmail.com. **Website:** www.tamuk.edu/artsci/langlit/writers_bloc.html. **Contact:** Dr. Michelle Johnson Vela. *Writer's Bloc*, published annually, prints poetry, short fiction, flash fiction, one-act plays, interviews, and essays. "About half of our pages are devoted to the works of Texas A&M University-Kingsville students and half to the works of writers and artists from all over the world." Wants quality poetry; no restrictions on content or form.

○ *Writer's Bloc* is 96 pages, digest-sized. Press run is 300. Reading period: February through May.

NEEDS Submit via e-mail or postal mail. Include cover letter with contact info, short bio. Accepts about 6 mss/year. Publishes short shorts. Also publishes literary essays, poetry. No pornography, genre fiction, or work by children. Length: up to 3,500 words. Average length is 2,500 words.

PAYMENT/TERMS Pays 1 contributor's copy.

THE WRITING DISORDER

A Literary Journal, P.O. Box 93613, Los Angeles CA 90093. **E-mail:** submit@thewritingdisorder.com. **Website:** www.writingdisorder.com. **Contact:** C.E. Lukather, editor; Paul Garson, managing editor; Julianna Woodhead, poetry editor. Estab. 2009. "*The Writing Disorder* is an online literary journal devoted to literature, art, and culture. Our mission is to showcase new and emerging writers—particularly those in writing programs—as well as established ones. We feature new fiction, poetry, nonfiction and art. Although we strive to publish original and experimental work, *The Writing Disorder* remains rooted in the classic art of storytelling. Send us your best work. Have someone proof your work before submitting. No limit on word count."

NEEDS Does not want to see romance, religious, or fluff. No limit.

HOW TO CONTACT Query.

PAYMENT/TERMS Pays contributor's copies.

TIPS "We are looking for work from new writers, writers in writing programs, and students and faculty of all ages."

XAVIER REVIEW

Xavier University of Louisiana, 1 Drexel Dr., Box 89, New Orleans LA 70125-1098. **Website:** www.xula.edu/review. **Contact:** Ralph Adamo, editor. Estab. 1980. "*Xavier Review* accepts poetry, fiction, translations, creative nonfiction, and critical essays. Content focuses on African American, Caribbean, and Southern literature, as well as works that touch on issues of religion and spirituality. We do, however, accept quality work on all themes. (Please note: This is not a religious publication.)"

NEEDS Has published work by Andrei Codrescu, Terrance Hayes, Naton Leslie, and Patricia Smith. Also publishes literary essays and literary criticism.

HOW TO CONTACT Send complete ms. Include 2-3 sentence bio and SASE. "We rarely accepts mss over 20 pages."

PAYMENT/TERMS Pays 2 contributor's copies; offers 40% discount on additional copies.

THE YALE REVIEW

The Yale Review, P.O. Box 208243, New Haven CT 06520-8243. (203)432-0499. **Fax:** (203)432-0510. **Website:** www.yale.edu/yalereview. **Contact:** J.D. McClatchy, editor. Estab. 1911. "Like Yale's schools of music, drama, and architecture, like its libraries and art galleries, *The Yale Review* has helped give the University its leading place in American education. In a land of quick fixes and short view and in a time of increasingly commercial publishing, the journal has an authority that derives from its commitment to bold established writers and promising newcomers, to both challenging literary work and a range of essays and reviews that can explore the connections between academic disciplines and the broader movements in American society, thought, and culture. With independence and boldness, with a concern for issues and ideas, with a respect for the mind's capacity to be surprised by speculation and delighted by elegance, *The Yale Review* proudly continues into its third century."

HOW TO CONTACT Submit complete ms with SASE. All submissions should be sent to the editorial office.

PAYMENT/TERMS Pays $400-500.

THE YALOBUSHA REVIEW

University of Mississippi, **E-mail:** yreditors@gmail.com. **Website:** yr.olemiss.edu. Estab. 1995.

NEEDS Length: up to 5,000 words for short stories; up to 1,000 words for flash fiction.

HOW TO CONTACT Submit 1 short story or up to 3 pieces of flash fiction via online submissions manager.

YEMASSEE

University of South Carolina, Department of English, Columbia SC 29208. **E-mail:** editor@yemasseejournal.com. **Website:** yemasseejournal.com. Estab. 1993. "*Yemassee* is the University of South Carolina's literary journal. Our readers are interested in exceptional fiction, poetry, creative nonfiction, and visual art. We publish in the fall and spring. We tend to solicit reviews and interviews but welcome unsolicited queries. We do not favor any particular aesthetic or school of writing."

NEEDS "We are open to a variety of subjects and writing styles. Our essential consideration for acceptance is the quality of the work." No romance, religious/inspirational, young adult/teen, children's/juvenile, erotica. We want more experimental work. Length: up to 5,000 words.

HOW TO CONTACT Send complete ms. Submissions for all genres should include a cover letter that lists the titles of the pieces included, along with your contact information (including author's name, address, e-mail address, and phone number). Yemassee Short Fiction Contest: $750 award. Check website for deadline.

PAYMENT/TERMS Pays 2 contributor's copies.

ZEEK

A Jewish Journal of Thought and Culture, 125 Maiden Ln., 8th Floor, New York NY 10038. (212)453-9435. **E-mail:** zeek@zeek.net. **Website:** www.zeek.net. **Contact:** Erica Brody, editor in chief. Estab. 2001. *ZEEK* "relaunched in late February 2013 as a hub for the domestic Jewish social justice movement, one that showcases the people, ideas, and conversations driving an inclusive and diverse progressive Jewish community. At the same time, we've reaffirmed our commitment to building on *ZEEK*'s reputation for original, ahead-of-the-curve Jewish writing and arts, culture and spirituality content, incubating emerging voices and artists, as well as established ones." *ZEEK* seeks "great writing in a variety of styles and voices, original thinking, and accessible content. That means we're interested in hearing your ideas for first-person essays, reflections and commentary, reporting, profiles, Q&As, analysis, infographics, and more. For the near future, *ZEEK* will focus on domestic issues. Our discourse will be civil."

NEEDS "Calls for fiction submissions are issued periodically. Follow *ZEEK* on Twitter @ZEEKMag for announcements and details."

🆂 ZOETROPE: ALL-STORY

Zoetrope: All-Story, The Sentinel Bldg., 916 Kearny St., San Francisco CA 94133. **Website:** www.all-story.com. **Contact:** fiction editor. Estab. 1997. Quarterly magazine specializing in the best of contemporary short fiction. Winner of the National Magazine Award for Fiction as the finest literary publication in the United States.

NEEDS Length: up to 7,000 words. Excerpts from larger works, screenplays, treatments, and poetry will be returned unread.

HOW TO CONTACT Writers should submit only one story at a time. We do not accept artwork or design submissions. We do not accept unsolicited revisions nor respond to writers who don't include an SASE. Send complete ms by postal mail.

PAYMENT/TERMS Pays $1,000.

🆂 ZYZZYVA

57 Post St., Suite 604, San Francisco CA 94104. (415)757-0465. **E-mail:** editor@zyzzyva.org. **Website:** www.zyzzyva.org. **Contact:** Laura Cogan, editor; Oscar Villalon, managing editor. Estab. 1985. "Every issue is a vibrant mix of established talents and new voices, providing an elegantly curated overview of contemporary arts and letters with a distinctly San Francisco perspective."

🅞   Accepts submissions January 1-May 31 and August 1-November 30. Does not accept online submissions.

NEEDS Length: no limit.

HOW TO CONTACT Send complete ms by mail. Include SASE and contact information.

PAYMENT/TERMS Pays $50.

TIPS "We are not currently seeking work about any particular theme or topic; that said, reading recent issues is perhaps the best way to develop a sense for the length and quality we are looking for in submissions."

BOOK PUBLISHERS

///

In this section, you will find many of the "big name" book publishers. Many of these publishers remain tough markets for new writers or for those whose work might be considered literary or experimental. Indeed, some only accept work from established authors, and then often only through an author's agent. Although having your novel published by one of the big commercial publishers listed in this section is difficult, it is not impossible. The trade magazine *Publishers Weekly* regularly features interviews with writers whose first novels are being released by top publishers. Many editors at large publishing houses find great satisfaction in publishing a writer's first novel.

Also listed here are "small presses," which publish four or more titles annually. Included among them are independent presses, university presses, and other nonprofit publishers. Introducing new writers to the reading public has become an increasingly important role of these smaller presses at a time when the large conglomerates are taking fewer chances on unknown writers. Many of the successful small presses listed in this section have built their reputations and their businesses in this way and have become known for publishing prize-winning fiction.

These smaller presses also tend to keep books in print longer than larger houses. And, since small presses publish a smaller number of books, each title is equally important to the publisher and each is promoted in much the same way and with the same commitment. Editors also stay at small presses longer because they have more of a stake in the business—often they own the business. Many smaller book publishers are writers themselves and know firsthand the importance of a close editor-author or publisher-author relationship.

⊘ ABBEVILLE FAMILY

Abbeville Press, 116 W. 23rd St., New York NY 10011. (646)375-2136. **Fax:** (646)375-2359. **E-mail:** abbeville@abbeville.com. **Website:** www.abbeville.com. Estab. 1977. Our list is full for the next several seasons. *Not accepting unsolicited book proposals at this time.*

NEEDS Picture books: animal, anthology, concept, contemporary, fantasy, folktales, health, hi-lo, history, humor, multicultural, nature/environment, poetry, science fiction, special needs, sports, suspense. Average word length 300-1,000 words.

HOW TO CONTACT Please refer to website for submission policy.

ABDO PUBLISHING CO.

8000 W. 78th St., Suite 310, Edina MN 55439. (800)800-1312. **Fax:** (952)831-1632. **E-mail:** nonfiction@abdopublishing.com. **E-mail:** fiction@abdopublishing.com; illustrations@abdopublishing.com. **Website:** www.abdopublishing.com. Estab. 1985. ABDO publishes nonfiction children's books (prekindergarten to 8th grade) for school and public libraries—mainly history, sports, biography, geography, science, and social studies. "Please specify each submission as either nonfiction, fiction, or illustration. Publishes hardcover originals. Guidelines online.

ABINGDON PRESS

Imprint of The United Methodist Publishing House, 201 Eighth Ave. S., P.O. Box 801, Nashville TN 37202. (615)749-6000. **Fax:** (615)749-6512. **E-mail:** submissions@umpublishing.org. **Website:** www.abingdonpress.com. Estab. 1789. Abingdon Press, America's oldest theological publisher, provides an ecumenical publishing program dedicated to serving the Christian community—clergy, scholars, church leaders, musicians, and general readers—with quality resources in the areas of Bible study, the practice of ministry, theology, devotion, spirituality, inspiration, prayer, music and worship, reference, Christian education, and church supplies. Publishes hardcover and paperback originals. Book catalog available free. Guidelines online.

NEEDS Publishes stories of faith, hope, and love that encourage readers to explore life.

HOW TO CONTACT Agented submissions only for fiction.

TERMS Pays 7½% royalty on retail price. Responds in 2 months to queries.

ACADEMY CHICAGO PUBLISHERS

814 N. Franklin St., Chicago IL 60610. (312)337-0747. **Fax:** (312)337-5985. **Website:** www.chicagoreviewpress.com. **Contact:** Yuval Taylor, senior editor. Estab. 1975. "We publish quality fiction and nonfiction. Our audience is literate and discriminating. No novelized biography, history, or science fiction. No electronic submissions." Publishes hardcover and some paperback originals and trade paperback reprints. Book catalog online. Guidelines online.

NEEDS "We look for quality work, but we do not publish experimental, avant garde, horror, science fiction, thrillers novels."

HOW TO CONTACT Submit proposal package, synopsis, 3 sample chapters, and short bio.

TERMS Pays 7-10% royalty on wholesale price. Responds in 3 months.

TIPS "At the moment, we are looking for good nonfiction; we certainly want excellent original fiction, but we are swamped. No fax queries, no disks. No electronic submissions. We are always interested in reprinting good out-of-print books."

◐⊘ ACE SCIENCE FICTION AND FANTASY

Imprint of the Berkley Publishing Group, Penguin Group (USA), Inc., 375 Hudson St., New York NY 10014. (212)366-2000. **Website:** www.us.penguingroup.com. Estab. 1953. Ace publishes science fiction and fantasy exclusively. Publishes hardcover, paperback, and trade paperback originals and reprints.

⊙   As imprint of Penguin, Ace is not open to unsolicited submissions.

NEEDS No other genre accepted. No short stories.

HOW TO CONTACT Due to the high volume of manuscripts received, most Penguin Group (USA) Inc. imprints do not normally accept unsolicited mss.

TERMS Pays royalty. Pays advance.

⊘ ALADDIN

Simon & Schuster, 1230 Avenue of the Americas, 4th Floor, New York NY 10020. (212)698-7000. **Website:** www.simonandschuster.com. **Contact:** Acquisitions Editor. Aladdin publishes picture books, beginning readers, chapter books, middle grade and tween fiction and nonfiction, and graphic novels and nonfiction in hardcover and paperback, with an emphasis on commercial, kid-friendly titles. Publishes hardcover/

paperback originals and imprints of Simon & Schuster Children's Publishing Children's Division.

HOW TO CONTACT Simon & Schuster does not review, retain or return unsolicited materials or artwork. "We suggest prospective authors and illustrators submit their mss through a professional literary agent."

⊘ ALGONQUIN BOOKS OF CHAPEL HILL

Workman Publishing, P.O. Box 2225, Chapel Hill NC 27515-2225. (919)967-0108. **Website:** www.algonquin.com. **Contact:** Editorial Department. Algonquin Books publishes quality literary fiction and literary nonfiction. Publishes hardcover originals. Guidelines online.

HOW TO CONTACT Does not accept unsolicited submissions at this time.

🌑 ALLEN & UNWIN

406 Albert St., East Melbourne VIC 3002, Australia. (61)(3)9665-5000. **E-mail:** fridaypitch@allenandunwin.com. **Website:** www.allenandunwin.com. Allen & Unwin publish over 80 new books for children and young adults each year, many of these from established authors and illustrators. "However, we know how difficult it can be for new writers to get their work in front of publishers, which is why we've decided to extend our innovative and pioneering Friday Pitch service to emerging writers for children and young adults. Guidelines online.

AMBERJACK PUBLISHING

P.O. Box 4668 #89611, New York NY 10163. (888)959-3352. **Website:** www.amberjackpublishing.com. Amberjack Publishing offers authors the freedom to write without burdening them with having to promote the work themselves. They retain all rights. "You will have no rights left to exploit, so you cannot resell, republish or use your story again."

NEEDS Amberjack Publishing is always on the lookout for the next great story. "We are interested in fiction, children's books, graphic novels, science fiction, fantasy, humor, and everything in between."

HOW TO CONTACT Submit via online query form with book proposal and first 10 pages of ms.

AMERICAN QUILTER'S SOCIETY

5801 Kentucky Dam Rd., Paducah KY 42003. (270)898-7903. **Fax:** (270)898-1173. **Website:** www.americanquilter.com. Estab. 1984. American Quilter's Society publishes how-to and pattern books for quilters (beginners through intermediate skill level). We are not the publisher for non-quilters writing about quilts. We now publish quilt-related craft cozy romance and mystery titles, series only. Humor is good. Graphic depictions and curse words are bad. Publishes trade paperbacks. Guidelines online.

🌑 Accepts simultaneous nonfiction submissions. Does not accept simultaneous fiction submissions.

HOW TO CONTACT Submit a synopsis and 2 sample chapters, plus an outline of the next 2 books in the series.

TERMS Pays 5% royalty on retail price for both nonfiction and fiction. Responds in 2 months to proposals.

🅐⊘ AMULET BOOKS

Imprint of Abrams, 115 W. 18th St., 6th Floor, New York NY 10001. **Website:** www.amuletbooks.com. Estab. 2004. *Does not accept unsolicited mss or queries.*

NEEDS Middle readers: adventure, contemporary, fantasy, history, science fiction, sports. Young adults/teens: adventure, contemporary, fantasy, history, science fiction, sports, suspense.

🌑 ANDERSEN PRESS

20 Vauxhall Bridge Rd., London SW1V 2SA, United Kingdom. **E-mail:** andersoneditorial@penguinrandomhouse.co.uk. **Website:** www.andersenpress.co.uk. Andersen Press is a specialist children's publisher. "We publish picture books, for which the required text would be approximately 500 words (maximum 1,000), juvenile fiction for which the text would be approximately 3,000-5,000 words and older fiction up to 75,000 words. We do not publish adult fiction, nonfiction, poetry, or short story anthologies." Guidelines online.

HOW TO CONTACT Send all submissions by post: Query and full ms for picture books; synopsis and 3 chapters for longer fiction.

ANKERWYCKE

American Bar Association, 321 N. Clark St., Chicago IL 60654. **Website:** www.ababooks.org. Estab. 1878. In 1215, the Magna Carta was signed underneath the ancient Ankerwycke Yew tree, starting the process which led to rule by constitutional law—in effect, giving rights and the law to the people. And today, the ABA's Ankerwycke line of books continues to bring the law to the people. With legal fiction, true crime books, popular legal histories, public policy handbooks, and prescriptive guides to current legal and business issues, Ankerwycke is a contemporary and innovative line of books for everyone from a trusted and vested authority. Publishes hardcover and trade paperback originals. Book catalog and ms guidelines online.

NEEDS "We're actively acquiring legal fiction with extreme verisimilitude."

HOW TO CONTACT Query with cover letter; outline or TOC; and CV/bio including other credits. Include e-mail address for response.

TERMS Responds in 1 month to queries and proposals; 3 months to mss.

☻⊘ ANNICK PRESS, LTD.

15 Patricia Ave., Toronto ON M2M 1H9, Canada. (416)221-4802. **Fax:** (416)221-8400. **Website:** www.annickpress.com. **Contact:** The Editors. Annick Press maintains a commitment to high quality books that entertain and challenge. Our publications share fantasy and stimulate imagination, while encouraging children to trust their judgment and abilities. *Does not accept unsolicited mss.* Publishes picture books, juvenile and YA fiction and nonfiction; specializes in trade books. Book catalog and guidelines online.

NEEDS Publisher of children's books. Not accepting picture books at this time.

TERMS Pays authors royalty of 5-12% based on retail price. Offers advances (average amount: $3,000). Pays illustrators royalty of 5% minimum.

☻ ANVIL PRESS

P.O. Box 3008 MPO, Vancouver BC V6B 3X5, Canada. (604)876-8710. **Fax:** (604)879-2667. **E-mail:** info@anvilpress.com. **Website:** www.anvilpress.com. Estab. 1988. Anvil Press publishes contemporary adult fiction, poetry, and drama, giving voice to up-and-coming Canadian writers, exploring all literary genres, discovering, nurturing, and promoting new Canadian literary talent. Currently emphasizing urban/suburban themed fiction and poetry; de-emphasizing historical novels. Canadian authors only. No e-mail submissions. Publishes trade paperback originals. Book catalog for 9×12 SAE with 2 first-class stamps. Guidelines online.

NEEDS Contemporary, modern literature; no formulaic or genre.

HOW TO CONTACT Query with 20-30 pages and SASE.

TERMS Pays advance. Average advance is $500-2,000, depending on the genre. Responds in 2 months to queries; 6 months to mss.

TIPS "Audience is informed, educated, aware, with an opinion, culturally active (films, books, the performing arts). No U.S. authors. Research the appropriate publisher for your work."

ARBORDALE PUBLISHING

612 Johnnie Dodds, Suite A2, Mt. Pleasant SC 29464. (843)971-6722. **Fax:** (843)216-3804. **E-mail:** submissions@arbordalepublishing.com. **Website:** www.arbordalepublishing.com. **Contact:** Acquisitions Editor. Estab. 2004. "The picture books we publish are usually, but not always, fictional stories with nonfiction woven into the story that relate to science or math. All books should subtly convey an educational theme through a warm story that is fun to read and that will grab a child's attention. Each book has a 4-page *'For Creative Minds'* section to reinforce the educational component. This section will have a craft and/or game as well as 'fun facts' to be shared by the parent, teacher, or other adult. Authors do not need to supply this information with their submission, but if their ms is accepted, they may be asked to provide additional information for this section. Mss should be less than 1,000 words and meet all of the following 4 criteria: fun to read—mostly fiction with nonfiction facts woven into the story; national or regional in scope; must tie into early elementary school curriculum; must be marketable through a niche market such as a zoo, aquarium, or museum gift shop." Publishes hardcover, trade paperback, and electronic originals. Book catalog and guidelines online.

NEEDS Picture books: animal, folktales, nature/environment, science- or math-related. No more than 1,000 words.

HOW TO CONTACT All mss should be submitted via e-mail to Katie Hall. Mss should be less than 1,000 words.

TERMS Pays 6-8% royalty on wholesale price. Pays small advance. Accepts electronic submissions only. Snail mail submissions are discarded without being opened.

Acknowledges receipt of ms submission within 1 month.

TIPS "Please make sure that you have looked at our website to read our complete submission guidelines and to see if we are looking for a particular subject.

Manuscripts must meet all four of our stated criteria. We look for fairly realistic, bright and colorful art-no cartoons. We want the children excited about the books. We envision the books being used at home and in the classroom."

ARCADE PUBLISHING

Skyhorse Publishing, 307 W. 36th St., 11th Floor, New York NY 10018. (212)643-6816. **Fax:** (212)643-6819. **E-mail:** arcadesubmissions@skyhorsepublishing.com. **Website:** www.arcadepub.com. **Contact:** Acquisitions Editor. Estab. 1988. Arcade prides itself on publishing top-notch literary nonfiction and fiction, with a significant proportion of foreign writers. Publishes hardcover originals, trade paperback reprints. Book catalog and ms guidelines for #10 SASE.

NEEDS No romance, historical, science fiction.

HOW TO CONTACT Submit proposal with brief query, 1-2 page synopsis, chapter outline, market analysis, sample chapter, bio.

TERMS Pays royalty on retail price and 10 author's copies. Pays advance. Responds in 2 months if interested.

ARCHAIA

Imprint of Boom! Studios, 5670 Wilshire Blvd., Suite 450, Los Angeles CA 90036. **Website:** www.archaia.com. Use online submission form.

NEEDS Looking for graphic novel submissions that include finished art. "Archaia is a multi-award-winning graphic novel publisher with more than 75 renowned publishing brands, including such domestic and international hits as *Artesia, Mouse Guard*, and a line of Jim Henson graphic novels including *Fraggle Rock* and *The Dark Crystal*. Publishes creator-shared comic books and graphic novels in the adventure, fantasy, horror, pulp noir, and science fiction genres that contain idiosyncratic and atypical writing and art. *Archaia does not generally hire freelancers or arrange for freelance work, so submissions should only be for completed book and series proposals.*"

ARCH STREET PRESS

1122 County Line Rd., Bryn Mawr PA 19010. (877)732-ARCH. **E-mail:** contact@archstreetpress.org. **Website:** www.archstreetpress.org. **Contact:** Robert Rimm, managing editor. Estab. 2010. Arch Street Press is an independent nonprofit publisher dedicated to the collaborative work of creative visionaries, social entrepreneurs and leading scholars worldwide. Arch Street Press is part of the Institute for Leadership Education, Advancement and Development, a Pennsylvania-based 501(c)(3) nonprofit with offices in Philadelphia and Bryn Mawr. It has served as a key force for community leadership development since 1995, fostering a degreed citizenry to tangibly improve and sustain the economic, civic and social well-being of communities throughout the United States. Please visit our website, www.archstreetpress.org, for further information, including our Innovate podcast series with international CEOs and leaders, current and upcoming books, wide-ranging blog et al. Publishes hardcover, trade paperback, mass market paperback, and electronic originals. Book catalog and guidelines online.

HOW TO CONTACT Query with SASE. Submit proposal package, including outline and 3 sample chapters.

TERMS Pays 6-20% royalty on retail price. Responds in 1-2 months.

ARROW PUBLICATIONS, LLC

7716 Bells Mill Rd., Bethesda MD 20817. (301)299-9422. **Fax:** (240)632-8477. **E-mail:** arrow_info@arrowpub.com. **Website:** www.arrowpub.com. **Contact:** Tom King, managing editor. Estab. 1987. No graphic novels until further notice. Guidelines online.

NEEDS "We are looking for outlines of stories heavy on romance with elements of adventure/intrigue/mystery. We will consider other romance genres such as fantasy, western, inspirational, and historical as long as the romance element is strong."

HOW TO CONTACT Query with outline first with SASE. Consult submission guidelines online before submitting.

TERMS Makes outright purchase of accepted completed scripts. Responds in 2 month to queries; 1 month to mss sent upon request.

TIPS "Our audience is primarily women 18 and older. Send query with outline only."

☉ ARSENAL PULP PRESS

#202-211 East Georgia St., Vancouver BC V6A 1Z6, Canada. (604)687-4233. **Fax:** (604)687-4283. **E-mail:** info@arsenalpulp.com. **Website:** www.arsenalpulp.com. **Contact:** Editorial Board. Estab. 1980. "We are interested in literature that traverses uncharted territories, publishing books that challenge and stimulate and ask probing questions about the world around us."

Publishes trade paperback originals, and trade paperback reprints. Book catalog for 9×12 SAE with IRCs or online. Guidelines online.

NEEDS No children's books or genre fiction, i.e., westerns, romance, horror, mystery, etc.

HOW TO CONTACT Submit proposal package, outline, clips, 2-3 sample chapters.

TERMS Responds in 2-4 months.

ARTE PUBLICO PRESS

University of Houston, 4902 Gulf Fwy, Bldg 19, Rm 100, Houston TX 77204-2004. **Fax:** (713)743-2847. **E-mail:** submapp@uh.edu. **Website:** artepublicopress.com. Estab. 1979. Arte Publico Press is the oldest and largest publisher of Hispanic literature for children and adults in the United States. "We are a showcase for Hispanic literary creativity, arts and culture. Our endeavor is to provide a national forum for U.S.-Hispanic literature." Publishes hardcover originals, trade paperback originals and reprints. Book catalog available free. Guidelines online.

NEEDS "Written by U.S.-Hispanics."

HOW TO CONTACT Submissions made through online submission form.

TERMS Pays 10% royalty on wholesale price. Provides 20 author's copies; 40% discount on subsequent copies. Pays $1,000-3,000 advance. Responds in 1 month to queries and proposals; 4 months to mss.

TIPS "Include cover letter in which you 'sell' your book—why should we publish the book, who will want to read it, why does it matter, etc. Use our ms submission online form. Format files accepted are: Word, plain/text, rich/text files. Other formats will not be accepted. Manuscript files cannot be larger than 5MB. Once editors review your ms, you will receive an e-mail with the decision. Revision process could take up to 4 months."

ASABI PUBLISHING

Asabi Publishing, **E-mail:** submissions@asabipublishing.com. **Website:** www.asabipublishing.com. **Contact:** Tressa Sanders, publisher. Estab. 2004. Publishes hardcover, mass market and trade paperback originals. Book catalog online. Guidelines online.

NEEDS "We will only consider publishing a fiction title if it is a part of a series." The series should not already exist (except for the first unpublished title). There should be a plan/outline for at least two more titles in the series beyond the initial title. Does not

want anything religious or spiritual, astrology, ghosts, aliens, vampires or werewolves.

HOW TO CONTACT Submit professional query letter.

TERMS Pays 40% royalty on wholesale or list price. Pays up to $500 advance. Responds in 1 month to queries and proposals, 2-6 months to mss.

⊘⊘ ATHENEUM BOOKS FOR YOUNG READERS

Simon & Schuster, 1230 Avenue of the Americas, New York NY 10020. **Website:** kids.simonandschuster.com. Estab. 1961. Publishes hardcover originals. Guidelines for #10 SASE.

NEEDS All in juvenile versions. "We have few specific needs except for books that are fresh, interesting and well written. Fad topics are dangerous, as are works you haven't polished to the best of your ability. We also don't need safety pamphlets, ABC books, coloring books and board books. In writing picture book texts, avoid the coy and 'cutesy,' such as stories about characters with alliterative names." Agented submissions only. No paperback romance-type fiction.

TIPS "Study our titles."

AUTUMN HOUSE PRESS

5530 Penn Ave., Pittsburgh PA 15206. (412)362-2665. **E-mail:** info@autumnhouse.org. **Website:** www.autumnhouse.org. **Contact:** Christine Stroud, editor-in-chief. Estab. 1998. A nonprofit literary publisher, Autumn House Press was launched in 1998 when prominent American publishers, driven by economic concerns, dramatically reduced their poetry lists. Since our launch, Autumn House has expanded to publish fiction (2008) and nonfiction titles (2010). These books receive the same attention to design and manufacturing as our award-winning poetry titles. Autumn House publications have received a great deal of recognition and acclaim. In 2011, we earned a Certificate of Appreciation from the Pennsylvania legislature recognizing our contribution to the arts. Our books are regularly reviewed in *Ploughshares*, *Brevity*, *London Grip Review*, *The Women's Review of Books*, *The Jewish Review of Books*, and *Poets Quarterly*. Many of our poems have been featured in *The New York Times Magazine*, on *The Writer's Almanac*, and Ted Kooser's *American Life in Poetry*. Our titles also circulate within the local Pittsburgh community, with reviews in *The Pittsburgh City Paper* and *The Pittsburgh Post-Gazette*. Our books have won numerous awards over the years, such as *Love for Sale and Other Essays* by Clifford Thompson, which won the 2013 Whiting Award. Publishes trade paperback and electronic originals. Format: acid-free paper; offset printing. Catalog online. Guidelines online.

HOW TO CONTACT Submit through our annual contest or open-call period. See guidelines online.

TERMS Pays 7% royalty on wholesale price. Pays $0-2,500 advance. Responds in 1-3 days on queries and proposals; 3 months on mss.

TIPS "Though we are open to all styles of poetry, fiction, and nonfiction, we suggest you familiarize yourself with previous Autumn House publications before submitting. We are committed not just to publishing the prominent voices of our age, but also to publishing first books and lesser-known authors who will become the important writers of their generation. Many of our past winners have been first-book authors. We encourage writers from all backgrounds to submit; it is our goal at Autumn House to develop a rich and varied literary tradition."

AVON ROMANCE

Harper Collins Publishers, 10 E. 53 St., New York NY 10022. **E-mail:** info@avonromance.com. **Website:** www.avonromance.com. Estab. 1941. Avon has been publishing award-winning books since 1941. It is recognized for having pioneered the historical romance category and continues to bring the best of commercial literature to the broadest possible audience. Publishes paperback and digital originals and reprints.

HOW TO CONTACT Submit a query and ms via the online submission form.

BAEN BOOKS

P.O. Box 1188, Wake Forest NC 27588. (919)570-1640. **E-mail:** info@baen.com. **Website:** www.baen.com. Estab. 1983. "We publish only science fiction and fantasy. Writers familiar with what we have published in the past will know what sort of material we are most likely to publish in the future: powerful plots with solid scientific and philosophical underpinnings are the sine qua non for consideration for science fiction submissions. As for fantasy, any magical system must be both rigorously coherent and integral to the plot, and overall the work must at least strive for originality."

NEEDS "Style: Simple is generally better; in our opinion good style, like good breeding, never calls attention to itself. Length: 100,000-130,000 words Generally we are uncomfortable with manuscripts under 100,000 words, but if your novel is really wonderful send it along regardless of length."

HOW TO CONTACT "Query letters are not necessary. We prefer to see complete manuscripts accompanied by a synopsis. We prefer not to see simultaneous submissions. Electronic submissions are strongly preferred. *We no longer accept submissions by e-mail.* Send ms by using the submission form at: http://ftp.baen.com/Slush/submit.aspx. No disks unless requested. Attach ms as a Rich Text Format (.rtf) file. Any other format will not be considered."

TERMS Responds to mss within 12-18 months.

BAEN PUBLISHING ENTERPRISES

P.O. Box 1188, Wake Forest NC 27588. (919)570-1640. **E-mail:** info@baen.com; toni@baen.com. **Website:** www.baen.com. Estab. 1983. Publishes hardcover, trade paperback and mass market paperback originals and reprints. Book catalog available free. Guidelines online.

HOW TO CONTACT Submit synopsis and complete ms. "Electronic submissions are strongly preferred. Attach manuscript as a Rich Text Format (.rtf) file. Any other format will not be considered." Additional submission guidelines online. Include estimated word count, brief bio. Send SASE or IRC. Responds in 9-12 months. No simultaneous submissions. Sometimes comments on rejected mss.

TERMS Responds in 9-12 months to mss.

TIPS "Keep an eye and a firm hand on the overall story you are telling. Style is important but less important than plot. Good style, like good breeding, never calls attention to itself. Read *Writing to the Point*, by Algis Budrys. We like to maintain long-term relationships with authors."

BAILIWICK PRESS

309 East Mulberry St., Fort Collins CO 80524. (970)672-4878. **Fax:** (970)672-4731. **E-mail:** info@bailiwickpress.com. **E-mail:** aldozelnick@gmail.com. **Website:** www.bailiwickpress.com. "We're a micro-press that produces books and other products that inspire and tell great stories. Our motto is 'books with something to say.' We are now considering submissions, agented and unagented, for children's and young adult fiction. We're looking for smart, funny, and layered writing that kids will clamor for. Authors who already have a following have a leg up. We are only looking for humorous children's fiction. Please do not submit work for adults. Illustrated fiction is de-

sired but not required. (Illustrators are also invited to send samples.) Make us laugh out loud, ooh and aah, and cry, 'Eureka!'"

HOW TO CONTACT "Please read the Aldo Zelnick series to determine if we might be on the same page, then fill out our submission form. Please do not send submissions via snail mail or phone calls. You must complete the online submission form to be considered. If, after completing and submitting the form, you also need to send us an e-mail attachment (such as sample illustrations or excerpts of graphics), you may e-mail them to aldozelnick@gmail.com."

TERMS Responds in 6 months.

Ⓐ BALLANTINE BOOKS

Imprint of Penguin Random House, Inc., 1745 Broadway, 18th Floor, New York NY 10019. (212)782-9000. **Website:** www.penguinrandomhouse.com. Estab. 1952. Ballantine Bantam Dell publishes a wide variety of nonfiction and fiction. Publishes hardcover, trade paperback, mass market paperback originals. Guidelines online.

HOW TO CONTACT Agented submissions only.

Ⓐ BALZER & BRAY

HarperCollins Children's Books, 10 E. 53rd St., New York NY 10022. **Website:** www.harpercollinschildrens.com. Estab. 2008. "We publish bold, creative, groundbreaking picture books and novels that appeal directly to kids in a fresh way."

NEEDS Picture Books, Young Readers: adventure, animal, anthology, concept, contemporary, fantasy, history, humor, multicultural, nature/environment, poetry, science fiction, special needs, sports, suspense. Middle readers, young adults/teens: adventure, animal, anthology, contemporary, fantasy, history, humor, multicultural, nature/environment, poetry, science fiction, special needs, sports, suspense.

HOW TO CONTACT Agented submissions only.

TERMS Offers advances. Pays illustrators by the project.

Ⓐ BANCROFT PRESS

P.O. Box 65360, Baltimore MD 21209-9945. (410)358-0658. **Fax:** (410)764-1967. **E-mail:** bruceb@bancroftpress.com. **Website:** www.bancroftpress.com. **Contact:** Bruce Bortz, editor/publisher (memoirs, health, investment, politics, history, humor, literary novels, mystery/thrillers, chick lit, young adult). Estab. 1992. "Bancroft Press is a general trade publisher. Our only

mandate is 'books that enlighten.' Our most recent emphasis, with 'The Missing Kennedy' and 'Both Sides of the Line,' has been on memoirs." Publishes hardcover and trade paperback originals as well as e-books and audiobooks. Guidelines online.

HOW TO CONTACT Submit complete ms.

TERMS Pays 8-15% royalty on retail price. Pays $750-2,500 advances. Responds in 6-12 months.

TIPS "We advise writers to visit our website and to be familiar with our previous work. Patience is the number one attribute contributors must have. It takes us a very long time to get through submitted material, because we are such a small company. Also, we only publish 4-6 books per year, so it may take a long time for your optioned book to be published. We like to be able to market our books to be used in schools and in libraries. We prefer fiction that bucks trends and moves in a new direction. We are especially interested in mysteries and humor (especially humorous mysteries)."

Ⓐ⊘ BANTAM BOOKS

Imprint of Penguin Random House, Inc., 1745 Broadway, New York NY 10019. (212)782-9000. **Website:** www.randomhousebooks.com. *Not seeking mss at this time.*

⊘ BARBOUR PUBLISHING, INC.

P.O. Box 719, Urichsville OH 44683. **E-mail:** submissions@barbourbooks.com. **Website:** www.barbourbooks.com. Estab. 1981. "Barbour Books publishes inspirational/devotional material that is nondenominational and evangelical in nature. We're a Christian evangelical publisher." Specializes in short, easy-to-read Christian bargain books. "Faithfulness to the Bible and Jesus Christ are the bedrock values behind every book Barbour's staff produces."

Ｑ "We no longer accept unsolicited submissions unless they are submitted through professional literary agencies. For more information, we encourage new fiction authors to join a professional writers organization like American Christian Fiction Writers."

FREDERIC C. BEIL, PUBLISHER, INC.

609 Whitaker St., Savannah GA 31401. (912)233-2446. **E-mail:** fcb@beil.com. **Website:** www.beil.com. **Contact:** Frederic Beil. Estab. 1982. Beil publishes books in the fields of biography, history, and fiction. While under way, Beil has published authors of meaningful

works and adhered to high standards in bookmaking craftsman. Publishes original titles in hardcover, softcover, and e-book. Catalog online. Upon agreement with author, Beil will provide guidelines to author.

HOW TO CONTACT Query with SASE.

TERMS Pays 7.5% royalty on retail price. Does not pay advance. Responds in 1 week to queries.

TIPS "Our objectives are to offer carefully selected texts, to adhere to high standards in the choice of materials and in bookmaking craftsmanship; to produce books that exemplify good taste in format and design; and to maintain the lowest cost consistent with quality."

BELLEBOOKS

P.O. Box 300921, Memphis TN 38130. (901)344-9024. **Fax:** (901)344-9068. **E-mail:** bellebooks@bellebooks. com. **Website:** www.bellebooks.com. Estab. 1999. BelleBooks began by publishing Southern fiction. It has become a "second home" for many established authors, who also continue to publish with major publishing houses. Guidelines online.

NEEDS "Yes, we'd love to find the next Harry Potter, but our primary focus for the moment is publishing for the teen market."

HOW TO CONTACT Query e-mail with brief synopsis and credentials/credits with full ms attached (RTF format preferred).

TIPS "Our list aims for the teen reader and the crossover market. If you're a 'Southern Louise Rennison,' that would catch our attention. Humor is always a plus. We'd love to see books featuring teen boys as protagonists. We're happy to see dark edgy books on serious subjects."

BELLEVUE LITERARY PRESS

Dept. of Medicine, NYU School of Medicine, 550 First Ave., OBV 612, New York NY 10016. (212)263-7802. **E-mail:** blpsubmissions@gmail.com. **Website:** blpress.org. **Contact:** Erika Goldman, publisher/editorial director. Estab. 2005. "Bellevue Literary Press is devoted to publishing literary fiction and nonfiction at the intersection of the arts and sciences because we believe that science and the humanities are natural companions for understanding the human experience. With each book we publish, our goal is to foster a rich, interdisciplinary dialogue that will forge new tools for thinking and engaging with the world." Guidelines available.

HOW TO CONTACT Submit complete ms.

TIPS "We are a project of New York University's School of Medicine and while our standards reflect NYU's excellence in scholarship, humanistic medicine, and science, our authors need not be affiliated with NYU. We are not a university press and do not receive any funding from NYU. Our publishing operations are financed exclusively by foundation grants, private donors, and book sales revenue."

🅐⊘ BERKLEY

Penguin Group (USA) Inc., 375 Hudson St., New York NY 10014. **Website:** penguin.com. Estab. 1955. The Berkley Publishing Group publishes a variety of general nonfiction and fiction including the traditional categories of romance, mystery and science fiction. Publishes paperback and mass market originals and reprints.

⊝   "Due to the high volume of manuscripts received, most Penguin Group (USA) Inc. imprints do not normally accept unsolicited mss. The preferred and standard method for having mss considered for publication by a major publisher is to submit them through an established literary agent."

NEEDS No occult fiction.

HOW TO CONTACT Prefers agented submissions.

⊘ BETHANY HOUSE PUBLISHERS

Division of Baker Publishing Group, 6030 E. Fulton Rd., Ada MI 49301. (616)676-9185. **Fax:** (616)676-9573. **Website:** bakerpublishinggroup.com/bethanyhouse. Estab. 1956. Bethany House Publishers specializes in books that communicate Biblical truth and assist people in both spiritual and practical areas of life. Considers unsolicited work only through a professional literary agent or through manuscript submission services, Authonomy or Christian Manuscript Submissions. Guidelines online. *All unsolicited mss returned unopened.* Publishes hardcover and trade paperback originals, mass market paperback reprints. Book catalog for 9 x 12 envelope and 5 first-class stamps.

TERMS Pays royalty on net price. Pays advance. Responds in 3 months to queries.

TIPS "Bethany House Publishers' publishing program relates Biblical truth to all areas of life—whether in the framework of a well-told story, of a challenging book for spiritual growth, or of a Bible reference work.

We are seeking high-quality fiction and nonfiction that will inspire and challenge our audience."

🅐🛇 BEYOND WORDS PUBLISHING, INC.

20827 NW Cornell Rd., Suite 500, Hillsboro OR 97124. (503)531-8700. **Fax:** (503)531-8773. **E-mail:** info@beyondword.com. **Website:** www.beyondword.com. **Contact:** Submissions Department (for agents only). Estab. 1984. "At this time, we are not accepting any unsolicited queries or proposals, and recommend that all authors work with a literary agent in submitting their work." Publishes hardcover and trade paperback originals and paperback reprints.

HOW TO CONTACT Agent should submit query letter with proposal, including author bio, 5 sample chapters, complete synopsis of book, market analysis, SASE.

BILINGUAL REVIEW PRESS

Hispanic Research Center, Arizona State University, P.O. Box 875303, Tempe AZ 85287-5303. (480)965-3867. **Fax:** (480)965-0315. **E-mail:** brp@asu.edu. **Website:** www.asu.edu/brp. **Contact:** Gary Francisco Keller, publisher. Estab. 1973. "We are always on the lookout for Chicano, Puerto Rican, Cuban American, or other U.S. Hispanic themes with strong and serious literary qualities and distinctive and intellectually important topics."

HOW TO CONTACT Query with SASE. Query should describe book, plot summary, sample chapter, and any other information relevant to the rationale, content, audience, etc., for the book.

TERMS Responds in 3-4 weeks for queries; 3-4 months on requested mss.

TIPS "Writers should take the utmost care in assuring that their manuscripts are clean, grammatically impeccable, and have perfect spelling. This is true not only of the English but the Spanish as well. All accent marks need to be in place as well as other diacritical marks. When these are missing it's an immediate first indication that the author does not really know Hispanic culture and is not equipped to write about it. We are interested in publishing creative literature that treats the U.S Hispanic experience in a distinctive, creative, revealing way. The kind of books that we publish we keep in print for a very long time irrespective of sales. We are busy establishing and preserving a U.S. Hispanic canon of creative literature."

🛇 BIRCH BOOK PRESS

Birch Brook Impressions, P.O. Box 81, Delhi NY 13753. **Fax:** (607)746-7453. **E-mail:** birchbrook@copper.net. **Website:** www.birchbrookpress.info. **Contact:** Tom Tolnay, editor/publisher; Leigh Eckmair, art & research editor; Joyce Tolnay, account services. Estab. 1982. Birch Brook Press "is a book printer/typesetter/designer that uses monies from these activities to publish several titles of its own each year with cultural and literary interest." Specializes in literary work, fly-fishing, baseball, outdoors, themed short fiction anthologies, and books about books. *Not considering any new mss in the foreseeable future.* Occasionally publishes trade paperback originals. Book catalog online.

NEEDS "Mostly we do anthologies around a particular theme generated inhouse. We make specific calls for fiction when we are doing an anthology." Currently, BBP is not seeking manuscripts on any subject. Overstocked.

HOW TO CONTACT *Not currently accepting any submissions.*

TERMS Pays modest royalty on acceptance. Responds in 3-6 months.

TIPS "Write well on subjects of interest to BBP, such as outdoors, flyfishing, baseball, music, literary stories, fine poetry, books about books."

BKMK PRESS

University of Missouri - Kansas City, 5101 Rockhill Rd., Kansas City MO 64110-2499. (816)235-2558. **Fax:** (816)235-2611. **E-mail:** bkmk@umkc.edu. **Website:** newletters.org/bkmk. Estab. 1971. "BkMk Press publishes fine literature. Reading period February-June." Publishes trade paperback originals. Guidelines online.

HOW TO CONTACT Query with SASE.

TERMS Responds in 4-6 months to queries.

TIPS "We skew toward readers of literature, particularly contemporary writing. Because of our limited number of titles published per year, we discourage apprentice writers or 'scattershot' submissions."

BLACK LAWRENCE PRESS

E-mail: editors@blacklawrencepress.com. **Website:** www.blacklawrencepress.com. **Contact:** Diane Goettel, executive editor. Estab. 2003. Black Lawrence press seeks to publish intriguing books of literature— novels, short story collections, poetry collections, chapbooks, anthologies, and creative nonfiction. Will also publish the occasional translation from German. Publishes 22-24 books/year, mostly poetry and fiction. Mss are selected through open submission and competition. Books are 20-400 pages, offset-printed or high-quality POD, perfect-bound, with 4-color cover.

HOW TO CONTACT Submit complete ms.

TERMS Pays royalties. Responds in 6 months to mss.

⊘ BLACK LYON PUBLISHING, LLC

P.O. Box 567, Baker City OR 97814. **E-mail:** info@blacklyonpublishing.com. **E-mail:** queries@blacklyonpublishing.com. **Website:** www.blacklyonpublishing.com. **Contact:** The Editors. Estab. 2007. "Black Lyon Publishing is a small, independent publisher. We are currently closed to all except existing Black Lyon authors through 2017." Publishes paperback and e-book originals. Guidelines online.

BLACK ROSE WRITING

P.O. Box 1540, Castroville TX 78009. **E-mail:** creator@blackrosewriting.com. **Website:** www.blackrosewriting.com/home. **Contact:** Reagan Rothe. Estab. 2006. Black Rose Writing is an independent publishing house that strongly believes in developing a personal relationship with their authors. The Texas-based publishing company doesn't see authors as clients or just another number on a page, but rather as individual people.. people who deserve an honest review of their material and to be paid traditional royalties without ever paying any fees to be published. Publishes fiction, nonfiction, and illustrated children's books. Book catalog online. Guidelines online.

HOW TO CONTACT "Our preferred submission method is via Authors.me, please click 'Submit Here' on our website."

TERMS Royalties start at 20%, e-book royalties 25% Responds in 3-6 weeks on queries; 3-6 months on mss.

BLACK VELVET SEDUCTIONS PUBLISHING

E-mail: ric@blackvelvetseductions.com. **E-mail:** submissions@blackvelvetseductions.com. **Website:** www.blackvelvetseductions.com. **Contact:** Richard Savage, CEO. Estab. 2005. "We publish across a wide range of romance sub-genres, from soft sweet romance to supernatural romance, domestic discipline to highly erotic romance stories containing D/s and BDSM relationships. We are looking for authors who take something ordinary and make it extraordinary. We want stories with well-developed multi-dimensional characters with back-stories, a high degree of emo-

tional impact, with strong sexual tension between the heroine and hero, and stories that contain strong internal conflict. We prefer stories told in the third person viewpoint, but will consider first person narratives. We put the emphasis on romance, rather than just the erotic. Although we will consider a high level of erotic content, it needs to be in the context of a romance story line. The plots may twist and turn and be full of passion, but please remember that our audience likes a happy ending. Do not be afraid to approach us with a non-traditional character or plot." Publishes trade paperback and electronic originals and reprints. Catalog free or online. Guidelines online.

NEEDS All stories must have a strong romance element. "There are very few sexual taboos in our erotic line. We tend to give our authors the widest latitude. If it is safe, sane, and consensual we will allow our authors latitude to show us the eroticism. However, we will not consider manuscripts with any of the following: bestiality (sex with animals), necrophilia (sex with dead people), pedophillia (sex with children)."

HOW TO CONTACT Only accepts electronic submissions.

TERMS Pays 10% royalty for paperbacks; 50% royalty for electronic books. Responds as swiftly as possible

TIPS "We publish romance and erotic romance. We look for books written in very deep point of view. Shallow point of view remains the number one reason we reject manuscripts in which the storyline generally works."

JOHN F. BLAIR, PUBLISHER

1406 Plaza Dr., Winston-Salem NC 27103. (336)768-1374. **Fax:** (336)768-9194. **E-mail:** editorial@blairpub.com. **Website:** www.blairpub.com. **Contact:** Carolyn Sakowski, president. Estab. 1954. No poetry, young adult, children's, science fiction. Fiction must be set in southern U.S. or author must have strong Southern connection. Catalog online. Guidelines online.

NEEDS "We specialize in regional books, with an emphasis on nonfiction categories such as history, travel, folklore, and biography. We publish only one or two works of fiction each year. Fiction submitted to us should have some connection with the Southeast. We do not publish children's books, poetry, or category fiction such as romances, science fiction, or spy thrillers. We do not publish collections of short stories, essays, or newspaper columns." Does not want fiction set outside southern U.S.

HOW TO CONTACT Accepts unsolicited mss. Any fiction submitted should have some connection with the Southeast, either through setting or author's background. Send a cover letter, giving a synopsis of the book. Include the first 2 chapters (at least 50 pages) of the ms. "You may send the entire ms if you wish. If you choose to send only samples, please include the projected word length of your book and estimated completion date in your cover letter. Send a biography of the author, including publishing credits and credentials."

TERMS Pays royalties. Pays negotiable advance. Responds in 3-6 months.

TIPS "We are primarily interested in nonfiction titles. Most of our titles have a tie-in with North Carolina or the southeastern United States, we do not accept short story collections. Please enclose a cover letter and outline with the ms. We prefer to review queries before we are sent complete mss. Queries should include an approximate word count."

BLAZEVOX [BOOKS]

131 Euclid Ave., Kenmore NY 14217. **E-mail:** editor@blazevox.org. **Website:** www.blazevox.org. **Contact:** Geoffrey Gatza, editor/publisher. Estab. 2005. "We are a major publishing presence specializing in innovative fictions and wide-ranging fields of innovative forms of poetry and prose. Our goal is to publish works that are challenging, creative, attractive, and yet affordable to individual readers. Articles of submission depend on many criteria, but overall items submitted must conform to one ethereal trait, your work must not suck. This put plainly, bad art should be punished; we will not promote it. However, all submissions will be reviewed and the author will receive feedback. We are human too." Guidelines online.

NEEDS Submit complete ms via e-mail.

TERMS Pays 10% royalties on fiction and poetry books, based on net receipts. This amount may be split across multiple contributors. "We do not pay advances."

TIPS "We actively contract and support authors who tour, read and perform their work, play an active part of the contemporary literary scene, and seek a readership."

BLIND EYE BOOKS

1141 Grant St., Bellingham WA 98225. **E-mail:** editor@blindeyebooks.com. **Website:** www.blindeyebooks.com. **Contact:** Nicole Kimberling, editor. Estab. 2007. "Blind Eye Books publishes science fiction, fantasy and paranormal romance novels featuring gay or lesbian protagonists. We do not publish short story collections, poetry, erotica, horror or nonfiction. We would hesitate to publish any manuscript that is less than 70,000 or over 150,000 words." Guidelines online.

HOW TO CONTACT Submit complete ms with cover letter. Accepts queries by snail mail. Send disposable copy of ms and SASE for reply only. Does not return rejected mss. Authors living outside the U.S. can e-mail the editor for submission guidelines.

Ⓐ⊘ BLOOMSBURY CHILDREN'S BOOKS

Imprint of Bloomsbury USA, 1385 Broadway, 5th Floor, New York NY 10018. **Website:** www.bloomsbury.com/us/childrens. No phone calls or e-mails. *Agented submissions only.* Book catalog online. Guidelines online.

HOW TO CONTACT *Agented submissions only.*

TERMS Pays royalty. Pays advance. Responds in 6 months.

BOA EDITIONS, LTD.

P.O. Box 30971, Rochester NY 14603. (585)546-3410. **Fax:** (585)546-3913. **E-mail:** contact@boaeditions.org. **Website:** www.boaeditions.org. **Contact:** Ron Martin-Dent, director of publicity and production; Peter Conners, publisher. Estab. 1976. BOA Editions, Ltd., a not-for-profit publisher of poetry, short fiction, and poetry-in-translation, fosters readership and appreciation of contemporary literature. By identifying, cultivating, and publishing both new and established poets and selecting authors of unique literary talent, BOA brings high quality literature to the public. Publishes hardcover, trade paperback, and digital e-book originals. Book catalog online. Guidelines online.

NEEDS BOA publishes literary fiction through its American Reader Series. While aesthetic quality is subjective, our fiction will be by authors more concerned with the artfulness of their writing than the twists and turns of plot. Our strongest current interest is in short story collections (and short-short story collections). We strongly advise you to read our published fiction collections. *BOA does not accept novel submissions.*

TERMS Negotiates royalties. Pays variable advance. Responds in 1 week to queries; 5 months to mss.

BOLD STROKES BOOKS, INC.

P.O. Box 249, Valley Falls NY 12094. (518)677-5127. **Fax:** (518)677-5291. **E-mail:** sandy@boldstrokesbooks. com. **E-mail:** submissions@boldstrokesbooks.com. **Website:** www.boldstrokesbooks.com. **Contact:** Sandy Lowe, senior editor. Estab. 2004. Publishes trade paperback originals and reprints; electronic originals and reprints. Guidelines online.

NEEDS "Submissions should have a gay, lesbian, transgendered, or bisexual focus and should be positive and life-affirming." We do not publish any nonlgbtqi focused works.

HOW TO CONTACT Submit completed ms with bio, cover letter, and synopsis—electronically only.

TERMS Sliding scale based on sales volume and format. Pays advance. Responds in 1 month to queries; 2 months to proposals; 4 months to mss.

TIPS "We are particularly interested in authors who are interested in craft enhancement, technical development, and exploring and expanding traditional genre definitions and boundaries and are looking for a long-term publishing relationship. LGBTQ-focused works only."

BOOKFISH BOOKS

E-mail: bookfishbooks@gmail.com. **Website:** bookfishbooks.com. **Contact:** Tammy Mckee, acquisitions editor. BookFish Books is looking for novel lengthed young adult, new adult, and middle grade works in all subgenres. Both published and unpublished, agented or unagented authors are welcome to submit. "Sorry, but we do not publish novellas, picture books, early reader/chapter books or adult novels." Responds to every query. Guidelines online.

HOW TO CONTACT Query via e-mail with a brief synopsis and first 3 chapters of ms.

TIPS "We only accept complete manuscripts. Please do not query us with partial manuscripts or proposals."

⊙ BOOKOUTURE

StoryFire Ltd., 23 Sussex Rd., Ickenham UB10 8P, United Kingdom. **Website:** www.bookouture.com. **Contact:** Oliver Rhodes, founder and publisher. Estab. 2012. Publishes mass market paperback and electronic originals and reprints. Book catalog online.

NEEDS "We are looking for entertaining fiction targeted at modern women. That can be anything from Steampunk to Erotica, Historicals to thrillers. A dis-

tinctive author voice is more important than a particular genre or ms length."

HOW TO CONTACT Submit complete ms.

TERMS Pays 45% royalty on wholesale price. Responds in 1 month.

TIPS "The most important question that we ask of submissions is why would a reader buy the next book? What's distinctive or different about your storytelling that will mean readers will want to come back for more. We look to acquire global English language rights for e-book and Print on Demand."

BOOKS FOR ALL TIMES, INC.

Box 202, Warrenton VA 20188. (540)428-3175. **E-mail:** staff@bfat.com. **Website:** www.bfat.com. **Contact:** Joe David, publisher & editor. Estab. 1981. One-man operation. Publishes paperback originals.

NEEDS Literary, mainstream/contemporary, short story collections. "No novels at the moment; hopeful, though, of publishing a collection of quality short stories. No popular fiction or material easily published by the major or minor houses specializing in mindless entertainment. Only interested in stories of the Victor Hugo or Sinclair Lewis quality."

HOW TO CONTACT Query with SASE. Responds in 1 month to queries. Sometimes comments on rejected mss. Joe David, publisher.

TERMS Pays negotiable advance. "Publishing/payment arrangement will depend on plans for the book."

TIPS Interested in "controversial, honest stories which satisfy the reader's curiosity to know. Read Victor Hugo, Fyodor Dostoyevsky and Sinclair Lewis for example."

BOTTOM DOG PRESS, INC.

P.O. Box 425, Huron OH 44839. (419)602-1556. **E-mail:** lsmithdog@smithdocs.net. **Website:** smithdocs. net. **Contact:** Larry Smith, director; Susanna Sharp-Schwacke, associate editor. Estab. 1985. Bottom Dog Press, Inc., "is a nonprofit literary and educational organization dedicated to publishing the best writing and art from the Midwest and Appalachia. Query via e-mail first with 2 paragraphs on book and author." Publishes fiction, poetry, and memoirs.

TERMS Pays 10 copies and 15% royalty. Does not pay advance.

GEORGE BRAZILLER, INC.

277 Broadway, Suite 708, New York NY 10007. **Website:** www.georgebraziller.com. Publishes hardcover and trade paperback originals and reprints.

NEEDS "We rarely do fiction but when we have published novels, they have mostly been literary novels."

HOW TO CONTACT Submit 4-6 sample chapter(s), SASE. Agented fiction 20%. Responds in 3 months to proposals.

❶❷ BROADWAY BOOKS

Penguin Random House, 1745 Broadway, New York NY 10019. (212)782-9000. **Fax:** (212)782-9411. **Website:** crownpublishing.com/imprint/broadway-books. Estab. 1995. "Broadway publishes high quality general interest nonfiction and fiction for adults." Publishes hardcover and trade paperback books.

HOW TO CONTACT *Agented submissions only.*

TERMS Pays royalty on retail price. Pays advance.

BRONZE MAN BOOKS

Millikin University, 1184 W. Main, Decatur IL 62522. (217)424-6264. **E-mail:** sfrech@millikin.edu. **Website:** www.bronzemanbooks.com. **Contact:** Dr. Randy Brooks, publisher; Stephen Frech, editorial board, Edwin Walker, editorial board. Estab. 2006. A student-owned and operated press located on Millikin University's campus in Decatur, Ill., Bronze Man Books is dedicated to integrating quality design and meaningful content. The company exposes undergraduate students to the process of publishing by combining the theory of writing, publishing, editing and designing with the practice of running a book publishing company. This emphasis on performance learning is a hallmark of Millikin's brand of education. Publishes hardcover, trade paperback, literary chapbooks and mass market paperback originals.

NEEDS Subjects include art, graphic design, exhibits, general.

HOW TO CONTACT Submit completed ms.

TERMS Outright purchase based on wholesale value of 10% of a press run. Responds in 1-3 months.

TIPS "The art books are intended for serious collectors and scholars of contemporary art, especially of artists from the Midwestern US. These books are published in conjunction with art exhibitions at Millikin University or the Decatur Area Arts Council. The children's books have our broadest audience, and the literary chapbooks are intended for readers of contemporary fiction, drama, and poetry."

❂ THE BRUCEDALE PRESS

P.O. Box 2259, Port Elgin ON N0H 2C0, Canada. (519)832-6025. **E-mail:** info@brucedalepress.ca. **Website:** brucedalepress.ca. Estab. 1994. The Brucedale Press publishes books and other materials of regional interest and merit, as well as literary, historical, and/or pictorial works. Accepts works by Canadian authors only. Book submissions reviewed November to January. Submissions to *The Leaf Journal* accepted in September and March only. Manuscripts must be in English and thoroughly proofread before being sent. Use Canadian spellings and style. Publishes hardcover and trade paperback originals. Book catalog online. "Unless responding to an invitation to submit, query first by Canada Post with outline and sample chapter to book-length manuscripts. Send full manuscripts for work intended for children." Guidelines online.

TERMS Pays royalty.

TIPS "Our focus is very regional. In reading submissions, I look for quality writing with a strong connection to the Queen's Bush area of Ontario. All authors should visit our website, get a catalog, and read our books before submitting. Except for contest entries, we do not review manuscripts sent from outside Canada."

BULLITT PUBLISHING

P.O. Box, Austin TX 78729. **E-mail:** bullittpublishing@yahoo.com. **E-mail:** submissions@bullittpublishing.com. **Website:** bullittpublishing.com. **Contact:** Pat Williams, editor. Estab. 2012. "Bullitt Publishing is a royalty-offering publishing house specializing in smart, contemporary romance. We are proud to provide print on demand distribution through the world's most comprehensive distribution channels. Whether this is your first novel or your 101st novel, Bullitt Publishing will treat you with the same amount of professionalism and respect. While we expect well-written entertaining manuscripts from all of our authors, we promise to provide high quality, professional product in return." Publishes trade paperback and electronic originals.

❸ BUSTER BOOKS

16 Lion Yard, Tremadoc Rd., London WA SW4 7NQ, United Kingdom. (020)7720-8643. **Fax:** (022)7720-

8953. **E-mail:** enquiries@mombooks.com. **Website:** www.busterbooks.co.uk. **Contact:** Buster Submissions. "We are dedicated to providing irresistible and fun books for children of all ages. We typically publish black & white nonfiction for children aged 8-12 novelty titles-including doodle books."

TIPS "We do not accept picturebook or poetry submissions. Please do not send original artwork as we cannot guarantee its safety." Visit website before submitting.

BY LIGHT UNSEEN MEDIA

325 Lakeview Dr., Winchendon MA 01475. (978)433-8866. **Fax:** (978)433-8866. **E-mail:** vyrdolak@bylightunseenmedia.com. **Website:** bylightunseenmedia.com. **Contact:** Inanna Arthen, owner/editor-in-chief. Estab. 2006. The only small press owned and operated by a recognized expert in vampire folklore, media and culture, By Light Unseen Media was founded in 2006. "Our mission is to explore and celebrate the variety, imagination and ambiguities of the vampire theme in fiction, history and the human psyche." Publishes hardcover, paperback and electronic originals. Catalog online. Ms guidelines online.

NEEDS "We are a niche small press that *only* publishes fiction relating in some way to vampires. Within that guideline, we're interested in almost any genre that includes a vampire trope, the more creative and innovative, the better. Restrictions are noted in the submission guidelines (no derivative fiction based on other works, such as Dracula, no gore-for-gore's-sake 'splatter' horror, etc.) We do not publish anthologies." Does not want anything that does not focus on vampires as the major theme.

HOW TO CONTACT Submit proposal package including synopsis, 3 sample chapters, brief author bio. "We encourage electronic submissions." *Unsolicited mss will not be considered.*

TERMS Pays royalty of 50-70% on net as explicitly defined in contract. Payment quarterly. No advance. Responds in 3 months.

TIPS "We strongly urge authors to familiarize themselves with the vampire genre and not imagine that they're doing something new and amazingly different just because they're not imitating the current fad."

⊘ CALAMARI PRESS

Via Titta Scarpetta #28, Rome 153, Italy. **E-mail:** derek@calamaripress.com. **Website:** www.calamaripress.com. **Contact:** Derek White. Calamari Press

publishes books of literary text and art. Mss are selected by invitation. Occasionally has open submission period—check website. Helps to be published in *SleepingFish* first. Publishes paperback originals. Guidelines online.

HOW TO CONTACT Query with outline/synopsis and 3 sample chapters. Accepts queries by e-mail only. Include brief bio. Send SASE or IRC for return of ms.

TERMS Pays in author's copies. Responds to mss in 2 weeks.

CALKINS CREEK

Boyds Mills Press, 815 Church St., Honesdale PA 18431. **Website:** www.boydsmillspress.com. Estab. 2004. "We aim to publish books that are a well-written blend of creative writing and extensive research, which emphasize important events, people, and places in U.S. history." Guidelines online.

HOW TO CONTACT Submit outline/synopsis and 3 sample chapters.

TERMS Pays authors royalty or work purchased outright.

TIPS "Read through our recently published titles and review our catalog. When selecting titles to publish, our emphasis will be on important events, people, and places in U.S. history. Writers are encouraged to submit a detailed bibliography, including secondary and primary sources, and expert reviews with their submissions."

⊘ CALYX BOOKS

P.O. Box B, Corvallis OR 97339-0539. (541)753-9384. **Fax:** (541)753-0515. **E-mail:** info@calyxpress.org. **E-mail:** editor@calyxpress.org. **Website:** www.calyxpress.org. **Contact:** The Editor. Estab. 1986.

"Due to the high volume of book manuscripts received, CALYX Books is currently closed for manuscript submissions until further notice except for the Sarah Lantz Poetry Book Prize."

HOW TO CONTACT Closed to submissions until further notice.

ⓐ⊘ CANDLEWICK PRESS

99 Dover St., Somerville MA 02144. (617) 661-3330. **Fax:** (617) 661-0565. **E-mail:** bigbear@candlewick.com. **Website:** www.candlewick.com. Estab. 1991. "Candlewick Press publishes high-quality, illustrated children's books for ages infant through young adult. We are a truly child-centered publisher." Publishes

hardcover and trade paperback originals, and reprints.

◯ *Candlewick Press is not accepting queries or unsolicited mss at this time.*

NEEDS Picture books: animal, concept, contemporary, fantasy, history, humor, multicultural, nature/environment, poetry. Middle readers, young adults: contemporary, fantasy, history, humor, multicultural, poetry, science fiction, sports, suspense/mystery.

HOW TO CONTACT "We currently do not accept unsolicited editorial queries or submissions. If you are an author or illustrator and would like us to consider your work, please read our submissions policy (online) to learn more."

TERMS Pays authors royalty of 2½-10% based on retail price. Offers advance.

TIPS *"We no longer accept unsolicited mss. See our website for further information about us."*

CANTERBURY HOUSE PUBLISHING, LTD.

4535 Ottawa Trail, Sarasota FL 34233. (941)312-6912. **Website:** www.canterburyhousepublishing.com. **Contact:** Sandra Horton, editor. Estab. 2009. "Our audience is made up of readers looking for wholesome fiction with good southern stories, with elements of mystery, romance, and inspiration and/or are looking for true stories of achievement and triumph over challenging circumstances. We are very strict on our submission guidelines due to our small staff, and our target market of Southern regional settings." Publishes hardcover, trade paperback, and electronic originals. Book catalog online. Guidelines online.

HOW TO CONTACT Query with SASE and through website.

TERMS Pays 10-15% royalty on wholesale price. Responds in 1 month to queries; 3 months to mss.

TIPS "Because of our limited staff, we prefer authors who have good writing credentials and submit edited manuscripts. We also look at authors who are business and marketing savvy and willing to help promote their books."

CARNEGIE MELLON UNIVERSITY PRESS

5032 Forbes Ave., Pittsburgh PA 15289. (412)268-2861. **Fax:** (412)268-8706. **E-mail:** carnegiemellonuniversitypress@gmail.com. **Website:** www.cmu.edu/universitypress/. **Contact:** Poetry Editor or Nonfiction Editor. Estab. 1972. Publishes hardcover and trade paperback originals. Book catalog and guidelines online.

CAROLINA WREN PRESS

120 Morris St., Durham NC 27701. (919)560-2738. **E-mail:** carolinawrenpress@earthlink.net. **Website:** www.carolinawrenpress.org. **Contact:** Robin Miura, Editor & Director. Estab. 1976. "We publish poetry, fiction, and memoirs by or about people of color, women, gay/lesbian issues, and work by writers from, living in, or writing about the U.S. South." Accepts simultaneous submissions, but "let us know if work has been accepted elsewhere." Guidelines online.

NEEDS "We are no longer publishing children's literature of any topic." Books: 6×9 paper; typeset; various bindings; illustrations. Distributes titles through John F. Blair, Amazon.com, Barnes & Noble, Baker & Taylor, and on their website. "We very rarely accept any unsolicited manuscripts, but we accept submissions for the Doris Bakwin Award for Writing by a Woman in Jan-June of even-numbered years and submissions for the Lee Smith Novel Prize in Jan-June of odd-numbered years."

HOW TO CONTACT "We will accept e-mailed queries—a letter in the body of the e-mail describing your project—but please do not send large attachments." All other submissions are accepted via Submittable as part of our annual contests.

TERMS We pay our authors an honorarium. Responds in 3 months to queries; 6 months to mss.

TIPS "Best way to get read is to submit to a contest."

Ⓐⵔ CARTWHEEL BOOKS

Imprint of Scholastic Trade Division, 557 Broadway, New York NY 10012. (212)343-6100. **Website:** www.scholastic.com. Estab. 1991. Cartwheel Books publishes innovative books for children, up to age 8. "We are looking for 'novelties' that are books first, play objects second. Even without its gimmick, a Cartwheel Book should stand alone as a valid piece of children's literature." Publishes novelty books, easy readers, board books, hardcover and trade paperback originals. Guidelines available free.

NEEDS Again, the subject should have mass market appeal for very young children. Humor can be helpful, but not necessary. Mistakes writers make are a reading level that is too difficult, a topic of no interest or too narrow, or mss that are too long.

HOW TO CONTACT *Accepts mss from agents only.*

CAVE HOLLOW PRESS

P.O. Drawer J, Warrensburg MO 64093. **E-mail:** gb-crump@cavehollowpress.com. **Website:** www.cave-hollowpress.com. **Contact:** G.B. Crump, editor. Estab. 2001. Publishes trade paperback originals. Catalog online. Guidelines available free.

NEEDS "We publish fiction by Midwestern authors and/or with Midwestern themes and/or settings. Our website is updated frequently to reflect the current type of fiction Cave Hollow Press is seeking."

HOW TO CONTACT Query with SASE.

TERMS Pays 7-12% royalty on wholesale price. Pays negotiable amount in advance. Responds in 1-2 months to queries and proposals; 3-6 months to mss.

TIPS "Our audience varies based on the type of book we are publishing. We specialize in Missouri and Midwest regional fiction. We are interested in talented writers from Missouri and the surrounding Midwest. Check our submission guidelines on the website for what type of fiction we are interested in currently."

CEDAR FORT, INC.

2373 W. 700 S, Springville UT 84663. (801)489-4084. **Website:** www.cedarfort.com. Estab. 1986. "Each year we publish well over 100 books, and many of those are by first-time authors. At the same time, we love to see books from established authors. As one of the largest book publishers in Utah, we have the capability and enthusiasm to make your book a success, whether you are a new author or a returning one. We want to publish uplifting and edifying books that help people think about what is important in life, books people enjoy reading to relax and feel better about themselves, and books to help improve lives. Although we do put out several children's books each year, we are extremely selective. Our children's books must have strong religious or moral values, and must contain outstanding writing and an excellent storyline." Publishes hardcover, trade paperback originals and reprints, mass market paperback and electronic reprints. Catalog and guidelines online.

HOW TO CONTACT Submit completed ms.

TERMS Pays 10-12% royalty on wholesale price. Pays $2,000-50,000 advance. Responds in 1 month on queries; 2 months on proposals; 4 months on mss.

TIPS "Our audience is rural, conservative, mainstream. The first page of your ms is very important because we start reading every submission, but good writing and plot keep us reading."

CHANGELING PRESS LLC

315 N. Centre St., Martinsburg WV 25404. **E-mail:** submissions.changelingpress@gmail.com. **Website:** www.changelingpress.com. **Contact:** Margaret Riley, publisher. Estab. 2004. Erotic romance, novellas only (10,000-30,000 words). "We're currently looking for contemporary and futuristic short fiction, single title, series, and serials in the following genres and themes: sci-fi/futuristic, dark and urban fantasy, paranormal, BDSM, action adventure, guilty pleasures (adult contemporary kink), new adult, menage, bisexual and more, gay, interracial, BBW, cougar (M/F), silver fox (M/M), men and women in uniform, vampires, werewolves, Elves, dragons and magical creatures, other shapeshifters, magic, dark desires (demons and horror), and hentai (tentacle monsters)." Publishes e-books. Catalog online. Guidelines online.

NEEDS Please read and follow our submissions guidelines available at http://changelingpress.com/submissions.php. All submissions which do not follow the submissions guidelines will be rejected unread. No lesbian fiction submissions without prior approval, please. Absolutely no lesbian fiction written by men.

HOW TO CONTACT E-mail submissions only. Please read and follow our submissions guidelines online. All submissions which do not follow the submissions guidelines will be rejected unread.

TERMS Pays 35% gross royalties on site, 50% gross off site monthly. Does not pay advance. Responds in 1 week to queries.

CHARLESBRIDGE PUBLISHING

85 Main St., Watertown MA 02472. (617)926-0329. **Fax:** (617)926-5720. **E-mail:** tradeeditorial@charlesbridge.com. **E-mail:** yasubs@charlesbridge.com. **Website:** www.charlesbridge.com. Estab. 1980. "Charlesbridge publishes high-quality books for children, with a goal of creating lifelong readers and lifelong learners. Our books encourage reading and discovery in the classroom, library, and home. We believe that books for children should offer accurate information, promote a positive worldview, and embrace a child's innate sense of wonder and fun. To this end, we continually strive to seek new voices, new visions, and new directions in children's literature. As of September 2015, we are now accepting young adult novels for consideration." Publishes hardcover and trade paperback nonfiction and fiction, children's books for the trade and library markets. Guidelines online.

NEEDS Strong stories with enduring themes. Charlesbridge publishes both picture books and transitional bridge books (books ranging from early readers to middle-grade chapter books). Our fiction titles include lively, plot-driven stories with strong, engaging characters. No alphabet books, board books, coloring books, activity books, or books with audiotapes or CD-ROMs.

HOW TO CONTACT Please submit only 1 ms at a time. For picture books and shorter bridge books, please send a complete ms. For fiction books longer than 30 ms pages, please send a detailed plot synopsis, a chapter outline, and 3 chapters of text. If sending a young adult novel, mark the front of the envelope with "YA novel enclosed." Please note, for YA, e-mail submissions are preferred to the following address; yasubs@charlesbridge.com. Only responds if interested. Full guidelines on site.

TERMS Pays royalty. Pays advance. Responds in 3 months.

TIPS "To become acquainted with our publishing program, we encourage you to review our books and visit our website where you will find our catalog."

CHILDREN'S BRAINS ARE YUMMY (CBAY) BOOKS

P.O. Box 670296, Dallas TX 75367. **E-mail:** submissions@cbaybooks.com. **Website:** www.cbaybooks. blog. **Contact:** Madeline Smoot, publisher. Estab. 2008. "CBAY Books currently focuses on quality fantasy and science fiction books for the middle grade and teen markets. We are not currently accepting unsolicited submissions. We do not publish picture books." "We are distributed by IPG. Our books can be found in their catalog at www.ipgbooks.com." Brochure and guidelines online.

TERMS Pays authors royalty 10%-15% based on wholesale price. Offers advances against royalties. Average amount $500. Pays advance. Responds in 2 months.

CHILD'S PLAY (INTERNATIONAL) LTD.

Child's Play, Ashworth Rd. Bridgemead, Swindon, Wiltshire SN5 7YD, United Kingdom. 01793 616286. **E-mail:** neil@childs-play.com; office@childs-play. com. **Website:** www.childs-play.com. **Contact:** Sue Baker, Neil Burden, manuscript acquisitions. Estab. 1972. Specializes in nonfiction, fiction, educational material, multicultural material. Produces 30 pic-

ture books/year; 10 young readers/year. "A child's early years are more important than any other. This is when children learn most about the world around them and the language they need to survive and grow. Child's Play aims to create exactly the right material for this all-important time."

- "Due to a backlog of submissions, Child's Play is currently no longer able to accept anymore manuscripts."

NEEDS Picture books: adventure, animal, concept, contemporary, folktales, multicultural, nature/environment. Young readers: adventure, animal, anthology, concept, contemporary, folktales, humor, multicultural, nature/environment, poetry. Average word length: picture books—1,500; young readers—2,000.

TIPS "Look at our website to see the kind of work we do before sending. Do not send cartoons. We do not publish novels. We do publish lots of books with pictures of babies/toddlers."

CHRISTIAN FOCUS PUBLICATIONS

Geanies House, Fearn, Tain Ross-shire Scotland IV20 1TW, United Kingdom. (44)1862-871-011. **Fax:** (44)1862-871-699. **E-mail:** submissions@christian-focus.com. **Website:** www.christianfocus.com. **Contact:** Director of Publishing. Estab. 1975. Specializes in Christian material, nonfiction, fiction, educational material.

NEEDS Picture books, young readers, adventure, history, religion. Middle readers: adventure, problem novels, religion. Young adult/teens: adventure, history, problem novels, religion. Average word length: young readers—5,000; middle readers—max 10,000; young adult/teen—max 20,000.

TERMS Responds to queries in 2 weeks; mss in 3-6 months.

TIPS "Be aware of the international market as regards writing style/topics as well as illustration styles. Our company sells rights to European as well as Asian countries. Fiction sales are not as good as they were. Christian fiction for youngsters is not a product that is performing well in comparison to nonfiction such as Christian biography/Bible stories/church history, etc."

CHRONICLE BOOKS

680 Second St., San Francisco CA 94107. **E-mail:** submissions@chroniclebooks.com. **Website:** www. chroniclebooks.com. "We publish an exciting range of books, stationery, kits, calendars, and novelty formats. Our list includes children's books and interac-

tive formats; young adult books; cookbooks; fine art, design, and photography; pop culture; craft, fashion, beauty, and home decor; relationships, mind-body-spirit; innovative formats such as interactive journals, kits, decks, and stationery; and much, much more." Book catalog for 9x12 SAE and 8 first-class stamps. Ms guidelines for #10 SASE.

NEEDS Only interested in fiction for children and young adults. No adult fiction.

HOW TO CONTACT Submit complete ms (picture books); submit outline/synopsis and 3 sample chapters (for older readers). Will not respond to submissions unless interested. Will not consider submissions by fax, e-mail or disk. Do not include SASE; do not send original materials. No submissions will be returned.

TERMS Generally pays authors in royalties based on retail price, "though we do occasionally work on a flat fee basis." Advance varies. Illustrators paid royalty based on retail price or flat fee. Responds to queries in 1 month.

CHRONICLE BOOKS FOR CHILDREN

680 Second St., San Francisco CA 94107. (415)537-4200. **Fax:** (415)537-4460. **Website:** www.chroniclekids.com. "Chronicle Books for Children publishes an eclectic mixture of traditional and innovative children's books. Our aim is to publish books that inspire young readers to learn and grow creatively while helping them discover the joy of reading. We're looking for quirky, bold artwork and subject matter." Publishes hardcover and trade paperback originals. Book catalog for 9x12 envelope and 3 first-class stamps. Guidelines online.

NEEDS Does not accept proposals by fax, via e-mail, or on disk. When submitting artwork, either as a part of a project or as samples for review, do not send original art.

TERMS Pays variable advance. Responds in 2-4 weeks to queries; 6 months to mss.

TIPS "We are interested in projects that have a unique bent to them—be it in subject matter, writing style, or illustrative technique. As a small list, we are looking for books that will lend our list a distinctive flavor. Primarily we are interested in fiction and nonfiction picture books for children ages up to 8 years, and nonfiction books for children ages up to 12 years. We publish board, pop-up, and other novelty formats as well as picture books. We are also interested in early

chapter books, middle grade fiction, and young adult projects."

CITY LIGHTS BOOKS

261 Columbus Ave., San Francisco CA 94133. (415)362-8193. **Fax:** (415)362-4921. **Website:** www.citylights.com. Estab. 1953. Publishes paperback originals. Plans 1-2 first novels this year. Averages 12 total titles, 4-5 fiction titles/year.

NEEDS Fiction, essays, memoirs, translations, poetry and books on social and political issues.

HOW TO CONTACT Submit one-page description of the book and a sample chapter or two with SASE. Does not accept unsolicited mss. Does not accept queries by e-mail. See website for guidelines.

CLARION BOOKS

Houghton Mifflin Co., 215 Park Ave. S., New York NY 10003. **Website:** www.hmhco.com. Estab. 1965. "Clarion Books publishes picture books, nonfiction, and fiction for infants through grade 12. Avoid telling your stories in verse unless you are a professional poet. *We are no longer responding to your unsolicited submission unless we are interested in publishing it. Please do not include a SASE. Submissions will be recycled, and you will not hear from us regarding the status of your submission unless we are interested. We regret that we cannot respond personally to each submission, but we do consider each and every submission we receive.*" Publishes hardcover originals for children. Guidelines online.

NEEDS "Clarion is highly selective in the areas of historical fiction, fantasy, and science fiction. A novel must be superlatively written in order to find a place on the list. Mss that arrive without an SASE of adequate size will *not* be responded to or returned. Accepts fiction translations."

HOW TO CONTACT Submit complete ms. No queries, please. Send to only *one* Clarion editor.

TERMS Pays 5-10% royalty on retail price. Pays minimum of $4,000 advance. Responds in 2 months to queries.

TIPS "Looks for freshness, enthusiasm—in short, life."

CLEIS PRESS

101 Hudson St., 37th Floor, Suite 3705, Jersey City NJ 07302. **Fax:** (510)845-8001. **Website:** www.cleispress.com. Estab. 1980. Cleis Press publishes provocative, intelligent books in the areas of sexuality, gay and lesbian studies, erotica, fiction, gender studies, and

human rights. Publishes books that inform, enlighten, and entertain. Areas of interest include gift, inspiration, health, family and childcare, self-help, women's issues, reference, cooking. "We do our best to bring readers quality books that celebrate life, inspire the mind, revive the spirit, and enhance lives all around. Our authors are practical visionaries; people who offer deep wisdom in a hopeful and helpful manner."

NEEDS "We are looking for high quality fiction and nonfiction."

HOW TO CONTACT Submit complete ms. Include brief bio, list of publishing credits. Send SASE for return of ms or send a disposable ms and SASE for reply only.

TERMS Responds in 2 month to queries.

TIPS "Be familiar with publishers' catalogs; be absolutely aware of your audience; research potential markets; present fresh new ways of looking at your topic; avoid 'PR' language and include publishing history in query letter."

✪ COACH HOUSE BOOKS

80 bpNichol Ln., Toronto ON M5S 3J4, Canada. (416)979-2217. **Fax:** (416)977-1158. **E-mail:** mail@chbooks.com. **E-mail:** editor@chbooks.com. **Website:** www.chbooks.com. **Contact:** Alana Wilcox, editorial director. Independent Canadian publisher of innovative poetry, literary fiction, nonfiction, and drama. Publishes trade paperback originals by Canadian authors. Guidelines online.

HOW TO CONTACT We much prefer to receive electronic submissions. Please put your cover letter and CV into one Word or PDF file along with the manuscript and e-mail it to editor@chbooks.com. We'd appreciate it if you would name your file following this convention: Last Name, First Name - MS Title. For fiction and poetry submissions, please send your complete manuscript, along with an introductory letter that describes your work and compares it to at least two current Coach House titles, explaining how your book would fit our list, and a literary CV listing your previous publications and relevant experience.

TERMS Pays 10% royalty on retail price. Responds in 6-8 months to queries.

TIPS "We are not a general publisher, and publish only Canadian poetry, fiction, select nonfiction and drama. We are interested primarily in innovative or experimental writing."

COFFEE HOUSE PRESS

79 13th Ave. NE, Suite 110, Minneapolis MN 55413. (612)338-0125. **Fax:** (612)338-4004. **Website:** www.coffeehousepress.org. Estab. 1984. This successful nonprofit small press has received numerous grants from various organizations including the NEA, the McKnight Foundation and Target. Books published by Coffee House Press have won numerous honors and awards. Example: *The Book of Medicines*, by Linda Hogan won the Colorado Book Award for Poetry and the Lannan Foundation Literary Fellowship. Publishes hardcover and trade paperback originals. Book catalog and ms guidelines online.

NEEDS Seeks literary novels, short story collections and poetry.

HOW TO CONTACT Query first with outline and samples (20-30 pages) during annual reading periods (March 1-31 and September 1-30).

TERMS Responds in 4-6 weeks to queries; up to 6 months to mss.

TIPS "Look for our books at stores and libraries to get a feel for what we like to publish. No phone calls, e-mails, or faxes."

✪❂✪✪ CONSTABLE & ROBINSON, LTD.

50 Victoria Embankment, London EC4Y 0DZ, United Kingdom. **E-mail:** info@littlebrown.co.uk. **Website:** https://www.littlebrown.co.uk/ConstableRobinson/about-constable-publisher.page. Publishes hardcover and trade paperback originals. Book catalog available free.

NEEDS Publishes "crime fiction (mysteries) and historical crime fiction." Length 80,000 words minimum; 130,000 words maximum.

HOW TO CONTACT *Agented submissions only.*

TERMS Pays royalty. Pays advance. Responds in 1-3 months.

✪ COTEAU BOOKS

Thunder Creek Publishing Co-operative Ltd., 2517 Victoria Ave., Regina SK S4P 0T2, Canada. (306)777-0170. **Fax:** (306)522-5152. **E-mail:** coteau@coteaubooks.com. **Website:** www.coteaubooks.com. **Contact:** Geoffrey Ursell, publisher. Estab. 1975. "Our mission is to publish the finest in Canadian fiction, nonfiction, poetry, drama, and children's literature, with an emphasis on Saskatchewan and prairie writers. De-emphasizing science fiction, picture books." Publishes chapter books for young readers aged 9-12 and novels for older kids ages 13-15 and for ages 15 and up. Publishes trade paperback originals and reprints. Book catalog available free. Guidelines online.

NEEDS No science fiction. No children's picture books.

HOW TO CONTACT Query.

TERMS Pays 10% royalty on retail price. Responds in 3 months.

TIPS "Look at past publications to get an idea of our editorial program. We do not publish romance, horror, or picture books but are interested in juvenile and teen fiction from Canadian authors. Submissions, even queries, must be made in hard copy only. We do not accept simultaneous/multiple submissions. Check our website for new submission timing guidelines."

COVENANT COMMUNICATIONS, INC.

Deseret Book Company, P.O. Box 416, American Fork UT 84003. (801)756-1041. **Fax:** (801)756-1049. **E-mail:** submissionsdesk@covenant-lds.com. **Website:** www.covenant-lds.com. **Contact:** Kathryn Gordon, managing editor. Estab. 1958. "Currently emphasizing inspirational, doctrinal, historical, biography, and fiction." Guidelines online.

NEEDS "Manuscripts do not necessarily have to include LDS/Mormon characters or themes, but cannot contain profanity, sexual content, gratuitous violence, witchcraft, vampires, and other such material." We do not accept nor publish young adult, middle grade, science fiction, fantasy, occult, steampunk, or gay/lesbian/bisexual/transgender themes.

HOW TO CONTACT Submit complete ms.

TERMS Pays 6-15% royalty on retail price. Responds in 1 month on queries; 4-6 months on mss.

TIPS "We are actively looking for new, fresh Regency romance authors."

CRAIGMORE CREATIONS

PMB 114, 4110 SE Hawthorne Blvd., Portland OR 97124. (503)477-9562. **E-mail:** info@craigmorecreations.com. **Website:** www.craigmorecreations.com. Estab. 2009.

HOW TO CONTACT Submit proposal package. See website for detailed submission guidelines.

🌙 CRESCENT MOON PUBLISHING

P.O. Box 1312, Maidstone Kent ME14 5XU, United Kingdom. (44)(162)272-9593. **E-mail:** cresmopub@yahoo.co.uk. **Website:** www.crmoon.com. **Contact:** Jeremy Robinson, director (arts, media, cinema, literature); Cassidy Hughes (visual arts). Estab. 1988. "Our mission is to publish the best in contemporary work, in poetry, fiction, and critical studies, and selections from the great writers. Currently emphasizing nonfiction (media, film, music, painting). De-emphasizing children's books." Publishes hardcover and trade paperback originals. Book catalog and ms guidelines free.

NEEDS "We do not publish much fiction at present but will consider high quality new work."

HOW TO CONTACT Query with SASE. Submit outline, clips, 2 sample chapters, bio.

TERMS Pays royalty. Pays negotiable advance. Responds in 2 months to queries; 4 months to proposals and mss.

TIPS "Our audience is interested in new contemporary writing."

CRESTON BOOKS

P.O. Box 9369, Berkeley CA 94709. **E-mail:** submissions@crestonbooks.co. **Website:** crestonbooks.co. Estab. 2013. Creston Books is author-illustrator driven, with talented, award-winning creators given more editorial freedom and control than in a typical New York house. Catalog online. Guidelines online.

HOW TO CONTACT Please paste text of picture books or first chapters of novels in the body of e-mail. Words of Advice for submitting authors listed on the site.

TERMS Pays advance.

CRIMSON ROMANCE

Simon & Schuster, Inc., 57 Littlefield St., Avon MA 02322. **E-mail:** crimsonsubmissions@simonandschuster.com. **Website:** crimsonromance.com. **Contact:** Tara Gelsomino, Executive Editor. Estab. 2012. Direct to e-book romance imprint of Simon & Schuster, Inc. Publishes electronic originals and print-on-demand copies. Guidelines online.

NEEDS Crimson seeks submissions featuring strong characters, smart stories, and satisfying romance in five popular subgenres: contemporary, historical, paranormal, romantic suspense, and spicy. We're looking for previously unpublished novellas (between 20,000 – 50,000 words) and full-length novels (between 50,000 – 90,000 words). All authors—agented or unagented, beginner or veteran writers—are welcome to submit any works that have not been previously published in whole or in part in any media, including self-publishing (Kindle, CreateSpace, etc.). **HOW TO CONTACT** Please see current submission guidelines online.

TERMS Does not pay advance.

CROSS-CULTURAL COMMUNICATIONS

Cross-Cultural Literary Editions, 239 Wynsum Ave., Merrick NY 11566-4725. (516)869-5635. **Fax:** (516) 379-1901. **E-mail:** info@cross-culturalcommunications.com; cccpoetry@aol.com. **Website:** www.crossculturalcommunications.com. **Contact:** Stanley H. Barkan; Bebe Barkan. Estab. 1971. Publishes hardcover and trade paperback originals. Book catalog (sample flyers) for #10 SASE.

HOW TO CONTACT Query with SASE.

TERMS Responds in 1 month to proposals; 2 months to mss.

TIPS "Best chance: poetry from a translation."

ⒶⓄ CROWN PUBLISHING GROUP

Penguin Random House, 1745 Broadway, New York NY 10019. (212)782-9000. **Website:** crownpublishing.com. Estab. 1933. Publishes popular fiction and nonfiction hardcover originals. *Agented submissions only.* See website for more details.

CRYSTAL SPIRIT PUBLISHING, INC.

P.O. Box 12506, Durham NC 27709. **E-mail:** crystalspiritinc@gmail.com. **Website:** www.crystalspiritinc.com. **Contact:** V. S. O'Neal, Senior Managing Editor. Estab. 2004. "Our readers are lovers of high-quality books that are sold as direct sales, in bookstores, gift shops and placed in libraries and schools. They support independent authors and they expect works that will provide them with entertainment, inspiration, romance, and education. Our audience loves to read and will embrace niche authors that love to write." Publishes hardcover, trade paperback, mass market paperback, and electronic originals. Book catalog and ms guidelines online. Submissions are only accepted via the website. Please see guidelines as stated on the website. Postal mail submissions are not allowed and will not be reviewed. We do not acknowledge or respond to queries.

HOW TO CONTACT Submissions are only accepted via the website. Please see guidelines as stated on the website. Postal mail submissions are not allowed and will not be reviewed. We do not acknowledge or respond to queries.

TERMS Pays 20-45% royalty on retail price. Responds in 15-30 days

TIPS "Submissions are accepted for publication throughout the year. Works should be positive and non-threatening. All submissions are accepted via the website only! Ensure that all contact information is correct, abide by the submission guidelines and do not send follow-up e-mails or calls." Do not send queries as they will not be acknowledged or receive a response.

CURIOSITY QUILLS

Whampa, LLC, P.O. Box 2160, Reston VA 20195. (800)998-2509. **Fax:** (800)998-2509. **E-mail:** editor@curiosityquills.com. **E-mail:** acquisitions@curiosityquills.com. **Website:** curiosityquills.com. **Contact:** Alisa Gus. Estab. 2011. Curiosity Quills is a publisher of hard-hitting dark sci-fi, speculative fiction, and paranormal works aimed at adults, young adults, and new adults. Firm publishes sci-fi, speculative fiction, steampunk, paranormal and urban fantasy, and corresponding romance titles under its new Rebel Romance imprint. Catalog available. Guidelines online.

NEEDS Looking for "thought-provoking, mind-twisting rollercoasters—challenge our mind, turn our world upside down, and make us question. Those are the makings of a true literary marauder."

HOW TO CONTACT Submit ms using online submission form or e-mail to acquisitions@curiosityquills.com.

TERMS Pays variable royalty. Does not pay advance. Responds in 1-6 weeks.

⬤ CURIOUS FOX

Brunel Rd., Houndmills, Basingstoke Hants RG21 6XS, United Kingdom. **E-mail:** submissions@curious-fox.com. **Website:** www.curious-fox.com. "Do you love telling good stories? If so, we'd like to hear from you. Curious Fox is on the lookout for UK-based authors, whether new talent or established authors with exciting ideas. We take submissions for books aimed at ages 3-young adult. If you have story ideas that are bold, fun, and imaginative, then please do get in touch!" Guidelines online.

HOW TO CONTACT "Send your submission via e-mail to submissions@curious-fox.com. Include the following in the body of the email, not as attachments: Sample chapters, Résumé, List of previous publishing credits, if applicable. We will respond only if your writing samples fit our needs."

DARK HORSE COMICS, INC.

10956 SE Main St., Milwaukie OR 97222. (503)652-8815. **Fax:** (503)654-9440. **E-mail:** dhcomics@darkhorse.com. **E-mail:** dhsubsproposals@darkhouse.com. **Website:** www.darkhorse.com. "In addition to publishing comics from top talent like Frank Miller, Mike Mignola, Stan Sakai and internationally-renowned humorist Sergio Aragonés, Dark Horse is recognized as the world's leading publisher of licensed comics."

NEEDS Comic books, graphic novels. Published *Astro Boy Volume 10 TPB*, by Osamu Tezuka and Reid Fleming; *Flaming Carrot Crossover #1* by Bob Burden and David Boswell.

HOW TO CONTACT Submit synopsis to dhcomics@darkhorse.com. See website (www.darkhorse.com) for detailed submission guidelines and submission agreement, which must be signed. Include a full script for any short story or single-issue submission, or the first eight pages of the first issue of any series. Submissions can no longer be mailed back to the sender.

TIPS "If you're looking for constructive criticism, show your work to industry professionals at conventions."

DAW BOOKS, INC.

Penguin Random House, 375 Hudson St., New York NY 10014. (212)366-2096. **Fax:** (212)366-2090. **E-mail:** daw@penguinrandomhouse.com. **Website:** www.dawbooks.com. **Contact:** Peter Stampfel, submissions editor. Estab. 1971. DAW Books publishes science fiction and fantasy. Publishes hardcover and paperback originals and reprints. Guidelines online.

NEEDS "Currently seeking modern urban fantasy and paranormals. We like character-driven books with appealing protagonists, engaging plots, and well-constructed worlds. We accept both agented and unagented manuscripts."

HOW TO CONTACT Submit entire ms, cover letter, SASE. "Do not submit your only copy of anything. The average length of the novels we publish varies but is almost never less than 80,000 words."

TERMS Pays in royalties with an advance negotiable on a book-by-book basis. Responds in 3 months.

KATHY DAWSON BOOKS

Penguin Random House, 375 Hudson St., New York NY 10014. (212)366-2000. **Website:** kathydawsonbooks.tumblr.com. **Contact:** Kathy Dawson, vice-president and publisher. Estab. 2014. Mission statement: Publish stellar novels with unforgettable characters for children and teens that expand their vision of the world, sneakily explore the meaning of life, celebrate the written word, and last for generations. The imprint strives to publish tomorrow's award contenders: quality books with strong hooks in a variety of genres with universal themes and compelling voices—books that break the mold and the heart. Guidelines online.

HOW TO CONTACT Accepts fiction queries via snail mail only. Include cover sheet with one-sentence elevator pitch, main themes, author version of catalog copy for book, first 10 pages of ms (double-spaced, Times Roman, 12 point type), and publishing history. No SASE needed. Responds only if interested.

TERMS Responds only if interested.

⊘ DC UNIVERSE

1700 Broadway, New York NY 10019. **Website:** www.dccomics.com. Imprints: Vertigo, Wildstorm, CMX Manga, DC Direct, Mad, DC Kids, Zuda.

HOW TO CONTACT *No unsolicited submissions.* Recycles unsolicited manuscripts. Artists should contact through Comic Con conventions. See submission guidelines on website for more information. International Comic-Cons.

TERMS Artist's guidelines on website.

⚠⊘ DELACORTE PRESS

an imprint of Random House Children's Books, a division of Penguin Random House LLC, New York, 1745 Broadway, New York NY 10019. (212)782-9000. **Website:** randomhousekids.com; randomhouseteens.com. Publishes middle grade and young adult fiction in hard cover, trade paperback, mass market and digest formats.

◑   All query letters and manuscript submissions must be submitted through an agent or at the request of an editor.

⚠⊘ DEL REY BOOKS

Penguin Random House, 1745 Broadway, 18th Floor, New York NY 10019. (212)782-9000. **Website:** www.penguinrandomhouse.com. Estab. 1977. Del Rey publishes top level fantasy, alternate history, and science fiction. Publishes hardcover, trade paperback, and mass market originals and mass market paperback reprints.

HOW TO CONTACT *Agented submissions only.*

TERMS Pays royalty on retail price. Pays competitive advance.

TIPS "Del Rey is a reader's house. Pay particular attention to plotting, strong characters, and dramatic, satisfactory conclusions. It must be/feel believable. That's what the readers like. In terms of mass market, we basically created the field of fantasy bestsellers. Not that it didn't exist before, but we put the mass into mass market."

DIAL BOOKS FOR YOUNG READERS

Imprint of Penguin Group (USA), 345 Hudson St., New York NY 10014. (212)366-2000. **Website:** www.penguin.com/children. Estab. 1961. "Dial Books for Young Readers publishes quality picture books for ages 18 months-6 years; lively, believable novels for middle readers and young adults; and occasional nonfiction for middle readers and young adults." Publishes hardcover originals. Book catalog and guidelines online.

NEEDS Especially looking for lively and well-written novels for middle grade and young adult children involving a convincing plot and believable characters. The subject matter or theme should not already be overworked in previously published books. The approach must not be demeaning to any minority group, nor should the roles of female characters (or others) be stereotyped, though we don't think books should be didactic, or in any way message-y. No topics inappropriate for the juvenile, young adult, and middle grade audiences. No plays.

HOW TO CONTACT Accepts unsolicited queries and up to 10 pages for longer works and unsolicited mss for picture books. Will only respond if interested.

TERMS Pays royalty. Pays varies advance. Responds in 4-6 months to queries.

TIPS "Our readers are anywhere from preschool age to teenage. Picture books must have strong plots, lots of action, unusual premises, or universal themes treated with freshness and originality. Humor works well in these books. A very well-thought-out and intelligently presented book has the best chance of being taken on. Genre isn't as much of a factor as presentation."

ⒶⓄ DIAL PRESS

1745 Broadway, New York NY 10019. **Website:** www.randomhouse.com/bantamdell/. Estab. 1924.

HOW TO CONTACT *Agented submissions only.*

DIGITAL MANGA PUBLISHING

1487 West 178th St., Suite 300, Gardenia CA 90248. **Website:** www.dmpbooks.com. "Submissions must be original and not infringe on copyrighted works by other creators. Please note that we are a manga publisher; we do not distribute Western style comics or literary novels. Completed works must contain a minimum of 90 pages of content. Submissions may be in black and white or full color. We accept submissions for all genres of manga which comply to US law and we only accept submissions from persons aged 18 and over. Please do not send your original copies as we cannot return them to you. If your work is published online elsewhere, please feel free to include a link for us to further view your portfolio."

DIVERTIR

P.O. Box 232, North Salem NH 03073. **E-mail:** info@divertirpublishing.com. **E-mail:** query@divertirpublishing.com. **Website:** www.divertirpublishing.com. **Contact:** Kenneth Tupper, Publisher. Estab. 2009. Divertir Publishing is an independent publisher located in Salem, NH. "Our goal is to provide interesting and entertaining books to our readers, as well as to offer new and exciting voices in the writing community the opportunity to publish their work. We seek to combine an understanding of traditional publishing with a unique understanding of the modern market to best serve both our authors and readers." Publishes trade paperback and electronic originals. Catalog online. Guidelines online.

NEEDS "We are particularly interested in the following: science fiction, fantasy, historical, alternate history, contemporary mythology, mystery and suspense, paranormal, and urban fantasy." Does not consider erotica or mss with excessive violence.

HOW TO CONTACT Electronically submit proposal package, including synopsis and query letter with author's bio.

TERMS Pays 10-15% royalty on wholesale price (for novels and nonfiction). Does not pay advance. Responds in 1-3 months on queries; 3-4 months on proposals and mss.

TIPS "Please see our Author Info page (online) for more information."

ⒶⒸ DOUBLEDAY CANADA

1 Toronto St., Suite 300, Toronto ON M5C 2V6, Canada. **Website:** www.randomhouse.ca. Random House of Canada, 1 Toronto Street, Suite 300, Toronto ON M5C 2V6 Canada. (416)364-4449. **Website:** www.randomhouse.ca. Publishes hardcover and paperback originals. Averages 50 total titles/year.

HOW TO CONTACT Does not accept unsolicited mss. *Agented submissions only.*

DOWN THE SHORE PUBLISHING

P.O. Box 100, West Creek NJ 08092. **Fax:** (609)812-5098. **E-mail:** info@down-the-shore.com. **Website:** www.down-the-shore.com. **Contact:** Acquisitions Editor. "Bear in mind that our market is regional-New Jersey, the Jersey Shore, the mid-Atlantic, and seashore and coastal subjects." Publishes hardcover and trade paperback originals and reprints. Book catalog online. Guidelines online.

HOW TO CONTACT Query with SASE. Submit proposal package, clips, 1-2 sample chapters.

TERMS Pays royalty on wholesale or retail price, or makes outright purchase. Responds in 3 months to queries.

TIPS "Carefully consider whether your proposal is a good fit for our established market."

Ⓒ DRAGON MOON PRESS

3521 43A Ave., Red Deer AB T4N 3E9, Canada. **Website:** www.dragonmoonpress.com. Estab. 1994. "Dragon Moon Press is dedicated to new and exciting voices in science fiction and fantasy." Publishes trade paperback and electronic originals. Books: 60 lb. offset paper; short run printing and offset printing. Average print order: 250-3,000. **Published several debut authors within the last year.** Plans 5 first novels this year. Averages 4-6 total titles, 4-5 fiction titles/year. Distributed through Baker & Taylor. Promoted locally through authors and online at leading retail bookstores like Amazon, Barnes & Noble, Chapters, etc.

NEEDS "At present, we are only accepting solicited manuscripts via referral from our authors and partners. All manuscripts already under review will still be considered by our readers, and we will notify you of our decision." For solicited submissions: Market: "We prefer manuscripts targeted to the adult market or the upper border of YA. No middle grade or children's literature, please. Fantasy, science fiction (soft/

sociological). No horror or children's fiction, short stories or poetry."

TIPS "First, be patient. Read our guidelines. Not following our submission guidelines can be grounds for automatic rejection. Second, be patient, we are small and sometimes very slow as a result, especially during book launch season. Third, we view publishing as a family affair. Be ready to participate in the process and show some enthusiasm and understanding in what we do. Remember also, this is a business and not about egos, so keep yours on a leash! Show us a great story with well-developed characters and plot lines, show us that you are interested in participating in marketing and developing as an author, and show us your desire to create a great book and you may just find yourself published by Dragon Moon Press."

DUFOUR EDITIONS

P.O. Box 7, 124 Byers Rd., Chester Springs PA 19425. (610)458-5005. **Website:** www.dufoureditions.com. Estab. 1948. "We publish literary fiction by good writers which is well received and achieves modest sales. De-emphsazing poetry and nonfiction." Publishes hardcover originals, trade paperback originals and reprints. Book catalog available free.

NEEDS "We like books that are slightly off-beat, different and well-written."

HOW TO CONTACT Query with SASE.

TERMS Pays $100-500 advance. Responds in 3-6 months.

Ⓒ THE DUNDURN GROUP

3 Church St., Suite 500, Toronto ON M5E 1M2, Canada. **Website:** www.dundurn.com. Estab. 1972. Dundurn prefers work by Canadian authors. First-time authors are welcome. Publishes hardcover and trade paperback originals and reprints.

HOW TO CONTACT Query with SASE or submit 3 sample chapter(s), synopsis. Accepts queries by mail. Include estimated word count. Responds in 3-4 months to queries. Accepts simultaneous submissions. No electronic submissions.

ⒶⓄ THOMAS DUNNE BOOKS

Imprint of St. Martin's Press, 175 Fifth Ave., New York NY 10010. (212)674-5151. **E-mail:** thomasdunnebooks@stmartins.com. **Website:** www.thomasdunnebooks.com. Estab. 1986. "Thomas Dunne Books publishes popular trade fiction and nonfiction. With an output of approximately 175 titles each year, his group covers a range of genres including commercial and literary fiction, thrillers, biography, politics, sports, popular science, and more. The list is intentionally eclectic and includes a wide range of fiction and nonfiction, from first books to international bestsellers." Publishes hardcover and trade paperback originals, and reprints. Book catalog and ms guidelines free.

HOW TO CONTACT *Accepts agented submissions only.*

Ⓐⵁ DUTTON ADULT TRADE

Penguin Random House, 375 Hudson St., New York NY 10014. (212)366-2000. **Website:** penguin.com. Estab. 1852. "Dutton currently publishes 45 hardcovers a year, roughly half fiction and half nonfiction." Publishes hardcover originals. Book catalog online.

HOW TO CONTACT Agented submissions only. *No unsolicited mss.*

TERMS Pays royalty. Pays negotiable advance.

TIPS "Write the complete ms and submit it to an agent or agents. They will know exactly which editor will be interested in a project."

DYNAMITE ENTERTAINMENT

113 Gaither Dr., Suite 205, Mt. Laurel NJ 8054. **E-mail:** submissions@dynamite.com. **Website:** www.dynamiteentertainment.com.

HOW TO CONTACT Query first. Does not accept unsolicited submissions. Include brief bio, list of publishing credits.

DZANC BOOKS

Dzanc Books, Inc., 2702 Lillian, Ann Arbor MI 48104. **Website:** www.dzancbooks.org.

NEEDS "We're an independent non-profit publishing literary fiction. We also set up writer-in-residence programs and help literary journals develop their subscription bases." Publishes paperback originals.

HOW TO CONTACT Query with outline/synopsis and 35 sample pages. Accepts queries by e-mail. Include brief bio. Agented fiction: 3%. Accepts unsolicited mss. Considers simultaneous submissions, submissions on CD or disk. Rarely critiques/comments on rejected mss. Responds to mss in 5 months.

TIPS "Every word counts—it's amazing how many submissions have poor first sentences or paragraphs and that first impression is hard to shake when it's a bad one."

Ⓐⵁ THE ECCO PRESS

195 Broadway, New York NY 10007. (212)207-7000. **Fax:** (212)702-2460. **Website:** www.harpercollins.com. Estab. 1970. Publishes hardcover and trade paperback originals and reprints.

NEEDS Literary, short story collections. "We can publish possibly 1 or 2 original novels a year."

HOW TO CONTACT *Does not accept unsolicited mss.*

TERMS Pays royalty. Pays negotiable advance.

TIPS "We are always interested in first novels and feel it's important that they be brought to the attention of the reading public."

ⵁ EDGE SCIENCE FICTION AND FANTASY PUBLISHING

Hades Publications, Box 1414, Calgary AB T2P 2L7, Canada. (403)254-0160. **E-mail:** publisher@hadespublications.com. **Website:** www.edgewebsite.com. **Contact:** Editorial Manager. Estab. 1996. EDGE publishes thought-provoking full length novels and anthologies of Science Fiction, Fantasy and Horror. Featuring works by established authors and emerging new voices, EDGE is pleased to provide quality literary entertainment in both print and pixels. Publishes trade paperback and e-book originals. Catalog online. Guidelines online.

NEEDS "We are looking for all types of fantasy, science fiction, and horror - except juvenile, erotica, and religious fiction. Short stories and poetry are only required for announced anthologies." Length: 75,000-100,000/words. Does not want juvenile, erotica, and religious fiction.

HOW TO CONTACT Submit first 3 chapters and synopsis. Check website for guidelines. Include estimated word count.

TERMS Pays 10% royalty on net price for distributed printed editions, 30% royalty on net price for eBook editions. Negotiable advance. Responds in 4-5 months to mss.

WILLIAM B. EERDMANS PUBLISHING CO.

2140 Oak Industrial Dr. NE, Grand Rapids MI 49505. (616)459-4591. **Fax:** (616)459-6540. **E-mail:** info@eerdmans.com. **E-mail:** submissions@eerdmans.com. **Website:** www.eerdmans.com. Estab. 1911. "The majority of our adult publications are religious and most of these are academic or semi-academic in character (as opposed to inspirational or celebrity books), though we also publish general trade books on the Christian life. Our nonreligious titles, most of them in regional history or on social issues, aim, similarly, at an educated audience." Publishes hardcover and paperback originals and reprints. Book catalog and ms guidelines free.

HOW TO CONTACT Query with SASE.

TERMS Responds in 4 weeks.

ELLYSIAN PRESS

E-mail: publisher@ellysianpress.com. **E-mail:** submissions@ellysianpress.com. **Website:** www.ellysianpress.com. **Contact:** Maer Wilson. Estab. 2014. "At Ellysian Press, we seek to create a sense of home for our authors, a place where they can find fulfillment as artists. Just as exceptional mortals once sought a place in the Elysian Fields, now exceptional authors can find a place here at Ellysian Press. We are accepting submissions in the following genres: Fantasy, Science Fiction, Paranormal, Paranormal Romance, Horror, along with Young/New Adult in these genres. Please submit polished manuscripts. It's best to have work read by critique groups or beta readers prior to submission." Publishes fantasy, science fiction, paranormal, paranormal romance, horror, young/new adult in these genres. Catalog online. Guidelines online.

HOW TO CONTACT "We accept online submissions only. Please submit a query letter, a synopsis and the first ten pages of your manuscript in the body of your e-mail."

TERMS Pays quarterly. Does not pay advance. Responds in 1 week for queries; 4-6 weeks for partials and fulls.

ELM BOOKS

1175 Hwy. 130, Laramie WY 82070. (610)529-0460. **E-mail:** leila.monaghan@gmail.com. **Website:** www.elm-books.com. **Contact:** Leila Monaghan, publisher. "We are eager to publish stories by new writers that have real stories to tell. We are looking for short stories (5,000-10,000 words) with real characters and true-to-life stories. Whether your story is fictionalized autobiography, or other stories of real-life mayhem and debauchery, we are interested in reading them!"

NEEDS "We are looking for short stories (1,000-5,000 words) about kids of color that will grab readers' attentions—mysteries, adventures, humor, suspense, set in the present, near past or near future that reflect the realities and hopes of life in diverse communi-

ties." Also looking for middle grade novels (20,000-50,000 words).

HOW TO CONTACT Send complete ms for short stories; synopsis and 3 sample chapters for novels.

TERMS Pays royalties.

ENTANGLED TEEN

Website: www.entangledteen.com. "Entangled Teen and Entangled digiTeen, our young adult imprints publish the swoonworthy young adult romances readers crave. Whether they're dark and angsty or fun and sassy, contemporary, fantastical, or futuristic. We are seeking fresh voices with interesting twists on popular genres."

NEEDS "We are seeking novels in the subgenres of romantic fiction for contemporary, upper young adult with crossover appeal."

HOW TO CONTACT E-mail using site. "All submissions must have strong romantic elements. YA novels should be 50K to 100K in length. Revised backlist titles will be considered on a case by case basis." Agented and unagented considered.

TERMS Pays royalty.

⬤ EYEWEAR PUBLISHING

E-mail: info@eyewearpublishing.com. **Website:** store.eyewearpublishing.com. **Contact:** Dr. Todd Swift, managing director and editor. Estab. 2012. Eyewear Publishing Ltd. is a small press founded in 2012 by Todd Swift, based in London, UK, with distribution in the USA. Our books have been recommended by such literary figures as Kaveh Akbar, Stephen Fry, Louis Theroux, Salman Rushdie, Clare Pollard, Vicki Feaver, Thomas Lux, Suhayl Saadi and The Rev. Jesse Jackson. We search for emerging talent, and neglected out-of-work authors, as well as well-established figures. We are welcoming, with a commitment to diversity. Firm publishes fiction, nonfiction, and poetry. Guidelines online.

TERMS Royalties vary from 10% to 20% Pays variable advance. Response time varies.

FAMILIUS

1254 Commerce Way, Sanger CA 93657. (559)876-2170. **Fax:** (559)876-2180. **E-mail:** bookideas@familius.com. **Website:** familius.com. **Contact:** Acquisitions. Estab. 2011. Familius is all about strengthening families. Collective, the authors and staff have experienced a wide slice of the family-life spectrum. Some come from broken homes. Some are married and in the throes of managing a bursting household. Some are preparing to start families of their own. Together, they publish books and articles that help families be happy. Publishes hardcover, trade paperback, and electronic originals and reprints. Catalog online and print. Guidelines online.

NEEDS All picture books must align with Familius values statement listed on the website footer.

HOW TO CONTACT Submit a proposal package, including a synopsis, 3 sample chapters, and your author platform.

TERMS Authors are paid 10-30% royalty on wholesale price. Responds in 1 month to queries and proposals; 2 months to mss.

FANTAGRAPHICS BOOKS, INC.

7563 Lake City Way NE, Seattle WA 98115. (206)524-1967. **Fax:** (206)524-2104. **Website:** www.fantagraphics.com. **Contact:** Submissions Editor. Estab. 1976. Publishes comics for thinking readers. Does not want mainstream genres of superhero, vigilante, horror, fantasy, or science fiction. Publishes original trade paperbacks. Book catalog online. Guidelines online.

NEEDS "Fantagraphics is an independent company with a modus operandi different from larger, factory-like corporate comics publishers. If your talents are limited to a specific area of expertise (i.e. inking, writing, etc.), then you will need to develop your own team before submitting a project to us. We want to see an idea that is fully fleshed-out in your mind, at least, if not on paper. Submit a minimum of 5 fully-inked pages of art, a synopsis, SASE, and a brief note stating approximately how many issues you have in mind."

TERMS Responds in 2-3 months to queries.

TIPS "Take note of the originality and diversity of the themes and approaches to drawing in such Fantagraphics titles as *Love & Rockets* (stories of life in Latin America and Chicano L.A.), *Palestine* (journalistic autobiography in the Middle East), *Eightball* (surrealism mixed with kitsch culture in stories alternately humorous and painfully personal), and *Naughty Bits* (feminist humor and short stories which both attack and commiserate). Try to develop your own, equally individual voice; originality, aesthetic maturity, and graphic storytelling skill are the signs by which Fantagraphics judges whether or not your submission is ripe for publication."

FARRAR, STRAUS & GIROUX

18 W. 18th St., New York NY 10011. (646)307-5151. **Website:** us.macmillan.com/fsg. **Contact:** Editorial Department. Estab. 1946. "We publish original and well-written material for all ages." Publishes hardcover originals and trade paperback reprints. Catalog available by request. Guidelines online.

NEEDS Do not query picture books; just send ms. Do not fax or e-mail queries or mss.

HOW TO CONTACT Send cover letter describing submission with first 50 pages.

TERMS Pays 2-6% royalty on retail price for paperbacks, 3-10% for hardcovers. Pays $3,000-25,000 advance. Responds in 2-3 months.

⊙ FAT FOX BOOKS

The Den, P.O. Box 579, Tonbridge TN9 9NG, United Kingdom. (44)(0)1580-857249. **E-mail:** hello@fatfoxbooks.com. **Website:** fatfoxbooks.com. "Can you write engaging, funny, original and brilliant stories? We are looking for fresh new talent as well as exciting new ideas from established writers and illustrators. We publish books for children from 3-14, and if we think the story is brilliant and fits our list, then as one of the few publishers who accepts unsolicited material, we will take it seriously. We will consider books of all genres." Guidelines online. Currently closed to submissions.

HOW TO CONTACT For picture books, send complete ms; for longer works, send first 3 chapters and estimate of final word count.

FATHER'S PRESS

590 N.W. 1921 St. Rd., Kingsville MO 64063. (816)550-1138. **E-mail:** mike@fatherspress.com. **Website:** www.fatherspress.com. **Contact:** Mike Smitley, owner (fiction, nonfiction, Christian). Estab. 2006. Publishes hardcover, trade paperback, and mass market paperback originals and reprints. Guidelines online.

HOW TO CONTACT Query with SASE. Unsolicited mss returned unopened. Call or e-mail first.

TERMS Pays 10-15% royalty on wholesale price. Responds in 1-3 months.

❶❷ FEIWEL AND FRIENDS

Macmillan Children's Publishing Group, 175 Fifth Ave., New York NY 10010. (646)307-5151. **Website:** us.macmillan.com. Feiwel and Friends is a publisher of innovative children's fiction and nonfiction literature, including hardcover, paperback series, and individual titles. The list is eclectic and combines quality and commercial appeal for readers ages 0-16. The imprint is dedicated to "book by book" publishing, bringing the work of distinctive and outstanding authors, illustrators, and ideas to the marketplace. This market does not accept unsolicited mss due to the volume of submissions; they also do not accept unsolicited queries for interior art. The best way to submit a ms is through an agent. Catalog online.

FENCE BOOKS

Science Library 320, Univ. of Albany, 1400 Washington Ave., Albany NY 12222. (518)591-8162. **E-mail:** jessp.fence@gmail.com. **Website:** www.fenceportal. org. **Contact:** Submissions Manager. "Fence Books publishes poetry, fiction, and critical texts and anthologies, and prioritizes sustained support for its authors, many of whom come to us through our book contests and then go on to publish second, third, fourth books." Publishes hardcover originals. Guidelines online.

HOW TO CONTACT Submit via contests and occasional open reading periods.

DAVID FICKLING BOOKS

31 Beamont St., Oxford OX1 2NP, United Kingdom. (018)65-339000. **Fax:** (018)65-339009. **Website:** www. davidficklingbooks.co.uk. **Contact:** Simon Mason, managing director. David Fickling Books is a story house."For nearly twelve years DFB has been run as an imprint—first as part of Scholastic, then of Random House. Now we've set up as an independent business." Guidelines online. Closed to submissions. Check website for when they open to submissions and for details on the Inkpot competition.

NEEDS Considers all categories.

HOW TO CONTACT Submit cover letter and 3 sample chapters as PDF attachment saved in format "Author Name_Full Title."

TERMS Responds to mss in 3 months, if interested.

TIPS "We adore stories for all ages, in both text and pictures. Quality is our watch word."

FILBERT PUBLISHING

Box 326, Kandiyohi MN 56251-0326. **E-mail:** filbertpublishing@filbertpublishing.com. **Website:** filbertpublishing.com. **Contact:** Maurice Erickson, acquisitions. Estab. 2001. "We really like to publish books that creative entrepreneurs can use to help them make a living following their dream. This includes books on marketing, books that encourage living a full life,

freelancing, self-help, we'll consider a fairly wide range of subjects under this umbrella. The people who purchase our titles (and visit our website) tend to be in their fifties, female, well-educated; many are freelancers who want to make a living writing. Any well-written manuscript that would appeal to that audience is nearly a slam dunk to get reviewed." Publishes trade paperback and electronic originals and reprints. Catalog online. Guidelines online.

NEEDS "We're thrilled when we find a story that sweeps us off our feet. Fiction queries have been very sparse the last couple of years, and we're keen on expanding our current mystery/suspense line in the coming year."

HOW TO CONTACT Query, include SASE with a proposal package, including a synopsis, 5 sample chapters, information regarding your web platform, and a brief mention of your current marketing plan. "If you'd like to submit a query via e-mail, that's fine. However, we get a lot of e-mail and if you don't receive a reply within a couple weeks, don't hesitate to resend."

TERMS Paperback authors receive 10% royalty on retail price. E-books receive 50% net. Responds in 1-2 months. Sometimes we get really behind on this. If after a couple months you haven't heard from us, feel free to resend.

TIPS "Get to know us. Subscribe to Writing Etc./The Creative Entrepreneur to capture our preferred tone. Dig through our website, you'll get many ideas of what we're looking for. We love nurturing new writing careers and most of our authors have stuck with us since our humble beginning. All new authors begin their journey with us with e-book publication. If that goes well, we move on to print. We love words. We enjoy marketing. We really love the publishing business. If you share those passions, feel free to query."

FIRST SECOND

Macmillan Children's Publishing Group, 175 5th Ave., New York NY 10010. **E-mail:** mail@firstsecondbooks. com. **Website:** www.firstsecondbooks.com. First Second is a publisher of graphic novels and an imprint of Macmillan Children's Publishing Group. First Second does not accept unsolicited submissions. Catalog online.

TERMS Responds in about 6 weeks.

FLASHLIGHT PRESS

527 Empire Blvd., Brooklyn NY 11225. (718)288-8300. **Fax:** (718)972-6307. **E-mail:** submissions@flashlight-

press.com. **Website:** www.flashlightpress.com. **Contact:** Shari Dash Greenspan, editor. Estab. 2004. Publishes hardcover original children's picture books for 4-8 year olds. Book catalog online. Guidelines online.

NEEDS Average word length: 1,000 words. Picture books: contemporary, humor, multicultural.

HOW TO CONTACT "Query by e-mail only, after carefully reading our submission guidelines online. Do not send anything by snail mail."

TERMS Pays 8-10% royalty on net. Pays advance. "Only accepts e-mail queries according to submission guidelines."

🟢 FLYING EYE BOOKS

62 Great Eastern St., London EC2A 3QR, United Kingdom. (44)(0)207-033-4430. **E-mail:** picturbksubs@nobrow.net. **Website:** www.flyingeyebooks.com. Estab. 2013. Flying Eye Books is the children's imprint of award-winning visual publishing house Nobrow. FEB seeks to retain the same attention to detail and excellence in illustrated content as its parent publisher, but with a focus on the craft of children's storytelling and nonfiction. Guidelines online.

FOLDED WORD

Website: https://folded.wordpress.com. Estab. 2008. Folded Word is a literary micro-press that explores the world, one voice at a time. "We publish single poems, short stories, and essays on our blog. Chapbook-length manuscripts are only solicited from regular contributors to our blog. We no longer publish full-length books." Catalog online. No longer accepting unsolicited submissions. Chapbook-length manuscripts only solicited from regular contributors to our blog. Please visit https://folded.wordpress.com/submissions/ for details.

TIPS "Chapbook-length manuscripts are only solicited from regular contributors to our blog. Unsolicited manuscripts will be discarded without reply."

FORWARD MOVEMENT

412 Sycamore St., Cincinnati OH 45202. (513)721-6659; (800)543-1813. **Fax:** (513)721-0729. **E-mail:** editorial@forwardmovement.org. **Website:** www.forwardmovement.org. Estab. 1934. "Forward Movement was established to help reinvigorate the life of the church. Many titles focus on the life of prayer, where our relationship with God is centered, death, marriage, baptism, recovery, joy, the Episcopal Church and more. Currently emphasizing prayer/spirituality." Book catalog free. Guidelines online.

TERMS Responds in 1 month.

TIPS "Audience is primarily Episcopalians and other Christians."

FOUR WAY BOOKS

Box 535, Village Station, New York NY 10014. **E-mail:** editors@fourwaybooks.com. **Website:** www.fourwaybooks.com. Estab. 1993. "Four Way Books is a not-for-profit literary press dedicated to publishing poetry and short fiction by emerging and established writers. Each year, Four Way Books publishes the winners of its national poetry competitions, as well as collections accepted through general submission, panel selection, and solicitation by the editors."

NEEDS Open reading period: June 1-30. Book-length story collections and novellas. Submission guidelines will be posted online at end of May. Does not want novels or translations.

FREE SPIRIT PUBLISHING, INC.

6325 Sandburg Rd., Suite 100, Minneapolis MN 55427-3674. (612)338-2068. **Fax:** (612)337-5050. **E-mail:** acquisitions@freespirit.com. **Website:** www. freespirit.com. Estab. 1983. "Free Spirit is the leading publisher of learning tools that support young people's social-emotional health and educational needs. We help children and teens think for themselves, overcome challenges, and make a difference in the world." Free Spirit does not accept general fiction, poetry or storybook submissions. Publishes trade paperback originals and reprints. Book catalog and guidelines online.

NEEDS "Please review catalog and author guidelines (both available online) for details before submitting proposal. If you'd like material returned, enclose a SASE with sufficient postage."

TERMS Responds to proposals in 2-6 months.

TIPS "Our books are issue-oriented, jargon-free, and solution-focused. Our audience is children, teens, teachers, parents and youth counselors. We are especially concerned with kids' social and emotional well-being and look for books with ready-to-use strategies for coping with today's issues at home or in school—written in everyday language. We are not looking for academic or religious materials, or books that analyze problems with the nation's school systems. Instead, we want books that offer practical, positive advice so kids can help themselves, and parents and teachers can help kids succeed."

GERTRUDE PRESS

P.O. Box 28281, Portland OR 97228. (503)515-8252. **E-mail:** editorgertrudepress@gmail.com. **Website:** www.gertrudepress.org. Estab. 2005. "Gertrude Press is a nonprofit organization developing and showcasing the creative talents of lesbian, gay, bisexual, trans, queer-identified and allied individuals. We publish limited-edition fiction and poetry chapbooks plus the biannual literary journal, *Gertrude*." Reads chapbook mss only through contests.

TIPS Sponsors poetry and fiction chapbook contest. Prize is $175 and 50 contributor's copies. Submission guidelines and fee information on website. "Read the journal and sample published work. We are not impressed by pages of publications; your work should speak for itself."

GIVAL PRESS

Gival Press, LLC, P.O. Box 3812, Arlington VA 22203. (703)351-0079. **E-mail:** givalpress@yahoo.com. **Website:** www.givalpress.com. **Contact:** Robert L. Giron, editor-in-chief (area of interest: literary). Estab. 1998. "We publish literary works: fiction, nonfiction (essays, academic), and poetry in English, Spanish, and French." Publishes trade paperback, electronic originals, and reprints. Book catalog online. Guidelines online.

HOW TO CONTACT Always query first via e-mail; provide description, author's bio, and supportive material.

TERMS Pays royalty. Per the contest prize, amount per the content. Outside of contests, Responds in 3-5 months. If we get behind, it's okay to remind us. Prefer submissions via Submittable or email (after query).

TIPS "Our audience is those who read literary works with depth to the work. Visit our website—there is much to be read/learned from the numerous pages."

THE GLENCANNON PRESS

P.O. Box 1428, El Cerrito CA 94530. (510)455-9027. **E-mail:** merships@yahoo.com. **Website:** www.glencannon.com. **Contact:** Bill Harris (maritime, maritime children's). Estab. 1993. "We publish quality books about ships and the sea." Average print order: 500. Member PMA, BAIPA. Distributes titles through Baker & Taylor. Promotes titles through direct mail, magazine advertising and word of mouth. Accepts unsolicited mss. Often comments on rejected mss. Publishes hardcover and paperback originals and hardcover reprints.

HOW TO CONTACT Submit complete ms. Include brief bio, list of publishing credits. Send SASE for return of ms or send a disposable ms and SASE for reply only.

TERMS Pays 10-20% royalty. Does not pay advance. Responds in 1 month to queries; 2 months to mss.

TIPS "Write a good story in a compelling style."

ⓐⓞ DAVID R. GODINE, PUBLISHER

15 Court Square, Suite 320, Boston MA 02108. (617)451-9600. **Fax:** (617)350-0250. **E-mail:** info@godine.com. **Website:** www.godine.com. Estab. 1970. "We publish books that matter for people who care." This publisher is no longer considering unsolicited mss of any type. Only interested in agented material.

ⓞ GOOSE LANE EDITIONS

500 Beaverbrook Ct., Suite 330, Fredericton NB E3B 5X4, Canada. (506)450-4251. **Fax:** (506)459-4991. **E-mail:** info@gooselane.com. **Website:** www.gooselane.com. Estab. 1954. "Goose Lane publishes literary fiction and nonfiction from well-read and highly skilled Canadian authors." Publishes hardcover and paperback originals and occasional reprints.

NEEDS Our needs in fiction never change: Substantial, character-centered literary fiction. No children's, YA, mainstream, mass market, genre, mystery, thriller, confessional or science fiction.

HOW TO CONTACT Query with SAE with Canadian stamps or IRCs. No U.S. stamps.

TERMS Pays 8-10% royalty on retail price. Pays $500-3,000, negotiable advance. Responds in 6 months to queries.

TIPS "Writers should send us outlines and samples of books that show a very well-read author with highly developed literary skills. Our books are almost all by Canadians living in Canada; we seldom consider submissions from outside Canada. We consider submissions from outside Canada only when the author is Canadian and the book is of extraordinary interest to Canadian readers. We do not publish books for children or for the young adult market."

ⓐⓞ GRAYWOLF PRESS

250 Third Ave. N., Suite 600, Minneapolis MN 55401. (651)641-0077. **Fax:** (651)641-0036. **Website:** www.graywolfpress.org. Estab. 1974. "Graywolf Press is an

independent, nonprofit publisher dedicated to the creation and promotion of thoughtful and imaginative contemporary literature essential to a vital and diverse culture." Publishes trade cloth and paperback originals. Book catalog free. Guidelines online.

NEEDS "Familiarize yourself with our list first." No genre books (romance, western, science fiction, suspense)

HOW TO CONTACT Agented submissions only.

TERMS Pays royalty on retail price. Pays $1,000-25,000 advance. Responds in 3 months to queries.

⚫⊘ GREENWILLOW BOOKS

HarperCollins Publishers, 10 E. 53rd St., New York NY 10022. (212)207-7000. **Website:** www.greenwillowblog.com. Estab. 1974. *Does not accept unsolicited mss.* "Unsolicited mail will not be opened and will not be returned." Publishes hardcover originals, paperbacks, e-books, and reprints.

HOW TO CONTACT *Agented submissions only.*

TERMS Pays 10% royalty on wholesale price for first-time authors. Offers variable advance.

⊘ GREY GECKO PRESS

565 S. Mason Rd., Suite 154, Katy TX 77450. **E-mail:** info@greygeckopress.com. **E-mail:** submissions@greygeckopress.com. **Website:** www.greygeckopress.com. **Contact:** Submissions Coordinator. Estab. 2011. Grey Gecko focuses on new and emerging authors and great books that might not otherwise get a chance to see the light of day. "We publish all our titles in hardcover, trade paperback, and e-book formats (both Kindle and ePub), as well as audiobook and foreign-language editions. Our books are available worldwide, for readers of all types, kinds, and interests." Not currently open for submissions; check website for updates. Publishes hardcover, trade paperback, audiobook, and electronic originals. Catalog online. Guidelines online.

NEEDS "We do not publish extreme horror, erotica, or religious fiction. New and interesting stories by unpublished authors will always get our attention. Innovation is a core value of our company." Does not want extreme horror (e.g. *Saw* or *Hostel*), religious, or erotica.

HOW TO CONTACT When open, use online submission page.

TERMS Pays 50-75% royalties on net revenue. Does not pay advance. Responds in 6-12 months.

TIPS "Be willing to be a part of the Grey Gecko family. Publishing with us is a partnership, not indentured servitude. Authors are expected and encouraged to be proactive and contribute to their book's success."

⚫⊘ GROSSET & DUNLAP PUBLISHERS

Penguin Random House, 345 Hudson St., New York NY 10014. **Website:** www.penguin.com. Estab. 1898. Grosset & Dunlap publishes children's books that show children that reading is fun, with books that speak to their interests, and that are affordable so that children can build a home library of their own. Focus on licensed properties, series and readers. "Grosset & Dunlap publishes high-interest, affordable books for children ages 0-10 years. We focus on original series, licensed properties, readers and novelty books." Publishes hardcover (few) and mass market paperback originals.

HOW TO CONTACT *Agented submissions only.*

TERMS Pays royalty. Pays advance.

◎ GROUNDWOOD BOOKS

128 Sterling Rd., Lower Level, Attention: Submissions, Toronto ON M6R 2B7, Canada. (416)363-4343. **Fax:** (416)363-1017. **E-mail:** submissions@groundwoodbooks.com. **Website:** groundwoodbooks.com. "We are always looking for new authors of novel-length fiction for children of all ages. Our mandate is to publish high-quality, character-driven literary fiction. We do not generally publish stories with an obvious moral or message, or genre fiction such as thrillers or fantasy." Publishes 19 picture books/year; 2 young readers/year; 3 middle readers/year; 3 young adult titles/year, approximately 2 nonfiction titles/year. Visit website for guidelines.

HOW TO CONTACT Submit a cover letter, synopsis and sample chapters via e-mail. "Due to the large number of submissions we receive, Groundwood regrets that we cannot accept unsolicited manuscripts for picture books."

TERMS Offers advances. Responds to mss in 6-8 months.

⚫⊘ GROVE/ATLANTIC, INC.

154 W. 14th St., 12th Floor, New York NY 10011. **E-mail:** info@groveatlantic.com. **Website:** www.groveatlantic.com. Estab. 1917. "Due to limited resources of time and staffing, Grove/Atlantic cannot accept manuscripts that do not come through a literary agent. In today's publishing world, agents are more impor-

tant than ever, helping writers shape their work and navigate the main publishing houses to find the most appropriate outlet for a project." Publishes hardcover and trade paperback originals, and reprints. Book catalog available online.

HOW TO CONTACT Agented submissions only.

TERMS Pays 7 ½-12 ½% royalty. Makes outright purchase of $5-500,000. Responds in 1 month to queries; 2 months to proposals; 4 months to mss.

GUERNICA EDITIONS

1569 Heritage Way, Oakville ON L6M 2Z7, Canada. (905)599-5304. **Fax:** (416)981-7606. **E-mail:** michaelmirolla@guernicaeditions.com. **Website:** www.guernicaeditions.com. **Contact:** Michael Mirolla, editor/publisher (poetry, nonfiction, short stories, novels). Estab. 1978. Guernica Editions is a literary press that produces works of poetry, fiction and nonfiction often by writers who are ignored by the mainstream. "We feature an imprint (MiroLand) which accepts memoirs, how-to books, graphic novels, genre fiction with the possibility of children's and cook books." A new imprint, Guernica World Editions, features writers who are non-Canadian. Publishes trade paperback originals and reprints. Book catalog online. Queries and submissions accepted via e-mail January 1-April 30.

NEEDS "We wish to open up into the literary fiction world and focus less on poetry." Does not want fantasy, YA.

HOW TO CONTACT E-mail queries only.

TERMS Pays 10% royalty on either cover or retail price. Pays $450-750 advance. Responds in 1 month to queries; 6 months to proposals; 1 year to mss.

HACHAI PUBLISHING

527 Empire Blvd., Brooklyn NY 11225. (718)633-0100. **Fax:** (718)633-0103. **E-mail:** info@hachai.com; dlr@hachai.com. **Website:** www.hachai.com. **Contact:** Devorah Leah Rosenfeld, editor. Estab. 1988. Hachai is dedicated to producing high quality Jewish children's literature, ages 2-10. Story should promote universal values such as sharing, kindness, etc. Publishes hardcover originals. Guidelines online.

> "All books have spiritual/religious themes, specifically traditional Jewish content. We're seeking books about morals and values; the Jewish experience in current and Biblical times; and Jewish observance, Sabbath and holidays."

NEEDS Picture books and young readers: contemporary, historical fiction, religion. Middle readers: adventure, contemporary, problem novels, religion. Does not want to see fantasy, animal stories, romance, problem novels depicting drug use or violence.

HOW TO CONTACT Submit complete ms.

TERMS Work purchased outright from authors for $800-1,000. Responds in 2 months to mss.

TIPS "We are looking for books that convey the traditional Jewish experience in modern times or long ago; traditional Jewish observance such as Sabbath and holidays and mitzvos such as mezuzah, blessings etc.; positive character traits (middos) such as honesty, charity, respect, sharing, etc. We are also interested in historical fiction for young readers (7-10) written with a traditional Jewish perspective and highlighting the relevance of Torah in making important choices. Please, no animal stories, romance, violence, preachy sermonizing. Write a story that incorporates a moral, not a preachy morality tale. Originality is the key. We feel Hachai publications will appeal to a wider readership as parents become more interested in positive values for their children."

HADLEY RILLE BOOKS

P.O. Box 25466, Overland Park KS 66225. **E-mail:** contact@hadleyrillebooks.com. **E-mail:** subs@hadleyrillebooks.com. **Website:** https://hadleyrillebks.wordpress.com. **Contact:** Eric T. Reynolds, editor/publisher. Estab. 2005. Currently closed to submissions. Check website for future reading periods.

TIPS "We aim to produce books that are aligned with current interest in the genres. Anthology markets are somewhat rare in SF these days, we feel there aren't enough good anthologies being published each year and part of our goal is to present the best that we can. We like stories that fit well within the guidelines of the particular anthology for which we are soliciting manuscripts. Aside from that, we want stories with strong characters (not necessarily characters with strong personalities, flawed characters are welcome). We want a sense of wonder and awe. We want to feel the world around the character and so scene description is important (however, this doesn't always require a lot of text, just set the scene well so we don't wonder where the character is). We strongly recommend workshopping the story or having it critiqued in some way by readers familiar with the genre. We prefer clichés be kept to a bare minimum in the prose and avoid re-working old story lines."

HAMPTON ROADS PUBLISHING CO., INC.

65 Parker St, Suite 7, Newburyport MA 01950. **E-mail:** submissions@rwwbooks.com. **Website:** www.redwheelweiser.com. Estab. 1989. "Our reason for being is to impact, uplift, and contribute to positive change in the world. We publish books that will enrich and empower the evolving consciousness of mankind. Though we are not necessarily limited in scope, we are most interested in manuscripts on the following subjects: Body/Mind/Spirit, Health and Healing, Self-Help. Please be advised that at the moment we are not accepting fiction or novelized material that does not pertain to body/mind/spirit, channeled writing." Publishes and distributes hardcover and trade paperback originals on subjects including metaphysics, health, complementary medicine, and other related topics. Guidelines online.

TERMS Pays royalty. Pays $1,000-50,000 advance. Responds in 2-4 months to queries; 1 month to proposals; 6-12 months to mss.

✪ HARLEQUIN BLAZE

225 Duncan Mill Rd., Don Mills ON M3B 3K9, Canada. (416)445-5860. **Website:** www.harlequin.com. **Contact:** Kathleen Scheibling, senior editor. "Harlequin Blaze is a red-hot series. It is a vehicle to build and promote new authors who have a strong sexual edge to their stories. It is also the place to be for seasoned authors who want to create a sexy, sizzling, longer contemporary story." Publishes paperback originals. Guidelines online.

NEEDS "Sensuous, highly romantic, innovative plots that are sexy in premise and execution. The tone of the books can run from fun and flirtatious to dark and sensual. Submissions should have a very contemporary feel—what it's like to be young and single today. We are looking for heroes and heroines in their early 20s and up. There should be a a strong emphasis on the physical relationship between the couples. Fully described love scenes along with a high level of fantasy and playfulness." Length: 55,000-60,000 words.

TIPS "Are you a *Cosmo* girl at heart? A fan of *Sex and the City*? Or maybe you have a sexually adventurous spirit. If so, then Blaze is the series for you!"

HARLEQUIN DESIRE

233 Broadway, Suite 1001, New York NY 10279. (212)553-4200. **Website:** www.harlequin.com. **Contact:** Stacy Boyd, senior editor. Always powerful, passionate, and provocative. "Desire novels are sensual reads and a love scene or scenes are still needed. But there is no set number of pages that needs to be fulfilled. Rather, the level of sensuality must be appropriate to the storyline. Above all, every Silhouette Desire novel must fulfill the promise of a powerful, passionate and provocative read." Publishes paperback originals and reprints. Guidelines online.

NEEDS Looking for novels in which "the conflict is an emotional one, springing naturally from the unique characters you've chosen. The focus is on the developing relationship, set in a believable plot. Sensuality is key, but lovemaking is never taken lightly. Secondary characters and subplots need to blend with the core story. Innovative new directions in storytelling and fresh approaches to classic romantic plots are welcome." Manuscripts must be 50,000-55,000 words.

TERMS Pays royalty. Offers advance.

✪ HARLEQUIN INTRIGUE

225 Duncan Mill Rd., Don Mills ON M3B 3K9, Canada. **Website:** www.harlequin.com. **Contact:** Denise Zaza, senior editor. Wants crime stories tailored to the series romance market packed with a variety of thrilling suspense and whodunit mystery. Word count: 55,000-60,000. Guidelines online.

HOW TO CONTACT Submit online.

✪ HARLEQUIN SUPERROMANCE

225 Duncan Mill Rd., Don Mills ON M3B 3K9, Canada. **Website:** www.harlequin.com. **Contact:** Victoria Curran, senior editor. "The Harlequin Superromance line focuses on believable characters triumphing over true-to-life drama and conflict. At the heart of these contemporary stories should be a compelling romance that brings the reader along with the hero and heroine on their journey of overcoming the obstacles in their way and falling in love. Because of the longer length relevant subplots and secondary characters are welcome but not required. This series publishes a variety of story types—family sagas, romantic suspense, Westerns, to name a few—and tones from light to dramatic, emotional to suspenseful. Settings also vary from vibrant urban neighborhoods to charming small towns. The unifying element of Harlequin Superromance stories is the realistic treatment of character

and plot. The characters should seem familiar to readers—similar to people they know in their own lives—and the circumstances within the realm of possibility. The stories should be layered and complex in that the conflicts should not be easily resolved. The best way to get an idea of we're looking for is to read what we're currently publishing. The aim of Superromance novels is to produce a contemporary, involving read with a mainstream tone in its situations and characters, using romance as the major theme. To achieve this, emphasis should be placed on individual writing styles and unique and topical ideas." Publishes paperback originals. Guidelines online.

NEEDS "The criteria for Superromance books are flexible. Aside from length (80,000 words), the determining factor for publication will always be quality. Authors should strive to break free of stereotypes, clichés and worn-out plot devices to create strong, believable stories with depth and emotional intensity. Superromance novels are intended to appeal to a wide range of romance readers."

HOW TO CONTACT Submit online.

TERMS Pays royalties. Pays advance.

TIPS "A general familiarity with current Superromance books is advisable to keep abreast of ever-changing trends and overall scope, but we don't want imitations. We look for sincere, heartfelt writing based on true-to-life experiences the reader can identify with. We are interested in innovation."

HARMONY INK PRESS

Dreamspinner Press, 5032 Capital Circle SW, Suite 2 PMB 279, Tallahassee FL 32305. (850)632-4648. **Fax:** (888)308-3739. **E-mail:** submissions@harmonyinkpress.com. **Website:** harmonyinkpress.com. **Contact:** Anne Regan. Estab. 2010. Teen and new adult fiction featuring at least 1 strong LGBTQ+ main character who shows significant personal growth through the course of the story.

NEEDS "We are looking for stories in all subgenres, featuring primary characters across the whole LGBTQ+ spectrum between the ages of 14 and 21 that explore all the facets of young adult, teen, and new adult life. Sexual content should be appropriate for the characters and the story."

HOW TO CONTACT Submit complete ms.

TERMS Pays royalty. Pays $500-1,000 advance.

HARPERCOLLINS

195 Broadway, New York NY 10007. (212)207-7000. **Website:** www.harpercollins.com. HarperCollins, one of the largest English language publishers in the world, is a broad-based publisher with strengths in academic, business and professional, children's, educational, general interest, and religious and spiritual books, as well as multimedia titles. Publishes hardcover and paperback originals and paperback reprints.

NEEDS "We look for a strong story line and exceptional literary talent."

HOW TO CONTACT Agented submissions only. *All unsolicited mss returned.*

TERMS Pays royalty. Pays negotiable advance.

TIPS "We do not accept any unsolicited material."

HARPERCOLLINS CANADA, LTD.

2 Bloor St. E., 20th Floor, Toronto ON M4W 1A8, Canada. (416)975-9334. **Fax:** (416)975-5223. **Website:** www.harpercollins.ca. Estab. 1989. *HarperCollins Canada is not accepting unsolicited material at this time.*

HARPERCOLLINS CHILDREN'S BOOKS/ HARPERCOLLINS PUBLISHERS

195 Broadway, New York NY 10007. (212)207-7000. **Website:** www.harpercollins.com. HarperCollins, one of the largest English language publishers in the world, is a broad-based publisher with strengths in academic, business and professional, children's, educational, general interest, and religious and spiritual books, as well as multimedia titles. Publishes hardcover and paperback originals and paperback reprints. Catalog online.

NEEDS "We look for a strong story line and exceptional literary talent."

HOW TO CONTACT Agented submissions only. *All unsolicited mss returned.*

TERMS Negotiates payment upon acceptance. Responds in 1 month, will contact only if interested. Does not accept any unsolicted texts.

TIPS "We do not accept any unsolicited material."

HARPER VOYAGER

Imprint of HarperCollins General Books Group, 195 Broadway, New York NY 10007. (212)207-7000. **Website:** www.harpercollins.com. Estab. 1998. Eos publishes quality science fiction/fantasy with broad appeal. Publishes hardcover originals, trade and mass market paperback originals, and reprints. Guidelines online.

NEEDS No horror or juvenile.

HOW TO CONTACT Agented submissions only. *All unsolicited mss returned.*

TERMS Pays royalty on retail price. Pays variable advance.

❶❷ HARVEST HOUSE PUBLISHERS

990 Owen Loop, Eugene OR 97402. (541)343-0123. **Fax:** (541)302-0731. **Website:** www.harvesthousepublishers.com. Estab. 1974. Publishes hardcover, trade paperback, and mass market paperback originals and reprints.

NEEDS *No unsolicited mss, proposals, or artwork.*

HOW TO CONTACT Agented submissions only.

TERMS Pays royalty.

TIPS "For first time/nonpublished authors we suggest building their literary résumé by submitting to magazines, or perhaps accruing book contributions."

HENDRICK-LONG PUBLISHING CO., INC.

10635 Tower Oaks, Suite D, Houston TX 77070. (832)912-READ. **Fax:** (832)912-7353. **E-mail:** hendrick-long@att.net. **Website:** hendricklongpublishing.com. Estab. 1969. "Hendrick-Long publishes historical fiction and nonfiction about Texas and the Southwest for children and young adults." Publishes hardcover and trade paperback originals and hardcover reprints. Book catalog available. Guidelines online.

HOW TO CONTACT Query with SASE. Submit outline, clips, 2 sample chapters.

TERMS Pays royalty on selling price. Pays advance. Responds in 3 months to queries.

HEYDAY BOOKS

c/o Acquisitions Editor, Box 9145, Berkeley CA 94709. **Fax:** (510)549-1889. **E-mail:** heyday@heydaybooks.com. **Website:** www.heydaybooks.com. **Contact:** Gayle Wattawa, acquisitions and editorial director. Estab. 1974. "Heyday Books publishes nonfiction books and literary anthologies with a strong California focus. We publish books about Native Americans, natural history, history, literature, and recreation, with a strong California focus." Publishes hardcover originals, trade paperback originals and reprints. Book catalog online. Guidelines online.

NEEDS Publishes picture books, beginning readers, and young adult literature.

HOW TO CONTACT Submit complete ms for picture books; proposal with sample chapters for longer works. include a chapter by chapter summary. Mark attention: Children's Submission. Reviews manuscript/illustration packages; but may consider art and text separately. Tries to respond to query within 12 weeks.

TERMS Pays 8% royalty on net price. Responds in 3 months.

HOLIDAY HOUSE, INC.

425 Madison Ave., New York NY 10017. (212)688-0085. **Fax:** (212)421-6134. **E-mail:** info@holidayhouse.com. **Website:** holidayhouse.com. Estab. 1935. "Holiday House publishes children's and young adult books for the school and library markets. We have a commitment to publishing first-time authors and illustrators. We specialize in quality hardcovers from picture books to young adult, both fiction and nonfiction, primarily for the school and library market." Publishes hardcover originals and paperback reprints. Guidelines for #10 SASE.

NEEDS Children's books only.

HOW TO CONTACT Query with SASE. No phone calls, please.

TERMS Pays royalty on list price, range varies. Responds in 4 months.

TIPS "We need manuscripts with strong stories and writing."

❶❷ HENRY HOLT

175 Fifth Ave., New York NY 10011. (646)307-5095. **Fax:** (212)633-0748. **Website:** www.henryholt.com. *Agented submissions only.*

HOPEWELL PUBLICATIONS

P.O. Box 11, Titusville NJ 08560. **Website:** www.hope-pubs.com. **Contact:** E. Martin, publisher. Estab. 2002. "Hopewell Publications specializes in classic reprints—books with proven sales records that have gone out of print—and new titles of interest. Our catalog spans from 1 to 60 years of publication history. We print fiction and nonfiction, and we accept agented and unagented materials. Submissions are accepted online only." Format publishes in hardcover, trade paperback, and electronic originals; trade paperback and electronic reprints. Catalog online. Guidelines online.

HOW TO CONTACT Query online using our online guidelines.

TERMS Pays royalty on retail price. Responds in 3 months to queries; 6 months to proposals; 9 months to mss.

HOUGHTON MIFFLIN HARCOURT BOOKS FOR CHILDREN

Imprint of Houghton Mifflin Trade & Reference Division, 222 Berkeley St., Boston MA 02116. (617)351-5000. **Fax:** (617)351-1111. **Website:** www.houghtonmifflinbooks.com. Houghton Mifflin Harcourt gives shape to ideas that educate, inform, and above all, delight. *Does not respond to or return mss unless interested.* Publishes hardcover originals and trade paperback originals and reprints. Guidelines online.

HOW TO CONTACT Submit complete ms.

TERMS Pays 5-10% royalty on retail price. Pays variable advance. Responds in 4-6 months to queries.

✪⊘ HOUSE OF ANANSI PRESS

128 Sterling Rd., Lower Level, Toronto ON M6R 2B7, Canada. (416)363-4343. **Fax:** (416)363-1017. **Website:** www.anansi.ca. Estab. 1967. House of Anansi publishes literary fiction and poetry by Canadian and international writers.

NEEDS Publishes literary fiction that has a unique flair, memorable characters, and a strong narrative voice.

HOW TO CONTACT Query with SASE.

TERMS Pays 8-10% royalties. Pays $750 advance and 10 author's copies.

IDW PUBLISHING

2765 Truxtun Rd., San Diego CA 92106. **E-mail:** letters@idwpublishing.com. **Website:** www.idwpublishing.com. Estab. 1999. IDW Publishing currently publishes a wide range of comic books and graphic novels including titles based on GI Joe, Star Trek, Terminator: Salvation, and Transformers. Creator-driven titles include Fallen Angel by Peter David and JK Woodward, Locke & Key by Joe Hill and Gabriel Rodriguez, and a variety of titles by writer Steve Niles including Wake the Dead, Epilogue, and Dead, She Said. Publishes hardcover, mass market and trade paperback originals.

ILIUM PRESS

2407 S. Sonora Dr., Spokane WA 99037. (509)701-8866. **E-mail:** iliumpress@outlook.com. **Contact:** John Lemon, owner/editor. Estab. 2010. "Ilium Press is a small, 1-person press that I created to cultivate and promote the relevance of epic poetry in today's world. My focus is book-length narrative poems in blank (non-rhyming) metered verse, such as iambic parameter or sprung verse. I am very selective about my projects, but I provide extensive editorial care to those projects I take on." Publishes trade paperback originals and reprints, electronic originals and reprints.

TERMS Pays 20-50% royalties on receipts. Does not pay advance. Responds in 6 months.

IMAGE COMICS

2701 NW Vaughn St., Suite 780, Portland OR 97210. **E-mail:** submissions@imagecomics.com. **Website:** www.imagecomics.com. Estab. 1992. Publishes creator-owned comic books, graphic novels. See this company's website for detailed guidelines. Does not accept writing samples without art.

HOW TO CONTACT Query with 1-page synopsis and 5 pages or more of samples. "We do not accept writing (that is plots, scripts, whatever) samples! If you're an established pro, we might be able to find somebody willing to work with you but it would be nearly impossible for us to read through every script that might find its way our direction. Do not send your script or your plot unaccompanied by art—it will be discarded, unread."

TIPS "We are not looking for any specific genre or type of comic book. We are looking for comics that are well written and well drawn, by people who are dedicated and can meet deadlines."

IMBRIFEX BOOKS

Flattop Productions, Inc., 8275 S. Eastern Ave., Suite 200, Las Vegas NV 89123. (702)309-0130. **E-mail:** acquisitions@imbrifex.com. **Website:** https://imbrifex.com. **Contact:** Mark Sedenquist. Estab. 2016. Based in Las Vegas, Nevada, Imbrifex Books publishes both fiction and nonfiction, with a particular interest in books for road trip aficionados and books that have a connection with Las Vegas and the desert Southwest. Titles are distributed world-wide through Pacific Group West, (PGW), and Audible.com. Guidelines online.

TERMS Pays advance. Responds in 2 months.

IMMEDIUM

P.O. Box 31846, San Francisco CA 94131. (415)452-8546. **Fax:** (360)937-6272. **Website:** www.immedium.com. **Contact:** Submissions Editor. Estab. 2005. "Immedium focuses on publishing eye-catching children's picture books, Asian-American topics, and contemporary arts, popular culture, and multicultural issues." Publishes hardcover and trade paperback originals. Catalog online. Guidelines online.

HOW TO CONTACT Submit complete ms.

TERMS Pays 5% royalty on wholesale price. Pays on publication. Responds in 1-3 months.

TIPS "Our audience is children and parents. Please visit our site."

☺ INSOMNIAC PRESS

520 Princess Ave., London ON N6B 2B8, Canada. (416)504-6270. **Website:** www.insomniacpress.com. Estab. 1992. Publishes trade paperback originals and reprints, mass market paperback originals, and electronic originals and reprints. Guidelines online.

NEEDS "We publish a mix of commercial (mysteries) and literary fiction."

HOW TO CONTACT Query via e-mail, submit proposal.

TERMS Pays 10-15% royalty on retail price. Pays $500-1,000 advance.

TIPS "We envision a mixed readership that appreciates up-and-coming literary fiction and poetry as well as solidly researched and provocative nonfiction. Peruse our website and familiarize yourself with what we've published in the past."

INTERLINK PUBLISHING GROUP, INC.

46 Crosby St., Northampton MA 01060. (413)582-7054. **E-mail:** info@interlinkbooks.com. **E-mail:** submissions@interlinkbooks.com. **Website:** www.interlinkbooks.com. Estab. 1987. Interlink is an independent publisher of general trade adult fiction and nonfiction with an emphasis on books that have a wide appeal while also meeting high intellectual and literary standards. "Our list is devoted to works of literature, history, contemporary politics, travel, art, and cuisine from around the world, often from areas underrepresented in Western media." Publishes hardcover and trade paperback originals. Book catalog and guidelines online.

NEEDS "We are looking for translated works relating to the Middle East, Africa or Latin America. The only fiction we publish falls into our 'Interlink World Fiction' series. Most of these books, as you can see in our catalog, are translated fiction from around the world. The series aims to bring fiction from other countries to a North American audience. In short, unless you

were born outside the United States, your novel will not fit into the series." No science fiction, romance, plays, erotica, fantasy, horror.

HOW TO CONTACT Query by e-mail. Submit outline, sample chapters.

TERMS Pays 6-8% royalty on retail price. Pays small advance. Responds in 3-6 months to queries.

TIPS "Any submissions that fit well in our publishing program will receive careful attention. A visit to our website, your local bookstore, or library to look at some of our books before you send in your submission is recommended."

INVERTED-A

P.O. Box 267, Licking MO 65542. **E-mail:** katzaya@gmail.com. **Website:** inverteda.com. **Contact:** Aya Katz, chief editor (poetry, novels, political); Nets Katz, science editor (scientific, academic). Estab. 1985. Books: POD. Distributes through Amazon, Bowker, Barnes Noble. Publishes paperback originals. Guidelines for SASE.

HOW TO CONTACT Does not accept unsolicited mss. Query with SASE. Reading period open from January 2 to March 15. Accepts queries by e-mail. Include estimated word count.

TERMS Pays 10 author's copies. Responds in 1 month to queries; 3 months to mss.

TIPS "Read our books. Read the *Inverted-A Horn*. We are different. We do not follow industry trends."

ITALICA PRESS

595 Main St., Suite 605, New York NY 10044. (917)371-0563. **E-mail:** inquiries@italicapress.com. **Website:** www.italicapress.com. Estab. 1985. "Italica Press publishes English translations of modern Italian fiction and medieval and Renaissance nonfiction." Publishes hardcover and trade paperback originals. Book catalog and guidelines online.

NEEDS "First-time translators published. We would like to see translations of Italian writers who are well-known in Italy who are not yet translated for an American audience."

HOW TO CONTACT Query via e-mail.

TERMS Pays 7-15% royalty on wholesale price; author's copies. Responds in 1 month to queries; 4 months to mss.

TIPS "We are interested in considering a wide variety of medieval and Renaissance topics (not historical fiction), and for modern works we are only interested in translations from Italian fiction by well-known Italian authors. *Only* fiction that has been previously published in Italian. A *brief* e-mail saves a lot of time. 90% of proposals we receive are completely off base—but we are very interested in things that are right on target."

JEWISH LIGHTS PUBLISHING

LongHill Partners, Inc., Sunset Farm Offices, Rt. 4, P.O. Box 237, Woodstock VT 05091. (802)457-4000. **Fax:** (802)457-4004. **E-mail:** submissions@turner-publishing.com. **Website:** www.jewishlights.com. Estab. 1990. "Jewish Lights publishes books for people of all faiths and all backgrounds who yearn for books that attract, engage, educate and spiritually inspire. Our authors are at the forefront of spiritual thought and deal with the quest for the self and for meaning in life by drawing on the Jewish wisdom tradition. Our books cover topics including history, spirituality, life cycle, children, self-help, recovery, theology and philosophy. We do not publish autobiography, biography, fiction, haggadot, poetry or cookbooks. At this point we plan to do only two books for children annually, and one will be for younger children (ages 4-10)." Publishes hardcover and trade paperback originals, trade paperback reprints. Book catalog and guidelines online.

NEEDS Picture books, young readers, middle readers: spirituality. "We are not interested in anything other than spirituality."

HOW TO CONTACT Query with outline/synopsis and 2 sample chapters; submit complete ms for picture books.

TERMS Pays authors royalty of 10% of revenue received; 15% royalty for subsequent printings. Responds in 6 months to queries.

TIPS "We publish books for all faiths and backgrounds that also reflect the Jewish wisdom tradition. Explain in your cover letter why you're submitting your project to us in particular. Make sure you know what we publish."

JOURNEYFORTH

Imprint of BJU Press, 1430 Wade Hampton Blvd., Greenville SC 29609. **E-mail:** journeyforth@bju-press.com. **Website:** www.journeyforth.com. **Contact:** Nancy Lohr. Estab. 1974. JourneyForth Books publishes fiction and nonfiction that reflect a worldview based solidly on the Bible and that encourages Christians to live out their faith. JourneyForth is an imprint of BJU Press. Publishes paperback originals. Book catalog available free in SASE or online. Guidelines online.

NEEDS "Our fiction is for the youth market only and is based on a Christian worldview. Our catalog ranges from first chapter books to YA titles." Does not want picture books, short stories, speculative fiction, poetry, or fiction for the adult market.

HOW TO CONTACT Submit proposal with synopsis, market analysis of competing works, and first 5 chapters. Will look at simultaneous submissions, but not multiple submissions.

TERMS Pays royalty. Pays advance. Responds in 1 month to queries; 3 months to mss.

TIPS "Study the publisher's guidelines. We are looking for engaging text and a biblical worldview. Will read hard copy submissions, but prefer e-mail queries/proposals/submissions."

JUST US BOOKS, INC.

P.O. Box 5306, East Orange NJ 07019. (973)672-7701. **Fax:** (973)677-7570. **Website:** justusbooks.com. Estab. 1988. "Just Us Books is the nation's premier independent publisher of Black-interest books for young people. Our books focus primarily on the culture, history, and contemporary experiences of African Americans." Guidelines online.

NEEDS Just Us Books is currently accepting queries for chapter books and middle reader titles only. "We are not considering any other works at this time."

TIPS "We are looking for realistic, contemporary characters; stories and interesting plots that introduce both conflict and resolution. We will consider various themes and story-lines, but before an author submits a query we urge them to become familiar with our books."

KAEDEN BOOKS

P.O. Box 16190, Rocky River OH 44116. **Website:** www.kaeden.com. Estab. 1986. "Children's book publisher for education K-3 market: reading stories, fiction/nonfiction, chapter books, science, and social studies materials." Publishes paperback originals. Book catalog and guidelines online.

NEEDS "We are looking for stories with humor, surprise endings, and interesting characters that will appeal to children in kindergarten through third grade." No sentence fragments. Please do not submit: queries, ms summaries, or résumés, mss that stereotype or demean individuals or groups, mss that present violence as acceptable behavior.

HOW TO CONTACT Submit complete ms. "Can be as minimal as 25 words for the earliest reader or as much as 2,000 words for the fluent reader. Beginning chapter books are welcome. Our readers are in kindergarten to third grade, so vocabulary and sentence structure must be appropriate for young readers. Make sure that all language used in the story is of an appropriate level for the students to read independently. Sentences should be complete and grammatically correct."

TERMS Work purchased outright from authors. Pays royalties to previous authors. Responds only if interested.

TIPS "Our audience ranges from kindergarten-third grade school children. We are an educational publisher. We are particularly interested in humorous stories with surprise endings and beginning chapter books."

Ⓐ **KANE/MILLER BOOK PUBLISHERS**

4901 Morena Blvd., Suite 213, San Diego CA 92117. (858)456-0540. **Fax:** (858)456-9641. **E-mail:** submissions@kanemiller.com. **Website:** www.kanemiller.com. **Contact:** Editorial Department. Estab. 1985. "Kane/Miller Book Publishers is a division of EDC Publishing, specializing in award-winning children's books from around the world. Our books bring the children of the world closer to each other, sharing stories and ideas, while exploring cultural differences and similarities. Although we continue to look for books from other countries, we are now actively seeking works that convey cultures and communities within the US. We are committed to expanding our picture book list and are interested in great stories with engaging characters, especially those with particularly American subjects. When writing about the experiences of a particular community, we will express a preference for stories written from a firsthand experience." Submission guidelines on site.

NEEDS Picture Books: concept, contemporary, health, humor, multicultural. Young Readers: contemporary, multicultural, suspense. Middle Readers: contemporary, humor, multicultural, suspense. "At this time, we are not considering holiday stories (in any age range) or self-published works."

TERMS If interested, responds in 90 days to queries.

TIPS "We like to think that a child reading a Kane/Miller book will see parallels between his own life and what might be the unfamiliar setting and characters of the story. And that by seeing how a character who is somehow or in some way dissimilar—an outsider—finds a way to fit comfortably into a culture or community or situation while maintaining a healthy sense of self and self-dignity, she might be empowered to do the same."

KAR-BEN PUBLISHING

Lerner Publishing Group, 1241 Washington Ave. N., Minneapolis MN 55401. **E-mail:** editorial@karben.com. **Website:** www.karben.com. Estab. 1974. Kar-Ben publishes exclusively children's books on Jewish themes. Publishes hardcover, trade paperback and e-books. Book catalog online; free upon request. Guidelines online.

NEEDS "We seek picture book mss 800-1,000 words on Jewish-themed topics for children." Picture books: Adventure, concept, folktales, history, humor, multicultural, religion, special needs; must be on a Jewish theme. Average word length: picture books–1,000.

HOW TO CONTACT Submit full ms. Picture books only.

TERMS Pays 5% royalty on NET sale. Pays $500-2,500 advance. Responds in 12 weeks.

TIPS "Authors: Do a literature search to make sure similar title doesn't already exist. Illustrators: Look at our online catalog for a sense of what we like—bright colors and lively composition."

KAYA PRESS

c/o USC ASE, 3620 S. Vermont Ave. KAP 462, Los Angeles CA 90089. (213) 740-2285. **E-mail:** info@kaya.com. **E-mail:** acquisitions@kaya.com. **Website:** www.kaya.com. Estab. 1994. Kaya is an independent literary press dedicated to the publication of innovative literature from the Asian Pacific diaspora. Publishes hardcover originals and trade paperback originals and reprints. Book catalog available free. Guidelines online.

HOW TO CONTACT Submit 2-4 sample chapters, clips, SASE.

TERMS Responds in 6 months to mss.

TIPS "Audience is people interested in a high standard of literature and who are interested in breaking down easy approaches to multicultural literature."

KELSEY STREET PRESS

Poetry by Women, 2824 Kelsey St., Berkeley CA 94705. **Website:** www.kelseyst.com. Estab. 1974. "A Berkeley,

California press publishing collaborations between women poets and artists. Many of the press's collaborations focus on a central theme or conceit, like the sprawl and spectacle of New York in *Arcade* by Erica Hunt and Alison Saar." Hardcover and trade paperback originals and electronic originals.

KENSINGTON PUBLISHING CORP.

119 W. 40th St., New York NY 10018. (212)407-1500. **Fax:** (212)935-0699. **E-mail:** jscognamiglio@kensingtonbooks.com. **Website:** www.kensingtonbooks.com. **Contact:** John Scognamiglio, editorial director, fiction (historical romance, Regency romance, women's contemporary fiction, gay and lesbian fiction and nonfiction, mysteries, suspense, mainstream fiction); Michaela Hamilton, editor-in-chief, Citadel Press (thrillers, mysteries, mainstream fiction, true crime, current events); Selena James, executive editor, Dafina Books (African American fiction and nonfiction, inspirational, young adult, romance); Peter Senftleben, assistant editor (mainstream fiction, women's contemporary fiction, gay and lesbian fiction, mysteries, suspense, thrillers, romantic suspense, paranormal romance). Estab. 1975. "Kensington focuses on profitable niches and uses aggressive marketing techniques to support its books." Publishes hardcover and trade paperback originals, mass market paperback originals and reprints. Book catalog and guidelines online.

NEEDS No science fiction/fantasy, experimental fiction, business texts or children's titles.

HOW TO CONTACT Query.

TERMS Pays 6-15% royalty on retail price. Makes outright purchase. Pays $2,000 and up advance. Responds in 1 month to queries and proposals; 4 months to mss.

TIPS "Agented submissions only, except for submissions to romance lines. For those lines, query with SASE or submit proposal package including 3 sample chapters, synopsis."

DENIS KITCHEN PUBLISHING CO., LLC

P.O. Box 2250, Amherst MA 01004. (413)259-1627. **Fax:** (413)259-1812. **E-mail:** help@deniskitchen.com. **Website:** www.deniskitchen.com. **Contact:** Denis Kitchen, publisher. Publishes hardcover and trade paperback originals and reprints.

This publisher strongly discourages e-mail submissions.

NEEDS "We do not want pure fiction. We seek cartoonists or writer/illustrator teams who can tell compelling stories with a combination of words and pictures." No pure fiction (meaning text only).

HOW TO CONTACT Query with SASE. Submit sample illustrations/comic pages. Submit complete ms.

TERMS Pays 6-10% royalty on retail price. Occasionally makes deals based on percentage of wholesale if idea and/or bulk of work is done in-house. Pays $1-5,000 advance. Responds in 4-6 weeks.

TIPS "Our audience is readers who embrace the graphic novel revolution, who appreciate historical comic strips and books, and those who follow popular and alternative culture. We like to discover new talent. The artist who has a day job but a great idea is encouraged to contact us. The pop culture historian who has a new take on an important figure is likewise encouraged. We have few preconceived notions about manuscripts or ideas, though we are decidedly selective. Historically, we have published many first-time authors and artists, some of whom developed into award-winning creators with substantial followings. Artists or illustrators who do not have confidence in their writing should send us self-promotional postcards (our favorite way of spotting new talent)."

KNOPF

Imprint of Random House, 1745 Broadway, New York NY 10019. **Fax:** (212)940-7390. **Website:** knopfdoubleday.com/imprint/knopf. Estab. 1915. Publishes hardcover and paperback originals.

NEEDS Publishes book-length fiction of literary merit by known or unknown writers. Length: 40,000-150,000 words.

HOW TO CONTACT Usually only accepts mss submitted by agents. However, writers may submit sample 25-50 pages with SASE.

TERMS Royalties vary. Offers advance. Responds in 2-6 months to queries.

KNOX ROBINSON PUBLISHING

Knox Robinson Holdings, LLC, 3104 Briarcliff RD NE #98414, Atlanta GA 30345. (404)478-8696. **E-mail:** info@knoxrobinsonpublishing.com. **Website:** www.knoxrobinsonpublishing.com. Estab. 2010. Knox Robinson Publishing began as an international, independent, specialist publisher of historical fiction, historical romance and fantasy. Now open to well-written literature in all genres. Publishes fiction and nonfiction. Catalog available. Guidelines online.

NEEDS "We are seeking historical fiction featuring obscure historical figures."

HOW TO CONTACT Submit first 3 chapters and author questionnaire found on website.

TERMS Pays royalty. Responds within 6 months to submissions of first 3 chapters. "We do not accept proposals."

⊘ KREGEL PUBLICATIONS

2450 Oak Industrial Dr. NE, Grand Rapids MI 49505. (616)451-4775. **Fax:** (616)451-9330. **E-mail:** kregelbooks@kregel.com. **Website:** www.kregelpublications.com. Estab. 1949. "Our mission as an evangelical Christian publisher is to provide—with integrity and excellence—trusted, Biblically based resources that challenge and encourage individuals in their Christian lives. Works in theology and Biblical studies should reflect the historic, orthodox Protestant tradition." Publishes hardcover and trade paperback originals and reprints. Guidelines online.

NEEDS Fiction should be geared toward the evangelical Christian market. Wants books with fast-paced, contemporary storylines presenting a strong Christian message in an engaging, entertaining style.

HOW TO CONTACT Finds works through The Writer's Edge and Christian Manuscript Submissions ms screening services.

TERMS Pays royalty on wholesale price. Pays negotiable advance. Responds in 2-3 months.

TIPS "Our audience consists of conservative, evangelical Christians, including pastors and ministry students."

◐ LANTANA PUBLISHING

London , United Kingdom. **E-mail:** info@lantanapublishing.com. **E-mail:** submissions@lantanapublishing.com. **Website:** www.lantanapublishing.com. Estab. 2014. Lantana Publishing is a young, independent publishing house producing award-winning picture books for children. Lantana's mission is to select outstanding writing from around the world, working with prize-winning authors and illustrators from many countries, while at the same time nurturing new writing talent. Lantana's cross-cultural collaborations have so far garnered high praise, described as 'dazzling', 'delectable', 'enchanting' and 'exquisite' by bloggers and reviewers, and receiving high commendations from awards-panels both at home and abroad. Lantana Publishing is hugely proud to bring UK children's publishing one step closer towards achieving a more diverse and inclusive children's book landscape for the next generation of young readers. Guidelines online.

NEEDS "We are currently focusing on picture books for 4-8 year-olds with text no longer than 500 words (and we prefer 200-400 words). We love writing that is contemporary and fun. We particularly like stories with modern-day settings in the UK or around the world, especially if they feature BAME families, and stories that lend themselves to great illustration."

TERMS Pays royalty. Pays advance. Responds in 6 weeks.

LEAPFROG PRESS

Box 505, Fredonia NY 14063. **E-mail:** leapfrog@leapfrogpress.com. **Website:** www.leapfrogpress.com. **Contact:** Nathan Carter, acquisitions editor; Lisa Graziano, publicity. Estab. 1996. Guidelines online. Submissions through Submittable only.

NEEDS "We search for beautifully written literary titles and market them aggressively to national trade and library accounts. We also sell film, translation, foreign, and book club rights." Publishes paperback originals. Books: acid-free paper; sewn binding. Print runs range from about 1,000 to 4,000. Distributes titles through Consortium Book Sales and Distribution, St. Paul, MN. Promotes titles through all national review media, bookstore readings, author tours, website, radio shows, chain store promotions, advertisements, book fairs. "Genres often blur; look for good writing. We are most interested in works that are quirky, that fall outside of any known genre,and of course well written and finely crafted. We are most interested in literary fiction."

HOW TO CONTACT Query with several chapters or stories through Submittable.

TERMS Pays 10% royalty on net receipts. Average advance: negotiable. Response time varies.

TIPS "We like anything that is superbly written and genuinely original. We like the idiosyncratic and the peculiar. We rarely publish nonfiction. Send only your best work, and send only completed work that is ready. That means the completed ms has already been through extensive editing and is ready to be judged. We consider submissions from both previously published and unpublished writers, and both agented and unagented submissions. We do not accept submissions through postal mail and cannot return physical letters or manuscripts."

LEE & LOW BOOKS

95 Madison Ave., #1205, New York NY 10016. (212)779-4400. **E-mail:** general@leeandlow.com. **Website:** www.leeandlow.com. Estab. 1991. "Our goals are to meet a growing need for books that address children of color, and to present literature that all children can identify with. We only consider multicultural children's books. Sponsors a yearly New Voices Award for first-time picture book authors of color. Contest rules online at website or for SASE." Publishes hardcover originals and trade paperback reprints. Book catalog available online. Guidelines available online or by written request with SASE.

NEEDS Picture books, young readers: anthology, contemporary, history, multicultural, poetry. Picture book, middle reader: contemporary, history, multicultural, nature/environment, poetry, sports. Average word length: picture books—1,000-1,500 words. "We do not publish folklore or animal stories."

HOW TO CONTACT Submit complete ms.

TERMS Pays net royalty. Pays authors advances against royalty. Pays illustrators advance against royalty. Photographers paid advance against royalty. Responds in 6 months to mss if interested.

TIPS "Check our website to see the kinds of books we publish. Do not send mss that don't fit our mission."

Ⓧ LES FIGUES PRESS

P.O. Box 7736, Los Angeles CA 90007. **E-mail:** info@lesfigues.com. **Website:** www.lesfigues.com. **Contact:** Teresa Carmody, director. Estab. 2005. Les Figues Press is an independent, nonprofit publisher of poetry, prose, visual art, conceptual writing, and translation. With amission is to create aesthetic conversations between readers, writers, and artists, Les Figues Press favors projects which push the boundaries of genre, form, and general acceptability. "We are currently closed to all submissions."

LETHE PRESS

118 Heritage Ave., Maple Shade NJ 8052. (609)410-7391. **Website:** www.lethepressbooks.com. Estab. 2001. "Welcomes submissions from authors of any sexual or gender identity." Guidelines online.

NEEDS "Named after the Greek river of memory and forgetfulness (and pronounced Lee-Thee), Lethe Press is a small press devoted to ideas that are often neglected or forgotten by mainstream, profit-oriented publishers." Distributes/promotes titles. Lethe Books are distributed by Ingram Publications and Bookazine, and are available at all major bookstores, as well as the major online retailers.

HOW TO CONTACT Query via e-mail.

ARTHUR A. LEVINE BOOKS

Scholastic, Inc., 557 Broadway, New York NY 10012. (212)343-4436. **Fax:** (212)343-6143. **Website:** www.arthuralevinebooks.com. Estab. 1996. Publishes hardcover, paperback, and e-book editions. Picture Books: Query letter and full text of pb. Novels: Send Query letter, first 2 chapters and synopsis. Other: Query letter, 10-page sample and synopsis/proposal.

NEEDS "Arthur A. Levine is looking for distinctive literature, for children and young adults, for whatever's extraordinary." Averages 18-20 total titles/year.

HOW TO CONTACT Query.

TERMS Responds in 1 month to queries; 5 months to mss.

LILLENAS PUBLISHING CO.

Imprint of Lillenas Drama Resources, P.O. Box 419527, Kansas City MO 64141. (800)877-0700. **Fax:** (816)412-8390. **E-mail:** drama@lillenas.com. **Website:** www.lillenasdrama.com. "We purchase only original, previously unpublished materials. Also, we require that all scripts be performed at least once before it is submitted for consideration. We do not accept scripts that are sent via fax or e-mail. Direct all manuscripts to the Drama Resources Editor." Publishes mass market paperback and electronic originals. Guidelines online.

NEEDS "Looking for sketch and monologue collections for all ages – adults, children and youth. For these collections, we request 12 - 15 scripts to be submitted at one time. Unique treatments of spiritual themes, relevant issues and biblical messages are of interest. Contemporary full-length and one-act plays that have conflict, characterization, and a spiritual context that is neither a sermon nor an apologetic for youth and adults. We also need wholesome so-called secular full-length scripts for dinner theatres and schools." No musicals.

TERMS Pays royalty on net price. Makes outright purchase. Responds in 4-6 months to material.

TIPS "We never receive too many manuscripts."

LITTLE, BROWN AND CO. ADULT TRADE BOOKS

1290 Avenue of the Americas, New York NY 10104. **Website:** www.littlebrown.com. Estab. 1837. "The general editorial philosophy for all divisions continues to be broad and flexible, with high quality and the promise of commercial success as always the first considerations." Publishes hardcover originals and paperback originals and reprints. Guidelines online.

HOW TO CONTACT *Agented submissions only.*

TERMS Pays royalty. Offer advance.

LITTLE, BROWN BOOKS FOR YOUNG READERS

Hachette Book Group USA, 1290 Avenue of the Americas, New York NY 10104. (212)364-1100. **Fax:** (212)364-0925. **Website:** littlebrown.com. Estab. 1837. "Little, Brown and Co. Children's Publishing publishes all formats including board books, picture books, middle grade fiction, and nonfiction YA titles. We are looking for strong writing and presentation, but no predetermined topics." *Only interested in solicited agented material.*

NEEDS Average word length: picture books—1,000; young readers—6,000; middle readers—15,000-50,000; young adults—50,000 and up.

HOW TO CONTACT *Agented submissions only.*

TERMS Pays authors royalties based on retail price. Pays illustrators and photographers by the project or royalty based on retail price. Sends galleys to authors; dummies to illustrators. Pays negotiable advance. Responds in 1-2 months.

TIPS "In order to break into the field, authors and illustrators should research their competition and try to come up with something outstandingly different."

LITTLE PICKLE PRESS

3701 Sacramento St., #494, San Francisco CA 94118. (415)340-3344. **Fax:** (415)366-1520. **E-mail:** info@march4thinc.com. **Website:** www.littlepicklepress.com. Little Pickle Press is a 21st Century publisher dedicated to helping parents and educators cultivate conscious, responsible little people by stimulating explorations of the meaningful topics of their generation through a variety of media, technologies, and techniques. Submit through submission link on site. Includes YA imprint Relish Media. Uses Author.me for submissions for Little Pickle and YA imprint Relish Media. Guidelines available on site.

TIPS "We have lots of manuscripts to consider, so it will take up to 8 weeks before we get back to you."

LITTLE SIMON

Imprint of Simon & Schuster, 1230 Avenue of the Americas, New York NY 10020. (212)698-1295. **Fax:** (212)698-2794. **Website:** www.simonandschuster.com/kids. "Our goal is to provide fresh material in an innovative format for preschool to age 8. Our books are often, if not exclusively, format driven." Publishes novelty and branded books only.

NEEDS Novelty books include many things that do not fit in the traditional hardcover or paperback format, such as pop-up, board book, scratch and sniff, glow in the dark, lift the flap, etc. Children's/juvenile. No picture books. Large part of the list is holiday-themed.

HOW TO CONTACT *Currently not accepting unsolicited mss.*

TERMS Offers advance and royalties.

LITTLE TIGER PRESS

1 The Coda Centre, 189 Munster Rd., London SW6 6AW, United Kingdom. (44)(20)7385-6333. **Website:** www.littletigerpress.com. Little Tiger Press is a dynamic and busy independent publisher. Also includes imprints: Caterpillar Books and Stripes Publishing.

NEEDS Picture books: animal, concept, contemporary, humor. Average word length: picture books—750 words or less.

HOW TO CONTACT "We are no longer accepting unsolicited manuscripts. We will however, continue to accept illustration submissions and samples."

LIVINGSTON PRESS

University of West Alabama, 100 N. Washington St., Station 22, University of West Alabama, Livingston AL 35470. **Fax:** (205)652-3717. **E-mail:** jwt@uwa.edu. **Website:** www.livingstonpress.uwa.edu. **Contact:** Joe Taylor, director. Estab. 1974. "Livingston Press, as do all literary presses, looks for authorial excellence in style. Currently emphasizing novels." Reading in June only. Check back for details. Publishes hardcover and trade paperback originals, plus Kindle. Book catalog online. Guidelines online.

NEEDS "We are interested in form and, of course, style." No genre fiction, please.

TERMS Pays 80 contributor's copies, after sales of 1,000, standard royalty. Responds in 4 months to queries; 6-12 months to mss.

TIPS "Our readers are interested in literature, often quirky literature that emphasizes form and style. Please visit our website for current needs."

LOOSE ID

P.O. Box 806, San Francisco CA 94104. **E-mail:** submissions@loose-id.com. **Website:** www.loose-id.com. **Contact:** Treva Harte, editor-in-chief. Estab. 2004. *"Loose Id* is love unleashed. We're taking romance to the edge." Publishes e-books and some print books. Distributes/promotes titles. "The company promotes itself through web and print advertising wherever readers of erotic romance may be found, creating a recognizable brand identity as the place to let your id run free and the people who unleash your fantasies. It is currently pursuing licensing agreements for foreign translations, and has a print program of 2 to 5 titles per month." Guidelines online.

○ "Loose Id is actively acquiring stories from both aspiring and established authors."

NEEDS Wants nontraditional erotic romance stories, including gay, lesbian, heroes and heroines, multiculturalism, cross-genre, fantasy, and science fiction, straight contemporary or historical romances.

HOW TO CONTACT Query with outline/synopsis and 3 sample chapters. Accepts queries by e-mail. Include estimated word count, list of publishing credits, and why your submission is love unleashed. "Before submitting a query or proposal, please read the guidelines on our website. Please don't hesitate to contact us by e-mail for any information you don't see there."

TERMS Pays e-book royalties of 40%. Responds to queries in 1 month.

MAGE PUBLISHERS, INC.

1780 Crossroads Dr., Odenton MD 21113. (202)342-1642. **Fax:** (202)342-9269. **E-mail:** as@mage.com. **Website:** www.mage.com. Estab. 1985. Mage publishes books relating to Persian/Iranian culture. Publishes hardcover originals and reprints, trade paperback originals. Book catalog available free. Guidelines online.

NEEDS Must relate to Persian/Iranian culture.

HOW TO CONTACT Submit outline, SASE. Query via mail or e-mail.

TERMS Pays royalty. Responds in 1 month to queries.

TIPS "Audience is the Iranian-American community in America and Americans interested in Persian culture."

MAGINATION PRESS

750 First St. NE, Washington DC 20002. (202)336-5618. **Fax:** (202)336-5624. **E-mail:** magination@apa.org. **Website:** www.apa.org. Estab. 1988. Magination Press is an imprint of the American Psychological Association. "We publish books dealing with the psycho/therapeutic resolution of children's problems and psychological issues with a strong self-help component." Submit complete ms. Full guidelines available on site. Materials returned only with SASE.

NEEDS All levels: psychological and social issues, self-help, health, parenting concerns and, special needs. Picture books, middle school readers.

TERMS Responds to queries in 1-2 months; mss in 2-6 months.

MANDALA PUBLISHING

Mandala Publishing and Earth Aware Editions, 800 A St., San Rafael CA 94901. **E-mail:** info@mandalapublishing.com. **Website:** www.mandalaeartheditions.com. Estab. 1989. "In the traditions of the East, wisdom, truth, and beauty go hand in-hand. This is reflected in the great arts, music, yoga, and philosophy of India. Mandala Publishing strives to bring to its readers authentic and accessible renderings of thousands of years of wisdom and philosophy from this unique culture-timeless treasures that are our inspirations and guides. At Mandala, we believe that the arts, health, ecology, and spirituality of the great Vedic traditions are as relevant today as they were in sacred India thousands of years ago. As a distinguished publisher in the world of Vedic literature, lifestyle, and interests today, Mandala strives to provide accessible and meaningful works for the modern reader." Publishes hardcover, trade paperback, and electronic originals. Book catalog online.

HOW TO CONTACT Query with SASE.

TERMS Pays 3-15% royalty on retail price. Responds in 6 months.

◐ MANOR HOUSE PUBLISHING, INC.

452 Cottingham Crescent, Ancaster ON L9G 3V6, Canada. (905)648-2193. **E-mail:** mbdavie@manor-house.biz. **Website:** www.manor-house.biz. **Contact:** Mike Davie, president (novels and nonfiction). Estab. 1998. Manor House is currently looking for new fully edited, ready-to-run titles to complete our spring-fall 2017 release lineup. This is a rare opportunity for authors, including self-published, to have existing or ready titles picked up by Manor House

and made available to retailers throughout the world, while our network of rights agents provide more potential revenue streams via foreign language rights sales. We are currently looking for titles that are ready or nearly ready for publishing to be released this fall. Such titles should be written by Canadian citizens residing in Canada and should be profitable or with strong market sales potential to allow full cost recovery and profit for publisher and author. Of primary interest are business and self-help titles along with other nonfiction, including new age. Publishes hardcover, trade paperback, and mass market paperback originals (and reprints if they meet specific criteria - best to inquire with publisher). Book catalog online. Guidelines available.

NEEDS Stories should mainly be by Canadian authors residing in Canada, have Canadian settings and characters should be Canadian, but content should have universal appeal to wide audience. In some cases, we will consider publishing non-Canadian fiction authors - provided they demonstrate publishing their book will be profitable for author and publisher.

HOW TO CONTACT Query via e-mail. Submit proposal package, clips, bio, 3 sample chapters. Submit complete ms.

TERMS Pays 10% royalty on retail price. Queries and mss to be sent by e-mail only. "We will respond in 30 days if interested-if not, there is no response. Do not follow up unless asked to do so."

TIPS "Our audience includes everyone-the general public/mass audience. Self-edit your work first, make sure it is well written and well edited with strong Canadian content and/or content of universal appeal (preferably with a Canadian connection of some kind)."

Ⓐ MARINER BOOKS

222 Berkeley St., Boston MA 2116. (617)351-5000. **Website:** www.hmco.com. Estab. 1997.

○ Mariner Books' *Interpreter of Maladies*, by debut author Jhumpa Lahiri, won the 2000 Pulitzer Prize for fiction and *The Caprices*, by Sabina Murray, received the 2003 PEN/Faulkner Award. Mariner Books' *Interpreter of Maladies*, by debut author Jhumpa Lahiri, won the 2000 Pulitzer Prize for fiction and *The Caprices*, by Sabina Murray, received the 2003 PEN/Faulkner Award.

NEEDS Literary, mainstream/contemporary. Recently published Timothy Egan, Donald Hall, Amitav Ghosh, and Edna O'Brien.

HOW TO CONTACT *Agented submissions only.* Responds in 4 months to mss.

TERMS Pays royalty on retail price or makes outright purchase. Average advance: variable.

MARTIN SISTERS PUBLISHING COMPANY, INC

P.O. Box 1154, Barbourville KY 40906-1499. **Website:** www.martinsisterspublishing.com. Estab. 2011. Firm/imprint publishes trade and mass market paperback originals; electronic originals. Catalog and guidelines online.

HOW TO CONTACT "Please place query letter, marketing plan and the first 5-10 pages of your manuscript (if you are submitting fiction) directly into your e-mail." Guidelines available on site.

TERMS Pays 7.5% royalty/max on print net; 35% royalty/max on e-book net. No advance offered. Responds in 1 month on queries, 2 months on proposals, 3-6 months on mss.

MARVEL COMICS

135 W. 50th St., 7th Floor, New York NY 10020. **Website:** www.marvel.com. Publishes hardcover originals and reprints, trade paperback reprints, mass market comic book originals, electronic reprints. Guidelines online.

NEEDS Our shared universe needs new heroes and villains; books for younger readers and teens needed.

HOW TO CONTACT Submit inquiry letter, idea submission form (download from website), SASE.

TERMS Pays on a per page work for hire basis or creator-owned which is then contracted. Pays negotiable advance. Responds in 3-5 weeks to queries.

Ⓢ MAVERICK MUSICALS AND PLAYS

17, Tarnkun St., Alexandra Headlands QLD 4572, Australia. Phone/**Fax:** (61)(7)5448 4093. **E-mail:** tahlia@maverickmusicals.com. **Website:** www.maverickmusicals.com. **Contact:** Tahlia Wilkins. Estab. 1978. Guidelines online.

NEEDS "Looking for two-act musicals and one- and two-act plays. See website for more details."

Ⓞ MCBOOKS PRESS

ID Booth Building, 520 N. Meadow St., Ithaca NY 14850. (607)272-2114. **E-mail:** mcbooks@mcbooks.

com. **E-mail:** alex@mcbooks.com. **Website:** www.mcbooks.com. **Contact:** Alexander G. Skutt, publisher. Estab. 1979. McBooks Press has been publishing books independently for over 30 years in Ithaca, New York. McBooks' extensive list of publications features works of historical fiction—including naval and military fiction in series. We continue to seek excellent historical naval adventures that are suitable for publication in series. In the past, we have also published nonfiction, including books on boxing, food and health, and the Finger Lakes Region of New York State. Publishes trade paperback and hardcover originals and reprints. Guidelines online.

○　"Currently not accepting submissions or queries for fiction or nonfiction." The only exceptions that we would look at are: 1) well-written nautical historical fiction that could grow into a series 2) great books about the Finger Lakes or adjacent regions of Upstate New York.

NEEDS Publishes Julian Stockwin, John Biggins, Colin Sargent, and Douglas W. Jacobson. Distributes titles through Independent Publishers Group.

TERMS Pays a percentage of cover price for physical books plus a percentage of net income for e-books. Pays advance. Responds in 2 months.

TIPS "We are currently only publishing authors with whom we have a pre-existing relationship. If this policy changes, we will announce the change on our website."

○ MCCLELLAND & STEWART, LTD.

The Canadian Publishers, 320 Front St. W., Suite 1400, Toronto ON M5V 3B6, Canada. (416)364-4449. **Fax:** (416)598-7764. **Website:** www.mcclelland.com. Publishes hardcover, trade paperback, and mass market paperback originals and reprints.

NEEDS "We publish work by established authors, as well as the work of new and developing authors."

HOW TO CONTACT Query. *All unsolicited mss* returned unopened.

TERMS Pays 10-15% royalty on retail price (hardcover rates). Pays advance. Responds in 3 months to proposals.

THE MCDONALD & WOODWARD PUBLISHING CO.

695 Tall Oaks Dr., Newark OH 43055. (740)641-2691. **Fax:** (740)641-2692. **E-mail:** mwpubco@mwpubco.com. **Website:** www.mwpubco.com. **Contact:** Jerry N. McDonald, publisher. Estab. 1986. McDonald & Woodward publishes books in natural history, cultural history, and natural resources. Currently emphasizing travel, natural and cultural history, and natural resource conservation. Publishes hardcover and trade paperback originals. Book catalog online. Guidelines free on request; by e-mail.

HOW TO CONTACT Query with SASE.

TERMS Pays 10% royalty. Responds in less than 1 month.

TIPS "Our books are meant for the curious and educated elements of the general population."

⊘ MARGARET K. MCELDERRY BOOKS

Imprint of Simon & Schuster Children's Publishing Division, 1230 Sixth Ave., New York NY 10020. (212)698-7200. **Website:** imprints.simonandschuster.biz/margaret-k-mcelderry-books. Estab. 1971. "Margaret K. McElderry Books publishes hardcover and paperback trade books for children from pre-school age through young adult. This list includes picture books, middle grade and teen fiction, poetry, and fantasy. The style and subject matter of the books we publish is almost unlimited. We do not publish textbooks, coloring and activity books, greeting cards, magazines, pamphlets, or religious publications." Guidelines for #10 SASE.

NEEDS *No unsolicited mss.*

HOW TO CONTACT *Agented submissions only.*

TERMS Pays authors royalty based on retail price. Pays illustrator royalty of by the project. Pays photographers by the project. Original artwork returned at job's completion. Offers $5,000-8,000 advance for new authors.

TIPS "Read! The children's book field is competitive. See what's been done and what's out there before submitting. We look for high quality: an originality of ideas, clarity and felicity of expression, a well organized plot, and strong character-driven stories. We're looking for strong, original fiction, especially mysteries and middle grade humor. We are always interested in picture books for the youngest age reader. Study our titles."

MELANGE BOOKS, LLC

White Bear Lake MN 55110-5538. **E-mail:** melange-books@melange-books.com. **E-mail:** submissions@melange-books.com. **Website:** www.melange-books.com. **Contact:** Nancy Schumacher, publisher and acquiring editor for Melange and Satin Romance; Caroline Andrus, acquiring editor for Fire and Ice for Young Adult.. Estab. 2011. Melange is a royalty-paying company publishing e-books and print books. Publishes trade paperback originals and electronic originals. Send SASE for book catalog. Guidelines online.

NEEDS Submit a clean mss by following guidelines on website.

HOW TO CONTACT Query electronically by clicking on "submissions" on website. Include a synopsis and 4 chapters.

TERMS Authors receive a minimum of 20% royalty on print sales, 40% on electronic book sales. Does not offer an advance. Responds in 1 month on queries; 2 months on proposals; 4-6 months on mss.

MERRIAM PRESS

489 South St., Hoosick Falls NY 12090. **E-mail:** ray@merriam-press.com. **Website:** www.merriam-press.com. **Contact:** Ray Merriam, owner. Estab. 1988. Merriam Press specializes in military history, particularly World War II history. We are also branching out into other genres, including fiction, historical fiction, poetry, children. Provide brief synopsis of ms. Never send any files in body of e-mail or as an attachment. Publisher will ask for full ms for review. Publisher requires unformatted mss. Mss must be thoroughly edited and error-free. Publishes hardcover and soft-cover trade paperback original works and reprints. Titles are also made available in e-book editions. Book catalog available in print and PDF editions. Author guidelines and additional information are available on publisher's website.

NEEDS Especially but not limited to military history.

HOW TO CONTACT Query with SASE or by e-mail first. Do not send ms (in whole or in part) unless requested to do so.

TERMS Pays 10% royalty for printed editions and 50% royalty for e-book editions. Royalty payment is based on the amount paid to the publisher, not the retail or list prices. Does not pay advance. Responds quickly (e-mail preferred) to queries.

TIPS "Our military history books are geared for military historians, collectors, model kit builders, wargamers, veterans, general enthusiasts. We now publish some historical fiction and poetry and will consider well-written books on a variety of non-military topics."

MESSIANIC JEWISH PUBLISHERS

6120 Day Long Ln., Clarksville MD 21029. (410)531-6644. **E-mail:** editor@messianicjewish.net. **Website:** www.messianicjewish.net. Publishes hardcover and trade paperback originals and reprints. Guidelines via e-mail.

NEEDS "We publish very little fiction. Jewish or Biblical themes are a must. Text must demonstrate keen awareness of Jewish culture and thought."

HOW TO CONTACT Query with SASE. Unsolicited mss are not return.

TERMS Pays 7-15% royalty on wholesale price.

METHUEN PUBLISHING LTD

Editorial Department, 35 Hospital Fields Rd., York YO10 4DZ, United Kingdom. **E-mail:** editorial@metheun.co.uk. **Website:** www.methuen.co.uk. Estab. 1889. Guidelines online.

No unsolicited mss; synopses and ideas welcome. Prefers to be approached via agents or a letter of inquiry. No first novels, cookery books or personal memoirs.

NEEDS No first novels.

HOW TO CONTACT Query with SASE. Submit proposal package, outline, outline/proposal, resume, publishing history, clips, bio, SASE.

TERMS Pays royalty.

TIPS "We recommend that all prospective authors attempt to find an agent before submitting to publishers and we do not encourage unagented submissions."

MICHIGAN STATE UNIVERSITY PRESS

1405 S. Harrison Rd., Suite 25, East Lansing MI 48823. (517)355-9543. **Fax:** (517)432-2611. **E-mail:** msupress@msu.edu. **Website:** msupress.org. **Contact:** Alex Schwartz and Julie Loehr, acquisitions. Estab. 1947. Michigan State University Press has notably represented both scholarly publishing and the mission of Michigan State University with the publication of numerous award-winning books and scholarly journals. In addition, they publish nonfiction that addresses, in a more contemporary way, social concerns, such as diversity and civil rights. They also publish literary fiction and poetry. Publishes hardcover and softcover originals. Book catalog and ms guidelines online.

NEEDS Publishes literary fiction.

HOW TO CONTACT Submit proposal.

TERMS Pays variable royalty.

MILKWEED EDITIONS

1011 Washington Ave. S., Suite 300, Minneapolis MN 55415. (612)332-3192. **Fax:** (612)215-2550. **Website:** www.milkweed.org. Estab. 1979. "Milkweed Editions publishes with the intention of making a humane impact on society, in the belief that literature is a transformative art uniquely able to convey the essential experiences of the human heart and spirit. To that end, Milkweed Editions publishes distinctive voices of literary merit in handsomely designed, visually dynamic books, exploring the ethical, cultural, and esthetic issues that free societies need continually to address." Publishes hardcover, trade paperback, and electronic originals; trade paperback and electronic reprints. Book catalog online. Only accepts submissions during open submission periods. See website for guidelines.

NEEDS Novels for adults and for readers 8-13. High literary quality. For adult readers: literary fiction, nonfiction, poetry, essays. Middle readers: adventure, contemporary, fantasy, multicultural, nature/environment, suspense/mystery. Average length: middle readers—90-200 pages. No romance, mysteries, science fiction.

HOW TO CONTACT "Please submit a query letter with three opening chapters (of a novel) or three representative stories (of a collection). Publishes YR."

TERMS Pays authors variable royalty based on retail price. Offers advance against royalties. Pays varied advance from $500-10,000. Responds in 6 months.

TIPS "We are looking for excellent writing with the intent of making a humane impact on society. Please read submission guidelines before submitting and acquaint yourself with our books in terms of style and quality before submitting. Many factors influence our selection process, so don't get discouraged. Nonfiction is focused on literary writing about the natural world, including living well in urban environments."

MONDIAL

203 W. 107th St., Suite 6C, New York NY 10025. 212-864-7095. **Fax:** (208)361-2863. **E-mail:** contact@mondialbooks.com. **Website:** www.mondialbooks.com; www.librejo.com. **Contact:** Andrew Moore, editor. Estab. 1996. Mondial publishes fiction and non-fiction in English, Esperanto, and Hebrew: novels, short stories, poetry, textbooks, dictionaries, books about history, linguistics, and psychology, among others. Since 2007, it has been publishing a literary magazine in Esperanto. Publishes hard cover, trade paperback originals and reprints. Guidelines online.

HOW TO CONTACT Query through online submission form.

TERMS Pays 10% royalty on wholesale price. Does not pay advance. Responds to queries in 3 months, only if interested.

MONSOON BOOKS

No.1 Duke of Windsor Suite, Burrough Court, Burrough on the Hill Leicestershire LE14 2QS, United Kingdom. **E-mail:** sales@monsoonbooks.co.uk. **Website:** www.monsoonbooks.co.uk. **Contact:** Philip Tatham, Publisher. Estab. 2002. Monsoon Books is a UK-based trade publisher of English-language fiction and narrative nonfiction relating to Asia. All titles have an Asian, usually a SE Asian, angle. Guidelines online.

HOW TO CONTACT Query with outline/synopsis and submit complete ms with cover letter. Accepts queries by snail mail, fax, and e-mail (submissions@monsoonbooks.com.sg. Please include estimated word count, brief bio, list of publishing credits, and list of three comparative titles. Send hard copy submissions to: Monsoon Books Pte Ltd, 71 Ayer Rajah Crescent #01-01, Mediapolis Phase, Singapore 139951. We are not able to return hard copy manuscripts. We do not encourage hand deliveries. Agented fiction 20%. Responds in 8 weeks to your submissions. If you do not hear from us by then, e-mail us. Accepts simultaneous submissions, submissions on CD or disk. Rarely comments on rejected manuscripts. Monsoon Books regularly works with literary agents from the UK and Australia (such as David Higham Associates in London and Cameron's Management in Sydney) and we are particularly keen to hear from agents with manuscripts set in Southeast or North Asia as well as mss written by authors from this region.

TIPS "Monsoon welcomes unsolicited manuscripts from agented and unagented authors writing books set in Asia, particularly Southeast Asia."

MOODY PUBLISHERS

Moody Bible Institute, 820 N. LaSalle Blvd., Chicago IL 60610. (800)678-8812. **Fax:** (312)329-4157. **Website:** www.moodypublishers.org. **Contact:** Acquisitions Coordinator. Estab. 1894. "The mission of Moody Publishers is to educate and edify the Christian and to evangelize the non-Christian by ethically publishing conservative, evangelical Christian literature and other media for all ages around the world, and to help provide resources for Moody Bible Institute in its training of future Christian leaders." Publishes hardcover, trade, and mass market paperback originals. Book catalog for 9×12 envelope and 4 first-class stamps. Guidelines online.

HOW TO CONTACT *Agented submissions only.*

TERMS Royalty varies. Responds in 2-3 months to queries.

TIPS "In our fiction list, we're looking for Christian storytellers rather than teachers trying to present a message. Your motivation should be to delight the reader. Using your skills to create beautiful works is glorifying to God."

NBM PUBLISHING

160 Broadway, Suite 700, East Bldg., New York NY 10038. **E-mail:** nbmgn@nbmpub.com. **Website:** nbmpub.com. **Contact:** Terry Nantier, editor. Estab. 1976. Publishes graphic novels for an audience of YA/adults. Types of books include fiction, mystery, biographies and social parodies. Catalog online.

TERMS Advance negotiable. Responds to e-mail 1-2 days; mail 1 week.

⊘⊘ THOMAS NELSON, INC.

HarperCollins Christian Publishing, Box 141000, Nashville TN 37214. (615)889-9000. **Website:** www.thomasnelson.com. Thomas Nelson publishes Christian lifestyle nonfiction and fiction, and general nonfiction. Publishes hardcover and paperback orginals.

NEEDS Publishes authors of commercial fiction who write for adults from a Christian perspective.

HOW TO CONTACT *Does not accept unsolicited mss.* No phone queries.

TERMS Rates negotiated for each project. Pays advance.

⊘ TOMMY NELSON

Imprint of Thomas Nelson, Inc., P.O. Box 141000, Nashville TN 37214-1000. (615)889-9000. **Fax:** (615)902-2219. **Website:** www.tommynelson.com. "Tommy Nelson publishes children's Christian nonfiction and fiction for boys and girls up to age 14. We honor God and serve people through books, videos, software and Bibles for children that improve the lives of our customers." Publishes hardcover and trade paperback originals. Guidelines online.

NEEDS No stereotypical characters.

HOW TO CONTACT *Does not accept unsolicited mss.*

TIPS "Know the Christian Booksellers Association market. Check out the Christian bookstores to see what sells and what is needed."

NEW DIRECTIONS

80 Eighth Ave., New York NY 10011. **Fax:** (212)255-0231. **E-mail:** editorial@ndbooks.com. **Website:** www.ndbooks.com. **Contact:** Editorial Assistant. Estab. 1936. "Currently, New Directions focuses primarily on fiction in translation, avant garde American fiction, and experimental poetry by American and foreign authors. If your work does not fall into one of those categories, you would probably do best to submit your work elsewhere." Hardcover and trade paperback originals. Book catalog and guidelines online.

NEEDS No juvenile or young adult, occult or paranormal, genre fiction (formula romances, sci-fi or westerns), arts & crafts, and inspirational poetry.

HOW TO CONTACT Brief query only.

TERMS Responds in 3-4 months to queries.

TIPS "Our books serve the academic community."

☯ NEWEST PUBLISHERS LTD.

201, 8540-109 St., Edmonton AB T6G 1E6, Canada. (780)432-9427. **Fax:** (780)433-3179. **E-mail:** info@newestpress.com. **E-mail:** submissions@newestpress.com. **Website:** www.newestpress.com. Estab. 1977. NeWest publishes Western Canadian fiction, nonfiction, poetry, and drama. Publishes trade paperback originals. Book catalog for 9×12 SASE. Guidelines online.

HOW TO CONTACT Submit complete ms.

TERMS Pays 10% royalty. Responds in 6-8 months to queries.

NEW ISSUES POETRY & PROSE

Western Michigan University, 1903 W. Michigan Ave., Kalamazoo MI 49008-5463. (269)387-8185. **E-mail:** new-issues@wmich.edu. **Website:** wmich.edu/newissues. **Contact:** Managing Editor. Estab. 1996. Guidelines online.

HOW TO CONTACT Only considers submissions to book contests.

NEW RIVERS PRESS

1104 Seventh Ave. S., Moorhead MN 56563. **Website:** www.newriverspress.com. **Contact:** Nayt Rundquist, managing editor. Estab. 1968. New Rivers Press publishes collections of poetry, novels, nonfiction, translations of contemporary literature, and collections of short fiction and nonfiction. "We continue to publish books regularly by new and emerging writers, but we also welcome the opportunity to read work of every character and to publish the best literature available nationwide. Each fall through the Many Voices Project competition, we choose 2 books: 1 poetry and 1 prose."

NEEDS Sponsors American Fiction Prize to find best unpublished short stories by American writers.

NIGHTSCAPE PRESS

P.O. Box 1948, Smyrna TN 37167. **E-mail:** info@nightscapepress.com. **E-mail:** submissions@nightscapepress.com. **Website:** www.nightscapepress.com. Estab. 2012. Nightscape Press is seeking quality book-length words of at least 50,000 words (40,000 for young adult). Guidelines online. Currently closed to submissions. Will announce on site when they re-open to submissions.

NEEDS "We are not interested in erotica or graphic novels."

HOW TO CONTACT Query.

TERMS Pays monthly royalties. Offers advance.

NORTIA PRESS

Santa Ana CA **E-mail:** acquisitions@nortiapress.com. **Website:** www.nortiapress.com. Estab. 2009. Publishes trade paperback and electronic originals.

NEEDS "We focus mainly on nonfiction as well as literary and historical fiction, but are open to other genres. No vampire stories, science fiction, or erotica, please."

HOW TO CONTACT Submit a brief e-mail query. Please include a short bio, approximate word count of book, and expected date of completion (fiction titles should be completed before sending a query, and should contain a sample chapter in the body of the e-mail). All unsolicited snail mail or attachments will be discarded without review.

TERMS Pays negotiable royalties on wholesale price. Responds in 1 month.

TIPS "We specialize in working with experienced authors who seek a more collaborative and fulfilling relationship with their publisher. As such, we are less likely to accept pitches form first-time authors, no matter how good the idea. As with any pitch, please make your e-mail very brief and to the point, so the reader is not forced to skim it. Always include some biographic information. Your life is interesting."

Ⓐ Ⓞ W.W. NORTON & COMPANY, INC.

500 Fifth Ave., New York NY 10110. (212)354-5500. **Fax:** (212)869-0856. **Website:** www.wwnorton.com. Estab. 1923. "W. W. Norton & Company, the oldest and largest publishing house owned wholly by its employees, strives to carry out the imperative of its founder to 'publish books not for a single season, but for the years' in fiction, nonfiction, poetry, college textbooks, cookbooks, art books and professional books. Due to the workload of our editorial staff and the large volume of materials we receive, *Norton is no longer able to accept unsolicited submissions.* If you are seeking publication, we suggest working with a literary agent who will represent you to the house."

Ⓢ NOSY CROW PUBLISHING

The Crow's Nest, 10a Lant St., London SE1 1QR, United Kingdom. (44)(0)207-089-7575. **Fax:** (44)(0)207-089-7576. **E-mail:** hello@nosycrow.com. **E-mail:** submissions@nosycrow.com. **Website:** nosycrow.com. "We publish books for children 0-14. We're looking for 'parent-friendly' books, and we don't publish books with explicit sex, drug use or serious violence, so no edgy YA or edgy cross-over. And whatever New Adult is, we don't do it. We also publish apps for children from 2-7, and may publish apps for older children if the idea feels right." Guidelines online.

NEEDS "As a rule, we don't like books with 'issues' that are in any way overly didactic."

HOW TO CONTACT Prefers submissions by e-mail, but post works if absolutely necessary.

TIPS "Please don't be too disappointed if we reject your work! We're a small company and can only publish a few new books and apps each year, so do try other publishers and agents: publishing is necessarily a hugely subjective business. We wish you luck!"

OCEANVIEW PUBLISHING

595 Bay Isles Rd., Suite 120-G, Longboat Key FL 34228. **E-mail:** mail@oceanviewpub.com. **E-mail:** submissions@oceanviewpub.com. **Website:** www.oceanviewpub.com. Estab. 2006. "Independent publisher of nonfiction and fiction, with primary interest in original mystery, thriller and suspense titles. Accepts new and established writers." Publishes hardcover and electronic originals. Catalog and guidelines online.

NEEDS Accepting adult mss with a primary interest in the mystery, thriller and suspense genres—from new and established writers. No children's or YA literature, poetry, cookbooks, technical manuals or short stories.

HOW TO CONTACT Within body of e-mail only, include author's name and brief bio (Indicate if this is an agent submission), ms title and word count, author's mailing address, phone number and e-mail address. Attached to the e-mail should be the following: A synopsis of 750 words or fewer. The first 30 pages of the ms. Please note that we accept only Word documents as attachments to the submission e-mail. Do not send query letters or proposals.

TERMS Responds in 3 months on mss.

OHIO UNIVERSITY PRESS

30 Park Place, Suite 101, Athens OH 45701. (740)593-1159. **Fax:** (740)593-4536. **E-mail:** berchowi@ohio.edu. **Website:** www.ohioswallow.com. **Contact:** Gillian Berchowitz, director. Estab. 1964. "In addition to scholarly works in African studies, Appalachian studies, US history, and other areas, Ohio University Press publishes a wide range of creative works as part of its Hollis Summers Poetry Prize (yearly deadline in December), its Modern African Writing series, and under its trade imprint, Swallow Press." Publishes hardcover and trade paperback originals and reprints. Catalog online. Guidelines online.

TERMS Responds in 1-3 months.

TIPS "Rather than trying to hook the editor on your work, let the material be compelling enough and well-presented enough to do it for you."

ONSTAGE PUBLISHING

190 Lime Quarry Rd., Suite 106-J, Madison AL 35758-8962. (256)542-3213. **Fax:** (256)542-3213. **E-mail:** submissions@onstagepublishing.com. **Website:** www.onstagepublishing.com. **Contact:** Dianne Hamilton, senior editor. Estab. 1999. "At this time, we only produce fiction books for ages 8-18. We have added an e-book only side of the house for mysteries for grades 6-12. See our website for more information. We will not do anthologies of any kind. Query first for nonfiction projects as nonfiction projects must spark our interest. We no longer are accepting written submissions. We want e-mail queries and submissions. For submissions: Put the first 3 chapters in the body of the e-mail. Do not use attachments! We will delete any submission with an attachment without acknowledgment."

Suggested ms lengths: Chapter books: 3,000-9,000 words, Middle Grade novels: 10,000-40,000 words, Young adult novels: 40,000-60,000 words. Guidelines online.

NEEDS Middle readers: adventure, contemporary, fantasy, history, nature/environment, science fiction, suspense/mystery. Young adults: adventure, contemporary, fantasy, history, humor, science fiction, suspense/mystery. Average word length: chapter books—4,000-6,000 words; middle readers—5,000 words and up; young adults—25,000 and up. Recently published *Mission: Shanghai* by Jamie Dodson (an adventure for boys ages 12+); *Birmingham, 1933: Alice* (a chapter book for grades 3-5). "We do not produce picture books."

TERMS Pays authors/illustrators/photographers advance plus royalties. Pays advance. Responds in 1-6 months.

TIPS "Study our titles and get a sense of the kind of books we publish, so that you know whether your project is likely to be right for us."

☼ OOLICHAN BOOKS

P.O. Box 2278, Lantzville BC V0B 1M0, Canada. (250)423-6113. **E-mail:** info@oolichan.com. **Website:** www.oolichan.com. Estab. 1974. Publishes hardcover and trade paperback originals and reprints. Book catalog online. Guidelines online.

◐ Only publishes Canadian authors.

NEEDS "We try to publish at least 2 literary fiction titles each year. We receive many more deserving submissions than we are able to publish, so we publish only outstanding work. We try to balance our list between emerging and established writers, and have published many first-time writers who have gone on to win or be shortlisted for major literary awards, both nationally and internationally."

HOW TO CONTACT Submit proposal package, publishing history, clips, bio, cover letter, 3 sample chapters, SASE.

TERMS Pays royalty on retail price. Responds in 1-3 months.

TIPS "Our audience is adult readers who love good books and good literature. Our audience is regional and national, as well as international. Follow our submission guidelines. Check out some of our titles at your local library or bookstore to get an idea of what we publish. Don't send us the only copy of your manuscript. Let us know if your submission is simultaneous, and inform us if it is accepted elsewhere. Above all, keep writing!"

OOLIGAN PRESS

369 Neuberger Hall, 724 SW Harrison St., Portland OR 97201. (503)725-9410. **E-mail:** acquisitions@ooliganpress.pdx.edu. **Website:** ooligan.pdx.edu. **Contact:** Acquisitions Co-Managers. Estab. 2001. "We seek to publish regionally significant works of literary, historical, and social value.

NEEDS "We seek to publish regionally significant works of literary, historical, and social value. We define the Pacific Northwest as Northern California, Oregon, Idaho, Washington, British Columbia, and Alaska."

HOW TO CONTACT Query with SASE. *"At this time we cannot accept science fiction or fantasy submissions."*

TERMS Pays negotiable royalty on retail price. Responds in 3 weeks for queries; 3 months for proposals.

TIPS "Search the blog for tips."

ORCA BOOK PUBLISHERS

1016 Balmoral Rd., Victoria BC V8T 1A8, Canada. (800)210-5277. **Fax:** (877)408-1551. **E-mail:** orca@orcabook.com. **Website:** www.orcabook.com. **Contact:** Amy Collins, editor (picture books); Sarah Harvey, editor (young readers); Andrew Wooldridge, editor (juvenile and teen fiction); Bob Tyrrell, publisher (YA, teen); Ruth Linka, associate editor (rapid reads).. Estab. 1984. Only publishes Canadian authors. Publishes hardcover and trade paperback originals, and mass market paperback originals and reprints. Book catalog for 8½x11 SASE. Guidelines online.

NEEDS Picture books: animals, contemporary, history, nature/environment. Middle readers: contemporary, history, fantasy, nature/environment, problem novels, graphic novels. Young adults: adventure, contemporary, hi-lo (Orca Soundings), history, multicultural, nature/environment, problem novels, suspense/mystery, graphic novels. Average word length: picture books—500-1,500; middle readers—20,000-35,000; young adult—25,000-45,000; Orca Soundings—13,000-15,000; Orca Currents—13,000-15,000. No romance, science fiction.

HOW TO CONTACT Query with SASE. Submit proposal package, outline, clips, 2-5 sample chapters, SASE.

TERMS Pays 10% royalty. Responds in 1 month to queries; 2 months to proposals and mss.

TIPS "Our audience is students in grades K-12. Know our books, and know the market."

ORCHARD BOOKS (US)

557 Broadway, New York NY 10012. **Website:** www.scholastic.com. *Orchard is not accepting unsolicited mss.*

NEEDS Picture books, early readers, and novelty: animal, contemporary, history, humor, multicultural, poetry.

TERMS Most commonly offers an advance against list royalties.

RICHARD C. OWEN PUBLISHERS, INC.

P.O. Box 585, Katonah NY 10536. (914)232-3903; (800)262-0787. **E-mail:** richardowen@rcowen.com. **Website:** www.rcowen.com. **Contact:** Richard Owen, publisher. Estab. 1982. "We publish child-focused books, with inherent instructional value, about characters and situations with which 5, 6, and 7-year-old children can identify—books that can be read for meaning, entertainment, enjoyment and information. We include multicultural stories that present minorities in a positive and natural way. Our stories show the diversity in America." Not interested in lesson plans, or books of activities for literature studies or other content areas. Submit complete ms and cover letter. Book catalog available with SASE. Ms guidelines with SASE or online.

"Due to high volume and long production time, we are currently limiting to nonfiction submissions only."

TERMS Pays authors royalty of 5% based on net price or outright purchase (range: $25-500). Offers no advances. Pays illustrators by the project (range: $100-2,000) or per photo (range: $50-150). Responds to mss in 1 year.

PETER OWEN PUBLISHERS

81 Bridge Rd., London N8 9NP, United Kingdom. (44)(208)350-1775. **Fax:** (44)(208)340-9488. **E-mail:** info@peterowen.com. **Website:** www.peterowen.com. "We are far more interested in proposals for nonfiction than fiction at the moment. No poetry or short stories." Publishes hardcover originals and trade paperback originals and reprints. Book catalog for SASE, SAE with IRC or on website.

NEEDS "No first novels. Authors should be aware that we publish very little new fiction these days."

HOW TO CONTACT Query with synopsis, sample chapters.

TERMS Pays 7½-10% royalty. Pays negotiable advance. Responds in 2 months to queries; 3 months to proposals and mss.

PACIFIC PRESS PUBLISHING ASSOCIATION

Trade Book Division, 1350 N. Kings Rd., Nampa ID 83687. (208)465-2500. **Fax:** (208)465-2531. **Website:** www.pacificpress.com. Estab. 1874. "We publish books that fit Seventh-day Adventist beliefs only. All titles are Christian and religious. For guidance, see www.adventist.org/beliefs/index.html. Our books fit into the categories of this retail site: www.adventistbookcenter.com." Publishes hardcover and trade paperback originals and reprints. Guidelines online.

NEEDS "Pacific Press rarely publishes fiction, but we're interested in developing a line of Seventh-day Adventist fiction in the future. Only proposals accepted; no full manuscripts."

TERMS Pays 8-16% royalty on wholesale price. Responds in 3 months to queries.

TIPS "Our primary audience is members of the Seventh-day Adventist denomination. Almost all are written by Seventh-day Adventists. Books that do well for us relate the Biblical message to practical human concerns and focus more on the experiential rather than theoretical aspects of Christianity. We are assigning more titles, using less unsolicited material—although we still publish manuscripts from freelance submissions and proposals."

PAGESPRING PUBLISHING

P.O. Box 2113, Columbus OH 43221. **E-mail:** sales@pagespringpublishing.com. **E-mail:** submissions@pagespringpublishing.com. **Website:** www.pagespringpublishing.com. **Contact:** Lucky Marble Books Editor or Cup of Tea Books Editor. Estab. 2012. PageSpring Publishing publishes women's fiction under the Cup of Tea Books imprint and YA/middle grade titles under the Lucky Marble Books imprint. Visit the PageSpring Publishing website for submission details. Publishes trade paperback and electronic originals. Catalog online. Guidelines online.

NEEDS Cup of Tea Books publishes women's fiction. Lucky Marble Books specializes in middle grade and young adult fiction.

HOW TO CONTACT Send submissions for both Cup of Tea Books and Lucky Marble Books to submissions@pagespringpublishing.com. Send a query, synopsis, and the first 30 pages of the manuscript in the body of the email. please. NO attachments.

TERMS Pays royalty on wholesale price. Endeavors to respond to queries within 3 months.

PAGESPRING PUBLISHING

PageSpring Publishing, P.O. Box 21133, Columbus OH 43221. **E-mail:** submissions@pagespringpublishing.com. **Website:** www.pagespringpublishing.com. Estab. 2012. PageSpring Publishing is a small independent publisher with two imprints: Cup of Tea Books and Lucky Marble Books. Cup of Tea Books publishes women's fiction, with particular emphasis on mystery and humor. Lucky Marble Books publishes young adult and middle grade fiction. "We are looking for engaging characters and well-crafted plots that keep our readers turning the page. We accept e-mail queries only; see our website for details." Publishes trade paperback and electronic originals. Guidelines online.

NEEDS Cup of Tea Books publishes women's fiction. Lucky Marble Books publishes middle grade and young adult novels. No children's picture books.

HOW TO CONTACT Submit proposal package via e-mail only. Include synopsis and 30 sample pages.

TERMS Pays royalty. Responds in 3 months.

TIPS "Cup of Tea Books is particularly interested in cozy mystery novels. Lucky Marble Books is looking for funny, age-appropriate tales for middle grade and young adult readers."

✪ PAJAMA PRESS

181 Carlaw Ave., Suite 207, Toronto ON M4M 2S1, Canada. 4164662222. **E-mail:** annfeatherstone@pajamapress.ca. **Website:** pajamapress.ca. **Contact:** Ann Featherstone, senior editor. Estab. 2011. "We publish picture books—both for the very young and for school-aged readers, as well as novels for middle grade readers and contemporary or historical fiction for young adults aged 12+. Our nonfiction titles typically contain a strong narrative element. Pajama Press is also looking for mss from authors of diverse backgrounds. Stories about immigrants are of special interest." Guidelines online.

NEEDS vampire novels; romance (except as part of a literary novel); fiction with overt political or religious messages

TERMS Pays advance. Responds in 6 weeks.

⚠⊘ PANTHEON BOOKS

Penguin Random House, 1745 Broadway, New York NY 10019. **Website:** www.pantheonbooks.com. Estab. 1942. Publishes hardcover and trade paperback originals and trade paperback reprints.

⊖ Pantheon Books publishes both Western and non-Western authors of literary fiction and important nonfiction. "We only accept mss submitted by an agent."

HOW TO CONTACT *Does not accept unsolicited mss.* Agented submissions only.

PANTS ON FIRE PRESS

2062 Harbor Cove Way, Winter Garden FL 34787. (863)546-0760. **E-mail:** submission@pantsonfire-press.com. **Website:** www.pantsonfirepress.com. **Contact:** Becca Goldman, senior editor; Emily Gerety, editor. Estab. 2012. Pants On Fire Press is an award-winning book publisher of picture, middle-grade, young adult, and adult books. Publishes hardcover originals and reprints, trade paperback originals and reprints, and electronic originals and reprints. Catalog online. Guidelines online.

NEEDS Publishes big story ideas with high concepts, new worlds, and meaty characters for children, teens, and discerning adults.

HOW TO CONTACT Submit a proposal package including a synopsis, 3 sample chapters, and a query letter via e-mail.

TERMS Pays 10-50% royalties on wholesale price. Responds in 3 months.

PAPERCUTZ

160 Broadway, Suite 700E, New York NY 10038. (646)559-4681. **Fax:** (212)643-1545. **E-mail:** papercutz@papercutz.com. **Website:** www.papercutz.com. Estab. 2004. Publisher of graphic novels for kids and teens. Publishes major licenses and author created comics.

NEEDS "Independent publisher of graphic novels including popular existing properties aimed at the teen and tween market."

TERMS Pays advance. Responds in 2-4 weeks.

TIPS "Be familiar with our titles—that's the best way to know what we're interested in publishing. If you are somehow attached to a successful tween or teen property and would like to adapt it into a graphic novel, we may be interested. We also take submissions for new series preferably that have already a following online."

PARADISE CAY PUBLICATIONS

P.O. Box 29, Arcata CA 95518-0029. (800)736-4509. **Fax:** (707)822-9163. **Website:** www.paracay.com. "Paradise Cay Publications, Inc. is a small independent publisher specializing in nautical books, videos, and art prints. Our primary interest is in manuscripts that deal with the instructional and technical aspects of ocean sailing. We also publish and will consider fiction if it has a strong nautical theme." Publishes hardcover and trade paperback originals and reprints. Book catalog and ms guidelines free on request or online.

NEEDS All fiction must have a nautical theme.

HOW TO CONTACT Query with SASE. Submit proposal package, clips, 2-3 sample chapters.

TERMS Pays 10-15% royalty on wholesale price. Makes outright purchase of $1,000-10,000. Does not normally pay advances to first-time or little-known authors. Responds in 1 month to queries/proposals; 2 months to mss.

TIPS "Audience is recreational sailors. Call Matt Morehouse (publisher)."

⊘ PAUL DRY BOOKS

1700 Sansom St., Suite 700, Philadelphia PA 19103. (215)231-9939. **Fax:** (215)231-9942. **E-mail:** editor@pauldrybooks.com. **E-mail:** pdry@pauldrybooks.com. **Website:** pauldrybooks.com. "We publish fiction, both novels and short stories, and nonfiction, biography, memoirs, history, and essays, covering subjects from Homer to Chekhov, bird watching to jazz music, New York City to shogunate Japan." Hardcover and trade paperback originals, trade paperback reprints. Book catalog online.

HOW TO CONTACT "We do not accept unsolicited manuscripts."

TIPS "Our aim is to publish lively books 'to awaken, delight, and educate'—to spark conversation. We publish fiction and nonfiction, and essays covering subjects from Homer to Chekhov, bird watching to jazz music, New York City to shogunate Japan."

PAULINE BOOKS & MEDIA

50 St. Paul's Ave., Boston MA 02130. (617)522-8911. **Fax:** (617)541-9805. **E-mail:** design@paulinemedia.

com; editorial@paulinemedia.com. **Website:** www. pauline.org. Estab. 1932. "Submissions are evaluated on adherence to Gospel values, harmony with the Catholic faith tradition, relevance of topic, and quality of writing." For board books and picture books, the entire manuscript should be submitted. For easy-to-read, young readers, and middle reader books and teen books, please send a cover letter accompanied by a synopsis and two sample chapters. "Electronic submissions are encouraged. We make every effort to respond to unsolicited submissions within 2 months." Publishes trade paperback originals and reprints. Book catalog online. Guidelines online.

NEEDS Children's and teen fiction only. "We are now accepting submissions for easy-to-read and middle reader chapter, and teen well documented historical fiction. We would also consider well-written fantasy, fairy tales, myths, science fiction, mysteries, or romance if approached from a Catholic perspective and consistent with church teaching. Please see our writer's guidelines."

HOW TO CONTACT "Submit proposal package, including synopsis, 2 sample chapters, and cover letter; complete ms."

TERMS Varies by project, but generally are royalties with advance. Flat fees sometimes considered for smaller works. Responds in 2 months.

TIPS "Manuscripts may or may not be explicitly catechetical, but we seek those that reflect a positive worldview, good moral values, awareness and appreciation of diversity, and respect for all people. All material must be relevant to the lives of readers and must conform to Catholic teaching and practice."

PAYCOCK PRESS

3819 N. 13th St., Arlington VA 22201. (703)525-9296. **E-mail:** rchrdpeabody9@gmail.com. **E-mail:** gargoyle@gargoylemagazine.com. **Website:** www.gargoylemagazine.com. **Contact:** Richard Peabody. Estab. 1976. "Too academic for the underground, too outlaw for the academic world. We tend to be edgy and look for ultra-literary work." Publishes paperback originals. Books: POD printing. Average print order: 500. Averages 1 total title/year. Member CLMP. Distributes through Amazon and website.

HOW TO CONTACT Accepts unsolicited mss. Accepts queries by e-mail. Include brief bio. Send SASE for return of ms or send a disposable ms and SASE for reply only.

TERMS Responds to queries in 1 month; mss in 4 months.

TIPS "Check out our website. Two of our favorite writers are Paul Bowles and Jeanette Winterson."

PEACHTREE PUBLISHERS

Peachtree Publishers, Ltd., 1700 Chattahoochee Ave., Atlanta GA 30318. (404)876-8761. **Fax:** (404)875-2578. **E-mail:** hello@peachtree-online.com. **Website:** www.peachtree-online.com. **Contact:** Helen Harriss, submissions editor. "We publish a broad range of subjects and perspectives, with emphasis on innovative plots and strong writing." Publishes hardcover and trade paperback originals. Book catalog for 6 first-class stamps. Guidelines online.

NEEDS Looking for very well-written middle grade and young adult novels. No adult fiction. No collections of poetry or short stories; no romance or science fiction.

HOW TO CONTACT Submit complete ms with SASE.

TERMS Pays royalty on retail price. Responds in 6 months and mss.

PEACHTREE PUBLISHERS, LTD.

1700 Chattahoochee Ave., Atlanta GA 30318. (404)876-8761. **Fax:** (404)875-2578. **E-mail:** hello@peachtree-online.com. **Website:** www.peachtree-online.com. Estab. 1977.

NEEDS Picture books, young readers: adventure, animal, concept, history, nature/environment. Middle readers: adventure, animal, history, nature/environment, sports. Young adults: fiction, mystery, adventure. Does not want to see science fiction, romance.

HOW TO CONTACT Submit complete ms or 3 sample chapters by postal mail only.

TERMS Responds in 6-7 months.

☼∅ PEDLAR PRESS

113 Bond St., St. John's NL A16 1T6, Canada. (709)738-6702. **E-mail:** feralgrl@interlog.com. **Website:** www.pedlarpress.com. **Contact:** Beth Follett, owner/editor. Estab. 1996. An award-winning independent Canadian literary publishing house, based in St John's NL, Pedlar Press was begun, and continues, with the following house vision: to acquire works of exceptional literary quality that also break silences regarding widespread failures of social and political systems: to make books with serious intellectual and emotional content, in other words, that are also works of art. So

much injustice cries out for attention, so much suffering, so many affronts to human dignity need to be met with strong literary force. Pedlar combines high aesthetic standards with a praxis of action; the press means to foster humane social and political ends. It has been possible, over the twenty-two years of Pedlar's existence, to combine an editorial vision that seeks out both works that are strong in literary quality and also distinctive, often avant-garde, and socially engaged. With everyone working together— author, publisher, editor, copyeditor and designer—the aim is to produce literary works of integrity that will make a pronounced difference in the lives of Pedlar's readers. Catalog online.

NEEDS Experimental, feminist, gay/lesbian, literary, short story collections. Canadian writers only.

HOW TO CONTACT Query with SASE, sample chapter(s), synopsis.

TERMS Pays 10% royalty on retail price. Average advance: $200-400.

TIPS "I select manuscripts according to my taste, which fluctuates. Be familiar with some if not most of Pedlar's recent titles."

● PENGUIN GROUP: SOUTH AFRICA

P.O. Box 9, Parklands 2121, South Africa. (27)(11)327-3550. **Fax:** (27)(11)327-3660. **E-mail:** fiction@penguinrandomhouse.co.za. **E-mail:** nonfiction@penguinrandomhouse.co.za. **Website:** www.penguinbooks.co.za. Seeks adult fiction (literary and mass market titles) and adult nonfiction (travel, sports, politics, current affairs, business). No children's, young adult, poetry, or short stories.

HOW TO CONTACT Submit intro letter, 3 sample chapters.

TERMS Pays royalty.

Ⓐ⊘ PENGUIN GROUP USA

375 Hudson St., New York NY 10014. (212)366-2000. **Website:** www.penguin.com. General interest publisher of both fiction and nonfiction. *No unsolicited mss.* Submit work through a literary agent. DAW Books is the lone exception. Guidelines online.

Ⓐ⊘ PENGUIN RANDOM HOUSE, LLC

Division of Bertelsmann Book Group, 1745 Broadway, New York NY 10019. (212)782-9000. **Website:** www.penguinrandomhouse.com. Estab. 1925. Penguin Random House LLC is the world's largest English-language general trade book publisher. *Agented submissions only. No unsolicited mss.*

THE PERMANENT PRESS

Second Chance Press, Attn: Judith Shepard, 4170 Noyac Rd., Sag Harbor NY 11963. (631)725-1101. **E-mail:** judith@thepermanentpress.com; shepard@thepermanentpress.com. **Website:** www.thepermanentpress.com. **Contact:** Judith and Martin Shepard, acquisitions/co-publishers. Estab. 1978. Mid-size, independent publisher of literary fiction. "We keep titles in print and are active in selling subsidiary rights." Average print order: 1,000-2,500. Averages 16 total titles. Accepts unsolicited mss. Pays 10-15% royalty on wholesale price. Offers $1,000 advance. *Will not accept simultaneous submissions.* Publishes hardcover originals. Catalog available.

NEEDS Promotes titles through reviews. Literary, mainstream/contemporary, mystery. Especially looking for high-line literary fiction, "artful, original and arresting." Accepts any fiction category as long as it is a "well-written, original full-length novel."

TERMS Pays 10-15% royalty on wholesale price. Offers $1,000 advance. Responds in weeks or months.

TIPS "We are looking for good books—be they 10th novels or first ones, it makes little difference. The fiction is more important than the track record. Send us the first 25 pages; it's impossible to judge something that begins on page 302. Also, no outlines—let the writing present itself."

PERSEA BOOKS

277 Broadway, Suite 708, New York NY 10007. (212)260-9256. **Fax:** (212)267-3165. **E-mail:** info@perseabooks.com. **Website:** www.perseabooks.com. Estab. 1975. The aim of Persea is to publish works that endure by meeting high standards of literary merit and relevance. "We have often taken on important books other publishers have overlooked, or have made significant discoveries and rediscoveries, whether of a single work or writer's entire oeuvre. Our books cover a wide range of themes, styles, and genres. We have published poetry, fiction, essays, memoir, biography, titles of Jewish and Middle Eastern interest, women's studies, American Indian folklore, and revived classics, as well as a notable selection of works in translation." Guidelines online.

HOW TO CONTACT Queries should include a cover letter, author background and publication history, a detailed synopsis of the proposed work, and a sample chapter. Please indicate if the work is simultaneously submitted.

TERMS Responds in 8 weeks to proposals; 10 weeks to mss.

◐⊘ PHILOMEL BOOKS

Imprint of Penguin Group (USA), Inc., 375 Hudson St., New York NY 10014. (212)414-3610. **Website:** www.penguin.com. **Contact:** Michael Green, president/publisher. Estab. 1980. "We look for beautifully written, engaging manuscripts for children and young adults." Publishes hardcover originals.

HOW TO CONTACT *No unsolicited mss.*

TERMS Pays authors in royalties. Average advance payment "varies." Illustrators paid by advance and in royalties. Pays negotiable advance.

PIANO PRESS

P.O. Box 85, Del Mar CA 92014. (619)884-1401. **Fax:** (858)755-1104. **E-mail:** pianopress@pianopress.com. **Website:** www.pianopress.com. **Contact:** Elizabeth C. Axford, editor. Estab. 1984. "We publish music-related books, either fiction or nonfiction, music-related coloring books, songbooks, sheet music, CDs, and music-related poetry." Book catalog online.

NEEDS Picture books, young readers, middle readers, young adults: folktales, multicultural, poetry, music. Average word length: picture books—1,500-2,000.

TERMS Pays authors, illustrators, and photographers royalties based on the retail price. Responds if interested.

TIPS "We are looking for music-related material only for the juvenile market. Please do not send non-music-related materials. Query by e-mail first before submitting anything."

◐●◑⊘ PIATKUS BOOKS

Little, Brown Book Group, Carmelite House, 50 Victoria Embankment, London EC4Y 0DZ, United Kingdom. (020)3122-7000. **Fax:** (020)3122-7000. **E-mail:** info@littlebrown.co.uk. **Website:** piatkus.co.uk. Estab. 1979. Publishes hardcover originals, paperback originals, and paperback reprints. Guidelines online.

NEEDS Romance fiction, women's fiction, bookclub fiction.

HOW TO CONTACT *Agented submissions only.*

◐⊘ PICADOR USA

MacMillan, 175 Fifth Ave., New York NY 10010. (212)674-5151. **Website:** us.macmillan.com/picador.

Estab. 1994. Picador publishes high-quality literary fiction and nonfiction. "We are open to a broad range of subjects, well written by authoritative authors." Publishes hardcover and trade paperback originals and reprints. Does not accept unsolicited mss. *Agented submissions only.*

TERMS Pays 7-15% on royalty. Advance varies.

PIÑATA BOOKS

Imprint of Arte Publico Press, University of Houston, 4902 Gulf Fwy., Bldg. 19, Room 100, Houston TX 77204-2004. (713)743-2845. **Fax:** (713)743-3080. **E-mail:** submapp@uh.edu. **Website:** www.artepublicopress.com. Estab. 1994. "Piñata Books is dedicated to the publication of children's and young adult literature focusing on U.S. Hispanic culture by U.S. Hispanic authors. Arte Publico's mission is the publication, promotion and dissemination of Latino literature for a variety of national and regional audiences, from early childhood to adult, through the complete gamut of delivery systems, including personal performance as well as print and electronic media." Publishes hardcover and trade paperback originals. Book catalog and guidelines online.

HOW TO CONTACT Submissions made through online submission form.

TERMS Pays 10% royalty on wholesale price. Pays $1,000-3,000 advance. Responds in 2-3 months to queries; 4-6 months to mss.

TIPS "Include cover letter with submission explaining why your manuscript is unique and important, why we should publish it, who will buy it, etc."

PINEAPPLE PRESS, INC.

P.O. Box 3889, Sarasota FL 34230. (941)706-2507. **Fax:** (800)746-3275. **Website:** www.pineapplepress.com. **Contact:** June Cussen, executive editor. Estab. 1982. "We are seeking quality nonfiction on diverse topics for the library and book trade markets. Our mission is to publish good books about Florida." Publishes hardcover and trade paperback originals. Book catalog for 9×12 SAE with $1.32 postage. Guidelines online.

NEEDS Picture books, young readers, middle readers, young adults: animal, folktales, history, nature/environment.

HOW TO CONTACT Query or submit outline/synopsis and 3 sample chapters.

TERMS Pays authors royalty of 10-15%. Responds in 2 months.

TIPS "Quality first novels will be published, though we usually only do one or two novels per year and they must be set in Florida. We regard the author/editor relationship as a trusting relationship with communication open both ways. Learn all you can about the publishing process and about how to promote your book once it is published. A query on a novel without a brief sample seems useless."

PLAYLAB PRESS

P.O. Box 3701, South Brisbane BC 4101, Australia. E-mail: info@playlab.org.au. **Website:** www.playlab.org.au. Estab. 1978. Guidelines online.

HOW TO CONTACT Submit 2 copies of ms, cover letter.

TERMS Responds in 3 months to mss.

TIPS "Playlab Press is committed to the publication of quality writing for and about theatre and performance, which is of significance to Australia's cultural life. It values socially just and diverse publication outcomes and aims to promote these outcomes in local, national, and international contexts."

PLEXUS PUBLISHING, INC.

143 Old Marlton Pike, Medford NJ 08055. (609)654-6500. **Fax:** (609)654-4309. **E-mail:** rcolding@plexuspublishing.com. **Website:** www.plexuspublishing.com. **Contact:** Rob Colding, Book Marketing Manager. Estab. 1977. Plexus publishes regional-interest (southern New Jersey and the greater Philadelphia area) fiction and nonfiction including mysteries, field guides, nature, travel and history. Publishes hardcover and paperback originals. Book catalog and book proposal guidelines for 10x13 SASE.

NEEDS Mysteries and literary novels with a strong regional (southern New Jersey) angle.

HOW TO CONTACT Query with SASE.

TERMS Pays $500-1,000 advance. Responds in 3 months to proposals.

POCKET BOOKS

Simon & Schuster, 1230 Avenue of the Americas, New York NY 10020. (212)698-7000. **Website:** www.simonandschuster.com. Estab. 1939. Pocket Books publishes commercial fiction and genre fiction (WWE, Downtown Press, Star Trek). Publishes paperback originals and reprints, mass market and trade paperbacks. Book catalog available free. Guidelines online.

HOW TO CONTACT *Agented submissions only.*

POCOL PRESS

Box 411, Clifton VA 20124. (703)830-5862. **Website:** www.pocolpress.com. **Contact:** J. Thomas Hetrick, editor. Estab. 1999. "Pocol Press is dedicated to producing high-quality print books and e-books from first-time, non-agented authors. However, all submissions are welcome. We're dedicated to good storytellers and to the written word, specializing in short fiction and baseball. Several of our books have been used as literary texts at universities and in book group discussions around the nation. Pocol Press does not publish children's books, romance novels, or graphic novels. Our authors are comprised of veteran writers and emerging talents." Publishes trade paperback originals. Book catalog and guidelines online.

NEEDS "We specialize in thematic short fiction collections by a single author, westerns, war stories, and baseball fiction. Expert storytellers welcome."

HOW TO CONTACT Does not accept or return unsolicited mss. Query with SASE or submit 1 sample chapter.

TERMS Pays 10-12% royalty on wholesale price. Responds in 1 month to queries; 2 months to mss.

TIPS "Our audience is aged 18 and over. Pocol Press is unique; we publish good writing and great storytelling. Write the best stories you can. Read them to you friends/peers. Note their reaction. Publishes some of the finest fiction by a small press."

POISONED PEN PRESS

4014 N. Goldwater Blvd., Suite 201, Scottsdale AZ 85251. **E-mail:** submissions@poisonedpenpress.com. **Website:** www.poisonedpenpress.com. **Contact:** Diane DiBiase, Assistant Publisher. Estab. 1997. "Our publishing goal is to offer well-written mystery novels of crime and/or detection where the puzzle and its resolution are the main forces that move the story forward." *Not currently accepting submissions. Check website.* Publishes hardcover and trade paperback originals, and hardcover and trade paperback reprints. Book catalog and guidelines online.

NEEDS Mss should generally be longer than 65,000 words and shorter than 100,000 words. Member Publishers Marketing Associations, Arizona Book Publishers Associations, Publishers Association of West. Distributes through Ingram, Baker & Taylor, Brodart. Does not want novels centered on serial killers, spousal or child abuse, drugs, or extremist groups, although we do not entirely rule such works out.

HOW TO CONTACT Accepts unsolicited mss. Electronic queries only. "Submit clips, first 3 pages. We must receive both the synopsis and ms pages electronically as separate attachments to an e-mail message."

TERMS Pays 9-15% royalty on retail price. Responds in 2-3 months to queries and proposals; 6 months to mss.

TIPS "Audience is adult readers of mystery fiction."

POLIS BOOKS

E-mail: info@polisbooks.com. **E-mail:** submissions@polisbooks.com. **Website:** www.polisbooks.com. Estab. 2013. "Polis Books is an independent publishing company actively seeking new and established authors for our growing list. We are actively acquiring titles in mystery, thriller, suspense, procedural, traditional crime, science fiction, fantasy, horror, supernatural, urban fantasy, romance, erotica, commercial women's fiction, commercial literary fiction, young adult and middle grade books." Guidelines online.

HOW TO CONTACT Query with 3 sample chapters and bio via e-mail.

TERMS Offers advance against royalties. Only responds to submissions if interested

PRESS 53

560 N. Trade St., Suite 103, Winston-Salem NC 27101. (336)770-5353. **E-mail:** editor@press53.com. **Website:** www.press53.com. **Contact:** Kevin Morgan Watson, publisher.. Estab. 2005. "Press 53 was founded in October 2005 and quickly earned a reputation for publishing remarkable short fiction and poetry collections." Poetry and short fiction collections only. Catalog online. Guidelines online.

NEEDS "We publish roughly 4-5 short fiction collections each year by writers who are active and earning recognition through publication and awards, plus the winner of our Press 53 Award for Short Fiction." Collections should be between 100 and 250 pages (give or take) with half or more of those stories previously published in journals, magazines, anthologies, etc. Does not want novels.

HOW TO CONTACT Finds mss through contest, referrals, and scouting magazines, journals, and contests.

TERMS Pays 10% royalty on gross sales. Pays advance only for contest winners.

TIPS "We are looking for writers who are actively involved in the writing community, writers who are submitting their work to journals, magazines and contests, and who are getting published, building readership, and earning a reputation for their work."

⚠️🚫 PRICE STERN SLOAN, INC.

Penguin Group, 375 Hudson St., New York NY 10014. (212)366-2000. **Website:** www.penguin.com. Estab. 1963. "Price Stern Sloan publishes quirky mass market novelty series for childrens as well as licensed movie tie-in books." Price Stern Sloan only responds to submissions it's interested in publishing. Book catalog online.

NEEDS Publishes picture books and novelty/board books.

HOW TO CONTACT *Agented submissions only.*

TIPS "Price Stern Sloan publishes unique, fun titles."

PRUFROCK PRESS, INC.

P.O. Box 8813, Waco TX 76714. (800)988-2208. **Fax:** (800)240-0333. **Website:** www.prufrock.com. "Prufrock Press offers award-winning products focused on gifted education, gifted children, advanced learning, and special needs learners, including trade non-fiction (not narrative nonfiction, however) for adults and children/teens. For more than 20 years, Prufrock has supported gifted children and their education and development. The company publishes more than 300 products that enhance the lives of gifted children and the teachers and parents who support them." Accepts simultaneous submissions, but must be notified about it. Book catalog available. Guidelines online.

NEEDS Prufrock Press "offers award-winning products focused on gifted education, gifted children, advanced learning, and special needs learners. For more than 20 years, Prufrock has supported gifted children and their education and development. The company publishes more than 300 products that enhance the lives of gifted children and the teachers and parents who support them." No picture books.

HOW TO CONTACT "Prufrock Press does not consider unsolicited manuscripts."

⚠️🚫 PUFFIN BOOKS

Imprint of Penguin Group (USA), Inc., 375 Hudson St., New York NY 10014. (212)366-2000. **Website:** www.penguin.com. "Puffin Books publishes high-end trade paperbacks and paperback reprints for preschool children, beginning and middle readers, and young adults." Publishes trade paperback originals and reprints.

HOW TO CONTACT *No unsolicited mss. Agented submissions only.*

TIPS "Our audience ranges from little children 'first books' to young adult (ages 14-16). An original idea has the best luck."

⚫⊘ G.P. PUTNAM'S SONS HARDCOVER

Imprint of Penguin Group (USA), Inc., 375 Hudson, New York NY 10014. (212)366-2000. **Fax:** (212)366-2664. **Website:** www.penguin.com. Publishes hardcover originals. Request book catalog through mail order department.

HOW TO CONTACT *Agented submissions only.*

TERMS Pays variable royalties on retail price. Pays varies advance.

⚫⊘ RANDOM HOUSE PUBLISHING GROUP

Division of Random House, Inc., 1745 Broadway, New York NY 10019. (212)782-9000. **Website:** www.penguinrandomhouse.com. Estab. 1925. Random House is the world's largest English-language general trade book publisher. It includes an array of prestigious imprints that publish some of the foremost writers of our time. Publishes hardcover and paperback trade books.

HOW TO CONTACT *Agented submissions only.*

RAZORBILL

Penguin Young Readers Group, 345 Hudson St., New York NY 10014. (212)414-3427. **E-mail:** asanchez@penguinrandomhouse.com; bschrank@penguinrandomhouse.com; jharriton@penguinrandomhouse.com. **Website:** www.razorbillbooks.com. **Contact:** Jessica Almon, executive editor; Casey McIntyre, associate publisher; Deborah Kaplan, vice president and executive art director, Marissa Grossman; assistant editor, Tiffany Liao; associate editor. Estab. 2003. "This division of Penguin Young Readers is looking for the best and the most original of commercial contemporary fiction titles for middle grade and YA readers. A select quantity of nonfiction titles will also be considered."

NEEDS Middle Readers: adventure, contemporary, graphic novels, fantasy, humor, problem novels. Young adults/teens: adventure, contemporary, fantasy, graphic novels, humor, multicultural, suspense, paranormal, science fiction, dystopian, literary, romance. Average word length: middle readers—40,000; young adult—60,000.

HOW TO CONTACT Submit cover letter with up to 30 sample pages.

TERMS Offers advance against royalties. Responds in 1-3 months.

TIPS "New writers will have the best chance of acceptance and publication with original, contemporary material that boasts a distinctive voice and well-articulated world. Check out website to get a better idea of what we're looking for."

⚪ REBELIGHT PUBLISHING, INC.

23-845 Dakota St., Suite 314, Winnipeg Manitoba R2M 5M3, Canada. **Website:** www.rebelight.com. **Contact:** Editor. Estab. 2014. Rebelight Publishing is interested in "crack the spine, blow your mind" manuscripts for middle grade, young adult and new adult novels. *Only considers submissions from Canadian writers.* Publishes paperback and electronic originals. Catalog online or PDF available via e-mail request. Guidelines online.

NEEDS All genres are considered, provided they are for a middle grade, young adult, or new adult audience. "Become familiar with our books. Study our website. Stick within the guidelines. Our tag line is 'crack the spine, blow your mind'—we are looking for well-written, powerful, fresh, fast-paced fiction. Keep us turning the pages. Give us something we just have to spread the word about."

HOW TO CONTACT Submit proposal package, including a synopsis and 3 sample chapters. Read guidelines carefully.

TERMS Pays 12-22% royalties on retail price. Does not offer an advance. Responds in 3 months to queries and mss. Submissions accepted via email only.

TIPS "Review your manuscript for passive voice prior to submitting! (And that means get rid of it.)"

⚪⊘ RED DEER PRESS

195 Allstate Pkwy., Markham ON L3R 4TB, Canada. (905)477-9700. **Fax:** (905)477-9179. **E-mail:** rdp@reddeerpress.com. **Website:** www.reddeerpress.com. **Contact:** Richard Dionne, publisher. Estab. 1975. Book catalog for 9 x 12 SASE.

⚪ Red Deer Press is an award-winning publisher of children's and young adult literary titles.

NEEDS Publishes young adult, adult science fiction, fantasy, and paperback originals "focusing on books by, about, or of interest to Canadians." Books: offset paper; offset printing; hardcover/perfect-bound. Average print order: 5,000. First novel print order: 2,500. Distributes titles in Canada and the US, the UK, Australia and New Zealand. Young adult (juvenile and early reader), contemporary. No romance or horror.

TERMS Pays 8-10% royalty.

TIPS "We're very interested in young adult and children's fiction from Canadian writers with a proven track record (either published books or widely published in established magazines or journals) and for manuscripts with regional themes and/or a distinctive voice. We publish Canadian authors exclusively."

RED HEN PRESS

P.O. Box 40820, Pasadena CA 91114. (626)356-4760. **Fax:** (626)356-9974. **Website:** www.redhen.org. **Contact:** Mark E. Cull, publisher/executive director. Estab. 1993. "At this time, the best opportunity to be published by Red Hen is by entering one of our contests. Please find more information in our award submission guidelines." Publishes trade paperback originals. Book catalog available free. Guidelines online.

HOW TO CONTACT Query with synopsis and either 20-30 sample pages or complete ms using online submission manager.

TERMS Responds in 1-2 months.

TIPS "Audience reads poetry, literary fiction, intelligent nonfiction. If you have an agent, we may be too small since we don't pay advances. Write well. Send queries first. Be willing to help promote your own book."

REDLEAF LANE

Redleaf Press, 10 Yorkton Ct., St. Paul MN 55117. (800)423-8309. **E-mail:** info@redleafpress.org. **E-mail:** acquisitions@redleafpress.org. **Website:** www. redleafpress.org. **Contact:** David Heath, director. Redleaf Lane publishes engaging, high-quality picture books for children. "Our books are unique because they take place in group-care settings and reflect developmentally appropriate practices and research-based standards." Guidelines online.

RED SAGE PUBLISHING, INC.

P.O. Box 4844, Seminole FL 33775. (727)391-3847. **E-mail:** submissions@eredsage.com. **Website:** www. eredsage.com. **Contact:** Alexandria Kendall. Estab. 1995. Publishes books of romance fiction, written for the adventurous woman. Guidelines online and all submissions via e-mail.

HOW TO CONTACT Read guidelines.

TERMS Pays author royalty.

🅐 ⊘ REVELL

Division of Baker Publishing Group, 6030 E. Fulton Rd., Ada MI 49301. (616)676-9185. **Fax:** (616)676-9573. **Website:** www.bakerbooks.com. Estab. 1870. "Revell publishes to the heart (rather than to the head). For 125 years, Revell has been publishing evangelical books for the personal enrichment and spiritual growth of general Christian readers." Publishes hardcover, trade paperback and mass market paperback originals. Book catalog and ms guidelines online.

🗨 *No longer accepts unsolicited mss.*

⊘ RING OF FIRE PUBLISHING LLC

6523 California Ave. SW #409, Seattle WA 98136. **E-mail:** contact@ringoffirebooks.com. **Website:** www. ringoffirebooks.com. Estab. 2011. "We are currently closed to submissions." Check website for updates. Publishes trade paperback and electronic originals. Book catalog and ms guidelines online.

TERMS Pays royalties.

RIPPLE GROVE PRESS

P.O. Box 910, Shelburne VT 05482. **E-mail:** submit@ ripplegrovepress.com. **Website:** www.ripplegrovepress.com. **Contact:** Rob Broder. Estab. 2013. Ripple Grove Press is an independent, family-run children's book publisher. "We started Ripple Grove Press because we have a passion for well-told and beautifully illustrated stories for children. Our mission is to bring together great writers and talented illustrators to make the most wonderful books possible. We hope our books find their way to the cozy spot in your home." Publishes hardcover originals. Catalog online. Guidelines online.

NEEDS We are looking for something unique, that has not been done before; an interesting story that captures a moment with a timeless feel. We are looking for picture driven stories for children ages 2-6. Please do not send early readers, middle grade, or YA mss. No religious stories. Please do not submit your story with page breaks or illustration notes. Do not submit a story with doodles or personal photographs.

HOW TO CONTACT Submit completed mss. Accepts submissions by mail and e-mail. E-mail preferred. Please submit a cover letter including a summary of your story, the age range of the story, a brief biography of yourself, and contact information.

TERMS Authors and illustrators receive royalties on net receipts. Pays negotiable advance. Given the volume of submissions we receive we are no longer able to individually respond to each. Please allow 5 months for us to review your submission. If we are interested in your story, you can expect to hear from us within that time. If you do not hear from us after that time, we are not interested in publishing your story. It's not you, it's us! We receive thousands of submissions and only publish a few books each year. Don't give up!

TIPS "Please read children's picture books. We create books that children and adults want to read over and over again. Our books showcase art as well as stories and tie them together in a unique and creative way."

RIVER CITY PUBLISHING

1719 Mulberry St., Montgomery AL 36106. **E-mail:** fnorris@rivercitypublishing.com. **Website:** www.rivercitypublishing.com. **Contact:** Fran Norris, editor. Estab. 1989. Midsize independent publisher. River City publishes literary fiction, regional, short story collections. No poetry, memoir, or children's books. We also consider narrative histories, sociological accounts, and travel; however, only biographies and memoirs from noted persons will be considered. Publishes hardcover and trade paperback originals.

NEEDS No poetry, memoir, or children's books.

HOW TO CONTACT Send appropriate-sized SASE or IRC, "otherwise, the material will be recycled." Also accepts queries by e-mail. "Please include your electronic query letter as inline text and not as an attachment; we do not open unsolicited attachments of any kind." No multiple submissions. Rarely comments on rejected mss.

TERMS Responds within 9 months.

TIPS "Only send your best work after you have received outside opinions. From approximately 1,000 submissions each year, we publish no more than 8 books and few of those come from unsolicited material. Competition is fierce, so follow the guidelines exactly. First-time novelists are also encouraged to send work."

ⒶⓄ RIVERHEAD BOOKS

Penguin Putnam, 375 Hudson St., New York NY 10014. **Website:** www.penguin.com.

HOW TO CONTACT *Submit through agent only. No unsolicited mss.*

ⒶⓄ ROARING BROOK PRESS

Macmillan Children's Publishing Group, 175 Fifth Ave., New York NY 10010. (646)307-5151. **Website:** us.macmillan.com. Estab. 2000. Roaring Brook Press is an imprint of MacMillan, a group of companies that includes Henry Holt and Farrar, Straus & Giroux. *Roaring Brook is not accepting unsolicited mss.*

NEEDS Picture books, young readers, middle readers, young adults: adventure, animal, contemporary, fantasy, history, humor, multicultural, nature/environment, poetry, religion, science fiction, sports, suspense/mystery.

HOW TO CONTACT *Not accepting unsolicited mss or queries.*

TERMS Pays authors royalty based on retail price.

TIPS "You should find a reputable agent and have him/her submit your work."

ⓞ RONSDALE PRESS

3350 W. 21st Ave., Vancouver BC V6S 1G7, Canada. (604)738-4688. **Fax:** (604)731-4548. **E-mail:** ronsdale@shaw.ca. **Website:** ronsdalepress.com. **Contact:** Ronald B. Hatch (fiction, poetry, nonfiction, social commentary); Veronica Hatch (YA novels and short stories). Estab. 1988. "Ronsdale Press is a Canadian literary publishing house that publishes 12 books each year, four of which are young adult titles. Of particular interest are books involving children exploring and discovering new aspects of Canadian history." Publishes trade paperback originals. Book catalog for #10 SASE. Guidelines online.

NEEDS Young adults: Canadian novels. Average word length: middle readers and young adults—50,000.

HOW TO CONTACT Submit complete MS if you are certain it is right for Ronsdale Press.

TERMS Pays 10% royalty on retail price. Responds to queries in 2 weeks; mss in 2 months.

TIPS "Ronsdale Press is a literary publishing house, based in Vancouver, and dedicated to publishing books from across Canada, books that give Canadians new insights into themselves and their country. We aim to publish the best Canadian writers."

SADDLEBACK EDUCATIONAL PUBLISHING

3120-A Pullman St., Costa Mesa CA 92626. (888)735-2225. **E-mail:** contact@sdlback.com. **Website:** www.sdlback.com. Saddleback is always looking for fresh, new talent. "Please note that we primarily publish books for kids ages 12-18."

NEEDS "We look for diversity for our characters and content."

HOW TO CONTACT Mail typed submission along with a query letter describing the work simply and where it fits in with other titles.

SAGUARO BOOKS, LLC

16201 E. Keymar Dr., Fountain Hills AZ 85268. **Fax:** (480)284-4855. **E-mail:** mjnickum@saguarobooks. com. **Website:** www.saguarobooks.com. **Contact:** Mary Nickum, CEO. Estab. 2012. Saguaro Books, LLC is a publishing company specializing in middle grade and young adult ficiton by first-time authors. Publishes trade paperback and electronic originals. Catalog online. Guidelines by e-mail.

NEEDS Ms should be well-written; signed letter by a professional editor is required. Does not want agented work.

HOW TO CONTACT Query via e-mail before submitting work. Any material sent before requested will be ignored.

TERMS Pays 20% royalties after taxes and publication costs. Does not offer advance. Responds within 3 months only if we're interested.

TIPS "Visit our website before sending us a query. Pay special attention to the For Authors Only page."

⊘⊘ ST. MARTIN'S PRESS, LLC

Holtzbrinck Publishers, 175 Fifth Ave., New York NY 10010. (212)674-5151. **Fax:** (212)420-9314. **Website:** www.stmartins.com. Estab. 1952. General interest publisher of both fiction and nonfiction. Publishes hardcover, trade paperback and mass market originals.

HOW TO CONTACT *Agented submissions only. No unsolicited mss.*

TERMS Pays royalty. Pays advance.

SAKURA PUBLISHING & TECHNOLOGIES

805 Lindaraxa Park North, Alhambra CA 91801. (330)360-5131. **E-mail:** skpublishing124@gmail.com. **Website:** www.sakura-publishing.com. **Contact:** Derek Vasconi, submissions coordinator. Estab. 2007. Visit our website for query guidelines. Mss that don't follow guidelines will not be considered. Sakura Publishing is a traditional, independent book publishing company that seeks to publish Asian-themed books, particularly Asian-Horror, or anything dealing with

Japan, Japanese culture, and Japanese horror. Publishes trade paperback, mass market paperback and electronic originals and reprints. Currently accepts only the following genres: Asian fiction, Japanese fiction (in English), Nonfiction, and horror. Please do not send queries for any other genres. Book catalog available for #10 SASE. Guidelines online.

NEEDS Only looking for Asian horror, with preference given to Japanese horror, as well as Japanese fiction, Japanese erotica, Asian erotica. Will consider other types of Asian-centered fiction, but top preference will be on fiction centered in or dealing with Japan or Japanese people living in America.

HOW TO CONTACT Follow guidelines online.

TERMS Royalty payments on paperback, e-book, wholesale, and merchandise Does not pay advance. Responds in 1 week.

TIPS "Please make sure you visit our submissions page at our website and follow all instructions exactly as written. Also, Sakura Publishing has a preference for fiction/nonfiction books specializing in Asian culture."

SALINA BOOKSHELF

1120 W. University Ave., Suite 102, Flagstaff AZ 86001. (877)527-0070. **Fax:** (928)526-0386. **Website:** www. salinabookshelf.com. Publishes trade paperback originals and reprints.

NEEDS Submissions should be in English or Navajo. "All our books relate to the Navajo language and culture."

HOW TO CONTACT Query with SASE.

TERMS Pays varying royalty. Pays advance. Responds in 3 months to queries.

SALVO PRESS

An imprint of Start Publishing, 101 Hudson St., 37th Floor, Suite 3705, Jersey City NJ 07302. **E-mail:** info@ salvopress.com. **Website:** www.salvopress.com. Estab. 1998. Salvo Press proudly publishes mysteries, thrillers, and literary books in e-book and audiobook formats. Book catalog and ms guidelines online.

NEEDS "We are a small press specializing in mystery, suspense, espionage and thriller fiction. Our press publishes in trade paperback and most e-book formats."

HOW TO CONTACT Query by e-mail.

TERMS Pays 10% royalty. Responds in 5 minutes to 1 month to queries; 2 months to mss.

SARABANDE BOOKS, INC.

822 E. Market St., Louisville KY 40206. (502)458-4028. **Fax:** (502)458-4065. **E-mail:** info@sarabandebooks.org. **Website:** www.sarabandebooks.org. **Contact:** Sarah Gorham, Editor-in-Chief. Estab. 1994. "Sarabande Books was founded to publish poetry, short fiction, and creative nonfiction. We look for works of lasting literary value. Please see our titles to get an idea of our taste. Accepts submissions through contests and open submissions." Publishes trade paperback originals. Book catalog available free. Contest guidelines for #10 SASE or on website.

◯ Charges $15 handling fee with alternative option of purchase of book from website (e-mail confirmation of sale must be included with submission).

NEEDS "We consider novels and nonfiction in a wide variety of genres. We do not consider genre fiction such as science fiction, fantasy, or horror. Our target length is 70,000-90,000 words."

HOW TO CONTACT Queries can be sent via e-mail, fax, or regular post.

TERMS Pays royalty. 10% on actual income received. Also pays in author's copies. Pays $500-1,000 advance.

TIPS "Sarabande publishes for a general literary audience. Know your market. Read-and buy-books of literature. Sponsors contests for poetry and fiction. Make sure you're not writing in a vacuum, that you've read and are conscious of contemporary literature. Have someone read your manuscript, checking it for ordering, coherence. Better a lean, consistently strong manuscript than one that is long and uneven. We like a story to have good narrative, and we like to be engaged by language."

SASQUATCH BOOKS

1904 Third Ave., Suite 710, Seattle WA 98101. (206)467-4300. **Fax:** (206)467-4301. **E-mail:** custserv@sasquatchbooks.com. **Website:** www.sasquatchbooks.com. Estab. 1986. "Sasquatch Books publishes books for and from the Pacific Northwest, Alaska, and California is the nation's premier regional press. Sasquatch Books' publishing program is a veritable celebration of regionally written words. Undeterred by political or geographical borders, Sasquatch defines its region as the magnificent area that stretches from the Brooks Range to the Gulf of California and from the Rocky Mountains to the Pacific Ocean. Our top-selling Best Places® travel guides serve the most popular destinations and locations of the West. We also publish widely in the areas of food and wine, gardening, nature, photography, children's books, and regional history, all facets of the literature of place. With more than 200 books brimming with insider information on the West, we offer an energetic eye on the lifestyle, landscape, and worldview of our region. Considers queries and proposals from authors and agents for new projects that fit into our West Coast regional publishing program. We can evaluate query letters, proposals, and complete mss." Publishes regional hardcover and trade paperback originals. Guidelines online.

NEEDS Young readers: adventure, animal, concept, contemporary, humor, nature/environment.

TERMS Pays royalty on cover price. Pays wide range advance. Responds to queries in 3 months.

TIPS "We sell books through a range of channels in addition to the book trade. Our primary audience consists of active, literate residents of the West Coast."

Ⓐ SCHOLASTIC PRESS

Imprint of Scholastic, Inc., 557 Broadway, New York NY 10012. (212)343-6100. **Fax:** (212)343-4713. **Website:** www.scholastic.com. Scholastic Press publishes fresh, literary picture book fiction and nonfiction; fresh, literary nonseries or nongenre-oriented middle grade and young adult fiction. Currently emphasizing subtly handled treatments of key relationships in children's lives; unusual approaches to commonly dry subjects, such as biography, math, history, or science. De-emphasizing fairy tales (or retellings), board books, genre, or series fiction (mystery, fantasy, etc.). Publishes hardcover originals.

NEEDS Looking for strong picture books, young chapter books, appealing middle grade novels (ages 8-11) and interesting and well-written young adult novels. Wants fresh, exciting picture books and novels—inspiring, new talent.

HOW TO CONTACT *Agented submissions only.*

TERMS Pays royalty on retail price. Pays variable advance. Responds in 3 months to queries; 6-8 months to mss.

TIPS "Read *currently* published children's books. Revise, rewrite, rework and find your own voice, style and subject. We are looking for authors with a strong and unique voice who can tell a great story and have the ability to evoke genuine emotion. Children's publishers are becoming more selective, looking for irresistible talent and fairly broad appeal, yet still very willing to take risks, just to keep the game interesting."

SCRIBE PUBLICATIONS

18-20 Edward St., Brunswick VIC 3056, Australia. (61) (3)9388-8780. **E-mail:** info@scribepub.com.au. **E-mail:** submissions@scribepub.com.au. **Website:** www.scribepublications.com.au. **Contact:** Anna Thwaites. Estab. 1976. Scribe has been operating as a wholly independent trade-publishing house for almost 40 years. What started off in 1976 as a desire on publisher Henry Rosenbloom's part to publish 'serious non-fiction' as a one-man band has turned into a multi-award-winning company with 20 staff members in two locations — Melbourne, Australia and London, England — and a scout in New York. Scribe publishes over 65 nonfiction and fiction titles annually in Australia and about 40 in the United Kingdom. "We currently have acquiring editors working in both our Melbourne and London offices. We spend each day sifting through submissions and manuscripts from around the world, and commissioning and editing local titles, in an uncompromising pursuit of the best books we can find, help create, and deliver to readers. We love what we do, and we hope you will, too." Guidelines online.

HOW TO CONTACT Submit synopsis, sample chapters, CV.

TIPS "We are only able to consider unsolicited submissions if you have a demonstrated background of writing and publishing for general readers."

SCRIBNER

Imprint of Simon & Schuster Adult Publishing Group, 1230 Avenue of the Americas, 12th Floor, New York NY 10020. (212)698-7000. **Website:** www.simonsays.com. Publishes hardcover originals.

HOW TO CONTACT *Agented submissions only.*

TERMS Pays 7-15% royalty. Pays variable advance. Responds in 3 months to queries

SECOND STORY PRESS

20 Maud St., Suite 401, Toronto ON M5V 2M5, Canada. (416)537-7850. **Fax:** (416)537-0588. **E-mail:** info@secondstorypress.ca. **Website:** www.secondstorypress.ca. "Please keep in mind that as a feminist press, we are looking for non-sexist, non-racist and non-violent stories, as well as historical fiction, chapter books, novels and biography."

NEEDS Considers non-sexist, non-racist, and non-violent stories, as well as historical fiction, chapter books, picture books.

SEEDLING CONTINENTAL PRESS

520 E. Bainbridge St., Elizabethtown PA 17022. (800)233-0759. **Website:** www.continentalpress.com. "Continental publishes educational materials for grades K-12, specializing in reading, mathematics, and test preparation materials. We are not currently accepting submissions for Seedling leveled readers or instructional materials."

NEEDS Young readers: adventure, animal, folktales, humor, multicultural, nature/environment. Does not accept texts longer than 12 pages or over 300 words. Average word length: young readers—100.

HOW TO CONTACT Submit complete ms.

TERMS Work purchased outright from authors. Responds to mss in 6 months.

TIPS "See our website. Follow writers' guidelines carefully and test your story with children and educators."

SEVEN STORIES PRESS

140 Watts St., New York NY 10013. (212)226-8760. **Fax:** (212)226-1411. **E-mail:** info@sevenstories.com. **Website:** www.sevenstories.com. **Contact:** Acquisitions. Estab. 1995. Founded in 1995 in New York City, and named for the seven authors who committed to a home with a fiercely independent spirit, Seven Stories Press publishes works of the imagination and political titles by voices of conscience. While most widely known for its books on politics, human rights, and social and economic justice, Seven Stories continues to champion literature, with a list encompassing both innovative debut novels and National Book Award–winning poetry collections, as well as prose and poetry translations from the French, Spanish, German, Swedish, Italian, Greek, Polish, Korean, Vietnamese, Russian, and Arabic. Publishes hardcover and trade paperback originals. Book catalog and ms guidelines free.

HOW TO CONTACT Submit cover letter with 2 sample chapters.

TERMS Pays 7-15% royalty on retail price. Pays advance. Responds in 1 month.

SEVERN HOUSE PUBLISHERS

Salatin House, 19 Cedar Rd., Sutton, Surrey SM2 5DA, United Kingdom. (44)(208)770-3930. **Fax:** (44)

(208)770-3850. **Website:** www.severnhouse.com. Severn House is currently emphasizing suspense, romance, mystery. Large print imprint from existing authors. Publishes hardcover and trade paperback originals and reprints. Book catalog available free.

HOW TO CONTACT *Agented submissions only.*

TERMS Pays 7-15% royalty on retail price. Pays $750-5,000 advance. Responds in 3 months to proposals.

SHAMBHALA PUBLICATIONS, INC.

4720 Walnut St., Boulder CO 80304. **E-mail:** submissions@shambhala.com. **Website:** www.shambhala.com. Estab. 1969. Publishes hardcover and trade paperback originals and reprints. Book catalog free. Guidelines online.

TERMS Pays 8% royalty on retail price. Responds in 4 months.

SHIPWRECKT BOOKS PUBLISHING COMPANY LLC

309 W. Stevens Ave., Rushford MN 55971. **E-mail:** contact@shipwrecktbooks.com. **Website:** www.shipwrecktbooks.com. **Contact:** Tom Driscoll, managing editor. Publishes trade paperback originals, mass market paperback originals, and electronic originals. Catalog and guidelines online.

HOW TO CONTACT E-mail query first. All unsolicited mss returned unopened.

TERMS Authors receive a maximum of 35% royalties. Responds to queries within 6 months.

TIPS "Quality writing. Query first. Development and full editorial services available."

Ⓐ⊘ SIMON & SCHUSTER

1230 Avenue of the Americas, New York NY 10020. (212)698-7000. **Website:** www.simonandschuster.com. *Accepts agented submissions only.*

✪ SIMPLY READ BOOKS

501-5525 W. Blvd., Vancouver BC V6M 3W6, Canada. **E-mail:** go@simplyreadbooks.com. **Website:** www.simplyreadbooks.com. Simply Read Books is current seeking mss in picture books, early readers, early chapter books, middle grade fiction, and graphic novels.

HOW TO CONTACT Query or submit complete ms.

SKINNER HOUSE BOOKS

The Unitarian Universalist Association, 24 Farnsworth St., Boston MA 02210. (617)742-2100, ext. 603. **Fax:** (617)948-6466. **E-mail:** bookproposals@

uua.org. **Website:** www.uua.org/publications/skinnerhouse. **Contact:** Betsy Martin. Estab. 1975. "We publish titles in Unitarian Universalist faith, liberal religion, history, biography, worship, and issues of social justice. Most of our children's titles are intended for religious education or worship use. They reflect Unitarian Universalist values. We also publish inspirational titles of poetic prose and meditations. Writers should know that Unitarian Universalism is a liberal religious denomination committed to progressive ideals. Currently emphasizing social justice concerns." Publishes trade paperback originals and reprints. Book catalog for 6×9 SAE with 3 first-class stamps. Guidelines online.

NEEDS Only publishes fiction for children's titles for religious instruction.

HOW TO CONTACT Query.

TERMS Responds to queries in 1 month.

TIPS "From outside our denomination, we are interested in manuscripts that will be of help or interest to liberal churches, Sunday School classes, parents, ministers, and volunteers. Inspirational/spiritual and children's titles must reflect liberal Unitarian Universalist values."

SKY PONY PRESS

307 W. 36th St., 11th Floor, New York NY 10018. (212)643-6816. **Fax:** (212)643-6819. **Website:** skyponypress.com. Estab. 2011. Sky Pony Press is the children's book imprint of Skyhorse Publishing. "Following in the footsteps of our parent company, our goal is to provide books for readers with a wide variety of interests." Guidelines online.

NEEDS "We will consider picture books, early readers, midgrade novels, novelties, and informational books for all ages."

HOW TO CONTACT Submit ms or proposal.

SLEEPING BEAR PRESS

2395 South Huron Parkway #200, Ann Arbor MI 48104. (800)487-2323. **Fax:** (734)794-0004. **E-mail:** submissions@sleepingbearpress.com. **Website:** www.sleepingbearpress.com. **Contact:** Manuscript Submissions. Estab. 1998. Book catalog available via e-mail.

NEEDS Picture books: adventure, animal, concept, folktales, history, multicultural, nature/environment, religion, sports. Young readers: adventure, animal, concept, folktales, history, humor, multicultural, nature/environment, religion, sports. Average word length: picture books—1,800.

HOW TO CONTACT Accepts unsolicited queries 3 times per year. See website for details. Query with sample of work (up to 15 pages) and SASE. Please address packages to Manuscript Submissions.

SMALL BEER PRESS

150 Pleasant St., #306, Easthampton MA 01027. (413)203-1636. **Fax:** (413)203-1636. **E-mail:** info@ smallbeerpress.com. **Website:** www.smallbeerpress. com. Estab. 2000. Small Beer Press also publishes the zine *Lady Churchill's Rosebud Wristlet*. "SBP's books have recently received the Tiptree and Crawford Awards."

HOW TO CONTACT Does not accept unsolicited novel or short story collection mss. Send queries with first 10-20 pages and SASE.

TERMS Advance and standard royalties.

TIPS "Please be familiar with our books first to avoid wasting your time and ours, thank you. E-mail queries will be deleted. Really."

SMITH AND KRAUS PUBLISHERS, INC.

177 Lyme Rd., Hanover NH 03755. (603)643-6431. **E-mail:** editor@smithandkraus.com. **E-mail:** carolb@ smithandkraus.com. **Website:** smithandkraus.com. Estab. 1990. Publishes hardcover and trade paperback originals. Book catalog available free.

NEEDS Does not return submissions.

HOW TO CONTACT Query with SASE.

TERMS Pays 7% royalty on retail price. Pays $500-2,000 advance. Responds in 1 month to queries; 2 months to proposals; 4 months to mss.

SOFT SKULL PRESS INC.

Counterpoint, 2650 Ninth St., Suite 318, Berkeley CA 94710. (510)704-0230. **Fax:** (510)704-0268. **E-mail:** info@counterpointpress.com. **Website:** www.softskull.com. "Here at Soft Skull we love books that are new, fun, smart, revelatory, quirky, groundbreaking, cage-rattling and/or otherwise unusual." Publishes hardcover and trade paperback originals. Book catalog and guidelines online.

NEEDS Does not consider poetry.

HOW TO CONTACT Soft Skull Press no longer accepts digital submissions. Send a cover letter describing your project in detail and a completed ms. For graphic novels, send a minimum of five fully inked pages of art, along with a synopsis of your storyline.

"Please do not send original material, as it will not be returned."

TERMS Pays 7-10% royalty. Average advance: $100-15,000. Responds in 2 months to proposals; 3 months to mss.

TIPS "See our website for updated submission guidelines."

SOHO PRESS, INC.

853 Broadway, New York NY 10003. (212)260-1900. **E-mail:** soho@sohopress.com. **Website:** www.sohopress.com. **Contact:** Bronwen Hruska, publisher; Mark Doten, senior editor. Estab. 1986. Soho Press publishes primarily fiction, as well as some narrative literary nonfiction and mysteries set abroad. No electronic submissions, only queries by e-mail. Publishes hardcover and trade paperback originals; trade paperback reprints. Guidelines online.

NEEDS Adventure, ethnic, feminist, historical, literary, mainstream/contemporary, mystery (police procedural), suspense, multicultural.

HOW TO CONTACT Submit 3 sample chapters and cover letter with synopsis, author bio, SASE. *No e-mailed submissions.*

TERMS Pays 10-15% royalty on retail price (varies under certain circumstances). Responds in 3 months.

TIPS "Soho Press publishes discerning authors for discriminating readers, finding the strongest possible writers and publishing them. Before submitting, look at our website for an idea of the types of books we publish, and read our submission guidelines."

SOURCEBOOKS CASABLANCA

Sourcebooks, Inc., 232 Madison Ave., Suite 1100, New York NY 10016. **E-mail:** romance@sourcebooks.com. **Website:** www.sourcebooks.com. **Contact:** Deb Werksman (deb.werksman@sourcebooks.com). "Our romance imprint, Sourcebooks Casablanca, publishes single title romance in all subgenres." Guidelines online.

NEEDS "Our editorial criteria call for: a heroine the reader can relate to, a hero she can fall in love with, a world gets created that the reader can escape into, there's a hook that we can sell within 2-3 sentences, and the author is out to build a career with us."

TERMS Responds in 2-3 months.

TIPS "We are actively acquiring single-title and single-title series romance fiction (90,000-100,000 words) for our Casablanca imprint. We are looking for strong writers who are excited about marketing their books and building their community of readers, and whose books have something fresh to offer in the genre of romance."

SOURCEBOOKS FIRE

1935 Brookdale Rd., Suite 139, Naperville IL 60563. (630)961-3900. **Fax:** (630)961-2168. **E-mail:** submissions@sourcebooks.com. **Website:** www.sourcebooks.com. "We're actively acquiring knockout books for our YA imprint. We are particularly looking for strong writers who are excited about promoting and building their community of readers, and whose books have something fresh to offer the ever-growing young adult audience. We are not accepting any unsolicited or unagented manuscripts at this time. Unfortunately, our staff can no longer handle the large volume of manuscripts that we receive on a daily basis. We will continue to consider agented manuscripts." See website for details.

HOW TO CONTACT Query with the full ms attached in Word doc.

SOURCEBOOKS LANDMARK

Sourcebooks, Inc., Sourcebooks, Inc., 232 Madison Ave., Suite 1100, New York NY 10016. **E-mail:** editorialsubmissions@sourcebooks.com. **Website:** www.sourcebooks.com. "Our fiction imprint, Sourcebooks Landmark, publishes a variety of commercial fiction, including specialties in historical fiction and Austenalia. We are interested first and foremost in books that have a story to tell."

NEEDS "We are actively acquiring contemporary, book club, and historical fiction for our Landmark imprint. We are looking for strong writers who are excited about marketing their books and building their community of readers."

HOW TO CONTACT Submit synopsis and full ms preferred. Receipt of e-mail submissions acknowledged within 3 weeks of e-mail.

TERMS Responds in 2-3 months.

SPENCER HILL PRESS

27 W. 20th St., Suite 1102, New York NY 10011. **Website:** www.spencerhillpress.com. Spencer Hill Press is an independent publishing house specializing in sci-fi, urban fantasy, and paranormal romance for young adult readers. "Our books have that 'I couldn't put it down!' quality." Guidelines online.

NEEDS "We are interested in young adult, new adult, and middle grade sci-fi, psych-fi, paranormal, or urban fantasy, particularly those with a strong and interesting voice."

HOW TO CONTACT Check website for open submission periods.

STAR BRIGHT BOOKS

13 Landsdowne St., Cambridge MA 02139. (617)354-1300. **Fax:** (617)354-1399. **E-mail:** info@starbrightbooks.com. **Website:** www.starbrightbooks.com. Star Bright Books does accept unsolicited mss and art submissions. "We welcome submissions for picture books and longer works, both fiction and nonfiction." Also beginner readers and chapter books. Query first. Catalog available.

TERMS Pays advance. Responds in several months.

STERLING PUBLISHING CO., INC.

1166 Avenue of the Americas, 17th Floor, New York NY 10036. (212)532-7160. **Website:** www.sterlingpublishing.com. "Sterling publishes highly illustrated, accessible, hands-on, practical books for adults and children. Our mission is to publish high-quality books that educate, entertain, and enrich the lives of our readers." Publishes hardcover and paperback originals and reprints. Catalog online. Guidelines online.

NEEDS Publishes fiction for children.

HOW TO CONTACT Submit to attention of "Children's Book Editor."

TERMS Pays royalty or work purchased outright. Offers advances (average amount: $2,000).

TIPS "We are primarily a nonfiction activities-based publisher. We have a picture book list, but we do not publish chapter books or novels. Our list is not trend-driven. We focus on titles that will backlist well. "

STONE ARCH BOOKS

1710 Roe Crest Rd., North Mankato MN 56003. **Website:** www.stonearchbooks.com. Catalog online.

NEEDS Imprint of Capstone Publishers.Young readers, middle readers, young adults: adventure, contemporary, fantasy, humor, light humor, mystery, science fiction, sports, suspense. Average word length: young readers—1,000-3,000; middle readers and early young adults—5,000-10,000.

HOW TO CONTACT Submit outline/synopsis and 3 sample chapters. Electronic submissions preferred. Full guidelines available on website.

TERMS Work purchased outright from authors.

TIPS "A high-interest topic or activity is one that a young person would spend their free time on without adult direction or suggestion."

STONE BRIDGE PRESS

P.O. Box 8208, Berkeley CA 94707. **E-mail:** sbp@stonebridge.com. **Website:** www.stonebridge.com. **Contact:** Peter Goodman, publisher. Estab. 1989. "Independent press focusing on books about Asia, primarily Japan and China, in English (business, language, culture, literature, animation)." Publishes hardcover and trade paperback originals. Books: 60-70 lb. offset paper; web and sheet paper; perfect bound; some illustrations. Distributes titles through Consortium. Promotes titles through Internet announcements, special-interest magazines and niche tie-ins to associations. Catalog online. Do not send children's books. Do not send proposals that are outside our key Asia-related subject areas.

NEEDS Experimental, gay/lesbian, literary, Asia-themed. "Primarily looking at material relating to Asia, especially Japan and China."

HOW TO CONTACT Does not accept unsolicited mss. Accepts queries by e-mail.

TERMS Pays royalty on wholesale price. Responds to queries in 4 months; mss in 8 months.

TIPS "Query first before submitting. Research us first and avoid sending mss not in our subject area. Generic and bulk submissions will be ignored. No poetry. Looking also for graphic novels, not manga or serializations."

STONESLIDE BOOKS

Stoneslide Media LLC, P.O. Box 8331, New Haven CT 06530. **Website:** www.stoneslidecorrective.com. Estab. 2012. "We like novels with strong character development and narrative thrust, brought out with writing that's clear and expressive." Publishes trade paperback and electronic originals. Book catalog and guidelines online.

NEEDS "We will look at any genre. The important factor for us is that the story use plot, characters, emotions, and other elements of storytelling to think and move the mind forward."

HOW TO CONTACT Submit proposal package via online submission form including: synopsis and 3 sample chapters.

TERMS Pays 20-80% royalty. Responds in 1-2 months.

TIPS "Read the Stoneslide Corrective to see if your work fits with our approach."

SUBITO PRESS

University of Colorado at Boulder, Dept. of English, 226 UCB, Boulder CO 80309-0226. **E-mail:** subitopressucb@gmail.com. **Website:** www.subitopress.org. Subito Press is a non-profit publisher of literary works. Each year Subito publishes one work of fiction and one work of poetry through its contest. Publishes trade paperback originals. Guidelines online.

HOW TO CONTACT Submit complete ms to contest.

TIPS "We publish 2 books of innovative writing a year through our poetry and fiction contests. All entries are also considered for publication with the press."

SUNBURY PRESS, INC.

PO Box 548, Boiling Springs PA 17007. **E-mail:** info@sunburypress.com. **E-mail:** proposals@sunburypress.com. **Website:** www.sunburypress.com. Estab. 2004. Sunbury Press, Inc., headquartered in Mechanicsburg, PA is a publisher of trade paperback, hard cover and digital books featuring established and emerging authors in many fiction and non-fiction categories. Sunbury's books are printed in the USA and sold through leading booksellers worldwide. "Please use our online submission form." Publishes trade paperback and hardcover originals and reprints; electronic originals and reprints. Catalog and guidelines online. Online submission form.

NEEDS "We are seeking manuscripts for our three fiction imprints: Milford House Press, Brown Posey Press, and Hellbender Books." Does not want vampires, zombies, erotica.

HOW TO CONTACT Please use our online submission service.

TERMS Pays 10% royalty on wholesale price. Responds in 3 months.

TIPS "We are a rapidly growing small press with six diverse imprints. We currently have over 250 authors and 500 works under management."

SUNSTONE PRESS

Box 2321, Santa Fe NM 87504. (800)243-5644. **Website:** www.sunstonepress.com. **Contact:** Submissions Editor. Sunstone's original focus was on nonfiction subjects that preserved and highlighted the richness of the American Southwest but it has expanded its view over the years to include mainstream themes and categories—both nonfiction and fiction—that have a more general appeal. Guidelines online.

HOW TO CONTACT Query with 1 sample chapter.

⬤ SWEET CHERRY PUBLISHING

Unit 36, Vulcan Business Complex, Vulcan Rd., Leicester Leicestershire LE5 3EF, United Kingdom. **E-mail:** info@sweetcherrypublishing.com. **E-mail:** submissions@sweetcherrypublishing.com. **Website:** www.sweetcherrypublishing.com. Estab. 2011. Sweet Cherry Publishing is an independent publishing company based in Leicester. "We specialize in middle-grade series. Our aim is to provide children with compelling worlds and engaging characters that they will want to revisit again and again." Send the first 3 chapters or 4,000 words along with a synopsis, author biography, and cover letter detailing your target audience and your plans for further books in the series.

TERMS Offers one-time fee for work that is accepted.

TIPS "Submit a cover letter and a synopsis with 3 sample chapters via post or e-mail. Please note that we strongly prefer e-mail submissions."

⬤ TAFELBERG PUBLISHERS

Imprint of NB Publishers, P.O. Box 879, Cape Town 8000, South Africa. (27)(21)406-3033. **Fax:** (27)(21)406-3812. **E-mail:** engela.reinke@nb.co.za. **Website:** www.tafelberg.com. **Contact:** Engela Reinke. General publisher best known for Afrikaans fiction, authoritative political works, children's/youth literature, and a variety of illustrated and nonillustrated nonfiction.

NEEDS Picture books, young readers: animal, anthology, contemporary, fantasy, folktales, hi-lo, humor, multicultural, nature/environment, scient fiction, special needs. Middle readers, young adults: animal (middle reader only), contemporary, fantasy, hi-lo, humor, multicultural, nature/environment, problem novels, science fiction, special needs, sports, suspense/mystery. Average word length: picture books—1,500-7,500; young readers—25,000; middle readers—15,000; young adults—40,000.

HOW TO CONTACT Submit complete ms.

TERMS Pays authors royalty of 15-18% based on wholesale price. Responds to queries in 2 weeks; mss in 6 months.

TIPS "Writers: Story needs to have a South African or African style. Illustrators: I'd like to look, but the chances of getting commissioned are slim. The market is small and difficult. Do not expect huge advances. Editorial staff attended or plans to attend the following conferences: IBBY, Frankfurt, SCBWI Bologna."

🅐⊘ NAN A. TALESE

Imprint of Doubleday, Random House, 1745 Broadway, New York NY 10019. (212)782-8918. **Fax:** (212)782-8448. **Website:** www.nanatalese.com. Nan A. Talese publishes nonfiction with a powerful guiding narrative and relevance to larger cultural interests, and literary fiction of the highest quality. Publishes hardcover originals.

NEEDS Well-written narratives with a compelling story line, good characterization and use of language. We like stories with an edge.

HOW TO CONTACT *Agented submissions only.*

TERMS Pays variable royalty on retail price. Pays varying advance.

TIPS "Audience is highly literate people interested in story, information and insight. We want well-written material submitted by agents only. See our website."

TANTOR MEDIA

Recorded Books, 6 Business Park Rd., Old Saybrook CT 06475. (860)395-1155. **Fax:** (860)395-1154. **E-mail:** rightsemail@tantor.com. **Website:** www.tantor.com. **Contact:** Ron Formica, director of acquisitions. Estab. 2001. Tantor Media, a division of Recorded Books, is a leading audiobook publisher, producing more than 100 new titles every month. We do not publish print or e-books. Publishes audiobooks only. Catalog online. Not accepting print or e-book queries. We only publish audiobooks.

TERMS Responds in 2 months.

TEXAS TECH UNIVERSITY PRESS

1120 Main St., Second Floor, Box 41037, Lubbock TX 79415. (806)742-2982. **Fax:** (806)742-2979. **E-mail:** ttup@ttu.edu. **Website:** www.ttupress.org. Estab. 1971. Texas Tech University Press, the book publishing office of the university since 1971 and an AAUP member since 1986, publishes nonfiction titles in the areas of natural history and the natural sciences; 18th century and Joseph Conrad studies; studies of modern Southeast Asia, particularly the Vietnam War; costume and textile history; Latin American literature and culture; and all aspects of the Great Plains and the American West, especially history, biography, memoir, sports history, and travel. In addition, the Press publishes several scholarly journals, acclaimed series for young readers, an annual invited poetry collection, and literary fiction of Texas and the West. Guidelines online.

NEEDS Fiction rooted in the American West and Southwest, Jewish literature, Latin American and Latino fiction (in translation or English).

⊕ THISTLEDOWN PRESS LTD.

410 2nd Ave., Saskatoon SK S7K 2C3, Canada. (306)244-1722. **Fax:** (306)244-1762. **E-mail:** editorial@thistledownpress.com. **Website:** www.thistledownpress.com. **Contact:** Allan Forrie, publisher. Estab. 1975. "Thistledown originates books by Canadian authors only, although we have co-published titles by authors outside Canada. We do not publish children's picture books." Book catalog on website. Guidelines online.

NEEDS Young adults: adventure, anthology, contemporary, fantasy, humor, poetry, romance, science fiction, suspense/mystery, short stories. Average word length: young adults—40,000.

HOW TO CONTACT Submit outline/synopsis and sample chapters. *Does not accept mss.* Do not query by e-mail. "Please note: we are not accepting middle years (ages 8-12) nor children's manuscripts at this time." See Submission Guidelines on Website.

TERMS Pays authors royalty of 10-12% based on net dollar sales. Pays illustrators and photographers by the project (range: $250-750). Rarely pays advance. Responds to queries in 6 months.

TIPS "Send cover letter including publishing history and SASE."

THUNDERSTONE BOOKS

6575 Horse Dr., Las Vegas NV 89131. **E-mail:** info@thunderstonebooks.com. **Website:** www.thunderstonebooks.com. **Contact:** Rachel Noorda, editorial director. Estab. 2014. "At ThunderStone Books, we aim to publish children's books that have an educational aspect. We are not looking for curriculum for learning certain subjects, but rather stories that encourage learning for children, whether that be learning about a new language/culture or learning more about science and math in a fun, fictional format. We want to help children to gain a love for other languages and subjects so that they are curious about the world around them. We are currently accepting fiction and nonfiction submissions. Picture books without accompanying illustration will not be accepted." Publishes hardcover, trade paperback, mass market pa-

perback, and electronic originals. Catalog available for SASE. Guidelines available.

NEEDS Interested in multicultural stories with an emphasis on authentic culture and language (these may include mythology).

HOW TO CONTACT "If you think your book is right for us, send a query letter with a word attachment of the first 50 pages to info@thunderstonebooks.com. If it is a picture book or chapter book for young readers that is shorter than 50 pages send the entire manuscript."

TERMS Pays 5-15% royalties on retail price. Pays $300-1,000 advance. Responds in 3 months.

⊙⊘ TIGHTROPE BOOKS

#207-2 College St., Toronto Ontario M5G 1K3, Canada. (416)928-6666. **E-mail:** tightropeasst@gmail.com. **Website:** www.tightropebooks.com. Estab. 2005. Publishes trade paperback originals. Catalog and guidelines online.

⊙ Accepting submissions for literary fiction, nonfiction and poetry from Canadian citizens and permanent Canadian residents only.

TERMS Pays 5-15% royalty on retail price. Pays advance of $200-300. Responds if interested.

TIPS "Audience is urban, literary, educated, unconventional."

⊙ TIN HOUSE BOOKS

2617 NW Thurman St., Portland OR 97210. (503)473-8663. **Fax:** (503)473-8957. **E-mail:** masie@tinhouse.com. **Website:** www.tinhouse.com. **Contact:** Masie Cochran, editor; Tony Perez, editor. "We are a small independent publisher dedicated to nurturing new, promising talent as well as showcasing the work of established writers." Distributes/promotes titles through W. W. Norton. Publishes hardcover originals, paperback originals, paperback reprints. Guidelines online.

HOW TO CONTACT *Agented mss only.* "We no longer read unsolicited submissions by authors with no representation. We will continue to accept submissions from agents."

TERMS Responds to queries in 2-3 weeks; mss in 2-3 months.

TITAN PRESS

5805 White Oak Ave. #17897, Encino CA 91316. **E-mail:** titan91416@yahoo.com. **Website:** https://www.facebook.com/RVClef. **Contact:** Romana Von Clef, editor. Estab. 1981. Little literary publisher. Publishes hardcover and paperback originals.

HOW TO CONTACT Does not accept unsolicited mss. Query with SASE. Include brief bio, list of publishing credits.

TERMS Pays 20-40% royalty. Responds to queries in 3 months.

TIPS "Look, act, sound, and *be* professional."

⊘ TOP COW PRODUCTIONS, INC.

3812 Dunn Dr., Culver City CA 90232. **Website:** www.topcow.com. Guidelines online.

HOW TO CONTACT *No unsolicited submissions.* Prefers submissions from artists. See website for details and advice on how to break into the market.

TOR BOOKS

Tom Doherty Associates, 175 Fifth Ave., New York NY 10010. **Website:** www.tor-forge.com. Tor Books is the "world's largest publisher of science fiction and fantasy, with strong category publishing in historical fiction, mystery, western/Americana, thriller, YA." Book catalog available. Guidelines online.

HOW TO CONTACT Submit first 3 chapters, 3-10 page synopsis, dated cover letter, SASE.

TERMS Pays author royalty. Pays illustrators by the project.

TORREY HOUSE PRESS

150 S. State St., #100, Salt Lake City UT 84111. **E-mail:** kirsten@torreyhouse.com. **Website:** www.torreyhouse.org. **Contact:** Kirsten Allen. Estab. 2010. Torrey House Press is an independent nonprofit publisher promoting environmental conservation through literature. Publishes hardcover, trade paperback, and electronic originals. Catalog online. Guidelines online.

NEEDS Torrey House Press publishes literary fiction and creative nonfiction about the world environment and the American West.

HOW TO CONTACT Submit proposal package including: synopsis, complete ms, bio.

TERMS Pays 5-15% royalty on retail price. Responds in 3 months.

TIPS Include writing experience (none okay).

☉ TOUCHWOOD EDITIONS

The Heritage Group, 103-1075 Pendergast St., Victoria BC V8V 0A1, Canada. (250)360-0829. **Fax:** (250)386-0829. **E-mail:** edit@touchwoodeditions.com. **Web**site: www.touchwoodeditions.com. **Contact:** Renée Layberry, Editor. Publishes trade paperback, originals and reprints. Book catalog and guidelines online.

HOW TO CONTACT Submit bio/CV, marketing plan, TOC, outline, word count.

TERMS Pays 15% royalty on net price. Responds in 6 months to queries.

TIPS "Our area of interest is western Canada. We would like more creative nonfiction and fiction from First Nations authors, and welcome authors who write about notable individuals in Canada's history. Please note we do not publish poetry."

☉ TRADEWIND BOOKS

202-1807 Maritime Mews, Granville Island, Vancouver BC V6H 3W7, Canada. (604)662-4405. **Website:** www.tradewindbooks.com. "Tradewind Books publishes juvenile picture books and young adult novels. Requires that submissions include evidence that author has read at least 3 titles published by Tradewind Books." Publishes hardcover and trade paperback originals. Book catalog and ms guidelines online.

NEEDS Average word length: 900 words.

HOW TO CONTACT Send complete ms for picture books. *YA novels by Canadian authors only. Chapter books by US authors considered.* For chapter books/Middle Grade Fiction, submit the first three chapters, a chapter outline and plot summary.

TERMS Pays 7% royalty on retail price. Pays variable advance. Responds to mss in 2 months.

TRIANGLE SQUARE

Seven Stories Press, 140 Watts St., New York NY 10013. (212)226-8760. **Fax:** (212)226-1411. **E-mail:** info@sevenstories.com. **Website:** https://www.sevenstories.com/imprints/triangle-square. Triangle Square is a children's and young adult imprint of Seven Story Press.

HOW TO CONTACT Send a cover letter with 2 sample chapters and SASE. Send c/o Acquisitions.

TRISTAN PUBLISHING

2355 Louisiana Ave. N, Golden Valley MN 55427. (763)545-1383. **Fax:** (763)545-1387. **E-mail:** info@tristanpublishing.com; manuscripts@tristanpublishing.com. **Website:** www.tristanpublishing.com. **Contact:** Brett Waldman, publisher. Estab. 2002. Publishes hardcover originals. Catalog and guidelines online.

HOW TO CONTACT Query with SASE; submit completed mss.

TERMS Pays royalty on wholesale or retail price; outright purchase. Responds in 3 months.

TIPS "Our audience is adults and children."

TU BOOKS

Lee & Low Books, 95 Madison Ave., Suite #1205, New York NY 10016. **Website:** www.leeandlow.com/imprints/3. **Contact:** Stacy Whitman, publisher. Estab. 2010. The Tu imprint spans many genres: science fiction, fantasy, mystery, contemporary, and more. We don't believe in labels or limits, just great stories. Join us at the crossroads where fantasy and real life collide. You'll be glad you did. Young adult and middle grade novels and graphic novels: science fiction, fantasy, contemporary realism, mystery, historical fiction, and more, with particular interest in books with strong literary hooks. Also seeking middle grade and young adult nonfiction. Catalog available online. Please see our full submissions guidelines online.

○   For new writers of color, please be aware of the New Visions Award writing contest, which runs every year from June-October. Previously unpublished writers of color and Native American writers may submit their middle grade and young adult novels. See submission guidelines for the contest at https://www.leeandlow.com/writers-illustrators/new-visions-award.

NEEDS At Tu Books, an imprint of Lee & Low Books, our focus is on well-told, exciting, adventurous fantasy, science fiction, and mystery novels and graphic novels starring people of color. We also selectively publish realism that explores the contemporary and historical experiences of people of color. We look for fantasy set in worlds inspired by non-Western folklore or culture, contemporary mysteries and fantasy set all over the world starring people of color, and science fiction that centers the possibilities for people of color in the future. We welcome intersectional narratives that feature LGBTQIA and disabled POC as heroes in their own stories. We are looking specifically for stories for both middle grade (ages 8-12) and young adult (ages 12-18) readers. Occasionally a manuscript might fall between those two categories; if your manuscript does, let us know. We are not looking for picture books, chapter books, or short stories at this time. Please do not send submissions in these categories. (See the Lee & Low Books guidelines for books for younger young readers.) Not seeking picture books or chapter books.

HOW TO CONTACT Please include a synopsis and first three chapters of the novel. Do not send the complete manuscript. Mss should be doubled-spaced. Mss should be accompanied by a cover letter that includes a brief biography of the author, including publishing history. The letter should also state if the ms is a simultaneous or an exclusive submission. "We're looking for middle grade (ages 8-12) and young adult (ages 12 and up) books. We are not looking for chapter books (ages 6 to 9) at this time. Be sure to include full contact information on the first page of the ms. Page numbers and your last name/title of the book should appear on subsequent pages." Unsolicited mss should be submitted online.

TERMS Advance against royalties. Pays advance. Responds only if interested.

TUMBLEHOME LEARNING

P.O. Box 71386, Boston MA 02117. **E-mail:** info@tumblehomelearning.com. **E-mail:** submissions@tumblehomelearning.com. **Website:** www.tumblehomelearning.com. **Contact:** Pendred Noyce, editor. Estab. 2011. Tumblehome Learning helps kids imagine themselves as young scientists or engineeers and encourages them to experience science through adventure and discovery. "We do this with exciting mystery and adventure tales as well as experiments carefully designed to engage students from ages 8 and up." Publishes hardcover, trade paperback, and electronic originals. Catalog available online. Guideliens available on request for SASE.

NEEDS "All our fiction has science at its heart. This can include using science to solve a mystery (see *The Walking Fish* by Rachelle Burk or *Something Stinks!* by Gail Hedrick), realistic science fiction, books in our Galactic Academy of Science series, science-based adventure tales, and the occasional picture book with a science theme, such as appreciation of the stars and constellations in *Elizabeth's Constellation Quilt* by Olivia Fu. A graphic novel about science would also be welcome."

HOW TO CONTACT Submit completed ms electronically.

TERMS Pays authors 8-12% royalties on retail price. Pays $500 advance. Responds in 1 month to queries and proposals, and 2 months to mss.

TIPS "Please don't submit to us if your book is not about science. We don't accept generic books about animals or books with glaring scientific errors in the first chapter. That said, the book should be fun to read and the science content can be subtle. We work closely with authors, including first-time authors, to edit and improve their books. As a small publisher, the greatest benefit we can offer is this friendly and respectful partnership with authors."

TUPELO PRESS

P.O. Box 1767, North Adams MA 01247. (413)664-9611. **Website:** www.tupelopress.org. **Contact:** Sarah Russell, administrative director. Estab. 2001. "We're an independent nonprofit literary press. We publish book-length poetry, poetry collections, translations, short story collections, novellas, literary nonfiction/memoirs and novels." Guidelines online.

NEEDS "For Novels—submit no more than 100 pages along with a summary of the entire book. If we're interested we'll ask you to send the rest. We accept very few works of prose (3 or 4 per year)."

HOW TO CONTACT Submit complete ms. **Charges a $45 reading fee.**

TERMS Standard royalty contract. Pays advance in rare instances.

☯ TURNSTONE PRESS

Artspace Building, 206-100 Arthur St., Winnipeg MB R3B 1H3, Canada. (204)947-1555. **Fax:** (204)942-1555. **Website:** www.turnstonepress.com. **Contact:** Submissions Assistant. Estab. 1976. "Turnstone Press is a literary publisher, not a general publisher, and therefore we are only interested in literary fiction, literary nonfiction—including literary criticism—and poetry. We do publish literary mysteries, thrillers, and noir under our Ravenstone imprint. We publish only Canadian authors or landed immigrants, we strive to publish a significant number of new writers, to publish in a variety of genres, and to have 50% of each year's list be Manitoba writers and/or books with Manitoba content." Guidelines online.

HOW TO CONTACT "Samples must be 40 to 60 pages, typed/printed in a minimum 12 point serif typeface such as Times, Book Antiqua, or Garamond."

TERMS Responds in 4-7 months.

TIPS "As a Canadian literary press, we have a mandate to publish Canadian writers only. Do some homework before submitting works to make sure your subject matter/genre/writing style falls within the publishers area of interest."

TWILIGHT TIMES BOOKS

P.O. Box 3340, Kingsport TN 37664. **E-mail:** publisher@twilighttimesbooks.com. **Website:** www.twilighttimesbooks.com. **Contact:** Andy M. Scott, managing editor. Estab. 1999. "We publish compelling literary fiction by authors with a distinctive voice." Published 5 debut authors within the last year. Averages 120 total titles; 15 fiction titles/year. Member: AAP, PAS, SPAN, SLF. Guidelines online.

HOW TO CONTACT Accepts unsolicited mss. Do not send complete mss. Queries via e-mail only. Include estimated word count, brief bio, list of publishing credits, marketing plan.

TERMS Pays 8-15% royalty. Responds in 4 weeks to queries; 2 months to mss.

TIPS "The only requirement for consideration at Twilight Times Books is that your novel must be entertaining and professionally written."

TWO DOLLAR RADIO

Website: www.twodollarradio.com. **Contact:** Eric Obenauf, editorial director. Estab. 2005. Two Dollar Radio is a boutique family-run press, publishing bold works of literary merit, each book, individually and collectively, providing a sonic progression that "we believe to be too loud to ignore." Targets readers who admire ambition and creativity. Range of print runs: 2,000-7,500 copies.

HOW TO CONTACT Submit entire, completed ms with a brief cover letter, via Submittable. No previously published work. No proposals. No excerpts. There is a $2 reading fee per submission. Accepts submissions every other month (January, March, May, July, September, November).

TERMS Advance: $500-1,000.

TIPS "We want writers who show an authority over language and the world that is being created, from the very first sentence on."

❶❷ TYNDALE HOUSE PUBLISHERS, INC.

351 Executive Dr., Carol Stream IL 60188. (800)323-9400. **Fax:** (800)684-0247. **Website:** www.tyndale.com. Estab. 1962. "Tyndale House publishes practical, user-friendly Christian books for the home and family." Publishes hardcover and trade paperback originals and mass paperback reprints. Guidelines online.

NEEDS "Christian truths must be woven into the story organically. No short story collections. Youth books: character building stories with Christian perspective. Especially interested in ages 10-14. We primarily publish Christian historical romances, with occasional contemporary, suspense, or standalones."

HOW TO CONTACT *Agented submissions only. No unsolicited mss.*

TERMS Pays negotiable royalty. Pays negotiable advance.

TIPS "All accepted manuscripts will appeal to Evangelical Christian children and parents."

⦸ TYRUS BOOKS

F+W Media, 1213 N. Sherman Ave., #306, Madison WI 53704. (508)427-7100. **Fax:** (508)427-6790. **Website:** tyrusbooks.com. "We publish crime and literary fiction. We believe in the life changing power of the written word."

HOW TO CONTACT Submissions currently closed; check website for updates.

UNBRIDLED BOOKS

8201 E. Highway WW, Columbia MO 65201. **E-mail:** michalsong@unbridledbooks.com. **Website:** unbridledbooks.com. **Contact:** Greg Michalson. Estab. 2004. "Unbridled Books is a premier publisher of works of rich literary quality that appeal to a broad audience."

HOW TO CONTACT Please query first by e-mail. "Due to the heavy volume of submissions, we regret that at this time we are not able to consider uninvited mss."

TIPS "We try to read each ms that arrives, so please be patient."

UNIVERSITY OF ALASKA PRESS

P.O. Box 756240, Fairbanks AK 99775-6240. (907)474-5831 or (888)252-6657. **Fax:** (907)474-5502. **Website:** www.uaf.edu/uapress. Estab. 1967. "The mission of the University of Alaska Press is to encourage, publish, and disseminate works of scholarship that will enhance the store of knowledge about Alaska and the North Pacific Rim, with a special emphasis on the circumpolar regions." Publishes hardcover originals, trade paperback originals and reprints. Book catalog available free. Guidelines online.

NEEDS Alaska literary series with Peggy Shumaker as series editor. Publishes 1-3 works of fiction/year.

HOW TO CONTACT Submit proposal.

TERMS Responds in 2 months to queries.

TIPS "Writers have the best chance with scholarly nonfiction relating to Alaska, the circumpolar regions and North Pacific Rim. Our audience is made up of scholars, historians, students, libraries, universities, individuals, and the general Alaskan public."

UNIVERSITY OF GEORGIA PRESS

Main Library, Third Floor, 320 S. Jackson St., Athens GA 30602. (706)369-6130. **Fax:** (706)369-6131. **Website:** www.ugapress.org. **Contact:** Mick Gusinde-Duffy, executive editor; Walter Biggins, executive editor; Pat Allen, acquisitions editor; Beth Snead, assistant acquisitions editor. Estab. 1938. University of Georgia Press is a midsized press that publishes fiction only through the Flannery O'Connor Award for Short Fiction competition. Publishes hardcover originals, trade paperback originals, and reprints. Book catalog and guidelines online.

NEEDS Short story collections published in Flannery O'Connor Award Competition.

TERMS Pays 7-10% royalty on net receipts. Pays rare, varying advance. Responds in 2 months to queries.

TIPS "Please visit our website to view our book catalogs and for all manuscript submission guidelines."

UNIVERSITY OF IOWA PRESS

100 Kuhl House, 119 W. Park Rd., Iowa City IA 52242. (319)335-2000. **Fax:** (319)335-2055. **E-mail:** james-mccoy@uiowa.edu. **Website:** www.uiowapress.org. **Contact:** James McCoy, director. Estab. 1969. The University of Iowa Press publishes both trade and academic work in a variety of fields. Publishes hardcover and paperback originals. Book catalog available free. Guidelines online.

NEEDS Currently publishes the Iowa Short Fiction Award selections. "We do not accept any fiction submissions outside of the Iowa Short Fiction Award. See www.uiowapress.org for contest details."

UNIVERSITY OF MICHIGAN PRESS

839 Greene St., Ann Arbor MI 48106. (734)764-4388. **Fax:** (734)615-1540. **Website:** www.press.umich.edu. **Contact:** Mary Francis, editorial director. "In partnership with our authors and series editors, we publish in a wide range of humanities and social sciences disciplines." Guidelines online.

NEEDS In addition to the annual Michigan Literary Fiction Awards, this publishes literary fiction linked to the Great Lakes region.

HOW TO CONTACT Submit cover letter and first 30 pages.

UNIVERSITY OF NORTH TEXAS PRESS

1155 Union Circle, #311336, Denton TX 76203. (940)565-2142. **Fax:** (940)565-4590. **E-mail:** karen.devinney@unt.edu. **Website:** untpress.unt.edu. **Contact:** Ronald Chrisman, director; Karen De Vinney, assistant director. Estab. 1987. "We are dedicated to producing the highest quality scholarly, academic, and general interest books. We are committed to serving all peoples by publishing stories of their cultures and experiences that have been overlooked. Currently emphasizing military history, Texas history, music, Mexican-American studies." Publishes hardcover and trade paperback originals and reprints. Book catalog for 8 ½×11 SASE. Guidelines online.

NEEDS "The only fiction we publish is the winner of the Katherine Anne Porter Prize in Short Fiction, an annual, national competition with a $1,000 prize, and publication of the winning ms each Fall."

TERMS Responds in 1 month to queries.

TIPS "We publish series called War and the Southwest; Texas Folklore Society Publications; the Western Life Series; Practical Guide Series; Al-Filo: Mexican-American studies; North Texas Crime and Criminal Justice; Katherine Anne Porter Prize in Short Fiction; and the North Texas Lives of Musicians Series."

UNIVERSITY OF TAMPA PRESS

The University of Tampa, 401 W. Kennedy Blvd., Tampa FL 33606. (813)253-6266. **E-mail:** utpress@ut.edu. **Website:** www.ut.edu/tampapress. **Contact:** Richard Mathews, editor. Estab. 1952. "We are a small university press publishing a limited number of titles each year, primarily in the areas of local and regional history, poetry, and printing history. We do not accept e-mail submissions." Publishes hardcover originals and reprints; trade paperback originals and reprints. Book catalog online.

TERMS Does not pay advance. Responds in 3-4 months to queries.

UNIVERSITY OF WISCONSIN PRESS

1930 Monroe St., 3rd Floor, Madison WI 53711. **E-mail:** kadushin@wisc.edu; gcwalker@wisc.edu. **Website:** uwpress.wisc.edu. **Contact:** Raphael Kadushin, executive editor; Gwen Walker, editorial director. Estab. 1937. See submission guidelines on our website.

HOW TO CONTACT Query with SASE or submit outline, 1-2 sample chapter(s), synopsis.

TERMS Pays royalty. Responds in 1-3 weeks to queries; 3-6 weeks to proposals. Rarely comments on rejected work.

TIPS "Make sure the query letter and sample text are well-written, and read guidelines carefully to make sure we accept the genre you are submitting."

ⒶⓈⓄ USBORNE PUBLISHING

83-85 Saffron Hill, London EC1N 8RT, United Kingdom. (44)207430-2800. **Fax:** (44)207430-1562. **E-mail:** mail@usborne.co.uk. **Website:** www.usborne.com. "Usborne Publishing is a multiple-award-winning, worldwide children's publishing company publishing almost every type of children's book for every age from baby to young adult."

NEEDS Young readers, middle readers: adventure, contemporary, fantasy, history, humor, multicultural, nature/environment, science fiction, suspense/mystery, strong concept-based or character-led series. Average word length: young readers—5,000-10,000; middle readers—25,000-50,000; young adult—50,000-100,000.

HOW TO CONTACT *Agented submissions only.*

TERMS Pays authors royalty.

TIPS "Do not send any original work and, sorry, but we cannot guarantee a reply."

⊕ VÉHICULE PRESS

P.O.B. 42094 BP Roy, Montreal QC H2W 2T3, Canada. (514)844-6073. **Fax:** (514)844-7543. **E-mail:** sd@vehiculepress.com. **E-mail:** admin@vehiculepress.com. **Website:** www.vehiculepress.com. **Contact:** Simon Dardick, nonfiction; Carmine Starnino, poetry; Dimitri Nasrallah, fiction. Estab. 1973. "Montreal's Véhicule Press has published the best of Canadian and Quebec literature-fiction, poetry, essays, translations, and social history." Publishes trade paperback originals by Canadian authors mostly. Book catalog for 9 x 12 SAE with IRCs.

NEEDS No romance or formula writing.

HOW TO CONTACT Query with SASE.

TERMS Pays 10-15% royalty on retail price. Pays $200-500 advance. Responds in 4 months to queries.

TIPS "Quality in almost any style is acceptable. We believe in the editing process."

VERTIGO

DC Universe, Vertigo-DC Comics, 1700 Broadway, New York NY 10019. **Website:** www.vertigocomics. com. At this time, DC Entertainment does not accept unsolicited artwork or writing submissions.

VIKING

Imprint of Penguin Group (USA), Inc., 375 Hudson St., New York NY 10014. (212)366-2000. **Website:** www.penguin.com. Estab. 1925. Viking publishes a mix of academic and popular fiction and nonfiction. Publishes hardcover and originals.

HOW TO CONTACT *Agented submissions only.*

TERMS Pays 10-15% royalty on retail price.

VILLARD BOOKS

Penguin Random House, 1745 Broadway, New York NY 10019. (212)572-2600. **Website:** www.penguin-randomhouse.com. Estab. 1983. "Villard Books is the publisher of savvy and sometimes quirky, best-selling hardcovers and trade paperbacks."

NEEDS Commercial fiction.

HOW TO CONTACT *Agented submissions only.*

TERMS Pays negotiable royalty. Pays negotiable advance.

VINTAGE ANCHOR PUBLISHING

Penguin Random House, 1745 Broadway, New York NY 10019. **Website:** www.penguinrandomhouse.com.

HOW TO CONTACT *Agented submissions only.*

TERMS Pays 4-8% royalty on retail price. Average advance: $2,500 and up.

VIVISPHERE PUBLISHING

675 Dutchess Turnpike, Poughkeepsie NY 12603. (845)463-1100, ext. 314. **Fax:** (845)463-0018. **E-mail:** cs@vivisphere.com. **Website:** www.vivisphere.com. **Contact:** Submissions. Estab. 1995. Vivisphere Publishing is now considering new submissions from any genre as follows: game of bridge (cards), nonfiction, history, military, new age, fiction, feminist/gay/lesbian, horror, contemporary, self-help, science fiction and cookbooks. Publishes trade paperback originals and reprints and e-books. Book catalog and ms guidelines online.

○ "Cookbooks should have a particular slant or appeal to a certain niche. Also publish out-of-print books."

HOW TO CONTACT Query with SASE.

TERMS Pays royalty. Responds in 6-24 months.

VIZ MEDIA LLC

P.O. Box 77010, San Francisco CA 94107. (415)546-7073. **Website:** www.viz.com. "VIZ Media, LLC is one of the most comprehensive and innovative companies in the field of manga (graphic novel) publishing, animation and entertainment licensing of Japanese content. Owned by three of Japan's largest creators and licensors of manga and animation, Shueisha Inc., Shogakukan Inc., and Shogakukan-Shueisha Productions, Co., Ltd., VIZ Media is a leader in the publishing and distribution of Japanese manga for English speaking audiences in North America, the United Kingdom, Ireland, and South Africa and is a global ex-Asia licensor of Japanese manga and animation. The company offers an integrated product line including magazines such as *Shonen Jump* and *Shojo Beat*, graphic novels, and DVDs, and develops, markets, licenses, and distributes animated entertainment for audiences and consumers of all ages."

HOW TO CONTACT "At the present, all of the manga that appears in our magazines come directly from manga that has been serialized and published in Japan."

WASHINGTON WRITERS' PUBLISHING HOUSE

P.O. Box 15271, Washington DC 20003. **Website:** www.washingtonwriters.org. Estab. 1975. Guidelines online.

NEEDS Washington Writers' Publishing House considers book-length mss for publication by fiction writers living within 75 driving miles of the U.S. Capitol, Baltimore area included, through competition only. Mss may include previously published stories and excerpts. "Author should indicate where they heard about WWPH."

HOW TO CONTACT Submit an electronic copy by e-mail (use PDF, .doc, or rich text format) or 2 hard copies by snail mail of a short story collection or novel (no more than 350 pages, double or 1-1/2 spaced; author's name should not appear on any ms pages). Include separate page of publication acknowledgments plus 2 cover sheets: one with ms title, poet's name, address, telephone number, and e-mail address, the other with ms title only. Include SASE for results only; mss will not be returned (will be recycled).

TERMS Offers $1,000 and 50 copies of published book plus additional copies for publicity use.

ⒶⓄ WATERBROOK MULTNOMAH PUBLISHING GROUP

10807 New Allegiance Dr., Suite 500, Colorado Springs CO 80921. (719)590-4999. **Fax:** (719)590-8977. **Website:** www.waterbrookmultnomah.com. Estab. 1996. Publishes hardcover and trade paperback originals. Book catalog online.

HOW TO CONTACT *Agented submissions only.*

TERMS Pays royalty. Responds in 2-3 months.

WHITAKER HOUSE

1030 Hunt Valley Circle, New Kensington PA 15068. **E-mail:** publisher@whitakerhouse.com. **Website:** www.whitakerhouse.com. **Contact:** Editorial Department. Estab. 1970. Publishes hardcover, trade paperback, and mass market originals. Book catalog online. Guidelines online.

NEEDS All fiction must have a Christian perspective.

HOW TO CONTACT Query with SASE.

TERMS Pays 5-15% royalty on wholesale price. Responds in 3 months.

TIPS "Audience includes those seeking uplifting and inspirational fiction and nonfiction."

Ⓒ WHITECAP BOOKS, LTD.

210 - 314 W. Cordova St., Vancouver BC V6B 1 E8, Canada. (604)681-6181. **Fax:** (905)477-9179. **Website:** www.whitecap.ca. "Whitecap Books is a general trade publisher with a focus on food and wine titles. Although we are interested in reviewing unsolicited ms submissions, please note that we only accept submissions that meet the needs of our current publishing program. Please see some of most recent releases to get an idea of the kinds of titles we are interested in." Publishes hardcover and trade paperback originals. Catalog and guidelines online.

NEEDS No children's picture books or adult fiction.

HOW TO CONTACT See guidelines.

TERMS Pays royalty. Pays negotiated advance. Responds in 2-3 months to proposals.

TIPS "We want well-written, well-researched material that presents a fresh approach to a particular topic."

WHITE MANE KIDS

73 W. Burd St., Shippensburg PA 17257. (717)532-2237. **Fax:** (717)532-6110. **E-mail:** marketing@whitemane.com. **Website:** www.whitemane.com. **Contact:** Harold Collier, acquisitions editor. Estab. 1987. Book catalog and writer's guidelines available for SASE.

NEEDS Middle readers, young adults: history (primarily American Civil War). Average word length: middle readers—30,000. Does not publish picture books.

HOW TO CONTACT Query.

TERMS Pays authors royalty of 7-10%. Pays illustrators and photographers by the project. Responds to queries in 1 month, mss in 6-9 months.

TIPS "Make your work historically accurate. We are interested in historically accurate fiction for middle and young adult readers. We do *not* publish picture books. Our primary focus is the American Civil War and some America Revolution topics."

THE WILD ROSE PRESS

P.O. Box 708, Adams Basin NY 14410-0708. (585)752-8770. **E-mail:** queryus@thewildrosepress.com. **Website:** www.thewildrosepress.com. **Contact:** Rhonda Penders, editor-in-chief. Estab. 2006. Publishes paperback originals, reprints, and e-books in a POD format. Guidelines online.

HOW TO CONTACT *Does not accept unsolicited mss.* Send query letter with outline and synopsis of up to 5 pages. Accepts all queries by e-mail. Include estimated word count, brief bio, and list of publishing credits. Agented fiction less than 1%. Always comments on rejected mss.

TERMS Pays royalty of 7% minimum; 40% maximum. Sends prepublication galleys to author. Responds to queries in 4 weeks; mss in 12 weeks.

TIPS "Polish your manuscript, make it as error free as possible, and follow our submission guidelines."

ⒶⓄ WILLIAM MORROW

HarperCollins, 195 Broadway, New York NY 10007. (212)207-7000. **Fax:** (212)207-7145. **Website:** www.harpercollins.com. Estab. 1926. "William Morrow publishes a wide range of titles that receive much recognition and prestige—a most selective house." Book catalog available free.

NEEDS Publishes adult fiction. Morrow accepts only the highest quality submissions in adult fiction. *No unsolicited mss or proposals.*

HOW TO CONTACT *Agented submissions only.*

TERMS Pays standard royalty on retail price. Pays varying advance.

WOODBINE HOUSE

6510 Bells Mill Rd., Bethesda MD 20817. (301)897-3570. **Fax:** (301)897-5838. **E-mail:** info@woodbinehouse.com. **Website:** www.woodbinehouse.com. **Contact:** Acquisitions Editor. Estab. 1985. Woodbine House publishes books for or about individuals with disabilities to help those individuals and their families live fulfilling and satisfying lives in their homes, schools, and communities. Publishes trade paperback originals. Guidelines online.

NEEDS Receptive to stories re: developmental and intellectual disabilities, e.g., autism and cerebral palsy.

HOW TO CONTACT Submit complete ms with SASE.

TERMS Pays 10-12% royalty. Responds in 3 months to queries.

TIPS "Do not send us a proposal on the basis of this description. Examine our catalog or website and a couple of our books to make sure you are on the right track. Put some thought into how your book could be marketed (aside from in bookstores). Keep cover letters concise and to the point; if it's a subject that interests us, we'll ask to see more."

WORLD WEAVER PRESS

Albuquerque NM 87154. **E-mail:** submissions@worldweaverpress.com. **Website:** www.worldweaverpress.com. **Contact:** WWP Editors. Estab. 2012. World Weaver Press publishes digital and print editions of speculative fiction at various lengths for adult, young adult, and new adult audiences. "We believe in great storytelling." Catalog online. Guidelines on website.

NEEDS "We believe that publishing speculative fiction isn't just printing words on the page — it's the act of weaving brand new worlds. Seeking speculative fiction in many varieties: protagonists who have strength, not fainting spells; intriguing worlds with well-developed settings; characters that are to die for (we'd rather find ourselves in love than just in lust)." Full list of interests on website. Does not want giant bugs, ghosts, post-apocalyptic and/or dystopia, angels, zombies, magical realism, surrealism, middle grade (MG) or younger.

HOW TO CONTACT Not currently open for queries. Full guidelines will be updated approximately one month before queries re-open. Frequently open for submissions for themed short story anthologies. Check website for details.

TERMS Average royalty rate of 39% net on all editions. No advance. Responds to query letters within 3 weeks. Responses to mss requests take longer.

TIPS "Use your letter to pitch us the story, not talk about its themes or inception."

YELLOW SHOE FICTION SERIES

LSU Press, P.O. Box 25053, Baton Rouge LA 70894. **Website:** www.lsu.edu/lsupress. **Contact:** Michael Griffith, editor. Estab. 2004.

"Looking first and foremost for literary excellence, especially good manuscripts that have fallen through the cracks at the big commercial presses. I'll cast a wide net."

HOW TO CONTACT Does not accept unsolicited mss. Accepts queries by mail, Attn: James W. Long.

TERMS Pays royalty. Offers advance.

ZEBRA BOOKS

Kensington, 119 W. 40th St., New York NY 10018. (212)407-1500. **E-mail:** esogah@kensingtonbooks.com. **Website:** www.kensingtonbooks.com. **Contact:** Esi Sogah, senior editor. Zebra Books is dedicated to women's fiction, which includes, but is not limited to romance. Publishes hardcover originals, trade paperback and mass market paperback originals and reprints. Book catalog online.

HOW TO CONTACT Query.

ZUMAYA PUBLICATIONS, LLC

3209 S. Interstate 35, Austin TX 78741. (512)330-4055. **Fax:** (512)276-6745. **E-mail:** business@zumayapublishing.com. **E-mail:** acquisitions@zumayapublications.com. **Website:** www.zumayapublications.com. **Contact:** Elizabeth K. Burton. Estab. 1999. Zumaya Publications is a digitally-based micro-press publishing mainly in on-demand trade paperback and e-book formats in an effort to reduce environmental impact. "We currently offer approximately 190 fiction titles in the mystery, SF/F, historical, romance, LGBTQ, horror, and occult genres in adult, young adult, and middle reader categories. In 2016, we plan to officially launch our graphic and illustrated novel imprint, Zumaya Fabled Ink. We publish approximately 10-15 new titles annually, at least five of which are from new authors. We do not publish erotica or graphic erotic romance at this time. We accept only electronic queries; all others will be discarded unread. A working knowledge of computers and relevant software is a necessity, as our production process is completely digital." Publishes trade paperback and electronic originals. Guidelines online. We do *not* accept hard-copy queries or submissions.

NEEDS "We are open to all genres, particularly GLBT and YA/middle grade, historical and western, New Age/inspirational (no overtly Christian materials, please), non-category romance, thrillers. We encourage people to review what we've already published so as to avoid sending us more of the same, at least, insofar as the plot is concerned. While we're always looking for good mysteries, especially cozies, mysteries with historical settings, and police procedurals, we want original concepts rather than slightly altered versions of what we've already published. We do not publish erotica or graphically erotic romance at this time." Does not want erotica, graphically erotic romance, experimental, literary (unless it fits into one of our established imprints).

HOW TO CONTACT A copy of our rules of submission is posted on our website and can be downloaded. They are rules rather than guidelines and should be read carefully before submitting. It will save everyone time and frustration.

TERMS Pay 20% of net on paperbacks, net defined as cover price less printing and other associated costs; 50% of net on all e-books. Does not pay advance. Responds in 3 months to queries and proposals; 6 months to mss.

TIPS "We're catering to readers who may have loved last year's best seller but not enough to want to read 10 more just like it. Have something different. If it does not fit standard pigeonholes, that's a plus. On the other hand, it has to have an audience. And if you're not prepared to work with us on promotion and marketing, particularly via social media, it would be better to look elsewhere."

CONTESTS & AWARDS

///

In addition to honors and, quite often, cash prizes, contests and awards programs offer writers the opportunity to be judged on the basis of quality alone, without the outside factors that sometimes influence publishing decisions. New writers who win contests may be published for the first time, while more experienced writers may gain public recognition for an entire body of work.

Listed here are contests for almost every type of fiction writing. Some focus on form, such as short stories, novels, or novellas, while others feature writing on particular themes or topics. Still others are prestigious prizes or awards for work that must be nominated.

SELECTING AND SUBMITTING TO A CONTEST

Use the same care in submitting to contests as you would sending your manuscript to a publication or book publisher. Deadlines are very important, and, where possible, we've included this information. For some contests, deadlines were only approximate at our press deadline, so be sure to write, call, or look online for complete information.

Follow the rules to the letter. If, for instance, contest rules require your name on a cover sheet only, you will be disqualified if you ignore this and put your name on every page. Find out how many copies to send. If you don't send the correct amount, by the time you are contacted to send more, it may be past the submission deadline. An increasing number of contests invite writers to query by e-mail, and many post contest information on their websites. Check listings for e-mail and website addresses.

One note of caution: Beware of contests that charge entry fees that are disproportionate to the amount of the prize. Contests offering a $10 prize and charging $7 in entry fees are a waste of your time and money.

AEON AWARD

Albedo One/Aeon Press, Aeon Award, Albedo One & Yellow Brick Road, 8 Bachelor's Walk, Dublin D1, Ireland. (353)1-8730177. **E-mail:** fraslaw@yahoo. co.uk. **Website:** www.albedo1.com. **Contact:** Frank Ludlow, event coordinator. Estab. 2004. Prestigious fiction writing competition for short stories in any speculative fiction genre, such as fantasy, science fiction, horror, or anything in-between or unclassifiable. Annual Deadline: November 30. Contest begins January 1. Grand Prize: €1,000; 2nd Prize: €200; and 3rd Prize: €100. The top 3 stories are guaranteed publication in *Albedo One*. Costs: €8.50 entry fee. Judged by Ian Watson, Juliet E. McKenna, Todd McCaffrey, and Michael Carroll.

AESTHETICA ART PRIZE

Aesthetica Magazine, P.O. Box 371, York YO23 1WL, United Kingdom. **E-mail:** info@aestheticamagazine. com; artprize@aestheticamagazine.com. **Website:** www.aestheticamagazine.com. The Aesthetica Art Prize is a celebration of excellence in art from across the world and offers artists the opportunity to showcase their work to wider audiences and further their involvement in the international art world. There are 4 categories: Photograpic & Digital Art, Three Dimensional Design & Sculpture, Painting & Drawing, Video Installation & Performance. See guidelines at Artwork & Photography, Fiction, and Poetry. See guidelines at www.aestheticamagazine.com. The Aesthetica Art Prize is a celebration of excellence in art from across the world and offers artists the opportunity to showcase their work to wider audiences and further their involvement in the international art world. Deadline: August 31. Prizes include: £5,000 main prize courtesy of Hiscox, £1,000 Student Prize courtesy of Hiscox, group exhibition and publication in the Aesthetica Art Prize Anthology. Entry is £15 and permits submission of 2 works in one category. Costs: £10 each category.

ALABAMA STATE COUNCIL ON THE ARTS INDIVIDUAL ARTIST FELLOWSHIP

201 Monroe St., Suite 110, Montgomery AL 36130. (334)242-4076, ext. 236. **Fax:** (334)240-3269. **E-mail:** anne.kimzey@arts.alabama.gov. **Website:** www.arts. state.al.us. **Contact:** Anne Kimzey, Literary Arts Program Manager. Recognizes the achievements and potential of Alabama writers. Deadline: March 1. Applications must be submitted online by eGRANT. Costs:

No entry fee. Judged by independent peer panel. Fellowship recipients notified by mail and announced on website in June.

MARIE ALEXANDER POETRY SERIES

English Department, 2801 S. University Ave., Little Rock AR 72204. **E-mail:** editor@mariealexanderseries.com. **Website:** mariealexanderseries.com. **Contact:** Nickole Brown. Annual contest for a collection of previously unpublished prose poems or flash fiction by a U.S. writer. Deadline: July 31. Open to submissions on July 1. Prize: $1,000, plus publication.

ALLIGATOR JUNIPER AWARD

Alligator Juniper/Prescott College, 220 Grove Ave., Prescott AZ 86301. (928)350-2012. **Fax:** (928)776-5102. **E-mail:** alligatorjuniper@prescott.edu. **Website:** www.prescott.edu/alligatorjuniper/national-contest/index.html. **Contact:** Skye Anicca, managing editor. Annual contest for unpublished fiction, creative nonfiction, and poetry. Open to all age levels. Each entrant receives a personal letter from staff regarding the status of their submission, as well as minor feedback on the piece. Deadline: October 1. Prize: $1,000 plus publication in all three categories. Finalists in each genre are recognized as such, published, and paid in copies. Costs: $15. Judged by the distinguished writers in each genre and Prescott College writing students enrolled in the Literary Journal Practicum course.

AMERICAN ASSOCIATION OF UNIVERSITY WOMEN AWARD IN JUVENILE LITERATURE

4610 Mail Service Center, Raleigh NC 27699-4610. (919)807-7290. **E-mail:** michael.hill@ncdcr.gov. **Website:** www.ncdcr.gov. **Contact:** Michael Hill, awards coordinator. Annual award. Book must be published during the year ending June 30. Submissions made by author, author's agent or publisher. SASE for contest rules. Recognizes the year's best work of juvenile literature by a North Carolina resident. Deadline: July 15. Prize: Awards a cup to the winner and winner's name inscribed on a plaque displayed within the North Carolina Office of Archives and History. Judged by three-judge panel.

THE AMERICAN GEM LITERARY FESTIVAL

FilmMakers Magazine / Write Brothers, FilmMakers Magazine (filmmakers.com), Beverly Hills CA 90210. **E-mail:** info@filmmakers.com. **Website:** http://filmmakers.com/contests/short_story/. **Contact:** Jennifer

Brooks. Estab. 2001. Worldwide contest to recognize excellent short screenplays and short stories. Deadlines: Early: Feb 29; Regular: April 30; Late: June 30; Final: July 31. Prize: Short Script: 1st Place: $1,000. Other cash and prizes to top 5. Costs: Ranges from $19-49, based on number of pages, entry type. Full details via website.

AMERICAN LITERARY REVIEW CONTESTS

American Literary Review, P.O. Box 311307, University of North Texas, Denton TX 76203-1307. (940)565-2755. **E-mail:** americanliteraryreview@gmail.com. **Website:** www.americanliteraryreview.com. Contest to award excellence in short fiction, creative nonfiction, and poetry. Multiple entries are acceptable, but each entry must be accompanied with a reading fee. Do not put any identifying information in the file itself; include the author's name, title(s), address, e-mail address, and phone number in the boxes provided in the online submissions manager. Short fiction: Limit 8,000 words per work. Creative nonfiction: Limit 6,500 words per work. Deadline: October 1. Submission period begins June 1. Prize: $1,000 prize for each category, along with publication in the Spring online issue of the *American Literary Review*. Costs: $15 reading fee for one short story, one creative nonfiction entry, or up to 3 poems.

AMERICAN-SCANDINAVIAN FOUNDATION TRANSLATION PRIZE

The American-Scandinavian Foundation, 58 Park Ave., New York NY 10016. (212)779-3587. **E-mail:** grants@amscan.org; info@amscan.org. **Website:** www.amscan.org. **Contact:** Carl Fritscher, Fellowships & Grants Officer. The annual ASF translation competition is awarded for the most outstanding translations of poetry, fiction, drama, or literary prose written by a Scandinavian author born after 1900. Deadline: June 15. Prize: The Nadia Christensen Prize includes a $2,500 award, publication of an excerpt in *Scandinavian Review*, and a commemorative bronze medallion; The Leif and Inger Sjöberg Award, given to an individual whose literature translations have not previously been published, includes a $2,000 award, publication of an excerpt in *Scandinavian Review*, and a commemorative bronze medallion.

SHERWOOD ANDERSON FICTION AWARD

Mid-American Review, Mid-American Review, Dept. of English, Box WM, BGSU, Bowling Green OH 43403. (419)372-2725. **Fax:** (419)372-4642. **E-mail:** mar@bgsu.edu. **Website:** www.bgsu.edu/midamericanreview. **Contact:** Abigail Cloud, editor-in-chief. Offered annually for unpublished mss (6,000 word limit). Contest is open to all writers not associated with a judge or *Mid-American Review*. Deadline: November 1. Prize: $1,000, plus publication in the spring issue of *Mid-American Review*. Four Finalists: Notation, possible publication. Costs: $10. Judged by editors and a well-known writer, i.e., Aimee Bender or Anthony Doerr. Judged by Charles Yu in 2017.

ARIZONA LITERARY CONTEST AND BOOK AWARDS

Arizona Authors' Association, 6939 East Chaparral Rd., Paradise Valley AZ 85253-7000. (602)554-8101. **E-mail:** azauthors@gmail.com. **Website:** www.azauthors.com. **Contact:** Lisa Aquilina, president. Estab. 1980. Arizona Authors' Association sponsors annual literary competition in poetry, short story, essay, unpublished novels, and published books (fiction, nonfiction, and children's literature) and Arizona Book of the Year. Cash prizes awarded ($500 Book of the Year) from Green Pieces Press and 1st, 2nd, and 3rd place in seven categories ($150, $75 and $50, respectively) from Vignetta Syndicate LLC. New category in 2017, New Drama Writing, with a grand prize of $250. All category winners are published in the *Arizona Literary Magazine*. NEW PRIZE in 2018 for Unpublished Novel category. Winner receives a standard, traditional publishing contract through IngramElliott Book Publishers. NEW CATEGORY in 2018 - Published Cookbooks! Must have 2017 or 2018 copyright date at time of submission. Deadline: July 2. Begins accepting submissions January 1. Finalists notified by Labor Day weekend. Prizes: Grand Prize, Arizona Book of the Year Award: $500. All categories except new drama writing: 1st Prize: $150 and publication; 2nd Prize: $75 and publication; 3rd Prize: $50 and publication. New drama writing grand prize $250 and publication. Features in *Arizona Literary Magazine* can be taken instead of money and publication. 1st and 2nd prize winners in poetry, essay, and short story are nominated for the Pushcart Prize. Costs: Each submission: Poetry-$20-member/$25-nonmember; Short Story and Essay/Article/True Story-$25-member/$30-nonmember; Unpublished novel/novella-$40-member/$50-nonmember; New drama writing-$30-member/$40-nonmember; and Published fiction, nonfiction, cookbooks, and children's literature books-$40-member/$50-nonmember.

Multiple entries by same author accepted in all categories except new drama writing. Judged by nationwide published authors, editors, literary agents, and reviewers. Winners announced at an awards dinner and ceremony held the first Saturday in November.

ARROWHEAD REGIONAL ARTS COUNCIL INDIVIDUAL ARTIST CAREER DEVELOPMENT GRANT

Arrowhead Regional Arts Council, 600 E Superior St., Suite 404, Duluth MN 55802. (218)722-0952 or (800)569-8134. **E-mail:** info@aracouncil.org. **Website:** www.aracouncil.org. Award is to provide financial support to regional artists wishing to take advantage of impending, concrete opportunities that will advance their work or careers. Deadline: October and April. Grant awards of up to $3,000. Candidates are reviewed by a panel of ARAC Board Members and Community Artists.

ARTIST TRUST FELLOWSHIP AWARD

1835 12th Ave., Seattle WA 98122. (209)467-8734, ext. 11. **Fax:** (866)218-7878. **E-mail:** info@artisttrust.org. **Website:** www.artisttrust.org. **Contact:** Miguel Guillen, program manager. Fellowships award $7,500 to practicing professional artists of exceptional talent and demonstrated ability. The Fellowship is a merit-based, not a project-based award. Recipients present a Meet the Artist Event to a community in Washington state that has little or no access to the artist and their work. Awards 14 fellowships of $7,500 and 2 residencies with $1,000 stipends at the Millay Colony. Deadline: January 17. Applications available December 3. Prize: $7,500.

ARTS & LETTERS PRIZES

Arts & Letters Journal of Contemporary Culture, Campus Box 89, GC&SU, Milledgeville GA 31061. (478)445-1289. **E-mail:** al.journal@gcsu.edu. **Website:** al.gcsu.edu. **Contact:** The Editors. Offered annually for unpublished work. Deadline: March 31. Prize: $1,000 prize for each of the four major genres. Fiction, poetry, and creative nonfiction winners are published in Fall or Spring issue. The prize-winning one-act play is produced at the Georgia College campus (usually in March). Costs: $20/entry (payable to GC&SU). Judged by the editors (initial screening); see website for final judges and further details about submitting work.

THE ATHENAEUM LITERARY AWARD

The Athenaeum of Philadelphia, 219 S. 6th St., Philadelphia PA 19106-3794. (215)925-2688. **Fax:** (215)925-3755. **E-mail:** jilly@PhilaAthenaeum.org. **Website:** http://www.philaathenaeum.org/literary.html. **Contact:** Jill LeMin Lee, Librarian. Estab. 1950. The Athenaeum Literary Award was established to recognize and encourage literary achievement among authors who are bona fide residents of Philadelphia or Pennsylvania living within a radius of 30 miles of City Hall at the time their book was written or published. Any volume of general literature is eligible; technical, scientific, and juvenile books are not included. Nominated works are reviewed on the basis of their significance and importance to the general public as well as for literary excellence. Deadline: All nominations must be submitted prior to December 1st of the year of publication. Costs: There is no fee to submit an entry.

AUTUMN HOUSE PRESS FULL-LENGTH FICTION PRIZE

Autumn House Press, 5530 Penn Ave., Pittsburgh PA 15206. **E-mail:** info@autumnhouse.org. **Website:** autumnhouse.org. Fiction submissions should be approximately 200-300 pages. All fiction sub-genres (short stories, short-shorts, novellas, or novels), or any combination of sub-genres, are eligible. All finalists will be considered for publication. Deadline: June 30. Prize: Winners will receive book publication, $1,000 advance against royalties, and a $1,500 travel grant to participate in the Autumn House Master Authors Series in Pittsburgh. Costs: $30. Judged by Dana Johnson (final judge).

AWP AWARD SERIES

Association of Writers & Writing Programs, George Mason University, 4400 University Drive, MSN 1E3, Fairfax VA 22030. **E-mail:** supriya@awpwriter.org. **Website:** www.awpwriter.org. **Contact:** Supriya Bhatnagar, director of publications. AWP sponsors the Award Series, an annual competition for the publication of excellent new book-length works. The competition is open to all authors writing in English regardless of nationality or residence, and is available to published and unpublished authors alike. Offered annually to foster new literary talent. Deadline: Postmarked between January 1 and February 28. Prize: AWP Prize for the Novel: $2,500 and publication by New Issues Press; Donald Hall Prize for Poetry: $5,500 and publication by the University of Pittsburgh Press; Grace Paley Prize in Short Fiction: $5,500 and publication by the University of Massachusetts Press; and AWP Prize for Creative Nonfiction: $2,500 and publication by the University of Georgia Press. Costs: $30 for non-members, $20 for members.

BALCONES FICTION PRIZE

Austin Commmunity College, Department of Creative Writing, 1212 Rio Grande St., Austin TX 78701. (512)584-5045. **E-mail:** joconne@austincc.edu. **Website:** http://www.austincc.edu/crw/html/balconescenter.html. **Contact:** Joe O'Connell. Awarded to the best book of literary fiction published the previous year. Books of prose may be submitted by publisher or author. Send three copies. Deadline: January 31. Prize: $1,500, winner is flown to Austin for a campus reading. Costs: $30 reading fee.

THE BALTIMORE REVIEW CONTESTS

The Baltimore Review, 6514 Maplewood Rd., Baltimore MD 21212. **E-mail:** editor@baltimorereview.org. **Website:** www.baltimorereview.org. **Contact:** Barbara Westwood Diehl, senior editor. Estab. 1996. Each summer and winter issue includes a contest theme (see submissions guidelines for theme). Prizes are awarded for first, second, and third place among all categories—poetry, short stories, and creative nonfiction. All entries are considered for publication. Deadline: May 31 and November 30. Prize: 1st Place: $500; 2nd Place: $200; 3rd Place: $100. All entries are considered for publication. Provides a small compensation to all contributors. Costs: $10 entry fee. Judged by the editors of *The Baltimore Review* and a guest, final judge.

BARD FICTION PRIZE

Bard College, P.O. Box 5000, Annandale-on-Hudson NY 12504-5000. (845)758-7087. **Fax:** (845)758-7917. **E-mail:** bfp@bard.edu. **Website:** www.bard.edu/bfp. **Contact:** Irene Zedlacher. Estab. 2001. The Bard Fiction Prize is awarded to a promising, emerging writer who is an American citizen aged 39 years or younger at the time of application. The Bard Fiction Prize is intended to encourage and support young writers of fiction to pursue their creative goals and to provide an opportunity to work in a fertile and intellectual environment. Deadline: June 15. Prize: $30,000 and appointment as writer-in-residence at Bard College for 1 semester. Judged by a committee of 5 judges (authors associated with Bard College).

MILDRED L. BATCHELDER AWARD

50 E. Huron St., Chicago IL 60611-2795. **Website:** http://www.ala.org/alsc/awardsgrants/. Estab. 1966.

The Batchelder Award is given to the most outstanding children's book originally published in a language other than English in a country other than the United States, and subsequently translated into English for publication in the US. The purpose of the award, a citation to an American publisher, is to encourage international exchange of quality children's books by recognizing US publishers of such books in translation. Deadline: December 31.

BELLEVUE LITERARY REVIEW GOLDENBERG PRIZE FOR FICTION

Bellevue Literary Review, NYU Dept of Medicine, 550 First Ave., OBV-A612, New York NY 10016. (212)263-3973. **E-mail:** info@blreview.org; stacy@blreview.org. **Website:** www.blreview.org. **Contact:** Stacy Bodziak, managing editor. The BLR prizes award outstanding writing related to themes of health, healing, illness, the mind and the body. Annual competition/award for short stories. Receives about 200-300 entries per category. Send credit card information or make checks payable to Bellevue Literary Review. Guidelines available in February. Accepts inquiries by e-mail, phone, mail. Submissions open in February. Results announced in December and made available to entrants with SASE, by e-mail, on website. Winners notified by mail, by e-mail. Deadline: July 1. Prize: $1,000 and publication in *The Bellevue Literary Review*. Honorable mention winners receive $250 and publication. Costs: $20, or $30 to include 1-year subscription. BLR editors select semi-finalists to be read by an independent judge who chooses the winner. Previous judges include Nathan Englander, Jane Smiley, Francine Prose, and Andre Dubus III.

GEORGE BENNETT FELLOWSHIP

Phillips Exeter Academy, 20 Main Street, Exeter NH 03833. **E-mail:** teaching_opportunities@exeter.edu. **Website:** www.exeter.edu/bennettfellowship. Annual award for fellow and family to provide time and freedom from material considerations to a person seriously contemplating or pursuing a career as a writer. Applicants should have a ms in progress which they intend to complete during the fellowship period. Ms should be fiction, nonfiction, novel, short stories, or poetry. Duties: To be in residency at the Academy for the academic year; to make oneself available informally to students interested in writing. Committee favors writers who have not yet published a book with a major publisher. Deadline: November 30. A choice will be made, and all entrants notified in mid-April. Prize: Cash stipend (currently $15,260), room and board. Costs: $15 application fee. Application form and guidelines on website. Judged by committee of the English department.

BEST LESBIAN EROTICA

BLE 2013, 31-64 21st St., #319, Long Island City NY 11106. **E-mail:** kwarnockble@gmail.com. **Website:** www.kathleenwarnock.com/best-lesbian-erotica. html. **Contact:** Kathleen Warnock, series editor. Call for submissions for *Best Lesbian Erotica*, an annual collection. Categories include: novel excerpts, short stories; poetry will be considered but is not encouraged. Accepts both previously published and unpublished material; will accept submissions that have appeared in other themed anthologies. Open to any writer. All submissions must include an e-mail address for response. No mss will be returned, so please do not include SASE. Deadline: April 1. Prize: $100 for each published story, plus 2 copies of the anthology.

BINGHAMTON UNIVERSITY JOHN GARDNER FICTION BOOK AWARD

Creative Writing Program, Binghamton University, Binghamton University, Department of English, General Literature, and Rhetoric, Library North Room 1149, P.O. Box 6000, Binghamton NY 13902-6000. (607)777-2713. **E-mail:** cwpro@binghamton.edu. **Website:** http://binghamton.edu/english/creative-writing/. **Contact:** Maria Mazziotti Gillan, director. Estab. 2001. Contest offered annually for a novel or collection of fiction published in previous year in a press run of 500 copies or more. Each book submitted must be accompanied by an application form. Publisher may submit more than 1 book for prize consideration. Send 2 copies of each book. Guidelines available on website. Deadline: March 1. Prize: $1,000. Judged by a professional writer not on Binghamton University faculty.

☻ JAMES TAIT BLACK MEMORIAL PRIZES

English Literature, University of Edinburgh, School of Literatures, Languages, and Cultures, 50 George Square, Edinburgh EH8 9LH, Scotland. (44-13)1650-3619. **E-mail:** s.strathdee@ed.ac.uk. **Website:** https://www.ed.ac.uk/events/james-tait-black. Estab. 1919. Open to any writer. Entries must be previously published. Winners notified by phone, via publisher. Contact department of English Literature for list of winners or check website. Accepts inquiries by e-mail or phone. Deadline: December 1. Prize: Two prizes each of £10,000 are awarded: one for the best work of fiction, one for the best biography or work of that nature, published during the calendar year January 1 to December 31. Judged by professors of English Literature with the assistance of teams of postgraduate readers.

THE BLACK RIVER CHAPBOOK COMPETITION

Black Lawrence Press, 279 Claremont Ave, Mount Vernon NY 10552. **E-mail:** editors@blacklawrence-press.com. **Website:** www.blacklawrence.com. **Contact:** Kit Frick, senior editor. Twice each year Black Lawrence Press will run the Black River Chapbook Competition for an unpublished chapbook of poems or short fiction between 16-36 pages in length. Spring deadline: May 31. Fall deadline: October 31. Prize: $500, publication, and 10 copies. Costs: $15. Judged by a revolving panel of judges, in addition to the Chapbook Editor and other members of the BLP editorial staff.

☻ THE BOARDMAN TASKER PRIZE FOR MOUNTAIN LITERATURE

The Boardman Tasker Charitable Trust, 8 Bank View Rd., Darley Abbey Derby DE22 1EJ, UK. 01332 342246. **E-mail:** steve@people-matter.co.uk. **Website:** www.boardmantasker.com. **Contact:** Steve Dean. Offered annually to reward a work with a mountain theme, whether fiction, nonfiction, drama, or poetry, written in the English language (initially or in translation). Subject must be concerned with a mountain environment. Previous winners have been books on expeditions, climbing experiences, a biography of a mountaineer, novels. Guidelines available in January by e-mail or on website. Entries must be previously published. Open to any writer. The award is to honor Peter Boardman and Joe Tasker, who disappeared on Everest in 1982. Deadline: August 1. Prize: £3,000 Judged by a panel of 3 judges elected by trustees.

BOSTON GLOBE-HORN BOOK AWARDS

The Boston Globe, Horn Book, Inc., 300 The Fenway, Palace Road Building, Suite P-311, Boston MA 02115. (617)278-0225. **Fax:** (617)278-6062. **E-mail:** bghb@hbook.com; info@hbook.com. **Website:** www.hbook.com/bghb/. Estab. 1967. Offered annually for excellence in literature for children and young adults (published June 1-May 31). Categories: picture book, fiction and poetry, nonfiction. Judges may also name up to 2 honor books in each category. Books must be published in the US, but may be written or illustrated by citizens of any country. The Horn Book Magazine publishes speeches given at awards ceremonies. Guidelines for submitting books online. Deadline: May 15. Prize: $500 and an engraved silver bowl; honor book recipients receive an engraved silver plate. Judged by a panel of 3 judges selected each year.

BOULEVARD SHORT FICTION CONTEST FOR EMERGING WRITERS

Boulevard Magazine, 6614 Clayton Rd., PMB #325, Richmond Heights MO 63117. (314)862-2643. **Website:** www.boulevardmagazine.org. **Contact:** Jessica Rogen, editor. Estab. 1985. Offered annually for unpublished short fiction to a writer who has not yet published a book of fiction, poetry, or creative nonfiction with a nationally distributed press. Holds first North American rights on anything not previously published. Open to any writer with no previous publication by a nationally known press. Guidelines for SASE or on website. Deadline: December 31. Prize: $1,500, and publication in 1 of the next year's issues. Costs: $16 fee/story, includes 1-year subscription to *Boulevard*.

THE BRIAR CLIFF REVIEW FICTION, POETRY, AND CREATIVE NONFICTION COMPETITION

The Briar Cliff Review, Briar Cliff University, 3303 Rebecca St., Sioux City IA 51104-0100. **E-mail:** tricia.currans-sheehan@briarcliff.edu (editor); jeanne.emmons@briarcliff.edu (poetry). **Website:** www.bcreview.org. **Contact:** Tricia Currans-Sheehan, editor. Estab. 1989. *The Briar Cliff Review* sponsors an annual contest offering $1,000 and publication to each 1st Prize winner in fiction, poetry, and creative nonfiction. Previous year's winner and former students of editors ineligible. Winning pieces accepted for publication on the basis of first-time rights. Considers simultaneous submissions, "but notify us immediately upon acceptance elsewhere. We guarantee a considerate reading." No mss returned. To reward good writers and showcase quality writing. Deadline: November 1. Prize: $1,000 and publication to each prize winner in fiction, poetry, and creative nonfiction. Costs: $20 per story/creative nonfiction piece or 3 poems. Judged by *Briar Cliff Review* editors.

THE BRIDPORT PRIZE

P.O. Box 6910, Dorset DT6 9QB, United Kingdom. **E-mail:** info@bridportprize.org.uk; kate@bridportprize. org.uk. **Website:** www.bridportprize.org.uk. **Contact:** Kate Wilson, Bridport Prize administrator. Estab. 1973. Award to promote literary excellence, discover new talent. Categories: Short stories, poetry, flash fiction, first novel. Deadline: May 31. Prize: £5,000; £1,000; £500; various runners-up prizes and publication of approximately 13 best stories and 13 best poems in anthology; plus 6 best flash fiction stories. 1st Prize of £1,000 for the best short, short story of under 250 words. £1,000 plus up to a year's mentoring for winner of Peggy Chapman-Andrews Award for a first novel. Costs: £9 for poems, £10 for short stories, £8 for flash fiction, and £20 for novels. Judged by 1 judge for short stories (in 2018, Monica Ali), 1 judge for poetry (in 2018, Daljit Nagra) and 1 judge for flash fiction (in 2018 Monica Ali). The Novel award is judged by a group comprising representatives from The Literary Consultancy, A.M. Heath Literary Agents, and (in 2018) judge Kamila Shamsie.

BRITISH CZECH AND SLOVAK ASSOCIATION WRITING COMPETITION

24 Ferndale, Tunbridge Wells Kent TN2 3NS, England. **E-mail:** prize@bcsa.co.uk. **Website:** www.bcsa.co.uk/specials.html. Estab. 2002. Annual contest for original writing (entries should be 1,500-2,000 words) in English on the links between Britain and the Czech/Slovak Republics, or describing society in transition in the Republics since 1989. Entries can be fact or fiction. Topics can include history, politics, the sciences, economics, the arts, or literature. Deadline: June 30. Winners announced in November. Prize: 1st Place: £300; 2nd Place: £100.

BURNABY WRITERS' SOCIETY CONTEST

E-mail: info@bws.ca. **Website:** www.bws.ca; www.burnabywritersnews.blogspot.com. **Contact:** Contest Committee. Offered annually for unpublished work. Open to all residents of British Columbia. Categories vary from year to year. Send SASE for current rules. For complete guidelines see website or burnabywritersnews.blogspot.com. Purpose is to encourage talented writers in all genres. Deadline: May 31. Prizes: 1st Place: $200; 2nd Place: $100; 3rd Place: $50; and public reading. Costs: $5/entry, or 3 entries for $10.

THE CAINE PRIZE FOR AFRICAN WRITING

51 Southwark St., London SE1 1RU, United Kingdom. **E-mail:** info@caineprize.com. **Website:** www.caine-

prize.com. **Contact:** Lizzy Attree. Estab. 1999. Entries must have appeared for the first time in the 5 years prior to the closing date for submissions, which is January 31 each year. Publishers should submit 6 copies of the published original with a brief cover note (no pro forma application). "Please indicate nationality or passport held." The Caine Prize is open to writers from anywhere in Africa for work published in English. Its focus is on the short story, reflecting the contemporary development of the African story-telling tradition. Deadline: January 31. Prize: £10,000. Judges change each year.

CALIFORNIA BOOK AWARDS

Commonwealth Club of California, 110 The Embarcadero, San Francisco CA 94105. (415)597-6700. **Fax:** (415)597-6729. **E-mail:** bookawards@commonwealthclub.org. **Website:** www.commonwealthclub.org/. **Contact:** Renee Miguel. Estab. 1931. Offered annually to recognize California's best writers and illuminate the wealth and diversity of California-based literature. Award is for published submissions appearing in print during the previous calendar year. Can be nominated by publisher or author. Open to California residents (or residents at time of publication). Deadline: December 22. Prize: Medals and cash prizes to be awarded at publicized event. Judged by 12-15 California professionals with a diverse range of views, backgrounds, and literary experience.

JOHN W. CAMPBELL MEMORIAL AWARD FOR BEST SCIENCE FICTION NOVEL OF THE YEAR

1445 Jayhawk Blvd, Suite 3001, University of Kansas, Lawrence KS 66045. (785)864-2518. **E-mail:** gunn.sf.center@gmail.com. **Website:** www.sfcenter.ku.edu/campbell.htm. **Contact:** Chris McKitterick. Estab. 1973. Honors the best science fiction novel of the year. Deadline: Check website. Prize: Campbell Award trophy. Winners receive an expense-paid trip to the Campbell Conference to receive their award. Their names are also engraved on a permanent trophy. Judged by a jury.

CANADIAN AUTHORS ASSOCIATION AWARD FOR FICTION

6 West St. N., Suite 203, Orilla ON L3X 5B8, Canada. **Website:** www.canadianauthors.org. **Contact:** Anita Purcell, executive director. Estab. 1975. Award for full-length, English language literature for adults by a Canadian author. Deadline: January 15. Prize: $1,000. Judging: Each year a trustee for each award appointed by the Canadian Authors Association selects up to 3 judges. Identities of the trustee and judges are confidential.

CANADIAN AUTHORS ASSOCIATION EMERGING WRITER AWARD

6 West St. N., Suite 203, Orilla ON L3X 5B8, Canada. **Website:** www.canadianauthors.org. **Contact:** Anita Purcell, executive director. Estab. 2006. Annual award for a writer under 30 years of age deemed to show exceptional promise in the field of literary creation. Deadline: January 15. Prize: $500. Judging: Each year a trustee for each award appointed by the Canadian Authors Association selects up to 3 judges. Identities of the trustee and judges are confidential.

CASCADE WRITING CONTEST & AWARDS

Oregon Christian Writers, 1075 Willow Lake Road N., Keizer Oregon 97303. **E-mail:** cascade@oregonchristianwriters.org. **E-mail:** cascade@oregonchristianwriters.org. **Website:** http://oregonchristianwriters.org/. **Contact:** Marilyn Rhoads and Julie McDonald Zander. The Cascade Awards are presented at the annual Oregon Christian Writers Summer Conference (held at the Red Lion on the River in Portland, Oregon, each August) attended by national editors, agents, and professional authors. The contest is open for both published and unpublished works in the following categories: contemporary fiction book, historical fiction book, speculative fiction book, nonfiction book, memoir book, young adult/middle grade fiction book, young adult/middle grade nonfiction book, children's chapter book and picture book (fiction and nonfiction), poetry, devotional, article, column, story, or blog post. Two additional special Cascade Awards are presented each year: the Trailblazer Award to a writer who has distinguished him/herself in the field of Christian writing; and a Writer of Promise Award for a writer who demonstrates unusual promise in the field of Christian writing. For a full list of categories, entry rules, and scoring elements, visit website. Annual multi-genre competition to encourage both published and emerging writers in the field of Christian writing. Deadline: March 31. Submissions period begins February 14. Prize: Award certificate and pin presented at the Cascade Awards ceremony during the Oregon Christian Writers Annual Summer Conference. Finalists are listed in the conference notebook and winners are listed online. Cascade Trophies are awarded to the recipients of the Trailblazer and Writer of Promise Awards. Costs: Published book entry: $35 (OCW member), $45 (nonmember); All other entries: $30 (OCW member), $40 (nonmember). Judged by published authors, editors, librarians, and retail book store owners and employees. Final judging by editors, agents, and published authors from the Christian publishing industry.

KAY CATTARULLA AWARD FOR BEST SHORT STORY

Texas Institute of Letters, P.O. Box 609, Round Rock TX 78680. **E-mail:** tilsecretary@yahoo.com. **Website:** www.texasinstituteofletters.org. Offered annually for work published January 1-December 31 of previous year to recognize the best short story. The story submitted must have appeared in print for the first time to be eligible. Writers must have been born in Texas, must have lived in Texas for at least 2 consecutive years, or the subject matter of the work must be associated with Texas. See website for guidelines. Deadline: January 10. Prize: $1,000.

G. S. SHARAT CHANDRA PRIZE FOR SHORT FICTION

BkMk Press, University of Missouri-Kansas City, BkMk Press, University of Missouri-Kansas City, 5100 Rockhill Rd., Kansas City MO 64110-2499. (816)235-2558. **Fax:** (816)235-2611. **E-mail:** bkmk@umkc.edu; newletters@umkc.edu. **Website:** www.umkc.edu/bkmk. **Contact:** Ben Furnish. Estab. 2002 (Chandra Prize established); 1971 (press established). Offered annually for the best book-length ms collection (unpublished) of short fiction in English by a living author. Translations are not eligible. Initial judging is done by a network of published writers. Final judging is done by a writer of national reputation. Guidelines for SASE, by e-mail, or on website. Deadline: January 15. Prize: $1,000, plus book publication by BkMk Press. Costs: $25 fee, $5 additional for online submission.

🖤 PEGGY CHAPMAN-ANDREWS FIRST NOVEL AWARD

P.O. Box 6910, Dorset DT6 9QB, United Kingdom. **E-mail:** info@bridportprize.org.uk. **Website:** www.bridportprize.org.uk. **Contact:** Kate Wilson, prize administrator. Estab. 1973. Award to promote literary excellence and new writers. Enter first chapters of novel, up to 8,000 words (minimum 5,000 words) plus 300 word synopsis. Deadline: May 31. Prize: 1st Place:

£1,000 plus mentoring & possible publication; Runner-Up: £500. Costs: £20. Judged by Kamila Shamsie with The Literary Consultancy & A.M. Heath Literary Agents.

THE CHARITON REVIEW SHORT FICTION PRIZE

Truman State University Press, 100 East Normal Ave., Kirksville MO 63501-4221. (660)785-7336. **Fax:** (660)785-4480. **E-mail:** chariton@truman.edu; tsup@truman.edu. **Website:** http://tsup.truman.edu. **Contact:** Barbara Smith-Mandell. Estab. 1975. An annual award for the best unpublished short fiction on any theme up to 5,000 words in English. Deadline: September 30. Prize: $500 and publication in *The Chariton Review* for the winner. Two or three finalists will also be published and receive $200 each. Costs: Include a nonrefundable reading fee of $20 for each ms submitted, make check payable to Truman State University Press. The final judge will be announced after the finalists have been selected in January.

⏱ THE CITY OF VANCOUVER BOOK AWARD

Cultural Services Dept., Woodward's Heritage Building, 111 W. Hastings St., Suite 501, Vancouver BC V6B 1H4, Canada. (604)871-6634. **Fax:** (604)871-6005. **E-mail:** marnie.rice@vancouver.ca; culture@vancouver.ca. **Website:** https://vancouver.ca/people-programs/city-of-vancouver-book-award.aspx. Estab. 1989. The annual City of Vancouver Book Award recognizes authors of excellence of any genre who contribute to the appreciation and understanding of Vancouver's history, unique character, or the achievements of its residents. The book must exhibit excellence in one or more of the following areas: content, illustration, design, format. Deadline: May 18. Prize: $3,000. Costs: $20/entry. Judged by an independent jury.

CLOUDBANK JOURNAL CONTEST

P.O. Box 610, Corvallis OR 97339. (541)752-0075. **E-mail:** michael@cloudbankbooks.com. **Website:** www.cloudbankbooks.com. **Contact:** Michael Malan. Estab. 2009. *Cloudbank* is a 96-page print journal published annually. Included are poems, flash fiction and book reviews. Regular submissions and contest submissions are accepted. An annual book contest, entitled the Vern Rutsala Book Prize, results in a published book of poetry and/or flash fiction. Deadline: *Cloudbank* contest due date is the last day in February. The Vern Rutsala Book contest due date is the last day in October. Prize: $200 and publication, plus an extra copy of the issue in which the winning poem appears. Two contributors' copies will be sent to writers whose work appears in the magazine. The book contest winner receives $1,000 and publication of the manuscript. Costs: To enter the journal contest there's a $15 entry fee. Make check out to *Cloudbank* or pay via Submittable. All writers who enter the contest will receive a 2-issue subscription to *Cloudbank* journal. To enter the Vern Rutsala Book Prize, the fee is $25 and submissions can be sent by mail or via Submittable. The *Cloudbank* contest is judged by Michael Malan and editorial staff. The Vern Rutsala Book contest is judged by an outside author.

COLORADO BOOK AWARDS

Colorado Humanities & Center for the Book, 7935 E. Prentice Ave., Suite 450, Greenwood Village CO 80111. (303)894-7951. **Fax:** (303)864-9361. **E-mail:** bess@coloradohumanities.org. **Website:** www.coloradohumanities.org. **Contact:** Bess Maher. Estab. 1991. An annual program that celebrates the accomplishments of Colorado's outstanding authors, editors, illustrators, and photographers. Awards are presented in at least ten categories including anthology/collection, biography, children's, creative nonfiction, fiction, history, nonfiction, pictorial, poetry, and young adult. Deadline: January 9.

THE CRUCIBLE POETRY AND FICTION COMPETITION

Crucible, Barton College, College Station, Wilson NC 27893. (800)345-4973 x6450. **E-mail:** crucible@barton.edu. **Website:** www.barton.edu. **Contact:** Terrence L. Grimes, editor. Open annually to all writers. Entries must be completely original, never published, and in ms form. Does not accept simultaneous submissions. Fiction is limited to 8,000 words; poetry is limited to 5 poems. Guidelines online or by email or for SASE. All submissions should be electronic. Deadline: May 1. Prize: 1st Place: $150; 2nd Place: $100 (for both poetry and fiction). Winners are also published in *Crucible*. Judged by in-house editorial board.

THE CUTBANK CHAPBOOK CONTEST

CutBank Literary Magazine, *CutBank*, University of Montana, English Dept., LA 133, Missoula MT 59812. **E-mail:** editor.cutbank@gmail.com. **Website:** www.cutbankonline.org. **Contact:** Kate Barrett, editor-in-chief. This competition is open to original English language mss in the genres of poetry, fiction, and creative nonfiction. While previously published stand-alone pieces or excerpts may be included in a ms, the ms as a whole must be an unpublished work. Looking for startling, compelling, and beautiful original work. "We're looking for a fresh, powerful manuscript. Maybe it will overtake us quietly; gracefully defy genres; satisfyingly subvert our expectations; punch us in the mouth page in and page out. We're interested in both prose and poetry—and particularly work that straddles the lines between genres." Deadline: March 31. Submissions period begins January1. Prize: $1,000 and 25 contributor copies. Costs: $20. Judged by a guest judge each year.

CWW ANNUAL WISCONSIN WRITERS AWARDS

Council for Wisconsin Writers, 4964 Gilkeson Rd, Waunakee WI 53597. **E-mail:** karlahuston@gmail.com. **Website:** www.wiswriters.org. **Contact:** Geoff Gilpin, president and annual awards co-chair; Karla Huston, secretary and annual awards co-chair; Sylvia Cavanaugh, annual awards co-chair; Edward Schultz, annual awards co-chair, Erik Richardson, annual awards co-chair. Estab. 1964. Offered annually for work published by Wisconsin writers during the previous calendar year. Nine awards: Major Achievement (presented in alternate years); short fiction; short nonfiction; nonfiction book; poetry book; fiction book; children's literature; Lorine Niedecker Poetry Award; Christopher Latham Sholes Award for Outstanding Service to Wisconsin Writers (presented in alternate years); Essay Award for Young Writers. Open to Wisconsin residents. Deadline: January 31. Submissions open on November 1. Prizes: First place prizes: $500. Honorable mentions: $50. Costs: $25 nonrefundable fee. List of judges available on website.

DANA AWARDS IN THE NOVEL, SHORT FICTION, AND POETRY

200 Fosseway Dr., Greensboro NC 27445. (336)644-8028. **E-mail:** danaawards@gmail.com. **Website:** www.danaawards.com. **Contact:** Mary Elizabeth Parker, chair. Estab. 1996. Three awards offered annually for unpublished work written in English. Works previously published online are not eligible. The Dana Awards are re-vamping. The Novel Award is now increased to $2,000, based on a new partnership with Blue Mary Books: Blue Mary has agreed to consider for possible publication not only the Novel Award winning manuscript, but the top 9 other Novel final-

ists, as well as the 30 top Novel semifinalists. The Short Fiction and Poetry Awards offer the traditional $1,000 awards each and do not offer a publishing option (currently, Blue Mary publishes only novels). See website for further updates. Purpose is monetary award for work that has not been previously published or received monetary award, but will accept work published simply for friends and family. Deadline: October 31 (postmarked). Prizes: $2,000 for the Novel Award; $1,000 each for the Short Fiction and Poetry awards awards. Costs: $30 per novel entry; $15 per short fiction entry; $15 per 5 poems.

THE DANAHY FICTION PRIZE

Tampa Review, University of Tampa, 401 W. Kennedy Blvd., Tampa FL 33606. 813-253-6266. **E-mail:** utpress@ut.edu. **Website:** www.ut.edu/TampaReview. Estab. 2006. Annual award for the best previously unpublished short fiction. Deadline: November 30. Prize: $1,000, plus publication in *Tampa Review*. Costs: $20.

✎ DEBUT DAGGER

Crime Writers' Association, Debut Dagger, Dea Parkin, CWA Secretary, The Writing House, 3 Dale View, Chorley Lancashire PR7 3QJ, United Kingdom. **E-mail:** secretary@thecwa.co.uk. **Website:** https://thecwa.co.uk/the-debuts/. **Contact:** Dea Parkin. Estab. 1998. Annual competition for unpublished crime writers. Submit the opening 3,000 words of a crime novel, plus a 500-1,000 word synopsis. Open to any writer who has not had a full-length novel traditionally published. Self-published only is acceptable, including the novel entry. Bring new writers to the attention of publishers. Deadline: February 28. Submission period begins October 1. Prize: £500. All shortlisted entrants will, with their permission, have their entry sent to UK literary agents, and receive brief feedback on their entries. Costs: £36. Judged by a panel of top crime editors and agents as well as the CWA's head of Criminal Critiques, and the shortlisted entries are sent to agents.

WILLIAM F. DEECK MALICE DOMESTIC GRANTS FOR UNPUBLISHED WRITERS

Malice Domestic, P.O. Box 8007, Gaithersburg MD 20898-8007. **E-mail:** malicegrants@comcast.net. **Website:** www.malicedomestic.org. **Contact:** Harriette Sackler. Estab. 1989. Offered annually for unpublished work in the mystery field. Malice awards one grant to unpublished writers in the Malice Domestic genre at its annual convention in May. The competition is designed to help the next generation of Malice authors get their first work published and to foster quality Malice literature. Malice Domestic literature is loosely described as mystery stories of the Agatha Christie type, i.e., traditional mysteries. These works usually feature no excessive gore, gratuitous violence, or explicit sex. Deadline: November 1. Prize: $2,500, plus a comprehensive registration to the following year's convention and two nights' lodging at the convention hotel.

DELAWARE DIVISION OF THE ARTS

820 N. French St., Wilmington DE 19801. (302)577-8278. **Fax:** (302)577-6561. **E-mail:** Roxanne.stanulis@state.de.us. **Website:** www.artsdel.org. **Contact:** Roxanne Stanulis. Award to help further careers of emerging and established professional artists. For Delaware residents only. Guidelines available after May 1 on website. Accepts inquiries by e-mail, phone. Results announced in December. Winners notified by mail. Results available on website. Deadline: August 1. Prize: $10,000 for masters; $6,000 for established professionals; $3,000 for emerging professionals. Judged by out-of-state, nationally recognized professionals in each artistic discipline.

DIAGRAM CHAPBOOK CONTEST

Department of English, University of Arizona, P.O. Box 210067, Tucson AZ 85721-0067. **E-mail:** nmp@thediagram.com; editor@thediagram.com. **Website:** www.thediagram.com/contest.html. **Contact:** Ander Monson, editor. Contest for prose, poetry, or hybrid manuscript between 18-44 pages. Deadline: April 28. Check website for more details. Prize: $1,000 and publication. Finalist essay also published. Costs: $20. Judged by editor Ander Monson.

DOBIE PAISANO WRITER'S FELLOWSHIP

The Graduate School, The University of Texas at Austin, Attn: Dobie Paisano Program, 110 Inner Campus Drive Stop G0400, Austin TX 78712-0531. (512)232-3609. **Fax:** (512)471-7620. **E-mail:** gbarton@austin.utexas.edu. **Website:** www.utexas.edu/ogs/Paisano. **Contact:** Gwen Barton. Sponsored by the Graduate School at The University of Texas at Austin and the Texas Institute of Letters, the Dobie Paisano Fellowship Program provides solitude, time, and a comfortable place for Texas writers or writers who have written significantly about Texas through fiction, nonfiction, poetry, plays, or other mediums. The Dobie

Paisano Ranch is a very rural and rustic setting, and applicants should read the guidelines closely to insure their ability to reside in this secluded environment. Deadline: January 15. Applications are accepted beginning December 1 and must be post-marked no later than January 15. The Ralph A. Johnston memorial Fellowship is for a period of 4 months with a stipend of $6,250 per month. It is aimed at writers who have already demonstrated some publishing and critical success. The Jesse H. Jones Writing Fellowship is for a period of approximately 6 months with a stipend of $3,000 per month. It is aimed at, but not limited to, writers who are early in their careers. Costs: Application fee: $20 for one fellowship; $30 for both fellowships.

THE JACK DYER FICTION PRIZE

Crab Orchard Review, Department of English, Mail Code 4503, Faner Hall 2380, Southern Illinois University Carbondale, 1000 Faner Drive, Carbondale IL 62901. (618)453-6833. **Fax:** (618)453-8224. **E-mail:** jtribble@siu.edu. **Website:** www.craborchardreview.siu.edu. **Contact:** Jon C. Tribble, managing editor. Estab. 1995 magazine/1997 fiction prize. Annual award for unpublished short fiction. Entries should consist of 1 story up to 6,000 words maximum in length. *Crab Orchard Review* acquires first North American serial rights to all submitted work. One winner and at least 2 finalists will be chosen. Deadline: May 17. Prize: $2,000, publication and 1-year subscription to *Crab Orchard Review*. Finalists are offered $500 and publication. Costs: $15/entry (up to 3 entries); entrants receive copy of the Winter/Spring issue of *Crab Orchard Review*, which will include the winner and finalists of this competition ($14 value; $1 for Submittable service) sent to a U.S. postal address for your first entry and extend your subscription beyond that according to the number of entries you have. Due to the extremely high cost of International Mail and uncertainty of successful delivery, individuals entering from overseas will need to provide a United States postal address to receive a copy of the issue.

MARY KENNEDY EASTHAM FLASH FICTION PRIZE

Category in the Soul-Making Keats Literary Competition, The Webhallow House, 1544 Sweetwood Dr., Broadmoor Village CA 94015-2029. **E-mail:** SoulKeats@gmail.com. **Website:** www.soulmakingcontest.us. **Contact:** Eileen Malone. Keep each story under 500 words. Three stories per entry. One story per page, typed, double-spaced, and unidentified. Deadline: November 30. Prizes: 1st Place: $100; 2nd Place: $50; 3rd Place: $25. Costs: $5.

EATON LITERARY AGENCY'S ANNUAL AWARDS PROGRAM

Eaton Literary Agency, P.O. Box 49795, Sarasota FL 34230-6795. (941)366-6589. **Fax:** (941)365-4679. **E-mail:** eatonlit@aol.com. **Website:** www.eatonliterary.com. **Contact:** Richard Lawrence, President. Estab. 1984. Offered biannually for unpublished mss. Entries must be unpublished. Open to any writer. Guidelines available for SASE, by fax, e-mail, or on website. Accepts inquiries by fax, phone, and e-mail. Results announced in April and September. Winners notified by mail. For contest results, send SASE, fax, e-mail, or visit website. Deadline: March 31 (short story); August 31 (book-length). Prize: $2,500 (book-length); $500 (short story). Judged by an independent agency in conjunction with some members of Eaton's staff.

THE EMILY CONTEST

West Houston RWA, Houston TX **E-mail:** emily.contest@whrwa.com. **Website:** www.whrwa.com. Annual award to promote publication of previously unpublished writers of romance. Open to any writer who has not published in a given category within the past 3 years. The mission of The Emily is to professionally support writers and guide them toward a path to publication. Deadline: October 7. Submission period begins September 1. Prize: $100. Costs: $20 for members of WHRWA, $30 for all others. Final judging done by an editor and an agent.

ETHEL ROHAN NOVEL EXCERPT PRIZE CATEGORY

Soul-Making Keats Literary Competition Category, The Webhallow House, 1544 Sweetwood Dr., Broadmoor Village CA 94015-2029. (650)756-5279. **Fax:** (650)756-5279. **E-mail:** soulkeats@mail.com. **Website:** www.soulmakingcontest.us. **Contact:** Eileen Malone. Open annually to any writer. Ongoing Deadline: November 30. Prize: 1st Place: $100; 2nd Place: $50; 3rd Place: $25. Costs: $5/entry (make checks payable to NLAPW).

FABLERS MONTHLY CONTEST

818 Los Arboles Lane, Santa Fe NM 87501. **Website:** www.fablers.net. **Contact:** W.B. Scott. Monthly contest for previously unpublished writers to help develop amateur writers. Guidelines posted online. No entry

fee. Open to any writer. Deadline: 14th of each month. Prize: $100. Judged by members of website.

☼ THE FAR HORIZONS AWARD FOR SHORT FICTION

The Malahat Review, University of Victoria, P.O. Box 1700, Stn CSC, Victoria BC V8W 2Y2, Canada. (250)721-8524. **Fax:** (250)472-5051. **E-mail:** malahat@uvic.ca. **E-mail:** horizons@uvic.ca. **Website:** www.malahatreview.ca. **Contact:** L'Amour Lisik, Marketing and Circulation Manager. Open to "emerging short fiction writers from Canada, the US, and elsewhere" who have not yet published their fiction in a full-length book (48 pages or more). Deadline: May 1 of odd numbered years. Prize: $1,000 CAD, publication in fall issue of *The Malahat Review*. Announced in fall on website, Facebook page, and in quarterly e-newsletter, *Malahat Lite*. Costs: $25 CAD for Canadian entries, $30 USD for US entries; $35 USD from Mexico and outside North America; includes a 1-year subscription to *The Malahat Review* $15 for additional entries, no limit.

THE VIRGINIA FAULKNER AWARD FOR EXCELLENCE IN WRITING

Prairie Schooner, 123 Andrews Hall, University of Nebraska-Lincoln, Lincoln NE 68588-0334. (402)472-0911. **Fax:** (402)472-1817. **E-mail:** PrairieSchooner@unl.edu. **Website:** www.prairieschooner.unl.edu. **Contact:** Kwame Dawes. Offered annually for work published in *Prairie Schooner* in the previous year. Categories: short stories, essays, novel excerpts, and translations. Prize: $1,000. Judged by editorial board.

THE WILLIAM FAULKNER-WILLIAM WISDOM CREATIVE WRITING COMPETITION

Faulkner - Wisdom Competition, Pirate's Alley Faulkner Society, Inc., The Pirate's Alley Faulkner Society, Inc., 624 Pirate's Alley, New Orleans LA 70116-3233. (504)586-1609. **E-mail:** faulkhouse@aol.com. **Website:** www.wordsandmusic.org. **Contact:** Rosemary James, award director. Estab. 1992. See guidelines posted at www.wordsandmusic.org. Deadline: May 15. Prizes: $750-7,500 depending on category. Costs: Charges $10-40, depending on category for entry fees. Judged by established authors, literary agents, and acquiring editors.

FINELINE COMPETITION FOR PROSE POEMS, SHORT SHORTS, AND ANYTHING IN BETWEEN

Mid-American Review, Dept. of English, Bowling Green State University, Bowling Green OH 43403. (419)372-2725. **E-mail:** mar@bgsu.edu. **Website:** www.bgsu.edu/midamericanreview. **Contact:** Abigail Cloud, editor-in-chief. Offered annually for previously unpublished submissions. Contest open to all writers not associated with current judge or *Mid-American Review*. Deadline: June 1. Prize: $1,000, plus publication in fall issue of *Mid-American Review*; 10 finalists receive notation plus possible publication. Costs: $10 for up to 3 prose poems or short shorts; all participants receive prize issue. Judge will be a contemporary writer of note.

FIRST NOVEL CONTEST

Harrington & Harrington Press, 3400 Yosemite, San Diego CA 92109. **E-mail:** press@harringtonandharrington.com. **Website:** www.harringtonandharrington.com. **Contact:** Laurie Champion, contest/award director. Annual contest for any writer who has not previously published a novel. Entries may be self-published. Accepts full-length works in literary fiction, creative nonfiction, memoir, genre fiction, and short story collections. No poetry. Guidelines available online. Harrington & Harrington Press aims to support writers, and the First Novel Contest will provide many ways to promote authors through networks and connections with writers, artists, and those involved in the technical production of art. Deadline: August 15. Prize: $500 advance royalty and publication by Harrington & Harrington Press. Costs: $20. Judged by the Harrington & Harrington staff for the preliminary round. A respected author with numerous publications will act as the final judge.

FIRSTWRITER.COM INTERNATIONAL SHORT STORY CONTEST

firstwriter.com, , United Kingdom. **Website:** https://www.firstwriter.com/competitions/short_story_contest/. **Contact:** J. Paul Dyson, managing editor. Accepts short stories up to 3,000 words on any subject and in any style. Deadline: April 1. The prize-money for first place is £200 (over $300). Ten special commendations will also be awarded, and all the winners will be published in firstwriter.magazine and receive a voucher that can be used to take out an annual subscription for free. Costs: $9.75 for 1 short story; $17.25

for 2; $22.50 for 3; and $30 for 5. Judged by firstwriter. magazine magazine editors.

🐟 FISH PUBLISHING FLASH FICTION COMPETITION

Durrus, Bantry, County Cork, Ireland. **E-mail:** info@fishpublishing.com. **Website:** www.fishpublishing.com. **Contact:** Clem Cairns. Estab. 2004. Annual prize awarding flash fiction. "This is an opportunity to attempt what is one of the most difficult and rewarding tasks—to create, in a tiny fragment, a completely resolved and compelling story in 300 words or less." Deadline: February 28. First Prize: $1,200. The 10 published authors will receive 5 copies of the Anthology and will be invited to read at the launch during the West Cork Literary Festival in July. Costs: $18. Judged by Nuala O'Connor.

🐟 FISH SHORT STORY PRIZE

Durrus, Bantry Co. Cork, Ireland. **E-mail:** info@fishpublishing.com. **Website:** www.fishpublishing.com. Estab. 1994. Annual worldwide competition to recognize the best short stories. Deadline: November 30. Prize: Overall prize fund: $6,000. 1st prize: $3,750. 2nd Prize: 1 week at Anam Cara Writers Retreat in West Cork and $350. 3rd Prize: $350. Closing date 30th November. The best 10 will be published in the Fish Anthology, launched in July at the West Cork Literary Festival. Winners announced March 17. Costs: $25 online, $27 postal.

FLASHCARD FLASH FICTION CONTEST

Sycamore Review, Department of English, 500 Oval Dr., Purdue University, West Lafayette IN 47907. **E-mail:** sycamore@purdue.edu; sycamorefiction@purdue.edu. **Website:** www.sycamorereview.com/contest/. **Contact:** Kara Krewer, editor-in-chief. Annual contest for unpublished flash fiction. Deadline: February 1.Submissions period begins January 1. Prize: $100, publication online, and publication on a flashcard to be distributed with *Sycamore Review* at AWP. Costs: $5 reading fee.

FOREWORD'S INDIES BOOK OF THE YEAR AWARDS

Foreword Magazine, 425 Boardman Ave, Traverse City MI 49684. (231)933-3699. **Website:** www.forewordreviews.com. **Contact:** Michele Lonoconus. Estab. 1998. Awards offered annually. In order to be eligible, books must have a current year copyright and be independently published which includes university

presses, privately held presses, and self-published authors. International submissions are welcome. Deadline: January 15th. Prize: $1,500 cash will be awarded to a Best Fiction and Best Nonfiction choice. Costs: We offer a $79 Early Bird entry fee for books registered before September 1st. Choose a second (or third, or fourth) category for the same book and the fee drops to $59 for each additional submission.

H.E. FRANCIS SHORT STORY COMPETITION

Ruth Hindman Foundation, University of Alabama in Huntsville, Department of English, Morton Hall Room 222, Huntsville AL 35899. **Website:** www.hefranciscompetition.com. Estab. 1990. Offered annually for unpublished work, not to exceed 5,000 words. Acquires first-time publication rights. Deadline: January 15. Prize: $2,000, publication as an Amazon Kindle Single, an announcement in Poets and Writers, and publication on the website. Costs: $20. Judged by a panel of nationally recognized, award-winning authors, directors of creative writing programs, and editors of literary journals.

SOEURETTE DIEHL FRASER AWARD FOR BEST TRANSLATION OF A BOOK

P.O. Box 609, Round Rock TX 78680. **E-mail:** tilsecretary@yahoo.com. **Website:** http://texasinstituteofletters.org. Offered every 2 years to recognize the best translation of a literary book into English. Translator must have been born in Texas or have lived in the state for at least 2 consecutive years at some time. Deadline: January 10. Prize: $1,000.

☁ FREEFALL SHORT PROSE AND POETRY CONTEST

Freefall Literary Society of Calgary, 922 9th Ave. SE, Calgary AB T2G 0S4, Canada. **E-mail:** editors@freefallmagazine.ca. **Website:** www.freefallmagazine.ca. **Contact:** Ryan Stromquist, managing editor. Offered annually for unpublished work in the categories of poetry (5 poems/entry) and prose (3,000 words or less). Recognizes writers and offers publication credits in a literary magazine format. Contest rules and entry form online. Acquires first Canadian serial rights; ownership reverts to author after one-time publication. Deadline: December 31. Prize: 1st Place: $500 (CAD); 2nd Place: $250 (CAD); 3rd Place: $75; Honorable Mention: $25. All prizes include publication in the spring edition of *FreeFall Magazine*. Winners will also be invited to read at the launch of that issue, if such a launch takes place. Honorable mentions in each category will be published and may be asked to read. Travel expenses not included. Costs: $25. Judged by current guest editor for issue (who are also published authors in Canada).

THE FRENCH-AMERICAN AND THE FLORENCE GOULD FOUNDATIONS TRANSLATION PRIZES

28 W. 44th St., Suite 1420, New York NY 10036. (646)588-6781. **E-mail:** tchareton@frenchamerican.org. **Website:** www.frenchamerican.org. **Contact:** Thibault Chareton. Annual contest to promote French literature in the United States by extending its reach beyond the first language and giving translators and their craft greater visibility among publishers and readers alike. The prize also seeks to increase the visibility of the publishers who bring these important French works of literature, in translation of exceptional quality, to the American market by publicizing the titles and giving more visibility to the books they publish. Deadline: January 15. Prize: $10,000 award. Jury committee made up of translators, writers, and scholars in French literature and culture.

THE GHOST STORY SUPERNATURAL FICTION AWARD

The Ghost Story, P.O. Box 601, Union ME 04862. **E-mail:** editor@theghoststory.com. **Website:** www.theghoststory.com. **Contact:** Paul Guernsey. Estab. 2015. Biannual contest for unpublished fiction. "Ghost stories are welcome, of course—but submissions may involve *any* paranormal or supernatural theme, as well as magic realism. What we're looking for is fine writing, fresh perspectives, and maybe a few surprises in the field of supernatural fiction." Deadline: April 30 and September 30. Winner receives $1,000 and publication. Honorable Mention wins $250 and publication, and Second Honorable Mention is awarded $100 and publication. Costs: $20. Judged by the editors of *The Ghost Story*.

GIVAL PRESS NOVEL AWARD

Gival Press, LLC, P.O. Box 3812, Arlington VA 22203. (703)351-0079. **E-mail:** givalpress@yahoo.com. **Website:** www.givalpress.submittable.com. **Contact:** Robert L. Giron. Estab. 2005. Offered every other year for a previously original unpublished novel (not a translation). Guidelines by phone, on website, via e-mail, or by mail with SASE. Results announced late fall of same year. Winners notified by phone. Results made

available to entrants with SASE, by e-mail, on website. Enter via portal: www.givalpress.submittable.com. Purpose is to award the best literary novel. Deadline: May 30. Prize: $3,000, plus publication of book with a standard contract and author's copies. Costs: $50. Final judge is announced after winner is chosen. Entries read anonymously.

GIVAL PRESS SHORT STORY AWARD

Gival Press, P.O. Box 3812, Arlington VA 22203. (703)351-0079. **E-mail:** givalpress@yahoo.com. **Website:** www.givalpress.submittable.com. **Contact:** Robert L. Giron, publisher. Estab. 2004. Annual literary, short story contest. Entries must be unpublished. Open to anyone who writes original short stories, which are not a chapter of a novel, in English. Receives about 100-150 entries per category. Guidelines available online, via e-mail, or by mail. Results announced in the fall of the same year. Winners notified by phone. Results available with SASE, by e-mail, and on website. Enter via portal: www.givalpress.submittable.com. Recognizes the best literary short story. Deadline: August 8. Prize: $1,000 and publication on website. Costs: $25 entry fee; make checks payable to Gival Press, LLC. Judged anonymously.

✪ JOHN GLASSCO TRANSLATION PRIZE

Literary Translators' Association of Canada, 620-03 Concordia University, 1455 boul. de Maisonneuve Ouest, Montréal QC H3G 1M8, Canada. (514)848-2424, ext. 8702. **E-mail:** info@attlc-ltac.org. **Website:** attlc-ltac.org/john-glassco-translation-prize. **Contact:** Glassco Prize Committee. Estab. 1981. Offered annually for a translator's first book-length literary translation into French or English, published in Canada during the previous calendar year. The translator must be a Canadian citizen or permanent resident. Eligible genres include fiction, creative nonfiction, poetry, and children's books. Deadline: July 31. Prize: $1,000.

GLIMMER TRAIN'S FAMILY MATTERS CONTEST

Glimmer Train, P.O. Box 80430, Portland OR 97280. (503)221-0836. **Fax:** (503)221-0837. **E-mail:** eds@glimmertrain.org. **Website:** www.glimmertrain.org. **Contact:** Susan Burmeister-Brown. Estab. 1990. This contest is now held once a year, during the months of November and December. Winners are contacted on March 1. Submit online at www.glimmertrain.org. Deadline: December 31. Prize: 1st Place: $2,500, publication in *Glimmer Train Stories*, and 10 copies of that issue; 2nd Place: $500 and consideration for publication; 3rd Place: $300 and consideration for publication. Costs: $18/story. The editors judge.

GLIMMER TRAIN'S FICTION OPEN

Glimmer Train, Inc., Glimmer Train Press, Inc., P.O. Box 80430, Portland OR 97280. (503)221-0836. **Fax:** (503)221-0837. **E-mail:** eds@glimmertrain.org. **Website:** www.glimmertrain.org. **Contact:** Susan Burmeister-Brown. Estab. 1990. Submissions to this category generally range from 3,000-8,000 words, but up to 20,000 is fine. Held twice a year: March 1 - April 30 and July 1 - August 31. Submit online at www.glimmertrain.org. Winners will be called 2 months after the close of the contest. Deadline: April 30 and August 31. Prize: 1st Place: $3,000, publication in *Glimmer Train Stories*, and 10 copies of that issue; 2nd Place: $1,000 and consideration for publication; 3rd Place: $600 and consideration for publication. Costs: $21/story. Judged by the editors.

GLIMMER TRAIN'S SHORT-STORY AWARD FOR NEW WRITERS

Glimmer Train Press, Inc., P.O. Box 80430, Portland OR 97280. (503)221-0836. **Fax:** (503)221-0837. **E-mail:** eds@glimmertrain.org. **Website:** www.glimmertrain.org. **Contact:** Susan Burmeister-Brown. Estab. 1990. Offered for any writer whose fiction hasn't appeared in a nationally distributed print publication with a circulation over 5,000. Submissions to this category generally range from 1,000–5,000 words, but up to 12,000 is fine. Held three times a year: January 1–February 28, May 1–June 30, September 1–October 31. Submit online at www.glimmertrain.org. Winners will be called 2 months after the close of the contest. Deadline: February 28, June 30, and October 31. Prize: 1st Place: $2,500, publication in *Glimmer Train Stories*, and 10 copies of that issue; 2nd Place: $500 and consideration for publication; 3rd Place: $300 and consideration for publication. Costs: $18/story.

GLIMMER TRAIN'S VERY SHORT FICTION CONTEST

Glimmer Train Press, Inc., P.O. Box 80430, Portland OR 97280. (503)221-0836. **Fax:** (503)221-0837. **E-mail:** eds@glimmertrain.org. **Website:** www.glimmertrain.org. **Contact:** Susan Burmeister-Brown. Estab. 1990. Offered to encourage the art of the very short story. Word count: 3,000 maximum. Held twice a year: March 1–April 30 and July 1–August 31. Submit on-

line at www.glimmertrain.org. Results announced 2 months after the close of the contest. To encourage the art of the very short story. Deadline: April 30 and August 31. Prize: 1st Place: $2,000, publication in *Glimmer Train Stories*, and 10 copies of that issue; 2nd Place: $500 and consideration for publication; 3rd Place: $300 and consideration for publication. Costs: $16 fee/story. Judged by the editors.

☼ GOVERNOR GENERAL'S LITERARY AWARDS

Canada Council for the Arts, 150 Elgin St., P.O. Box 1047, Ottawa ON K1P 5V8, Canada. (800)263-5588, ext. 5573. **Website:** ggbooks.ca. Estab. 1937. The Canada Council for the Arts provides a wide range of grants and services to professional Canadian artists and art organizations in dance, media arts, music, theatre, writing, publishing, and the visual arts. The Governor General's Literary Awards are given annually for the best English-language and French-language work in each of 7 categories, including fiction, non-fiction, poetry, drama, young people's literature (text), young people's literature (illustrated books), and translation. Deadline: Depends on the book's publication date. See website for details. Prize: Each GG winner receives $25,000. Non-winning finalists receive $1,000. Publishers of the winning titles receive a $3,000 grant for promotional purposes. Evaluated by fellow authors, translators, and illustrators. For each category, a jury makes the final selection.

☼ MARJORIE GRABER-MCINNIS SHORT STORY AWARD

ACT Writers Centre, Gorman House Arts Centre, Ainslie Ave., Braddon ACT 2612, Australia. (61)(2)6262-9191. **Fax:** (61)(2)6262-9191. **E-mail:** admin@actwriters.org.au. **Website:** www.actwriters.org.au. Open theme for a short story with 1,500-3,000 words. Guidelines available on website. Open only to unpublished emerging writers residing within the ACT or region. Deadline: September 18. Submissions period begins in early September. Prize: $600 and publication. Five runners-up receive book prizes. All winners may be published in the ACT Writers Centre newsletter and on the ACT Writers Centre website. Costs: $7.50 for nonmembers; $5 for members.

SUE GRANZELLA HUMOR PRIZE

Category in the Soul-Making Keats Literary Competition, The Webhallow House, 1544 Sweetwood Dr., Broadmoor Village CA 94015-2029. (650)756-5279.

Fax: (650)756-5279. **E-mail:** soulkeats@mail.com. **Website:** www.soulmakingcontest.us. **Contact:** Eileen Malone. Deadline: November 30. Prize: First Place: $100; Second Place: $50; Third Place: $25. Costs: $5. Judged by Sue Granzella.

GREAT LAKES COLLEGES ASSOCIATION NEW WRITERS AWARD

The Great Lakes Colleges Association, 535 W. William St., Suite 301, Ann Arbor MI 48103. (734)661-2350. **Fax:** (734)661-2349. **E-mail:** wegner@glca.org. **Website:** glca.org/program-menu/new-writers-award. **Contact:** Gregory R. Wegner, Director of Program Development: wegner@glca.org.. Estab. 1970. The Great Lakes Colleges Association (GLCA) is a consortium of 13 independent liberal arts colleges in Ohio, Michigan, Indiana, and Pennsylvania. The Award's purpose is to celebrate literary achievement in a writer's first-published volume of fiction, poetry, or nonfiction. Deadline: June 25, 2018. Prize: Honorarium of at least $500 from each member college that invites a winning to give a reading on its campus. Each award winner receives invitations from several of the 13 colleges of the GLCA to visit campus. At these campus events an author will give readings, meet students and faculty, and occasionally visit college classes. In addition to the $500 honorarium for each campus visit, travel costs to colleges are paid by GLCA and its member colleges. Costs: No entry fee. Publisher must submit four copies of the submitted volume to be considered by judges. Judged by professors of literature and writers in residence at GLCA colleges.

GUGGENHEIM FELLOWSHIPS

John Simon Guggenheim Memorial Foundation, 90 Park Ave., New York NY 10016. (212)687-4470. **E-mail:** fellowships@gf.org. **Website:** www.gf.org. Estab. 1925. Often characterized as "midcareer" awards, Guggenheim Fellowships are intended for men and women who have already demonstrated exceptional capacity for productive scholarship or exceptional creative ability in the arts. Fellowships are awarded through two annual competitions: one open to citizens and permanent residents of the United States and Canada, and the other open to citizens and permanent residents of Latin America and the Caribbean. Candidates must apply to the Guggenheim Foundation in order to be considered in either of these competitions. The Foundation receives between 3,500 and 4,000 applications each year. Although no one who applies is guaranteed success in the competition, there is no prescreening: all applications are reviewed. Approximately 200 Fellowships are awarded each year. Deadline: September 15.

LYNDALL HADOW/DONALD STUART SHORT STORY COMPETITION

Fellowship of Australian Writers (WA), P.O. Box 6180, Swanbourne WA 6910, Australia. (61)(8)9384-4771. **Fax:** (61)(8)9384-4854. **E-mail:** fellowshipaustralianwriterswa@gmail.com. **Website:** www.fawwa.org. Annual contest for unpublished short stories (maximum 3,000 words). Reserves the right to publish entries in a FAWWA publication or on website. Guidelines online or for SASE. Deadline: June 1. Submissions period begins April 1. Prize: 1st Place: $1,00; 2nd Place: $300; 3rd Place: $100. Costs: $10/story (maximum of 3).

HAMMETT PRIZE

International Association of Crime Writers, North American Branch, 243 Fifth Avenue, #537, New York NY 10016. **E-mail:** mfrisque@igc.org. **Website:** www.crimewritersna.org.. **Contact:** Mary A. Frisque, executive director, North American Branch. Award for crime novels, story collections, nonfiction by one author. "Our reading committee seeks suggestions from publishers and they also ask the membership for recommendations." Nominations announced in January; winners announced in fall. Winners notified by e-mail or mail and recognized at awards ceremony. For contest results, send SASE or e-mail. Award established to honor a work of literary excellence in the field of crime writing by a US or Canadian author. Deadline: December 15. Prize: Trophy. Judged by a committee of members of the organization. The committee chooses 5 nominated books, which are then sent to 3 outside judges for a final selection. Judges are outside the crime writing field.

WILDA HEARNE FLASH FICTION CONTEST

Big Muddy: A Journal of the Mississippi River Valley, WHFF Contest, Southeast Missouri State University Press, One University Plaza, MS 2650, Cape Girardeau MO 63701. (573) 651-2044. **E-mail:** sswartwout@semo.edu. **Website:** www.semopress.com. **Contact:** Susan Swartwout, publisher. Annual competition for flash fiction, held by Southeast Missouri State University Press. Deadline: October 1. Prize: $500 and publication in *Big Muddy: A Journal of the Mississippi River Valley.* Costs: $15.

DRUE HEINZ LITERATURE PRIZE

University of Pittsburgh Press, 7500 Thomas Blvd., Pittsburgh PA 15260. **Fax:** (412)383-2466. **E-mail:** info@upress.pitt.edu. **Website:** www.upress.pitt.edu. Estab. 1981. Offered annually to writers who have published a book-length collection of fiction or a minimum of 3 short stories or novellas in commercial magazines or literary journals of national distribution. Does not return mss. Deadline: June 30. Open to submissions on May 1. Prize: $15,000. Judged by anonymous nationally known writers such as Robert Penn Warren, Joyce Carol Oates, and Margaret Atwood.

LORIAN HEMINGWAY SHORT STORY COMPETITION

P.O. Box 2011 c/o Cynthia. D. Higgs: Key West Editorial, Key West FL 33045. **E-mail:** shortstorykeywest@hushmail.com. **Website:** www.shortstorycompetition.com. **Contact:** Eva Eliot, editorial assistant. Estab. 1981. Offered annually for unpublished short stories up to 3,500 words. Guidelines available via e-mail, or online. Award to encourage literary excellence and the efforts of writers whose voices have yet to be heard. Deadline: May 15. Prizes: 1st Place: $1,500, plus publication of his or her winning story in *Cutthroat: A Journal of the Arts*; 2nd-3rd Place: $500; honorable mentions will also be awarded. Costs: $15/story postmarked by May 1; $20/story postmarked by May 15. Judged by a panel of writers, editors, and literary scholars selected by author Lorian Hemingway. Lorian Hemingway is the competition's final judge.

TONY HILLERMAN PRIZE

Wordharvest, 1063 Willow Way, Santa Fe NM 87507. (505)471-1565. **E-mail:** wordharvest@wordharvest.com. **Website:** www.wordharvest.com. **Contact:** Anne Hillerman and Jean Schaumberg, co-organizers. Estab. 2006. Awarded annually, and sponsored by St. Martin's Press, for the best first mystery set in the Southwest. Murder or another serious crime or crimes must be at the heart of the story, with the emphasis on the solution rather than the details of the crime. Honors the contributions made by Tony Hillerman to the art and craft of the mystery. Deadline: June 1. Prize: $10,000 advance and publication by St. Martin's Press. Nominees will be selected by judges chosen by the editorial staff of St. Martin's Press, with the assistance of independent judges selected by organizers of the Tony Hillerman Writers Conference

(Wordharvest), and the winner will be chosen by St. Martin's editors.

✎ THE HODDER FELLOWSHIP

Lewis Center for the Arts, 185 Nassau St., Princeton NJ 08544. (609)258-6926. **E-mail:** ysabelg@princeton.edu. **Website:** arts.princeton.edu. **Contact:** Ysabel Gonzalez, fellowships assistant. The Hodder Fellowship will be given to writers of exceptional promise to pursue independent projects at Princeton University during the current academic year. Typically the fellows are poets, playwrights, novelists, creative nonfiction writers and translators who have published one highly acclaimed work and are undertaking a significant new project that might not be possible without the "studious leisure" afforded by the fellowship. Deadline: October 1. Open to applications in July. Prize: $75,000 stipend.

ERIC HOFFER AWARD

Hopewell Publications, LLC, P.O. Box 11, Titusville NJ 08560-0011. **Fax:** (609)964-1718. **E-mail:** info@hopepubs.com. **Website:** www.hofferaward.com. **Contact:** Dawn Shows, EHA Coordinator. Annual contest for previously published books. Recognizes excellence in independent publishing in many unique categories: Art (titles capture the experience, execution, or demonstration of the arts); Poetry (all styles); Chapbook (40 pages or less, artistic assembly); General Fiction (nongenre-specific fiction); Commercial Fiction (genre-specific fiction); Children (titles for young children); Young Adult (titles aimed at the juvenile and teen markets); Culture (titles demonstrating the human or world experience); Memoir (titles relating to personal experience); Business (titles with application to today's business environment and emerging trends); Reference (titles from traditional and emerging reference areas); Home (titles with practical applications to home or home-related issues, including family); Health (titles promoting physical, mental, and emotional well-being); Self-help (titles involving new and emerging topics in self-help); Spiritual (titles involving the mind and spirit, including relgion); Legacy Fiction and Nonfiction (titles over 2 years of age that hold particular relevance to any subject matter or form); E-book Fiction; E-book Nonfiction. Open to any writer of published work within the last 2 years, including categories for older books. This contest recognizes excellence in independent publishing in many unique categories. Also awards the Montaigne Medal for most though-provoking book, the Da Vinci Eye for best cover, and the First Horizon Award for best new authors. Results published in the US Review of Books. Deadline: January 21. Grand Prize: $2,500; honors (winner, runner-up, honorable mentions) in each category, including the Montaigne Medal (most thought-provoking), da Vinci Art (cover art), First Horizon (first book), and Best in Press (small, academic, micro, self-published). Costs: Charges $60; $40 for chapbook.

TOM HOWARD/JOHN H. REID FICTION & ESSAY CONTEST

Winning Writers, 351 Pleasant St., PMB 222, Northampton MA 01060-3961. (866)946-9748. **Fax:** (413)280-0539. **E-mail:** adam@winningwriters.com. **Website:** www.winningwriters.com. **Contact:** Adam Cohen, president. Estab. 1993. Since 2001, Winning Writers has provided expert literary contest information to the public. Sponsors four contests. One of the "101 Best Websites for Writers" (*Writer's Digest*). Open to all writers. Submit any type of short story or essay. Both published and unpublished works are welcome. If you win a prize, requests nonexclusive rights to publish your submission online, in e-mail newsletters, in e-books, and in press releases. Deadline: April 30. Prizes: Two 1st prizes of $2,000 will be awarded, plus 10 honorable mentions of $100 each. Top 12 entries published online. Costs: $20. Judged by Dennis Norris II, assisted by Lauren Singer.

THE JULIA WARD HOWE/BOSTON AUTHORS AWARD

The Boston Authors Club, The Boston Authors Club, 36 Sunhill Lane, Newton Center MA 02459. **E-mail:** bostonauthors@aol.com;. **Website:** www.bostonauthorsclub.org. **Contact:** Alan Lawson. Estab. 1900. This annual award honors Julia Ward Howe and her literary friends who founded the Boston Authors Club in 1900. It also honors the membership over 110 years, consisting of novelists, biographers, historians, governors, senators, philosophers, poets, playwrights, and other luminaries. There are 2 categories: trade books and books for young readers (beginning with chapter books through young adult books). Deadline: January 15. Prize: $1,000. Costs: $25/title. Judged by the members.

HENRY HOYNS & POE/FAULKNER FELLOWSHIPS

Creative Writing Program, 219 Bryan Hall, P.O. Box 400121, University of Virginia, Charlottesville VA 22904-4121. (434)924-6074. **Fax:** (434)924-1478. **E-mail:** creativewriting@virginia.edu. **Website:** creativewriting.virginia.edu. **Contact:** Barbara Moriarty, administrative assistant. Two-year MFA program in poetry and fiction; all students receive fellowships and teaching stipends that total $20,000 in both years of study. Sample poems/prose required with application. Deadline: December 15.

L. RON HUBBARD'S WRITERS OF THE FUTURE CONTEST

Author Services, Inc., 7051 Hollywood Blvd., Los Angeles CA 90028. (323)466-3310. **Fax:** (323)466-6474. **E-mail:** contests@authorservicesinc.com. **Website:** www.writersofthefuture.com. **Contact:** Joni Labaqui, contest director. Estab. 1983. Foremost competition for new and amateur writers of unpublished science fiction or fantasy short stories or novelettes. Offered to find, reward and publicize new speculative fiction writers so they may more easily attain professional writing careers. Open to writers who have not professionally published a novel or short novel, more than 2 novelettes, or more than 3 short stories. Entry stories must be unpublished. Limit 1 entry per quarter. This is an international contest. Results announced quarterly in e-newsletter. Winners notified by phone. Contest has 4 quarters. There shall be 3 cash prizes in each quarter. In addition, at the end of the year, the 4 first-place, quarterly winners will have their entries rejudged, and a grand prize winner shall be determined. Deadline: December 31, March 31, June 30, September 30. Prize (awards quarterly): 1st Place: $1,000; 2nd Place: $750; and 3rd Place: $500. Annual grand prize: $5,000. Costs: No entry fee. Judged by David Farland (initial judge), then by a panel of 4 professional authors.

CAROL OTIS HURST CHILDREN'S BOOK PRIZE

Westfield Athenaeum, 6 Elm St., Westfield MA 01085. (413)568-7833. **Fax:** (413)568-0988. **Website:** www.westath.org. **Contact:** Pamela Weingart. Estab. 2007. The Carol Otis Hurst Children's Book Prize honors outstanding works of fiction and nonfiction, including biography and memoir, written for children and young adults through the age of eighteen that exemplify the highest standards of research, analysis, and authorship in their portrayal of the New England Experience. The prize will be presented annually to an author whose book treats the region's history as broadly conceived to encompass one or more of the following elements: political experience, social development, fine and performing artistic expression, domestic life and arts, transportation and communication, changing technology, military experience at home and abroad, schooling, business and manufacturing, workers and the labor movement, agriculture and its transformation, racial and ethnic diversity, religious life and institutions, immigration and adjustment, sports at all levels, and the evolution of popular entertainment. The public presentation of the prize will be accompanied by a reading and/or talk by the recipient at a mutually agreed upon time during the spring immediately following the publication year. Deadline: December 31. Prize: $500.

INDEPENDENT PUBLISHER BOOK AWARDS

Jenkins Group/Independent Publisher Online, 1129 Woodmere Ave., Ste. B, Traverse City MI 49686. (231)933-0445. **Fax:** (231)933-0448. **E-mail:** jimb@bookpublishing.com. **Website:** www.independentpublisher.com. **Contact:** Jim Barnes. Honors the year's best independently published English language titles from around the world. The IPPY Awards reward those who exhibit the courage, innovation, and creativity to bring about change in the world of publishing. Independent spirit and expertise comes from publishers of all areas and budgets, and they judge books with that in mind. Entries will be accepted in over 80 categories, visit website to see details. Open to any published author. Deadline: Late February. Price of submission rises in September and December. Prize: Gold, silver and bronze medals for each category; foil seals available to all. Costs: $75-$95, based on entry date. Judged by a panel of experts representing the fields of design, writing, bookselling, library, and reviewing.

INDIVIDUAL EXCELLENCE AWARDS

Ohio Arts Council, 30 E. Broad St., 33rd Floor, Columbus OH 43215-2613. (614)466-2613. **E-mail:** olgahelpdesk@oac.state.oh.us. **Website:** www.oac.state.oh.us. The Individual Excellence Awards program recognizes outstanding accomplishments by artists in a variety of disciplines. The awards give the artists who receive them the time and resources to experiment, explore and reflect as they develop their skills and advance their art form. They also provide affirmation and acknowledgment of the excellent work

of Ohio artists. Deadline: September 1. Prize: $5,000. Judged by 3-person panel of out-of-state panelists, anonymous review.

INK & INSIGHTS WRITING CONTEST

Critique My Novel, 1802 S Lincoln, Amarillo TX 79102. **E-mail:** contest@inkandinsights.com. **Website:** https://inkandinsights.com. **Contact:** Catherine York, contest administrator. Estab. 2012. Ink & Insights is a writing contest geared toward strengthening the skills of independent writers by focusing on feedback. Each entry is assigned four judges who specialize in the genre of the manuscript. They read, score, and comment on specific aspects of the segment. The top three mss in the Master and Nonfiction categories move on to the Agent Round and receive a guaranteed read and feedback from a panel of agents. Deadline: May 30 (regular entry), June 30 (late entry). Prize: Prizes vary depending on category. Every novel receives personal feedback from 4 judges. Costs: Early bird entry: $35; Regular entry: $40; Late entry: $45. Judges listed on website, including the agents who will be helping choose the top winners this year.

✪ INTERNATIONAL 3-DAY NOVEL CONTEST

210-111 West Hastings Street, Vancouver BC V6B 1H4, Canada. **E-mail:** info@3daynovel.com. **Website:** www.3daynovel.com. **Contact:** Brittany Huddart, managing editor. Estab. 1977. "Can you produce a masterwork of fiction in three short days? The 3-Day Novel Contest is your chance to find out. Each Labour Day weekend, fueled by adrenaline and the desire for literary nirvana, hundreds of writers step up to the challenge. It's a thrill, a grind, a 72-hour kick in the pants and an awesome creative experience. How many crazed plotlines, coffee-stained pages, pangs of doubt and moments of genius will next year's contest bring forth? And what will you think up under pressure?" Entrants write in whatever setting they wish, in whatever genre they wish, anywhere in the world. Entrants may start writing as of midnight on Friday night, and must stop by midnight on Monday night. Then they print entry and mail it in to the contest for judging. Deadline: Friday before Labor Day weekend. Prize: 1st place receives publication; 2nd place receives $500; 3rd place receives $100. Costs: $55.

INTERNATIONAL LITERACY ASSOCIATION CHILDREN'S AND YOUNG ADULT'S BOOK AWARDS

P.O. Box 8139, 800 Barksdale Rd., Newark DE 19714-8139. (302)731-1600, ext. 221. **E-mail:** kbaughman@reading.org. **E-mail:** committees@reading.org. **Website:** www.literacyworldwide.org. **Contact:** Kathy Baughman. The ILA Children's and Young Adults Book Awards are intended for newly published authors who show unusual promise in the children's and young adults' book field. Awards are given for fiction and nonfiction in each of three categories: primary, intermediate, and young adult. Books from all countries and published in English for the first time during the previous calendar year will be considered. Deadline: January 15. Prize: $1,000.

THE IOWA REVIEW AWARD IN POETRY, FICTION, AND NONFICTION

308 EPB, University of Iowa, Iowa City IA 52242. **E-mail:** iowa-review@uiowa.edu. **Website:** www.iowareview.org. The Iowa Review Award in Poetry, Fiction, and Nonfiction presents $1,500 to each winner in each genre and $750 to runners-up. Winners and runners-up published in The Iowa Review. Deadline: January 31. Submission period begins January 1. Costs: $20. Make checks payable to The Iowa Review. Enclose additional $10 (optional) for year-long subscription. Judged by Joyelle McSweeney, Amy Gray, and Charles D'Ambrosio in 2017.

THE IOWA SHORT FICTION AWARD & JOHN SIMMONS SHORT FICTION AWARD

Iowa Writers' Workshop, 507 N. Clinton St., 102 Dey House, Iowa City IA 52242-1000. **Website:** www.uiowapress.org. **Contact:** James McCoy, director. Annual award to give exposure to promising writers who have not yet published a book of prose. Open to any writer. Current University of Iowa students are not eligible. No application forms are necessary. Announcement of winners made early in year following competition. Winners notified by phone. No application forms are necessary. Do not send original ms. Include SASE for return of ms. Deadline: September 30. Submission period begins August 1. Prize: Publication by University of Iowa Press. Judged by senior Iowa Writers' Workshop members who screen mss; published fiction author of note makes final selections.

JAPAN-U.S. FRIENDSHIP COMMISSION PRIZE FOR THE TRANSLATION OF JAPANESE LITERATURE

Japanese Literary Translation Prize, Donald Keene Center of Japanese Culture, Columbia University, 507 Kent Hall

1140 Amsterdam Ave., New York NY 10027, USA. **Website:** http://www.keenecenter.org/. **Contact:** Yoshiko Niiya, Program Coordinator. Estab. 1979. The Donald Keene Center of Japanese Culture at Columbia University annually awards Japan-U.S. Friendship Commission Prizes for the Translation of Japanese Literature. A prize is given for the best translation of a modern work or a classical work, or the prize is divided between equally distinguished translations. Deadline: June 1. Prize: $6,000.

JERRY JAZZ MUSICIAN NEW SHORT FICTION AWARD

Jerry Jazz Musician, 2207 NE Broadway, Portland OR 97232. **E-mail:** jm@jerryjazz.com. **Website:** www.jerryjazzmusician.com. Three times a year, Jerry Jazz Musician awards a writer who submits the best original, previously unpublished work of approximately 1,000-5,000 words. The winner will be announced via a mailing of the Jerry Jazz newsletter. Publishers, artists, musicians, and interested readers are among those who subscribe to the newsletter. Additionally, the work will be published on the home page of Jerry Jazz Musician and featured there for at least 4 weeks. The Jerry Jazz Musician reader tends to have interests in music, history, literature, art, film, and theater—particularly that of the counter-culture of mid-20th century America. Guidelines available online. Deadline: September, January, and May. See website for specific dates. Prize: $100. Judged by the editors of Jerry Jazz Musician.

JESSE H. JONES AWARD FOR BEST WORK OF FICTION

P.O. Box 609, Round Rock TX 78680. **E-mail:** tilsecretary@yahoo.com. **Website:** http://texasinstituteofletters.org. Offered annually by Texas Institute of Letters for work published January 1-December 31 of year before award is given to recognize the writer of the best book of fiction entered in the competition. Writers must have been born in Texas, have lived in the state for at least 2 consecutive years at some time, or the subject matter of the work should be associated with the state. Deadline: January 10. Prize: $6,000.

JAMES JONES FIRST NOVEL FELLOWSHIP

Wilkes University, Creative Writing Department, Wilkes University, 84 West South Street, Wilkes-Barre PA 18766. (570)408-4547. **Fax:** (570)408-3333. **E-mail:** jamesjonesfirstnovel@wilkes.edu. **Website:** www.wilkes.edu/. Offered annually for unpublished novels (must be works-in-progress). This competition is open to all U.S. citizens who have not previously published novels. The award is intended to honor the spirit of unblinking honesty, determination, and insight into modern culture exemplified by the late James Jones. Deadline: March 15. Submission period begins October 1. Prize: $10,000; 2 runners-up get $1,000 honorarium. Costs: A $30 check/money order, payable to Wilkes University, not to James Jones First Novel Fellowship, must accompany each entry. For online submissions add a $3.00 processing fee.

JUNIPER PRIZE FOR FICTION

University of Massachusetts Press, East Experiment Station, 671 North Pleasant St., Amherst MA 01003. (413)545-2217. **Fax:** (413)545-1226. **E-mail:** info@umpress.umass.edu; kfisk@umpress.umass.edu. **E-mail:** fiction@umpress.umass.edu. **Website:** www.umass.edu/umpress. **Contact:** Karen Fisk, competition coordinator. Estab. 2004. Award to honor and publish outstanding works of literary fiction. Deadline: September 30. Submissions period begins August 1. Winners announced online in April on the press website. Prize: $1,000 cash and publication. Costs: $30.

THE LAWRENCE FOUNDATION AWARD

Prairie Schooner, 123 Andrews Hall, University of Nebraska-Lincoln, Lincoln NE 68588-0334. (402)472-0911. **Fax:** (402)472-9771. **E-mail:** prairieschooner@unl.edu. **Website:** www.prairieschooner.unl.edu. Offered annually for the best short story published in Prairie Schooner in the previous year. Only work published in *Prairie Schooner* in the previous year is considered. Work is nominated by editorial staff. Results announced in the Spring issue. Winners notified by mail in February or March. Prize: $1,000. Judged by editorial staff of *Praire Schooner*.

LAWRENCE FOUNDATION PRIZE

Michigan Quarterly Review, 0576 Rackham Bldg., 915 E. Washington Street, Ann Arbor MI 48109-1070. (734)764-9265. **E-mail:** mqr@umich.edu. **Website:** www.michiganquarterlyreview.com. **Contact:** Vicki Lawrence, managing editor. Estab. 1978. This annual prize is awarded by the *Michigan Quarterly Review* editorial board to the author of the best short story published in *MQR* that year. The prize is sponsored by University of Michigan alumnus and fiction writer Leonard S. Bernstein, a trustee of the Lawrence Foundation of New York. Approximately 20 short stories are published in *MQR* each year. Prize: $1,000. Judged by editorial board.

✪ THE STEPHEN LEACOCK MEMORIAL MEDAL FOR HUMOUR

149 Peter St. N., Orillia ON L3V 4Z4, Canada. (705)326-9286. **E-mail:** bettewalkerca@gmail.com. **Website:** www.leacock.ca. **Contact:** Bette Walker, award committee, Stephen Leacock Associates. The Leacock Associates awards the prestigious Leacock Medal for the best book of literary humor written by a Canadian and published in the current year. The winning author also receives a cash prize of $15,000 thanks to the generous support of the TD Financial Group. 2 runners-up are each awarded a cash prize of $1,500. Deadline: December 31. Prize: $15,000. Costs: $200.

LEAGUE OF UTAH WRITERS CONTEST

The League of Utah Writers, The League of Utah Writers, P.O. Box 64, Lewiston UT 84320. (435)755-7609. **E-mail:** luwcontest@gmail.com; luwriters@gmail.com. **Website:** www.luwriters.org. Open to any writer, the LUW Contest provides authors an opportunity to get their work read and critiqued. Multiple categories are offered; see website for details. Entries must be the original and unpublished work of the author. Winners are announced at the Annual Writers Round-Up in September. Those not present will be notified by e-mail. Deadline: June 15. Submissions period begins March 15. Prize: Cash prizes are awarded. Judged by professional authors and editors from outside the League.

LES FIGUES PRESS NOS BOOK CONTEST

P.O. Box 7736, Los Angeles CA 90007. (323)734-4732. **E-mail:** info@lesfigues.com. **Website:** www.lesfigues.com. **Contact:** Teresa Carmody, director. Les Figues Press creates aesthetic conversations between writers/artists and readers, especially those interested in innovative/experimental/avant-garde work. The Press intends in the most premeditated fashion to champion the trinity of Beauty, Belief, and Bawdry. Deadline: September 15. Prize: $1,000, plus publication by Les Figues Press. Each entry receives LFP book. Costs: $25.

LET'S WRITE LITERARY CONTEST

The Gulf Coast Writers Association, P.O. Box 4808, Biloxi MS 39535. **E-mail:** writerpllevin@gmail.com. **Website:** www.gcwriters.org/contest.html. **Contact:** Philip Levin. The Gulf Coast Writers Association sponsors this nationally recognized contest, which accepts unpublished poems, prose, and short stories from authors all around the US. This is an annual event which has been held for 29 years. Deadline: April 10. Prize: 1st Prize: $80; 2nd Prize: $60; 3rd Prize: $40. Costs: $8 for prose, $8 for 3 poems.

FENIA AND YAAKOV LEVIANT MEMORIAL PRIZE IN YIDDISH STUDIES

Modern Language Association of America, 85 Broad Street, suite 500, New York NY 10004-2434. (646)576-5141. **Fax:** (646)458-0030. **E-mail:** awards@mla.org. **Website:** www.mla.org. **Contact:** Coordinator of book prizes. Offered in even-numbered years for an outstanding English translation of a Yiddish literary work or the publication of a scholarly work. Cultural studies, critical biographies, or edited works in the field of Yiddish folklore or linguistic studies are eligible to compete. See website for details on which they are accepting. Deadline: May 1. Prize: A cash prize, and a certificate, to be presented at the Modern Language Association's annual convention in January.

LITERAL LATTÉ FICTION AWARD

Literal Latté, 200 E. 10th St., Suite 240, New York NY 10003. **E-mail:** litlatte@aol.com. **Website:** www.literal-latte.com. **Contact:** Edward Estlin, contributing editor. Estab. 1994. Award to provide talented writers with 3 essential tools for continued success: money, publication, and recognition. Offered annually for unpublished fiction (maximum 20,000 words). Guidelines online. Open to any writer. Deadline: January 30. Prize: 1st Place: $1,000 and publication in *Literal Latté*; 2nd Place: $300; 3rd Place: $200; also up to 7 honorable mentions. All winners published in *Literal Latté*. Costs: $10 per story; $15 for two.

LITERAL LATTE SHORT SHORTS CONTEST

Literal Latté, 200 E. 10th St., Suite 240, New York NY 10003. **E-mail:** litlatte@aol.com. **Website:** www.literal-latte.com. **Contact:** Jenine Gordon Bockman, editor. Estab. 1994. Keeping free thought free since 1994. Deadline: June 30. Prize: $500. Costs: $10 for up to three shorts. Judged by the editors.

THE HUGH J. LUKE AWARD

Prairie Schooner, 123 Andrews Hall, University of Nebraska-Lincoln, Lincoln NE 68588-0334. (402)472-0911. **Fax:** (402)472-1817. **E-mail:** prairieschooner@unl.edu. **Website:** www.prairieschooner.unl.edu. **Contact:** Kwame Dawes. Offered annually for work published in *Prairie Schooner* in the previous year. Results announced in the Spring issue. Winners notified by mail in February or March. Prize: $250. Judged by editorial staff of *Prairie Schooner*.

THE MARY MACKEY SHORT STORY PRIZE CATEGORY

Soul-Making Keats Literary Competition, The Webhallow House, 1544 Sweetwood Dr., Broadmoor Village CA 94015-2029. (650)756-5279. **Fax:** (650)756-5279. **E-mail:** soulkeats@mail.com. **Website:** www.soulmakingcontest.us. **Contact:** Eileen Malone. Open annually to any writer. Deadline: November 30. Prize: Cash prizes. Costs: $5/entry (make checks payable to NLAPW).

✪ THE MALAHAT REVIEW NOVELLA PRIZE

The Malahat Review, University of Victoria, P.O. Box 1700 STN CSC, Victoria BC V8W 2Y2, Canada. (250)721-8524. **E-mail:** malahat@uvic.ca. **E-mail:** novella@uvic.ca. **Website:** malahatreview.ca. **Contact:** L'Amour Lisik, marketing and circulation manager. Held in alternate (even numbered) years with the Long Poem Prize. Offered to promote unpublished novellas. Obtains first world rights. After publication rights revert to the author. Open to any writer. Deadline: February 1 (even years). Prize: $1,500 CAD and one year's subscription. Winner published in summer issue of *The Malahat Review* and announced on website, Facebook page, and in quarterly e-newsletter, *Malahat Lite*. Costs: $35 CAD for Canadian entrants; $40 US for American entrants; $45 US for entrants from elsewhere (includes a 1-year subscription to *Malahat*). $15 for additional entries, no limit. Three recognized literary figures are assigned to judge the contest each year.

✪ THE MAN BOOKER PRIZE

Four Colman Getty PR, 20 St Thomas Street, London SE1 9BF, United Kingdom. (44)(207)697 4200. **Website:** www.themanbookerprize.com. **Contact:** Four Colman Getty PR. Estab. 1968. Books are only accepted through UK publishers. However, publication outside the UK does not disqualify a book once it is published in the UK. Open to any full-length novel (published October 1-September 30). No novellas, collections of short stories, translations, or self-published books. Open to citizens of the Commonwealth or Republic of Ireland. Deadline: July. Prize: £50,000. Judges appointed by the Booker Prize Management Committee.

🔾 MANITOBA BOOK AWARDS

Manitoba Writers' Guild, c/o Manitoba Writers' Guild, 218-100 Arthur St., Winnipeg MB R3B 1H3, Canada. (204)944-8013. **E-mail:** events@mbwriter.mb.ca. **Website:** www.manitobabookawards.com. **Contact:** Ellen MacDonald. Estab. 1983. The awards honor books written by Manitobans, published in Manitoba or about Manitoba. More than $30,000 in prizes is awarded each year to Manitoba writers. The Manitoba Book Awards celebrates literary excellence, originality and diverse talent. Some of Canada's best writers have springboarded to national and international acclaim after winning the Manitoba Book Awards. Previous winners include: Carol Shields (1993), David Bergen (1993,1996, 2009), Miriam Toews (1998, 2000), Margaret Sweatman (1991, 2001), Sandra Birdsell (1992), Jake MacDonald (2002), Allan Levine (2010), Barbara Huck (2014) and Wab Kinew (2016). The 18 awards to be presented at the 29th annual Manitoba Book Awards include Alexander Kennedy Isbister Award for Non-Fiction/Prix Alexander-Kennedy-Isbister pour les études et les essais, Beatrice Mosionier Aboriginal Writer of the Year Award /Prix Beatrice-Mosionier pour l'écrivain.e autochtone de l'année (English/Français/Indigenous Languages), Carol Shields Winnipeg Book Award/Prix littéraire Carol-Shields de la ville de Winnipeg, The Chris Johnson Award for Best Play by a Manitoba Playwright / Prix Chris-Johnson pour la meilleure pièce par un dramaturge manitobain, Eileen McTavish Sykes Award for Best First Book, John Hirsch Award for Most Promising Manitoba Writer/Prix John-Hirsch pour l'écrivain manitobain le plus prometteur, Lansdowne Prize for Poetry / Prix Lansdowne de poésie, Le Prix Littéraire Rue-Deschambault, Manuela Dias Book Design and Illustration Awards/Prix Manuela—Dias de conception graphique et d'illustration en édition—4 categories, Margaret Laurence Award for Fiction, Mary Scorer Award for Best Book by a Manitoba Publisher/Prix Mary-Scorer pour le meilleur livre par un éditeur du Manitoba, McNally Robinson Books for Young People Awards—2 categories, McNally Robinson Book of the Year Award, and Lifetime Achievement Award—English/Français. Deadline: December 1 and January 15. Prize: Several prizes up to $5,000 (Canadian). Costs: $25 per category. Jurors selected by the Manitoba Writers' Guild.

🌑 MARSH AWARD FOR CHILDREN'S LITERATURE IN TRANSLATION

The English-Speaking Union, Dartmouth House, 37 Charles St., London En W1J 5ED, United Kingdom. 020 7529 1590. **E-mail:** emma.coffey@esu.org. **Website:** www.marshchristiantrust.org; www.esu.org. **Contact:** Emma Coffey, education officer. Estab. 1996. The Marsh Award for Children's Literature in Translation, awarded biennially, was founded to celebrate the best translation of a children's book from a foreign language into English and published in the UK. It aims to spotlight the high quality and diversity of translated fiction for young readers. The Award is administered by the ESU on behalf of the Marsh Christian Trust.

MASS CULTURAL COUNCIL ARTIST FELLOWSHIP PROGRAM

Mass Cultural Council, 10 St. James Ave., 3rd Floor, Boston MA 02116-3803. (617)727-3668. **Fax:** (617)727-0044. **E-mail:** mcc@art.state.ma.us. **Website:** www.massculturalcouncil.org; http://artsake.massculturalcouncil.org. **Contact:** Dan Blask, program officer. Awards in poetry, fiction/creative nonfiction, and dramatic writing (among other discipline categories) are given in recognition of exceptional original work (check website for award amount). Looking to award artistic excellence and creative ability, based on work submitted for review. Judged by independent peer panels composed of artists and arts professionals.

MARY MCCARTHY PRIZE IN SHORT FICTION

Sarabande Books, 2234 Dundee Rd., Suite 200, Louisville KY 40205. (502)458-4028. **Fax:** (502)458-4065. **E-mail:** info@sarabandebooks.org. **Website:** www.sarabandebooks.org. **Contact:** Sarah Gorham, Editor-in-Chief. Annual competition to honor a collection of short stories, novellas, or a short novel. Deadline: February 15. Submission period begins January 1. Prize: $2,000 and publication (standard royalty contract). Costs: $28.

THE MCGINNIS-RITCHIE MEMORIAL AWARD

Southwest Review, Southern Methodist University, P.O. Box 750374, Dallas TX 75275-0374. (214)768-1037. **Fax:** (214)768-1408. **E-mail:** swr@mail.smu.edu. **Website:** www.smu.edu/southwestreview. **Contact:** Greg Brownderville, editor-in-chief. The McGinnis-Ritchie Memorial Award is given annually to the best works of fiction and nonfiction that appeared in the magazine in the previous year. Mss are submitted for publication, not for the prizes themselves. Guidelines for SASE or online. Prize: $500. Judged by Greg Brownderville and Preston Hutcherson.

MCKNIGHT ARTIST FELLOWSHIPS FOR WRITERS, LOFT AWARD(S) IN CHILDREN'S LITERATURE/CREATIVE PROSE/POETRY

The Loft Literary Center, 1011 Washington Ave. S., Suite 200, Open Book, Minneapolis MN 55415. (612)215-2575. **Fax:** (612)215-2576. **E-mail:** loft@loft.org. **Website:** www.loft.org. **Contact:** Bao Phi. "The Loft administers the McKnight Artists Fellowships for Writers. Five $25,000 awards are presented annually to accomplished Minnesota writers and spoken word artists. Four awards alternate annually between creative prose (fiction and creative nonfiction) and poetry/spoken word. The fifth award is presented in children's literature and alternates annually for writing for ages 8 and under and writing for children older than 8." The awards provide the writers the opportunity to focus on their craft for the course of the fellowship year. Prize: $25,000.

MEMPHIS MAGAZINE FICTION CONTEST

Memphis Magazine, co-sponsored by booksellers of Laurelwood and Burke's Book Store, Fiction Contest, c/o *Memphis* magazine, P.O. Box 1738, Memphis TN 38101. (901)521-9000, ext. 451. **Fax:** (901)521-0129. **E-mail:** sadler@memphismagazine.com. **Website:** www.memphismagazine.com. **Contact:** Marilyn Sadler. Annual award for authors of short fiction living within 150 miles of Memphis. Deadline: February 15. Prize: $1,000 grand prize, along with being published in the annual Cultural Issue; two honorable-mention awards of $500 each will be given if the quality of entries warrants. Costs: $20/story.

DAVID NATHAN MEYERSON PRIZE FOR FICTION

Southwest Review, Southern Methodist University, P.O. Box 750374, Dallas TX 75275-0374. (214)768-1037. **Fax:** (214)768-1408. **E-mail:** swr@smu.edu. **Website:** www.smu.edu/southwestreview. **Contact:** Greg Brownderville, editor-in-chief. Annual award given to a writer who has not published a first book of fiction, either a novel or collection of stories. Deadline: May 1 (postmarked). Prize: $1,000 and publication in the *Southwest Review*. Costs: $25/story.

A MIDSUMMER TALE

E-mail: editors@toasted-cheese.com. **Website:** www.toasted-cheese.com. **Contact:** Theryn Fleming, editor. Estab. 2002. A Midsummer Tale is open to non-genre fiction and creative nonfiction. There is a different theme each year. Entries must be unpublished. Accepts inquiries by e-mail. Deadline: June 21. Results announced on July 31. Winners notified by e-mail. List of winners on website. Prize: Amazon gift certificates and publication in Toasted Cheese. Entries are blind-judged by at least one Toasted Cheese editor

MILKWEED NATIONAL FICTION PRIZE

1011 Washington Ave. S., Suite 300, Minneapolis MN 55415. (612)332-3192. **Fax:** (612)215-2550. **E-mail:** editor@milkweed.org. **Website:** www.milkweed.org. **Contact:** Patrick Thoman, editor and program manager. Annual award for unpublished works. Mss should be one of the following: a novel, a collection of short stories, one or more novellas, or a combination of short stories and one or more novellas. Deadline: Rolling submissions. Check website for details of when they're accepting mss. Prize: Publication by Milkweed Editions and a cash advance of $5,000 against royalties, agreed upon in the contractual arrangement negotiated at the time of acceptance. Judged by the editors.

MILKWEED PRIZE FOR CHILDREN'S LITERATURE

Milkweed Editions, 1011 Washington Ave. S., Suite 300, Minneapolis MN 55415. (612)332-3192. **Fax:** (612)215-2550. **E-mail:** editor@milkweed.org. **Website:** www.milkweed.org. Milkweed Editions will award the Milkweed Prize for Children's Literature to the best mss for young readers that Milkweed accepts for publication during the calendar year by a writer not previously published by Milkweed. All mss for young readers submitted for publication by Milkweed are automatically entered into the competition. Recognizes an outstanding literary novel for readers ages 8-13 and encourage writers to turn their attention to readers in this age group. Prize: $10,000 cash prize in addition to a publishing contract negotiated at the time of acceptance. Judged by the editors of Milkweed Editions.

THE MILTON CENTER POSTGRADUATE FELLOWSHIP

3307 Third Ave. W, Seattle WA 98119. **Website:** www.imagejournal.org/milton. **Contact:** Tyler McCabe, director of programs. Award to bring emerging writers of Christian commitment to the Center, where their primary goal is to complete their first book-length manuscript in fiction, poetry or creative nonfiction. Guidelines on website. Open to any writer. Deadline: March 15. Prize: $16,000 stipend. Costs: $25 application fee.

MINNESOTA BOOK AWARDS

The Friends of the Saint Paul Public Library, 1080 Montreal Ave., Suite 2, St. Paul MN 55116. (651)222-3242. **Fax:** (651)222-1988. **E-mail:** mnbookawards@thefriends.org. **Website:** www.mnbookawards.org. Estab. 1988. A year-round program celebrating and honoring Minnesota's best books, culminating in an annual awards ceremony. Recognizes and honors achievement by members of Minnesota's book and book arts community. Deadline: Books should be entered by 5 p.m. on the third Friday in November.

MISSISSIPPI REVIEW PRIZE

Mississippi Review, 118 College Dr., #5144, Hattiesburg MS 39406-0001. (601)266-4321. **Fax:** (601)266-5757. **E-mail:** msreview@usm.edu. **Website:** www.mississippireview.com. Annual contest starting August 1 and running until January 1. Winners and finalists will make up next spring's print issue of the national literary magazine *Mississippi Review*. Each entrant will receive a copy of the prize issue. Deadline: January 1. Prize: $1,000 in fiction and poetry. Costs: $15 mail submission; $16 online submission. Judged by Andrew Malan Milward in fiction, and Angela Ball in poetry.

MONTANA PRIZE IN FICTION

Cutbank Literary Magazine, *CutBank*, University of Montana, English Dept., LA 133, Missoula MT 59812. **E-mail:** editor.cutbank@gmail.com. **Website:** www.cutbankonline.org. **Contact:** Allison Linville, editor-in-chief. The Montana Prize in Fiction seeks to highlight work that showcases an authentic voice, a boldness of form, and a rejection of functional fixedness. Deadline: January 15. Submissions period begins November 9. Prize: $500 and featured in the magazine. Costs: $20. Judged by a guest judge each year.

JENNY MCKEAN MOORE VISITING WRITER

English Department, George Washington University, Rome Hall, 801 22nd St. NW, Suite 760, Washington DC 20052. (202)994-6180. **Fax:** (202)994-7915. **E-mail:** tvmallon@gwu.edu. **Website:** https://english.columbian.gwu.edu/activities-events. **Contact:** Lisa Page, Acting Director of Creative Writing. The position is filled annually, bringing a visiting writer to The George Washington University. During each semester the Writer teaches 1 creative-writing course at the university as well as a community workshop. Seeks someone specializing in a different genre each year—fiction, poetry, creative nonfiction. Annual stipend between $50,000 and $60,000, plus reduced-rent townhouse on campus (not guaranteed). Application deadline: December 12. Annual stipend varies, depending on endowment performance; most recently, stipend was $60,000, plus reduced-rent townhouse (not guaranteed).

THE HOWARD FRANK MOSHER SHORT FICTION PRIZE

Vermont College, 36 College St., Montpelier VT 05602. (802)828-8517. **E-mail:** hungermtn@vcfa.edu. **Website:** www.hungermtn.org. **Contact:** Samantha Kolber, managing editor. Estab. 2002. The Howard Frank Mosher Short Fiction Prize is an annual contest for short fiction. Deadline: March 1 Prize: One first place winner receives $1,000 and publication. Two honorable mentions receive $100 each, and are considered for publication. Costs: $20. Judged by Janet Burroway in 2016 and Caitlyn Horrocks in 2017.

NATIONAL BOOK AWARDS

The National Book Foundation, 90 Broad St., Suite 604, New York NY 10004. (212)685-0261. **E-mail:** nationalbook@nationalbook.org; agall@nationalbook.org. **Website:** www.nationalbook.org. **Contact:** Amy Gall. The National Book Foundation and the National Book Awards celebrate the best of American literature, expand its audience, and enhance the cultural value of great writing in America. The contest offers prizes in 4 categories: fiction, nonfiction, poetry, and young people's literature. Books should be published between December 1 and November 30 of the past year. Deadline: Submit entry form, payment, and a copy of the book by July 1. Prize: $10,000 in each category. Finalists will each receive a prize of $1,000. Costs: $135/title. Judged by a category specific panel of 5 judges for each category.

NATIONAL OUTDOOR BOOK AWARDS

921 S. 8th Ave., Stop 8128, Pocatello ID 83209. (208)282-3912. **E-mail:** wattron@isu.edu. **Website:** www.noba-web.org. **Contact:** Ron Watters. Nine categories: History/biography, outdoor literature, instructional texts, outdoor adventure guides, nature guides, children's books, design/artistic merit, natural history literature, and nature and the environment. Additionally, a special award, the Outdoor Classic Award, is given annually to books which, over a period of time, have proven to be exceptionally valuable works in the outdoor field. Application forms and eligibility requirements are available online. Applications for the Awards program become available in early June. Deadline: August 23. Prize: Winning books are promoted nationally and are entitled to display the National Outdoor Book Award (NOBA) medallion. Costs: $75.

NATIONAL READERS' CHOICE AWARDS

Oklahoma Romance Writers of America (OKRWA), **E-mail:** nrca@okrwa.com. **Website:** www.okrwa.com. **Contact:** Kathy L Wheeler. Estab. 1990. "To provide writers of romance fiction with a competition where their published novels are judged by readers." See the website for categories and descriptions. Additional award for best first book. All entries must have an original copyright date during the current contest year. Entries will be accepted from authors, editors, publishers, agents, readers, whoever wants to fill out the entry form, pay the fee, and supply the books. No limit to the number of entries, but each title may be entered only in one category. Open to any writer published by an RWA approved non-vanity/non-subsidy press. For guidelines, send e-mail or visit website. Deadline: December 1st. Prize: Plaques and finalist certificates awarded at the awards banquet hosted at the Annual National Romance Writers Convention. Costs: $30 per entry, plus $5 for Best First Book Category. Judged by readers.

NATIONAL WRITERS ASSOCIATION NOVEL WRITING CONTEST

The National Writers Association, 10940 S. Parker Rd. #508, Parker CO 80134. **E-mail:** natlwritersassn@hotmail.com. **Website:** www.nationalwriters.com. **Contact:** Sandy Whelchel, director. Open to any genre or category. Contest begins December 1. Open to any writer. Annual contest to help develop creative skills, to recognize and reward outstanding ability, and to increase the opportunity for the marketing and subsequent publication of novel mss. Deadline: April 1. Prize: 1st Place: $500; 2nd Place: $250; 3rd Place: $150. Costs: $35. Judged by editors and agents.

NATIONAL WRITERS ASSOCIATION SHORT STORY CONTEST

10940 S. Parker Rd., #508, Parker CO 80134. **E-mail:** natlwritersassn@hotmail.com. **Website:** www.nationalwriters.com. Estab. 1971. The purpose of the National Writers Assn. Short Story Contest is to encourage the development of creative skills, recognize and reward outstanding ability in the area of short story writing. Prize: 1st Prize: $250; 2nd Prize: $100; 3rd Prize: $50; 4th-10th places will receive a book. 1st-3rd place winners may be asked to grant one-time rights for publication in *Authorship* magazine. Honorable Mentions receive a certificate. Costs: $15. Judging will be based on originality, marketability, research, and reader interest. Copies of the judges evaluation sheets will be sent to entrants furnishing an SASE with their entry.

THE NELLIGAN PRIZE FOR SHORT FICTION

Colorado Review/Center for Literary Publishing, Colorado State University, 9105 Campus Delivery, Dept. of English, Colorado State University, Ft. Collins CO 80523-9105. (970)491-5449. **E-mail:** creview@colostate.edu. **Website:** http://nelliganprize.colostate.edu. **Contact:** Stephanie G'Schwind, editor. Annual competition/award for short stories. Receives approximately 900 stories. All entries are read blind by Colorado Review's editorial staff. Ten to fifteen entries are selected to be sent on to a final, outside judge. Stories must be unpublished and between 10 and 50 pages. "The Nelligan Prize for Short Fiction was established in memory of Liza Nelligan, a writer, editor, and friend of many in Colorado State University's English Department, where she received her master's degree in literature in 1992. By giving an award to the author of an outstanding short story each year, we hope to honor Liza Nelligan's life, her passion for writing, and her love of fiction." Deadline: March 14. Prize: $2,000 and publication of story in *Colorado Review*. Costs: $15, send checks payable to Colorado Review; payment also accepted via our online submission manager link from website. Judged by a different writer each year. 2017 judge is Richard Bausch.

THE NEUTRINO SHORT-SHORT CONTEST

Passages North, Dept. of English, Northern Michigan University, 1401 Presque Isle Ave., Marquette MI 49855. (906)227-1203. **Fax:** (906)227-1096. **E-mail:** passages@nmu.edu. **Website:** www.passagesnorth. com. **Contact:** Jennifer Howard. Offered every 2 years to publish new voices in literary fiction, nonfiction, hybrid-essays and prose poems (maximum 1,000 words). Guidelines available for SASE or online. Deadline: April 15. Submission period begins February 15. Prize: $1,000, and publication for the winner; 2 honorable mentions also published; all entrants receive a copy of *Passages North*. Costs: $15 for up to 3 pieces. Judged by T Fleischmann in 2018.

NEW ENGLAND BOOK AWARDS

1955 Massachusetts Ave., #2, Cambridge MA 02140. (617)547-3642. **Fax:** (617)547-3759. **E-mail:** nan@ neba.org. **Website:** www.newenglandbooks.org/ programs/awards-scholarships/new-england-book-awards/. **Contact:** Nan Sorensen, administrative coordinator. Estab. 1990. All books must be either written by a New England based author or be set in New England. Eligible books must be published between September 1, 2017 and August 31, 2018 in either hardcover or paperback. Submissions made by New England booksellers; publishers. Submit written nominations only; actual books should not be sent. $25 fee per title for non-member submissions. Award is given to a specific title, fiction, non-fiction, children's. The titles must be either about New England, set in New England or by an author residing in the New England. The titles must be hardcover, paperback original or reissue that was published between September 1 and August 31. Entries must be still in print and available. Deadline: June 8. Prize: Winners will receive $250 for literacy to a charity of their choice. Judged by NEIBA membership.

NEW LETTERS LITERARY AWARDS

New Letters, University of Missouri-Kansas City, 5101 Rockhill Rd., Kansas City MO 64110-2499. (816)235-1168. **Fax:** (816)235-2611. **Website:** www.newletters. org/writers-wanted/writing-contests. **Contact:** Ashley Wann. Estab. 1986. Award has 3 categories (fiction, poetry, and creative nonfiction) with 1 winner in each. Offered annually for previously unpublished work. For guidelines, send an SASE to *New Letters*, or

visit http://www.newletters.org/writers-wanted/writing-contests. Deadline: May 18. 1st place: $1,500, plus publication in poetry and fiction category; 1st place: $2,500, plus publication in essay category. Costs: $24 entry fee. Judged by regional writers of prominence and experience. Final judging by someone of national repute. Previous judges include Maxine Kumin, Albert Goldbarth, Charles Simic, and Janet Burroway.

NEW LETTERS PRIZE FOR FICTION

New Letters, University of Missouri-Kansas City, *New Letters* Awards for Writers, UMKC, University House, 5101 Rockhill Rd., Kansas City MO 64110-2499. (816)235-1168. **Fax:** (816)235-2611. **E-mail:** newletters@umkc.edu. **Website:** www.newletters.org/writers-wanted/writing-contests. **Contact:** Ashley Wann. Estab. 1986. Offered annually for the best short story to discover and reward new and upcoming writers. Buys first North American serial rights. Open to any writer. Deadline: May 18. 1st Place: $1,500 and publication in a volume of *New Letters*. Costs: $24 entry fee.

NEW MILLENNIUM AWARDS FOR FICTION, POETRY, AND NONFICTION

New Millennium Writings, 4021 Garden Dr., Knoxville TN 37918. (865)254-4880. **Website:** www.newmillenniumwritings.org. **Contact:** Alexis Williams, Editor and Publisher. Estab. 1996. No restrictions as to style, content or number of submissions. Previously published pieces acceptable if online or under 5,000 print circulation. Simultaneous and multiple submissions welcome. Deadline: Postmarked on or before January 31 for the Winter Awards and July 31 for the Summer Awards. Prize: $1,000 for Best Poem; $1,000 for Best Fiction; $1,000 for Best Nonfiction; $1,000 for Best Short-Short Fiction. Costs: $20.

NEW SOUTH WRITING CONTEST

English Department, Georgia State University, P.O. Box 3970, Atlanta GA 30302-3970. **E-mail:** newsoutheditors@gmail.com. **Website:** newsouthjournal. com/contest. **Contact:** Anna Sandy, editor-in-chief. Offered annually to publish the most promising work of up-and-coming writers of poetry (up to 3 poems) and fiction (9,000 word limit). Rights revert to writer upon publication. Guidelines online. Deadline: March 21. Prize: 1st Place: $1,000 in each category; 2nd Place: $250; and publication to winners. Costs: $15. Judged by Safiya Sinclair in poetry and Alissa Nutting in prose.

NORTH CAROLINA ARTS COUNCIL REGIONAL ARTIST PROJECT GRANTS

North Carolina Arts Council, Dept. of Natural and Cultural Resources, MSC #4632, Raleigh NC 27699-4634. (919)807-6512. **Fax:** (919)807-6532. **E-mail:** david.potorti@ncdcr.gov. **Website:** www.ncarts.org. **Contact:** David Potorti, literature and theater director. See website for contact information for the consortia of local arts councils that distribute these grants. Deadline: Dates vary in fall/spring. Prize: $500-3,000 awarded to writers to pursue projects that further their artistic development. These grants are awarded through consortia of local arts councils. See our website for details.

NORTH CAROLINA WRITERS' FELLOWSHIPS

North Carolina Arts Council, NC Department of Natural and Cultural Resources, North Carolina Arts Council, Mail Service Center #4632, Raleigh NC 27699-4632. (919)807-6512. **E-mail:** david.potorti@ncdcr.gov. **Website:** www.ncarts.org. **Contact:** David Potorti, literature and theater director. The North Carolina Arts Council offers fellowship grants to support writers of fiction, creative non-fiction, poetry, spoken word, playwrighting, screenwriting and literary translation. Offered every even-numbered year to support writers of fiction, creative non-fiction, poetry, spoken word, playwriting, screenwriting and literary translation. See website for guidelines and other eligibility requirements. Deadline: November 1 of even-numbered years. Prize: $10,000 grant. Reviewed by a panel of literature professionals (writers and editors).

NORTHERN CALIFORNIA BOOK AWARDS

Northern California Book Reviewers Association, c/o Poetry Flash, 1450 Fourth St. #4, Berkeley CA 94710. (510)525-5476. **E-mail:** ncbr@poetryflash.org; editor@poetryflash.org. **Website:** www.poetryflash.org. **Contact:** Joyce Jenkins, executive director. Estab. 1981. Annual Northern California Book Award for outstanding book in literature, open to books published in the current calendar year by Northern California authors. NCBR presents annual awards to Bay Area (northern California) authors annually in fiction, nonfiction, poetry and children's literature. Encourages writers and stimulates interest in books and reading. Deadline: December 28. Prize: $100 honorarium and award certificate. Judging by voting members of the Northern California Book Reviewers.

NOVA WRITES COMPETITION FOR UNPUBLISHED MANUSCRIPTS

Writers' Federation of Nova Scotia, 1113 Marginal Rd., Halifax NS B3H 4P7. (902)423-8116. **Fax:** (902)422-0881. **E-mail:** programs@writers.ns.ca. **Website:** www.writers.ns.ca. **Contact:** Robin Spittal, communications and development officer. Estab. 1975. Annual program designed to honor work by unpublished writers in all 4 Atlantic Provinces. Entry is open to writers unpublished in the category of writing they wish to enter. Prizes are presented in the fall of each year. Categories include: short form creative nonfiction, long form creative nonfiction, novel, poetry, short story, and writing for children/young adult novel. Judges return written comments when competition is concluded. Deadline: December 13. Prizes vary based on categories. See website for details. Costs: $35 fee for novel ($30 for WFNS members); $25 fee for all other categories ($20 for WFNS members).

SEAN O'FAOLAIN SHORT STORY COMPETITION

The Munster Literature Centre, Frank O'Connor House, 84 Douglas Street, Cork , Ireland. +353-0214319255. **E-mail:** munsterlit@eircom.net. **Website:** www.munsterlit.ie. **Contact:** Patrick Cotter, artistic director. Purpose is to reward writers of outstanding short stories. Deadline: July 31. Prize: 1st prize €2,000; 2nd prize €500. Four runners-up prizes of €100 (approx $146). All six stories to be published in *Southword Literary Journal*. First-Prize Winner offered week's residency in Anam Cara Artist's Retreat in Ireland. Costs: $20.

FRANK O'CONNOR AWARD FOR SHORT FICTION

descant, Texas Christian University's literary journal, TCU Box 298300, Fort Worth TX 76129. **E-mail:** descant@tcu.edu. **Website:** www.descant.tcu.edu. **Contact:** Matthew Pitt, editor. Offered annually for an outstanding story accepted for publication in the current edition of the journal. Publication retains copyright but will transfer it to the author upon request. Deadline: March 31. Open to submissions September 1. Prize: $500.

THE FLANNERY O'CONNOR AWARD FOR SHORT FICTION

The University of Georgia Press, Main Library, 3rd Floor, 320 S. Jackson St., Athens GA 30602. (706)369-6130. **Fax:** (706)369-6131. **Website:** www.ugapress.org.

Estab. 1981. This competition welcomes short story or novella collections. Stories may have been published singly, but should not have appeared in a book-length collection of the author's own work. Length: 40,000-75,000 words. Deadline: April 1-May 31. 2 winners receive $1,000 and book contracts from the University of Georgia Press. Costs: $25.

OHIOANA BOOK AWARDS

Ohioana Library Association, 274 E. First Ave., Suite 300, Columbus OH 43201-3673. (614)466-3831. **Fax:** (614)728-6974. **E-mail:** ohioana@ohioana.org. **Website:** www.ohioana.org. **Contact:** David Weaver, executive director. Estab. 1942. Offered annually to bring national attention to Ohio authors and their books, published in the last year. (Books can only be considered once.) Categories: Fiction, nonfiction, juvenile, poetry, and books about Ohio or an Ohioan. Deadline: December 31. Prize: $1,000 cash prize, certificate, and glass sculpture. Judged by a jury selected by librarians, book reviewers, writers and other knowledgeable people.

OHIOANA WALTER RUMSEY MARVIN GRANT

Ohioana Library Association, 274 E. First Ave., Suite 300, Columbus OH 43201. (614)466-3831. **Fax:** (614)728-6974. **E-mail:** ohioana@ohioana.org. **Website:** www.ohioana.org. **Contact:** David Weaver, executive director. Award to encourage young, unpublished writers 30 years of age or younger. Competition for short stories or novels in progress. Deadline: January 31 Prize: $1,000.

OKLAHOMA BOOK AWARDS

200 NE 18th St., Oklahoma City OK 73105. (405)521-2502. **Fax:** (405)525-7804. **E-mail:** connie.armstrong@libraries.ok.gov. **Website:** www.odl.state.ok.us/ocb. **Contact:** Connie Armstrong, executive director. Estab. 1989. This award honors Oklahoma writers and books about Oklahoma. Awards are presented to best books in fiction, nonfiction, children's, design and illustration, and poetry books about Oklahoma or books written by an author who was born, is living or has lived in Oklahoma. SASE for award rules and entry forms. Winner will be announced at banquet in Oklahoma City. The Arrell Gibson Lifetime Achievement Award is also presented each year for a body of work. Deadline: January 10. Prize: Awards a medal. Costs: $25. Judging by a panel of 5 people for each category, generally a librarian, a working writer in the genre, booksellers, editors, etc.

ON THE PREMISES CONTEST

On The Premises, LLC, 4323 Gingham Court, Alexandria VA 22310. **E-mail:** questions@onthepremises.com. **Website:** www.onthepremises.com. **Contact:** Tarl Kudrick or Bethany Granger, co-publishers. *On the Premises* aims to promote newer and/or relatively unknown writers who can write creative, compelling stories told in effective, uncluttered, and evocative prose. Each contest challenges writers to produce a great story based on a broad premise that the editors supply as part of the contest. Deadline: Short story contests held twice a year; smaller mini-contests held four times a year; check website for exact dates. Prize: 1st Prize: $220; 2nd Prize: $160; 3rd Prize: $120; Honorable Mentions receive $60. All prize winners are published in *On the Premises* magazine in HTML and PDF format. Costs: There are no fees for entering our contests. Judged by a panel of judges with professional editing and writing experience.

◑ OPEN SEASON AWARDS

The Malahat Review, University of Victoria, P.O. Box 1700, Stn CSC, Victoria BC V8V 2Y2, Canada. (250)721-8524. **Fax:** (250)472-5051. **E-mail:** malahat@uvic.ca. **Website:** www.malahatreview.ca. **Contact:** L'Amour Lisik, publicity manager. The Open Season Awards accepts entries of poetry, fiction, and creative nonfiction. Winners published in spring issue of *Malahat Review* announced in winter on website, facebook page, and in quarterly e-newsletter, *Malahat lite*. Deadline: November 1. Prize: $6,000 over three categories (poetry, fiction, creative nonfiction) and publication in *The Malahat Review* in each category. Costs: $35 CAD for Canadian entries; $40 USD for US entries ($45 USD for entries from Mexico and outside North America). $15 for each additional entry, any genre, no limit to how many times you can send in additional entries. Includes a 1-year subscription to *The Malahat Review*.

OREGON BOOK AWARDS

925 SW Washington St., Portland OR 97205. (503)227-2583. **Fax:** (503)241-4256. **E-mail:** la@literary-arts.org. **Website:** www.literary-arts.org. **Contact:** Susan Denning, director of programs and events. The annual Oregon Book Awards celebrate Oregon authors in the areas of poetry, fiction, nonfiction, drama and young readers' literature published between August

1 and July 31 of the previous calendar year. Awards are available for every category. See website for details. Deadline: August 26. Prize: Grant of $2,500. (Grant money could vary.) Judged by writers who are selected from outside Oregon for their expertise in a genre. Past judges include Mark Doty, Colson Whitehead and Kim Barnes.

OREGON LITERARY FELLOWSHIPS

925 S.W. Washington, Portland OR 97205. (503)227-2583. **E-mail:** susan@literary-arts.org. **Website:** www.literary-arts.org. **Contact:** Susan Moore, Director of programs and events. Oregon Literary Fellowships are intended to help Oregon writers initiate, develop, or complete literary projects in poetry, fiction, literary nonfiction, drama, and young readers literature. Writers in the early stages of their career are encouraged to apply. The awards are merit-based. Deadline: Last Friday in June. Prize: $3,000 minimum award, for approximately 8 writers and 2 publishers. Judged by out-of-state writers

KENNETH PATCHEN AWARD FOR THE INNOVATIVE NOVEL

Eckhard Gerdes Publishing, 1110 Varsity Blvd., Apt. 221, DeKalb IL 60115. **E-mail:** egerdes@experimentalfiction.com. **Website:** www.experimentalfiction.com. **Contact:** Eckhard Gerdes. This award will honor the most innovative novel submitted during the previous calendar year. Kenneth Patchen is celebrated for being among the greatest innovators of American fiction, incorporating strategies of concretism, asemic writing, digression, and verbal juxtaposition into his writing long before such strategies were popularized during the height of American postmodernist experimentation in the 1970s. Deadline: All submissions must be postmarked between January 1 and July 31. Prize: $1,000 and 20 complimentary copies. Costs: $25 entry fee. Judged by novelist Dominic Ward.

THE PATERSON FICTION PRIZE

The Poetry Center at Passaic Community College, One College Blvd., Paterson NJ 07505. (973)684-6555. **Fax:** (973)523-6085. **E-mail:** mgillan@pccc.edu. **Website:** www.pccc.edu/poetry. **Contact:** Maria Mazziotti Gillan, executive director. Offered annually for a novel or collection of short fiction published the previous calendar year. For more information, visit the website or send SASE. Deadline: February 1. Prize: $1,000.

JUDITH SIEGEL PEARSON AWARD

Judith Siegel Pearson Award, c/o Department of English, Wayne State University, Attn: Royanne Smith, 5057 Woodward Ave., Ste. 9408, Detroit MI 48202. **E-mail:** fm8146@wayne.edu. **Website:** https://wsuwritingawards.submittable.com/submit. **Contact:** Donovan Hohn. Offers an annual award for the best creative or scholarly work on a subject concerning women. The type of work accepted rotates each year: nonfiction in 2018; fiction in 2019; drama in 2020, poetry in 2021. Open to all interested writers and scholars. Only submit the appropriate genre in each year. Deadline: February 22. Prize: $500. Judged by members of the writing faculty of the Wayne State University English Department.

WILLIAM PEDEN PRIZE IN FICTION

The Missouri Review, 357 McReynolds Hall, Columbia MO 65211. (573)882-4474. **Fax:** (573)884-4671. **E-mail:** mutmrcontestquestion@moreview.com. **Website:** www.missourireview.com. **Contact:** Michael Nye, managing editor. Offered annually for the best story published in the past volume year of the magazine. All stories published in *The Missouri Review* are automatically considered. Guidelines online or for SASE. Prize: $1,000 and a reading/reception.

PEN CENTER USA LITERARY AWARDS

PEN Center USA, P.O. Box 6037, Beverly Hills CA 90212. (323)424-4939. **E-mail:** awards@penusa.org. **E-mail:** awards@penusa.org. **Website:** www.penusa.org. Offered for work published or produced in the previous calendar year. Open to writers living west of the Mississippi River. Award categories: fiction, poetry, research nonfiction, creative nonfiction, translation, young adult, graphic literature, drama, screenplay, teleplay, journalism. Deadline: See website for details. Prize: $1,000. Costs: $35 entry fee per submission.

PEN/FAULKNER AWARDS FOR FICTION

PEN/Faulkner Foundation, 201 E. Capitol St. SE, Washington DC 20003. (202)898-9063. **E-mail:** awards@penfaulkner.org. **Website:** www.penfaulkner.org. **Contact:** Emma Snyder, executive director. Offered annually for best book-length work of fiction by an American citizen published in a calendar year. Deadline: October 31. Prize: $15,000 (one Winner); $5,000 (4 Finalists).

PENGUIN RANDOM HOUSE CREATIVE WRITING AWARDS

One Scholarship Way, P.O. Box 297, St. Peter MN 56082. (212)782-9348. **Fax:** (212) 782-5157. **E-mail:** creativewriting@penguinrandomhouse.com. **Website:** www.penguinrandomhouse.com/creativewriting. **Contact:** Melanie Fallon Hauska, director. Offered annually for unpublished work to NYC public high school seniors. 72 awards given in literary and nonliterary categories. Four categories: poetry, fiction/drama, personal essay, and graphic novel. Applicants must be seniors (under age 21) at a New York high school. No college essays or class assignments will be accepted. Deadline: February 3 for all categories. Graphic Novel extended deadline: March 1st. Prize: Awards range from $500-10,000. The program usually awards just under $100,000 in scholarships.

PHOEBE WINTER FICTION CONTEST

Phoebe, MSN 2D6, George Mason University, 4400 University Dr., Fairfax VA 22030. (703)993-2915. **E-mail:** phoebe@gmu.edu. **Website:** http://www.phoebejournal.com/. Offered annually for an unpublished story (25 pages maximum). Guidelines online or for SASE. First serial rights if work is accepted for publication. Purpose is to recognize new and exciting fiction. Deadline: March 19. Prize: $400 and publication in the Spring online issue. Costs: $9. Judged by a recognized fiction writer, hired by *Phoebe* (changes each year). For 2016, the fiction judge will be Patricia Park.

THE PINCH LITERARY AWARDS

Literary Awards, The Pinch, Department of English, The University of Memphis, Memphis TN 38152-6176. (901)678-4591. **Website:** www.pinchjournal.com. Offered annually for unpublished short stories of 5,000 words maximum or up to three poems. Guidelines on website. Cost: $20, which is put toward one issue of *The Pinch*. Deadline: March 15. Prize: 1st place Fiction: $1,500 and publication; 1st place Poetry: $1,000 and publication. Offered annually for unpublished short stories and prose of up to 5,000 words and 1-3 poems. Deadline: March 15. Open to submissions on December 15. Prizes: $1,000 for 1st place in each category. Costs: $20 for initial entry, $10 each for subsequent entries.

PNWA LITERARY CONTEST

Pacifc Northwest Writers Association, PMB 2717, 1420 NW Gilman Blvd., Suite 2, Issaquah WA 98027. (452)673-2665. **Fax:** (452)961-0768. **E-mail:** pnwa@pnwa.org. **Website:** www.pnwa.org. Annual literary contest with 12 different categories. See website for details and specific guidelines. Each entry receives 2 critiques. Winners announced at the PNWA Summer Conference, held annually in mid-July. Deadline: February 20. Prize: 1st Place: $600; 2nd Place: $300; 3rd Place: $100. Costs: $35 for PNWA members; $50 for non-members. Judged by an agent or editor attending the conference.

POCKETS FICTION-WRITING CONTEST

P.O. Box 340004, Nashville TN 37203-0004. (615)340-7333. **Fax:** (615)340-7267. **E-mail:** pockets@upperroom.org. **Website:** www.pockets.upperroom.org. **Contact:** Lynn W. Gilliam, senior editor. Designed for 6- to 12-year-olds, *Pockets* magazine offers wholesome devotional readings that teach about God's love and presence in life. The content includes fiction, scripture stories, puzzles and games, poems, recipes, colorful pictures, activities, and scripture readings. Freelance submissions of stories, poems, recipes, puzzles and games, and activities are welcome. The primary purpose of *Pockets* is to help children grow in their relationship with God and to claim the good news of the gospel of Jesus Christ by applying it to their daily lives. *Pockets* espouses respect for all human beings and for God's creation. It regards a child's faith journey as an integral part of all of life and sees prayer as undergirding that journey. Deadline: August 15. Submission period begins March 15. Prize: $500 and publication in magazine.

EDGAR ALLAN POE AWARD

1140 Broadway, Suite 1507, New York NY 10001. (212)888-8171. **E-mail:** mwa@mysterywriters.org. **Website:** www.mysterywriters.org. Estab. 1945. Mystery Writers of America is the leading association for professional crime writers in the United States. Members of MWA include most major writers of crime fiction and nonfiction, as well as screenwriters, dramatists, editors, publishers, and other professionals in the field. Purpose of the award: Honor authors of distinguished works in the mystery field. Previously published submissions only. Submissions should be made by the publisher. Work must be published/produced the year of the contest. Deadline: November 30. Prize: Awards ceramic bust of "Edgar" for winner; certificates for all nominees. Judged by active status members of Mystery Writers of America (writers).

THE KATHERINE ANNE PORTER PRIZE FOR FICTION

Nimrod International Journal, The University of Tulsa, 800 S. Tucker Dr., Tulsa OK 74104. (918)631-3080. **Fax:** (918)631-3033. **E-mail:** nimrod@utulsa.edu. **Website:** www.utulsa.edu/nimrod. **Contact:** Eilis O'Neal. Estab. 1978. Postmark Deadline: April 30. Prizes: 1st Place: $2,000 and publication; 2nd Place: $1,000 and publication. Costs: $20, includes a 1-year subscription (2 issues) to *Nimrod*; make checks payable to *Nimrod*. Judged by the *Nimrod* editors, who select the finalists, and a recognized author, who selects the winners.

KATHERINE ANNE PORTER PRIZE IN SHORT FICTION

The University of North Texas Press, 1155 Union Cir., #311336, Denton TX 76203-5017. (940)565-2142. **Fax:** (940)565-4590. **Website:** web3.unt.edu/untpress. **Contact:** Laura Kopchick, editor, University of Texas at Arlington. Contest is offered annually. Prize is awarded to a collection of short fiction. The University of North Texas Press announces the 2012 Katherine Anne Porter Prize in Short Fiction. Entries will be judged by an eminent writer. Entries can be a combination of short-shorts, short stories, and novellas, from 100 to 200 book pages in length (word count between 27,500 and 50,000). Material should be previously unpublished in book form. Once a winner is declared and contracted for publication, UNT Press will hold the rights to the stories in the winning collection. They may no longer be under consideration for serial publication elsewhere and must be withdrawn by the author from consideration. Please include two cover sheets: one with title only, and one with title, your name, address, e-mail, phone, and acknowledgment of any previously published material. Your name should not appear anywhere on the ms except on the one cover page. The winning manuscript will be announced in January 2012. Manuscripts cannot be returned and must be accompanied by a $25 entry fee (payable to UNT Press) and a letter-sized SASE for notification. Costs: $25.

PRAIRIE SCHOONER BOOK PRIZE

Prairie Schooner and the University of Nebraska Press, Prairie Schooner Prize Series, 123 Andrews Hall, Lincoln NE 68588-0334. (402)472-0911. **E-mail:** PSBookPrize@unl.edu. **Website:** prairieschooner.unl.edu. **Contact:** Kwame Dawes, editor. Annual competition/ award for poetry and short story collections. Deadline: March 15. Prize: $3,000 and publication through the University of Nebraska Press. Costs: $25.

PRAIRIE SCHOONER GLENNA LUSCHEI AWARDS

201 Andrews Hall, P.O. Box 880334, Lincoln NE 68588-0334. (402)472-0911. **Fax:** (402)472-9771. **E-mail:** jengelhardt2@unl.edu. **Contact:** Hilda Raz, editor-in-chief. Awards to honor work published the previous year in Prairie Schooner, including poetry, essays and fiction. Prize: $250 in each category. Judged by editorial staff of Prairie Schooner. No entry fee. For guidelines, send SASE or visit website. "Only work published in Prairie Schooner in the previous year is considered." Work nominated by the editorial staff. Results announced in the Spring issue. Winners notified by mail in February or March.

PRESS 53 AWARD FOR SHORT FICTION

Press 53, 560 N. Trade St., Suite 103, Winston-Salem NC 27101. (336)770-5353. **E-mail:** kevin@press53.com. **Website:** www.press53.com. **Contact:** Kevin Morgan Watson, Publisher. Estab. 2014. Awarded to an outstanding, unpublished collection of short stories. Deadline: December 31. Submission period begins September 1. Finalists and winner announced no later than May 1. Publication in October. Prize: Publication of winning short story collection, $1,500 cash advance and 10 copies of the book. Costs: $30 via Submittable or by mail. Judged by Press 53 publisher Kevin Morgan Watson.

PRIME NUMBER MAGAZINE AWARDS

Press 53, 560 N. Trade St., Suite 103, Winston-Salem NC 27101. (336)770-5353. **Fax:** N/A. **E-mail:** kevin@press53.com. **Website:** www.press53.com. **Contact:** Kevin Morgan Watson, Publisher. Awards $1,000 in poetry and short fiction. Deadline: April 15. Submission period begins January 1. Finalists and winners announced by August 1. Winners published in Prime Number Magazine in October. Prize: $1,000 cash. All winners receive publication in Prime Number Magazine online. Costs: $15 via Submittable. Judged by industry professionals to be named when the contest begins.

○ PRISM INTERNATIONAL ANNUAL SHORT FICTION, POETRY, AND CREATIVE NONFICTION CONTESTS

PRISM International, Creative Writing Program, UBC, Buch. E462, 1866 Main Mall, Vancouver BC

V6T 1Z1, Canada. **E-mail:** promotions@prismmagazine.ca. **Website:** www.prismmagazine.ca. **Contact:** Claire Matthews. Estab. 1959. Offered annually for unpublished work to award the best in contemporary fiction, poetry, drama, translation, and nonfiction. Works of translation are eligible. Guidelines are available on website. Acquires first North American serial rights upon publication, and limited web rights for pieces selected for website. Open to any writer except students and faculty in the Creative Writing Department at UBC, or people who have taken a creative writing course at UBC within 2 years of the contest deadline. Entry includes subscription. Deadlines: Creative Nonfiction: July 15; Fiction: January 15; Poetry: October 15. Prize: All grand prizes are $1,500, $600 for first runner up, and $400 for second runner up. Winners are published. Costs: $35 Canadian entries, $40 US entries, and $45 International entries; $5 each additional entry. Entries accepted via Submittable at http://prisminternational.submittable.com/submit or by mail.

☺ PRISM INTERNATIONAL ANNUAL SHORT FICTION CONTEST

Creative Writing Program, UBC, Buch. E462 - 1866 Main Mall, Vancouver BC V6T 1Z1, Canada. (604)822-2514. **Fax:** (604)822-3616. **Website:** prismmagazine.ca/contests. **Contact:** Jessica Johns, executive editor, promotions. Offered annually for unpublished work to award the best in contemporary fiction. Works of translation are eligible. Guidelines by SASE, by e-mail, or on website. Acquires first North American serial rights upon publication, and rights to publish online for promotional or archival purposes. Open to any writer except students and faculty in the Creative Writing Department at UBC, or people who have taken a creative writing course at UBC with the 2 years prior to the contest deadline. Deadline: January 31. Prize: 1st Place: $1,500; 1st Runner-up: $600; 2nd Runner-up: $400; winner is published. Costs: $35 CAD entries; $40 US entries; $45 international entries; $5 each additional entry (outside Canada, pay US currency); includes subscription.

PURPLE DRAGONFLY BOOK AWARDS

Story Monsters LLC, 4696 W Tyson St, Chandler AZ 85226-2903. (480)940-8182. **Fax:** (480)940-8787. **E-mail:** linda@storymonsters.com. **Website:** www. dragonflybookawards.com. **Contact:** Cristy Bertini, contest coordinator. The Purple Dragonfly Book Awards are designed with children in mind. Awards are divided into 54 distinct subject categories, ranging from books on the environment and cooking to sports and family issues. The Purple Dragonfly Book Awards are geared toward stories that appeal to children of all ages. We now offer new Marketing/Promotion Categories: Book Trailer, Bookmark, Flyer, Media Kit, and Press Release. Deadline: May 1. The grand prize winner will receive a $500 cash prize, a certificate commemorating their accomplishment, 100 Grand Prize seals, a one-hour marketing consulting session with Linda F. Radke, a news release announcing the winners sent to a comprehensive list of media outlets, and a listing on the Dragonfly Book Awards website. All first-place winners of categories will be put into a drawing for a $100 prize. In addition, each first-place winner in each category receives a certificate commemorating their accomplishment, 25 foil award seals, and mention on Dragonfly Book Awards website. All winners receive certificates and are listed in Story Monsters Ink magazine. Costs: Early bird pricing: $60/category before March 1. Fee is $65/category after March 1. Judged by industry experts with specific knowledge about the categories over which they preside.

PUSHCART PRIZE

Pushcart Press, P.O. Box 380, Wainscott NY 11975. (631)324-9300. **Website:** www.pushcartprize.com. **Contact:** Bill Henderson. Estab. 1976. Published every year since 1976, The Pushcart Prize - Best of the Small Presses series "is the most honored literary project in America. Hundreds of presses and thousands of writers of short stories, poetry and essays have been represented in the pages of our annual collections." Little magazine and small book press editors (print or online) may make up to six nominations from their year's publicatoins by the deadline. The nominations may be any combination of poetry, short fiction, essays or literary whatnot. Editors may nominate self-contained portions of books — for instance, a chapter from a novel. Deadline: December 1.

☺ QUEBEC WRITERS' FEDERATION BOOK AWARDS

1200 Atwater, Westmount QC H3Z 1X4, Canada. (514)933-0878. **Website:** www.Qwf.org. Award "to honor excellence in writing in English in Quebec." Prize: $2,000 (Canadian) in each category. Categories: fiction, poetry, nonfiction, first book, translation, and children's and young adult. Each prize judged by panel of 3 jurors, different each year. $20 entry fee. Guidelines for submissions sent to Canadian publishers and posted on website in March. Accepts inquiries by e-mail. Deadline: May 31, August 15. Entries must be previously published. Length: must be more than 48 pages. "Writer must have resided in Quebec for 3 of the previous 5 years." Books may be published anywhere. Winners announced in November at Annual Awards Gala and posted on website.

✪ THOMAS H. RADDALL ATLANTIC FICTION AWARD

Writers' Federation of Nova Scotia, 1113 Marginal Rd., Halifax NS B3H 4P7, Canada. (902)423-8116. **Fax:** (902)422-0881. **E-mail:** director@writers.ns.ca. **Website:** www.writers.ns.ca. **Contact:** Marilyn Smulders, executive director. Estab. 1990. The Thomas Head Raddall Atlantic Fiction Award is awarded for a novel or a book of short fiction by a full-time resident of Atlantic Canada. Deadline: First Friday in December. Prize: Valued at $25,000 for winning title.

DAVID RAFFELOCK AWARD FOR PUBLISHING EXCELLENCE

National Writers Association, 10940 S. Parker Rd., #508, Parker CO 80134. **E-mail:** natlwritersassn@hotmail.com. **Website:** www.nationalwriters.com. **Contact:** Sandy Whelchel. Contest is offered annually for books published the previous year. Published works only. Open to any writer. Guidelines for SASE, by e-mail, or on website. Winners will be notified by mail or phone. List of winners available for SASE or visit website. Purpose is to assist published authors in marketing their works and to reward outstanding published works. Deadline: May 15. Prize: Publicity tour, including airfare, valued at $5,000. Costs: $100.

✪ THE RBC BRONWEN WALLACE AWARD FOR EMERGING WRITERS

The Writers' Trust of Canada, 460 Richmond St. W., Suite 600, Toronto ON M5C 1P1, Canada. (416)504-8222. **Fax:** (416)504-9090. **E-mail:** info@writerstrust.com. **Website:** www.writerstrust.com. **Contact:** Amanda Hopkins. Presented annually to a Canadian writer under the age of 35 who is not yet published in book form. The award, which alternates each year between poetry and short fiction, was established in memory of Bronwen Wallace. Deadline: March 5. Prize: $10,000. Two finalists receive $2,500 each.

◐ THE RED HOUSE CHILDREN'S BOOK AWARD

Red House Children's Book Award, 123 Frederick Road, Cheam, Sutton, Surrey SM1 2HT, United Kingdom. **E-mail:** info@rhcba.co.uk. **Website:** www.redhousechildrensbookaward.co.uk. **Contact:** Sinead Kromer, national coordinator. Estab. 1980. The Red House Children's Book Award is the only national book award that is entirely voted for by children. A shortlist is drawn up from children's nominations and any child can then vote for the winner of the three categories: Books for Younger Children, Books for Younger Readers and Books for Older Readers. The book with the most votes is then crowned the winner of the Red House Children's Book Award. Deadline: December 31.

RHODE ISLAND ARTIST FELLOWSHIPS AND INDIVIDUAL PROJECT GRANTS

Rhode Island State Council on the Arts, State of Rhode Island, One Capitol Hill, 3rd Floor, Providence RI 02908. (401)222-3880. **Fax:** (401)222-3018. **E-mail:** Cristina.DiChiera@arts.ri.gov. **Website:** www.arts.ri.gov. **Contact:** Cristina DiChiera, director of individual artist programs. Annual fellowship competition is based upon panel review of poetry, fiction, and playwriting/screenwriting manuscripts. Project grants provide funds for community-based arts projects. Rhode Island artists who have lived in the state for at least 12 consecutive months may apply without a nonprofit sponsor. Applicants for all RSCA grant and award programs must be at least 18 years old and not currently enrolled in an arts-related degree program. Online application and guidelines can be found at www.arts.ri.gov/grants/guidelines/. Deadline: April 1 and October 1. Fellowship awards: $5,000 and $1,000. Grants range from $500-5,000, with an average of around $1,500. Judged by a rotating panel of artists.

HAROLD U. RIBALOW PRIZE

Hadassah Magazine, Hadassah WZOA, 40 Wall St., 8th Floor, New York NY 10005. (212)451-6286. **Fax:** (212)451-6257. **E-mail:** magtemp3@hadassah.org. **Website:** www.hadassahmagazine.org. **Contact:** Deb Meisels, coordinator. Offered annually for English-language (no translation) books of fiction (novel or short stories) on a Jewish theme published the previous year. Books should be submitted by the publisher. Administered annually by *Hadassah Magazine*. Deadline: April 15. The official announcement of the winner will be made in the fall.

○ THE ROGERS WRITERS' TRUST FICTION PRIZE

The Writers' Trust of Canada, 460 Richmond St. W., Suite 600, Toronto ON M5V 1Y1, Canada. (416)504-8222. **Fax:** (416)504-9090. **E-mail:** info@writerstrust.com. **Website:** www.writerstrust.com. **Contact:** Amanda Hopkins. Awarded annually to the best novel or short story collection published within the previous year. Presented at the Writers' Trust Awards event held in Toronto each fall. Open to Canadian citizens and permanent residents only. Deadline: July 18. Prize: $50,000 and $5,000 to 4 finalists.

LOIS ROTH AWARD

Modern Language Association, 85 Broad Street, suite 500, New York NY 10004-2434. (646)576-5141. **Fax:** (646)458-0030. **E-mail:** awards@mla.org. **Website:** www.mla.org. Offered in odd-numbered years for an outstanding translation into English of a book-length literary work. Translators need not be members of the MLA. Deadline: April 1. Prize: A cash award and a certificate to be presented at the Modern Language Association's annual convention in January.

ERNEST SANDEEN PRIZE IN POETRY AND THE RICHARD SULLIVAN PRIZE IN SHORT FICTION

University of Notre Dame, Dept. of English, 356 O'Shaughnessy Hall, Notre Dame IN 46556-5639. (574)631-7526. **Fax:** (574)631-4795. **E-mail:** creativewriting@nd.edu. **Website:** http://english.nd.edu/creative-writing/publications/sandeen-sullivan-prizes. **Contact:** Director of Creative Writing. Estab. 1994. The Sandeen & Sullivan Prizes in Poetry and Short Fiction is awarded to the author who has published at least one volume of short fiction or one volume of poetry. Awarded biannually, but judged quadrennially. Submissions Period: May 1 - September 1. Prize: $1,000, a $500 award and a $500 advance against royalties from the Notre Dame Press. Costs: $15.

SANTA FE WRITERS PROJECT LITERARY AWARDS PROGRAM

Santa Fe Writers Project, 369 Montezuma Ave., #350, Santa Fe NM 87501. **E-mail:** info@sfwp.com. **Website:** www.sfwp.com. **Contact:** Andrew Gifford. Estab. 1998. Annual contest seeking fiction and nonfiction of any genre. The Literary Awards Program was founded by a group of authors to offer recognition

for excellence in writing in a time of declining support for writers and the craft of literature. Past judges have included Richard Currey, Jayne Anne Phillips, Chris Offutt, Emily St. John Mandel, and David Morrell. Deadline: July 20th. Prize: $3,300 and publication. Costs: $30. Judged by Benjamin Percy and Mat Johnson in 2017.

○ SASKATCHEWAN BOOK AWARDS

315-1102 8th Ave., Regina SK S4R 1C9, Canada. (306)569-1585. **E-mail:** director@bookawards.sk.ca. **Website:** www.bookawards.sk.ca. **Contact:** Courtney Bates-Hardy, executive director. Estab. 1993. Saskatchewan Book Awards celebrates, promotes, and rewards Saskatchewan authors and publishers worthy of recognition through 14 awards, granted on an annual or semiannual basis. Awards: Fiction, Nonfiction, Poetry, Scholarly, First Book, Prix du Livre Français, Regina, Saskatoon, Indigenous Peoples' Writing, Indigenous Peoples' Publishing, Publishing in Education, Publishing, Children's Literature/Young Adult Literature, Book of the Year. November 1. Prize: $2,000 (CAD) for all awards except Book of the Year, which is $3,000 (CAD). Costs: $50 per award entered. Juries are made up of writing and publishing professionals from outside of Saskatchewan.

THE SATURDAY EVENING POST GREAT AMERICAN FICTION CONTEST

The Saturday Evening Post Society, 1100 Waterway Blvd., Indianapolis IN 46202. **E-mail:** fictioncontest@saturdayeveningpost.com. **Website:** www.saturdayeveningpost.com/fiction-contest. "In its nearly 3 centuries of publication, *The Saturday Evening Post* has included fiction by a who's who of American authors, including F. Scott Fitzgerald, William Faulkner, Kurt Vonnegut, Ray Bradbury, Louis L'Amour, Sinclair Lewis, Jack London, and Edgar Allan Poe. The *Post*'s fiction has not just entertained us; it has played a vital role in defining who we are as Americans. In launching this contest, we are seeking America's next great, unpublished voices." Deadline: July 1. The winning story will receive $500 and publication in the magazine and online. Five runners-up will be published online and receive $100 each. Costs: $10.

ALDO AND JEANNE SCAGLIONE PRIZE FOR A TRANSLATION OF A LITERARY WORK

Modern Language Association, 85 Broad Street, suite 500, New York NY 10004-2434. (646)576-5141. **Fax:**

(646)458-0030. **E-mail:** awards@mla.org. **Website:** www.mla.org. **Contact:** Coordinator of Book Prizes. Offered in even-numbered years for an outstanding translation into English of a book-length literary work. Deadline: April 1. Prize: A cash award and a certificate to be presented at the Modern Language Association's annual convention in January.

THE SCARS EDITOR'S CHOICE AWARDS

Scars Publications, **E-mail:** editor@scars.tv. **Website:** http://scars.tv (contest direct link http://scars.tv/contests.htm). **Contact:** Janet Kuypers, editor/publisher (whom all reading fee checks need to be made out to). Estab. annually. Award to showcase good writing in an annual book. Prize: Publication of story/essay and 1 copy of the book. Costs: $19/short story and $15/poem.

THE MONA SCHREIBER PRIZE FOR HUMOROUS FICTION & NONFICTION

3940 Laurel Canyon Blvd., #566, Studio City CA 91604. **E-mail:** brad.schreiber@att.net. **Website:** www.bradschreiber.com. **Contact:** Brad Schreiber. Estab. 2000. Established in 2000, to honor Mona Schreiber, a writer and teacher. Entry fees are the same as in 2000 and money from entries helps pay for prizes. The purpose of the contest is to award the most creative humor writing, in any form, under than 750 words, in either fiction or nonfiction, including but not limited to stories, articles, essays, speeches, shopping lists, diary entries, and anything else writers dream up. Complete rules and previous winning entries On website. Deadline: December 1. Prize: 1st Place: $500; 2nd Place: $250; 3rd Place: $100. Costs: $5 fee per entry (checks payable to Mona Schreiber Prize). Foreign entries may include US currency or checks drawn on US banks. Judged by Brad Schreiber, journalist, consultant, instructor, author of among other books, the humor writing how-to *What Are You Laughing At?*

SCREAMINMAMAS MAGICAL FICTION CONTEST

1911 Cleveland St., Hollywood FL 33020. **E-mail:** screaminmamas@gmail.com. **Website:** www.screaminmamas.com/contests. **Contact:** Darlene Pistocchi, editor/managing director. This contest celebrates moms and the magical spirit of the holidays. If you had an opportunity to be anything you wanted to be, what would you be? Transport yourself! Become that character and write a short story around that charac-

ter. Can be any genre. Length: 800-3,000 words. Open only to moms. Deadline: June 30. Prize: Publication.

SCREAMINMAMAS VALENTINE'S DAY CONTEST

1911 Cleveland St., Hollywood FL 33020. **E-mail:** screaminmamas@gmail.com. **Website:** www.screaminmamas.com/contests. **Contact:** Darlene Pistocchi, editor/managing director. "Looking for light romantic comedy. Can be historical or contemporary—something to lift the spirits and celebrate the gift of innocent romance that might be found in the everyday life of a busy mom." Length: 600-1,200 words. Open only to moms. Deadline: June 30. Prize: Publication. Costs: $5.

MARY WOLLSTONECRAFT SHELLEY PRIZE FOR IMAGINATIVE FICTION

Rosebud, ROSEBUD MAGAZINE; ROSEBUD, INC., C/O Rosebud Magazine, N3310 Asje Rd., Cambridge WI 53523. (608)423-9780. **E-mail:** jrodclark@rsbd.net. **Website:** www.rsbd.net. **Contact:** J. Roderick Clark, editor. Estab. 1993. Publishes eclectic mix of poetry, fiction and nonfiction. Genres with a literary feel okay. The Shelley Award is presented for any kind of unpublished imaginative fiction/short stories, 4,000 words or less. Entries are welcome any time. Acquires first rights. Open to any writer. Deadline: June 15 in even years. Prize: Grand Prize: $1,000. 4 runner-ups receive $100. All winners published in *Rosebud*. Costs: $30/story. Judged by editor Rod Clark in 2016.

☯ SHORT GRAIN CONTEST

P.O. Box 3986, Regina SK S4P 3R9, Canada. (306)791-7749. **E-mail:** grainmag@skwriter.com. **Website:** www.grainmagazine.ca/short-grain-contest. **Contact:** Jordan Morris, business administrator (inquiries only). The annual Short Grain Contest includes a category for poetry of any style up to 100 lines and fiction of any style up to 2,500 words, offering 3 prizes. Deadline: April 1. Prize: $1,000, plus publication in *Grain Magazine*; 2nd Place: $750; 3rd Place: $500. Costs: $40 CAD; $50 for US and $60 for international entrants, in US or CAD funds; includes 1-year subscription to *Grain Magazine*.

SKIPPING STONES HONOR (BOOK) AWARDS

P.O. Box 3939, Eugene OR 97403, USA. (541)342-4956. **Fax:** (541)342-4956. **E-mail:** editor@skippingstones. org. **Website:** www.skippingstones.org. **Contact:** Arun N. Toké. Estab. 1994. *Skipping Stones* is a well respected, multicultural literary magazine now in its 29th year. Annual award to promote multicultural and/or nature awareness through creative writings for children and teens and their educators. Seeks authentic, exceptional, child/youth friendly books that promote intercultural, international, intergenerational harmony, or understanding through creative ways. Deadline: February 29. Prize: Honor certificates; gold seals; reviews; press release/publicity. Costs: $50. Judged by a multicultural committee of teachers, librarians, parents, students and editors.

THE BERNICE SLOTE AWARD

Prairie Schooner, 123 Andrews Hall, PO Box 880334, Lincoln NE 68588-0334. (402)472-0911. **Fax:** (402)472-1817. **E-mail:** PrairieSchooner@unl.edu. **Website:** www.prairieschooner.unl.edu. **Contact:** Kwame Dawes. Offered annually for the best work by a beginning writer published in *Prairie Schooner* in the previous year. Celebrates the best and finest writing that they have published for the year. Prize: $500. Judged by editorial staff of *Prairie Schooner*.

BYRON CALDWELL SMITH BOOK AWARD

The University of Kansas, Hall Center for the Humanities, 900 Sunnyside Ave., Lawrence KS 66045. (785)864-4798. **E-mail:** vbailey@ku.edu. **Website:** www.hallcenter.ku.edu. **Contact:** Victor Bailey, director. Offered in odd years. To qualify, applicants must live or be employed in Kansas and have written an outstanding book published within the previous 2 calendar years. Translations are eligible. Guidelines for SASE or online. Deadline: March 1. Prize: $1,500.

JEFFREY E. SMITH EDITORS' PRIZE IN FICTION, ESSAY AND POETRY

The Missouri Review, 357 McReynolds Hall, UMC, Columbia MO 65211. (573)882-4474. **Fax:** (573)884-4671. **E-mail:** contest_question@moreview.com. **Website:** www.missourireview.com. **Contact:** Editor. Offered annually for unpublished work in 3 categories: fiction, essay, and poetry. Guidelines online or for SASE. Deadline: October 15. Prize: $5,000 and publication for each category winner. Costs: $20, includes a 1-year print or digital subscription.

KAY SNOW WRITING CONTEST

Willamette Writers, Willamette Writers, 2108 Buck St., West Linn OR 97068. (503)305-6729. **Fax:** (503)344-6174. **E-mail:** reg@willamettewriters.com. **Website:** www.willamettewriters.org. Willamette

Writers is the largest writers' organization in Oregon and one of the largest writers' organizations in the United States. It is a non-profit, tax-exempt Oregon corporation led by volunteers. Elected officials and directors administer an active program of monthly meetings, special seminars, workshops, and an annual writing conference. Continuing with established programs and starting new ones is only made possible by strong volunteer support. The purpose of this annual writing contest, named in honor of Willamette Writer's founder, Kay Snow, is to help writers reach professional goals in writing in a broad array of categories and to encourage student writers. Deadline: April 23. Submission deadline begins January 15. Prize: One first prize of $300, one second place prize of $150, and a third place prize of $50 per winning entry in each of the six categories. Student first prize is $50, $20 for second place, $10 for third. Costs: $10-$15, no fee for student entries (grades 1-12).

SOCIETY OF MIDLAND AUTHORS AWARD

Society of Midland Authors, Society of Midland Authors, P.O. Box 10419, Chicago IL 60610-0419. **E-mail:** marlenetbrill@comcast.net. **Website:** www.midlandauthors.com. **Contact:** Marlene Targ Brill, awards chair. Since 1957, the Society has presented annual awards for the best books written by Midwestern authors. The Society began in 1915. The Society of Midland Authors (SMA) Award is presented to one title in each of 6 categories: adult nonfiction, adult fiction, adult biography and memoir, children's nonfiction, children's fiction, and poetry. There may be honor book winners as well. Books and entry forms must be mailed to the 3 judges in each category; for a list of judges and the entry and payment forms, visit the SMA website. Do not mail books to the society's P.O. box. The fee can be sent to the SMA P.O. box or paid via Paypal. Deadline: The first Saturday in January for books from the previous year. Prize: $500 and a plaque that is awarded at the SMA banquet in May in Chicago. Honorary winners receive a plaque. Costs: $10 entry fee. Check the SMA website for each year's judges.

SPUR AWARDS

1080 Mesa Vista Hall MSC06 3770, 1 University of New Mexico, Alberquerque NM 87131. (615)791-1444. **E-mail:** wwa@unm.edu. **Website:** www.westernwriters.org. Purpose of award is "to reward quality in the fields of western fiction and nonfiction." Prize: Trophy. Categories: short stories, novels, poetry, songs, scripts and nonfiction. No entry fee. **Deadline: January 10.** Entries must be published during the contest year. Open to any writer. Guidelines available in Sept./Oct. for SASE, on website or by phone. Inquiries accepted by e-mail or phone. Results announced annually in Summer. Winners notified by mail. For contest results, send SASE.

JOHN STEINBECK FICTION AWARD

Reed Magazine. San Jose State University, Dept. of English, One Washington Square, San Jose CA 95192. **E-mail:** reed@email.sjsu.edu. **Website:** www.reed-mag.org/drupal/. **Contact:** Nick Taylor, editor. "Award for an unpublished short story of up to 6,000 words." Annual. Competition/award for short stories. Prize: $1,000 prize and publication in Reed Magazine. Receives several hundred entries per category. Entries are judged by a prominent fiction writer; 2007 judge was Tobias Wolff. Entry fee: $15 (includes issue of Reed). **Submission period is June 1 - November 1.** Anyone may enter contest. "Do not submit any pornographic material, science fiction, fantasy, or children's literature. The work must be your own, (no translations)." Results announced in April.

STORY MONSTER APPROVED BOOK AWARDS

Story Monsters LLC, 4696 W. Tyson St., Chandler AZ 85226. (480)940-8182. **Fax:** (480)940-8787. **E-mail:** linda@storymonsters.com. **E-mail:** cristy@storymonsters.com. **Website:** www.dragonflybookawards.com. **Contact:** Cristy Bertini. Recognizes and honors accomplished authors in the field of children's literature who inspire, inform, teach, or entertain. A Story Monsters seal of approval on your book tells teachers, librarians, and parents they are giving children the very best. Offered on an annual basis, we have expanded our program to include 23 distinct categories which cover a variety of genres and target ages. Deadline: December 1. The Book of the Year winner will receive an advertorial, which includes a feature interview and a full-page ad in Story Monsters Ink® magazine (a $1,600 value), a certificate commemorating their accomplishment, and 50 Story Monsters Approved! seals. All books earning a Story Monsters Approved! Gold Medal Honor receive a gold medal, a certificate, and 25 award seals. All books earning a Story Monsters Approved! designation receive a certificate and 15 award seals. All winners are listed in a news release sent to a comprehensive list of media outlets, on the Dragonfly Book Awards website, and in Story Monsters Ink® magazine. Costs: $65 per entry, per category. Our judging panel includes industry experts in specific fields as well as experts in education and publishing.

STORYSOUTH MILLION WRITERS AWARD

E-mail: terry@storysouth.com. **Website:** www.storysouth.com. **Contact:** Terry Kennedy, editor. Estab. 2003. Annual award to honor and promote the best fiction published in online literary journals and magazines during the previous year. Most literary prizes for short fiction have traditionally ignored web-published fiction. This award aims to show that world-class fiction is being published online and to promote to the larger reading and literary community. Deadline: August 15. Nominations of stories begins on March 15. Prize: Prize amounts subject to donation. Check website for details.

THEODORE STURGEON MEMORIAL AWARD FOR BEST SHORT SF OF THE YEAR

Center for the Study of SF, 1445 Jayhawk Blvd, Room 3001, University of Kansas, Lawrence KS 66045. (785)864-2518. **Fax:** (785)864-1159. **E-mail:** cssf@ku.edu. **Website:** sfcenter.ku.edu/sturgeon.htm. **Contact:** Kij Johnson, professor and associate director. Estab. 1987. Award to "honor the best science fiction short story of the year." Prize: Trophy. Winners receive expense-paid trip to the University and have their names engraved on the pernmanent trophy.

◯ SUBTERRAIN MAGAZINE'S LUSH TRIUMPHANT LITERARY AWARDS COMPETITION

P.O. Box 3008 MPO, Vancouver BC V6B 3X5, Canada. (604)876-8710. **Fax:** (604)879-2667. **E-mail:** subter@portal.ca. **Website:** www.subterrain.ca. Estab. Magazine est. 1988; Lush Triumphant est. 2002. Entrants may submit as many entries in as many categories as they like. Fiction: Max of 3,000 words. Poetry: A suite of 5 related poems (max of 15 pages). Creative Nonfiction (based on fact, adorned with fiction): Max of 4,000 words. Deadline: May 15. Prize: Winners in each category will receive $1,000 cash (plus payment for publication) and publication in the Winter issue. First runner-up in each category will be published in the Spring issue of *subTerrain*. Costs: $30.00/entry includes a 1-year subscription to *subTerrain*.

SYDNEY TAYLOR MANUSCRIPT COMPETITION

Association of Jewish Libraries, Sydney Taylor Manuscript Award Competition, 204 Park St., Montclair NJ 07042-2903. **E-mail:** stmacajl@aol.com. **Website:** www.jewishlibraries.org/main/Awards/SydneyTaylorManuscriptAward.aspx. **Contact:** Aileen Grossberg. Estab. 1985. This competition is for unpublished writers of juvenile fiction. Material should be for readers ages 8-13. The manuscript should have universal appeal and reveal positive aspects of Jewish life that will serve to deepen the understanding of Judaism for all children. To encourage new fiction of Jewish interest for readers ages 8-13. Deadline: September 30. Prize: $1,000. Judging by qualified judges from within the Association of Jewish Libraries.

THE TEXAS INSTITUTE OF LETTERS LITERARY AWARDS

E-mail: Betwx@aol.com. **Website:** www.texasinstituteofletters.org. Estab. 1936. The Texas Institute of Letters gives annual awards for books by Texas authors and writers who have produced books about Texas, including Best Books of Poetry, Fiction, and Nonfiction. Awards are also given for best Short Story, Magazine or Newspaper Article, Essay, and best Books for Children and Young Adults. Work submitted must have been published in the year stipulated, and entries may be made by authors or by their publishers. Complete guidelines and award information is available on the Texas Institute of Letters website.

THREE CHEERS AND A TIGER

E-mail: editors@toasted-cheese.com. **Website:** tclj.toasted-cheese.com. **Contact:** Stephanie Lenz, editor. Contestants are to write a short story (following a specific theme) within 48 hours. Contests are held first weekend in Spring (mystery) and first weekend in Fall (science fiction/fantasy). Word limit announced at the start of the contest, 5 pm ET. Contest-specific information is announced 48 hours before the contest submission deadline. Results announced in April and October. Winners notified by e-mail. List of winners on website. Prize: Amazon gift certificates and publication. Costs: Contest is free to enter. Blind-judged by *Toasted Cheese* editors. Each judge uses his or her own criteria to choose entries.

THRILLER FICTION CONTEST

P.O. Box 1001, Reynoldsburg OH 43068. **E-mail:** dianaperry@DianaPerryBooks.com. **Website:** diana-perrybooks.com. **Contact:** Diana Perry. Estab. 2014. "Tell a suspenseful story in the thriller genre; can be viral/disease thriller, legal thriller, espionage thriller, adventure thriller, suspense thriller, technical thriller." Rules on website. Length: up to 20 pages or 5,000 words. Purpose: "To give exposure to beginning poets trying to break in to the business and get noticed." Deadline: March 31. 1st Place: $300, trophy, mention on website, t-shirt, press releases in your local newspapers; 2nd Place: $200, trophy, mention on website, t-shirt, press releases in your local newspapers; 3rd Place: $100, trophy, mention on website, t-shirt, press releases in your local newspapers; 4th/5th places: $50/$25, plaque, mention on website, t-shirt, press releases in your local newspapers. "We also list names of next 25 honorable mentions on website. Contest guidelines and entry form on website. CHECK WEBSITE FOR GUEST JUDGES. Mail entry form, your story, and a $15 money order only to Thriller Fiction Contest at above address postmarked no later than March 31. Winners announced both on website and via snail mail May 1. Prizes mailed within 10 days of announcement. Judged by Diana Perry and guest judge.

THE THURBER PRIZE FOR AMERICAN HUMOR

77 Jefferson Ave., Columbus OH 43215. **Website:** www.thurberhouse.org. This award recognizes the art of humor writing. Deadline: March 31. Prize: $5,000 for the finalist, non-cash prizes awarded to two runners-up. Judged by well-known members of the national arts community.

TOMMY AWARD FOR EXCELLENCE IN WRITING

International Book Management Corporation, 3468 Babcock Blvd., Pittsburgh PA 15237-2402. (412)837-2423. **E-mail:** info@internationalbookmanagement.com; editor@writersnewsweekly.com. **Website:** writersnewsweekly.com. **Contact:** Christopher Stokum and Sarah Schiavoni. Estab. 2004. The Tommy Award For Writing Excellent recognizes and rewards excellence in full length literary works in adult fiction and nonfiction. Books must be published in the U.S. between June 1 and May 31 of the following year. Textbooks, e-books, children's books, young adult books, poetry and audio-books will not be considered, nor will manuscripts. Judges will selected one winner and may designate up to two Honorable Mention books in each of the following categories: fiction, nonfiction, shosrt story collection. Books can be submitted by the publisher or the author. A copy of each book submitted should be mailed directly to: International Book Management Corporation, 3468 Babcock Blvd., Pittsburgh, PA 15237. Please send submissions as soon as possible after publication. No books will be accepted after May 21, 2011. There will be no extensions to this deadline. Winners and honorable mentions will be announced on August 15th. The awards are presented in October. Winners receive a certificate and trophy. An author interview and book review of the winning submission will appear on WritersNewsWeekly. Entries will not be returned. International Book Management Corp. reserves the right to donate or dispose of entries. No entry fee. More more information contact International Management at: info@ internationalbookmanagement.com. "The Tommy Award honors and encourages outstanding novelists and short story authors by separating them from the bulk of contemporary fiction writers for recognition. Authors may submit previously published novels or unpublished short stories for consideration." May 21 The winning novelist will receive a trophy and a certificate. WritersNewsWeekly will feature a review of his/her book and indicate where the book can be purchased. The winning short story author will also receive a trophy and a certificate, and his/her winning story will be featured on WritersNewsWeekly. Novelists retain all rights to their submitted material. Short Story authors agree to a one-time online publication upon submitting their work but retain all rights. Costs: No entry fee. Judged by the combined staff of WritersNewsWeekly and International Book Management Corportation.

☼ TORONTO BOOK AWARDS

City of Toronto c/o Toronto Arts & Culture, Cultural Partnerships, City Hall, 9E, 100 Queen St. W., Toronto ON M5H 2N2, Canada. **E-mail:** shan@toronto.ca. **Website:** www.toronto.ca/book_awards. Estab. 1974. The Toronto Book Awards honor authors of books of literary or artistic merit that are evocative of Toronto. Deadline: April 30. Prize: Each finalist receives $1,000 and the winning author receives$10,000 ($15,000 total in prize money available).

STEVEN TURNER AWARD FOR BEST FIRST WORK OF FICTION

6335 W. Northwest Hwy., #618, Dallas TX 75225. **Website:** www.texasinstituteofletters.org. Offered annually for work published January 1-December 31 for the best first book of fiction. Deadline: normally first week in January; see website for specific date. Prize: $1,000.

ANNUAL VENTURA COUNTY WRITERS CLUB SHORT STORY CONTEST

Ventura County Writers Club Short Story Contest, P.O. Box 3373, Thousand Oaks CA 91362. **E-mail:** vcwc.contestchair@gmail.com. **Website:** www.venturacountywriters.com. **Contact:** Contest Chair. Estab. 1999. Annual short story contest for youth and adult writers. High school division for writers still in school. Adult division for those 18 and older. Club membership not required to enter and entries accepted worldwide as long as fees are paid, story is unpublished and in English. Enter through website. Winners get cash prizes and are published in club anthology. Deadline: November 15. Adult Prizes: 1st Place: $500; 2nd Place: $250; 3rd Place: $125. High School Prizes: 1st Place: $100; 2nd Place: $75; 3rd Place: $50. Costs: Submission fee for each story submitted: $15 U.S. for adult VCWC members; $25 U.S. for adult non-members; and $10 for high school students. PayPal, credit or debit cards are accepted.

WAASNODE SHORT FICTION PRIZE

Passages North, Department of English, Northern Michigan University, 1401 Presque Isle Ave., Marquette MI 49855. (906)227-1203. **Fax:** (906)227-1096. **E-mail:** passages@nmu.edu. **Website:** www.passagesnorth.com. **Contact:** Jennifer Howard. Offered every 2 years to publish new voices in literary fiction (maximum 10,000 words). Guidelines for SASE or online. Submissions accepted online. Deadline: April 15. Submission period begins February 15. Prize: $1,000 and publication for winner; 2 honorable mentions are also published; all entrants receive a copy of *Passages North*. Costs: $15 reading fee/story, make checks payable to Northern Michigan University. Judged by Anne Valente in 2018.

WABASH PRIZE FOR FICTION

Sycamore Review, Department of English, 500 Oval Dr., Purdue University, West Lafayette IN 47907. **E-mail:** sycamore@purdue.edu; sycamorefiction@purdue.edu. **Website:** www.sycamorereview.com/contest/. **Contact:** Kara Krewer, editor-in-chief. Annual contest for unpublished fiction. Deadline: November 15. Prize: $1,000 and publication. Costs: $20 reading fee; $5 for each additional story.

THE JULIA WARD HOWE AWARD

The Boston Authors Club, 33 Brayton Road, Brighton MA 02135. (617)783-1357. **E-mail:** alan.lawson@bc.edu. **Website:** www.bostonauthorsclub.org. **Contact:** Alan Lawson, president. Julia Ward Howe Prize offered annually in the spring for books published the previous year. Two awards are given: one for adult books of fiction, nonfiction, or poetry, and one for children's books, middle grade and young adult novels, nonfiction, or poetry. No picture books or subsidized publishers. There must be two copies of each book submitted. Deadline: January 15. Prize: $1,000 in each category. Several books will also be cited with no cash awards as Finalists or Highly Recommended. Costs: $25/title.

THE WASHINGTON WRITERS' PUBLISHING HOUSE FICTION PRIZE

Washington Writers' Publishing House, P.O. Box 15271, Washington DC 20003. **E-mail:** wwphpress@gmail.com. **Website:** www.washingtonwriters.org. Fiction writers living within 75 miles of the Capitol are invited to submit a ms of either a novel or a collection of short stories (no more than 350 pages, double-spaced). Deadline: November 15. Submission period begins July 1. Prize: $1,000 and 50 copies of the book. Costs: $25 reading fee.

THE ROBERT WATSON LITERARY PRIZE IN FICTION AND POETRY

The Robert Watson Literary Prizes, *The Greensboro Review*, MFA Writing Program, 3302 MHRA Building, Greensboro NC 27402-6170. (336)334-5459. **E-mail:** jlclark@uncg.edu. **Website:** www.greensbororeview.org. **Contact:** Jim Clark, editor. Offered annually for fiction (up to 25 double-spaced pages) and poetry (up to 10 pages). Entries must be unpublished. Open to any writer. Deadline: September 15. Prize: $1,000 each for best short story and poem. Costs: $14. Judged by editors of *The Greensboro Review*.

◐ WESTERN AUSTRALIAN PREMIER'S BOOK AWARDS

State Library of Western Australia, Perth Cultural Centre, 25 Francis St., Perth WA 6000, Australia. (61)(8)9427-3151. **E-mail:** premiersbookawards@slwa.wa.gov.au. **Website:** pba.slwa.wa.gov.au. **Contact:** Karen de San Miguel. Estab. 1982. Annual competition for Australian citizens or permanent residents of Australia, or writers whose work has Australia as its primary focus. Categories: children's books, digital narrative, fiction, nonfiction, poetry, scripts, writing for young adults, West Australian history, and Western Australian emerging writers. Deadline: January 31. Prize: Awards $25,000 for Premier's Prize; awards $15,000 each for the Children's Books, Digital Narrative, Fiction, and Nonfiction categories; awards $10,000 each for the Poetry, Scripts, Western Australian History, Western Australian Emerging Writers, and Writing for Young Adults; awards $5,000 for People's Choice Award.

WESTERN HERITAGE AWARDS

National Cowboy & Western Heritage Museum, 1700 NE 63rd St., Oklahoma City OK 73111-7997. (405)478-2250. **Fax:** (405)478-4714. **Website:** www.nationalcowboymuseum.org. **Contact:** Jessica Limestall. Estab. 1961. The National Cowboy & Western Heritage Museum Western Heritage Awards were established to honor and encourage the legacy of those whose works in literature, music, film, and television reflect the significant stories of the American West. Accepted categories for literary entries: western novel, nonfiction book, art book, photography book, juvenile book, magazine article, or poetry book. The WHA are presented annually to encourage the accurate and artistic telling of great stories of the West through 16 categories of western literature, television, film and music; including fiction, nonfiction, children's books and poetry. See website for details and category definitions. Deadline: November 30. Prize: Awards a Wrangler bronze sculpture designed by famed western artist, John Free. Costs: $50. Judged by a panel of judges selected each year with distinction in various fields of western art and heritage.

WESTERN WRITERS OF AMERICA

271CR 219, Encampment WY 82325. (307)329-8942. **E-mail:** wwa.moulton@gmail.com. **Website:** www.westernwriters.org. **Contact:** Candy Moulton, executive director. Estab. 1953. Eighteen Spur Award categories in various aspects of the American West. The nonprofit Western Writers of America has promoted and honored the best in Western literature with the annual Spur Awards, selected by panels of judges. Awards, for material published last year, are given for works whose inspirations, image and literary excellence best represent the reality and spirit of the American West. Deadline: January 4. Costs: No fee.

WESTMORELAND POETRY & SHORT STORY CONTEST

Westmoreland Arts & Heritage Festival, 252 Twin Lakes Road, Latrobe PA 15650-9415. (724)834-7474. **Fax:** (724)850-7474. **E-mail:** info@artsandheritage. com. **Website:** www.artsandheritage.com. **Contact:** Diane Shrader. Offered annually for unpublished work. Two categories: Poem and Short Story. Short story entries no longer than 4,000 words. Family-oriented festival and contest. Deadline: February 17. Prizes: Award: $200; 1st Place: $125; 2nd Place: $100; 3rd Place: $75. Costs: $10/story or for 2 poems; both categories may be entered for $20.

WILLA LITERARY AWARD

Women Writing the West, 8547 East Arapaho Rd., #J-541, Greenwood Village CO 80112-1436. **E-mail:** jcpeone@gmail.com. **Website:** www.womenwritingthewest.org. **Contact:** Carmen Peone. The WILLA Literary Award honors the year's best in published literature featuring women's or girls' stories set in the West. Women Writing the West (WWW), a nonprofit association of writers and other professionals writing and promoting the Women's West, underwrites and presents the nationally recognized award annually (for work published between January 1 and December 31). The award is named in honor of Pulitzer Prize winner Willa Cather, one of the country's foremost novelists. The award is given in 8 categories: historical fiction, contemporary fiction, original softcover fiction, creative nonfiction, scholarly nonfiction, poetry, children's fiction and nonfiction and young adult fiction/nonfiction. Entry forms available on the website. Deadline: November 1–February 1. Prize: $150 and a trophy. Finalist receives a plaque. Both receive digital and sticker award emblems for book covers. Also, the eight winners will participate in a drawing for 2 two week all expenses paid residencies donated by Playa at Summer Lake in Oregon. Costs: $65. Judged by professional librarians not affiliated with WWW.

TENNESSEE WILLIAMS/NEW ORLEANS LITERARY FESTIVAL CONTESTS

Tennessee Williams/New Orleans Literary Festival, 938 Lafayette St., Suite 514, New Orleans LA 70113. (504)581-1144. **E-mail:** info@tennesseewilliams.net. **Website:** www.tennesseewilliams.net/contests. **Contact:** Paul J. Willis. Annual contests for: Unpublished One Act, Unpublished Short Fiction, Unpublished Flash Fiction, and Unpublished Poem. "Our competitions provide writers a large audience during one of the largest literary festivals in the nation." Deadline: October 1 (One Act, Fiction); October 15 (Poetry, Very Short Fiction) Prize: One Act: $1,500, staged read at the next festival, VIP All-Access Festival pass, and publication in Bayou. Poetry: $1,000, public reading at next festival, VIP all-access pass, publication in Louisiana Cultural Vistas Magazine. Fiction: $1,500, public reading at next festival, publication in Louisiana Literature, VIP all-access pass. Very Short Fiction: $500, publication in the New Orleans Review, VIP all-access past. Costs: $25 entry fee for One Act and Fiction submissions; $20 entry fee for Poetry submissions; $10 entry fee for Very Short Fiction. Judged by special guest judges, who change every year.

WISCONSIN INSTITUTE FOR CREATIVE WRITING FELLOWSHIP

6195B H.C. White Hall, 600 N. Park St., Madison WI 53706. **E-mail:** rfkuka@wisc.edu. **Website:** creativewriting.wisc.edu/fellowships.html. **Contact:** Sean Bishop, graduate coordinator. Estab. 1986. Fellowship provides time, space and an intellectual community for writers working on first books. Receives approximately 300 applicants a year for each genre. Judged by English Department faculty and current fellows. Candidates can have up to one published book in the genre for which they are applying. Open to any writer with either an M.F.A. or Ph.D. in creative writing. Please enclose a SASE for notification of results. Results announced on website by May 1. Deadline: Last day of February. Open to submissions on December 15. Prize: $30,000 for a 9-month appointment. Costs: $45, payable to the Dept. of English; see website for payment instructions.

THOMAS WOLFE PRIZE AND LECTURE

North Carolina Writers' Network, Thomas Wolfe Fiction Prize, Great Smokies Writing Program, Attn: Nancy Williams, CPO #1860, UNC, Asheville NC 28805. **Website:** englishcomplit.unc.edu/wolfe. Estab. 1999. The Thomas Wolfe Fiction Prize honors internationally celebrated North Carolina novelist Thomas Wolfe. The prize is administered by Tommy Hays and the Great Smokies Writing Program at the University of North Carolina at Asheville. Deadline: January 30. Submissions period begins December 1. Prize: $1,000 and potential publication in *The Thomas Wolfe Review*. Costs: $15 fee for members of the NC Writers' Network, $25 for non-members.

TOBIAS WOLFF AWARD FOR FICTION

Bellingham Review, Mail Stop 9053, Western Washington University, Bellingham WA 98225. (360)650-4863. **E-mail:** bellingham.review@wwu.edu. **Website:** www.bhreview.org. **Contact:** Susanne Paola Antonetta, editor-in-chief; Mike Oliphant, managing editor. Offered annually for unpublished work. Guidelines available on website; online submissions only. Categories: novel exceprts and short stories. Deadline: March 15. Submissions period begins December 1. Prize: $1,000, plus publication and subscription. Costs: $20 entry fee for 1st entry; $10 for each additional entry. Judged by Debra Dean.

⊙ THE WORD AWARDS

The Word Guild, The Word Guild, Suite # 226, 245 King George Rd, Brantford ON N3R 7N7, Canada. 800-969-9010 x 1. **E-mail:** info@thewordguild.com. **E-mail:** info@thewordguild.com. **Website:** www. thewordguild.com. **Contact:** Karen deBlieck. The Word Guild is an organization of Canadian writers and editors who are Christian, and who are committed to encouraging one another and to fostering standards of excellence in the art, craft, practice and ministry of writing. Memberships available for various experience levels. Yearly conference Write Canada (please see website for information) and features keynote speakers, continuing classes and workshops. Editors and agents on site. The Word Awards is for work published in the past year, in almost 30 categories including books, articles, essays, fiction, nonfiction, novels, short stories, songs, and poetry. Please see website for more information. Deadline: January 15. Prize $50 CAD for article and short pieces; $100 CAD for book entries. Finalists book entries are eligible for the $5,000 Grace Irwin prize. Costs: Short Piece Entries: Members: $30 CAD + HST (per short piece entered); Non Members: $60 CAD + HST (per short piece entered). Book Entries: Members: $55 CAD + HST (per title entered); Non Members: $110 + HST (per title entered). Judged by industry leaders and professionals.

WORLD FANTASY AWARDS

P.O. Box 43, Mukilteo WA 98275. **E-mail:** sfexecsec@gmail.com. **Website:** www.worldfantasy.org. **Contact:** Peter Dennis Pautz, president. Offered annually for previously published work in several categories, including life achievement, novel, novella, short story, anthology, collection, artist, special award-pro and special award-nonpro. Works are recommended by attendees of current and previous 2 years' conventions and a panel of judges. Awards to recognize excellence in fantasy literature worldwide. Deadline: June 1. Prize: Trophy. Judged by panel.

WORLD'S BEST SHORT-SHORT STORY CONTEST, NARRATIVE NONFICTION CONTEST & SOUTHEAST REVIEW POETRY CONTEST

The Southeast Review, Florida State University, English Department, Tallahassee FL 32306. **E-mail:** southeastreview@gmail.com. **Website:** www.southeastreview.org. **Contact:** Erin Hoover, editor. Estab. 1979. Annual award for unpublished short-short stories (500 words or less), poetry, and narrative nonfiction (6,000 words or less). Visit website for details. Deadline: March 15. Prize: $500 per category. Winners and finalists will be published in *The Southeast Review*. Costs: $16 reading fee for up to 3 stories or poems, or 1 narrative essay.

WOW! WOMEN ON WRITING QUARTERLY FLASH FICTION CONTEST

WOW! Women on Writing, P.O. Box 2832, Winnetka CA 91396. **E-mail:** contestinfo@wow-womenonwriting.com. **Website:** www.wow-womenonwriting.com/contest.php. **Contact:** Angela Mackintosh, editor. Contest offered quarterly. "We are open to all themes and genres, although we do encourage writers to take a close look at our literary agent guest judge for the season if you are serious about winning." Deadline: August 31, November 30, February 28, May 31. Prize: 1st place: $400 cash prize, $25 Amazon gift certificate, story published on WOW! Women On Writing, interview on blog; 2nd place: $300 cash prize, $25 Amazon gift certificate, story published on WOW! Women On Writing, interview on blog; 3rd place: $200 cash prize, $25 Amazon gift certificate, story published on WOW! Women On Writing, interview on blog; 7 runners up: $25 Amazon gift certificate, story published on WOW! Women on Writing, interview on blog; 10 honorable mentions: $20 gift certificate from Amazon, story title and name published on WOW!Women On Writing. Costs: $10. Judged by a different guest every season, who is either a literary agent, acquiring editor or publisher.

WRITER'S DIGEST WRITING COMPETITION

Writer's Digest, a publication of F+W Media, Inc., 10151 Carver Rd., Suite 300, Cincinnati OH 45242.

(715)445-4612, ext. 13430. **E-mail:** writing-competition@fwmedia.com. **Website:** www.writersdigest.com. Writing contest with 9 categories: Inspirational Writing (spiritual/religious, maximum 2,500 words); Memoir/Personal Essay (maximum 2,000 words); Magazine Feature Article (maximum 2,000 words);Children's/Young Adult Fiction (maximum 2,000 words) Short Story (genre, maximum 4,000 words); Short Story (mainstream/literary, maximum 4,000 words); Rhyming Poetry (maximum 32 lines); Nonrhyming Poetry (maximum 32 lines); Stage Play/TV/Movie Script (first 15 pages and 1-page synopsis). Entries must be original, in English, unpublished/unproduced (except for Magazine Feature Articles), and not accepted by another publisher/producer at the time of submission. Writer's Digest retains one-time publication rights to the winning entries in each category. Deadline: May (early bird); June. Grand Prize: $5,000 and a trip to the Writer's Digest Conference to meet with editors and agents; 1st Place: $1,000 and $100 of Writer's Digest Books; 2nd Place: $500 and $100 of Writer's Digest Books; 3rd Place: $250 and $100 of Writer's Digest Books; 4th Place: $100 and $50 of Writer's Digest Books; 5th Place:$50 and $50 of Writer's Digest Books; Sixth through Tenth place winners in each category:$25; and more. Costs: **Early-Bird Deadline: May 4, 2018.** Poetry entry—$20 for the first entry; $15 for each additional poetry entry. Manuscript entry—$30 for the first entry; $25 for each additional manuscript entry. **Deadline: June 1, 2018.** Poetry entry—$25 for the first entry; $20 for each additional poetry entry. Manuscript entry—$35 for the first entry; $30 for each additional manuscript entry.

WRITER'S DIGEST SELF-PUBLISHED BOOK AWARDS

Writer's Digest, 10151 Carver Road, Suite 300, Blue Ash OH 45242. (715)445-4612, ext. 13430. **E-mail:** writersdigestselfpublishingcompetition@fwmedia.com. **Website:** www.writersdigest.com. **Contact:** Nicole Howard. Estab. 1992. Contest open to all English-language, self-published books for which the authors have paid the full cost of publication, or the cost of printing has been paid for by a grant or as part of a prize. Categories include: Mainstream/Literary Fiction, Genre Fiction, Nonfiction, Inspirational (spiritual/new age), Life Stories (biographies/autobiographies/family histories/memoirs), Children's Books, Reference Books (directories/encyclopedias/guide books), Poetry, and Middle-Grade/Young Adult

Books. Judges reserve the right to re-categorize entries. Judges reserve the right to withhold prizes in any category. All winners will be notified in October. Early bird deadline: April 2. Prizes: Grand Prize: $8,000, a trip to the Writer's Digest Conference, promotion in *Writer's Digest*, 10 copies of the book will be sent to major review houses, and a guaranteed review in *Midwest Book Review*; 1st Place (9 winners): $1,000 and promotion in *Writer's Digest*; Honorable Mentions: $50 worth of Writer's Digest Books and promotion on writersdigest.com. All entrants will receive a brief commentary from one of the judges. Costs: $99; $85/additional entry.

WRITER'S DIGEST SELF-PUBLISHED E-BOOK AWARDS

Writer's Digest, 10151 Carver Road, Suite 300, Blue Ash OH 45242. (715)445-4612, ext. 13430. **E-mail:** writersdigestselfpublishingcompetition@fwmedia.com. **Website:** www.writersdigest.com. **Contact:** Nicole Howard. Estab. 2013. Contest open to all English-language, self-published e-books for which the authors have paid the full cost of publication, or the cost of publication has been paid for by a grant or as part of a prize. Categories include: Mainstream/Literary Fiction, Genre Fiction, Nonfiction (includes reference books), Inspirational (spiritual/new age), Life Stories (biographies/autobiographies/family histories/memoirs), Children's Books, Poetry, and Middle-Grade/Young Adult Books. Judges reserve the right to re-categorize entries. Judges reserve the right to withhold prizes in any category. All winners will be notified by December 31. Early bird deadline: August 1; Deadline: September 4. Prizes: Grand Prize: $5,000, promotion in *Writer's Digest*, $200 worth of Writer's Digest Books, and more; 1st Place (9 winners): $1,000 and promotion in *Writer's Digest*; Honorable Mentions: $50 worth of Writer's Digest Books and promotion on writersdigest.com. All entrants will receive a brief commentary from one of the judges. Costs: $99; $85/additional entry.

WRITER'S DIGEST SHORT SHORT STORY COMPETITION

Writer's Digest, 10151 Carver Road, Suite 300, Blue Ash OH 45242. (715)445-4612; ext. 13430. **E-mail:** WritersDigestShortShortStoryCompetition@fwmedia.com. **Website:** www.writersdigest.com. **Contact:** Nicole Howard. Looking for fiction that's bold, brilliant, and brief. Send your best in 1,500 words or fewer. All entries must be original, unpublished, and not submitted elsewhere at the time of submission. *Writer's Digest* reserves one-time publication rights to the 1st-25th winning entries. Winners will be notified by Feb. 28. Early bird deadline: November 15. Final deadline: December 15. Prize: 1st Place: $3,000 and a trip to the Writer's Digest Conference; 2nd Place: $1,500; 3rd Place: $500; 4th-10th Place: $100; 11th-25th Place: $50 gift certificate for writersdigestshop.com. Costs: $25.

WRITERS-EDITORS NETWORK INTERNATIONAL WRITING COMPETITION

CNW Publishing, P.O. Box A, North Stratford NH 03590-0167. **E-mail:** contestentry@writers-editors. com. **E-mail:** info@writers-editors.com. **Website:** www.writers-editors.com. **Contact:** Dana K. Cassell, executive director. Annual award to recognize publishable talent. New categories and awards for 2018: Nonfiction (unpublished or self-published; may be an article, blog post, essay/opinion piece, column, nonfiction book chapter, children's article or book chapter); fiction (unpublished or self-published; may be a short story, novel chapter, Young Adult [YA] or children's story or book chapter); poetry (unpublished or self-published; may be traditional or free verse poetry or children's verse). Guidelines available online. Deadline: March 15. Prize: 1st Place: $150 plus one year Writers-Editors membership; 2nd Place: $100; 3rd Place: $75. All winners and Honorable Mentions will receive certificates as warranted. Most Promising entry in each category will receive a free critique by a contest judge. Costs: $10 (active or new WEN/FFWA members) or $20 (nonmembers) for each fiction or nonfiction entry; $3 (members) or $5 (nonmembers) for each poem; or $10 for 3 poems (members), $15 for 3 poems (nonmembers). Judged by editors, librarians, and writers.

☼ WRITERS' GUILD OF ALBERTA AWARDS

Writers' Guild of Alberta, Percy Page Centre, 11759 Groat Rd., Edmonton AB T5M 3K6, Canada. (780)422-8174. **Fax:** (780)422-2663. **E-mail:** mail@ writersguild.ca. **Website:** writersguild.ca. **Contact:** Executive Director. Offers the following awards: Wilfrid Eggleston Award for Nonfiction; Georges Bugnet Award for Fiction; Howard O'Hagan Award for Short Story; Stephan G. Stephansson Award for Poetry; R. Ross Annett Award for Children's Literature; Gwen Pharis Ringwood Award for Drama; Jon Whyte Memorial Essay Award; James H. Gray Award for Short

Nonfiction. Deadline: December 31. Prize: Winning authors receive $1,500; short piece prize winners receive $700.

WRITERS' LEAGUE OF TEXAS BOOK AWARDS

Writers' League of Texas, 611 S. Congress Ave., Suite 200A-3, Austin TX 78704. (512)499-8914. **Fax:** (512)499-0441. **E-mail:** sara@writersleague.org. **Website:** www.writersleague.org. **Contact:** Sara Kocek. Open to Texas authors of books published the previous year. To enter this contest, you must be a Texas author. "Texas author" is defined as anyone who (whether currently a resident or not) has lived in Texas for a period of 3 or more years. This contest is open to indie or self-published authors as well as traditionally-published authors. Deadline: February 28. Open to submissions October 7. Prize: $1,000 and a commemorative award. Costs: $60/title; $40 for WLT members.

☼ THE WRITERS' TRUST ENGEL/FINDLEY AWARD

The Writers' Trust of Canada, 460 Richmond St. W., Suite 600, Toronto ON M5V 1Y1, Canada. (416)504-8222. **Fax:** (416)504-9090. **E-mail:** info@writerstrust. com. **Website:** www.writerstrust.com. **Contact:** Amanda Hopkins. The Writers' Trust Engel/Findley Award is presented annually at The Writers' Trust Awards Event, held in Toronto each fall, to a Canadian writer for a body of work in hope of continued contribution to the richness of Canadian literature. Open to Canadian citizens and permanent residents only. Prize: $25,000.

WRITERSWEEKLY.COM'S QUARTERLY 24-HOUR SHORT STORY CONTEST

WritersWeekly.com, BookLocker.com, Inc., 200 2nd Ave. S., #526, St. Petersburg FL 33701. (305)768-0261. **Fax:** (305)768-0261. **E-mail:** writersweekly@writersweekly.com. **Website:** 24hourshortstorycontest. com/. **Contact:** Angela Hoy, publisher. Estab. 2001. A popular and fun quarterly contest in which registered entrants receive an assigned topic at start time (usually noon Central Time on a Saturday), and have 24 hours to write and submit a story on that topic. All submissions must be returned via e-mail. Each contest is limited to 500 people. Upon registration, entrant will receive guidelines and details on competition, including submission process. All past topics and winners are listed on the website, as well as the contest rules and hints for winning. Deadline: Quarterly—see website for dates. Prize: 1st Place: $300; 2nd Place: $250; 3rd Place: $200. There are also 20 honorable mentions and 60 door prizes (randomly drawn from all participants). The top 3 winners' entries are posted on WritersWeekly.com (non-exclusive electronic rights only). Writers retain all rights to their work. See website for full details on prizes. Costs: $5. Judged by Angela Hoy (publisher of WritersWeekly.com and Booklocker.com).

LAMAR YORK PRIZE FOR FICTION AND NONFICTION CONTEST

The Chattahoochee Review, Georgia Perimeter College, 2101 Womack Rd., Dunwoody GA 30338-4497. (770)274-5479. **E-mail:** gpccr@gpc.edu. **Website:** thechattahoocheereview.gpc.edu. **Contact:** Anna Schachner, Editor. Offered annually for unpublished creative nonfiction and nonscholarly essays and fiction up to 5,000 words. *The Chattahoochee Review* buys first rights only for winning essay/ms for the purpose of publication in the summer issue. Deadline: January 31. Submission period begins October 1. Prize: 2 prizes of $1,000 each, plus publication. Costs: $15 fee/entry; subscription included in fee. Judged by the editorial staff of *The Chattahoochee Review*.

ZOETROPE: ALL-STORY SHORT FICTION COMPETITION

Zoetrope: All-Story, Zoetrope: All-Story, Attn: Fiction Editor, 916 Kearny St., San Francisco CA 94133. (415)788-7500. **E-mail:** contests@all-story.com. **Website:** www.all-story.com/contests.cgi. Acclaimed annual short fiction competition. Considers submissions of short stories no longer than 5,000 words. Deadline: October 1. Su
bmission period begins July 1. Prizes: 1st place: $1,000 and publication on website; 2nd place: $500; 3rd place: $250. Costs: $25.

ZONE 3 FICTION AWARD

Zone 3, Austin Peay State University, P.O. Box 4565, Clarksville TN 37044. (931)221-7031. **Fax:** (931)221-7149. **E-mail:** wallacess@apsu.edu. **Website:** www.apsu.edu/zone3/contests. **Contact:** Susan Wallace, Managing Editor. Annual contest for unpublished fiction. Open to any fiction writer. Deadline: April 1. Prize: $250 and publication.

CONFERENCES & WORKSHOPS

//

Why are conferences so popular? Writers and conference directors alike tell us it's because writing can be such a lonely business—at conferences writers have the opportunity to meet (and commiserate) with fellow writers, as well as meet and network with publishers, editors, and agents. Conferences and workshops provide some of the best opportunities for writers to make publishing contacts and pick up valuable information on the business, as well as the craft, of writing.

The bulk of the listings in this section are for conferences. Most conferences last from one day to one week and offer a combination of workshop-type writing sessions, panel discussions, and a variety of guest speakers. Topics may include all aspects of writing from fiction to poetry to scriptwriting, or they may focus on a specific type of writing, such as those conferences sponsored by the Romance Writers of America (RWA) for writers of romance or by the Society of Children's Book Writers and Illustrators (SCBWI) for writers of children's books.

Workshops, however, tend to run longer—usually one to two weeks. Designed to operate like writing classes, most require writers to be prepared to work on and discuss their fiction while attending. An important benefit of workshops is the opportunity they provide writers for an intensive critique of their work, often by professional writing teachers and established writers.

Each of the listings here includes information on the specific focus of an event as well as planned panels, guest speakers, and workshop topics. It is important to note, however, some conference directors were still in the planning stages for 2019 when we contacted them. If it was not possible to include 2019 dates, fees, or topics, we provided the most up-to-date information available so you can get an idea of what to expect. For the most current information, it's best to check the conference website about three months before the date(s) listed.

AGENTS & EDITORS CONFERENCE

Writers' League of Texas, 611 S. Congress Ave., Suite 200 A-3, Austin TX 78704. (512)499-8914. **E-mail:** michael@writersleague.org. **Website:** www.writersleague.org/38/conference. **Contact:** Michael Noll, program director. Estab. 1982.

COSTS Registration for the 2018 conference: $409 for Writers' League members and $469 for non-members through April 2, 2018. Registrations through April 2 include a one-on-one consultation with an agent or editor. After April 2: $449 for members and $409 for non-members, with consultations available for individual purchase.

ACCOMMODATIONS Discounted rates are available at the conference hotel.

ADDITIONAL INFORMATION Register before April 3 to receive a free consultation with an agent or editor.

ALABAMA WRITERS' CONCLAVE

AL **Website:** www.alabamawritersconclave.org. **Contact:** T.K. Thorne, president. Estab. 1923.

COSTS Previous fees for the conference: $175 for members and $225 for non-members. Discount $30 for seniors/students. Includes 2 meals. Critique fee: $25 for members and $30 for non-members.

ADDITIONAL INFORMATION "We have major speakers and faculty members who conduct intensive, energetic workshops. Our annual writing contest guidelines and all other information are available online."

ALASKA WRITERS CONFERENCE

Alaska Writers Guild, P.O. Box 670014, Chugiak AK 99567. **E-mail:** alaskawritersguild.awg@gmail.com. **Website:** alaskawritersguild.com.

ALGONKIAN FIVE DAY NOVEL CAMP

2020 Pennsylvania Ave. NW, Suite 443, Washington DC 20006. **E-mail:** info@algonkianconferences.com. **Website:** algonkianconferences.com.

ALTERNATIVE PRESS EXPO (APE)

Comic-Con International, P.O. Box 128458, San Diego CA 92112. (619)491-2475. **Fax:** (619)414-1022. **E-mail:** cci-info@comic-con.org. **Website:** www.alternativepressexpo.com. **Contact:** Eddie Ibrahim, director of programming.

AMERICAN CHRISTIAN WRITERS CONFERENCES

P.O. Box 110390, Nashville TN 37222. (800)219-7483 or (615)331-8668. **E-mail:** acwriters@aol.com. **Website:** www.acwriters.com. **Contact:** Reg Forder, director. Estab. 1981.

COSTS Costs vary and may depend on type of event (conference or mentoring retreat).

ACCOMMODATIONS Special rates are available at the host hotel (usually a major chain like Holiday Inn).

ADDITIONAL INFORMATION E-mail or call for conference brochures.

ANTIOCH WRITERS' WORKSHOP

Antioch Writers' Workshop, c/o Antioch University Midwest, 900 Dayton St., Yellow Springs OH 45387. (937)769-1803. **E-mail:** info@antiochwritersworkshop.com. **Website:** www.antiochwritersworkshop.com. **Contact:** Sharon Short, director. Estab. 1986.

ACCOMMODATIONS Accommodations are available at local hotels and bed-and-breakfasts.

ADDITIONAL INFORMATION The easiest way to contact this event is through the website's contact form.

ARKANSAS WRITERS' CONFERENCE

1815 Columbia Dr., Conway AR 72034. (501)833-2756. **E-mail:** breannacone1@yahoo.com. **Website:** www.arkansaswritersconference.org.

ARTIST-IN-RESIDENCE NATIONAL PARKS

E-mail: acadia_information@nps.gov. **Website:** www.nps.gov/subjects/arts/air.htm. **Contact:** Artist-In-Residence Coordinator.

ADDITIONAL INFORMATION See website for contact information for individual parks.

ART WORKSHOPS IN GUATEMALA

4758 Lyndale Ave. S., Minneapolis MN 55419. (612)825-0747. **E-mail:** info@artguat.org. **Website:** www.artguat.org. **Contact:** Liza Fourre, director. Estab. 1995.

COSTS See website. Includes tuition, lodging, breakfast, and ground transportation.

ADDITIONAL INFORMATION For brochure/guidelines, visit website, e-mail, or call.

ASPEN SUMMER WORDS LITERARY FESTIVAL & WRITING RETREAT

Aspen Words, 110 E. Hallam St., Suite 116, Aspen CO 81611. (970)925-3122. **Fax:** (970)925-5700. **E-mail:** aspenwords@aspeninstitute.org. **Website:** www.aspenwords.org. **Contact:** Caroline Tory. Estab. 1976.

COSTS $1,375. Includes some meals. Financial aid is available on a limited basis.

ADDITIONAL INFORMATION To apply for a juried workshop, submit up to 10 pages of prose with a $30 application fee by February. Registration to nonjuried workshops (Beginning Fiction and Playwriting) is first-come, first-served. Call, e-mail, or visit the website for an application and complete guidelines.

ASSOCIATION OF WRITERS & WRITING PROGRAMS CONFERENCE & BOOKFAIR

Association of Writers & Writing Programs, University of Maryland, 5700 Rivertech Court, Suite 225, Riverdale Park MD 20737-1250. (301)226-9711. **Fax:** (301)226.9797. **E-mail:** conference@awpwriter.org; events@awpwriter.org. **Website:** www.awpwriter.org/awp_conference. Estab. 1973.

ADDITIONAL INFORMATION Upcoming conference locations include Washington, DC (February 8-11, 2017) and Tampa, Florida (March 7-10, 2018).

ATLANTA WRITERS CONFERENCE

Atlanta Writers Club, Westin Atlanta Airport Hotel, 4736 Best Rd., Atlanta GA 30337. **E-mail:** awconference@gmail.com. **Website:** www.atlantawritersconference.com/about. **Contact:** George Weinstein. Estab. 2008.

COSTS Manuscript critiques are $170 each (2 spots/waitlists maximum). Pitches are $70 each (2 spots/waitlists maximum). There's no charge for waitlists unless a spot opens. Query letter critiques are $70 (1 spot maximum). Other workshops and panels may also cost extra; see website. The "all activities" option is $620 and includes 2 manuscript critiques, 2 pitches, and 1 of each remaining activity.

ACCOMMODATIONS A block of rooms is reserved at the conference hotel. Booking instructions will be sent in the registration confirmation e-mail.

ADDITIONAL INFORMATION A free shuttle runs between the airport and the hotel.

AUSTIN FILM FESTIVAL & CONFERENCE

1801 Salina St., Suite 210, Austin TX 78702. (512)478-4795 or (800)310-3378. **Fax:** (512)478-6205. **Website:** www.austinfilmfestival.com. **Contact:** Conference Director. Estab. 1994.

COSTS Austin Film Festival offers 4 badge levels for entry, and access to the conference depends on the badge level. Go online for offers and to view the different options available with each badge.

AWP ANNUAL CONFERENCE AND BOOKFAIR

MS 1E3, George Mason Univ., Fairfax VA 22030. (703)993-4317. **E-mail:** conference@awpwriter.org. **Website:** https://www.awpwriter.org/awp_conference/overview. Estab. 1967.

COSTS Early registration fees: $40 student; $140 AWP member; $160 non-member.

ACCOMMODATIONS Provides airline discounts and rental-car discounts.

ADDITIONAL INFORMATION AWP Annual Conference & Bookfair, Los Angeles, CA 2016. Annual. Conference duration: 4 days. AWP holds its Annual Conference in a different region of North America in order to celebrate the outstanding authors, teachers, writing programs, literary centers, and small press publishers of that region. The Annual Conference typically features 350 presentations: readings, lectures, panel discussions, and forums plus hundreds of book signings, receptions, dances, and informal gatherings. The conference attracts more than 8,000 attendees and more than 500 publishers. All genres are represented. "We will offer 175 panels on everything from writing to teaching to critical analysis." In 2009, Art Spiegelman was the keynote speaker. Others readers were Charles Baxter, Isaiah Sheffer, Z.Z. Packer, Nareem Murr, Marilynne Robinson; 2008: John Irving, Joyce Carol Oates, among others.

BACKSPACE AGENT-AUTHOR SEMINAR

P.O. Box 454, Washington MI 48094. (732)267-6449. **Fax:** (586)532-9652. **E-mail:** admin@bksp.org. **Website:** www.backspacewritersconference.com. **Contact:** Christopher Graham and Karen Dionne, organizers. Estab. 2006.

COSTS Each workshop is $225. Attendance limited to 10. Writerws can register for as many workshops as they wish.

BALTIMORE COMIC-CON

Baltimore Convention Center, 1 West Pratt St., Baltimore MD 21201. (410)526-7410. **E-mail:** general@baltimorecomiccon.com. **Website:** www.baltimorecomiccon.com. **Contact:** Marc Nathan. Estab. 1999.

COSTS General admission, VIP, celebrity, and Ringo Awards tickets are available at baltimorecomiccon.com/tickets.

ACCOMMODATIONS Does not offer overnight accommodation. Provides list of area hotels and lodging options offering associated discounts.

ADDITIONAL INFORMATION For brochure, visit website.

BALTIMORE WRITERS' CONFERENCE

English Department, Liberal Arts Bldg., Towson University, 8000 York Rd., Towson MD 21252. (410)704-5196. **E-mail:** prwr@towson.edu. **Website:** baltimorewritersconference.org. Estab. 1994.

ACCOMMODATIONS Hotels are close by, if required.

ADDITIONAL INFORMATION Writers may register through the website. Send inquiries via e-mail.

BAY TO OCEAN WRITERS CONFERENCE

P.O. Box 1773, Easton MD 21601. (410)482-6337. **E-mail:** info@baytoocean.com. **Website:** www.baytoocean.com. Estab. 1998.

COSTS Adults: $100-120. Students: $55. A paid ms review is also available; details on website. Includes continental breakfast and networking lunch.

ADDITIONAL INFORMATION Registration is on website. Pre-registration is required; no registration at door. Conference usually sells out 1 month in advance. Conference is for all levels of writers.

BLOCKBUSTER PLOT INTENSIVE WRITING WORKSHOPS (SANTA CRUZ)

Santa Cruz CA **E-mail:** contact@blockbusterplots.com. **Website:** www.blockbusterplots.com. **Contact:** Martha Alderson (also known as the Plot Whisperer), instructor. Estab. 2000.

COSTS Costs vary based on the time frame of the retreat/workshop.

ACCOMMODATIONS Updated website provides list of area hotels and lodging options.

ADDITIONAL INFORMATION Accepts inquiries by e-mail.

JAMES BONNET'S STORYMAKING: THE MASTER CLASS

Santa Monica CA (310)451-5418. **E-mail:** bonnet@storymaking.com. **Website:** www.storymaking.com. **Contact:** James Bonnet. Estab. 1990.

ACCOMMODATIONS Provides a list of area hotels or lodging options.

ADDITIONAL INFORMATION For brochure, e-mail, visit website, or call. Accepts inquiries by e-mail, phone, and fax. James Bonnet is the author of *Stealing Fire From the Gods: The Complete Guide to Story for Writers and Filmmakers.*

BOOKS-IN-PROGRESS CONFERENCE

Carnegie Center for Literacy and Learning, 251 W. Second St., Lexington KY 40507. (859)254-4175. **E-mail:** ccll1@carnegiecenterlex.org. **Website:** carnegiecenterlex.org. **Contact:** Laura Whitaker, program director. Estab. 2010.

ACCOMMODATIONS See website for list of area hotels.

BOOMING GROUND MENTORSHIP PROGRAM & MANUSCRIPT EVALUATION SERVICE

Buch E462, 1866 Main Mall, University of British Columbia, Vancouver British Columbia V6T 1Z1, Canada. **E-mail:** contact@boomingground.com. **Website:** www.boomingground.com.

BREAD LOAF IN SICILY WRITERS' CONFERENCE

Middlebury College, Middlebury College, Middlebury VT 05753. (802)443-5286. **Fax:** (802)443-2087. **E-mail:** blsicily@middlebury.edu. **Website:** www.middlebury.edu/bread-loaf-conferences/blsicily. Estab. 2011.

COSTS $3,020. Includes the conference program, transfer to and from Palermo Airport, 6 nights of lodging, 3 meals daily (except for Wednesday), wine reception at the readings, and an excursion to the ancient ruins of Segesta. The charge for an additional person is $1,750. There is a $15 application fee an a $300 deposit.

ACCOMMODATIONS Accommodations are single rooms with private bath. Breakfast and lunch are served at the hotel, and dinner is available at select Erice restaurants. A double room is possible for those who would like to be accompanied by a spouse or significant other.

ADDITIONAL INFORMATION Application deadline for 2017 conference: April 15. Rolling admissions. Space is limited.

BREAD LOAF ORION ENVIRONMENTAL WRITERS' CONFERENCE

Middlebury College, Middlebury College, Middlebury VT 05753. (802)443-5286. **Fax:** (802)443-2087. **E-mail:** blorion@middlebury.edu. **Website:** www.middlebury.edu/bread-loaf-conferences/blorion. Estab. 2014.

COSTS $2205 for full participants and $1875 for auditors. Both options include room and board.

ACCOMMODATIONS Mountain campus of Middlebury College in Vermont.

ADDITIONAL INFORMATION The event is designed to hone the skills of people interested in producing literary writing about the environment and the natural world. The conference is co-sponsored by the Bread Loaf Writers' Conference, Orion magazine, and Middlebury College's Environmental Studies Program. Application deadline for 2017 conference: February 15. Rolling admissions. Space is limited.

BREAD LOAF WRITERS' CONFERENCE

Middlebury College, Middlebury College, Middlebury VT 05753. (802)443-5286. **Fax:** (802)443-2087. **E-mail:** blwc@middlebury.edu. **Website:** www.middlebury.edu/bread-loaf-conferences/bl_writers. Estab. 1926.

COSTS $3,395 for general contributors and $3,255 for auditors. Both options include room and board.

ACCOMMODATIONS Bread Loaf campus of Middlebury College in Ripton, Vermont.

ADDITIONAL INFORMATION The application deadline for the 2018 event is February 15; there is $15 application fee.

◐ BYRON WRITERS FESTIVAL

Northern Rivers Writers' Centre, P.O. Box 1846, Byron Bay New South Wales 2481, Australia. (61)(02)6685-5115. **Website:** www.byronwritersfestival.com. **Contact:** Edwina Johnson, director. Estab. 1997.

COSTS See website for details. Costs vary for early bird registration, NRWC members, students, and children.

CALIFORNIA CRIME WRITERS CONFERENCE

Sisters in Crime Los Angeles and Southern California Mystery Writers of America, DoubleTree by Hilton Los Angeles—Westside, 6161 W. Centinela Avenue, Culver City CA 90230, USA. **E-mail:** ccwconference@gmail.com. **E-mail:** ccwconference@gmail.com. **Website:** www.ccwconference.org. **Contact:** Rochelle Staab and Sue Ann Jaffarian, 2017 co-chairs. Estab. 1995.

COSTS Early bird registration through January 31: $265. Registration February 1-April 30: $300. Registration May 1-31: $335. Onsite registration: $350.

CAMPBELL CONFERENCE

University of Kansas Gunn Center for the Study of Science Fiction, Wesoce Hall, 1445 Jayhawk Blvd., Lawrence KS 66045. (785)864-2508. **E-mail:** cmckit@ku.edu; cssf@ku.edu. **Website:** www.sfcenter.ku.edu/campbell-conference.htm. Estab. 1985.

ACCOMMODATIONS Housing information is available. Several airport shuttle services offer reasonable transportation from the Kansas City International Airport to Lawrence.

ADDITIONAL INFORMATION Admission to the workshop is by submission of an acceptable story. Two additional stories are submitted by the middle of June. These 3 stories are distributed to other participants for critiquing and are the basis for the first week of the workshop. One story is rewritten for the second week, when students also work with guest authors. See website for guidelines. This workshop is intended for writers who have just started to sell their work or need that extra bit of understanding or skill to become a published writer.

CAPE COD WRITERS CENTER ANNUAL CONFERENCE

P.O. Box 408, Osterville MA 02655. (508)420-0200. **E-mail:** writers@capecodwriterscenter.org. **Website:** www.capecodwriterscenter.org. **Contact:** Nancy Rubin Stuart, executive director.

COSTS Costs vary, depending on the number of courses selected, beginning at $125. Several scholarships are available.

ACCOMMODATIONS Resort and Conference Center of Hyannis, Massachusetts.

CELEBRATION OF SOUTHERN LITERATURE

Southern Lit Alliance, 301 E. 11th St., Suite 301, Chattanooga TN 37403. (423)267-1218. **Fax:** (866)483-6831. **Website:** www.southernlitalliance.org.

CENTRAL OHIO FICTION WRITERS ANNUAL CONFERENCE

Romance Writers of America, P.O. Box 4213, Newark OH 43058. **E-mail:** susan_gee_heino@yahoo.com; msgigimorgan@gmail.com. **Website:** www.cofw.org. **Contact:** Susan Gee Heino, president; Gigi Morgan, conference chair. Estab. 1990.

CENTRUM'S PORT TOWNSEND WRITERS' CONFERENCE

P.O. Box 1158, Port Townsend WA 98368. (360)385-3102. **E-mail:** info@centrum.org. **Website:** centrum.

org/the-port-townsend-writers-conference. **Contact:** Jordan Hartt, director of programs. Estab. 1974. P.O. Box 1158, Port Townsend, WA 98368. (360)385-3102. **Fax:** (360)385-2470. **E-mail:** info@centrum.org; jhartt@centrum.org. **Website:** www.centrum.org. Estab. 1974. Annual. Conference held mid-July. Average attendance: 180. Conference to promote poetry, fiction, and creative nonfiction "featuring many of the nation's leading writers." Two different workshop options: "New Works" and "Works-in-Progress." Site: The conference is held at Fort Worden State Park on the Strait of Juan de Fuca. "The site is a Victorian-era military fort with miles of beaches, wooded trails, and recreation facilities. The park is within the limits of Port Townsend, a historic seaport and arts community, approximately 80 miles northwest of Seattle, on the Olympic Peninsula." Guest speakers participate in addition to full-time faculty.

COSTS Tuition for the conference is $200-700. Admission to afternoon workshops is $200-300. Register online.

ACCOMMODATIONS "Modest room and board facilities on site." Provides list of area lodging options.

ADDITIONAL INFORMATION Brochures/guidelines available for SASE or on website. "The conference focus is on the craft of writing and the writing life, not on marketing."

CHRISTOPHER NEWPORT UNIVERSITY WRITERS' CONFERENCE & WRITING CONTEST

(757)269-4368. **E-mail:** eleanor.taylor@cnu.edu. **Website:** writers.cnu.edu. Estab. 1981.

ACCOMMODATIONS Provides list of area hotels.

CLARION SCIENCE FICTION AND FANTASY WRITERS' WORKSHOP

Arthur C. Clarke Center for Human Imagination, University of California, San Diego, 9500 Gilman Dr., #0445, La Jolla CA 92093. (858)534-2115. **E-mail:** clarion@ucsd.edu. **Website:** clarion.ucsd.edu. **Contact:** Program Coordinator. Estab. 1968.

COSTS See website for current costs. Application fee is $50 before February 15 and $65 after. "Financial aid is awarded based on a combination of merit, need, and the criteria established by donors for particular funds. They range in size from $100 to over $3000, though most are between $500 and $1500."

ACCOMMODATIONS Participants make their own travel arrangements to and from the campus.

Campus residency is required. Participants are housed in semi-private accommodations (private bedroom, shared bathroom) in student apartments. The workshop fee includes room and board and 3 meals a day at a campus dining facility.

ADDITIONAL INFORMATION "Workshop participants are selected on the basis of their potential for highly successful writing careers. Applications are judged by a review panel composed of the workshop instructors. Applicants submit an application and 2 complete short stories, each between 2,500 words and 6,000 words. The application deadline (typically, March 1) is posted on the Clarion website." Information available in September. For additional information, visit website.

CLARION WEST WRITERS WORKSHOP

P.O. Box 31264, Seattle WA 98103. (206)322-9083. **E-mail:** info@clarionwest.org. **Website:** www.clarionwest.org. **Contact:** Neile Graham, workshop director.

COSTS $4,200 (for tuition, housing, most meals). Numerous scholarships are available. Students can apply by mail or e-mail and must submit 20-30 pages of ms with four-page biography and $60 fee ($35 if received by February 10).

ACCOMMODATIONS Students stay on-site in workshop housing near the University of Washington.

ADDITIONAL INFORMATION Conference information available in fall. For brochure/guidelines, send SASE, visit website, e-mail, or call.

DETROIT WORKING WRITERS ANNUAL WRITERS CONFERENCE

Detroit Working Writers, P.O. Box 82395, Rochester MI 48308. **E-mail:** conference@detworkingwriters.org. **Website:** dww-writers-conference.org. Estab. 1961.

COSTS Costs vary, depending on early bird registration and membership status within the organization.

EMERALD CITY COMICON

3333 184th St. SW. Suite G, Lynnwood WA 98037. (425)744-2767. **Fax:** (425)675-0737. **E-mail:** info@emeraldcitycomicon.com; ksalierno@reedexpo.com. **Website:** www.emeraldcitycomicon.com. **Contact:** Kristen Salierno, operations manager. Estab. 2002.

COSTS Prices vary based on day.

ACCOMMODATIONS Offers discounted rate at Roosevelt Hotel, Crowne Plaza, and Red Lion in Seattle.

FESTIVAL OF FAITH AND WRITING

Department of English, Calvin College, 1795 Knollcrest Circle SE, Grand Rapids MI 49546. (616)526-6770. **E-mail:** ffw@calvin.edu. **Website:** festival.calvin.edu. Estab. 1990.

ACCOMMODATIONS Shuttles are available to and from local hotels. Shuttles are also available for overflow parking lots. A list of hotels with special rates for attendees is available on the conference website. High school and college students can arrange on-campus lodging by e-mail.

FLORIDA CHRISTIAN WRITERS CONFERENCE

Word Weavers International, Inc., P O Box 520224, Longwood FL 32752. (407)615-4112. **E-mail:** floridacwc@aol.com. **Website:** floridacwc.net. **Contact:** Eva Marie Everson and Mark T. Hancock. Estab. 1988.

COSTS Ranges: $275 (daily rate—in advance, includes lunch and dinner; specify days) to $1,495 (attendee and participating spouse/family member in same room). Scholarships offered. For more information or to register, go to the conference website.

ACCOMMODATIONS Offers private rooms and double occupancy as well as accommodations for participating and non-participating family members. Meals provided, including awards dessert banquet Saturday evening. For those flying into Orlando or Sanford airports, FCWC provides a shuttle to and from the conference center.

FLORIDA ROMANCE WRIITERS FUN IN THE SUN CONFERENCE

Florida Romance Writers, P.O. Box 550562, Fort Lauderdale FL 33355. **E-mail:** frwfuninthesun@yahoo.com. **Website:** frwfuninthesunmain.blogspot.com. Estab. 1986.

THE GLEN WORKSHOP

Image Journal, St. John's College, 1160 Camino Cruz Blanca, Santa Fe NM 87505. (206)281-2988. **Fax:** (206)281-2335. **E-mail:** glenworkshop@imagejournal.org. **Website:** glenworkshop.com. Estab. 1995.

COSTS See costs online. "Lodging and meals are included with registration at affordable rates. A low-cost 'commuter' rate is also available for those who wish to camp, stay with friends, or otherwise find their own food and lodging." A limited number of partial scholarships are available.

ACCOMMODATIONS Offers dorm rooms, dorm suites, and apartments.

ADDITIONAL INFORMATION "Like *Image*, the Glen is grounded in a Christian perspective, but its tone is informal and hospitable to all spiritual wayfarers. Depending on the teacher, participants may need to submit workshop material prior to arrival (usually 10-25 pages)."

GOTHAM WRITERS' WORKSHOP

writingclasses.com, 555 Eighth Ave., Suite 1402, New York NY 10018. (212)974-8377. **Fax:** (212)307-6325. **E-mail:** contact@gothamwriters.com. **Website:** www.writingclasses.com. Estab. 1993.

ADDITIONAL INFORMATION See the website for courses, pricing, and instructors.

GREAT LAKES WRITERS FESTIVAL

Lakeland College, P.O. Box 359, Sheboygan WI 53082. **E-mail:** elderk@lakeland.edu. **Website:** www.greatlakeswritersfestival.org. **Contact:** Karl Elder. Estab. 1991.

COSTS Free and open to the public. Participants may purchase meals and must arrange for their own lodging.

ACCOMMODATIONS Does not offer overnight accommodations. Provides list of area hotels and lodging options.

ADDITIONAL INFORMATION All participants who would like to have their writing considered as an object for discussion during the festival workshops should submit to Karl Elder electronically by October 15. Participants may submit material for workshops in 1 genre only (poetry, fiction, or creative nonfiction). Sponsors contest. Contest entries must contain the writer's name and address on a separate title page, typed, and be submitted as a clear, hard copy on Friday at the festival registration table. Entries may be in each of 3 genres per participant, yet only 1 poem, 1 story, and/or 1 nonfiction piece may be entered. There are 2 categories—high school students and adults—of cash awards for first place in each of the 3 genres. The judges reserve the right to decline to award a prize in 1 or more of the genres. Judges will be the editorial staff of *Seems* (a.k.a. Word of Mouth Books), excluding the festival coordinator, Karl Elder. Information available in September. For brochure, visit website.

GREEN LAKE CHRISTIAN WRITERS' CONFERENCE

W2511 State Rd. 23, Green Lake Conference Center, Green Lake WI 54941. (920)294-3323. **E-mail:** program@glcc.org. **E-mail:** kriswood@glcc.org. **Website:** glcc.org. **Contact:** Kris Wood, conference director. Estab. 1948.

COSTS Check website for updated pricing.

ACCOMMODATIONS Hotels, lodges, and all meeting rooms are air conditioned. Affordable rates, excellent meals.

ADDITIONAL INFORMATION Brochure and scholarship info available online, or contact Kris Wood.

GREEN MOUNTAIN WRITERS CONFERENCE

47 Hazel St., Rutland VT 05701. (802)236-6133. **E-mail:** ydaley@sbcglobal.net. **E-mail:** yvonnedaley@me.com. **Website:** vermontwriters.com. **Contact:** Yvonne Daley, director. Estab. 1998.

COSTS $525 before April 15; $575 before May 15; $600 before June 1. Partial scholarships are available.

ACCOMMODATIONS Dramatically reduced rates at the Mountain Top Inn and Resort for attendees. Close to other area hotels and bed-and-breakfasts in Rutland County, Vermont.

ADDITIONAL INFORMATION Participants' mss can be read and commented on at a cost. Sponsors contests and publishes a literary magazine featuring work of participants. Brochures available on website or e-mail.

HAMPTON ROADS WRITERS CONFERENCE

Hampton Roads Writers, P.O. Box 56228, Virginia Beach VA 23456. (757)639-6146. **E-mail:** hrwriters@cox.net. **Website:** hamptonroadswriters.org. Estab. 2008.

COSTS Costs vary. There are discounts for members, for early bird registration, for students, and more.

HEDGEBROOK

P.O. Box 1231, Freeland WA 98249. (360)321-4786. **Fax:** (360)321-2171. **Website:** www.hedgebrook.org. **Contact:** Vito Zingarelli, residency director. Estab. 1988.

ADDITIONAL INFORMATION Takes applications 6 months in advance.

HIGHLAND SUMMER CONFERENCE

P.O. Box 7014, Radford University, Radford VA 24142. **E-mail:** tburriss@radford.edu; rbderrick@radford.edu. **Website:** tinyurl.com/q8z8ej9. **Contact:** Dr. Theresa Burriss; Ruth Derrick. Estab. 1978.

HIGHLIGHTS FOUNDATION FOUNDERS WORKSHOPS

814 Court St., Honesdale PA 18431. (877)288-3410. **Fax:** (570)253-0179. **E-mail:** klbrown@highlightsfoundation.org. **E-mail:** jo.lloyd@highlightsfoundation.org. **Website:** highlightsfoundation.org. **Contact:** Kent L. Brown, Jr.. Estab. 2000.

COSTS Prices vary based on workshop. Check website for details.

ACCOMMODATIONS Coordinates pickup at local airport. Offers overnight accommodations. Participants stay in guest cabins on the wooded grounds surrounding Highlights Founders' home adjacent to the house/conference center.

ADDITIONAL INFORMATION Some workshops require pre-workshop assignment. Brochure available for SASE, by e-mail, on website, by phone, by fax. Accepts inquiries by phone, fax, e-mail, SASE. Editors attend conference.

HIGHLIGHTS FOUNDATION WRITERS WORKSHOPS

814 Court St., Honesdale PA 18431. (570)253-1192. **Fax:** (570)253-0179. **E-mail:** jo.lloyd@highlightsfoundation.org. **Website:** highlightsfoundation.org. Estab. 1985.

ACCOMMODATIONS Private lodging on-site, included in workshop tuition.

ADDITIONAL INFORMATION Most workshops offer attendees the option of submitting a ms for review at the conference. Workshop brochures/guidelines are available upon request.

TONY HILLERMAN WRITERS CONFERENCE

1063 Willow Way, Santa Fe NM 87505. (505)795-1590. **E-mail:** wordharvest@wordharvest.com. **Website:** www.wordharvest.com. **Contact:** Anne Hillerman and Jean Schaumberg, cofounders. Estab. 2004.

COSTS Check website for current pricing.

ACCOMMODATIONS Hilton Santa Fe Historic Plaza.

IDAHO WRITERS LEAGUE WRITERS' CONFERENCE

601 W. 75 St., Blackfoot ID 83221. (208)684-4200. **Website:** www.idahowritersleague.org. Estab. 1940.

COSTS Pricing varies. Check website for more information.

INDIANA UNIVERSITY WRITERS' CONFERENCE

470 Ballantine Hall, 1020 E. Kirkwood Ave., Bloomington IN 47405. (812)855-1877. **E-mail:** writecon@indiana.edu. **Website:** http://www.iuwc.indiana.edu/. Estab. 1940.

COSTS The cost for the Poetry, Fiction Workshops is $645 (which includes all classes). For classes only, the cost is $385.

ACCOMMODATIONS Information on accommodations available on website.

ADDITIONAL INFORMATION Follow the conference on Twitter at @iuwritecon.

INTERNATIONAL COMIC-CON

Comic-Con International, P.O. Box 128458, San Diego CA 92112. (619)491-2475. **Fax:** (619)414-1022. **E-mail:** cci-info@comic-con.org. **Website:** www.comic-con.org/cci. **Contact:** Gary Sassaman, director of print/publications. Comic-Con International, P.O. Box 128458, San Diego, CA 92112-8458. (619)491-2475. **Fax:** (619)414-1022. **E-mail:** cci-info@comic-con.org. **Website:** www.comic-con.org/cci/. Annual. Conference duration: 4 days. Average attendance: 104,000. "The comics industry's largest expo, hosting writers, artists, editors, agents, publishers, buyers and sellers of comics and graphic novels." Site: San Diego Convention Center. "Nearly 300 programming events, including panels, seminars and previews, on the world of comics, movies, television, animation, art, and much more. We're also, of course, featuring Golden and Silver Age creators, sf/fantasy writers and artists, and longtime Comic-Con friends." Previous special guests included Ray Bradbury, Forrest J. Ackerman, Sergio Aragones, John Romita Sr., J. Michael Straczynski, Daniel Clowes, George Perez.

COSTS Prices vary. Check website for full costs.

ACCOMMODATIONS Does not offer overnight accommodations. Provides list of area hotels or lodging options. Special conference hotel and airfare discounts available. See website for details.

ADDITIONAL INFORMATION For brochure, visit website. Agents and editors participate in conference.

INTERNATIONAL MUSIC CAMP CREATIVE WRITING WORKSHOP

111 11th Ave. SW, Minot ND 58701. (701)838-8472. **Fax:** (701)838-1351. **E-mail:** info@internationalmusiccamp.com. **Website:** www.internationalmusic-camp.com. **Contact:** Christine Baumann and Tim Baumann, camp directors. Estab. 1956.

COSTS Fees vary based on activities. Check website for full details.

ACCOMMODATIONS Airline and depot shuttles are available upon request. Housing is included in the fee.

ADDITIONAL INFORMATION Conference information is available on the website. Welcomes questions via e-mail.

◑ INTERNATIONAL WOMEN'S FICTION FESTIVAL

Via Cappuccini 8E, Matera , Italy. (39)0835-312044. **Fax:** (39)333-5857933. **E-mail:** contact@womensfictionfestival.com. **Website:** www.womensfictionfestival.com. **Contact:** Elizabeth Jennings. Estab. 2004.

COSTS Registration costs vary. Check website for full details.

ACCOMMODATIONS The conference is held at Le Monacelle, a restored 17th century convent. Conference travel agency will find reasonably priced accommodation. A paid shuttle is available from the Bari Airport to the hotel in Matera.

IOWA SUMMER WRITING FESTIVAL

The University of Iowa, 250 Continuing Education Facility, University of Iowa, Iowa City IA 52242. (319)335-4160. **Fax:** (319)335-4039. **E-mail:** iswfestival@uiowa.edu. **Website:** www.iowasummerwritingfestival.org. Estab. 1987.

ACCOMMODATIONS Accommodations available at area hotels. Information on overnight accommodations available by phone or on website.

ADDITIONAL INFORMATION Brochures are available in February. Inquire via e-mail or on website. "Register early. Classes fill quickly."

IWWG ANNUAL SUMMER CONFERENCE

(917)720-6959. **E-mail:** iwwgquestions@gmail.com. **Website:** https://iwwg.wildapricot.org/events. **Contact:** Dixie King, executive director. Estab. 1976. 2017 dates: July 7-14. Location: Pennsylvania. More information to come. Average attendance: 500 maximum.

Open to all women. Around 65 workshops offered each day.

ACCOMMODATIONS Check website for updated pricing.

ADDITIONAL INFORMATION Choose from 30 workshops in poetry, fiction, memoir and personal narrative, social action/advocacy, and mind-body-spirit. Critique sessions; book fair; salons; open readings. No portfolio required.

JACKSON HOLE WRITERS CONFERENCE

P.O. Box 1974, Jackson WY 83001. (307)413-3332. **E-mail:** connie@blackhen.com. **Website:** jacksonholewritersconference.com. Estab. 1991.

COSTS $375 thru May 12, 2018; critiques additional.

ACCOMMODATIONS Accommodations not included.

ADDITIONAL INFORMATION Held at the Center for the Arts in Jackson, Wyoming, and online.

JAMES RIVER WRITERS CONFERENCE

2319 E. Broad St., Richmond VA 23223. (804)433-3790. **E-mail:** info@jamesriverwriters.org. **Website:** www.jamesriverwriters.org. **Contact:** Katharine Herndon. Estab. 2003.

COSTS Check website for updated pricing.

JOURNEY INTO THE IMAGINATION: A FIVE-DAY WRITING RETREAT

995 Chapman Rd., Yorktown Heights NY 10598. (914)962-4432. **E-mail:** emily@emilyhanlon.com. **Website:** www.thefictionwritersjourney.com/pendle-hill-spring-writers-retreat.html. **Contact:** Emily Hanlon. Estab. 2004.

COSTS See website for current costs.

ACCOMMODATIONS All rooms are private with shared bath.

ADDITIONAL INFORMATION For brochure, visit website.

KACHEMAK BAY WRITERS' CONFERENCE

Kachemak Bay Campus—Kenai Peninsula College/University of Alaska Anchorage, Kenai Peninsula College—Kachemak Bay Campus, 533 E. Pioneer Ave., Homer AK 99603. (907)235-7743. **E-mail:** iyconf@uaa.alaska.edu. **Website:** writersconf.kpc.alaska.edu.

COSTS See the website. Some scholarships available.

ACCOMMODATIONS Homer is 225 miles south of Anchorage, Alaska, on the southern tip of the Kenai Peninsula and the shores of Kachemak Bay. There are multiple hotels in the area.

KENTUCKY WOMEN WRITERS CONFERENCE

University of Kentucky College of Arts & Sciences, 232 E. Maxwell St., Lexington KY 40506. (859)257-2874. **E-mail:** kentuckywomenwriters@gmail.com. **Website:** kentuckywomenwriters.org. **Contact:** Julie Wrinn, director. Estab. 1979.

COSTS $200 for general admission and a workshop and $125 for admission with no workshop.

ADDITIONAL INFORMATION Sponsors prizes in poetry ($300), fiction ($300), nonfiction ($300), playwriting ($500), and spoken word ($500). Winners are also invited to read during the conference. Pre-registration opens May 1.

KENTUCKY WRITERS CONFERENCE

Southern Kentucky Book Fest, WKU South Campus, 2355 Nashville Rd., Bowling Green KY 42101. (270)745-4502. **E-mail:** sara.volpi@wku.edu. **Website:** www.sokybookfest.org. **Contact:** Sara Volpi.

KENYON REVIEW WRITERS WORKSHOP

Kenyon Review, Kenyon College, Gambier OH 43022. (740)427-5208. **Fax:** (740)427-5417. **E-mail:** kenyonreview@kenyon.edu; writers@kenyonreview.org. **Website:** www.kenyonreview.org/workshops. **Contact:** Anna Duke Reach, director. Estab. 1990.

COSTS Fiction, literary nonfiction, poetry, nature writing, translation: $2,295. Teachers: $1,495. All rates include tuition and room and board.

ACCOMMODATIONS The workshop operates a shuttle to and from Gambier and the airport in Columbus, Ohio. Offers overnight accommodations. Participants are housed in Kenyon College student housing.

ADDITIONAL INFORMATION Application includes a writing sample. Admission decisions are made on a rolling basis. Starting in November, workshop information is available online. For a brochure, send e-mail, visit website, call, or fax. Accepts inquiries by SASE, e-mail, phone, fax.

KILLER NASHVILLE

P.O. Box 680759, Franklin TN 37068. (615)599-4032. **E-mail:** contact@killernashville.com. **Website:** www.killernashville.com. Estab. 2006.

COSTS $375 for general registration. Includes network lunches on Friday and Saturday and special sessions with best-selling authors and industry professionals.

ADDITIONAL INFORMATION Additional information about registration is provided online.

LAS VEGAS WRITER'S CONFERENCE

Henderson Writers' Group, P.O. Box 92032, Henderson NV 89009. (702)953-5675. **E-mail:** info@lasvegaswritersconference.com. **Website:** www.lasvegaswritersconference.com. Estab. 2001.

COSTS Costs vary depending on the package. See the website. There are early bird rates through January 31.

ADDITIONAL INFORMATION Agents and editors participate in conference.

LEAGUE OF UTAH WRITERS' ANNUAL WRITER'S CONFERENCES

Spring Conference and Quills Conference, 1042 East Fort Union Blvd. #443, Midvale UT 84047. (385)434-0355. **E-mail:** president@leagueofutahwriters.org. **Website:** https://www.leagueofutahwriters.com. **Contact:** Johnny Worthen. Estab. 1935.

COSTS Spring Conference is $50 for members. Quills Conference is $250 for members.

THE MACDOWELL COLONY

100 High St., Peterborough NH 03458. (603)924-3886. **Fax:** (603)924-9142. **E-mail:** admissions@macdowellcolony.org. **Website:** www.macdowellcolony.org. Estab. 1907.

COSTS Artists are responsible for travel to and from the Colony. Travel reimbursement and stipends are available for participants of the residency, based on need. There are no residency fees.

ACCOMMODATIONS Exclusive use of a private studio and bedroom are provided for each artist in residence.

MAGNA CUM MURDER

Magna Cum Murder Crime Writing Festival, E.B. and Bertha C. Ball Center, Ball State University, 400 Minnetrista Pkwy., Muncie IN 47306. (765)285-8975. **Fax:** (765)747-9566. **E-mail:** magnacummurder@yahoo.com;. **Website:** www.magnacummurder.com. Estab. 1994.

COSTS Check website for updates.

MENDOCINO COAST WRITERS' CONFERENCE

P.O. Box 2087, Fort Bragg CA 95437. (707)485-4031. **E-mail:** info@mcwc.org. **Website:** www.mcwc.org.

Contact: Shirin Bridges, Executive Director. Estab. 1989.

COSTS $575 early bird registration includes morning intensives, afternoon panels and seminars, social events, and most meals. Scholarships available. Opt-in for consultations and Publishing Boot Camp. Early application advised.

ACCOMMODATIONS Many lodging options in the scenic coastal area.

ADDITIONAL INFORMATION "Take your writing to the next level with encouragement, expertise, and inspiration in a literary community where authors are also fantastic teachers." General registration opens March 1. Apply now for a scholarship or for the Master Class, deadline is February 15.

MIDWEST WRITERS WORKSHOP

Muncie IN 47306. (765)282-1055. **E-mail:** midwestwriters@yahoo.com. **Website:** www.midwestwriters.org. **Contact:** Jama Kehoe Bigger, director.

COSTS $155-400. Most meals included.

ADDITIONAL INFORMATION Offers scholarships. See website for more information. Keep in touch with the MWW at facebook.com/midwestwriters and twitter.com/midwestwriters.

MISSOURI WRITERS' GUILD CONFERENCE

St. Louis MO **E-mail:** mwgconferenceinfo@gmail.com. **Website:** www.missouriwritersguild.org. **Contact:** Tricia Sanders, vice president/conference chair.

ADDITIONAL INFORMATION The primary contact individual changes every year, because the conference chair changes every year. See the website for contact info.

MONTEVALLO LITERARY FESTIVAL

Comer Hall, Station 6420, University of Montevallo, Montevallo AL 35115. (205)665-6420. **Fax:** (205)665-6420. **E-mail:** murphyj@montevallo.edu. **Website:** www.montevallo.edu/arts-sciences/college-of-arts-sciences/departments/english-foreign-languages/student-organizations/montevallo-literary-festival. **Contact:** Dr. Jim Murphy, director. Estab. 2003.

MONTROSE CHRISTIAN WRITERS' CONFERENCE

Montrose Bible Conference, 218 Locust St., Montrose PA 18801. (570)278-1001 or (800)598-5030. **Fax:** (570)278-3061. **E-mail:** mbc@montrosebible.org. **Website:** www.montrosebible.org. Estab. 1990.

COSTS Tuition is $195.

ACCOMMODATIONS Will meet planes in Binghamton, New York, and Scranton, Pennsylvania. On-site accommodations: room and board $360-490/conference, including food (2018 rates). RV court available.

ADDITIONAL INFORMATION "Writers can send work ahead of time and have it critiqued for a small fee." The attendees are usually church related. The writing has a Christian emphasis. Conference information available in April. For brochure, visit website, e-mail, or call. Accepts inquiries by phone or e-mail.

MOONLIGHT AND MAGNOLIAS WRITER'S CONFERENCE

Georgia Romance Writers, 3741 Casteel Park Dr., Marietta GA 30064. **Website:** www.georgiaromancewriters.org/mm-conference. Estab. 1982.

JENNY MCKEAN MOORE COMMUNITY WORKSHOPS

English Department, George Washington University, 801 22nd St. NW, Rome Hall, Suite 760, Washington DC 20052. (202)994-6180. **Fax:** (202)994-6637. **E-mail:** lpageinc@aol.com. **Website:** www.gwu.edu/~english/creative_jennymckeanmoore.html. **Contact:** Lisa Page, director of creative writing. Estab. 1976.

ADDITIONAL INFORMATION Admission is competitive and by decided by the quality of a submitted ms.

MOUNT HERMON CHRISTIAN WRITERS CONFERENCE

P.O. Box 413, Mount Hermon CA 95041. **E-mail:** info@mounthermon.org. **Website:** writers.mounthermon.org. Estab. 1970.

MUSE AND THE MARKETPLACE

Grub Street, 162 Boylston St., 5th Floor, Boston MA 02116. (617)695-0075. **E-mail:** info@grubstreet.org. **Website:** museandthemarketplace.com. **ACCOMMODATIONS** Boston Park Plaza Hotel.

NAPA VALLEY WRITERS' CONFERENCE

Napa Valley College, 1088 College Ave., St. Helena CA 94574. (707)967-2900 ext. 4. **E-mail:** info@napawritersconference.og. **Website:** www.napawritersconference.org. **Contact:** Catherine Thorpe, managing director. Estab. 1981.

COSTS $975; $25 application fee.

NATIONAL WRITERS ASSOCIATION FOUNDATION CONFERENCE

10940 S. Parker Rd., #508, Parker CO 80138. **E-mail:** natlwritersassn@hotmail.com. **Website:** www.nationalwriters.com. **Contact:** Sandy Whelchel, executive director. Estab. 1926.

ADDITIONAL INFORMATION Awards for previous contests will be presented at the conference. Brochures/guidelines are available online or by SASE.

NETWO WRITERS CONFERENCE

Northeast Texas Writers Organization, P.O. Box 962, Mt. Pleasant TX 75456. (469)867-2624 or (903)573-6084. **E-mail:** jimcallan@winnsboro.com. **Website:** www.netwo.org. Estab. 1987.

COSTS $90 for members before February 29th, and $100 after. $112.50 for non-members before February 29th, and $125 after.

ACCOMMODATIONS See website for information on area motels and hotels.The conference is held at the Titus County Civic Center in Mt. Pleasant, Texas.

ADDITIONAL INFORMATION Conference is co-sponsored by the Texas Commission on the Arts. See website for current updates.

NEW JERSEY ROMANCE WRITERS PUT YOUR HEART IN A BOOK CONFERENCE

P.O. Box 513, Plainsboro NJ 08536. **Website:** www.njromancewriters.org/conference.html. Estab. 1984.

NIMROD JOURNAL'S CONFERENCE FOR READERS AND WRITERS

800 S. Tucker Dr., Tulsa OK 74104. (918)631-3080. **E-mail:** nimrod@utulsa.edu. **Website:** www.utulsa.edu/nimrod. **Contact:** Eilis O'Neal, editor-in-chief. Estab. 1978.

COSTS $60. Lunch provided. Scholarships are available for students.

ADDITIONAL INFORMATION *Nimrod International Journal* sponsors the Katherine Anne Porter Prize for fiction and the Pablo Neruda Prize for poetry. Poetry and fiction prizes: $2,000 each and publication (top prize); $1,000 each and publication (other winners). Deadline: must be postmarked no later than April 30.

NORTH CAROLINA WRITERS' NETWORK FALL CONFERENCE

P.O. Box 21591, Winston-Salem NC 27120. (336)293-8844. **E-mail:** mail@ncwriters.org. **Website:** www.ncwriters.org. Estab. 1985.

COSTS Approximately $250 (includes 4 meals).

ACCOMMODATIONS Special rates are usually available at the conference hotel, but attendees must make their own reservations.

NORTHERN COLORADO WRITERS CONFERENCE

407 Cormorant Court, Fort Collins CO 80525. (970)227-5746. **E-mail:** april@northerncoloradowriters.com. **Website:** www.northerncoloradowriters.com. Estab. 2006.

COSTS Prices vary depending on a number of factors. See website for details.

ACCOMMODATIONS Conference hotel may offer rooms at a discounted rate.

NORWESCON

100 Andover Park W. Suite 150-165, Tukwila WA 98188. (425)243-4692. **E-mail:** info@norwescon.org. **Website:** www.norwescon.org. Estab. 1978.

ACCOMMODATIONS Conference is held at the Doubletree Hotel Seattle Airport.

ODYSSEY FANTASY WRITING WORKSHOP

P.O. Box 75, Mont Vernon NH 03057. (603)673-6234. **E-mail:** jcavelos@odysseyworkshop.org. **Website:** www.odysseyworkshop.org. **Contact:** Jeanne Cavelos. Estab. 1996.

COSTS $2,025 tuition, $195 textbook, $892 housing (double room), $1,784 housing (single room), $40 application fee, $600 food (approximate), $950 optional processing fee to receive college credit.

ACCOMMODATIONS Most students stay in Saint Anselm College apartments to get the full Odyssey experience. Each apartment has 2 bedrooms and can house a total of 2 to 3 people (with each bedroom holding 1 or 2 students). The apartments are equipped with kitchens, so you may buy and prepare your own food, which is a money-saving option, or you may eat at the college's Coffee Shop or Dining Hall. Wireless internet access and use of laundry facilities are provided at no cost. Students with cars will receive a campus parking permit.

ADDITIONAL INFORMATION Students must apply and include a writing sample. Application deadline: April 8. Students' works are critiqued throughout the 6 weeks. Workshop information available in October. For brochure/guidelines, send SASE, e-mail, visit website, or call.

OHIO KENTUCKY INDIANA CHILDREN'S LITERATURE CONFERENCE

Northern Kentucky University, 405 Steely Library, Highland Heights KY 41099. (859)572-6620. **Fax:** (859)572-5390. **E-mail:** smithjen@nku.edu. **Website:** www.dearbornhighlandsarts.org/oki-conference-registration. **Contact:** Jennifer Smith.

COSTS $85; includes registration/attendance at all workshop sessions, continental breakfast, lunch, and author/illustrator signings. Manuscript critiques are available for an additional cost. E-mail or call for more information.

OREGON CHRISTIAN WRITERS SUMMER CONFERENCE

1075 Willow Lake Rd. N., Keizer OR 97303. **E-mail:** summerconference@oregonchristianwriters.org. **Website:** www.oregonchristianwriters.org. **Contact:** Lindy Jacobs, summer conference director. Estab. 1989.

COSTS $550 for OCW members, $595 for nonmembers. Registration fee includes all classes, workshops, and 2 lunches and 3 dinners. Lodging additional. Full-time registered attendees may also pre-submit 3 proposals for review by an editor (or agent) through the conference, plus sign up for a half-hour mentoring appointment with an author.

ACCOMMODATIONS Conference is held at the Red Lion on the River Hotel. Attendees wishing to stay at the hotel must make a reservation through the hotel. A block of rooms is reserved at a special rate and held until mid-July. The hotel reservation link is posted on the website in late spring. Shuttle bus transportation is provided from Portland Airport (PDX) to the hotel, which is 20 minutes away.

ADDITIONAL INFORMATION Conference details posted online beginning in January. All conferees are welcome to attend the Cascade Awards ceremony, which takes place Wednesday evening during the conference. For more information about the Cascade Writing Contest for published and unpublished writers—opens February 14. Please check the website for details.

OUTDOOR WRITERS ASSOCIATION OF AMERICA ANNUAL CONFERENCE

615 Oak St., Suite 201, Missoula MT 59801. (406)728-7434. **E-mail:** info@owaa.org. **Website:** owaa.org. **Contact:** Jessica Seitz, conference and membership coordinator. Estab. 1927.

COSTS Before April 28, $225 for members and $425 for non-members. After April 28, $249 for members and $449 for non-members. Single-day rates are also available.

PACIFIC COAST CHILDREN'S WRITERS WHOLE-NOVEL WORKSHOP: FOR ADULTS AND TEENS

P.O. Box 244, Aptos CA 95001. **Website:** www.childrenswritersworkshop.com. Estab. 2003.

COSTS Visit website for tiered fees (includes lodging, meals), schedule, and more; e-mail Director Nancy Sondel via the contact form.

WILLIAM PATERSON UNIVERSITY SPRING WRITER'S CONFERENCE

English Department, Preakness Hall 349, 300 Pompton Rd., Wayne NJ 07470. (973)720-3067. **Fax:** (973)720-2189. **E-mail:** parrasj@wpunj.edu. **Website:** wpunj.edu/mfa. **Contact:** John Parras.

COSTS $22-66

PENNWRITERS CONFERENCE

P.O. Box 685, Dalton PA 18414. **E-mail:** conference-co@pennwriters.org; info@pennwriters.org. **Website:** pennwriters.org/conference. Estab. 1987.

ACCOMMODATIONS Costs vary. Pennwriters members in good standing get a slightly reduced rate.

ADDITIONAL INFORMATION Sponsors contest. Published authors judge fiction in various categories. Agent/editor appointments are available on a first-come, first-served basis.

PHILADELPHIA WRITERS' CONFERENCE

P.O. Box 7171, Elkins Park PA 19027. (215)619-7422. **E-mail:** info@pwcwriters.org. **Website:** pwcwriters.org. Estab. 1949.

ACCOMMODATIONS See website for details. Hotel may offer discount for early registration.

ADDITIONAL INFORMATION Accepts inquiries by e-mail. Agents and editors attend the conference. Many questions are answered online.

PIKES PEAK WRITERS CONFERENCE

Pikes Peak Writers, P.O. Box 64273, Colorado Springs CO 80962. (719)244-6220. **E-mail:** registrar@pikespeakwriters.com. **Website:** www.pikespeakwriters.com/ppwc. Estab. 1993.

COSTS $395-465 (includes all 7 meals).

ACCOMMODATIONS Marriott Colorado Springs holds a block of rooms at a special rate for attendees until late March.

ADDITIONAL INFORMATION Readings with critiques are available on Friday afternoon. Registration forms are online; brochures are available in January. Send inquiries via e-mail.

RETREAT TO THE SPRINGS!

Beckman Communications, 2836 Westbrook Dr., Cincinnati OH 45211. **E-mail:** whbeckman@gmail.com. **Website:** https://wendyonwriting.com/2017/03/31/write-in-yellow-springs/. **Contact:** Wendy Hart Beckman. Estab. 2000.

COSTS $195 for instruction. Participants procure their own lodging and meals.

ACCOMMODATIONS John Bryan Community Center (http://www.yellowspringsohio.org/venue/john-bryan-community-center/) for classes. Many hotels available in the area with numerous restaurants within walking distance.

ADDITIONAL INFORMATION The 2018 retreat features Ann Hagedorn (creative nonfiction), Donna MacMeans (romance), Jason Sanford (sci-fi/fantasy), and Valerie Coleman (self-publishing).

ROCKY MOUNTAIN FICTION WRITERS COLORADO GOLD CONFERENCE

Rocky Mountain Fiction Writers, Denver Renaissance Hotel, Denver CO **E-mail:** conference@rmfw.org. **Website:** www.rmfw.org. **Contact:** Pamela Nowak and Susan Brooks. Estab. 1982.

COSTS Available on website.

ACCOMMODATIONS Special rates will be available at conference hotel.

ADDITIONAL INFORMATION Pitch appointments available at no charge. Add-on options include agent and editor critiques, master classes, pitch coaching, query letter coaching, special critiques, and more.

ROMANCE WRITERS OF AMERICA NATIONAL CONFERENCE

14615 Benfer Rd., Houston TX 77069. (832)717-5200. **Fax:** (832)717-5201. **E-mail:** info@rwa.org. **Website:** www.rwa.org/conference. Estab. 1981.

COSTS $450-675 depending on your membership status as well as when you register.

ADDITIONAL INFORMATION Annual RTA awards are presented for romance authors. Annual

Golden Heart awards are presented for unpublished writers.

☾ SAGE HILL WRITING EXPERIENCE

324-1831 College Avenue, Regina Saskatchewan S4P 4V5, Canada. (306)537-7243. **E-mail:** sage.hill@sasktel.net. **Website:** sagehillwriting.ca.

ACCOMMODATIONS Located at Lumsden, 45 kilometers outside Regina.

ADDITIONAL INFORMATION See the website for pricing and current course offerings.

☽ SALT CAY WRITERS RETREAT

Salt Cay , Bahamas. (732)267-6449. **E-mail:** admin@saltcaywritersretreat.com. **Website:** www.saltcaywritersretreat.com. **Contact:** Karen Dionne and Christopher Graham.

COSTS $2,450 through May 1; $2,950 after.

ACCOMMODATIONS Comfort Suites, Paradise Island, Nassau, Bahamas.

SAN DIEGO STATE UNIVERSITY WRITERS' CONFERENCE

SDSU College of Extended Studies, 5250 Campanile Dr., San Diego State University, San Diego CA 92182. (619)594-2099. **Fax:** (619)594-8566. **E-mail:** sdsuwritersconference@mail.sdsu.edu. **Website:** ces.sdsu.edu/writers. Estab. 1984.

COSTS $495-549. Extra costs for consultations.

ACCOMMODATIONS Attendees must make their own travel arrangements. A conference rate for attendees is available at the event hotel (Marriott Mission Valley Hotel).

2019 SAN FRANCISCO WRITERS CONFERENCE

Hyatt Regency Embarcadero, San Francisco CA 94111. (925)420-6223. **E-mail:** barbara@sfwriters.org; www.sfwriters.org. **E-mail:** See website at www.SFWriters.org for writing contest and scholarship submissions and other details.. **Website:** sfwriters.org. **Contact:** Barbara Santos, marketing director. Estab. 2003.

COSTS Full registration is $895 (as of the 2018 event) with early bird registration discounts through February 1.

ACCOMMODATIONS The Hyatt Regency Embarcadero offers a discounted SFWC rate (based on availability). Call directly: (415) 788-1234. Across from the Ferry Building in San Francisco, the hotel is located so that everyone arriving at the Oakland or San Francisco airport can take the BART to the Embarcadero exit, directly in front of the hotel.

ADDITIONAL INFORMATION "Present yourself in a professional manner, and the contacts you will make will be invaluable to your writing career. Fliers, details, and registration information are online."

SANTA BARBARA WRITERS CONFERENCE

27 W. Anapamu St., Suite 305, Santa Barbara CA 93101. (805)568-1516. **E-mail:** info@sbwriters.com. **Website:** www.sbwriters.com. Estab. 1972.

COSTS Early conference registration is $575, and regular registration is $650.

ACCOMMODATIONS Hyatt Santa Barbara.

ADDITIONAL INFORMATION Register online or contact for brochure and registration forms.

SCBWI WINTER CONFERENCE ON WRITING AND ILLUSTRATING FOR CHILDREN

4727 Wilshire Blvd #301, Los Angeles CA 90010. (323)782-1010. **Fax:** (323)782-1892. **E-mail:** scbwi@scbwi.org. **Website:** www.scbwi.org. **Contact:** Stephen Mooser. Estab. 2000.

COSTS See website for current cost and conference information.

ADDITIONAL INFORMATION SCBWI also holds an annual summer conference in August in Los Angeles.

SEWANEE WRITERS' CONFERENCE

735 University Ave., 119 Gailor Hall, Stamler Center, Sewanee TN 37383. (931)598-1654. **E-mail:** swc@sewanee.edu. **Website:** www.sewaneewriters.org. **Contact:** Adam Latham. Estab. 1990.

COSTS $1,100 for tuition, and $700 for room, board, and activity costs.

ACCOMMODATIONS Participants are housed in single rooms in university dormitories. Bathrooms are shared by small groups.

SITKA CENTER FOR ART AND ECOLOGY

56605 Sitka Dr., Otis OR 97368. (541)994-5485. **Fax:** (541)994-8024. **E-mail:** info@sitkacenter.org. **Website:** www.sitkacenter.org. **Contact:** Mindy Chaffin, program manager. Estab. 1970.

COSTS Workshops are generally $25-505; they do not include meals or lodging.

ACCOMMODATIONS Does not offer overnight accommodations. Provides a list of area hotels or lodging options.

ADDITIONAL INFORMATION Brochure available in February of each year; request a copy by e-mail or phone, or visit website for listing. Accepts inquiries in person or by e-mail, phone, or fax.

SOUTHMPTON CHILDREN'S LITERATURE CONFERENCE

Stony Brook Southampton MFA in Creative Writing, 239 Montauk Hwy., Southampton NY 11968. (631)632-5007. **Fax:** (631)632-2578. **Website:** www.stonybrook.edu/mfa/clc/. **Contact:** Christian McLean, director of summer and special programs. Estab. 2007. 239 Montauk Hwy., Southampton NY 11968-6700. (631)632-5030. **Fax:** (631)632-2578. **E-mail:** southamptonwriters@notes.cc.sunysb.edu. **Website:** www.stonybrook.edu/writers. Annual conference held in July. "The seaside campus of Stony Brook Southampton is located in the heart of the Hamptons, a renowned resort area only 70 miles from New York City. During free time, participants can draw on inspiration from the Atlantic beaches or explore the charming seaside towns."

COSTS Fees vary. 2017 fees will be available online.

ACCOMMODATIONS On-campus housing, doubles and small singles with shared baths, is modest but comfortable. Supplies list of lodging alternatives.

ADDITIONAL INFORMATION Applicants must complete an application and submit a writing sample of original, unpublished work. Details available online. Accepts inquiries by e-mail, phone.

THE SOUTHAMPTON WRITERS CONFERENCE

Stony Brook Southampton MFA in Creative Writing Program, 239 Montauk Hwy., Southampton NY 11968. (631)632-5007. **E-mail:** christian.mclean@stonybrook.edu. **Website:** www.stonybrook.edu/southampton/mfa/summer/cwl_home.html. **Contact:** Christian McLean. Estab. 1976.

COSTS 12-day master class: $600 (does not include afternoon faculty-led workshop). 5-day workshop only: $1,395. 5-day workshop plus residency: $1,995 (12 days total). 12-day workshop: $1,995. 12-day residency: $600. (2017 prices not finalized at time of printing.)

ACCOMMODATIONS Participants can stay on campus in air-conditioned dorms.

SOUTH COAST WRITERS CONFERENCE

Southwestern Oregon Community College, P.O. Box 590, 29392 Ellensburg Ave., Gold Beach OR 97444. (541)247-2741. **Fax:** (541)247-6247. **E-mail:** scwc@socc.edu. **Website:** www.socc.edu/scwriters. **Contact:** Karim Shumaker. Estab. 1996.

COSTS Friday workshop cost is $55. Saturday conference cost is $60 before January 31 and $70 after. Fish fry lunch is $14 if purchased in advance, or $15 at the door.

ACCOMMODATIONS List of local motels that offer discounts to conference participants is available on request.

SOUTHEASTERN WRITERS ASSOCIATION— ANNUAL WRITERS WORKSHOP

E-mail: purple@southeasternwriters.org. **Website:** www.southeasternwriters.org. Estab. 1975.

COSTS Cost of workshop: $445 for 4 days or lower prices for daily tuition or early bird special. (See website for tuition pricing.)

ACCOMMODATIONS Lodging at Epworth and throughout St. Simons Island. Visit website for more information.

SPACE (SMALL PRESS AND ALTERNATIVE COMICS EXPO)

Back Porch Comics, P.O. Box 20550, Columbus OH 43220. **E-mail:** bpc013@gmail.com. **Website:** www.backporchcomics.com/space.htm. **Contact:** Bob Corby, founder.

COSTS Admission is free.

ADDITIONAL INFORMATION For brochure, visit website. Editors participate in conference.

COMMUNITY OF WRITERS AT SQUAW VALLEY

Community of Writers at Squaw Valley, P.O. Box 1416, Nevada City CA 95959. (530)470-8440 or (530)583-5200 (summer). **E-mail:** info@communityofwriters.org. **Website:** www.communityofwriters.org. **Contact:** Brett Hall Jones, Executive Director. Estab. 1969.

COSTS Tuition is $1,150, which includes 6 dinners. Limited financial aid is available.

ACCOMMODATIONS The Community of Writers rents houses and condominiums in the Squaw Valley for participants to live in during the week of the conference. Single room (1 participant): $700/week. Double room (twin beds, room shared by conference participant of the same gender): $465/week. Multiple room (bunk beds, room shared with 2 or more participants of the same gender): $295/week. All rooms subject to availability; early requests are recommended. Can arrange airport shuttle pickups for a fee.

SUMMER WRITING PROGRAM

Naropa University, 2130 Arapahoe Ave., Boulder CO 80302. (303)245-4862. **Fax:** (303)546-5287. **E-mail:** swp@naropa.edu. **Website:** www.naropa.edu/swp. **Contact:** Kyle Pivarnik, special projects manager. Estab. 1974.

ADDITIONAL INFORMATION Writers can elect to take the Summer Writing Program for noncredit, graduate credit, or undergraduate credit. The registration procedure varies, so participants should consider which option they are choosing. All participants can elect to take any combination of the first, second, third, and fourth weeks. To request a catalog of upcoming programs or to find additional information, visit the website. Naropa University welcomes participants with disabilities.

TAOS SUMMER WRITERS' CONFERENCE

Department of English Language and Literature, MSC 03 2170, 1 University of New Mexico, Albuquerque NM 87131. (505)277-5572. **E-mail:** nmwriter@unm.edu. **Website:** taosconf.unm.edu. **Contact:** Sharon Oard Warner, founding director. Estab. 1999.

COSTS Week-long workshop registration: $700. Weekend workshop registration: $400. Master classes: $1,350-1,625. Publishing consultations: $175.

◗ THE UNIVERSITY OF WINCHESTER WRITERS' FESTIVAL

University of Winchester, Winchester Hampshire S022 4NR, United Kingdom. (44)(0)1962-827238. **E-mail:** judith.heneghan@winchester.ac.uk. **Website:** www.writersfestival.co.uk. **Contact:** Judith Heneghan, festival director. Estab. 1980.

COSTS See festival program.

ACCOMMODATIONS On-site student single ensuite accommodation available. Also, a range of hotels and bed and breakfasts nearby in the city.

ADDITIONAL INFORMATION Lunch, and tea/coffee/cake included in the booking cost. Dinner can be booked separately. All dietary needs catered for.

THRILLERFEST

P.O. Box 311, Eureka CA 95502. **E-mail:** kimberlyhowe@thrillerwriters.org; infocentral@thrillerwrit-

ers.org. **Website:** www.thrillerfest.com. **Contact:** Kimberley Howe, executive director. Estab. 2006.

COSTS $475-1,199, depending on which events are selected. Various package deals are available, and early bird pricing is offered beginning September of each year.

TIN HOUSE SUMMER WORKSHOP

Tin House, 2601 NW Thurman St., Portland OR 97210. (503)219-0622. **E-mail:** lance@tinhouse.com. **Website:** www.tinhouse.com/workshop. **Contact:** Lance Cleland. Estab. 2003.

COSTS $40 application fee; $1,200 for tuition; $600 for room & board; $350 to Audit. Payment plans are available.

ACCOMMODATIONS "The Tin House Summer Writers Workshop is held at Reed College, located on 100 acres of rolling lawns, winding lanes, and magnificent old trees in the southeast area of Portland, Oregon, just minutes from downtown and 12 miles from the airport."

ADDITIONAL INFORMATION Attendees must apply; all information available online.

TMCC WRITERS' CONFERENCE

Truckee Meadows Community College, 7000 Dandini Blvd., Reno NV 89512. (775)673-7111. **E-mail:** wdce@tmcc.edu. **Website:** wdce.tmcc.edu. Estab. 1991.

ACCOMMODATIONS Contact the conference manager to learn about accommodation discounts.

ADDITIONAL INFORMATION "The conference is open to all writers, regardless of their level of experience. Brochures are available online and mailed in January. Send inquiries via e-mail."

UCLA EXTENSION WRITERS' PROGRAM

10995 Le Conte Ave., Suite 440, Los Angeles CA 90024. (310)825-9415. **Fax:** (310)206-7382. **E-mail:** writers@uclaextension.edu. **Website:** www.uclaextension.edu/writers. Estab. 1891. 10995 Le Conte Avenue, #440, Los Angeles CA 90024. (310)825-9415. **Fax:** (310)206-7382. **E-mail:** writers@uclaextension.edu. **Website:** www.uclaextension.edu/writers. **Contact:** Cindy Lieberman, program manager. Courses held year-round with one-day or intensive weekend workshops to 12-week courses. Writers Studio held in February. Nine-month master classes are also offered every fall. "The diverse offerings span introductory seminars to professional novel and script completion workshops.

The annual Writers Studio and a number of one-, two- and four-day intensive workshops are popular with out-of-town students due to their specific focus and the chance to work with industry professionals. The most comprehensive and diverse continuing education writing program in the country, offering over 550 courses a year, including screenwriting, fiction, writing for the youth market, poetry, nonfiction, playwriting and publishing. Adult learners in the UCLA Extension Writers' Program study with professional screenwriters, fiction writers, playwrights, poets, and nonfiction writers, who bring practical experience, theoretical knowledge, and a wide variety of teaching styles and philosophies to their classes." Site: Courses are offered in Los Angeles on the UCLA campus, in the 1010 Westwood Center in Westwood Village, at the Figueroa Courtyard in downtown Los Angeles, as well as online.

COSTS Depends on length of the course.

ACCOMMODATIONS Students make their own arrangements. Out-of-town students are encouraged to take online courses.

ADDITIONAL INFORMATION Some advanced-level classes have ms submittal requirements; see the UCLA Extension catalog or visit website.

UNICORN WRITERS CONFERENCE

17 Church Hill Rd., Redding CT 06896, USA. (203)938-7405. **E-mail:** unicornwritersconference@ gmail.com. **Website:** www.unicornwritersconference. com. **Contact:** Jan L. Kardys, chair. Estab. 2010.

COSTS $325 includes all workshops (6 every hour to select on the day of the conference), gift bag, and 3 meals. Additional cost for manuscript reviews: $60 each.

ACCOMMODATIONS Held at Reid Castle, Purchase, New York. Directions available on event website.

ADDITIONAL INFORMATION The first self-published authors will be featured on the website, and the bookstore will sell their books at the event.

UNIVERSITY OF WISCONSIN AT MADISON WRITERS INSTITUTE

21 N. Park St., Madison WI 53715. (608)265-3972. E-mail: laurie.scheer@wisc.edu. **Website:** uwwritersinstitute.wisc.edu. Estab. 1990.

COSTS $250-375, depending on discounts and if you attend one day or multiple days.

VERMONT STUDIO CENTER

P.O. Box 613, 80 Pearl Street, Johnson VT 05656. (802)635-2727. **Fax:** (802)635-2730. **E-mail:** info@ vermontstudiocenter.org. **Website:** www.vermontstudiocenter.org. **Contact:** Gary Clark, writing program director. Estab. 1984. P.O. Box 613, Johnson VT 05656. (802)635-2727. **Fax:** (802)635-2730. **E-mail:** info@vermontstudiocenter.org. **Website:** www.vermontstudiocenter.org. **Contact:** Gary Clark, writing program director. Estab. 1984. Ongoing residencies. Conference duration: From 2-12 weeks. Average attendance: 55 writers and visual artists/month. Visiting writers have included Ron Carlson, Donald Revell, Jane Hirshfield, Rosanna Warren, Chris Abani, Bob Shacochis, Tony Hoagland, and Alice Notley.

COSTS The cost of a 4-week residency is $3,950. Generous fellowship and grant assistance is available.

ACCOMMODATIONS Accommodations available on site. "Residents live in single rooms in 10 modest, comfortable houses adjacent to the Red Mill Building. Rooms are simply furnished and have shared baths. Complete linen service is provided. The Studio Center is unable to accommodate guests at meals, overnight guests, spouses, children, or pets."

ADDITIONAL INFORMATION Fellowships application deadlines are February 15, June 15, and October 1. Writers are encouraged to visit website for more information. May also e-mail, call, fax.

WESLEYAN WRITERS CONFERENCE

Wesleyan University, 294 High St., Room 207, Middletown CT 06459. (860)685-3604. **Fax:** (860)685-2441. **E-mail:** agreene@wesleyan.edu. **Website:** www.wesleyan.edu/writing/conference. **Contact:** Anne Greene, director. Estab. 1956.

ACCOMMODATIONS Meals are provided on campus. Lodging is available on campus or in town.

ADDITIONAL INFORMATION Ms critiques are available but not required.

WESTERN RESERVE WRITERS & FREELANCE CONFERENCE

Cuyahoga County Public Library, South Euclid-Lyndhurst Branch, 4645 Mayfield Road, South Euclid OH 44121. (216)382-4880. **E-mail:** deanna@deannaadams.com. **Website:** www.deannaadams.com. **Contact:** Deanna Adams, director/conference coordinator. Estab. 1983.

COSTS The conference is now free but does not include lunch.

ADDITIONAL INFORMATION Brochures for the conferences are available by January. Also accepts inquiries by e-mail and phone. Check Deanna Adams' website for all updates. Editors always attend the conferences. Agents, occasionally. Private editing consultations are available as well.

WHIDBEY ISLAND WRITERS' CONFERENCE

P.O. Box 1289, Langley WA 98260. (360)331-0307. **E-mail:** http://writeonwhidbey.org. **Website:** http:// writeonwhidbey.org.

COSTS Cost: $395; early bird and member discounts available

WILDACRES WRITERS WORKSHOP

233 S. Elm St., Greensboro NC 27401. (336)255-8210. **E-mail:** judihill@aol.com. **Website:** www.wildacres-writers.com. **Contact:** Judi Hill, director. Estab. 1985.

COSTS The current price is $830. Check the website for more info.

ADDITIONAL INFORMATION Include a one-page writing sample with registration.

WILLAMETTE WRITERS CONFERENCE

2108 Buck St., West Linn OR 97068. (503)305-6729. **Fax:** (503)344-6174. **Website:** willamettewriters.com/ wwcon/. Estab. 1981.

COSTS Pricing schedule available online.

ACCOMMODATIONS If necessary, arrangements can be made on an individual basis through the conference hotel. Special rates may be available. 2015 location is the Lloyd Center DoubleTree Hotel.

ADDITIONAL INFORMATION Brochure/guidelines are available for a catalog-sized SASE.

WINTER POETRY & PROSE GETAWAY

Murphy Writing of Stockton University, 35 S. Dr. Martin Luther King Blvd., Atlantic City NJ 08401, USA. (609)626-3596. **E-mail:** info@murphywriting. com. **Website:** www.stockton.edu/wintergetaway. **Contact:** Amanda Murphy. Estab. 1994.

COSTS See website or call for current fee information.

ACCOMMODATIONS Room packages at the historic Stockton Seaview Hotel are available.

ADDITIONAL INFORMATION Previous faculty has included Julianna Baggott, Christian Bauman, Laure-Anne Bosselaar, Kurt Brown, Mark Doty (National Book Award winner), Stephen Dunn (Pulitzer Prize winner), Dorianne Laux, Carol Plum-Ucci,

James Richardson, Mimi Schwartz, Terese Svoboda, and more.

WISCONSIN WRITERS ASSOCIATION

Wisconsin Writers Association, Inc., WI **E-mail:** karinss1945@outlook.com. **Website:** www.wiwrite. org. **Contact:** Karin Schmidt, president. Estab. 1948. 9708 Idell Ave., Sparta WI 54656. (608)269-8541. **E-mail:** registration@wrwa.net. **Website:** www.wrwa. net. **Contact:** Nate Scholze, Fall Conference Coordinator; Roxanne Aehl, Spring Conference Coordinator. Estab. 1948. Annual. Conferences held in May and September "are dedicated to self-improvement through speakers, workshops and presentations. Topics and speakers vary with each event." Average attendance: 100-150. "We honor all genres of writing. Fall conference is a two-day event featuring the Jade Ring Banquet and awards for six genre categories. Spring conference is a one-day event."

COSTS $80-100.

ACCOMMODATIONS Rooms available at the host conference center.

WOMEN WRITERS WINTER RETREAT

Steele Mansion B&B, 348 Mentor Avenue, Painesville OH 44077. (440)463-4633. **E-mail:** deencr@aol.com. **Website:** www.deannaadams.com. Estab. 2007.

COSTS Single room: $395; shared room: $295 (includes complete weekend package, with B&B stay in this historic mansion, breakfast and workshops); weekend commute: $165; Saturday only: $135.

ADDITIONAL INFORMATION Brochures for the writers retreat are available by December. Accepts inquiries and reservations by e-mail or phone. See Deanna's website for additional information and updates.

WRITEAWAYS

Durham NC **E-mail:** writeawaysinfo@gmail.com. **Website:** https://www.writeaways.com. **Contact:** Mimi Herman. Estab. 2013.

COSTS North Carolina workshop: $395 single room/ bath, $345 shared bath. North Carolina retreat: $160/ night; $145/night workshop participants. France and Italy: $2,350 single room, $2,100 shared rooms. The Grand Tour (France and Italy): $4,200 each single room, $4,000 each shared room.

ACCOMMODATIONS North Carolina: The Whitehall, Camden, North Carolina. France: Chateau du Pin, near Champtocé-sur Loire (18 miles west of Angers). Italy: Villas Cini and Casanova, near Bucine, between Siena and Arezzo.

WRITE IT OUT

P.O. Box 704, Sarasota FL 34230. (941)359-3824. **E-mail:** rmillerwio@aol.com. **Website:** www.writeitout. com. **Contact:** Ronni Miller, director. Estab. 1997.

COSTS Costs vary by workshop.

ADDITIONAL INFORMATION Conference information available year round. For brochures/guidelines e-mail, call, or visit website. Accepts inquiries by phone, e-mail.

WRITE ON THE RIVER

8941 Kelsey Lane, Knoxville TN 37922. **E-mail:** bob@ bobmayer.org. **Website:** www.bobmayer.org. **Contact:** Bob Mayer. Estab. 2002.

COSTS Varies; depends on venue. Please see website for any updates.

ADDITIONAL INFORMATION Limited to 4 participants, and focused on their novel and marketability.

WRITE ON THE SOUND

WOTS, City of Edmonds Arts Commission, Frances Anderson Center, 700 Main St., Edmonds WA 98020. (425)771-0228. **E-mail:** wots@edmondswa.gov. **Website:** www.writeonthesound.com. **Contact:** Laurie Rose, Conference Organizer or Frances Chapin, Edmonds Arts Commission Mgr. Estab. 1985.

COSTS $85-285 (not including optional fees).

ACCOMMODATIONS Best Western Plus/Edmonds Harbor Inn is a conference partner.

ADDITIONAL INFORMATION Schedule posted on website late spring/early summer. Registration opens mid-July. Attendees are required to select the sessions when they register. Waiting lists for conference and manuscript appointments are available.

WRITERS@WORK WRITING RETREAT

P.O. Box 711191, Salt Lake City UT 84171. (801)996-3313. **E-mail:** jennifer@writersatwork.org. **Website:** www.writersatwork.org. Estab. 1985.

COSTS $650-1,000, based on housing type and consultations.

ACCOMMODATIONS Onsite housing available. Additional lodging information is on the website.

WRITER'S DIGEST ANNUAL CONFERENCE

F+W Media, Inc., 10151 Carver Rd., Suite 200, Blue Ash OH 45242. (877)436-7764 (option 2). **E-mail:** writersdigestconference@fwmedia.com. **E-mail:** phil. sexton@fwmedia.com. **Website:** www.writersdigest-conference.com. **Contact:** Taylor Sferra. Estab. 1995.

COSTS Cost varies by location and year. There are typically different pricing options for those who wish attend the pitch slam and those who just want to attend the conference education.

ACCOMMODATIONS A block of rooms at the event hotel is reserved for guests. See the travel page on the website for more information.

WRITERS IN PARADISE

Eckerd College, 4200 54th Ave. S., St. Petersburg FL 33711. (727)386-2264. **E-mail:** wip@eckerd.edu. **Website:** writersinparadise.com. Estab. 2005.

ADDITIONAL INFORMATION Application materials are due in November and required of all attendees.

WRITERS OMI AT LEDIG HOUSE

55 Fifth Ave., 15th Floor, New York NY 10003. (212)206-6114. **E-mail:** writers@artomi.org. **Website:** www.artomi.org.

ACCOMMODATIONS Residents provide their own transportation. Offers overnight accommodations.

ADDITIONAL INFORMATION "Agents and editors from the New York publishing community are invited for dinner and discussion. Bicycles, a swimming pool, and nearby tennis court are available for use."

WRITERS STUDIO AT UCLA EXTENSION

1010 Westwood Blvd., Los Angeles CA 90024. (310)825-9415. **E-mail:** writers@uclaextension.edu. **Website:** writers.uclaextension.edu/programs-services/writers-studio. **Contact:** Katy Flaherty. Estab. 1997.

ADDITIONAL INFORMATION For more information, call or e-mail.

THE WRITERS' WORKSHOP

THE RENBOURNE EDITORIAL AGENCY, 387 Beaucatcher Rd., Asheville NC 28805. (828)254-8111. **E-mail:** writersw@gmail.com. **Website:** www.twwoa. org. Estab. 1985.

COSTS For editorial services: usually $4 per page (double spaced) for a thorough editing, or $3 per page for a read-through and revision suggestions.

ADDITIONAL INFORMATION Also sponsors annual contests in poetry, literary fiction, memoirs, and essay. For guidelines, see website.

WRITE-TO-PUBLISH CONFERENCE

WordPro Communication Services, 9118 W. Elmwood Dr., Suite 1G, Niles IL 60714. (847)296-3964. **E-mail:** lin@writetopublish.com. **Website:** www.writetopublish.com. **Contact:** Lin Johnson, director. Estab. 1971.

COSTS See the website for current costs.

ACCOMMODATIONS Campus residence hall rooms available. See the website for current information and costs.

ADDITIONAL INFORMATION Conference information available in late January or early February. For details, visit website, or e-mail brochure@writetopublish.com. Accepts inquiries by e-mail, phone.

WRITING AND ILLUSTRATING FOR YOUNG READERS CONFERENCE

1480 E. 9400 S., Sandy UT 84093. **E-mail:** staff@wifyr.com. **Website:** www.wifyr.com. Estab. 2000. BYU, conferences and workshops, 348 HCEB, BYU, Provo UT 84602-1532. (801)422-2568. **Fax:** (801)422-0745. **E-mail:** cw348@byu.edu. **Website:** http://wifyr.byu.edu. **Contact:** Conferences & Workshops. Estab. 2000. Annual. 5-day workshop held in June of each year. The workshop is designed for people who want to write or illustrate for children or teenagers. Participants focus on a single market during daily four-hour morning writing workshops led by published authors or illustrators. Afternoon workshop sessions include a mingle with the authors, editors and agents. Workshop focuses on fiction for young readers: picture books, book-length fiction, fantasy/science fiction, nonfiction, mystery, illustration and general writing. Site: Conference Center at Brigham Young University in the foothills of the Wasatch Mountain range.

ACCOMMODATIONS A block of rooms is available at the Best Western Cotton Tree Inn in Sandy, UT, at a discounted rate. This rate is good as long as there are available rooms.

ADDITIONAL INFORMATION There is an online form to contact this event.

THE HELENE WURLITZER FOUNDATION

P.O. Box 1891, Taos NM 87571. (575)758-2413. **Fax:** (575)758-2559. **E-mail:** hwf@taosnet.com. **Website:** www.wurlitzerfoundation.org. **Contact:** Michael A. Knight, executive director. Estab. 1954.

ACCOMMODATIONS Provides individual housing in fully furnished studios/houses (casitas), rent and utility free. Artists are responsible for transportation to and from Taos, their meals, and materials for their work. Bicycles are provided upon request.

GLOSSARY

ADVANCE. Payment by a publisher to an author prior to the publication of a book, to be deducted from the author's future royalties.

ADVENTURE STORY. A genre of fiction in which action is the key element, overshadowing characters, theme, and setting. The conflict in an adventure story is often man against nature. A secondary plot that reinforces this kind of conflict is sometimes included.

ALL RIGHTS. The rights contracted to a publisher permitting a manuscript's use anywhere and in any form without additional payment to the writer.

AMATEUR SLEUTH. The character in a mystery, usually the protagonist, who does the detection but is not a professional private investigator or police detective.

ANTHOLOGY. A collection of selected writings by various authors.

ASSOCIATION OF AUTHORS' REPRESENTATIVES (AAR). An organization for literary agents committed to maintaining excellence in literary representation.

AUCTION. Publishers sometimes bid against each other for the acquisition of a manuscript that has excellent sales prospects.

BACKLIST. A publisher's books not published during the current season but still in print.

BIOGRAPHICAL NOVEL. A life story documented in history and transformed into fiction through the insight and imagination of the writer. This type of novel melds the elements of biographical research and historical truth into the framework of a novel, complete with dialogue, drama, and mood. A biographical novel resembles historical fiction, save for one aspect: Characters in a historical novel may be fabricated and then placed into an authentic setting; characters in a biographical novel have actually lived.

BOOK PRODUCER/PACKAGER. An organization that may develop a book for a publisher based upon the publisher's idea or may plan all elements of a book, from its initial concept to writing and marketing strategies, and then sell the package to a book publisher and/or movie producer.

CLIFFHANGER. Fictional event in which the reader is left in suspense at the end of a chapter or episode, so that interest in the story's outcome will be sustained.

CLIP. Sample, usually from a newspaper or magazine, of a writer's published work.

CLOAK-AND-DAGGER. A melodramatic, romantic type of fiction dealing with espionage and intrigue.

COMMERCIAL. Publishers whose concern is salability, profit, and success with a large readership.

CONTEMPORARY. Material dealing with popular current trends, themes, or topics.

CONTRIBUTOR'S COPY. Copy of an issue of a magazine or published book sent to an author whose work is included.

CO-PUBLISHING. An arrangement in which the author and publisher share costs and profits.

COPYEDITING. Editing a manuscript for writing style, grammar, punctuation and factual accuracy.

COPYRIGHT. The legal right to exclusive publication, sale, or distribution of a literary work.

COVER LETTER. A brief letter sent with a complete manuscript submitted to an editor.

"COZY" (OR "TEACUP") MYSTERY. Mystery usually set in a small British town, in a bygone era, featuring a somewhat genteel, intellectual protagonist.

ELECTRONIC RIGHTS. The right to publish material electronically, either in book or short story form.

ELECTRONIC SUBMISSION. A submission of material by e-mail or on computer disk.

ETHNIC FICTION. Stories whose central characters are black, Native American, Italian-American, Jewish, Appalachian, or members of some other specific cultural group.

EXPERIMENTAL FICTION. Fiction that is innovative in subject matter and style; avant-garde, non-formulaic, usually literary material.

EXPOSITION. The portion of the story line, usually the beginning, where background information about character and setting is related.

E-ZINE. A magazine that is published electronically.

FAIR USE. A provision in the copyright law that says short passages from copyrighted material may be used without infringing on the owner's rights.

FANTASY (TRADITIONAL). Fantasy with an emphasis on magic, using characters with the ability to practice magic, such as wizards, witches, dragons, elves, and unicorns.

FANZINE. A noncommercial, small-circulation magazine usually dealing with fantasy, horror or science-fiction literature and art.

FIRST NORTH AMERICAN SERIAL RIGHTS. The right to publish material in a periodical before it appears in book form, for the first time, in the United States or Canada.

FLASH FICTION. *See* short short story.

GALLEY PROOF. The first typeset version of a manuscript that has not yet been divided into pages.

GENRE. A formulaic type of fiction such as romance, western, or horror.

GOTHIC. This type of category fiction dates back to the late eighteenth and early nineteenth centuries. Contemporary gothic novels are characterized by atmospheric, historical settings and feature young, beautiful women who win the favor of handsome, brooding heroes—simultaneously dealing successfully with some life-threatening menace, either natural or supernatural. Gothics rely on mystery, peril, romantic relationships, and a sense of foreboding for their strong, emotional effect on the reader. A classic early gothic novel is Emily Brontë's *Wuthering Heights*.

GRAPHIC NOVEL. A book (original or adapted) that takes the form of a long comic strip or heavily illustrated story of forty pages or more, produced in paperback. Though called a novel, these can also be works of nonfiction.

HARD-BOILED DETECTIVE NOVEL. Mystery novel featuring a private eye or police detective as the protagonist; usually involves a murder. The emphasis is on the details of the crime, and the tough, unsentimental protagonist usually takes a matter-of-fact attitude toward violence.

HARD SCIENCE FICTION. Science fiction with an emphasis on science and technology.

HIGH FANTASY. Fantasy with a medieval setting and a heavy emphasis on chivalry and the quest.

HISTORICAL FICTION. A fictional story set in a recognizable period of history. As well as telling the stories of ordinary people's lives, historical fiction may involve political or social events of the time.

HORROR. Howard Phillips (H.P.) Lovecraft, generally acknowledged to be the master of the horror tale in the twentieth century and the most important American writer of this genre since Edgar Allan Poe, distinguishes horror literature from fiction based entirely on physical fear and the merely gruesome. It is that atmosphere—the creation of a particular sensation or emotional level—that, according to Lovecraft, is the most important element in the creation of horror literature. Contemporary writers enjoying considerable success in horror fiction include Stephen King, Robert Bloch, Peter Straub, and Dean Koontz.

HYPERTEXT FICTION. A fictional form, read electronically, that incorporates traditional elements of storytelling with a nonlinear plot line, in which the reader determines the direction of the story by opting for one of many author-supplied links.

IMPRINT. Name applied to a publisher's specific line (e.g., Owl, an imprint of Henry Holt).

INTERACTIVE FICTION. Fiction in book or computer-software format where the reader determines the path the story will take by choosing from several alternatives at the end of each chapter or episode.

INTERNATIONAL REPLY COUPON (IRC). A form purchased at a post office and enclosed with a letter or manuscript to an international publisher, to cover return postage costs.

JUVENILES, WRITING FOR. This includes works intended for an audience usually between the ages of two and eighteen. Categories of children's books are usually divided in this way: (1) picture books and storybooks (ages two to eight); (2) young readers or easy-to-read books (ages five to eight); (3) middle readers or middle grade (ages nine to eleven); (4) young adult books (ages twelve and up).

LIBEL. Written or printed words that defame, malign, or damagingly misrepresent a living person.

LITERARY AGENT. A person who acts for an author in finding a publisher or arranging contract terms on a literary project.

LITERARY FICTION. The general category of fiction that employs more sophisticated technique, driven as much or more by character evolution than action in the plot.

MAINSTREAM FICTION. Fiction that appeals to a more general reading audience, versus literary or genre fiction. Mainstream is more plot-driven than literary fiction and less formulaic than genre fiction.

MALICE DOMESTIC NOVEL. A mystery featuring a murder among family members, such as the murder of a spouse or a parent.

MANUSCRIPT. The author's unpublished copy of a work, usually typewritten, used as the basis for typesetting.

MASS MARKET PAPERBACK. Softcover book on a popular subject directed to a general audience and sold in drugstores and groceries as well as in bookstores.

MIDDLE READER. Also called *middle grade*. Juvenile fiction for readers aged nine to eleven.

MS(S). Abbreviation for *manuscript(s)*.

MULTIPLE SUBMISSION. Submission of more than one short story at a time to the same editor. *Do not make a multiple submission unless requested.*

MYSTERY. A form of narration in which one or more elements remain unknown or un-explained until the end of the story. The modern mystery story contains elements of the mainstream novel: a convincing account of a character's struggle with various physical and psychological obstacles in an effort to achieve his goal, good characterization, and sound motivation.

NARRATION. The account of events in a story's plot as related by the speaker or the voice of the author.

NARRATOR. The person who tells the story, either someone involved in the action or the voice of the writer.

NEW AGE. A term including categories such as astrology, psychic phenomena, spiritual healing, UFOs, mysticism, and other aspects of the occult.

NOIR. A style of mystery involving hard-boiled detectives and bleak settings.

NOM DE PLUME. French for "pen name"; a pseudonym.

NONFICTION NOVEL. A work in which real events and people are written [about] in novel form, but are not camouflaged, as they are in the roman à clef.

NOVELLA (ALSO NOVELETTE). A short novel or long story, approximately 20,000–50,000 words.

#10 ENVELOPE. 4" × 9½" envelope, used for queries and other business letters.

OFFPRINT. Copy of a story taken from a magazine before it is bound.

ONETIME RIGHTS. Permission to publish a story in periodical or book form one time only.

OUTLINE. A summary of a book's contents, often in the form of chapter headings with a few sentences outlining the action of the story under each one; sometimes part of a book proposal.

OVER THE TRANSOM. A phrase referring to unsolicited manuscripts, or those that come in "over the transom."

PAYMENT ON ACCEPTANCE. Payment from the magazine or publishing house as soon as the decision to print a manuscript is made.

PAYMENT ON PUBLICATION. Payment from the publisher after a manuscript is printed.

PEN NAME. A pseudonym used to conceal a writer's real name.

PERIODICAL. A magazine or journal published at regular intervals.

PLOT. The carefully devised series of events through which the characters progress in a work of fiction.

POPULAR FICTION. Generally, a synonym for category or genre fiction; i.e., fiction intended to appeal to audiences for certain kinds of novels. Popular, or category, fiction is defined as such primarily for the convenience of publishers, editors, reviewers, and booksellers who must identify novels of different areas of interest for potential readers.

PRINT ON DEMAND (POD). Novels produced digitally one at a time, as ordered.

PROOFREADING. Close reading and correction of a manuscript's typographical errors.

PROOFS. A typeset version of a manuscript used for correcting errors and making changes, often a photocopy of the galleys.

PROPOSAL. An offer to write a specific work, usually consisting of an outline of the work and one or two completed chapters.

PROTAGONIST. The principal or leading character in a literary work.

PSYCHOLOGICAL NOVEL. A narrative that emphasizes the mental and emotional aspects of its characters, focusing on motivations and mental activities rather than on exterior events. The psychological novelist is less concerned about relating what happened than about exploring why it happened. The term is most often used to describe twentieth-century works that employ techniques such as interior monologue and stream of consciousness. Two examples of contemporary psychological novels are Judith Guest's *Ordinary People* and Mary Gordon's *The Company of Women*.

PUBLIC DOMAIN. Material that either was never copyrighted or whose copyright term has expired.

PULP MAGAZINE. A periodical printed on inexpensive paper, usually containing lurid, sensational stories or articles.

QUERY. A letter written to an editor to elicit interest in a story the writer wants to submit.

READER. A person hired by a publisher to read unsolicited manuscripts.

READING FEE. An arbitrary amount of money charged by some agents and publishers to read a submitted manuscript.

REGENCY ROMANCE. A subgenre of romance, usually set in England between 1811 and 1820.

REMAINDERS. Leftover copies of an out-of-print book, sold by the publisher at a reduced price.

REPORTING TIME. The number of weeks or months it takes an editor to report back on an author's query or manuscript.

REPRINT RIGHTS. Permission to print an already published work whose rights have been sold to another magazine or book publisher.

ROMAN À CLEF. French "novel with a key." A novel that represents actual living or historical characters and events in fictionalized form.

ROMANCE NOVEL. A type of category fiction in which the love relationship between a man and a woman pervades the plot. The story is often told from the viewpoint of the heroine, who meets a man (the hero), falls in love with him, encounters a conflict that hinders their relationship, then resolves the conflict. Romance is the overriding element in this kind of story: The couple's relationship determines the plot and tone of the book.

ROYALTIES. A percentage of the retail price paid to an author for each copy of the book that is sold.

SASE. Self-addressed stamped envelope.

SCIENCE FICTION (VS. FANTASY). It is generally accepted that, to be science fiction, a story must have elements of science in either the conflict or setting (usually both). Fantasy, on the other hand, rarely utilizes science, relying instead on magic, mythological and neomythological beings, and devices and outright invention for conflict and setting.

SECOND SERIAL (REPRINT) RIGHTS. Permission for the reprinting of a work in another periodical after its first publication in book or magazine form.

SELF-PUBLISHING. In this arrangement, the author keeps all income derived from the book, but he pays for its manufacturing, production, and marketing.

SERIAL RIGHTS. The rights given by an author to a publisher to print a piece in one or more periodicals.

SERIALIZED NOVEL. A book-length work of fiction published in sequential issues of a periodical.

SETTING. The environment and time period during which the action of a story takes place.

SHORT SHORT STORY. A condensed piece of fiction, usually under 1,000 words.

SIMULTANEOUS SUBMISSION. The practice of sending copies of the same manuscript to several editors or publishers at the same time. Some editors refuse to consider such submissions.

SLANT. A story's particular approach or style, designed to appeal to the readers of a specific magazine.

SLICE OF LIFE. A presentation of characters in a seemingly mundane situation that offers the reader a flash of illumination about the characters or their situation.

SLUSH PILE. A stack of unsolicited manuscripts in the editorial offices of a publisher.

SOCIAL FICTION. Fiction written with the purpose of bringing positive changes in society.

SOFT/SOCIOLOGICAL SCIENCE FICTION. Science fiction with an emphasis on society and culture versus scientific accuracy.

SPACE OPERA. Epic science fiction with an emphasis on good guys versus bad guys.

SPECULATION (OR SPEC). An editor's agreement to look at an author's manuscript with no promise to purchase.

SPECULATIVE FICTION (SPECFIC). The all-inclusive term for science fiction, fantasy, and horror.

SUBSIDIARY. An incorporated branch of a company or conglomerate (e.g., Alfred Knopf, Inc., a subsidiary of Random House, Inc.).

SUBSIDIARY RIGHTS. All rights other than book publishing rights included in a book contract, such as paperback, book club, and movie rights.

SUBSIDY PUBLISHER. A book publisher who charges the author for the cost of typesetting, printing, and promoting a book. Also called a *vanity publisher*.

SUBTERFICIAL FICTION. Innovative, challenging, nonconventional fiction in which what seems to be happening is the result of things not so easily perceived.

SUSPENSE. A genre of fiction where the plot's primary function is to build a feeling of anticipation and fear in the reader over its possible outcome.

SYNOPSIS. A brief summary of a story, novel or play. As part of a book proposal, it is a comprehensive summary condensed in a page or page and a half.

TABLOID. Publication printed on paper about half the size of a regular newspaper page (e.g., the *National Enquirer*).

TEARSHEET. Page from a magazine containing a published story.

THEME. The dominant or central idea in a literary work; its message, moral, or main thread.

THRILLER. A novel intended to arouse feelings of excitement or suspense. Works in this genre are highly sensational, usually focusing on illegal activities, international espionage, sex, and violence. A thriller is often a detective story in which the forces of good are pitted against the forces of evil in a kill-or-be-killed situation.

TRADE PAPERBACK. A softbound volume, usually around 5" × 8", published and designed for the general public, available mainly in bookstores.

UNSOLICITED MANUSCRIPT. A story or novel manuscript that an editor did not specifically ask to see.

URBAN FANTASY. Fantasy that takes magical characters, such as elves, fairies, vampires, or wizards, and places them in modern-day settings, often in the inner city.

VANITY PUBLISHER. See subsidy publisher.

VIEWPOINT. The position or attitude of the first- or third-person narrator or multiple narrators, which determines how a story's action is seen and evaluated.

WESTERN. Genre with a setting in the West, usually between 1860 and 1890, with a formula plot about cowboys or other aspects of frontier life.

WHODUNIT. Genre dealing with murder, suspense, and the detection of criminals.

WORK-FOR-HIRE. Work that another party commissions you to do, generally for a flat fee. The creator does not own the copyright and therefore cannot sell any rights.

YOUNG ADULT (YA). The general classification of books written for readers twelve and up.

ZINE. A small, noncommercial magazine, often one- or two-person operations run from the home of the publisher/editor. Themes tend to be specialized, personal, experimental, and often controversial.

GENRE GLOSSARY

Definitions of Fiction Subcategories

///

The following were provided courtesy of The Extended Novel Writing Workshop, created by the staff of Writers Online Workshops (www.writersonlineworkshops.com).

MYSTERY SUBCATEGORIES

The major mystery subcategories are listed below, each followed by a brief description and the names of representative authors, so you can sample each type of work. Note that we have loosely classified "suspense/thriller" as a mystery category. While these stories do not necessarily follow a traditional "whodunit" plot pattern, they share many elements with other mystery categories.

AMATEUR DETECTIVE. As the name implies, the detective is not a professional detective (private or otherwise), but is almost always a professional something. This professional association routinely involves the protagonist in criminal cases (in a support capacity), gives him or her a special advantage in a specific case, or provides the contacts and skills necessary to solve a particular crime. (Jonathan Kellerman, Patricia Cornwell, Jan Burke)

CLASSIC MYSTERY (WHODUNIT). A crime (almost always a murder) is solved. The detective is the viewpoint character; the reader never knows any more or less about the crime than the detective, and all the clues to solving the crime are available to the reader.

COURTROOM DRAMA. The action takes place primarily in the courtroom; protagonist is generally a defense attorney out to prove the innocence of his or her client by finding the real culprit.

COZY. A special class of the amateur detective category that frequently features a female protagonist. (Agatha Christie's Miss Marple stories are the classic example.) There is less onstage violence than in other categories, and the plot is often wrapped up in a final scene where the detective identifies the murderer and explains how the crime was solved. In contemporary stories, the protagonist can be anyone from a chronically curious housewife to a mystery-buff clergyman to a college professor, but he or she is usually quirky, even eccentric. (Susan Isaacs, Andrew Greeley, Lillian Jackson Braun)

ESPIONAGE. The international spy novel is less popular since the end of the Cold War, but stories can still revolve around political intrigue in unstable regions. (John le Carré, Ken Follett)

HEISTS AND CAPERS. The crime itself is the focus. Its planning and execution are seen in detail, and the participants are fully drawn characters that may even be portrayed sympathetically. One character is the obvious leader of the group (the "brains"); the other members are often brought together by the leader specifically for this job and may or may not have a previous association. In a heist, no matter how clever or daring the characters are, they are still portrayed as criminals, and the expectation is that they will be caught and punished (but not always). A caper is more lighthearted, even comedic. The participants may have a noble goal (something other than personal gain) and often get away with the crime. (Eric Ambler, Tony Kenrick, Leslie Hollander)

HISTORICAL. May be any category or subcategory of mystery, but with an emphasis on setting, the details of which must be diligently researched. But beyond the historical details (which must never overshadow the story), the plot develops along the lines of its contemporary counterpart. (Candace Robb, Caleb Carr, Anne Perry)

JUVENILE/YOUNG ADULT. Written for the 8–12 age group (middle grade) or the 12 and up age group (young adult), the crime in these stories may or may not be murder, but it is serious. The protagonist is a kid (or group of kids) in the same age range as the targeted reader. There is no graphic violence depicted, but the stories are scary and the villains are realistic. (Mary Downing Hahn, Wendy Corsi Staub, Cameron Dokey, Norma Fox Mazer)

MEDICAL THRILLER. The plot can involve a legitimate medical threat (such as the outbreak of a virulent plague) or the illegal or immoral use of medical technology. In the former scenario, the protagonist is likely to be the doctor (or team) who identifies the virus and procures the antidote; in the latter he or she could be a patient (or the relative of a victim) who uncovers the plot and brings down the villain. (Robin Cook, Michael Palmer, Michael Crichton, Stanley Pottinger)

POLICE PROCEDURALS. The most realistic category, these stories require the most meticulous research. A police procedural may have more than one protagonist since cops rarely work alone. Conflict between partners, or between the detective and his or her superiors, is a common theme. But cops are portrayed positively as a group, even though there may be a couple of bad or ineffective law enforcement characters for contrast and conflict. Jurisdictional disputes are still popular sources of conflict as well. (Lawrence Treat, Joseph Wambaugh, Ridley Pearson, Julie Smith)

PRIVATE DETECTIVE. When described as "hard-boiled," this category takes a tough stance. Violence is more prominent, characters are darker, the detective—while almost always licensed by the state—operates on the fringes of the law, and there is often open resentment between the detective and law enforcement. More "enlightened" male detectives and a crop of contemporary females have brought about new trends in this category. (For female P.I.s: Sue Grafton, Sara Paretsky; for male P.I.s: John D. MacDonald, Lawrence Sanders)

SUSPENSE/THRILLER. Where a classic mystery is always a whodunit, a suspense/thriller novel may deal more with the intricacies of the crime, what motivated it, and how the villain (whose identity may be revealed to the reader early on) is caught and brought to justice. Novels in this category frequently employ multiple points of view and have broader scopes than more traditional murder mysteries. The crime may not even involve murder— it may be a threat to global economy or regional ecology; it may be technology run amok or abused at the hands of an unscrupulous scientist; it may involve innocent citizens victimized for personal or corporate gain. Its perpetrators are kidnappers, stalkers, serial killers, rapists, pedophiles, computer hackers, or just about anyone with an evil intention and the means to carry it out. The protagonist may be a private detective or law enforcement official, but is just as likely to be a doctor, lawyer, military officer, or other individual in a unique position to identify the villain and bring him or her to justice. (James Patterson, John J. Nance)

TECHNO-THRILLER. These are replacing the traditional espionage novel and feature technology as an integral part of not just the setting but the plot as well.

WOMAN IN JEOPARDY. A murder or other crime may be committed, but the focus is on the woman (and/or her children) currently at risk, her struggle to understand the nature of the danger, and her eventual victory over her tormentor. The protagonist makes up for her lack of physical prowess with intellect or special skills and solves the problem on her own or with the help of her family (but she runs the show). Closely related to this category is romantic suspense. But, while the heroine in a romantic suspense is certainly a "woman in jeopardy,'" the mystery or suspense element is subordinate to the romance. (Mary Higgins Clark, Mary Stewart, Jessica Mann)

ROMANCE SUBCATEGORIES

These categories and subcategories of romance fiction have been culled from the *Romance Writer's Sourcebook* (Writer's Digest Books) and Phyllis Taylor Pianka's *How to Write Romances* (Writer's Digest Books). We've arranged the "major" categories below, with the subcategories beneath them, each followed by a brief description and the names of authors who write in each category, so you can sample representative works.

CATEGORY OR SERIES. These are published in "lines" by individual publishing houses (such as Harlequin); each line has its own requirements as to word length, story content, and amount of sex. (Debbie Macomber, Nora Roberts, Glenda Sanders)

CHRISTIAN. With an inspirational Christian message centering on the spiritual dynamic of the romantic relationship and faith in God as the foundation for that relationship; sensuality is played down. (Janelle Burnham, Ann Bell, Linda Chaikin, Catherine Palmer, Dee Henderson, Lisa Tawn Bergen)

GLITZ. So called because they feature generally wealthy characters with high-powered positions in careers that are considered glamorous—high finance, modeling/acting, publishing, fashion—and are set in exciting or exotic (often metropolitan) locales, such as Monte Carlo, Hollywood, London, or New York. (Jackie Collins, Judith Krantz)

HISTORICAL. Can cover just about any historical (or even prehistorical) period. Setting in the historical is especially significant, and details must be thoroughly researched and accurately presented. For a sampling of a variety of historical styles, try Laura Kinsell (*Flowers from the Storm*), Mary Jo Putney (*The Rake and the Reformer*), and Judy Cuevas (*Bliss*). Some currently popular periods/themes in historicals are:

- **GOTHIC:** Historical with a strong element of suspense and a feeling of supernatural events, although these events frequently have a natural explanation. Setting plays an important role in establishing a dark, moody, suspenseful atmosphere. (Phyllis Whitney, Victoria Holt)
- **HISTORICAL FANTASY:** With traditional fantasy elements of magic and magical beings, frequently set in a medieval society. (Amanda Glass, Jayne Ann Krentz, Kathleen Morgan, Jessica Bryan, Taylor Quinn Evans, Carla Simpson, Karyn Monk)
- **EARLY AMERICAN:** Usually Revolution to Civil War, set in New England or the South, but "frontier" stories set in the American West are quite popular as well. (Robin Lee Hatcher, Ann Maxwell, Heather Graham)

- **NATIVE AMERICAN:** Where one or both of the characters are Native Americans; the conflict between cultures is a popular theme. (Carol Finch, Elizabeth Grayson, Karen Kay, Kathleen Harrington, Genell Dellim, Candace McCarthy)
- **REGENCY:** Set in England during the Regency period from 1811 to 1820. (Carol Finch, Elizabeth Elliott, Georgette Heyer, Joan Johnston, Lynn Collum)

MULTICULTURAL. Most currently feature African-American or Hispanic couples, but editors are looking for other ethnic stories as well. Multiculturals can be contemporary or historical and fall into any subcategory. (Rochelle Alers, Monica Jackson, Bette Ford, Sandra Kitt, Brenda Jackson)

PARANORMAL. Containing elements of the supernatural or science fiction/fantasy. There are numerous subcategories (many stories combine elements of more than one) including:

- **TIME TRAVEL:** One or more of the characters travels to another time—usually the past—to find love. (Jude Deveraux, Linda Lael Miller, Diana Gabaldon, Constance O'Day-Flannery)
- **SCIENCE FICTION/FUTURISTIC:** S/F elements are used for the story's setting: imaginary worlds, parallel universes, Earth in the near or distant future. (Marilyn Campbell, Jayne Ann Krentz, J.D. Robb [Nora Roberts], Anne Avery)
- **CONTEMPORARY FANTASY:** From modern ghost and vampire stories to "New Age" themes such as extraterrestrials and reincarnation. (Linda Lael Miller, Anne Stuart, Antoinette Stockenberg, Christine Feehan)

ROMANTIC COMEDY. Has a fairly strong comic premise and/or a comic perspective in the author's voice or the voices of the characters (especially the heroine). (Jennifer Crusie, Susan Elizabeth Phillips)

ROMANTIC SUSPENSE. With a mystery or psychological thriller subplot in addition to the romance plot. (Mary Stewart, Barbara Michaels, Tami Hoag, Nora Roberts, Linda Howard, Catherine Coulter)

SINGLE TITLE. Longer contemporaries that do not necessarily conform to the requirements of a specific romance line and therefore feature more complex plots and nontraditional characters. (Mary Ruth Myers, Nora Roberts, Kathleen Gilles Seidel, Kathleen Korbel)

YOUNG ADULT (YA). Focus is on first love with very little, if any, sex. These can have bittersweet endings, as opposed to the traditional romance happy ending, since first loves are often lost loves. (YA historical: Nancy Covert Smith, Louise Vernon; YA contemporary: Kathryn Makris)

SCIENCE FICTION SUBCATEGORIES

Peter Heck, in his article "Doors to Other Worlds: Trends in Science Fiction and Fantasy," which appears in the 1996 edition of *Science Fiction and Fantasy Writer's Sourcebook* (Writer's Digest Books), identifies some science fiction trends that have distinct enough characteristics to be defined as categories. These distinctions are frequently the result of marketing decisions as much as literary ones, so understanding them is important in deciding where your novel idea belongs. We've supplied a brief description and the names of authors who write in each category. In those instances where the author writes in more than one category, we've included titles of appropriate representative works.

ALTERNATE HISTORY. Fantasy, sometimes with science fiction elements, that changes the accepted account of actual historical events or people to suggest an alternate view of history. (Ted Mooney, *Traffic and Laughter*; Ward Moore, *Bring the Jubilee*; Philip K. Dick, *The Man in the High Castle*)

CYBERPUNK. Characters in these stories are tough outsiders in a high-tech, generally near-future society where computers have produced major changes in the way society functions. (William Gibson, Bruce Sterling, Pat Cadigan, Wilhelmina Baird)

HARD SCIENCE FICTION. Based on the logical extrapolation of real science to the future. In these stories the scientific background (setting) may be as, or more, important than the characters. (Larry Niven)

MILITARY SCIENCE FICTION. Stories about war that feature traditional military organization and tactics extrapolated into the future. (Jerry Pournelle, David Drake, Elizabeth Moon)

NEW AGE. A category of speculative fiction that deals with subjects such as astrology, psychic phenomena, spiritual healing, UFOs, mysticism, and other aspects of the occult. (Walter Mosley, *Blue Light*; Neil Gaiman)

SCIENCE FANTASY. Blend of traditional fantasy elements with scientific or pseudoscientific support (genetic engineering, for example, to "explain" a traditional fantasy creature like the dragon). These stories are traditionally more character driven than hard science fiction. (Anne McCaffrey, Mercedes Lackey, Marion Zimmer Bradley)

SCIENCE FICTION MYSTERY. A cross-genre blending that can either be a more-or-less traditional science fiction story with a mystery as a key plot element, or a more-or-less traditional whodunit with science fiction elements. (Philip K. Dick, Lynn S. Hightower)

SCIENCE FICTION ROMANCE. Another genre blend that may be a romance with science fiction elements (in which case it is more accurately placed as a subcategory within the romance genre) or a science fiction story with a strong romantic subplot. (Anne McCaffrey, Melanie Rawn, Kate Elliott)

SOCIAL SCIENCE FICTION. The focus is on how the characters react to their environments. This category includes social satire. (George Orwell's *1984* is a classic example.) (Margaret Atwood, *The Handmaid's Tale*; Ursula K. Le Guin, *The Left Hand of Darkness*; Marge Piercy, *Woman on the Edge of Time*)

SPACE OPERA. From the term "horse opera," describing a traditional good-guys-versus-bad-guys western, these stories put the emphasis on sweeping action and larger-than-life characters. The focus on action makes these stories especially appealing for film treatment. (The Star Wars series is one of the best examples; also Samuel R. Delany.)

STEAMPUNK. A specific type of alternate-history science fiction set in Victorian England in which characters have access to 20th-century technology. (William Gibson; Bruce Sterling, *The Difference Engine*)

YOUNG ADULT. Any subcategory of science fiction geared to a YA audience (12–18), but these are usually shorter novels with characters in the central roles who are the same age as (or slightly older than) the targeted reader. (Jane Yolen, Andre Norton)

FANTASY SUBCATEGORIES

Before we take a look at the individual fantasy categories, it should be noted that, for purposes of these supplements, we've treated fantasy as a genre distinct from science fiction. While these two are closely related, there are significant enough differences to warrant their separation for study purposes. We have included here those science fiction categories that have strong fantasy elements, or that have a significant amount of crossover (these categories appear in both the science fiction and the fantasy supplements), but "pure" science fiction categories are not included below. If you're not sure whether your novel is fantasy or science fiction, consider this definition by Orson Scott Card in *How to Write Science Fiction and Fantasy* (Writer's Digest Books): "Here's a good, simple, semi-accurate rule of thumb: If the story is set in a universe that follows the same rules as ours, it's science fiction. If it's set in a universe that doesn't follow our rules, it's fantasy. Or in other words, science fiction is about what could be but isn't; fantasy is about what couldn't be."

But even Card admits this rule is only "semi-accurate." He goes on to say that the real boundary between science fiction and fantasy is defined by how the impossible is achieved: "If you have people do some magic, impossible thing [like time travel] by stroking a talisman or praying to a tree, it's fantasy; if they do the same thing by pressing a button or climbing inside a machine, it's science fiction."

Peter Heck, in his article "Doors to Other Worlds: Trends in Science Fiction and Fantasy," which appears in the 1996 edition of the *Science Fiction and Fantasy Writer's Sourcebook* (Writer's Digest Books), does note some trends that have distinct enough characteristics to be defined as separate categories. These categories are frequently the result of marketing decisions as much as literary ones, so understanding them is important in deciding where your novel idea belongs. We've supplied a brief description and the names of authors who write in each category, so you can sample representative works.

ARTHURIAN. Reworking of the legend of King Arthur and the Knights of the Round Table. (T.H. White, *The Once and Future King*; Marion Zimmer Bradley, *The Mists of Avalon*)

CONTEMPORARY (ALSO CALLED "URBAN") FANTASY. Traditional fantasy elements (such as elves and magic) are incorporated into an otherwise recognizable modern setting. (Emma Bull, *War for the Oaks*; Mercedes Lackey, *The SERRAted Edge*; Terry Brooks, the Word & Void series)

DARK FANTASY. Closely related to horror but generally not as graphic. Characters in these stories are the "darker" fantasy types: vampires, witches, werewolves, demons, etc. (Anne Rice; Clive Barker, *Weaveworld*, *Imajica*; Fred Chappell)

FANTASTIC ALTERNATE HISTORY. Set in an alternate historical period (in which magic would not have been a common belief) where magic works, these stories frequently feature actual historical figures. (Orson Scott Card, *Alvin Maker*)

GAME-RELATED FANTASY. Plots and characters are similar to high fantasy, but are based on a particular role-playing game. (Dungeons and Dragons; Magic: The Gathering; World of Warcraft)

HEROIC FANTASY. The fantasy equivalent to military science fiction, these are stories of war and its heroes and heroines. (Robert E. Howard, the Conan the Barbarian series; Elizabeth Moon, *Deed of Paksenarrion*; Michael Moorcock, the Elric series)

HIGH FANTASY. Emphasis is on the fate of an entire race or nation, threatened by an ultimate evil. J.R.R. Tolkien's Lord of the Rings trilogy is a classic example. (Terry Brooks, David Eddings, Margaret Weis, Tracy Hickman)

HISTORICAL FANTASY. The setting can be almost any era in which the belief in magic was strong; these are essentially historical novels where magic is a key element of the plot and/or setting. (Susan Schwartz, *Silk Roads and Shadows*; Margaret Ball, *No Earthly Sunne*; Tim Powers, *The Anubis Gates*)

JUVENILE/YOUNG ADULT. Can be any type of fantasy, but geared to a juvenile (8–12) or YA audience (12–18); these are shorter novels with younger characters in central roles. (J.K. Rowling, Christopher Paolini, C.S. Lewis)

SCIENCE FANTASY. A blend of traditional fantasy elements with scientific or pseudoscientific support (genetic engineering, for example, to "explain" a traditional fantasy creature like the dragon). These stories are traditionally more character driven than hard science fiction. (Anne McCaffrey, Mercedes Lackey, Marion Zimmer Bradley)

HORROR SUBCATEGORIES

Subcategories in horror are less well defined than in other genres and are frequently the result of marketing decisions as much as literary ones. But being familiar with the terms used to describe different horror styles can be important in understanding how your own novel might be best presented to an agent or editor. What follows is a brief description of the most commonly used terms, along with names of authors and, where necessary, representative works.

DARK FANTASY. Sometimes used as a euphemistic term for horror in general, but also refers to a specific type of fantasy, usually less graphic than other horror subcategories, that features more "traditional" supernatural or mythical beings (vampires, werewolves, zombies, etc.) in either contemporary or historical settings. (Contemporary: Stephen King, *Salem's Lot*; Thomas Tessier, *The Nightwalker*. Historical: Brian Stableford, *The Empire of Fear* and *Werewolves of London*)

HAUNTINGS. "Classic" stories of ghosts, poltergeists, and spiritual possessions. The level of violence portrayed varies, but many writers in this category exploit the reader's natural fear of the unknown by hinting at the horror and letting the reader's imagination supply the details. (Peter Straub, *Ghost Story*; Richard Matheson, *Hell House*)

JUVENILE/YOUNG ADULT. Can be any horror style, but with a protagonist who is the same age as, or slightly older than, the targeted reader. Stories for middle grades (8–12 years old) are scary, with monsters and violent acts that might best be described as "gross," but stories for young adults (12–18) may be more graphic. (R.L. Stine, Christopher Pike, Carol Gorman)

PSYCHOLOGICAL HORROR. Features a human monster with horrific, but not necessarily supernatural, aspects. (Thomas Harris, *The Silence of the Lambs*, *Hannibal*; Dean Koontz, *Whispers*)

SPLATTERPUNK. Very graphic depiction of violence—often gratuitous—popularized in the 1980s, especially in film. (*Friday the 13th*, *Halloween*, *Nightmare on Elm Street*, etc.)

SUPERNATURAL/OCCULT. Similar to the dark fantasy, but may be more graphic in its depiction of violence. Stories feature satanic worship, demonic possession, or ultimate evil incarnate in an entity or supernatural being that may or may not have its roots in traditional mythology or folklore. (Ramsey Campbell; Robert McCammon; Ira Levin, *Rosemary's Baby*; William Peter Blatty, *The Exorcist*; Stephen King, *Pet Sematary*)

TECHNOLOGICAL HORROR. "Monsters" in these stories are the result of science run amok or technology turned to purposes of evil. (Dean Koontz, *Watchers*; Michael Crichton, *Jurassic Park*)

PROFESSIONAL ORGANIZATIONS

///

AGENTS' ORGANIZATIONS

ASSOCIATION OF AUTHORS' AGENTS (AAA) Curtis Brown, Haymarket House, 28-29 Haymarket, London SW1Y 4SP. (020)7393-4420. E-mail: wiseoffice@curtisbrown.co.uk. Website: www.agentsassoc.co.uk.

ASSOCIATION OF AUTHORS' REPRESENTATIVES (AAR) 302A West 12th Street, #122, New York, NY 10014. E-mail: administrator@aaronline.org. Website: aaronline.org.

ASSOCIATION OF TALENT AGENTS (ATA) 9255 Sunset Blvd., Suite 930, Los Angeles, CA 90069. (310)274-0628. Fax: (310)274-5063. E-mail: info@agentassociation.com. Website: www.agentassociation.com.

WRITERS' ORGANIZATIONS

ACADEMY OF AMERICAN POETS 75 Maiden Lane, Suite 901, New York, NY 10038. (212)274-0343. Fax: (212)274-9427. E-mail: academy@poets.org. Website: www.poets.org.

AMERICAN CRIME WRITERS LEAGUE (ACWL) E-mail: info@acwl.org. Website: www.acwl.org.

AMERICAN MEDICAL WRITERS ASSOCIATION (AMWA) 30 West Gude Drive, Suite 525, Rockville, MD 20850-4347. (240)238-0940. Fax: (301)294-9006. E-mail: amwa@amwa.org. Website: www.amwa.org.

AMERICAN SCREENWRITERS ASSOCIATION (ASA) E-mail: info@americanscreenwriters.com. Website: www.americanscreenwriters.com.

AMERICAN TRANSLATORS ASSOCIATION (ATA) 225 Reinekers Lane, Suite 590, Alexandria, VA 22314. (703)683-6100. Fax: (703)683-6122. E-mail: ata@atanet.org. Website: www.atanet.org.

EDUCATION WRITERS ASSOCIATION (EWA) 3516 Connecticut Avenue NW, Washington, DC 20008. (202)452-9830. Website: www.ewa.org.

THE ASSOCIATION OF GARDEN COMMUNICATORS (GWA) 355 Lexington Avenue, 15th Floor, New York, NY 10017. (212)297-2198. Fax: (212)297-2149. E-mail: info@garden writers.org. Website: www.gardenwriters.org.

HORROR WRITERS ASSOCIATION (HWA) P.O. Box 56687, Sherman Oaks, CA 91413. (818)220-3965. E-mail: hwa.contact@gmail.com. Website: www.horror.org.

THE INTERNATIONAL WOMEN'S WRITING GUILD (IWWG) 5 Penn Plaza, PMB #19059, New York, NY 10001. (917)720-6959. E-mail: iwwgquestions@gmail.com Website: iwwg. wildapricot.org.

MYSTERY WRITERS OF AMERICA (MWA) 1140 Broadway, Suite 1507, New York, NY 10001. (212)888-8171. Fax: (212)888-8107. Website: www.mysterywriters.org.

NATIONAL ASSOCIATION OF SCIENCE WRITERS (NASW) P.O. Box 7905, Berkeley, CA 94707. (510)647-9500. E-mail: editor@nasw.org. Website: www.nasw.org.

ORGANIZATION OF BLACK SCREENWRITERS (OBS) 3010 Wilshire Boulevard, #269, Los Angeles, CA 90010. E-mail: contactus@obswriter.com. Website: www.obswriter.com.

OUTDOOR WRITERS ASSOCIATION OF AMERICA (OWAA) 615 Oak Street, Suite 201, Missoula, MT 59801. (406)728-7434. E-mail: info@owaa.org. Website: www.owaa.org.

POETRY SOCIETY OF AMERICA (PSA) 15 Gramercy Park, New York, NY 10003. (212)254-9628. Website: www.poetrysociety.org.

POETS & WRITERS 90 Broad St., Suite 2100, New York, NY 10004. (212)226-3586. Fax: (212)226-3963. Website: www.pw.org.

ROMANCE WRITERS OF AMERICA (RWA) 14615 Benfer Road, Houston, TX 77069. (832)717-5200. E-mail: info@rwa.org. Website: www.rwa.org.

SCIENCE FICTION AND FANTASY WRITERS OF AMERICA (SFWA) P.O. Box 3238, Enfield, CT 06083-3238. Website: www.sfwa.org.

SOCIETY OF AMERICAN BUSINESS EDITORS AND WRITERS (SABEW) Walter Cronkite School of Journalism and Mass Communication, Arizona State University, 555 North Central Avenue, Suite 406E, Phoenix, AZ 85004-1248 (602)496-7862. E-mail: sabew@sabew.org. Website: www.sabew.org.

SOCIETY OF AMERICAN TRAVEL WRITERS (SATW) 1 Parkview Plaza, Suite 800, Oakbrook Terrace, IL 60181. E-mail: info@satw.org. Website: www.satw.org.

SOCIETY OF CHILDREN'S BOOK WRITERS & ILLUSTRATORS (SCBWI) 4727 Wilshire Boulevard, Suite 301, Los Angeles, CA 90010. (323)782-1010. E-mail: scbwi@scbwi.org. Website: www.scbwi.org.

WESTERN WRITERS OF AMERICA (WWA) E-mail: wwa.moulton@gmail.com. Website: www.westernwriters.org.

INDUSTRY ORGANIZATIONS

AMERICAN BOOKSELLERS ASSOCIATION (ABA) 333 Westchester Avenue, Suite S202, White Plains, NY 10604. (914)406-7500. Fax: (914)417-4013. E-mail: info@bookweb.org. Website: www.bookweb.org.

AMERICAN SOCIETY OF JOURNALISTS & AUTHORS (ASJA) 355 Lexington Avenue, 15th Floor, New York, NY 10017-6603. (212)997-0947. Website: www.asja.org.

THE ASSOCIATION FOR CHRISTIAN RETAIL (CBA) 1365 Garden of the Gods Road, Suite 105, Colorado Springs, CO 80907. (800)252-1950. Fax: (719)272-3510. E-mail: info@cbaonline. org. Website: cbaonline.org.

THE ASSOCIATION FOR WOMEN IN COMMUNICATIONS (AWC) 1717 East Republic Road, Suite A, Springfield, MO 65804. (417)886-8606. Fax: (417)886-3685. E-mail: becky@club-managementservices.com. Website: www.womcom.org.

ASSOCIATION OF AMERICAN PUBLISHERS (AAP) 71 Fifth Avenue, Second Floor, New York NY 10003. (212)255-0200. Fax: (212)255-7007. Or: 455 Massachusetts Avenue NW, Suite 700, Washington, DC 20001. (202)347-3375. Fax: (202)347-3690. Website: publishers.org.

ASSOCIATION OF WRITERS & WRITING PROGRAMS (AWP) George Mason University, 4400 University Drive, MSN 1E3, Fairfax, VA 22030. (703)993-4301. Fax: (703)993-4302. E-mail: awp@awpwriter.org. Website: www.awpwriter.org.

THE AUTHORS GUILD 31 East 32nd Street, Seventh Floor, New York, NY 10016. (212)563-5904. Fax: (212)564-5363. E-mail: staff@authorsguild.org. Website: www.authorsguild.org.

CANADIAN AUTHORS ASSOCIATION (CAA) 6 West Street North, Suite 203, Orilla, ON L3V 5B8 Canada. (705)325-3926. E-mail: admin@canadianauthors.org. Website: www.canadianauthors.org.

DRAMATISTS GUILD OF AMERICA 1501 Broadway, Suite 701, New York, NY 10036. (212)398-9366. Fax: (212)944-0420. Website: www.dramatistsguild.com.

NATIONAL LEAGUE OF AMERICAN PEN WOMEN (NLAPW) Pen Arts Building and Art Museum, 1300 17th St. NW, Washington DC 20036-1973. (202)785-1997. Fax: (202)452-8868. E-mail: contact@nlapw.org. Website: www.nlapw.org.

NATIONAL WRITERS ASSOCIATION (NWA) 10940 South Parker Road, #508, Parker, CO 80134. E-mail: natlwritersassn@hotmail.com. Website: www.nationalwriters.com

NATIONAL WRITERS UNION (NWU) 256 West 38th Street, Suite 703, New York, NY 10018. (212)254-0279. Fax: (212)254-0673. E-mail: nwu@nwu.org. Website: www.nwu.org.

PEN AMERICA 588 Broadway, Suite 303, New York, NY 10012. (212)334-1660. E-mail: info@pen.org. Website: www.pen.org.

PLAYWRIGHTS GUILD OF CANADA (PGC) 401 Richmond Street West, Suite 350, Toronto, ON M5V 3A8 Canada. (416)703-0201. Fax: (416)703-0059. E-mail: info@playwrightsguild.ca. Website: www.playwrightsguild.ca.

VOLUNTEER LAWYERS FOR THE ARTS (VLA) 1 East 53rd Street, New York, NY 10022. (212)319-2787, ext.1. E-mail: vlany@vlany.org. Website: www.vlany.org.

WOMEN IN FILM (WIF) 6100 Wilshire Boulevard, Suite 710, Los Angeles, CA 90048. (323)935-2211. Fax: (323)935-2212. E-mail: info@wif.org. Website: www.wif.org.

WOMEN'S NATIONAL BOOK ASSOCIATION (WNBA) P.O. Box 237, FDR Station, New York NY 10150. (866)610-9622. Fax: (212)208-4629. E-mail: info@wnba-books.org. Website: www.wnba-books.org.

WRITERS' GUILD OF ALBERTA (WGA) Main Floor, Percy Page Centre, 11759 Groat Road NW, Edmonton AB T5M 3K6 Canada. (780)422-8174. Fax: (780)422-2663 (Attn: Writers' Guild of Alberta). E-mail: mail@writersguild.ca. Website: writersguild.ab.ca.

WRITERS GUILD OF AMERICA, EAST (WGA) 250 Hudson Street, Suite 700, New York, NY 10013. (212)767-7800. Fax: (212)582-1909. E-mail: gbynoe@wgaeast.org. Website: www.wgaeast.org.

WRITERS GUILD OF AMERICA, WEST (WGA) 7000 West Third Street, Los Angeles, CA 90048. (323)951-4000, (800)548-4532. Website: www.wga.org.

THE WRITERS' UNION OF CANADA (TWUC) 600-460 Richmond Street West, Toronto, ON M5V 1Y1 Canada. (416)703-8982. Fax: (416)504-9090. E-mail: info@writersunion.ca. Website: www.writersunion.ca.

LITERARY AGENTS SPECIALTIES INDEX

CATEGORY INDEX

Magazines

GENERAL INDEX

507

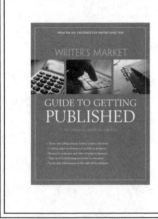